Applied Mergers and Acquisitions Workbook

Founded in 1807, John Wiley & Sons is the oldest independent publishing company in the United States. With offices in North America, Europe, Australia and Asia, Wiley is globally committed to developing and marketing print and electronic products and services for our customers' professional and personal knowledge and understanding.

The Wiley Finance series contains books written specifically for finance and investment professionals as well as sophisticated individual investors and their financial advisors. Book topics range from portfolio management to e-commerce, risk management, financial engineering, valuation and financial instrument analysis, as well as much more.

For a list of available titles, please visit our Web site at www.WileyFinance.com.

Applied Mergers and Acquisitions Workbook

ROBERT F. BRUNER

WILEY

John Wiley & Sons, Inc.

Published by John Wiley & Sons, Inc., Hoboken, New Jersey.
Published simultaneously in Canada.

For general information on our other products and services, or technical support, please contact our Customer Care Department within the United States at 800-762-2974, outside the United States at 317-572-3993 or fax 317-572-4002.

Wiley also publishes its books in a variety of electronic formats. Some content that appears in print may not be available in electronic books.

For more information about Wiley products, visit our web site at www.wiley.com.

ISBN: 978-0-471-39585-0

10 9 8 7 6 5 4

With gratitude, I dedicate this workbook to my students.

Acknowledgments

I am greatly thankful for the contributions of my able research assistants, who prepared questions for this workbook under my direction. The principal assistant for this project was Jessica Chan. Bright, patient, and a tenacious researcher, her work showed great care and dedication. Jessica led a team consisting of herself, Christine Shim, and Baocheng Yang. Christine was especially creative in framing financial problems in realistic terms; she is a champion wordsmith. Baocheng was the champion quant, contributing analytic care, modeling, and real option valuation. The complementary efforts of the three assistants lent flair and precision to the book. I must also recognize Frank Wilmot, Research Librarian at Darden, who gave excellent support in obtaining sometimes obscure data and references. I am truly grateful to them for the creativity and exceptionally hard work they brought to the project. Many of the illustrations in this book draw on the efforts of my earlier research assistants

I am very grateful to the staff of the Darden School for its support in this project. Excellent editorial assistance at Darden was provided by Stephen Smith (Darden's unflappable editor) and Sherry Alston. Betty Sprouse gave stalwart secretarial support. Outstanding library research support was given by Karen Marsh and Frank Wilmot. The patience, care, and dedication of these people are richly appreciated.

I must also acknowledge the great support and encouragement given by my editors (and now friends) at John Wiley & Sons: Bill Falloon, Senior Editor, Finance and Investments; Melissa Scuereb, Editorial Assistant; Robin Factor, Managing Production Editor; and Todd Tedesco, Senior Production Editor. I thank the staff at Cape Cod Compositors as well for their fine attention to detail. Also at Wiley, Pamela Van Giessen, Executive Editor; Joan O'Neil, Publisher, Finance and Investment; and Will Pesce, President, were decisive in my commitment to embark on this project. For the vision and enthusiasm of the Wiley organization, I am very thankful.

Lewis O'Brien of HPS Permissions read everything and gave very helpful advice regarding editorial presentation and support in obtaining permissions.

Of all the contributors, my wife, Barbara McTigue Bruner, and two sons, Jonathan and Alexander, have endured some of the greatest sacrifices to see this book appear. I owe this to them.

All these acknowledgments notwithstanding, responsibility for the final product is mine. I welcome suggestions for its enhancement. Please let me know of your experience with this book either through Wiley or contact me directly.

—Robert F. Bruner
Distinguished Professor of Business Administration
and Executive Director of the Batten Institute
Darden Graduate Business School
University of Virginia
E-mail: brunerr@virginia.edu.

About the Author

Robert F. Bruner is Distinguished Professor of Business Administration and Executive Director of the Batten Institute at the Darden Graduate School of Business Administration, University of Virginia. He teaches the course, "Mergers and Acquisitions" in Darden's MBA program, and is the faculty director of Darden's executive education program, "Mergers and Acquisitions." He has received numerous awards for teaching and casewriting in the United States and Europe. *BusinessWeek* magazine cited him as one of the "masters of the MBA classroom." He is the author or co-author of over 400 case studies and notes, and of *Case Studies in Finance: Managing for Corporate Value Creation*, now in its fourth edition. His research has been published in journals such as *Financial Management*, *Journal of Accounting and Economics*, *Journal of Applied Corporate Finance*, *Journal of Financial Economics*, *Journal of Financial and Quantitative Analysis*, and *Journal of Money, Credit, and Banking*. Industrial corporations, financial institutions, and government agencies have retained him for counsel and training. He has served the Darden School, professional groups, and community organizations in various positions of leadership. Copies of his papers and essays may be obtained from his website, http://faculty.darden.edu/brunerb/. He may be reached via e-mail at brunerr@virginia.edu.

Contents

Introduction to the Workbook

This *Workbook* aims to help you learn faster and more deeply from *Applied Mergers and Acquisitions* by Robert F. Bruner. Its mission is to promote self-instruction about M&A. Its chapters track exactly the content of the chapters in the main book. The problems and answers in this book carry the reader beyond the end-of-chapter questions on the CD-ROM, offering more exercise, stimulating further reflection, and exploring the topics in more depth. Specifically, each chapter in this book can help you:

- **Review** the main ideas in each chapter and a few focused problems and questions.
- **Survey** the ideas in a forthcoming class and chapter reading assignment.
- **Track** the quantitative analysis of M&A issues in a step-by-step fashion.
- **Exercise** spreadsheet models in hands-on fashion.
- **Test** your own grasp of tools and concepts.

Activities such as these are valuable in the effort to gain a solid mastery of M&A.

The *Workbook* has four key features supporting the study of each chapter:

1. *Introduction to the chapter.* Stated in a few sentences, the introduction conveys the main focus of the chapter.
2. *Key ideas.* These are listed at the start of each review chapter in bullet-point fashion to summarize and express key learning points.
3. *Worked-through problems and questions.* These are useful to illustrate key concepts and to test your grasp of lessons.
4. *References to Excel spreadsheet files.* Found on the CD-ROM, these contain the actual models underlying the worked-through problems. You can study these files for the structure of the models and the logic of the analysis.

Chapter 38 of the main book emphasizes the importance of active learning to support one's study. It is not enough simply to *read*: one must *do*. The spirit of this *Workbook* is to help you convert ideas into *best practice* in your daily work.

PART One

Questions

CHAPTER 1

Introduction and Executive Summary

M&A (mergers and acquisitions) is one of the most important means by which companies respond to changing conditions. Many firms have no alternative but to merge, acquire, or be acquired.

Although M&A is often portrayed as a gamble that one cannot win, it is possible to succeed in M&A. However, competitive forces may limit the chances of success.

- M&A is a world of contingencies. There are few universal absolute truths about M&A success. For the M&A professional, therefore, there will always be a market for diligent research, sound judgment, and artful execution.
- Success in M&A is driven by both the *structure* of the M&A opportunity one faces and the *conduct* by which one pursues it.
- Elements of *structure* of the M&A environment include:
  - *Economics.* This refers to quantitative drivers of the attractiveness of the opportunity: revenues, costs (both fixed and variable), risk, and required rates of return—these determine cash flow and the net present value of an M&A transaction. They also drive the financial stability and future growth of Newco. Best practitioners in M&A are rigorous analysts of the economics of an opportunity.
  - *Strategy.* Strategic strengths, weaknesses, opportunities, and threats are part of the structure of the M&A environment. Many M&A transactions are motivated by a need to respond to the strategic environment. Careful strategic planning is crucial to success in M&A.
  - *Organization.* Culture, leadership, talent, and organizational architecture of the merging firms have a major influence on the ability of Newco to achieve benefits of the deal. M&A practitioners must therefore lend careful thought to postmerger organizational structure.
  - *Brand.* Large intangible influences in the setting of the M&A opportunity are the reputations of buyer and target. As a brand name affects the thinking of consumers, reputations can shape the expectations and behavior of participants in a merger. Best practitioners seek to create and preserve brand value, and to understand the sources of the counterparty's brand.

  - *Law.* Laws and regulations limit the actions of buyer and target firms. M&A practitioners must manage legal risk exposure and to consider opportunities to shape legislation.
  - *Ethics.* Ethical norms surround everything one does in M&A and are often discovered only after they are broken. Best practitioners in M&A consciously address the ethical dimension in deal development.

- *Conduct* is the behavior of managers in the pursuit of good M&A outcomes and appears in M&A in the form of creativity, interpersonal skills, and elements of personality. Behavior is important because it filters and interacts with the structural elements of a deal. Behavior affects M&A outcomes in areas such as the following:

  - ***Search for partners.*** Discovery of partners may rely on "networking," which relies on social skills.
  - ***Due diligence.*** Success in due diligence is tied to the investigator's attitude and personal attributes such as stamina, care, and capacity for critical thinking.
  - ***Negotiation and bidding.*** Psychology and self-discipline affect the outcomes of negotiation and bidding. Attitudes, appetites, and negotiation tactics have a large influence on deal prices and terms.
  - ***Dealing with laws, regulations, and the justice system.*** Although laws and regulations may seem like constraints on actions, the M&A practitioner can strive to actually *shape* the structure of the M&A situation.
  - ***Deal design.*** Deal design entails searching for trade-offs that will result in a win-win deal for both buyer and seller. Often, such a search requires flexibility and creativity from the deal negotiators.
  - ***Postmerger integration.*** It takes managerial skill to successfully implement postmerger integration.
  - ***Deal development process.*** Good *process* is one of the key drivers of good outcomes. Conscientiousness in developing a process mind-set lends discipline to thinking and increases the likelihood of a successful M&A outcome.

- The framework reminds us that successful *outcomes* have many dimensions. Best practitioners think in terms of the entire range of outcomes rather than narrowly in just one or two dimensions. One can benchmark the success of a deal against at least seven measures:

  1. ***Creation of market value.*** This is necessarily the first measure of success because of the obligation of managers and directors to serve the welfare of shareholders. But it is rarely sufficient by itself—to take an extreme example, value created unethically or illegally would be unacceptable.
  2. ***Financial stability.*** Another measure of success is whether a deal strengthens the financial structure of the firm. Some deals have been so aggressively financed that they led to bankruptcy shortly after closing.
  3. ***Improved strategic position.*** The deal should serve the mission and strategic objectives of the firm. Best practitioners look for a solid strategic rationale.

4. ***Organizational strength.*** The acquisition of talent, rejuvenation of a worn-out or defeatist culture, improvement of learning or technology transfer, and transformation of the organizational architecture of a firm are examples of ways in which a deal can strengthen the organization.
5. ***Enhanced brand.*** A successful deal may strengthen the esteem for the firm in the eyes of competitors, suppliers, customers, and employees.
6. ***Observance of the letter and spirit of ethical norms and laws.*** Success means more than avoiding criminal indictment: Best practitioners understand that it is important not only to do deals well, but also to do them *right.*
7. ***Improved process.*** Every transaction should sharpen a firm's leadership and business processes. This happens when one conducts a deal with a learning mind-set.

- The *practice* of M&A is continually changing. The chapter outlines several disruptive ideas that will affect the ongoing development of practice:
  - ***A deal is a system.*** Internal consistency is important; one must negotiate the pieces of the deal with a view toward the whole. There may be unanticipated side effects; practitioners must look out for these. There may be many attractive structures, rather than a single best structure, that satisfy the objectives of all parties.
  - ***Find and use optionality.*** Options are pervasive in M&A.
  - ***Study market inefficiency.*** Where markets are integrated and efficient, decision makers can and should refer to market prices for signals about behavior. However, some markets may be inefficient—where this is true, the best practitioner modifies the tools and concepts to adapt to the market circumstances.
  - ***Good governance pays.*** Good governance increases the chances of successful M&A outcomes, though the practices of good governance are still evolving.
  - ***A deal is more than price.*** The practitioner faces a host of choices in designing a transaction, most of which have consequences for the buyer and target company shareholders. Deal design choices can create or destroy value.
  - ***Behaviorism.*** M&A bidding processes, negotiations, and deal design can influence *and* be influenced by behavior.
  - ***No silos.*** The M&A effort will be more successful the more integrated it is across deal design, strategy, and implementation.

CHAPTER 1—WORKBOOK QUESTIONS

Explain why each of the following statements is false:

1. *Success in M&A is determined solely by structural factors.*

2. *In the behavioral realm, success in postmerger integration is influenced more by the conduct and interpersonal skills of managers than by organizational structure.*

3. *Best practice in the legal area of M&A emphasizes only the avoidance of violating laws or regulations so that the pre- and postmerger firms involved in the M&A transaction are not exposed to any legal jeopardy.*

4. *Actions in M&A that are not clearly ethical or that even are unethical will not lead to outright failure as long as they do not violate the law.*

5. *Being able to negotiate and consummate a deal is the hallmark of success in M&A.*

6. *Planning everything with painstaking care ensures a successful outcome.*

7. *The best due diligence processes are those that simply verify facts.*

8. *In M&A, outcomes are more important than processes.*

9. *For every M&A deal, there is one "best" deal design.*

10. *Decision makers should always refer to market prices for signals about behavior.*

CHAPTER 2

Ethics in M&A

Ethical dilemmas are pervasive in M&A.

Unethical business practices are unsustainable; they do not provide a strong foundation for long-term corporate or professional success.

- Companies that are committed to ethical behavior build trust and add meaningful value to their brand. A strong corporate reputation attracts active buyers, intermediaries, advisers, repeat business, and price premiums that ultimately yield attractive profits and higher returns.
- Ethical business practices promote strong leadership and teamwork in organizations. Ethical behavior aligns a company's human capital around a set of shared values, which in turn enhance business processes and capabilities.
- A company committed to ethics will look above and beyond the law to set its standards for good business practices. The law is the lowest common denominator of social norms; it enforces punishment only for illegal behavior.
- Professionals who are guided by their consciences and commitment to ethical standards understand that personal pride and self-respect are invaluable, intangible assets.
- In most, if not all, cases, M&A professionals act as agents on behalf of a company's stockholders and/or stakeholders.
  - The *stockholder theory*, advanced by Milton Friedman (1962), holds that a company must act in the best interests of its owners and strive to maximize shareholders' returns.
  - Alternatively, Edward Freeman's *stakeholder theory* (1984) prescribes a broader view: management should act in the interests of all of its stakeholders, which include constituent groups such as customers, buyers, and employees.
- Moral philosophy offers at least three bases for assessing what is right versus wrong.

  1. *Consequences.* The first perspective asks who will be affected, and how. This branch of philosophy argues that the "right actions" are those that produce the greatest good for the greatest number. Its best-known proponents include philosophers Jeremy Bentham (1748–1832) and John Stuart Mill (1806–1873).

2. ***Duties or intentions.*** The second perspective focuses on the matrix of duties surrounding the manager and the consistency of one's intentions to fulfill them. An action is deemed as moral if it is intended to benefit and respect others and it is done out of a sense of duty, not self-gain. Perhaps the best-known deontologist is Immanuel Kant (1724–1804).
3. ***Virtues.*** The third perspective asks how an action will affect one's virtue, either in one's own or in others' eyes. A simple test is to imagine how you would feel if the contemplated action were published on the front page of tomorrow's newspaper. Rather than following rules, people are best guided by considering what a paragon of virtue would do. The Greek philosopher Aristotle (384–322 B.C.) prescribed this view.

- Business leadership involves more than an understanding of ethics; it also entails the promotion and practice of ethical behavior, active discussion, and reflection.
- Developing a high-performing culture that is also ethical can be achieved by adopting and enacting personal, corporate, and professional codes of ethics.

CHAPTER 2—WORKBOOK QUESTIONS

Analysis of the 1984 Disney Case

Imagine a conversation among three student philosophers: David, who is focused on duties; Ulyssa, focused on consequences; and Vera, a virtue-ethicist. They are debating the Disney Company's decision to pay greenmail. (For more information about this, see Chapter 2 of the main text.)

1a. *What do you think the three philosophers would say about Ron Miller and the 1984 greenmail situation?*

1b. *In your opinion, which philosopher could most successfully convince you as to whether paying greenmail was ethical and why? How might one philosopher's line of reasoning supersede the others?*

Applying Ethics to Real Business Situations

Case #1

Former majority owners of a manufacturing company, Power Electronics, have filed a lawsuit in federal district court against Systems Integration Corporation (SIC), to whom they recently sold Power Electronics. The plaintiffs claim that the buyer, SIC, ended up paying them about $20 million less than the agreed-upon $220 million for the company after accountants supposedly manipulated the post-closing account. That account included $17 million held in escrow and $4 million in receivables.

The two companies entered into a purchase agreement a year ago. As is standard practice, the seller filed a financial statement at the time of the contract. At the closing, the usual practice is for the buyer to hold back a portion of the agreed-upon price and put it in escrow while it checks the acquired company's books. The acquirer takes possession of the business and produces a final accounting of inventory, receivables, and other assets and liabilities, then often makes a final adjustment to the purchase price from the escrow money.

In the agreement, both companies agreed to use the same rules that conformed to generally accepted accounting principles (GAAP) to avoid any discrepancies regarding inventory and other issues. The two sides hired separate well-known accounting firms. In the event of a dispute, they agreed to use one of the internationally recognized accounting firms as an arbiter.

According to the claimants, the buyer's accountants were intent on finding ways to reduce the purchase price. They claim that the accountants found ways to show that the inventory was lower and that the tax credits would not be fully used because the company's future earnings would be lower than expected.

They are now suing SIC for $25 million, plus legal fees. The plaintiffs have declined to use an arbiter, arguing that they believe that it would be difficult to find one that was objective since many have had dealings with SIC.

On the side of the defense, Systems Integration Corporation's accountants say the company doesn't owe anything to the sellers. According to their audit, the company should not only keep the $17 million in escrow, but should also inform the sellers that they owe another $6 million to SIC.

2. *What ethical issues does this dispute raise? Set aside the legal question of the lawsuit and focus on the frameworks outlined in the chapter.*

Case #2

> *Hershey was a sweet target stuck in a bitter controversy. Dealmakers and M&A lawyers say that there probably never was a controversy of this type plaguing an acquisition, and there may never be again.*
>
> —*Mergers & Acquisitions*, October 2002

On July 25, 2002, the Hershey Trust Company—the primary owner of Hershey Foods and holder of 77 percent of Hershey Foods' voting stock—publicly announced that it wanted Hershey Foods to explore a sale of the entire company. The trust's primary financial and social responsibility is to operate the Milton Hershey School. It had decided that exploring a possible sale of the company "was the most prudent course of action" consistent with its diversification objectives, claiming it needed to diversify its portfolio in order to protect the assets of its beneficiary. When rival food firms like Wrigley and Nestlé inquired about buying the entire stake, the trustees also liked the prospect of receiving a large premium for their control of the company. Wrigley and Nestlé bid $12.5 billion and $11.2 billion, respectively, for Hershey Foods.

Richard Lenny, CEO of Hershey Foods, proposed to buy back the trust's shares over time at a small premium, but Robert Vowler, CEO and president of the Hershey Trust Company, rejected the offer. Robert Vowler released a statement in mid-August 2002 saying, "The board continues to believe this course [of selling its shares in Hershey Foods] is in keeping with its fiduciary responsibility to protect and preserve the Trust, which through the Milton Hershey School serves children in need. We're not talking about making more money. That's not what this is all about. This is about protecting the trust fund in perpetuity, protecting it from risk." But members of the school's alumni association criticized the trust for careless spending, exorbitant salaries, and inadequate oversight of the student facility. Alumni of the Milton Hershey School contended that "modern business temptations, mismanagement, and conflicts of interest have diverted Hershey trustees from the philanthropic and educational mission set down a century ago."

3. *What ethical issues emerge in the controversy over the Hershey Trust's decision to put Hershey Foods up for sale?*

CHAPTER 3

Does M&A Pay?

The degree of success or failure of M&A transactions is of the utmost importance to CEOs, business planners, investors, and government regulators. "Success" can be defined in many ways, but *profitability* from an economic standpoint is the most rigorous and measurable definition. The scientific evidence suggests that M&A *does* pay.

- The best measurable benchmark for evaluating any investment is the investors' required return, also known as the return that investors could have earned on other investment opportunities of similar risk.
  - Value is created when the returns on the investment exceed the required rate of return.
  - Value is destroyed when the investment returns fall short of the return rate required by investors.
  - Value is conserved when investors earn the "required rate of return": that which they expect to receive.
- The primary parties to an M&A transaction are the buying and selling companies. To evaluate value creation, one must consider the economic consequences of M&A transactions on the shareholders of both of the primary parties. These consequences are measured by researchers in four main ways from the standpoint of buyers and sellers.

  1. Event studies
  2. Accounting studies
  3. Surveys of executives
  4. Clinical studies

- Each research method has strengths and weaknesses, and some arguably offer more robust findings than others. The M&A scholar would be well served to look at various studies, using different methods and approaches, in order to glean some patterns of confirmation.
- Event studies, which examine the abnormal returns to shareholders in the period surrounding the announcement of an M&A transaction, yield insights about market-based returns to shareholders of target, buyer, and combined companies. The results of these studies provide the following key findings:
  - Shareholders of target firms receive "average abnormal" positive returns in the 20 to 30 percent range.

  - In the aggregate, market-adjusted returns to buyer shareholders essentially break even and value is conserved. In more than two-thirds of the studies, the buyer shareholders receive zero or positive event returns at the announcements of mergers. This suggests that most of the time the market thinks the investment will at least pay its way.
  - Shareholders who invest in the *combined* entity formed by an M&A transaction receive positive returns. This suggests that the transaction does create new value.

- Accounting studies, which analyze reported financial results of acquiring companies before and after acquisitions against comparable companies that did not make acquisitions, have brought to bear some enlightening points. These include:

  - Buyers outperform their benchmark leading up to an acquisition, which seems to occur near or at the peak of their financial performance.
  - After making an acquisition, buyers tend to perform worse than their peer benchmark on measures such as profit margins, growth rates, and returns on assets.
  - Targets tend to be profitable firms.
  - Anticipated gains of postmerger operating performance drive share prices at the time of a deal's announcement.

- The determinants of M&A profitability can be gleaned from cross-sectional research studies. Some key insights are:

  - Expected synergies are important drivers of wealth creation through merger.
  - When analysts and investors expect synergies, they price the benefits in their valuation.
  - Increased market share achieved through M&A does not create value.
  - Paying with stock is costly; paying with cash is neutral.
  - Hostile deals create more value for buyers than do friendly deals.
  - When managers have a greater economic interest, more value is created.

- The research findings of clinical studies underscore the importance of context and company-specific circumstances that can affect buyers and/or sellers. The role of strategic and organizational issues as well as financial implications should be considered in the evaluation of M&A deals.

- On balance, M&A is economically profitable for buyers, targets, and merging companies combined. M&A does pay. But buyers should be cautious. Though the averages suggest that most deals cover their cost of capital, there is a wide variation in results. Buyers should avoid overpaying and work very hard to achieve projected synergies.

CHAPTER 3—WORKBOOK QUESTIONS

Part I: Short Answer

1. *There are several different research methods of M&A profitability. Please briefly describe four examples, and the advantages and limitations of each method.*

2. *Will accounting-based studies and market return analyses reveal the same information regarding the value created by a merger? Why or why not?*

Part II: Questions on Real Business Situations

Case #1[1]

In October 2001, the J. M. Smucker Co.[2] agreed to purchase Jif peanut butter and Crisco cooking oil and shortening brands from Procter & Gamble[3] for $810 million in stock. P&G shareholders would receive one share of new Smucker stock for every 50 shares they held in P&G. This would shift 53 percent of Smucker stock into the hands of P&G shareholders, and would roughly double its total shares outstanding. However, the new arrangement called for existing Smucker shareholders to retain control over major decisions despite holding a minority share in the company.

Adding Jif and Crisco was expected to double Smucker's projected revenues to an estimated $1.3 billion in fiscal 2003. Due to the acquisition, Smucker's market share would rise to 41 percent in jam, 38 percent in peanut butter, and 24 percent in cooking oils.

At the time of the acquisition, Smucker did not have its own sales force. Because of its small size, it sold its products through brokers. Smucker had recently finished a three-year $35 million overhaul in its inventory and customer-service systems.

Analysts suspected that this would not be Smucker's last acquisition. The company held a cash balance of $67 million and was believed to have borrowing capacity for a further $500 million to $1 billion in debt.

Many expected P&G shareholders to sell their new Smucker shares. Because P&G was heavily owned by many index funds, this large constituent of P&G shareholders would have to unload Smucker stock because unlike P&G, Smucker was not in the Standard & Poor's 500-stock index. Other institutional investors, too, might sell if they believed Smucker would not be actively traded or enjoy good growth prospects.

The deal closed in June 2002. The chart shows the historical price of Smucker between September 2001 and June 2002.

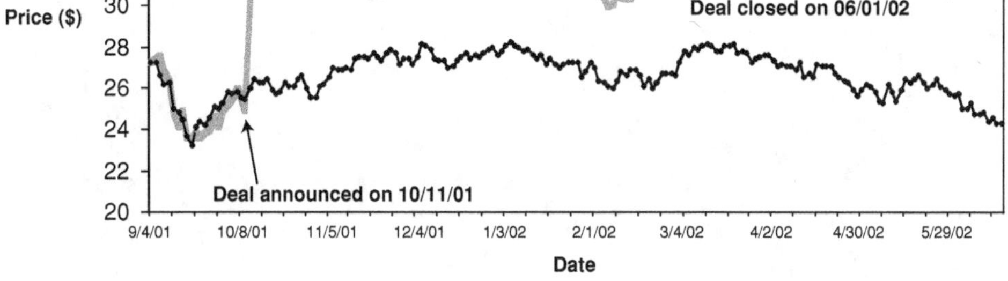

1. *Based solely on the information provided here and the general findings about acquisition returns in Chapter 3 of the main text, do you think this was a good acquisition for Smucker? Why or why not?*

Case #2

In 1997, Quaker Oats Co. agreed to sell Snapple Beverage Corp. to Triarc Cos. for $300 million—a little over two years after it had spent $1.7 billion to acquire the specialty drink maker. Three years later, in October 2000, Triarc sold the Snapple brand to Cadbury Schweppes for approximately $1 billion.

When Quaker made this purchase in 1994, the company believed it would be able to increase the value of the independent beverage producer and to enhance its revenue streams. At the time, however, the growth of the specialty beverage market was slowing, and huge rivals, such as Coca-Cola Co. and PepsiCo, were unleashing new products to compete against Snapple.

After Quaker completed the acquisition, Snapple had more than half of its sales at convenience stores, gas stations, and similar outlets, primarily on the East and West Coasts. Quaker decided to move beyond working with Snapple's small independent distributors in order to leverage its prowess in large-scale market distribution (i.e., supermarkets, mass merchants). Since Quaker's Gatorade drink had been selling well through mass distribution, the company expected that Snapple would meet similar success through those channels.

2. *How did the acquisition of Snapple turn out for Quaker and Triarc, respectively? What might explain Quaker's experience with Snapple? Is past success a good indicator of future experience?*

NOTES

1. *Source: Wall Street Journal*, October 11, 2001.
2. Smucker is the number one U.S. producer of jams, jellies, and preserves, and also makes dessert toppings, peanut butter, juices, and specialty fruit spreads under brand names.
3. Procter & Gamble is a large consumer-goods manufacturer that markets over 250 brands to nearly five billion consumers in over 140 countries. These brands include Tide, Crest, Pantene, Always, Pringles, Pampers, Olay, Folgers, Cover Girl, Downy, Dawn, Bounty, and Charmin.

CHAPTER 4

M&A Activity

This chapter explores the drivers of M&A activity in the economy. Of the many possible explanations, the role of "shocks" or economic turbulence offers the greatest traction for the practitioner seeking to understand why M&A appears in waves. The chapter surveys approaches for listening for the forces that drive M&A activity.

- Reflecting on M&A deals of the past helps us to learn and understand the drivers of M&A activity. While past M&A activity does not necessarily reflect the present or predict the future, it does provide key lessons that should be learned and analyzed for future application.
- M&A activity appears in waves, which follow a random walk and show no regularity in terms of period length or amplitude.
- Key points of each M&A wave in the preceding century include:

  Wave 1: 1895–1904
  - Characterized by horizontal mergers.
  - Coincided with a period of economic and capital market growth.
  - Firms sought to build market power in response to overcapacity.
  - Touched a wide variety of manufacturing industries.

  Wave 2: 1925–1929
  - Characterized by vertical integration mergers.
  - Coincided with a booming stock market, ended with the crash of 1929.
  - When large public utility holding companies emerged.
  - U.S. government increased its antitrust enforcement following passage of the Clayton Act of 1914.

  Wave 3: 1965–1970
  - Characterized by conglomerate or diversifying combinations.
  - Concentrated activity among a group of conglomerates and oil companies.
  - Coincided with a strong economy and the 1960s bull market.

  Wave 4a: 1981–1987
  - More hostile takeovers, leveraged deals, and going-private transactions than in prior waves.
  - Broad-based activity: touched virtually all sectors of the U.S. economy.
  - Financial and international buyers became more prominent players.

- Complexity of deals mirrored growing capital market innovation and sophistication.

Wave 4b: 1992–2000

- High M&A activity in banking, health care, defense, and high technology.
- Signaled a paradigm shift with new rules regarding M&A deal design and size.
- Significance of strategic buyers looking for synergies with target companies.

- Explanations for M&A activity are various; any explanation will entail a complicated, multifaceted story. Basically, these stories cluster into four categories:

1. ***Markets are rational but managers are irrational.*** An example of this view would be the "hubris hypothesis," which holds that managers know that great success in M&A is elusive, but do deals anyway out of sheer arrogance or in the belief that *they* have special capabilities. Markets know better, and punish the share prices of acquirers.
2. ***Markets and managers are irrational.*** By this view, M&A activity is simply herdlike behavior, much like the swarming of bees or flights of geese.
3. ***Markets are irrational but managers are rational.*** Share prices occasionally get overvalued. When managers, who have better inside information, see this, they use stock to make acquisitions. At other times they use cash. By this view, the stock market cycle drives M&A activity, an association confirmed by research.
4. ***Markets and managers are rational.*** M&A activity is driven by profit-seeing behavior on the part of managers and investors. For instance, periodically stimuli like new products, processes, or technologies "shock" the balance of competition in the industry. These shocks stimulate M&A activity. By this view, one should pay attention to forces of turbulence (shocks), such as deregulation, technological innovation, demographic change, trade liberalization, and so on.

- Of the four approaches, only the fourth lends much traction to the practitioner seeking to understand developments and do business. The other three may have some explanatory power at certain times and under certain conditions. But the fourth view, *turbulence*, stimulates an ongoing critical evaluation that can yield useful insights.

- Chapter 4 of the main text describes the turbulence perspective through the writings of four observers of M&A.

Entrepreneurs: Joseph Schumpeter and "Creative Destruction"

- Focuses on the role of the entrepreneur, who seeks to profit from new opportunities. This generates "creative destruction" in markets and ensures that market economies are self-renewing.
- Waves of creative destruction create business cycles.
- Similarly, creative destruction, in the form of industry "stocks" creates waves of M&A activity. This implies that to understand M&A activity, we should listen for shocks and turbulence at the level of firms and markets, not at the level of the economy.

Naomi Lamoreaux's History of the First Great Merger Wave

- M&A activity was triggered by the entry of new and more powerful technology. This technology hit capital intensive and mass-production firms the hardest.
- Large trusts emerged in response to industry shocks.
- Antitrust policy should have been aimed at minimizing the erection of entry barriers.

Reduction of Agency Costs: Michael Jensen's Explanation

- The wave of M&A activity in the 1980s and 1990s had its roots in problems that built up in the 1960s and 1970s, especially the accumulated effects of inflation, regulation, and the conglomerate merger wave.
- Cited the importance of deregulation, globalization of trade, and organizational innovation as triggers of recent M&A waves.

Practitioners' View: Bruce Wasserstein

- Five pistons drive the merger process: regulatory and political reform, technological change, fluctuations in financial markets, role of leadership, and tension between scale and focus.
- Booms in M&A can be traced to turbulence caused by one or more of the five pistons.

- In order to identify the role of turbulence in stimulating M&A activity, one should look for forms of economic shocks (deregulation, technology change, etc.) in specific industries.
- Capital markets (equity, debt, and derivative markets) are reliable messengers of economic turbulence.

CHAPTER 4—WORKBOOK QUESTIONS

1. *What might explain the association between the cycle of M&A activity and the cycle of the stock market?*

2. *Consider the following quotation from Schumpeter:*

   The fundamental impulse that sets and keeps the capitalist engine in motion comes from the new consumers, goods, the new methods of production or transportation, the new markets, the new forms of industrial organization that capitalist enterprise creates."

   —Joseph Schumpeter, *Capitalism, Socialism and Democracy*, 1942, pp. 82–83

What role does the entrepreneur play in keeping the capitalist engine in motion?

3. *According to Schumpeter:*

   Railroads did not emerge because any consumers took the initiative in displaying an effective demand for their service in preference to the services of the mail

> *coaches. Railroads were forced by producers on consumers who, most often than not, have resisted the change and have had to be educated.*
>
> —Joseph Schumpeter, *Business*, p. 73

Do innovations arise because of consumers' needs or wants, or because the producers force the innovations on the consumer? What are the implications for the entrepreneur?

4. *Read the following fictional case and answer the questions that follow.*

Case

Mara Davis, a broadcast journalist, is interviewing Matthew Adams, the CEO of High Tech Telecom, Inc., an acquisitive telecom company that has been engaged in a few mergers in the past few years.

Background

In 1999, Adams, the CEO of Long Lines Telephone, spent $80 billion to acquire two giant cable companies, Wire Squires and Best Brand Broadband, in order to put Long Lines in the broadband business. Since Long Lines was facing declining margins in its core long-distance business, its stated goal was to achieve operational synergies which could bundle cable, Internet, wireless, and telephone services.

A year later, Long Lines' stock price plummeted with the Internet collapse. Adams decided to restructure the company and break up the consolidated businesses back into separate units, which were sold.

Now, CEO Adams is proposing another mega-merger with another cable giant, Power-line, Inc., which would give Long Lines access to a significant share of the U.S. cable customer base. However, the deal is uniquely designed: The merger would be structured so that the combined cable unit would be spun off as a separate venture. The CEO of Power-line, David Rollins, would be the CEO of this spun-off entity, with Adams at his side as the chairman. Rollins would get 33 percent of the new voting shares.

Shortly after Adams' announcement of this deal, journalist Davis conducted the following interview of Adams:

Interview

JOURNALIST: *A common view that people hold is that M&A activity is dictated by forces of change in the economy that enable companies to take advantage of particularly favorable circumstances and opportunities. However, some people claim that mergers happen because CEOs and senior management really push to complete deals for more personal reasons. What is your take on this?*

CEO: I can say with certainty that my company's acquisitions are motivated by economic and strategic reasons. In fact, I believe that most company mergers are driven for the purpose of creating value, regardless of the hearsay that circulates the market. In particular, acquisitive companies like my own will not put in the time, energy, and resources to complete a deal that does not enhance their business operations and financial results. All it takes is one bad merger to set a company back, and then make it more difficult in the future to transact successful subsequent acquisitions.

JOURNALIST: *Three years ago, you made two significant acquisitions of two cable companies. A year after the acquisitions, you reversed your decision by break-*

ing up the assets of your company. Why did you do this, if you claim your acquisitions are based on sound economic and strategic reasons?

CEO: The two acquisitions we made three years back were made in favorable economic conditions: the stock market was at a peak, interest rates were low, and GDP [gross domestic product] was strong. I expected that the mergers would help us realize significant synergies, better margins, and ultimately, better profits.

However, the economy took an unexpected turn for the worse when the technology bubble burst. Our industry was certainly one that experienced particularly great pains and repercussions of the technology market tumbling. Even though the two acquisitions were made on sound economic and strategic reasoning, conditions changed dramatically. Sometimes drastic changes will dictate that other actions be taken to preserve value. That is what I did when I broke up the assets of the company.

JOURNALIST: *But isn't it possible that managers of acquisitive companies make merger decisions based on their own personal agendas, and just stand behind other outward claims for why a merger is taking place?*

CEO: Good M&A initiatives are based on strategic business goals, not the personal agendas of managers. At Long Lines, we employ strategies for long-term success and value creation. We also realize that our shareholders and the public eye scrutinize all of our M&A transactions and for that reason alone we would not make false outward claims to justify merger decisions.

JOURNALIST: *So explain the reasons for this new proposed merger. Why are you proposing an acquisition of another cable company when you already tried buying two cable companies and ended up selling them shortly after?*

CEO: Well, the circumstances in our industry and the overall economy have changed, and we believe that Long Lines is now in a position to make a successful cable acquisition that will create meaningful value for our company. We do not expect to see another market disruption like the 2001 technology bubble burst. Since 2001, investors have taken on a much more conservative and skeptical view about technology stocks. Even though we would like to restore investor confidence, we believe that the events of the past few years have taken the extreme volatility out of the capital markets. While we may never again see valuations of technology stocks rise at the speed and magnitude of the late 1990s, we also doubt we will see them fall in the same manner.

The proposed merger with Power-line is based on value creation, plain and simple. Cable continues to be a high-margin business, whereas the more mature long-distance telephone and wireless services have been experiencing lower growth and profitability.

4a. *Analyze the interview between the journalist and the CEO. What views or sentiments do the journalist's questions convey? What is the CEO's stance on M&A activity, as revealed in his answers?*

4b. *Which view of M&A activity do you think holds more credence? If you were to enter the conversation, what position would you take? How would you explain what drives M&A activity?*

5. *Read the following case and answer the question that follows. This is drawn from an actual situation.*

Case

In November 2002, Level 3 Communications announced that it would acquire nearly all of Genuity Inc.'s assets. To facilitate the transaction, Genuity filed voluntary petitions for reorganization under Chapter 11 of the Bankruptcy Code.

In December, Level 3 Communications received approval from the U.S. Department of Justice and the Federal Trade Commission to acquire Genuity Inc. Under the Telecommunications Act of 1996, any entity may enter a telecommunications market.

As a result of the transaction, which was completed in February 2003, Level 3 now operates one of the largest Internet backbones in the world and is the primary provider of Internet connectivity for millions of dial-up and broadband subscribers. As of March 2003, the company had a total of 73 markets in service: 57 in the United States and 16 in Europe. This was up sharply from December 2002, when the company had operational facilities in 27 U.S. markets and 9 European markets.

Level 3's CEO attested, "There is a unique and compelling fit between Genuity and Level 3. The transaction combines the assets and operations of Genuity, the company that helped invent the Internet, with Level 3, the company that built the first network fully optimized for Internet Protocol–based communications. . . . Genuity operates an international IP network. Its largest customers are Verizon Communications and America Online. . . . The transaction adds substantial new revenue from high-quality customers and creates value by generating significant network and operating cost synergies for the combined business, as well as reductions in capital expenditures."

The CEO also noted that the agreement with Genuity was consistent with Level 3's overall acquisition strategy, "As we have said in the past, we evaluate every potential acquisition according to its ability to generate positive cash flow from high-quality customers. We look for opportunities to acquire recurring revenues that come predominantly from services we already provide in geographic areas that we already serve, with customers consistent with our existing customer base. Above all we are committed to remaining fully funded to free cash flow breakeven and improving our financial position."

The acquisition was believed to accelerate Level 3's projected time to positive free cash flow to early 2004.

Company Information

Level 3 is an international communications and information services company. It operates the world's first international network optimized end-to-end for IP packet switching technology. Genuity is a leading provider of managed IP networking services for businesses. The company offers a full portfolio of services, including Internet access, Internet security, and Virtual Private Networks (VPNs).

As of July 2002, Genuity Inc. had doubted its ability to stay in business: The company had recently defaulted on a $2 billion line of credit and a $1.15 billion loan from Verizon Communications Corp. The default came after Verizon decided not to exercise its option to take a controlling stake in Genuity.

5. *Identify one or more potential sources of turbulence for Level 3's acquisition of Genuity, Inc., and briefly explain how the turbulence may have created a merger opportunity.*

CHAPTER 5

Cross-Border M&A

Countries differ in important ways that will affect the values of firms. Beneath every cross-border valuation analysis is some hidden assumption or "bet" about the future of a country market. Given the ubiquity of cross-border deals, a good M&A practitioner should seek to master cross-border analysis.

- Research has found that cross-border transactions have a different profile compared to domestic deals: Cross-border transactions tend to:
  - Be more related to the buyer's core industry.
  - Be paid for mainly in cash. Many cross-border buyers do not have shares listed for trading in the foreign market. Thus, buyers tend to pay with cash rather than stock.
  - Involve targets that are mainly manufacturing firms with low intangible assets.
- Following are some of the forces that drive cross-border M&A activity:
  - Exploiting market imperfections. Buyers may recognize profitable opportunities to take advantage of cheap labor and raw materials, unmet consumer demand, deregulation, trade liberalization, and country integration of capital and product markets into global markets.
  - Extending the reach of intangible assets. Firms with significant intangible assets such as brand name and patents may want to broaden the scale of their use and preempt others who might be tempted to imitate or appropriate those intangible assets.
  - Reducing tax expense through arbitrage across different tax jurisdictions.
  - Reducing risk through diversification. If economic activity across countries is less than perfectly correlated, geographic diversification can reduce risk.
  - Exploiting differences in capital market and currency conditions.
  - Improving governance. M&A is a means by which companies can exit from a poor governance environment.
- The M&A practitioner must have a "view" about a country in which an acquisition is contemplated. Such a view will be informed by insights about:
  - Expected economic growth in the country and region.
  - Foundations of the country's competitive advantage.
  - Outlook for inflation, interest rates, and exchange rates.

- Relative valuation of assets.
- Risks.

- Macroeconomic analysis of a country should cover the following aspects:
  - Fiscal policy.
  - Monetary policy.
  - Exchange rate policy.
  - Intervention policy.
  - Trade policy.
  - Employment and welfare policy.
- Microeconomic analysis of a country considers activity at the level of industries and firms. Michael Porter argues that country performance is essentially a matter of microeconomic performance. His "diamond model" of competitive advantage asserts that the ability to innovate and to improve productivity resides in the following:
  - ***Factor conditions.*** These regard the inputs of production, such as labor, land, natural resources, physical facilities, infrastructure, human resources, and intellectual capital. The analyst should assess how specialized a nation's factors are, and how tailored they are to the needs of the acquisition target.
  - ***Demand conditions.*** The home-market demand for the goods or services of an industry will heavily influence the international success of that industry. The best home demand arises from discerning and sophisticated customers.
  - ***Related or supporting industries.*** Porter maintains that the presence of strong upstream and downstream industries can create industry clusters that in turn enhance a nation's competitive advantage.
  - ***Domestic rivalry.*** Competition tends to strengthen the international competitiveness of local industries. The level of competition can be assessed by measuring concentration ratios, evaluating entry barriers, and analyzing the patterns of competition within an industry/country.
- Institutional economics emphasizes the important role played in national economic growth by a range of institutions that are not direct producers of growth. These institutions include:
  - Banking.
  - Stock markets and investment regulations.
  - Watchdogs: auditors, free press, opposition political parties.
  - Independent judiciary, rule of law, respect for contracts and property rights.
  - Educational system.
- Economic growth may also be influenced by cultural factors such as willingness to pay and receive interest, respect for entrepreneurs, consumerism, emphasis on education, and saving.

CHAPTER 5—WORKBOOK QUESTIONS

1. You are the head of strategic planning for a large U.S. telecommunications firm. In early 2003, you held a planning session with your firm's executive committee in order to flesh out a 10-year vision for your company. The conclusion from that session was that your firm needs to expand overseas if it wants to grow. After analyzing the demographics in several regions, you decide that Southeast Asia offers the greatest growth prospects: It is young, has underserved telecommunications needs, and presents less competition as opposed to the U.S. market.

   You are contemplating either a 100 percent acquisition or a joint venture agreement with a local firm. From having been in the business many years, you have established good relationships with a couple of telecommunications firms in the Philippines and in Thailand. These two countries would therefore be a logical start to your Southeast Asian strategy.

   To begin, you gather some social and economic data as of 2001 and recent economic reports, on the two countries. Now you are ready to perform a preliminary analysis. Here are summary tables of comparative information between the Philippines and Thailand, followed by individual reports and statistics on each country.

1a. *Based on the information here, provide a comparative analysis of both countries.*

1b. *Which country would you invest in? Why? Would you do a 100 percent acquisition or a joint venture? Why?*

1c. *What other information would you like to have, to complete the framework shown in Exhibit 5.12 of the main text?*

	Philippines	Thailand	East Asia & Pacific (Where Available)
Poverty and social			
Population (millions)	85.0	62.0	1,826.0
Surface area (thousand sq. km.)	300.0	513.1	
Population per sq. km.	283.3	119.0	
Population growth	1.90%	0.80%	1.10%
Life expectancy	69	69	69
Population below national poverty line	26%	16.10%	
Urban population as % of total	59	20	37
Infant mortality (per 1,000 live births)	31	28	36
Child malnutrition	32	18	12
Illiteracy (% of population age 15+)	5%	4%	14%
Economics			
GDP (US$ billions)	71	115	
GNI per capita (US$)	1,050	1,970	

(Continued)

	Philippines	Thailand	East Asia & Pacific (Where Available)
Gross domestic investment/GDP	18.0	24.0	
Exports of goods and services/GDP	49.3	66.3	
Gross domestic savings/GDP	19.4	30.1	
Gross national savings/GDP	26.0	28.7	
Current account balance/GDP	6.3	5.4	
Interest payments/GDP	3.5	3.0	
Total debt/GDP	73.3	58.5	
Total debt service/exports	18.7	20.5	
Other			
Form of government	Republic	Constitutional monarchy	
Corruption perceptions index, 2002 (rank out of 102 countries, 1 being the highest)	77.0	64.0	

Sources of data: World Bank web site, "Countries and Regions" section; Transparency International.

Infrastructure	Thailand	Philippines
Telecommunications:		
General assessment	Service to general public adequate but investment in technological upgrades reduced by recession	Good international radiotelephone and submarine cable services; domestic service adequate
Telephone—main lines in use	5.6 million (2000)	3.1 million (2000)
Telephone—mobile cellular	3.1 million (2002)	6.5 million (2000)
Number of Internet users	1.2 million (2001)	4.5 million (2002)
Transportation:		
Railways (km)	4,071	897
Highways (km)		
Total	64,000	199,950
Paved	62,985	39,590
Unpaved	1,615	160,360
Airports (number)	110	275
Number of towns/cities with ports and harbors	7	15

Source of data: CIA web site.

[These spreadsheets can be found in the folder "Key Spreadsheets from the Workbook" located on the CD-ROM.]

The Philippines

Development Progress
The Philippines made significant progress in reducing poverty between 1990 and 1997, when the incidence of poverty fell sharply from 34 percent in 1991 to 25 percent in 1997. Much of this improvement occurred in 1994–1997 when economic growth averaged 5 percent per annum. In contrast, from 1998 to 2001 economic growth averaged only 2.5 percent and poverty reduction stagnated; preliminary data suggest that poverty incidence in 2000 is about 26 percent.

. . .

Recent Developments and Current Challenges
The Philippines had gone through a turbulent political period from 1999 to early 2001, with modest economic growth, weak poverty reduction performance, and faltering investor confidence, undermined by governance concerns. Since a new administration assumed power in January 2001, public confidence has increased with the pursuit of sound macroeconomic policies, and governance and structural reforms. The new administration has also emphasized a "peace and development" approach to conflict-affected Mindanao,* since the resurgence of violence there in 2000.

The Philippines' main challenge for the medium term remains poverty reduction. Poverty is still largely a rural phenomenon, attributed to: high dependence on agriculture where productivity has been declining and per capita economic growth is low; lack of adequate social safety nets, especially for poor women and children; and low educational attainment due to relatively high dropout rates and poor educational quality. Population pressures and a declining natural resource base have exacerbated these problems.

Despite lackluster performance in financial markets domestically and abroad, the real economy has enjoyed relatively robust performance during the first half of 2002 with GDP growing at 4.1 percent annually. Agriculture, trade, and telecommunications performed particularly strongly. The first semester of 2002 saw exports grow by 4.3 percent (year-on-year), while imports grew 3.4 percent, reflecting renewed growth in electronic exports and domestic demand for capital replenishment and consumer durables. Meanwhile, buoyed by strong workers remittances, consumption has played a key role in supporting domestic demand.

Aided by a steady decline in the inflation rate (2.6 percent in July 2002, year-on-year), the monetary authorities were able to lower key interest rates by 800 basis points since the end of 2000, and this has allowed banks to lower lending rates. Moreover, portfolio investment for the first four months of 2002 showed a turnaround from a net negative position of $884 million in 2001 to $1.7 billion this year. Net foreign direct investment also increased (by 86 percent) in the first four months of 2002, to $1.5 billion compared to $808 million for the same period in 2001.

Recent data on the financial market, however, is not as upbeat. Nonperforming

---

*Mindanao is the southern region of the Philippines.

Source of the Philippines country description: World Bank web site, "Countries and Regions" section. *Note:* ". . ." indicates portions taken out. World Bank Online by World Bank.

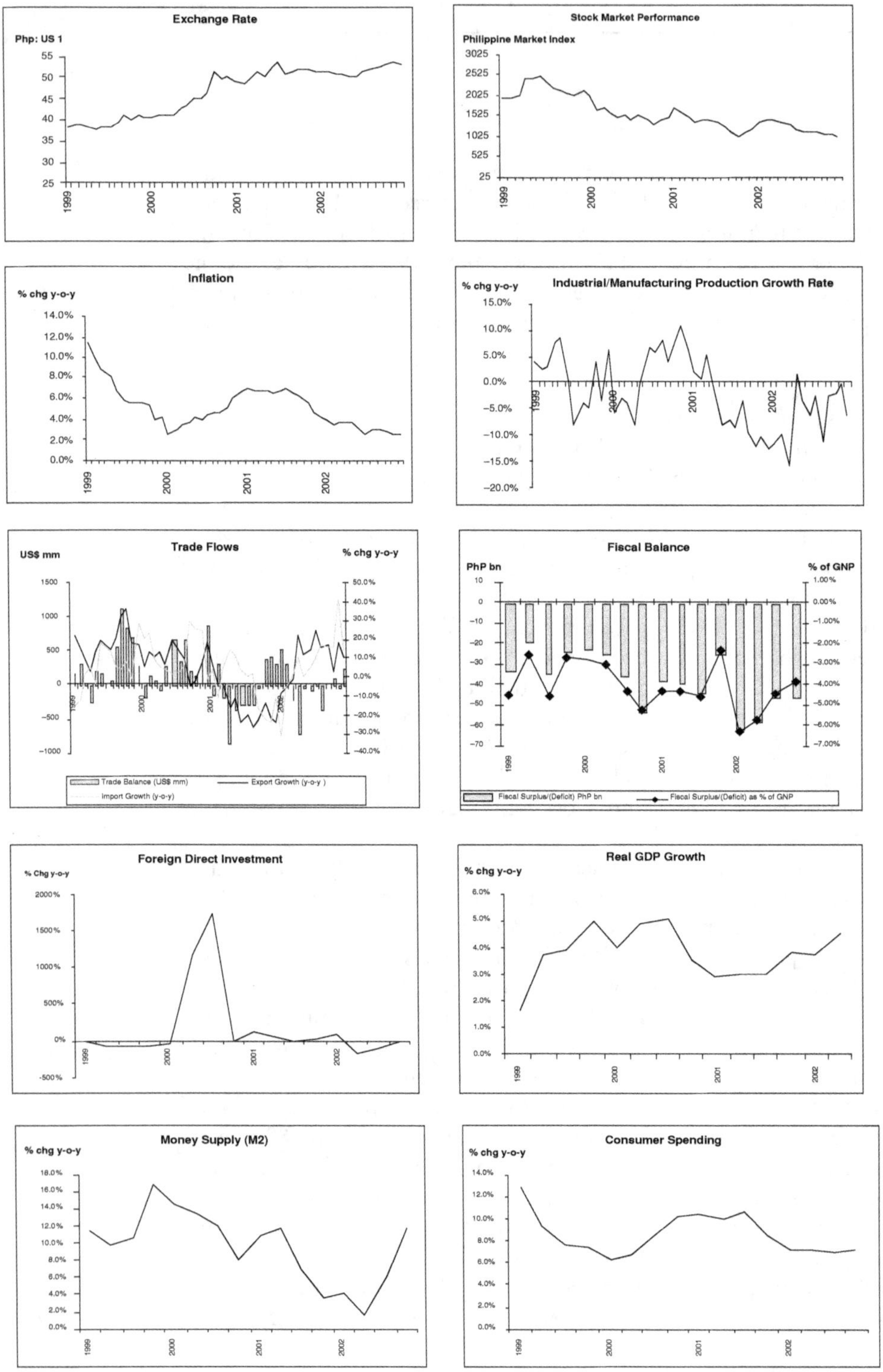

The Philippines Economic Indicators

[This spreadsheet can be found in the folder "Key Spreadsheets from the Workbook" located on the CD-ROM.]

loans (NPLs) of the banking sector have risen to 18 percent in June 2002, from 17 percent a year ago. The Philippine stock market composite index has fallen by 23 percent over the March–August 2002 period, under very thin volumes (average of $5.8 million a day). Spreads on government bonds have also gone up in recent months (e.g., spreads on Eurobonds maturing in 2008 have risen to 460 basis points, after having fallen from 644 in December 2000 to 305 basis points in May 2002). Also, the peso has depreciated slightly since mid-2002.

At the heart of the financial market's concern is fiscal policy discipline. The government budget deficit for the first seven months of 2002 (P133 billion) has already breached its full-year target of P130 billion. Higher spending during the first half of the year to support economic recovery and to maintain the needed basic social expenditures and weak revenue collection have both contributed to the deficit. This revenue shortfall is a key concern of government. Without an improvement in revenue collection, the government will find it hard to sustain the needed expenditures for health, education, and other basic social services, and it will find it hard to absorb increased Official Development Assistance.

In an effort to strengthen fiscal management, the government has continued to work on longer-term structural reforms and efforts to reverse the slide in revenues. In particular, the procurement bill is now at advanced stages of deliberation in the Senate. This will lend strong support to efforts to strengthen expenditure management and to make every peso count. Second, key leaders of Congress recently sponsored a bill to create an Internal Revenue Management Authority (IRMA). The bill proposes to establish an organization that will increase managerial flexibility and strengthen performance review and accountabilities of the primary revenue collection agency of government. These two proposed legislations will help support government's efforts to strengthen fiscal management.

Thailand

Progress in the Last Decade

Following the crisis,* Thailand began to implement deep reform of the financial sector, corporate governance, the secured lending regime, and competition policy to strengthen the incentive for owners of banks and firms to move toward their competitive frontiers. The resilience of the Thai economy facilitated a quick recovery of economic growth and the numbers in poverty began to fall. After contracting by more than 10 percent in 1998, Thailand's economy grew at over 4 percent in 1999 and 2000—and stayed positive at 1.8 percent in 2001, in spite of the global slowdown.

In 1999–2000, aided by the fiscal stimulus and increased external demand, poverty fell by 2 percentage points. Nearly a million people bounced back out of poverty following the recovery of economic growth.

Thailand Government, led by the Prime Minister's Thai Rak Thai party, which has a majority in the Parliament, won the national election on a pro-poor, pro-rural,

---

*The Asian financial crisis that began in 1997.

Source of the Thailand country description: World Bank web site, "Countries and Regions" section. *Note:* ". . ." indicates portions taken out.

and pro-Thailand platform. Notably, this administration is the first to be elected to office under the new Constitution. . . . The Government is in the process of putting forward its medium-term strategies through the Ninth Plan, which focuses on poverty reduction and balanced development.

Thailand's Monarch has set out an agenda for the nation to address the problems of the poor by promoting the idea of a community-driven, self-sufficiency economy. The King has also spoken out against corruption and for the improved management of natural resources. The Senate is playing an increasingly important role as is the new National Social and Economic Council in providing more checks and balances as the country moves forward under the new Constitution.

Current Challenges

Thailand, however, faces a considerably unfinished agenda. With the downturn in the United States and Japan, the country's economic growth has not returned to precrisis levels, although 2002 growth rates are expected to be in the range of 3.5 to 4 percent, assisted by strong domestic consumption. Progress in financial and corporate sector reform has been affected by lagging corporate debt restructuring. . . .

Thailand also faces the challenge of implementing the new Constitution. The Constitution considerably strengthens democratic and accountability institutions such as the National Counter-Corruption Commission, Electoral Commission, and Administrative Courts, but many of those institutions have come under attack. The electoral process has been revamped with a directly elected Senate and a reformed system of parliamentary representation. Civil society has gained greater recognition and voice and is becoming a more powerful participant in the policy debate, and the media is among the freest in the region. However, the public continues to regard weak governance—and in particular corruption—as a major impediment to economic and social development.

The problems of the poor have also been compounded by the crisis. Until the onset of the crisis in 1997, high growth rates in Thailand had pulled poverty rates down from 32.6 percent of the population in 1988 to 11.4 percent in 1996, lifting nearly a million people out of poverty every year. But much of this progress came to a halt in 1997. In a total population of 61 million, the number of poor increased during the crisis from 6.8 million in 1996 to 9.8 million in 1999. The Northeast, the poorest region of the country, experienced a drop in income that was twice the national average.

Substantial environmental damage, a by-product of Thailand's rapid development over the last 30 years and weak environmental institutions, has also hurt the poor disproportionately. One-third of the surface water is unsuitable for human consumption or agricultural use. Half of the forest cover has been lost. Air pollution in Bangkok exceeds standards twofold, and industrial hazardous waste generation has hit 1.6 million tons per year.

The poor in Thailand could also benefit greatly from faster progress in the area of governance, affording them more security, opportunity, and greater voice. Governance is one of the four pillars of the Government's Ninth Plan, which is underpinned by a multifaceted poverty reduction strategy that operates through the four pillars of social protection, competitiveness, governance, and environmental protection in a holistic framework.

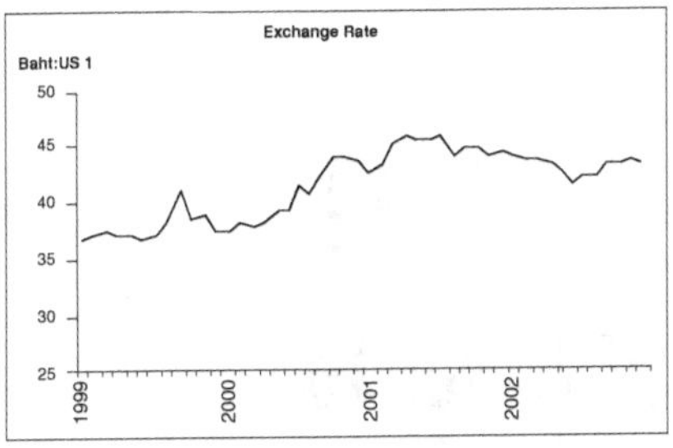

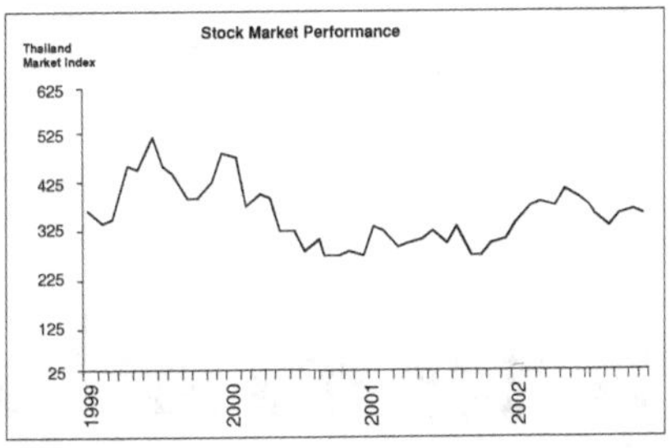

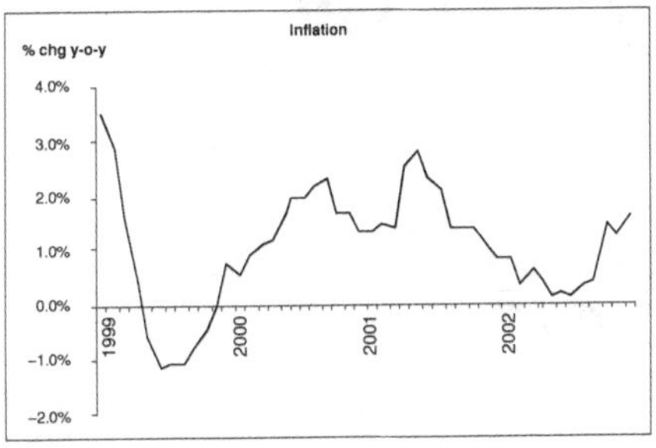

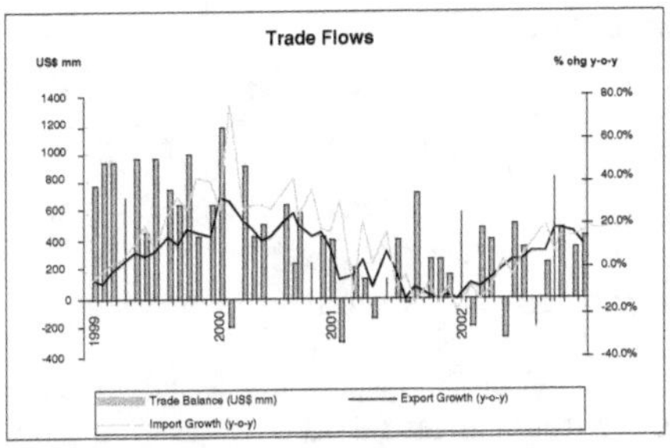

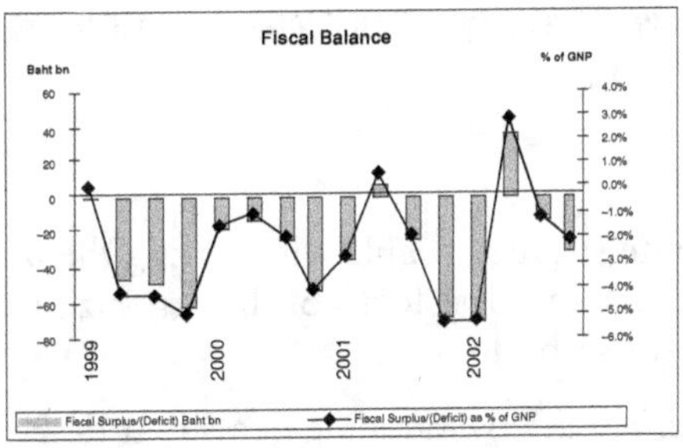

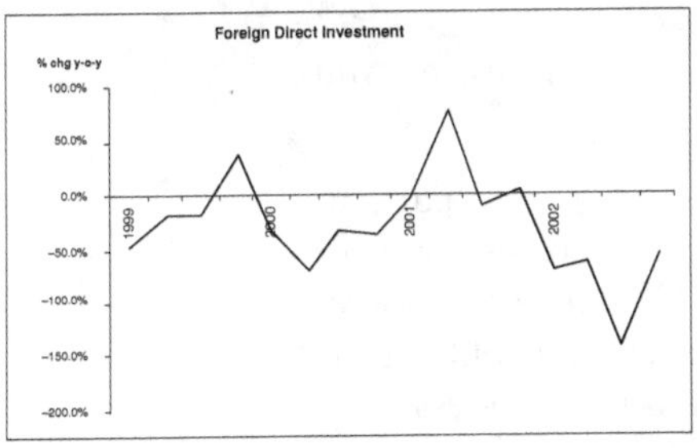

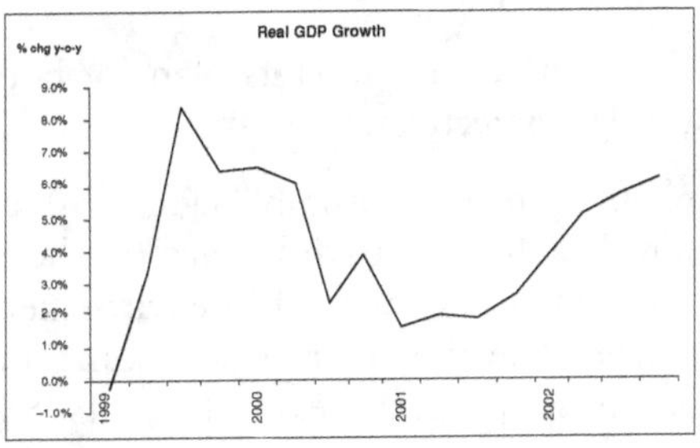

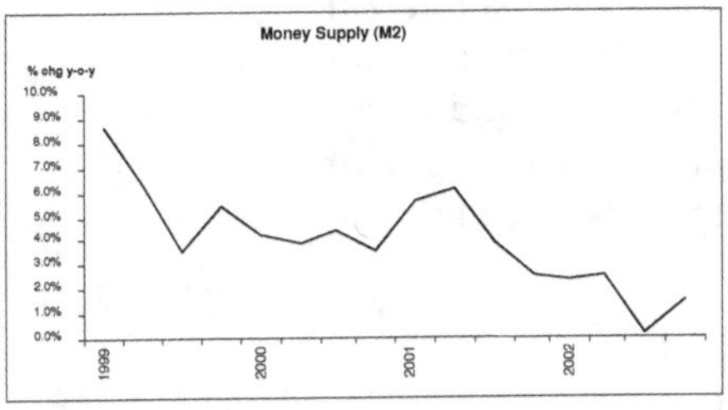

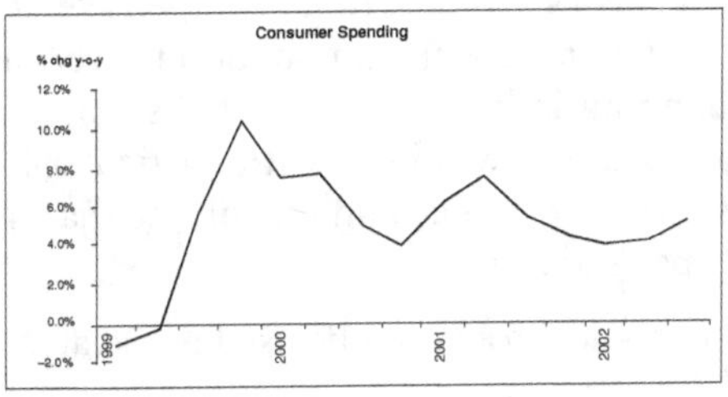

Thailand Economic Indicators

[This spreadsheet can be found in the folder "Key Spreadsheets from the Workbook" located on the CD-ROM.]

CHAPTER 6

Strategy and the Uses of M&A to Grow or Restructure the Firm

M&A is one of the tactical instruments by which a company can pursue an inorganic growth strategy (growth outside of the firm). The various alternatives in addition to M&A include contractual agreements, alliances, joint ventures, and minority investments.

The choice among these alternatives is driven by strategic decisions. Furthermore, the design of good M&A transactions always takes root in good strategy.

- Setting corporate strategy begins with setting the *mission* for the enterprise. A mission defines the business focus of the organization, and implicitly tells what the enterprise does *not* do.
- *Strategic objectives* are overarching goals that flesh out the strategic intent and set the direction of the firm.
- The *corporate strategy* for a firm is its plan for both fulfilling its mission and achieving its strategic objectives.
- The strategic planning process usually begins with an *assessment* of a particular business unit. This focuses both inward on the condition and resources of the unit, and outward on the shape of its environment and the unit's position in the competitive field. The aim of strategic assessment is to draw a profile of the strengths, weaknesses, opportunities, and threats (SWOT) of the business.
- Determining the firm's *position* in its competitive environment and its *internal resources and capabilities* is the foundation for setting strategy. This assessment includes profiling an industry (especially, its competitive structure) and determining a firm's position within it, with particular attention to the intensity of firm rivalry, sources of change and turbulence that may trigger a shift in the industry landscape, and so on.
- A number of analytical tools can be used for strategic planning:
  - The *growth-share matrix* is used to determine and analyze the relative positions of firms in an industry or divisions within a firm along three dimensions: size, growth, and relative share of market. The matrix delineates four broad categories of industry positions: cash cow, star, dog, and problem child (also known as "question mark").

- *Michael Porter's framework* characterizes industry structure and competitive conduct as drivers of competitive success in an industry. Specifically, he highlights the role of *five forces* as driving/influencing economic attractiveness of an industry: (1) barriers to entry, (2) customer power, (3) supplier power, (4) threat of substitutes, and (5) rivalry conduct.
- A *strategic map*, like a growth-share matrix, positions the players in an industry on the basis of size and two other dimensions that are strategically meaningful.
- A *strategic canvas* illustrates in graphic form the similarity or difference among competitors' strategies.
- The *attractiveness-strength matrix* is a tool used to assess both the attractiveness of an industry and the attractiveness of a position in the industry. It addresses the question: "How do returns vary with industry position and industry attractiveness?"
- The *self-sustainable growth rate (SSGR)* is a test of fit between the firm's current capabilities and its aspirations, and the maximum internally sustainable rate of asset growth will be a direct result of the firm's profitability and retention rate.

- All of the strategic analytic tools are *judgment-intensive*. They depend crucially upon proper definition of the "business" and the "peer group" being studied.
- There are *three classic strategies* that seem to yield competitive advantage: low-cost leadership, differentiation, and focus or specialization.
- In considering how to expand a business, executives first must make the classic "make versus buy" decision. They need to decide whether to grow *organically* (i.e., through internal investment) or *inorganically* (i.e., by investing or structuring an affiliation outside the firm).
- Inorganic growth may be employed to:
  - Grow in the context of a maturing product line.
  - Grow by circumventing regulatory or antitrust limits.
  - Create value through horizontal or vertical integration.
  - Acquire unique resources and capabilities.
  - Create value through diversification.
- Diversification might pay if it promotes knowledge transfer across divisions, reduces costs, creates critical mass for facing the competition, and/or exploits better transparency and monitoring through internal capital markets. Diversifying mergers may also have a greater likelihood of success with the following conditions: When there is high relatedness in terms of industry focus between the target and buyer, when managers are properly motivated and rewarded, where the local capital market is less effective, where product markets are experiencing an episode of deregulation or other turbulence, and when one or both firms have significant information-based assets.

- While considering growth by M&A, the executive should also regard the relative costs and benefits of at least four other avenues for inorganic growth: contractual relationships, strategic alliances, joint ventures, and minority stakes.

    1. ***Contractual relationships*** are the simplest of all inorganic expansions. These relationships can take many forms: licensing agreements, co-marketing agreements, co-development agreements, joint purchasing agreements, franchising, and long-term supply or toll agreement.
    2. ***Strategic alliances*** are typically more complicated and express a more serious commitment between the parties. Sometimes alliances entail cross-shareholding agreements between the allies.
    3. ***A joint venture (JV)*** creates a separate entity in which a firm and the counterparty will invest.
    4. A ***minority investment*** is the direct investment into the counterparty firm, rather than into an intermediate firm (like the joint venture).

- Research findings about joint ventures, alliances, and minority equity investments indicate:

    - Alliances are more likely than acquisitions where the risk of the venture is greater than the risk of the partner's core business.
    - Whole ownership is most common when firms coordinate integrated production activities across different locations, transfer technology, and benefit from worldwide tax planning.
    - Like M&A, joint ventures, alliances, and minority equity investments are, on average, profitable for targets, a break-even proposition for purchasers, and, for both target and purchaser combined, an economically positive activity.
    - Joint venture partners do better when buyers have good investment opportunities, the JV increases focus for the buyer, and/or the JV reduces agency costs and returns.

- *Restructuring* is a lengthy process that may entail selling assets, closing plants, streamlining operations, or exiting an industry entirely—all with a goal of improving returns and the prospects for the firm's survival. *Industry turbulence* of the kinds outlined in Chapter 4 of the main text typically stimulates restructuring activity. Other motives could be: to sharpen strategic focus, to correct "mistakes" and harvest "learning," to correct the market valuation of assets, to improve the internal capital market, to reduce tax expenses, to strengthen managerial incentives/align them with the interests of shareholders, to respond to capital market discipline, and to gain financing when external funds are limited.

- The possible transactions to restructure, redeploy, or sell also span a wide range of alternatives: sale of minority interest, sale of joint venture interest, divestiture or asset sale, carve-out, spin-off, split-off or exchange, tracking stock, and financial recapitalization.

- Research studies on the profitability of unit divestitures, asset sales, and liquidation indicate:

- Announcements of divestitures create value for shareholders of sellers, on the order of a 1 to 3 percent significant abnormal return.
- It is the redeployment of assets that matters, not merely the sale. The market seems to reward divestitures that focus the firm. Firms selling assets tend to suffer from lower profitability or high leverage.

- Research on the profitability of carve-outs, spin-offs, split-offs, and tracking stock indicates:
  - Investment behavior and financial performance of firms improves following the spin-off.
  - Relatedness matters in the choice of transaction. The more unrelated the unit, the greater the likelihood that it will be separated from the parent.
  - The findings are consistent with benefits of increased focus.
  - The types of transactions do differ in their effects.
  - As with divestitures, deployment of funds raised in these transactions makes a difference.
  - The restructuring has an impact on the rivals of the firm.
  - Firms will favor carve-outs over divestitures when the parent's shares are relatively undervalued and the subsidiary's shares are relatively overvalued. Thus, a sale of equity in the subsidiary would become a signal to investors of the parent's undervaluation.
- Some key considerations in choosing a *decision path for inorganic growth*: (1) benefits from a relationship: learning and coordination gains, (2) need for ownership and control, and (3) management of risk exposure. These three criteria convey the complexity of the choice. These considerations illustrate the following common lessons: one kind of transaction does not fit all needs, the choice among the alternatives is a logical result of balancing important considerations, retain a bias for simplicity, consider starting small, and remember value creation.
- The selection among *alternatives for restructuring* should be influenced by the following considerations: relationship to the core business of the parent, need for control, and whether the business or asset can operate as an independent entity. To complete any strategic analysis of alternatives, one must assess the implications of each choice for shareholder value.
- One of the robust debates today deals with whether and how the strategic efforts to diversify or focus the firm pay. Profitability varies by type of diversification strategy: As firms have moved from great focus (a "single business" strategy) to great diversity (an "unrelated business" strategy), the accounting returns of firms have varied materially by type of strategy. Early studies showed that a strategy of relatedness in diversification yielded higher accounting returns. Recent studies offer a more complicated judgment still somewhat in favor of the benefits of focus and relatedness.
- The practical implication of research is that one should diversify only where there is a sound economic rationale: strong relatedness, strong internal capital markets, where local capital markets are less effective, where there is significant

turbulence in the industry, and/or where one or both firms have significant information-based assets. Overall, the value creation discipline is vital.

- The design of good M&A transactions takes root in good strategy. Analysis of positions and capabilities should underpin the effort to profile your firm's strengths, weaknesses, opportunities, and threats (SWOT).
- Restructuring activity is a significant source of M&A activity, but divestiture is only one of the tactical instruments of a strategy of restructuring. Other alternatives include liquidations, minority investments, spin-offs, carve-outs, split-offs, and tracking stock.
- The survey of research establishes that restructuring creates value: divestiture, spin-offs, carve-outs, and tracking stock are associated with significant positive returns at the announcement of those transactions.
- The practitioner should think critically about blanket assertions made about whether there is more value in a strategy of diversification or one of focus. Perhaps the most value is created by responding appropriately (with diversification or focusing) as the situation requires.

CHAPTER 6—WORKBOOK QUESTIONS

1. *What is strategy and why is it important in M&A? How does one use strategy in M&A?*

2. *You are the head of strategic planning for your firm. You are currently trying to analyze three different projects. What strategic analysis tools would you use for each?*

    1. *Your firm has decided to enter a new market to expand the business. You need to assess the ability to earn high returns in that market.*
    2. *You are reassessing the market position of your product relative to its competitors as you prepare to launch an advertising campaign.*
    3. *You are trying to decide whether to keep or sell one of your business units. The decision will depend on your view of how well the unit can compete in its industry, and whether it will survive the competition.*

3. *Identify drivers of value that would influence the choice of diversification versus focus. How do these drivers create value for diversified companies?*

4. *Define organic and inorganic growth. What are the circumstances under which each growth method is particularly appropriate?*

5. *Conventional wisdom says that diversification destroys value. Why has this view been challenged? What evidence is there that shows that diversification may actually create value?*

6. You are the CEO of a publicly listed fast-food chain with both domestic and international operations. Protection and growth of the brand are vitally important to your firm. Therefore, quality control of food and service is paramount. Strength of relationship with the operating units is important as a basis for transferring technology and best practices that build the brand. Domestically, your chain has a presence in every state, and in virtually all profitable locations. You therefore believe that it will be difficult to grow the chain organically, at least in the domestic scene.

   Internationally, there is plenty of growth potential in developing countries. However, high risks of political and economic instability may make greenfield expansion (that is, the construction of brand-new facilities) unfeasible. The need for total control is lower where a local partner can help to manage risks and adapt your firm's best practices.

   In both cases (domestic and international) please recommend alternatives for the company to grow inorganically, and evaluate each. (See Exhibit 6.20 in the main text for a framework for considering the alternatives.)

7. *You are the CEO of a diversified holding company. For a long time you have believed that your stock is undervalued primarily because of a diversification discount. How might you restructure the company to address your perception of the problem? (See Exhibit 6.21 in the main text for a framework that might be of use.)*

8. *What is the framework to be used for choosing a strategy of inorganic growth? Once you arrive at possible inorganic growth alternatives, what guidelines can you use to help make your decision?*

9. *Suppose you are the head of business strategy at Olivia Inc., a consumer foods company. You feel that the company should adopt a focused strategy and shed some of its businesses—right now it has six divisions. A tool that you can use to evaluate strategic issues is the growth-share matrix. Suppose the divisions have the following characteristics; evaluate each using the matrix. Which divisions would you keep, and which ones would you shed? Why? (See the spreadsheet template "Growth Share.xls" found on the CD-ROM.)*

	Growth Rate	Relative Share of Market	Revenues ($ MM)
Division 1	32%	1.50	50
Division 2	15%	0.70	70
Division 3	20%	0.50	150
Division 4	4%	2.00	200
Division 5	24%	0.30	120
Division 6	6%	0.80	100

10. You are the head of a biotech company and have just received the license to manufacture a vaccine to protect from a contagious disease. You estimate that market demand for this product will be explosive. In order to evaluate the financial viability of this product, you need to know accurate information about the cost of manufacturing the vaccine. Because of the difficulty of the process, you plan to start with a low production level, gradually increasing to a higher level. Your intended schedule of production is as follows, where each time period is one month:

Time Period	Cumulative Production (000)
0	0
1	5
2	10
3	20
4	40
5	80
6	160

The base cost for 1,000 doses of vaccine is estimated at $120. Assuming you can reduce the cost by 5 percent, 10 percent, or 15 percent, if your cumulative production doubles, calculate the cost for each period under each scenario and graph the results. What kind of impact will "learning" have on your cost of production?

11. Suppose the CEO of Joy Company, a private company, is determined to achieve 16 percent growth annually in order to compete effectively and to survive in its industry. The following table summarizes the modeling assumptions and results:

Joy Company Self-Sustainable Growth Rate Analysis	Assumptions and Result
Dividend payout ratio	40%
Target debt/equity ratio	30%
Expected return on equity	15.00%
Expected return on total capital	12.46%
Expected after-tax cost of debt	4%
New issues of common equity	Nil
Self-sustainable growth rate	9.00%

But Joy Company can self-sustain a growth rate of only 9 percent. How can the CEO increase the firm's self-sustainable growth rate? Assume you are hired by the CEO as a consultant, list several possible alternatives. Which would you recommend to the CEO?

12. You are the CEO of a diversified company that has three divisions in different industries. The following table shows each division's annual sales, and the industry average ratio of total capital to sales:

	($ MM)	Total Capital/Sales (Industry Average)
Division 1 sales	12	2.00
Division 2 sales	44	1.28
Division 3 sales	30	1.76
Total capital	120	

Based on market capitalization, the total value of your company's capital is $120 million. Is there a diversification discount? If so, how much is it?

CHAPTER 7

Acquisition Search and Deal Origination: Some Guiding Principles

M&A transactions may spring from a *search* process by a buyer or from an *origination* process by an intermediary, such as a banker. The acquisition search process is essentially an intelligence-gathering operation. As such, the search process needs to be structured so as to enhance the quality of information acquired.

- It is helpful to keep the following ideas in mind with respect to the acquisition search process:
  - The most valuable information is private.
  - Networks are valuable. Networking can be profitable.
  - Investing in building a search network is like investing in options.
  - Information about deal opportunities is often dispersed through the market. As such, studies of the speed and impact of dispersion may yield insights about the pathway of information that can help buyers in the search process.
- In performing an acquisition search, focus on *information*, rather than on transactions. This is another variation on a theme that is repeatedly offered in this book—focus on *process*, rather than outcomes.
- Markets discount ambiguous information. In contrast, what the market knows clearly is fully priced. Public information gets impounded into security prices rapidly and without bias—this is the cornerstone of the efficient markets hypothesis. Therefore, private knowledge of high return opportunities is a crucial ingredient for creating value through M&A. Deal searches should be structured to generate private information before it becomes widely known.
- In a world of adverse selection (where the seller has an incentive to misrepresent the item to be sold), costly attributes (such as a promise to pay dividends) will tell buyers things that mere words will not.
- Usual acquisition screening criteria include:
  - Industry and buyer's and target's position in it.
  - Strategic capabilities.

  - Size of the business (usually in terms of sales or assets).
  - Profitability.
  - Risk exposure.
  - Asset type.
  - Management quality.
  - Prospective control.
  - Organizational fit.
  - Prospective control.
- Acquisition search involves dynamic learning by doing. The searcher *learns* through experience, revising targets and expectations over time. One must allow for a certain degree of opportunism, since opportunities help clarify strategy.
- Invest in social networks: They make search more efficient and effective. What you seek may be closer than you think. Through social connections, the research on the "small world" phenomenon suggests that we are separated from distant strangers by a relatively small number of connections. Paradoxically, there is strength in weak ties: The connections most likely to help you are those people who are least like you.
- Information first disseminates slowly, then spreads explosively. For this reason, the searcher should seek to position him/herself early or "upstream" in the flow of news about investment opportunities. *Primary* research is the best and safest way of positioning oneself upstream.
- Cultivating strong relationships with "navigators" helps position a searcher upstream. Navigators are intermediaries in the flow of information. They include:
  - *Gatekeepers*—those who provide access to information and deals. Investment bankers who have an exclusive engagement to sell a firm are among the most important gatekeepers.
  - *River guides*—industry or regional specialists who highlight emerging trends that might affect the availability of investment opportunities.
- Attributes of the best navigators include:
  - Control over an existing base of customers or suppliers.
  - Intellectual property rights.
  - Ability to innovate better than other navigators.
  - First-mover advantages.
  - Low-cost provider of search services.
  - Reputation and brand name image.
- A search or origination team that is flexible and consistent with the complex external environment has the highest probability of succeeding in a rapidly changing world.

- Persistence and repeated effort in acquisition search pays. The probability of a positive payoff from an acquisition search can be increased by:
  - Choosing promising arenas—those where there is uncertainty about who knows what information.
  - Increasing the total number of deal opportunities reviewed.
  - Increasing the frequency of reviews.
  - Optimizing the network infrastructure to yield valuable information.
- The acquisition search process requires proactivity.

CHAPTER 7—WORKBOOK QUESTIONS

Part I: True or False

1. *Asymmetry and ambiguity of information about an asset can affect the price of that asset.*

2. *In performing an acquisition search, one should focus on information rather than on transactions.*

3. *What the market knows clearly is fully priced.*

4. *High-quality information is costly.*

5. *If information about an acquisition opportunity is fully public, there is a high likelihood that the opportunity is fully priced.*

6. *If information about an acquisition opportunity is fully public, there is a high likelihood that the buyer can tailor the pricing and terms to greater advantage.*

7. *It is all right for some acquisition searchers to look for unusual capabilities rather than market positions.*

8. *Focusing on distressed targets can be a search strategy.*

9. *There is no place for opportunism in acquisitions. Every acquisition must be a result of careful reflection on strategy, rather than the availability of a target.*

10. *Deal-rich information is public.*

Part II: Short Answer

1. *Go to www.cs.virginia.edu/oracle. Play the "Oracle of Bacon" game. Type in names of actors or actresses to see how close their connection is to Kevin Bacon; include international actors and actresses in your experiment, too! Were you surprised by the results? What does this game tell you about connectivity? How can you tie this idea in to the M&A search process?*

2. *What implications does the Granovetter study on how people find jobs have for the M&A search process?*

3. *Navigators are intermediaries of information—people like investment bankers, consultants, lawyers, and accountants. What are some attributes of the best navigators in the realm of M&A?*

Part III: Target Assessment Cases

In May 2003, a large food and beverage manufacturer is searching for an acquisition target. This buyer is a manufacturer of a variety of carbonated and noncarbonated drinks, and of snack foods. In general, its products are in the convenience and impulse foods category. Annual revenues are over $20 billion. The buyer, which has operations all over the world, believes that the U.S. market is mature and that foreign markets offer greater growth potential.

The buyer's ideal target would have the following characteristics:

- At least $50 million in sales.
- At least 12 percent in operating margins.
- Accretive to EPS in the first year.
- Products that fit the buyer's ambient and/or chilled distribution system.
- Products that are in the "good for you" food category.

1. *Suppose you are a business developer just hired by the buyer for this assignment. Draw up a short list of potential targets, and assess each according to the criteria provided by the buyer. Also consider other issues such as industry position, shareholder structure, and so on—you may want to use the discussion in Chapter 7 of the main text as reference. Do not focus on pricing, valuation, or accounting issues for now. Concentrate on the rationale.*

CHAPTER 8

Due Diligence

"Know what you are buying." The lack of knowledge of potential problems in an acquisition is one of the more common causes of failure in M&A.

- "Due diligence" is research. Traditionally, it has been aimed at revealing risks in the target company that a diligent buyer should understand. This chapter defines due diligence to include a search for *both* risks and opportunities.
- Excellence in due diligence begins with the *right mind-set.* The essence of the mind-set can be summarized in the following elements:
  - *Avoid a compliance mentality and adopt an investor mentality.* One of the recurrent themes in the book is *think like an investor.*
  - *Generally, one should conduct due diligence broadly.* Broad due diligence will reveal more about risk and opportunity than will narrow due diligence. Ultimately, the trade-offs between broad and narrow due diligence boil down to "surprises now" versus "surprises later."
  - *Be fact-based but knowledge-oriented.* Due diligence builds from the bottom up—from data to information, to knowledge.
  - *Communication should be clear and documented.* Communicate the output in plain-language briefings for managers, but leave a detailed paper trail.
  - *Leadership matters.* The due diligence process requires strong skills of leadership and process management. Link the process and conclusions to the valuation, negotiation, and postmerger integration processes.
- Broad due diligence encompasses knowledge of:
  - Risks *and* opportunities.
  - The past, present, *and* future.
  - The firm *and* its partners such as key customers and suppliers.
  - The financial condition *and* the business that generated it.
  - Internal conditions of the firm *and* external conditions of the firm's environment.
  - The basic data of the target *and* the refined opinions of the experts.
- Within the buyer's due diligence team there must be formalized understanding of deadlines, assignments of responsibility, and objectives of specific tasks, through memos or other written messages. Progress must be monitored, and quality checked.

- From the target's side, management of the due diligence process entails organizing, planning, and controlling the process to satisfy the buyer's due diligence needs with least disruption to the target's operations. An important means for this is the "data room," a location where the requested documents are placed for inspection by the buyer's diligence team.
- Some important issues to explore as part of the due diligence process are:

Legal issues	Proper incorporation, legal standing, compliance with laws, shareholding/voting structure, procedures for electing directors, involvement in legal proceedings, and potential litigation issues.
Accounting issues	Compliance with GAAP, any unusual accounting practices, any unusual trends in the target's financial results, and comparison of target's accounting processes and results with peers.
Tax issues	Compliance with tax laws, accrued unpaid taxes, and opportunities for tax reduction.
Information technology	Adequacy of target's management information systems and compatibility with buyer's, and investments necessary to achieve compatibility.
Risk and insurance issues	Adequacy of target's insurance policies and liability coverage, possible exposures to natural hazards, business interruption, technological change, and change in government policy.
Environmental issues	Compliance with environmental laws, and possible exposures to environmental liabilities.
Market presence and sales issues	General image of the firm, strength of its brand franchise, compatibility of market segment with buyer's, competitors, strength of target's sales and marketing organizations, and outlook for revenues and future trends.
Operations	Strength of target's operational processes in terms of cost, quality, efficiency, and flexibility; compatibility of target's operational processes with buyer's; streamlining for cost synergies; exposure to technological change; and labor issues.
Intellectual and intangible assets	Value of intangible assets, how well they are protected, and potential exposures to infringement claims.
Finance	Soundness of financial policies, creditworthiness and solvency, and likelihood of cash flow problems.
Cross-border issues	Exposure to foreign currency fluctuations and to foreign laws and regulations, and cultural differences.
Human resources	Depth of talent and leadership pool, compensation policies, levels of turnover and employee satisfaction, union issues, and pension liabilities.
Cultural issues	The target's beliefs, mission, values, norms, and traditions; leadership and communication styles; and cultural compatibility with buyer.
Ethics	Compatibility of ethical norms and practices between target and buyer.

- Cultural due diligence should assess congruence on three dimensions:
  1. Between actions and aspirations (i.e., as expressed in statements about mission and values). Is the culture of the target company consistent with the aims of the firm?
  2. Between the cultures of buyer and target.
  3. Between the target's culture and its strategic threats and opportunities. Acquisitions fail when the buyer makes demands on the target inconsistent with the target's culture. The main text summarizes the research of Christopher Luis, who finds that strategic cultures tend to cluster around:
     - Customer service cultures
     - Product uniqueness cultures
     - Cost orientation cultures
     - Preeminence cultures
- Public sources can be used to help:
  - Obtain basic financial information about a target and assess the target's industry and peer firms.
  - Identify economic forces affecting the target, such as deregulation, technological change, demographic change, and trade liberalization.
  - Gauge the view of peers and investors about the target.
  - Develop a basic factual foundation about the target.
- In summary, excellent due diligence is:
  - *Fact-based.* Avoids guesses or opinions.
  - *Inquisitive.* Avoids a compliance or checklist mentality.
  - *Knowledge-focused.* Goes beyond mere data.
  - *Systems-focused.* Seeks the links to valuation, negotiation, and closing.
  - *Undertaken with initiative.* Begins as soon as the possibility of a transaction arises.
  - *Managed to take enough time.* Plans ahead and avoids errors from too little time.
  - *Multidisciplinary.* Seeks to understand the target firm in all its aspects.
  - *Drawn from both formal and informal resources.*
  - *Careful to avoid surprises.* Due diligence is, in part, risk management. If you must have surprises, you should want them early rather than later.
  - *Written.* Good due diligence creates a careful written record of findings that can be retrieved if disputes arise later.

CHAPTER 8—WORKBOOK QUESTIONS

Part I: Concept Questions

1. *Why is it important to think like an investor when conducting due diligence?*
2. *Discuss the tension between broad and narrow due diligence.*

3. *Why is it important to focus on knowledge when conducting due diligence? How are data, information, and knowledge different from each other?*

Part II: Mini-Cases

CUC-HFS[1]

In December 1997, Cendant Corporation was created by a $14 billion merger between HFS Inc. and CUC International Inc. HFS was run by a well-known deal maker, Henry Silverman, and owned hotel brands Ramada, Days Inn, and Howard Johnson, car-rental company Avis, and real estate brokers Coldwell Banker and Century 21. CUC was in the business of selling memberships in clubs that offered travel, shopping, and dining discounts. The merger was predicated on cross-selling products and services to the combined (massive) customer database of the two companies. However, just four months later, it was discovered that CUC had been engaging in accounting fraud since 1995: About $500 million of revenues reported from 1995 to 1997 was made up, and 61 percent of CUC's 1997 net income was fictitious.

> *In sworn affidavits taken by Cendant investigators . . . [two former CUC managers] said they had been told to record millions of dollars of phony orders. Mr. Sabatino said he had been told to arbitrarily adjust revenue up or expenses down. He had raided reserves set up for merger costs to cover revenue shortfalls. In short, the men alleged that they had cooked the books to order for CUC executives, and specifically named . . . CUC's former senior vice president of finance and controller . . . [and] CUC's chief financial officer.*[2]

CUC had had accounting problems before. In 1989, it changed its accounting methods after being criticized by investors for "spreading out the cost of recruiting new members over three years instead of reflecting those costs right away. In 1991, the SEC questioned the completeness of CUC's financial documents and required numerous amendments to them."[3]

After the merger was announced, Henry Silverman began requiring daily cash reports and detailed monthly financial statements about operations, which had not been required at CUC. These were slow in coming. Frustrated, Silverman finally assigned two HFS finance officials to CUC's case. It was at this point that anomalies began to be discovered, prompting further investigations that ultimately revealed evidence of fraud since 1995. Tactics employed by CUC had included making up or reclassifying revenues, overstating membership renewal rates, claiming bogus merger reserves, falsifying expenses, and delaying recognition of insurance claims. One investigation uncovered "several million dollars in questionable expenses over three years, including about $550,000 in undocumented cash advances between . . . 1995 and 1997."[4] In addition, CUC, despite being a large company, appeared not to have highly automated accounting systems. For instance, most revenues and expenses had to be entered manually.[5]

Silverman's due diligence on CUC had been based almost purely on public information. Although the merger deal was friendly, CUC had refused to share some nonpublic data. Silverman has insisted many times that there was no way he could have known about the fraud at the time of merger negotiations.

1. *In light of the facts given, do you think the problems associated with this deal could have been uncovered with due diligence? If so, how? Or do you agree with Mr. Silverman's position?*

Quaker Oats–Snapple

On November 2, 1994, Quaker Oats announced it had agreed to acquire Snapple Beverage Corp. for $1.7 billion. Quaker believed it could build Snapple into a vibrant, growing brand, just as it had done with Gatorade. It believed that synergies could be exploited by integrating the Snapple operation into its Gatorade organization. Just two years and five months later, Quaker agreed to sell Snapple for $300 million, taking a $1.4 billion charge on the loss.

Quaker had planned to streamline distribution in order to exploit cross-selling opportunities between Snapple and Gatorade—in fact, reconfiguring distribution had been a basic tenet of the postmerger plan. Snapple had employed a distribution scheme that relied on more than 300 independent distributors to service supermarkets, restaurants, gas stations, and other "convenience chains and mom-and-pop markets" within their respective territories (to which they had exclusive rights). Gatorade, in contrast, distributed its product directly from its bottling plants to the warehouses of supermarket chains. The postmerger plan aimed to swap distribution rights: Quaker would grant Snapple's independent distributors rights to deliver Gatorade to the convenience chains and mom-and-pop stores. In exchange, Quaker wanted the distributors to hand over their supermarket accounts and let Quaker sell Snapple directly to the supermarkets.

A journalist wrote, "The uproar was immediate. The plan gave Quaker the benefit of an already established Snapple supermarket business in exchange for a small-store Gatorade trade that had yet to be built."[6] Further, the independent distributors were making $4-per-case margins on Snapple—double what they would have been able to make on Gatorade. Quaker was forced to shelve its plans to streamline distribution, a linchpin of its merger program. *Forbes* magazine wrote, "Only after it bought Snapple did it [Quaker] fully realize that Snapple's distribution system is completely different from Gatorade's."[7]

Other problems appeared after the merger. For one, it was discovered that much of Snapple's growth before the acquisition had come from cramming its distribution pipeline full of inventory. In addition, Quaker ran into problems with Snapple's manufacturing systems. Snapple had employed a production scheme whereby it outsourced bottling operations to independent contractors. This procedure not only slowed production, but also locked Snapple into contracts that required minimum bottling quotas even when sales slowed. Quaker had to take a $30 million charge to buy out these bottling contracts. In addition, Quaker encountered stock-out problems at Snapple, where it took weeks rather than days to fill orders.

Finally, there was the problem of slowing sales, signs of which emerged *before* the definitive agreement had been signed. Late in the merger discussions, Snapple revealed to Quaker that sales and profits for the year had plummeted, and that weakness was expected to continue throughout the year. In addition, Snapple's owners insisted on an all-cash deal despite the stock-and-cash plan originally put forward.[8] Despite this, Quaker agreed to buy Snapple for $1.7 billion in cash.

2. *Do you think faulty due diligence was a cause of merger failure in this case? Explain.*

Medical Care–Critical Care

On September 9, 1992, Medical Care America was formed by a merger between two of the largest and fastest-growing providers of outpatient health care services in the United States: Medical Care International, Inc. (MCI), an operator of outpatient surgery centers, and Critical Care America, Inc. (CCA), a provider of "home-infusion therapies" (i.e., programs in which outpatients are supplied with equipment and training to administer their own drugs, therapies, and recovery programs at home). Examples of infusion therapies include chemotherapy, nutrition support, IV antibiotics, and so forth.

The merger received overwhelming shareholder approval, with at least 80 percent of each company's shareholders voting in favor. Analysts lauded the deal as well. But merely 16 days after the merger announcement, the new company declared that its third-quarter earnings would be flat, as opposed to market expectations of 30 percent profit growth. On that day, Medical Care stock dropped 57 percent. Two months later, the chairman of Medical Care resigned.

More bad news was to come: In the fourth quarter of 1992, Medical Care's earnings fell 25 percent below the previous year. In the first quarter of 1993, net income dropped 32 percent from the previous year's comparable period. The surgery centers—that portion of the business contributed by the former Medical Care International—were doing well; revenues were growing briskly. It was the infusion business (formerly of Critical Care) that was faltering.

Only after the merger was it learned just how badly competitive pressures were pushing prices down in the infusion industry, and how badly Critical Care had been falling behind in the changing health-care environment. Its prices were as much as 26 percent higher than those of its rivals, due to its propensity to "provide high-level service regardless of the cost. . . . Founder Patrick S. Smith . . . had been so eager to prove that his company could provide many of the same services available in hospitals that he spared no expense in assembling the staff and equipment needed to treat medical problems such as cancer, cardiac disease and bone-marrow transplants."[9] In addition, Critical Care's sales force had focused almost solely on marketing to physicians (who would then send their patients to Critical Care's centers) rather than to managed-care networks and insurance companies, which increasingly dominated the health market, and whose profit margins depended on low costs. Because of Critical Care's uncompetitive prices and its refusal even to negotiate them, it often was bypassed by HMOs and insurers.

After the earnings disappointments were revealed, 15 shareholders filed a lawsuit against Medical Care, charging that "Critical Care's problems were so severe that managers had to have known about them."[10] But a senior vice president of Medical Care asserted, "We were very surprised by the problem and had no idea of the problem on September 9."

3. *Do you think the problems would have been uncovered with better due diligence?*

NOTES

1. This account draws from Emily Nelson and Joann Lublin, "Buy the Numbers? How Whistle-Blowers Set off a Fraud Probe That Crushed Cendant," *Wall Street Journal*, August 13, 1998, p. A1. *Wall Street Journal.* Eastern Edition [staff produced copy only] by Emily Nelson and Joann Lublin. Copyright © 1998 by Dow Jones & Co. Inc. Reproduced with permission of Dow Jones & Co. Inc. in the format textbook via Copyright Clearance Center.
2. Ibid.
3. Ibid.
4. Ibid.
5. Amy Barrett, "Cendant: Who's to Blame? A Loose Accounting Culture May Lie at the Core of the Debacle," *BusinessWeek*, August 17, 1998, p. 70.
6. Nancy Millman, "Quaker Stumbles over Snapple," *Raleigh News and Observer*, September 12, 1996, p. C7.
7. Zina Moukheiber, "He Who Laughs Last: Was Quaker Oats Taken When It Paid $1.7 Billion for Snapple?" *Forbes*, January 1, 1996, p. 42.
8. Millman, "Quaker Stumbles over Snapple," p. C7.
9. Robert Tomsho, "Medical Care America Tries to Regain Investor Faith," *Wall Street Journal*, November 2, 1992, p. B6.
10. Stephanie Anderson Forest, "Operating Room Mishap—A "Brilliant Idea" Led to Medical Care America. So What Happened?" *BusinessWeek*, September 20, 1993, p. 77.

CHAPTER 9

Valuing Firms

Mastery of valuation is important, not only because it is a primary concern in M&A, but also because an understanding of valuation can guide managerial action. This chapter introduces techniques for valuing firms on a stand-alone basis, and outlines the mind-set necessary for creating value.

- In valuation, remember:
  - Think like an investor; that is, focus on economic reality, focus on future expectations, focus on cash flow, get paid for risks, account for the time value of money and for opportunity cost, consider any information advantages, and diversify efficiently.
  - Intrinsic value is unobservable; it can only be estimated. One should therefore triangulate from many estimates. One should also work with ranges of value, rather than with point estimates.
  - An opportunity to create value exists where price and intrinsic value differ—in other words, when the concept of value additivity is violated. Value additivity means that the value of the whole should equal the sum of the values of the parts.
  - Have a view about the various estimators of value. Understand the strengths and weaknesses of each and how relevant each is to your situation.
  - Find key value drivers and the inherent bets in the acquisition. Some tools for helping to find the key value drivers are sensitivity analysis, scenario analysis, break-even analysis, and Monte Carlo simulation.
  - Think critically; triangulate carefully. To "triangulate" is to converge on a range of value within which intrinsic value probably resides.
  - Focus on process, not on product. Thoughtfully attend to the steps of valuation analysis rather than trying to push the analysis to justify an outcome.
- Some of the methods ("estimators") used to estimate value are:
  - *Accounting book value.* Value is based on amounts recorded in the financial statements.
  - *Liquidation value.* Sums the values that might be realized in a liquidation of the firm today.
  - *Replacement cost valuation.* Value is estimated by determining the cost to replace the assets of the firm piecemeal today.
  - *Current trading or market value.* Sum of the market values of debt and equity.

- *Trading multiples.* Applies the valuation multiples of peer firms to the target.
- *Transaction multiples.* Multiples based on actual prices paid for firms in comparable transactions are applied to the target firm.
- *Discounted cash flow approaches.* Value is based on the present value of cash flows discounted at an appropriate cost of capital.
- *Venture capital/private equity approach.* Value of the business is equal to the present value of the target's exit value.
- *Option valuation.* Value of business is based on the value of equity as a call option on the value of the business.

- *Enterprise value* is the value of the whole firm, while *equity value* is the value of the residual claim on the firm's assets.
- There are three types of discounted cash flow approaches. Theoretically, each approach should yield the same firm value, but in practice it is rare to obtain the same answer under all three approaches due to imperfections in data, models, or procedures.

	Discounted Cash Flow (DCF) Method	Residual Cash Flow (RCF) Method	Adjusted Present Value (APV) Method
Cash flows discounted	Cash flows before financing effects (i.e., flows available to both debt and equity holders)	Cash flows to equity	Free cash flows assuming 100% equity financing, adjusted for the value of debt tax shields
Discount rate used	Weighted average cost of capital (WACC)	Cost of equity	Unlevered cost of equity for free cash flows; cost of debt for debt tax shields

- Two general approaches for estimating the cost of equity are the *dividend growth model* and the *capital asset pricing model*:
  - Dividend growth model: $K_e = \frac{DIV_1}{P_0} + g\infty$
  - CAPM: $K_e = R_f + \beta\,(R_m - R_f)$
- If an acquirer intends to lever up or lever down the target significantly, beta should be unlevered and then relevered.

$$\beta_{\text{Unlevered}} = \frac{\beta_{\text{Levered}}}{\left[1 + (1 - t)\frac{D}{E}\right]}$$

$$\beta_{\text{Levered}} = \beta_{\text{Unlevered}}\left[1 + (1 - t)\frac{D}{E}\right]$$

- When bidding, the opening bid is typically bounded on the low side by the recent market price range of the target. The walk-away bid should be bounded on the high side by the intrinsic value of the target. The intrinsic value of the target to the buyer should include synergies.

CHAPTER 9—WORKBOOK QUESTIONS

1. Sober Brews Corporation is a holding company composed of the following subsidiaries:

   - *Sober Brews Beer Corporation* produces, markets, and sells various beer products. Beers produced appeal to a wide range of consumer taste and price preferences.
   - *Sober Brews Foods Corporation* produces, markets, and sells meat products for household consumption.
   - *SBC Brews Packaging Corporation* produces, markets, and sells packaging products, including bottles, aluminum cans, and cardboard boxes.
   - *SBC Properties, Inc.* develops and sells commercial and residential properties.
   - *SBC International, Inc.* acts as the holding company for all of Sober Brews' international operations, which are concentrated in Eastern Europe and China.

   You have performed a DCF analysis on each of the subsidiaries, with the following results:

	Equity Value ($ MM)
Sober Brews Beer Corporation	713.70
Sober Brews Foods Corporation	396.50
Sober Brews Packaging Corporation	237.90
SBC Properties, Inc.	95.16
SBC International, Inc.	142.74
Total	1,586.00

   Sober Brews currently trades on the New York Stock Exchange at $32.8 a share, and has 36.2 million shares outstanding. Debt on Sober Brews' balance sheet totals $396 million.

   Would you recommend taking any action with regard to Sober Brews? If so, what course of action would you take?

2. *What is wrong with each of these statements?*

   a. *Value can be created when price and intrinsic value are the same.*
   b. *All estimators must be used when determining a company's value.*
   c. *To arrive at a company's value, one must pick a point estimate arrived at after using the various estimators.*

d. Intrinsic value can be observed by looking at a company's stock market price.

3. Red Hill Vinegar Company is going out of business due to fierce competition in the condiments industry. Jack Mueller, an independent appraiser, has been hired to estimate the liquidation value of Red Hill's assets.

   How much will be left to the owner of Red Hill after liquidation?

	Book Value ($000)	Percent Recoverable
Cash	$ 123.8	100
Receivables	619.0	75
Inventory	309.5	55
PPE	879.0	60
Other assets	92.9	90
	$2,024.1	
Debt	$1,763.3	
Equity	$4,114.7	

[This spreadsheet can be found in the folder "Key Spreadsheets from the Workbook" located on the CD-ROM.]

4. Pellagia Inc. is a nationwide retail chain specializing in women's apparel. The company's most popular lines are Aura and Home. Aura offers executive wear for women in the middle to high-end markets, and Home features casual but stylish clothes, also targeted at women in the middle to high-end markets. The company has 135 million shares outstanding, 30 percent of which are publicly traded with a current market price of $5.63 per share. The company is expected to net $38 million in the next 12 months. Forecast sales and EBITDA are $633 million and $57 million, respectively. Debt outstanding is $120 million.

   a. What is the current enterprise market value of Pellagia?

   b. Suppose you are asked to value Pellagia Inc. given the following information. What is your estimate of equity value? Of enterprise value?

	Price to Earnings	Price to Sales
Abercrombie & Fitch	13.04	1.58
Ann Taylor Stores Corp.	26.10	0.78
Bebe Stores Inc.	15.36	1.41
Gap Inc.	N/A	0.76
Limited Brands Inc.	18.59	0.96
Talbots Inc.	14.11	1.06

[This spreadsheet can be found in the folder "Key Spreadsheets from the Workbook" located on the CD-ROM.]

5. *What is wrong with the following equations?*

a.

$$V_{\text{Enterprise}} = \frac{\text{FCF}}{K_e}$$

b.

$$V_{\text{Equity}} = \frac{\text{Dividends}}{\text{WACC}}$$

6. Tel-Talk Inc. is a company that provides domestic and international long distance, regional and local communications services, cable (broadband) television, and Internet communications services. For the past two years, it has paid an annual dividend of $2.31 per share; however, the compound rate of growth in dividends per share over the past 10 years has been 6.2 percent. The beta of Tel-Talk stock measured over the past three years is 1.10. Its debt, which makes up 32 percent of total capital, currently yields 7.28 percent, while long-term Treasury bonds are yielding 5.63 percent. The market risk premium (geometric) is at 5.9 percent. Tel-Talk shares are currently trading at $46.25 per share.

   Calculate Tel-Talk's cost of equity using both the CAPM and the dividend growth model.

7. Trigeorgis Partners, a leveraged buyout firm, is considering an investment in a national retail bookseller. The target is attractive to Trigeorgis because of its low level of debt, which at present makes up just 9.5 percent of the company's total capital. The partners at Trigeorgis believe that the debt level can be raised to as much as 30 percent of capital. Although this might mean a lowering of the credit rating from AAA to AA, or even to A, the Trigeorgis partners believe that the interest tax shields would more than offset higher costs of borrowing. The bookseller's average beta for the past year has been 0.98, and its marginal tax rate is 35 percent.

   How would beta change if Trigeorgis completed the acquisition and raised the bookseller's debt to 30 percent?

8. The following is a five-year discounted cash flow (DCF) forecast for Middlestates Electric, Inc., an electric utility company:

($ MM)	Year 1	Year 2	Year 3	Year 4	Year 5
Operating income	2,039	2,325	2,169	2,430	2,615
Taxes	712	813	777	870	937
Depreciation and amortization	1,299	1,413	1,470	1,527	1,584
Change in working capital	(169)	294	(223)	163	(205)
Capital expenditures/asset sales	(1,754)	(3,432)	1,180	(2,720)	(2,133)
Free cash flow	703	(213)	3,819	530	924

[This spreadsheet can be found in the folder "Key Spreadsheets from the Workbook" located on the CD-ROM.]

Cash flows over the next five years are expected to fluctuate significantly due to key acquisitions and restructuring measures planned by Middlestates. After the fifth year, however, cash flow is expected to stabilize. Economists expect the long-term inflation rate to stabilize at 1.5 percent, and Middlestates expects real growth in sales to be 1.5 percent or less. Management has determined that the cost of capital is 9.28 percent.

Estimate Middlestates' enterprise value.

9. Vanguard Office Supplies is a nationwide retail chain that offers office supplies and office furniture. Company management has decided that, from both a competitive and a cost-cutting standpoint, Vanguard should offer its own private-label brands for products like student notebooks, fillers, ledgers and journals, bond and linen paper, and other products. To accomplish this objective, Vanguard is considering the purchase of Omega Paper, a manufacturer of paper products and notebooks. A five-year income forecast for Omega is given, along with other pertinent information. Vanguard plans to keep Omega's debt-equity ratio at its current level.

Calculate the equity value per share of Omega using the discounted cash flow method.

Five-Year Forecast ($ MM)	Year 1	Year 2	Year 3	Year 4	Year 5
Revenue	957.9	972.2	986.8	1,001.6	1,016.6
Cost of goods sold	862.1	875.0	888.1	901.4	915.0
SG&A	67.0	68.1	69.1	70.1	71.2
EBIT	28.7	29.2	29.6	30.0	30.5
Interest expense	12.5	13.4	13.8	14.1	14.4
EBT	16.2	15.7	15.8	16.0	16.1
Taxes	5.5	5.3	5.4	5.4	5.5
Net Income	10.7	10.4	10.5	10.5	10.6
Other projections:					
Change in net working capital	(5.7)	(5.8)	(5.9)	(6.0)	(6.1)
Capital expenditures	28.7	29.2	80.3	62.2	30.5
Depreciation	52.7	53.5	54.3	55.1	55.9
Tax rate	34.0%				
Book value of debt ($MM)	192.3				
Book value of equity ($MM)	364.9				
Share price ($)	10.5				
Beta	0.76				
Shares outstanding (MM)	51.5				
Interest rate on company debt	6.5%				
Current bond yields on similarly rated companies	6.1%				
10-year T-bond rate	5.0%				
Inflation	2.5%				
Market risk premium	6.0%				

[This spreadsheet can be found in the folder "Key Spreadsheets from the Workbook" located on the CD-ROM.]

10. Refer to problem 7. See the forecasts for the next five years given here. Assume that the new debt level will total $400 million at an interest rate of 6 percent and that this debt will be the perpetual amount of debt of the firm.

    Calculate the equity value of the bookseller to Trigeorgis using the adjusted present value approach.

($ MM)	Year 1	Year 2	Year 3	Year 4	Year 5
Sales	3,271.2	3,387.9	3,537.4	3,777.5	3,966.4
EBIT	171.4	191.9	210.3	235.9	238.0
Depreciation and amortization	83.5	95.3	96.2	103.0	112.0
Changes in working capital	(32.7)	(37.3)	(17.7)	(41.6)	(39.7)
Capital expenditures	(159.2)	(141.2)	(90.7)	(100.0)	(120.0)
Risk-free rate	5%				
Risk premium	6%				
Terminal value growth rate	3%				
Shares outstanding	75 million				

[This spreadsheet can be found in the folder "Key Spreadsheets from the Workbook" located on the CD-ROM.]

CHAPTER 10

Valuing Options

The world of M&A has been influenced greatly by options concepts; these concepts help explain behavior and deal features that were previously difficult to understand. There are six important determinants of an option's value: asset price, exercise price, volatility, time to expiration, interest rate, and dividends. The value of options can be calculated by analytical and numerical methods. Option-pricing theory can be used to value securities as different as loan guarantees, bonds, common stock, and real assets.

- Some terminology:
  - An *option* is the right, not the obligation, to do something.
  - A *call* option is the right to buy and a *put* option is the right to sell an asset at certain price within a certain time period.
  - An *American option* can be exercised at any moment before expiration; a *European option* can be exercised only at expiration.
  - A *long position* gives the investor the *right* to exercise an option; a *short position commits* the investor to perform if the option is exercised.
  - A call option is *in the money* if the current stock price is higher than the exercise price; it is *out of the money* if the stock price is lower than the exercise price. A put option is *in the money* if the stock price is lower than the exercise price; it is *out of the money* if the stock price is higher than the exercise price.
- The value of a firm consists of its stand-alone value plus the value of options. Long options are assets; short options are liabilities.

$$V_{\text{Enterprise, option-adjusted}} = V_{\text{DCF of enterprise}} + V_{\text{Long options}} - V_{\text{Short options}}$$

- A *payoff* is the flow of cash to the parties to an option contract at the time of exercise of the option. Profit differs from payoff by recognizing the outlay necessary to establish the option position. Payoffs are not to be confused with profits—profits reflect the cost of buying (or the revenue from selling) the option while payoffs do not. Payoffs for different option positions are:

	Call	Put
Long	Payoff = Max(S – Ex, 0)	Payoff = Max(Ex – S, 0)
Short	Payoff = – Max(S – Ex, 0)	Payoff = – Max(Ex – S, 0)

S = Underlying asset price; Ex = Exercise price.

By using various combinations of these four simple positions, one can achieve more complex payoff structures.

- *Put-call parity* refers to the relationship between the price of a put option and the price of a call option on the same underlying asset with the same expiration date. The equality of the two sides hypothesizes that at equilibrium there will be no arbitrage opportunities.

$$P_t - C_t = E/(1 + R_f)^{T-t} - S_t$$

- Option value consists of two parts: *intrinsic value* and *time value*. Intrinsic value refers to the payoffs that can be obtained by exercising an option. Time value derives from the chance that the option will be in the money at some point in the future. As long as the option holder does not have to exercise the option immediately, the option will have some time value.
- The *Black-Scholes option pricing model* estimates the value of an option. The basis of the model is that a risk-free hedge is created, and once the risk-free hedge is created we can then set the cost of the hedge equal to the present value of the hedge payoff discounted at the risk-free rate, in order to arrive at an option value. The Black-Scholes model is popular because of its simplicity.
- The table describes the drivers of option values:

Increase In	Call Option Value	Put Option Value
Underlying asset price	Increase	Decrease
Exercise price	Decrease	Increase
Time to expiration	Increase	Increase
Risk (volatility)	Increase	Increase
Dividend yield	Decrease	Increase
Risk-free rate	Increase	Decrease

- Some applications of option-pricing theory include:
  - Value the residual claim on a firm's assets. Equity can be treated as an option on the assets of the firm, with the exercise price equal to the par value of the debt, and expiration equal to the maturity of the debt.
  - Value a firm's debt, which should be equal to the present value of a risk-free zero coupon bond less the value of a put option written on the firm's assets:

$$V_{\text{Bond}} = Ee^{-rt} - V_{\text{Put}}$$

  - Value loan guarantees, subordinated debt, and equity-linked debt, to design securities and to assess capital investments, too.
- Options permeate M&A transactions and affect the attractiveness of a deal. Good analysis based on an appropriate consideration of options drives good deal design and helps both parties converge to a better deal.

CHAPTER 10—WORKBOOK QUESTIONS

1. Mr. Jones holds a biotech stock in his portfolio. The stock has been a highflier for several years, and Mr. Jones thinks it will continue to go up in value because it has a couple of drugs in the pipeline. But he also worries about the uncertainty of future Food and Drug Administration (FDA) approvals. Therefore, he is thinking about using options to hedge his position. He wants a minimum return of 30 percent and is willing to give up any returns above 50 percent in two years. The stock trades at $80 today.

   a. Draw the payoff diagram illustrating Jones' objectives.

   b. Decompose this into discrete option positions (long/short; put/call) and cite the exercise prices that will allow Jones to meet his goals.

2. *Mrs. Chelsea is a business manager at Company ABC, and is considering purchasing the right to drill an oil well. The right will allow ABC to drill the well anytime in the next five years and then extract any oil in perpetuity. The initial cost for drilling will be around $8 million. The expected value for the total sales from the well is estimated at $10 million with a standard deviation of 40 percent. Given a 7 percent risk-free rate for five-year government bonds, what is the value of this right?*

3. Suppose a stock has an equal chance of moving up by 20 percent or down by 15 percent over the next year—the probability of either outcome is 50 percent. The current stock price is $100.

   a. Calculate the one-year at-the-money call and put option payoff at the expiration, assuming exercise prices for both at $100.

   b. Estimate the appropriate risk-free rate that makes put-call parity hold.

4. Suppose a stock is trading at $50 today. A one-month call option on this stock with an exercise price of $55 is quoted at $.50, and a one-month put option at the same exercise price is quoted at $6.00. The annualized one-month Treasury-bill rate is 8 percent.

   Is there an arbitrage opportunity? If so, what position should you take to exploit it?

5. *In words, explain:*

   a. Why an investor would exercise an American call option before expiration if the stock pays a dividend.

   b. Why put-call parity does not hold for American options.

6. *List the six drivers of option value and illustrate the corresponding price movements for call and put options with the decrease of each driver.*

7. *You can use beta to characterize the risk of stocks; can you calculate the beta of an option? If so, how would it compare to the beta of the underlying stock?*

8. *Consider stock ABC, trading at $80 with an historical volatility of 25 percent annually. The one-year risk-free rate is 9 percent. Calculate the value of the following investment alternatives:*

   a. *Call option with an exercise price of $90, expiring in one year.*

   b. *Put option with an exercise price of $75, expiring in one year.*

   c. *The combination of a call and a put option with an exercise price of $80, expiring in one year. What is the purpose of combining the two options this way?*

   d. *Assuming stock ABC pays a $3 dividend next year, recalculate the prices for a, b, and c.*

9. *Mr. Brian, a loan officer at a midsize local bank, is reviewing the file for Acme Programs, a computer software company. Acme is applying for a $5 million subordinated long-term loan from Mr. Brian's bank. The company has a market capitalization of $30 million and already has $10 million of senior debt on its balance sheet. The book value of assets is only $10 million. What is your recommendation to Mr. Brian about this loan? Please state your reasons and concerns qualitatively and illustrate your recommendation using a graph.*

CHAPTER **11**

Valuing Synergies

The word "synergy" refers to an increased result from the combination of efforts compared to what could be obtained from the two efforts alone. In M&A, the defining feature of a synergistic transaction is that it creates value for shareholders that they would be unable to create on their own through combination of shares in a portfolio.

- *Synergies* can be of two kinds: synergies "in place" and synergies that are contingent (i.e., that have optionlike characteristics).
- Payoffs on *in-place synergies* are reasonably predictable. Discounted cash flow valuation is well suited for valuing synergies of this kind. In-place synergies include:
  - Revenue enhancement synergies.
  - Cost reduction synergies.
  - Asset reduction synergies such as through the disposal of idle or redundant assets.
  - Tax reduction synergies such as through an increase in depreciation tax shields or through a transfer of net operating losses.
  - Weighted average cost of capital (WACC) reduction synergies.
- WACC reduction synergies may occur in two ways, neither of which is necessarily a straightforward path to value creation.
  - Optimization of debt tax shields (i.e., increasing the use of interest-bearing debt). But unless there are imperfections in capital markets, tax shield optimization may not be doing something for shareholders that they cannot already do on their own through "homemade leverage."
  - Coinsurance effects (i.e., combining two cash flow streams that are less than perfectly correlated to produce a joint stream that is less risky and that will therefore reduce capital costs). Shareholders can duplicate the effect of coinsurance on WACC through their own portfolio changes; therefore, it likely does not do something for shareholders they cannot already do on their own. However, coinsurance may expand the debt capacity of the firm, permitting greater exploitation of debt tax shields, and therefore the creation of value.
- *Contingent synergies* are those that depend on a triggering event—a right that is exercised—to produce payoffs. Examples of contingent synergies include growth option synergies, exit option synergies, and options to switch.

- When valuing synergies, one must:
  - Choose a discount rate consistent with the risk of the synergy. One size does not fit all: Riskless synergies should be discounted at the risk-free rate; highly speculative synergies should be discounted at a high rate, such as the return required by venture capitalists. Synergy cash flows as risky as earnings before interest and taxes (EBIT) could be discounted at the cost of debt; synergies as risky as dividends could be discounted at the cost of equity.
  - Reflect inflation, real growth, taxes, and a reasonable life span.
  - Use a terminal value to reflect life of the synergies beyond the forecast horizon.
- Back-solving for required synergies is useful for decision makers. In back-solving, one asks what synergies are necessary in order for a deal to be economically attractive, given a certain price.
- Synergies are:
  - Highest in horizontal deals; middling in vertical combinations; lowest in conglomerate deals.
  - Highest in "in-market" deals; lower in market extension deals.

CHAPTER 11—WORKBOOK QUESTIONS

1. *What discount rates would you choose to value the following synergy cash flows? Please explain for each whether you would use WACC, K_e, K_d, or R_f as the discount rate, and why.*

   a. *The merger between Pfizer and Pharmacia in July 2002 created a pharmaceutical giant with combined annual revenue of $48 billion. Potential cost savings were the biggest impetus for the merger: The combined company was expected to realize $2.5 billion in annual savings by 2005.*[1]

   b. *In June 2000, the French water supplier Vivendi S.A. announced its plans to acquire Seagram. Vivendi was also in the television and telecommunications businesses, and intended to bolster its presence in these areas by combining them with Seagram's Universal Studios. Vivendi intended to deliver Universal's entertainment through its (Vivendi's) digital delivery systems (i.e., wireless telephones and Internet). What discount rate would you use to value possible revenue synergies from this business combination?*

   c. *In June 1998, the Canadian Imperial Bank of Commerce (CIBC) and Toronto Dominion Bank announced a $14 billion merger. Executives of both companies said that the banks' complementary strengths made for a good fit: CIBC was strong in retail and investment banking, while Toronto Dominion had strong discount-broker and mutual-fund operations. The ability to cross-sell products of the two banks would result in revenue synergies. The executives also said that they anticipated eventual cost savings of about 10 percent a year.*[2]

2. UniMart and Harry's were two big supermarket chains operating in the southeastern United States. The two chains recently agreed to merge in response to increased competition within the industry. The feasibility of the merger hinged very much on the potential cost savings that could be achieved through greater purchasing power. The CFOs of both chains agreed that cost savings of 2 percent of annual revenue could be achieved. Around $50 million would have to be spent on redecorating the stores and putting up new signs. Revenues were expected to grow at an annual nominal rate of 4 percent. Both chains' cost of debt currently stood at 6.5 percent. Profits were taxed at a rate of 35 percent.
   What is the value of the synergies?

3. April 6, 1998, saw the announcement of the then biggest merger in history: the $83 billion deal between Travelers Group Inc. and Citicorp. The deal "brought forth a colossus—Citigroup—with a commercial bank (Citibank), an insurance company (Travelers), an investment bank (Salomon Brothers) and a retail brokerage firm (Smith Barney) all under one roof."[3] Executives at both companies bet that the one-stop-shop format would lure customers in. Cost savings were also an important part of the deal: An estimated 8,000 employees were to be laid off by the completion date. Given are stand-alone earnings forecasts for Travelers and Citicorp. Suppose that revenue synergies were forecast at 5 percent of projected revenue, that annual cost savings of $400 million were expected, and that operating margins were forecast at 12.2 percent of revenue.

Stand-Alone Summary Earnings Models

	1998F	1999F	2000F	2001F	2002F	2003F
Revenues						
Travelers	41,829	43,653	46,804	49,847	52,837	56,008
Citicorp	23,525	26,139	28,194	30,449	32,733	35,188
	65,354	69,792	74,998	80,296	85,570	91,196
Operating earnings						
Travelers	4,035	4,420	5,035	5,234	5,548	5,881
Citicorp	4,273	4,806	4,973	5,329	5,728	6,158
	8,308	9,226	10,008	10,563	11,276	12,039

Note: 1998–2000 figures taken from report by Judah Kraushaar and Amy Butte, "Citigroup: A New Model for the Millennium," Merrill Lynch, July 10, 1998. F = Forecast.

Calculate the present value of the expected synergies. (Assume a tax rate of 35 percent, a discount rate of 10 percent suitable for the cost and revenue synergies combined, and inflation of 3 percent. Assume also that the transaction is completed at the end of 1998.)

4. On behalf of Bridgewater Corporation you are negotiating to acquire Coastal Inc., a large competitor. The two sides cannot agree on price. However, the negotiator for the other side argues that the combination of the two firms will produce financial synergies that will make Newco worth $2.5 billion more than your analysis suggests. The negotiator hands you the following table in support of her analysis.

	Buyer (Before)	Target (Before)	Sum of Buyer and Target (Before)	Newco	Value Impact
Weighted average cost of capital, before the acquisition	9.1%	11.1%	9.1%		
Newco's weighted average cost of capital, after the acquisition				8.3%	
Total capital of buyer and target, before the acquisition	$26,723	$581		$27,304	
Dollar cost of capital	$ 2,424	$ 64	$2,488	$ 2,278	$ 210
Implied Present Value of Financial Synergies from Acquistion					**$2,521**
Calculation of Newco's Cost of Capital after Acquistion					
Cost of equity estimate =	**10.6%**	**14.2%**		**9.8%**	
Beta of buyer, before the acquisition	1.02				
Beta of target, before the acquisition		1.62			
Unleverered beta	0.84	1.13		0.84	
Adjustment in Newco asset beta because of covariance unanticipated by market				–0.15	
Market value weight of buyer in Newco (%)	98%				
Market value weight of target in Newco (%)		2%			
Beta of Newco				0.89	
Risk-free rate of return	4.5%	4.5%		4.5%	
Equity market risk premium	6.0%	6.0%		6.0%	
Cost of equity from CAPM	10.6%	14.2%		9.8%	
Cost of debt estimate =	**4.4%**	**6.3%**		**4.9%**	
Current *pre-tax* yields on debt, at rating and tenor of Newco	6.8%	9.8%		7.5%	
Marginal tax rate for Newco	35.0%	35.0%		35.0%	
After-tax cost of debt for Newco	4.4%	6.3%		4.9%	
Weights in target capital structure for Newco					
Targeted weight of debt (%)	25%	40%		30%	
Targeted weight of equity (%)	75%	60%		70%	

What questions or observations might you raise?

5. Phantom Computing and Ghostly Notebooks, formerly competitors in the computing industry, have agreed to merge. Phantom's management is fairly certain that the projected cost synergies—mostly to come from layoffs and restructuring—are achievable. It is less certain about the achievability of the revenue enhancements, which are expected to come from greater market power and from cross-selling the products and services of both firms. Management estimates that the net present value (NPV) of revenue synergies, discounted at a WACC of 10 percent, should be worth at least $1.2 billion in order to ensure that the deal is value enhancing.

   Based on the following information, how much should the annual revenue enhancements (in constant dollars) be in order to achieve the desired NPV?

Expected inflation rate	2%
Growth rate of FCF (nominal), in perpetuity	3%
Discount rate	10%
Ongoing investment revenue (year 1+)	2%
Operating cost revenues	90%
Tax rate	38%

6. Two auto parts manufacturers have agreed to merge. By streamlining operations, the merger is projected to generate pretax cost savings of $63 million in the first year, $118 million in the second year, $183 million in the third year, and thereafter growing at the rate of inflation. To achieve these cost savings an investment of $480 million must be made at the outset. Sales of redundant equipment and property are expected to bring in pretax gains of $63 million in the first year and $48 million in the second year. There is a high probability that these projections will materialize. The merged company's cost of capital is forecast at 9.6 percent; borrowing cost is expected to be 7.8 percent. Inflation is 2.5 percent.

   What is the present value of savings? (Assume a marginal tax rate of 35 percent.)

7. Sirius Technologies, a manufacturer of personal digital assistants (PDAs), is looking to acquire Leonid Corporation, a weaker competitor. Sirius believes Leonid's PDAs are of inferior quality, but is optimistic about a technology being developed by Leonid that would allow PDAs to measure human body temperatures and pulse rates. Sirius estimates the present value of cash flows from this new technology to be $388 million. Leonid is roughly eight months away from bringing this new technology to market. To launch the product, Sirius would need to spend approximately $272 million. The CFO of Sirius has qualms about the Leonid acquisition. He believes that while the new technology could give Sirius a first-mover advantage, it is not sophisticated enough and will be easily replicated/improved upon by competitors. Accordingly, he thinks the projected $871 million in cash flows may have a standard deviation of as much as 90 percent.

   If the current risk-free rate is 4.5 percent, what would be the value of this new technology to Sirius?

8. Refer to problem 7. Leonid wants Sirius to pay $270 million for the company. The CFO of Sirius believes that revenue synergies will be insignificant, while cost synergies will be merely $8 million a year. Here is a forecast of Leonid's financial performance, excluding the new technology:

	Year 1	Year 2	Year 3	Year 4	Year 5
Revenue	$58.00	$75.40	$90.48	$99.53	$104.50
Cost of goods sold and operating expenses	51.62	67.86	82.34	92.56	97.19
Operating income	$ 6.38	$ 7.54	$ 8.14	$ 6.97	$ 7.32
Taxes	2.23	2.64	2.85	2.44	2.56
Net income	$ 4.15	$ 4.90	$ 5.29	$ 4.53	$ 4.75
Other items:					
Capex			(20.00)		
Depreciation	1.74	2.26	2.71	2.99	3.14
Change in net working capital	(2.32)	(3.02)	(3.62)	(3.98)	(4.18)

Assuming a tax rate of 35 percent, discount rate of 12 percent, and inflation of 2.5 percent, is Leonid worth $270 million to Sirius?

NOTES

1. Scott Gotlieb, "Mergers Won't Cure Diseases," *Wall Street Journal*, July 17, 2002, p. A16.
2. Mark Heinzl, "CIBC to Merge with Toronto Dominion," *Wall Street Journal*, April 20, 1998, p. A3.
3. Ron Chernow, "The Birth of a Bureaucratic Mastodon?" *Wall Street Journal*, April 9, 1998, p. A22.

CHAPTER 12

Valuing the Firm across Borders

Going across borders affects many of the valuation assumptions in M&A. Analysts must think carefully about factors such as inflation, exchange rates, tax rates, the timing of cash remittances, political risk, market segmentation, governance, accounting principles, and social/cultural issues. Analysts must have a view, not merely about the forecast assumptions for the target firm, but also about the country and local market in which the target firm competes.

- The Fisher Equation decomposes nominal rates into inflation and a real growth rate:

$$(1+R_{\text{Nom}})^n = (1+R_{\text{Real}})^n(1+Inf)^n$$

where R_{Nom} = Nominal interest rate.
R_{Real} = Real interest rate.
Inf = Inflation rate.

- The spot rate is the exchange rate today between two currencies. The forward rate is the expected exchange rate at some future point in time. Forward exchange rates can be projected using the idea of interest rate parity, using these formulas. The relation between them supposes a constant real rate of return as suggested in the Fisher Equation.

$$\frac{SPOT_{\frac{\text{Foreign currency}}{\text{Dollar}}}}{FWD_{\frac{\text{Foreign currency}}{\text{Dollar}}}} = \frac{(1+R_{\text{Dollar}})}{(1+R_{\text{Foreign currency}})}$$

$$FWD_{\frac{\text{Foreign currency}}{\text{Dollar}}} = SPOT_{\frac{\text{Foreign currency}}{\text{Dollar}}}\left[\frac{\left(1+Inf_{\text{Foreign currency}}\right)^n}{\left(1+Inf_{\text{Dollar}}\right)^n}\right]$$

- Different countries have different tax and accounting systems. With respect to tax systems, some countries may use the territorial tax system; others may use the worldwide tax credit system. Accounting treatments may be very different from U.S. GAAP.

- There are two ways to adjust DCF calculations for higher political risk in a foreign market than your home market: (1) by "haircutting" the cash flow estimates, or (2) by raising the discount rate.
- Segmented markets are those that have a low degree of integration with the global markets. Segmentation may be created by a variety of factors such as foreign exchange controls, controls on investment by foreigners, high and variable inflation, lack of a high-quality regulatory and accounting framework, lack of country funds or cross-listed securities that provide benchmarks for arbitrage, small size of market, poor credit ratings, or absence of credit ratings. In segmented markets, a beta versus the global equity market index will poorly explain returns.
- Research suggests that equity markets of emerging markets exhibit (1) higher average returns and higher volatility than developed markets, (2) lower correlations with developed market returns, and (3) variable volatility and correlation across time.
- Cross-border DCF valuations may be approached in two ways:
    1. Convert local currency flows into dollars using forward exchange rates, and discount such flows at a dollar rate.
    2. Forecast in local currency and discount at a local WACC.

    Note: The two approaches will produce identical estimates only if assumptions are consistent.
- Nominal cash flows must be discounted at nominal rates; real cash flows must be discounted at real rates. Note that under the nominal cash flow/nominal discount rate approach, the distortion of historical cost assets causes cash flows to be less than they would be with current cost assets. The real/real approach ignores this distortion.
- Aside from the simple CAPM, other methods can be used to estimate the cost of equity:
    - ***Multifactor model*** considers the exposure of a stock to various factors, both macroeconomic and firm-specific, such as world stock market price risk, country stock market risk, industry risk, foreign exchange rate risk, political risk, and liquidity risk.

$$(R_i - R_f) = \alpha_i + \beta_{i/W}(R_W - R_f) + \beta_{i/C}(R_C - R_f) + \beta_{i/I}(R_I - R_f) + \beta_{Ex}(R_{Ex} - R_f) + \beta_D(R_C^D - R_{AAA}) + \beta_L(R_L^{Lo} - R_L^{Hi}) + \varepsilon$$

where:

R = Return.
β = Regression coefficient.
i = Specific company.
f = Risk-free.
W = Global equity market portfolio.
C = Country equity market portfolio.
I = Industry equity market portfolio.
Ex = Portfolio of foreign currency deposits.
D = Sovereign debt instrument of home country, C.
AAA = Highest-rated sovereign debt instrument.
L = Portfolio of low or high liquidity bonds.
ε = Regression residual indicating company-specific variability of returns (unsystematic risk).

- *CAPM*, the capital asset pricing model, suggests that the relevant measure of a stock's risk is how it covaries with the equity market portfolio. This can be expressed in its domestic or global versions (the ICAPM). The domestic version is based on the home equity market portfolio; the global version is based on the global equity market portfolio.

$$\text{CAPM: } k_e = R_f + \beta_i \cdot (R_{\text{Market}} - R_f)$$

$$\text{ICAPM: } k_e = R_f + \beta_i^W \cdot (R_m^W - R_f)$$

- *Credit model* relies on non–equity market measures.

$$K_{i,t+1} = \gamma_0 + \gamma_1 \times \ln(\text{Country credit risk rating}_{it}) + \varepsilon_{it+1}$$

- *Adjusted CAPM* adjusts cost of equity for segmentation and political risks.

$$k_e = R_f^{US} + \pi + (\beta_i^{Foreign} \cdot \beta_{Foreign}^{US}) \cdot (R_m^{US} - R_f^{US})$$

CHAPTER 12—WORKBOOK QUESTIONS

1. Following is an income statement projection for an acquisition target in a developing nation. The forecasts are in the local currency, and have been projected using an expected real rate of growth of 5 percent, which is also the expected perpetual growth rate. The local sovereign debt yields are currently at 8 percent, which factors in expected inflation of 3 percent.

   What is the NPV of these cash flows?

   Assume that the cost of capital for this company is a nominal 13 percent, and that net working capital requirements will increase by 0.5 percent of sales each year, and that depreciation and capital expenditures offset each other. Depreciation is based on historical book values.

($ MM)	Year 1	Year 2	Year 3	Year 4	Year 5
Sales	68,776	72,215	75,826	79,617	83,598
Cost of goods sold (65.5% of sales)	45,048	47,301	49,666	52,149	54,756
Gross profit	23,728	24,914	26,160	27,468	28,841
Operating expenses (24.5% of sales)	16,850	17,693	18,577	19,506	20,481
Operating income	6,878	7,221	7,583	7,962	8,360
Interest expense	741	631	712	753	771
Income before taxes	6,137	6,590	6,871	7,209	7,589
Taxes (@34%)	1,964	2,109	2,199	2,307	2,428
Net income	4,173	4,482	4,672	4,902	5,160

[This spreadsheet can be found in the folder "Key Spreadsheets from the Workbook" located on the CD-ROM.]

2. On September 1, 1997, the exchange rate between the U.S. dollar and the Philippine peso was US$1:PhP30.4. The one-year Philippine Treasury bill rate at this time was 15 percent, while the yield on the one-year U.S. Treasury was 5.52 percent. The expected inflation rate for the Philippines was 8 percent, and for the United States it was 2.5 percent.

   a. *Using interest rate parity, what is your estimate of the peso-dollar exchange rate one year hence as implied by the Treasury bill yields in the two countries?*

   b. *Use equation (5) in Chapter 12 of main text to estimate the forward rate one year hence as implied by the expected exchange rates in the two countries.*

$$FWD_{\frac{\text{Peso}}{\text{Dollar}}} = SPOT_{\frac{\text{Peso}}{\text{Dollar}}} \left[\frac{(1+Inf_{\text{Peso}})^n}{(1+Inf_{\text{Dollar}})^n} \right]$$

   c. *Did you get the same answers to a and b? Why or why not?*

3. Assume you have acquired manufacturing equipment for $500 million, and that it has a useful life of 10 years. Depreciation, calculated on a straight-line basis, will be $50 million per year. Inflation is 3 percent, the real discount rate is 4.85 percent, and the tax rate is 40 percent.

   a. *What would be the present value of the depreciation tax shields from year 1 to year 5? Use the nominal discount rate to calculate present value.*

   b. *Now assume that you can inflate depreciation expense at a rate of 3 percent annually. Using the same discount rate, what is the present value of depreciation tax shields from year 1 to year 5?*

   c. *Go back to (a). This time, use the real discount rate to calculate the present value of the tax shields. What do you observe? How would you interpret the results?*

4. Following is a free cash flow estimate and valuation for a Brazilian company. Values are given in Brazilian reals (R$), and the NPV is translated into U.S. dollars at the current exchange rate of US$1:R$3.54.

(R$, in millions)		2003	2004	2005	2006	2007	2008
Free cash flows		R$1,505	1,990	2,674	3,153	3,780	8,219
Terminal value						103,247	
Cash flows including terminal value		R$1,505	1,990	2,674	3,153	107,028	
Present value in reals	R$62,578		32.21%	34.37%	17.95%	19.88%	
Present value in U.S. Dollars	$17,677						

[This spreadsheet can be found in the folder "Key Spreadsheets from the Workbook" located on the CD-ROM.]

Translate the cash flows into U.S. dollars and find their present value. Assume the following:

Inflation rate, United States	2.4%
Inflation rate, Brazil	8.4%
Exchange rate at time 0 (reals per dollar)	R$3.54
Real discount rate	5.0%

Did you come up with the same present value? What rate did you use to discount the U.S. dollar flows? What assumptions are necessary to obtain equivalency between the approach of converting local flows into dollars and discounting at a dollar rate and the approach of forecasting in local currency and discounting at a local rate?

5. You are trying to determine the cost of equity for a target located in a developing country whose cash flows you have projected in dollars. You have the following data:

10-year rate, U.S. dollar denominated sovereign bonds	7.25%
Beta of target versus foreign country stock index	0.97
Beta of foreign country stock index versus U.S. index	1.28
Market risk premium, United States	6.00%
Market risk premium, foreign country	8.00%

[The spreadsheet can be found in the folder "Key Spreadsheets from the Workbook" located on the CD-ROM.]

What would be your estimate of this firm's cost of equity?

6. In late April 2003, you are attempting to determine Singapore Airlines' cost of equity for valuing cash flows in Singapore dollars. Its beta versus the global equity portfolio was 1.02 over the past 12 months. You estimate, based on the past 17 years of data, that the equity market premium on the global portfolio is 5.8 percent. Currently, the Singaporean Treasury bond yield is at 4.5 percent.

   a. *What is your estimate of Singapore Airlines' cost of equity based on the preceding data?*
   b. *Estimate the cost of equity for Southwest Airlines and American Airlines using a risk premium of 5.6 percent for the United States. Based on stock price performance over the past 12 months, the betas for the two companies versus the S&P 500 index are 1.10 and 2.16 respectively. The yield on the 10-year U.S. Treasury bond in April 2003 is 3.8 percent.*
   c. *Are the costs of equity among the three airlines comparable? What are the drivers of the differences among their costs of equity?*

7. *For each of the following situations, what method(s) might you use for calculating the cost of equity? Write out the equation for each method you choose, and explain why you think it is appropriate.*

a. You work for a large conglomerate that has holdings in companies in more than 50 different countries; most of the investments are in consumer goods manufacturers. Currently your firm is evaluating a potential Malaysian target. What method would you use to calculate the cost of equity for the Malaysian company?

b. You have just set up your own private equity firm in Canada and are evaluating your first investment—in the United States. The target is small and privately held. What method would you use to calculate the cost of equity for this company?

8. Telekom Malaysia BHD is a provider of telecommunication and related services in Malaysia.

   Calculate the U.S. dollar cost of equity for the company under the different approaches. You are given the data you will need for each approach.

   a. ICAPM:

U.S. risk-free rate	5.43%
World risk premium	5.70%
Telekom Malaysia beta vs. world portfolio	0.31

   b. CAPM adjusted for segmentation and political risk:

Return on U.S. 10-year T-bond	5.43%
U.S. equity market premium	5.70%
Beta, Malaysia vs. S&P	0.39
Beta, Telekom Malaysia vs. Malaysia market	1.34
Country credit spread	1.47%

   c. Compare your results from the two methods. How do you interpret the differences?

CHAPTER 13

Valuing the Highly Levered Firm, Assessing the Highly Levered Transaction

High leverage presents special challenges for M&A practitioners and analysts. Because of the relatively low volume of highly leveraged transactions (HLTs), this is an area of M&A in which sound judgment comes at a super-premium. Having a rigorous view of the way to analyze these deals and their wealth-transfer possibilities is vital.

- Highly levered transactions appear in corporate finance in three classic forms:

  1. *Leveraged buyout (LBO).* In this transaction a private group of investors acquire a company (or division) financed with a mixture of high-ratio debt and equity. In the LBO, the management of the target is usually retained, and often takes an equity interest in Newco—hence the alternative name for this transaction, management buyout. In addition, it is also called a going-private transaction. A typical LBO candidate would have most of the following features: (1) strong cash flow, (2) low level of capital expenditures, (3) strong market position, (4) stable industry, (5) low rate of technological change (and low R&D expense), (6) proven management with no anticipated changes, (7) relatively low (or under-) valuation in the stock market, and (8) no major change in strategy.
  2. *Leveraged recapitalization.* In a "recap" the company dramatically levers itself and uses the proceeds of the financing to pay an extraordinary dividend or to repurchase shares. The leveraged recapitalization is similar to the LBO except that the company continues to be publicly owned.
  3. *Reorganization in distress or bankruptcy.* In bankruptcy the value of the firm's assets is less than the value of its debt. Under protection of a court, the firm reorganizes its debt and equity claims.

- The buyout boom gained momentum in the early 1980s, peaked in 1988 with the massive buyout of RJR Nabisco, and receded somewhat in the 1990s.

- Typically the LBO offers a sizable abnormal return to shareholders of target companies. Also, shareholders of the buyer group typically earn large absolute returns. The large returns to target and buyer shareholders stem from significant improvements in operating efficiency.

- Leverage has two offsetting effects on firm value. The first is the benefit of *debt tax shields*—literally, the savings in free cash flow owing to a lower tax bill. The second effect is the *default risk*, which will offset the value created by borrowing as the borrowing of the firm increases.
- It is difficult to value highly levered firms because costs of bankruptcy and distress are unobservable. There is no fluid market in which these costs are isolated, priced, and may be observed from one day to the next. The analyst can look for some guidance from two sources: debt market yields and put option valuation. The difficulty of estimating the value of the highly levered firm poses two chief implications for the M&A practitioner. First, analytic rigor is even more important in the instance of highly levered transactions (HLTs), not less. Second, the ambiguities about valuing the highly levered firm mean that there will be many opportunities to transfer value from some players (e.g., creditors) to others (e.g., equity holders) in the design of the transaction.
- To use the adjusted present value approach to valuation, follow these steps:
    1. Project the book value balance sheets before and after the transaction.
    2. Estimate the market value of the enterprise before the transaction by adding together the book value of liabilities and the market value of equity of the firm.
    3. Estimate the present value of the firm's debt tax shields before the HLT.
    4. Solve for the implied market value of the firm's long-term business assets before the HLT.
    5. Solve for the market value of equity of the firm after the HLT including new debt tax shields.
    6. Estimate the new price per share as equal to the new market value of equity, plus any extraordinary dividend to be received, divided by the number of shares.
- The key lesson of the highly levered transaction is the need for a "*whole deal*" perspective, which looks at the risks and returns to all the players in the transaction. The whole deal perspective includes asking four kinds of questions:
    1. Is the purchase price for the target appropriate? Begin by valuing the target of the HLT. If the price is greater than intrinsic value, one should go no further with the HLT.
    2. What are the sources of positive NPV? If the first step suggests that the intrinsic value of the target is greater than purchase price, one should scrutinize the assumptions to identify *key value drivers*.
    3. Can the firm sustain the debt it will assume? This third question focuses on *financial feasibility*, as measured by analyses of asset coverage, interest coverage, and covenant coverage.
    4. What are the prospective returns to various providers of funds in the deal? Too often analysts focus only on the NPVs or internal rates of return (IRRs) of their own firm's investment in the target, rather than on the allocation of

profits among all the players. This final analysis focuses on possible *wealth transfers* among participants.

- The methodology and results of the risk analysis offer some important lessons about debt capacity and capital adequacy. Capital adequacy should be measured by the ability of expected cash flows to cover debt service requirements. In setting capitalization targets, point estimates of coverage are of limited value. What matters is the *probability of default*.
- Highly levered transactions are a prominent fixture on the M&A landscape. The analysis of HLTs uses discounted cash flow based on rates reflecting the classic risk-and-return relationship of modern financial theory. Yet these transactions require careful scrutiny for nonlinearities in the estimation of beta, for circularities in respect to capital structure assumptions, and for changing capital structures.

CHAPTER 13—WORKBOOK QUESTIONS

Case: Deep-Sea Tuna[1]

In 1984, Laurel Everett, the managing lending officer of Drake and Hollinger Bank (D&H Bank) was approached by Crawford & Co. to help finance $59 million for a management-led leveraged buyout of Deep-Sea Tuna Inc. from its parent company, Felicity Foods, Inc.

Crawford was looking to find an institutional investor to purchase $7 million in senior subordinated debt, which included the right to buy a 20 percent equity stake in the new company for an additional $1 million. The remaining $2.3 million in equity would be divided between the Felicity management team and Crawford. D&H Bank would be the sole creditor; thus, Felicity agreed to take back $15 million in junior subordinated notes.

Proposed Financing Structure

Senior Secured Bank Notes

Amount:	$37 million
Rate:	16%
Maturity:	7 years
Amortization:	Debt to be paid down as quickly as profits allow

Senior Subordinated Notes (Institutional Investor)

Amount:	$7 million
Rate:	16%
Maturity:	15 years
Amortization:	20% of face amount in years 11 through 15
Security:	Inventory and receivables, no trademarks

Junior Subordinated Notes

Amount:	$15 million
Rate:	12%
Maturity:	5 years
Amortization:	End of: 6 months, $1.5mm; 12 months, $1.5mm; 18 months, $2.0mm; 3 years, $2.5mm; 4 years, $2.5mm; 5 years, $5.0mm
Security:	Trademarks, Puerto Rican cannery leasehold, inventory, and receivables
Subordination:	Subordinated to principal and interest payments of senior bank debt and interest payments of senior subordinated notes

Common Equity

Amount:	$3.3 million
Investors:	Institutional investor of senior subordinated notes ($1.0mm buys 20%) Crawford & Co. ($2.0mm buys 40%) Management ($0.3mm buys 40%)

In early 1984, the managers of Felicity Foods decided to divest Deep-Sea Tuna because the tuna operation did not fit well with the company's overall business strategy. Felicity managers approached Deep-Sea Tuna to propose a possible management buyout. In addition, Felicity Foods hired/retained an investment bank to solicit bids from other interested buyers. None of their bids, however, exceeded Deep-Sea's net book value and therefore Felicity Foods decided to focus its efforts on the Deep-Sea management group. To facilitate the deal, the parent company even agreed to charge only the risk-free interest rate of 12 percent on the $15 million junior subordinated debt. To reduce the risk, the junior notes were scheduled to retire in five years, significantly sooner than the retirement of the senior subordinated notes.

Two years earlier, Deep-Sea had begun to experience difficulties after Felicity management had decided to expand capacity by entering into long-term contracts and by purchasing the largest tuna fleet in the industry. Felicity's strategic intent was to gain market share nationally. However, Felicity's decision unfortunately coincided with a period of overcapacity and stable demand in the tuna industry. Deep-Sea managers had to take cost-cutting measures soon thereafter, thus relinquishing the goal of capturing national market share in order to maintain their foothold in traditional markets. They also contracted their business by discontinuing certain operations and closing down plants. After the company incurred some initial losses due to discontinued operations, the overall cost cuts began to improve its bottom line.

Management believed that they could help continue this positive trend and that further improvement would follow. In particular, the proposed new managers estimated that $9.6 million in annual savings would be realized.

Refer to the following exhibits before answering the questions.

DEEP-SEA TUNA, INC.
Pro Forma Balance Sheets
(in millions $)

	1985	1986	1987	1988	1989	1990	1991	1992
Cash	0.0	0.0	0.0	0.0	0.0	0.0	0.0	0.0
Other receivables	1.1	1.1	1.1	1.1	1.1	1.1	1.1	1.1
Accounts receivable	0.0	10.9	11.0	10.9	10.9	11.7	11.7	11.7
Inventory	54.7	56.6	57.4	56.6	56.8	61.2	61.2	61.2
Other current assets	4.0	4.0	4.0	4.0	4.0	4.0	4.0	4.0
Total current assets	$59.8	$72.6	$73.5	$72.5	$72.8	$78.0	$78.0	$78.0
Plant, prop., and equip.	0.5	0.8	1.1	1.6	2.1	2.6	2.9	3.2
Other assets	2.0	2.0	2.0	2.0	2.0	2.0	2.0	2.0
Total assets	$62.3	$75.4	$76.6	$76.1	$76.9	$82.6	$82.9	$83.2
Accruals and payables	0.0	10.5	10.6	10.5	10.5	11.3	11.3	11.3
Current portion LTD	3.0	2.0	2.5	2.5	5.0	0.0	0.0	0.0
Total current liab.	$ 3.0	$12.5	$13.1	$13.0	$15.5	$11.3	$11.3	$11.3
Debt: Sr. bank	37.0	36.4	32.8	27.7	22.7	22.4	11.9	0.0
Sr. sub. notes	7.0	7.0	7.0	7.0	7.0	7.0	7.0	7.0
Jr. sub. notes	12.0	10.0	7.5	5.0	0.0	0.0	0.0	0.0
Total liabilities	$59.0	$65.9	$60.4	$52.7	$45.2	$40.7	$30.3	$18.4
Equity	3.3	3.3	3.3	3.3	3.3	3.3	3.3	3.3
Retained earnings	0.0	6.2	12.9	20.1	28.4	38.6	49.3	61.5
Total liabilities and owners' equity	$62.3	$75.4	$76.6	$76.1	$76.9	$82.6	$82.9	$83.2
Capital expenditures		$0.6	$0.8	$1.1	$1.1	$1.1	$1.1	$1.1
Depreciation		$0.3	$0.5	$0.6	$0.6	$0.6	$0.8	$0.8

DEEP-SEA TUNA, INC.
Pro Forma Income Statement
(in millions $)

	1986	1987	1988	1989	1990	1991	1992
Sales	$208.9	$211.9	$208.7	$209.5	$225.7	$225.7	$225.7
Cost of goods sold	169.2	171.6	169.0	169.7	182.8	182.8	182.8
Gross profit	$ 39.7	$ 40.3	$ 39.7	$ 39.8	$ 42.9	$ 42.9	$ 42.9
Distribution	5.0	5.1	5.0	5.0	5.4	5.4	5.4
Selling	10.2	10.4	10.2	10.3	11.1	11.1	11.1
General and admin.	8.4	8.5	8.3	8.4	9.0	9.0	9.0
Operating income	$ 16.1	$ 16.3	$ 16.1	$ 16.1	$ 17.4	$ 17.4	$ 17.4
Interest expense	8.8	8.4	7.6	6.5	5.4	4.7	3.0
Profit before taxes	7.2	7.9	8.5	9.7	12.0	12.7	14.4
Income taxes	1.1	1.2	1.3	1.5	1.8	1.9	2.2
Net income	$ 6.2	$ 6.7	$ 7.2	$ 8.2	$ 10.2	$ 10.8	$ 12.2
Assumed interest rates:							
U.S. bank debt	16.0%	Tax rate			15%		
Junior debt	12.0%						

Calculation of Cash Flows to Equity

	1986	1987	1988	1989	1990	1991	1992
Net income	$ 6.2	$ 6.7	$ 7.2	$ 8.2	$ 10.2	$ 10.8	$ 12.2
Plus depreciation	0.3	0.5	0.6	0.6	0.6	0.8	0.8
Less capital expenditures	(0.6)	(0.8)	(1.1)	(1.1)	(1.1)	(1.1)	(1.1)
Less additions to working capital	(2.3)	(0.8)	0.9	(0.2)	(4.4)	0.0	0.0
Less debt amortization	(3.6)	(5.6)	(7.6)	(7.5)	(5.3)	(10.5)	(11.9)
Cash flow to equity[1]	$ 0.0	$ 0.0	$ 0.0	$ 0.0	$ 0.0	$ 0.0	$ 0.0

1. Leveraged buyouts are usually designed so that debt service absorbs virtually all of the cash flow of the firm.

[These spreadsheets can be found in the folder "Key Spreadsheets from the Workbook" located on the CD-ROM.]

1. *Estimate the equity value of Deep-Sea Tuna Company. Refer to Exhibit 13.4 in the main text and to the Chapter 13 Questions and Answers located on the CD-ROM as guides for your calculations. Use a terminal (perpetual) growth rate of 2.5 percent.*

2. *Is the deal attractive from the perspective of a senior mezzanine investor?*

3. *Is the deal attractive from the perspective of a senior-secured debt investor?*

4. *What is your overall analysis of this deal? With all relevant parties in mind, is it a well-structured management buyout?*

NOTE

1. This problem is a disguised synopsis of an actual leveraged buyout case study prepared by Robert Bruner and Peter Hennessy.

CHAPTER 14

Real Options and Their Impact on M&A

Real options are usually unique, derived from nonfinancial assets such as land, plant and machinery, patents, and artistic property. These are usually challenging to value. Nonetheless, having a real options mind-set (i.e., looking for real optionality in any business situation) can lend important insights into the structure and valuation of deals.

- Analysts and executives should strive to master real options thinking for at least four reasons:
  1. Real options are pervasive in the business environment.
  2. Real options can have a material influence on firm value.
  3. One can easily create and destroy real option value.
  4. Discounted cash flow and other cash flow methods alone fail to capture qualities about an asset that are not reflected in the projected cash flows.
- Real options can be difficult to value because the parameters are not always clear. For instance, the exercise price, expiration date, and underlying value of the asset may be contingent. Or the option may actually consist of a cluster of options.
- Best practice in M&A draws on real option theory to:
  - Refine estimates of value.
  - Structure thinking about M&A opportunities, particularly for setting strategy and planning integration.
  - Guide deal design and negotiation problem solving.
- Some generic types of real options include:
  - Entry or growth options.
  - Exit or abandonment options.
  - Timing options: rights to delay or accelerate.
  - Switching options.
- Real options may appear in the field of M&A in strategic planning, deal design, and postmerger integration:
  - In strategy, real options appear in decisions about flexibility versus irreversibility of actions; insurance; learning and competencies (e.g., the acquisition of

strategic capabilities); and planning. Possible applications of real options in strategy might focus on:

    - Buying a minority interest versus total control.
    - Buying a built-up company versus building up the same assets yourself.
    - Moving first, as opposed to following.
    - Rights to exploit an uncertain resource.
    - Acquisition search.
  - Real options often appear in deal design through the exchange offer, breakup terms, liquidity and control features, contingent payment schemes, transaction risk management, and the adoption of takeover tactics.
  - In postmerger integration, real options may appear in the organizational design and operational architecture of the firm, the structuring of contracts for human resources, and the selection among competing capabilities.
- Despite the pervasiveness of "rights," not all of them are options—some rights are better classified as "opportunities" rather than options. You may have the right to sell lemonade at the curbside in front of your house, but it's an opportunity rather than an option. Options exist where asset values are uncertain, the rights are exclusive, the decision can be freely and rationally made, and the rights are costly to acquire.
- Chapter 14 of the main text outlined steps to assess the impact of real options:
  1. Find and specify the option. Anything that creates the right to "get" is a *call* option. The right to give away in return for payment is a *put* option. Anything that provides flexibility is a *long* position. Any commitment is a *short* position.
  2. Options and their values can be assessed for three considerations:
     - ***Direction.*** Who holds the option? Who is the counterparty? Does the option create or destroy value for your position?
     - ***Materiality.*** Will the option make a material difference? Where the decision is important, the valuation analysis based on discounted cash flow seems close, and/or the assets under option are sizable, the option values will make a difference.
     - ***Key value drivers.*** What attributes of the asset are its main value drivers?
  3. Model and value the option. There are four possible approaches for valuing options:
     - Value the real option in the framework of an existing equation (e.g., the *Black-Scholes option pricing model*).
     - Fit the option in the framework of a *binomial* lattice.
     - Fit the option in a *decision tree* framework.
     - Value the option using *simulation analysis*.
  4. Interpret the results and develop implications.
     - Examine real option estimates against some test of reasonableness.
     - Examine one's confidence level in the estimated values.
     - Ask "so what?"

CHAPTER 14—WORKBOOK QUESTIONS

1. *Where can you find real options in the field of M&A?*

2. *List four methods of estimating real option value, and consider where each method could be used.*

3. *Assume you are a general manager of a professional sports club. You have just built a new stadium for the club, with $5 million remaining in your budget. Your architect proposes four ways to use the $5 million: upgrading a section of seats to private luxury rooms; building a multimedia center that will hold more than 50 journalists; upgrading the court to a multifunction one so that it can be used for basketball, ice hockey, and even arena football matches; and installing a flexible lighting and sound system that allows the stadium to be used for concerts or other events. Among these, which one seems like an option to you? Please explain why.*

4. Mr. Jones is a top professional basketball player. His agent just signed a deal with the New York Knicks. He will be given $25 million for the next three years, with an option to extend his contract for one more year at a salary of $8 million. Normally, after two years, if he plays well, he will get a contract extension for several years and forfeit the one-year extension. Based on current market demand and on his health, he estimates that the possibility of getting a contract extension is about 60 percent. If he does not get the contract extension, he thinks there is a 50 percent chance that he will be able to sign a contract with another team for a yearly salary of $10 million, and a 50 percent chance of getting a contract for $5 million a year. In the first instance, he will definitely forfeit his extension option and go for the $10 million. And in the latter instance, he may exercise his extension option in order to get the $8 million salary.

   From this information, draw a decision tree and value the extension option for Mr. Jones. (Do not consider the time value of the money.)

5. Referring to problem 4, assume that there is another clause in the agreement that allows the club to buy out the last two years of Mr. Jones' contract for $10 million after the first year or buy out the last year of his contract for $6 million if he does not perform well. The total value of the contract was $25 million—the payout schedule being $7.5 million, $8.5 million, and $9 million respectively for years 1, 2, and 3. Given his track record and the current team structure, there is a 75 percent chance that Mr. Jones will play well in the first year. If that happens, the probability of playing well in the second year will be 80 percent.

   Assuming there is no monetary benefit to the team keeping him if he does not perform well, what is the value of the club's option to buy out Mr. Jones' contract? Use a discount rate of 10 percent and assume that the payment is made in the beginning of each year. (Consider the time value of money.)

6. Your company is considering acquiring a patent for an innovative hard drive from a computer hardware company. The seller agrees to give you the right to purchase the patent after three years for $10 million. Based on market research data, the estimated value of the patent today is $8 million. But uncertainty about

this patent's success leads you to conclude that its value has a future volatility of 25 percent.

Given a three-year risk-free rate of 7.5 percent, please value this right. (Use the file "Option Valuation.xls," found on the CD-ROM, for your calculations.)

7. Bockhaus Industries is developing a joint venture deal with a local company in an emerging market. Due to industry regulations, Bockhaus Industries can own only 50 percent of this joint venture at the moment. The gradual deregulation of the domestic industry will allow Bockhaus Industries to have a maximum 75 percent share after three years and 100 percent ownership in five years. Therefore, Bockhaus Industries is planning to sign an agreement with its partner to give it the right to buy the rest of the company at its current market price of $20 million. The annual volatility of the venture is 20 percent, and the risk-free rate is 5 percent (assume this is constant).

   What is the maximum value that Bockhaus Industries should be willing to pay? (Using the binomial method, draw the tree and fold it back to calculate the present value of this portfolio of European options.)

8. Company ABC, a leading chip maker, is considering engaging in a joint venture deal with a semiconductor company XYZ, which just developed an innovative photolithography technology. Due to the complexity and uncertainty of this new technology, the deal is structured in the following way:

   Stage one: ABC will pay $10 million up front to fund R&D for one year.

   Stage two: After XYZ develops the first prototype of chips using this technology, ABC agrees to pay another $10 million as milestone payment. Developing the first prototype will take one year.

   Stage three: If the beta test of this technology is successful, ABC will pay another $10 million. Beta testing will take one year.

   Stage four: Finally, if test marketing is successful ABC will pay $25 million. It will take half a year to finish test marketing.

   Based on market research data and responses to this technology, the management team made four estimates about the probabilities of success and size of profits:

   1. XYZ has an 80 percent chance of successfully developing the prototype.
   2. XYZ has a 75 percent chance of passing the beta test if stage one is completed.
   3. There is a 90 percent chance that test marketing will be successful if stage two is completed.
   4. Based on forecasts of the market, there is a 70 percent chance of earning a profit of $200 million and a 30 percent chance of earning $100 million if stage three is completed.

   If ABC is seeking 60 percent of the joint venture, how much, in terms of NPV, will it earn from this investment? Draw the decision tree and calculate the NPV of the project assuming a 10 percent discount rate.

9. Consider the following expansion project. Utility company ABC can sign a deal with the Chinese government to build an oil-based power plant. An investment of $10 million will be required today. During the first three years, company ABC is entitled to 100 percent of the profits from the power plant. After three years, it will hand the plant back to the Chinese government. Forecasted revenue for the first year follows a normal distribution with a mean of $50 million and a standard deviation of $25 million. Revenues are projected to increase by 5 percent annually for years 2 and 3. The expected profit margin is 20 percent. A discount rate of 25 percent has been assigned to this project.

   a. *Should the company invest in this project? Explain using both quantitative and qualitative reasons.*

   b. *Suppose the Chinese government allows company ABC to increase its capacity after the first year if revenues reach $50 million. An investment of $1.5 million will be needed to increase capacity. If this additional investment is made, any revenues in excess of $50 million will grow by 20 percent, on top of the 5 percent natural growth of the industry. (The original $50 million will still grow by 5 percent annually.) In addition, the profit margin for the entire operation will increase to 21 percent. Under these conditions, how much is this project worth to company ABC?*

CHAPTER 15

Valuing Liquidity and Control

Liquidity and control can have sizable effects on shareholder value. They are rights that may be assessed for their option value. Illiquidity requires a discount from liquid values, and minority status requires a discount from value with control. Volatility and time produce material variations in estimates of the premiums and discounts.

- The value of a target firm consists of its stand-alone value plus synergy value plus a premium or discount for liquidity and control:

$$\text{Maximum payment for target} = V_{\text{Stand-alone}} + V_{\text{Synergies}} + \pi_{\text{Liquidity and control}}$$

- "Liquidity" implies the ability to find a ready price and counterparty for a transaction to purchase or sell an asset. Illiquidity commands a discount sufficient to induce investors to buy the nonmarketable asset rather than an identical marketable asset.
- Liquidity is valuable. This is found in many studies of illiquid securities such as letter stock, entrepreneurs' restricted shares, private placements before public transactions, initial public offerings, and so on. Its value varies with volatility, time to maturity, and other factors.
- The value of liquidity can be modeled as the value of a European put option with a strike price equal to the share price at date of issue. Volatility, the length of the restriction period, the risk-free rate, and the stock's dividend yield significantly determine the discount.
- "Control" is the right to direct the strategy and activities of the firm, to allocate resources, and to distribute the economic wealth of the firm.
- When shares are widely dispersed among shareholders, effective control may be achieved with a relatively small block of shares. Voting power (that determines control) is determined by the likelihood that a stockholder or group of stockholders might become the decisive factor in the outcome of a vote. Voting power can be estimated using the Shapley Value, which measures the number of times each player in a contest would be pivotal to the voting outcome.
- Research tells us that owning a controlling interest commands a premium; owning a minority interest commands a discount relative to the controller. Some research findings provide evidence of the value of controlling power:

- ***Dual-class shares.*** Research finds that the class with superior voting rights trades at a material premium relative to the junior class for firms that have two classes of common stock outstanding.
- ***Block trades.*** Studies show that trades of large blocks of stock can alter the ownership structure of a firm. Blocks have been found to trade at a 20 percent premium, reflecting the voting power of the block.
- ***The private benefits of control, pyramids, and cross-shareholdings.*** One reason that control might be valuable is that it presents the opportunity for the majority to expropriate wealth of the minority. Benefits not shared by all shareholders are private benefits. Private benefits can be achieved through control, pyramids, and cross-shareholdings.
- ***M&A transactions.*** Research suggests that acquiring a majority position commands a premium 20 to 30 percent higher than the price paid for a minority position.

- The conventional multiplicative approach for estimating the joint impact of illiquidity and lack of control is:

$$V_{\text{With discount}} = V_{\text{Base}}\,[(1 - d_L) \times (1 - d_C) - 1]$$

where V_{Base} = Value of the firm without accounting for illiquidity or lack of control.
d_L = Percentage discount for illiquidity.
d_C = Percentage discount (premium) for lack of control (control).

- The discounts or premiums are typically determined by studying a sample of comparable transactions. Given the dissimilarity among transactions, considerable judgment is involved in developing a suggested discount or premium. Chapter 15 of the main text emphasizes that since control and liquidity are options, their effects may well interact. The conventional adjustment outlined earlier assumes no such interaction.

- Discounts or premiums have meaning only relative to some base case. It is vital to clearly describe the base case when discussing any discount or premium. Chapter 15 assumes as a convention that the base case would be a firm whose shares are actively traded on a public stock exchange (and therefore "liquid"), and among whose shareholders there was no *control asymmetry*, meaning that no shareholder or group of shareholders had controlling power over the firm and that therefore no control premium or discount could be applied to the value of the shares.

- Four reasons why liquidity and control may interact are:

1. Liquidity may bring with it transparency, which may reduce the value of control.
2. Liquidity may be associated with more dispersed shareholdings.
3. Control positions tend to be sticky. Controlling shareholders tend not to trade shares actively, and if they decide to sell control intact, may experience delays in selling. Thus, liquidation of a control position occurs only after

you have tried to create value through strategic choice. This time sequencing of control and liquidation choices suggests that the decision to liquidate depends on the prior choice of strategy.

4. With control, any decision to liquidate is complicated by the right to choose the most attractive strategy.

- If, as Chapter 15 argues, control and liquidity are options, then using a standard discount or premium for all transactions is inappropriate. Such adjustments should be tailored carefully to the situation of the specific target company. One size does not fit all.

CHAPTER 15—WORKBOOK QUESTIONS

1. Not only do liquidity discounts and control premiums permeate the M&A world, they are everywhere in our daily lives, from baseball card trading to your election bid for the student body president position and so on. Think about examples in your personal life when you have had to pay a premium or discount for something.

   Why did you have to pay the premium/discount?

2. Suppose you are purchasing a private company that has a value of $50 million today. The acquisition agreement does not allow you to sell the equity until the end of the third year. Your estimated volatility of the firm's value for the next three years is 22 percent, and the risk-free rate is 3 percent.

   Should you ask for a liquidity discount from the owner? If so, by how much? Assuming risk neutrality, use the binomial pricing model to value the discount. Assume that the length of each period in the binomial model is one year.

3. Refer to problem 2. Assume that you can sell your equity stake only after five years. Assume the same volatility and risk-free rate for the next five years.

   How much of a discount should you deduct from the base value? Compare your result to that in problem 2 and explain the difference.

4. You are the CEO of a private company and are negotiating a deal with a potential buyer. The base value of your firm using the DCF method assuming full liquidity is around $10 million. Based on current market conditions, you and the buyer agree that it would be very difficult for the buyer to resell your firm to another party or to launch a public offering in two years. You are asking for $9 million for your firm and the buyer wants to pay only $8.5 million. Given a two-year Treasury bond yield of 5 percent, explain the difference in asking prices between buyer and seller. Assume that both estimate the same base values for your firm, and that no synergies are considered.

   Use the Black-Scholes model to find the implicit volatility in your asking price and the bidder's offering price.

5. Assume you have just been hired as the CEO of a public company. The board of directors offers you a compensation package that includes call options on

100,000 shares of the company's stock at an exercise price equivalent to today's trading price of $40. The options expire in five years and cannot be exercised in the first two years, which is a "lockup" period for you. You find some data from several sources: The two-year Treasury rate is at 6 percent, the six-year T-note yields 7.5 percent, the historical volatility for the stock is 20 percent, and the company does not plan to pay any dividends in the near future.

How much are the options worth? Use the Black-Scholes model to find an approximate value.

6. In Chapter 15 of the main text, the Shapley Value is introduced to assess the voting power of any given type of shareholder. The file "Power.xls," found on the CD-ROM, can be used to calculate the power index and power ratio for scenarios where there are two major shareholders and the rest are oceanic shareholders.

   a. Assume the oceanic shareholders have 50 percent control of the company; by varying the ratio between the two major shareholders, calculate the corresponding power index.

      What conclusion can be drawn from the results?

   b. Assume the oceanic shareholders have 10 percent control of the company; by varying the ratio between the two major shareholders, calculate the corresponding power index.

      What conclusion can be drawn from the results?

7. You are the CEO of a trading firm considering a merger with another trading firm. After the merger you will have full control of the company, so you start thinking about how to implement your aggressive strategy in the target company. The target has $100 million in capital. By acquiring control of the target, you gain the right to impose a new strategy on the firm. At present, the new strategy is economically unattractive. But if conditions improve sufficiently, the new strategy would be very attractive. Specifically, if the S&P 500 index's annual return is 15 percent or lower, the target's $100 million in capital will increase by whatever the return on the index is. However, if the S&P 500 return exceeds 15 percent, the $100 million capital will increase by 15 percent plus twice the excess returns beyond 15 percent.

   Assuming 20 percent historical volatility for the return of S&P 500, a 13.5 percent historical return for the past 10 years, a three-year time horizon, and a risk-free rate of 7 percent, use the binomial pricing method to value the control right over the strategy of this firm.

8. *Refer to problem 7. Use the Monte Carlo simulation method to value control. Compare the results from problems 7 and 8 and explain the difference.*

9. As the CEO of a leading children's toy company, you are considering a 100 percent acquisition of a midsize children's clothing company. You believe that by co-branding the toys and clothes, it might be possible to create synergy value with a mean present value of $20 million and a volatility of 25 percent. Your CFO indicates that the investment necessary to co-brand is $25 million, pro-

ducing a negative NPV ($20 – $25 million) for the co-branding project. Nevertheless, you believe the control right for co-branding is valuable. You have a two-year window in which to launch this product.

Assuming a risk-free rate of 8 percent, use the Black-Scholes model to estimate the value of control in this case. (Also assume there is no difference between the value of a European call option and an American call option.)

10. You are the CEO of a private company and want to buy it. There is one major shareholder who owns 51 percent of the firm. The remaining 49 percent is held by oceanic shareholders. Based on a DCF model, you estimate the base value of the firm to be $100 million. This excludes any liquidity discount and/or control premium. Based on your observations of the market, liquidity discounts are about 25 percent and control premiums are about 20 percent for similar deals. Your firm has 50 million shares outstanding.

    What would you offer to pay per share to the controlling shareholder? To the oceanic shareholders?

CHAPTER 16

Financial Accounting for Mergers and Acquisitions

Accounting rules can shape the conduct of firms in M&A. Because there is some latitude in the interpretation and implementation of accounting rules, firms may engage in earnings management that can be either conservative (to produce the appearance of smooth and stable performance) or aggressive (to produce the appearance of supernormal financial results). In either case, earnings management is wrong. Best practitioners seek to tell the truth. Investors should exercise caution in interpreting financial results surrounding an acquisition.

- The Financial Accounting Standards Board (FASB) issued Financial Accounting Statements 141 and 142, which became effective after June 30, 2001. These landmark rules changed the method of accounting in the United States for mergers and acquisitions, most significantly by:
  - *Eliminating the pooling-of-interests method of accounting.* Today, all business combinations must be accounted for by the purchase method, whereby the target firm is recorded on the buyer's books at the purchase price. No retroactive restatement of the buyer's past financial results is permitted.
  - *Eliminating amortization of goodwill.* Instead, the FASB now requires that goodwill be tested at least annually for impairment. In addition, goodwill must first be allocated to a reporting unit.
  - *Tightening the recognition of intangible assets.* The new accounting standards require intangible assets to be recognized apart from goodwill if they meet the contractual-legal criterion and/or the separability criterion.
  - *Revising rules on amortization of intangible assets.* Intangible assets may have indefinite useful lives and need not be amortized under the new rules. However, intangible assets whose lives are finite must be amortized over their useful lives.
- Depending on the percentage of shares acquired, there are three methods of accounting for acquisitions under purchase accounting:

Method of Accounting	Ownership Percentage of Shares	Particulars
Consolidation method	>50%	• The buyer records 100% of the target company's assets at fair market value. A "Minority Interest" account is created on the liabilities side representing the portion of the firm not owned by the buyer. • Any portion of the difference between purchase price and book value that is not allocable to any other asset is recorded as goodwill. • 100% of the target's income statement flows would be reflected on the buyer's income statement, with a deduction for the minority investors' interest in the profits or losses of the target.
Equity method	20 to 50%	• The buyer records its acquisition of the target in an account called "Investment in Target Company," which shows up as an asset on the balance sheet. The amount recorded reflects the cost of purchasing the shares. • The buyer's share in the target's earnings/losses is reflected on its income statement in an account called "Income from Minority Interest," as well as on its balance sheet as an addition/deduction from the "Investment in Target Company" account.
Cost method	Less than 20%	• The buyer records the investment on the balance sheet sheet, typically in an account called "Investment in Affiliate," as the cost of acquisition. The investment is revalued regularly, and any unrealized gains or losses are reflected not in the income statement, but rather in the buyer's owner's equity account. Dividends, however, are recorded in the buyer's income statement.

- Accounting choices may affect the long-term value of the firm. For instance, asset allocation choices will affect the future depreciation/amortization tax shields, which in turn will affect the value of the firm.
- Managers of a buyer firm will often evaluate an acquisition by comparing the buyer's expected earnings per share (EPS) for the current year to the pro forma EPS for the same year, assuming consummation of an acquisition. A reduction in EPS is *dilution*, and an increase is *accretion*. The extent of dilution or accretion can be influenced by accounting choices. Sometimes, excessive focus on EPS dilution/accretion may distract managers from focusing on value creation and the real economic effects of a deal instead.
- M&A accounting choices can also affect and likewise be influenced by:
  - *Measures of financial leverage*. Measures such as debt/equity ratios, interest coverage, and so on can in turn affect the ability of the firm to borrow funds in the future.

   - *Profit margins.* The allocation of the purchase price to different asset categories can affect margins.
   - *Measures of asset efficiency.* Recording the acquisition of a target using the consolidation method versus the equity method will have different results in terms of returns on assets and equity.
   - *Liquidity.* Larger allocations of the target purchase price to current assets will enhance the appearance of liquidity of Newco.
- Managers may employ accounting tactics to engage in earnings and EPS enhancement games, credit enhancement games, price maximization games, and tax management games. Such games can raise serious ethical questions.
- Successive discoveries of accounting fraud at large corporations led to the drafting of the Sarbanes-Oxley Act in 2002. The Act seeks to discourage fraud by:
   - Requiring the CEO and CFO to certify financial reports.
   - Requiring public companies to appoint independent directors to audit committees within their boards of directors.
   - Requiring enhanced financial disclosures by corporations.
   - Prohibiting auditors from providing ancillary services such as consulting, legal, and corporate financial advisory services.

CHAPTER 16—WORKBOOK QUESTIONS

Exercises in Accounting for Acquisitions

Suppose Bed Bath & Beyond, a chain of stores selling bed linens, bath items, and home and kitchen furnishings, decides to acquire Pier 1 Imports, Inc., a retail chain that sells furniture and home furnishings, dining and kitchen goods, and bath and bedding accessories. At the end of fiscal year 2001, Pier 1 has 96.3 million shares outstanding, currently trading at $17.05 apiece. Suppose Bed, Bath & Beyond pays $21.31 per Pier 1 share. At its current share price of $33.90, Bed Bath & Beyond will have to issue 60.5 million shares to pay for the acquisition. Here are income statements and balance sheets for both companies.

Bed Bath & Beyond

Income Statement ($ Millions)	**2002**	**2001**
Net Sales	2,928.0	2,396.7
Cost of sales	1,720.4	1,410.2
Gross profit	1,207.6	986.5
SG&A	861.5	713.6
Operating profit	346.1	272.8
Interest income (expense)	11.0	9.0
Earnings before taxes	357.1	281.8
Provision for taxes	137.5	109.9
Net earnings	219.6	171.9
Earnings per share	0.76	0.61
Weighted average shares outstanding	289.7	283.9

Balance Sheet ($ Millions)	**2002**	**2001**
Assets		
Current assets:		
Cash and equivalents	429.5	239.3
Merchandise inventories	754.0	606.7
Other current assets	43.2	39.7
Total current assets	1,226.7	885.7
Investment securities	51.9	—
Property and equipment, net	361.7	302.7
Other assets	7.2	7.4
Total assets	1,647.5	1,195.7
Liabilities and Shareholders' Equity		
Current liabilities:		
Accounts payable	270.9	192.4
Accrued expenses and other current liabilities	190.9	128.8
Income taxes payable	49.4	32.0
Total current liabilities	511.3	353.2
Deferred rent and other liabilities	41.9	25.5
Total liabilities	553.2	378.7
Shareholders' equity:		
Common stock	241.6	183.9
Retained earnings	852.8	633.2
Total shareholders' equity	1,094.4	817.0
Total liabilities and shareholders' equity	1,647.5	1,195.7

Pier 1 Imports, Inc.

Income Statement ($ Millions)	2002	2001
Net sales	1,548.6	1,411.5
Operating costs and expenses:		
Cost of sales	898.8	817.0
SG&A	448.1	399.8
Depreciation and amortization	42.8	43.2
	1,389.7	1,260.0
Operating income	158.8	151.5
Nonoperating income and expenses:		
Interest and investment income	2.5	1.9
Interest expense	(2.3)	(3.1)
	0.2	(1.3)
Income before taxes	159.0	150.2
Provision for taxes	58.8	55.6
Net income	100.2	94.7
Earnings per share	1.06	0.98
Average shares outstanding	94.4	96.3

Balance Sheet ($ Millions)	2002	2001
Assets		
Current assets:		
Cash and equivalents	235.6	46.8
Other accounts receivable, net	6.2	8.4
Inventories	275.4	310.7
Prepaid expenses and other current assets	87.9	111.2
Total current assets	605.2	477.1
Properties, net	210.0	212.1
Other noncurrent assets	47.6	46.6
	862.7	735.7
Liabilities and Shareholders' Equity		
Current liabilities:		
Current portion of long-term debt	0.4	—
Accounts payable and accrued liabilities	208.0	144.1
Total current liabilities	208.4	144.1
Long-term debt	25.4	25.0
Other noncurrent liabilities	43.3	34.7
Total liabilities	277.0	203.8
Shareholders' equity:		
Common stock	100.8	100.8
Additional paid-in capital	140.2	139.4
Retained earnings	429.9	344.8
Cumulative other comprehensive income	(4.7)	(3.2)
Treasury stock	(80.5)	(49.9)
Total shareholders' equity	585.7	531.9
Total liabilities and shareholders' equity	862.7	735.7

[These spreadsheets can be found in the folder "Key Spreadsheets from the Workbook" located on the CD-ROM.]

1. Assume Bed Bath & Beyond acquires 100 percent of Pier 1, and that the transaction takes place at fiscal year end 2001.

   Prepare a consolidated balance sheet to reflect the acquisition. Then, prepare an income statement for fiscal year 2002, the year following the acquisition.

   Assume that:

   - The book values of Pier 1's assets and liabilities are equal to their fair market values.
   - There is a total of $500 million in identifiable intangible assets, which will be amortized for 20 years using the straight-line method.
   - The tax rate is 38 percent.

2. *Compute the following for Bed Bath & Beyond, pre- and postmerger, and fill in the appropriate parts of the table that follows:*

   - *Gross margin*
   - *Operating margin*
   - *Net margin*
   - *EPS*

		With Merger	
Ratios for Bed Bath & Beyond	Without Merger	100% Stock	60% Stock, 40% Cash
Gross margin			
Operating margin			
Net margin			
EPS			
% Dilution (accretion)			

3. Now assume that the terms of the deal have changed—that Bed Bath & Beyond will pay 60 percent of the consideration price in stock and the rest in cash, to be funded with a 10-year debt obligation at a fixed annual rate of 7 percent. It will also assume Pier 1's existing liabilities.

   Redo the consolidated balance sheet and income statement to reflect this new structure.

4. *Compute the following for Bed Bath & Beyond, postmerger, and fill in the rest of the table in problem 2:*

   - *Gross margin*
   - *Operating margin*
   - *Net margin*
   - *EPS*

Think about the following:

- *Do the ratios improve following the deal?*
- *Is the deal accretive or dilutive to Bed Bath & Beyond's EPS?*
- *How do the ratios differ between the all-stock deal versus the part-stock, part-cash deal? Can you explain the differences?*

5. Now assume that Bed Bath & Beyond acquires a 40 percent stake in Pier 1 at the same price ($21.31 per share), and pays for its investment by issuing shares. Assume that the transaction takes place at fiscal year end 2001.

   Use the equity method of accounting to prepare a balance sheet reflecting the acquisition. Then, prepare an income statement for fiscal year 2002, the year following the acquisition. Use the same assumptions given in problem 1.

CHAPTER 17

Momentum Acquisition Strategies: An Illustration of Why Value Creation Is the Best Financial Criterion

The strategy of momentum acquisition has appeared episodically over the years, most recently in the late 1990s. Some of the telltales of this strategy are a focus on EPS (or revenues), a relatively large number of acquisitions increasing in size over time, an aggressive growth trajectory, and a high price/earnings multiple reflecting investor expectations of continued growth. Regardless of the temporary attractiveness of momentum acquisition approaches, growth strategies based on momentum end in disappointment. Focusing on value creation rather than earnings momentum better promotes the survival and prosperity of the firm.

- Momentum acquisition strategies commonly focus on EPS and revenue momentum.
  - EPS has been the traditional focus of momentum acquirers, based on the belief that stock prices are driven by changes in EPS and that therefore steady and aggressive growth in EPS will result in high stock prices (and high P/E multiples).
  - In some industries, the momentum focus is on revenues instead of earnings per share due to the fact that a significant portion of the market value of firms in these industries derives from their growth options; some analysts therefore advocate using revenue multiples as a basis for valuing these firms.
- The common argument for momentum acquiring is that stock market investors appear to reward momentum. It appears that firms with momentum enjoy higher valuation multiples than other firms. And "momentum investing" attracted specialist investment managers in the 1990s. But the existence of such specialists was no proof of the superiority of momentum investing. And, in fact, the research evidence tends to reject the ability of momentum investors to earn supernormal returns. Arguments *against* momentum acquiring include the following:
  - Momentum is unsustainable indefinitely because the annual acquisition volume cannot get bigger forever; the world is finite, and unexpected events can happen at any time in the future to halt growth.

- Momentum invites a focus on accounting cosmetics rather than on economic reality. Central to the momentum acquisition approach is the maintenance of a steady path of growth in EPS, revenues, or assets. Because of the difficulties of maintaining the growth trajectory, the incentives to use accounting cosmetics increase. Purchase accounting for M&A transactions entails various judgments about the fair market value of assets, the allocation of purchase price, the creation of reporting units, and the impairment of assets. Finally, momentum acquirers will be highly sensitive to the factors that drive EPS dilution: the growth rate of the buyer's shares relative to the target's percentage addition to the buyer's earnings, the P/E ratio embedded in the bid relative to the P/E ratio of the buyer, and the size of the target relative to the size of the bidder.
- Momentum strategies can promote uneconomic deals and reject good ones.
- Value creation is the best criterion for acquisition strategies because it focuses on the longer-term future, accounts for the time value of money, focuses on economic reality, focuses on risk and return, and accounts for opportunity costs. Further, the use of NPV directly measures changes in investors' welfare. Although difficult to apply, value-based acquisition strategies have the ultimate virtue of weeding out bad deals more effectively than other approaches.
- Momentum acquiring is a dangerous path for both corporate managers and their investors. On the contrary, value maximization is a superior foundation for acquisition planning.

CHAPTER 17—WORKBOOK QUESTIONS

1. In Chapter 17 of the main text, Tyco International, Ltd., is introduced to illustrate the application of a momentum acquisition strategy. After the restructuring announcement on January 22, 2002, by CEO Dennis Kozlowski, various market participants had different responses.

   Using the critique of momentum acquiring in the chapter, what prompted Tyco to stop acquiring more companies and restructure? How did the market respond?

2. The strategy of momentum acquisition has swung in and out of favor over the years.

   What are the arguments for and against momentum acquiring? What should be the criteria used to evaluate the success of an acquisition strategy?

3. The momentum acquisition approach focuses on the maintenance of a steady path of growth in EPS, revenue, or assets. Therefore, how to manage the earnings dilution or accretion is essential to the success of this strategy.

   Please briefly explain how dilution (or accretion) occurs and identify the factors that drive EPS dilution.

4. Assume that a buyer and target agree to a stock-for-stock acquisition. The buyer has 1.5 million shares outstanding and $3 million in earnings. Its current

P/E ratio is 25. The target has one million shares outstanding and $1 million in earnings. The target's current P/E ratio is 20. Suppose the buyer is willing to offer a 20 percent premium for the target, and a purchase-related transaction charge of 0.5 percent of total purchase price is expected. (You will find the Excel file, "Momentum.xls," on the CD-ROM to automate your calculations on this problem.)

a. *Calculate the earnings per share for Newco after the merger and the percentage change in the buyer's EPS.*
b. *Assuming the deal is paid by cash, which is funded by an issue of new debt by the buyer at an annual interest rate of 5 percent, calculate the EPS for Newco after the merger and percentage change in the buyer's EPS assuming a tax rate of 35 percent.*
c. *Refer to problem 4a. By changing the bid price for the target, the buyer can avoid dilution. Please calculate the percentage dilution or accretion for purchase premiums of 0 percent, 5 percent, 15 percent, 25 percent, 35 percent, and 45 percent. Now recalculate the percentage dilution or accretion, varying the target's earnings according to the following schedule: $500,000, $1,000,000, $1,500,000, $2,000,000, $2,500,000, $3,000,000, and $3,500,000. Explain the results.*

5. Assume you as the CEO of a publicly listed company are considering an acquisition. There are two opportunities available. Company A is a high-growth firm that invests heavily in R&D. But it also demands a higher premium than Company B, which has lower growth potential. Both companies have 2 million shares outstanding, and projected earnings for this year for both companies are the same at $3 million. Company A's stock trades at $40, and Company B's stock trades at $18. After due diligence research, you estimate that earnings of Company A will grow at a rate of 25 percent and those of Company B will grow at only 5 percent. You estimate your own firm's earnings will grow at 10 percent. Assume that the earnings of Newco after the merger will be just the simple arithmetic addition of the forecasted earnings of your firm and the target. There are 5 million shares outstanding for your firm; projected earnings for this year are $6.5 million. Your firm's stock trades at $28.

   If Company A asks for a 60 percent premium over its market price and Company B asks for only a 20 percent premium, which company would you acquire? Use quantitative evidence to back up your decision. (Refer to "Momentum.xls" on the CD-ROM for calculating your answers.)

CHAPTER 18

An Introduction to Deal Design in M&A

Designing a deal is more than setting a price. As Bruce Wasserstein says, "Implementing a deal is a blend of psychology, business judgment, and technical dexterity. While taxes, accounting, and corporate law provide the skeletal frame of a transaction, *optimizing position* is the purpose of direct negotiation."[1] One must optimize across a range of goals, and within a series of constraints.

- Deals are solutions to economic problems. To design deal terms, begin with an understanding of the economic problems: the constraints and competing objectives under which the deal designer must try to "optimize position."
- Classic objectives of M&A deal design include:
  - Creating value.
  - Improving reported financial results; avoiding EPS dilution.
  - Improving control; avoiding voting dilution.
  - Building financial flexibility.
  - Hedging security price risk.
  - Improving competitive standing.
  - Managing signals to the capital markets.
  - Managing incentives.
  - Shaping impact on employees and communities.
- Some deal terms and how they can be used to achieve objectives:
  - *Price* is a key instrument for claiming value. Be careful, however, not to focus exclusively on price—multi-issue bargaining generally leads to more successful outcomes than does single-issue bargaining.
  - *Form of payment* considers whether the payment should be "fixed" or "contingent." There may also be "side" payments.
  - *Fixed payments* use cash or senior debt securities. They can resolve uncertainty for the target shareholders about the value they will receive; however, they could also have an adverse signaling effect—their use could be interpreted as a lack of confidence by target shareholders in the buyer's future management of the enterprise (i.e., thus prompting them to demand fixed payments).

- *Contingent payments* use mezzanine or "junk" debt securities, preferred stock, and common stock. These permit target investors to participate in the combined entity's upside potential, and may also be used when the buyer does not have the cash or senior debt capacity to finance the acquisition. Earnouts, warrants, convertible bonds, contingent value rights, puts, guarantees, caps, collars, and floors are usually used to resolve strong disagreements about the value of the target firm, and to limit the adverse effects of stock price changes between announcement and consummation of a deal.
- *Side payments* are payments to parties other than the owners of the target firm, parties that may have some influence on the success of the firm post-merger. Examples of side payments are golden parachutes, warrants, bonuses, buyouts of employment contracts, and consulting commitments to managers of the target firm. Sometimes, side payments might also be made to municipal, state, and national governments.
- *Timing and deadlines* are important, as the speed of closing will affect the present value of cash flows to investors. Acquisitions might be full and immediate, or partial and staged over time.
- *Commitments* are promises by the target and/or buyer to make good on previous agreements; for instance, the buyer commits to assuming the target's liabilities, the target commits to handing over all tangible and intangible assets to the buyer, and so on. Commitments may also include warranties from either side to the other that certain conditions exist, and that if not, reparations will be made.
- *Control and governance* affect the balance of power among the shareholders of the firm, as well as the degree of managerial discretion. Important deal terms with respect to control and governance include the relative proportions of share ownership and voting rights, and the makeup of the new board and executive management.
- *Transaction hedges* are special terms that mitigate risks that the transaction may not be consummated. For instance, walk-away fees when either party reneges are usually part of the deal terms.
- The *form of transaction* (e.g., merger of equals, "type A" reorganization, etc.) has implications for tax exposure, exposure to liabilities, control, and value creation.
- The *form of financing* has implications for tax shields, default risk, and the financial flexibility of the firm.
- *Social issues* include agreements about the composition of the board, executive management, headquarters, corporate name, and so on.

- Each deal is a system—deal terms are linked to one another. The terms of an M&A transaction cannot be set independently of each other.

- Some important concepts for the deal designer to remember:
  - *There is no single best feasible deal.* Rather, there is an *area* within which feasible deals exist for both buyer and seller. This area is called the zone of potential agreement (ZOPA).

- *Deal design involves trade-offs.* The process of optimization is simply a matter of comparing the desirability of one set of terms against another. Desirability is measured in terms of the value attached to each attribute.
- *Deal design is a learning process.* Trial and error and feedback are intrinsic to the learning process.

CHAPTER 18—WORKBOOK QUESTIONS

Part I: Mini-Problems

1. Genesis Corp., a biotech company, has approached R_x Pharmaceuticals, a large drug manufacturer, to acquire a minority equity interest in Genesis for funding drug development. In return for the equity investment, Genesis will commit to a co-marketing agreement with R_x for those drugs. R_x thinks Genesis has a promising lineup of drugs, but all are still in Phase II clinical trials, meaning that there remains a substantial risk that the drugs might not receive approval for release to the public. Also, R_x has a strategic interest in the drugs that Genesis is proposing to bring to market, and would be disadvantaged if a competitor bought a stake in Genesis. The CEO of Genesis is optimistic about the prospects for regulatory approval and for sales revenue of the new drugs.

    a. *What are the deal design problems here? Where might R_x and Genesis find helpful trade-offs that produce a win-win deal to both?*

    b. *Suppose R_x decides to make an equity investment in Genesis, but buyer and target differ widely in their valuation of the target. How might the parties bridge the gap?*

2. Company B has agreed to be acquired by Company A. However, Company B shareholders are only willing to accept cash payment. However, paying in cash would affect Company A's credit ratings.

    a. *Can a deal be designed such as to satisfy both parties' requirements?*

    b. *Suppose Company B agrees to a stock acquisition, but wants to protect the value of stock against fluctuations in Company A's stock price. How might Company B protect itself? On the other hand, Company A wants to ensure it does not give away too much value. How can Company A do this? What is the resulting structure called?*

    c. *Although Company B has agreed to be acquired by Company A, the latter knows that the former continues to be pursued by several other interested parties. What can Company A do to prevent Company B from reneging on its agreement?*

    d. *Company A needs to retain the top managers at Company B because their knowledge of the business is key to postmerger success. What provisions might Company A include in the deal terms to increase the chances that the target's managers will stay?*

Part II: Mini-Case

During the 1980s, the economy of Texas nearly collapsed due to a prolonged downward spiral in oil prices. This downturn severely affected Texas' banking industry, causing many local banks to fail. One of the most serious cases involved the $41 billion First Republic Bank, the largest bank in Texas. The Federal Deposit Insurance Corporation (FDIC) chose not to bail out First Republic Bank, and invited large financial institutions to take over the bank. North Carolina National Bank (NCNB) won the takeover contest over rivals such as Citicorp and Chase Manhattan by coming up with a creative structure for the deal. As a result, in August 1988, NCNB acquired 20 percent of First Republic, with the FDIC acquiring the remaining 80 percent. Some of the key deal terms were:[2]

Control	• NCNB's 20 percent equity interest is composed of 100 percent of the voting stock. • The FDIC's 80 percent equity interest is in the form of nonvoting common stock.
Option to purchase	• NCNB has an exclusive option to purchase stock owned by the FDIC immediately or at any time within the next five years.
Option purchase prices:	
First year	The pro rata amount of the FDIC's original investment plus 115 percent of the net increase in book value of the acquired entity.
Second year	The pro rata amount of the FDIC's original investment plus 120 percent of the net increase in book value of the acquired entity.
Third to fifth year	The pro rata amount of the FDIC's original investment plus 125 percent of the net increase in book value of the acquired entity.
Sale by FDIC	• The FDIC is not permitted to sell its shares other than to NCNB until after November 22, 1993. • In the event that NCNB has not raised its ownership percentage to 51 percent or more by the end of the fifth year, the FDIC may sell its shares to whomever it chooses.
Special Asset Division	A Special Asset Division was created within Newco to absorb substandard loans acquired or originated prior to August 29, 1988, or loans that had been charged off prior to November 22, 1988. • Through December 31, 1989, NCNB could transfer to the division, *in unlimited amounts*, loans acquired prior to August 29, 1988. • During 1990, NCNB could designate additional loans as division assets subject to a $750 million limitation. • The FDIC would provide as assistance the estimated loss amount. The FDIC would also reimburse NCNB for the costs of funding and administering division assets. • Neither NCNB or any of its subsidiaries would share losses that might be suffered by the Special Asset Division, but NCNB would be entitled, in the event of gains by the division, to receive incentive payments that could range from 3 percent to 20 percent of such gains.

1. *Was the control structure advantageous for NCNB? What were the reasons for why the control structure was designed the way it was? Why would the FDIC agree to this structure?*

2. *Describe NCNB's purchase option. What advantages did NCNB gain from this structure? What risks did this structure protect NCNB against? Why did the purchase option price ratchet up over time?*

3. *What was the purpose of the Special Asset Division? What did it effectively do for NCNB? What kind of economic rewards did NCNB get from administering the Special Asset Division?*

4. *Putting aside price considerations, was this an attractive deal for NCNB? Why or why not?*

NOTES

1. Quoted from Bruce Wasserstein, *Big Deal* (New York: Free Press, 1998). (Emphasis added.)
2. *Source:* NCNB Form 10-K as filed with the Securities and Exchange Commission (SEC) on March 31, 1989, modified for instructional purposes. (Emphasis added.)

CHAPTER 19

Choosing the Form of Acquisitive Reorganization

Mergers and acquisitions often result in a *legal reorganization* of one or both of the partners to the deal. There are several forms of reorganization, each with peculiar advantages and qualifying conditions. Transactions are designed in ways to meet those qualifying conditions and to achieve desired outcomes. Through an understanding of the forms of organization, one can see that transaction design has big implications for issues that concern deal designers and senior executives, such as taxes, control, transfer of liability, risk exposure, form of payment, legal standing, and other issues. A careful understanding of the buyer's and seller's goals should drive the choice of the reorganization structure.

- The choice of reorganization structure will affect and be affected by at least five considerations:

  1. *Taxation.* Is this proposed deal taxable or tax deferred? To whom is it taxable? What are the tax consequences for the buyer and seller? How large is the tax exposure? Will the seller be subject to double taxation?
  2. *Risk exposure.* Will this structure isolate the hidden liabilities of the target from the buyer?
  3. *Control.* Will this require a vote of shareholders of the target and/or the buyer? How will the voting control of Newco be affected by this structure?
  4. *Continuity.* Which, if any, firm survives as an ongoing entity? What implications does this have for the ability to assign leases and licenses, for corporate identity, and for social issues such as headquarters location?
  5. *Form of payment.* What form of payment is required to achieve objectives for taxation, risk exposure, control, and continuity?

- The possible types of acquisitive reorganization and their definitions follow along with a summary providing more detailed information pertaining to each structure.

Type of Reorganization	Description
Cash purchase of assets	The buyer exchanges its cash for the assets of the target. The target's liabilities are not transferred to the buyer without explicit agreement. After the transaction, the target may or may not liquidate.
Cash purchase of stock	The buyer exchanges its cash for shares of the target's voting common stock. The target company remains in existence. The buyer will be shielded from the target's known and unknown liabilities.
Reverse triangular cash merger	The buyer forms a subsidiary (Newco) and capitalizes it with cash sufficient to acquire the target's stock. Newco merges into the target. The target company survives, as do its tax attributes and liabilities.
Forward triangular cash merger	The buyer forms a subsidiary (Newco) and capitalizes it with cash sufficient to acquire the target's stock. The target merges into Newco and ceases to exist, although its liabilities have been transferred to Newco.
Statutory merger ("A" reorganization)	In a statutory merger one company absorbs the other. Target shareholders exchange their shares for the buyer's stock and other consideration. The target company ceases to exist. The buyer assumes the liabilities of the target.
Statutory consolidation ("A" reorganization)	In a statutory consolidation, two or more corporations combine into one new corporation. The preexisting corporations cease to exist as legal entities.
Forward triangular merger ("A" reorganization)	The target company merges into a subsidiary of the buyer (Newco). Payment must consist of at least 50 percent of the parent corporation stock to qualify as "tax-free."
Reverse triangular merger ("A" reorganization)	The buyer's subsidiary (Newco) merges into the target, leaving the target company in existence as a subsidiary of the buyer. At least 80 percent of the consideration must be paid in the buyer's parent corporation voting stock to qualify as "tax-free."
Voting stock-for-stock ("B" reorganization)	To qualify as "tax-free" the buyer must exchange only voting stock and afterward control at least 80 percent of the votes. No merger occurs, as the target is retained as a wholly (or partially) owned subsidiary.
Voting stock-for-assets ("C" reorganization)	The buyer offers shares of its voting stock in return for substantially all of the assets of the target company. The target company must liquidate after the transaction.

Note: "Tax-free" is common usage for "tax deferred until disposition or sale of the stock."

Summary of Features of Various Transaction Types

	Tax Implication for Seller	Buyer's Exposure to Target's Liabilities	Need for Target Shareholder Vote	Need for Buyer Shareholder Vote	Minority Freeze-Out?[1]	Does the Target Company Survive?	Form of Payment
Cash purchase of assets	Immediately taxable	Low	Maybe	No	No minority	Uncertain	No restriction; usually cash
Cash purchase of stock	Immediately taxable	High	No	No	No	Yes	No restriction; usually cash
Cash merger	Immediately taxable	Low if target merged into a subsidiary	Yes	Maybe	Yes	No if forward triangular merger Yes if reverse triangular merger	No restriction; usually cash
Statutory merger or consolidation ("A" reorganization)	Tax-free[2]	High	Yes	Yes	Yes	No	Buyer's stock and typically no more than 50% "boot"
Forward triangular merger ("A" reorganization)	Tax-free[2]	Low—limited by sub	Yes	No[3]—unless need to authorize more shares	Yes	No	Buyer's stock and typically no more than 50% "boot"
Reverse triangular merger ("A" reorganization)	Tax-free[2]	Low—limited by sub	Yes	No[3]—unless need to authorize more shares	Yes	Yes	Buyer's voting stock of at least 80% and the rest in "boot"
Voting stock-for-stock ("B" reorganization)	Tax-free[2]	Low	Maybe	No[3]—unless need to authorize more shares	No	Yes	100% in buyer's voting stock
Voting stock-for-assets ("C" reorganization)	Tax-free[2]	Low	Maybe	No[3]—unless need to authorize more shares	No minority	No	At least 80% buyer's voting stock in value and the rest in "boot"

1. A "minority freeze-out" seeks to eliminate *direct* interests in the target firm held by a minority of shareholders (who are possibly dissidents) following the completion of the deal. This is ordinarily accomplished by merging the target into the buyer.
2. "Tax-free" is common usage for "tax deferred until disposition or sale of the stock." Also, any "boot" in the tax-free transactions may create an immediate tax liability to the extent of any gain implicit in the boot.
3. Stock exchanges and legal counsel may require a vote of the buyer's shareholders on material transactions. Asset sales and spin-offs could create adverse tax consequences.

CHAPTER 19—WORKBOOK QUESTIONS

1. Sam Goodman, founder and CEO of fast-food chain Uncle Sam's Fried Chicken, is set to retire in a few months. Two parties have approached him offering to buy the chain. Party A has offered an all-cash deal, while party B has offered an all-stock deal. Sam reckons that the nominal value of the two offers is about the same, so he wants to base his decision on which of the deals would be more tax-efficient.

   Which deal would you advise Sam to take? Why?

2. Phil Welch, owner of a midsize trucking service, recently purchased some secondhand trucks and containers for cash. His discount rate for these assets was 10 percent. The assets, which were on the seller's books for $483,000, were sold to him for $511,000. Phil estimated that the new equipment had a useful life of eight years, and expected annual tax savings of $20,528 on a marginal tax rate of 34 percent.

   Is Phil correct that the expected annual tax savings is $20,528? What is the present value of the tax shields?

3. Escape Cruise Lines is seeking to expand its operations in the Caribbean by acquiring Grupo Viva Cruise Lines in either a stock-and-cash deal, or an all-stock deal. Escape's risk-averse CEO is concerned above all about keeping Escape insulated from Grupo Viva's liabilities.

   Knowing this, what forms of reorganization might you recommend to Escape's CEO? Please explain.

4. Refer to problem 3. Escape's CEO wants to make sure that the deal qualifies as tax-free, and wants to "freeze out" a troublesome shareholder of Grupo Viva.

   For each type of reorganization that you suggested in problem 3, what requirements must be met for the deal to qualify as tax-free? Knowing these requirements, does any form of reorganization from among those you suggested stand out as being most favorable?

5. Refer to problems 3 and 4.

   If Grupo Viva's shareholders want some cash, can the transaction be structured to meet their requirements and still be tax-free? If so, what types of reorganization are possible?

6. Consumer products manufacturer Holden & Caulfield wants to acquire Sally's Delectable Dinners, a manufacturer of frozen microwave dinners. Holden & Caulfield plans to integrate Sally's into its own microwave dinner operating division, and then spin the division off within two years. The shareholders of Sally's want a tax-free deal.

   What forms of acquisitive reorganizations are possible in light of these conditions?

7. Refer to problem 6. It turns out that Holden & Caulfield had earlier purchased a toehold position in Sally's Delectable Dinners.

Does this narrow down the possible forms of reorganization you suggested in problem 6?

8. Decadence, a manufacturer of premium ice cream, wants to acquire Bright Ice, a specialty maker of sherbets. Bright Ice is 82 percent owned by the O'Shaughnessy family, who are willing to sell only their shares of stock, not the assets of the company. Eight years ago, the company underwent financial difficulties, prompting founder Maurice O'Shaughnessy to sell 15 percent of the company to a multimillionaire, Leonardo Fox. (Other shareholders own the remaining 3 percent.) Over the years, Fox has repeatedly badgered the O'Shaughnessy family, asking for increasing dividend payments or constantly criticizing Maurice O'Shaughnessy's decisions. Therefore, Decadence wants to make sure it gets rid of Fox when it purchases Bright Ice. Also, Decadence wants to isolate the liabilities of Bright Ice in a subsidiary.

   What acquisition structures would you recommend to Decadence?

9. *What is a "minority freeze-out"?*

CHAPTER 20

Choosing the Form of Payment and Financing

Form of payment and financing are major deal design dimensions that have implications for each other, and for returns to shareholders. Choices along these dimensions merit careful analysis.

- The form of payment chosen in an M&A transaction can lead to large differences in shareholder returns. Studies find that:
  - Payment in cash is associated with lower (but still large and positive) returns to targets, and close to zero returns to buyers.
  - Payment in stock is associated with higher returns to targets and significantly negative returns to buyers.
- Over the years following a deal, share-for-share transactions yield lower returns to investors than do cash deals.
- Stock payments tend to be used when:
  - A deal is friendly.
  - The buyer's stock price is buoyant.
  - Ownership is not concentrated.
  - Deals are larger in size.
  - The buyer has less cash.
- Stock payments are used with greater frequency when the stock market is buoyant. This contributes to the appearance of merger waves during economic booms. This phenomenon supports the notion that overvaluation is an important motive for using stock as a medium of payment.
- Choice of form of payment is driven by a range of considerations:
  - *Perspectives of buyer and seller.* To the selling shareholder, form of payment is an *investment* issue; to the buyer, form of payment is a *financing* issue. The form of payment must result in a good investment decision from the seller's standpoint and a good financing decision from the buyer's standpoint.
  - *Possibility of competing bidders.* The form of payment can strongly influence the target and thus preempt competing bidders. The form of payment chosen must be consistent with the probability of entry by competitors.

- *Taxes.* Cash and stock deals differ in their tax exposures for the target shareholders and buyer firm. The decision maker must consider the interests of the selling shareholders, as well as opportunities for value creation arising from tax shields or deferred taxes.
- *Control.* Cash and stock differ in their impact on the voting control of Newco.
- *Financing.* The choice of form of payment must consider the impact on present and future funding capacities of both buyer and target. The type of financing employed will also have future implications for taxes and control.
- *Transaction costs.* Different forms of payment may entail a wide variety of transaction costs. Generally, a cash payment made directly from the buyer's cash accounts entails the least costs, while a stock payment made by issuance of new equity will be the most costly.
- *Size.* The absolute and relative sizes of target and buyer can have implications for the form of payment, transaction costs, financing, control, and expected synergy value.
- *Asymmetric information.* The managers of the buyer and target may each have differing views on the values of their own firms and of any expected synergies. Such views will have an impact on the form of payment chosen.

- Seven dimensions describe transaction financing:

  1. *Classes of capital.* The mix of classes of capital to be used for acquisition financing may be influenced by several factors, such as the firm's current debt-equity mix; the CFO's preference for different kinds of financing (pecking order); opportunistic responses to hot, cold, or segmented markets; and the asset base of the firm.
  2. *Maturity.* A risk-neutral maturity structure would equate the life of the firm's assets with the life of the firm's liabilities to reduce exposure to reinvestment risk and refinancing risk.
  3. *Basis for the yields.* Management's outlook for interest rates will determine whether rates of payment on debt will be fixed or floating. Whether the issuer's returns vary with fluctuations in interest rates will also affect this choice.
  4. *Currency.* A firm's exposure to foreign exchange rate fluctuations, unusual financing possibilities in global capital markets, and management's views about the future movement of exchange rates will affect the choice of currency used to finance a deal.
  5. *Exotic terms.* Securities can be highly tailored in cases where there is some disagreement between issuers and investors about a firm's prospects.
  6. *Control features.* Financing choices will affect issues surrounding control, such as *who* might exercise control (e.g., creditors or shareholders); the *degree* of control exercised by various players; and the *control trigger* (e.g., tightness of loan covenants, default on a loan covenant, etc.).
  7. *Distribution.* Choices about distribution of securities include retail versus institutional, domestic versus international, and full commitment versus best efforts. The decision is influenced by (1) how the firm wants to mar-

ket itself through its securities (e.g., where the shares are sold, how liquid the shares are) and (2) how the firm delivers value (i.e., returns capital) to its investors.

- A framework that is helpful for evaluating financing alternatives is the *FRICTO* framework:
  - F lexibility—the ability to meet unforeseen financing requirements as they arise.
  - Risk—the predictable variability in the firm's operating cash flow.
  - Income—the effect of financing choice on value creation.
  - Control—the effect on financing choices on ownership.
  - Timing—the suitability of the financing choice given current capital market conditions.
  - Other—examples include issues like signaling effects, investment liquidity of the owners, estate-planning considerations, and so on.

CHAPTER 20—WORKBOOK QUESTIONS

Part I: True or False

1. *Form of payment is often related to the size of a deal.*

2. *Payment in cash is associated with higher returns to targets than payment in stock.*

3. *Choices in form of payment and financing vary with the economic cycle.*

4. *Taxable deals are for stock, and "tax-deferred" deals are for cash.*

5. *From the seller's standpoint, cash deals are more likely to be more tax efficient.*

6. *Issuing new debt of higher seniority can allow buyers to bid more than their assessment of the intrinsic value of the target.*

7. *The more highly levered the target, the lower will be the total payment required to acquire the target's equity.*

8. *Financing choices can have effects on taxes and control.*

9. *When a target firm knows its value better than does the acquirer, the acquirer will prefer to offer cash.*

10. *Bidders that are optimistic about the value of merger synergies will tend to offer cash.*

11. *The fraction of the acquisition value funded by bank debt has no effect on announcement returns.*

Part II: Questions

1. Company A is thinking of acquiring Company B. The CEO of Company A is optimistic about the value of merger synergies, but less confident about the stand-alone value of Company B. With respect to Company A's own shares, the CEO thinks they are currently fairly valued. The ratio of Company A's debt to total capital is currently 20 percent. At present, interest rates are attractive.

   What are the advantages of using cash or stock as the form of payment for the acquisition?

2. Company A has been eyeing Company B for some time, and believes now is the time to complete an acquisition. Company A's stock is at an all-time high. At the same time, it has a large cash reserve and substantial debt capacity.

   Given his outlook on the economic cycle, the CEO of Company A believes that the valuation of Company A's stock may soon recede. Would you recommend a cash or stock payment? If the latter, how do you think the market might react, assuming the purchase price is reasonable? Why?

3. Company A wants to acquire Company B. Fifty percent of Company A is owned by its founder, Jeff Smith. Twenty percent is owned by another major stockholder, and the remaining portion is held in small amounts by individual shareholders (also called "oceanic shareholders"). Company B is 80 percent owned by its founder, Angus Pierce, who is known to be brilliant, but hotheaded. The remaining 20 percent is owned by oceanic shareholders. Jeff Smith values Pierce's talent, but is wary of Pierce owning a large enough block of shares that might upset the balance of power. Smith insists on controlling a stake in Newco that is at least twice as large (in percentage terms) as Pierce's.

   Assuming 0.5 shares of Company A are exchanged for each share of Company B, and that A and B have 100 million shares and 60 million shares outstanding, respectively, would a share-for-share deal be acceptable to Smith?

4. Company A wants to launch a hostile bid for Company B. A competitor analysis leads the CEO of Company A to conclude that two other bidders may jump into the fray after Company A announces its bid.

   What strategy would you advise for the CEO of Company A in terms of price, form of payment, and financing so that the likelihood of a successful bid increases?

5. *Explain how the cost of overpaying for a target might be borne by creditors.*

6. The table at the top of the opposite page lists the number of cash and stock transactions in the United States for deals above $100 million for two different time periods: 1990–1992, and 1998–2000.

   What do you think might explain the change in proportion between cash and stock deals from the earlier period to the latter?

	1990–1992	1998–2000
Completed deals > $100 million:		
Cash	691	2,558
Stock	196	1,343
	887	3,901
% of cash deals	78%	66%
% of stock deals	22%	34%

Source of data: Thomson Financial Securities Data Corporation.

7. Going back to our example in Chapter 16 of this workbook ("Financial Accounting for Mergers and Acquisitions"), suppose Bed Bath & Beyond wants to acquire Pier 1 Imports. Let's examine the impact of choosing a 100 percent stock payment versus a 100 percent cash payment that is funded entirely with debt.

   Note: A spreadsheet has already been built for you, showing primary data for Bed Bath & Beyond (BB&B), Pier 1, results for a 100 percent stock deal, and results for a 100 percent cash deal. Please see it in "Chapter 20 Workbook.xls" on the CD-ROM, and answer the following questions.

   a. *Assuming a 25 percent purchase premium, fill in the following table. What observations can you make about the impact of form of payment on the ratios?*

		With Merger	
Ratios for BB&B	Without Merger	100% Stock	100% Cash
Gross margin			
Operating margin			
Net margin			
EPS			
% Accretion/(dilution)			
Debt-equity ratio			
Interest cover (EBIT/Interest expense)			

   b. *Build data tables that show the EPS impact of purchase premiums of 20 percent, 25 percent, 30 percent, 35 percent, and 40 percent under both the all-stock and all-cash transactions. Calculate the percentage accretion/dilution for all cases. What do you observe?*

   c. *Under the 100 percent stock transaction, build a data table showing how the exchange ratio, number of new shares issued, and control change under purchase premiums of 20 percent, 25 percent, 30 percent, 35 percent, and 40 percent.*

CHAPTER 21

Framework for Structuring the Terms of Exchange: Finding the "Win-Win" Deal

In an M&A transaction, neither the buyer nor the seller wants to be worse off financially after the deal. A range of exchange ratios can be derived such that both buyer and seller will be better off after the deal, though this may not always be possible.

- The exchange ratio is the number of shares of the buyer's stock to be received for each share of the target firm's stock:
  - The buyer will set a *maximum* exchange ratio, below which the buyer will be willing to acquire the target.
  - The seller will have a *minimum* exchange ratio, above which it will be willing to be acquired.

  It is possible that in a deal negotiation there will be a range of exchange ratios between the buyer's maximum and the seller's minimum that will allow both parties to emerge better off after the deal. This is the win-win zone of outcomes.
- The maximum and minimum exchange ratios of buyer and seller, respectively, depend on the estimated value of Newco. But because the value of Newco is uncertain, the analyst needs to assess the minimum and maximum exchange ratios across a range of possible values for Newco. Two ways to do this are by: (1) focusing on the likely price/earnings ratio of Newco and (2) estimating the likely discounted cash flow (DCF) value of the equity of Newco. Refer to Chapter 21 of the main text for the formulas for calculating minimum and maximum exchange ratios under different parameters.
- Deal boundaries have three important applications:
  1. Given a view about the DCF value or P/E of Newco, one can identify a negotiation range and some likelihood of agreement.
  2. Given a proposed exchange ratio, one can identify P/E or DCF break-even assumptions necessary to permit a mutually beneficial deal.
  3. Given both a proposed exchange ratio and view of DCF value or P/E of Newco, one can evaluate the adequacy of a proposal.
- There are four possible outcomes based on the deal boundaries:
  1. Both win; the exchange ratio is below the buyer's maximum and above the seller's minimum. Here, the deal creates value for the buyer and seller.

2. Target wins, buyer loses.
3. Both lose. Here, the deal destroys value for the buyer and seller.
4. Buyer wins, target loses.

- In situations where the zone of potential agreement (the win-win region) is large, the following are the factors that tend to determine the outcomes:
  - Bargaining power.
  - Control premium in comparable transactions.
  - Focal points based on relative contribution of the two firms.
  - Social issues.
- Synergies create flexibility for the deal designer. Value creation through synergies can raise the buyer's maximum exchange ratio boundary and lower the target's minimum.

CHAPTER 21—WORKBOOK QUESTIONS

1. Suppose Microsoft Corporation (MSFT), the largest software company in the world, wants to acquire ExxonMobil (XOM), the largest oil and gas company in the world. Microsoft is currently trading at $25.96, and ExxonMobil, at $38.31 per share. Microsoft's earnings are at $9.6 billion, and Exxon's, at $15.4 billion. Synergies of $1.25 billion are expected. Shares outstanding are 10.7 billion and 6.68 billion for Microsoft and Exxon, respectively.

   What minimum price/earnings ratio for Newco will make a deal just feasible for both parties?

2. Suppose ExxonMobil thinks Newco will trade at a P/E ratio of 22 times and that Bill Gates says, "How can Exxon think that by merging with us it can raise its P/E to 22 times? Microsoft thinks Newco will trade only at 18 times. If ExxonMobil wants to make the deal work, it needs to convince Microsoft to increase its P/E estimate for Newco." This is a test of negotiating skills!

   Without changing its own view that the postmerger P/E will be 22 times, what P/E level must ExxonMobil convince Microsoft that Newco will trade at in order for Microsoft to agree to a deal?

3. Suppose Microsoft wants to acquire ExxonMobil and thinks that Newco's DCF value will be $550 billion. (Currently, Microsoft and ExxonMobil's market capitalizations are at $278 billion and $256 billion, respectively.) Suppose ExxonMobil thinks, however, that because the two companies' businesses are so unrelated, Newco will suffer a diversification discount, and will have a DCF value of only $500 billion—even *less* than the sum of the two companies' current market capitalizations.

   What is the minimum DCF value for Newco that Microsoft must convince Exxon is possible in order for there to be a possibility for a win-win deal?

4. Assume that the hypothetical Microsoft-ExxonMobil deal is going to be a cash-for-stock deal.

   Calculate the minimum and maximum exchange ratios for P/E ratios ranging from 19 to 25 times. Graph the results. What P/E ratio must Newco trade at in order for the deal to be economically attractive to both firms?

5. *Still assuming a cash-for-stock deal, calculate the exchange ratios for the hypothetical Microsoft-Exxon deal using the DCF method, and graph the results. (Assume DCF values ranging from $400 billion to $800 billion.) What DCF value will make a deal between Microsoft and Exxon feasible?*

6. *Why is it that the minimum acceptable payment in a cash-for-stock transaction is constant regardless of the expected P/E or DCF value of Newco?*

7. Two companies are in merger negotiations. The buyer's and target's share prices are currently trading at $35 and $20, respectively. The buyer is projected to earn $200 million, and the target, $150 million. Synergies of $10 million are expected from the deal. Each party has 80 million shares outstanding. Both buyer and target expect Newco to trade at a price/earnings ratio of 11 times.

   Is a deal attractive to both parties feasible at this P/E ratio? Calculate the maximum and minimum exchange ratios for P/E ratios from 11 to 17 times and graph your results.

8. *Refer to problem 7. Still assuming that Newco will trade at a P/E ratio of 11 times, what amount of synergies would make a deal feasible? Using this new amount of synergies, calculate the maximum and minimum exchange ratios for P/E ratios ranging from 9 to 15 times. Graph your results, superimposed on the graph you drew in problem 7. Interpret the results.*

9. Two companies are in merger negotiations. The buyer's and target's shares are currently trading at $35 and $20, respectively. The buyer is projected to earn $200 million, and the target, $150 million. No synergies are expected from the deal. Each party has 80 million shares outstanding.

   Calculate the maximum and minimum exchange ratios for DCF values ranging from $3 billion to $7 billion and graph your results. If the projected stand-alone DCF value is $5 billion, can a deal be feasible?

10. Refer to problem 9. Assume that the DCF value of synergies of $1 billion is expected from the deal.

    Will the graph that you drew in problem 9 change? Explain. What does change?

11. On June 6, 2003, Oracle Corporation, a provider of software solutions, announced a hostile tender offer for PeopleSoft, a company specializing in software solutions for business. PeopleSoft's stock was trading at $15.11; Oracle offered to pay $16.00 per share. Oracle's own stock was trading at $13.36 a share. Some data about the two companies follows:

Data for Fiscal Year 2002 (in Millions)	Oracle	PeopleSoft	% Contribution Oracle	% Contribution PeopleSoft
Revenues	$ 9,673	$1,949	83.2%	16.8%
Operating expense	$ 6,102	$1,696	78.2%	21.8%
Operating income	$ 3,571	$ 253	93.4%	6.6%
Net income	$ 2,224	$ 183	92.4%	7.6%
Operating margin	36.9%	13.0%		
Net margin	23.0%	9.4%		
Total assets	$10,800	$2,849	79.1%	20.9%
Total shareholders' equity	$ 6,117	$1,956	75.8%	24.2%
Outstanding shares	5,518	311		
Market capitalization on May 15, 2003	$71,237	$5,038	93.4%	6.6%

[This spreadsheet can be found in the folder "Key Spreadsheets from the Workbook" located on the CD-ROM.]

Use contribution analysis to calculate the exchange ratios, assuming the contributions are based on each company's net income. Is a deal feasible?

12. On June 16, 2003, Oracle raised its bid for PeopleSoft to $19.50 a share.

Would a deal be feasible now?

CHAPTER 22

Structuring and Valuing Contingent Payments in M&A

Earnouts are options. The option analogy highlights two important design aspects that are worth careful attention by the negotiators: the time period and triggers (exercise prices) for the earnout. Ultimately the design and evaluation of earnouts depend on the assessment of uncertainty. Incentive payment plans can be extremely useful devices for breaking deadlocks by bridging the perspectives for both buyer and seller.

- Incentive payments are pervasive in M&A activities. They can take many forms: bonus payments to sellers, escrowed funds, holdback allowances, stock options, targeted stock, and earnout plans. In this chapter, "earnout" refers generically to all forms of incentive payments.
- Earnouts are used mostly in the acquisitions of privately held targets, of service businesses, and of high-tech companies. Smaller acquirers are more likely to use earnouts than larger acquirers.
- Although earnouts are quite useful in bridging the valuation gap and retaining and motivating shareholders or managers, they also pose challenges in postacquisition integration and in defining the earnout formulas and performance goals.
- Earnout provisions are call options on the benefits of future performance by the target firm. Like the more standardized option, the earnout can be described in terms of some of its key value drivers: exercise price, price of the underlying asset, interim payout, term, and uncertainty. It must be tailored to the specific deal and therefore can help in bridging the differences in perspectives between an optimistic seller and a pessimistic buyer.
- To structure an effective earnout, the following key elements must be tailored to the expectations of the two sides:
  - *Earnout amount.* Most earnout values range from 20 percent to 70 percent of the total purchase price.
  - *Earnout period.* Earnouts typically run for a period of between one and five years.
  - *Performance goals.* Common performance milestones are cast in terms of revenues, gross margin, pretax profit, cash flow, or earnings before interest, taxes, depreciation, and amortization (EBITDA). Often the goals are tailored to rise over time.

- *Payment schedule.* This can be structured as periodic payments or a lump-sum payment at the end of the earnout period. Different schedules have different motivational effects on the sellers.
- *Operational integration.* The earnout contract must clearly define the business criteria being measured, and the responsibilities of decision makers.
- *Accounting rules and performance measurement.* The earnout agreement should specify the accounting policies that will be followed when measuring the target's performance.
- *Additional issues.* Availability of financing, management process, change in control, liquidity, and impact on the buyer's financial structure should be considered.

- Under purchase accounting for M&A, the earnout must be included as part of the total consideration paid to acquire the target. It brings up a series of legal and accounting implications. Careful consideration of the tax implication of earnout structure is important to reduce friction between the parties.
- The right approach to valuing earnouts is to value them as derivative instruments rather than as predictable streams of cash. The Monte Carlo simulation method is a simple and effective numerical valuation approach. Under this method, the buyer and seller are allowed to input their own assessments of key value drivers, leading to different valuations of the same earnout structure for the two parties and therefore giving both parties a negotiating window.
- An acceptable earnout will satisfy both sides. To the buyer, the earnout and fixed payment will be *equal to or less than* the value of the target to the buyer. To the seller, the earnout and fixed payment will be *equal to or greater than* the target's value. Stated mathematically, a satisfactory deal should meet both equations simultaneously:

$$\text{Enterprise value according to buyer} \geq \text{Dollars at closing} + \text{Buyer valuation of earnout}$$

$$\text{Enterprise value according to seller} \leq \text{Dollars at closing} + \text{Seller valuation of earnout}$$

CHAPTER 22—WORKBOOK QUESTIONS

1. Earnouts are very useful in bridging differences between buyers and sellers. However, they are also difficult to implement.

   Please briefly explain the advantages and disadvantages of using earnouts in M&A.

2. Suppose you as CEO of your firm are negotiating an acquisition deal with Company ABC. The deal structure is proposed as follows: You will pay $5 million in cash to ABC's shareholders now; if ABC's profit reaches $1.5 million after five years, ABC's shareholders will be awarded any amount that exceeds $1.5 million. By checking ABC's financial statements over the past several years, you estimate that the revenues of the firm have a volatility of 35 percent.

ABC has $10 million in revenue this year, and its profit margin is estimated at 10 percent for the next five years.

Given a 6 percent risk-free rate, how much is the value of the earnout plan? Use a binomial tree to value the earnout.

3. Refer to problem 2. Different assessments of volatilities and future profit margins will create huge discrepancies in the valuation of the firm.

   What is the value of the earnout plan assuming sales volatilities of 25 percent, 30 percent, 35 percent, 40 percent, and 45 percent?

   What is the value of the earnout plan assuming profit margins of 8 percent, 9 percent, 10 percent, 11 percent, and 12 percent?

   Build a matrix with the different profit margins and sales volatilities and calculate the corresponding earnout values. What do you observe?

4. *Refer to problem 2. If the earnout begins after three years rather than five years, how does the value of the deal change assuming all other parameters are the same?*

5. *Refer to problem 3. Changing the start of the earnout from five years to three years, build the matrix with the different profit margins and sales volatilities, and calculate the different values of the earnout. Give your observations.*

6. Assume a buyer plans to acquire a target company that has $12 million in sales. The buyer's estimation of the enterprise value of the target firm is $5 million, while the target values itself at $7 million. To bridge the gap between the target and buyer, an earnout plan is proposed: The buyer will pay $2 million at closing; the earnout, which is based on the target's profit, will be good for five years. In the first year, the earnout will be triggered when the firm reaches a profit of $500,000—any profit in excess will be paid to the target shareholders. The same procedure will be followed every year for five years, except that the earnout trigger will increase by $500,000 every year; therefore, for year 2, for instance, target shareholders will be paid any profit in excess of $1 million, for year 3, $1.5 million, and so forth. Sales growth follows a normal distribution with a mean of 12 percent and a standard deviation of 3 percent. The profit margin also follows a normal distribution with a mean of 12 percent and a standard deviation of 2 percent. The five-year risk-free rate is 7 percent.

   What is the economic cost of the earnout to the buyer?

7. *Refer to problem 6. The target estimates that sales growth will follow a normal distribution with a mean of 20 percent and a standard deviation of 5 percent, and profit margins will follow a normal distribution with a mean of 14 percent and a standard deviation of 3 percent. What is the economic value of the earnout to the seller?*

8. Refer to problems 6 and 7. Different assessments of revenue growth rates and profit margins will lead to completely different valuations.

Do a sensitivity analysis using means of 10 percent, 11 percent, 12 percent, 13 percent, and 14 percent for revenue growth, and means of 10 percent, 11 percent, 12 percent, 13 percent, and 14 percent for profit margins. In what combinations will the buyer not take this deal?

9. *Now from the seller's perspective, do a sensitivity analysis using means of 16 percent, 18 percent, 20 percent, 22 percent, and 24 percent for revenue growth, and means of 12 percent, 13 percent, 14 percent, 15 percent, and 16 percent for profit margins. In what combinations will the seller not take this deal?*

CHAPTER 23

Risk Management in M&A

M&A is risky activity. The appropriate goal for investors should be to at least get paid for the risk one does take. The advice to novices and seasoned practitioners is to pay attention to the uncertainties embedded in a transaction, and use risk management devices where warranted.

- The value at risk in the failure of a deal is not trivial and probably grows over time, reaching its maximum at the closing. Strategic options, synergies, and other opportunity costs amplify the value at risk. For the frequent buyer or participant in M&A activity, reputation considerations will amplify the value at risk.
- Some sources of risk to the transaction:
  - Decline in the buyer's share price or financial performance.
  - Preemption by a competing bidder.
  - Disappointed sellers.
  - Appearance of formerly hidden product liabilities.
  - Loss of key customers by the target.
  - Problems in the target's accounting statements.
  - Regulatory intervention.
  - Litigation by competitors.
  - Disagreements over social issues.
  - Failure to get shareholder approvals.
  - Controversy or lack of credibility.
- Risk management devices that are available to the deal designer appear in three time periods around an M&A transaction:
  1. Before the public announcement of the deal: The investment in cash and attention by each side is relatively small.
     - Toehold stake.
     - Antitakeover defenses.
  2. Between announcement and consummation: The investment of the two sides grows dramatically during this period.
     - Breakup and "topping" fees.
     - Lockup options.
     - Exit clauses.

- Representations and warranties.
- Due diligence research.
- Caps, floors, and collars.

3. After consummation:
   - Escrow accounts and post-transaction price adjustments.
   - Contingent value rights.
   - Earnouts and other contingent payments.
   - Staged investing.
   - Cash payment.

- A collar is simply a way to hedge uncertainty about the value of the buyer. Deals that incorporate collars are significantly more likely to succeed (i.e., to close) than are straight stock or cash offers. In addition, the announcement returns to the buyer's shareholders are not materially affected by the use of collars.
- Stock-for-stock deals may be grouped into four classic profiles:
  1. *Fixed exchange ratio deal.* No matter what happens, the target shareholder receives X *shares* of the buyer per target share.
  2. *Fixed value deal.* No matter what happens, the target shareholder receives X *dollars* of value in buyer stock per target share.
  3. *Floating collar.* Within limits, the value the target shareholder receives varies with changes in the buyer's stock price.
  4. *Fixed collar.* Within limits, the value the target shareholder receives is fixed and does not vary with changes in the buyer's stock price.
- A collar mitigates the impact of uncertainty about the buyer's share price through either a transfer of cash or an adjustment in the exchange ratio. To value a collar, as in the AT&T/MediaOne case given in Chapter 23 of the main text, simulate the expected value based on the three factors:
  1. *The life of the collar.* This depends on the closing date for the transaction. Uncertainty about regulatory approvals, shareholder votes, and the absence of potential competitors make the closing date and the life of the collar uncertain.
  2. *The expected future share price at the date of the consummation of the deal.* The buyer's shares are the assets underlying the collar. The price of the buyer's shares is uncertain and can be modeled using the estimated volatility of the buyer's shares.
  3. *The risk-free rate of return.*
- Contingent value rights (CVRs) (see the case of Rhône-Poulenc's acquisition of Rorer given in Chapter 23 of the main text) may be regarded as *fixed collars* that live well beyond the closing date of the transaction. Contingent payments tended to appear in acquisitions involving a large potential difference between the target transaction prices of buyers and sellers or when the sellers were seeking some protection for the remaining minority shareholders against unfair treatment by the acquirer.

- Staged investing structures a series of options over time. The Genzyme/GelTex deal described in Chapter 23 of the main text illustrates the use of *staged investing* (as opposed to lump-sum investing) as a means of hedging the risk associated with FDA approval.
- Risk management in M&A will be more valuable while the value at risk is greater; the ability of buyer or seller to bear those risks is lower; the uncertainty is greater; they create the right incentives for behavior; and they create reasonable signals of expectations to employees and the capital markets.

CHAPTER 23—WORKBOOK QUESTIONS

1. *What are some possible sources of risk to the M&A transaction?*

2. Assume you are the CEO of a publicly listed company who is considering a purchase of a manufacturing company, Fine-Machinery. The most attractive asset in Fine-Machinery is its newly updated Baltimore factory, which has a book value of $15 million and a market value of $20 million. You estimate that extensive due diligence research on Fine-Machinery and other deal development expenses have amounted to almost $3 million. To mitigate your risk, you propose a lockup option to be incorporated into the purchase agreement. This lockup option allows you purchase the Baltimore factory at $15 million if another bidder comes in and acquires the target. You estimate the probability of a competing bid to be 25 percent.

   Please identify the type of this option and calculate its value.

3. As the CEO of a big information technology (IT) consulting firm, you are considering acquiring several small financial consulting firms to enter the financial services market. You reached a tentative agreement with one of the potential targets. You will pay a 25 percent premium over its market value of $24 million for the target's equity. After extensive due diligence, you conclude that the acquisition will generate $10 million present value of synergies. Because the major asset of the financial consulting firm is human capital, you and the target also agree on an exit clause, which allows you to cancel the deal if more than 30 percent of the target's key employees decide to leave the firm before the closing of the deal—loss of these employees would make the target worth $5 million less. The probability of its happening is estimated at 20 percent.

   Please identify the optionality of this exit clause and calculate its value.

4. As the CEO of a hotel chain management firm, you are considering a potential purchase. After preliminary study, you identified one target that suits your overall market positioning and strategy very well. The rough estimate of the value of the target is $50 million. But there are some uncertainties around its accounting methodologies employed for the past several years' financial statements that are used to determine the value of the target. You are considering hiring an independent auditing firm to conduct a thorough audit of its financial reports. The estimated cost of an audit is $500,000. Assuming the accounting

is okay, you believe the deal will generate an NPV of $20 million. You believe that there is an 85 percent chance that the accounting is okay. But if the accounting is as bad as rumored, it would not only wipe out the synergies, but create an NPV (negative) of –$10 million. The agreement allows you to exit from the deal if an audit uncovers accounting irregularities.

If you invest in an audit of the target, what kind of option are you acquiring? What is the option worth?

5. Assume the fixed exchange ratio in a deal is 1.4:1. The buyer and seller agree to a floating collar, which has a low trigger of $20 and a high trigger of $40. Thus, the exchange ratio is 1.4 to 1, unless the buyer's stock price falls below $20, in which case the exchange ratio will be equal to $28 divided by the buyer's share price; if the buyer's share price is greater than $40, the exchange ratio will equal $56 divided by the buyer's share price.

   Calculate and graph the number of shares issued for one share of the seller's stock, assuming the following share prices for the buyer: $0.01, $10.00, $15.00, $20.00, $30.00, $40.00, and $50.00. Also calculate and graph the value of the bid with the collar at these prices. (Use the spreadsheet "Collars Analysis.xls" found on the CD-ROM.)

6. Assume a seller and buyer have agreed on an acquisition, in which the seller will receive a payment in buyer's stock worth $40 per seller share. In addition, buyer and seller agree to a collar, which has a low trigger of $20 and a high trigger of $60. Thus, the cash payment will be $40 for each share of the seller's stock, unless the buyer's stock price falls below $20, in which case the exchange ratio would be equal to two shares of buyer stock; or unless the buyer's share price is greater than $60, in which case the exchange ratio will equal 0.67 shares of stock.

   Please calculate and graph the number of shares issued for each share of the seller's stock, assuming the following share prices for the buyer: $0.01, $10.00, $20.00, $30.00, $40.00, $50.00, $60.00, and $70.00. Also calculate and graph the value of the bid with the collar at these prices. (Use the Excel spreadsheet "Collars Analysis.xls" found on the CD-ROM.)

7. Assume that you—the CEO of a big pharmaceutical company—have been approached by a small biotech company to discuss an acquisition. After preliminary research, you and the target reach a tentative agreement on a $20 million purchase price for the target's equity although there is some disagreement on the value of the promising product of the target, a potential cancer treatment drug. Because the drug is still in the early development stage and the target cannot provide detailed information to you, it is very hard to estimate the drug's true value. Therefore, you propose a staged investment: You will pay $15 million in cash now; later, if the value of the drug is proved, you will pay another $5 million if its value is above $50 million in present value terms (you will pay no more if its value is below $50 million).

   Assume that the probability distribution for the value of the drug is a normal distribution with a mean of $60 million and a standard deviation of $15 million. What is the total cost of the deal to you, and what is the probability of paying the added $5 million?

8. Assume you are negotiating a deal with Company ABC. The tentative agreement proposed is:

   - You will pay ABC shareholders $45 cash for each ABC share right now, which equals 1.5 shares of your stock.
   - Besides the cash payment, each share of ABC stock will also get 1.5 share contingent value rights, which will give ABC's shareholders the right to some cash payment at the end of one year if Newco's stock does not perform well during this period. Assume one share of Newco is worth $30 today. The contingent value right will permit a holder of Newco to receive a cash payment equal to the difference between $42 and the stock price of Newco after two years, *if* Newco's stock trades below $42. The cash payment will be capped at $10 for each share of Newco's stock.

   Use the Excel spreadsheet "Collars Analysis.xls," found on the CD-ROM, to estimate values using Monte Carlo simulation for the questions.

   a. *Given a risk-free rate of 4.8 percent with a 16 percent volatility and estimated volatility of 15 percent for Newco's stock, what does the deal cost the buyer in terms of each share of ABC's stock?*
   b. *Assuming the time period for this contingent value right is not certain and has a triangular distribution, the best guess is two years with a minimum of one year and maximum of three years. The volatility of interest rates is 16 percent. What is the expected value of this right?*

9. Company Macrosofft, a leading computer software developing company, is considering engaging in a joint venture deal with a small software firm Red Dragon, which just developed an innovative voice recognition software package. Macrosofft believes this technology, using the digitalization of voice patterns, may have application to ultra-secure computing environments. For instance, voice recognition might be a substitute for complex passwords or scans of retinas or thumbprints. Due to the complexity and uncertainty of this new technology, the deal is structured in the following way:

   Stage one: Macrosofft will pay $20 million up front to fund continuous R&D to expand its application to security market. Upon Red Dragon's completion of the first prototype of its security system using this technology, Macrosofft will invest another $10 million as a milestone payment. Developing the first prototype will take a half year.

   Stage two: If the beta test of this technology is successful, Macrosofft will pay another $10 million. Beta testing will take another half year.

   Stage three: Finally, if test marketing is successful, Macrosofft will pay another $5 million, which is the final payment. It will take three months to finish test marketing.

   Based on market research data and responses to this technology, the management team made four estimates about the probabilities of success and size of profits:

   1. Red Dragon has a 75 percent chance of successfully developing the prototype.

2. Red Dragon has an 85 percent chance of passing the beta test if stage one is completed.
3. There is a 90 percent chance that test marketing will be successful if stage two is completed.
4. Based on forecasts of the market, the projected profit follows a normal distribution with a mean of $250 million and a standard deviation of $50 million if stage three is completed.

If Macrosofft is seeking 75 percent of the joint venture, how much, in terms of NPV, will it earn from this investment? Please draw the decision tree and calculate the NPV of the project assuming a 15 percent discount rate.

CHAPTER 24

Social Issues

The term *social* is meant to distinguish a set of issues and deal terms from economic issues such as price, form of payment, and generally the returns to shareholders. These issues define the management and governance of Newco, including designation of the CEO and senior management team, makeup of the board of directors, and location of the headquarters. In many cases, social issues have a complicated impact on the buyer, target, and newly combined company.

- Deal-related social issues are often the first terms to be negotiated in a friendly acquisition. The likelihood of consummating a deal is typically contingent on the settlement of social issues.
- While they are sometimes difficult to quantify, social issues can have an economic impact. They can impose a direct cost on the buyer and/or target firm's shareholders. And they may stimulate side payments and complex trade-offs with other terms of the acquisition.
- Social issues cluster into at least nine categories:
  1. Designation of the management team of Newco.
  2. Payments to retain key employees.
  3. Severance payments.
  4. Leadership succession.
  5. Organization design of Newco.
  6. Control options and the composition of the new board of directors.
  7. Structure of transactions: merger of equals (MOE) or other.
  8. Corporate name for the new company.
  9. Geographic location of headquarters.
- Research shows that top management turnover increases significantly following an M&A transaction. In particular, studies have revealed a correlation between the degree of firm underperformance and management changes following merger transactions. Problems arising from corporate culture differences between buyer and target firms explain a significant variation of the top management turnover rate in the first year after the transactions.
- *Retention payments* are the terms of compensation for managers continuing with the new company.

  - They come in varying forms: increased salaries, extraordinary retention bonuses, and so on.
  - They are intended to keep key executives and employees from leaving the firm prior to the completion of the deal. To that end, they usually include contingencies regarding continued employment for a set period of time after the merger closes.
- *Severance payments* are given to departing managers in lump sum, usually according to some predetermined formula set by the firm. Sometimes severance payments are accompanied by *perquisites*: nonmonetary benefits like the use of a company office, car and/or airplane; administrative assistance; country club membership; and so on.
- Regarding the organization design of the new company, the lines of reporting and accountability will convey the degree of the target's independence.
- The determination of the new board of directors will be of particular interest for the directors of the buyer and target firms. The composition of the new board will convey the relative influence of the buyer and target firm's shareholders.
- Structuring a transaction as a merger of equals seeks to give the buyer and target firms equal influence in Newco. MOEs usually involve an exchange of shares with low or zero implied acquisition premiums.
- Naming the new company is no small task; it may signal the relative power and continuity of the buyer and target firms.
- The new headquarters location is often dictated by the firm with more dominance or greater size. Because a buyer is usually much larger than the target, it most likely will endeavor to retain its existing headquarters while closing that of the target firm. Sometimes the two firms will maintain different regional headquarters, in which they share the various headquarters functions.
- In order to understand the transfer of value in a deal, it is important to determine all the relevant parties who will benefit from the resources spent on social terms. These include shareholders, managers, and employees of the buyer and target firms.
- Incentives provided by social terms can influence the present value of expected cash flows, attributable to better operating performance. The business practitioner should not double-count the incentive effect if it is already priced in with estimates of synergy cash flows.
- Adding social terms to the deal may affect the price, reflecting the trade-off between economic and social issues.

CHAPTER 24—WORKBOOK QUESTIONS

1. In early 1998, the CEOs for Daimler-Benz and Chrysler met to discuss a potential merger between the two companies. Study the case ("Daimler and Chrysler: Cross-Border Merger of Equals") outlined in Chapter 24 of the main text and respond to the following questions:

a. *In addition to structuring the transaction as a merger of equals, what were the key social issues included in the DaimlerChrysler merger agreement?*
b. *Did these issues reflect a merger of equals? Why or why not?*
c. *What were issues that were controversial in negotiations?*
d. *Do you think that there were any particular issues that could become problematic after the merger closed? If so, which one(s) and why?*

2. *How can social issues create value? How can social issues destroy value?*

3. Roberta has been working for nine years as a managing architect in the landscaping division of Best Homes, Inc., which has recently become a target for acquisition by Urban Living, Inc. Both companies are home design and decorating firms; Best Homes mainly serves a rural and suburban clientele, while Urban Living caters to city dwellers. If Best Homes is acquired by Urban Living, there is a high probability that Roberta's job will be eliminated. However, there is also a chance that Roberta will continue with the new company in a different job role. Roberta has been one of the best-performing managing executives at her firm.

   How might a golden parachute and severance package induce Roberta to stay with the target firm, even if her future at the firm is threatened by a merger?

4. In February 1997, investment bank Morgan Stanley and brokerage firm Dean Witter announced their plans to merge; their combination would represent the biggest ever in the securities business. Each firm was to have equal representation on the board of the new company. Dean Witter chief executive Philip Purcell would become chairman and chief executive of the new firm, to be called Morgan Stanley Dean Witter Discover (MSDWD). John Mack, current president of Morgan Stanley, would be the new company's president.

   The cultural integration was expected to be critical to the success of the merger. Some say the deal would not have been consummated had Mack not agreed to let Purcell be CEO. One thing Mack would have going for him was that most of the firm's business would report to him. In the new MSDWD, Purcell would directly control Dean Witter's mutual funds and its credit card operations. Mack would oversee all of Morgan Stanley's former businesses as well as Dean Witter's retail sales force of 9,000 brokers.

   Reconciling the two firms' cultural differences would involve sorting out compensation issues, because Morgan Stanley executives tended to make much more than their Dean Witter counterparts. The employees of the investment bank wanted to make sure it would get to pick the chair of the new company's compensation committee.

   The proposed transaction received large majority approval from the two company's shareholders. At Morgan Stanley, shareholders representing about 83 percent of the common shares outstanding approved the merger; at Dean Witter, the merger was approved by stockholders representing about 87 percent of the shares outstanding. Both stocks rose on the merger announcement.

The deal carried a $250 million termination fee, according to an SEC filing. If either Dean Witter or Morgan Stanley should strike a better deal with another partner, that firm must immediately pay the other $250 million.

In addition to the breakup fee, each firm would give the other an option to acquire a substantial amount of its own stock—equal to 19.9 percent of its currently outstanding shares—if a higher bidder came along. Dean Witter gave Morgan Stanley an option to buy 63.9 million shares of Dean Witter's stock at $38.13 a share. Morgan Stanley gave Dean Witter an option to buy 31.5 million shares of Morgan Stanley's stock at $62.92 a share.

The two companies said that they were not going to integrate everything. For example, Dean Witter would keep its headquarters in the World Trade Center, while Morgan Stanley would remain in its offices in Times Square.

Based on the information given, do you think the proposed merger was a merger of equals? Why or why not?

CHAPTER 25

How a Negotiated Deal Takes Shape

The key to understanding best practice in shaping a deal is the concept of *risk management*. The shaping process is riddled with uncertainties. Anecdotal evidence from seasoned M&A professionals suggests that only small percentages of M&A proposals result in a consummated deal. The process of striking a deal is more like a game of poker than an engineering problem. Law structures the game. Economics adds powerful incentives and motivates strategic behavior. Psychology influences how the game is played.

- Good deal process management involves using the legal framework to hedge risk exposure and stimulate good behavior. In general, a deal takes shape through the following process:

1. *Strategic planning, search, and target identification.* Months, or maybe years, of purposeful search culminates in an internal decision by the buyer's managers to approach the target firm. Often this decision entails a formal presentation and discussion supported by strategic and financial analysis.
2. *The initial contact.* The CEO or other senior representative of the buyer approaches the target firm's CEO with a proposal to talk. This brief discussion must give a compelling reason for the combination of two firms that speaks to the needs of target shareholders and management. If the target responds positively to the initial contact, further talks will be scheduled. At the top of the agenda will be social issues.
3. *Confidentiality agreement and related documents.* Very early in the discussions, the two sides will negotiate agreements that outline the behavior of the two sides in the deal shaping process. These agreements address respect for the confidentiality of information, exclusivity of discussions, standstill in the purchase of target shares, and the conditions for terminating discussions.
4. *Term sheet and letter of intent.* When the two sides reach a sufficient degree of alignment on the general terms of a deal, they may memorialize their understanding in a term sheet and/or a letter of intent. These serve to confirm a growing level of commitment and guide the lawyers in drafting a definitive agreement.
5. *Due diligence and negotiation of a definitive agreement.* The next phase entails drafting a definitive agreement that will depend on detailed assertions about the condition of the target, and perhaps the buyer. The defini-

tive agreement binds the two sides to consummate a transaction. Due diligence research becomes a vital step underlying both the definitive agreement and the closing.

6. ***Affirmative vote by the board of directors.*** The definitive agreement likely requires approval of the target's board of directors, and may require approval by the buyer's board as well. If a vote of the shareholders is required, the board can only recommend that they approve the deal. Usually around this stage, the merger negotiations are disclosed to the public and to regulators.
7. ***Disclosure to the public and to regulators.*** Securities regulations and court decisions require firms to disclose to shareholders news about events that is material and probable. When to make the announcement and what to say are matters of judgment, and therefore two of the most delicate issues faced in managing the deal shaping process.
8. ***Antitrust filings and permission.*** Part of the process of releasing information about the deal entails required disclosure to antitrust authorities as part of gaining their permission to consummate the transaction. Filings under the Hart-Scott-Rodino Act (HSR) must reveal the likely degree of Newco's industry concentration following the deal.
9. ***Informing the shareholders and gaining an affirmative vote.*** Merger proposals require the approval of shareholders. Thus, the target and sometimes the buyer will issue a merger prospectus that informs shareholders about the deal, and a proxy statement that requests their votes in support of the deal. The document preparation and voting process take three to six months.
10. ***Closing.*** The M&A agreement commits the two firms to conclude a transaction under various terms and conditions, such as gaining shareholder votes and regulatory approvals. At the closing the two sides document that they have met the representations, warranties, and covenants outlined in the agreement. Payment is made and ownership is assumed by the buyer.
11. ***Postmerger integration.*** Except for terms of the definitive agreement that specifically extend beyond closing, the focus thereafter is on combining the two companies to realize the economic benefits hypothesized at the outset. Indifference to integration is a leading cause of M&A failure. Planning for integration ideally commences early in the process such as at the signing of the letter of intent.

- Factors that may derail the deal process are:
  - *Bad chemistry.* CEOs/management teams do not get along.
  - *Social issues, control.* Disagreements arise about who becomes CEO or chairman of the board; there are culture clashes.
  - *Pricing.* Target and buyer do not agree on the purchase price/valuation.
  - *Market trends.* Adverse moves in the stock market or interest rates may affect the value of the buyer's offer or ability to finance the transaction.
  - *Skeletons in the closet.* Previously unknown or undisclosed facts or events relating to either party surface during negotiations.

  - *Material adverse change.* There are sudden changes in the businesses of the buyer or target.
  - *Regulatory or antitrust constraints.* Regulatory bodies may not approve merger for antitrust reasons.
  - *Competing bidder.*
  - *Shareholders vote "no."*
- First-round documents help deal designers manage risks such as leakage of information, double-dealing, buyer backing out, and so on. Examples of first-round documents include the term sheet, exclusivity agreement, engagement letter, confidentiality agreement, standstill agreement, and letter of intent.
- Generally, executives and boards are obligated to disclose material news to investors. "Materiality" will depend on:
  - Significance of the transaction to the company.
  - Probability of the transaction occurring.
- An attitude of risk management should guide the deal shaping process. One must focus on good process and trust that in doing so a good outcome will emerge.

CHAPTER 25—WORKBOOK QUESTIONS

1. Family Mart, a medium-sized supermarket chain in the Carolinas, has been approached by Mighty Mart, the largest supermarket chain in the Southeast, for a possible merger. In his excitement, the CEO of Family Mart says during the initial meeting, "This sounds like a winner! I will instruct my CFO and chief auditor to provide all the information you need. You can start immediately!"
   Comment on the action of the CEO of Family Mart.

2. Refer to problem 1. At the conclusion of the initial meeting, the CEO of Family Mart tells the CEO of Mighty Mart, "Our bylaws require board approval for these kinds of transactions. But don't worry—I give you my word that the directors will vote in favor of our merger."
   Comment on the action of the CEO of Family Mart.

3. Camelot, Inc., a large publisher, is planning to acquire Little Pete's House, a specialty publisher of children's books. Based on his business development team's analysis, the CEO of Camelot, Hans Olsen, believes that the acquisition will be a big win for his company. Confident that Camelot's directors will agree with him, he proceeds to make a presentation to Little Pete's management without first informing his own board. The two CEOs agree to a merger, and go through the necessary procedures (e.g., signing of confidentiality agreements, due diligence, discussion of tax and accounting treatment, etc.).
   If you were in Olsen's shoes and likewise believed that the acquisition would be a big win, would you go about the deal process in the same fashion as Olsen?

4. Refer to problem 3. Suppose that Little Pete's CEO vehemently opposes Olsen's proposal to merge. Olsen, however, continues to believe that a merger would be favorable to both companies, and refuses to give up.
   What alternatives does Olsen have? Explain.

5. Refer to problem 4. Suppose word gets out that Little Pete's has been approached by Camelot, and that this results in unusual trading activity in Little Pete's.
   Does Little Pete's have an obligation to disclose that it has received an unwanted offer?

6. *What risk does a standstill agreement manage?*

7. Two large telecommunications companies have agreed in principle to a merger of equals. Both companies think that the merger may be challenged by outside parties (competitors and activist shareholders), and therefore want to keep discussions private for as long as they can. Many of the main merger terms (i.e., price, form of payment, structure, social issues) have already been worked out.
   Should the companies formalize their understanding with a letter of intent?

CHAPTER **26**

Governance in M&A: The Board of Directors and Shareholder Voting

"Governance" is the action of controlling or directing. In a corporate setting, governance entails a system of oversight and delegation of decisions that reaches from the owners of the firm (the shareholders) to the board of directors, and from there to senior, middle, and front-line managers. While good governance may be challenging to achieve because of complexity, size, diffuse ownership, conflicting interests of owners and agents, and moral hazard, the evidence suggests that good governance pays.

- The board of directors plays a key role in promoting shareholder interests in the management of the firm. A company's board of directors exercises governance through the processes of executive hiring and firing, compensation, auditing, review of financial performance, and approval of major decisions.
- Agency costs arise when managements promote their own interests at the expense of shareholders. Good governance is necessary for the minimization of agency costs.
- Governance reduces agency costs by:
  - *Designing compensation structures* that align the interests of managers and shareholders.
  - *Monitoring financial performance* and taking actions necessary to improve shareholder wealth.
  - Binding managers through contracts aimed at achieving goals. This is known as *financial contracting*.
  - Building a coalition among directors and shareholders to influence managers. This is known as *jawboning*.
- Shareholders exercise their influence through votes, lawsuits, and jawboning. Foundational documents (e.g., articles of incorporation and bylaws) lay out guidelines such as procedures for voting, creation of new shares of stock, how resolutions may be presented to shareholders, and so on, and are therefore also a means by which shareholders can exercise their influence. Bylaws, in particular, can be changed only by a vote of the shareholders. Provisions such as supermajority voting requirements, and straight or cumulative voting for directors all influence the potency of shareholder votes.

- Good governance pays in the sense of being associated with higher returns to shareholders, higher corporate valuation, and higher financial performance. Alignment of the interests of managers and shareholders is associated with shareholder value creation.
- The corporate charter and bylaws specify how shareholders can vote. The two classic approaches are *straight voting*, in which shareholders wield votes equal to the number of shares on each candidate independently, and *cumulative voting*, in which a shareholder is granted votes equal to the number of shares held times the number of directors to be elected, and can allocate votes at will (in the extreme giving all his or her *cumulative* votes to just one director). The cumulative voting system makes it easier for cohesive, but minority, groups of shareholders to gain representation on the board.
- The actions of directors are measured against three doctrines of rising degrees of intervention by courts: the business judgment rule, enhanced scrutiny, and entire fairness.
  1. ***Business judgment rule.*** This rule holds that courts are unlikely to intervene if directors and officers fulfill their duties in good faith—that is, if they are not conflicted, are informed, and act in rational belief. Directors must adhere to the duties of loyalty and care.
  2. ***Enhanced scrutiny.*** In certain instances, such as hostile tender offers and auctions, the courts have acknowledged that some business problems may warrant a higher level of judicial scrutiny. Before applying the business judgment rule, the court will first examine the directors' decision-making process and the reasonableness of the action. The *Revlon duties* fall under enhanced scrutiny, and require the directors to auction the firm when the firm is for sale and more than one bidder is competing to acquire it.
  3. ***Entire fairness.*** The highest level of court intervention occurs when an actual conflict of interest affects a majority of directors approving a transaction. In these cases, the defendants (directors) must show that the challenged action was entirely fair to the corporation and its shareholders: fair in terms of "fair dealing" and fair price.

CHAPTER 26—WORKBOOK QUESTIONS

1. *For challenging the decision of directors to sell a firm, which laws govern?*
   - *Laws of the state in which the company is headquartered.*
   - *Laws of the state in which the company is incorporated.*
   - *Delaware state laws.*
2. *What is the difference between straight voting and cumulative voting?*
3. The Addams family owns 70 percent of Addams' Apple, a manufacturer of apple juice, apple cider, apple chips, and other apple-related products. The remaining 30 percent is publicly traded, with Gordon Echo, a raider, owning 100,000 of the publicly traded shares. The company has 1 million shares out-

standing and eight directors on its board. A shareholders' meeting is coming up, and Gordon wants to get at least one of his nominees on the board.

a. *Under straight voting, does Echo have a chance?*
b. *What about under cumulative voting?*

4. The directors of XYZ Corporation met for 20 minutes to discuss the sale of the company, and then voted.
   Assuming they held no other meetings or viewed no other reports, which duty would this violate?

5. The CEO of Starstruck Corporation submitted a management buyout proposal to his board of directors, offering to buy the company at a small premium to current market value. Privately, the CEO promised each board member they would remain on the board of the company, and that directors' salaries would be raised.
   Does voting to approve this transaction violate any of the rules that govern directors' conduct?

6. Tom Kane sits on the board of Walking Shoes, Inc. He has headed the board's audit committee for seven years, and has been instrumental in designing Walking Shoes' financial reporting and monitoring systems. He has great confidence in the system of checks and balances he has built, and has therefore become more relaxed in his review of financial results. Lately he has limited his involvement to reading the firm's quarterly financial statements.
   Under which duty might Tom have an obligation to do more?

7. Special Delivery, Inc., offers domestic courier services via ground transportation across the United States. Its board of directors has just voted to approve the sale of the company to Fly-by-Night, Inc., a provider of overnight courier service throughout the country. There are compelling synergies in support of the merger. The financial advisers believe that Special Delivery is receiving a fair price at $55 per share. The price represents nearly a 30 percent premium to the current market price of $43.50.
   Upon learning of the deal, Jet Courier, a competitor, quickly assembles an offer to buy Special Delivery at $60 per share. Jet Courier expects to realize even greater synergies.
   Is it possible that Special Delivery, Inc. is in "Revlon mode" at this point in time?

8. The directors of Pizza Joe's, a nationwide fast-food chain, have agreed to a merger of equals with Mexican Delight, another nationwide fast-food chain. The directors of both boards believe that significant cost synergies can be achieved through economies of scale in purchasing ingredients and equipment, and through savings in rent and leases by having both franchises in each location. Both boards have reviewed internal studies exhaustively and have consulted independent financial and legal advisers. Fairness opinions have been obtained, and the directors believe that the terms of agreement are fair to both parties.
   Are courts likely to intervene in this case? Why or why not?

CHAPTER 27

Rules of the Road: Securities Law, Issuance Process, Disclosure, and Insider Trading

The practice of M&A is vastly influenced by securities laws and regulations. The aim of these laws is to inform investors, prevent manipulation, produce more efficient markets, and achieve a level playing field. M&A practitioners should be knowledgeable about these laws. Ignorance of the laws is no defense for failing to observe them.

- Key rules of disclosure include these:
  - If a deal is material and probable to investors in public firms, one must disclose the proposed transaction to the public.
  - One must control information about a deal and avoid insider trading.
  - One must observe correct procedures regarding deadlines and filings.
- The *Securities Act of 1933* requires that new securities be registered with the Securities and Exchange Commission (SEC), grants the SEC rule-making authority, and sharply limits the trading of unregistered securities. The significance of this act lies in the concept of *registration*, through which the SEC can impose standards of disclosure of information by means of a prospectus.
- The *Securities Exchange Act of 1934* lays out rules regulating securities exchanges and the securities traded in the public markets. It also requires corporations with assets greater than $10 million and more than 500 shareholders to register with the SEC. These companies are called reporting companies.
- The *Williams Amendment* requires hostile bidders to disclose information to the public and target shareholders in connection with a bid. The Williams Amendment imposes four important rules of the road:

  1. *Early warning.* A buyer must notify the SEC within 10 days upon the accumulation of 5 percent or more of a target's shares.
  2. *Open for 20 days.* The buyer's tender offer must be open for 20 business days before shares may be purchased.
  3. *Equal treatment.* All target shareholders must be treated equally by the buyer.
  4. *Cash offers, too.* Cash tender offers are also subject to the antifraud and registration requirements that govern share-for-share exchanges.

- Private placements are exempt from registration under certain rules.
- States are permitted to have jurisdiction over securities registration as long as they don't conflict directly with the provisions of the 1934 Act.
- Court law directs the decision maker to consider the following disclosure guidelines:
  - ***Materiality.*** Do not omit material facts. The Supreme Court states, "An omitted fact is material if there is a substantial likelihood that a reasonable shareholder would consider it important in deciding how to vote."
  - ***Probability.*** Disclosure of merger negotiations is not required if the merger is unlikely to go through.
  - ***Commit and disclose.*** When an agreement has been reached, release a definitive agreement or a letter of intent to the public.
  - ***Expectations in the market.*** A firm has a "duty to update" where recent actions depart from past pronouncements.
  - ***"No comment."*** Do not deny rumors if negotiations are serious.
  - ***Abstain from trading or disclose.*** Abstain from trading during merger negotiations. If abstention is not possible, disclose merger negotiations.

CHAPTER 27—WORKBOOK QUESTIONS

1. *Joe says to John, "The aim of securities law is to build security for companies and individuals." Is Joe right?*

2. *You are adviser to Pearl Ronaldman, a raider. She wants to commence a hostile tender offer for Mary Stuart Living, Inc., a producer and marketer of products for homemakers and other consumers. Pearl already purchased 4.99 percent of Mary Stuart in the open market 15 days ago. She has four friends, consciously acting together, who have each purchased another 4.99 percent of the company. Pearl is planning to offer higher prices to shareholders who tender more than 100,000 shares apiece and lower prices to those who tender less. Her offer will be open for 10 days because she wants to try to stampede investors into tendering. Will her strategy create any legal exposure?*

3. *In another situation, Pearl makes a hostile two-tier offer for a furniture company. The offer is as follows: $50 in cash to investors who tender the first 50 percent, and in the second stage, five shares of Ronaldman Corp. stock, which is currently trading at $10 per share. Does this violate the Williams Amendment?*

4. *Fitness Buff, Inc., a maker of fitness equipment, is in serious talks to be acquired by Olympic Life, a company that operates fitness centers across the United States. The two parties are very close to signing a merger agreement. Rumors that Fitness Buff is for sale begin to spread. In response to journalists' questions, the company issues a press release denying it is for sale. By means of its public denial, has Fitness Buff created any legal exposure for itself? Explain.*

5. *Jack Siegel tells his long-time friend Sam Denver in confidence that his (Siegel's) company has been approached by a competitor wishing to initiate friendly merger discussions. Siegel also tells Denver that he believes a well-known raider is accumulating a significant percentage of shares in his company, and that a bidding war might ensue between the raider and the "friendly" competitor. The next day Denver asks his broker to buy 20,000 shares in Siegel's company. Do Denver and Siegel have any legal exposure? Explain.*

6. *Myer-Goodwill-Milo wants to acquire independent filmmaker La Primavera Pictures, and approaches the latter's 22,000 shareholders with an offer for a share-for-share exchange. Myer-Goodwill-Milo's shares are privately held and unregistered, but the firm will file a registration with the SEC in two months. Is Myer-Goodwill-Milo in any legal trouble?*

7. *Myer-Goodwill-Milo wants to acquire 18th Century Fox. Myer-Goodwill-Milo offers the five wealthy people who own 18th Century a share-for-share exchange. Myer-Goodwill-Milo does not intend to register its shares issued in this exchange. Is it in any legal trouble?*

CHAPTER 28

Rules of the Road: Antitrust Law

The goal of antitrust law in the United States is to preserve and promote competition within industries, reflecting the public policy view that active competition produces efficiency, innovation, and prices that are fair to consumers. It is important for M&A practitioners to gain familiarity with current antitrust attitudes, to anticipate possible objections, and to creatively work to revise a deal to satisfy regulators.

- According to the Federal Trade Commission (FTC), for a merger to be ruled *anticompetitive* it must substantially concentrate the market for a product and make it difficult for new firms to enter.
- The *Sherman Act* outlaws anticompetitive behavior. It considers illegal (1) contracts that attempt to restrain trade or commerce among the different states and foreign countries, and (2) attempts to monopolize trade among the states or with foreign nations. Violations of the Sherman Act are punished by fines and/or imprisonment. The Antitrust Division of the Department of Justice (DOJ) handles violations of the Sherman Act.
- The *Clayton Act* specifically addresses mergers and acquisitions, preventing combinations that would restrain trade. The Clayton Act forbids acquisitions whose effect may be "substantially to lessen competition or tend to create a monopoly."
- The *Hart-Scott-Rodino Act* requires combinations above a certain size threshold to submit information to the DOJ and FTC in advance of consummating the deal. This law grants the federal government a right of advance regulatory refusal on M&A deals.
- *Horizontal mergers* occur among peer competitors in an industry, and are motivated by the potential for greater market power and increased economies of scale. *Vertical mergers* occur among firms within the value chain. Vertical mergers may help firms increase revenue through greater product offerings and reduce costs through greater control of the supply chain. *Conglomerate mergers* occur among firms unrelated by value chain or peer competition. They help buyer firms grow in size. They may also be motivated by the belief that the central office has key know-how in allocating capital and running the disparate businesses better than they can be run independently.
- Regulatory agencies use two quantitative measures when assessing the impact of horizontal mergers. These are the *cross elasticity of demand* and the

Herfindahl-Hirschman Index (HHI). The cross elasticity of demand measures how closely related demand is for two different goods. The relationship is measured as the change in demand for one good in response to a change in the price of another good. The Herfindahl-Hirschman Index measures market concentration based on market shares of players in the relevant market.

$$\text{Elasticity} = \frac{\%\ \text{Change in quantity demanded of good B}}{\%\ \text{Change in price of good A}}$$

$$HHI = \sum_{i}^{n}\left(\frac{\text{Sales or output of Firm } i}{\text{Total sales or output of market}}\times 100\right)^2$$

- Regulatory agencies also use other guidelines to decide whether to approve or disapprove horizontal mergers:
  - Whether the merger will forestall entry by other firms.
  - Whether the merger efficiency gains are credible.
  - Whether either of the merger partners is a failing firm.
- Antitrust agencies challenge nonhorizontal mergers under two theories:
  1. ***Theory of potential competition.*** Nonhorizontal mergers may have adverse effects on competition in indirect ways by eliminating potential entrants into a market.
  2. ***Barriers to entry from vertical mergers.*** Some vertical mergers could reduce competition in a market through the erection of significant barriers to entry.

CHAPTER 28—WORKBOOK QUESTIONS

1. *Goods X and Y have a cross elasticity of −1.2. If the price of X increases, what do you think will happen to the demand for Y? Provide examples of goods with negative cross elasticities. How would you characterize the relationship between such goods?*

2. Firm A, a large processor of beefsteaks, wants to acquire Firm B, a processor of lamb chops. The Federal Trade Commission wants to determine the economic relationship between beef and lamb. A review of prices over the past 10 years reveals that demand for lamb chops rises 0.25 percent for every 1 percent increase in the price of beefsteaks.

   Calculate the cross elasticity of demand and interpret the results

3. Listed are the 10 largest U.S. electronics, audio, and appliance stores, ranked according to fiscal year 2000 revenue:[1]

	FY 2000 Revenues ($ MM)
Best Buy Co. Inc.	12,494.0
Circuit City Stores Inc.	10,599.4
RadioShack Corporation	4,794.7
The Good Guys Inc.	860.5
Intertan Inc.	484.2
Rex Stores Corp.	464.3
Tweeter Home Entertainment	404.7
Ultimate Electronics Inc.	385.0
Sound Advice Inc.	177.3
Harvey Electronics Inc.	34.4

Suppose RadioShack Corporation wanted to acquire The Good Guys, Inc. Here are descriptions of both companies:

RadioShack Corporation

RadioShack operates 5,109 company-owned stores located throughout the United States. These stores . . . are located in major malls and strip centers, as well as individual storefronts. Product lines include electronic parts and accessories, cellular and conventional telephones, audio and video equipment, direct-to-home satellite systems, and personal computers. . . . In addition, the company has a network of 2,090 dealer/franchise outlets, including 54 located outside of the U.S.[2]

The Good Guys, Inc.

The Good Guys, Inc. is a leading specialty retailer of consumer electronics products. The company currently operates 72 stores in California, Nevada, Oregon, and Washington. These stores offer some 4,600 products from 240 vendors. The company's merchandising strategy is to provide shoppers with a broad selection of brand name consumer electronics products, with an emphasis on more fully featured merchandise.[3]

Calculate the Herfindahl-Hirschman Indexes premerger and postmerger. Do you think the FTC would approve this acquisition?

4. In December of 2000, PepsiCo agreed to acquire Quaker Oats. By doing so, PepsiCo gained access to Gatorade, which controlled 84.1 percent of the sports-drink market. Coca-Cola's Powerade was second, with a share of 10.9 percent, while PepsiCo's All Sport was third at 2.8 percent. Other brands accounted for the remaining 2.2 percent.[4] Total market revenues were $2.658 billion.

   Compute the HHI in terms of revenue before and after the deal, determine the change in the index, and interpret the results.

5. *Firm A wants to acquire Firm B. Firm A has assets of $398 million; Firm B has assets of $82 million. Is Firm A required to file a report with the DOJ and FTC in advance of the acquisition? Why?*

6. Blue Skies Airways wants to acquire Eagle Airlines. This combination would make the airline industry even more highly concentrated than it already is: Together the two airlines would control 38 percent of the air travel market. The post-transaction HHI would be 2,738 and the change in HHI would be 137 points. Eagle, which has a workforce of approximately 18,000, is teetering on the edge of bankruptcy.
   Is there a chance that the FTC might approve this deal?

7. Satellite Communications Inc. and The Alpha Digital Group have agreed to a merger of equals. The companies submitted filings to the FTC and the DOJ on July 5, 2002. A month later they had not received a response from either of the agencies.
   Can Satellite and Alpha proceed to consummate their merger?

NOTES

1. Jack W. Plunkett, *Plunkett's Entertainment & Media Industry Almanac 2002–2003*, Houston, TX: Plunkett Research Ltd. p. 89.
2. Ibid., p. 391.
3. Ibid., p. 250.
4. Skip Wollenberg, "Gatorade-plus: PepsiCo Snack Foods, Juice Sales to Be Sweeter after Quaker Deal," *Houston Chronicle*, December 5, 2000.

CHAPTER 29

Documenting the M&A Deal

First-round documents lay out terms of engagement among parties privy to a deal. The purpose of first-round documents is to address risks that may arise before a definitive agreement can be reached. First-round documents include confidentiality agreements, engagement letters, exclusivity/termination agreements, standstill agreements, a term sheet, and a letter of intent. In contrast to first-round documents, the definitive agreement contractually binds the buyer and target to consummate the deal. This agreement is a device for managing risks that may arise between signing the contract and actually consummating the deal.

- *Engagement letters* for advisory work must deal with the following considerations:
  - Scope of the engagement.
  - Compensation.
  - Tail provision (whether the obligation to compensate extends to events after possible cessation of talks).
  - Indemnification of adviser against liabilities.
  - Length of engagement.
  - Method of terminating the engagement.
- A *confidentiality agreement* commits the buyer to hold in confidence all nonpublic information received from the target and to use it for no other purpose than consummating the transaction. The agreement also lays out the information to be provided and the channels through which it is to be accessed. The target may seek relief in the event that the agreement is violated.
- An *exclusivity agreement* binds a target to not share information or seek discussions with other potential buyers over a specified period of time during which the merger agreement is being negotiated and the buyer is performing due diligence.
- A *standstill agreement* prevents a buyer from purchasing more target shares without approval from the target's board of directors. Its objective is to prevent the buyer from pressuring the target by short-circuiting merger negotiations through open market purchases or a direct tender offer to shareholders.
- A *term sheet* contains a brief summary of terms of the deal such as price, form of payment, structure, and social issues. Although not a binding agreement, the

term sheet establishes a sense of alignment between the two parties, and provides a framework on which to draft the definitive agreement.

- A *letter of intent* is an agreement on the intent of the deal negotiations up to that point. Some M&A advisers advise against signing an LOI because it is not contractually binding, and because it may trigger some disclosure obligations. On the other hand, it can serve the following useful purposes:
  - Confirm understanding between the two parties.
  - Express commitment.
  - Preempt market rumors.
  - Test investor sentiment.
  - Help get financing for a deal.
  - Start to shape integration efforts.
  - Deter competitors.
- Most *definitive agreements* contain the following sections/information:
  - ***Parties to the deal.*** This section defines who the parties to the transaction are, thereby ensuring clarity about who has commitments to perform under the agreement. Defining the parties to the deal also establishes exclusivity.
  - ***Recitals.*** These tell the reader what the parties want to accomplish, and are easily identified by clauses that begin with "Whereas." The risk management aspect of the "Recitals" section is to frame the transaction as being in the best interests of shareholders.
  - ***Definition of terms.*** The risk management content of the "Definitions" section is to prevent or reduce misunderstanding. Formal definitions also help reduce the length and complexity of the document.
  - ***Description of the basic transaction: purchase or sale of assets or equity, or merger.*** The "Transactions" section lays out the terms of the merger and contains information about how the deal will be consummated. Details provided in this section will usually include the form of exchange, the price or the exchange ratio, information about the treatment of options and warrants, the merger structure, the targeted closing date, and social issues.
  - ***Representations and warranties.*** This section contains disclosures about the condition of the buyer and seller at the time of the transaction. In effect, this section provides a snapshot of the buyer and seller as of a certain date. A representation is a statement of fact, while a warranty is a commitment that a fact is or will be true. The reps and warranties can trigger an exit with no liability if the other party's representations and warranties are shown to be false. By the same token, this section gives a foundation for indemnities after the closing of the deal.
  - ***Covenants.*** Covenants are promises, forward-looking commitments. In the covenants section, the buyer and seller promise to do or not do certain things between the signing of the agreement and the closing date. Covenants prevent opportunistic behavior by either party.
  - ***Conditions to closing.*** This section lists the conditions that each side must observe in order to consummate the transaction. Standard closing conditions

include shareholder approvals, regulatory approvals, absence of material litigation, and consents from third parties (such as landlords and creditors where necessary).
- *Termination.* This gives the circumstances under which the parties can unilaterally or mutually terminate the transaction. These may include mutual consent to terminate, the failure to receive regulatory or shareholder approvals, the expiration of a completion date, material adverse change in the business, or breach of reps, warranties, or covenants.
- *Indemnifications.* The "Indemnifications" section specifies damage payments in the event of losses discovered after closing, or even breach of provisions in the agreement. Typical structures of indemnification are "basket," threshold, ceiling, clawback, and escrow or deferred payment.
- *Miscellaneous items.*

- Corporations and shareholder groups send out solicit proxies from shareholders to gain authority to vote on behalf of shareholders.
- In the context of a vote to approve a merger, the proxy statement chiefly aims to disclose the terms, history, and effects of the merger. At their most basic level, merger proxy statements contain information about terms of the proposed deal (e.g., price, form of exchange, organizational structure), rationale and background of the deal, financial and tax impact of the deal, requirements for consummation, proof of financing for buyer, fairness opinions, regulatory matters, and conditions of termination.
- Merger proxy statements do not tell investors everything they want to know. The proxy statement is drafted in a way to help stockholders vote wisely, yet not divulge valuable information to competitors. Merger proxy statements contain very few forward-looking statements. Careful scrutiny of the merger proxy statement and independent analysis are needed to make wise decisions about deals.

CHAPTER 29—WORKBOOK QUESTIONS

1. Harry, the president of a stock brokerage and research firm called Motley Players, has initiated merger talks with Close Call, another stock brokerage firm. Sally, the president of Close Call, is interested in continuing discussions, but is worried that Motley Players, which already has an 11 percent stake in Close Call, will preempt negotiations and launch a tender offer.

   What can Sally do to address this? Explain.

2. In view of problem 1, Sally insists early in the negotiations that Harry sign a standstill agreement, as well as a confidentiality agreement. Harry tells his financial adviser, "That's outrageous!" to which the financial adviser replies, "Not if we can get something in return."

   What might the financial adviser be thinking of?

3. Predator Bank has been hired to act as financial adviser for Close Call. In the engagement letter proposed by Predator, the latter asks for the right to be com-

pensated even if the deal is not consummated. The clause states that Predator has the right to receive the agreed-upon fees as long as Close Call consummates a merger (with any party) within four years of termination of its engagement with Predator. Sally blows up when she reads this clause.

Is Sally's reaction reasonable? Explain.

4. The engagement letter between Predator Bank and Close Call includes the following terms:

   - Compensation: 5 percent of the first $1 million (or part thereof) of the total purchase price, 4 percent of the second $1 million (or part thereof) of the total purchase price, 3 percent of the third $1 million (or part thereof) of the total purchase price, 2 percent of the fourth $1 million (or part thereof) of the total purchase price, and 1 percent of the remainder of the total purchase price.
   - Length of engagement: 120 days.
   - Tail provision: Close Call agrees to remunerate Predator for the fees cited above if Close Call consummates a merger with any other party within four years of termination of its engagement with Predator.
   - Indemnification: Predator shall be indemnified against possible liabilities arising from the engagement.

   Is the engagement letter missing any important features?

5. Harry has requested a period of 60 days to conduct due diligence research. Sally is in a hurry to consummate the transaction and insists on completing due diligence within two weeks. Sally's company conducts business in 15 countries, sometimes through wholly owned subsidiaries and other times through joint ventures with local partners.

   Comment on this situation.

6. After conducting due diligence, Harry presents Sally with a first draft of the definitive agreement. The portion on "Merger Consideration" reads:

   Each share of the Common Stock, par value $0.001 per share of Close Call . . . shall be converted into, and become exchangeable for 0.42 shares of Motley Players, subject to the following adjustment: If the average of the Motley Players market price 20 days before the closing date is greater than $38.6522, the exchange ratio shall be adjusted to 0.41 shares, and shall decrease by 0.01 for each subsequent 5 percent upward movement.

   Sally is outraged upon reading this. She tells Harry, "We never said anything in our preliminary term sheet and letter of intent about adjusting the exchange ratio!"

   Is Harry under any obligation to adhere to the terms set out in the earlier documents?

Answer the following questions based on the eBay/PayPal merger agreement found at this web address: www.sec.gov/Archives/edgar/data/1065088

/000089161802003151/0000891618-02-003151.txt (You'll have to scroll down a little to get to the merger agreement.)

7. *Who are the parties to the deal?*

8. *Fill in the following term sheet:*

Purchase Price
- Implied price per share
- Resulting PayPal ownership of eBay
- Transaction fees
- Exchange ratio
- Cap

Format of Payment
- Consideration
- Number of shares to be issued

Form of Transaction and Tax Considerations

Transaction Process Requirements
- Termination penalties
- Shareholder vote
- Closing date

Social Issues
- Organization structure
- Executives
- Board seats
- Headquarters
- Name
- Workforce

---

9. *When was the merger agreement dated? What defines the closing date? What defines the effective date?*

   Explain the organizational structure of the merger. Please also diagram the transaction.

10. *What information can you glean from the Recitals section?*

11. *Whose bylaws will apply to the surviving entity?*

12. *Who will serve as the directors of the surviving entity? Who will serve as the company officers? What is the impact of this structure?*

13. *In what form will the target receive payment? What are the terms of exchange?*

14. Go over the "Representations and Warranties" section briefly.

    What do you observe as the most common or most important issues addressed? Why are these issues included?

15. *Describe some of the covenants in the merger agreement and how they serve as risk-management tools.*

16. *What are some of the conditions deemed by eBay and PayPal to be necessary for the consummation of the merger? How do these conditions manage risk?*

17. *When is termination of the agreement possible?*

The following material contains excerpts from a merger proxy statement. Read this material and then address questions 18 to 31 that follow. [Note that ". . ." indicates the intentional omission of material not deemed relevant to this chapter.]

SCHEDULE 14A

(Rule 14a-101)
INFORMATION REQUIRED IN PROXY STATEMENT

SCHEDULE 14A INFORMATION

Proxy Statement Pursuant to Section 14(a) of the Securities Exchange Act of 1934

Filed by the Registrant [ ]

Filed by a Party other than the Registrant [X]

Check the appropriate box:

[ ] Preliminary Proxy Statement

[X] Definitive Proxy Statement

[ ] Definitive Additional Materials

[ ] Soliciting Material Pursuant to

240.14a-11(c) or 240.14a-12

[ ] Confidential, for Use of the Commission Only (as Permitted by Rule 14a-6(e)(2))

Echlin Inc. (Name of Registrant as Specified In Its Charter)

SPX Corporation (Name of Person(s) Filing Proxy Statement, if other than Registrant)

SPX CORPORATION

Solicitation Statement

to Call a Special Meeting of Shareholders

of

ECHLIN INC.

SPX Corporation, a Delaware corporation ("SPX"), is asking you to help it call a special meeting of shareholders (a "Special Meeting") of Echlin Inc., a Connecticut corporation (the "Company"), for the purpose of voting to remove the current members of the Board of Directors of the Company and replace them with SPX's nominees.

On February 17, 1998, SPX delivered a letter to the Company containing a proposal for a strategic business combination of the Company with SPX (the "Proposed Business Combination"), in which shareholders of the Company would receive for each of their shares of common stock, par value $1.00, of the Company ("Shares") (together with the associated preferred stock purchase right (the "Rights")), the amount of $12.00 net in cash and 0.4796 share of SPX's common stock, par value $10.00 ("SPX Common Stock") (the "Consideration"). The SPX Common Stock component had a value of $36.00, and the total Consideration had a value of $48.00, based on the $75-1/16 closing price on the New York Stock Exchange of a share of SPX Common Stock on February 13, 1998, the last trading date preceding the date of the public announcement of the Proposed Business Combination, and the SPX Common Stock component had a value of $36.12, and the total Consideration had a value of $48.12, based on the $75-5/16 closing price on the New York Stock Exchange of a share of SPX Common Stock on March 5, 1998, the last trading date preceding the date of this Solicitation Statement. At the time the Proposed Business Combination is consummated, the transaction may have a market value that is greater or less than either of those two amounts depending upon the market price of a share of SPX Common Stock at such time. At a total value of $48.12, the Consideration represents a 24% premium over the $38-7/8 price at which a Share closed on the New York Stock Exchange on February 13, 1998, and a 32% premium over the average trading price at which a Share closed on the New York Stock Exchange during the 30 trading days preceding February 17, 1998, the date of the public announcement of the Proposed Business Combination. Immediately following the consummation of the Proposed Business Combination and after giving effect to the issuance of the SPX Common Stock in the transaction, shareholders of the Company (other than SPX) would own approximately 70% of the then outstanding shares of SPX Common Stock.

SPX believes that the Proposed Business Combination would be advantageous to the shareholders of both companies. See "The Proposed Business Combination, the Exchange Offer, and the Merger." The Company, however, in past meetings and correspondence with SPX, has consistently advised SPX that the Company and its Board of Directors have no interest in pursuing discussions with SPX.

The Company has Rights outstanding, issued pursuant to a Rights Agreement dated as of June 30, 1989, between the Company and The Connecticut Bank and Trust Company, N.A., as rights agent (the "Rights Agreement"), which purports to prevent SPX from consummating the Proposed Business Combination without the approval of the Company's Board of Directors. Likewise, Sections 840-845 of the Connecticut Business Corporation Act (the "Connecticut Business Act") governing business combinations (the "Business Combination Statutes") present certain obstacles to the consummation of the Proposed Business Combination absent Board approval. See "Reason to Call a Special Meeting" below.

Consequently, SPX is asking its fellow shareholders to join SPX in executing written demands upon the Company that a special meeting be called and held ("Demands") in order to remove the entire Board of Directors of the Company and elect SPX's nominees to the Board in their place. SPX expects that if SPX's nominees are elected, they will act to facilitate the consummation of the Proposed Business Combination, subject to their fiduciary duties as directors of the Company and the general statutory standards applicable to any person serving as a director of a Connecticut corporation as required by Section 756 of the Connecticut Business Act. In particular, the provisions of Section 756(d) of the Connecticut Business Act require directors of a Connecticut corporation, when considering a business combination such as a plan of merger or share exchange, to consider the interests of constituencies other than shareholders, including creditors, customers, suppliers, employees and the communities in which any office or other facility of the corporation is located. SPX's three nominees who are also executive officers of SPX, if elected to the Company's Board of Directors, may find themselves faced with a potential conflict of interest due to their current positions with SPX. If that occurs, such directors will act in compliance with law, including the aforementioned provisions of the Connecticut Business Act and the provisions of the Connecticut Business Act relating to directors' conflicting interest transactions.

Under applicable law, the Special Meeting must be held if holders of outstanding Shares representing in the aggregate at least 35% of all the votes entitled to be cast on any issue proposed to be considered at the Special Meeting demand in writing that a special meeting of shareholders be held. According to a shareholder list provided to SPX by the Company, as of February 17, 1998, the Company had 63,248,939 Shares outstanding. SPX owns 1,150,150 Shares, or approximately 1.82% of the outstanding Shares.

This Solicitation Statement and the GOLD DEMAND CARD are first being mailed or furnished to the Company's shareholders on or about March 6, 1998.

AT THIS TIME SPX IS SOLICITING YOUR WRITTEN DEMAND THAT A SPECIAL MEETING OF SHAREHOLDERS BE CALLED AND HELD. SPX IS NOT SOLICITING YOUR PROXY TO VOTE ON THE REMOVAL OF THE EXISTING DIRECTORS OR THE ELECTION OF SPX'S NOMINEES IN THEIR PLACE. ONCE THE SPECIAL MEETING HAS BEEN CALLED, YOU WILL BE SENT SEPARATE PROXY MATERIALS URGING YOU TO TAKE SUCH ACTION. THOSE PROXY MATERIALS WILL CONTAIN SIGNIFICANTLY

MORE DETAILED INFORMATION CONCERNING THE PROPOSED BUSINESS COMBINATION, INCLUDING RELEVANT PRO FORMA FINANCIAL INFORMATION.

IMPORTANT NOTE: If you hold your shares in the name of one or more brokerage firms, banks or nominees, only they can exercise the right with respect to your Shares to make a written demand that the Special Meeting be called and held, and only upon receipt of your specific instructions. Accordingly, it is critical that you promptly sign and date the GOLD DEMAND CARD and mail it in the envelope provided by your broker, bank, or nominee so that they can exercise the right to make a Demand on your behalf.

A registration statement relating to the securities of SPX to be issued in connection with the Exchange Offer has been filed with the Securities and Exchange Commission but has not yet become effective. Such securities may not be sold nor may offers to buy be accepted prior to the time the registration statement becomes effective. This Solicitation Statement shall not constitute an offer to sell or the solicitation of an offer to buy nor shall there be any sale of these securities in any state in which such offer, solicitation or sale would be unlawful prior to registration or qualification under the securities laws of any such state.

. . .

SPX Common Stock trades on the New York Stock Exchange and the Pacific Stock Exchange under the symbol "SPW." On March 5, 1998, the last trading day before the date of this Solicitation Statement, the closing price of a share of SPX Common Stock was $75-5/16.

THE PROPOSED BUSINESS COMBINATION

SPX has proposed to enter into the Proposed Business Combination with the Company pursuant to which the shareholders of the Company would receive for each Share (together with the associated Right) the Consideration in the amount of $12.00 net in cash and 0.4796 share of SPX Common Stock. The Consideration had a total value of $48.00, based on the $75-1/16 closing price on the New York Stock Exchange of a share of SPX Common Stock on February 13, 1998, the last trading date preceding the date of the public announcement of the Proposed Business Combination, and a total value of $48.12, based on the $75-5/16 closing price on the New York Stock Exchange of a share of SPX Common Stock on March 5, 1998, the last trading date preceding the date of this Solicitation Statement. At the time the Proposed Business Combination is consummated, the transaction may have a market value that is greater or less than either of those two amounts depending upon the market price of a share of SPX Common Stock at such time. At a total value of $48.12, the Consideration represents a 24% premium over the $38-7/8 price at which a Share closed on the New York Stock Exchange on February 13, 1998, and a 32% premium over the average trading price at which a Share closed on the New York Stock Exchange during the 30 trading days preceding February 17, 1998, the date of the public announcement of the Proposed Business

Combination. Immediately following the consummation of the Proposed Business Combination and after giving effect to the issuance of SPX Common Stock in the transaction, shareholders of the Company (other than SPX) would own approximately 70% of the then outstanding shares of SPX Common Stock.

At present, it is contemplated that the Proposed Business Combination would be effected by means of (i) an exchange offer in which SPX is offering to pay the Consideration in exchange for each Share (together with the associated Right) validly tendered and not properly withdrawn (the "Exchange Offer"), and (ii) a subsequent merger of a subsidiary of SPX into the Company (the "Merger") in which each Share (together with the associated Right) not purchased in the Exchange Offer would be converted into the right to receive the Consideration. The transaction would be taxable to exchanging shareholders. The Exchange Offer is conditioned upon, among other things, the amendment by the Company of the Rights Agreement to render it inapplicable to the Proposed Business Combination, the Exchange Offer and the Merger, and the inapplicability of the restrictions contained in the Business Combination Statutes to the Proposed Business Combination, the Exchange Offer and the Merger. The Merger would be conditioned, among other things, on the consummation of the Exchange Offer. See "The Proposed Business Combination, the Exchange Offer, and the Merger." SPX has filed exchange offer materials with the Securities and Exchange Commission and will commence the Exchange Offer as soon as the registration statement included in those materials has become effective. With its letter to the Board of Directors of the Company setting forth the Proposed Business Combination, SPX delivered a proposed merger agreement to the Company in contemplation of arriving at a negotiated transaction. That agreement provides for a single-step "cash election" merger of the Company into a subsidiary of SPX in which each outstanding Share would be converted into the right to receive the Consideration (with shareholders able, instead, to elect to receive all cash, in the amount of $48.00 per Share, or all stock, in the amount of 0.6395 share of SPX Common Stock per Share, subject to proration) in a partially tax-free reorganization.

The Merits of the Proposed Business Combination

In SPX's letters to the Company, SPX set forth various benefits of the Proposed Business Combination to the shareholders, customers, suppliers, and employees of the Company and to the constituencies of both companies. See "Background."

Demand for a Special Meeting.

SPX is asking the Company's shareholders to demand a Special Meeting for the following purposes: (i) to repeal any provision of the Company's By-Laws or amendment to the Company's By-Laws adopted by the Board of Directors of the Company or any Committee thereof at any time after April 3, 1997 (the date of the last set of By-Laws publicly filed by the Company) and before the effectiveness of the last of the proposals to be voted on at the Special Meeting; (ii) to vote upon a proposal to remove all of the members of the Board of Directors of the Company; (iii) to vote upon a proposal to amend the By-Laws of the Company to fix the number of directors of the Company at five; and (iv) to elect SPX's five nominees to the Board of Directors of the Company.

Reasons for the Demand.

Despite repeated urgings by SPX to the Chief Executive Officer of the Company and then directly to the Board of Directors of the Company, the Company has steadfastly turned down requests by SPX to meet with and make a presentation to the Company's Board of Directors to discuss any and all aspects of a proposed business combination. The Company has informed SPX that it and its Board of Directors have no interest in pursuing a business combination.

In its February 17, 1998 letter to the Company's Board of Directors, SPX reaffirmed its desire to enter into a negotiated transaction with, rather than to effect a unilateral acquisition of, the Company. However, if the Company's Board of Directors remains adamant in its refusal to enter into discussions with SPX, the only way that the Proposed Business Combination can proceed is for the present members of the Board of Directors of the Company to be removed and SPX's nominees to be elected in their place. See "Reason to Call a Special Meeting." SPX expects that SPX's nominees, if elected as the new Board of Directors, will act to facilitate the consummation of the Proposed Business Combination, subject to their fiduciary duties as directors of the Company and the general statutory standards applicable to any person serving as a director of a Connecticut corporation as required by Section 756 of the Connecticut Business Act.

Proposed Shareholder Action

SPX's Exchange Offer to the Company's shareholders and the merger proposal to the Company are conditioned upon, and will not be effected without, certain action being taken by the Company's Board of Directors. If the current Board of Directors persists in its position that it will not enter into a negotiated transaction with SPX, the only way that SPX's Proposed Business Combination can be effected is for the existing Board to be replaced with SPX's nominees.

Under applicable law, holders of outstanding Shares representing in the aggregate at least 35% of all the votes entitled to be cast on any issue proposed to be considered at the Special Meeting have the right to demand that a Special Meeting be held. By signing and sending the GOLD DEMAND CARD, you are merely demanding that a Special Meeting be called and held. Signing and sending the GOLD DEMAND CARD will NOT give SPX the right to vote your Shares at the Special Meeting.

SPX is not asking in this solicitation that the Company's shareholders remove the existing Board and replace it with its nominees. Thus, the current Board members may still reverse their position and determine to enter into discussions with the Company for a negotiated transaction. HOWEVER, THE FAILURE TO SIGN AND RETURN THE GOLD DEMAND CARD WILL HAVE THE SAME EFFECT AS OPPOSING THE CALL OF A SPECIAL MEETING, IN WHICH EVENT THE PROPOSED BUSINESS COMBINATION WILL NOT BE ABLE TO PROCEED.

Timing; Assistance

We ask that you sign and date the GOLD DEMAND CARD and mail it in the enclosed envelope as soon as possible and, preferably, before March 31, 1998. If you have any questions or need assistance, please call D.F. King & Co., Inc. at (212) 269-5550 (collect) or (800) 758-5378 (toll free).

PURPOSE OF THE SOLICITATION

SPX is soliciting Demands for the Company to call and hold a Special Meeting. SPX has made a proposal for a business combination with the Company, which SPX believes would provide exceptional value to the Company's shareholders. See "The Proposed Business Combination, the Exchange Offer, and the Merger." The Proposed Business Combination, the Exchange Offer and the Merger are conditioned upon, among other things, the Board of Directors of the Company amending the Rights Agreement so as to render it inapplicable to the Proposed Business Combination, the Exchange Offer and the Merger, and the Board taking such other action as may be necessary so that the restrictions contained in the Business Combination Statutes are not applicable thereto. See "Reason to Call a Special Meeting" and "The Proposed Business Combination, the Exchange Offer, and the Merger." The Company has advised SPX that the Company and its Board have no interest in pursuing discussions with SPX. Accordingly, if the Proposed Business Combination is to proceed, the present members of the Company's Board of Directors will have to be removed and new directors elected in their place who will take all action necessary to facilitate the consummation of the Proposed Business Combination, the Exchange Offer and the Merger, subject to their fiduciary duties as directors of the Company and the general statutory standards applicable to any person serving as a director of a Connecticut corporation as required in Section 756 of the Connecticut Business Act.

The purpose of this Solicitation Statement is to solicit Demands from the shareholders of the Company holding outstanding Shares representing in the aggregate at least 35% of all the votes entitled to be cast on any issue proposed to be considered at the Special Meeting, demanding that the Company call and hold a Special Meeting. According to a shareholder list provided to SPX by the Company, as of February 17, 1998, there were 63,248,939 Shares outstanding; based on that number, Demands from holders of an aggregate of 22,137,129 Shares would be required. SPX owns 1,150,150 Shares or 1.82% of the outstanding Shares.

If SPX is successful in this solicitation, the Company will be required to call and hold a Special Meeting at which the shareholders will be asked (i) to repeal any provision of the Company's By-Laws or amendment to the Company's By-Laws adopted by the Board of Directors of the Company or any Committee thereof at any time after April 3, 1997 (the date of the last set of By-Laws publicly filed by the Company) and before the effectiveness of the last of the proposals to be voted on at the Special Meeting (the "By-Law Repeal Proposal"); (ii) to vote upon a proposal to remove all of the members of the Board of Directors of the

Company (the "Proposal to Remove the Directors"); (iii) to vote upon a proposal to amend the By-Laws of the Company to fix the number of directors of the Company at five (the "Proposal to Amend the By-Laws of the Company"); and (iv) to elect SPX's five nominees (the "SPX Nominees") to the Board of Directors of the Company.

. . .

REASON TO CALL A SPECIAL MEETING

The reason to demand that a Special Meeting be called and held is simple. Unless the Board of Directors of the Company takes action to remove certain obstacles, described below, to the Proposed Business Combination, the Proposed Business Combination, the Exchange Offer, and the Merger will not proceed. Thus far, the present Board of Directors of the Company has indicated that it has no interest in pursuing discussions with SPX.

Rights Agreement. Under the Rights Agreement, if SPX were to acquire beneficial ownership of 20% or more of the Shares, unless the Rights are redeemed or invalidated or are otherwise inapplicable to the Proposed Business Combination, each holder of record of a Right (other than SPX) would, upon exercise of the Right, have the right to purchase, at the exercise price of the Right, Shares having a value at the time equal to twice the exercise price. As a result, the Rights could make SPX's acquisition of the Company prohibitively expensive by severely diluting SPX's equity interest and voting power.

The Rights Agreement provides that the Board of Directors may redeem the Rights at any time prior to a person becoming an "Acquiring Person." An Acquiring Person generally means a person who, together with his or her Affiliates and Associates (each term as defined in the Rights Agreement), beneficially owns 20% or more of the Shares outstanding, subject to certain exceptions. Once a person has become an Acquiring Person the Board of Directors may only redeem the Rights if there are "Continuing Directors" in office and a majority of such "Continuing Directors" concur in authorizing redemption of the Rights. A "Continuing Director" means a director, while a member of the Board, who either (A) was a member of the Board prior to an Acquiring Person becoming such or (B) subsequently became a member of the Board, is not an Acquiring Person or its Affiliate or Associate, representative or nominee, and whose nomination for election or election to the Board was recommended or approved by a majority of the Continuing Directors. In any event, the Board of Directors may not redeem the Rights after the tenth day following the day on which a person has become an Acquiring Person.

The Board of Directors may amend the Rights Agreement prior to the earlier of (i) the first date a public announcement is made that a person has become an Acquiring Person, or (ii) the close of business on the tenth business day (or such later date as the Board may determine prior to such time as any person becomes an Acquiring Person) following the commencement of a tender offer or exchange offer which would result in a person becoming an Acquiring Person). Neither of those events has yet occurred. The commencement of the Exchange Offer will result in the Board of Directors of the Company no longer being able to amend the Rights Agreement after the end of the ten business day period unless the Board of Directors takes action to extend such period.

If elected to the Board of Directors of the Company, the SPX Nominees intend to amend the Rights Agreement so that the Rights Agreement will not be applicable to the Proposed Business Combination, the Exchange Offer or the Merger, or, if the Rights Agreement can no longer be amended, to cause the redemption of the Rights, in each case subject to their fiduciary duties as directors of the Company and the general statutory standards applicable to any person serving as a director of a Connecticut corporation as required in Section 756 of the Connecticut Business Act.

Business Combination Statutes. Pursuant to Section 844 of the Business Combination Statutes, a corporation may not engage in any business combination with an "Interested Shareholder" (defined as the beneficial owner of 10% or more of the voting power of a company) for five years following the date on which the Interested Shareholder became such (the "Stock Acquisition Date") unless the acquisition which resulted in the Interested Shareholder becoming such (the "10% Acquisition"), or the business combination, is approved by the board of directors and by a majority of the non-employee directors, of which there shall be at least two, before the date of the 10% Acquisition.

Pursuant to Sections 841 and 842 of the Business Combination Statutes, any business combination with an Interested Shareholder that was not approved by the board of directors prior to the 10% Acquisition must be approved by the board of directors, 80% of the voting power and two-thirds of the voting power not controlled by the Interested Shareholder or meet certain conditions regarding minimum price and type of consideration.

On March 4, 1998, Raised Bill No. 5695 was introduced into the Connecticut House of Representatives, which, if enacted, would (i) amend the Connecticut Business Act to restrict the ability of shareholders of a public company to remove directors, (ii) amend Section 844 of the Business Combination Statutes to require the approval of a majority of "continuing directors," rather than the approval of the board of directors, and (iii) amend Section 842 of the Business Combination Statutes to provide that the failure to obtain approval of a majority of "continuing directors", rather than the failure to obtain the approval of the board of directors, would trigger the requirements of Section 842 discussed above.

If elected to the Board of Directors of the Company, the SPX Nominees intend to approve the Proposed Business Combination, the Exchange Offer and the Merger or seek to take such other action so that the restrictions contained in the Business Combination Statutes will not be applicable thereto, subject to their fiduciary duties as directors of the Company and the general statutory standards applicable to any person serving as a director of a Connecticut corporation as required in Section 756 of the Connecticut Business Act.

Shareholders of the Company are urged to execute the GOLD DEMAND CARD to demand that the Special Meeting be called and held. Making a Demand and causing the Special Meeting to be called and held is not a vote at the Special Meeting or a vote in favor of the Proposed Business Combination. Shareholders will have the opportunity to vote on the Proposal to Remove the Directors and the election of the SPX Nominees at the Special Meeting. Moreover, shareholders will be able to elect whether or not to tender their Shares into the Exchange Offer; execution of a Demand does not constitute a tender of the shareholder's Shares or obligate the shareholder to tender his or her Shares in the Exchange Offer. However, the failure to obtain Demands from holders of the requisite 35% of the outstanding Shares to call the Special Meeting is a dispositive vote against the Proposed Business Combination because without the Special Meeting, the shareholders will not be able to override the Board's refusal to negotiate with SPX and enter into the Proposed Business Combination. THE FAILURE TO SIGN, DATE, AND MAIL A GOLD DEMAND CARD HAS THE SAME EFFECT AS OPPOSING THE DEMAND FOR A SPECIAL MEETING TO BE CALLED AND HELD.

THE PROPOSED BUSINESS COMBINATION, THE EXCHANGE OFFER AND THE MERGER

By letter dated February 17, 1997 to the Company's Board of Directors, SPX has proposed a business combination with the Company. In the Proposed Business Combination, shareholders of the Company would receive for each of their Shares (together with the associated Right) Consideration in the amount of $12.00 net in cash and 0.4796 share of SPX Common Stock, for a total value of $48.00 based on the $75-1/16 closing price on the New York Stock Exchange of a share of SPX Common Stock on February 13, 1998, the last trading date preceding the date of the public announcement of the Proposed Business Combination, and a total value of $48.12 based on the $75-5/16 closing price on the New York Stock Exchange of a share of SPX Common Stock on March 5, 1998, the last trading date preceding the date of this Solicitation Statement. At the time the Proposed Business Combination is consummated, the transaction may have a market value that is greater or less than either of those two amounts depending upon the market price of a share of SPX Common Stock at such time. At a total value of $48.12, the Consideration represents a 24% premium over the $38-7/8 price at which a Share closed on the New York Stock Exchange on February 13, 1998, and a 32% premium over the average trading price at which a Share closed on the New York Stock Exchange during the 30 trading days preceding February 17, 1998, the date of the public announcement of the Proposed Business Combination. Immediately following the consummation of the Proposed Business Combination and after giving effect to the issuance of the SPX Common Stock in the transaction, shareholders of the Company (other than SPX) would own approximately 70% of the then outstanding shares of SPX Common Stock.

The Proposed Business Combination would be effected by means of (i) the Exchange Offer, in which SPX is offering to pay the Consideration in exchange for each Share (together with the associated Right) validly tendered and not withdrawn, and (ii) the Merger, in which each Share (together with the associated Right) not purchased in the Exchange Offer would be converted into the right to receive the Consideration.

SPX has today filed Exchange Offer materials with the Securities and Exchange Commission and intends to make the Exchange Offer as soon as its registration statement has been declared effective by the Securities and Exchange Commission.

The Exchange Offer will be conditioned, among other things, upon the following:

The Minimum Condition. The number of Shares validly tendered and not withdrawn before the expiration date of the Exchange Offer, together with the Shares owned by SPX and its affiliates as of such time, must represent at least 66-2/3% of the Shares outstanding on a fully diluted basis (the "Minimum Condition"). According to a shareholder list provided to SPX by the Company, as of February 17, 1998, there were 63,248,939 Shares outstanding. Based on publicly available information, as of December 31, 1997, options to acquire 2,044,284 Shares were also outstanding. SPX owns 1,150,150 Shares. See Schedule II. For purposes of the Exchange Offer, "fully-diluted basis" assumes that all outstanding stock options are presently exercisable and exercised.

Based on the foregoing and assuming no additional Shares have been or will be issued after February 17, 1998 (other than Shares issued pursuant to the exercise of the stock options referred to above), and no options, warrants or rights exercisable for, or securities convertible into, Shares have been or will be issued after December 31, 1997, the Minimum Condition would be satisfied if at least 42,378,666 Shares were validly tendered into and not withdrawn from the Exchange Offer.

The Rights Condition. SPX must be satisfied, in its sole discretion, that a Distribution Date has not occurred under the Rights Agreement, and that the Rights have been invalidated or are otherwise inapplicable to the Exchange Offer and the Merger (the "Rights Condition"). See "Reason to Call a Special Meeting - Rights Agreement."

The Business Combination Statutes Condition. SPX must be satisfied, in its sole discretion, that the restrictions contained in the Business Combination Statutes will not apply to the Proposed Business Combination, the Exchange Offer, the Merger or any other business combination to which SPX and the Company are directly or indirectly parties (the "Business Combination Condition").

The Business Combination Condition may be satisfied if the Board of Directors of the Company duly approved the Exchange Offer and the Merger prior to consummation of the Exchange Offer, or if SPX, in its sole discretion, were satisfied that the Business Combination Statutes were invalid or their restrictions were otherwise inapplicable to SPX in connection with the Exchange Offer and the Merger for any reason, including, without limitation, those specified in the Business Combination Statutes.

Financing Condition. SPX must have obtained, on terms satisfactory to it in its sole discretion, sufficient financing to enable the Exchange Offer and the Merger to be consummated. SPX estimates that the total amount of financing that will be required to pay the cash component of the Consideration in the Proposed Business Combination, to refinance outstanding debt of SPX and of the Company, to pay fees and expenses related to the Proposed Business Combination and to provide working capital will be approximately $2.4 billion. SPX has received a "highly confident" letter from Canadian Imperial Bank of Commerce and its affiliate CIBC Oppenheimer Corp. ("CIBC Oppenheimer"), dated February 13, 1998, in which the two entities state that they are highly confident of their ability to raise the financing in the credit markets in an amount sufficient to consummate the acquisition of the Company, refinance existing debt of SPX and the Company, pay fees and expenses related to the Proposed Business Combination and provide working capital. SPX has not had access to, and therefore has not been able to review, any of the documents governing any indebtedness of the Company. Some or all of these documents may contain provisions for acceleration of the Company's indebtedness upon a change in control of the Company. In determining the amount of financing necessary to effect the Proposed Business Combination and in arranging for receipt of the "highly confident" letter with respect thereto, SPX has assumed that all of the indebtedness of the Company would need to be refinanced.

SPX Stockholder Approval Condition. Pursuant to the rules promulgated by the New York Stock Exchange, approval by stockholders of SPX is required prior to the issuance of additional shares of SPX Common Stock if the number of shares to be issued is or will be equal to 20% or more of the number of shares of SPX Common Stock outstanding before the issuance of the additional shares. Since the number of shares of SPX Common Stock that would be required to be issued in the Exchange Offer exceeds such 20%, consummation of the Exchange Offer will be conditioned upon receipt of the requisite approval by SPX's stockholders of the issuance of the shares of SPX Common Stock in the Exchange Offer and the Merger (the "SPX Stockholder Approval Condition"). Under the rules of the New York Stock Exchange, assuming there is a quorum present at the stockholders meeting at which the matter is being considered (consisting of over 50% of the stock issued and outstanding and entitled to be voted at the stockholders meeting), the issuance of the additional shares must be approved by a majority of the votes entitled to be cast by the holders of SPX Common Stock that are present or represented by proxy at the stockholders meeting. SPX has not commenced a solicitation of its stockholders to approve the issuance of the shares in the Exchange Offer and the Merger and does not intend to do so at least until the required number of Demands have been received to call the Special Meeting.

The timing of the consummation of the Exchange Offer and the Merger will depend on a variety of factors and legal requirements, the actions of the Board of Directors of the Company, and whether the Minimum Condition, the Rights Condition, the Business Combination Statutes Condition, the Financing Condition and the SPX Stockholder Approval Condition are satisfied or (if permissible) waived. On January 6, 1998, SPX made its HSR Filing under the HSR Act.

The waiting period under the HSR Act expired at 11:59 p.m. on February 5, 1998. Accordingly, satisfaction of the pre-merger notification and waiting period requirements of the HSR Act is not a condition of either the Exchange Offer or the Merger.

SPX reserves the right to amend the terms of the Exchange Offer and/or the Merger (including amending the number of Shares to be purchased in the Exchange Offer, the nature or amount of the Consideration to be paid in the Exchange Offer and/or in the Merger, and the surviving entity in the Merger) at any time, including upon entering into a merger agreement with the Company. SPX further reserves the right to negotiate and enter into a merger agreement with the Company (and has delivered a draft of such a merger agreement with its February 17, 1998 letter to the Board of Directors (See "Background")) pursuant to which there would be no Exchange Offer but rather a "single-step" merger in which the Shares would be converted into the right to receive the Consideration, or all cash, in the amount of $48.00 per Share, or all stock, in the amount of 0.6395 share of SPX Common Stock per Share, subject to proration, or cash and SPX Common Stock in such other amounts as are negotiated between SPX and the Company; provided that SPX does not presently intend to reduce the aggregate amount of the consideration to be paid in respect of the Shares from the amount of the Consideration proposed to be paid in the Exchange Offer and the Merger, although the taking of certain actions by the Company's current Board of Directors, such as an extraordinary dividend, might lead SPX to reduce the amount of consideration to be paid. SPX has repeatedly stated to the Company's Board and management, including in its February 17, 1998 letter to the Board, that if the Company is able to substantiate more value in the Company, SPX is prepared to recognize such additional value in the context of a negotiated transaction.

A registration statement relating to the shares of SPX Common Stock to be issued in connection with the Exchange Offer has been filed with the Securities and Exchange Commission but has not yet become effective. Such securities may not be sold nor may offers to buy be accepted prior to the time the registration statement becomes effective. This Solicitation Statement shall not constitute an offer to sell or the solicitation of an offer to buy nor shall there be any sale of these securities in any state in which such offer, solicitation or sale would be unlawful prior to registration or qualification under the securities laws of any such state.

In the February 17, 1998 press release announcing the Proposed Business Combination and in certain slides utilized by SPX regarding the Proposed Business Combination, copies of which were filed as supplemental materials to the Preliminary Solicitation Materials of SPX, certain cautions were given regarding the forward-looking statements contained therein. To the extent these materials are deemed issued in connection with the proposed Exchange Offer, it should be noted that the safe harbor provisions of the Private Securities Litigation Reform Act of 1995 do not apply to tender or exchange offers.

SPECIAL MEETING PROPOSALS

If SPX is successful in its solicitation of Demands and a Special Meeting is called and held, the following matters will be proposed for action by the shareholders at the Special Meeting:

Repeal of By-Laws Adopted Subsequent to April 3, 1997. The By-Law Repeal Proposal is designed to prevent the Board of Directors of the Company or a Committee thereof from taking actions, by means of amending the Company's By-Laws, to attempt to nullify the actions to be voted on by the shareholders at the Special Meeting or to create obstacles to the consummation of the Proposed Business Combination, the Exchange Offer and the Merger. According to publicly available information, the most recent version of the Company's By-Laws was adopted on April 3, 1997 and no amendments subsequent to that date have been publicly disclosed. If the Board of Directors of the Company or any Committee thereof has adopted since April 3, 1997, or adopts prior to the effectiveness of the proposals that are to be voted on at the Special Meeting, any amendment to the Company's By-Laws, this proposal would repeal such amendment. The purpose of this amendment is to remove any existing undisclosed obstacles, and to prevent the Board or any Committee thereof from creating new obstacles, to the consummation of the Proposed Business Consummation, the Exchange Offer, and the Merger. Assuming there is a quorum (consisting of a majority of the votes entitled to be cast on the matter (a "Quorum")) at the Special Meeting, the By-Law Repeal Proposal will be adopted, and the By-Laws and By-Law amendments covered thereby will be repealed, if the number of votes cast in favor of adopting the proposal exceeds the number of votes cast against such proposal.

Removal of Directors of the Company. Unless the Board of Directors of the Company takes action to remove certain obstacles, the Proposed Business Combination, the Exchange Offer, and the Merger will not proceed. Thus far, the current Board has shown no interest in negotiating with SPX. . . .

Amendment of the By-Laws of the Company. The Company's By-Laws currently provide that the Board shall consist of not less than three members and not more than 12 members, with the exact number of directors to be determined from time to time by a resolution of the Board. According to publicly available information, the Company currently has nine directors. At the Special Meeting, SPX will propose that the By-Laws of the Company be amended to fix the number of directors of the Company at five by replacing the first sentence of Article II, Section 1, which currently provides that

"The Board of Directors shall consist of not less than three nor more than twelve members, the number to be as the directors shall from time to time direct.",

with the following sentence:

"The Board of Directors of the Corporation shall consist of five members."

Assuming there is a Quorum at the Special Meeting, the By-Laws will be amended if the number of votes cast in favor of amending the By-Laws exceeds the number of votes cast against the amendment.

Election of SPX Nominees as Directors. SPX will propose at the Special Meeting that the shareholders of the Company elect the following persons, all of whom are nominees of SPX, to the Board of Directors of the Company: . . . If the SPX Nominees are elected, SPX anticipates that the SPX Nominees will act to facilitate the consummation of the Proposed Business Combination, including the actions with respect to the Rights Agreement and Business Combination Statutes discussed above (see "Reason to Call a Special Meeting"), subject to their fiduciary duties as directors of the Company and the general statutory standards applicable to any person serving as a director of a Connecticut corporation as required by Section 756 of the Connecticut Business Act. Assuming there is a Quorum at the Special Meeting, directors are elected by a plurality of the votes cast by the shareholders entitled to vote at the Special Meeting. Shareholders of the Company do not have cumulative voting rights.

Each SPX Nominee, other than the three executive officers of SPX, will receive $25,000 from SPX for his services as a nominee for election as a director of the Company, and, if elected, as a director of the Company, and each SPX Nominee will be reimbursed his reasonable out-of-pocket expenses incurred in the performance of his service as a nominee and, if elected, as a director of the Company. SPX has agreed to indemnify each SPX Nominee from and against any losses, claims, charges, liabilities, costs or expenses (including reasonable legal fees and expenses) arising out of any claim, action, suit or proceeding to which the SPX Nominee is or is threatened to be made a party (i) by reason of his being a nominee and a "participant in a solicitation" (as defined in the Securities Exchange Act of 1934) or (ii) arising out of or in connection with his service as a Company director. SPX may, but is not obligated to, obtain insurance policies covering any portion of such indemnification.

SPX does not expect that any of the SPX Nominees will be unable to stand for election if the Special Meeting is held, but, in the event that any vacancy in the slate of SPX Nominees should occur, SPX will name a substitute nominee. In addition, SPX reserves the right (i) to nominate additional nominees to fill any director positions created by the Board of Directors of the Company prior to or at the Special Meeting and (ii) to nominate substitute or additional persons if the Company makes or announces any changes to its By-Laws or takes or announces any other action that has, or if consummated would have, the effect of disqualifying any or all of the SPX Nominees.

If the Special Meeting is called, shareholders of the Company will be furnished proxy materials relating to the foregoing proposals. These proxy materials will contain significantly more detailed information concerning the Proposed Business Combination, including relevant pro forma financial information.

DEMAND PROCEDURES

Under the Connecticut Business Act and the Company's By-Laws, a special meeting of the Company's shareholders may be called by one or more holders of Shares representing in the aggregate at least 35% of all the votes entitled to be cast on any issue proposed to be considered at the Special Meeting. According to the Company's By-Laws, each holder of Shares is entitled to one vote per Share held. According to a shareholder list provided to SPX by the Company, as of February 17, 1998, there were 63,248,939 Shares outstanding. Based on such number and the fact that SPX owns 1,150,150 Shares, Demands from holders of an aggregate of at least 20,986,979 Shares in addition to SPX will be required to call the Special Meeting. The By-Laws of the Company provide that, upon written request of the requisite holders, the President of the Company shall call a Special Meeting. Following receipt of the requisite Demands, SPX will deliver the Demands to the Secretary of the Company and request that officer forthwith to cause appropriate notice of the Special Meeting to be given to the Company's shareholders entitled thereto.

Under the Connecticut Business Act, a company's by-laws may fix or provide the manner of fixing the record date for one or more voting groups in order to determine, among other things, the shareholders entitled to demand a special meeting (the "Demand Record Date"). The Connecticut Business Act provides that, if not otherwise fixed by the by-laws or the board of directors, the record date for determining shareholders entitled to demand a special meeting is the date the first shareholder signs the demand. On February 17, 1998, SPX delivered its written Demand to the Secretary of the Company. Accordingly, SPX believes that the Demand Record Date is February 17, 1998.

You may revoke a previously executed Demand at any time before the delivery of Demands from holders of Shares representing in the aggregate the requisite 35% vote to the Secretary of the Company by delivering a written notice of revocation to SPX, care of D.F. King & Co., Inc. ("D.F. King"), 77 Water Street, 20th Floor, New York, New York 10005. Although such a revocation is also effective if delivered to the Secretary of the Company or to such other recipient as the Company may designate as its agent, SPX requests that either the original or photostatic copies of all revocations be mailed or faxed to SPX, care of D.F. King, so that SPX will be aware of all revocations and can more accurately determine if and when enough Demands have been received from requisite holders.

Under the Connecticut Business Act, the Connecticut Superior Court may summarily order a special meeting to be held if notice of the special meeting is not given within 30 days after the date the demand is delivered to the corporation's secretary or if the special meeting is not held in accordance with the notice. Moreover, a corporation must notify shareholders of the date, time, and place of the special meeting no fewer than ten nor more than 60 days before the meeting date. The Demands contain a request that the Special Meeting be scheduled 35 days after delivery of the Demands so as to provide shareholders the opportunity to vote on the Special Meeting proposals in a reasonably prompt timeframe.

BY EXECUTING THE GOLD DEMAND CARD AND RETURNING IT TO SPX, YOU ARE NOT COMMITTING TO CAST ANY VOTE IN FAVOR OF OR AGAINST, NOR ARE YOU GRANTING ANY PROXY TO VOTE ON, ANY OF

THE PROPOSALS TO BE BROUGHT BEFORE THE SPECIAL MEETING. MOREOVER, EXECUTION AND DELIVERY OF THE GOLD DEMAND CARD WILL NOT OBLIGATE YOU IN ANY WAY TO SELL YOUR SHARES PURSUANT TO THE EXCHANGE OFFER OR ANY OTHER OFFER.

SOLICITATION OF DEMANDS

This solicitation of Demands is being made by SPX. Demands may be solicited by mail, facsimile, telephone, telegraph, the internet, in person and by advertisements. Solicitations may be made by certain directors, officers, and employees of SPX, none of whom will receive additional compensation for such solicitation.

SPX has retained D.F. King for solicitation and advisory services in connection with this solicitation, for which D.F. King will receive a fee not to exceed $50,000, together with reimbursement for its reasonable out-of-pocket expenses. SPX has also agreed to indemnify D.F. King against certain liabilities and expenses, including liabilities and expenses under federal securities laws. D.F. King will solicit Demands from individuals, brokers, banks, bank nominees and other institutional holders. SPX is requesting banks, brokerage houses and other custodians, nominees and fiduciaries to forward all solicitation materials to the beneficial owners of the Shares they hold of record. SPX will reimburse these record holders for their reasonable out-of-pocket expenses in so doing.

CIBC Oppenheimer is acting as financial advisor to SPX in connection with the Proposed Business Combination, and will act as Dealer Manager of the Exchange Offer, for which services SPX has paid a fee of $500,000 and has agreed to pay additional fees, up to a maximum of $8,500,000 in the aggregate (in addition to any fees which may be paid to it in connection with arranging or participating in the financing of the transaction), a substantial portion of which is contingent upon the consummation of the Proposed Business Combination. SPX has also agreed to reimburse CIBC Oppenheimer for its reasonable out-of-pocket expenses, including reasonable legal fees up to a specified maximum, and to indemnify CIBC Oppenheimer and certain related persons against certain liabilities and certain expenses in connection with its engagement, including certain liabilities under the federal securities laws. In connection with CIBC Oppenheimer's engagement as financial advisor, officers and employees of CIBC Oppenheimer may communicate in person, by telephone or otherwise with a limited number of institutions, brokers or other persons who are shareholders of the Company for the purpose of assisting in the solicitation of Demands for the Special Meeting. In addition, CIBC Oppenheimer, together with CIBC, has issued a "highly confident" letter regarding the financing of the Proposed Business Combination. See "The Proposed Business Combination, the Exchange Offer, and the Merger - Financing Condition." CIBC Oppenheimer will not receive any fee for or in connection with such solicitation activities or for the issuance of such letter apart from the fees which it is otherwise entitled to receive as described above.

The entire expense of soliciting Demands is being borne by SPX. SPX does not currently intend to seek reimbursement of the costs of this solicitation from the Company. Costs of this solicitation of Demands, including the fees referred to above, are expected to be approximately $2,000,000 (exclusive of costs represented by salaries and wages of regular officers and employees) of which approximately $1,150,000 have been incurred to date.

. . .

IMPORTANT

Your action is important. No matter how many Shares you own, please join SPX in demanding that the Special Meeting be called and held by:

MAILING the enclosed GOLD DEMAND CARD TODAY in the envelope provided (no postage is required if mailed in the United States).

If you hold your Shares in the name of one or more brokerage firms, banks, nominees or other institution, only they can exercise the right with respect to your Shares to make a written demand that the Special Meeting be called and held, and only upon receipt of your specific instructions. Accordingly, it is critical that you promptly sign and date the GOLD DEMAND CARD and mail it in the envelope provided by your broker, bank or other nominee so that they can exercise the right to make a Demand on your behalf.

If you have any questions or require any additional information concerning this Solicitation Statement, please contact D.F. King at the address set forth below.

D.F. King & Co., Inc. 77 Water Street New York, New York 10005 Call Toll Free (800) 758-5378 Banks and Brokers Call (212) 269-5550 (Collect)

DEMAND TO CALL A SPECIAL MEETING OF SHAREHOLDERS OF ECHLIN INC.

THIS REVOCABLE DEMAND AND REQUEST IS SOLICITED BY SPX CORPORATION

To the President and Secretary of Echlin Inc.:

The undersigned is a shareholder of common stock, par value $1.00 per share (the "Shares"), of Echlin Inc., a Connecticut corporation (the "Company"). Pursuant to Article I, Section 3 of the Company's By-Laws and Section 696 of the Connecticut Business Corporation Act, the undersigned hereby requests and demands that the President of the Company call a special meeting of the shareholders of the Company (a "Special Meeting") for the purposes described below, fix the date, time and place of the Special Meeting and give notice of the Special Meeting (together with a description of the purposes for which the Special Meeting is being called) to shareholders of the Company entitled to vote thereat.

A. To repeal any provision of the Company's By-Laws or amendments thereto adopted by the Company's Board of Directors or any Committee thereof subsequent to April 3, 1997 and prior to the effectiveness of the last of the proposals to be voted on at the Special Meeting.

B. To consider and vote upon a proposal to remove all of the directors of the Company.

C. To consider and vote upon a proposal to amend the By-Laws of the Company to fix the number of directors of the Company at five.

D. To consider and vote upon a proposal to elect five persons nominated by SPX Corporation to the Board of Directors of the Company.

The undersigned further requests that the Special Meeting be held 35 days after such date as the Company has received demands to call a Special Meeting for the purposes listed above from shareholders who, in the aggregate, hold at least 35% of the Company's outstanding Shares, unless such 35th day is not a business day in Connecticut, in which case it is requested that the Special Meeting be called for the first such business day after such 35th day.

The undersigned hereby authorizes SPX Corporation or any agent thereof to collect and deliver this demand to the Company.

This demand supersedes, and the undersigned hereby revokes, any earlier dated revocation which the undersigned may have submitted to SPX Corporation, the Company or any designee of either.

Dated:_________________, 1998

____

(Signature)

____

(Signature, if held jointly)

Title: ________________________

Please sign exactly as your shares are registered. When Shares are held by joint tenants, both should sign. When signing as an attorney-in-fact, executor, administrator, trustee or guardian, give full title as such. If a corporation, sign in full corporate name by president or other authorized officer. If a partnership, sign in partnership name by authorized person. This demand will represent all Shares held in all capacities.

PLEASE SIGN, DATE, AND MAIL IN THE ENCLOSED ENVELOPE PROMPTLY.

[______________________ **end of proxy statement** ______________________]

18. *Who is filing the proxy statement, the target or the buyer?*

19. *What specifically is SPX asking Echlin's shareholders to vote for in the proxy statement? What percent of votes does SPX need?*

20. *What class/classes of Echlin securities has/have voting rights?*

21. *What condition(s) of the Business Combination Statutes must be met for SPX to be able to acquire Echlin? How do these impact SPX?*

22. *What defense mechanism does Echlin have against unwanted takeover attempts? How do these hinder SPX's attempt to acquire Echlin?*

23. *Do you think Connecticut is a state friendly to hostile takeovers? Why or why not?*

24. *What organizational form is SPX proposing for its acquisition of Echlin?*

25. *What form of payment is SPX proposing? Is the deal going to be taxable for Echlin's shareholders? At SPX's current share price, how big a premium is it paying to Echlin shareholders? Has SPX filed a registration statement with the SEC? Is its registration effective?*

26. *If the merger is consummated as described, what percent of SPX stock will Echlin shareholders hold?*

27. *The SPX offer is conditioned upon certain things. What are these conditions? For each condition, explain the risk that SPX is trying to mitigate.*

28. *How much financing does SPX estimate it needs to consummate the deal? Has SPX received confirmation that it has access to such funding?*

29. *What is the significance of this clause?*

> *SPX further reserves the right to negotiate and enter into a merger agreement with the Company . . . pursuant to which there would be no Exchange Offer but rather a "single-step" merger in which the Shares would be converted into the right to receive the Consideration, or all cash, in the amount of $48.00 per Share, or all stock, in the amount of 0.6395 share of SPX Common Stock per Share, subject to proration, or cash and SPX Common Stock in such other amounts as are negotiated between SPX and the Company.*

30. *What matters will SPX propose for action if a special shareholders' meeting is called? Why is SPX proposing each of these actions?*

31. *What will it take to get one of Echlin's current directors removed from the board?*

CHAPTER 30

Negotiating the Deal

The bargaining entailed in designing the agreement to merge or acquire can have a material influence on the outcome. Success in M&A is not determined solely by excellent analysis. One must also master the processes of negotiation by which deals are obtained. This chapter outlines some of the considerations in setting a negotiating strategy for the deal.

- To prepare for a merger negotiation:
  - Assess the current strategic position and alternative strategic actions for buyer and target.
  - Value the target using a variety of approaches.
  - Explore your best alternative to a negotiated agreement (BATNA).
  - Decide on an opening and a reservation price—these bound the *range* in which you aim to settle on price.
  - Identify the relevant players and their interests.
  - Anticipate trade-offs.
  - Consider motivations and aspirations.
  - Work through possible negotiation scenarios in advance.
  - Assess the impact of bargaining costs.
  - Check the reputation of your counterparty.
  - Reflect on persuasion, its sources, and its impact.
- The midpoint between the opening and asking prices is often a fair predictor of the settlement price, as long as it falls within the zone of potential agreement (ZOPA). Knowing this effect, a seller might seek to *anchor* the buyer's thinking by quoting a high asking price—this has the effect of elevating the range of prices within which the buyer believes a deal is possible. The use of tactics such as anchoring can influence outcomes.
- How to manage a negotiation:
  - Conduct multi-issue, parallel bargaining, not single-issue, serial bargaining.
  - Distinguish claiming value from creating value.
  - Look for trade-offs.
  - Consider using a strategy of openness.
  - Don't let stalemates simmer.

- Master the tactics (anchoring, making offers, ultimatums, number and rate of change of offers).
- Remember that time matters.
- Turn negotiation into a corporate capability.
- Use contingent payments to bridge a gap between two positions.
- Respect the other party's culture.
- Manage the politics within your own team.

CHAPTER 30—WORKBOOK QUESTIONS

Identify the mistakes in the following situations based on what you have learned about negotiations:

1. *Nova Water is in talks to acquire Seattle Springs, a small water bottler in the Pacific Northwest. Nova and its financial advisers have come to the conclusion that the target is worth between $290 million to $330 million. Seattle Springs and its advisers have settled on a range of $320 million to $350 million. During the negotiations, Nova opens with an offer of $80 million. Seattle Springs' chief gets up without a word and leaves the room. What happened? Why?*

2. *Refer to problem 1. Suppose that instead of opening at $80 million, Nova opens at $330 million. Is this a good strategy?*

3. *Suppose that two other bidders are competing with Nova for Seattle Springs. The sale is to take place through a sealed-bid first-price auction. Nova has hired an investment bank to do a competitor analysis. The bankers are closely acquainted with the bottled water industry and are almost certain that Rings of Saturn, one of the other bidders, will offer a price close to $350 million. The bankers have come to this conclusion based on Rings of Saturn's past bidding patterns and on the value that the bankers think Rings of Saturn can derive from Seattle Springs. Thinking of the amount Nova has already spent putting its bid together, its CEO says, "We've put so much work into this that it would be stupid to abandon the deal now. Go ahead and bid $360 million." As an adviser to the CEO of Nova, what would be your counsel?*

4. *Sea Horse Inc., a large cargo shipping company, is looking to expand its presence in Asia by acquiring a majority position in a Taiwanese shipping concern. Arthur Sprouse, CEO of Sea Horse, flies to Taiwan to meet with CEO Te-Hua Chang. Their meetings go well enough that Sprouse decides to leave the negotiations to his CFO and financial advisers, despite having been advised in advance that Asians place particular importance on rank. Is there any problem with this?*

5. *The CEO and CFO of a large pharmaceutical company are preparing to negotiate with a target. The CFO insists that price, form of payment, and issues regarding the makeup of the board can all be negotiated as a bundle. The CEO*

disagrees, and orders the CFO to negotiate only the price first. Is there any problem with this?

6. *A large soft drink company, fearful of being left behind by the competition, wanted to quickly create a presence in the fast-growing noncarbonated beverages segment. It estimated the cost of building a noncarbonated beverages business was $400 million invested annually over five years. Its cost of capital was 10 percent. However, when word went around that one of the players in the noncarbonated beverages business was looking to sell, the soft drink company initiated discussions. The soft drink company ended up paying $2 billion for the target. Has the soft drink company ignored a basic tenet?*

7. *Dan Settles wanted to acquire a string of distributorships in the Southeastern United States in a "roll-up" strategy. In his first negotiation he behaved in an intimidating, aggressive manner, and was able to acquire the target for a cheap price—the target was a weak player in the market with an owner eager to sell. Settles thought, "The intimidating approach worked pretty well. I am going to adopt that approach in my next negotiations." He boasted to the local newspaper, "I always get the terms I want." The next week, a local trade magazine referred to Settles in an uncomplimentary fashion. What may be the result?*

8. *John Bailey negotiated a definitive agreement that was within the bounds of the range his CEO had instructed him. The seller and Bailey shook hands on the deal. Bailey's CEO had offered no other guidance. When Bailey finished presenting the acquisition terms to the CEO, the latter erupted, "They'll be moving the headquarters to Toledo, Ohio! I can't stand that place! Get that fixed or you're fired."*

CHAPTER 31

Auctions in M&A

An understanding of the basics of corporate auctions is vital to successful bidding in M&A. Different types of auctions will affect the behaviors of buyers and sellers in different ways. M&A practitioners must not only see auctions as rational processes driven by price, but must also be alert to the dynamics of strategy and psychology inherent in auctions.

- An auction is a public event at which an asset is sold through a bidding process to the highest bidder. Auctions in M&A can vary dramatically from this conventional definition of auctions.
- Five methods of sale and their advantages and disadvantages are:

Method	Description	Advantages	Disadvantages
Beauty contest	Interested buyers are invited to present themselves to the target. Choice of buyer is made behind closed doors.	Judges have greater ability to obtain information from buyers.	Slow, opaque, and vulnerable to lobbying.
Lottery	Seller specifies sale price; winner is selected by random drawing.	Speed: quick to set up and conclude.	No price discovery by seller. No chance to evaluate buyer on other criteria such as fit, competence, and so on.
First come, first served	First buyer to show up gets to acquire target.	Straightforward to conclude.	No price discovery or chance to evaluate buyer on other criteria.
Auction	Sale is awarded to highest bidder.	Reveals prices, transparent, fast, draws more potential buyers.	Likely is costly to buyer.
Friendly, noncompetitive negotiation	Buyer persuades target to sell in friendly negotiations.	No hostility or nettlesome events that might hinder integration. Target has greater say in structuring the deal.	No price discovery.

- Auctions may be open versus sealed, single versus double, and common value versus private value. In an open auction bids are made public, while in a sealed-bid auction, only the seller sees the bids. In a single auction, only the buyers bid, while in a double auction, buyers bid and sellers offer prices at which they would be willing to consummate a deal. In a common value auction, the asset being sold has similar use to all buyers. In a private value auction, values differ depending on their uses to the buyer.
- Types of auctions include the English auction, the Dutch auction, the first-price sealed-bid auction, and the second-price sealed-bid auction.

Method	Description	Advantages	Disadvantages
English auction	Open bidding. Asset is sold to highest bidder.	• Price discovery and revenue maximization for seller. • Transparency. • Speed.	• Bidding frenzy may result in overpayment by buyer. • Reduces flexibility for seller. No chance to evaluate buyer on other criteria such as fit, competence, and so on. • Vulnerable to collusion. • "Winner's curse."
Dutch auction	Seller begins with arbitrarily high price and reduces it until a bidder accepts.	• Does not "leave money on the table." • Speed.	• Reduces flexibility for seller. No chance to evaluate buyer on other criteria.
First-price sealed-bid auction	Each bidder has only one chance to offer—and outside the view of other bidders.	• Price discovery. • Speed.	• Bidders have no chance to counteroffer. • Revenues to seller are not maximized.
Second-price sealed-bid auction	Same as first-price sealed-bid auction, but winner pays second-highest price rather than highest price.	• May encourage more bidders and higher prices. • Speed.	• Bidders have no chance to counteroffer. • Revenues to seller are not maximized.

- Auctions can be advantageous because they allow sellers to maximize revenue, motivate buyers to bid with speed and at higher prices, and are relatively fast, fair, and transparent. But the disadvantage of auction is that it reduces the flexibility and discretion of the seller by committing the seller to a specific process. Auctions may also be subject to manipulation by buyers. Finally, auctions may discourage entry by prospective bidders because auctions are so successful in maximizing revenue to the seller.
- In an auction sellers rationally seek to reduce uncertainty about the process and to draw many bidders into the contest. Buyers rationally seek to bend or break the rules to gain some special advantage in the process, using tactics such as pressure, aggressive bids, use of the press, and bluffing and threats.

- An auction is an advisable method of sale if the asset for sale is limited or unique.
- Auctions are not always settled solely by price. Price is just one consideration within the bundle of attributes that constitutes the M&A deal.

CHAPTER 31—WORKBOOK QUESTIONS

1. *If bidders are affiliated with or know each other, what auction method is most advisable to use? Explain.*

2. *Plexus Energy has decided to focus solely on electricity distribution and to wind down its business in power generation. Hence it is selling its generation assets that serve the New York and New Jersey areas. Management believes that given the high concentration of population and businesses in these areas, the assets will be highly coveted by several bidders. What method of sale would you recommend? Explain.*

3. *Selectiv, Inc., seeks to sell a minority equity stake and can identify only two other firms that might be interested in making the investment. Factors other than price are important to the founders: reputation, cultural fit, and past experience. The CEO of Selectiv wonders whether an auction would be the best approach to making the sale. What would you recommend?*

4. *What advantage does a Dutch auction have over an English auction? Explain.*

5. *Why might a second-price sealed-bid auction be more advantageous than a first-price sealed-bid auction?*

6. *An English auction was held recently for the sale of Culpeper, Inc. The winning bidder, Virginia, Inc., wound up paying a very high price—beyond even its reservation price. What is it about auctions that might lead to this outcome?*

7. *Refer to problem 6. After Virginia, Inc. was defined as the winner in the English auction, the two sides entered negotiation of the definitive agreement. What is the power of each side at this round of deal design?*

8. *What would be the strategy of a target that wants to hold an auction? What would be the strategy of a bidder that is faced with the announcement of an auction?*

CHAPTER 32

Hostile Takeovers: Preparing a Bid in Light of Competition and Arbitrage

A hostile tender offer ("takeover") begins with an unsolicited offer by a bidder to purchase a majority or all of the target firm's shares. The bidder will set the offer for a particular period of time, price, and form of payment, and may attach conditions to the offer. Economic motives for hostile takeovers may include redirection of underperforming firms and exploitation of synergies.

- An unsolicited offer is one of several tactics aimed at motivating the target's management and board of directors to negotiate with the bidder. Thus, it is part of a buyer's bargaining strategy.
- Takeovers are *games*: This lends the foundation for understanding, analyzing, and designing or repelling hostile tender offers. One can understand these events and the behavior of their participants by studying them as a game. One should try to gain the perspective of the various players in the takeover scenario, their motives and behaviors; master important rules and defenses that constrain the players; and anticipate the paths that outcomes may take.
- The outcome of takeover attempts is highly uncertain. A quarter of takeover attempts succeed; another 45 percent result in the target remaining independent; and the final 30 percent result in the target being acquired by another firm.
- A target may seek to defend itself by searching for a white knight buyer, developing a recapitalization plan, or mounting other defenses.
- A hostile takeover often involves more than just the bidder and the target. Other players include arbitrageurs, free riders, other potential buyers (e.g., white knights and white squires), and factions within the target firm (e.g., managers versus directors, inside versus outside directors, large versus small shareholders).
- The arbitrageur is the consummate economic actor. The arb's outlook is rationalistic, impatient, and always oriented toward value maximization. Once a takeover is announced, arbs become a major influence on the outcome of the contest, typically absorbing available shares in the market and betting that the target's share price will rise.
- Arbs evaluate the likelihood of a deal being consummated and structure an investment position based on that view. The arb will seek to create a hedged position whose risk is determined by the deal rather than by general market

conditions. A typical arbitrage position following a hostile takeover announcement would be to take a "long" position in the shares of the target company and a "short" position in the shares of the bidder—this reflects the typical movement of share prices at the announcement of hostile bids, but the structure also cushions the arb against general movements in the stock market.

- An arb's returns are highly sensitive to the length of the waiting period and the size of the payoff.
- In a takeover attempt with a two-tiered offer, bidders benefit and target shareholders lose by the asymmetric structure of payoffs and the difficulty of taking joint action among target shareholders.
- Target shareholders should be willing to accept a tender offer if the value of tendering is greater than the expected value of not tendering (EVNT).
- EVNT is the expected value of share prices under all possible "not tendering" outcomes, though for illustration we focus on two uncertain outcomes: (1) no shares are tendered to the raider, the takeover fails, and share prices subside to the *ex ante* price; and (2) no shares are tendered to the raider, but they are tendered to a higher competing bidder who buys the firm.
- Hostile bidders should take actions that shorten the time to outcome, that forestall collaboration among target shareholders, that preempt potential competitors, that reduce investor uncertainty about the value of the bid, and that generally pressure the target board to cooperate. The target firm should do the opposite: delay, explore restructuring and white knight bidders, cast uncertainty on the hostile bidder and its bid, and generally pressure the target board not to cooperate.

CHAPTER 32—WORKBOOK QUESTIONS

1. *On October 8, 2002, Arthur Knight announced an unsolicited bid for the Empire State Construction Company. On October 20, a competing bidder entered the contest with a bid that was significantly higher than Knight's. Shareholders who had previously tendered to Knight now wanted to back out. Is this possible? Explain.*

2. *Will an M&A arbitrageur always tender to the bidder with the highest offer?*

3. *What is a two-tiered offer? Why might a bidder resort to a two-tiered offer?*

4. *Explain how a two-tiered offer can be likened to the "prisoner's dilemma."*

5. *As a shareholder, what strategy is best when faced with a two-tiered offer?*

6. In the face of a hostile bid, the restaurant chain Bacon and Eggs announced a recapitalization plan to buy back 30 percent of its shares at $58 per share pro rata among all shares. The stub shares (the shares that remain outstanding after

a share buy-back) are estimated to trade at approximately $52 per share after the recapitalization is completed. An arb holds 10,000 shares of the company with an average cost of $51.50.

What is the value of the arb's shares based on the recapitalization plan?

7. *What is a leveraged recapitalization? How does it fend off a hostile bid?*

8. Scott Siegel, manager of an M&A hedge fund, picked up his copy of the *Wall Street Journal* on September 4, 2001, and was greeted by a front-page headline reading "H-P Reaches Accord to Acquire Compaq for $25 Billion in Stock."[1] The article reported that Hewlett-Packard had agreed to acquire Compaq in a merger-of-equals all-stock deal that valued the latter at around $25 billion. Each Compaq share would be exchanged for 0.63 share of Hewlett-Packard. The previous trading day, Hewlett-Packard shares had declined 19 cents to $23.32, while Compaq fell 34 cents to $12.35.

   a. *Calculate the effective purchase price. What do you think of the acquisition premium?*
   b. *The acquisition involved a fierce proxy fight and was not completed until eight months after the date of announcement. Hewlett-Packard's share price on the closing date was $18.22. Assume that Siegel had purchased 125,000 shares of Compaq at $12.35 per share, and shorted 32,000 shares of Hewlett-Packard at $23.32 each on the day the acquisition was announced. Assuming a borrowing cost of 6 percent, calculate the return on Siegel's investment for the holding period and on an annualized basis.*

9. CleanPack, Inc., a manufacturer of flexible packaging solutions, wants to acquire its fiercest rival, EasyPack. CleanPack has determined that its purchase price should not exceed $114.40 per EasyPack share. The shares currently trade at $74.10 apiece. EasyPack's officers occupy all board seats and are determined to keep the company within their control. They have drawn up a restructuring plan that, by their estimates, could raise the value of EasyPack to $117 a share—over a period of two years. An aggressive raider named Lou Barrymore is reportedly going to join the bidding contest. CleanPack thinks Barrymore will place a bid of $91. CleanPack estimates a 50 percent chance that EasyPack will win the bid, a 30 percent chance that Barrymore will win, and a 20 percent chance that neither scenario will materialize.

   Should CleanPack put in a bid? If so, for how much? Draw a decision diagram facing the investor.

NOTES

1. Nikhil Deogun, Gary McWilliams, and Molly Williams, "Computer Deal: H-P Reaches Accord to Acquire Compaq for $25 Billion in Stock—Hit by Global PC Slowdown, Firms Aim for Growth in the Services Business—Carly Fiorina Places Her Bet," *Wall Street Journal*, September 4, 2001, p. A1.

CHAPTER 33

Takeover Attack and Defense

Firms employ certain tactics for both takeover attack and defense. In general, the power of tactics is derived from their ability to: (1) accelerate or delay a takeover deal, (2) increase/decrease the costs to the buyer, and (3) change the perceptions of certainty to the investor.

- Use of defensive tactics is widespread: Over 80 percent of public companies have adopted some kind of defenses to deter potential bidders from making hostile takeover attacks.
- Defense tactics empower a target firm's board of directors and management team with increased control options. These are call options on the strategy of the target firm. Defensive tactics increase in value with longer delay and greater uncertainty.
- Tactics of attack attempt to neutralize or nullify defense control options by accelerating outcomes and removing uncertainties.
- The most persuasive takeover attack is a high offering bid; the best defense against takeovers is a high stock price.
- There are two views about the targets of takeovers. The first is that they are underperforming firms that have attracted capital market discipline—this is the *inefficiency hypothesis*, which holds that takeovers are motivated by a desire to correct and profit from target company inefficiency. Another view, the *investment opportunities hypothesis*, suggests that targets simply offer investment and growth opportunities to prospective buyers.
- Many studies portray a strong relationship between the strength of the target's corporate governance and the market reaction to the announcement of takeover defenses. Where the board of directors is strong, independent, and effective, the reaction is positive. Where corporate governance is weak, the reaction is negative.
- Studies also reveal a positive correlation between the alignment of a CEO's interests and the market reaction to takeover defenses. The market reaction is positive when CEO's interests are strongly aligned with shareholders, and negative when they are not.
- Tactics of takeover attack:
  - Purchase of shares directly in the market.
  - Offer directly to the target board of directors.

- Tender offer directly to target shareholders.
- Coercive tender offer structures.
- Proxy contest and consent solicitation.
- Challenge the target's defenses through litigation.

- Tactics of takeover defense:

  Proactive Defenses
  - Charter amendments.
  - Golden parachutes.
  - Employee stock ownership plans (ESOP) and labor agreements.
  - Poison pills.

  Deal-Embedded Defenses
  - Breakup and topping fees.
  - Toehold stakes.
  - Asset lockup options: the "crown jewels."
  - Stock lockup options.

  Reactive Defenses
  - Litigation.
  - Counter tender offer: "Pac Man."
  - Share repurchases and leveraged recapitalization.
  - Asset restructuring.
  - White knight or white squire.
  - Going-private transaction/leveraged buyout.
  - Greenmail or targeted share repurchase.

- Having a combination of different defenses leads to better defense success than having just one defense tactic.

CHAPTER 33—WORKBOOK QUESTIONS

1. *Why are takeover defenses likely to help shareholders of well-managed "good" firms, and why might takeover defenses harm shareholders of poorly managed "bad" firms? What is the reason for the discrepancy, and what can you deduce from this difference?*

2. *Describe the various forms of charter amendments. What, if any, findings have there been regarding their effects on shareholder wealth, and on the probability of takeovers?*

3. Company A is considering a hostile takeover of Company B. After some initial due diligence, Company A estimates that the intrinsic value of Company B is \$460 million. Company A's investment bank advisory fee is 2 percent of the total deal, and the legal fees are fixed at \$10 million. Based on Company A's

planned bid price of $450 million, it estimates the probability of a successful takeover to be 60 percent.

Given this information, is it profitable for Company A to make an offer for Company B?

4. K-Wells Industries is a target company with a $30 stock price and 1.5 million shares outstanding. Currently, it has a poison pill in place, which allows investors to buy $200 worth of shares for each share that they own. The shares could be purchased at an 80 percent discount to the prevailing the market price of the stock. The poison pill will be triggered when a shareholder purchases 12 percent or more of K-Wells Industries' stock.

   Please estimate the total economic dilution to the raider from triggering the poison pill. (The Excel spreadsheet "Poison Pill Dilution.xls," found on the CD-ROM, can assist in computing the raider's dilution.)

CHAPTER 34

The Leveraged Restructuring as a Takeover Defense: The Case of American Standard

The leveraged restructuring is a classic defensive response to hostile takeover bids. The aggressive use of debt financing can create value through the exploitation of debt tax shields. But it also increases default risk. The net impact of the restructuring on the takeover attempt is to raise the floor for bidding. Used in combination with other defenses, the restructuring can help to form an effective deterrent to takeover.

- Successful defense against hostile takeover attempts does not depend entirely on preestablished defenses. How well a target company employs defensive tactics *in response* to the attack has a large influence on the overall success of the defense. A company can protect itself against a hostile takeover bid with various defense tactics that can be employed simultaneously or in succession.
- As outlined in Chapter 33 of the main text, the panoply of defensive tactics includes defenses that can be established in advance, such as the poison pill and golden parachute. Leveraged restructurings include leveraged recapitalizations and leveraged buyouts—these are typically undertaken in response to an announced attack. As Black & Decker Company's hostile takeover attack of American Standard illustrates, defense strategies such as parachutes, pension lockups, and poison pills are not "bullet-proof" because they are all subject to judicial review. These "shark repellent" defenses do buy time for a target's management to develop other alternatives to the raider's bid.
  - To date, a golden parachute has never defeated a hostile bid. Nevertheless, more than 350 firms of the Fortune 500 have golden parachutes. Having a golden parachute marginally raises the takeover cost, creating an additional hurdle for a buyer. And it keeps management on board during difficult times. A company making a hostile takeover attempt can sue to disarm a golden parachute. Black & Decker made such a suit against American Standard, which resulted in a temporary immobilization of the parachute.
  - There has been no instance thus far in which the target of a hostile raid has swallowed a poison pill. Like the golden parachute, the poison pill can be contested. Black & Decker sued to challenge American Standard's poison pill and successfully disarmed this defense tool in court. Thus, while poison pills

are "showstoppers" in the sense that they have never been deliberately triggered, they are not invulnerable.

- A management buyout (MBO) is a going-private transaction whereby a company's management team purchases the company with funds that are mainly borrowed. MBOs allow companies to keep information private and save on public reporting costs. With MBOs, equity shares become illiquid securities. Evidence shows that the announcement of MBOs and leveraged recaps is associated with positive abnormal returns to target shareholders. A few sources of value creation include:
  - Substantial increase in corporate leverage, which affords the company the benefits of increased debt (i.e., tax shield).
  - Reduction in agency costs through the realignment of interests between managers and shareholders.
  - Improvements in operating efficiency and sale of redundant assets.
- Leveraged recapitalizations (discussed in Chapters 13 and 20 of the main text) can be viewed as synthetic MBOs that provide similar benefits to shareholders without taking the company private. The prerequisites for executing a leveraged recapitalization include these:
  - The target company must have substantial unused debt capacity.
  - The proposed restructuring must be able to provide the value that the target might have realized through synergies with takeover bidding companies.
  - The target management team must be highly effective.
- With all forms of leveraged restructuring, the target company must be able to finance a sizable amount of debt. For the recapitalization, the debt finances an extraordinary dividend or share repurchase. In a leveraged buyout, the company must be able to sustain the debt financing, *and* management must be able to finance its equity purchase and assume the related risks.

CHAPTER 34—WORKBOOK QUESTIONS

1. *Why did American Standard decide to restructure?*
2. *Why can one view a leveraged recapitalization as a "synthetic MBO"?*
3. *Why are the wealth effects for shark repellent defenses and leveraged restructurings vastly different?*
4. *Some corporate advisers argue that it is important for companies to erect elaborate defenses as a precaution against unforeseen takeover bids. Is the case of American Standard consistent with this view? Why or why not? What might be a counterargument?*

5. This question is based on the American Standard case, discussed in Chapter 34 of the main text. In order to solve this problem, you will need to make the following assumptions:

- Suppose that management contemplates a defensive leveraged restructuring under which it issues debt and pays a one-time dividend in cash equal to the amount of the new borrowing.
- American Standard can borrow $1,486,201,000 in new debt.
- The maximum amount of debt the firm might be able to borrow is equal to six times its market value of equity outstanding.
- The firm's marginal tax rate is 37.5 percent.
- The tax shield equals the tax rate times total debt resulting from the deal.
- American Standard's shares were trading at $50 before the takeover announcement.

Also suppose the following financial information:

American Standard's Balance Sheet
Prior to Black & Decker's Hostile Bidding
for American Standard (January 1988)

Current assets	$1,347,954
Property, plant, and equipment	$ 912,772
Goodwill	$ 55,700
Other assets	$ 81,812
Total assets	$2,398,238
Current liabilities	$ 897,790
Long-term debt	$ 279,506
Deferred taxes	$ 370,316
Total liabilities	$1,547,612
Preferred stock	$ 1,046
Common stock	$ 837,722
Other	$ 11,858
Total shareholder equity	$ 850,626
Total shareholder equity and liabilities	$2,398,238
Number of outstanding shares	30,962,513
Share price	$ 50.00
Tax rate	37.5%

[This spreadsheet can be found in the folder "Key Spreadsheets from the Workbook" located on the CD-ROM.]

With this information, complete the following:

a. *Calculate the value of the restructuring to American Standard's shareholders.*

b. *Next, recalculate the amount of debt that American Standard must borrow in order to fund a recapitalization plan that will defend against Black & Decker's various increasing bids (of $65, $68, $73, $77) after the initial bid of $56.*

c. *In light of your answers to problem 5b, to what extent is it true that a firm's unused debt capacity is an antitakeover defense?*

CHAPTER 35

Communicating the Deal: Gaining Mandates, Approval, and Support

Effective deal presentation promotes good corporate governance. Failure to communicate a transaction effectively to investors and decision makers may result in uneconomic deal outcomes. The timing, depth, and focus of deal presentations affect investor perceptions, as well as the ability of senior managers and boards of directors to evaluate the transaction.

- There are four classic kinds of deal presentations: (1) a "concept" presentation to a CEO or senior executive seeking approval to begin negotiations; (2) a formal presentation to a firm's board of directors seeking approval for negotiated terms; (3) an announcement of the deal to the financial markets; and (4) presentation of the deal to employees.
- Usual challenges to effective presentation include:
  - *Conflicting objectives.* Start with a clear sense of what you are trying to accomplish with the deal presentation. Often you will uncover aims that may conflict, such as achieving transparency and preserving flexibility.
  - *Differing perspectives.* You and your audience may bring different points of view to the presentation. It is important to anticipate the impact of these differences.
  - *Balancing secrecy and disclosure.* Secrecy is important in the early stages of transaction development in order to preempt competitors (e.g., rival bidders) and to avoid unnecessary volatility in the capital markets. However, secrecy until consummation of the deal is not advisable. Instead, target and buyer firms ought to disclose the transaction at the point in time that the consummation of the deal looks probable. Deal presenters need to balance between telling too much and too little.
  - *Bandwidth.* Humans are limited in their ability to absorb information. Therefore, a deal presenter should edit information about the deal, and focus on the aspects that matter.
  - *Objectivity versus advocacy.* Sometimes, deal presenters become invested in the goal of gaining acceptance for their particular deal rather than in ensuring that the right decision is made or that the deal is value-enhancing.
  - *Market expectations.* In presenting a deal to shareholders, one has an opportunity to communicate with investors and shape expectations in the public arena.

- All communications should be guided by prudence, ethical norms, and the law.

Summary Comparison of Types of Deal Communications

	Concept Proposal	Board Presentation	Public Announcement	Employee Communication
Key audience	CEO	Independent directors	"Lead steer" investors	Managers, supervisors, rank-and-file employees
Predominant interest of the audience	Fit with his/her vision; resource allocation.	Execute well duties of loyalty and care.	Economic insight on which to base trading intentions.	"Me issues"; rationale for the deal: Why us? Why now?
Focus of communication	An opportunity; themes; the payoff. Key issues are strategy, valuation, and setting negotiation goals.	A definitive agreement. Key issues are valuation, implications for stakeholders, and strategy.	Either letter of intent or definitive agreement. Key issues are deal terms, motives, and probabilities.	Letter of intent or definitive agreement, eventually followed by integration plan for the two organizations; maintaining a customer focus during the transition.
Objective	To gain a mandate to proceed, with targets for negotiation.	Board approval to consummate the deal.	Shape capital market reaction.	Resolve uncertainty; build support for the merger; motivate.
Special challenges	Balance analysis and advocacy: presenter needs approval and joint thinking on goals.	Can't say too much; limited bandwidth; risk of lawsuit for carelessness, disloyalty.	Can't say enough; risk of lawsuit for misrepresentation.	Greed and fear: dealing with threats and opportunities to employees posed by the merger. Rumors. Distraction caused by the deal, and resulting effect on productivity.
Tactics	Focus on the optionality in the concept development effort: explore uncertainty and its drivers, along with valuation.	Focus on the board's stakeholder perspectives, and their natural concern for risk exposure.	Speak to concerns of the lead steers, not just the average investor or other interested groups.	Build trust. Address concerns of employees through many channels; intervention by direct managers. Respond promptly to rumors. Be proactive in communicating facts.

CHAPTER 35—WORKBOOK QUESTIONS

Part I: What's Wrong with This Picture?

1. Consider the following:

   a. *At an industrial corporation, a senior associate in the strategic planning group is about to present to the CEO a proposal to acquire what he thinks is the "perfect target." He has worked hard all week to finally be ready with his presentation—a PowerPoint slide show containing 100 slides. In addition, a few days ago he submitted to the CEO a 387-page "pitch book" containing details about the target.*

   b. *At another company, a planner from the strategic business group has just started presenting his proposal to the CEO and other executive officers of the firm. He begins his presentation with a brief background about the potential target, followed by valuation, pricing, financial impact of the deal, and then its strategic rationale.*

Part II: Vignettes

1. You are the director of business development for Perra Delight, a consumer products company, and you have developed a merger idea. A month ago, the former CEO, Leroy Lazar, with whom you had worked for 10 years, retired and left the firm. The new CEO, Hillary Madison, whom you did not know prior to her arrival at the company, comes from a successful competitor firm. Madison has a good reputation and credibility in the industry, but she is younger than the prior CEO and thus perhaps a bit more ambitious—someone with her eye on becoming one of the "best CEOs."

   a. *What challenges might you face in presenting your merger idea to the new CEO?*

   b. *Could there be any greater opportunity for a successful deal presentation to Madison (versus one that would have been made to Lazar)? Why or why not?*

   c. *What could you do to increase the probability of a successful deal presentation to Madison?*

2. You are the director of business development for the Wermelt Wonders Corporation, which will be coming out with a press release announcing its merger with Daneker Diamonds. Right now, you are in a meeting with Wermelt's CEO, the CFO, director of investor relations, and the company's PR director. Collectively, you are deciding what to put in the press release, and specifically how much to include. The director of PR would like to limit the amount of information in the release. The CFO and the CEO are in disagreement on whether they should disclose certain financials; furthermore, the CEO believes the CFO's projections are overly conservative.

   What would you advise?

Part III: Cases

Hewlett-Packard and Compaq

On September 4, 2001, Compaq and Hewlett-Packard (HP) held their first joint investor presentation, in which they announced the merger between the two companies. The presentation—made in person and also available via conference call and webcast[1]—was delivered primarily for the investment community rather than for press reporters and the general public.

The intent of the investor presentation was to build on the press release from the previous day and to highlight what a few of the two companies' top executives (namely Carly Fiorina, HP chairman and CEO, and Compaq's chairman, Michael Cappellas) believed to be important aspects of the deal.

Read the following informal excerpts from the presentation (commentary from Carly Fiorina and Michael Cappellas) and then answer the questions that follow.

CARLY FIORINA: Michael and I first met at a public policy conference . . . and we figured out quickly that not only did we agree on public policy . . . but we also had a common vision of where the [technology] industry was going.

MICHAEL CAPPELLAS: Yes, I actually remember we were in such agreement. . . .

CARLY FIORINA: And we agreed on just about everything, I recall. . . .

MICHAEL CAPPELLAS: As [we] started to look at the vision of what we were doing, where we believe the Internet is going fundamentally, what the strategies were—it was clear that they overlapped. Then [we got] to the cultural issues—that the two companies believe in innovation, really painting the foundation, engineering excellence and a real drive. So in addition to the strategies, it was pretty clear that the culture was the same.

CARLY FIORINA: I think we realized very early on that we saw eye to eye, that we liked and respected each other, and I think it's going to be a terrific team. Not just at the top, but throughout the entire organization.

Michael mentioned culture. And, of course, culture is essential to a successful integration. There has been much written about the culture and the values of both of our companies. And, in fact, I think we've seen how closely those cultures and values are aligned just in how our teams worked together over the last several months.

I think as well I mentioned we share a commitment to innovation, to invention, to engineering excellence and prowess. We share a deep contribution to communities, and we share common values of how you ought to treat people: with respect, trust, and integrity.

We have a common strategy—this is not about a change in strategy. This is about a leapfrog move to accelerate our ability to continue on the strategy that we have been on, and the one Compaq has been on for the last two years as well.

If you go back and look at the presentations each company has made separately to the financial community over the last 18 months in particular, I think you will see a great deal of commonality. . . .

I want you to know that we take the integration challenge exceptionally seriously. This is a massive integration effort. One could argue it is the largest integration effort in the technology industry. And we are trying to integrate in a very difficult overall environment. . . .

We have a comprehensive integration plan in place. We've thought carefully about organizational rationalization. And we intend to be decisive. We intend to be disciplined and aggressive. And we intend to move with speed.

We have a set of early decisions already made, and we've identified the managers that we think are absolutely critical to this going forward. We already have retention plans in place. We will be appropriately leveraging outside expertise. . . . Each of us worked with McKinsey and Accenture to lay out what a mathematical model of the deal would look like. So we've done a lot of work and a lot of detailed planning before we ever said that this is a transaction that we were prepared to do.

We have chosen our executives very carefully.

We are helped by the fact that we have similar organizational models already in place: a go-to-market or front-end organization and a product development or back-end organization. And we are helped by the fact that our sales forces are structured around country management.

We have the same kind of structure around what we would call customer business managers, lead account reps to a customer, and then product specialization and technical consulting support underneath.

That helps with integration.

MICHAEL CAPPELLAS: And one of the interesting things as you think about the potential of this company, remember, both of us have not been sitting still for the last weeks and quarters. There is an awful lot of work being done, and what will now start to show up is the work we've accomplished. And I actually believe and think you'll start to see the things we've done as we've been bringing the companies together; you'll start to see not only the benefit of what we will do, but the benefit of what we have done. . . .

1. *Analyze the comments made by Fiorina and Cappellas. Based on the excerpts, what do you think they tried to convey to their shareholders, and how do you think they tried to "sell" the deal in the investor presentation?*

2. *The HP-Compaq merger was announced on September 4, 2001. Between the opening and closing of stock trading that day, HP's stock price fell from $20.40 to $18.33, a 10 percent drop in value. Does the drop in stock value convey a failure of HP-Compaq's deal presentation on September 4?*

Smucker

1. *Here is a press release from the J. M. Smucker Company[2] announcing its acquisition of the Jif and Crisco brands from the Procter & Gamble Company. As a shareholder, would you have thought this press release to be effective? Why? What does it do well or not do well? What themes and expectations are created in investors' minds as a result of these announcements?*

2. *The day the deal was announced, the chairman and president of Smucker also issued a memo to employees, informing them of the deal. The memo is reproduced here following the press release. What do you think of this move by the Smucker executives? What do you think of the memo?*

J.M. SMUCKER ANNOUNCES STOCK DEAL WITH P&G FOR JIF AND CRISCO[3]

—Smucker combines three #1 classic food brands—

ORRVILLE, Ohio and CINCINNATI, Ohio, October 10—The J.M. Smucker Company (NYSE: SJM) and The Procter & Gamble Company (NYSE: PG) today announced a definitive agreement to merge the JIF peanut butter and CRISCO cooking oils businesses into The J.M. Smucker Company in an all-stock transaction.

Prior to completion, the JIF and CRISCO brands and the associated assets will be spun off from the existing P&G Company and then immediately merged with The J.M. Smucker Company. Procter & Gamble shareholders will receive one share of new J.M. Smucker stock for every 50 shares they hold in Procter & Gamble in a tax-free transaction. Based on Smucker's closing stock price of $25.89 on October 9, 2001, this represents a pre-tax equivalent cash price of $1.0 billion or approximately 1.7 times net sales.

With successful closing of the transaction, Smucker expects its sales to approximately double, to $1.3 billion. For fiscal 2003, the first full year of integration, Smucker projects net earnings before one time costs associated with the transaction to be in the range of $95–105 million, almost three times current levels. This includes a provision for increased marketing support focused on the JIF and CRISCO brands.

Additionally, the Smucker Company said it expects the combined earnings power of the three brands to allow it both to continue its historic strong dividend practice, typically in the range of 40 to 50 percent of earnings, and to pursue new product development and acquisition opportunities while maintaining its investment grade rating profile.

For P&G, the transaction is expected to be slightly dilutive in fiscal 2002, but the company is comfortable with the current range of estimates. Dilution in fiscal 2003 is estimated at 6 cents per share. However, with the potential accretive impact of the pending Clairol transaction, P&G still expects to achieve its earnings goal of double-digit growth in 2003.

EXECUTIVE COMMENTS:

"The combination of these icon brands, SMUCKER'S, JIF and CRISCO—all with number one market positions—creates a new and exciting company with the strongest of positions in both the minds of consumers and in the center aisles of the nation's retail outlets," said Timothy Smucker, Smucker Chairman and Co-CEO.

"Not only is this transaction very accretive to earnings, it provides significant cash flows when coupled with our already strong balance sheet," said Richard Smucker, Smucker President and Co-CEO. "Just as important, it will strengthen our position to acquire other complementary leading food brands, providing opportunity for greater top- and bottom-line growth and clearly enhancing shareholder value."

"JIF and CRISCO are strong U.S. brands but they're no longer a strategic fit for P&G as we focus on building our big brands in core categories," said A.G. Lafley, President and CEO of Procter & Gamble. "At Smucker they will continue to enjoy a prominent position in another one of America's most admired companies, with an over 100-year proven track record of quality brand management."

According to Mr. Lafley, "This structure builds shareholder value very efficiently—a spin-off of JIF and CRISCO assets directly to our shareholders, and the opportunity for them to participate in the future growth of the new J.M. Smucker Company."

"Both these brands are an outstanding fit for Smucker," said Timothy Smucker. "CRISCO is very profitable and our singular focus on food will accrue to CRISCO'S benefit, and provide us an enabling platform leading to new categories and enhancing vertical integration."

"Combining JIF and SMUCKER'S," Richard Smucker explained, "brings number one brands together in the original, All-American comfort food—peanut butter and jelly. JIF also offers a broad and exciting menu of possibilities for product development and growth."

"In addition to the brands being market leaders, our companies possess similar management and employee cultures, common focus on customers, dedication to the highest standards of quality for consumers, and commitment to continually enhancing shareholder value. That is why both Richard and I, along with our entire board and management team, are so enthusiastic about this deal," Timothy Smucker concluded.

TRANSACTION DETAILS:

This spin-off and merger transaction (a "Revised Morris Trust" structure) effectively manages the tax implications to the parties. Procter & Gamble shareholders will own approximately 53 percent of the newly combined company, which will have approximately 49.3 million shares outstanding. The transaction is subject to regulatory and Smucker shareholder approvals, and the receipt of a ruling from the Internal Revenue Service that the transaction is tax-free to both companies and their shareholders. The transaction is expected to close during the second calendar quarter of 2002.

Following the completion of the transaction, the expanded company will include the JIF and CRISCO manufacturing plants in Lexington, Kentucky, and Cincinnati, Ohio, respectively, in addition to the existing Smucker facilities. Smucker will offer employment to all employees at these facilities 100% dedicated to these businesses.

TO: All Employees

FROM: Tim Smucker and Richard Smucker

DATE: October 10, 2001

AGREEMENT REACHED FOR JIF AND CRISCO BRANDS[4]

Today The J. M. Smucker Company reached a significant growth milestone in its more than 100-year history. We announced an all-stock transaction with Procter & Gamble for their JIF peanut butter and CRISCO cooking oil brands.

We are extremely excited about the combination of these three American icon brands (SMUCKER'S, JIF, and CRISCO), each with the number one market share position in their respective categories. It will create an even stronger company, doubling our sales to $1.3 billion and more than doubling our profits. Most importantly, this will provide us with a platform for even greater growth in the future.

The JIF and CRISCO brands are extremely compatible with our business. They have the same distribution channels and consumer appeal. All three brands are sold in the "center of the retail store" and complement our existing broker network giving us greater critical mass to serve our customers.

Included in this transaction are the CRISCO production facility located in Cincinnati, Ohio, and the JIF peanut butter plant located in Lexington, Kentucky. These facilities, along with support staff, will add about 450 new employees to the "family" of Smucker.

As we look to the future with this family of leading brands, we would expect our growth to continue to be generated from three major areas: (1) growing the core business and respective share of market of each of the brands, (2) the development of new products, and (3) the acquisition of additional brands. Since this is an all-stock transaction, we are not taking on any new debt, which positions us well for future acquisitions.

The closing of the transaction requires shareholder and regulatory approval, in addition to a private letter ruling from the IRS; therefore, we don't anticipate the transaction will close until our fiscal year's fourth quarter. As you would expect, this has and will require a great deal of effort by many people to complete. We would like to thank everyone involved for their efforts thus far and for the future efforts that will be required for a successful integration into our business.

As noted in our press release, there will be an investor relations conference call and Web cast later this morning. There will be many communication opportunities for our employees, and we would request that you not dial in to the call.

We are very excited to welcome JIF and CRISCO and the employees making these quality products into our family at Smucker.

TIM RICHARD

Raytheon

1. *Here is a press release issued by Raytheon Company, a large defense contractor, announcing a recent acquisition. How does it compare to the Smucker press release? Can you offer an explanation for the differences?*

RAYTHEON ACQUIRES HONEYWELL AEROSPACE AND DEFENCE SERVICES BUSINESS UNIT IN AUSTRALIA[5]

LEXINGTON, Mass., July 25/PRNewswire-FirstCall/—Raytheon Company (NYSE: RTN) announced today that it has acquired the Honeywell Aerospace and Defence Services (HADS) business unit of Honeywell (NYSE: HON) in Australia. With U.S. $20 million in revenue, HADS is a provider to the Australian Defence Forces of aviation life-cycle support operations in the form of avionics maintenance, logistics, and depot operations for fixed wing platforms.

"This acquisition establishes Raytheon as a principal provider of integrated aerospace support services to the Australian Defence Forces," said William H. Swanson, Raytheon chief executive officer and president. "It enhances our capabilities in two of our strategic business areas-Intelligence, Surveillance and Reconnaissance and Precision Engagement."

The terms of the transaction were not disclosed. HADS has become part of Raytheon Australia Pty Ltd, and is aligned with Raytheon Technical Services Company in Reston, Va.

Raytheon Company, with 2002 sales of $16.8 billion, is an industry leader in defense, government and commercial electronics, space, information technology, technical services, and business and special mission aircraft. With headquarters in Lexington, Mass., Raytheon employs more than 76,000 people worldwide.

NOTES

1. *References:* Link to full audiocast/webcast transcript: http://h18020.www1.hp.com/newsroom/presspaq/090401/transcript_investor.html; link to supporting PowerPoint presentation: http://h18020.www1.hp.com/newsroom/presspaq/090401/Investor_Doc.ppt.
2. A global manufacturer of food products. Its primary products are fruit spreads, dessert toppings, peanut butters, frozen peanut butter and jelly sandwiches, industrial fruit products, fruit and vegetable juices, beverages, syrups, condiments, and gift packages. (*Source:* Yahoo! Finance)
3. Press release as filed by Smucker with the SEC on October 10, 2003. Source: www.sec.gov/Archives/edgar/data/91419/000095015201504915/0000950152-01-504915.txt.
4. www.sec.gov/Archives/edgar/data/91419/000095015201504916/0000950152-01-504916.txt.
5. www.prnewswire.com/cgi-bin/micro_stories.pl?ACCT=149999&TICK=RTN&STORY=/www/story/07-25-2003/0001989212&EDATE=Jul+25,+2003.

CHAPTER 36

Framework for Postmerger Integration

Postmerger integration is where expectations are fulfilled or broken. Failing to recognize integration issues at the bargaining table or in the analytic phase of the work can create enormous problems later on. More importantly, knowing what to do after the definitive agreement is signed is vital to the success of the deal.

- One must decide on an *integration strategy* early in the merger proceedings. Integration strategy must follow business strategy. The business strategy and merger rationale should be used as guides for designing integration strategy. Consider the strategic setting, turbulence, and motives for the deal. Integration strategy entails making a choice as to the level of autonomy, interdependence, and control of the target:
  - Autonomy is often reflected in the preservation of a culture, the continuation of a leadership team, and independence of decision making.
  - Interdependence is reflected in how closely the target meshes with the buyer's value chain and operations.
  - Control is reflected in the degree to which systems are imposed—financial control systems, quality control systems, governance mechanisms, and so on.

  Chapter 36 of the main text offers four integration strategies based on the choices made about autonomy, interdependence, and control. (See graphic on following page.)

- Integration planning is the first phase in integration implementation. Some factors to consider are:

Talent and intellectual capital	Who are the key employees? How do we retain them? What layoffs are necessary to achieve synergies and economies of scale from the combination? What strategic capabilities will be required by the firm for the future? How do we retain the knowledge base necessary for those capabilities? Should workforces be kept separate or be combined?
Production, logistics, and supply chain management	Where can we achieve cost reductions? How we can streamline operations to achieve those reductions? Should facilities be shut down? Should production processes be integrated or kept separate? Will suppliers be retained? What improvements can be made in the supply chain? Can customer service be integrated? How? What investments are necessary to achieve cost reductions?

(Continued)

Financial controls and management information systems	Are the reporting systems of the target congruent with ours? Do their reporting systems provide the information we need to advance our strategy? What must be done to align their systems with ours? What investments are necessary to achieve alignment? Which systems need to be phased out?
Compensation systems	Are our compensation systems aligned with those of the target? Do we want our compensation systems to be aligned with those of the target—might their culture be more responsive to a different compensation system than ours? How do we communicate any necessary adjustments in compensation?
Space	Should work spaces be integrated? What factors must we consider in work space design? What atmosphere do we want the work spaces to have?

- Execution is the second phase of integration implementation. Its success depends on:
  - Speed and decisiveness.
  - Communication.
- Seven deadly sins to avoid in postmerger integration, according to Michael Sweeney of UBS:[1]
  1. Poor due diligence (financial and human capital).
  2. Delay the start of integration and drag out the finish.
  3. Allow divergent initiatives.
  4. Take too long to answer "me" issues.

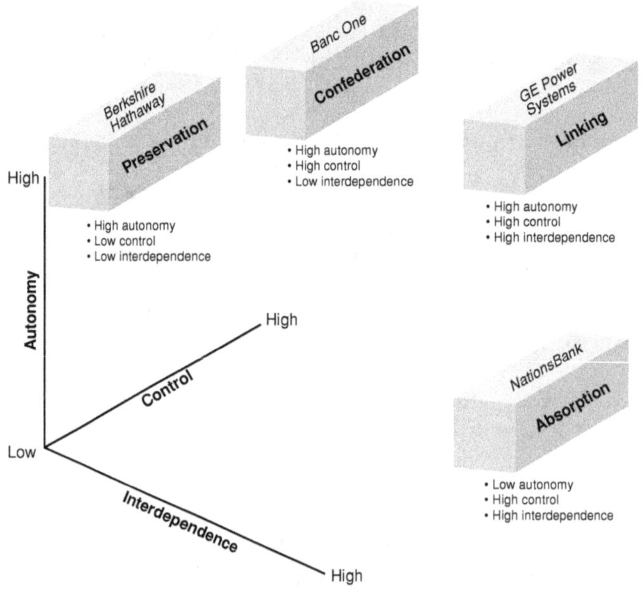

5. Undercommunicate.
6. Put no one in charge.
7. Ignore project management disciplines.

CHAPTER 36—WORKBOOK QUESTIONS

Part I: Integration Strategy

Chapter 36 of the main text discusses four integration strategies for postmerger integration: preservation, confederation, linking, absorption.

In each of the following cases, what would you recommend as the best integration strategy? What considerations about autonomy, interdependence, and control led to your recommendation?

1. In 1983, Brown-Forman Distillers, a U.S.-based manufacturer of top-selling whiskey brands, acquired in a hostile takeover Lenox China & Crystal, a maker of tabletop and other consumer products. Brown-Forman's strategy was to assemble a portfolio of businesses around the focus of high-quality consumer products with strong brands. John Chamberlin, chairman and CEO of Lenox, cited the acquisition as a poor fit, saying, "Lenox is a design company with 'aesthetics and mystique' that sells durables with a long purchase cycle and substantial department store distribution channels. . . . In contrast . . . Brown-Forman is a 'packaging and taste' company that makes consumable products with repeat-purchase cycles and liquor-store distribution channels."[2]

2. In September 2001, Hewlett-Packard Co. (HP) announced it would acquire Compaq Computer Corp. in a $25 billion stock swap transaction. The deal would bring together the world's second (Compaq) and third (HP) largest computer makers. Both companies were struggling to keep costs down and to stay competitive amidst a PC industry that had become commoditized. Cost savings were therefore a major rationale for the deal. The savings were to come from layoffs, office closures, shedding duplicate product lines, and consolidating supply chains. Some observers noted that it would be hard to create a unified culture within the merged entity. HP was known to have an entrepreneurial, "shoot-from-the-hip" culture, whereas Compaq had a reputation as a bureaucracy. During one HP reception an observer commented, "I could tell H-P folks from the Compaq folks right away. The former Compaq employees, in suits and ties, huddled on one side of the room. Polo-shirted H-P staffers stood on the other." The observer joked, "Those guys are going to kill each other."[3] However, Carly Fiorina, CEO of the combined company, asserted that melding the two cultures would "go smoothly, because there are many parallels between them."[4]

3. In May 1998, German firm Daimler-Benz AG and U.S.-based Chrysler Corp. announced a merger of equals that would create the fifth largest automotive company in the world by sales. A primary motive for the deal was the potential for cross-selling—the merger would enable Chrysler to sell more cars in Europe,

and Daimler to sell more Mercedes cars in the United States, where it had a less than 1 percent share.[5] The merger would create a global manufacturer with products ranging from economy cars to luxury sedans to sport utility vehicles to minivans—the merging companies had distinctly different product lines whose identities the CEOs would seek to maintain. Due to the different product lineups, assembly lines would be kept separate, no plants would be closed, and dealerships would not be combined. Dual headquarters would be maintained in Stuttgart, Germany, and Auburn Hills, Michigan. Cost reductions would be achieved by utilizing economies of scale in manufacturing, purchasing, new product development, and logistics. Jürgen Schrempp and Robert Eaton, chief executives of Daimler and Chrysler respectively, would be co-chairmen and chief executives of the merged company, with Eaton stepping down after three years. Many observers commented that melding the cultures would be difficult. Said one newspaper, "[Daimler] has been fed fat on success. . . . [Chrysler] still sees itself as scrappy following a brush with bankruptcy."[6] Other differences included corporate structures and the role of labor unions.

4. In July 1995, Walt Disney Co. announced it would acquire Capital Cities/ABC Inc., in what was then the second-largest merger in U.S. history. The motive for the deal was to integrate entertainment programming with distribution. Walt Disney would bring to the table its movies and television productions among others, while Capital Cities/ABC would bring its number one rated television network, which distributed programming to 225 affiliates reaching 99.9 percent of U.S. television households. Capital Cities/ABC also owned 80 percent of sports channel ESPN, which reached 67 million local households and 100 million households overseas.[7] An observer commented, "With one stroke of the pen, the ABC network is now assured [of] its supply of programming . . . and at the same time Disney has assured shelf spaces for its TV production."[8] Because the two companies' businesses were complementary, there were to be neither staff reductions nor shedding of assets. Michael Eisner, CEO of Disney, said, "None of the assets are duplicative; they all mesh together."[9]

5. In August 1995, Pharmacia AB (Stockholm, Sweden) and Upjohn Co. (Kalamazoo, Michigan) announced a merger of equals that would create the ninth largest pharmaceutical company in terms of worldwide drug sales. The firms had previously ranked 19th and 20th, respectively. Pharmacia was a niche drug manufacturer specializing in cancer and cardiovascular, infectious, and neurobiological diseases,[10] while Upjohn had several high-profile products including antibaldness treatment Rogaine, anti-anxiety drugs Xanax and Halcion, and pain reliever Motrin.

   Of late, Upjohn had been in a worrisome situation due to both a weak pipeline of drugs and patent expirations—four of its top drugs had lost U.S. patent protection in the prior three years.[11] In contrast, Pharmacia had a strong research pipeline, with a host of new products nearing the end of clinical trials and poised for launches. Marketwise, Upjohn had only a small presence in Europe, and Pharmacia had a relatively small presence in the United States. Jan Ekberg, chairman of Pharmacia, said, "Through the merger, Pharmacia gains access to Upjohn's strong U.S. sales, marketing, and distribution infrastructure to fully exploit the sale of Pharmacia products, while Upjohn gains additional sales and marketing support in Europe."[12] The merged company would be headquartered in London, although there would also be operational headquarters in Stockholm, Kalamazoo, and Milan. Only the chief executive and corporate officers would be based in London.[13]

Part II: Integration Implementation

1. *You are managing the postmerger integration for a company and notice that the progress in one division seems a bit behind schedule. The division manager pleads with you to understand—after all, the integration process just started one month ago; one must plan these things carefully and work out the details before moving. Do you agree with the manager? Why or why not? If you do not agree, what would you tell him?*

2. *You are part of a team of consultants hired to make sure integration is kept on target for a newly merged company. Several days into the job, you notice a palpable difference between two sales divisions. In division A, the atmosphere is optimistic and jovial, the team members are excited about the new direction of the company, and people from both the old target and buyer firms blend well. In division B, morale seems to be low, especially among employees of the target firm. They say they have no idea as to how the merger will impact their division. They also have neither seen nor been addressed by the new CEO. What might have gone wrong here?*

3. *Bank A (buyer) and Bank B (target) recently announced a merger. Each had been highly successful on its own, but trends in the banking industry led each to conclude that merging was the only way to survive. Most of the value would be created from cost synergies—financial and operating control procedures would be harmonized, and duplicate operations would be shed. Both banks had top-of-the-line information systems, but it was important to have only one unified system. The head of the postmerger integration team decided to test both systems for a few months to see which would work better. Do you agree with his strategy? Why or why not?*

NOTES

1. UBS AG internal document, Michael Sweeney, May 31, 2000.
2. "Lenox Rebuffs Brown-Forman Takeover Offer, Adopts Defense," *Dow Jones News Service*, June 15, 1983.
3. Pui-Wing Tam, "Merger by Numbers: An Elaborate Plan Forces H-P Union to Stay on Target," *Wall Street Journal*, April 28, 2003, p. A1.
4. Molly Williams, "H-P's Deal for Compaq Has Doubters As Value of Plan Falls to $20.52 Billion," *Wall Street Journal*, September 5, 2001, p. A3.
5. Brandon Mitchener and Steven Lipin, "Deal Sparks Enthusiasm for 'Global Reach'—Analysts See Team with Little Overlap and Synergies to Exploit," *Wall Street Journal Europe*, May 7, 1998, p. 6.

6. Ibid.
7. "Disney, Capital Cities/ABC Agree to Merge; $19 Billion Transaction Will Enhance Shareholder Value by Creating World's Leading Entertainment and Communications Company," *Business Wire*, July 31, 1995.
8. Laura Landro et al., "That's Show-Biz: Walt Disney's Merger with Cap Cities/ABC Stuns Global Industry," *Wall Street Journal Europe*, August 1, 1995, p. 1.
9. "News Roundup: Walt Disney–Cap Cities Merger Developments," *Dow Jones Newswires*, July 31, 1995.
10. "Pharmacia-Upjohn to Merge: Everybody Seems Happy," *Genesis Report-Rx*, vol. 4, no. 5, August 1, 1995.
11. Nigel Cope, "Pharmacia and Upjohn Merge," *Independent* (London), August 21, 1995, p. 15.
12. David Lawder, "Upjohn Co., Sweden's Pharmacia to Merge," *Reuters News*, August 20, 1995.
13. Eric Reguly, "Upjohn in $13Bn Swedish Merger—Pharmacia & Upjohn Inc.," *Times* (London), August 21, 1995.

CHAPTER 37

Corporate Development as a Strategic Capability: The Approach of GE Power Systems

A significant development in the field of M&A is that active buyers are investing increasingly in business processes, human capital, and information technology to elevate the quality of their business development activities. The resulting infrastructure can contribute significantly to the successful execution of the corporate development strategy.

General Electric Power Systems illustrates how the business development function of a company can become a strategic capability.

- A *strategic capability* integrates a set of resources (such as human capital, financial capital, and physical property) in a special way to generate competitive advantages, yield high returns, and create organizational agility. Strategic capabilities are difficult to imitate.
- Chapter 37 of the main text presents a profile of General Electric's Power Systems (GEPS) division as an example of business development viewed as a strategic capability. The main strategy of GEPS was to survey the whole energy chain, focusing on oil and gas, power generation, and energy management technologies. From 1995 to 2000, GEPS was highly acquisitive. Key attributes of GEPS' business development contributed to both its overall excellence and to the high success rate of its mergers and acquisitions. Noteworthy examples include:
  - *Consistency of processes.* This included using common valuation models, presentation templates, and analytical frameworks that were applied to all business development projects. GEPS developed structured and standardized processes to provide a strong foundation and even playing field for comparative acquisition analysis and consistent, streamlined deal execution.
  - *Active knowledge management.* Strong electronic data systems allowed for an integrated M&A process, organized archiving of important materials, and strong communication between employees.
  - *Continuous improvement mind-set.* A strong dedication to process improvement, especially in deal origination, deal cycle time, due diligence, acquisition integration, and synergies, characterized GEPS. Five percent of the group's staff was focused solely on process improvement.

- *Top-down and bottom-up pipeline.* By taking this double-pronged approach, GEPS was able to develop rich business development ideas from various sources of the firm.
- *Senior management engagement.* Senior executives at GEPS personally reviewed the deals in progress and postacquisition integration activities on a weekly basis. The CEO of General Electric himself dedicated material time each month to review the business development process.
- *Careful and systematic acquisition screening* of potential targets, with a particular focus on:
  - *Strategic fit.* Acquisition to get better, not bigger.
  - *Technology.* Target should provide enhancing capabilities.
  - *Quality of human resources.* Significantly influenced the acquisition decision.
  - *Financial considerations.* Predetermined requirements (i.e., EBIT operating margins of 15 percent or more, accretive to GE earnings in the first year, double-digit revenue growth, etc.).
- *Integration of experts in a broad array of functional backgrounds.* Experts in areas such as intellectual property, environmental issues, human resources, finance, law, sales, technology, sourcing and manufacturing are immersed in GE's intense due diligence efforts.
- *Postmerger integration and audit.* GEPS was highly cognizant of the fact that a deal's success was contingent on the postmerger integration efforts.
  - Assigned integration team leaders.
  - Established Centers of Excellence (COEs) that focused on guiding integration in each function.

CHAPTER 37—WORKBOOK QUESTIONS

1. *What are the attributes that characterize business development at GEPS? Please identify and describe them.*

2. One of the hallmarks of GEPS' success in business development is its systematic processes. The division has built an M&A "factory" for business development that reduces variation.

   a. *Please describe GEPS' M&A factory. What components or features have contributed to the factory-like processes?*

   b. *Do you think there could be any drawbacks to GEPS' systematic process-focused approach? If yes, please explain.*

3. *Suppose you are the CEO of a company division similar to GEPS, and you have been mandated to hire three new employees: a black belt six sigma practitioner, a technology trainer, and a knowledge-management learning specialist. What are the important benefits that each professional would bring to your organizational division?*

4. *In GEPS' deal development process, a business development professional or operating unit CEO initiates contact with a top executive at a prospective target firm. If the response from the target firm is negative, would it make sense for GEPS to pursue further discussions, or would further solicitation be a waste of time? Explain.*

5. You are a management consultant who has just finished a six-week project on-site at GEPS. While you had been hired specifically to work on the integration of a recently acquired company, part of your project entailed learning more about GEPS' entire approach to making acquisitions.

   You have been asked by your manager, a senior consultant, to make a presentation about how a corporate business development process can become a strategic capability for a firm. Based on your close observance at GEPS, what would you highlight in your presentation?

CHAPTER 38

M&A "Best Practices": Some Lessons and Next Steps

Effective M&A practitioners take a proactive stance in understanding M&A and develop views about future cycles.

Learning about the different aspects of M&A is necessary but not sufficient for becoming a true deal leader. Deal leadership is achieved only when a business practitioner can synthesize the different parts of the M&A deal into a successful, integrated whole.

- Good M&A practices can be identified and adopted—and if employed well they can become part of a masterful repertoire of *best practices*. However, the field is too complicated and rapidly changing to offer a definitive expression of a single best practice approach. Rather, best practitioners commit to a process of ongoing study and learning in order to define for themselves the outlines of good practice.
- Some elements of best practice include:
  - Think like an investor.
  - Take a "whole deal" perspective.
  - Aim to create value rather than claim value.
  - Develop a view and play the game.
  - Find and use optionality.
  - Resist earnings management and momentum-acquiring.
  - Temper determinism with behaviorism.
  - Focus on process first, then outcome.
  - Master the tools and concepts, but also get help.
  - Practice with integrity.
- Our understanding of M&A remains imperfect. Chapter 38 of the main text outlines 10 areas for further research:
  1. The profitability of M&A.
  2. The relative merits of strategies of focus and diversification.
  3. Herd behavior of acquirers in producing cycles of M&A activity.
  4. The role of information asymmetries in M&A.
  5. The efficiency of trade-offs among terms in the design of deals.

6. The "management" of financial reports: why and how it happens.
7. The defining features of "good governance."
8. The costs and benefits of antitakeover defenses.
9. The costs and benefits of merger regulation.
10. The estimation of appropriate costs of capital for discounting in M&A.

- Many businesspeople will argue that *learning by doing* is the best process for ongoing professional development in M&A. But while the lessons obtained from learning by doing are usually highly instructive, they can also be costly. Chapter 38 of the main text emphasizes the benefits of professional development from other sources:
  - *Learning by watching.* Observing other M&A professionals at work conveys a great deal of tacit learning about the field.
  - *Learning by reading.* Chapter 38 offers a list of recommended books and articles. One could initiate a reading program, possibly in concert with others.
  - *Learning from current events.* Chapter 38 offers an approach to studying newly announced deals. This centers around valuing the target, interpreting stock price movements, and constructing a term sheet for the deal.

CHAPTER 38—WORKBOOK QUESTIONS

1. *The continuous increase in the automation of M&A analytical techniques allows for the deal designer to focus less on number crunching and more on the shaping of deals. What are the possible benefits and drawbacks of this? Please explain.*

2. *Victoria Nakagawa is the newly appointed managing director of a business development group at Best Ensemble Inc. Looking at its historical performance, she has concluded that the group has been slow to conclude deals and uneven in the quality of work completed on various deals, and has lost a number of acquisition opportunities to competitors. She has noticed that the professionals in the group define their contributions very narrowly: accounting, valuation, due diligence, law, and so on. Based on the reading in this and previous chapters, in what directions might she pursue the development of this group?*

3. *What can you learn from current events in M&A?*

PART Two

Answers

CHAPTER 1

Introduction and Executive Summary

1. Success in M&A is determined not only by structural factors, but also by conduct.
2. Organizational structure is just as important as managerial conduct and interpersonal skills. Organizational structure can have great impact on the ability of target and buyer to mesh, and as such affects postmerger success.
3. Managing legal exposure is important. But best practitioners also watch for opportunities to proactively *shape* laws and regulations in ways that benefit the public interest.
4. Success means more than avoiding criminal indictment: Best practitioners understand that it is important not only to do deals well, but also to do them *right*. For this to happen, best practitioners consciously promote the development of an ethical environment in their firms.
5. Success in M&A goes beyond being able to negotiate and consummate a deal. The ultimate measure of success in M&A is whether a deal is able to create value. Value creation entails being successful on many fronts—strategic planning, search, due diligence, deal design, negotiations, postmerger integration, communication, and process management.
6. Careful planning increases the likelihood of success in M&A. But human behavior and luck can also play a role.
7. Good due diligence goes beyond simply checking facts. An inquisitive mind-set that looks for patterns, synthesizes facts into valuable information, and answers "why" questions is important to the due diligence process.
8. Good process is crucial to developing good M&A practice because it lends discipline to thinking, provokes analysis, and invites reflection. Merely focusing on outcomes does not motivate the development of a mind-set that synthesizes, learns from past lessons, and continually builds on a body of knowledge.
9. It is unlikely that there is a single "best" design for each M&A deal. Instead, there may be several feasible designs because of the complex trade-offs among the many dimensions of a deal.
10. Market prices are useful data for valuation where markets are integrated and efficient. But where markets are inefficient and/or segmented, prices may be less helpful as indicators of intrinsic value.

CHAPTER 2

Ethics in M&A

1a. The following are hypothetical expressions consistent with the three perspectives:

- *David:* Disney should not have paid the greenmail to either Saul Steinberg or Irwin Jacobs. By paying greenmail, the company neglected its duty to maximize the wealth of its shareholders. Furthermore, if paying greenmail were actually ethical, it could be made into a universal rule. Such is not the case, however. If all corporations paid greenmail as a routine response to objections from shareholders about corporate policies, it would stifle debate and dissent, divert corporate resources away from the business mission of the firm, and create an environment of rule by intimidation. The investing public would lose confidence in companies neglecting their duty to maximize the wealth of shareholders.
- *Ulyssa:* David, I don't think greenmail can be deemed as a universal unethical act; whether it is good or bad depends on its consequences for those affected by the payment. Look at the positive outcome of paying greenmail in this particular case. I think the potential benefits here outweighed the drawbacks. Paying greenmail was the best action because Disney was preserved and left intact, which in the long run benefited the shareholders, the corporation, and employees. Now consider what could have happened if Disney had not paid greenmail: The company could have been handed over to a raider with less management experience and commitment to Disney's artistic and corporate visions. This in turn could have weakened the Disney brand and negatively altered company's operations, marketing, and corporate culture. This could have caused the stock to plummet, which would have destroyed value for shareholders.
- *Vera:* I think both of you are focusing on the wrong issues. You are not ethical simply because you follow your duties and evaluate the consequences of your actions. What we really need to consider is what paying greenmail portrays about Ron Miller and the Disney Company. Do you think that Miller could look at himself in a mirror or publicly address an audience of Disney's shareholders with pride, and feel confident that he did the right thing? I don't think he could. A person who pays greenmail disregards the fundamental virtues of fairness and equality. Greenmail is not what a person of character would do.

1b. This is not a math problem for which there is a strictly correct answer. A critical thinker would offer these observations:

- Did David weigh all of Ron Miller's duties? The duty to the welfare of shareholders is a legal obligation. But CEOs carry other duties as well, even though they may not have the blessing of law: These might include a duty to preserve and develop the artistic vision of Disney and a duty to promote the welfare of employees. Also, even if shareholder welfare is the highest responsibility, paying greenmail *might* best promote shareholder welfare, as Chapter 2 of the main text argued.
- Does Ulyssa really intend to suggest that an end justifies any means? A positive end might explain the means, but it neither justifies nor makes the means ethical. An additional flaw stems from the difficulty of assessing the probabilities of future results and consequences. The sequence of events requires making a decision with unpredictable outcomes before knowing the consequences in advance. Another time-based flaw concerns the trade-off between short-term and long-term consequences. A decision that considers "the greatest good for the greatest number" in the short term could be harmful to an even larger group of people in the long term. Consider an example that we see often in practice. A corporation may adopt certain operational or accounting policies to meet Wall Street analysts' earnings expectations and thus make its shareholders happy without careful consideration of the potential negative long-term consequences for the corporate entity, its shareholders, its employees, and other stakeholders.
- Vera's virtues-based approach urges one to think beyond duty, compliance, and results. She believes that ethics is about being a virtuous person. Vera's approach to making sound decisions emphasizes our ability to reason and judge based on our expectations of ourselves and of others. But whose virtues matter here? Is it sufficient to take a simply personal view, or are there overarching virtues that one should serve?

2. *Case #1: Power Electronics/SIC.* Settlement of escrow accounts is fertile ground for ethical issues. The postmerger audit may have exposed systematic "earnings management" by the target firm that the buyer justifiably wants to correct—and for which the buyer does not want to overpay. But the buyer could be playing an aggressive game of earnings management as well: essentially taking write-offs at the seller's expense that will make the buyer look good later on. The seller's abandonment of the arbitration process agreed upon in the contract is not consistent with the duty to fulfill contracts.

The *consequences* are pretty clear: One side's gain in this dispute is the other side's loss. The argument for *duties* seems to favor SIC: The contract specifies how disputes might be resolved through arbitration. Perhaps Power Electronics is trying to get SIC's attention with the lawsuit. The *virtues* consideration invites more information. What was the real situation at Power Electronics? Was SIC justified in withholding the payment from escrow or did Power Electronics really hide conditions at the firm?

(*Note:* This is based on an actual business case; names have been disguised.)

3. *Case #2: Hershey.* The controversy over the Hershey Trust's proposal to sell the company generated international attention. While the synopsis necessarily omits detailed information one might like to have, and though the ethical dilemmas in this case are not given to straightforward resolution, the perspectives raised in Chapter 2 of the main text suggest a number of ethical issues:

   - ***Duties.*** The directors of the Hershey Trust were obliged to preserve the financial standing of the trust and promote its mission—the proposed sale seems consistent with these duties. Even taking a stakeholder perspective, it is not clear that the sale of the company would impair the directors' obligation to other groups. A sale of the company could have been conditional upon guarantees of employment in the company's current locations. The loss of independence by senior management of Hershey Foods seems to be the most likely casualty—any formal or implied contract between the trust and management would need to be carefully weighed.
   - ***Consequences.*** The sale of Hershey Foods would probably generate a healthy premium for the trust's investment in the company and diversify its endowment base. The consequence for the company would be a loss of independence, which mattered particularly to management. The loss of independence triggered some fears that acquisition of Hershey Foods by another company might cause a shift of manufacturing to other locations, hurting the employees and community with a loss of jobs—there was no evidence to suggest that this was likely, but opponents of the sale made much of the speculation. On balance, it seems that the Hershey Trust (and other shareholders) would have gained from the sale, and management would have lost.
   - ***Virtues.*** The fight seems to have been toughest here. Promoting the survival and prosperity of a philanthropic organization seems virtuous. But opponents presented the proposal as an abandonment of a trust with the community. They argued that the Hershey Trust was unethical because it was acting out of self-interest and self-aggrandizement.

CHAPTER 3

Does M&A Pay?

PART I: SHORT ANSWER

1. *Event studies.* These studies look at value creation for a firm and its shareholders surrounding the announcement of a merger transaction by examining its abnormal returns. The abnormal return of the merger is simply the raw return (the change in share price plus any dividend paid, divided by the closing share price of the previous day) less a benchmark of what investors required that day, such as the return on a large market index like the S&P 500.

   Advantages: These studies provide direct measures of value created for investors, and are forward looking.

   Drawbacks: This method assumes "capital market efficiency," which research finds is valid in developed financial markets on average and over time. But occasional anomalies can distort the returns. The analyst should seek to draw inferences from many studies with large samples on the assumption that many observations will overcome the effect of possible anomalies.

   Accounting Studies. These studies examine the reported financial results (i.e., quarterly or annual earnings reports) of acquirers before, during, and after acquisitions to see how financial performance changed. The focus of these studies could include: net income, return on equity, returns on assets, earnings per share (EPS), leverage, and liquidity of the firm. The best accounting studies compare acquiring firms with their nonacquirer peer firms.

   Advantages: These are based on financial statements that have been audited and certified. They are widely used by investors and considered a good indirect source of information regarding value creation. Also, they reflect the financial position of the company (leverage and liquidity, to name a couple of aspects).

   Drawbacks: Financial statements are backward looking in that they rely on historical data. Also, the data are based on accounting values, not market values. The reporting practices and structure of a company's financial statements can change over time, leading to noncomparable data for different reporting periods. Furthermore, companies and auditors have been known to "manage" financial reports (as discussed in the preceding chapter). In addition, the analysis of financial statements does not account for the value of intangible assets, and is sensitive to inflation and deflation because of the historic cost approach.

Surveys. These entail administering and analyzing the results of a standardized questionnaire, which asks a diverse pool of managers to answer whether particular acquisitions created value.

Advantages: As a form of primary research, these can offer more direct and insightful information relevant to specific deals.

Drawbacks: Surveys can be biased by managers' subjective views. Also, their recollections may not be entirely accurate. Furthermore, the worth and validity of surveys is often dependent on the level of response. M&A surveys typically yield a low rate of participation (2 to 10 percent).

Clinical studies. These are the most focused of all the research methods. Each clinical study examines in great depth either one deal exclusively or a small number of deals. These studies generally involve conversational, face-to-face primary research—field interviews with executives and knowledgeable observers.

Advantages: A clinical study can offer the most detailed and insightful information regarding specific deals. Given its inductive approach, much detail and factual background information can be gathered.

Drawbacks: Given the extremely focused nature of this approach, it is not well suited for hypothesis testing or other statistical analysis. The extreme specificity and potentially idiosyncratic results of these studies can make it difficult to draw insightful "big picture" conclusions.

2. The two approaches evaluate different metrics, and at different times. The accounting-based study looks at a company's financial reports, which reflect a company's operation results, highlight its financing and investing activities. The market return analysis, however, focuses more on a company's stock price (or market capitalization), a measure of what investors believe to be the present value of the firm's future cash flows. Market return analyses, therefore, are forward looking.

   As for differences in timing: Event studies look at market returns before, during, and after a deal *announcement*: This can be over any length of time, even measured in a short time frame of a few days. Accounting studies, however, compare reported data that are at least three months apart (quarterly reports).

PART II: QUESTIONS ON REAL BUSINESS SITUATIONS

1. Yes. The deal appears to have created new economic value for Smucker. This is evident in the sustained positive difference between Smucker's share price and the benchmark, the S&P 500 index. Smucker's positive returns could be due to several reasons:

   - *A focusing, not diversifying, investment for Smucker.* The buyer was familiar with consumer packaged foods. Jif and Crisco would complement the rest of the line.
   - *Synergies through economies of scale and purchasing.* For example, Smucker did not have a direct sales force and dealt solely with brokers. If Jif and Crisco already had a direct sales force, Smucker could leverage that new dis-

tribution channel and use it for a broader array of products. Even if Jif and Crisco did not have direct sales forces, the additional volume of these products would allow Smucker to spread its distribution costs, which should in turn still improve profit margins.

- *Increased market power for Newco owing to its greater size.* With larger size, Smucker might enjoy greater ability to position its products more favorably on retailers' shelves. Another concern about this deal is that it might have been executed to build market share. Research studies have shown that efforts to enhance market position through M&A yield flat to worse financial performance compared to predeal financial metrics. However, it is possible that M&A growth could actually enhance organic growth, and that the real warning from research is that M&A growth is *not a substitute* for organic growth.
- *Advantageous price.* Perhaps P&G simply sold cheap.
- *Issuance of shares by Smucker builds debt capacity for the firm.* There were a few aspects of this deal that could be seen as cautionary signs. One was the all-stock payment method. Studies referenced in Chapter 3 of the main text have shown that stock-based deals are associated with negative returns at deal announcements. In most cases, this is a logical result following theories that managers issue stock at the high point in the cycle of a company's market capitalization or in the overall stock market cycle. However, in the aftermath of September 11, Smucker's shares were trading at historically low points. As pointed out in the chapter, the announcement of an all-stock deal signals that management of the buying firm believe their shares are expensive and overvalued. In this particular case, however, it is questionable that Smucker's management or investors viewed the shares as overpriced.

2. In undiscounted terms, Quaker lost $1.4 billion on Snapple, while Triarc gained $700 million. Quaker's loss is notable especially in light of the expected synergies. Like Smucker's acquisition of Jif and Crisco, Quaker Oats was making a focused investment. In this instance, M&A did not pay off for Quaker.

   Quaker's effort to reposition Snapple in grocery stores and away from convenience stores was a flop. Resistance by independent bottlers and competitive responses by Coke and Pepsi turned a moneymaker into a money loser.

   Past success (such as Quaker's with Gatorade) is no indicator of future performance. M&A is not a profit machine that will automatically create value for the buyer. The buyer should enter each new deal with few preconceptions about success.

CHAPTER 4

M&A Activity

1. The cycle of M&A activity and the cycle of the stock market are both driven by the same fundamental forces in the economy. When the stock market is buoyant, the economic activity in markets is probably good—at such times, companies may have more cash to spend on acquisitions, and CEOs may be more optimistic about the payoff from acquisitions. Also, companies might acquire with stock if they think their stock is overvalued. When stock prices rise, buyers can more easily offer stock as a form of payment over cash. Thus, a company's sheer ability to pay in stock rather than cash can stimulate and influence its decision to engage in M&A activity. Rapid development of a capital market in countries where it had been previously underdeveloped may spur M&A activity.

2. The entrepreneur is the key figure in keeping the capitalist engine in motion. He or she seeks to exploit profitable opportunities and thus becomes a steady agent of change. By exploiting an invention, new technology, or other type of innovation, entrepreneurs trigger new patterns of behavior in the business landscape. Changes spurred by the entrepreneur can relate to production, consumer behavior, distribution, and so on.

3. Innovations do arise because of consumers' needs or wants, although those needs or wants can be latent (not realized) or not yet developed in consumers. For example, the invention of the television was not a response to an existing demand from consumers, but rather a forward-looking anticipation of demand that could be created for the product. While producers may need to educate consumers on the attributes and benefits of new products and services, they do not force the products onto consumers. Because consumers often do resist change, producers have the burden of showing and convincing them of the worthiness of an innovation.

   Entrepreneurs, therefore, have the task of identifying and envisioning needs and wants that may not yet be met, realized, or developed. In addition, entrepreneurs can identify not only unmet demands, but also alternative methods for meeting existing demands. The railroad was not invented because consumers "took the initiative in displaying an effective demand for their service in preference to the services of the mail coaches." However, the railroad was an alternative method of meeting the demand for transportation, and the entrepreneur responsible for its invention envisioned a future demand for the railroad: a "want" and "need" for a faster transportation service that offered new advantages.

4a. The journalist's questions ask the CEO to respond to the view that M&A activity could be a product of self-serving managers who make deals happen if and when they are in their favor. Her questions convey skepticism about the reasons given by executives to explain M&A activity.

In contrast, the CEO's stance portrays the straight economic turbulence view: M&A activity is a product of market and industry conditions and turbulence, which all present attractive investment opportunities.

4b. While the journalist's questions raise some concerns about the motivations behind M&A activity, she has no more than anecdotal evidence to ground the argument that M&A activity is a product of self-serving managers. The deal process itself involves justification for the reasons of a merger. From extensive documentation, discussions, and due diligence, a company must convey the business reasons behind any merger.

The CEO's view that economic conditions and turbulence are the leading drivers of M&A is based on facts about macroeconomic conditions and turbulence in the communications industry. Much evidence supports the "turbulence view," which explains well the M&A activity across various industries and across time.

5. Potential sources of turbulence include:

1. ***Overcapacity and collapsed demand for Internet services.*** Providers of Internet capacity seriously overinvested in plant and equipment. Falling demand bankrupted many companies whose businesses were predicated on rapid growth of the digital economy. Genuity's bankruptcy provided Level 3 with an opportunity to acquire capacity that would seem to fit well with Level 3's business strategy.
2. ***Deregulation: the Telecommunications Act of 1996.*** The Act provided opportunities for "any entity to compete in the telecommunications market." This allowed companies like Level 3 Communications to enter, grow, and compete in a market that was previously much more regulated and restrictive. The Act was a source of turbulence in that it changed the landscape of the entire communications industry and provided growth and acquisition opportunities that were previously not possible.
3. ***Globalization: international expansion.*** The globalization of communication services itself is a source of turbulence that likely motivated Level 3 to significantly expand in international markets through acquisitive growth. Before acquiring Genuity, the company had operational facilities in 27 U.S. markets and nine European markets. After the acquisition the company nearly doubled its number of markets: As of March 2003, it had 57 markets in the United States and 16 markets in Europe.
4. ***Technological change: evolution and changing landscape of the Internet.*** Level 3 identified Genuity as a pioneer in the Internet, and realized that Genuity's assets and intellectual capital would complement its own, which were based more on later Internet developments (optical and IP-based services).

CHAPTER 5

Cross-Border M&A

1a. *Analysis:* A business manager must have a "view" about a country in which an investment is contemplated. To get a view on where the best place to invest is and how to invest, one needs to perform a strategic analysis of countries. The strategic analysis for a country should include macroeconomic conditions and trends, microeconomic strength, the health of institutions, and so on. The following commentary gives a strategic overview of Thailand and the Philippines. Its conclusions are that *Thailand is a better investment site for the business manager described in the case, and a joint venture is a practical and safer approach for entering the Thai market.*

Thailand

As reported in the World Bank write-up, Thailand began to implement deep reforms in the financial sector, corporate governance, and competition policy after the financial crisis in 1997. These reforms have helped the economy to hold up in spite of the global downturn. After the major crisis in 1998, Thailand's economy started the recovery process and grew at over 4 percent in 1999. The graph of real GDP growth shows that after the sudden slowdown in 2000 and the first half of 2001, which coincided with the global economic recession, economic growth showed a strong turnaround. Real GDP growth increased from lower than 2 percent in the third quarter of 2001 to almost 6 percent in fourth quarter 2002. A positive trade balance kept boosting foreign exchange reserves, which strengthen foreign investors' confidence and capital market stability. Although the fiscal budget turned to a slight deficit in 2002, in general the balance is healthy both in absolute terms and as a percentage of GDP. The Thai government implemented a slightly contractionary monetary policy to keep inflation at bay starting in mid-2001. But the overall inflation level over the past several years is definitely in control compared to the 1998 level. At the same time, the exchange rate between the Thai baht and the U.S. dollar has stabilized at around 40 to 45 due to the stability of inflation. Although foreign direct investment has not returned to the same level as before the crisis, domestic spending, consumer spending, and net exports have pushed overall GDP to grow at an accelerated level. Domestic industrial production growth also picked up its pace after 2002. Overall, economic recovery is under way and the government's fiscal and monetary policies continue to support growth and reduce external vulnerability.

As with most developing nations, Thailand seems to be undergoing a change from being an agricultural country to being a manufacturing country. After strong efforts by the government to help the poor and focus on education, Thailand's illiteracy rate dropped to 4 percent, which is among the lowest in this region. The high-savings habit of the Thais also helps to maintain a high level of investment that is essential to the country's long-term growth. After the 1998 crisis, the Thai government proactively kept foreign debt at a maintainable level. Besides financial industry reforms, structural reforms were also implemented in other areas as part of a broader strategy to improve the nation's competitiveness. The government strove to formulate a comprehensive strategy and to initiate new measures to promote productivity growth. Poverty reduction and balanced development are set forth as medium-term strategies in the government's Ninth Plan. Thailand's monarch has also attacked corruption and has advocated for the improved management of natural resources. In the telecom industry, Thailand seems to be lagging in terms of technological investment and wireless coverage, which offers a great opportunity for foreign investors to bring in much needed investment and technology, especially in the wireless sector. Although the government is devoted to battling poverty and corruption, the challenge remains for the government to convince the general public about governance and social stability. The move toward strengthening democratic institutions is, however, a step in the right direction.

The Thai government also advocated several industrial reforms to improve transparency in the banking industry (and although not mentioned in the information provided, to increase the speed of privatization and support several niche industries). The stock market has stagnated for several years, suggesting that this is a time of attractive valuations in terms of asset pricing compared to the mid-1990s' high-flying real estate prices.

Overall, Thailand is on the verge of economic recovery and has a stable government that has prioritized poverty reduction, which is essential for social stability and long-term domestic demand growth. GDP growth mainly relies on domestic demand and investment, which is the result of a high savings rate. A current account surplus boosts foreign exchange reserves and reduces total debt, which relieves the pressure on fiscal policy and capital investment by the private sector. A healthy macroeconomic environment, supportive microeconomic conditions, and efforts to improve corporate governance and government regulation all offer a great opportunity for foreign investors to enter the Thai market. The relatively well-integrated capital market, reasonable asset pricing levels, and growing industry demand make the timing favorable, too.

The Philippines

Similar to Thailand, the Philippines made much progress in reducing poverty during the early to mid-1990s. However, the Philippines went through a turbulent political period from 1999 to early 2001, leading to slowdowns in both economic growth and poverty reduction. However, public confidence was restored somewhat with the ascendance of a new administration in January 2001. This administration has attempted to pursue sound macroeconomic policies as well as governance and structural reforms.

Although several macroeconomic indicators show some bright spots, the overall economy in 2003 does not look very optimistic. Real GDP growth over the past three years has been around 3 to 5 percent, which indicates that the Philippines did not suffer as much as Thailand from the Asian crisis. Inflation was reduced from 12 percent in 1999 to less than 4 percent in 2002, because of an aggressive contractionary monetary policy. The Philippine government seems to have reversed this policy in the second quarter of 2002 to encourage private investment and consumer spending. Although the current account is in surplus, most of that is coming from positive net income received from abroad, whereas the other major component of the current account—the trade balance—is flat to negative. In addition, foreign direct investment has been erratic. As opposed to Thailand, the Philippines' GDP growth is mainly caused by consumer spending and government spending; the latter has resulted in a persistent budget deficit and increasing debt burden. The industrial production growth rate decreased to a negative level, which is not a promising sign.

The key challenge for the Philippines is to address its chronic fiscal deficit. But in order to do this while sustaining growth at the same time, private demand will have to take the lead. This will be possible if the government takes steps to create a favorable investment climate and to be persistent in its financial and corporate restructuring efforts. Although the Philippine government has done a great job managing inflation, the peso continues to weaken against major currencies, presenting another obstacle to foreign investors. Overall, the Philippines has shown modest growth in the past several years and did not experience a dramatic downturn, which may suggest it is a less integrated market.

The Philippines, like Thailand, undertook efforts to reduce poverty and to focus on education. The illiteracy rate is at 5 percent, which is low in this region. However, educational attainment is low, and the quality of education is poor. The Philippines also has a modest savings rate. Because of a long period of budget deficit, the country's debt-to-GDP ratio has increased to 74 percent, which imposes an annual interest burden amounting to 3.5 percent of GDP. To improve its fiscal position, the government is working on longer-term structural reforms, including finding ways to reverse the slide in revenues.

Nonperforming loans (NPLs) of the banking sector rose to 18 percent in June 2002 versus 17 percent in 2001. The Philippine government has been trying to improve the banking system, though efforts to deal with nonperforming loans have yet to bear fruit. The Philippine stock market has not done well, and volumes have been thin. Spreads on government bonds have risen. Although the low level of the stock market helps bring down overall asset pricing, the increasing credit spread indicates that there is a higher risk level associated with uncertainty in the future. In the telecommunications industry, the Philippines has adequate domestic service, which may mean stiffer competition for new entrants.

Overall, a moderate recovery is under way. However, the boost from the demand side has been from public spending, and income from abroad. Indications of increasing financial risk suggest that this may not be the right time to invest in the Philippines. Furthermore, political instability poses a challenge to foreign investors.

1b. ***Preliminary choice:*** Comparing the two countries, in mid-2003 one could conclude that Thailand is economically and politically more attractive as a country for investment than the Philippines. Economically, Thailand seems to have greater potential for sustainable economic growth supported by positive trends such as a higher savings rate, higher investment growth, net export growth, and so on. Nonetheless, Thailand still sustains some degree of political and economic risk; in addition, there is some uncertainty as to how government regulation will play out: Will reform efforts be successful? Because of these uncertainties, a joint venture investment may make more sense than a 100 percent acquisition. In fact, this is a very common method of investment for many cross-border deals in developing countries.

1c. The information obtained by your analyst has focused primarily on macroeconomic and institutional factors. While these areas lend important insights, the country analysis framework summarized in Exhibit 5.12 of the main text suggests research in two additional areas:

- *Microeconomy:* industry structure, the role of foreign direct investment, infrastructure, and factors suggested by Porter's "diamond" of country competitiveness.
- *Culture:* norms and practices in areas such as work ethic, risk bearing, leadership, and entrepreneurship.

Country analysis draws on the wide range of insights offered by macroeconomics, microeconomics, institutional analysis, and cultural analysis.

CHAPTER 6

Strategy and the Uses of M&A to Grow or Restructure the Firm

1. Strategy is a plan for fulfilling the mission and achieving the strategic objectives of a company. It is the road map that guides the day-to-day actions of a firm. To achieve a firm's objectives, then, strategy should be the engine driving M&A search, analysis, and implementation. M&A is a tactical instrument of strategy. Strategy should therefore influence decisions on issues like whether to grow organically or inorganically, how to grow, whether and how to restructure a company, and whether and how to exit a business.

2. Strategic analysis tools include:

    1. The Porter model is a useful guide and discipline for industry and competitor analysis. Based on your analysis of the five forces, you should be able to assess how fast a market will grow and how competitive the market will be.
    2. The strategic map and growth-share matrix are useful in this case, since they can help illustrate the relative positions of competitors. The map is helpful for identifying any areas that are unoccupied by competitors.
    3. The strategic canvas and the attractiveness-strength matrix can both be used in this case. The strategic canvas will allow you to compare the strategies of competitors on a number of dimensions in order for you to assess how well your business unit can compete. The attractiveness-strength matrix will allow you to evaluate the business unit relative to other units in your firm on the basis of industry attractiveness and the competitive strength of the unit within that industry.

3. Drivers of value include:

    - ***High relatedness, in terms of industry of buyer and target.*** Studies by Rumelt (1974, 1982) found that strategies motivated by "related" diversification purposes had higher returns on equity than strategies for unrelated diversification or for single-business focus. Perhaps a good example for this would be a company that strategically decides to acquire another company that is a supplier for the company. Acquiring a supplier could eliminate costs and improve operating efficiencies in the company's value chain, thus creating value and higher returns.
    - ***Deregulation.*** In industries experiencing deregulation, companies may seek to create value by merging with companies that they previously were not

able to—for example, the deregulation of the commercial banking industry allowed for convergence (mergers) between commercial banks and insurance companies.

- ***Efficiency or inefficiency of internal capital markets.*** Research studies have shown that some diversification mergers (of conglomerates) have realized greater efficiencies because their ability to allocate resources was better than that of the external capital market. Thus, a diversifying merger would be a more likely driver of value when the external capital markets are inefficient (i.e., where the more diversified company could create more efficiency and value internally than the capital markets would be able to do externally).
- ***Special information-based assets.*** There is evidence that when one or both firms in a diversifying merger have significant information-based assets, the diversified firm can transfer knowledge and intellectual capital more efficiently than the public markets could.

4. Organic growth is that which is "home grown" inside of a firm through internal investment. Inorganic growth, in contrast, is growth through investing or structuring an affiliation outside of the firm.

   Organic growth is particularly appropriate if a firm has a unique competitive advantage that will allow for superior returns on investment, such as patents/patent rights, proprietary technology, unique know-how, and core competencies (i.e., strategic capabilities that translate resources into special advantages for a firm). Organic growth is particularly appropriate if a firm has unique resources or capabilities, that are difficult to imitate and thus something the firm does not want to share or dilute by combining with another company.

   Inorganic growth is particularly appropriate for a company that does not currently have, but would like to acquire and benefit from, a unique competitive advantage of another firm. For example, a pharmaceutical company might want to buy another firm in the same industry that has a patent to develop/produce a new drug that the company believes will be very successful and profitable. Inorganic growth may be the best/only way a company can attain resources that are vital to its continued success. In fields such as biotechnology, computer software, defense electronics, and filmed entertainment, corporations may need to reach beyond their internal operations to acquire intellectual property, patents, creative talent, and managerial know-how. Also, inorganic growth is particularly appropriate if it gives a company significantly greater access to suppliers and buyers (which, not surprisingly, are two of Porter's five forces).

5. The conventional view that mergers for diversification destroy value has been challenged by critics who offer both theories and evidence to prove otherwise—that at least in some cases, diversification can and does create value.

   Salter and Weinhold (1979) argued that corporate diversification could do things that shareholder portfolio formation could not, such as: promote knowledge transfer across divisions, reduce costs, aggregate resources that can be shaped into core competencies that create competitive advantage, and exploit better transparency and monitoring through internal capital markets. The diversified firm "internalizes" the capital market by acting as an allocator of resources among its businesses.

Rumelt (1974) found that profitability varied by type of diversification strategy—that not all mergers driven by diversification motives have the same returns. Rumelt's findings reveal that a strategy of close relatedness in diversification yields the best returns. While his research was instrumental in demonstrating that strategic focus is important and creates value, it also shows that there is a wide range of returns that can result from diversification strategy, and that some types of diversification can create more value than others.

Four studies by Kruse (2002), Healey, Palepu, and Ruback (1992), Parrino and Harris (1999), and Cornett and Tehranian (1992) found improvements in operating performance following diversifying acquisitions.

Anslinger and Copeland (1996) performed research that found that some firms pursuing a conscious strategy of unrelated diversification have realized high abnormal returns for sustained periods.

6. Domestically, the main options for inorganic growth would include (1) a majority acquisition, (2) joint venture, or (3) minority investment. The majority acquisition, for instance, might entail buying out a different fast-food chain or some other business. Or, since location is important in this business, you may want to buy out those other restaurants or commercial establishments that are in prime spots in those locales where you don't have the best locations. Purchase of a direct competitor may encounter sharp antitrust restrictions. With joint venture or minority investments you could grow through partial engagement with other firms that would still carry influence for the protection of the brand and mitigation of risks.

   In developing countries the choices are broader where there is a strong local partner: franchising, strategic alliance, joint venture, and purchasing a minority stake. Among the four, franchising and joint venture agreements are the most attractive strategies. Depending on the particular conditions of a country, one can be more appropriate than the other. For instance, in a country where the political and economic risk is relatively high and consumer acceptance of foreign brands is high, franchising would be a better alternative because it would not require a large capital investment. It would also allow you to expand very fast, thereby capitalizing on the high customer acceptance of foreign brands. In contrast, in a country that is more economically and politically stable, but where people are not as open to foreign brands, a joint venture might be the better choice because it allows you more direct operational control necessary for promoting quality and brand image.

7. Restructuring the company in a way that creates more transparency about its business divisions may help reduce the diversification discount. Setting a division up as a separate entity from the holding company can help increase transparency. There are four ways of organizing a division as a separate entity: partial carve-out, partial spin-off, partial split-off, and tracking stock. The four differ from each other in terms of who ends up owning the shares in the new entity, and the degree of the control the parent retains. The specific choice will therefore depend on the strategy of the firm. For instance, if the firm wants to retain a high degree of control, issuing tracking stock may be the best option.

   Another way that restructuring can create value is by preventing the cross-subsidization of "loser" business units by successful units. This could be achieved by divesting the losers and by carve-out, spin-off, or split-off.

8. The framework for choosing an inorganic growth strategy would require the following steps:

   1. Identify the benefits from a relationship with the target business.
   2. Assess the need for ownership and control.
   3. Manage risk exposure.

   The thought process can be laid out in a decision tree format: The first question leads to an answer that sets up the second question, and the second to the third. By following the path of answers, one should be able to arrive at the inorganic growth strategy that best fits the company's needs. (Refer to Exhibit 6.20 in the main text.) In some cases, one may identify more than one attractive strategy. To decide which strategy is best, one can use these guidelines: retain a bias for simplicity, consider starting small, and remember value creation!

9. Input the data into the growth-share matrix in the Excel spreadsheet model "Growth Share.xls," which is found on the CD-ROM. You should come up with the following chart:

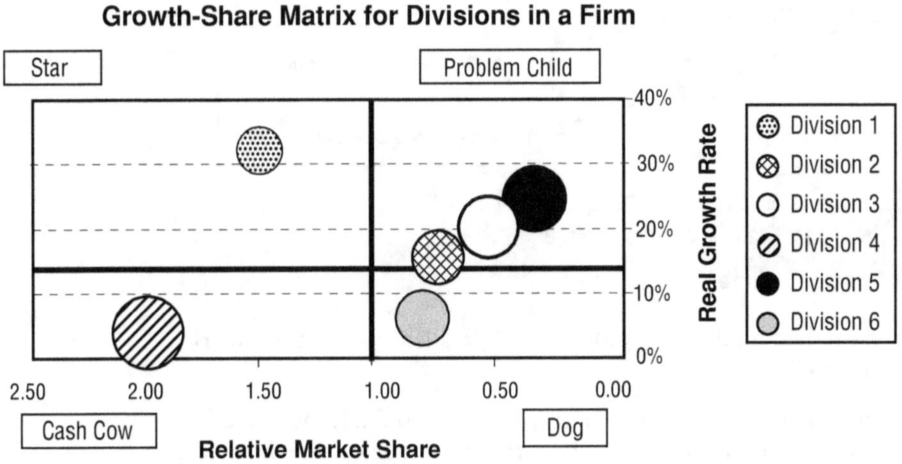

   [This spreadsheet can be found in the folder "Key Spreadsheets from the Workbook" located on the CD-ROM.]

   As can be seen from the graph, division 6 is a "dog" and would be the prime candidate for shedding. There may be hope for the "problem children" if the company can find a way to increase market shares of those divisions—they would then become stars. Division 4 is the cash cow, which can provide for the financial needs of your company.

10. Input the data into the spreadsheet model "Learning Curve.xls," found on the CD-ROM. The results should be:

		5% Cost Reduction	10% Cost Reduction	15% Cost Reduction
Slope		0.05	0.10	0.15
Base cost		$120.00	$120.00	$120.00
Time Period	Cumulative Production (000s)			
0	0	$120.00	$120.00	$120.00
1	5	$114.00	$108.00	$102.00
2	10	$108.30	$ 97.20	$ 86.70
3	20	$102.89	$ 87.48	$ 73.70
4	40	$ 97.74	$ 78.73	$ 62.64
5	80	$ 92.85	$ 70.86	$ 53.24
6	160	$ 88.21	$ 63.77	$ 45.26

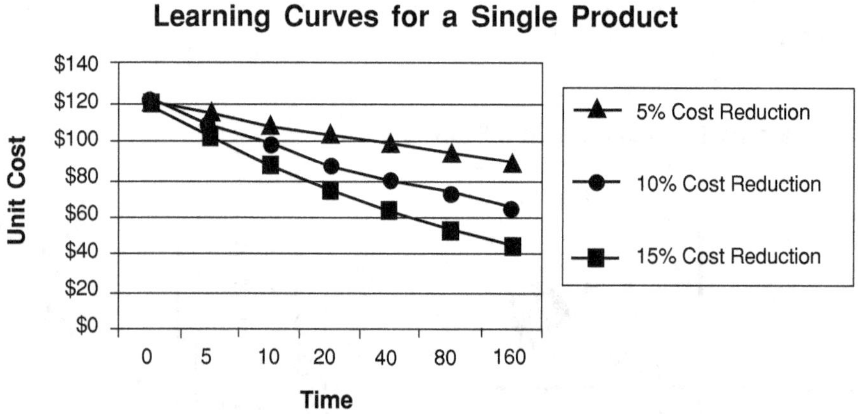

[This spreadsheet can be found in the folder "Key Spreadsheets from the Workbook" located on the CD-ROM.]

As the table shows, as the number of units produced doubles, the reduction in cost proceeds at a different rate under the different scenarios. For instance, for the 5 percent cost reduction scenario in time period 2, cumulative production doubles from 5,000 to 10,000, and the cost per thousand decreases from $114 to $108.30—a 5 percent reduction. In the 15 percent cost reduction scenario in time period 2, cumulative production doubles from 5,000 to 10,000, and the cost per thousand decreases from $102 to $86.70—a 15 percent reduction. Another important thing to note is the compounding effect of the learning curve. As time progresses and cumulative production increases, the difference in cost between different scenarios increases, too, due to the compounding effect. For instance, in time period 1, the difference in cost under the 5 percent and 10 percent reduction scenarios—$114 vs. $108—is 5 percent. By the time we get to time period 6, the difference in cost under these two scenarios is 28 percent ($88.21 vs. $63.77)!

11. The following are several alternatives for increasing Joy Company's self-sustainable growth rate, although there may be many more combinations of different strategies that will produce the targeted 16 percent rate of growth:

Change in Policy	New Policy Target	Existing Policy	Required Change
1. Increase debt/equity ratio. Finance the growth with debt.	D/E = 1.68	D/E = .30	Fivefold relevering
2. Sell equity.	DPO = –107% (i.e., sell about as much equity each year as you generate internally)	DPO = 40% (i.e., no equity sales)	Drop the dividend. Sell equity.
3. Improve internal profitability.	ROE = 26.77% ROTC = 21.44%	ROE = 15% ROTC = 12.46%	Margins almost double.
4. Improve internal profitability *and* increase debt/equity ratio.	ROTC = 17.33% D/E = .70	ROTC = 12.46% D/E = .30	Increase margins and leverage a lot.
5. Cut dividend payout ratio *and* improve internal profitability *and* increase debt/equity ratio.	DPO = 20% ROTC = 14.67% D/E = .50	DPO = 40% ROTC = 12.46% D/E = .30	Cut dividend in half. Increase leverage. Increase margins.

[This spreadsheet can be found in the folder "Key Spreadsheets from the Workbook" located on the CD-ROM.]

As can be seen in the table, the CEO can increase the sustainable growth rate to 16 percent by increasing leverage, selling equity or improving internal profitability. In addition, the CEO can combine these strategies to achieve the targeted growth rate. Comparing the different alternatives, some have advantages and some have disadvantages. For instance, increasing the debt ratio to 1.68 can achieve the goal, but is difficult to implement and also increases financial risks associated with huge increases in leverage. Or, although improving internal profitability can help achieve the target, it may be very difficult to implement. So among the five alternatives, the fifth choice may be the most reasonable because it balances the different approaches by reducing the dividend payout, modestly improving internal profitability, and increasing the debt equity ratio to a reasonable level.

12. The diversification discount can be calculated by comparing the company's total capital to the sum of the implied total capital of its divisions, which in turn can be estimated individually using the data on industry averages. The implied total capital of the divisions comes out to $133 million; therefore, there is a diversification discount of 9.86 percent:

	Implied Capital ($ MM)
Division 1	24.0
Division 2	56.3
Division 3	52.8
Total capital	133.1
Discount	9.86%

[This spreadsheet can be found in the folder "Key Spreadsheets from the Workbook" located on the CD-ROM.]

CHAPTER 7

Acquisition Search and Deal Origination: Some Guiding Principles

PART I: TRUE OR FALSE

1. True.
2. True.
3. True.
4. True.
5. True.
6. False. If information about an acquisition opportunity is fully public, it will be difficult for the buyer to tailor the terms to greater advantage.
7. True.
8. True.
9. False. In some cases, an ideal target may become available unexpectedly. If there is a compelling argument for doing a deal, the unexpectedness of the target's appearance should not hinder a deal.
10. False. Deal-rich information is private.

PART II: SHORT ANSWER

1. The "Oracle of Bacon" game illustrates the "small world" concept. It is difficult to find actors/actresses separated by more than four links to Kevin Bacon. In fact, the average number of links is 2.94. The point is that people are more connected to each other than we may think. As an M&A practitioner, therefore, part of the game in acquisition search is to get good connections. Potential targets may very well come the M&A practitioner's way through such connections.
2. In studying how people find jobs, Granovetter discovered that personal connections were decisive. Granovetter found that three-quarters of successful connections to job offers were through "weak ties," people whom the job seeker saw occasionally or rarely. The point is that there is strength in weak ties, and that

the diversity and breadth of the network matter. The implication for an M&A practitioner is that it pays to build a network that extends beyond people in one's own circle. If an M&A practitioner limits his connections to people in the same circles, it may limit his chances of being in the "sweet spot"—finding a target that not many competitors know about.

3. The best navigators:
   - Have proprietary information, know-how, and connections.
   - Can innovate better than others.
   - Discover trends and sweet spots before others.
   - Enjoy a cost advantage over competitors.
   - Have positive reputations.

PART III: TARGET ASSESSMENT CASES

1. *Possible Answers:* Nine groups of students conducted this exercise in May 2003 and separately came up with the companies discussed here. Your results, of course, do not necessarily have to match what is in the list—in fact, they may not match at all. Go ahead and read about the suggested targets nonetheless. You may pick up some useful ideas regarding the acquisition search process/criteria/issues. You will also find for each suggested target how the buyer reacted to the proposal.

Campbell Soup Company

Profile

Campbell manufactures soups, juice beverages, sauces, crackers, and confectionery products. It operates under four business segments: North America Soup and Away from Home, North America Sauces and Beverages, Biscuits and Confectionery, and International Soup and Sauces. Popular brands are Campbell's and Swanson's for soups, Prego and Pace for sauces, Franco-American for pasta, V8 for vegetable juice, Pepperidge Farm for baked goods, and Godiva for premium chocolate.

2002 Revenues	$6.46 billion
2002 Operating margins	17.1%

Campbell's 2002 Revenue and Earnings Distribution

	Revenues	Earnings
North America Soup and Away from Home	41%	55%
North America Sauces and Beverages	19%	21%
Biscuits and Confectionery	25%	16%
International Soup and Sauces	15%	8%

Why Campbell's?

- Products fit the fast and portable meal kit concept (will fit the buyer's distribution system).
- Lines of "good for you" products: Campbell's Soup, Swanson, V8 vegetable juice.
- Growth opportunities in soup market: "ready to serve" market growth of 16 percent; Campbell's Soup's growth only 9 percent. Over 90 percent of consumers eat soup of some form.
- Dominance in North America.
- Strong presence in Europe.

Deal Rationale

- Synergies in the product line and distribution channels.
- Opportunities to grow Campbell's business internationally using the buyer's distribution capabilities.
- Expansion and diversification of the buyer's product line.
- Access to strong "ready to serve" and "good for you" brands.
- Opportunity to purchase undervalued company and change management to improve operations (Campbell's was undergoing some restructuring measures during this time).

Ownership Structure

Family trust and insiders	45.1%
Barclays Bank	2.7%
State Street Corp.	2.6%
Capital Guardian	2.3%
Mellon Bank	2.1%
Other institutions	23.0%
Free float	22.2%

Risks

- Ability to convince majority stock owners to sell.
- Regulatory approval. However, this risk was thought to be low because the product portfolios were complementary.
- Integration risk: Campbell's was founded in 1869, so there is a strong culture and sense of pride.

Buyer's Reaction

The buyer had already been monitoring this potential target and knew that the family was not interested in selling. However, the buyer said it would keep Campbell's on its watch list to be alert for possible interest in selling by the insiders.

Lifeway Foods

Profile

Lifeway Foods, Inc., manufactures probiotic, cultured, dairy, and nondairy health food products. The company's primary products are kefir, a dairy beverage similar to yogurt; a line of various drinkable yogurts under the name La Fruta and Tuscan, and a dairy-based immune-supporting dietary supplement beverage, Basics Plus. It also produces a soy-based alternative to dairy kefir. Finally, the company manufactures a line of various farmer cheeses sold under the name Lifeway Farmer Cheese.[1]

2002 Revenues	$12.2 million
2002 Operating margins	21.1%

Why Lifeway?

- Proprietary probiotic formula.
- The only product known in the kefir category.
- Growing brand names.
- Innovative product offerings.
- Consistent revenue and net income growth versus industry.
- High margins.
- High quality management.

Deal Rationale

- Enables the buyer to gain foothold in "good for you"/organics market, to participate in the trend toward health-consciousness.
- Provides opportunity for the buyer to enter high margin dairy and gut health sector.
- Provides stable of morning meal products and microsnacks.

Ownership Structure

Family	54.3%
Danone	20.4%
Institutional	1.3%
Other	24.0%

Risks

- Ability to convince major stockholders to sell.
- Cultural fit.
- Integration risk.
- Noncompetition agreement with Danone.

Buyer's Reaction

The buyer considered the target too small.

Hansen Natural Corporation

Profile

Hansen Natural Corporation is an alternative beverage company with products in several categories: natural sodas, fruit juices, soy smoothies, energy drinks, "functional drinks," sparkling lemonades and orangeades, noncarbonated ready-to-drink iced teas, children's multivitamin juice drinks, and noncarbonated lightly flavored energy waters.[2] It also sells nutrition bars and cereals under the Hansen's brand name.

2002 Revenues	$95.5 million
2002 Operating margins	5.8%

Why Hansen's?

- Seventy years in the natural beverage industry.
- Has 20 percent market share in energy drinks market.
- Five-year sales compound average growth rate of 16.5 percent.
- Was 2002 sales leader in new age carbonated beverages within California market.
- Leading brand in Southern California natural soda market for more than 25 years.
- Low-asset business—third-party suppliers.

Deal Rationale

- Allows buyer entry into fast-growing organic, soy, juice, and energy drinks markets:
  - Energy drinks are fastest-growing segment of beverage market.
  - Growth in sales of soy food in 2001 was 27 percent.
  - Organic beverage sales are expected to grow 24 percent annually until 2005.
  - Shelf-stable juices expected to grow 26 percent annually until 2005.
- Buyer has opportunity to grow the brand.

Ownership Structure

Insiders and 5%+ owners	42.0%
Institutional	14.0%
Other	44.0%

Risks

- Ability to convince majority stock owners to sell.
- Integration risk.

Buyer's Reaction

Hansen and its operating margins are too small.

Lance, Inc.

Profile

Lance manufactures, markets, and distributes a variety of snack-food products that include sandwich crackers, potato chips, nuts, popcorn, and other salty snacks, as well as cookies, cakes, and candy. Lance uses its own fleet of tractors and trailers to make weekly deliveries to sales territories. Lance also operates approximately 39,000 company-owned vending machines.

2002 Revenues	$538.4 million
2002 Operating margins	12.0%

Why Lance?

- Highly recognized brand name.
- Proven management team.

Deal Rationale

- Products complement the buyer's own snack foods lines.
- Feasible to push target's product lines through buyer's distribution channels.
- Buyer's product lines can be pushed through Lance's vending machines.

Ownership Structure

Top five shareholders:

Van Every Lance	5.4%
Philip Van Every	4.8%
Barclays Global	4.1%
PIMCO Equity	3.9%
American Century Investments	2.6%

Risks

- Ability to convince family members to sell stock.
- Regulatory approval.
- Cannibalization of buyer's own snack food brands.
- Potential perceived dilution of high-powered stable of buyer's brands.

Buyer's Reaction

Buyer felt that target's products too heavily overlapped with its own, and could not justify cannibalizing its own products, which were generating higher profit margins than those of the target.

Group Danone

Profile

Group Danone is a producer of fresh dairy products and packaged water, biscuits, and cereal products.[3]

2002 Revenues	$14 billion
2002 Operating margins	10.8%

Danone's Revenue Breakdown by Product	
Fresh dairy products	46%
Beverages	27%
Biscuits	24%
Other	3%

Danone's Revenue Breakdown by Geography	
France	23%
Rest of European Union	34%
Rest of world	43%

Why Group Danone?

- Global leader in cultured dairy products.
- Second largest producer of biscuits.
- Second largest bottled water producer.
- Strong international presence.
- Strong R&D.
- Little product overlap.

Deal Rationale

- Product line expansion.
- Fulfill buyer's objective of expanding into "good for you" products.
- Gain access to Danone's European and Asian distribution channels.
- Acquire expertise in chilled and refrigerated markets.

Ownership Structure

Danone has no large controlling shareholder; 40 percent of shares are held by shareholders outside of France.

Risks

- Willingness of foreign shareholders to sell to a U.S. company.
- Antitrust issues.
- Integration concerns—significant time might be required to realize gains due to size, with respect to both distribution channels and management structure.
- Supplier relationships for Danone products must be managed due to EU structure.

Buyer's Reaction

Interested. Margins are thinner than targeted, but would like to know more about possibilities to increase margins.

Lindt

Profile

Lindt is a company with more than 150 years of experience making premium Swiss chocolate.

2002 Revenues	$1.2 billion
2002 Operating margins	10.1%

Lindt's Revenue Breakdown by Geography

Europe	72%
United States	20%
North and South America (excluding U.S.)	4%
Rest of world	4%

Why Lindt?

- Strong brand awareness.
- Strong market share in Europe.
- Premium pricing.
- More than a 150 years of experience.
- Opportunity to improve market share in United States, where it has less than 1 percent of the market.

Deal Rationale

- Buyer would gain a new product line with captive premium markets.
- Buyer would gain exposure to European market.
- Lindt would provide a new platform for product innovation.
- Lindt's R&D capabilities could be used to develop buyer's line of snack-food products.
- Buyer could build Lindt into a strong brand, just like Campbell's has done with Godiva.

Ownership Structure

Fonds fur Pensionserganzungen der Chocoladefabriken Lindt & Sprugli AG owns 22.3 percent of shares. It is the only shareholder that owns more than 5 percent of the company.

Risks

- Willingness of foreign shareholders to sell to a U.S. company.
- Lindt operates in a mature, low-growth market.
- Chocolate would be a new market for the buyer, with new technologies and production processes.
- Failure of retail expansion of Lindt in the United States.

Buyer's Reaction

Margins are thinner than targeted, but strong brand may present opportunities for improvement in margins. Also, dedicated retail system may be too asset intensive for buyer's preferences. Still, buyer wanted to know more.

Tingyi (Cayman Islands) Holding Corp.

Profile

Tingyi is the best-known food and beverage company in China. It specializes in the production and distribution of instant noodles, beverages, and bakery products.

2002 Revenues	$1.2 billion
2002 Operating margins	12.6%

Revenue Breakdown by Product

Instant noodles	54%
Beverages	38%
Bakery	7%
Other	1%

Why Tingyi?

- Strong brand:
  - Number one in instant noodles, with 35 percent market share.
  - Fifty-one percent market share in ready-to-drink tea market.
  - Number three player in fruit juice market, with 15 percent market share.
- Well-developed distribution network.
- Nationwide network of production.
- Instant noodles business is a cash cow.

Deal Rationale

- Acquisition will allow buyer to have a strong presence in China.
- Opportunity to push buyer's products through target's well-established distribution network.
- Expansion of buyer's product lines—major revenue enhancement.
- Little product overlap—new products can be source of growth.

Ownership Structure

Ting Hsin Holdings	33% (This parent company of Tingyi is a Taiwanese company.)
Sanyo Foods	33%
Public	34%

Risks

- Ability to convince major shareholders to sell.
- Lack of familiarity doing business in China.
- Oversupply of low-end products in China may lead to price wars.
- Stiff competition: There are many well-established local brands in China.
- Scalability of products in the Western world is questionable.
- Regulatory approval.
- Differences in management style and culture.
- Chinese consumers may not accept buyer's Western products.

Buyer's Reaction
Strong interest. Wants to know more about the "country bet" implicit in this acquisition.

Maruchan, Inc.

Profile
Maruchan, Inc., is a noodles manufacturer with $500 million in sales. It is a wholly owned subsidiary of Toyo Susian, a Japanese company.

2002 Revenues	$ 500 million
2002 Operating margins	9.4%

Why Maruchan?

- Strong brand—dominant market share in North America.
- Double-digit growth in North America.
- Leading low-cost capabilities.
- Has two manufacturing plants in the United States: one in Virginia and one in California.

Deal Rationale

- Instant noodles fit the buyer's desired product characteristics: convenient, ready to go, "good for you/better for you."
- Appeal to ethnic groups in the United States.
- Growth potential for instant noodle market in the United States (currently, Asia accounts for 88 percent of the market for instant noodles).
- About 42 percent of U.S. population is below 30 years old; thus, there is a large number of potential consumers of instant noodles.
- Revenue enhancement through extension of buyer's product line.

Risks

- Ability to convince Toyo Susian to sell.
- Instant noodles would be a new product/new market for the buyer.
- Instant noodle product line may not be compatible with buyer's products.
- Differences in management style and culture.

Buyer's Reaction

Low interest because of margins and strength of competition.

Yakult Honsha Co. Ltd.

Profile

Yakult Honsha makes the leading brand of probiotic drinks worldwide. It also manufactures other juices, sports drinks, teas, and coffees.

2001 Revenues	$1.9 billion
2001 Operating margins	9.9%

Revenue Breakdown by Product

Food and beverages	85%
Cosmetics	6%
Pharmaceuticals and life sciences	9%

Why Yakult?

- Leading brand in probiotic drinks worldwide.
- Innovative technology.
- Product has proven medical benefits.

Deal Rationale

- Secure a strong international brand in a growing category (probiotics).
- Enhance good-for-you product portfolio.
- Growth potential through chilled distribution capabilities.
- Secure revenue streams from outside North America.
- Opportunity to build Yakult brand in the United States.

Ownership Structure

Top five shareholders:

Fedian PTE Ltd. (Danone)	19.3%
Fidelity Investments	7.5%
Matsusho Co.	6.5%
Chase Manhattan	5.5%
Capital Research Management	4.5%

It must be noted, however, that Yakult's ownership remains predominantly Japanese:

Japanese financial institutions	24%
Japanese individuals	21%
Other Japanese corporations	20%
Foreign institutions and others	35%

Risks

- Ability to convince Japanese shareholders to sell.
- Ability to manage cultural integration.
- Yakult may not "click" with American consumers—it has a very distinct taste.
- M&A rules in Japan may pose difficulties—for instance, share for share exchanges by non-Japanese firms are prohibited; thus, payment would need to be in cash.

Buyer's Reaction

Low interest because of low margins and likely demands of sellers.

NOTES

1. *Source:* Yahoo! Finance.
2. Ibid.
3. Ibid.

CHAPTER 8

Due Diligence

PART I: CONCEPT QUESTIONS

1. An investor mentality goes beyond mere data-fetching and list-checking. It seeks to gauge the risk exposure and investment attractiveness of the target. Thinking like an investor therefore expands due diligence toward a critical assessment of risk and returns.

2. A narrow due diligence review is brief, contained, and focused only on issues needed to get the deal done, such as legal and accounting issues. In a competitive setting, this may be the only feasible strategy. However, it does not serve the investor mentality very well; its main focus is simply deal consummation. In contrast, a broad review looks everywhere, takes the time it needs, and makes material demands on the target. A choice between narrow or broad due diligence often equates to a choice between "surprises now" and "surprises later." "Surprises now" entails higher expenditures for due diligence, but yields greater insight about the target.

3. The best due diligence efforts focus on acquiring knowledge rather than just amassing information or data. Knowledge is information that has been processed in order to be usable. Data are simply raw facts, and information consists of data that is concentrated and improved. Knowledge, in contrast, examines, ruminates on, and synthesizes data and information in order to extract patterns, trends, and insights. Knowledge presupposes *understanding*.

PART II: MINI-CASES

1. It seems reasonable to conclude that the due diligence process for this deal was wanting in no small measure. Given the size of the deal, it is surprising that the buyer was content to simply base due diligence on public information. Of course, no one can say for sure whether going beyond the public domain would have uncovered the fraud, even though the nature of the problems uncovered, the length of the time period during which fraud had been taking place, and the massiveness of the deception suggest that a discovery might have been possible with some digging. At the very least, it would have been known that CUC's accounting systems were outdated, and that might have raised some alarm bells.

2. Due diligence was probably one cause of the Quaker/Snapple merger failure, albeit not the only one. Hubris certainly seems to have been a factor in this case—it would explain why Quaker went forward with the deal in spite of clear indications that sales were much weaker than expected. But with respect to the distribution, excess inventory, and production problems, it appears that greater due diligence efforts might have prevented surprises. For instance, given the crucial role distribution would play in the success of the merger, could Quaker have consulted with Snapple's independent distributors to ensure their agreement with Quaker's distribution plan? Could interviews with Snapple's customers have helped uncover the slow turnaround time and the stuffing of the distribution pipeline with inventory? Could interviews with suppliers have revealed the contracts that required minimum quotas? Doing the legwork on these issues may have brought about more "surprises now" rather than "surprises later."

3. Although no definitive evidence can be given, it seems in this case that the acquirers failed to conduct enough due diligence on the infusion industry and on Critical Care's competitive position within it. The huge disparity between expectations of 30 percent earnings growth versus the actual results (flat earnings) suggests how little Medical Care's executives knew. It is difficult to understand how Medical Care could not have known about pricing pressures in the industry given how drastic they were. Careful industry study should have uncovered information such as this. Presumably, too, discussions with other players in the industry, such as competitors, insurers, and HMOs, might have led to the discovery that Critical Care was charging fees well above market and losing share because of it.

CHAPTER 9

Valuing Firms

1. The recommended action should be to buy shares of Sober Brews. At $32.8 apiece, Sober's market capitalization comes out to only $1,187.70, 25 percent lower than the estimated equity value of $1,586. This is a violation of value additivity (i.e., $V_{\text{Sum of parts}} > V_{\text{Market}}$). Securities analysts and corporate raiders are known to conduct this kind of analysis.

2. Corrected statements are:

   a. An opportunity to create value exists when price and intrinsic value differ.

   b. It is not necessary that *all* estimators be used. Indeed, it may be an inefficient use of your time. Only those that are applicable are relevant. One must not mechanically apply all estimators; rather, one should carefully select the most relevant estimators to use.

   c. Using point estimates ignores the fact that these values are estimated with uncertainty. It is better to pick a *range* of value within which the intrinsic value is believed to reside.

   d. Intrinsic value is unobservable; it can only be estimated.

3. Nothing will be left to the owner of Red Hill because the liquidation value of assets is less than debt outstanding. The resulting equity value is minus $394.1:

	Book Value ($000)	Percent Recoverable	Liquidation Value
Cash	$ 123.8	100	$ 123.8
Receivables	619.0	75	464.3
Inventory	309.5	55	170.2
PPE	879.0	60	527.4
Other assets	92.9	90	83.6
	$2,024.1		$1,369.2
Debt	1,763.3		1,763.3
Equity	$4,114.7		$ (394.1)

[This spreadsheet can be found in the folder "Key Spreadsheets from the Workbook" located on the CD-ROM.]

4a. The current enterprise market value of Pellagia is $880.05 million:

Shares outstanding	135.00
Price per share	$ 5.63
Equity market value	$760.05
Debt market value	120.00
Enterprise market value	$880.05

[This spreadsheet can be found in the folder "Key Spreadsheets from the Workbook" located on the CD-ROM.]

4b. Based on simple averages of the comparable firms' multiples (17.44 P/E and 1.09 P/S), the equity value using price-earnings is $662.7 million, and the enterprise value using price-sales is $690.4 million.

5a. The proper discount rate for free cash flows is the weighted average cost of capital (WACC), not the cost of equity.

5b. The proper discount rate for cash flows to equity holders is the cost of equity.

6. Calculating Tel-Talk's cost of equity:

$$\begin{aligned} K_e \text{ using CAPM} &= R_f + \text{Beta} \times \text{Market risk premium} \\ &= 5.63\% + 1.10 \times 5.9\% \\ &= 12.12\% \end{aligned}$$

$$\begin{aligned} K_e \text{ using the dividend growth model} &= \$2.31/\$46.25 + 6.2\% \\ &= 5.0\% + 6.2\% \\ &= 11.2\% \end{aligned}$$

The two methods yield estimated costs of equity that differ by 92 basis points. This is a common problem in valuation. If both estimators are credible, one should triangulate toward an estimate from them. To triangulate means to critically evaluate the assumptions behind each method, and to weigh each method according to its relevance to the company under consideration. For instance, the dividend growth model assumes a constant growth rate in dividends and ignores risk. One must ask whether such assumptions are reflective of the reality of the company being valued.

7. The bookseller's current beta reflects its current capital structure; therefore, beta has to be unlevered first:

$$\begin{aligned} \beta_u &= \frac{\beta_L}{1 + \dfrac{(1-T)D}{E}} \\ &= \frac{.98}{1 + \dfrac{(1-.35).095}{.905}} \\ &= .92 \end{aligned}$$

Now the unlevered beta has to be relevered to reflect Trigeorgis' desired capital structure:

$$\beta_L = \beta_U\left[1+(1-t)\frac{D}{E}\right]$$

$$= .92\ [1 + (1 - 0.35) \times .30/.70]$$

$$= 1.18$$

In short, Trigeorgis' beta will rise from 0.98 to 1.18 if the firm increases its leverage as suggested.

8. Middlestates' free cash flows given in the problem need to be discounted at the cost of capital. In addition, terminal value has to be estimated.

   Terminal value comes out to $15,213, calculated as follows:

$$\text{Terminal value} = \frac{CF \times (1+g_{\infty})}{K - g_{\infty}}$$

$$= \frac{924 \times (1+3.0\%)}{9.28\% - 3.0\%}$$

$$= 15{,}213$$

Where g is calculated using the Fisher formula:

$$g^{\infty}_{\text{Nominal}} = \left[(1+g^{\infty}_{\text{Units}}) \times (1+g^{\infty}_{\text{Inflation}})\right] - 1$$

$$= [(1 + 1.5\%) \times (1 + 1.5\%)] - 1$$

$$= 3.0\%$$

The enterprise value, calculated by discounting the yearly free cash flows (given in the problem) and the terminal value ($15,213) at the cost of capital, comes out to $14,117. A valuable insight is that the terminal value makes up most of the enterprise value.

9.

	Year 1	Year 2	Year 3	Year 4	Year 5
EBIT	28.74	29.17	29.60	30.05	30.50
Taxes	9.77	9.92	10.07	10.22	10.37
NOPAT	18.97	19.25	19.54	19.83	20.13
Less: additions to net working capital	(5.75)	(5.83)	(5.92)	(6.01)	(6.10)
Less: capital expenditures	(28.74)	(29.17)	(80.30)	(62.20)	(30.50)
Plus: depreciation	52.68	53.47	54.27	55.09	55.91
Free cash flow	37.16	37.72	(12.41)	6.71	39.45
Terminal value					720.93
Total free cash flows	37.16	37.72	(12.41)	6.71	760.37
Discounted at WACC	34.38	32.28	(9.82)	4.91	514.91
Enterprise value	576.66				
Less debt	192.30				
Equity value	384.36				

(Continued)

	Year 1	Year 2	Year 3	Year 4	Year 5
Equity value per share	7.46				
Calculation of WACC:					
K_d	6.1%				
After-tax K_d	4.0%				
K_e	9.6%				
Market value of debt	192.30				
Market value of equity	540.75				
% debt	26.2%				
% equity	73.8%				
WACC	8.1%				

[This spreadsheet can be found in the folder "Key Spreadsheets from the Workbook" located on the CD-ROM.]

The equity value per share, according to this valuation, is $7.46.

10. The equity value of the bookseller is $1.865 billion or $24.88 per share.

Step 1: Unlever the beta:

.98(1+((1-.35) × (.095))/.905 = 0.92

Note: This step has already been performed in the answer to Problem 7.

Step 2: Compute the CAPM for unlevered K_e 10.50%

Step 3: Discount free cash flows at the unlevered cost of equity.

	1	2	3	4	5
EBIT	171.4	191.9	210.3	235.9	238.0
Plus: depreciation and amortization	83.5	95.3	96.2	103.0	112.0
Less: additions to net working capital	(32.7)	(37.3)	(17.7)	(41.6)	(39.7)
Less: capital expenditures	(159.2)	(141.2)	(90.7)	(100.0)	(120.0)
Subtotal	63.0	108.7	198.1	197.3	190.3
Terminal value					2,612.2
Free cash flows	62.99	108.73	198.11	197.35	2,802.49
Discounted at unlevered ke	57.00	89.04	146.82	132.35	1,700.77
Enterprise value, unlevered	$2,126.0				

Step 4: Evaluate financing effects.	
Total debt:	400.0
Interest rate:	6.0%
Annual interest expense	$ 24.0
Tax shield	$8.4
PV of perpetual debt tax shields	$ 140.0

Total enterprise value = Value of enterprise (unlevered) + Value of debt tax shields

= $2,126.0 + $140 = $2,265.98

Less debt	400.00
Equity value	$1,865.98
Equity value per share	$ 24.88

[This spreadsheet can be found in the folder "Key Spreadsheets from the Workbook" located on the CD-ROM.]

CHAPTER 10
Valuing Options

1a. To calculate the payoff, one needs to translate Mr. Jones' requirement into numerical cash flows. The minimum return of 30 percent means that he wants a payoff of at least \$104 [\$80 × (1 + 30%)]. Because he is willing to give up the excess returns over 50 percent, the maximum payoff for Mr. Jones will be \$120 [\$80 × (1 + 50%)]. Therefore, if the stock trades at between \$104 and \$120 at the end of two years, he will get an amount equivalent to whatever the stock price is.

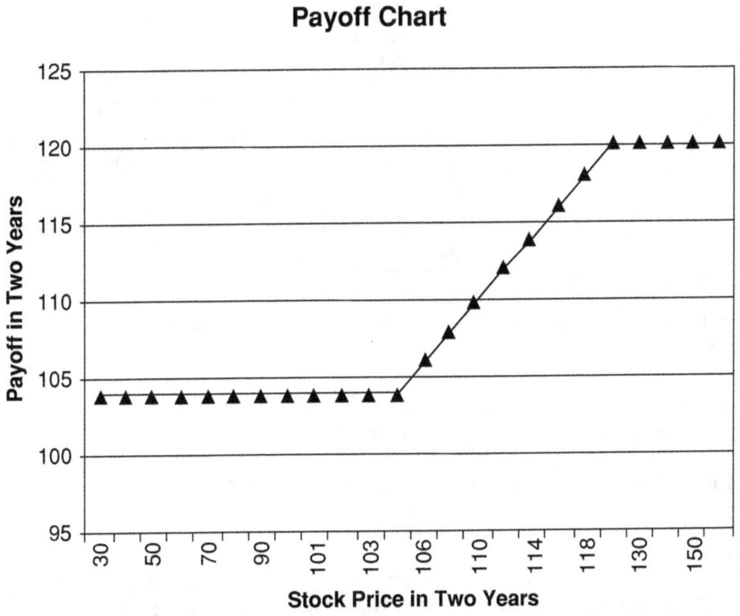

[This spreadsheet can be found in the folder "Key Spreadsheets from the Workbook" located on the CD-ROM.]

1b. From the payoff chart, one can recognize a "bull spread" as discussed in Chapter 10 of the main text. To hedge his position, Mr. Jones has to buy a put option to protect himself from downside risk if the stock trades below \$104. At the same time, he can sell a call option with a strike price of \$120, giving up some upside but also reducing the cost he incurs to protect himself from the downside risk (i.e., the cost of his put option). This payoff can therefore be decomposed into a combination of a short call option with an exercise price of $120 and a long put option with an exercise price of $104.

2. Black-Scholes is a common approach to valuing European options when the distribution of the value of the underlying asset is lognormal, in which case the binomial method is not appropriate. Here, the uncertainty of the value of the underlying asset—the total sales from the well—follows a normal distribution. Therefore, the Black-Scholes model is a useful approach in this example.

Step 1	Insert parameters into the model	
Stock price		$10,000,000
* The expected value of the well.		
Exercise price		$8,000,000
* The cost to exercise the option.		
Risk-free rate		7%
Volatility		40%
Time (years)		5
Step 2	Calculate the option value using template.	
Call value		$5,365,623

Black-Scholes ***European: No Dividend***	
Call value	$5,365,623
Call delta (hedge ratio)	0.862
Call elasticity	1.606
Using put-call parity	
Put value	$1,003,127
Delta	–0.138
Elasticity	–1.379
S underlying asset price	$10,000,000
X exercise price	$8,000,000
rf risk-free rate	7%
sd volatility	40%
t years to expiration	5
Cumulative Standard Normal Function	
d1 from Black-Scholes	1.088
N(d1)	0.862
d2 from Black-Scholes	0.194
N(d2)	0.577

[This spreadsheet can be found in the folder "Key Spreadsheets from the Workbook" located on the CD-ROM.]

The right to drill is a call option that has an expected value of $10 million (the underlying asset price). The value of the option is $5,365,623.

3a. Draw the tree and calculate the payoff of options at the expiration.

	Time: Now		Time: One Year Later	Probability	Call Option Payoff Ex. Price: $100	Put Option Payoff Ex. Price: $100
		Up 20%	$120.00	50%	$20.00	$–
Stock price	$100.00					
		Down 15%	$85.00	50%	$–	$15.00

3b. Then, use the Goal Seek feature in Excel to find the appropriate risk-free rate that makes C – P – [S – Ex × exp(–rt)] equal to zero. In this case, the implied risk-free rate is 2.47 percent.

Expected call option payoff at expiration	\$ 10.00
Expected put option value at expiration	\$ 7.50
Stock price	\$100.00
Exercise price	\$100.00
Call value	\$ 9.76
Put value	\$ 7.32
$C - P$	\$ 2.44
$S - \text{Ex} \times \exp(-rt)$	\$ 2.44
$C - P - [S - \text{Ex} \times \exp(-rt)]$	\$ (0.00)
Risk-free rate	2.47%

[This spreadsheet can be found in the folder "Key Spreadsheets from the Workbook" located on the CD-ROM.]

4. The way to find an arbitrage opportunity is to identify a violation of put-call parity. The simple way to do this is to estimate the value of the put option using the three other components of put-call parity. If the estimated price is the same as the quoted price, then there is no arbitrage opportunity.

   Using put-call parity, the value of the put option in this case can be calculated as:

$$P = C + \text{Ex} \times \exp(-r \times t) \times S$$
$$? = 0.50 + \$55 \times \exp(\times 8\% \text{ x } 1/12) \times \$50$$
$$? = \$5.13$$

   This indicates that the put option (quoted at \$6.00) is overvalued. By selling one put option and shorting one stock, you can get \$56.00 cash. Use this money to buy one call option (\$0.50) and put the rest (\$55.50) in Treasury bills to earn the risk-free rate of return, and you will lock in a return of \$0.87 in one month without any cost and risk.

Payoff Diagram

Decomposed position
One short put option
One short stock
One long call option
One long Treasury bill

Stock Price in One Month	Payoff of Short Put	Payoff of Short Stock	Payoff of Long Call	Payoff of T-bills	Net Payoff
\$35.00	\$(20.00)	\$(35.00)	\$ —	55.87124	\$0.87
\$40.00	\$(15.00)	\$(40.00)	\$ —	55.87124	\$0.87
\$45.00	\$(10.00)	\$(45.00)	\$ —	55.87124	\$0.87
\$50.00	\$ (5.00)	\$(50.00)	\$ —	55.87124	\$0.87
\$55.00	\$ —	\$(55.00)	\$ —	55.87124	\$0.87
\$60.00	\$ —	\$(60.00)	\$ 5.00	55.87124	\$0.87
\$65.00	\$ —	\$(65.00)	\$10.00	55.87124	\$0.87
\$70.00	\$ —	\$(70.00)	\$15.00	55.87124	\$0.87
\$75.00	\$ —	\$(75.00)	\$20.00	55.87124	\$0.87
\$80.00	\$ —	\$(80.00)	\$25.00	55.87124	\$0.87
\$85.00	\$ —	\$(85.00)	\$30.00	55.87124	\$0.87

[This spreadsheet can be found in the folder "Key Spreadsheets from the Workbook" located on the CD-ROM.]

Under parity, you should get the same payoff no matter whether the price of the underlying asset rises or falls. You can demonstrate this with a table of payoff results as shown.

5a. When a call option is deep in the money, with little chance of the stock moving back below the strike price before expiration, the option might be exercised early. This generally occurs where the dividend the investor would receive on the underlying stock, if he were to exercise the option, is greater than the interest expense incurred in buying the shares ahead of the expiration date. Generally this exercising of the call option occurs only in the period right before the ex-dividend date.

5b. Let's take a non-dividend-paying stock as an example. In this case, call option values for both American and European options will be the same because it would never be optimal to exercise the American option early. But in the case of put options, an American put option might be exercised early if it is deep in the money because of a put option's insurance purpose. Therefore, an American put option has greater value than a European put option with the same terms. Putting these two values in the put-call parity equation, one will find that one side of the equation changes in value while the other side doesn't. Therefore, put-call parity will not hold.

6. Drivers of option values:

Decrease In	Call Option Value Will	Put Option Value Will
Underlying asset price	Decrease	Increase
Exercise price	Increase	Decrease
Time to expiration	Decrease	Decrease
Risk (volatility)	Decrease	Decrease
Dividend yield	Increase	Decrease
Risk-free rate	Decrease	Increase

7. The beta of an option can be calculated by using the same regression method used for stocks. As with stocks, the beta of an option is a measure of movement relative to the market—but it is not the same as volatility (which is the standard deviation of returns). Generally speaking, the beta of an option is much greater than that of the corresponding underlying stock because the option offers a much greater return for the same market movement—this is a more levered return, is riskier, and will have a higher beta than the underlying stock.

8. The option values can be calculated using the Black-Scholes equation. The example illustrates the calculation for the call option in problem 8a using "Option Valuation.xls."

Step 1 Insert parameters into the model

Stock price	$80.00
Exercise price	$90.00
Risk-free rate	9%
Volatility	25%
Time (years)	1
Call value	$6.99

Black-Scholes ***European: No Dividend***	
Call value	$6.99
Call delta (hedge ratio)	0.506
Call elasticity	5.783
Using put-call parity	
Put value	$9.25
Delta	–0.494
Elasticity	–4.278
S underlying asset price	$80.00
X exercise price	$90.00
rf risk-free rate	9%
sd volatility	25%
t years to expiration	1
Cumulative Standard Normal Function	
d1 from Black-Scholes	0.014
N(d1)	0.506
d2 from Black-Scholes	–0.236
N(d2)	0.407

[This spreadsheet can be found in the folder "Key Spreadsheets from the Workbook" located on the CD-ROM.]

a. $6.99.

b. $3.02.

c. $16.20, which is made up of the call option value of $11.54 and the put option value of $4.66. This kind of portfolio can be used to capture the returns from an increase in volatility of the stock. If the stock swings more than $16.20 (the likely price of the position) in either direction in the next year, the holder of this portfolio will earn a profit.

d. $5.59 for call, $3.76 for put, $15.26 total.

9. First, calculate the payoff from senior and junior debt for a range of different asset market values. Then, graph the payoffs:

Book value of assets	$10,000,000.00	New Debt	$5,000,000.00
Market value of equity	$30,000,000.00		
Book value of debt	$10,000,000.00		
Market value of asset	$40,000,000.00		

Asset Value (in Millions)	Senior Debt Payoff	Junior Debt Payoff
$ —	$ —	$ —
$ 2.50	$ 2.50	$ —
$ 5.00	$ 5.00	$ —
$ 7.50	$ 7.50	$ —

(Continued)

Asset Value (in Millions)	Senior Debt Payoff	Junior Debt Payoff
$10.00	$10.00	$ —
$12.50	$10.00	$2.50
$15.00	$10.00	$5.00
$17.50	$10.00	$5.00
$20.00	$10.00	$5.00
$22.50	$10.00	$5.00
$25.00	$10.00	$5.00
$27.50	$10.00	$5.00
$30.00	$10.00	$5.00
$32.50	$10.00	$5.00
$35.00	$10.00	$5.00
$37.50	$10.00	$5.00
$40.00	$10.00	$5.00

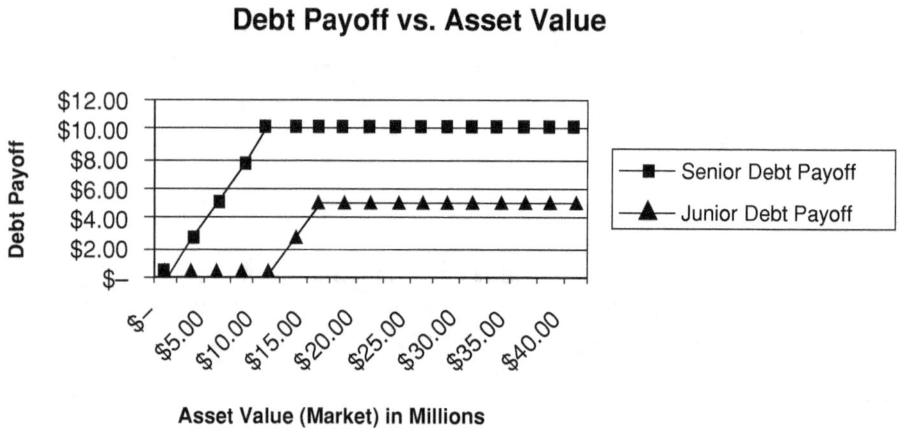

[These spreadsheets can be found in the folder "Key Spreadsheets from the Workbook" located on the CD-ROM.]

From the graph, it is clear that a positive payoff on junior debt begins when the asset value exceeds the obligation to senior creditors, and that the junior debt payoff behaves like a bond when asset value exceeds the combined obligations to senior and subordinated creditors. Note that the sloping portions of the senior and junior debt functions in the graph suggest that, over some range, the creditors will feel like equity holders. When the asset value drops below $15 million, junior debt creditors will have a payoff similar to a short put option—

this short put estimates the default risk discount for the debt. Therefore, when Mr. Brian is considering this loan, he needs to price this option into the terms of the loan. One way to do so is to find the quoted price for a put option with an exercise price for total assets at $15 million and add that into the yield. In addition, Mr. Brian's risk level will affect his decision. Even if this loan offers a higher return because of the extra discount caused by the embedded put option, it also brings higher risk.

CHAPTER 11

Valuing Synergies

1. Preferred discount rates:
   a. Cost-saving synergies are typically considered to be fairly predictable, with a level of risk about as variable as EBIT; therefore, K_d could be used as the discount rate.
   b. The revenue synergies are speculative. Other mergers of content providers and channels of distribution (such as AOL/Time-Warner and Sony/Columbia) that were premised on revenue synergies failed to deliver them. Even K_e may not be high enough to capture the risk. A venture capitalist's required rate of return may be appropriate.
   c. Again, cost synergies are considered to be fairly predictable and might be discounted at K_d; revenue synergies are less certain, so a higher discount rate such as the cost of equity may be more appropriate.

2.	Year 0	Year 1	Year 2	Year 3	Year 4	Year 5
Revenues		297.0	308.9	321.2	334.1	347.4
Cost savings		5.9	6.2	6.4	6.7	6.9
Cost savings after tax		3.9	4.0	4.2	4.3	4.5
Initial investment	(50.0)					
Terminal value						187.9
Free cash flows	(50.0)	3.9	4.0	4.2	4.3	192.4
Net present value	**$98.1**					

3. The present value of after-tax synergies is $8.2 billion:[1]

	1999F	2000F	2001F	2002F	2003F
Revenue enhancements	3,489.6	3,749.9	4,014.8	4,278.5	4,559.8
Operating income from revenue enhancements	425.8	457.5	489.8	522.0	556.3
Cost savings	400.0	412.0	424.4	437.1	450.2
Total incremental operating income	825.8	869.5	914.2	959.1	1,006.5
Taxes	289.0	304.3	320.0	335.7	352.3
After-tax incremental income	536.7	565.2	594.2	623.4	654.3
Terminal cash flow					9,626.8
Total incremental income	536.75	565.19	594.23	623.42	10,281.09
Present value	$8,211.06				

4. The entire gain is predicated upon a reduction in cost of capital that stems from lower-than-anticipated covariance in returns between the two firms. Specific questions to ask are:

   - Why is this covariance *unanticipated* by investors? The merging companies are both public and have a sizable analyst following. What makes you suppose that the analysts are not already aware of this?
   - Is there some *information asymmetry* between insiders and the public? Is there something you would like to tell me that I don't already know?
   - What is the basis for your estimated covariance reduction? Why is it likely to be –0.15, and not –0.20 or –0.10? Is there some rigor behind this estimate, or is it just a guess?
   - What prevents public shareholders from creating this value on their own by combining the two firms in a securities portfolio?
   - If public shareholders can create this value on their own, why should my firm pay your shareholders for the right to create this value?

5. By trial and error or the Excel "solver" function, back-solve to find that annual revenue enhancements should be at least $2.7 billion:

Year		0	1	2	3	4	5
Revenue enhancements, constant dollars			$2,702	$2,702	$2,702	$2,702	$2,702
Expected inflation rate			2%	2%	2%	2%	2%
Growth rate of FCF (nominal), in perpetuity	3%						
Discount rate	10%						
Ongoing investment revenue (year 1+)	2%						
Operating cost revenue	90%						
Revenue enhancements, current dollars			$2,756	$2,812	$2,868	$2,925	$2,984
Operating costs to support revenue enhancements			(2,481)	(2,530)	(2,581)	(2,633)	(2,685)
Tax expense (@ .38)			(105)	(107)	(109)	(111)	(113)
After-tax cost savings			171	174	178	181	185
Less: investment necessary to realize the added revenue		$ (400)	(55)	(56)	(57)	(59)	(60)
Subtotal		(400)	116	118	120	123	125
Terminal value							1,844
Free cash flow		$ (400)	$ 116	$ 118	$ 120	$ 123	$1,969
Net present value of cost savings		**$1,200**					

6. The present value of savings is $2.6 billion. See the following chart:

Year		0	1	2	3	4	5
Pretax cost savings, constant dollars			$ 63	$118	$183	$183	$ 183
Expected inflation rate	2.5%						
Discount rate	6.0%						
Tax rate	35.0%						
Pretax cost savings, current dollars			$ 63	$118	$183	$188	$ 192
Gain on sale of assets			$ 63	$ 48			
			$126	$166	$183	$188	$ 192
Tax expense			(44)	(58)	(64)	(66)	(67)
After-tax cost savings			19	60	119	122	125
Less: investment necessary to realize the savings		$ (480)					
Subtotal		(480)	19	60	119	122	125
Terminal value							3,660
Free cash flow		$ (480)	$ 19	$ 60	$119	$122	$3,785
Net present value of cost savings		**$2,616**					

7. An investment in Leonid could be regarded as an option on uncertain product development activities. This investment could be valued as a European option. Inserting the following inputs into the Black-Scholes option pricing model yields a value of $167.3 million.

Underlying asset value	$388
Strike price	$272
Term	.667 years
Volatility	90%
Risk-free rate	4.5%

8. No, Leonid is not worth $270 million to Sirius. The expected value of cash flows from existing operations is $88.9 million. Adding to that the value of the contingent synergies, $167.3 million, totals only $256.2 million, less than the asking price.

	Year 1	Year 2	Year 3	Year 4	Year 5
Operating income	$ 6.38	$ 7.54	$ 8.14	$ 6.97	$ 7.32
Cost savings	8.00	8.41	9.05	9.99	11.30
	$ 14.38	$15.95	$17.19	$16.96	$ 18.62
Taxes	5.03	5.58	6.02	5.94	6.52
	$ 9.35	$10.36	$11.18	$11.02	$ 12.10
Capex	—	—	(20.00)	—	—
Depreciation	1.74	2.26	2.71	2.99	3.14

	Year 1	Year 2	Year 3	Year 4	Year 5
Change in net working capital	(2.32)	(3.02)	(3.62)	(3.98)	(4.18)
	$ 8.77	$ 9.61	$ (9.73)	$10.03	$ 11.06
Terminal value					119.30
	$ 8.77	$ 9.61	$(9.73)	$10.03	$130.36
Present value of cash flows	88.91				
Add value of contingent synergies	167.30				
Value of Leonid to Pritzker	$256.21				

NOTE

1. On announcement day, shares of both Citicorp and Travelers soared, adding roughly $30 billion to the combined market value of the two companies.

CHAPTER 12

Valuing the Firm across Borders

1. The problem here is a mismatch between the growth rate of cash flows (stated to be in real terms) and the discount rate (nominal). The rates and cash flows should be expressed in consistent terms, either real/real or nominal/nominal. In ideal settings the two approaches should yield the same NPV. But where depreciation expense is based on historical asset values, the two approaches will differ. Chapter 12 in the main text argues that the nominal/nominal approach gives a correct estimate of NPV where depreciation expense is based on historical book values.

   To complete the valuation, the cash flow forecast must be expressed in nominal terms to be consistent with the cost of capital. The sales growth rate must therefore be adjusted to reflect a nominal rate. Using the Fisher equation, the rate would be $[(1.05 \times 1.03) - 1] = 8.15$ percent, and the NPV would be 89,338.

		Year 1	Year 2	Year 3	Year 4	Year 5
Sales		68,776	74,381	80,443	86,999	94,090
Cost of goods sold		45,048	48,720	52,690	56,985	61,629
Gross profit		23,728	25,662	27,753	30,015	32,461
Operating expenses		16,850	18,223	19,709	21,315	23,052
EBIT		6,878	7,438	8,044	8,700	9,409
Taxes		2,201	2,380	2,574	2,784	3,011
After-tax EBIT		4,677	5,058	5,470	5,916	6,398
Change in net working capital		(344)	(372)	(402)	(435)	(470)
Subtotal		4,333	4,686	5,068	5,481	5,928
Perpetual growth rate	8.15%					
Terminal value						132,181
Free cash flows		4,333	4,686	5,068	5,481	138,108
Discount rate	13.0%					
Discounted cash flows		3,834	3,670	3,512	3,362	74,960
NPV	89,338					

[This spreadsheet can be found in the folder "Key Spreadsheets from the Workbook" located on the CD-ROM.]

2a. The one-year forward rate would be US\$1:PhP33.1. The solution is obtained from the no-arbitrage condition:

$$\$1 \times (1 + R_{\text{Dollar}}) = \$1 \times SPOT_{\frac{\text{Peso}}{\text{Dollar}}} \times (1 + R_{\text{Peso}}) \times \frac{1}{FWD_{\frac{\text{Peso}}{\text{Dollar}}}}$$

$$\text{One-year rate: } (1 + .0552) = \text{PhP}30.4 \times (1 + .15) \times 1/FWD_{\text{1-yr}}$$

$$FWD_{\text{1-yr}} = \text{PhP}33.1$$

(The actual rate one year later was US\$1:PhP43.56—a 32 percent difference from the rate projected. In fact, the Asian crisis broke out in September 1997 and set off rounds of devaluations across Southeast Asia.)

2b. One-year forward rate:

$$FWD_{\frac{\text{Peso}}{\text{Dollar}}} = SPOT_{\frac{\text{Peso}}{\text{Dollar}}} \left[\frac{(1 + Inf_{\text{Peso}})^n}{(1 + Inf_{\text{Dollar}})^n} \right]$$
$$= \text{PhP}30.4 \times (1.08/1.025)$$
$$= \text{PhP}32.0 \text{ one year from now}$$

2c. The modest difference between the two estimates of forward exchange rates is due to the large difference in the implied real rates of return in the two countries. The equation implicitly assumes that the two rates are equal. However, the real rates of return implied when one works backward using the Fisher equation are 2.9 percent for the United States and 6.5 percent for the Philippines; hence the nonequivalency of results. It is not unusual for developing countries to offer higher real rates of return than developed countries—it is by this means that capital is attracted from developed to developing countries.

3. This is an illustration of the equivalence of the nominal/nominal and real/real approaches:

	Year 1	Year 2	Year 3	Year 4	Year 5
a. Without inflation, at nominal rate					
Depreciation	50	50	50	50	50
Depreciation tax shield	20	20	20	20	20
NPV of depreciation tax shields	\$79.85				
b. With inflation, at nominal rate					
Depreciation	51.5	53.0	54.6	56.3	58.0
Depreciation tax shield	20.6	21.2	21.9	22.5	23.2
NPV of depreciation tax shields	\$86.94				
c. Without inflation, at real estate					
Depreciation	50	50	50	50	50
Depreciation tax shield	20	20	20	20	20
NPV of depreciation tax shields	\$86.94				

[This spreadsheet can be found in the folder "Key Spreadsheets from the Workbook" located on the CD-ROM.]

Note: The nominal discount rates in both (a) and (b) were calculated using the Fisher equation: $(1.03 \times 1.0485) - 1 = 8.0$ percent.

Notice that the answers to (b) and (c) are the same. In effect, when one discounts depreciation tax shields at the real rate, it is as if the historical cost basis of depreciation was actually allowed to inflate. This is why we say that the real/real approach of discounting cash flows ignores the distortion of using historical cost assets as the basis of depreciation.

4.

(U.S.$, in Millions)		2003	2004	2005	2006	2007	2008
Exchange rate (reals per dollar)	R$3.54	3.75	3.97	4.20	4.45	4.71	4.98
Free cash flows		$402	$502	$637	$709	$803	$1,650
Terminal value						$21,940	
Cash flows including terminal value		$402	$502	$637	$709	$22,743	
Present value in U.S. dollars	$17,677						

[This spreadsheet can be found in the folder "Key Spreadsheets from the Workbook" located on the CD-ROM.]

First, forecast forward exchange rates using the given inflation rates. Then, use the forecasted forward rates to convert the Brazilian cash flows into U.S. dollar cash flows. To come up with the same values between the approaches, the dollar flows must be discounted at the nominal discount rate in U.S. dollars, which is equal to 7.52 percent, calculated as [(1 + 5%) × (1 + 2.4%) – 1]. The key underlying assumptions are that inflation is the only differing variable between the U.S. and Brazilian nominal discount rates, and that the real discount rate in Brazilian reals is the same as that in U.S. dollars. Inflation is already reflected in the exchange rate and in the U.S. dollar cash flows; therefore it is necessary only to discount the U.S. dollar cash flows using the real rate of return. These assumptions are consistent with interest rate parity.

5. Based on the data provided, one could use the adjusted CAPM to estimate K_e:

$$k_e = R_f^{US} + \pi + (\beta_i^{Foreign} \cdot \beta_{Foreign}^{US}) \cdot (R_m^{US} - R_f^{US})$$

$[R_f$(US) + Country credit spread] = R_f(foreign country)	7.25%
Beta of target versus foreign country stock index	0.97
Beta of foreign country stock index versus U.S. index	1.28
Market risk premium, U.S.	6.00%
k_e	**14.7%**

[This spreadsheet can be found in the folder "Key Spreadsheets from the Workbook" located on the CD-ROM.]

6a. The cost of equity of Singapore Airlines is estimated to be 10.4 percent, based on the following calculations:

Singapore Airlines	
R_f	4.5%
$R_m - R_f$	5.8%
Beta	1.02
K_e	10.4%

6b. The costs of equity of Southwest Airlines and American Airlines are estimated to be 9.8 percent and 13.7 percent respectively based on the following calculations:

Southwest Airlines	
R_f	3.8%
$R_m - R_f$	5.6%
Beta	1.07
K_e	9.8%
American Airlines	
R_f	3.8%
$R_m - R_f$	5.6%
Beta	1.77
K_e	13.7%

[These spreadsheets can be found in the folder "Key Spreadsheets from the Workbook" located on the CD-ROM.]

6c. In general, the costs of equity between Singapore Airlines and the two U.S. airlines are not comparable because the numbers are denominated in different currencies, and their betas are against different indexes. Also, the equity market risk premiums are slightly different. In short, this is an apples-versus-oranges comparison.

7. Calculating U.S. dollar cost of equity:

a. The globally diversified nature of the investment firm's holdings would argue for the use of the international CAPM (ICAPM), where the beta of the firm is measured against a global index, and the risk premium used is a world risk premium as opposed to a country risk premium:

$$k_e = R_f + \beta_i^w \times (R_m^w - R_f)$$

b. Using a CAPM estimate based on a country equity market risk premium might be reasonable if the country is a major component of the global equity market portfolio (as is the United States) and one believes that the global and country equity market risk premiums are similar (as is the case between the United States and Canada). A U.S.-based CAPM could be used if there are comparable U.S. companies that are actively traded on which to base an estimate of beta. Otherwise, given the integration of the United States and Canada, one could estimate a cost of equity from CAPM using Canadian data, or the ICAPM, with betas of comparable companies (making adjustments, where necessary for differences in inflation).

8a. 7.18 percent.

8b. 9.84 percent.

8c. Comparing the results between (a) and (b), the K_e using the adjusted CAPM method is higher because of the country credit spread and also because Telekom Malaysia has a much higher beta against its home market than against the world market, which itself is probably due to a low correlation between equity returns in Malaysia and the global market.

CHAPTER 13

Valuing the Highly Levered Firm, Assessing the Highly Levered Transaction

1. To calculate Deep-Sea Tuna's terminal value, you first need to calculate the residual cash flows. Assume that no more debt is repaid. The terminal value for 1992 is derived from the residual cash flow in 1993, capitalized at $K_e - g$. Assume the residual cash flow in 1993 is equal to the net income in 1992 multiplied by $(1 + g)$ (or \$12.2mm × 1.025). Other assumptions are $g = 2.5\%$; $K_e = 13.93\%$.

Solution 1: DCF Analysis Using Circularity Method

	1985	1986	1987	1988	1989	1990	1991	1992
Risk-free rate	12.00%	12.00%	12.00%	12.00%	12.00%	12.00%	12.00%	12.00%
Market premium (equity)	6.00%	6.00%	6.00%	6.00%	6.00%	6.00%	6.00%	6.00%
Book value of the debt ($ MM)	$59.0	$55.4	$49.8	$42.2	$34.7	$29.4	$18.9	$7.0
DCF value of equity ($ MM)	$32.7	$38.6	$45.3	$52.9	$61.6	$71.6	$82.9	$95.8
D/E (market)	180.30%	143.57%	109.91%	79.72%	56.29%	41.06%	22.81%	7.33%
Unlevered beta	0.57	0.57	0.57	0.57	0.57	0.57	0.57	0.57
Levered beta	1.10	1.00	0.90	0.81	0.74	0.69	0.64	0.59
Cost of equity	18.63%	17.97%	17.37%	16.84%	16.42%	16.15%	15.83%	15.55%
Cumulative cost of equity								**16.84%**
Discount factor	84.30%	71.46%	60.88%	52.10%	44.76%	38.53%	33.27%	28.79%
Residual cash flows	$ —	$ —	$ —	$ —	$ —	$ —	$ —	$ —
Terminal value							Note 1	$95.8
Net present value ($ MM)	**$27.6**						Perpetual growth =	2.50%

Note 1: Assumes no more debt is repaid. The terminal value for 1992 was calculated as the residual cash flow in 1993, capitalized at $K_e - g$. The residual cash flow in 1993 was assumed equal to the net income in 1989 times $(1 + g)$ (or 12.2 × 1.025).
Other assumptions: $g = 2.5\%$; $K_e = 13.93\%$.

Using the circularity method illustrated in Exhibit 13.4 of the main text, you can start with an (approximate) fixed equity value (this can be hard-coded in the cell) and then derive the debt-to-equity ratio.

With the unlevered beta of 0.57 (given), you can determine the levered beta (B_L) for the equity as well as the cost of equity.

$$B_L = B_U \times [1 + (1 - t) \times (\text{Debt}_{\text{Book}}/\text{Equity}_{\text{Market}})]$$

The resulting estimated levered beta varies from 1.10 in 1985 to 0.59 in 1992—this is due entirely to the changing mix of debt and equity over time. With estimates of the levered beta, it is now possible to estimate the cost of equity using the CAPM model.

The terminal value can be estimated using the cost of equity in the final year[1] (15.55 percent), the residual cash flow, and the perpetual growth rate (2.50 percent), based on the following equation:

$$\text{Terminal value} = \text{Equity cash flow}_{1992} \times (1 + g)/(k_e - g)$$

From this end point, you can iterate back to the present with circularity calculations to determine the various years' discount rates and annual equity values. Finally, you arrive at the net present value of the equity valuation equal to $27.59 million.

2. To determine what the deal is worth to a senior mezzanine investor, lay out the expected cash flows of the equity, principal, and interest for each year from 1985 to 2000 (as in the Solution 2 chart) and then determine the internal rate of return (IRR) from the total cash flows, which equals 26.67 percent.

Solution 2: Valuing the Senior Mezzanine Participation

Year	Equity	Principal	Interest	Total Cash Flow
1985	$ (1.00)	$ (7.00)		$(8.00)
1986	$ —	$ —	$1.12	$ 1.12
1987	$ —	$ —	$1.12	$ 1.12
1988	$ —	$ —	$1.12	$ 1.12
1989	$ —	$ —	$1.12	$ 1.12
1990	$ —	$ —	$1.12	$ 1.12
1991	$ —	$ —	$1.12	$ 1.12
1992	$19.16	$ —	$1.12	$20.28
1993	$ —	$ —	$1.12	$ 1.12
1994	$ —	$ —	$1.12	$ 1.12
1995	$ —	$ —	$1.12	$ 1.12
1996	$ —	$ 1.40	$1.12	$ 2.52
1997	$ —	$ 1.40	$0.90	$ 2.30
1998	$ —	$ 1.40	$0.67	$ 2.07
1999	$ —	$ 1.40	$0.45	$ 1.85
2000	$ —	$ 1.40	$0.22	$ 1.62
NPV of 20% equity:				**$ 4.52**
IRR				**26.67%**
Benchmark for evaluating IRR			Weight	
	K_e	16.84%	12.50%	
	i	16.00%	87.50%	
	Weighted average		**16.11%**	

Then determine a hurdle rate against which to compare this IRR by taking a weighted average of the geometric mean cost of equity, 16.84 percent (estimated across time from the equity costs found in the first part of the analysis) and the required return on the notes (assume this is 16 percent, for the purpose of this example), weighted according to their proportion in the strip (i.e., 1/8 for equity and 7/8 for notes. The hurdle rate is 16.11 percent. In comparison, the IRR on the strip is larger by about 10 percent.

3.

Solution 3: Valuing the Bank Participation

Year	Equity	Principal	Interest	Total Cash Flow
1985	$ (2.00)	$(37.00)		$(39.00)
1986		$ 0.57	$5.92	$ 6.49
1987		$ 3.62	$5.83	$ 9.45
1988		$ 5.10	$5.25	$ 10.35
1989		$ 5.01	$4.43	$ 9.44
1990		$ 0.30	$3.63	$ 3.94
1991		$ 10.47	$3.58	$ 14.06
1992	$38.33	$ 11.90	$1.91	$ 52.13
NPV of 40% equity:				**$ 9.03**
IRR				**22.93%**
Benchmark for evaluating IRR			Weight	
K_e		16.84%	5.13%	
i		16.00%	94.87%	
Weighted average			**16.04%**	

You can take the same approach as the one used in answer 2. The difference between hurdle rate of 16.04 percent and the IRR on the strip (22.93%) is about 7 percent.

4. The following chart summarizes both the investment and expected returns of each of the parties involved in this case:

Party	Investment ($ MM)		Return of Equity ($ MM)	IRR	Required Rate of Return
Management	Equity	$ 0.30	$38.30	12,675.0%	16.8%
Senior	Equity	$ 1.00	$19.16	1,816.0%	16.8%
subordinated	Debt	$ 7.00		16.0%	16.0%
notes investors	Total	$ 8.00		26.7%	16.1%
Bank	Equity	$ 2.00	$38.30	1,816.0%	16.8%
	Debt	$37.00		16.0%	16.0%
	Total	$39.00		22.9%	16.0%

Under the assumptions they set forth, the management team of Felicity will earn the highest rate of return on the buyout of Deep-Sea Tuna, which is consistent with the fact that they also bear the highest risk in this investment. The

IRR on the investment is astonishingly high. As argued in Chapter 13 of the main text, there is no straightforward quantitative benchmark against which to assess the adequacy of this IRR—the geometric mean of 16.8 percent is imperfect because the levered beta model assumes no default risk. However, on the basis of sheer size one might conclude that the management team is capturing most of the profit in this investment.

The investors in the senior subordinated (mezzanine) notes take on more risk than the bank does because their debt is junior to that of the bank: They have secondary claims on the repayment of debt. In order to compensate for this additional risk, these investors would receive an opportunity to purchase 20 percent of the equity in Deep-Sea Tuna. So the overall returns on their investment are higher than those for the bank's investment.

From the perspective of the bank, having a mezzanine investor creates a buffer of sorts; to these senior lenders, the mezzanine layers look like equity.

Overall, this case illustrates the different grades of investment based on risk levels; the higher the risks, the higher the returns. The senior subordinated note seems to be the "plug" security in the transaction, designed to supply the financing and meet investors' required returns without overburdening the firm financially.

[The spreadsheets in this chapter can be found in the folder "Key Spreadsheets from the Workbook" located on the CD-ROM.]

NOTE

1. By implication, using the final year's cost of equity to estimate the terminal value suggests no further changes in the mix of debt and equity for the firm. The analyst should test this assumption for reasonableness. But in general, it is not an unreasonable assumption: The firm is unlikely to reduce its debt to zero.

CHAPTER 14

Real Options and Their Impact on M&A

1. Real options may appear in the field of M&A in strategic planning, deal design, and postmerger integration:
   - In strategy, real options appear in decisions about flexibility versus irreversibility of actions; insurance; learning and competencies; and corporate strategic planning. Possible applications of real options in strategy might be buying a minority interest before completing the acquisition; buying a built-up company versus building up the same assets yourself; choosing to be a second mover; acquiring the rights to exploit an uncertain resource; and searching for acquisition targets.
   - Real options often appear in deal design through the exchange offer, breakup terms, liquidity and control features, contingent payment schemes, transaction risk management, and takeover tactics.
   - In postmerger integration, real options may appear in the organizational design and operational architecture of the firm, the structuring of contracts for human resources, and selection among competing capabilities.
2. There are four possible approaches for valuing options:
   1. Value the real option in the framework of an existing equation.
   2. Value the option using the framework of a binomial lattice.
   3. Value the option in a decision tree framework.
   4. Value the option using simulation analysis.

   The Black-Scholes option pricing model is the simplest to use. It can be helpful when the parameters are easy to define and the assumptions for underlying asset returns are met. The binomial lattice is more flexible than the Black-Scholes equation; therefore it can be best used for simplified staging problems. But it is tedious to use it to model many periods, and use of the binomial distribution may result in oversimplification. The decision tree method is the most commonly used model for real option valuation because of its flexibility and transparency. Its drawbacks are that it is difficult to use for more complex problems, and it entails estimating probabilities accurately. Finally, Monte Carlo simulation is the most advanced and comprehensive method. It not only values options, but it also provides a complete risk profile. Similar to the decision tree and binomial methods, the difficulty of assessing the appropriate distribution function to use makes it a subjective method, too.

3. Among the four choices, the court upgrade and flexible lighting and sound system give you options. They have extra value compared to the seating upgrade and the multimedia center because they give you the *flexibility* to change the use of the stadium. The luxury rooms and the multimedia center projects do not provide the same flexibility.

4.

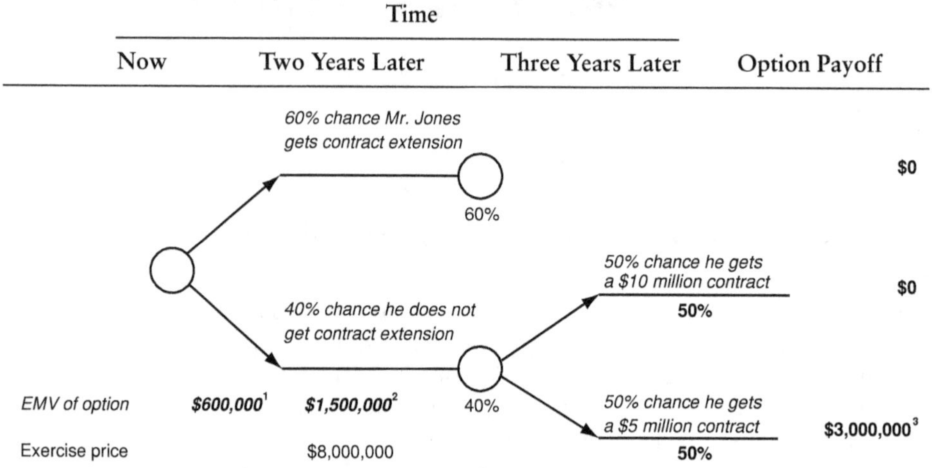

1. $600,000 = 60% × $0 + 40% × $1,500,000.
2. $1,500,000 = 50% × $0 + 50% × $3,000,000. $1.5 million is the expected monetary value of this option after two years.
3. $3,000,000 = $8,000,000 – $5,000,000. If Mr. Jones manages to get only the $5 million contract, he would want to exercise his extension option with the current team to earn a salary of $8 million. Therefore, the payoff of the option is the difference between the $5 million contract he could get and the $8 million guaranteed extension contract.

Folding back the tree to the present, we come up with a value of $600,000 for the extension option.

5.

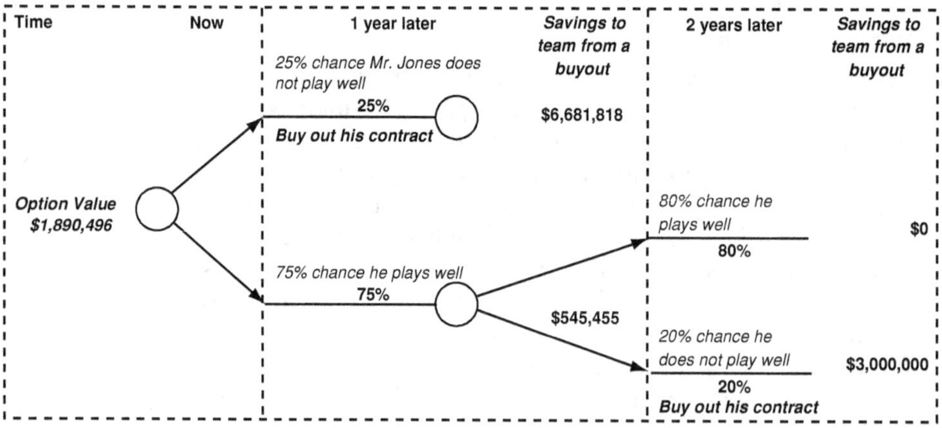

(Continued)

The payoff of $3,000,000 at the end of two years is calculated based on the fact that the team will buy his contract out at $6 million instead of paying him $9 million. The savings of $6,681,818 after the first year is calculated by following the same logic and accounting for the time value of money.

$6,681,818 = $9,000,000/(1 + 10%) + $8,500,000 – $10,000,000
$545,455 = (80% × $0 + 20% × $3,000,000)/(1 + 10%)
$1,890,496 = (25% × $6,681,818 + 75% × $545,455)/(1 + 10%)

Payment schedule: Discount rate 10%

Year	Salary		
1	$7,500,000	Exercise price in year 1	$10,000,000
2	$8,500,000	Exercise price in year 2	$ 6,000,000
3	$9,000,000		

Based on the preceding calculation, the total present value of the buyout option = $1,890,496.

6.

Step 1 ***Insert parameters***

Underlying asset value	**$8,000,000**
(The current value of the patent)	
Exercise price	**$10,000,000**
(The purchase price for the patent after three years.)	
Risk-free rate	**7.5%**
Volatility	**25.0%**
Time (years)	**3**
Resulting call value	**$1,377,415**

Black-Scholes
European: No Dividend

Call value	**$ 1,377,415**
Call delta (hedge ratio)	0.587373404
Call elasticity	3.411454722
Using put-call parity	
Put value	$ 1,362,577
Delta	–0.412626596
Elasticity	–2.422625293
S underlying asset price	$ 8,000,000
X exercise price	$10,000,000
rf risk-free rate	7.5%
sd volatility	25.0%
t years to expiration	3
Cumulative Standard Normal Function	
d1 from Black-Scholes	0.220793636
N(d1)	0.587373404
d2 from Black-Scholes	–0.212219066
N(d2)	0.415968097

7.

Step 1 ***Grow the tree***

Parameters needed:

Volatility (annualized)	20%	
Length of period (year)	1	
Up percentage (u)	1.221402758	
Down percentage (d)	0.818730753	

Now	Year 1	Year 2	Year 3	Year 4	Year 5
					$ 54,365,637
				$44,510,819	
			$ 36,442,376		**$ 36,442,376**
	A	$ 29,836,494		$29,836,494	
	$24,428,055		**$ 24,428,055**		**$ 24,428,055**
$ 20,000,000		$ 20,000,000		$20,000,000	
	$16,374,615		$16,374,615		$16,374,615
		$ 13,406,401		$13,406,401	
			$10,976,233		$10,976,233
				$ 8,986,579	
					$7,357,589

A: $24,428,055 = $20,000,000 × U (1.221)

The binomial approach assumes that each year, the value of the firm will move up by *u* (*u*= e^(1 × 20%) = 1.221) or down by *d* (*d* = e^(–1 × 20%) = 1/*u* = 0.818). This means that at the end of the first year, the value of the joint venture will be either $24,428,055 (*u* × $20,000,000) or $16,374,615 (*d* × $20,000,000)

Step 2 ***Assess the probabilities of an up or down movement***

— These will be used in step 5 to fold back the tree.

Pu = [(1 + Rf)–d)]/(u–d) 0.574336542— 57.43% chance of moving up

Pd = [u–(1 + Rf)]/(u–d) 0.425663458— 42.57% chance of moving down

Rf = 5%

Step 3 ***Assess the states in which the options will be exercised***

In the table above, the shaded numbers indicate when the option will be exercised. In these cases, the value of the joint venture is greater than the exercise price — $20,000,000 for 100% ownership or $5,000,000 for 25% of the joint venture.

Step 4 ***Estimate the payoffs associated with these end-states.***

Exercise price $20,000,000 for 100% 25% 25%

Now	Year 1	Year 2	Year 3	Year 4	**Year 5**
					$8,591,409
				—	
			$4,110,594		**$4,110,594**
		—		—	
	—		**$1,107,014**		**$1,107,014**
		—		—	
—					
	—		—		—
		—		—	
			—		—
				—	
			—		—

Step 5 ***Calculate the present expected value of future payoffs.***

Now	Year 1	Year 2	Year 3	Year 4	Year 5
			B		
					$8,591,409
				$6,365,800	
			$8,686,041		**$4,110,594**
		$5,897,539		**$2,697,219**	
	$3,907,369		**$2,827,833**		**$1,107,014**
$2,539,822		**$1,681,060**		**$605,522**	
	$992,963		**$331,213**		—
		$181,169		—	
			—		—
				—	
					—

$8,686,041 = ($6,365,800 × Pu + $2,697,219 × Pd)/(1 + rf) + $4,110,594

(B): Taking the example of $8,686,041, one would take the expected value of the *Pu* × *$6,365,800* + *Pd* × *$2,697,219*, or (.5743 × $6,365,800) + (0.4257 × $2,697,219) to yield $4,804,219—discounting this by one year at the risk-free rate, 0.05 yields $3,814,374, then add $4,110,594 from Step 4 for a total option payoff in year 3 of $8,686,041. This process is repeated for each cell to arrive at a value of $2,539,822 for the option portfolio.

8.

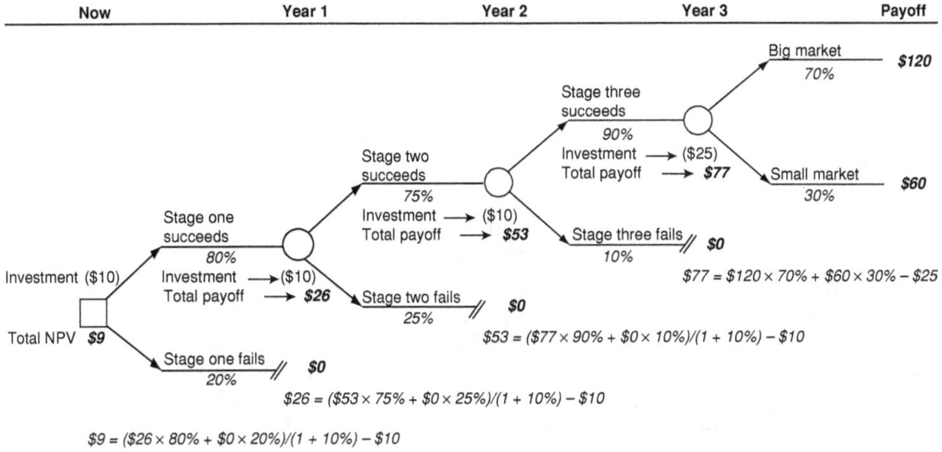

Percentage of venture	60%
Discount rate	10%
Big market	$200
Small market	$100

(All Numbers in Millions)

In the decision tree, the terminal payoffs are calculated by multiplying 60 percent by the forecasted profits because ABC is purchasing 60 percent of XYZ. Then, the payoffs are discounted according to the corresponding time period to obtain the expected monetary value (EMV). The investment for each period is deducted from EMV to obtain the net present value for each period.

9a. To arrive at the conclusion about whether to invest in this project, one needs to calculate the net present value. First, the cash flow model is built as shown. Then, the uncertainty distribution about the revenues is specified: a normal distribution with a mean of $50 million and a standard deviation of $25 million. (Revenues have a minimum value of zero as sales cannot be negative.) NPV is calculated by discounting all cash flows by 25 percent, and the probability distribution of NPV is simulated by running the model 5,000 times. The results reveal a mean NPV of $10.58 million for company ABC.

			Now	Year 1	Year 2	Year 3
Capital expenditure	10 in millions					
Period	3 years	Capex	−10.0			
Mean of year 1 revenue	50 in millions	Revenues		39.5	41.4	43.5
Standard deviation of revenue	25 in millions	Profit		7.9	8.3	8.7
Revenue growth for years 2 and 3	5%	Total cash flows	−10.0	7.9	8.3	8.7
Profit margin	20%	NPV of project		6.1		
Discount rate	25%					

Statistics	Value
Trials	5,000
Mean	$10.58
Median	$10.21
Mode	—
Standard deviation	$ 9.63
Variance	$92.67
Skewness	0.25
Kurtosis	2.74
Coefficient of variability	0.91
Range minimum	($9.98)
Range maximum	$44.70
Range width	$54.68
Mean standard error	$ 0.14

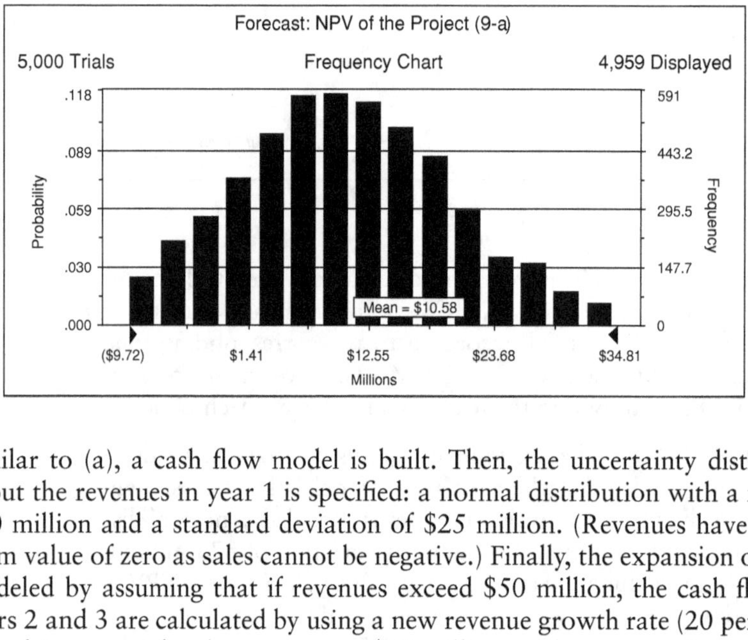

9b. Similar to (a), a cash flow model is built. Then, the uncertainty distribution about the revenues in year 1 is specified: a normal distribution with a mean of $50 million and a standard deviation of $25 million. (Revenues have a minimum value of zero as sales cannot be negative.) Finally, the expansion option is modeled by assuming that if revenues exceed $50 million, the cash flows for years 2 and 3 are calculated by using a new revenue growth rate (20 percent on top of 5 percent) for the excess over $50 million, and a new profit margin (21 perent). NPV is calculated by discounting all cash flows by 25 percent. Running the model 5,000 times, the simulation generates a mean NPV of $11.18 million for company ABC. Compared to the result in (a), it indicates a $0.50 million increase in the project NPV, the value of this expansion option.

			Now	Year 1	Year 2	Year 3
Capital expenditure	10 in millions					
Extra capital expenditure for expansion	1.5 in millions	Capex	−10.0	0.0		
Period	3 years	Revenues		26.9	28.3	29.7
Mean of year 1 revenue	50 in millions	Profit		5.4	5.7	5.9

			Now	Year 1	Year 2	Year 3
Standard deviation of revenue	25 in millions	Total cash flow	−10.0	5.4	5.7	5.9
Revenue growth for years 2 and 3	5%	NPV of project		1.0		
Extra revenue growth from expansion for years 2 and 3	20%					
Profit margin (without expansion)	20%					
Profit margin (with expansion)	21%					
Discount rate	25%					

Statistics	Value
Trials	5,000
Mean	$ 11.18
Median	$ 10.17
Mode	—
Standard deviation	$ 10.11
Variance	$102.16
Skewness	0.37
Kurtosis	2.90
Coefficient of variability	0.90
Range minimum	($ 9.99)
Range maximum	$ 49.11
Range width	$ 59.11
Mean standard error	$ 0.14

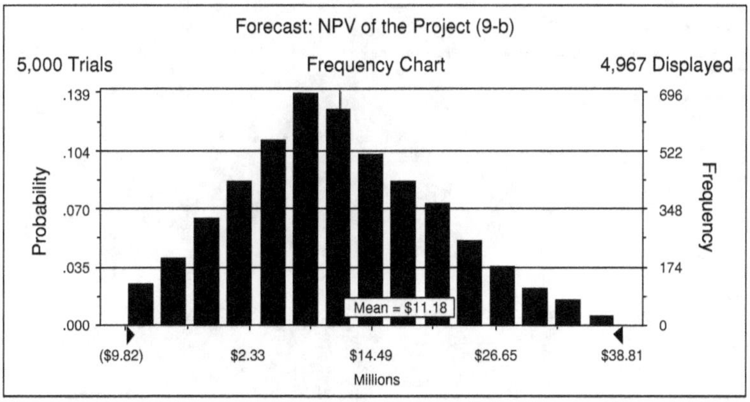

[All spreadsheets in this chapter can be found in the folder "Key Spreadsheets from the Workbook" located on the CD-ROM.]

CHAPTER 15

Valuing Liquidity and Control

1. Liquidity and control are rights, and as option theory shows, rights are valuable. You paid a premium or discount because of the presence or absence of these rights.

2. The following table gives the calculations based on the binomial option-pricing model. The inability to exit is like forgoing the value of a put option for the next three years. The calculation estimates the value of this put option to be $5.85 million, or 11.7 percent of the value of the company.

Step 1 Grow the tree

Parameters needed:		Now	Year 1	Year 2	Year 3
			(A)		$96.74
				$77.64	
Volatility (annualized)	22%		$62.30		$62.30
Length of period (year)	1	$50.00		$50.00	
			$40.13		**$40.13**
Up percentage (u)	1.2460767			$32.20	
Down percentage (d)	0.8025188				**$25.84**

(A) – $62.30 = $50 × U = $50 × 1.246

The binomial approach assumes that each year, the value of the firm will move up by *u* (*u* = e^(1 × 22%) = 1.246) or down by *d* (*d* = e^(–1 × 22%) = 1/*u* = 0.803). This means that at the end of the first year, the firm's value will be worth either $62.30 million (*u* × $50 milllion) or $40.13 (*d* × $50 million)

Step 2 Assess the probabilities of an up or down movement. (These probabilities will be used in step 5 to fold back the tree.)

Pu = [(1 + Rf) – d)]/(u – d)	51.29%	= chance of the firm value moving up
Pd = [u – (1 + Rf)]/(u – d)	48.71%	= chance of the firm value moving down
(Rf = 3%)		

Step 3 Assess the states in which the options will be exercised

In the above table, the shaded numbers indicate when the put option will be exercised. In these cases, the payoff is less than the exercise price of $50,000,000.

Step 4 Estimate the payoffs associated with these end-states.

Now	Year 1	Year 2	Year 3	
			—	
		—		
	—		—	
—		—		
	—		$9.87	($50 – $40.13)
		—		
			$24.16	($50 – $25.84)

Step 5 Calculate the present value of expected future payoffs.

Now	Year 1	Year 2	Year 3
			—
		—	
			—
	$2.21		
$5.85		$4.67	
	$10.05		$9.87
		$16.34	
	(B)		$24.16

(B) — $10.05 = ($4.67 × Pu + $16.34 × Pd)/(1 + Rf)

For instance, to arrive at (B), $10.05 million, one would take the expected value of (*Pu* × *$4.67* + *Pd* × *$16.34*), or (.513 × $4.67) + (0.487 × $16.34) to yield $10.35. Discounting this by one year at the risk-free rate, 3%, yields $10.05. This process is repeated for the other cells. Folding the expected values back to the present, we arrive at a value of $5.85 million for this put option.

Step 6 Calculate the liquidity discount.

Net value of the firm (Value of the firm – Put option value)	$44.15
Liquidity discount	11.7%

3. The solution is similar to problem 2, except that the binomial tree is grown out to five years instead of three years. Now the put option is worth $6.39 million or 12.8 percent of the base value of the firm. See the chart:

Step 1 Grow the tree

		Now	Year 1	Year 2	Year 3	Year 4
						$120.54
Parameters needed:		(A)			$96.74	
				$77.64		$77.64
Volatility (annualized)	22%		$62.30		$62.30	
Length of period (year)	1	$50.00		$50.00		$50.00
			$40.13		$40.13	
Up percentage (u)	1.2460767			$32.20		$32.20
Down percentage (d)	0.8025188				$25.84	
(A) — $62.30 = $50 × U = $50 × 1.246						$20.74

The binomial approach assumes that each year, the value of the firm will move up by *u* (*u* = e^(1 × 22%) = (1.246)or down by *d* (*d* = e^ (–1 × 22%) = 1/*u*= 0.803). This means that at the end of the first year, the firm's value will be worth either $62.30 million (*u* × $50 milllion) $40.13 (*d* × $50 million)

Step 2 Assess the probabilities of an up or down movement. (These probabilities will be used in step 5 to fold back the tree.)

Pu = [(1+Rf)-d)]/(u–d)	51.29%	= chance of the firm value moving up
Pd = [u–(1+Rf)]/(u–d)	48.71%	= chance of the firm value moving down
Rf = 3%		

Step 3 Assess the states in which the options will be exercised

In the above table, the shaded numbers indicate when the put option will be exercised. In these cases, the payoff is less than the exercise price of $50,000,000.

Step 4 Estimate the payoffs associated with these end-states.

Exercise price $50

Now	Year 1	Year 2	Year 3	Year 4	Year 5	
					—	
				—		
			—		—	
		—		—		
	—		—		—	
—		—		—		
	—		—		**$9.87**	($50 – $40.13)
		—		—		
			—		**$24.16**	($50 – $25.84)
				—		
					$33.36	($50 – $16.64)

Step 5 Calculate the present value of expected future payoffs.

	Now	Year 1	Year 2	Year 3	Year 4	Year 5
						—
					—	
				—		—
			$1.04		—	
		$3.29		***$2.21***		—
	$6.39		**$5.85**		***$4.67***	
		$10.04		***$10.05***		**$9.87**
			$15.07		***$16.34***	
				$21.29		**$24.16**
(B) — $10.04 = ($5.87 × Pu + $15.07 × Pd)/(1 + Rf)		*(B)*			***$27.80***	
						$33.36

For instance, to arrive at (B), $10.04 million, one would take the expected value of (*Pu* × *$5.85* + *Pd* × *$15.07),* or (.513 × $5.85) + (0.487 × $15.07) to yield $10.35. Discounting this by one year at the risk-free rate, 3%, yields $10.04. This process is repeated for the other cells. Folding the expected values back to the present, we arrive at a value of $6.39 million for this put option.

Step 6 Calculate the liquidity discount.

Net value of the firm (Value of the firm – Put option value)	$43.61
Liquidity discount	12.8%

Extending the term of illiquidity will result in a higher liquidity discount. The liquidity option becomes more valuable because of the longer term. However, although you will pay less now, the risk is also greater due to more uncertainty for a longer term.

4. The implied volatility can be found using Excel's Goal Seek function, but to do so, one must first know the value of the option:

Step 1 Determine the implied option values for both buyer and seller.

			Implied option value for each party:
DCF valution:	$10,000,000		
Buyer's bid price:	$8,500,000	***Buyer***	***$1,500,000***
Seller's ask price:	$9,000,000	***Seller***	***$1,000,000***

Step 2 Insert the parameters into the model and then use Goal Seek to calculate implied volatility. (The illustration below calculates the implied volatility from the point of view of the seller. To calculate the implied volatility from the buyer's viewpoint, simply replace the put value of the seller with that of the buyer.)

Stock price	$10,000,000
* DCF value of the company.	
Exercise price	$10,000,000
* The cost to exercise the option.	
Risk-free rate	7%
Put value	$1,000,000
Time (years)	1
Implied volatilities:	
Buyer's view:	47.6%
Seller's view:	34.2%

Black-Scholes ***European: No Dividend***	
Call value	$1,676,062
Call delta (hedge ratio)	0.646431209
Call elasticity	3.856845901
Using put-call parity	
Put value	$1,000,000
Delta	–0.353568791
Elasticity	–3.535687914
S underlying asset price	$10,000,000
X exercise price	$10,000,000
rf risk-free rate	7%
sd volatility	34.2%
t years to expiration	1
Cumulative Standard Normal Function	
d1 from Black-Scholes	0.375703313
N(d1)	0.646431209
d2 from Black-Scholes	0.033955554
N(d2)	0.51354376

The implied volatility from the buyer's valuation is greater than that for seller. As the results show, the volatility implied by the buyer's view is 47.6 percent and by the seller's view is 34.2 percent. Therefore, the buyer's assessment of the risk level of the company is higher than that of the seller. Thus, the value of the put option is greater to the buyer than to the seller.

[The spreadsheets for questions 1 to 4 can be found in the folder "Key Spreadsheets from the Workbook" located on the CD-ROM.]

5. Your options position can be decomposed into two options: a long call option expiring in five years and a short put option expiring in two years. Therefore, the value of your options is the difference between the call and put option values.

Valuation of Call		
Assumptions:		
Stock price	$	40
Exercise price	$	40
Risk-free rate		8%
Volatility		20%
Time (years)		5
Call value	**$**	**14.15**

(Continued)

Valuation of Put		
Assumptions:		
Stock price	$	40
Exercise price	$	40
Risk-free rate		6%
Volatility		20%
Time (years)		2
Put value	**$**	**2.36**
Long call	$	14.15
Short put	$	2.36
Net value of one share	$	11.79
Total value of options		$1,179,000.00

[This spreadsheet can be found in the folder "Key Spreadsheets from the Workbook" located on the CD-ROM.]

6a. The Shapley Values for the oceanic shareholders are given in the following table—this table assumes that the oceanic shareholders own 50 percent of the votes.

A

% Voting Control Shareholder 2	% Voting control shareholder 1: 5	10	15	20	25	30	35	40	45
45	0.18	0.20	0.22	0.24	0.28	0.32	0.38	0.44	0.50
40		0.32	0.35	0.38	0.41	0.44	0.48	0.50	0.44
35			0.42	0.44	0.47	0.49	0.50	0.48	0.38
30				0.48	0.49	0.50	0.49	0.44	0.32
25					0.50	0.49	0.47	0.41	0.28
20						0.48	0.44	0.38	0.24
15							0.42	0.35	0.22
10								0.32	0.20
5									0.18

Notice that the power index for oceanic shareholders is highest when the balance of shares is divided equally between the major shareholders; for example, each has 25 percent. Notice also that the increase or loss in power is not linear. Going from a 25–25 split between shareholders 1 and 2 to a 20–30 split results in a .02 decrease in power for the oceanic shareholders. However, going from a 20–30 split between shareholders 1 and 2, to a 15–35 split results in a greater decrease in power—.06—for the oceanic shareholders. In general, the more lopsided the balance between shareholders 1 and 2 becomes, the higher the rate at which the oceanic shareholders lose power.

6b. The following table assumes that the oceanic shareholders own only 10 percent of the votes.

B

% Voting Control Shareholder 2	% Voting control shareholder 1: 41	42	43	44	45	46	47	48	49
49	0.18	0.20	0.22	0.24	0.28	0.32	0.38	0.44	0.50
48		0.32	0.35	0.38	0.41	0.44	0.48	0.50	0.44
47			0.42	0.44	0.47	0.49	0.50	0.48	0.38
46				0.48	0.49	0.50	0.49	0.44	0.32
45					0.50	0.49	0.47	0.41	0.28
44						0.48	0.44	0.38	0.24
43							0.42	0.35	0.22
42								0.32	0.20
41									0.18

Notice that the power indexes for the oceanic shareholders in this scenario follow the same pattern as in problem 6a. This illustrates that voting power derives from *relative* distribution of votes rather than the absolute percentage held.

7.

			Percentage Return				Total Capital			
			Now	Year 1	Year 2	Year 3	Now	Year 1	Year 2	Year 3
Step 1	Grow the tree									
	Parameters needed:		(A)			**24.60%**				$174.37
					20.14%				$139.95	
	Volatility (annualized)	20%		**16.49%**		**16.49%**		$116.49		$146.83
	Length of period (year)	1	13.50%		13.50%		$100.00		$126.05	
				11.05%		11.05%		$111.05		$139.98
	Up percentage (u)	1.221403			9.05%				$121.10	
	Down percentage (d)	0.818731				7.41%				$130.07

(A) – 16.49% = 13.5% × u = 13.5% × 1.221

The binomial approach assumes that each year, the index return will move up by *u*(*u* = e^(1 × 20%) = 1.221) or down by *d* (*d* = e^ (–1 × 20%) = 1/*u* = 0.818). This means that at the end of the first year, the S&P 500's return will be either 16.49% (*u* × 13.5%) or 11.05% (*d* × 13.5%)

Step 2 Assess the probabilities of an up or down movement. (These probabilities will be used in step 5 to fold back the tree.)

Pu = [(1 + Rf) – d)]/(u – d) 62.40% = chance of index return moving up
Pd = [u – (1 + Rf)]/(u – d) 37.60% = chance of index return moving down
Rf = 7%

Step 3 Assess the states in which the options will be exercised

In the above table, the shaded numbers indicate when the incremental benefit will be obtained. In these cases, the return on the S&P 500 index is greater than the "exercise percentage" of 15%.

Step 4 Estimate the percentage and monetary payoffs associated with these states.

Trigger percentage 15%

Percentage payoff				Monetary payoff			
Now	Year 1	Year 2	Year 3	Now	Year 1	Year 2	Year 3
			9.60%				**$13.43**
		5.14%				**$5.99**	
	1.49%		**1.49%**		**$1.49**		**$1.88**
—		—		—		—	
	—		—		—		—
		—				—	
			—				—

The percentage return is calculated by deducting the trigger return — 15% — from the return on the S&P 500. The monetary pay off is calculated by multiplying the percentage payoff with the corresponding year's beginning total capital.

Step 5 Calculate the present value of expected future payoffs.

Now	Year 1	Year 2	Year 3
		(B)	
			$13.43
		$14.48	
	$10.32		**$1.88**
$6.24		**$1.09**	
	$0.64		—
		—	
			—

(B) — $14.48 = ($13.43 × Pu + $1.88 × Pd)/(1 + Rf) + $5.99

For instance, to arrive at (B), $14.48 million, one would take the expected value of (*Pu* × *$13.43* + *Pd* × *$1.88*), or (.6240 × $13.43) + (0.3760 × $1.88) to yield $9.09. Discounting this by one year at the risk-free rate, 7%, yields $8.49, to which we add $5.99 to arrive at the value of $14.48 million for year 2. This process is repeated for the other cells. Folding the expected values back to the present, we arrive at a value of $6.24 million for control. This is the present value of the incremental benefits from the aggressive trading strategy.

8.

Step 1 Build an Excel spreadsheet model. A finished model, "SP 500 CHPT15.xls," can be found on the CD-ROM.

S&P 500 Return	
Mean	13.50%
Volatility	20%

Starting capital	$100.00
Risk-free rate	7%
Trigger return	15%

Time	Now	Year 1	Year 2	Year 3
SP 500 return	13.50%	15.27%	11.82%	10.48%
Standard deviation	2.700%	3.053%	2.364%	2.095%
Total capital	$100.00	$115.27	$128.89	$142.39
Incremental profit		$0.27	$ —	$ —
Present value of incremental profit				$0.25

Step 2 Go to cells with uncertain distributions and specify the distribution. In this problem, this has been done for you: The distribution is normal with a mean of 13.5% and a standard deviation of 2.7%.

Step 3 Run Crystal Ball 5,000 times (or any number of times you want), and you will get a result like the following:
Forecast: PV of incremental profit

Summary:
Display range is from $0.00 to $16.95 million.
Entire range is from $0.00 to $43.97 million.
After 5,000 trials, the Standard error of the mean is $0.07.

Statistics	Value
Trials	5,000
Mean	$2.84
Median	$0.00
Mode	$0.00
Standard deviation	$5.20
Variance	$27.07
Skewness	2.60
Kurtosis	10.85
Coefficient of variability	1.83
Range minimum	$0.00
Range maximum	$43.97
Range width	$43.97
Mean standard error	$0.07

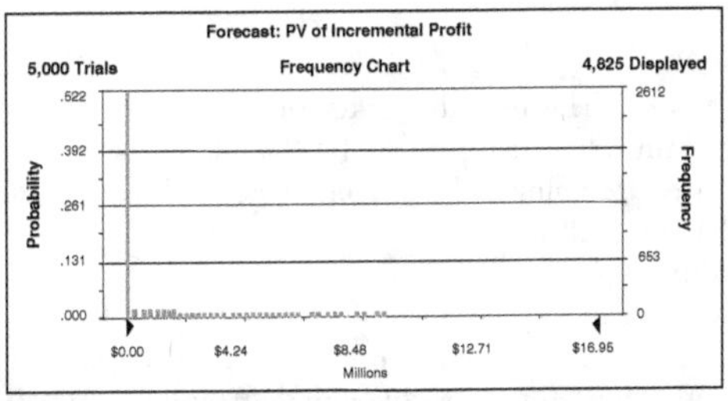

In this particular run, the value of control is calculated at $2.84 million with a standard deviation of $5.20 million. This mean is much lower than the result calculated using the binomial model because of the smoothing effect of a normal distribution. In addition, we obtain a risk profile by using Monte Carlo simulation as opposed to the binomial model. Our simulation tells us that the payoff has a very high standard deviation, indicating that the value of the control right will be very uncertain.

Note that simulation results will not always return the exact numbers. However, in general, the results should be pretty consistent.

9.

Step 1 Insert parameters into the model

Stock price	$20
Exercise price	$25
Risk-free rate	8%
Volatility	25%
Time (years)	2
Call value	***$2.22***

Control gives the owner the right to take on this co-branding project. The total value of the control right is $2.22 million. Therefore, the buyer can pay $2.22 million for this "control" premium.

Black-Scholes European: No Dividend	
Call value	$2.22
Call delta (hedge ratio)	0.487992
Call elasticity	4.405481
Using put-call parity	
Put value	$3.73
Delta	−0.512008
Elasticity	−2.743084
S underlying asset price	$20
X exercise price	$25
rf risk-free rate	8%
sd volatility	25%
t years to expiration	2
Cumulative Standard Normal Function	
d1 from Black-Scholes	−0.030105
N(d1)	0.487992
d2 from Black-Scholes	−0.383658
N(d2)	0.350616

10.

Base case value of the equity[1] (in millions)	$100.00
Adjustment for illiquidity[2]	−25%
Value of equity adjusted for possible illiquidity[3] (in millions)	$ 75.00
% premium for control	20%
Size of controlling block[4]	51%
Value of controlling block[5] (in millions)	$ 45.90
Value of minority block[6] (in millions)	$ 29.10
Value of equity adjusted for control asymmetry and illiquidity[7] (in millions)	$ 75.00
Total share outstanding in millions	50
Controlling block price per share[8]	$ 1.80
Minority block price per share[9]	$ 1.19

1. The base value of the company is the value of the firm with marketable shares but without any control blocks. This is in effect the value of the firm calculated from the DCF model.
2. When you take the firm private, the shares are going to be illiquid, hence a discount—in this case, 25%. Illiquidity is assumed to affect all shares equally.
3. Base value × (1 − % discount for illiquidity).
4. Percentage ownership of the major shareholder.
5. Value of equity adjusted for possible illiquidity × (1 + Control premium) × Size of controlling block.
6. The difference between the value of equity adjusted for possible illiquidity and the value of the control block.
7. The law of conservation of value requires that the value of minority and control blocks sum up to the value of equity adjusted for possible illiquidity.
8. Value of the controlling block divided by the number of shares for the controlling block.
9. Value of the minority block divided by the number of shares for the minority block.

The price per share for the controlling block is $1.80, and the price per share for the minority block is $1.19.

[The spreadsheets for questions 6 to 10 can be found in the folder "Key Spreadsheets from the Workbook" located on the CD-ROM.]

Financial Accounting for Mergers and Acquisitions

1. Consolidated statements for 100 percent stock transaction:

Consolidated Balance Sheet (FY 2001)	BB&B	Entries	Consolidated
Assets			
Current assets:			
Cash and equivalents	239.3	46.8	286.2
Merchandise inventories	606.7	310.7	917.4
Other current assets	39.7	119.5	159.2
Total current assets	885.7	477.1	1,362.8
Investment securities	—	—	—
Property and equipment, net	302.7	212.1	514.7
Identifiable intangible assets		500.0	500.0
Goodwill		1,020.6	1,020.6
Other assets	7.4	46.6	53.9
Total assets	1,195.7	2,256.4	3,452.1
Liabilities and Shareholders' Equity			
Current liabilites:			
Accounts payable, accrued expenses and other current liabilities	321.2	144.1	465.3
Current portion of long-term debt		—	—
Income taxes payable	32.0	—	32.0
Total current liabilities	353.2	144.1	497.3
Long-term debt		25.0	25.0
Deferred rent and other liabilities	25.5	34.7	60.2
Total liabilities	378.7	203.8	582.5
Shareholders' equity:			
Common stock	183.9	2,052.5	2,236.4
Retained earnings	633.2	—	633.2
Cumulative other comprehensive income			
Treasury stock			
Total shareholders' equity	817.0	2,052.5	2,869.5
Total liabilities and shareholders' equity	1,195.7	2,256.4	3,452.1

All accounts on the balance sheet simply add the preexisting balances for BB&B and Pier 1, except for "Identifiable intangible assets," "Goodwill," and "Common Stock."

Identifiable intangible assets: Given in the problem

Goodwill is calculated as follows:

Implied market value of firm (bid price + Pier 1's liabilities)	2,256.35
Book value of Pier 1 assets	735.71
Identifiable intangible assets	500.00
Goodwill	1,020.64

Common stock: Pier 1's equity accounts do not appear in the consolidated statement. Additional common stock is recorded based on the value of the new shares issued by BB&B for the acquisition.

Consolidated Income Statement (FY 2002) ($ Millions)	BB&B	Entries	Consolidated
Net sales	2,928.0	1,548.6	4,476.5
Cost of sales	1,720.4	898.8	2,619.2
Gross profit	1,207.6	649.8	1,857.3
SG&A (incl. depreciation & amortization)	861.5	490.9	1,352.4
Extra depreciation & amortization		25.0	25.0
Operating profit	346.1	133.8	479.9
Interest income (expense)	11.0	0.2	11.2
Earnings before taxes	357.1	134.0	491.1
Provision for taxes	137.5		186.6
Net income	219.6		304.5
EPS	0.76		0.87
Shares outstanding	289.7	60.5	350.2

All accounts on the income statement are simply added together, except for the line that shows amortization expense for "Identifiable intangible assets."

Provision for taxes: Taxes are based on the 38% tax rate applied to earnings before taxes.

[These spreadsheets can be found in the folder "Key Spreadsheets from the Workbook" located on the CD-ROM.]

2. See answer 4.

3. Consolidated statements for 60 percent stock, 40 percent cash transaction:

Consolidated Balance Sheet (FY 2001)	BB&B	Entries	Consolidated
Assets			
Current assets:			
Cash and equivalents	239.3	46.8	286.2
Merchandise inventories	606.7	310.7	917.4
Other current assets	39.7	119.5	159.2
Total current assets	885.7	477.1	1,362.8
Investment securities	—	—	—
Property and equipment, net	302.7	212.1	514.7
Identifiable intangible assets		500.0	500.0
Goodwill		1,020.6	1,020.6
Other assets	7.4	46.6	53.9
Total assets	1,195.7	2,256.4	3,452.1
Liabilities and Shareholders' Equity			
Current liabilites:			
Accounts payable, accrued expenses and other current liabilities	321.2	144.1	465.3
Current portion of long-term debt		—	—
Income taxes payable	32.0	—	32.0
Total current liabilities	353.2	144.1	497.3
Long-term debt (Pier 1 existing debt)		25.0	25.0
Long-term debt (for acquisition payment)		821.0	821.0
Deferred rent and other liabilities	25.5	34.7	60.2
Total liabilities	378.7	1,024.8	1,403.5
Shareholders' equity:			
Common stock	183.9	1,231.5	1,415.4
Retained earnings	633.2	—	633.2
Cumulative other comprehensive income			
Treasury stock			
Total shareholders' equity	817.0	1,231.5	2,048.5
Total liabilities and shareholders' equity	1,195.7	2,256.4	3,452.1

In coming up with the balance sheet, all procedures are the same as with the 100% stock transaction, except for the addition of debt used to fund the acquisition.

Debt assumed is 40% of the total purchase price.

Pier 1's equity accounts do not appear in the consolidated statement. Additional common stock is recorded based on 60% of the total purchase price.

Consolidated Income Statement (FY 2002) ($ Millions)	BB&B	Entries	Consolidated
Net sales	2,928.0	1,548.6	4,476.5
Cost of sales	1,720.4	898.8	2,619.2
Gross profit	1,207.6	649.8	1,857.3
SG&A (incl. depreciation & amortization)	861.5	490.9	1,352.4
Extra depreciation & amortization		25.0	25.0
Operating profit	346.1	133.8	479.9
Interest income (expense)	11.0	(57.3)	(46.3)
Earnings before taxes	357.1	76.5	433.6
Provision for taxes	137.5		164.8
Net income	219.6		268.8
EPS	0.76		0.82
Shares outstanding	289.7	36.3	326.0

For the income statement, all procedures are the same as with the 100% stock transaction, except for the interest expense on the debt used to fund the acquisition.

4. Answers to problems 2 and 4:

		With Merger	
Ratios for Bed Bath & Beyond	Without Merger	100% Stock	60% Stock, 40% Cash
Gross margin	41.2%	41.5%	41.5%
Operating margin	11.8%	10.7%	10.7%
Net margin	7.5%	6.8%	6.0%
EPS	0.76	0.87	0.82
% Dilution/(accretion)	—	14.7%	8.8%

- Gross margins increase slightly, but operating margins decrease due to the amortization of intangible assets. Remember, however, that we have not factored in any synergies. Synergy can trump dilution!
- Net margin declines much more significantly in the part-stock, part-cash transaction owing to the interest expense associated with the debt raised for the acquisition.

5. Financial statements for 40 percent stake:

Bed Bath & Beyond **Balance Sheet**		**2001**	
Assets			
Current assets:			
Cash and equivalents	429.5		429.5
Merchandise inventories	754.0		754.0
Other current assets	43.2		43.2
Total current assets	1,226.7		1,226.7
Investment securities	51.9		51.9
Investment in Pier 1	—	821.0	821.0 ←
Property and equipment, net	361.7		361.7
Other assets	7.2		7.2
Total assets	1,647.5		2,468.5
Liabilities and Shareholders' Equity			
Current liabilites:			
Accounts payable	270.9		270.9
Accrued expenses and other current liabilities	190.9		190.9
Income taxes payable	49.4		49.4
Total current liabilities	511.3		511.3
Deferred rent and other liabilities	41.9		41.9
Total liabilities	553.2		553.2
Shareholders' equity:			
Common stock	241.6	821.0	1,062.6 ←
Retained earnings	852.8		852.8
Total shareholders' equity	1,094.4		1,915.4
Total liabilities and shareholders' equity	1,647.5		2,468.5

Under the equity method, the buyer's investment in the target is reflected on the balance sheet at the buyer's acquisition cost. This investment is captured in an "Investment" account on the asset side.

The common stock account is increased by the value of shares issued to acquire 40% of the target.

Bed Bath & Beyond Income Statement ($ Millions)	BB&B	2002 Entries	New Balance
Net sales	2,928.0		2,928.0
Cost of sales	1,720.4		1,720.4
Gross profit	1,207.6		1,207.6
SG&A	861.5		861.5
Operating profit	346.1		346.1
Interest income/(expense)	11.0		11.0
Earnings before taxes	357.1		397.2
Provision for taxes	137.5		137.5
Income from equity investment		40.1	40.1
Net earnings	219.6		259.7
EPS	0.76		0.83
Shares outstanding	289.7	24.2	313.9

Under the equity method, the buyer's share in the target's earnings is simply reflected in one line, "Income from equity investment."

This is calculated by multiplying the target's *net* income by the buyer's proportionate share.

[These spreadsheets can be found in the folder "Key Spreadsheets from the Workbook" located on the CD-ROM.]

CHAPTER 17

Momentum Acquisition Strategies: An Illustration of Why Value Creation Is the Best Financial Criterion

1. Tyco probably stopped acquiring because it "hit the wall," having realized that the pace of growth by acquisition was unsustainable. Tyco had experienced tremendous growth since the 1980s through aggressive acquisitions. The firm's stock price fell sharply when investors realized that the firm's growth momentum was ending.

   The alleged fraud at the company offers a related explanation. Like unrealistic earnings momentum, tax and accounting fraud are eventually discovered. The restructuring may have been an attempt to cover the accounting trail. Both motives (momentum or fraud) spring from the exploitation of illusion and should be condemned by best practitioners.

2. Corporate managers and directors sometimes argue that investors want earnings momentum, and that all they are doing is giving investors what they want. But what investors want is the creation of value, not momentum. Research finds that momentum produces no supernormal returns for investors. Momentum is unsustainable indefinitely; it invites a focus on accounting cosmetics rather than on economic reality. And finally, momentum distracts management from focusing on value creation.

3. In simple terms, dilution occurs when shares outstanding increase faster than earnings in an acquisition; also, dilution occurs if the P/E ratio paid for the target exceeds the P/E ratio of the buyer. Accretion, on the other hand, occurs where the offered P/E ratio is smaller. Large size amplifies the dilution/accretion effect; small size dampens it. The factors that drive EPS dilution are the growth rate of the buyer's shares relative to the target's percentage addition to the buyer's earnings, the P/E ratio embedded in the bid relative to the P/E ratio of the buyer, and the size of the target relative to the size of the bidder.

4.

Financial Data on Merging Firms		Before Merger Buyer	Before Merger Target	After Merger Newco	After Merger % Change	Cash Deal Newco
1 Purchase-related charges (in thousands)	0.5%			$(120)		$(120)
2 Net income (in thousands)		$3,000	$1,000	$3,880	29%	$2,710.00
3 Number of shares (in thousands)		1,500	1,000	1,980	32%	1,500
4 Earnings per share (EPS)		$2.00	$1.00	$1.96	−2%	$1.81
5 Current stock price		$50.00	$20.00			$43.36
6 Price/earnings ratio		25.00	20.00			24.00
7 Ratio of earnings of target to buyer			0.33			
Terms of share-for-share offer						**In Cash**
8 Dollar value of bid				$24.00		$24.00
9 Premium over target's prebid price				20%		20%
10 Ratio of P/E paid to P/E of buyer				0.96		0.96
Dilution to the buyer resulting from the deal						
11 Dollar accretion (dilution) in buyer EPS				$(0.04)		$(0.19)
12 Percentage accretion (dilution)				−2.0%		−9.7%
					Interest rate	5%
					Tax rate	35%

a. As seen in the table, the earnings per share for Newco after the merger is $1.96 (line 4). This implies dilution of 2.0 percent from the buyer's EPS before the merger.

b. Note that the EPS for Newco is estimated to be $1.81, which indicates a 9.7 percent dilution.

c. As seen in the following table, an increase in the target's earnings will reduce dilution and enhance accretion when premiums are low. As premiums grow larger, deals become *more* dilutive as target earnings increase—this reflects the "double whammy" of a bigger target and higher premium, both of which require more shares to be issued.

Dilution/Accretion for the Buyer in a Share-for-Share Deal

		Premium over Target's Prebid Price (%)						
		0%	5%	15%	20%	25%	35%	45%
Earnings of the target (in thousands)	$ 500	1.5%	0.8%	−0.5%	−1.1%	−1.8%	−3.0%	−4.3%
	$1,000	2.6%	1.4%	−0.9%	−2.0%	−3.1%	−5.3%	−7.3%
	$1,500	3.6%	1.9%	−1.2%	−2.7%	−4.2%	−7.0%	−9.7%
	$2,000	4.3%	2.4%	−1.4%	−3.3%	−5.0%	−8.3%	−11.5%
	$2,500	5.0%	2.7%	−1.7%	−3.7%	−5.7%	−9.4%	−12.9%
	$3,000	5.6%	3.0%	−1.8%	−4.1%	−6.3%	−10.3%	−14.1%
	$3,500	6.0%	3.2%	−2.0%	−4.4%	−6.7%	−11.1%	−15.1%

5. From the tables and chart following, it can be seen that a deal with Company A is immediately dilutive (–23.7 percent) and a deal with Company B is immediately accretive (16.3 percent). But the deal with Company A offers faster growth in earnings after the merger. In roughly six years, it will yield the higher EPS. Valuation analysis should determine which target creates more value for shareholders. It may be that Company A creates more value even though it would dilute earnings.

	Buyer Before	Target A Before	Buyer after Acquiring Target A	Target B Before	Buyer after Acquiring Target B
Financial Data on Merging Firms					
Number of shares	5,000	2,000	9,571	2,000	6,286
Net income	$6,500	$3,000	$9,500	$3,000	$9,500
Earnings per share	$ 1.30	$ 1.50	$ 0.99	$ 1.50	$ 1.51
Current stock price	$28.00	$40.00	$64.00	$15.00	$18.00
Price/earnings ratio	21.54	26.67	64.48	10.00	11.91
Ratio of earnings of target to buyer		0.462		0.462	
Earnings growth rate	10%	25%		5%	
Terms of share-to-share offer					
Dollar value of bid			$64.00		$18.00
Premium over target's prebid price			60%		20%
Ratio of P/E paid to P/E of buyer			1.98		0.56
Resulting accretion (dilution)					
Dollar accretion (dilution) in buyer EPS			($ 0.31)		$ 0.21
Percentage accretion (dilution)			–23.7%		16.3%

Earnings forecasts

	Now	Year 1	Year 2	Year 3	Year 4	Year 5	Year 6	Year 7	Year 8	Year 9	Year 10
Income for buyer before	$6,500	$7,150	$7,865	$8,652	$9,517	$10,468	$11,515	$12,667	$13,933	$15,327	$16,859
EPS for buyer alone	$1.30	$1.43	$1.57	$1.73	$1.90	$2.09	$2.30	$2.53	$2.79	$3.07	$3.37
Target A before	$3,000	$3,750	$4,688	$5,859	$7,324	$9,155	$11,444	$14,305	$17,881	$22,352	$27,940
Income for buyer after acquiring target A	$9,500	$10,900	$12,553	$14,511	$16,841	$19,624	$22,959	$26,972	$31,815	$37,678	$44,799
EPS after merger	$0.99	$1.14	$1.31	$1.52	$1.76	$2.05	$2.40	$2.82	$3.32	$3.94	$4.68
Growth rate for Newco		14.74%	15.16%	15.60%	16.06%	16.52%	17.00%	17.48%	17.96%	18.43%	18.90%
Target B before	$3,000	$3,150	$3,308	$3,473	$3,647	$3,829	$4,020	$4,221	$4,432	$4,654	$4,887
Income for buyer after acquiring target B	$9,500	$10,300	$11,173	$12,124	$13,163	$14,297	$15,535	$16,888	$18,366	$19,981	$21,746
EPS after merger	$1.51	$1.64	$1.78	$1.93	$2.09	$2.27	$2.47	$2.69	$2.92	$3.18	$3.46
Growth rate for Newco		8.42%	8.47%	8.52%	8.57%	8.61%	8.66%	8.71%	8.75%	8.79%	8.84%

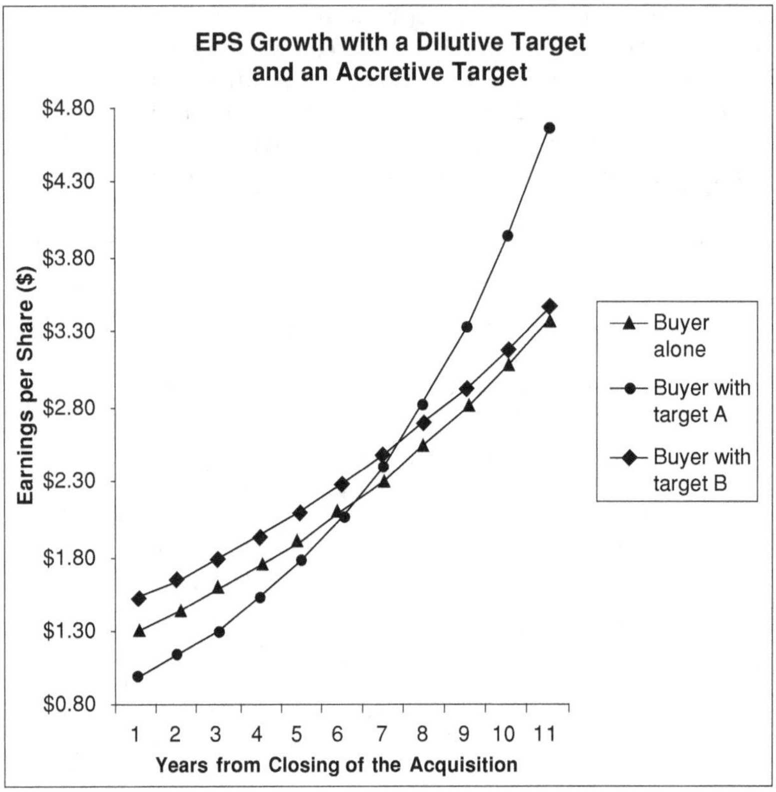

[All spreadsheets in this chapter can be found in the folder "Key Spreadsheets from the Workbook" located on the CD-ROM.]

CHAPTER 18

An Introduction to Deal Design in M&A

PART I: MINI-PROBLEMS

1a. Both sides have strong motivations for doing a deal: R_x wants the co-marketing rights to the new drugs for strategic reasons. Genesis needs funding. But the uncertainty surrounding approval of the drugs puts an equity investment at risk. The CEO of Genesis is optimistic, but approval and success of the drug are not certain. The design problem is one of how to deal with different assessments of risk. There are at least two design solutions:

1. Genesis could issue a convertible bond to R_x rather than shares of equity. The proceeds of a convertible bond issue could provide Genesis the funding it needs, while granting some downside protection to R_x in the event that the drugs do not receive approval. Later, if the drugs succeed, R_x could convert the debt to equity. The option embedded in the convertible bond helps to bridge the differing views of risk.
2. R_x could purchase Genesis equity in stages, after Genesis passes the various milestones of regulatory approval. Staged investing commits R_x to providing additional funds as uncertainty about the new drugs is resolved. This scheme amounts to creating a stream of options—these help to bridge the differing views of risk.

1b. The parties could bridge the gap through the use of an earnout, an arrangement where a portion of the purchase price would be paid by R_x only if Genesis attains agreed-upon performance goals within some time frame.

2a. If maintaining its credit rating is valuable to Company A, then A could extend a choice to the shareholders of B: accept a fully valued offer, paid in stock, or a less than fully valued offer in cash—the discount would be equivalent to the loss in value sustained by A arising from any damage to its credit rating.

2b. Company B can insist on a floor. If Company A's stock price falls below a certain level, the exchange ratio ought to be adjusted upward, or Company B must be remunerated in some other form. Company A in turn can insist on a cap. If its stock rises beyond a certain level, it can ask for a downward readjustment of the exchange ratio. The resulting structure—one with both a cap and a floor—is called a collar.

2c. Company A can use a variety of methods to keep Company B in the deal. One solution is to impose a walk-away or termination fee if Company B withdraws from the agreement. Another solution might be to agree on a "lock-up" option, where Company A gains the right to buy a block of shares in Company B should the latter enter into a merger agreement with another party. (Usually, both parties are subject to these terms—in this case, Company A would most likely be subject to the walk-away fee or lock-up option too if it withdraws from the deal agreement.)

2d. Company A could negotiate private agreements with Company B's managers. These agreements might entail commitments about titles, perquisites, and side payments (in the form of options, bonuses, employment contracts, consulting contracts, golden parachutes, etc.).

PART II: MINI-CASE

1. The control structure was highly advantageous to NCNB. Despite being a minority shareholder and putting up only 20 percent of equity, NCNB obtained control as the only shareholder to hold voting shares. One can guess that the FDIC accepted this structure because its main interest lay in saving First Republic from failing rather than in actively running the bank.
2. NCNB not only had a staggered purchase option, it also had exclusive rights to acquire more equity in Newco within the next five years. The staggered purchase terms effectively gave NCNB a number of long call options on Newco. NCNB had the right, but not the obligation to buy more stock. Having the staggered purchase option allowed NCNB to have more *time* to gain more *information* on Newco. The advantage of time was offset somewhat by the ratcheting price, which served as an incentive for NCNB to complete its acquisition of Newco earlier rather than later. The exclusivity clause bought NCNB time to bring Newco back to health without threat of a competitor or some other outside party benefiting from ownership of Newco.
3. NCNB was allowed to transfer bad loans originated under old management to the Special Asset Division, and was reimbursed by the FDIC for these loan losses. In addition, the FDIC paid NCNB the costs of administering the division. NCNB did not share in any losses suffered by the Special Asset Division, but did share in any gains made by the division. For NCNB, the agreements with respect to the Special Asset Division virtually eliminated any exposure to bad loans originated under previous management.
4. It was an attractive deal from NCNB's viewpoint. NCNB obtained title to the largest bank in Texas, with plenty of protection from the FDIC. NCNB virtually had no exposure to First Republic's bad loans. The control structure allowed NCNB 100 percent control over Newco, yet NCNB was never required to commit to buying the whole company. The staggered payment option gave NCNB the chance to opt out of the deal if its attempt to restructure First Republic did not work out. The deal design insulated NCNB from many risks.

CHAPTER 19

Choosing the Form of Acquisitive Reorganization

1. Sam should take party B's offer. The all-cash deal is not tax-efficient since it would require Sam and his shareholders to pay taxes immediately on the gain from the sale of shares. In contrast, the all-stock deal can be organized to be tax-free under any of the following structures:

   Statutory merger ("A" reorganization).
   Forward triangular merger ("A" reorganization).
   Reverse triangular merger ("A" reorganization).
   Voting stock-for-stock ("B" reorganization).
   Voting stock for assets ("C" reorganization).

2. No. Mr. Welch used the book value of the assets as the basis for his tax calculation. He should have used market value (as long as he can justify to the IRS that the economic value of the assets is $511,000). The correct answers are:

Market value	$511,000
Useful life	8
Depreciation expense	$ 63,875
Tax savings	**$ 21,718**
Discount rate	10%
Present value of savings	**$115,861**

3. The possible forms of reorganization are those in which the target (or the Newco into which the target merges) becomes a subsidiary of Escape. Since the deal will definitely involve some exchange of stock, the possible forms of reorganization are:

   Forward triangular merger ("A" type reorganization).
   Reverse triangular merger ("A" type reorganization).
   Voting stock-for-stock acquisition ("B" type reorganization).
   Voting stock-for-assets acquisition ("C" type reorganization).

4.

Type of Reorganization	Requirements for Tax-Free Qualification
Forward triangular merger ("A" type reorganization)	• Escape must acquire at least 70 percent of the fair market value of Grupo Viva's gross assets, and 90 percent of the FMV of net assets. • Payment must consist of at least 50 percent of Escape's parent corporation stock.
Reverse triangular merger ("A" type reorganization)	• At least 80 percent of the consideration must be paid in Escape's parent corporation voting stock. • As in the forward triangular merger, Escape must control "substantially all" of the Grupo Viva's assets.
Voting stock-for-stock acquisition ("B" type reorganization)	• Escape must pay only in voting stock, and afterward control at least 80 percent of the votes.
Voting stock-for-assets acquisition ("C" type reorganization)	• Escape must pay at least 80 percent of the consideration in voting stock. • Escape must not have had an ownership interest in Grupo Viva prior to the transaction. • At least 70 percent of the fair market value of the gross assets and 90 percent of the FMV of net assets of Grupo Viva must be transferred to Escape.

All of these forms of reorganization are tax-free to the seller. The two "A" type reorganizations dominate the others by permitting freeze-outs.

5. Under the forward triangular merger ("A" type reorganization), Escape cannot pay more than 50 percent of the consideration in cash. Under the reverse triangular merger ("A" type reorganization) Escape cannot pay more than 20 percent of the consideration in cash. Thus the forward triangular merger appears to offer the greatest design flexibility.

6. The possible forms of reorganization are:

   Statutory merger ("A" type reorganization).
   Voting stock-for-assets acquisition ("C" type reorganization).

7. Yes. The voting stock-for-assets acquisition does not allow tax-free status if the buyer had an ownership interest in the target prior to the transaction. Therefore, the only remaining option is a statutory merger (the "A" type reorganization).

8. To force Leonardo Fox out, Decadence should acquire Bright Ice for cash, thus leaving no shares in Fox's ownership. This entails a two-step transaction, an acquisition of a voting majority of Bright Ice shares for cash, followed by a "minority freeze-out" merger of Bright Ice with a subsidiary of Decadence, also for cash. Thus, the transaction should be structured using cash as the form of payment and entailing a merger with a subsidiary of Decadence. A triangular cash merger, either reverse or forward, would achieve Decadence's goal. As long as the buyer can attract a voting majority of the target's shares, the merger can be effected and the dissenting shareholders can be forced to exit.
9. A minority freeze-out seeks to eliminate direct interests in the target firm held by minority shareholders following the completion of the deal. This is ordinarily accomplished by merging the target into the buyer or a subsidiary of the buyer.

CHAPTER 20

Choosing the Form of Payment and Financing

PART I: TRUE OR FALSE

1. True.
2. False. Payment in stock is associated with higher returns to targets.
3. True.
4. False. Taxable deals are for cash, and "tax-deferred" deals are for stock.
5. False. In cash deals, target shareholders must pay taxes immediately on their capital gains, whereas in stock deals, taxes can be deferred until shares are sold.
6. True. This is called expropriating creditor wealth. A bidder can bid aggressively if part of the cost of possible overpayment is borne by the creditors of the firm.
7. True.
8. True.
9. False. The acquirer will prefer to offer stock (due to its contingent-pricing characteristics) if it thinks the target knows more than it does.
10. True.
11. False. Because the discipline imposed by creditors presumably results in better performance, bidders' announcement returns have been found to be positively related to the fraction of acquisition value funded by bank debt.

PART II: QUESTIONS

1. Factors that favor either a cash or a stock payment are present. On one hand, one could argue for a cash payment on the grounds of the CEO's optimism about the value of synergies, available debt capacity, and favorable interest rate environment. On the other hand, one could say a stock payment is better given the uncertainty about the target's stand-alone value.

2. Given the CEO's view that current market valuations may not last, this seems to be an opportune time to use stock as a medium of currency. However, an issuance of stock may signal a belief that the stock is overvalued, and may produce a negative reaction from the market.

3. If Company A issues shares to pay for the acquisition, Smith would still be the largest shareholder by far, though Pierce would also hold a sizable stake. Smith would own a percentage stake slightly more than twice as large as Pierce's; on the grounds of Smith's requirement that his stake be *at least* twice that of Pierce, the stock payment would be acceptable to Smith.

	% Ownership in Newco
Smith	38.5%
Pierce	18.5%
Other major stockholder of Company A	15.4%
Oceanic shareholders	27.7%

4. Offer to pay as high a premium for the target as consistent with the buyer's analysis of the target's intrinsic value, offer to pay in cash, and use internal sources of funds (such as cash on hand or unused debt capacity). These will increase Company A's chance of success in its hostile bid.

5. Issuing new debt of higher seniority than current creditors enjoy can allow buyers to bid more than their assessment of the intrinsic value of the target. This imposes part of the cost of possible overpayment on the creditors of the firm; it represents an expropriation of creditor wealth.

6. The period 1998–2000 was a period of economic strength and a buoyant stock market, whereas 1990–1992 represented a period of economic weakness. As discussed in the chapter, stock payments tend to be used with greater frequency during economic booms.

7a.

		With Merger	
Ratios	Without Merger	100% Stock	100% Cash
Gross margin	41.2%	41.5%	41.5%
Operating margin	11.8%	10.7%	10.7%
Net margin	7.5%	6.8%	4.8%
EPS	$0.76	$0.87	$0.66
% Accretion/(dilution)		14.7%	–12.8%
Debt-equity ratio	—	0.9%	251.2%
Interest cover (EBIT/Interest expense)	Net interest income	Net interest income	3.6×

- Gross and operating margins are the same regardless of the form of payment chosen.
- Net margins are much lower under the 100 percent cash transaction due to interest expense on the debt used for funding the acquisition.
- EPS is accretive under the 100 percent stock transaction, suggesting that the incremental income from the merger is more than enough to offset the impact of new share issuance. However, EPS is dilutive under the 100 percent cash payment scenario, suggesting that the additional income from the synergies of the deal is not high enough to offset interest expense on the acquisition debt.
- Obviously, under the all-cash transaction, Bed Bath & Beyond's debt-equity ratio shoots up, and it moves to a net interest expense rather than net interest income situation. (Interest coverage of 3.6×, however, is still respectable.)

7b.

100% Cash

Purchase Premium	EPS ($)	% Dilution
20%	0.675	–11.0%
25%	0.661	–12.8%
30%	0.647	–14.7%
35%	0.633	–16.5%
40%	0.620	–18.3%

100% Stock

Purchase Premium	EPS ($)	% Accretion
20%	0.875	15.5%
25%	0.869	14.7%
30%	0.863	13.9%
35%	0.858	13.1%
40%	0.852	12.3%

In general, the higher the purchase premium, the lower the accretion (in the all-stock transaction) and the greater the dilution (in the all-cash transaction). In addition, EPS is more sensitive to changes in the purchase premiums under the 100 perent cash transaction.

7c.

100% Stock

Purchase Premium	Exchange Ratio	New Shares Issued	% Ownership by BB&B Shareholders	% Ownership by Pier 1 Shareholders
20%	0.60	58.12	83.3%	16.7%
25%	0.63	60.55	82.7%	17.3%
30%	0.65	62.97	82.1%	17.9%
35%	0.68	65.39	81.6%	18.4%
40%	0.70	67.81	81.0%	19.0%

The higher the purchase premium, the higher the exchange ratio required, and thus the greater the number of shares that need to be issued. Accordingly, a higher purchase premium means Bed Bath & Beyond will need to give up more control.

[All spreadsheets for problem 7 can be found in the folder "Key Spreadsheets from the Workbook" located on the CD-ROM.]

CHAPTER 21

Framework for Structuring the Terms of Exchange: Finding the "Win-Win" Deal

1. The task here is to find the crossover point for the deal boundaries because that is the minimum point of the win-win region. By preparing a graph or table of the deal boundaries, one can identify the crossover point. In this case, Newco must trade at around 21 times or higher in order for there to exist the possibility of a deal acceptable to both parties.

	P/E Model Assumptions	
Buyer's share price	P1	$ 25.96
Target's share price	P2	$ 38.31
Buyer's net income	E1	$ 9,600
Target's net income	E2	$15,400
Net income from synergies	Es	$ 1,250
Buyer's shares outstanding	S1	10,700
Target's shares outstanding	S2	6,680

Results Based on P/E of Newco		
	Maximum Acceptable ER1	Minimum Acceptable ER2
16	0.82	2.50
17	0.97	2.15
18	1.12	1.89
19	1.27	1.69
20	1.43	1.52
21	1.58	1.39
22	1.73	1.27
23	1.88	1.18
24	2.03	1.10
25	2.18	1.02

2. As can be seen from the following hypothetical numbers, right now Microsoft is willing to pay a maximum exchange ratio of 1.12, but the minimum ExxonMobil will accept is 1.27. To make the deal work, Microsoft must be convinced to increase the exchange ratio to 1.27—which means ExxonMobil must convince Microsoft that Newco will trade at a minimum of 19 times.

MSFT

	P/E Model Assumptions	
Buyer's share price	P1	$ 25.96
Target's share price	P2	$ 38.31
Buyer's net income	E1	$ 9,600
Target's net income	E2	$15,400
Net income from synergies	Es	$ 1,250
Buyer's shares outstanding	S1	10,700
Target's shares outstanding	S2	6,680
Expected P/E ratio of Newco	PE12	18.00

Results Based on P/E of Newco		
	Maximum Acceptable **ER1**	
	1.12	

The maximum that Microsoft is willing to pay given its view that Newco will trade at a P/E of 18x

XOM

	P/E Model Assumptions	
Buyer's share price	P1	$ 25.96
Target's share price	P2	$ 38.31
Buyer's net income	E1	$ 9,600
Target's net income	E2	$15,400
Net income from synergies	Es	$ 1,250
Buyer's shares outstanding	S1	10,700
Target's shares outstanding	S2	6,680
Expected P/E ratio of Newco	PE12	22.00

Results Based on P/E of Newco		
		Minimum Acceptable **ER2**
		1.27

The minimum that Exxon is willing to accept given its view that Newco will trade 22x

Feasible Deal for Microsoft

	P/E Model Assumptions	
Buyer's share price	P1	$ 25.96
Target's share price	P2	$ 38.31
Buyer's net income	E1	$ 9,600
Target's net income	E2	$15,400
Net income from synergies	Es	$ 1,250
Buyer's shares outstanding	S1	10,700
Target's shares outstanding	S2	6,680
Expected P/E ratio of Newco	PE12	19.00

Microsoft must believe that Newco will trade at 19x before it will be willing to pay Exxon's asking price. This P/E ratio can be found by using Goal Seek to solve for the P/E ratio that will give a maximum acceptable exchange ratio of 1.27.

Results Based on P/E of Newco		
	Maximum Acceptable **ER1**	
	1.27	

3. As can be seen from the following hypothetical numbers, Microsoft is willing to pay a maximum exchange ratio of 1.57, but the minimum ExxonMobil will accept is 1.68. To make the deal work, Microsoft must convince ExxonMobil to lower its minimum to 1.57. This means Microsoft must convince ExxonMobil that Newco will have a DCF value of at least $517 billion.

MSFT

DCF Model Assumptions	
P1	$ 25.96
P2	$ 38.31
S1	10,700
S2	6,680
DCF12	$550,000

Maximum Acceptable ER1
1.57

← Microsoft is willing to pay at most an exchange ratio of 1.57 given its view that Newco will have a DCF value of $550 billion . . .

XOM

DCF Model Assumptions	
P1	$ 25.96
P2	$ 38.31
S1	10,700
S2	6,680
DCF12	$500,000

Minimum Acceptable ER2
1.68

← . . . but Exxon thinks Newco will have a DCF value of only $500 billion. As a result, its minimum acceptable payment is above what Microsoft is willing to pay.

XOM

DCF Model Assumptions	
P1	$ 25.96
P2	$ 38.31
S1	10,700
S2	6,680
DCF12	$516,997

← Microsoft must convince Exxon that Newco will have a DCF value of $517 billion in order for Exxon to accept Microsoft's maximum offer. This DCF value is found by using Goal Seek to find the DCF value that will result in a minimum acceptable ratio of 1.57.

Minimum Acceptable ER2
1.57

4. This is still the same deal; only the currency used for the acquisition has changed. Newco must still trade at around 21 times or higher in order for a deal to be attractive. (See problem 1.)

	P/E Model Assumptions	
Buyer's share price	P1	$ 25.96
Target's share price	P2	$ 38.31
Buyer's net income	E1	$ 9,600
Target's net income	E2	$15,400
Net income from synergies	Es	$ 1,250
Buyer's shares outstanding	S1	10,700
Target's shares outstanding	S2	6,680

Results Based on P/E of Newco

PE12	Maximum Acceptable ER1	Minimum Acceptable ER2
19	33.08	38.31
20	37.01	38.31
21	40.94	38.31
22	44.87	38.31
23	48.80	38.31
24	52.73	38.31
25	56.66	38.31

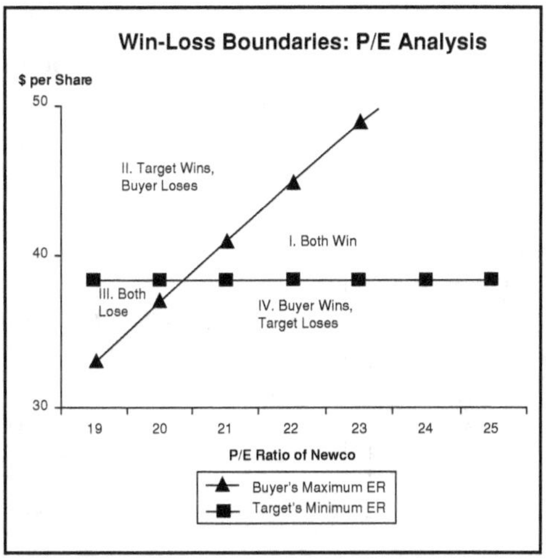

5. The crossover point can be found by preparing a data table of the deal boundaries. In this case, the data table reveals that the deal becomes feasible at a DCF value of between $500 and $550 billion. The exact number is $537 billion.

DCF Model Assumptions	
P1	$ 25.96
P2	$ 38.31
S1	10,700
S2	6,680
DCF12	$550,000

DCF	Maximum Acceptable ER1	Minimum Acceptable ER2
$400,000	$18.30	$38.31
$450,000	$25.78	$38.31
$500,000	$33.27	$38.31
$550,000	$40.75	$38.31
$600,000	$48.24	$38.31
$650,000	$55.72	$38.31
$700,000	$63.21	$38.31
$750,000	$70.69	$38.31
$800,000	$78.18	$38.31

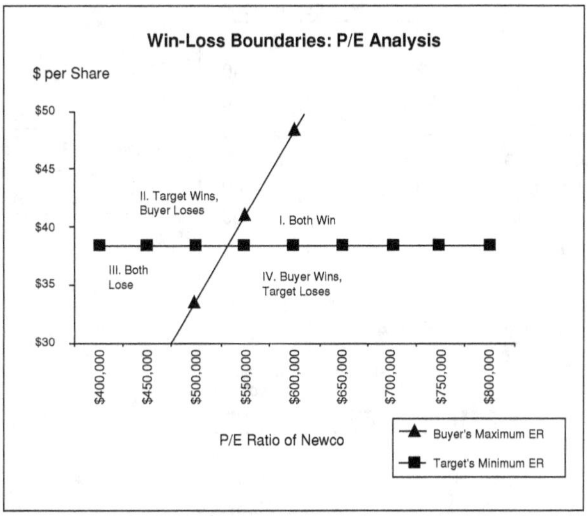

6. In a cash-for-stock transaction, the minimum price paid is the target's market price.

7. A win-win deal is not feasible at an expected P/E ratio of 11 times.

	P/E Model Assumptions	
Buyer's share price	P1	$35.00
Target's share price	P2	$20.00
Buyer's net income	E1	$ 200
Target's net income	E2	$ 150
Net income from synergies	Es	$ 10
Buyer's shares outstanding	S1	80
Target's shares outstanding	S2	80
Expected P/E ratio of Newco	PE12	11

Results Based on the P/E of Newco

PE12	Maximum Acceptable ER1	Minimum Acceptable ER2
11	0.41	0.68
12	0.54	0.59
13	0.67	0.52
14	0.80	0.47
15	0.93	0.42
16	1.06	0.38
17	1.19	0.35

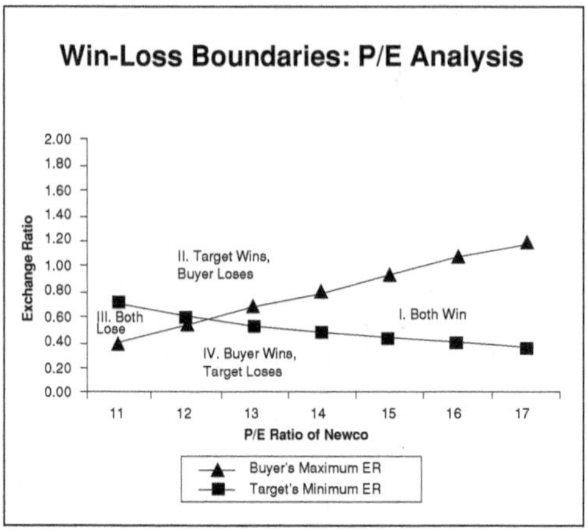

8. They must achieve $50 million in synergies in order to make this a win-win deal at a P/E ratio for Newco of 11 times. The impact of synergies can be seen in the graph: with only $10 million in synergies, there is no zone of potential agreement at a P/E ratio of 11 times; the seller's maximum is below the target's minimum. The deal will become feasible only if the P/E is at around 13 times or higher. With the increase in synergy value, a deal becomes possible at a P/E of 11 times.

	P/E Model Assumptions	
Buyer's share price	P1	$35.00
Target's share price	P2	$20.00
Buyer's net income	E1	$ 200
Target's net income	E2	$ 150
Net income from synergies	Es	$ 50
Buyer's shares outstanding	S1	80
Target's shares outstanding	S2	80
Expected P/E ratio of Newco	PE12	11

Use Goal Seek to find the value of synergies that will make the deal work if Newco trades at 11x.

Results Based on the P/E of Newco

PE12	Maximum Acceptable ER1	Minimum Acceptable ER2
9	0.29	0.80
10	0.43	0.67
11	0.57	0.57
12	0.71	0.50
13	0.86	0.44
14	1.00	0.40
15	1.14	0.36

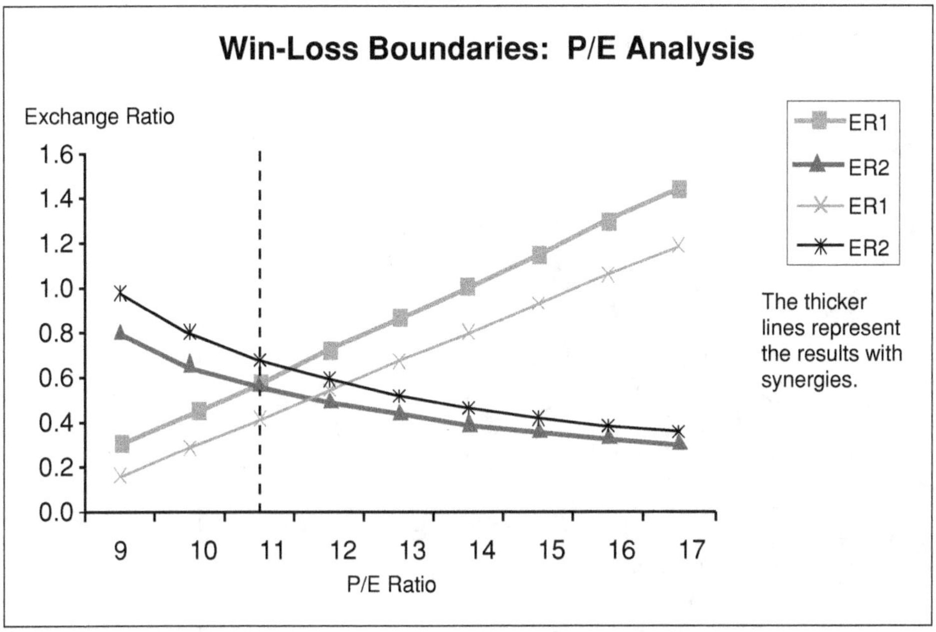

[The spreadsheets for problem 1 to 8 can be found in the folder "Key Spreadsheets from the Workbook" located on the CD-ROM.]

9. A deal is feasible if DCF value is projected at $5 billion.

DCF Model Assumptions	
P1	$35.00
P2	$20.00
S1	80
S2	80

DCF12	Maximum Acceptable ER1	Minimum Acceptable ER2
$3,000	0.0714	1.1429
$3,500	0.2500	0.8421
$4,000	0.4286	0.6667
$4,500	0.6071	0.5517
$5,000	0.7857	0.4706
$5,500	0.9643	0.4103
$6,000	1.1429	0.3636
$6,500	1.3214	0.3265
$7,000	1.5000	0.2963

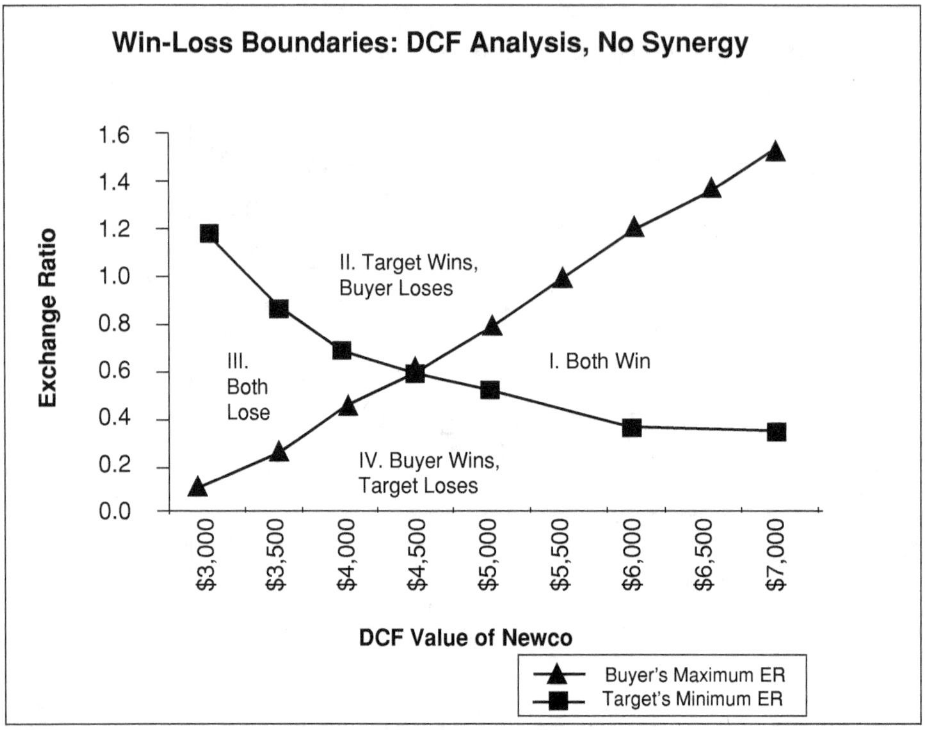

10. The graph in problem 9 does not change. Only the positions of the parties change: Looking at the x-axis, the parties are now at a DCF value for Newco of $6 billion due to the addition of the $1 billion in synergies. As can be seen from the graph, the zone of potential agreement widens as the DCF value of Newco increases.

11. The proportion of Oracle's net income in Newco is 92.4 percent. This contribution ratio for Oracle would imply an exchange ratio of 1.36 Newco shares for each PeopleSoft share. This number can be calculated using the following formula:

$$ER = \frac{\frac{N_{\text{Buyer}}}{C_{\text{Buyer}}} - N_{\text{Buyer}}}{N_{\text{Target}}}$$

However, based on Oracle's bid price and its current market price, the implied exchange ratio is 1.2. The difference is due to the fact that the exchange ratio of 1.36 is based on accounting values, whereas the exchange ratio of 1.2 is based on market prices. These two differing perspectives may suggest why PeopleSoft chose not to accept this offer: It underestimates the contribution of PeopleSoft to Newco's earnings.

12. At this new bid price, the implied exchange ratio is 1.46—higher than what is implied by the contribution analysis. Therefore, this bid is more attractive from PeopleSoft's point of view—but there remain the knotty *social* issues created by Oracle's hostile bid.

CHAPTER 22

Structuring and Valuing Contingent Payments in M&A

1. An earnout can provide a number of benefits to both parties if it is properly structured. For the seller, an earnout can provide additional payments if the acquired business does as well as expected. In addition, an earnout will benefit the buyer by making additional payments necessary only if the business does significantly better than expected. Although earnouts are quite useful in bridging the valuation gap and retaining and motivating shareholders or managers, they also pose challenges in postacquisition integration and in the definitions of the earnout formulas and performance goals.

2.

		Now	Year 1	Year 2	Year 3	Year 4	Year 5
Step 1 Grow the tree							
							$57.55
						$40.55	
Parameters needed:		(A)			$28.58		$28.58
				$20.14		$20.14	
Volatility (annualized)	35%		$14.19		$14.19		$14.19
Length of period (year)	1	$10.00		$10.00		$10.00	
			$7.05		$7.05		$7.05
Up percentage (u)	1.419068			$4.97		$4.97	
Down percentage (d)	0.704688				$3.50		$3.50
(A) – $14.19 = $10 × U = $10 × 1.419						$2.47	
							$1.74

The binomial approach assumes that each year, the value of the firm will move up by u (u = e^(1 × 35%) = 1.419) or down by d (d = e^(–1 × 35%) = 1/u = 0.705). This means that at the end of the first year, firm value will be worth either $14.19 million ($u$ × $10 milllion) or $7.05 ($d$ × $10 million).

	Now	Year 1	Year 2	Year 3	Year 4	Year 5
Profit margin	10%	10%	10%	10%	10%	10%
						$5.75
					$4.06	
				$2.86		$2.86
			$2.01		$2.01	
		$1.42		$1.42		$1.42
	$1.00		$1.00		$1.00	
		$0.70		$0.70		$0.70
			$0.50		$0.50	
				$0.35		$0.35
					$0.25	
						$0.17

Step 2 Assess the probabilities of an up or down movement. (These probabilities will be used in step 5 to fold back the tree.)

Pu = [(1 + Rf) – d)]/(u – d)	49.74%	= chance of the firm value moving up
Pd = [u – (1 + Rf)]/(u – d)	50.26%	= chance of the firm value moving down
Rf = 6%		

(Continued)

Step 3 Assess the states in which the options will be exercised.

In the table, the shaded numbers indicate when the earnout will be awarded.
In these cases, the profit is more than the exercise price of $1,500,000.

Step 4 Estimate the payoffs associated with these end-states.

Exercise price $1.50

Now	Year 1	Year 2	Year 3	Year 4	Year 5	
					$4.25	(= $5.75 – $1.50)
				—		
			—		$1.36	(= $ 2.86 – $1.50)
		—		—		
	—		—		—	
—		—		—		
	—		—		—	
		—		—		
			—		—	
				—		
					—	

Step 5 Calculate the present value of expected future payoffs.

Now	Year 1	Year 2	Year 3	Year 4	Year 5
				(B)	
					$4.25
				$2.64	
			$1.54		**$1.36**
		$0.86		**$0.64**	
	$0.47		**$0.30**		—
$0.25		**$0.14**		—	
	$0.07		—		—
		—		—	
			—		—
				—	
					—

(B) — $2.64 = ($4.25 × Pu + $1.36 × Pd)/(1 + Rf)

For instance, to arrive at (B), $2.64 million, one would take the expected value of (*Pu × $4.25 + Pd × $1.36),* or (.4974 × $4.25) + (0.5026 × $1.36) to yield $2.80. Discounting this by one year at the risk-free rate, 6%, yields $2.64. This process is repeated for the other cells. Folding the expected values back to the present, we arrive at a value of $0.25 million for this earnout plan. Although in this case, the total value of the earnout plan is just about 5% of the value of the total deal, it is a good illustration of how to value the earnout plan by the binomial approach. In reality, the earnout plan will generally be a much greater percentage of the value of the deal.

[This spreadsheet can be found in the folder "Key Spreadsheets from the Workbook" located on the CD-ROM.]

3. As with problem 2, build a binomial lattice laying out the outcomes. Then calculate the payoffs for each outcome. Fold back the expected value of the payoffs to arrive at the value of the option. The answers are:

Profit	Volatility of Revenue Growth				
Margin	25%	30%	35%	40%	45%
8%	$0.082	$0.124	$0.161	$0.194	$0.225
9%	$0.130	$0.171	$0.207	$0.240	$0.272
10%	$0.178	$0.217	$0.253	$0.287	$0.333
11%	$0.225	$0.263	$0.313	$0.364	$0.413
12%	$0.283	$0.338	$0.392	$0.443	$0.493

From the table, it is clear that the value of the earnout increases directly with volatility and profit margins.

4. The solution is the same as in problem 2, except that the binomial tree goes only as far as three rather than five periods.

			Now	Year 1	Year 2	Year 3
Step 1	Grow the tree					
	Parameters needed:		(A)			**$28.58**
					$20.14	
	Volatility (annualized)	35%		$14.19		$14.19
	Length of period (year)	1	$10.00		$10.00	
				$7.05		$7.05
	Up percentage (u)	1.419068			$4.97	
	Down percentage (d)	0.704688				$3.50

(A) – $14.19 = $10 × U = $10 × 1.419

The binomial approach assumes that each year, the value of the firm will move up by *u* (*u* = e^(1 × 35%) = 1.419) or down by *d* (*d* = e^(–1 × 35%) = 1/*u* = 0.705). This means that at the end of the first year, firm value will be worth either $14.19 million (*u* × $10 milllion) or $7.05 (*d* × $10 million).

	Now	Year 1	Year 2	Year 3
Profit margin	**10%**	**10%**	**10%**	**10%**
				$2.86
			$2.01	
		$1.42		$1.42
	$1.00		$1.00	
		$0.70		$0.70
			$0.50	
				$0.35

Step 2 Assess the probabilities of an up or down movement. (These probabilities will be used in step 5 to fold back the tree.)

Pu = [(1 + Rf) – d)]/(u – d) 49.74% = chance of the firm value moving up
Pd = [u – (1 + Rf)]/(u – d) 50.26% = chance of the firm value moving down
Rf = 6%

Step 3 Assess the states in which the options will be exercised.

In the above table, the shaded numbers indicate when the earnout will be awarded. In these cases, the profit is more than the exercise price of $1,500,000.

Step 4 Estimate the payoffs associated with these end-states.

Now	Year 1	Year 2	Year 3
			$1.36 (= $2.86 – $1.50)
		—	
	—		—
—		—	
	—		—
		—	
			—

Step 5 Calculate the present value of expected future payoffs.

Now	Year 1	Year 2	Year 3
		(B)	
			$1.36
		$0.64	
	$0.30		—
$0.14		—	
	—		—
		—	
			—

(B) — $0.64 = ($1.36 × Pu + 0 × Pd)/(1 + Rf)

For instance, to arrive at (B), $0.64 million, one would take the expected value of (*Pu × $1.36 + Pd × $0)*, or (.4974 × $1.36) + (0.5026 × $0) to yield $0.675. Discounting this by one year at the risk-free rate, 6%, yields $0.64. This process is repeated for the other cells. Folding the expected values back to the present, we arrive at a value of $0.14 million for this earnout plan.

[This spreadsheet can be found in the folder "Key Spreadsheets from the Workbook" located on the CD-ROM.]

5. The results are:

Profit Margin	Volatility of Revenue Growth 25%	30%	35%	40%	45%
8%	$0.028	$0.057	$0.081	$0.104	$0.124
9%	$0.059	$0.086	$0.111	$0.133	$0.155
10%	$0.089	$0.116	$0.140	$0.163	$0.185
11%	$0.120	$0.146	$0.170	$0.193	$0.215
12%	$0.151	$0.175	$0.199	$0.223	$0.246

From this table, it is clear that the value of the earnout increases with increases in volatility and profit margins. At the same time, as compared to problem 3, notice that the value of the earnout plan decreases with the shortening of the earnout period.

6. Build the five-year forecast as shown, and model the uncertainties about revenue growth and profit margins as normal distributions. Running Crystal Ball 5,000 times, the result is shown. From the buyer's point of view, the value of the proposed deal has an expected value of $4.56 million ($2 million cash and $2.56 million expected value of the earnout); this is lower than the buyer's estimation of the value of the firm. Therefore, it is an attractive deal to the buyer.

Buyer Valuation

				Year 1	Year 2	Year 3	Year 4	Year 5
Base Year Sales			$12,000					
Earnout Period, in Years			5					
Sales				$13,849	$15,429	$17,092	$18,021	$19,547
	Growth Rate	Mean	12%					
		Standard deviation	3%	15%	11%	11%	5%	8%
Profit				$1,510	$1,885	$1,917	$2,091	$2,790
	Profit Margin	Mean	12%	11%	12%	11%	12%	14%
		Standard deviation	2%					
Earnout Target for Profits				$500	$1,000	$1,500	$2,000	$2,500
Annual Earnout Value				$1,010	$885	$417	$91	$290
	Present Value of Earnout, Discounted at 7%			**$2,333**				
	Dollars at Closing			$2,000				
	Enterprise Valuation of Proposed Earnout			**$4,333**				

[This spreadsheet can be found in the folder "Key Spreadsheets from the Workbook" located on the CD-ROM.]

Note that this result is a deterministic estimate of value, which differs from the probabilistic estimate given in the next table. Because the probabilistic estimate accounts for the entire range of outcomes, it is superior to the deterministic estimate.

Summary:
Display range is from $2,995 to $6,129 thousands
Entire range is from $2,605 to $7,063 thousands
After 5,000 trials, the standard error of the mean is $9

Statistics	Value
Trials	5,000
Mean	$ 4,557
Median	$ 4,519
Mode	—
Standard deviation	$ 609
Variance	$371,107
Skewness	0.29
Kurtosis	3.01
Coefficient of variability	0.13
Range minimum	$ 2,605
Range maximum	$ 7,063
Range width	$ 4,458
Mean standard error	$ 8.62

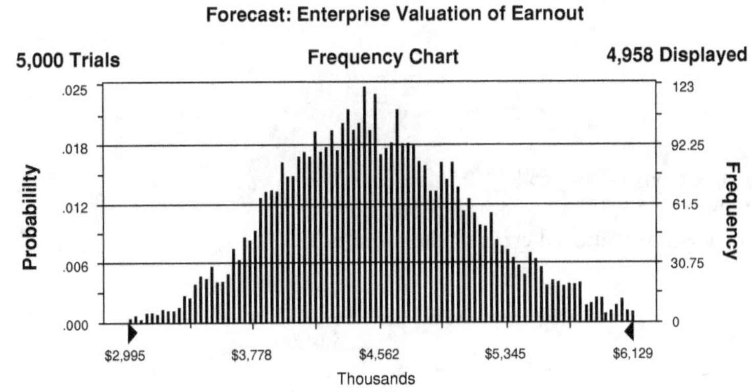

In conclusion, the deterministic approach yields an estimated value of $4,333, while the probabilistic approach gives a mean estimate of $4,557.

7. Build the five-year forecast as shown, and model the uncertainties about revenue growth and profit margins as normal distributions. Running Crystal Ball 5,000 times, the result is shown. From the seller's point of view, the valuation of the proposed earnout has a mean of $8.14 million, which is higher than the seller's estimation of the value of the firm. Therefore, it is an attractive deal to the seller.

Seller Valuation

				Year 1	Year 2	Year 3	Year 4	Year 5
Base Year Sales			$12,000					
Earnout Period, in Years			5					
Sales				$13,364	$15,506	$18,606	$21,854	$26,126
	Growth Rate	Mean	20%					
		Standard deviation	5%	11%	16%	20%	17%	20%
Profit				$2,027	$2,210	$2,376	$3,790	$3,920
	Profit Margin	Mean	14%	15%	14%	13%	17%	15%
		Standard deviation	3%					
Earnout Target for Profits				$500	$1,000	$1,500	$2,000	$2,500
Annual Earnout Value				$1,527	$1,210	$876	$1,790	$1,420
	Present Value of the Earnout, Discounted at 7%							
				$5,576				
	Dollars at Closing			$2,000				
	Enterprise Valuation of Proposed Earnout			**$7,576**				

[This spreadsheet can be found in the folder "Key Spreadsheets from the Workbook" located on the CD-ROM.]

Note that this result is a deterministic estimate of value, which differs from the probabilistic estimate given in the next table. Because the probabilistic estimate accounts for the entire range of outcomes, it is superior to the deterministic estimate.

Summary:
Display range is from $4,440 to $11,951 thousands
Entire range is from $3,538 to $14,334 thousands
After 5,000 trials, the standard error of the mean is $20

Statistics	Value
Trials	5,000
Mean	$ 8,137
Median	$ 8,079
Mode	—
Standard deviation	$ 1,406
Variance	$1,977,696
Skewness	0.26
Kurtosis	3.15
Coefficient of variability	0.17
Range minimum	$ 3,538
Range maximum	$ 14,334
Range width	$ 10,796
Mean standard error	$ 19.89

(Continued)

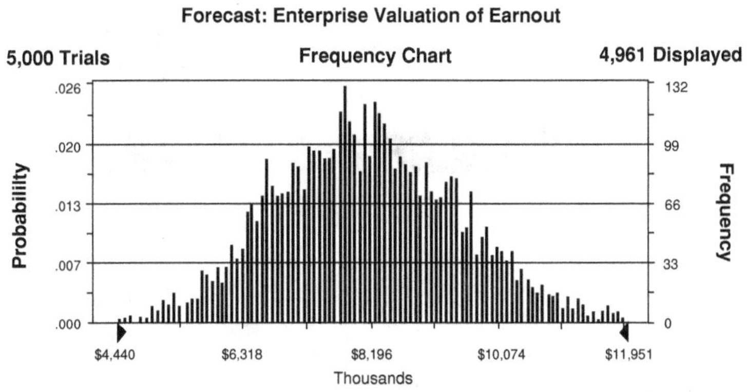

8. Use the model you built in problem 6, using the Decision Table tool in Crystal Ball to estimate the value of the earnout plan under different revenue growth rates and profit margins. The results will be similar to those shown in the following table:

Mean Profit Margin	Mean Revenue Growth				
	10%	11%	12%	13%	14%
10%	$3,376	$3,462	$3,552	$3,675	$3,779
11%	$3,771	$3,875	$4,023	$4,172	$4,340
12%	$4,229	$4,393	$4,579	$4,756	$4,953
13%	$4,753	$4,965	**$5,185**	**$5,405**	**$5,629**
14%	**$5,345**	**$5,560**	**$5,800**	**$6,090**	**$6,344**

Shaded portions are where the buyer will not take the deal.

9. Use the model you built in problem 7, using the Decision Table tool in Crystal Ball to estimate the value of the earnout plan under different revenue growth rates and profit margins. The results will be similar to those shown in the following table:

Mean Profit Margin	Mean Revenue Growth				
	16%	18%	20%	22%	24%
12%	**$5,503**	**$5,760**	**$5,989**	**$6,248**	**$6,515**
13%	**$6,231**	**$6,496**	**$6,751**	$7,054	$7,283
14%	**$6,919**	$7,210	$7,546	$7,849	$8,158
15%	$7,697	$8,012	$8,301	$8,672	$9,001
16%	$8,454	$8,766	$9,096	$9,485	$9,827

Shaded portions are where the seller will not take the deal.

[These spreadsheets from problems 8 and 9 can be found in the folder "Key Spreadsheets from the Workbook" located on the CD-ROM.]

CHAPTER 23

Risk Management in M&A

1. There are many kinds of transaction risks in M&A:
   - Decline in the buyer's share price or financial performance.
   - Preemption by a competing bidder.
   - Disappointed sellers.
   - Appearance of formerly hidden product liabilities.
   - Loss of key customers by the target.
   - Problems in the target's accounting statements.
   - Regulatory intervention.
   - Litigation by competitors.
   - Disagreements over social issues.
   - Failure to get shareholder approvals.
   - Controversy or lack of credibility.
2. The lockup option gives the buyer the right to buy the Baltimore factory if another bidder acquires Fine-Machinery. Therefore, it is a call option with a payoff of $5 million (value of $20 million, less the exercise price of $15 million) if there is a competing successful bid, and zero if there is no competing successful bid. The decision tree is drawn as follows, and the value of this call option is calculated at $1,250,000.

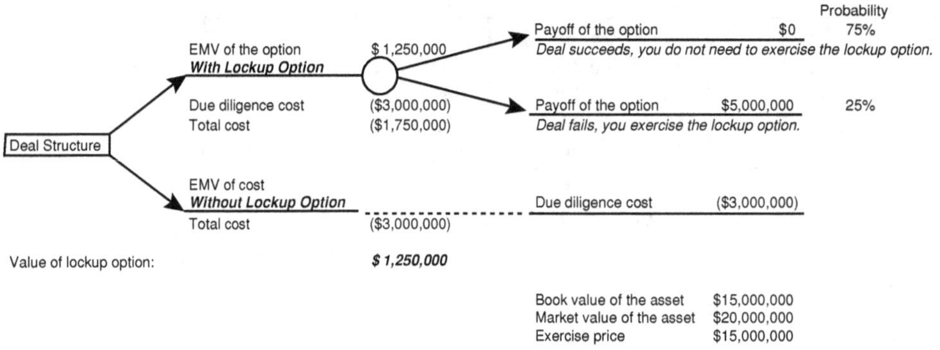

3. An exit clause is a very common risk management tool to reduce the buyer's risk. In this problem, the exit clause gives the buyer the right, not the obligation, to abandon the purchase if the deal becomes unattractive. The value of the exit clause is $1 million, computed as the difference between the expected monetary value (EMV) of the deal with, and without, the exit clause.

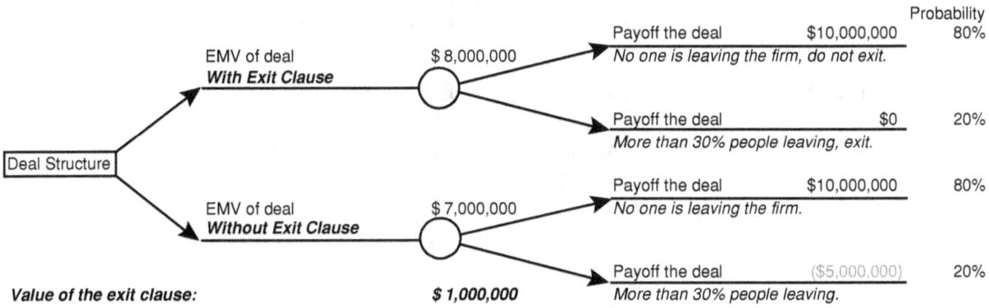

4. As noted in Chapter 8 of the main text, due diligence is a risk management device. In combination with the exit clause, investing in due diligence acquires a *put option* in this case; the audit provides more accurate information about the accounting of the target, which gives the buyer the right to withdraw from an economically unattractive deal. By drawing the decision tree, one can compute the value of this option at $1.5 million. After deducting the cost of option from the value of the option, the net value of the option is estimated to be $1 million.

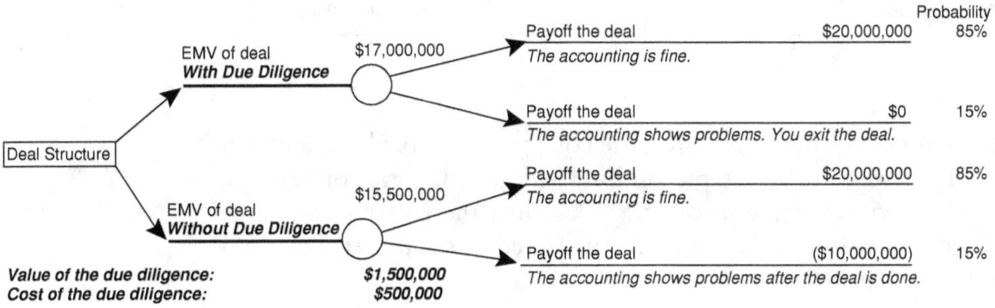

5. Insert the parameters into the model. You should obtain the following results:

		Buyer's Stock Price	Value of Bid with Collar	Number of Buyer Shares Issued per Target Share with Stock Collar
Fixed exchange ratio	1.40	$ 0.01	$28.00	2,800.00
Collar upper strike	$40.00	$ 5.00	$28.00	5.60
		$10.00	$28.00	2.80
Exchange ratio above upper strike	Upper strike/buyer's stock price	$15.00	$28.00	1.87

(Continued)

		Buyer's Stock Price	Value of Bid with Collar	Number of Buyer Shares Issued per Target Share with Stock Collar
Collar lower strike	$20.00	$20.00	$28.00	1.40
		$25.00	$35.00	1.40
Exchange ratio below lower strike	Lower strike/buyer's stock price	$30.00	$42.00	1.40
		$35.00	$49.00	1.40
		$40.00	$56.00	1.40
		$45.00	$56.00	1.24
		$50.00	$56.00	1.12

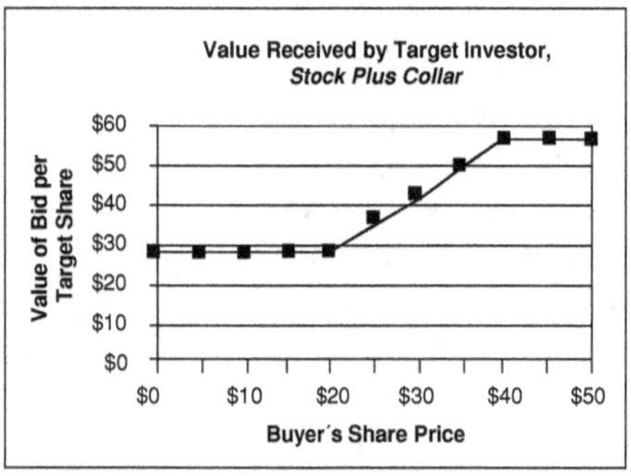

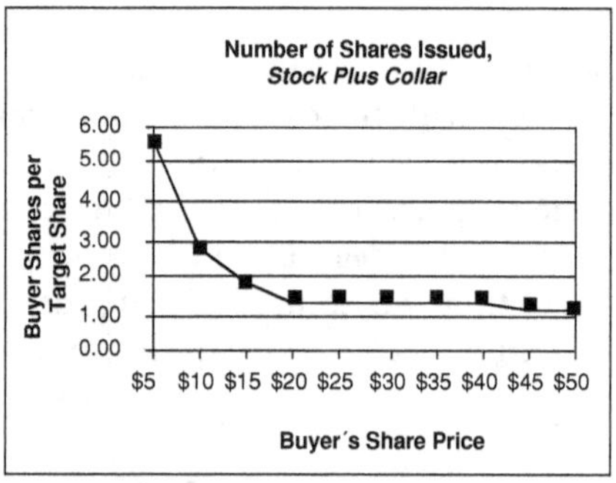

From the standpoint of the target investor, the collar for this fixed exchange ratio deal essentially consists of a long put option (with a strike price of $20) and a short call option (with a strike price of $40). When the collar is combined with the stock position, the graph of payoffs presented to the target shareholders corresponds to the floating collar.

6. Insert the parameters into the model. You should obtain the following results:

		Buyer's Stock Price	Value of Bid with Collar	Number of Buyer Shares Issued per Target Share with Stock Collar
Fixed value per target share	$40.00	$ 0.01	$ 0.02	2.00
Collar upper strike	$60.00	$10.00	$20.00	2.00
Exchange ratio above upper strike	0.667	$20.00	$40.00	2.00
Collar lower strike	$20.00	$30.00	$40.00	1.33
Exchange ratio below lower strike	2.00	$40.00	$40.00	1.00
		$50.00	$40.00	0.80
		$60.00	$40.00	0.67
		$70.00	$46.67	0.67

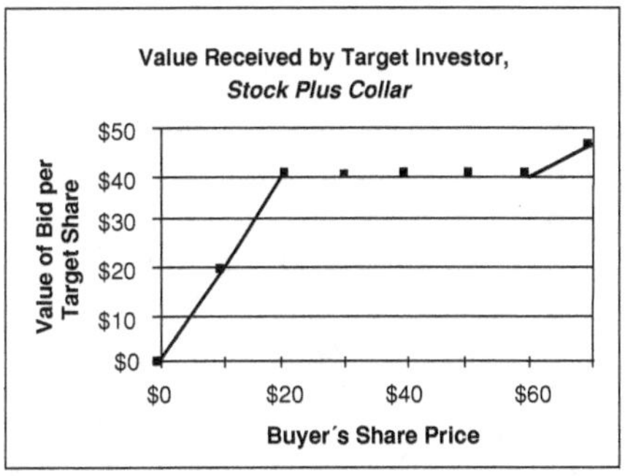

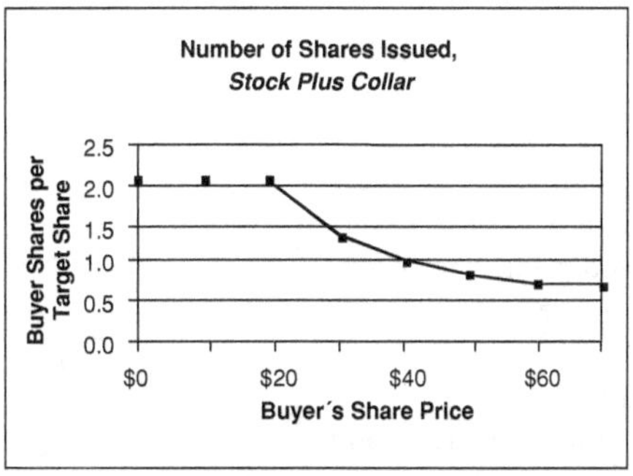

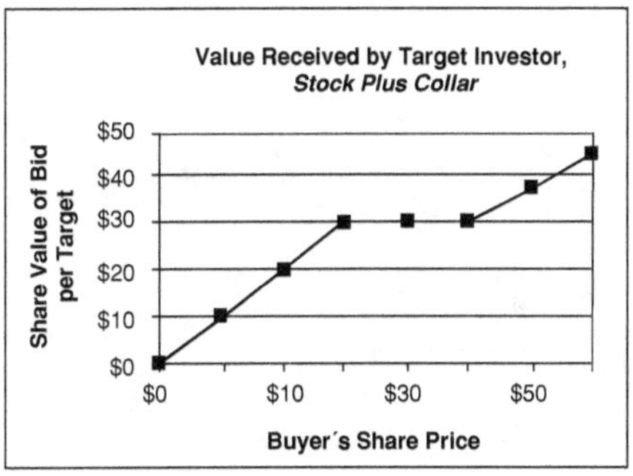

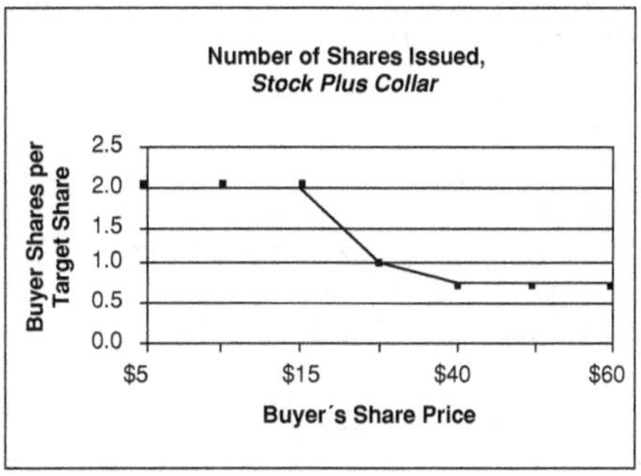

The diagrams of the combined position given in the preceding charts correspond to the fixed collar.

7. This problem is a simple illustration of how the Monte Carlo simulation can be used to calculate the value of a staged investment. The distribution of the value of the potential drug follows a normal distribution as shown:

	Time		
	Now	After More Information	Total
Payment	$15	$5	$20
Uncertainty		61.55518	
Trigger price		$50	

Running Crystal Ball 5,000 times, a $19 million mean total payment is obtained. It indicates that the buyer can save an expected value of $1 million by structuring the acquisition as a staged payment plan.

Statistics	Value
Trials	5,000
Mean	$ 19
Median	$ 20
Mode	$ 20
Standard deviation	$ 2
Variance	$ 5
Skewness	–1.20
Kurtosis	2.43
Coefficient of variability	0.11
Range minimum	$ 15
Range maximum	$ 20
Range width	$ 5
Mean standard error	$0.03

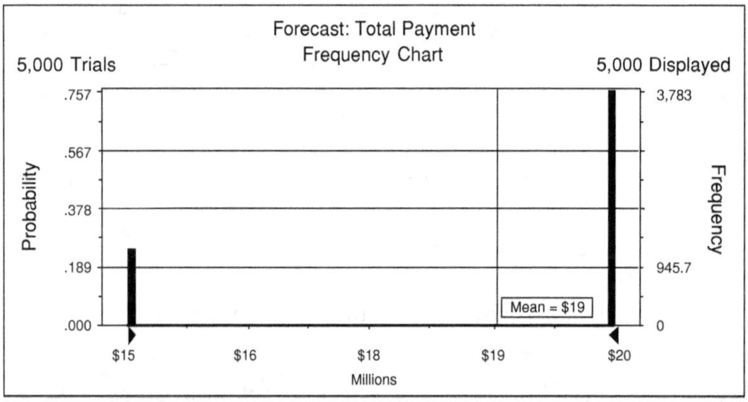

Source: Output as produced from Crystal Ball software simulation.

8a. To arrive at the true value of the deal, one needs to calculate the value of the contingent value right—the CVR is essentially a collar that lives beyond the closing of the acquisition. This collar consists of a long put with the strike price at $42 and a short put with the strike price at $32, which allows a maximum cash payment of $10 ($42 – $32). By using "Collars Analysis.xls" in the CD-ROM, one can arrive at the option value of the individual put options. The net value of one collar comes out to $7.88. Since each target share will be exchanged for two shares of your firm's stock, the offer in terms of one target's share is worth $55.89, which is equal to $45.00 + $10.89 (cash plus the value of the collar times 1.4).

Life of collar:	365
Structure of collar:	
If one component is a long call:	
Strike price:	$ —
Payoff formula (text):	Maximum of (stock price minus strike price) or zero
Payoff calculated:	0
If one component is a short call:	
Strike price:	$ —
Payoff formula (text):	Zero minus the maximum of (stock price minus strike price) or zero
Payoff calculated:	$ —
If one component is a long put:	
Strike price:	$42.00
Payoff formula (text):	Maximum of (strike price minus stock price) or zero
Payoff calculated:	$ 7.89
If one component is a short put:	
Strike price:	$32.00
Payoff formula (text):	Zero minus the maximum of (strike price minus stock price) or zero
Payoff calculated:	$ —
Buyer's share price today	$30.00
Annualized volatility of buyer's share price	15.0%
Forecast of return of buyer's share price at closing of deal	12.84%
Forecast of buyer's share price at closing of deal	$34.11
Risk-free rate of return today	4.8%
Annualized volatility of risk-free rate of return	16%
Standard deviation of annualized risk-free rate of return	0.8%
Forecast of risk-free rate of return	7%
Calculated value of the collar (sum of four payoffs)	$7.39

Note: The calculated value in this table reflects just one draw from the various distributions. Please refer to the next table for an estimate of the mean of the entire distribution.

Forecast: Value of Collar

Statistics	Value
Trials	5,000
Mean	$7.88
Median	$9.46
Mode	$0.00
Standard deviation	$2.61
Variance	$6.81
Skewness	–1.60
Kurtosis	4.56
Coefficient of variability	0.33
Range minimum	$0.00
Range maximum	$9.80
Range width	$9.80
Mean standard error	$0.04

(Continued)

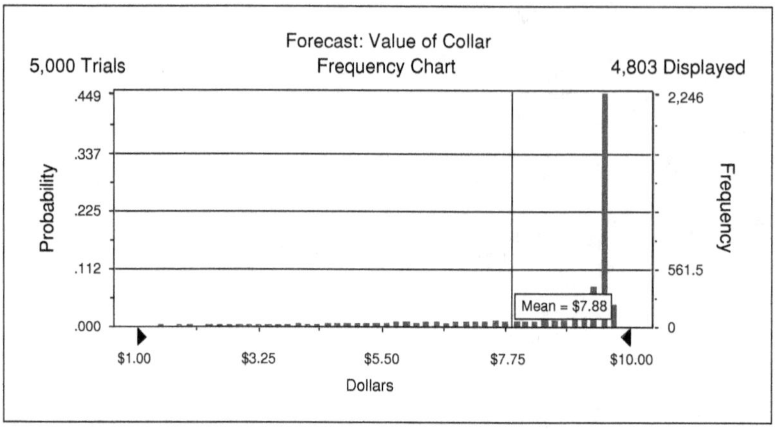

8b.

Life of the collar:	
Best guess days	730
Maximum days	1,095
Minimum days	365
Forecast of life of collar:	628.1783
Structure of the collar:	
If one component is a long call:	
Strike price:	$ —
Payoff formula (text):	Maximum of (stock price minus strike price) or zero
Payoff calculated:	0
If one component is a short call:	
Strike price:	$ —
Payoff formula (text):	Zero minus the maximum of (stock price minus strike price) or zero
Payoff calculated:	$ —
If one component is a long put:	
Strike price:	$50.00
Payoff formula (text):	Maximum of (strike price minus stock price) or zero
Payoff calculated:	$15.89
If one component is a short put:	
Strike price:	$35.00
Payoff formula (text):	Zero minus the maximum of (strike price minus stock price) or zero
Payoff calculated:	(0.89)
Buyer's share price today	$40.00
Annualized volatility of buyer's share price	18.0%
Forecast of return of buyer's share price at closing of deal	7.50%
Forecast of buyer's share price at closing of deal	$43.12
Risk-free rate of return today	6%
Annualized volatility of risk-free rate of return	20%
Standard deviation of annualized risk-free rate of return	1.2%
Forecast of risk-free rate of return	6%
Calculated value of the collar (sum of four payoffs)	$13.63

Note: The calculated value in this table reflects just one draw from the various distributions. Please refer to the next table for an estimate of the mean of the entire distribution.

Forecast: Value of Collar

Statistics	Value
Trials	5,000
Mean	$12.65
Median	$13.22
Mode	$ 0.00
Standard deviation	$ 1.79
Variance	$ 3.22
Skewness	–2.93
Kurtosis	13.45
Coefficient of variability	0.14
Range minimum	$ 0.00
Range maximum	$14.55
Range width	$14.55
Mean standard error	$ 0.03

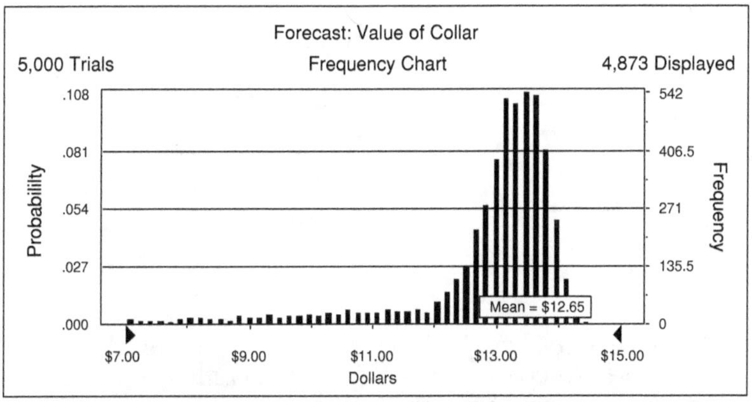

By using a triangular distribution for the time period of the option, the value of the collar can be calculated. A trial run of 5,000 times results in a mean value of the collar of $12.65 per buyer's share. Therefore, the total payment for one share of the target's stock is $62.71 ($45 + 1.4 × $12.65).

9.

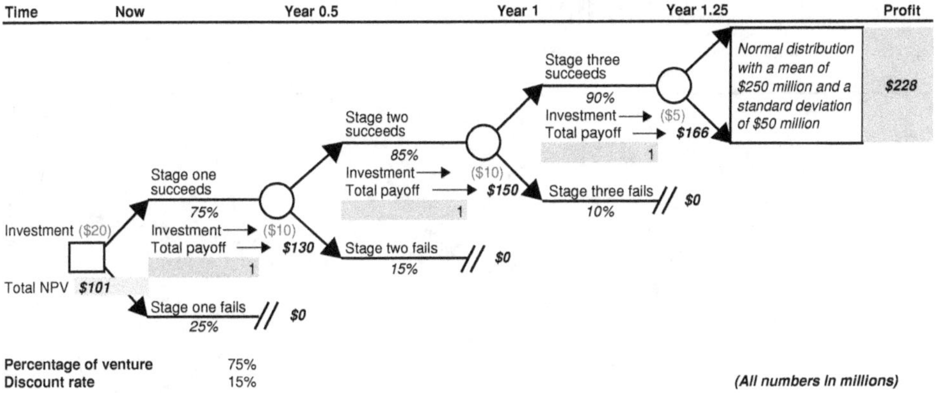

In the tree, the terminal payoffs are calculated by multiplying 75 percent by the forecasted profits, which follows a normal distribution with a mean of $250 million and a standard deviation of $50 million because Macrosofft is purchasing 75 percent of Red Dragon. Then, the payoffs are discounted according to the corresponding time period to obtain the expected monetary value (EMV). The investment for each period is deducted from EMV to obtain the net present value for each period. Given that the profit at the end of year 1.25 ($228 million) is uncertain, it should be simulated to generate a distribution and an expected value. The following table completes this analysis, and finds the expected NPV today is $57 million.

Statistics	Value
Trials	5,000
Mean	$ 57
Median	$ 82
Mode	($ 20)
Standard deviation	$ 73
Variance	$5,402
Skewness	–0.05
Kurtosis	1.38
Coefficient of variability	1.28
Range minimum	($ 38)
Range maximum	$ 223
Range width	$ 261
Mean standard error	$ 1.04

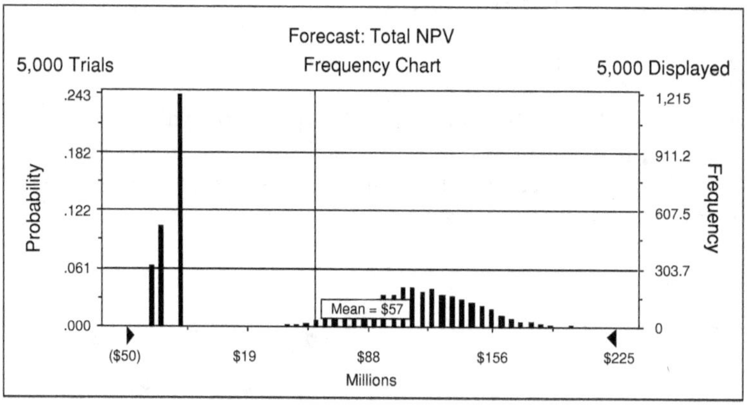

CHAPTER 24

Social Issues

1a. There were several key social issues included in the DaimlerChrysler merger agreement:

- *Joint name:* DaimlerChrysler.
- *Country of incorporation:* Germany.
- *Operational Headquarters:* in Germany and the United States.
- *Common language:* English.
- *CEO:* A structure of two co-CEOs.
- *Board seats:* Chrysler and Daimler would each hold half of the board seats of the Newco board of directors.
- *Executive compensation:* The compensation for German executives was significantly lower than that for their American counterparts. It was known that the CEO of Daimler made the equivalent of $2.5 million a year, while Chrysler's CEO made $16 million in 1997. However, Daimler disclosed pay only on an aggregate basis.

1b. By and large, these terms reflect a merger of equals. Two headquarters, two co-CEOs, and a board of directors for Newco with equal representation from both Daimler and Chrysler are strong indications of this.

1c. The issue of the new company name was a point of contention that became resolved only in the final merger discussions. CEO Jürgen Schrempp really wanted the Newco name to be Daimler-Benz; Robert Eaton, the CEO of Chrysler, insisted on having his company name included. The issue of the new company name appeared to be one that would make or break the deal.

The choice of English as the common language was controversial among German DaimlerChrysler employees. But English was widely used in business across Europe and DaimlerChrysler wanted to be a truly global firm.

1d. There is always a risk that any social issue can create problems after a merger deal closes. In this case, an issue that could become problematic is the discrepancies between German and U.S. executive compensation structures. The differences could make German employees feel they are not being treated fairly. Furthermore, the structure of co-CEOs could become problematic as each CEO may be accustomed to taking the lead, rather than conceding and negotiating decisions with a partner on equal footing.

2. Social issues can create value. Spending on social issues may be positively correlated with incentive effects: The more a company spends on social issues, the better the returns from improved employee motivation.

   Social issues can also destroy value: Because negotiations on social issues may give a prospective buyer favorable consideration by a target firm, other potential bidders may be discouraged from making a higher competing bid. A target firm may end up settling on an acquisition price with the favored buyer that is lower than what target shareholders might have received from another bidder. The difference in value represents an opportunity cost to the target shareholders.

3. Best Homes, Inc., may have a golden parachute program in place that would give Roberta a sizable sum of money if there were a change in corporate control (i.e., if Urban Living acquired the company). Even if Best Homes did not have golden parachute provisions, its severance package could be significant for Roberta, and something that she believes is worth receiving if her job is indeed terminated. The formula for severance packages at Best Homes is a month's salary for every year worked at the firm; this means that Roberta would receive a severance payment worth 75 percent of her current annual salary. Given that Roberta is very marketable and skilled, she could stay until she receives a severance payment and then easily get a comparable job if and when she leaves Best Homes.

4. The merger bears many of the characteristics of a merger of equals:

   - Each firm was to have equal representation on the board of the new company.
   - The former CEOs would occupy the top two executive positions.
   - Each firm was bound to a $250 million breakup fee.
   - Each firm would give the other an option to acquire 19.9 percent of its currently outstanding shares if a higher bidder came along.
   - The proposed new blended name, Morgan Stanley Dean Witter Discover, conveyed an appearance of equality.
   - The two firms would retain their respective headquarters locations.
   - The deal was structured as a merger with an exchange of shares.
   - The acquisition premium was low.

CHAPTER 25

How a Negotiated Deal Takes Shape

1. The CEO of Family Mart may be exposing his company to risk by showing the buyer the books before signing a confidentiality agreement. If the parties do not intend to sign a confidentiality agreement, it may be advisable for the CEO of Family Mart to release private information in stages.
2. The CEO of Family Mart is making a promise before even discussing the transaction with his directors. Such a commitment may expose the CEO to legal liability. The advisable procedure is to gain approval of the board first.
3. It is not uncommon for CEOs to engage in preliminary discussions prior to informing a larger group. However, Olsen is taking an unnecessary risk by going far along the process without informing his directors. No matter how attractive the deal seems to him, the board may not grant its approval, and Olsen may end up wasting precious time and resources.

   This happened in merger discussions between Coca-Cola and Quaker. Coca-Cola had begun negotiations with Quaker without informing its board. Coca-Cola delivered a written proposal to Quaker discussing the terms of its offer, and the two parties signed a confidentiality agreement, conducted due diligence reviews, and even got an auditing firm's opinion that the merger could be accounted for under the pooling method. When Coca-Cola brought the matter up for approval in a board meeting, the directors unanimously rejected the combination.
4. Olsen could resort to either a bear hug or a hostile tender offer. In a bear hug, Olsen would send a merger proposal directly to Little Pete's board of directors, bypassing the CEO. In a hostile tender offer Olsen would send the proposal directly to Little Pete's shareholders.
5. If the acquisition is material and probable, Little Pete's has an obligation to disclose.
6. A standstill agreement protects the target against the buyer gaining control or accumulating voting power in the target in the open market while negotiations are proceeding.
7. A letter of intent would probably trigger the need to make a public announcement (because the deal is certainly material and highly probable). Given the concern that outside parties may derail the deal, the two parties might simply proceed to negotiate the definitive agreement, gain support of the two firms' boards of directors, and simultaneously issue a merger proxy statement, submit the antitrust filings with the government, and make a public announcement. This approach leaves as little time as possible for potentially hostile parties to react.

CHAPTER 26

Governance in M&A: The Board of Directors and Shareholder Voting

1. The laws of the state of incorporation govern when challenging directors' decision to sell a firm.

2. Under straight voting, the shareholder wields votes equal to the number of shares held. Under cumulative voting, a shareholder is granted votes equal to the number of shares held times the number of directors to be elected.

3a. Echo has no chance under straight voting. The Addams family can outvote Echo 700,000 to 100,000 for each director.

3b. Assuming that the public does not vote straight for Addams' Apple directors, Echo has a chance under cumulative voting. The Addams family has a total of 5.6 million votes, which when divided by eight comes out to 700,000 votes per director. Echo can vote his nominee in if he votes all of his 800,000 shares for his nominee.

4. The duty of care is violated. See Smith vs. Van Gorkom.pdf on the CD-ROM for description of an instance similar to this.

5. The directors have a clear conflict of interest in this situation and would arguably violate the duty of loyalty in approving the proposal.

6. Tom Kane has an obligation to do more under the duty of care. Financial statements are detailed presentations requiring careful and thorough attention. Tom should not slacken in his oversight of Walking Shoes' financial systems.

7. The Revlon duties are probably triggered in this case. Directors must commence an auction unless strong strategic reasons exist (as in *Time Warner v. Paramount*) as to why the directors should "just say no" to a superior bid.

8. Under the business judgment rule, courts are unlikely to intervene if directors and officers have fulfilled their duties in good faith, are not conflicted, are informed, and act in rational belief, all of which seem to be true in this case.

CHAPTER 27

Rules of the Road: Securities Law, Issuance Process, Disclosure, and Insider Trading

1. Joe is not right. The aim of securities laws is to inform investors, prevent manipulation, produce more efficient markets, and achieve a level playing field.

2. Pearl has already violated the Williams Amendment. Although she personally did not cross the 5 percent threshold, the investor group of which she is a part owns 24.95 percent. The Williams Amendment states that upon crossing the 5 perent threshold, the buyer (the pool) has to file notice with the SEC within 10 days. She will also violate the Williams Amendment by discriminating among the shareholders, and by keeping her offer open for less than 20 business days.

3. This does not violate the Williams Amendment since both back-end and front-end offers have equal economic value. A court challenge may succeed if a plaintiff can argue that Ronaldman's shares are worth less than $10 each.

4. Fitness Buff should have disclosed the merger negotiations or responded, "We do not comment on rumors in the market." By denying the rumor, Fitness Buff went against the SEC pronouncement that "If the issuer is aware of nonpublic information concerning acquisition discussions . . . at the time the statement is made, the issuer has an obligation to disclose sufficient information concerning the discussions to prevent the statements made from being materially misleading."

5. Denver has clearly violated the laws of insider trading by misappropriating the information provided by Siegel. Siegel, although he may not have been intending to, may have also violated regulations for disclosure of information by providing confidential information to one outsider and not the public.

6. Yes. Myer-Goodwill-Milo is engaging in a public offering of unregistered stock, in violation of the 1933 Act. Myer-Goodwill-Milo has jumped the gun by making an offering before the registration of securities is effective.

7. No, not if the issuance qualifies as a private placement. To qualify as a private placement, there must be a small circle of offerees (which there is in this case), and 18th Century's five owners would need to qualify as "accredited investors" for which status as high-net-worth individuals is a key criterion.

CHAPTER 28

Rules of the Road: Antitrust Law

1. If the price of X increases, demand for Y will decrease. Some examples of products that might exhibit negative cross elasticities are:

   - *DVD player prices and DVDs*. If the prices of DVD players fall, demand for DVDs increases.
   - *Gasoline prices and cars*. If gasoline prices rise, demand for cars may fall.
   - *Mobile phone usage rates and handsets*. If charges for mobile phone usage increase, demand for mobile phone handsets may fall.

   Goods that exhibit negative cross elasticities tend to be complementary; that is, they tend to be used together.

2.

% Change in demand for lamb chops(*a*)	0.0025
% Change in price of beefsteaks (*b*)	0.01
Cross elasticity of demand (*a*/*b*)	**0.25**

   The positive cross elasticity suggests that lamb chops and beefsteaks are substitutes rather than complements. But demand for lamb chops is not very sensitive to changes in the price of beef.

3. The calculation of pre- and post-transaction HHI indexes is:

Summary	
Market HHI before the deal	3,108.8
Market HHI after the deal	3,196.4
Change in market HHI	87.6

HHI Indexes before the Contemplated Transaction

	Based on Revenues		
Market Players	FY 2000 Revenue ($ MM)	% Market Share	(Market Share)^2
Best Buy Co. Inc.	12,494.0	40.7	1,656.4
Circuit City Stores Inc.	10,599.4	34.5	1,192.1
RadioShack Corporation	4,794.7	15.6	243.9

(Continued)

Market Players	Based on Revenues FY 2000 Revenue ($MM)	% Market Share	(Market Share)^2
The Good Guys Inc.	860.5	2.8	7.9
Intertan Inc.	484.2	1.6	2.5
Rex Stores Corp.	464.3	1.5	2.3
Tweeter Home Entertainment	404.7	1.3	1.7
Ultimate Electronics Inc.	385.0	1.3	1.6
Sound Advice Inc.	177.3	0.6	0.3
Harvey Electronics Inc.	34.4	0.1	0.0
Total	30,698.5	100.0	3,108.8 HHI

HHI Indexes after the Contemplated Transaction

Market Players	Based on Revenues Revenues	% Market Share	(Market Share)^2
Best Buy Co. Inc.	12,494.0	40.7	1,656.4
Circuit City Stores Inc.	10,599.4	34.5	1,192.1
Intertan Inc.	484.2	1.6	2.5
Rex Stores Corp.	464.3	1.5	2.3
Tweeter Home Entertainment	404.7	1.3	1.7
Ultimate Electronics Inc.	385.0	1.3	1.6
Sound Advice Inc.	177.3	0.6	0.3
Harvey Electronics Inc.	34.4	0.1	0.0
RadioShack & Good Guys	5,655.2	18.4	339.4
Total	30,698.5	100.0	3,196.4 HHI

Note: "(Market Share)^2" indicates the resulting value when "% market share" has been raised to the second power.

The merger certainly increases the already high concentration among the sample of firms selected. But it might be argued that RadioShack and The Good Guys operate in different market segments. One specializes in the do-it-yourself private-label market, while the other specializes in brand-name systems. The problem here illustrates that market definition is at least as important as the calculation of HHIs.

4.

Market HHI before the deal	7,204
Market HHI after the deal	7,675
Change in market HHI	471

These results show the sports-drink market as being highly concentrated. The HHI is well above the 1,800 threshold, and the change in market HHI is also well above the 50-point mark. The FTC commissioners were actually split on this issue. Two of the commissioners voted to investigate further the proposed merger between PepsiCo and Quaker Oats, while two others voted against taking any further action.

5. Yes, Firm A is required to file a report. The Hart-Scott-Rodino Act requires a filing if a buyer has assets over $100 million and a target has assets over $10 million.

6. Yes. The post-transaction concentration may be very high, but because Eagle is a failing firm, the FTC might approve the deal. Specifically, if the effect of the deal on competition (if the two companies merge) is less deleterious than the effect of letting Eagle go bankrupt, the FTC may approve the deal. This is the "failing company defense" to possible antitrust objections.

7. Yes, Satellite and Alpha can consummate the deal. No response from the FTC or the DOJ within 30 days of filing gives clearance for firms to complete mergers and acquisitions.

CHAPTER 29

Documenting the M&A Deal

1. Sally can ask Harry to sign a standstill agreement, which seeks a commitment on Harry's part not to purchase more target shares without the approval of Close Call's board. By limiting the Motley Players' shares, the standstill agreement prevents Motley Players from accumulating voting power. A standstill agreement helps Close Call prevent loss of control during negotiations.
2. The financial adviser may have been thinking that in exchange for signing a confidentiality agreement, Harry could ask Sally to sign an exclusivity agreement to prevent competitors from entering the picture. The financial adviser could also be thinking of having Sally sign a termination agreement in which Close Call would pay a fee or reimburse Motley's expenses if it terminated negotiations. This would increase the chances of a successful negotiation.
3. Predator's insistence on a "tail provision" is common practice, though the four-year time frame that Predator requests seems rather long.
4. The engagement letter has not included a provision that specifies the scope of the engagement. The services sought by the client can cover a potentially wide range, from providing a fairness opinion to advising on deal structure and even performing other services up to and including closing. The scope of the adviser's services should be clearly laid out in the engagement letter.
5. The complexity of the target in terms of scope of operations would dictate a longer due diligence period than two weeks. Harry's request is more reasonable.
6. No, Harry has no obligation to comply with the terms set out in the earlier documents. The term sheet and the letter of intent are nonbinding.
7. The parties to the deal are PayPal, Inc. (the target), eBay Inc. (the buyer), and Vaquita Acquisition Corp. (a wholly owned subsidiary of eBay).
8.

Purchase Price	
Implied price per share	No share price given for eBay
Resulting PayPal ownership of eBay	7.6% (students will need to calculate)
Transaction fees	Not given
Exchange ratio	0.39
Cap	None

(Continued)

Form of Payment	
Consideration	100% stock
Number of shares to be issued	26.14 million shares (you will need to calculate)
Form of Transaction and Tax Considerations	Section 368(a) Reverse Triangular Merger. Tax-deferred to the sellers.
Transaction Process Requirements	
Termination penalties	PayPal pays eBay $5 million if the agreement is terminated by eBay. PayPal pays eBay $45 million pursuant to conditions set out in Section 8.5(c).
Shareholder vote	PayPal shareholders must approve the deal. Shareholder approval is not required for eBay.
Closing date	No specific date given. "Occurs after all the conditions in the merger agreement have been fulfilled."
Social Issues	
Organization structure	PayPal becomes a stand-alone subsidiary of eBay.
Executives	The officers of the company at the effective time shall, from and after the effective time, be the officers of the surviving corporation until their successors have been duly elected or appointed and qualified.
Board seats	The directors of merger subsidiary at the effective time shall, from and after the effective time, be the directors of the surviving corporation until their successors have been duly elected or appointed and qualified.
Headquarters	Not mentioned.
Name	Subsidiary will remain PayPal Inc.
Workforce	eBay and PayPal shall work together to retain selected key employees of PayPal, including new employment terms as appropriate.

9. The merger agreement was dated July 7, 2002. The closing date occurs after all the conditions in the merger agreement have been fulfilled. The effective date is when a certificate of merger has been filed with and accepted by the secretary of state of Delaware (the state in which both buyer and target are incorporated).

   The merger is a reverse triangular merger. PayPal will merge into the eBay subsidiary Vaquita, and will emerge as the surviving entity.

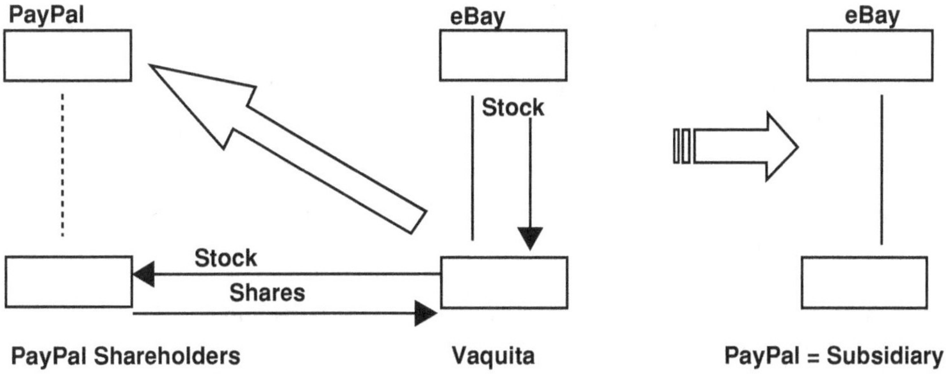

10. The "Recitals" section tells us that the boards of both target and acquirer have already approved the deal, and that they deem the deal to be in the best interest of shareholders. The "Recitals" section also suggests that certain conditions—such as stockholders' agreements and employment agreements—have been put in place. These agreements make it more difficult for each party to back out of the deal.
11. PayPal's bylaws will apply.
12. The directors will be those of Vaquita Acquisition Corp., and the officers will be those of PayPal. As a result, eBay retains control of the board and keeps PayPal management in place.
13. The deal is a share-for-share exchange. Each PayPal share will be exchanged for 0.39 shares of eBay.
14. The chief representations and warranties issues include:
    - Proper incorporation and valid existence of the company, and warranty of good standing. (This prevents fraud.)
    - Class and number of shares outstanding, including any options outstanding. (This fixes the number of shares to be included in the exchange, preventing unexpected dilution.)
    - No violations of governmental filings. (This prevents surprise over violations of rules and laws.)
    - Integrity of financial statements. (This prevents surprise due to accounting fraud or error.)
    - Existing and expected litigation and liabilities. (This prevents surprise over unexpected lawsuits and legal obligations.)
    - Employee benefit plans and labor matters. (This prevents surprise over labor matters.)
    - Compliance with company bylaws and any contracts entered into. (This prevents unexpected lawsuits due to noncompliance.)

- Potential environmental litigation. (This limits exposure arising from unexpected environmental liabilities.)
- Sufficiency of corporate authority for merger approval. (This prevents corporate authorities from obstructing the deal.)

15. Examples of covenants are:

- The agreement to conduct business as usual until the effective date protects both buyer and target from material adverse effects arising from business disruption.
- Agreements prohibiting the target from doling out additional awards under employee benefit plans, from selling any capital stock and/or paying extraordinary dividends, and from commencing litigation all protect the buyer from potential additional liabilities.
- The agreement by the target not to solicit any other merger offers protects the buyer from competing bids.
- Prohibitions against making misleading statements and omitting material facts protect both the target and buyer from potential liabilities arising from fraud or from consummating a bad deal.
- Agreements to convene shareholder meetings, to file registration/proxy statements promptly, and to take any actions needed to consummate the merger protect both parties from any foot-dragging.
- Agreements to provide target employees with benefits no less favorable than those previously provided and to retain key employees protect the target's employees and ensure smoother consummation of the deal.

16. Some of the conditions include:

- Obtaining the necessary stockholder approval.
- Expiration of the waiting period under the Hart-Scott-Rodino Act.
- No governmental litigation prohibiting the consummation of the merger.
- S-4 registration statements (these register with the SEC new shares to be issued) should have become effective.
- Blue-sky approvals should have been obtained.

The preceding conditions give the buyer and/or target an exit in the event that some outside party (e.g., shareholders, government) fail to complete important prerequisites.

- Reps and warranties made by buyer and target should be true as of agreement and closing dates.
- Both buyer and target should have performed all obligations agreed upon in the merger agreement.
- Submission of "comfort letters" from accountants.

The preceding conditions manage risk by preventing fraud and by allowing either party to exit in the event that the other party fails to complete an important condition for the merger.

- No material changes in financial condition, business, or results of operations of both buyer and target.
- Submission of tax opinions stating that the merger will be treated for federal income tax purposes as desired by the parties.

The preceding conditions manage risk by allowing the target or buyer to exit if outside conditions render the merger unable to bring about the expected financial benefits.

17. Termination is possible when:
    - There is mutual written consent by the respective boards of eBay and PayPal.
    - The merger is not consummated by December 31, 2002, or, if an extension is needed, by March 31, 2002, at the latest.
    - There has been a breach of any representation, warranty, covenant, or other term of agreement by either party.
18. The buyer, SPX Corporation, is filing the proxy statement.
19. SPX wants Echlin's shareholders to call for a special shareholders' meeting. SPX needs at least 35 percent of the votes for a special meeting to be called.
20. Common stock.
21. According to the Business Combination Statutes,

    a. a corporation may not engage in any business combination with an "Interested Shareholder" (defined as the beneficial owner of 10% or more of the voting power of a company) for five years following the date on which the Interested Shareholder became such unless the acquisition which resulted in the Interested Shareholder becoming such or the business combination is approved by the board of directors and by a majority of the non-employee directors, of which there shall be at least two, before the date of the 10% acquisition.

    b. any business combination with an Interested Shareholder that was not approved by the board of directors prior to the 10% Acquisition must be approved by the board of directors, 80% of the voting power and two-thirds of the voting power not controlled by the Interested Shareholder or meet certain conditions regarding minimum price and type of consideration.

    These conditions limit the ability of SPX to accumulate shares if board approval is not obtained. If SPX accumulates 10 percent *before* board approval is obtained, SPX will need to gain approval from an even wider constituency.
22. Echlin has a "Rights Agreement" that allows each right holder (in Echlin's case, all common stockholders except the potential buyer) to buy Echlin shares at a predetermined exercise price once a potential buyer obtains 20 percent or more of Echlin's shares. Once a potential buyer has accumulated 20 percent of shares, the rights may be redeemed only if there are "Continuing Directors" in office and a majority of such "Continuing Directors" concurs in

authorizing redemption of the rights. If a potential buyer commences a tender offer, Echlin's board of directors will no longer be able to amend the Rights Agreement after the 10-business-day period after commencement of the tender offer, unless the board of directors takes action to extend such period.

The Rights Agreement hinders SPX's attempt to acquire Echlin by severely diluting SPX's equity stake and voting power. The provision that only continuing directors can redeem the rights makes it virtually impossible for SPX to revoke the Rights Agreement unless it can get its own nominees on the board before it accumulates 20 percent of Echlin's shares, or before it commences a tender offer.

23. Probably Connecticut is not friendly to hostile takeovers. According to the proxy statement, the Connecticut House of Representatives recently introduced a bill that would (1) restrict the ability of shareholders of a public company to remove directors, (2) require the approval of a majority of "continuing directors," rather than the approval of the board of directors, and (3) provide that approval of a majority of "continuing directors," rather than the board of directors, would be required.

24. SPX is proposing a reverse triangular merger in which a subsidiary of SPX would be merged into Echlin. However, SPX reserves the right to amend the terms of the exchange, including the surviving entity in the merger.

25. SPX is proposing a part-stock, part-cash deal where Echlin shareholders would receive for each Echlin share $12.00 in cash and 0.4796 share of SPX common stock. The transaction will be taxable to exchanging shareholders. The offer represents around a 32 percent premium to Echlin's share price. SPX has filed a registration statement with the SEC, but the registration is not yet effective.

26. Echlin shareholders will own 70 percent of SPX if the deal is consummated. The deal is a reverse takeover, in effect.

27. SPX's conditions:

- *Minimum condition.* The number of shares tendered must represent at least $66^2/_3$ percent of the shares outstanding on a fully diluted basis.
- *Rights condition.* The Rights Agreement must have been suspended or otherwise be inapplicable to the exchange offer. The rights condition is to prevent triggering the poison pill, which would allow Echlin shareholders to acquire shares cheaply, thereby diluting SPX's equity stake.
- *Business Combination Statutes condition.* SPX must be satisfied that the restrictions contained in the Business Combination Statutes (see problem 21) will not apply to the proposed business combination. This is to relieve SPX of having to overcome inordinate obstacles (e.g., approval of directors/continuing directors, 80 percent vote, etc.).
- *Financing condition.* SPX must have obtained sufficient financing to enable the exchange offer and the merger to be consummated. This is to avoid the risk that the merger cannot be consummated due to lack of funding.
- *SPX stockholder approval condition.* Since SPX needs to issue more than 20 percent of its outstanding common stock to consummate the exchange offer,

it needs the approval of its stockholders. This is in compliance with New York Stock Exchange rules.

28. SPX estimates it will need $2.4 billion in funding and has received a "highly confident" letter from CIBC Oppenheimer that the necessary financing will be raised.

29. This is an escape clause that would allow SPX to start negotiating again if the opportunity arises. In effect, this clause prevents SPX from being compelled to go through with its offer if it changes its mind.

30. SPX is proposing:

    - *Repeal of bylaws adopted subsequent to April 3, 1997.* SPX wants to repeal Echlin's bylaws to prevent its directors from taking action permitted by its bylaws to block SPX's acquisition of Echlin.
    - *Removal of directors of the company and replacement with SPX nominees.* SPX wants to remove all of Echlin's current directors from the board and replace them with its own nominees. SPX needs to remove Echlin's directors because they have shown no interest in pursuing a merger with SPX and are likely to prevent SPX from consummating its offer. SPX has put up five nominees for election to the board.
    - *Amendment of the bylaws of the company.* SPX wants to amend Echlin's bylaws to reduce the number of directors from nine at present to five.

31. There must be a quorum at the special meeting, and the number of votes cast in favor of removal of a director must exceed the number of votes cast against removal.

CHAPTER 30

Negotiating the Deal

1. Nova was trying to "anchor" at a price that was clearly too low and probably insulting to the CEO of Seattle Springs. Anchoring works as long as the quoted price is credible.
2. Maybe not. Opening at one's reservation price commits one to a "take it or leave it" strategy—you retain no flexibility for further bargaining. Furthermore, such a strategy ignores the fact that bargaining is a process of *discovery* of prices and other terms. Nova might have anchored at a lower price. By opening right at the high end of its estimate of the target's value, Nova may be setting itself up for overpayment.
3. The CEO of Nova Water should get a grip on reality. The CEO's reason for continuing to bid is "sunk cost" logic—economics teaches that this is a bad basis for making financial decisions. If, as assumed in problem 1, Nova's reservation price was $330 million, how does the entry of Rings of Saturn into the bidding change that? Without further sound justification, the CEO of Nova should be counseled to drop out of the bidding.
4. Sprouse is ignoring cultural influences on bargaining outcomes. Given what he has been advised, to leave the CEO of the Taiwanese concern negotiating with anyone less than the CEO of Sea Horse may be considered disrespectful.
5. The CEO is using single-issue serial bargaining rather than multi-issue parallel bargaining. In general, single-issue serial bargaining is associated with greater likelihood of deadlocks. Multi-issue parallel bargaining allows the parties greater room for finding mutually agreeable trade-offs.
6. The soft drink company may have ignored its BATNA. The $2 billion acquisition of the target was clearly more expensive in present value terms than building its own noncarbonated beverages business.
7. Settles is not paying attention to the fact that he is a repeated buyer in a small market and that he depends on positive rapport with sellers. His reputation may cost him deals in the future.
8. Bailey did not manage the approval process on his side effectively. He could have called the CEO to report that the other side insisted on locating headquarters in Toledo. He could have insisted on going over a list of points with the CEO prior to the negotiations. He could have avoided shaking hands on the agreement until he got the approval of his CEO.

CHAPTER 31

Auctions in M&A

1. The English auction method is most advisable if bidders are affiliated. Although it may be vulnerable to collusion, it is less vulnerable than other methods and is the most transparent method.
2. The asset is unique/scarce; hence, an auction is preferred over other methods. If the bidders know each other, an English auction would be most advisable.
3. An auction is *not* recommended. There are only two potential bidders—if one decides not to bid, Selectiv will suffer loss of reputation by trying to hold a competitive auction and failing. Also, the goal of the founders is clearly not just revenue maximization, but also fit, stability, and ability to help the company grow. A private negotiated sale seems more appropriate.
4. A Dutch auction does not "leave money on the table," as opposed to an English auction. Because prices start from the top in a Dutch auction, the seller can fetch the highest price that any of the bidders is willing to pay. In an English auction, the winning bid is not necessarily the maximum price that the winner is willing to pay.
5. Because a second-price sealed-bid auction lets the winning bidder pay the second highest bid instead of the winning bid, it gives bidders an incentive to raise their bids. Thinking that they will never have to pay what they bid, bidders may be willing to bid their maximum or even beyond. In a first-price sealed-bid auction, bidders are unlikely to go beyond their maximum, or even to bid at maximum, for fear of the "winner's curse." Thus, a second-price sealed bid auction may have greater potential to fetch higher prices.
6. Two effects seem to have a role in this outcome. First, Virginia, Inc., may have been victimized by the "winner's curse." Winning an auction reveals that everyone else estimated the value of the asset to be less than the winner estimated—thus, the implication is that the buyer may have overpaid. Second, the fact that Virginia, Inc., bid higher than its reservation price suggests that it succumbed to bidding frenzy.
7. In theory, Virginia, Inc., has the power to abandon the negotiation at this point, though to do so might damage Virginia's reputation. Abandonment is threatening to the target, as it may signal new negative information about the target that may turn other interested parties away. Culpeper, Inc., though, has the advantage of still having other interested parties (bidders), the monopoly on the assets being sold, and inside information about the target.

8. A target's strategy would be to maximize revenues and the number of bidders. To do so the target must build credibility about the auction; that is, the target must disclose all rules clearly, and stick to them at all costs.

   The strategy of a bidder upon learning of an auction would be to pressure the target board to negotiate directly with it. This may be done through a host of tactics such as "bear hugs," "Saturday night specials," and others. The bidder will aim to drag the target away from an auction, or if that is not possible, to break down the rules of the auction.

CHAPTER 32

Hostile Takeovers: Preparing a Bid in Light of Competition and Arbitrage

1. Yes, under Rule 14d-7(a)(1) target shareholders may withdraw their tenders for any reason in the first 15 days of a tender offer.
2. Not necessarily. If the highest offer is associated with a longer expected time to consummation, the arbitrageur may achieve higher *annualized returns* by taking a lower offer and a shorter holding period.
3. A two-tiered offer is one in which the terms of the offer are different for shareholders who tender earlier than for those who tender later. The difference might be in the actual value of the offer or in the form of payment (e.g., cash versus stock). The first tier often receives more value than the second tier as an incentive to compel shareholders to tender, such as when there are competing bids or time is of the essence, or if it is necessary to gain majority control quickly.
4.

	Two-Tiered Offer	Prisoner's Dilemma
The Incentive	The first tier in a two-tier offer is usually more attractive than the second tier (e.g., cash in first tier and stock in second tier). This creates an incentive for shareholders to tender as soon as they can.	The prisoner (let's call him Prisoner A) who confesses gets a shorter time in jail.
The Dilemma	If shareholders hold out, they may get a better deal through a competing offer. But at the same time, if they hold out, they may end up having no choice but to accept the less attractive part of the deal (the second tier) if other shareholders completely take up the first tier. As a result, the shareholders may choose to tender in order to receive the more attractive part of the deal. As with a prisoner's dilemma, a two-tiered offer exploits the shareholders' (prisoners') inability to work in concert with each other and to communicate.	If Prisoner A confesses he will get a shorter sentence *as long as* Prisoner B does not implicate him. However, Prisoner A cannot tell what Prisoner B will do. If Prisoner A does not confess (shareholders hold out) and Prisoner B squeals on him (other shareholders tender), he will get a longer sentence than Prisoner B (shareholders that held out will get the less attractive part of the deal).

5. Shareholders should communicate and collaborate, such as by forming ad hoc committees of target shareholder groups, and by taking action together to achieve a maximum bid. Shareholders could also try to buy more time. This will allow the target to search for a white knight, develop a recapitalization plan, or mount other defenses.

6. Blended value per share = (.30 × \$58.00) + (.70 × \$52.00) = \$53.80

   Times number of shares × 10,000

   \$538,000

   [This spreadsheet can be found in the folder "Key Spreadsheets from the Workbook" located on the CD-ROM.]

7. A leveraged recapitalization entails borrowing substantially and paying a large one-time dividend to shareholders and/or executing a large one-time share repurchase. The result is a highly levered acquisition target that is probably less attractive to a hostile bidder.

8a. Based on the last closing, the effective purchase price for Compaq would be \$14.69, representing a 19 percent premium to its market price. The premium seems modest and consistent with the merger-of-equals tone of the transaction.

8b. According to the following calculations, Siegel's holding period return and annualized return were 105 percent and 160 percent respectively.

Days in Holding Period		240
Assumptions		
Position and Payoff in Target Shares		
Buy target shares at		\$ 12.35
Payoff on target shares at end (exchange ratio × price of buyer's shares)		\$ 11.48
Gross spread per share on target shares		\$ (0.87)
Total value of gross spread on target shares (times # shares =	125,000	\$(108,925.00)
Position and Payoff in Buyer Shares		
Short buyer shares at		\$ 23.32
Payoff on buyer shares at end		\$ 18.22
Gross spread per share on buyer shares		\$ 5.10
Total value of gross spread on buyer shares	32,000	\$ 637,500.00
Total Assets of the Arbitrage Position		\$1,543,750.00
Short position in buyer shares		\$ 746,240.00
Borrowed shares of buyer		\$(746,240.00)
Debt @ % assets	70%	\$1,080,625.00
Capital employed		\$ 463,125.00
Total Liabilities and Capital of the Arbitrage Position		\$1,543,750.00
Net Spread Calculation		
Gross spread		\$ 528,575.00
– Interest @	6%	\$ (42,632.88)
– Short dividends forgone		\$ —

(Continued)

+ Long dividends received	$	—
Net spread	$	485,942.12
Days in holding period		240
Results		
Return on capital for holding period only		105%
Return on capital annualized		160%

[This spreadsheet can be found in the folder "Key Spreadsheets from the Workbook" located on the CD-ROM.]

9. To decide on its bid price, CleanPack should consider things from the investor's point of view. The investor has to decide whether to tender to CleanPack. If the investor decides not to tender to CleanPack, she is faced with three scenarios, as illustrated in the following investor's decision diagram:

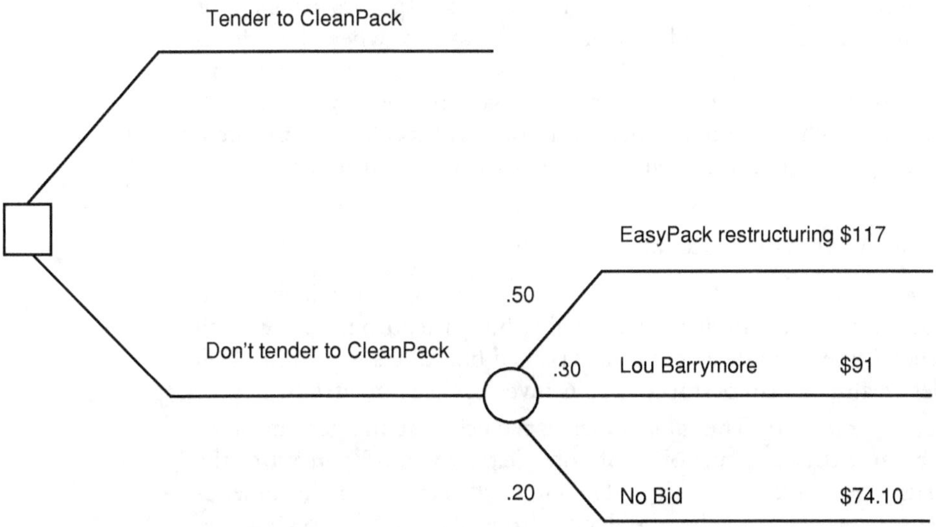

The expected value of not tendering (EVNT) = (.50 × $117) + (.30 × 91) + (.20 × 74.10) = $100.62.

Therefore, CleanPack must bid a price above $100.62 to attract shares into its tender offer.

CHAPTER 33

Takeover Attack and Defense

1. "Good" firms are those with not only strong financial performance, but also strong corporate governance and company management teams. Takeover defenses can leverage the bargaining power of good firms' managing executives for extracting high prices from bidders. However, takeover defenses more deeply entrench managers of "bad" firms—those whose managers are inept or pursuing private benefits; shareholders will react negatively when these firms announce antitakeover defenses. The primary implication is ironic: The firms that are most vulnerable to takeover (poorly managed and poorly performing firms) are those in which shareholders may be most hurt by defenses instituted, whereas the strong firms become even better guarded when takeover defenses are adopted.

2. There are four main types of charter amendments:

    1. *Classified board.* A classified board is a "staggered" one, in which board members are not elected all at once annually, but instead only a few each year. In general, the announcement of a classified board has little impact on shareholder wealth or firm performance, as investors react neutrally.
    2. *Supermajority provision.* This amendment specifies that mergers must be approved by an extra-large majority of votes (e.g., 75 to 85 percent of the votes, versus a 51 percent majority). The intended purpose of this amendment is to give a minority of shareholders a stronger voice to veto a merger, as well as delay a merger from being consummated. Scholars (Johnson and Rao 1999; Ambrose and Megginson 1992) have found that putting a supermajority provision in place has little effect on firms and shareholder value.
    3. *Fair price provision.* This provision requires that all selling shareholders receive the same price from the buyer. This prevents discriminatory practices like greenmail, where a bidder may seek to buy a majority of shares by offering a more attractive purchase price. Many states in the United States now require a takeover bid to carry a "fair price" for all shareholders. Some early research suggested that adopting a fair price amendment has a neutral to slightly negative effect on stock price. Ambrose and Megginson (1992) found that firms with fair price amendments are not much more likely to attract takeover bids.
    4. *Dual-class recapitalization.* This amendment creates two classes of stock with different voting rights (weightings): Class A stockholders may have five votes per share, whereas Class B stockholders may have one vote per share.

Some research on dual-class recapitalization shows a statistically negative impact on shareholder wealth, due to the loss of voting rights. However, Shum, Davidson, and Glascock (1995) found neutral to positive market reaction due to the loss of voting rights, provided that the shareholders received some form of compensation (e.g., increased dividends). Ambrose and Megginson (1992) found that dual-class recapitalization does not decrease the likelihood of a takeover bid.

3. You can use the following equation to test the profitability to the buyer of a takeover attack.

$$[\pi \text{ (Intrinsic value} - \text{Price} - \text{Transaction costs)} + (1 - \pi)\text{Transaction costs}] > 0$$

Probability of successful takeover	60%
Target intrinsic value (in $ millions)	$460.00
Investment banking adviser fee	2%
Legal fee	$ 10.00
Total transaction cost	$ 19.00
Buyer's planned bid price (in $ millions)	$450.00
Test	$ (1.40)

From the calculation the test gives a negative value, which indicates that the takeover attack would not create value for the buyer.

4.

Estimate of Dilution Imposed on the Bidder from a Poison Pill

Assumptions		
Stock price of target before pill is triggered	$30.00	
Number of shares outstanding before attempted raid:	1,500,000	
Discount at which nonraider shareholders have the right to purchase shares:	80%	
Purchase shares worth	$200	
By paying	$40	
Poison pill "trigger":	12%	
Assumption about whether pill exercise proceeds will be dividended to shareholders	No Dividend	Dividend
Market value of equity before trigger	$ 45,000,000	$ 45,000,000
Cash received upon exercise of poison pill rights	$ 52,800,000	$ 52,800,000
Dividend paid	$ —	$(52,800,000)
Market value of equity after trigger	$ 97,800,000	$ 45,000,000
Number of shares held by the raider when the pill is triggered	180,000	180,000
Number of shares held by investors other than the raider after the pill is triggered	10,120,000	10,120,000
Total number of shares outstanding after the pill is triggered	10,300,000	10,300,000
Price per share after trigger	$ 9.50	$ 4.37
Dilution in price per share	68%	85%

(Continued)

Estimate of Dilution Imposed on the Bidder from a Poison Pill *(Continued)*

Analysis of voting dilution imposed on raider			
Raider voting interest just before pill is triggered		12%	
Raider voting interest after pill is triggered		2%	
Economic dilution imposed on raider if pill is triggered and bid fails			
Change in raider's value of shares after pill is triggered		$ (3,690,874)	$ (4,613,592)
Raider's share of dividend from pill exercise proceeds		$ —	$ 922,718
Raider's total economic dilution after pill is triggered		$ (3,690,874)	$ (3,690,874)
Raider's total economic dilution as a percent of outlay		–68%	–68%
Economic dilution imposed on raider if pill is triggered and bid succeeds			
Value of nonraider shares before pill is triggered	$39,600,000		
Value of nonraider shares after pill is triggered	$96,090,874		
Change in raider's cost to acquire rest of shares		$(56,490,874)	$ (4,613,592)
Raider's share of dividend from pill exercise proceeds			$ 922,718
Raider applies cash from rights toward purchase price		$ 52,800,000	$ —
Raider's total economic dilution after pill is triggered		$ (3,690,874)	$ (3,690,874)
Raider's total economic dilution as a percent of outlay pretrigger		–68%	–68%
Change in cost to acquire remaining 88%		8%	8%

[This spreadsheet can be found in the folder "Key Spreadsheets from the Workbook" located on the CD-ROM.]

Using the model "Poison Pill Dilution.xls," you will need to input the assumptions at the top of the spreadsheet, namely the stock price before the pill is triggered, the number of shares outstanding before the attempted raid, the trigger percentage, the discount at which the nonraider shareholders have the right to purchase shares, and the total dollar worth of possible shares, that each share is eligible to buy.

As a result of triggering the poison pill, the raider's wealth in the target is diluted 68 percent. The raider's voting interest drops from 12 percent to 2 percent. And the raider will need to pay 8 percent more to acquire the remaining shares of the target.

CHAPTER 34

The Leveraged Restructuring as a Takeover Defense: The Case of American Standard

1. American Standard (AS) decided to restructure when its prearranged takeover defenses were breached by court intervention. Originally, the company contemplated a leveraged recapitalization. But as the raider's bid price rose, AS signed a merger agreement with Kelso & Company, a white knight. The deal was effectively an LBO with an ESOP investment made with excess pension assets. It was only after American Standard had undergone this drastic restructuring that Black & Decker (B&D) retreated.

2. A leveraged recapitalization could be considered a synthetic MBO because it yields similar benefits to shareholders as those provided by an MBO, but without taking a firm private. Both MBOs and leveraged recaps provide preexisting shareholders with a large one-time cash payout, which is financed by a dramatic releveraging of the company. In addition, both restructurings also involve a significant change in operations and management incentive compensation.

3. Announcements of a company's shark repellent defenses are sometimes followed by declines in stock price because investors may suspect that incumbent management is adopting such provisions to protect their own interests over those of shareholders. Announcements of leveraged recaps and MBOs, however, are followed by substantial rises in share prices. Both involve a dramatic increase in corporate leverage, which can add value to a company in various ways: the value of debt tax shields, greater alignment of managers with shareholder interests, and improved operational efficiency. Furthermore, shareholders receive direct cash payouts from recaps and MBOs, which provide them with a quantitative, tangible method to value the company.

4. Being proactive is generally better than being reactive. But making a precautionary commitment to a full line of defense can have several disadvantages. First, it can lull management and the board into a false sense of security. As Chapter 32 of the main text noted, well over half of all targets of takeover attempts lose their independence. Second, defenses can entrench poor management to the disadvantage of shareholders: Takeover defenses may not al-

ways be in the interests of shareholders. And third, as the American Standard case suggests, success depends in large part on defensive reaction while the takeover contest is in progress. What matters most is *how you play the game*.

5a. You can set up a spreadsheet model like the following one, as outlined in Chapter 13 of the main text. In this base-case assumption, the value per American Standard share (line 24) rises from $50 to $68 (see line 24).

	Before Recapitalization	Changes	After Recapitalization
Book Value Balance Sheet			
1 Net working capital	$ 450,164		$ 450,164
2 Fixed assets & goodwill	$ 968,472		$ 968,472
3 Other	$ 81,812		$ 81,812
4 Total assets	$1,500,448		$1,500,448
5 Long-term debt	$ 279,506	$ 1,486,201	$1,765,707
6 Deferred tax, etc.	$ 370,316		$ 370,316
7 Preferred stock	$ 1,046		$ 1,046
8 Common equity	$ 837,722	$(1,486,201)	$ (648,479)
9 Other	$ 11,858		$ 11,858
10 Total capital	$1,500,448		$1,500,448
Market Value Balance Sheet			
11 Net working capital	$ 450,164		$ 450,164
12 Fixed assets & goodwill	$1,574,061		$1,574,061
13 Other	$ 81,812		$ 81,812
14 Tax shield	$ 104,815		$ 662,140
15 Total assets	$2,210,852		$2,768,177
16 Long-term debt	$ 279,506	$ 1,486,201	$1,765,707
17 Deferred tax, etc.	$ 370,316		$ 370,316
18 Preferred stock	$ 1,046		$ 1,046
19 Common equity	$1,548,126		$ 619,250
20 Other	$ 11,858		$ 11,858
21 Total capital	$2,210,852		$2,768,177
22 Cash	$ —		$ 48.00
23 Value of the share	$ 50.00		$ 20.00
24 Total per share	$ 50.00		$ 68.00

[This spreadsheet can be found in the folder "Key Spreadsheets from the Workbook" located on the CD-ROM.]

5b. By using the Goal Seek feature of Excel, you can back-solve for the new debt required to offer a restructuring value equal to Black & Decker's successively higher bids. The resulting findings show that beyond $68 per share, American Standard exceeds its maximum amount of external new borrowings.

	B&D's Bid	AS New Borrowing Required to Produce Total Value Equal to B&D's Bid	Value per Stub Share	Ratio of Long-Term Debt to Market Value of Common Equity
Prebid	$50.00	N/A	N/A	0.18
B&D's Bid	$65.00	$1,238,501	$25.00	1.96
	$68.00	$1,486,201	$20.00	2.85
	$73.00	$1,899,034	$11.67	6.03
	$77.00	$2,229,301	$ 5.00	16.21

[This spreadsheet can be found in the folder "Key Spreadsheets from the Workbook" located on the CD-ROM.]

These results are roughly consistent with the facts of the case: AS was able to boost its recapitalization plan to a total value of $74 to $75, but when Black & Decker raised its bid to $73, AS moved to formulate a leveraged buyout proposal that would pay AS shareholders $78. Operating as a public company, AS had less debt capacity than as a private firm.

5c. Unused debt capacity is an instrument of takeover defense used in the context of a restructuring or leveraged buyout proposal. But large unused debt capacity may be an inducement for the raider to attack in the expectation of a profit whether the target restructures or sells to the raider. Thus, unused debt capacity is a two-edged sword.

CHAPTER 35

Communicating the Deal: Gaining Mandates, Approval, and Support

PART I: WHAT'S WRONG WITH THIS PICTURE?

1a. Keep the presentation simple. Too much material can obscure one's message. Most CEOs will probably not have the time (or the patience) to sit through a 100-slide presentation, much less read a nearly 400-page pitch book. The message has to be presented in a convincing but *concise* form.

1b. A deal presentation should emphasize its strategic rationale before getting into financial details. It would be difficult for a CEO (or anyone else for that matter) to absorb financial details without first understanding why and how a deal might fit with the company's overall business strategy.

PART II: VIGNETTES

1a. You have the challenge of communicating an idea to someone you do not know well and have not worked with in the past. Without a strong frame of reference (e.g., having already made other merger pitches to her) you probably do not have a sense of what aspects of a merger deal could be important to her and what kinds of ideas would be unattractive. Furthermore, even though you have a long tenure at the firm, you do not necessarily have buy-in or credibility with the new CEO. Perhaps you have done a good job at establishing yourself at the firm, but you have not yet personally proven yourself to Madison.

If you had a good relationship and working history with former CEO Lazar, it would probably be less difficult to present a merger deal to him, if only because you and he would have already had extensive conversations and communication on other matters. You probably would already know some of Lazar's ideas and viewpoints on different business matters (and what his important issues were) even before you pitched your specific merger idea to him.

1b. Yes, the circumstances could actually yield a better opportunity for deal approval. Consider this: The absence of a preexisting relationship with the new CEO may motivate or require you to take more formal preparation time to develop your merger idea and to sharpen your presentation skills. The extra time and effort could pay off if they result in a better overall presentation, which would in turn increase your chances of successfully getting the merger idea approved by Madison.

There could be another reason for an increased probability for making a successful deal presentation, one in which your idea is approved. If Madison were very eager to make her mark at the new company and biased toward doing a merger even before seeing the specifics of a deal, you may have a greater opportunity for success. (This would be a clear example of managerial hubris at play in the merger decision-making process.)

1c. To improve your chances for making a successful deal presentation to the new CEO, you could do research on Madison and read about her background. If Madison does indeed have a good reputation and credibility in the industry, you would probably be able to find some good sources of information about her. In addition, you could just spend some time getting to know the new CEO before making a merger deal pitch to her. If you were to talk with Madison informally and develop a relationship with her, you would have a better sense of how to present your merger idea(s) in a way that would be successful.

2. Public disclosures of mergers should be prepared with legal counsel. It is important to disclose pertinent terms of the deal (such as the deal size, payment form, expected financial implications and synergies, etc.). While there may be an argument that "less is more" with respect to an initial press release about a merger for liability reasons as well as others, investors also have a right to learn the important facts about the deal up front. If shareholders are the ones whose votes you need to win, they will not likely support the deal if they do not have enough information, or if they learn about the deal in a piecemeal fashion well after the initial press release. The firms involved should use the press release as an opportunity to see how investors react up front, so they can gauge what they are up against as they prepare a formal deal presentation to shareholders.

   At the same time, the company must at all times be conscious of managing legal exposure and minimizing risk. Given the inherent risk of changing deal conditions, it would be wise to *not* include more information than necessary, and to *not* say anything that might be misleading or even construed/claimed to be misleading.

PART III: CASES

Hewlett-Packard and Company

1. The excerpts have two strong themes that Fiorina and Cappellas both convey repeatedly to market the deal as an attractive one.

   First and foremost, they both speak of the two companies as having a great deal "in common," including cultures, organizational models, sales force design, structures of customer support and account management, strategies, visions, and values. The two CEOs also speak of sharing a similar commitment to innovation, invention, and engineering excellence, as well as a deep contribution to communities. The two executives delineate the firms as two parts of an (already) integrated whole, and with all the descriptions of what the two companies have in common, the impression one gets is that they are in many ways the same company.

Second, both Fiorina and Cappellas speak about their comprehensive integration plan. What is particularly noteworthy in their commentaries is not the discussion of what they intend to do, but rather their testimonies about the great deal *that they have already done*.

Fiorina stated, "We have a set of early decisions already made. . . . We've done a lot of work and a lot of detailed planning before we ever said that this is a transaction that we were prepared to do."

Along the same lines, Cappellas noted, "I actually believe and think you'll start to see the things we've done as we've been bringing the companies together; you'll start to see not only the benefit of what we will do, but the benefit of what we have done. . . ."

What is particularly effective about these commentaries is that they make a strong impression and reinforce that a great deal of work has already been done, and that therefore the deal is far along and very much under way. This could have a strong influence on how shareholders decide to vote (i.e., for versus against the merger). It would be easier to vote for a merger that had already made a great deal of progress versus one that seemed to be in its infancy. Likewise, it would be much harder (presumably) to vote against a merger that is further developed than against one in which the wheels have barely been put into motion.

2. The drop in HP's stock value does not necessarily convey a failure on the part of HP and Compaq in communicating and presenting the deal to the investing community. An investor's decisions to buy or sell HP may be completely independent of the HP-Compaq press release and deal presentation. Some of those shareholders may have decided to sell even without spending (much) time reading the release or attending/listening to the investor presentation by the two companies. Regarding the investors who decided to sell HP after having taken a more active role in evaluating the deal—reading the news, listening to the investor presentation, and paying attention to Wall Street analysts' views—they did not necessarily sell because HP-Compaq management did a poor job of presenting the deal. The actual quality of the deal presentation will not always dictate the shareholders' reactions or receptivity to the deal, even though it seeks to influence them in a positive way. The quality of the presentation should enhance the probability and level of investors' receptivity to the deal, but even a good presentation will not suffice when a deal is perceived to destroy value.

Smucker

1. The Smucker press release on the Jif/Crisco acquisition is short and clear, provides enough detail, and has an upbeat tone. It has all the elements of a good press release.

   - *Provides the strategic rationale for the deal:*

     SMUCKER

     "Combining JIF and SMUCKER'S," Richard Smucker explained, "brings number one brands together in the original, All-American

comfort food—peanut butter and jelly. JIF also offers a broad and exciting menu of possibilities for product development and growth."

"Just as important, it will strengthen our position to acquire other complementary leading food brands, providing opportunity for greater top- and bottom-line growth. . . ."

"Both these brands are an outstanding fit for Smucker."

P&G

"JIF and CRISCO are strong U.S. brands but they're no longer a strategic fit for P&G as we focus on building our big brands in core categories."

- *Gives details on price, form of payment, reorganization plan, and the resulting shareholder structure:*

  Prior to completion, the JIF and CRISCO brands and the associated assets will be spun off from the existing P&G Company and then immediately merged with The J.M. Smucker Company. Procter & Gamble shareholders will receive one share of new J.M. Smucker stock for every 50 shares they hold in Procter & Gamble in a tax-free transaction. Based on Smucker's closing stock price of $25.89 on October 9, 2001, this represents a pre-tax equivalent cash price of $1.0 billion or approximately 1.7 times net sales.

  This spin-off and merger transaction (a "Revised Morris Trust" structure) effectively manages the tax implications to the parties. Procter & Gamble shareholders will own approximately 53 percent of the newly combined company, which will have approximately 49.3 million shares outstanding.

- *Describes the financial impact of the transaction and the EPS impact for both Smucker and P&G shareholders:*

  With successful closing of the transaction, Smucker expects its sales to approximately double, to $1.3 billion. For fiscal 2003, the first full year of integration, Smucker projects net earnings before one time costs associated with the transaction to be in the range of $95–105 million, almost three times current levels. . . .

  Additionally, the Smucker Company said it expects the combined earnings power of the three brands to allow it both to continue its historic strong dividend practice, typically in the range of 40 to 50 percent of earnings. . . .

  "Not only is this transaction very accretive to earnings, it provides significant cash flows when coupled with our already strong balance sheet," said Richard Smucker.

  For P&G, the transaction is expected to be slightly dilutive in fiscal 2002, but the company is comfortable with the current range of estimates. Dilution in fiscal 2003 is estimated at 6 cents per share.

However, with the potential accretive impact of the pending Clairol transaction, P&G still expects to achieve its earnings goal of double-digit growth in 2003.

- *Discusses the expected timing of deal consummation, and the approvals required:*

  The transaction is subject to regulatory and Smucker shareholder approvals, and the receipt of a ruling from the Internal Revenue Service that the transaction is tax-free to both companies and their shareholders. The transaction is expected to close during the second calendar quarter of 2002.

- *Conveys a focus on creating shareholder value:*

  Smucker

  "Just as important, it [the transaction] will strengthen our position to acquire other complementary leading food brands, providing opportunity for greater top- and bottom-line growth and clearly enhancing shareholder value."

  P&G

  "This structure builds shareholder value very efficiently—a spin-off of JIF and CRISCO assets directly to our shareholders, and the opportunity for them to participate in the future growth of the new J.M. Smucker Company."

  Both

  "In addition to the brands being market leaders, our companies possess . . . commitment to continually enhancing shareholder value."

- *Addresses social issues:*

  "In addition to the brands being market leaders, our companies possess similar management and employee cultures, common focus on customers, dedication to the highest standards of quality for consumers, and commitment to continually enhancing shareholder value."

  Smucker will offer employment to all employees at these facilities 100% dedicated to these businesses.

- *Conveys enthusiasm:*

  ". . . both Richard and I, along with our entire board and management team, are so enthusiastic about this deal," Timothy Smucker concluded.

2. Issuing a memo to employees to inform them of a transaction may help to improve the chances of getting their buy-in. The Smucker memo conveys enthusiasm and starts out with a strong message: that the deal is beneficial for the company and therefore for its employees.

   It will create an even stronger company, doubling our sales to $1.3 billion and more than doubling our profits. Most importantly, this will provide us with a platform for even greater growth in the future.

The memo also briefly discusses the strategic rationale for the deal. In addition, the memo emphasizes that the employees are key to the success of this transaction; it recognizes and thanks the employees for their past and future efforts:

> *As you would expect, this has and will require a great deal of effort by many people to complete. We would like to thank everyone involved for their efforts thus far and for the future efforts that will be required for a successful integration into our business.*

Finally, there is a tacit message to Smucker employees to welcome their new colleagues into the "family":

> *Included in this transaction are the CRISCO production facility located in Cincinnati, Ohio, and the JIF peanut butter plant located in Lexington, Kentucky. These facilities, along with support staff, will add about 450 new employees to the "family" of Smucker.*

Raytheon

1. In contrast to the Smucker press release, the Raytheon release is very short and does not provide much detail. However, this is understandable since the target is small: $20 million in revenue. This makes up only 0.1 percent of Raytheon's $16.8 billion in revenue. The key point is that the quality and degree of disclosure need not be belabored if a transaction is relatively immaterial.

CHAPTER 36

Framework for Postmerger Integration

PART I: INTEGRATION STRATEGY

1. Preservation would seem to be an appropriate integration strategy in this case:

   - *Low interdependence.* The two companies have such different businesses that there would be scant opportunity for meshing the target's and the buyer's operations.
   - *Low control.* Likewise, the unrelated nature of the two businesses' operations would warrant separate financial, quality, and other operational control systems.
   - *High autonomy.* Given Brown-Forman's lack of experience in Lenox's business area, it would be advisable to keep Lenox's leadership team intact and allow them relatively wide discretion/independence in decision making.

2. Absorption into a new culture would be the best integration strategy in this case:

   - *Low autonomy.* Given that a key rationale for the deal is to achieve cost savings by integrating duplicate businesses, a unified culture is probably necessary. As Chapter 36 in the main text states, some researchers have concluded that in scale-driven deals (typically focused intently on improving efficiency), the successful acquirers tended to impose their culture on the target company.
   - *High control.* Because integration is key to the success of this deal, there needs to be a unified system of controls. Also, because the businesses of the two companies are similar, it is possible to operate under a unified system of controls.
   - *High interdependence.* Again, because the two companies operate in similar business areas, there are many opportunities for integrating operations.

3. The need for economies of scale would argue for an integration strategy of absorption. Yet the CEOs seek to maintain lines of differentiated products, which would suggest the need for some autonomy in product design and development. Linking might be an appropriate integration strategy:

- *High autonomy.* The wide divergence between Daimler's and Chrysler's product lines, the vast cultural gap, and the existence of dual headquarters and dual CEOs all call for each party to have a high degree of autonomy.
- *High control.* Being both automobile manufacturers, quality control systems, purchase control systems, asset allocation processes, and other logistical control systems could be unified.
- *High interdependence.* Coordinated business processes, especially in purchasing and manufacturing is necessary to achieve synergies contemplated in the deal.

4. This is a vertical merger with Disney the supplier and Cap Cities/ABC the distribution channel. Linking is a classic strategy for integrating firms in a value chain: high control, high interdependence, and high autonomy. The high control and interdependence are warranted where high coordination within the value chain is necessary to achieve economies of scale and high quality. But also, high autonomy may be justified where the businesses are different enough to warrant separate managerial oversight.

5. An integration strategy of confederation seems to be consistent with the business strategy and rationale for this deal:

   - *High autonomy.* The areas of specialty of the two drug firms seem to have little in common; in addition, the two companies are based in countries with significantly different cultural heritages. These would warrant a high degree of autonomy for both companies.
   - *High control.* Being both drug manufacturers, it seems plausible that control systems such as accounting and financial controls, quality controls, laboratory and resource allocation procedures would easily render themselves to unified systems.
   - *Low interdependence.* Although cross-selling using each other's sales and marketing forces was one of the main merger arguments, in terms of manufacturing operations little interdependence can be achieved, at least initially, due to the divergence in product specializations and the geographic distance.

PART II: INTEGRATION IMPLEMENTATION

1. Speed is crucial to the success of postmerger integration. This is not to say that integration should not be planned carefully—rather, the planning should be completed before the deal is consummated. Once integration is begun, it needs to be implemented quickly. Delay breeds uncertainty, and uncertainty paralyzes the course of business. It also often drains morale. Some consultants have argued that a merger is won or lost within the first 90 days after the merger announcement.

2. The difference in morale between the two divisions could be due to many things (differences in layoffs and other "me issues" are prime candidates). But confusion about the strategic direction of division B also suggests a

communication problem. Has the rationale for the merger been explained there? Have the new organization and strategy been communicated? Above all, is management *listening* to the employees?

3. The manager's approach ignores the need for speed and determination in completing postmerger integration. Not only will the duplicate systems hamper the unification of the two banks in various operational ways, but the strategy also signals to the organization the acceptability of redundancy and delay.

CHAPTER 37

Corporate Development as a Strategic Capability: The Approach of GE Power Systems

1. Business development at GEPS is characterized by:

   - *Consistency of processes.* GEPS streamlined its approach to deals by using common valuation models, presentation templates, and common decision frameworks.
   - *Active knowledge management.* GEPS was committed to sharing knowledge across staff and across time. Data retrieval system and Web-based tools helped to manage business planning, the deal process, and work coordination.
   - *Continuous improvement mind-set.* GEPS (and GE at large) was committed to Total Quality Management and made use of the six sigma approach to map processes and to encourage ongoing process improvement.
   - *Top-down and bottom-up deal pipeline.* GEPS took these two different approaches to generate deals: The bottom-up approach started with ideas from sales and marketing, and worked its way up to senior management, and the top-down approach began with ideas from senior management and moved down the hierarchical chain.
   - *Senior management engagement.* GEPS senior leadership actively participated in weekly meetings, and the CEO of GE reviewed GEPS' business development activities monthly.

2a. The GEPS M&A "factory" is a metaphorical description of its streamlined and standardized business development processes. The "factory" eliminated variation and used the same methods across different deals.

The electronic digitization of information was a key contribution to the factory-like processes. These included:

- An e-deal room, which was a Web-based system that tracked deal progress and allowed for chat room conversations among professionals.
- A company tracker system of "wish list" target companies and their competitors.
- An equity tracker system that allowed executives to follow GEPS' equity investments and to see board meeting and deal progress notes.

- Due diligence tools, such as a question bank to promote an effective and thorough due diligence process.

2b. While GEPS' systematic processes have proved to be highly effective, there is perhaps an inherent risk that the factory-like approach could limit or discourage independent thinking that could be beneficial. When processes become so systematic, people may be prone to think uniformly, rather than creatively and "out of the box." Active, independent thinking may be highly important for working through the intricacies and nuances that are specific to different deals. Just because a standardized system can help streamline the processes for various deals does not mean that all of the deals should always be handled in exactly the same way.

3. A black belt six sigma practitioner is a full-time team leader who is responsible for measuring, analyzing, improving, and controlling key processes that contribute to Total Quality Management. A black belt would help create an environment and mind-set for continuous process improvement and operational efficiency.

   A technology trainer and knowledge-management learning specialist would add value to your division by training employees on how to use and master technological tools. A trainer and learning specialist would increase the value of your human capital by improving employees' skill sets and know-how.

4. It depends on the particular target company and the circumstances, and also on the judgment of the GEPS' business development team. It is logical to assume that if a cold call—an initial conversation with a potential target—is negative, it would be better to move on to other cold calls that might lead to better prospects.

   However, sometimes circumstances change such that an unlikely prospect becomes a strong candidate for a deal. For example, the mini-case describing GEPS' acquisition of Alpha Company (in Chapter 37 of the main text) depicts a situation where a follow-up call was worth making. The first call received a negative response from an elderly owner who was the original inventor of Alpha's proprietary technology. Three years after an initial cold call, GEPS contacted Alpha Company again and spoke to a different executive at the firm: a co-owner who was interested in possibly selling the company. The new circumstances ultimately allowed GEPS to make a successful acquisition.

5. You could describe the key attributes of GEPS' business development process, which, when executed well and taken collectively, translate to a strategic capability. These include:

   - *Strategic mind-set.* Effective, value-creating business development begins with a strategic view that guides the entire process. At GEPS, the business development efforts were highly focused and strategic in nature, as manifested in their matrix grid for deal sourcing.
   - *Integrated teams.* As depicted by GEPS, a "best practice" business development approach is integrating the work of individuals through team formation and integrating the efforts across teams.

- *Strong commitment.* A key component of good business development is commitment-building and commitment-giving. Notable at GEPS is the commitment and involvement of the CEO of GE.
- *Good information technology (IT) infrastructure.* GEPS shows the advantage of having good IT systems and know-how.
- *Knowledge management.* Often used in conjunction with IT systems, knowledge management allows for learning and information sharing across business units and across different deals. This was instrumental for GEPS business development processes.
- *A disciplined process focus.* Systematic process focus leads to great operating efficiency and total quality management. According to Dave Tucker at GEPS, a process discipline did not lead to a rigid and robotic mind-set; it actually allowed for great flexibility in creating deal design.
- *Early integration planning.* GEPS shows the effectiveness of early integration planning—which can help to make smoother transitions and to realize synergies.

CHAPTER 38

M&A "Best Practices": Some Lessons and Next Steps

1. Possible benefit(s) of automation include allowing the deal designer to spend more time on the creative aspects of the deal, and producing multiple and more varied quantitative analyses (i.e., employing different valuation techniques for comparison) in a short period of time.

   A possible drawback could be an overreliance on "opaque box" tools to do quantitative analyses—M&A practitioners should all have a strong conceptual understanding of the analytics and tools and should be able to question quantitative data and even perform some basic modeling and number crunching to test results and findings from more complex systems.

2. The group lacks process leaders—professionals who are in charge of pursuing a deal from beginning to end—and a "whole deal" perspective. She might begin with mapping the deal development processes and engaging professional counsel in improving the process at Best Ensemble. Also, hiring some process managers to carry the deals along and complement the work of the specialists might generate some improvement in performance.

3. Current events in M&A can be instructive in certain areas:

   - *Turbulence and activity:* As discussed in Chapters 3, 4, 5, and 6, the M&A practitioner will benefit greatly from "listening" not only to individual firms but also to different markets: the capital markets, industry markets, and the macro economy at large. Listening to both firms and markets is important in the process for identifying the drivers of economic turbulence and, in turn, good opportunities for mergers and acquisitions.

     The relationship between listening to firms and listening to markets is straightforward: The events and conditions of individual firms may reflect or have an impact on their industries and the capital markets, while the events and conditions of a particular industry (deregulation, consolidation) or the economy at large (interest rates, stock market) will have an impact on individual firms.

   - *Valuation analysis and deal design.* These two activities are highly interrelated. The target valuation will directly affect certain aspects of the deal design—the price, payment, and financing method. At the same time, certain aspects of the deal design such as social issues—side payments, golden parachutes, a "merger of equals" deal structure—will often dictate adjustments to initial valuation analysis.

A deal leader could enhance the transaction development process by assigning cross-functional roles to employees or by creating small deal teams comprised of members working on the different discrete parts of the deal. These small teams could share information and connect the different discrete transaction activities and results. In order to promote fluidity and dynamic interaction, a deal leader should try to break down barriers that divide different functional groups without disturbing the efficient processes in place within the various functional areas.

www.ingramcontent.com/pod-product-compliance
Lightning Source LLC
LaVergne TN
LVHW060937210926
848354LV00004B/139

Applied Mergers and Acquisitions

Founded in 1807, John Wiley & Sons is the oldest independent publishing company in the United States. With offices in North America, Europe, Australia and Asia, Wiley is globally committed to developing and marketing print and electronic products and services for our customers' professional and personal knowledge and understanding.

The Wiley Finance series contains books written specifically for finance and investment professionals as well as sophisticated individual investors and their financial advisors. Book topics range from portfolio management to e-commerce, risk management, financial engineering, valuation and financial instrument analysis, as well as much more.

For a list of available titles, please visit our Web site at www.WileyFinance.com.

Applied Mergers and Acquisitions

ROBERT F. BRUNER

WILEY

John Wiley & Sons, Inc.

Published by John Wiley & Sons, Inc., Hoboken, New Jersey.
Published simultaneously in Canada.

For general information on our other products and services, or technical support, please contact our Customer Care Department within the United States at 800-762-2974, outside the United States at 317-572-3993 or fax 317-572-4002.

Wiley also publishes its books in a variety of electronic formats. Some content that appears in print may not be available in electronic books.

For more information about Wiley products, visit our web site at www.wiley.com.

Library of Congress Cataloging-in-Publication Data:

Bruner, Robert F, 1949–
Applied mergers and acquisitions / Robert F. Bruner.
p. cm.
Includes index.
ISBN 0-471-39506-4 (cloth/CD-ROM) — ISBN 0-471-39505-6 (cloth) —
0-471-395064 (university)
1. Consolidation and merger of corporations. I. Title.
HD2746.5.B783 2004
658.1'62—dc22

2003020246

Printed in the United States of America.

22 21 20 19

To
Jonathan E. Bruner
and
Alexander W. Bruner

1221 Hafast þū gefēred, þæt ðē feor ond nēah
Ealne wīde-ferhð weras ehtigað,
Efne swā sīde swā sæ bebūgeð
Wind-geard, weallas. Wes, þenden þū lifige,
Æþeling, ēadig! Ic þē an tela
Sinc-gestrēona. Bēo þū suna mīnum
Dædum gedēfe, drēam-healdende!
Hēr is æghwylc eorl ōþrum getrŷwe,
mōdes milde, man-drihtne hold;

1841 þē þā word-cwydas wigtig Drihten
On sefan sende;

Bēowulf

About the Author

Robert F. Bruner is Distinguished Professor of Business Administration and Executive Director of the Batten Institute at the Darden Graduate School of Business Administration, University of Virginia. He teaches the course "Mergers and Acquisition" in Darden's MBA program, and is the faculty director of Darden's executive education program, "Mergers and Acquistions." He has received numerous awards for teaching and casewriting in the United States and Europe. *BusinessWeek* magazine cited him as one of the "masters of the MBA classroom." He is the author or co-author of over 400 case studies and notes, and of *Case Studies in Finance: Managing for Corporate Value Creation,* now in its fourth edition. His research has been published in journals such as *Financial Management*, *Journal of Accounting and Economics*, *Journal of Applied Corporate Finance*, *Journal of Financial Economics*, *Journal of Financial and Quantitative Analysis*, and *Journal of Money, Credit, and Banking*. Industrial corporations, financial institutions, and government agencies have retained him for counsel and training. He has served the Darden School, professional groups, and community organizations in various positions of leadership. Copies of his papers and essays may be obtained via his web site, http://faculty.darden.edu/brunerb/. He may be reached by e-mail at brunerr@virginia.edu.

Contents

Foreword

Joseph R. Perella
Chairman of Institutional Securities Group
Morgan Stanley

The Chinese expression for crisis—*wei ji*—combines the character "risk" with the character "opportunity." Mergers and acquisitions (M&A) transactions are opportunities that bear some considerable risk. For more than 30 years as an M&A professional, I have encountered many opportunities and risks; but I am still as excited about my work as when I started in this business in 1972. Nonetheless, things have changed since then.

The M&A environment has always been a fast-paced, highly complex world where transactions can be arranged in a matter of days and where the values involved often exceed billions of dollars. For more than two decades, M&A activities have captured the general attention of the public and motivated many young, intelligent, and ambitious people to pursue careers as M&A professionals at investment banks, consulting companies, and law firms across the world. In fact, the flow of M&A business reached unprecedented levels in the late 1990s. In 2000, the dollar volume of worldwide M&A activities reached approximately \$3.2 trillion through over 3,000 transactions. Of these, approximately half involved U.S. parties and seven transactions had values of \$10 billion or more, including the Time Warner/America Online transaction valued at \$182 billion. Two years later, the dollar volume of worldwide M&A activity was one-third of the 2000 peak, at approximately \$1.0 trillion.[1] It is uncertain if we will revisit the levels attained in 2000 again, but no one doubts that M&A activity is an integral part of corporate strategy.

It is important to realize that popular images are often mistaken. The M&A world is not full of Gordon Gecko types expounding that "greed is good." The real M&A world is built upon hard analysis and research, continuous dialogue among corporate officers, board members, and in many cases external advisers. It is also a world of excitement and innovation, based on transforming transactions that have a major impact on both domestic and global economies.

I prefer to take a more holistic view of molding two organizations together. In many respects, a merger is like a marriage between two companies. It cannot be a surrender followed by constant surveillance; but rather it must result in gains for both sides. Companies unite to forge strengths without necessarily losing individuality, while creating a new and better organization. A merger always involves imperfections, but these imperfections are offset by the potential that the new organization can achieve. Even though we tend to focus on the decision to merge and its prerequisite analysis, it is often the integration and execution processes afterward that matter the most. A successful merger is not the result of the contracts and documents binding organizations together; rather, it is a function of the implicit agreements governing the conduct of all individuals involved and the effects the new organization will have on these individuals. And never fear a tough transaction or a difficult negotiation. To prevail in an M&A negotiation is to see the future value of the possibilities created, not the immediate price paid or initial valuation.

That is what excites me most about such a well written and comprehensive journey into M&A. *Applied Mergers and Acquisitions* by Robert Bruner will surely become an essential reference for any M&A practitioner. Throughout the book, you will find a practical overview of the M&A world and a summary of the theoretical and academic work done on a variety of topics, as well as further questions not yet answered. But this isn't just a book about great thoughts and process, but rather how to turn insight into deals, and deals into lasting value. Read it, absorb its concepts and ideas, question its conclusions, and develop your own way of thinking. Bruner has provided you with the framework and the freedom to forge your own point of view. As W. H. Auden more eloquently put it in "The Managers":

The last word on how we may live or die
Rests today with such quiet
Men, working too hard in rooms that are too big,
Reducing to figures
What is the matter, what is to be done.[2]

NOTES

1. Thompson Financial. Includes announced transactions each with an aggregate value of US$100 MM or more. Includes transactions with estimated values. Excludes terminated transactions.
2. W. H. Auden, *Collected Shorter Poems 1927–1957*, New York: Random House, 1966, page 301.

Preface

Mark Twain barely contained his use of profanity, a problem his wife abhorred and sought to cure. One evening, he and she were dressing for a formal dinner when a button popped off his shirt. He launched a tirade against buttons, formal shirts, and evening wear. After a few minutes, the profanity subsided. Twain's wife decided to use the moment to remind her husband to govern his language. Calmly, and in a flat voice, she repeated, word for word, the entire tirade. Twain replied, "It would pain me to think that when I swear it sounds like that. You got the words right, Livy, but you don't know the tune."[1]

Thus it is in conversations about mergers and acquisitions (M&A) between scholars and practitioners. Each thinks the other has, at best, the words but not the tune. I wrote this book to blend both views. It all began when I needed written notes with which to teach MBA students and practitioners about the analysis and design of M&A deals. I had studied M&A for my entire career, producing a number of research articles and monographs, and numerous case studies. Over the years, so many students and practitioners had shared with me their struggles to learn M&A that I gained a clear sense of the development challenge. And early in my career, I worked briefly as an analyst for a large financial institution, assessing, implementing, and financing M&A deals. Based on this, I thought I had something to say. Plus, I cared enough to want to say it. Motivated by the astonishing M&A boom of the 1990s and the subsequent bust spangled with some prominent M&A-related corporate collapses, I wanted to help practitioners redefine *best practice* in the field of M&A and to highlight how one might actually apply it. I sought to remind the many critics of M&A that it is a vital instrument of industrial renewal and that we stifle the disruptions of M&A only at our peril. I aimed to caution the optimists in M&A to take very great care because M&A is no simple road to success. And I hoped that my writing might nudge my scholarly colleagues toward greater insights.

Therefore, I started to write and to use these notes in my teaching. I tried to blend the conceptual world of the scholar and the "how to do it" view of the practitioner. I gave greater attention to research where the issues were important and when I thought it had something important to say. The chapters present ideas refined in my work with practitioners and MBA students at Darden, INSEAD, and IESE. As the chapters developed, more questions appeared. The interdependent nature of M&A deals meant that a narrow focus would not be appropriate—simply to discuss valuation and value creation without covering the management processes and practices on which they rely would be to tell only part of the story. Thus, I became convinced that the subject had to be presented *comprehensively* or not at all. Also, I found that *learning by doing* was the best way to absorb the tools and concepts of best practice. Therefore, I determined to give the reader software in the form of Excel spreadsheet programs that would enable hands-on experimentation with the ideas and tools presented in the chapters. The CD-ROM, which may be purchased as a bundle with this book or separately at a later date for those who want that option, contains that software. Also, the CD-ROM has prepared questions and problems that can help cement ideas from the chapters for those who want the self-study challenge of answering them, and some M&A deal documentation and reading materials that should aid the *learning by doing* process. And, finally, the companion workbook contains summaries and more self-training questions and problems, a few of which will require the CD-ROM, for highly motivated students of M&A best practices. What started as a small project has now, thousands of manuscript pages later, become the item in front of you.

Through a focus on ideas and their application, this book aims to help the practitioner improve his or her practice of M&A. Thus, the idea-based approach preempts a number of attributes common to the professional literature. This is not a handbook in the sense of providing recipes, wiring diagrams, or assembly instructions. Wherever possible, I have tried to offer examples that can be carried over to other cases and some guidance on how to translate analysis to other situations. Exhibit P.1 gives a list of the actual mergers and acquisitions presented as case studies; these illustrate tools, concepts, and processes discussed in the book. "About the CD-ROM" on page 939 lists the template spreadsheet files on the CD-ROM—you can use these to start exercising your intuition and apply the ideas to your own deals. The field of M&A is too complicated to distill into a simple "to do" list. Rather, I hope to arm the thoughtful practitioner with a wide range of powerful tools and concepts (along with suitable warnings about their use and limitations) and trust that one will adapt them to the specifics of one's circumstances. This book outlines responses to the four classic questions:

1. ***How should I understand M&A activity?*** Broadly stated, what you see happening around you is the result of economic forces at work. But economics is only a necessary (but not sufficient) explanation for what you see. Psychology plays a significant role as well. This book will illustrate how psychology intervenes through conduct.
2. ***What drives success in M&A?*** Lucky structure of the environment combined with good conduct. The book will also offer details about how to measure success.
3. ***What do I need to know?*** The executive and M&A professional should have a competent foundation in all areas of M&A practice. This includes being able to assess the structure of the environment as well as the ability to shape the right conduct on your side (and anticipate the varieties of conduct on the other side).
4. ***What is best practice in M&A?*** Best practices enhance the probability that you will deliver successful outcomes. The book will highlight good approaches in each of the areas of structural analysis and conduct. Ultimately, the secret to best practice is the development of *good processes*. This book highlights process management considerations that might enhance the performance of your organization.

In answering these classic questions, this book insists that the reader should "get a view." On some issues, the research findings and conventional wisdom are in alignment—there, getting a view is not so hard. But on other issues they are in flux or wide disagreement and the reader will need to work to get a view. I'll sketch my

EXHIBIT P.1 Merger and Acquistion Cases Illustrating Practical Ideas in This Book

Chapter	Case
2	Walt Disney Company (ethics of greenmail)
6, 9, 11, 24, 25	Daimler-Benz A.G. and Chrysler Corporation (strategic analysis, valuation, analysis of synergies, social issues, and deal process)
7, 29	Kestrel Ventures (acquisition search)
12	Westmoreland Energy (cross-border joint venture)
12	Continental Cablevision (cross-border joint venture)
13	MediMedia International (leveraged buyout)
13	Revco Drug Stores (leveraged buyout)
13	Koppers Company (leveraged recapitalization)
14	Lucent (spin-off, real options)
14	Agouron Pharmaceuticals (valuing a biotech firm with real options)
14	NCNB/First Republic (staged investing, real options)
14	EM.TV/SLEC (setting acquisition terms, real options)
15	Volvo/Renault (valuing liquidity and control)
17	"Automatic" Sprinkler (momentum acquiring)
17	Ling-Temco-Vought (conglomerate strategy, momentum acquiring)
17	U.S. Office Products (industry roll-up, momentum acquiring)
17	Tyco International (conglomerate strategy, momentum acquiring)
22	Lilly/Hybritech (contingent payment unit)
23	AT&T/MediaOne (collar)
23	Rhône-Poulenc/Rorer (contingent value right)
23	Genzyme/GelTex (staged investing)
24	First Union/Wachovia (social issues)
24	Hewlett-Packard/Compaq (social issues)
24	Fleet Bank/BankBoston (social issues)
31	RJR Nabisco (leveraged buyout, auction)
34	American Standard (leveraged recapitalization)
36	Union Bank of Switzerland/Swiss Banking Corp. (postmerger integration)
37	GE Power Systems (business development process management)

own positions when doing so is instructive. But at the end of the day, you learn best that which you teach yourself.

How can you use this book to best advantage? The following points lend some practical guidance to these and other questions:

- *Read.* It is hard to get the gist of the ideas presented here without some concentration and dedicated effort. To get the maximum benefit, it makes sense to follow the advice of Lewis Carroll's Mad Hatter: "Start at the beginning and when you come to the end, stop."
- *Test your knowledge.* There are some questions and problems for each chapter on the CD-ROM. One could work through these and then examine the suggested solutions given for each on the CD-ROM. A companion, *Applied Mergers and Acquisitions Workbook*, gives summaries of each chapter and worked-through problems available on the CD-ROM.
- *Exercise your skills.* The spreadsheet programs in the software pack enable the reader to use the tools and concepts discussed in the text—this is a good way to

strengthen one's intuition. Also, the models can be applied to cases or problems with which one is familiar.

- *Browse intentionally.* The use of bullet points facilitates a quick survey of topics so that one can focus in on areas of special interest. Corporate executives will find the sections on strategy, laws, communication, integration, and process management to be meaningful. Front-line analysts will find the chapters on valuation and research to offer direct guidance. The manager who is parachuting into a business development assignment will find the chapters on deal development and process management to offer a kick start to one's thinking.
- *Revisit and refer.* This book affords a ready reference on specific questions one might have. One could keep this on the shelf as an ongoing resource for questions about terms, tools, concepts, and processes.
- *Springboard to further study.* One could use this book as an embarkation for other readings about M&A. Chapter 38 gives my list of "best bet" readings for continued study in M&A. In chapter endnotes throughout and in the extensive list of references at the end of the book, I have offered suggestions of other readings.

ACKNOWLEDGMENTS

Of course, I owe a very great debt of thanks to colleagues, friends, assistants, and students who have contributed to this work. First, I thank greatly those who read and commented on chapters. Professor Andrew Wicks of Darden commented on Chapter 2. Professor April Triantis of the University of Virginia School of Law, Professor Diane Denis of the Krannert School of Management, Purdue University, and Frank M. Conner III of Alston and Bird LLP commented on chapters dealing with legal issues. Chris Meyer, an antitrust lawyer, commented on the chapter on antitrust. Professor Gary Blemaster of Georgetown University commented on some of the valuation chapters. Messrs. Norman Siegel and D. French Slaughter, and Professors Luann Lynch, Paul Simko, and Robert Sack commented on various editions of the tax and accounting chapters. Professor Dana Clyman gave helpful suggestions on the chapters dealing with negotiations and auctions. Miguel Palacios commented on chapters on liquidity and control, and cross-border valuation. Professor Bernard Dumas of INSEAD gave helpful comments on the chapters on cross-border valuation. Michael McCloskey and Bill Snider of Legent Corporation commented on the chapters on search and due diligence. Professor Ben Esty of Harvard offered helpful comments on the materials related to contingent forms of payment. Bart Crawford, Dave Edinger, and Jim Kingdon supported the development of materials on merger search and graciously allowed the presentation of some of their materials in Chapters 7 and 29. Ali Fatemi and Keith Howe, editors of *Journal of Applied Finance*, permitted me to excerpt and expand on my article published in their journal (Bruner 2002) that has emerged as Chapter 3. Similarly, Joseph O'Donoghue and Donald Grunewald permitted the republication of an article by Donald Benson, Robert Harris, and myself (1990) as Chapter 34—this article appeared in their book.[2] Marcel Ospel, Peter Wuffli, and their colleagues at UBS A.G. cooperated in my field research that produced Chapter 36 on post-merger integration. And David Tucker cooperated in the development of the case study on General Electric in Chapter 37.

I am very thankful for the contributions of my able research assistants, who read and commented on the chapters and prepared questions for the book and associated workbook under my direction. The principal assistant for this project was Jessica Chan. Bright, patient, and a tenacious researcher, she showed great care and dedication in her work. Jessica led a team consisting of herself, Christine Shim, and Baocheng Yang. Christine was especially creative in framing financial problems in realistic terms; she is a champion wordsmith. Baocheng was the champion quant, contributing analytic care, modeling, and real option valuation. The complementary efforts of the three assistants lent flair and precision to the book. I must also recognize Frank Wilmot, research librarian at Darden, who gave excellent support in obtaining sometimes obscure data and references. I am truly grateful to them for the creativity and exceptionally hard work they brought to the project. Many of the illustrations in this book draw on the efforts of my earlier research assistants.[3]

I especially recognize Kristen S. Huntley, formerly managing director at Morgan Stanley, where she served clients in the Financial Institutions Group and was executive director of mergers, acquisitions, and restructurings in London. She suggested a number of the topics that appear here and also read and commented on many chapters. Since 2001, she and I have co-taught Darden's MBA course on mergers and acquisitions.

Thanks go to co-authors whose work with me appears directly or in summary form here: Donald Benson, Samuel Bodily, Richard Brownlee, Susan Chaplinsky, Petra Christmann, Robert Conroy, Kenneth Eades, Gregory Fairchild, Robert Harris, Pierre Jacquet, Lynn Paine, Miguel Palacios, Robert Spekman, and Scott Stiegler. A number of students and assistants wrote case studies under my direction; they are recognized in each chapter. All these colleagues contributed both stimulating ideas and encouragement to this volume.

This project would not have been possible without the financial support of the University of Virginia Darden School Foundation and the Batten Institute. In particular, I thank Professor S. Venkataraman, director of research, and associate dean Mark Reisler for their timely assistance. I was encouraged and stimulated by many colleagues: Yiorgos Allayannis, Karl-Adam Bonnier, Susan Chaplinsky, John Colley, Bob Fair, Jim Freeland, Sherwood Frey, Jud Reis, Michael Schill, and William Sihler. Darden's deans have been especially supportive: John Rosenblum, Lee Higdon, Ted Snyder, and Bob Harris. I am grateful to the staff of the Batten Institute for their excellent professional support during preparation of the manuscript: Robert Carraway, Trienet Coggeshall, Melissa Collier, Debbie Fisher, Susie Gainer, Donna Gowen, Steve Mendenhall, Gayle Noble, Elizabeth O'Halloran, C. Ray Smith, and S. Venkataraman.

Colleagues at other schools gave insights and encouragement. I am grateful to the following persons (listed with the schools with which they were associated at the time of my correspondence or work with them):

Raj Aggarwal, John Carroll
James Ang, Florida State
Paul Asquith, M.I.T.
Carliss Baldwin, Harvard
Geert Bekaert, Stanford

Gary Blemaster, Georgetown
Rick Boebel, Univ. Otago, New Zealand
Andrew Boynton, IMD
Michael Brennan, UCLA
Duke Bristow, UCLA
Kirt Butler, Michigan State
Richard Caves, Harvard
Don Chance, VPI&SU
Andrew Chen, Southern Methodist
Donald Chew, Stern, Stewart
John Coates, Harvard Law
Thomas E. Copeland, McKinsey
Chuck Cory, Morgan Stanley
Dave Daetz, Symantec
Jean Dermine, INSEAD
Michael Dooley, UVA Law
Bernard Dumas, INSEAD
Klaus Durrer, UBS
Peter Eisemann, Georgia State
Javier Estrada, IESE
Ben Esty, Harvard
Thomas H. Eyssell, Missouri
Ali Fatemi, DePaul
Pablo Fernandez, IESE
Kenneth Ferris, Thunderbird
John Finnerty, Fordham
Steve Foerster, Western Ontario
Jon Freedman, GE
Bill Fulmer, George Mason
Louis Gagnon, Queens
Dan Galai, Jerusalem
Ronald Gilson, Stanford and Columbia
Stuart Gilson, Harvard
Robert Glauber, Harvard
Mustafa Gultekin, North Carolina
Benton Gup, Alabama
Jim Haltiner, William & Mary
Rob Hansen, VPI&SU
Larry Harris, SEC and USC
Philippe Haspeslagh, INSEAD
Pekka Hietala, INSEAD
Rocky Higgins, Washington
Pierre Hillion, INSEAD
Laurie Simon Hodrick, Columbia
Keith Howe, DePaul
John Hund, Texas
Daniel Indro, Kent State
Thomas Jackson, UVA Law

Pradeep Jalan, Regina
Michael Jensen, Harvard
Sreeni Kamma, Indiana
Steven Kaplan, Chicago
Andrew Karolyi, Western Ontario
Carl Kester, Harvard
Herwig Langohr, INSEAD
Ken Lehn, Pittsburgh
Josh Lerner, Harvard
Saul Levmore, UVA Law
Scott Linn, Oklahoma
Dennis Logue, Dartmouth
Timothy Luehrman, Harvard
Paul Mahoney, UVA Law
Paul Malatesta, Washington
Felicia Marston, UVA (McIntire)
Ronald Masulis, Vanderbilt
Stewart Mayhew, SEC
John McConnell, Purdue
Catherine McDonough, Babson
Wayne Mikkelson, Oregon
Michael Moffett, Thunderbird
Nancy Mohan, Dayton
Ed Moses, Rollins
Charles Moyer, Wake Forest
David W. Mullins Jr., Harvard
James T. Murphy, Tulane
Chris Muscarella, Penn State
Robert Nachtmann, Pittsburgh
Ralph Norwood, Polaroid
Robert Parrino, Texas (Austin)
Luis Pereiro, Universidad Torcuato di Tella
Pamela Peterson, Florida State
Gordon Philips, Maryland
Tom Piper, Harvard
Michael Porter, Harvard
John Pringle, North Carolina
Jack Rader, South Florida and FMA
Ahmad Rahnema, IESE
Al Rappaport, Northwestern
Raghu Rau, Purdue
David Ravenscraft, North Carolina
Henry B. Reiling, Harvard
Lee Remmers, INSEAD
Jay Ritter, Michigan
Richard Ruback, Harvard
Art Selander, Southern Methodist
Israel Shaked, Boston

Dennis Sheehan, Penn State
Betty Simkins, Oklahoma State
Scott Smart, Indiana
Luke Sparvero, Texas
Michael Spence, Harvard
Laura Starks, Texas
Jerry Stevens, Richmond
John Strong, William & Mary
Marti Subrahmanyam, NYU
Sudi Sudarsanam, City University
Anant Sundaram, Thunderbird
Rick Swasey, Northeastern
Bob Taggart, Boston College
Anjan Thakor, Indiana
Thomas Thibodeau, Southern Methodist
Walter Torous, UCLA
Max Torres, IESE
Nick Travlos, ALBA
Alex Triantis, Maryland
George Triantis, UVA Law
Lenos Trigeorgis, Cyprus
Suzanne Trimbath, Milken Institute
George Tsetsekos, Drexel
Peter Tufano, Harvard
Nick Varaiya, San Diego State
Theo Vermaelen, INSEAD
Michael Vetsuypens, Southern Methodist
Claude Viallet, INSEAD
Ralph Walkling, Ohio State
Ingo Walter, NYU
J. F. Weston, UCLA
Kent Womack, Dartmouth
Karen Wruck, Ohio State
Marc Zenner, North Carolina
Luigi Zingales, Chicago

I am also grateful to the following practitioners (listed here with affiliated companies at the time of my work with them):

Tanja Aalto, Houlihan, Lokey
Max Boot, *Wall Street Journal*
W. L. Lyons Brown, Brown-Forman
Bliss Williams Browne, First Chicago
Daniel Cohrs, Marriott
Dan Coleman, Fleet Boston
Chuck Cory, Morgan Stanley
Klaus Durrer, UBS
Ty Eggemeyer, McKinsey

Geoffrey Elliott, Morgan Stanley
Catherine Friedman, Morgan Stanley
James Gelly, General Motors
Ed Giera, General Motors
Denis Hamboyan, Bank Boston
Betsy Hatfield, Bank Boston
David Herter, Fleet Boston
Tod Hibbard, Fleet Boston
Christopher Howe, Kleinwort Benson
Thomas Jasper, Salomon Brothers
Scott Johnson, Ober Kaler
Andrew Kalotay, Salomon Brothers
Eric Linnes, Kleinwort Benson
Hugh McColl, Bank of America
Mary McDaniel, SNL Securities
Jean McTighe, BankBoston
Angelo Messina, United Technologies
David Meyer, J.P. Morgan
Dennis Morgan, Yahoo!
Lin Morison, BankBoston
John Muleta, PSINet
John Newcomb, BankBoston
Ralph Norwood, Polaroid
Tim Opler, Lehman Brothers
Michael Pearson, McKinsey
Nancy Preis, Kleinwort Benson
Christopher Reilly, S.G. Warburg
Gerry Rooney, NationsBank
Emilio Rottoli, Glaxo
Jonathan Rouner, CSFB
Craig Ruff, AIMR
Barry Sabloff, First Chicago
Katrina Sherrerd, AIMR
Kirsten Spector, BankBoston
Martin Steinmeyer, MediMedia
Stephanie Summers, Lehman Brothers
Sven-Ivan Sundqvist, Dagens Nyheter
Peter Thorpe, Citicorp
Katherine Updike, Excelsior
Carlos Valle, Merrill Lynch
Manoj Verma, Yahoo!
David Wake Walker, Kleinwort Benson
Elizabeth Wells, SNL Securities
Ulrich Wiechmann, UWINC
Scott Williams, McKinsey
Bill Wright, Morgan Stanley
Harry You, Salomon Brothers
Marc Zenner, Salomon Smith Barney

I am very grateful to the staff of the Darden School for its support in this project. Excellent editorial assistance at Darden was provided by Stephen Smith (Darden's unflappable editor) and Sherry Alston. Betty Sprouse gave stalwart secretarial support. Outstanding library research support was given by Karen Marsh and Frank Wilmot. The patience, care, and dedication of these people are richly appreciated.

I must also acknowledge the great support and encouragement given by my editors (and now friends) at John Wiley & Sons: Bill Falloon, senior editor, finance and investments; Melissa Scuereb, editorial assistant; Robin Factor, managing production editor; and Todd Tedesco, senior production editor. I also thank the staff at Cape Cod Compositors, who worked with the Wiley team, for their fine attention to detail. Pamela Van Giessen, executive editor, Joan O'Neil, publisher, finance and investment, and Will Pesce, president, were decisive in my commitment to embark on this project. For the vision and enthusiasm of the Wiley organization, I am very thankful.

Lewis O'Brien, permissions consultant, makes the author's life immeasurably easier. He checked the manuscript, offered editorial advice, and ferreted out some elusive permissions to quote the material of other authors.

Of all the contributors, my wife, Barbara McTigue Bruner, and two sons, Jonathan and Alexander, have endured the greatest sacrifices for this volume. It is significantly a product of their faith, hope, and charity.

All these acknowledgments notwithstanding, responsibility for the final product is mine. I welcome suggestions for its enhancement. Please let me know of your experience with this book either through Wiley or at the coordinates given below.

Robert F. Bruner
Distinguished Professor of Business Administration and
Executive Director of the Batten Institute
Darden Graduate School of Business
University of Virginia
Post Office Box 6550
Charlottesville, Virginia 22906
United States of America
E-mail: brunerr@virginia.edu
Web site: http://faculty.darden.edu/brunerb/

NOTES

1. Quoted from Albert Bigelow Paine's authorized biography, *Mark Twain*, 1912, page 559.
2. *How to Resist Hostile Takeovers*, edited by Joseph O'Donoghue and Donald Grunewald (International University Press, 1991).
3. Darren Berry, Anne Campbell, David Eichler, Dennis Hall, Jerry Halpin, Peter Hennessy, Brian Kannry, Doug Leslie, Andrew Meiman, Reed Menefee, Casey Opitz, Katarina Paddack, Thien Pham, Chad Rynbrandt, Michael Schill, John Sherwood, Jane Sommers-Kelly, Carla Stiassni, Sanjay Vakharia, Larry Weatherford, and Steve Wilus.

PART One

Introduction and Key Themes

CHAPTER 1

Introduction and Executive Summary

AN URGENT PROBLEM: HOW CAN MY TEAM DO BETTER THAN THE AVERAGES?

M&A (*mergers* and *acquisitions*)[1] is no easy path to riches or career advancement. On average, it looks like buyers earn just the going rate of return on their acquisitions. However, around the average is a wide variance. We learn about the stupendously bad deals from the media: They make lurid reading and sell copy. Unfortunately, we know less about the real winners, probably because successful buyers do not want to alert the competition. Nevertheless, we know enough to say that it *is possible* to succeed through M&A.

Most firms have no better alternative. M&A is one of the most important means by which companies respond to changing conditions. It is an instrument of macroeconomic renewal. And even if you did opt out of M&A, the odds are that your competitors would use it to reach for strategic or financial advantage, with consequences that might be disastrous for your firm in the long run. Simply opting out of M&A is not feasible.

Some writers portray M&A as the kind of losing proposition that compulsive gamblers face in Las Vegas: You can't win; you can't break even; and you can't get out of the game. This is unduly pessimistic. Though M&A is a very competitive business activity, it *is* possible to succeed. But competitive forces limit true success to a fortunate few.

So here's the problem: How do you succeed at an activity in which you must participate and in which the odds of great success are slim? The problem manifests itself in four ways:

1. ***Getting a handle on the subject.*** Good practice begins with a good grasp of what is happening. "How can I make sense of what's going on around me?" M&A is one of the most aggressive change agents in the business economy: volatile and disruptive. The volume of deals and their dollar value grew explosively over the past 30 years. Journalists, legislators, and consumers have watched this activity with fascination and concern. Those inside the firms have felt elation or anxiety as they watched deals hatch. The thoughtful practitioner needs an objective grasp of M&A to serve as an anchor amidst the emotional froth.

2. *Setting goals and benchmarks.* As one executive asked me, "What drives success in M&A? What will it take for my firm to do better than the averages?" The mystery about M&A deepens if one has no clear definition of success. The decision maker needs a guideline for action.
3. *Getting prepared.* Succeeding in M&A has a personal perspective. As an educator I am often asked, "What do *I* need to know? How can I best prepare myself to be effective, or at least survive, in the M&A arena?" Executives and analysts new to the field rarely know how to launch a program of personal development.
4. *Adopting best practice.* Most M&A professionals have some influence on the policies and practices of those who work with them. Executives, particularly, want to know, "What expectations should I set for the development of our M&A business processes? If I wanted to raise the bar in any dimensions, where should I do it?"

This book speaks to these problems. First, the book takes a pragmatic approach, highlighting useful insights wherever they are to be found. As a result, the discussion here synthesizes a range of perspectives rather than just focusing on one silo of ideas. Second, the book highlights seven important ideas that open fresh insights on subjects previously thought to be too narrow or confusing for meaningful commentary. Finally, the discussion here emphasizes that M&A is a world of contingencies and that therefore the M&A professional needs to become competent at forming a view for him- or herself. One finds few universal absolute truths about M&A success. While that frustrates the seeker of hard answers, it is good news to the professional adviser and business developer, for it dictates that there will always be a market for diligent research, sound judgment, and artful execution.

OVERVIEW OF A FRAMEWORK FOR M&A SUCCESS

"Success" in M&A is not so different from "success" achieved by value-style investing and created by the perfection of an analysis discipline that allows good judgment. The winners follow it over and over, and never deviate from the discipline. An aim of this book is to bring M&A analysis discipline to the forefront, in much the same way that Benjamin Graham and David Dodd did for securities analysis and Warren Buffett put into practice.

Even though success in M&A is uncertain, research and practice suggest the outlines of its key drivers. The perspective developed in this book is that success is driven by both the *structure* of the M&A opportunity one faces, as well as the *conduct* by which one pursues it. This venerable[2] model is useful for sorting out the determinants of success in M&A. Exhibit 1.1 summarizes the direction of influence: Structure drives conduct and *outcomes*; and conduct shapes structure[3] and drives outcomes. This has intuitive appeal when you consider the simple idea that where you wind up is a matter of the resources, opportunities, and constraints you began with, and of what you did along the way. The random strokes of good or bad luck also have an influence; therefore, your conduct of M&A needs to anticipate the possibility of both.

The structure of the M&A situation is like the setup of a game, the resources

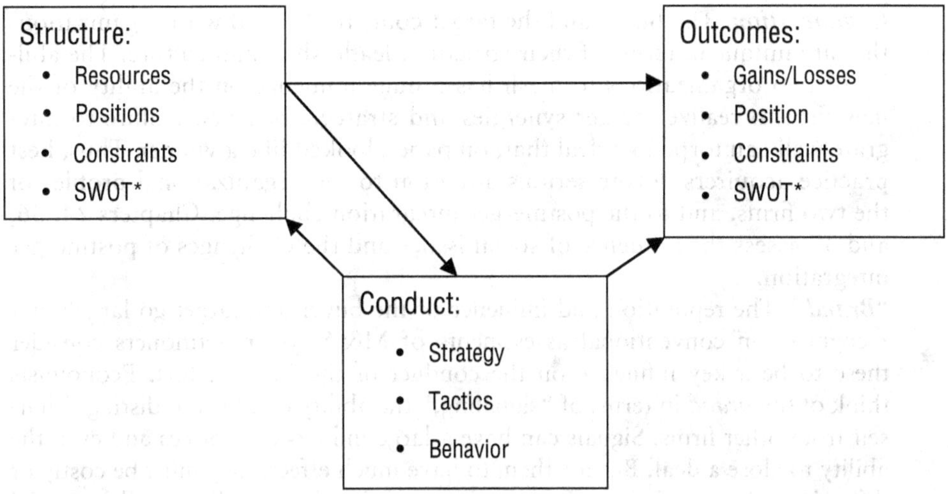

EXHIBIT 1.1 A Model of the Drivers of Outcomes
*"SWOT" stands for strengths, weaknesses, opportunities, and threats. The use of SWOT analysis to develop strategy is discussed in Chapter 6.

(the sports equipment you have), opportunities (the team you recruit), and constraints (the rules) under which you operate. In M&A, the elements of structure include:

- ***Economics of the opportunity.*** This is simply the distribution of costs and revenues that determine cash flows, and ultimately net present values of investment. The "economics" also refers to the financial impact of the transaction on the buyer and target shareholders. From the buyer's standpoint, the financial impact consists of the potential value to be created (as measured by net present value) as well as the effects of deal financing. Synergies are a key driver of the economic impact of the deal. Valuation analysis is the cluster of tools that enables one to assess the likelihood of the deal to create value. Best practitioners in M&A are rigorous analysts of the *economics of an opportunity.* In short, "economics" embraces the factors determining the financial risk and return of a deal. Chapters 9 through 17 outline the economic analysis of M&A opportunities; Chapters 18 through 24 present an economic lens through which to assess the design of transactions.
- ***Strategy.*** The recognition of a strategic threat or opportunity in the firm's competitive arena motivates most deals. The industry positions of the buyer and target are important determinants of the attractiveness of a deal. The firm may want to engage in M&A activity to acquire special capabilities and to improve its strategic position. *Strategy* is not only a direct driver of deal success, but also a driver of the economics, organization, and reputational structure of the deal. Successful acquirers are critical analysts of the strategic positions of the buyer and the target. Chapters 4 through 7 explore the strategic perspective and present several tools with which to assess the position of a firm and the strategic attractiveness of a deal.

- *Organization.* The buyer and the target come to the deal with organizations that are unique in terms of their structure, leadership, and culture. The ability of two organizations to mesh has a huge influence on the ability of the new firm to realize merger synergies and strategic benefits. Failure to integrate well can torpedo a deal that, on paper, looked like a winner. Thus, best practice acquirers devote serious attention to the organizational profiles of the two firms, and to the postmerger integration challenge. Chapters 24, 36, and 37 assess the influence of social issues and the challenges of postmerger integration.
- *"Brand."* The reputation and influence of the buyer and target go largely unrecognized in conventional assessments of M&A, yet practitioners consider these to be a key influence on the conduct of the M&A effort. Economists think of the *brand* in terms of "signaling," the ability of a firm to distinguish itself from other firms. Signals can have a large influence on prices and even the ability to close a deal. But for them to have much effect, they must be costly or difficult, and unambiguous. Brand names are signals of quality or other special attributes. Brands and signals have special influence where interaction with customers or counterparties is repeated over time. Best practitioners seek to create and preserve brand value, and to understand the sources of the counterparty's brand. Worth noting is that in M&A *personal brand* is also important: The aura of a CEO, financial adviser, or operating manager has been known to advance or stall a deal. Chapters 30 through 33 explore some of the implications of reputation in M&A.
- *Law.* The matrix of laws and regulations in the business environment constrain the actions of the buyer and target firms and of specific players such as CEOs, directors, accountants, analysts, and insiders. The businessperson must ask, "What is our legal exposure in this situation and how can we manage it?" Chapters 26 through 29 explore the structural influence of laws and regulations in M&A.
- *Ethics.* In the professional literature on M&A, very little has been written about ethical dilemmas. Yet practitioners struggle through these virtually daily. Chapter 2 argues that the best practitioners consciously address the ethical dimension in deal development and assiduously avoid taint that might accrue from an ethical lapse.

To focus only on structure is to be a determinist: "If X is the condition, Y is the outcome." Yet to be a determinist is to settle for a limited view of the world. Causality might be more complicated than initially believed, as the followers of Karl Marx and Sigmund Freud discovered. Human behavior is *uncertain.* This uncertainty muddies the causal effects of structure. For instance, a machine can hit a tennis ball over the net with great predictability. Humans, on the other hand, are less predictable—differences in skill, strength, and strategy can force opponents to make bets about the behavior of each other. Such is also the case in M&A, a game in which one's conduct has a large influence on outcomes. *Conduct* intervenes in the pursuit of good outcomes anytime one must make a strategic choice or adopt tactics for behavior. In short, best practice requires that we augment the *deterministic* focus on structure with a *probabilistic* focus on conduct, in areas such as the following:

- ***Search for partners.*** Chapter 6 argues that the search for acquisition targets is one part structured research and another part serendipity: In the modern jargon, good discovery relies on networking, which itself relies on social skills that are not readily given to deterministic description.
- ***Due diligence.*** This is the structured search for risk. Here again, we have a discovery *process* that depends on both organized inquiry and agile thinking. Chapter 8 argues that *due diligence* is least successful when reduced to rote fact checking. Instead, the right way to discover hidden risks is to research curious details, anomalies, inconsistencies, and discontinuities—all under tight time pressure and efforts by the seller to put a gloss on things. Here, the uncertainty of conduct arises from the investigator's stamina, care, and capacity for critical thinking.
- ***Negotiation and bidding.*** The probabilistic influence of psychology and self-discipline appear most vividly in settings where M&A parties grapple with one another. Chapter 30 reviews research that shows that attitudes, appetites, and negotiation tactics have a large influence on deal prices and terms. Chapter 31 shows that auctions and deal frenzy can prompt a bidder to make an offer beyond the rational maximum—this results in the "winner's curse." Chapters 32 and 33 emphasize that hostile takeovers are games in which psychology and beliefs about competitors have huge influences on the step-by-step movements of the competitors.
- ***Dealing with laws, regulations, and the judicial system.*** Laws and regulations may seem like constraints on actions, though to the artful practitioner they may raise new opportunities and/or mitigate threats. Lobbying regulators and legislators and appealing to the courts for relief are means by which the practitioner might actually *shape* the structure of the M&A situation. Chapters 26 through 29, 32, and 33 survey the dimensions in which laws, regulations, and the courts may affect M&A conduct.
- ***Deal design.*** Chapters 18 and 25 frame the deal design effort as a search for trade-offs that can accumulate to a winning outcome for both buyer and target, the so-called win-win deal. This search is yet another discovery process, more like a dance than an engineering problem. And as dancers know, it takes skill and coordination to come to an end with graceful bow and applause rather than stumbles and embarrassed gasps.
- ***Postmerger integration.*** William Blake once said, "Execution is the chariot of genius." No matter how good the deal design, implementing the merger integration is where the hypothesized deal benefits are won or lost. Choosing the right integration strategy is a matter of judgment; implementing it well is a matter of managerial skill. Chapter 36 argues that acquisitions trigger fear and anxiety among employees in the target firm and that these emotions can torpedo efforts to realize benefits from the deal.
- ***Leadership and communication.*** As adept public speakers know, it is not merely what you say, but also *how* you say it, that counts. Differences in expression are some of the most subtle and powerful ways in which conduct can intervene in the realization of outcomes. Communication issues permeate the deal process. This book addresses them in numerous areas, including ethics (Chapter 2), deal search (Chapter 7), due diligence (Chapter 8), accounting (Chapter 16), social issues (Chapter 24), disclosure to markets (Chapter 27),

negotiation (Chapter 30), auctions (Chapter 31), hostile takeovers (Chapters 32 and 33), the presentation of proposals (Chapter 35), postmerger integration (Chapter 36), and the leadership of the deal process (Chapter 37).

- ***Managing the deal development process.*** A special perspective of this book is an emphasis on the importance of good *process* as one of the key drivers of good outcomes. Best practitioners make deal management into a strategic capability. Process lends discipline to one's thinking, fights the psychological trap of deal frenzy, and helps to motivate the creative search for solutions to thorny problems. How one might structure good M&A process is the subject of discussion in chapters on deal search (7), due diligence (8), valuation (9), deal development (25), negotiation (30), communication (35), and best practice (38).

The final element of the structure-conduct-outcomes framework is *outcomes*, the whole point of the M&A effort. Quite simply, this could be measured in terms of the fulfillment of one's intentions for doing the deal. The thoughtful practitioner will benchmark the deal's outcomes against at least seven measures:

1. ***Creation of market value.*** As Chapter 9 suggests, one needs to think like an investor, which means harnessing the perspective of the providers of capital. The creation of *market value* is measured straightforwardly by the change in share values, net of changes in the stock market.
2. ***Financial stability.*** Some of the saddest M&A deals are those that, rather than making the buyer stronger, actually destabilize it. In most of these cases, the buyer overreaches its financial capacity. Financial stability can be measured by changes in debt ratings, default risk, or other measures of financial capacity outlined in Chapters 13 and 20.
3. ***Improved strategic position.*** Many M&A transactions are motivated by a strategic purpose that seeks to improve the firm's competitive position, acquire new capabilities, improve agility, or obtain resources that are vital to future prosperity. Chapter 6 sketches these considerations. Also, many deals respond directly to turbulent forces in the firm's environment—these are surveyed in Chapters 4 and 5.
4. ***Organizational strength.*** Knitting together two firms is especially challenging from an organizational perspective. Most CEOs would agree with the old slogan "People are our most important asset." Chapters 36 and 37 survey what this might mean in practice. In essence, one could measure organizational strength in terms of depth of talent and leadership, effectiveness of business processes, and the transmission of culture and values.
5. ***Enhanced "brand."*** The deal should improve the reputation of the acquirer and its deal architects. Usually, the realization of these other aims will do just that. But one can imagine deals that depend on acrimony, subterfuge, and win-lose mentality—in a world of repeated play, the executive must consider how these qualities might affect one's M&A success in future deals.
6. ***Observance of the letter and spirit of ethical norms and laws.*** You can gain financial, organizational, and strategic objectives in M&A, but in ways that violate norms such as equity, duty, honesty, and lawful observance. After the corporate scandals of recent years, any assessment of outcomes would be incomplete without consideration of laws (Chapters 25 through 29) and *ethics* (Chapter 2).

7. *Improved process.* The process orientation of this book emphasizes the importance of learning from each deal. As illustrated in Chapter 37, good practitioners try to capture the lessons of each deal in an effort to accumulate an improvement of practice for the next time around. This is the way a firm turns mere skills into truly strategic capabilities.

Exhibit 1.2 summarizes the success framework for M&A. It suggests that one must first assess the structure of the business environment and deal opportunity. The structure will suggest the outlines of a deal design. Next, the thoughtful practitioner must tailor a deal development process and conduct the process in ways that achieve an attractive outcome. In other words, Exhibit 1.2 summarizes a way for practitioners to organize and execute good deal development. Think of Exhibit 1.2 as a bull's-eye target, useful for practicing your aim at various points in the merger process. The balance of this book adds the details.

SEVEN DISRUPTIVE IDEAS WORTHY OF BEST PRACTITIONERS

This book advises business practitioners and students about the best ways to analyze, design, and implement mergers and acquisitions. The "best," of course, are always moving targets. Therefore, students of best practices can never rest. In the

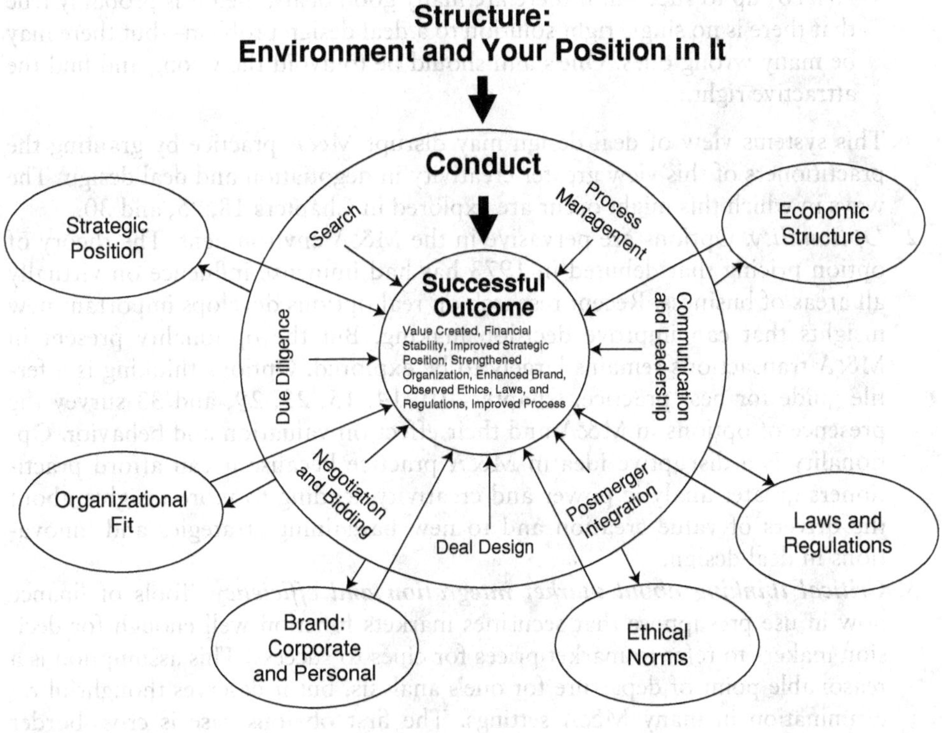

EXHIBIT 1.2 Drivers of Success in M&A

marketplace for ideas, the tried-and-true notions are constantly being elbowed aside by disruptive new ideas that reshape the landscape. This book sketches that jockeying: It aims to synthesize the enduring and upstart ideas into a comprehensive perspective on best practice in M&A. While many of these ideas originated in academia, the book emphasizes their practical application—hence, the name *Applied Mergers and Acquisitions*. This book heralds seven important ideas that have received scant attention in M&A practice. Yet they yield valuable insights. I highlight them because they have the capacity to disrupt conventional practice.

1. ***A deal is a system.*** This presentation discusses the systemic nature of M&A transactions. In this, it draws on basic concepts from systems engineering to illuminate the trade-offs that occur within the design of a deal. Chapter 18 outlines several important implications for the practitioner, including the following:

   - *Internal consistency.* If a deal is a system, then the parts need to fit together in a sensible way. One must negotiate the pieces of the deal with a view toward an integrated whole.
   - *Unanticipated side effects.* The systems view gives a wide-angle perspective. It encourages the deal designer to look out for the cumulative effect of tinkering. Just as a balloon squeezed in the middle will bulge at the ends, it is likely that hard bargaining on one point will lead to stress somewhere else.
   - *What "best" means.* A systems view admits the possibility that there may be *many* great deal structures that satisfy the objectives of all parties and set *Newco*[4] up to succeed. If there are many good deals, then it is probably true that there is no single right solution to a deal design problem—but there may be many wrong ones. One's aim should be to avoid the wrong and find the attractive right.

   This systems view of deal design may disrupt M&A practice by granting the practitioners of this view greater creativity in negotiation and deal design. The ways in which this might occur are explored in Chapters 18, 25, and 30.
2. ***Optionality.*** Options are pervasive in the M&A environment. The theory of option pricing that debuted in 1973 has had immense influence on virtually all areas of business. Recent research on real options develops important new insights that can improve decision making. But the optionality present in M&A transactions remains largely to be explored. Options thinking is a fertile guide for best practice. Chapters 10, 14, 15, 23, 29, and 33 survey the presence of options in M&A and their effect on valuation and behavior. Optionality is a disruptive idea in M&A practice because it can afford practitioners greater analytic power and creativity, leading to more insights about the drivers of value creation and to new bargaining strategies and innovations in deal design.
3. ***Critical thinking about market integration and efficiency.*** Tools of finance now in use presuppose that securities markets function well enough for decision makers to refer to market prices for clues to success. This assumption is a reasonable point of departure for one's analysis, but it deserves thoughtful reexamination in many M&A settings. The first obvious case is cross-border

M&A. Chapters 5 and 12 suggest that differences between one's home country and the country of the target firm may be large enough to warrant careful adjustment in the use of financial tools. The second obvious case is the world of very high leverage. Chapters 13, 20, and 34 explore this world and suggest that it requires thoughtful judgment rather than blind application of tools. Finally, the third case is the world of the privately owned firm. Here, control and liquidity of the investment may differ materially from that of the publicly held large corporation. Chapter 15 explores the impact of those differences on firm value. At issue in these three cases is the extent to which asset markets are integrated and efficient. An ability to think critically about integration and efficiency is potentially disruptive to conventional M&A practice because it arms the practitioner with tools to view markets more insightfully.

4. ***Good governance is valuable.*** Recent corporate scandals remind us of the importance of good systems of corporate oversight and control. Indeed, a growing body of research finds that good governance pays. Chapter 26 considers the role for systems of governance in the world of M&A, giving particular attention to duties of the board of directors, laws and regulations, accounting, and takeover defense. Chapter 17 on momentum acquisition explores the potential destruction of value when managers focus on the wrong aims. As this is being written, it seems that a revolution in corporate governance is merely beginning. Changes in governance will inevitably disrupt old practices in M&A.
5. ***Valuation and value creation through deal design.*** Financial economics teaches that prices should drive managerial decisions, which in turn affect shareholder wealth. Valuation is the practice by which we assess the actual fairness of prices. Numerous chapters in this book survey the state of the art in valuation and extend those tools to discrete new problems of particular importance to practitioners: valuation of synergies, valuation of real options, and valuation of assets across borders. This book also emphasizes the normative implications of managers' duty to create shareholder wealth, and carefully details how deal design choices can create or destroy value. Better valuation practices will disrupt older M&A approaches by arming future deal designers with greater insight into the risks and economic potential in a deal.
6. ***Behavioral effects.*** We know from extensive anecdotal evidence and the emerging field of behavioral finance that decision makers can deviate from value-creating choices, owing to a variety of personal and group behavioral influences. Chapters 30 through 33 and 36 discuss behavioral influences in M&A, especially as they appear in negotiations, auctions, competitive bidding, hostile takeovers, and process leadership.
7. ***Integration among deal design, strategy, and implementation.*** The process orientation in this book reinforces a central theme: the need to integrate the M&A effort across disciplines. The failure of the right hand to let the left hand know what is going on is one of the oldest administrative problems in history. Yet the revolution of business process reengineering over the past 20 years lends new urgency and sophistication to the integration message—you cannot afford to neglect the effort to integrate across M&A specialties, because, in all probability, your competitors and counterparties are doing it already. Business excellence depends on it.

CONCLUSION

"What *were* you thinking?" is a favorite tag line of comedians. Best practitioners use it more seriously in reference to M&A deals. The following chapters give you the frameworks, tools, and processes with which to anticipate that question and/or critique the conclusions of others. Rigorous thinking about M&A is indispensable. This book highlights new ideas, the diffusion of which will shape best practice in coming years and raise our understanding about M&A success.

NOTES

1. The *Oxford English Dictionary* defines "merger" as the "consolidation or combination of one firm or trading company with another." The French have a good word for it: *fusion*—this conveys the emergence of a new structure out of two old ones. An "acquisition," on the other hand, is simply a purchase. Generally, the terms are used interchangeably. But where one is negotiating, drafting legal documents, managing tax exposure, or reporting financial results, it pays to mince words. More on this follows in later chapters.
2. Joseph Bain, a founder of the field of industrial organization economics, bequeathed the notion that the structure of an industry and conduct of competition within that industry drive investment returns.
3. How you behave can affect your position in the competitive arena.
4. "Newco" designates the new firm that emerges from a merger or acquisition.

CHAPTER 2

Ethics in M&A

INTRODUCTION

Ethics and economics were once tightly interwoven. The patriarch of economics, Adam Smith, was actually a scholar of moral philosophy. Though the linkage between the two fields may have worn thin in the twentieth century, they remain strong complements.[1] Morality concerns norms and teachings. Ethics concerns the process of making morally *good* decisions, or as Andrew Wicks writes, "Ethics has to do with pursuing—and achieving—laudable ends."[2] The *Oxford English Dictionary* defines "moral" as "Of knowledge, opinions, judgments, etc.; Relating to the nature and application of the distinction between right and wrong."[3] "Ethics," on the other hand, is defined as "The science of morals."[4]

Ethical dilemmas pervade the field of mergers and acquisitions. For instance, consider these five cases:

1. The CEO of a firm sought to prepare the firm for sale. Part of this entailed the use of accounting policies to improve the financial track record of the firm. The practice of "prettying up" a target company for sale may be widespread—is this unethical?
2. A firm pursued an aggressive strategy of growth by acquisition that relied on creating the appearance of high growth, when in fact the companies acquired were mature and growing slowly. The appearance fueled expectations of prolonged growth, granting the firm a high share price, and therefore a strong acquisition currency with which to do more deals. Was this strategy of momentum acquiring unethical? Many companies aim to persuade investors of good growth prospects even when that growth is uncertain. Is such persuasion unethical?
3. The directors of a public corporation approved without much analysis or discussion a leveraged buyout proposal from the CEO at a relatively low price. A number of the directors were friends or affiliates of the CEO. Was the behavior of the directors unethical? Most directors develop a personal or social acquaintance with the CEOs they employ. Is this affiliation unethical?
4. A large investment bank refused to provide acquisition financing for a deal unless it was to be listed as the lead underwriter, ahead of its rival, another firm also in the underwriting syndicate. Is the use of bargaining power unethical?

5. In response to a hostile takeover attempt, a CEO considered paying "*greenmail*" to make the raider go away. The CEO had a strong self-interest in the outcome of the takeover attempt, as the retention of his position hinged on it. Is the payment of greenmail unethical?

The ethical dilemmas in M&A are rarely clear—or, if they are, they may entail a violation of the law. The field of business ethics offers no easy answers to dilemmas. But a failure to reflect seriously on them easily leads to unhappy outcomes. The long tradition in Western civilization says that ethical behavior promotes sustainable life; unethical behavior does not. The aim in this chapter is to sound a strong cautionary note and stimulate the M&A professional to reflect carefully on the ethical dilemmas embedded in the field.

WHY SHOULD ONE CARE?

The scant attention to ethics in books and articles on M&A is arresting, given the prevalence of ethical dilemmas in the field. One hears numerous explanations for this: We have no training in business ethics; it is embarrassing to discuss these things; we're too busy making money; it's a dog-eat-dog world; it's not in my job description; and so on. If all this is true, why should we pause here at the start of a treatise on M&A to dwell on ethics? Consider these interrelated reasons.

Sustainability

Unethical practices are not a foundation for an enduring sustainable, enterprise. This first consideration focuses on the *legacy* one creates through one's M&A deals. What legacy do you want to leave? To incorporate ethics into our M&A mind-set is to think about the kind of world that we would like to live in, and that our children will inherit.

One might object that in a totally anarchic world, unethical behavior might be the only path to life. But this only begs the point: We don't live in such a world. Instead, our world of norms and laws ensures a corrective process against unethical behavior.

Trust

Ethical behavior builds trust; trust rewards. The branding of products seeks to create a bond between producer and consumer: a signal of purity, performance, or other attributes of quality. This bond is built by trustworthy behavior. As markets reveal, successfully branded products command a premium price. Bonds of trust tend to pay. If the field of M&A were purely a world of one-off transactions, it would seem ripe for opportunistic behavior. But in the case of repeated entry into M&A, for instance by active buyers, intermediaries, and advisers, reputation can count for a great deal in shaping the expectations of counterparties. This implicit bond, trust, or reputation can translate into more effective and economically attractive mergers and acquisitions.

The objection to this line of reasoning is that ethical behavior should be an end in itself. If you are behaving ethically only to get rich, then you are hardly committed to that behavior; being ethical for pay is inauthentic. This is true. But it is a useful encouragement to all of us that ethical behavior need not entail pure sacrifice. Some might even see this as an imperfect means by which justice expresses itself.

Team Building

Ethical behavior builds teams and leadership, which underpin process excellence. This book emphasizes the importance of good process as a driver of good outcomes. Stronger teams and leaders result in more agile and creative responses to problems. Ethical behavior contributes to the strength of teams and leadership by aligning employees around shared values, and building confidence and loyalty.

An objection to this argument is that in some settings promoting ethical behavior is no guarantee of team building. Indeed, teams might blow apart over disagreement about what is ethical or what action is appropriate to take. Yet typically this is not the fault of ethics, but rather of team processes for handling disagreements.

Higher Standard

Ethics sets a higher standard than laws and regulations. Several chapters in this book highlight the boundaries on managerial action set by laws and regulations. But to a large extent, the law is a crude instrument: It tends to trail rather than anticipate behavior; it contains gaps that become recreational exploitation for the aggressive businessperson; justice may be neither swift nor proportional to the crime; and as Andrew Wicks said, it "puts you in an adversarial posture with respect to others, which may be counterproductive to other objectives in facing a crisis."[5] To use only the law as a basis for ethical thinking is to settle for the lowest common denominator of social norms. As former chairman of the Securities and Exchange Commission (SEC) Richard Breeden said, "It is not an adequate ethical standard to want to get through the day without being indicted."[6]

Some might object to this line of thinking by claiming that in a pluralistic society, the law is the only baseline of norms on which society can agree. Therefore, isn't the law a "good enough" guide to ethical behavior? Lynn Sharpe Paine (1999) argues that this leads to a "compliance" mentality and that ethics takes one farther. She writes, "Attention to law, as an important source of managers' rights and responsibilities, is integral to, but not a substitute for, the ethical point of view—a point of view that is attentive to rights, responsibilities, relationships, opportunities to improve and enhance human well-being, and virtue and moral excellence."[7]

Reputation and Conscience

Motivating ethical behavior by appealing solely to benefits and avoiding costs is inappropriate. After all, the average annual income for a lifetime of car thievery (even counting years spent in prison) is large—so it seems that crime *does* pay. If income were all that mattered, most of us would switch into this lucrative field.

The business world features enough cheats and scoundrels to offer any professional the opportunity to break promises, or worse, for money. Ethical professionals decline these opportunities for reasons having to do with the kind of people they want to be. Amar Bhide and Howard H. Stevenson (1990) write, "The answer lies firmly in the realm of social and moral behavior, not in finance. The businesspeople we interviewed set great store on the regard of their family, friends, and the community at large. They valued their reputations, not for some nebulous financial gain but because they took pride in their good names. Even more important, since outsiders cannot easily judge trustworthiness, businesspeople seem guided by their inner voices, by their consciences. . . . We keep promises because it is right to do so, not because it is good business."[8]

The reflective practitioner will summon more reasons, or more interesting variations on these. Other writers—see, for instance, Carroll (1999) and Kidder (1997)—give explanations generally rooted in the expectations of society and the self-interest of firms.

IN WHOSE INTERESTS ARE YOU WORKING?

Generally, the M&A executive or deal designer is an agent acting on behalf of others. For whom are you the agent? Two classic schools of thought emerge.

1. *Stockholders.* The U.S. legal framework generally requires directors and managers to operate a company in the interests of its shareholders—Chapter 26 discusses this in more detail. The shareholder focus lends a clear objective: Do what creates wealth for shareholders. This would seem to limit charitable giving, "living wage" programs, voluntary reduction of pollution, and enlargement of pension benefits for retirees—all of these loosely gather under the umbrella of the "social responsibility" movement in business. Milton Friedman (1962), perhaps the most prominent exponent of the *stockholder* school of thought, argues that the objective of business is to return value to its owners and that to divert the objective to other ends is to expropriate shareholder value and threaten the survival of the enterprise. Also, the stockholder view would argue that if all companies deviated, the price system would cease to function well as a carrier of information about the allocation of resources in the economy. The stockholder view is perhaps dominant in the United States, United Kingdom, and other countries in the Anglo-Saxon sphere.
2. *Stakeholders.* The alternative view admits that stockholders are an important constituency of the firm, but that other groups such as employees, customers, suppliers, and the community also have a stake in the activities and success of the firm. Edward Freeman (1984) argues that the firm should be managed in the interest of the broader spectrum of constituents. The manager would necessarily be obligated to account for the interests and concerns of the various constituent groups in arriving at business decisions, the aim being to satisfy them all, or at least the most concerned *stakeholders* on each issue. The complexity of this kind of decision making can be daunting and slow. In addition, it is not always clear which stakeholder interests are relevant in making specific decisions. Such a definition seems to depend highly on the specific context, which

would seem to challenge the ability to achieve equitable treatment of different stakeholder groups. But the important contribution of this view is to suggest a relational view of the firm and to stimulate the manager to consider the diversity of those relationships.

Adding complexity to the question of whose interests one serves is the fact that often one has many allegiances—not only to the firm or client, but also (as a person) faithful to one's community, family, and so on. Obligations that one has as an employee or professional are only a subset of obligations one has on the whole.

WHAT IS "GOOD"? CONSEQUENCES, DUTIES, VIRTUES

One confronts ethical issues when one must choose among alternatives on the basis of right versus wrong. The ethical choices may be stark where one alternative is truly right and the other truly wrong. But in professional life, the alternatives typically differ more subtly, as in choosing which alternative is *more* right or *less* wrong. Ernest Hemingway said that what is moral is what one feels good after and what is immoral is what one feels bad after. Since feelings about an action could vary tremendously from one person to the next, this simplistic test would seem to admit moral relativism as the only course, an ethical "I'm okay, you're okay" approach. Fortunately, 3,000 years of moral reasoning lend frameworks for greater definition of what is "right" and "wrong."

"Right" and "Wrong" Defined by *Consequences*

An easy point of departure is to focus on outcomes. An action might be weighed in terms of its utility[9] for society. Who is hurt or helped must be taken into consideration. Utility can be assessed in terms of the pleasure or pain for people. People choose to maximize utility. Therefore, right action is that which produces the greatest good for the greatest number of people.

Utilitarianism has proved to be controversial. Some critics feared that this approach might endorse gross violations of norms that society holds dear including the right to privacy, the sanctity of contracts, and property rights, when weighed in the balance of *consequences* for all. And the calculation of utility might be subject to special circumstances or open to interpretation, making the assessment rather more situation-specific than some philosophers could accept.

Utilitarianism was the foundation for modern neoclassical economics. Utility has proved to be difficult to measure rigorously and remains a largely theoretical idea. Yet utility-based theories are at the core of welfare economics and underpin analyses of phenomena varying as widely as government policies, consumer preferences, and investor behavior.

"Right" and "Wrong" Defined by *Duty or Intentions*

Immoral actions are ultimately self-defeating. A practice of writing bad checks, for instance, if practiced universally, would result in a world without check writing and probably very little credit. Therefore, you should act on rules that you would require to be applied universally.[10] You should treat a person as an end, never as a means. It is vital to ask whether an action would show respect for other persons and whether that action was something a rational person would do—"If everyone behaved this way, what kind of world would we have?"

Critics of this perspective argue that its universal view is too demanding—indeed, impossible for a businessperson to observe. For instance, the profit motive focuses on the manager's duty to just one company. But N. E. Bowie responds, "Perhaps focusing on issues other than profits . . . will actually enhance the bottom line. . . . Perhaps we should view profits as a consequence of good business practices rather than as the goal of business."[11]

"Right" and "Wrong" Defined by *Virtues*

Finally, a third tradition[12] in philosophy argues that the debate over "values" is misplaced: The focus should be on *virtues* and the qualities of the actor. The attention to consequences or duty is fundamentally a focus on *compliance*. Instead, one should consider whether it is consistent with being a virtuous person. This view argues that personal happiness flows from being virtuous, and not merely from comfort (utility) or observance (duty). It acknowledges that vices are corrupting. And it focuses on personal pride: "If I take this action would I be proud of what I see in the mirror? If it were reported tomorrow in the newspaper, would I be proud of myself?" A journalist reported that this is the stance of Warren Buffett, CEO of Berkshire Hathaway and one of the most successful investors in modern history:

> *Every year, Buffett reminds his CEOs how important personal integrity is to him. "He sends out this letter, and the opening paragraph is always the same," [manager Melvyn] Wolff says. "I've seen it enough times by now that I've got it memorized: 'We can afford to lose money. We can afford to lose a lot of money. But we cannot afford to lose one shred of our reputation. Make sure everything you do can be reported on the front page of your local newspaper written by an unfriendly, but intelligent reporter.' Those comments were written long before the recent corporate scandals."*[13]

In the gray areas of business ethics, rules can be faulty guides; one might gain clearer guidance from reasoning what a person of character would do.

Critics of virtue-based ethics raise two objections. First, a virtue to one person may be a vice to another. Solomon (1999) points out that Confucius and Friedrich Nietzsche, two other virtue ethicists, held radically different visions of virtue: Confucius extolled virtues such as respect and piety. In contrast, Nietzsche extolled risk taking, war making, and ingenuity. Thus, virtue ethics may be context-specific. Second, virtues can change over time. What may have been regarded as gentlemanly behavior (i.e., formal politeness) in the nineteenth century might have been seen by feminists in the late twentieth century as insincere and manipulative.

Discrete definition of "right" and "wrong" remains a subject of ongoing discourse. But the practical person can abstract from these and other perspectives useful guidelines toward ethical work:

- How will my action affect others? What are the consequences?
- What are my motives and my duty here? How does this decision affect them?
- Does this action serve the best that I can be?

PROMOTING ETHICAL BEHAVIOR

The leadership of a team or organization entails shaping a high-performance culture that is ethical. Lynn Sharpe Paine (1999, 2003) has argued that ethical failure and success have their roots in the culture of an organization. The leader can take a number of steps to shape an ethical culture.

Adopt a Code of Ethics

One dimension of ethical behavior is to acknowledge some code by which one intends to live.

- *Personal.* Various religious and secular traditions afford the basis for a personal code of ethics, the foundation for all ethical behavior. But ethical values vary from one person to the next, perhaps creating dissonance and ensuring that one person's assumptions about his or her colleague's values may not be valid. To focus only on personal ethics is inward looking and ignores values on which a team, company, or society might agree.
- *Corporate.* Firms recognize the "problem of the commons" inherent in unethical behavior by one or a few employees. In 1909, the U.S. Supreme Court decided that a corporation could be held liable for the actions of its employees.[14] Since then, companies have sought to set expectations for employee behavior, including codes of ethics.[15] Exhibit 2.1 gives an example of one such code, from General Electric Company. These norms are merely the first page of a 32-page document outlining the code, to whom it applies, special responsibilities for employees and leaders, specific codes of conduct with respect to customers and suppliers, government business, competition, health, safety, employment, and protection of GE assets. Corporate codes are viewed by some critics as

EXHIBIT 2.1 General Electric's "Code of Conduct"

- Obey the applicable laws and regulations governing our business conduct worldwide.
- Be honest, fair, and trustworthy in all your GE activities and relationships.
- Avoid all conflicts of interest between work and personal affairs.
- Foster an atmosphere in which fair employment practices extend to every member of the diverse GE community.
- Strive to create a safe workplace and to protect the environment.
- Through leadership at all levels, sustain a culture where ethical conduct is recognized, valued, and exemplified by all employees.

Source: "Integrity: The Spirit and Letter of Our Commitment," General Electric Company, October 2000, page 3. A longer version of this resource is also available on the company's web site at www.integrity.ge.com.

cynical efforts that seem merely to respond to executive liability that might arise from white-collar and other economic crimes. Companies and their executives may be held liable for employee behavior, even if the employee acted contrary to instructions. In 1991, the U.S. Sentencing Commission handed down seven mitigating factors[16] that may reduce the likelihood of criminal prosecution of companies; among these is promulgating a code of behavior against which the firm should conduct internal investigations. Mere observance of guidelines in order to reduce liability is a legalistic approach to ethical behavior. In contrast, Lynn Sharpe Paine (1994) urges firms to adopt an "integrity strategy" that uses ethics as the driving force within a corporation. Deeply held values would become the foundation for decision making across the firm and would yield a frame of reference that would integrate functions and businesses. By this view, ethics defines what a firm stands for.

- ***Professional or industry.*** Some professional groups organize codes of ethics. One example relevant for M&A professionals is the code of ethics of the Association for Investment Management and Research (AIMR), the group that confers the Chartered Financial Analyst (CFA) designation on professional securities analysts and portfolio managers. Excerpts from the AIMR Code of Ethics and AIMR Standards of Professional Conduct are given in Exhibit 2.2. In a public advertisement, AIMR wrote, "Just as each and every investment professional is hurt by the scandals, so must each and every one of us work to

EXHIBIT 2.2 Excerpts from AIMR Code of Ethics and AIMR Standards of Professional Conduct

AIMR Code of Ethics

- Act with integrity, competence, dignity, and in an ethical manner. . . .
- Practice and encourage others to practice in a professional and ethical manner. . . .
- Strive to maintain and improve our competence and the competence of others in the profession.
- Use reasonable care and exercise independent professional judgment.

AIMR Standards of Professional Conduct *(in part)*

- . . . Act for the benefit of our [investing] clients and place their interests before our own.
- Use reasonable care and judgment to achieve and maintain independence and objectivity.
- . . . Have a reasonable and adequate basis, supported by appropriate research and investigation, in making investment recommendations or taking investment actions.
- Avoid any material misrepresentation in any research report or investment recommendation.
- Disclose to clients and prospects all matters that reasonably could be expected to impair our ability to make unbiased and objective recommendations.
- Deal fairly and objectively with all clients and prospects.
- Not engage in any professional conduct involving dishonesty, fraud, deceit, or misrepresentation.
- Exercise reasonable supervision to prevent any violation of the Code and Standards by those subject to our supervision and authority.

Source: Thomas A. Bowman, "An Open Letter to Leaders of the Investment Community," *Wall Street Journal*, January 23, 2003, page C3.

repair the damage to our professional and to the financial markets. It will not be enough simply to abide by all the requirements of the law. We must demonstrate that we are committed to the highest standards of professional conduct if we are going to restore investor confidence and trust. This cannot be a one-time commitment or a passing response to recent events. For example, as CFA charter holders and AIMR members, we attest annually in writing to our continued adherence to the AIMR Code and Standards. . . . Violations can and do bring enforcement actions that can lead to revocations of AIMR membership and the right to use the CFA designation."[17]

Codes of ethics are easily reduced to a mentality of compliance (e.g., observance of checklists and other external reminders that can be monitored). The flaw with the mentality of compliance is that it is fundamentally mindless. Ethical issues are subtle and demand mindful engagement to be detected and resolved.

Talk about Ethics within Your Team and Firm

The sound approach builds upon a mentality of commitment or mindfulness. One's objective as a team or enterprise leader should be to create a culture of integrity that promotes reflection and discussion. Many firms introduce such a culture with a program of seminars and training in ethical reasoning. Companies such as Sun Microsystems, Boeing, United Technologies, and Johnson & Johnson have launched comprehensive ethics training programs for executives. A reporter noted, "Most corporations have long had codes of conduct and have publicized them in employee handbooks and elsewhere. But now, [one expert] said, they are 'looking to create ethical athletes out of their managers' who are capable of navigating the gray areas."[18] Part of leadership should be to make ethical issues a legitimate point of discussion in both informal and formal ways within the working group.

A leader can stimulate reflection through informal discussion of ethical developments (e.g., indictments, convictions, civil lawsuits) in the industry or profession or of ethical issues that the team may be facing. This kind of discussion (without preaching) signals that it is on the leader's mind and is a legitimate focus of discussion. One executive regularly raises issues such as these informally over lunch and morning coffee. Leaders believe ethical matters are important enough to be the focus of team discussions.

Find and Reflect on Your Dilemmas

The showstopper for many business professionals is that ethical dilemmas are not readily given to structured analysis, as one values a firm or balances the books. Nevertheless, one can harness the questions raised in the field of ethics to lend some rigor to one's reflections. Laura Nash (1981) abstracted a list of 12 questions on which the thoughtful practitioner might reflect in grappling with an ethical dilemma:

1. Have I defined the problem correctly and accurately?
2. If I stood on the other side of the problem, how would I define it?
3. What are the origins of this dilemma?

4. To whom and what am I loyal, as a person and as a member of a firm?
5. What is my intention in making this decision?
6. How do the likely results compare with my intention?
7. Can my decision injure anyone? How?
8. Can I engage the affected parties in my decision before I decide or take action?
9. Am I confident that my decision will be valid over the long-term future?
10. If my boss, the CEO, the directors, my family, or community learned about this decision, would I have misgivings?
11. What signals (or symbols) might my decision convey, if my decision were understood correctly? If misunderstood?
12. Are there exceptions to my position, "special circumstances" under which I might make an alternative decision?

In addition to analysis, you can bring *moral imagination* to the reflection on ethical dilemmas. Mark Johnson defines moral imagination as "an ability to imaginatively discern various possibilities for acting within a given situation and to envision the potential help and harm that are likely to result from a given action."[19] Patricia Werhane lists four qualities necessary for moral imagination: "(1) a disengagement from an individual's role, particular situation, or context; (2) an awareness of the kind of scheme one has adopted or that is operating in a particular kind of context; (3) a creative vision of new possibilities—fresh ways to frame experiences and new solutions to present dilemmas; and (4) an evaluation of the old context, scope or range of conceptual schemes at work, and new possibilities."[20]

Act on Your Reflections

This may be the toughest step of all. The field of ethics can lend structure to one's thinking but has less to say about the action to be taken. Confronting a problem of ethics within a team or organization, one can consider a hierarchy of responses, from questioning and coaching to "whistle blowing" (either to an internal ombudsperson or if necessary to an outside source) and, possibly, to exit from the organization.

MINI-CASE: GREENMAIL PAYMENT BY WALT DISNEY PRODUCTIONS, 1984

Some of the most interesting reflections on ethics in business emerge in dilemmas between two "bads" (i.e., asking which is less bad) or two "goods" (i.e., asking which is better). Choosing one ultimately impinges on another good, or perhaps commits a bad in the process. Consider the case of the attempted takeover of Walt Disney Productions by the corporate raider Saul Steinberg in June 1984. Disney's CEO, Ronald Miller, faced the dilemma of whether to fight the takeover or pay "greenmail" to make Steinberg go away. The case discussion here highlights the kind of ethical considerations that Laura Nash's framework can address.

Assessment of the Problem

Greenmail is the payment of a premium share price by a takeover target to a hostile buyer for the buyer's accumulated shares in the target. Paying greenmail could be considered unethical for four reasons. First, it is a discriminatory payment; not all public shareholders enjoy the right to sell their shares to the company at the price paid to the greenmailer. It violates an implied *duty* of fairness to *all* shareholders. Second, it is viewed as the triumph of certain agents' self-interest: senior managers rarely welcome the consequences of a hostile takeover and, so it is argued, sacrifice shareholders' wealth by paying greenmail to preserve their jobs. Third, it is believed to effect significant transfers of wealth from the remaining public shareholders to a more powerful raider. Research finds that the rest of the shareholders are poorer after greenmail; thus, the *consequences* are bad. Fourth, greenmail payments (like blackmail) are actions not freely conceived and may set the pattern for further intimidation; expediency is a bad precedent. From a *virtues* perspective, greenmail is like a flashing sign that says, "We are weak." Against such a list, no conditions appear to exist under which management would be justified in paying greenmail. Do the considerations in the case of Walt Disney's greenmailing by Saul Steinberg warrant such a conclusion?

Origins of the Problem

In large part, Disney brought the unsolicited tender offer upon itself. Since the death of the founder, Walt Disney, in 1966, the firm had invested heavily in projects that failed to provide an adequate return. This led to a depressed share price. But the firm also retained assets such as a film library and valuable raw land in Florida that might be sold at a high profit. Steinberg saw this opportunity to buy Disney, restructure the firm, and earn a sizable return.

One significant influence in this problem was the intrinsic value of Disney. Before the hostile bid, Disney's shares were trading around $47.50 apiece. Steinberg revealed in a filing with the SEC that he paid an average of $63.25 per share to acquire a toehold stake in Disney before mounting his hostile bid. This suggested that he estimated the true value of Disney to be something greater than his cost basis. The estimates of securities analysts at C. J. Lawrence ($64.00 to $99.00/share) and Goldman Sachs ($75.00/share) supported the views that Steinberg did not overpay for his shares and that the shares might be worth considerably more than his cost. The disparity among the valuations existed simply because Disney was worth one thing on a business-as-usual basis and something much higher if restructured.

Duties of Disney's CEO and Board

Ron Miller, the CEO of Disney, was Walt Disney's son-in-law. He was seen by many as the torchbearer for his father-in-law's artistic and corporate vision. Unfortunately, as neither an artist nor an experienced theme-park professional, he carried none of the cachet of Walt Disney's persona. Miller was a former professional football player who as CEO was greatly expanding the firm's activities in real estate development. In the hostile tender offer, Miller confronted the dilemma of whether to serve Walt's vision or the interests of shareholder value maximization. Legal obligation of the board and CEO rested on the latter.

Consequences

It is uncertain how employees or suppliers might fare after a takeover by Saul Steinberg, but his predilection to break the linkage between films and theme parks might lower the enjoyment for customers. On balance, greenmail to preserve the status quo might serve the interests of these groups. As for shareholders, circumstances might exist in which they would be better off after the greenmail payment *even if* they were discriminated against, their agents acted in self-interest, and the action was not freely taken. A decision involves weighing the evident costs of greenmail versus the potential benefits. One might argue that to place a price on discrimination or the loss of free choice is impossible and that managerial self-interest is always bad. Yet, in many ways every day, individuals submit to discrimination or loss of choice to enhance their own welfare. Furthermore, managerial self-interest is not harmful per se to shareholders; managerial and shareholder self-interest undoubtedly coincide in a wide range of decisions.

The key question is whether Disney's shareholders would receive any benefits to offset the costs of greenmail. The facts in the Disney case imply that management may have had an estimate of the intrinsic value of the firm that was materially higher than the *ex ante* share price or than a potential greenmail price per share. Under this circumstance, any repurchase of shares at a price less than intrinsic value will transfer wealth from the selling shareholders (i.e., the greenmailer) *to* the remaining public shareholders. The total wealth transferred depends on the difference between what the greenmailer (e.g., Steinberg) would have received had he bought and held versus what he actually received. If the wealth transfer is positive and material, Ron Miller might be justified in paying greenmail.

Possible Engagement with the Other Side

U.S. securities laws limit the extent to which the opposing sides in a hostile takeover contest can engage each other. Material developments mentioned in any conversation with the counterparty may need to be disclosed in public filings with the SEC. This constrains what can be said directly. But through emissaries, it was possible to negotiate a disengagement of the hostile action through a greenmail payment.

Long-Term Validity of the Action

The consequences judged over the long term probably appeared stark for employees and suppliers. If Miller fought and lost the firm to Steinberg, the company would be restructured, possibly ending the creative marriage of animated films and theme parks that Walt Disney consummated. As a believer in Walt's vision, Miller probably felt that this would be a net loss for consumers and the entertainment industry. Greenmail, if it purchased sufficient time and operating flexibility, might grant the firm space in which to restructure itself and improve shareholder welfare. Doing so would give the CEO and directors discretion over how to restructure and realize greater shareholder value without sacrificing the unique operating virtues of the firm.

Alternatives

Miller had at least two alternatives to paying greenmail. One was to announce and execute a restructuring of the firm along the lines the raider would have to do to unlock latent value. This move would allow both the raider and the public to participate in the benefits. The second alternative was to offer to repurchase shares from the public instead of the greenmailer, as happened in the case of T. Boone Pickens's attempted raid on Unocal. This would siphon cash to the public at the expense of the raider and enhance the freedom of choice of the public shareholder: He or she could elect to receive the greenmailer's price per share or hold onto the shares in hopes of eventually receiving the intrinsic value per share. The decision to pay greenmail versus the alternatives ultimately depends on the wealth-creation/wealth-transfer effects each choice may have.

Public Reaction

The payment of greenmail is routinely condemned by analysts, investors, editorial writers, and public officials. Stock prices usually *fall* after greenmail is paid. Greenmail payment takes a target company "out of play" (i.e., it removes the immediate threat of takeover). Terminating the takeover process induces frantic selling by arbitrageurs. The market in the firm's stock is equilibrating away from highly opportunistic clientele back toward long-term investors. Moreover, investors cannot know as much as managers about a firm's prospects. The problem is essentially one of signaling or investor relations, which, by and large, firms do poorly. Even if management *never* talks to shareholders, however, and instead waits for intrinsic value eventually to become manifest in operating performance, paying greenmail still makes economic sense if the wealth transfer to the remaining shareholders is positive.

Conclusion

Should Disney pay greenmail to Saul Steinberg? Various perspectives would seem to support it. Focusing on shareholder welfare, assume that (1) the price paid by Walt Disney Productions per Steinberg share is less than the intrinsic value, (2) Disney makes realizing the intrinsic value for remaining shareholders a top priority (via operational changes and better investor relations), and (3) the effect on share price is superior to restructuring or other defenses; the result then is an economic gain for the remaining shareholders of Disney. What should the price be? It should be as low as possible, consistent with an incentive for Steinberg to sell—certainly no higher than the estimated intrinsic value. Raiders and arbitrageurs look for annualized rates of return above 50 percent. Assuming Steinberg bought his shares on March 1, 1984, his holding period to the date of the case was 103 days. Thus, he would seek an interim gain of 14 percent in order to achieve an annualized gain of 50 percent. Steinberg's apparent cost basis was $63.25, suggesting a greenmail price of $72.11 (114 percent of cost).

The decision to pay greenmail is difficult because of the ambiguity and conflicting tugs of various arguments; but wrestling with these inenviable problems is what chief executives are paid to do. Although the economic analysis outlined here sheds light on the consequences of paying greenmail, nothing in the analysis should be construed as suggesting that the decision can be reduced to a simple rule.

Outcome

On June 12, 1984, Disney's chief executive officer announced an agreement to buy Steinberg's shares for $77.45 per share, yielding a 78 percent annualized return on investment to him. On that day, Disney shares closed at $49.00, down $5.25, or 9.7 percent, from the previous close. Two days later, the first of many shareholder lawsuits protesting the payment was filed.

Then, on July 17, Irwin Jacobs, another raider, mounted a hostile bid for Disney. The Bass family, wealthy investors who had gained a significant stake in Disney as a result of an earlier transaction with Disney, undertook a series of actions to defuse Jacobs. First, the Bass group purchased large blocks of stock from Michael Milken and Ivan Boesky, and then purchased Jacobs' shares, in effect paying a second round of greenmail. With Jacobs' departure, the directors could focus their attention on underlying problems at the company. Apparently sensing that the two raids indicated fundamental problems in management, the board of directors fired Ronald Miller as CEO; other senior managers soon left the company as well. A major management housecleaning took place following the raids.

More importantly, the focus of the firm's strategy shifted from real property back to creative capital with the hiring of the new chief executive officer, Michael Eisner, from Paramount. While campaigning for the CEO position, Eisner is reported to have said to Sid Bass, "It's going to take a creative person to run this company. Look at the history of American companies. They have always gotten into trouble when the creative people are replaced by the managers. Walt Disney Productions can't allow that to happen to it."[21]

Eisner's strategy of returning to the creative core of the company was successful. For the next 10 years, Disney showed a ninefold increase in net income. The compound annual growth in stock price from June 1984 to May 1993 was 34 percent.

CONCLUSION

Analysis of ethical issues in M&A is important but not easy. Ethical issues pervade the M&A environment. And as I argued in Chapter 1, ethics is one of the pillars on which stands success in M&A. Therefore, the M&A deal designer must learn to identify, analyze, and act on ethical issues that may arise.

This chapter has sketched a framework of reflection that draws on the long literature of ethics. Consequences, duties, and virtues stand out as three important reference points for reflection. Nevertheless, the results of such analysis are rarely clear-cut. Indeed, the five cases outlined in the introduction to this chapter will find rational arguments on each side of the question and raise classic problems for further consideration:

1. ***Prettying up a firm for sale.*** In general, this book takes a strong stance *against* earnings management. Chapters 16 and 17 spell out why. As usually practiced, earnings management fails all three ethical tests: It breaks duties to shareholders and society; it hurts shareholders and employees; and it seems to corrupt those who practice it. In the mid-1980s, the CEO of CUC Inc. sought to prepare the firm for sale. Part of this entailed the use of aggressive accounting policies to improve the financial track record of the firm. Ultimately, the firm fraudulently booked nonexistent sales. After acquiring CUC in late 1997, Cendant Corporation discovered an estimated $500 million in fraudulent revenue booked at CUC over the previous three years. The CEO was indicted (and pleaded not guilty). The practice of prettying up a target company for sale in less dramatic ways is thought to be widespread. Is this unethical? One issue here is *intent*: Is it to clarify or deceive? Another issue is *consequences*: Who will be helped or hurt? A study by William Shafer (2002) found that *materiality* of the fraud would influence the likelihood of committing fraud by financial executives: The less material, the greater the likelihood.
2. ***Persuasion of growth prospects.*** Like the problem of prettying up, the ethical judgment on conveying growth prospects hinges significantly on questions of intent and consequences for the other party. Through the 1990s, Tyco International pursued an aggressive strategy of growth by acquisition that relied on creating the appearance of high growth, when in fact the companies acquired were mature and growing slowly. The appearance fueled expectations of prolonged growth, granting Tyco a high share price, and therefore a strong acquisition currency with which to do more deals. The limits to high rates of growth are obvious. (This kind of "momentum acquiring" is discussed in detail in Chapter 17.) Suddenly, in January 2002, Tyco announced that it would not only stop acquiring, but also split up the firm. This burst the bubble of growth expectations, leading ultimately to a collapse in the share price, investigations, indictment of the CEO and CFO, and write-offs for accounting errors. Tyco is a strong cautionary tale against momentum growth. Many companies aim to persuade investors of good growth prospects even when that growth is uncertain. Be cautious about how the effort to persuade investors affects others, how it ignores or respects duties, and how it corrupts or strengthens the persuader.
3. ***Selling at a low price and directors' conflicts of interest.*** In 1980, the directors of Trans Union Corporation approved without much analysis or discussion a leveraged buyout proposal from the CEO at a relatively low price. A number of the directors were friends or affiliates of the CEO. Details of this case are given in Chapter 26 and in the excerpts of the court's opinion, found on the CD-ROM. The core issue here is the directors' faithfulness to their duty to shareholders. It may be that competing higher bids are unrealistic, not credible, or unlikely to gain financial backing, in which case a sure thing at a lower price may actually be in the shareholders' best interests. But directors have a strong obligation to make such a decision at arm's length, free of conflicts or even the *appearance* of conflict arising from affiliation with the CEO. On its face, the sweetheart deal for the CEO would have adverse consequences for the public shareholders. And one could be concerned about

the corrupting effect of the conflict of interest on the CEO and directors. The court judged the directors to be personally liable for the shareholders' opportunity cost in the Trans Union case.

4. ***Bargaining power.*** As an end in itself, the exercise of power would be condemned by many ethicists. But power is rarely exercised in a vacuum. Many companies cultivate and exercise power consistently with duty toward shareholders, customers, or other stakeholders, and conscious of the consequences imposed on other parties. In 1988, Salomon Brothers, the leading bond-trading house in the world, refused to provide acquisition financing for the takeover of RJR Nabisco unless it was to be listed as the lead underwriter, ahead of its rival, Drexel Burnham Lambert. This killed a proposal that would have united warring parties in the deal. More details on this case are given in Chapter 31. In this instance, the warring parties were *all* powerful players, and the banker-client relationship was unclear and shifting rapidly; the effect on duties is ambiguous. And the effect on RJR Nabisco's public shareholders was positive: They received a much higher payment for their shares.
5. ***Greenmail.*** On the surface, paying greenmail seems to give in to coercive power, and possibly to serve the interests of management of the target firm, rather than its shareholders. But the discussion of Walt Disney's case suggests that doing so preserved and increased value for Disney's shareholders, employees, customers, and suppliers.

These and other ethical themes will appear throughout M&A. The thoughtful practitioner is counseled to reflect carefully and do what is right.

NOTES

1. Sen (1987) and Werhane (1999) have argued that Smith's masterpiece, *Wealth of Nations*, is incorrectly construed as a justification for self-interest, and that it speaks more broadly about virtues such as prudence, fairness, and cooperation.
2. Wicks (2003), page 5.
3. *Oxford English Dictionary* (1989), Vol. IX, page 1068.
4. Ibid., Vol. V, page 421.
5. Wicks (2003), page 11.
6. Quoted in K. V. Salwen, "SEC Chief's Criticism of Ex-managers of Salomon Suggests Civil Action Is Likely," *Wall Street Journal*, November 20, 1991, page A10.
7. Paine (1999), pages 194–195.
8. Bhide and Stevenson (1990), pages 127–128.
9. The utilitarian philosophers, Jeremy Bentham (1748–1832), James Mill (1773–1836), and John Stuart Mill (1806–1873), argued that the utility (or usefulness) of ideas, actions, and institutions could be measured in terms of their consequences.
10. The philosopher Immanuel Kant (1724–1804) sought a foundation for ethics in the purity of one's motives.
11. Bowie (1999), page 13.

12. This view originates in ancient Greek philosophy, starting from Socrates, Plato, and Aristotle.
13. Russ Banham, "The Warren Buffett School," *Chief Executive*, December 2002, downloaded from www.robertpmiles.com/BuffettSchool.htm, May 19, 2003.
14. See *New York Central v. United States*, 212 US 481.
15. Murphy (1997) compiles 80 exemplary ethics statements.
16. The seven steps include:

    1. Tailor ethics standards to be appropriate to a company's particular business and demands.
    2. Appoint "high-level personnel" to monitor compliance with the standards.
    3. Take care not to delegate "substantial discretionary authority" to anyone with a tendency toward illegal conduct.
    4. Communicate the ethics standards to all employees.
    5. Take reasonable steps to achieve compliance with the ethics standards, including a system by which employees might report the misconduct of others.
    6. Consistly enforce the ethics program through "appropriate disciplinary mechanisms."
    7. Respond to the infractions appropriately and in a way to prevent similar offenses.

17. Thomas A. Bowman, "An Open Letter to Leaders of the Investment Community," *Wall Street Journal*, January 23, 2003, page C3.
18. Melinda Ligos, "Boot Camps on Ethics Ask the 'What Ifs,' " *New York Times*, January 8, 2003, page 12 BU.
19. Johnson (1993), page 202.
20. Werhane (1997), page 4.
21. Ron Grover, *The Disney Touch*, Homewood, IL: Business One Irwin, 1991, page 23.

CHAPTER 3

Does M&A Pay?

INTRODUCTION

Having a view on the profitability of M&A is a foundation for effective practice. This view should shape one's expectations and approach. Researchers have generated a small mountain of studies on the profitability of M&A activity over the past 30 years. With each passing decade, more scientific evidence emerges, permitting us to sharpen our conclusions. It is appropriate to consider the latest findings along with earlier studies to synthesize some insights from the literature. Reviews of the scientific evidence were published in 1979, 1983, 1987, 1989, and 1992. In the wake of the largest merger wave in history, spanning the years 1992 to 2000, a fresh review of the findings is appropriate. The 14 informal surveys and 120 scientific studies surveyed here include a blend of the classic most-cited research, and some of the newer and notable work.

A review of the evidence is also warranted by the view, grown popular in circles of executives, consultants, and journalists, that M&A destroys value. Consider some statements culled from a recent work by consultants in M&A:

> *The sobering reality is that only about 20 percent of all mergers really succeed. Most mergers typically erode shareholder wealth . . . the cold, hard reality that most mergers fail to achieve any real financial returns . . . very high rate of merger failure . . . rampant merger failure. . . .*[1]

A manager should find these assertions alarming, not least because of the large business- and public-policy implications they might have. But the findings of a broad range of scientific studies are not consistent with the language quoted here if one uses definitions of "success" and "failure" rooted in economics, and tested using conventional statistical methods. One possible reason for the disparity between popular perception and scientific findings is confusion about what it means for an investment "to pay."

This book uses a specific benchmark for measuring performance: investors' required returns, commonly defined as the return investors could have earned on other investment opportunities of similar risk. Against this benchmark, we can define three possible outcomes:

1. *Value conserved.* Here, investment returns equal the required returns. Shareholders get just what they required. The investment has a net present value of

zero; it breaks even in present value terms. This does *not* indicate an investment failure. If the investor requires a return of 15 percent, and gets it, his or her invested wealth will double in five years. Under this scenario, wealth will grow at the rate the investor requires. Economically speaking, the investor earns "normal" returns. The investor should be satisfied.

2. ***Value created.*** This occurs where the returns on the investment exceed the returns required. This investment bears a positive net present value; the investor's wealth grew higher than was required. The investor must be very happy. Given competition in markets, it is difficult to earn "supernormal" returns, and very difficult to earn them on a sustained basis over time.
3. ***Value destroyed.*** In this case, investment returns are less than required. The investor could have done better investing in another opportunity of similar risk. The investor is justifiably unhappy here.

Notions of success or failure should be linked to these measurable economic outcomes. In economic terms, an investment is successful if it does anything other than destroy value.

Why should we focus so narrowly on economics? Many managers describe a complex set of motives for acquisitions—shouldn't the benefit of M&A activity be benchmarked against all of these? The use of broader benchmarks is debatable for at least two reasons. First, the managers' motives may be inappropriate, or the managers themselves foolhardy. One hears of M&A deals that are struck for vague strategic benefits, the creation of special capabilities, the achievement of competitive scale, or because two organizations or CEOs are especially friendly. But the only way one can prove that these are actually beneficial is by measuring the economic outcomes rigorously. Second, special deal-specific definitions of success limit generalizing from the research findings. Enhancing the welfare of shareholders is a fundamental objective of all firms—indeed, in the United States, corporate directors are required to implement policies consistent with shareholder welfare, usually synonymous with creating value. Fortunately, benchmarking against value creation *does* permit generalizations to be drawn. Indeed, the definition of M&A success and its drivers is a fertile area for further research. I pursue the narrow economic question here in hope of saying something meaningful and tangible that is grounded in scientific research.

There are two primary parties to an M&A transaction: the buyer and the seller of the target company. In addition, there are numerous ancillary economic interests in the deal, those of advisors, creditors, suppliers, customers, employees, communities, governments, and so on. This survey will focus mainly on the consequences for the *shareholders* of the two primary parties. This is not to deny the relevance of other interests, but to acknowledge the fiduciary responsibility of boards of directors to their shareholders (above all others). The possible transfer of wealth among shareholders and other groups in a deal is a very interesting topic, on which there is little rigorous research. Of course, private and social interests can diverge, as the "problem of the commons" illustrates.[2] M&A activity may affect a variety of influences on the common good, including industry concentration and monopolies, international competitiveness, productivity growth, and technology transfer. The research literature on these aspects, however, parallels the more narrow discussion here about shareholder welfare.

For brevity, therefore, the discussion here does not survey the impact on other stakeholders.

MEASUREMENT OF M&A PROFITABILITY: BETTER THAN WHAT?

There is no free lunch, said Nobel laureate Milton Friedman. One of the basic conclusions of economics is that where markets are reasonably competitive, players will earn just a "fair" rate of return; you just get paid for the risk you take. The intuition for this is simple: Where information is free-flowing and entry is easy, a firm earning very high returns will draw competitors, as honey draws flies. The entry of these other firms will drive returns down to a point at which the marginal investor just gets a fair rate of return. This idea has been tested extensively in financial markets and leads to the concept of market efficiency, that prices will reflect what is known quickly and without bias. Whether a free lunch exists in M&A hinges on returns to investors, and like the tests of capital market efficiency, could be gauged in three classes of measures, sketched in Exhibit 3.1:

1. *Weak form.* Did the share price rise? Are the shareholders better off after the deal than they were before? For instance, this would compare whether the buyer's stock price was higher after the deal than before. This before-and-after comparison is widespread, especially in the writings of journalists and consultants. But it is a weak test because it fails to control for other factors that might have triggered a price change, unrelated to the deal. Stock prices are driven by random noise, marketwide effects, and other firm-specific events, of which

EXHIBIT 3.1 Classes of Tests of M&A Profitability

Test	Structure: M&A Pays If:	Description and Comments
Weak form	$P_{\text{After}} > P_{\text{Before}}$	Does the firm's share price improve from before to after the deal? A comparison widely used by consultants and journalists. Unreliable. Vulnerable to confounding events at the firm and marketwide effects.
Semistrong form	$\%R_{\text{M\&A Firm}} > \%R_{\text{Benchmark}}$	Does the return on the firm's shares exceed that of a benchmark? Widely used by academic researchers. Depends for its integrity on good benchmark selection and large samples of observations.
Strong form	$\%R_{\text{Firm with M\&A}} > \%R_{\text{Firm without M\&A}}$	Does the return on the firm's shares exceed what it would have been without the deal? The "gold standard" test, but unobservable.

firms generate a lot. As an exercise, pick a merger announcement, and then do a scan of all the news stories that pertain to the firm for several months or years afterward. The odds are that the merger will be a minute portion of the news that drove your firm's share prices. For this reason, weak form tests are notoriously unreliable.

2. *Semistrong form.* Did the firm's returns exceed a benchmark? Are shareholders better off compared to the return on a benchmark investment? Introducing a benchmark like the return on the S&P 500 index, or the return on a matched sample of peers that did not merge, strengthens the analysis. This kind of test, widespread in academic research, dominates the weak form tests because it controls for the possibility that the observed returns were actually driven by factors in the industry or entire economy, rather than due to the merger. But this kind of test is at best *semi*strong because benchmarks are imperfect. For instance, which firm would have been a good benchmark comparison to Walt Disney at the time of its acquisition of ABC Cap Cities? We could name some entertainment and real estate firms, but at the end of the comparison, we should still harbor some unease about noise and confounding effects. Taking care to choose good benchmarks and using large samples, researchers hope to minimize the weaknesses of semistrong form tests.
3. *Strong form.* Are shareholders better off after the deal than *they would have been if the deal had not occurred?* This question poses the true test of the cost of lost opportunity, the economists' "gold standard" of comparison. And it is what most people *think* they are finding when they look at weak and semistrong form test results. But the true strong form test will tell a sharper story. Consider the case of AOL's acquisition of Time-Warner in January 2000. The weak and semistrong tests will reveal sizable losses to AOL's shareholders over the years following the deal. But given the implosion of the Internet industry after 2000, it seems likely that AOL's shareholders would have been much worse off without the merger. It would appear that AOL's acquisition of Time-Warner was shrewd and successful for the buyer,[3] despite what the weak and semistrong results show. The problem is that strong form results are unobservable.

The distinction among these three kinds of tests is important to bear in mind. The studies summarized in this chapter are, at best, semistrong. Therefore, we must exercise humility in drawing conclusions about performance against economic opportunity. We are looking through a glass darkly.

Four research approaches offer findings relevant to forming a view about M&A profitability:

1. *Event studies.* These examine the abnormal returns to shareholders in the period surrounding the announcement of a transaction. The raw return for one day is the change in share price and any dividends paid, divided by the closing share price the day before. The *abnormal return* is simply the raw return less a benchmark of what investors required that day—typically, the benchmark is the return dictated by the capital asset pricing model (CAPM) or quite simply the return on a large market index, such as the S&P 500. These studies are regarded to be *forward-looking* on the assumption that share prices equal the

present value of expected future cash flows to shareholders. Since the 1970s, these studies have dominated the field.[4]

2. *Accounting studies.* These examine the reported financial results (i.e., accounting statements) of acquirers before, and after, acquisitions to see how financial performance changed. The focus of these studies ranges across net income, return on equity or assets, earning per share (EPS), leverage, and liquidity of the firm. The best studies are structured as matched-sample comparisons, benchmarking acquirers against nonacquirers based on industry and size of firm. In these studies, the question is whether the acquirers outperformed their nonacquirer peers.
3. *Surveys of executives.* Simply asking managers whether an acquisition created value seems like an obvious course. These present a sample of executives with a standardized questionnaire, and aggregate across the results to yield generalizations from the sample.
4. *Clinical studies.* These focus on one transaction or on a small sample in great depth, usually deriving insights from field interviews with executives and knowledgeable observers. This is inductive research. By drilling down into the detail and factual background of a deal, the researchers often induce new insights.

Exhibit 3.2 summarizes the approach, strengths, and weaknesses of each research method. Plainly, no research approach is fault-free, though some command more respect of scientific researchers than do others. The task must be to look for patterns of confirmation across approaches and studies, much as one sees an image in a mosaic of stones.

If "scientific inquiry" means anything, it is to frame a hypothesis and test it rigorously against the possibility that the result is merely due to chance. Strictly speaking, one never proves the hypothesis, one only disproves the "null hypothesis" that the phenomenon is due to chance. The event studies and accounting studies are excellent examples of the scientific method applied to social phenomena. Surveys and clinical studies are usually not tests of hypotheses; they aim to describe, rather than test. The key test by which an event study or accounting study proves its finding is with the "t-statistic." The derivation and history of this statistic are beyond the scope of this discussion. But the novice in this field must note that the t-statistic indicates the probability that the result was due to chance—the higher the t value, the lower the probability of a chance occurrence.[5] By informal convention, many financial economists look for t-values in excess of 2.0, generally indicating significance at the 95 percent level of confidence that the result could not be due to chance. There is, however, nothing magical about the 95 percent level of significance; a confidence level of 90 percent ($t = 1.67$) is still relatively rare. Statistical studies never prove a phenomenon with certainty; at best, we can say that a result is probably not due to chance.

A final comment: *Statistical significance* is not the same as economic materiality. To say that M&A transactions create or destroy value on average, one needs not only the proof of significance (i.e., that the result is not due to chance) but also *materiality*, that the wealth effect is something that shareholders or society should worry about. Many of the *significant* abnormal returns reported in event studies are as low as 1 or 2 percent—one might ask whether this is enough to care about.

EXHIBIT 3.2 Comparison of Research Approaches Regarding the Profitability of M&A

	Strengths	Weaknesses
Market-based returns to shareholders (event studies)	• A direct measure of value created for investors. • A *forward-looking* measure of value creation. In theory stock prices are the present value of expected future cash flows.	• Requires significant assumptions about the functioning of stock markets: efficiency, rationality, and absence of restrictions on arbitrage. Research suggests that for most stocks these are not unreasonable assumptions, on average and over time. • Vulnerable to confounding events, which could skew the returns for specific companies at specific events. Care by the researcher and law of large numbers deal with this.
Accounting studies: returns estimated from reported financial statements	• Credibility. Statements have been certified. Accounts have been audited. • Used by investors in judging corporate performance. An indirect measure of economic value creation.	• Possibly noncomparable data for different years. Companies may change their reporting practices. Reporting principles and regulations change over time. • Backward-looking. • Ignores value of intangible assets. • Sensitive to inflation and deflation because of historic cost approach. • Possibly inadequate disclosure by companies. Great latitude in reporting financial results. • Differences among companies in accounting policies adds noise. • Differences in accounting principles from one country to the next make cross-border comparison difficult.
Surveys of managers	• Yields insights into value creation that may not be known in the stock market. • Benefits from the intimate familiarity with the actual success of the acquisition.	• Gives the perspectives of managers who may or may not be shareholders, and whose estimates of value creation may or may not be focused on *economic* value. • Recall of historical results can be hazy, or worse, slanted to present results in the best light. • Typically surveys have a low rate of participation (2–10%) that makes them vulnerable to criticisms of generalizability.
Clinical research (case studies)	• Objectivity and depth in reconstructing an actual experience. • Inductive research. Ideal for discovering new patterns and behaviors.	• Ill-suited to hypothesis testing because the small number of observations limits the researcher's ability to generalize from the case(s). • The research reports can be idiosyncratic making it difficult for the reader to abstract larger implications from one or several reports.

Source: Author's analysis.

The answer is emphatically "yes." Usually these returns occur over a few days. Abnormal returns of this magnitude in a short period of time are enough to cause concern or elation among institutions or other sophisticated investors whose performance in turn can be greatly affected by these kinds of events. One also needs to compare apples to apples: the M&A event returns must be *annualized* to compare them to other rates of return that investors experience. For instance, a 1 percent abnormal positive return to announcements by buyers that occurs over a week should be annualized by compounding one percent across 52 weeks to yield a 68 percent annualized gain.[6] This is merely theoretical: Reinvestment risk will frustrate attempts to invest in a way that reliably yields a 68 percent abnormal return each year. But in order to make fair comparisons of the materiality of M&A activity with other investing activity by corporations and institutions, it is necessary to adjust for differences in time frame.

FINDINGS BASED ON THE ANALYSIS OF MARKET-BASED RETURNS TO SHAREHOLDERS

Event studies yield insights about market-based returns to target firm shareholders, buyers, and a combination of both.

Returns to Target Firms

Target firm shareholders enjoy returns that are significantly and materially positive. Exhibit 3.3 summarizes the findings of 25 studies, which reveal returns that are material and significant, despite variations in time period, type of deal (merger vs. tender offer), and observation period. In short, the M&A transaction delivers a premium return to target firm shareholders.

Returns to Buyer Firms

The pattern of findings about market-based returns to buyer firms' shareholders is more problematical.

- There are 22 studies that report negative returns with 14 of the 22 significantly negative (see Exhibit 3.4). The significantly negative returns vary between 1 and 4 percent.
- There are 32 studies (see Exhibit 3.5) that report positive returns—23 of these report significantly positive returns.
- The studies of returns to buyer firm shareholders around the time of announcement are distributed with a slight positive bias: 26 percent (14) show value destruction (significantly negative returns); 31 percent (17) show value conservation (insignificantly different from zero): and 43 percent (23) show value creation (positively significant returns).

EXHIBIT 3.3 Summary of Shareholder Return Studies for M&A: Returns to the Target Firm Shareholders

Study	Cumulative Abnormal Returns (% or avg$/acq)	Sample Size	Sample Period	Event Window (Days)	% Positive Returns	Notes
Langetieg (1978)	+10.63%*	149	1929–1969	(–120,0)	71.6%	Mergers; uses effective date as event date.
Bradley, Desai, Kim (1988)	+31.77%*	236	1963–1984	(–5,5)	95%	Tender offers only; subperiod data available for 7/63–6/68, 7/68–12/80, 1/81–12/84; acquirer returns have increased from +19% to +35% over time.
Dennis, McConnell (1986)	+8.56%*	76	1962–1980	(–1,0)	70%	
Jarrell, Poulsen (1989)	+28.99%*	526	1963–1986	(–20,10)	N/A	Tender offers only.
Lang, Stulz, Walkling (1989)	+40.3%*	87	1968–1986	(–5,5)	N/A	Tender offers only.
Franks, Harris, Titman (1991)	+28.04%*	399	1975–1984	(–5,5)	N/A	Mergers and tenders offers; segment data available on means of payment and competition.
Servaes (1991)	+23.64%*	704	1972–1987	(–1,close)	N/A	Mergers and tender offers; segment data by payment method.
Bannerjee, Owers (1992)	+$137.1 MM*	33	1978–1987	(–1,0)	85%	White knight bids.
Healy, Palepu, Ruback (1992)	+45.6%*	50	1979–1984	(–5,5)	N/A	Largest U.S. mergers during period.
Kaplan, Weisbach (1992)	+26.9%*	209	1971–1982	(–5,5)	94.7%	Mergers and tender offers.
Berkovitch, Narayanan (1993)	+$130.1 MM*	330	1963–1988	(–5,5)	95.8%	Tender offers.
Smith, Kim (1994)	+30.19%* +15.84%*	177	1980–1986	(–5,5) (–1,0)	96.0% 91.3%	Successful and unsuccessful tender offers.

(Continued)

EXHIBIT 3.3 *(Continued)*

Study	Cumulative Abnormal Returns (% or avg$/acq)	Sample Size	Sample Period	Event Window (Days)	% Positive Returns	Notes
Schwert (1996)	+26.3%*	666	1975–1991	(–42,126)	N/A	Mergers, tenders offers; segment data available for various transaction attributes.
Loughran, Vijh (1997)	+29.6%* merger +126.9%* tender +47.9* combined	419 135	1970–1989	(–2,1,250)	N/A	Five-year postacquisition returns; segment data also available on form of payment.
Maquieira, Megginson and Nail (1998)	+41.65%* conglomerate +38.08% * nonconglomerate	47 55	1963–1996	(–60,60)	61.8% 83.0%	Study of returns for conglomerate and nonconglomerate stock-for-stock mergers.
Eckbo, Thorburn (2000)	+7.45%*	332	1964–1983	(–40,0)	N/A	Canadian targets only.
Leeth, Borg (2000)	+13.27%*	72	1919–1930	(–40,0)	N/A	
Mulherin, Boone (2000)	+21.2%*	376	1990–1999	(–1,+1)	N/A	
Mulherin (2000)	+10.14%*	202	1962–1997	(–1,0)	76%	A sample of incomplete acquisitions.
DeLong (2001)	+16.61%*	280	1988–1995	(–10,1)	88.6%	Studied deals where at least one party is a bank.
Houston et al. (2001)	+15.58% * (1985–90) +24.60%* (1991–96) +20.80%* (all)	27 37 64	1985–1996	(–4,1)	N/A	Deals in which both parties are banks.
Beitel et al. (2002)	+10.48%*	98	1985–2000	(–1,0)	53%	Sample of European bank mergers.
Kuipers, Miller, Patel (2003)	+23.07%*	181	1982–1991	(–1,0)	N/A	U.S. targets of foreign acquirers.
Renneboog, Goergen (2003)	+9.01%*	136	1993–2000	(–1,0)	N/A	European transactions.
Billett, King, Mauer (2003)	+22.15%*	265	1979–1997	(–1,0 month)	N/A	

Unless otherwise noted, event date is announcement date of merger/bid.
*Significant at the 0.95 confidence level or better.

EXHIBIT 3.4 Studies Reporting Negative Returns to Acquirers

Study	Cumulative Abnormal Returns	Sample Size	Sample Period	Event Window (Days)	% Positive Returns	Notes
Langetieg (1978)	–1.61%	149	1929–1969	(–120,0)	47.6%	Mergers; uses effective date as event date.
Dodd (1980)	–1.09%* successful	60	1970–1977	(–1,0)	N/A	Mergers only. Daily data.
	–1.24%* unsuccessful	66				
Asquith, Bruner, Mullins (1987)	–0.85%*	343	1973–1983	(–1,0)	41%	
Varaiya, Ferris (1987)	–2.15%*	96	1974–1983	(–1,0)	N/A	
	–3.9%*	96	1974–1983	(–20,80)	42%	
Morck, Shleifer, Vishny (1990)	–0.70%	326	1975–1987	(–1,1)	41.4%	Measured return by comparing change in bidder market value to market value of target's equity.
Franks, Harris, Titman (1991)	–1.45%	399	1975–1984	(–5,5)	N/A	Mergers and tenders offers; segment data available on means of payment and competition.
Servaes (1991)	–1.07%*	384	1972–1987	(–1,close)	N/A	Mergers and tender offers; segment data by payment method.
Jennings, Mazzeo (1991)	–0.8%*	352	1979–1985	(–1,0)	37%	
Bannerjee, Owers (1992)	–3.3%*	57	1978–1987	(–1,0)	21%	White knight bids.
Byrd, Hickman (1992)	–1.2%**	128	1980–1987	(–1,0)	33%	
Healy, Palepu, Ruback (1992)	–2.2%	50	1979–1984	(–5,5)	N/A	50 largest U.S. mergers during period.
Kaplan, Weisbach (1992)	–1.49%*	271	1971–1982	(–5,5)	38%	Mergers and tender offers.

(Continued)

EXHIBIT 3.4 *(Continued)*

Study	Cumulative Abnormal Returns	Sample Size	Sample Period	Event Window (Days)	% Positive Returns	Notes
Berkovitch, Narayanan (1993)	−$10 MM	330	1963–1988	(−5,5)	49.4%	Tender offers.
Sirower (1994)	−2.3%*	168	1979–1990	(−1,1)	35%	
Eckbo, Thorburn (2000)	−0.30%	390	1964–1983	(−40,0)	N/A	U.S. acquirers of Canadian targets.
Mulherin, Boone (2000)	−0.37%	281	1990–1999	(−1,+1)	N/A	
Mitchell, Stafford (2000)	−0.14%*†	366	1961–1993	(−1,0)	N/A	Fama and French three-factor model, applied to monthly returns.
	−0.07%	366				
Walker (2000)	−0.84%*‡	278	1980–1996	(−2,+2)	41.4%	
	−0.77%	278			46.4%	
DeLong (2001)	−1.68%*	280	(1988–1995)	(−10,1)	33.6%	Deals in which at least one party is a bank.
Houston et al. (2001)	−4.64%* (1985–1990)	27	(1985–1996)	(−4,1)	N/A	Deals in which both parties are banks.
	−2.61% (1991–1996)	37				
	−3.47%* (all)	64				
Ghosh (2002)	−0.96%	1,190	(1985–1999)	(−5,0)	N/A	
Kuipers, Miller, Patel (2003)	−0.92%*	138	(1982–1991)	(−1,0)	N/A	Foreign acquirers of U.S. targets.

Unless otherwise noted, event date is announcement date of merger/bid.
*Significant at the 0.95 confidence level or better.
†Top return is based on an equal-weighted benchmark portfolio. Bottom return is based on a value-weighted benchmark portfolio.
‡Top return is a return adjusted for market average returns. Bottom return is adjusted for return on a matched firm.

EXHIBIT 3.5 Studies Reporting Positive Returns to Acquirers

Study	Cumulative Abnormal Returns	Sample Size	Sample Period	Event Window (Days)	% Positive Returns	Notes
Dodd, Ruback (1977)	+2.83%* successful +0.58% unsuccessful	124 48	1958–1978	(0,0)	N/A	Tender offers only. Monthly data.
Kummer, Hoffmeister (1978)	+5.20%*successful	17	1956–1970	(0,0)	N/A	Tender offers only. Monthly data.
Bradley (1980)	+4.36%* successful –2.96% unsuccessful	88 46	1962–1977	(–20,+20)	N/A	Tender offers only. Daily data.
Jarrell, Bradley (1980)	+6.66%*	88	1962–1977	(–40,+20)	N/A	Tender offers only. Daily data.
Bradley, Desai, Kim (1982)	+2.35* successful	161	1962–1980	(–10,+10)	N/A	Tender offers only. Daily data.
Asquith (1983)	+0.20% successful +0.50% unsuccessful	196 89	1962–1976	(–1,0)	N/A	Mergers only. Daily data.
Asquith, Bruner, Mullins (1983)	+3.48%* successful +0.70% unsuccessful	170 41	1963–1979	(–20,+1)	N/A	Mergers only. Daily data.
Eckbo (1983)	+0.07% successful +1.20%* unsuccessful	102 57	1963–1978	(–1,0)	N/A	Mergers only. Daily data.
Malatesta (1983)	+0.90% successful	256	1969–1974	(0,0)	N/A	Mergers only. Monthly data.
Wier (1983)	+3.99% unsuccessful	16	1962–1979	(–10, cancellation date)	N/A	Unsuccessful mergers only. Daily data.
Dennis, McConnell (1986)	–0.12% (–1,0) +3.24% (–6,+6)*	90	1962–1980	(–1,0)	52%	
Jarrell, Brickley, Netter (1987)	+1.14%*	440	1962–1985	(–10,5)	N/A	Tender offers only; subperiod data available for 1962–69, 70–79, 80–85; acquirer returns have decreased from +4% to –1%

(*Continued*)

EXHIBIT 3.5 *(Continued)*

Study	Cumulative Abnormal Returns	Sample Size	Sample Period	Event Window (Days)	% Positive Returns	Notes
Sicherman, Pettway (1987)	+4.026%* related +0.047% unrelated	49 98	1983–1985	(–10,+10)	N/A	Compared returns to buyers of divested assets in related and unrelated industries.
Bradley, Desai, Kim (1988)	+1%*	236	1963–1984	(–5,5)	47%	Tender offers only; subperiod data available for 7/63–6/68, 7/68–12/80, 1/81–12/84; acquirer returns have decreased from +4% to –3% over time.
Jarrell, Poulsen (1989)	+0.92%*	461	1963–1986	(–5,5)	N/A	Tender offers only.
Lang, Stulz, Walkling (1989)	0%	87	1968–1986	(–5,5)	N/A	Tender offers only.
Loderer, Martin (1990)	+1.72%* 1966–1968 +0.57%* 1968–1980 –0.07% 1981–1984	970 3,401 801	1966–1984	(–5,0)	N/A	Mergers and tenders offers; segment data available on size of acquisition.
Smith, Kim (1994)	+0.50% –0.23%	177	1980–1986	(–5,5) (–1,0)	49.2% 76.2%	Successful and unsuccessful tender offers.
Schwert (1996)	+1.4%	666	1975–1991	(–42,126)	N/A	Mergers, tenders offers; segment data available for various transaction attributes.
Maquieira et al. (1998)	+6.14%* nonconglomerate deals –4.79% conglomerate	55 47	1963–1996	(–60,60)	61.8% 36.2%	Study of returns in conglomerate and nonconglomerate stock-for-stock deals.

Lyroudi, Lazardis, Subeniotis (1999)	0%	50	1989–1991	(–5,5)	N/A	International acquisitions by European and Japanese firms.
Eckbo, Thorburn (2000)	+1.71%*	1,261	1964–1983	(–40,0)	N/A	Canadian acquirers of Canadian targets.
Leeth, Borg (2000)	+3.12%*	466	1919–1930	(–40,0)	N/A	
Kohers, Kohers (2000)	1.37%* cash deals 1.09%* stock 1.26% whole sample	961 673 1,634	1987–1996	(0,1)	N/A	Sample of mergers among high-tech firms.
Mulherin (2000)	+0.85%*	161	1962–1997	(–1,0)	49%	Sample of incomplete acquisitions.
Floreani, Rigamonti (2001)	+2.63%*	56	1996–2000	(–5,+5)	N/A	Sample of European insurance company mergers.
Kohers, Kohers (2001)	+0.92%*	304	1984–1995	(–1,0)	N/A	Sample of technology mergers.
Beitel et al. (2002)	+0.06%	98	1985–2000	(–1,0)	53%	Sample of European bank mergers.
Fuller, Netter, Stegemoller (2002)	+1.77%*all +2.74%* 1st time bidders	3,135	1990–2000	(–2, +2)	N/A	
Billett, King, Mauer (2003)	+0.15%	831	1979–1997	(–1,0 month)	N/A	
Moeller, Schlingemann, Stulz (2003)	+1.13%* all +1.496%* private –1.020%* public +2.003%* subsidiary	12,023	1980–2001	(0, 36 months)	N/A	Tested the difference in bidder's returns at acquiring private company, public company, or subsidiary of public company.
Renneboog, Goergen (2003)	+0.70%*	142	1993–2000	(–1,0)	N/A	European transactions.

Unless otherwise noted, event date is announcement date of merger/bid.
*Significant at the 0.95 confidence level or better.

- There are 16 studies that consider returns well *after* the consummation of the transaction (see Exhibit 3.6). Eleven of these studies report negative and significant returns. Caves (1989) infers that these findings are due to "second thoughts" by bidders' shareholders, and/or the release of new information about the deal. But interpretation of longer-run returns following the transaction is complicated by possibly confounding events that have nothing to do with the transaction. Consistent with this, two streams of recent research suggest plausible explanations for the postmerger declines. The first is overvaluation of the buyer's shares; Shleifer and Vishny (2001) suggest that buying firms tend to acquire with stock when they believe their shares are overvalued. Thus, the postmerger decline is not a reflection of the success of the merger, but rather a correction in the market's valuation of the buyer. The second is the effect of industry shocks. Mitchell and Mulherin (1996) argue that the poor performance following acquisition is often the signal of economic turbulence in the industry rather than the acquisition itself. More is said about both theories in Chapters 4 and 20.
- When the welfare of creditors *and* stockholders in the buyer firm are considered, three studies suggest that the value of the buyer firm increases by a statistically significant amount.[7] This suggests that the gains from acquisition are not isolated to stockholders.

A reasonable conclusion from these studies is that in the aggregate, abnormal (or market-adjusted) returns to buyer shareholders from M&A activity are essentially zero. Buyers basically break even (i.e., acquisitions tend to offer zero net present values, or, equivalently, investors earn their required return).

Any inferences about the typical returns to buyers based on returns must grapple with the difficult issue of the size difference between buyers and targets. Buyers are typically much larger than targets. Thus, even if the dollar gains from merger were divided equally between the two sides, the percentage gain to the buyer's shareholders would be smaller than to the target's. Asquith, Bruner, and Mullins (1983) reported results consistent with the size effect. For instance, in mergers where the target's market value was equal to 10 percent or more of the buyer's market value, the return to the buyer was 4.1 percent ($t = 4.42$). But where the target's value was less than 10 percent, the return to the buyer was only 1.7 percent. Numerous other studies have confirmed the significance of the relative size of the target in explaining variations in returns. The practical implication of this is that the impact of smaller deals (which constitute the bulk of M&A activity) *gets lost in the noise*. In other words, what we know about M&A profitability is a blend of noise and large deals.

Returns to Buyer and Target Firms Combined

Findings of positive abnormal returns to the seller and breakeven returns to the buyer raise the question of *net economic gain* from this event. The challenge here stems from the size difference between buyer and target: typically, the buyer is substantially larger. Hence, a large percentage gain to the target shareholders could be more than offset by a small percentage loss to the buyer shareholders. A number of studies have examined this by forming a portfolio of the buyer and

EXHIBIT 3.6 Studies Reporting Long-Term Returns to Acquirers

Study	Cumulative Abnormal Returns	Sample Size	Sample Period	Event Window (Days)	% Positive Returns	Notes
Mandelker (1974)	−1.32% successful bids only	241	1941–1963	(0,365)	N/A	Mergers only. Event date is date of consummation of the deal.
Dodd, Ruback (1977)	−1.32% successful −1.60% unsuccessful	124 48	1958–1978	(0,365)	N/A	Tender offers only. Event date is date of offer.
Langetieg (1978)	−6.59%* successful bids only	149	1929–1969	(0,365)	N/A	Mergers only.
Asquith (1983)	−7.20%* successful −9.60%* unsuccessful	196 89	1962–1976	(0,240)	N/A	Mergers only.
Bradley, Desai, Kim (1983)	−7.85%* unsuccessful bids only	94	1962–1980	(0,365)	N/A	Tender offers only.
Malatesta (1983)	−2.90% whole sample −13.70% *after 1970 −7.70% smaller bidders	121 75 59	1969–1974	(0,365)	N/A	Mergers only. Event date is date of approval.
Agrawal, Jaffe, Mandelker (1992)	−10.26%*	765	1955–1987	(0,1,250)	43.97%	Mergers only; five-year postmerger performance; tender offer postacquisition performance is not significantly different from zero.
Loderer, Martin (1992)	+1.5%	1,298	1966–1986	(0,1,250)	N/A	Mergers and tender offers; five-year postacquisition performance.

(Continued)

EXHIBIT 3.6 *(Continued)*

Study	Cumulative Abnormal Returns	Sample Size	Sample Period	Event Window (Days)	% Positive Returns	Notes
Gregory (1997)	–12% to –18%*	452	1984–1992	(0,500)	31% to 37%	Uses six variations of the event study methodology; U.K. mergers and tender offers; two-year postacquisition performance.
Loughran, Vijh (1997)	–14.2% merger +61.3%* tender –0.1% combined	434 100	1970–1989	(1,1,250)	N/A	Five-year postacquisition returns; segment data also available on form of payment.
Rau, Vermaelen (1998)	–4%* mergers +9%* tender offers	3,968 348	1980–1991	(0,36 months)	N/A	Three-year postacquisition returns, with insights into value and glamour investing strategies.
Louis (undated)	–7.3%* successful –18.4%* unsuccessful	1,297 308	1981–1998	(0,3 years)	N/A	Comparison of successful and unsuccessful acquirers.
Pettit (2000)	–25.41%*	216	1977–1993	(0,3 years)	N/A	Tender offers, French sample.
Ferris and Park (2001)	–19.80%*	56	1990–1993	(1,+60 months)	N/A	Sample of mergers in the telecommunications industry.
Kohers, Kohers (2001)	–37.39%	304	1984–1995	(1,1,250)	N/A	Sample of technology mergers.
Moeller, Schlingemann, Stulz (2003)	–4.1%	12,023	1980–2001	(0,36 months)	N/A	

Unless otherwise noted, event date is announcement date of merger/bid.
*Significant at the 0.95 confidence level or better.

target firms and examining either their weighted average returns (weighted by the relative sizes of the two firms) or by examining the absolute dollar value of returns. Exhibit 3.7 reports the findings of 24 studies. Almost all of the studies report positive combined returns, with 14 of the 24 being significantly positive. The findings suggest that M&A *does* pay the investors in the combined buyer and target firms.

FINDINGS BASED ON THE ANALYSIS OF REPORTED FINANCIAL PERFORMANCE

A second important stream of research on M&A returns is found in 15 studies of profit margins, growth rates, and returns on assets, capital, and equity, summarized in Exhibit 3.8. Scanning the column of results yields the observation that two studies report significantly negative performance postacquisition, four report significantly positive performance, and the rest are in the nonsignificant middle ground. Four studies illuminate interesting aspects of postacquisition performance.

Geoffrey Meeks (1977) explored the gains from merger for a sample of transactions in the United Kingdom between 1964 and 1971. This study draws upon a relatively large sample (233 observations), and tests the change in profitability following the merger. Meeks looks at the change in return on assets[8] (ROA) compared to the change in ROA for the buyer's industry. His chief finding is excerpted in Exhibit 3.9. Meeks' findings reveal a decline in ROA for acquirers following the transaction, with performance reaching the nadir five years after. For nearly two-thirds of acquirers, performance is below the standard of the industry. He concludes that the mergers in his sample suffered a "mild decline in profitability" (page 25).

Mueller (1980) edited a collection of studies of M&A profitability across seven nations (Belgium, Germany, France, Netherlands, Sweden, United Kingdom, and United States). All the studies applied standard tests and data criteria and therefore afford an unusually rich cross-border comparison of results across parts of Europe and the United States. The research tested theories about changes in size, risk, leverage, and profitability. Profitability was measured three ways: (1) profit divided by equity; (2) profit divided by assets, and (3) profit divided by sales. The changes in profitability for an acquirer (measured as the difference between the postacquisition performance and the average profitability for five years before the transaction) were compared to similar measures for two benchmark groups: firms matched on the basis of size and industry and who made no acquisitions, and a general sample of firms that neither made acquisitions nor were acquired during the observation period. Consistent with Meeks' finding, Mueller's work finds that acquirers are significantly larger than targets, acquirers have been growing faster than their peers and than their targets, and are more highly leveraged than targets and peers. Regarding profitability, acquirers show no significant differences—the specific data for the United States are generally representative of the findings across many nations. Exhibit 3.10 on page 53 gives an excerpt of these findings.

EXHIBIT 3.7 Summary of Shareholder Return Studies for M&A: Combined Returns to Shareholders of Acquiring Firm and Target Firm

Study	Cumulative Abnormal Returns	Sample Size	Sample Period	Event Window (Days)	% Positive Returns	Notes
Halpern (1973)	+$27.35 MM	77	1950–1965	(–140,0)	N/A	Mergers.
Langetieg (1978)	0%	149	1929–1969	(0,60)	46%	Mergers; uses effective date as event baseline.
Firth (1980)	–£36.6 MM	434	1969–1975	(–20,0)	N/A	U.K. acquisitions.
Bradley, Desai, Kim (1982)	+$17 MM	162	1962–1980	(–20,5)	N/A	Tender offers; referenced through Jensen, Ruback (1983).
Bradley, Desai, Kim (1983)	+$33.9 MM	161	1963–1980	(–20,5)	N/A	Referenced through Weidenbaum, Vogt (1987).
Malatesta (1983)	+$32.4 MM*	30	1969–1974	(–20,20)	N/A	Mergers.
Varaiya (1985)	+$60.7 MM	N/A	N/A	(–60,60)	N/A	Referenced through Weidenbaum, Vogt (1987).
Bradley, Desai, Kim (1988)	+$117 MM (7.43%)*	236	1963–1984	(–5,5)	75%	Tender offers only; subperiod data available for 7/63–6/68, 7/68–12/80, 1/81–12/84; combined returns have not changed significantly over time.
Lang, Stulz, Walkling (1989)	+11.3%*	87	1968–1986	(–5,5)	N/A	Tender offers only.
Franks, Harris, Titman (1991)	+3.9%*	399	1975–1984	(–5,5)	N/A	Mergers and tender offers.
Servaes (1991)	+3.66%*	384	1972–1987	(–1,close)	N/A	Mergers and tender offers.
Bannerjee, Owers (1992)	+$9.95MM	33	1978–1987	(–1,0)	N/A	White knight bids.
Healy, Palepu, Ruback (1992)	+9.1%*	50	1979–1984	(–5,5)	N/A	Largest U.S. mergers during period.

Kaplan, Weisbach (1992)	+3.74%*	209	1971–1982	(–5,5)	66%	Mergers and tender offers.
Berkovitch, Narayanan (1993)	+$120 MM*	330	1963–1988	(–5,5)	75%	Tender offers only.
Smith, Kim (1994)	+8.88%* +3.79%*	177	1980–1986	(–5,5) (–1,0)	79.1% 73.8%	Tender offers only.
Leeth, Borg (2000)	+$86 MM	53	1919–1930	(–40,0)	56.6%	In 1998 dollars.
Mulherin (2000)	+2.53%*	116	1962–1997	(–1,0)	66%	A sample of incomplete acquisitions.
Mulherin, Boone (2000)	+3.56%	281	1990–1999	(–1,+1)	N/A	
Houston et al. (2001)	+0.14% (1985–1990) +3.11%* (1991–1996) +1.86%* all	27 37 64	1985–1996	(–4,1)	N/A	Deals in which both parties are banks.
Beitel et al. (2002)	+1.2%*	98	1985–2000	(–1,0)	65%	Sample of European bank mergers.
Fan, Goyal (2002)	+1.9%*	2,162	1962–1996	(–1,+1)	N/A	
Kuipers, Miller, Patel (2003)	+2.99%*	120	1982–1991	(–1,0)	N/A	Foreign acquirers and U.S. targets.
Gupta, Misra (undated)	+7.06 MM	393	1980–1998	(–1,0)	53%	Sample of acquirers and targets in the financial sector.

Unless otherwise noted, event date is announcement date of merger/bid.
*Significant at the 0.95 confidence level or better.

EXHIBIT 3.8 Summary of Studies of Financial Statement Data

Author, Sample Period, and Sample Size	Major Findings
Meeks (1977) 1964–1972 233 mergers	ROA for acquiring firms in the United Kingdom consistently declined in postmerger years.
Salter, Weinhold (1979) Sample period unknown 16 acquirers	Average ROE for acquirers was 44% below the NYSE ROE, and the ROA was 75% below the NYSE.
Mueller (1980) 1962–1972 287 mergers	Using measures such as ROE, ROA, and ROS, U.S. firms engaging in merger activity were less profitable, although not significantly so, than comparable firms. Similar conclusions were reached for representative European countries.
Mueller (1985) 1950–1992 100 firms involved in mergers	The largest 100 firms in the United States involved in merger, both conglomerate and horizontal, suffer significant losses in market share.
Ravenscraft, Scherer (1987 article) 1950–1977 471 mergers	Significant negative relationships between operating ROA and tender offer activity. Other things being equal, firms with tender offer activity were 3.1% less profitable than firms without the activity.
Ravenscraft, Scherer (1987 book) 1950–1977 471 mergers	ROA declined on average 0.5% per year for target companies that were merged under pooling accounting.
Herman, Lowenstein (1988) 1975–1983 56 hostile takeovers	ROC for acquirers (using tender offers) increased from 14.7% to 19.6% postmerger in 1975–1978. A similar measure for the 1981–1983 period showed a decrease in ROC.
Seth (1990) 1962–1979 102 tender offers	Using a modeled (rather than a market) value of equity based on expected cash flows and a required rate of return, acquisitions returned 9.3% in additional equity value. Operational synergies, in the form of additional cash flows, returned 12.9%, and financial synergies, from changes in the required rate of return, were –3.6%.
Healy, Palepu, Ruback (1992) 1979–1984 50 mergers	In 50 largest U.S. mergers, merged firms showed significant abnormal improvements in asset productivity (asset turnover), but no significant abnormal increases in operating cash flow margins.
Chatterjee, Meeks (1996) 1977–1990 144 mergers	Before 1985, U.K. mergers showed no significant increase in profitability after merger. Between 1985 and 1990, firms showed significant improvement in accounting profitability returns (13–22%) in years following merger, presumably because of changes in accounting policy.

EXHIBIT 3.8 *(Continued)*

Author, Sample Period, and Sample Size	Major Findings
Dickerson, Gibson, Tsakalotos (1997) 1948–1977 613 mergers	For the first five years, postacquisition, ROA for acquirers is 2% lower than ROA for nonacquirers.
Healy, Palepu, Ruback (1997) 1979–1984 50 mergers	Based on the 50 largest U.S. mergers, operating cash flow returns as a result of merger met but did not exceed the premium paid for target; therefore M&A is a zero net present value (NPV) activity. Stock price activity at time of announcement was related to postacquisition cash flow performance.
Parrino, Harris (1999) and Parrino, Harris (2001) 1982–1987 197 mergers	Buyers experienced a significant +2.1% operating cash flow return after merger. This return is defined as operating cash flow divided by market value of assets. Postmerger returns were significantly higher where the buyer and target shared at least one common business line, or merged to take advantage of technology.
Ghosh (2001) 1981–1995 315 mergers	Buyers experienced returns on assets no different from a control sample following acquisitions. But cash flows increased significantly following acquisitions made with cash, and declined for stock acquisitions.
Carline, Linn, Yadav (2001) 1985–1994 86 mergers	Buyers and targets, combined, underperformed their industry peers in five years before merger, and outperformed their peers in five years after. Median change in performance of industry adjusted operating cash flows was +6.39%.*
Sharma, Ho (2002) 1986–1991 36 mergers, Australian sample	Comparing the three years before merger to the three years after, buyers showed significantly lower return on equity, return on assets, profit margin, and earnings per share.

ROE = Return on equity.
ROA = Return on assets.
ROS = Return on sales.
ROC = Return on capital.
*Significant at the 0.99 confidence level.

EXHIBIT 3.9 Excerpted Findings about the Change in Profitability of British Acquirers Following Acquisition

	Change in Profitability versus Industry and versus Predeal Performance	Percentage of Observations in Which Change in Profitability Is Negative
Year of transaction	0.148*	0.338†
Year +1	–0.015	0.536
Year +2	–0.010	0.517
Year +3	–0.058*	0.527
Year +4	–0.098*	0.660†
Year +5	–0.110*	0.642†
Year +6	–0.067	0.523
Year +7	–0.073	0.619

*Significantly different from zero at 1%.
†Significantly different from 0.5 at 5%.
Source: Meeks (1977), page 25.

The main observation from Mueller's findings is that acquirers reported worse returns in the years after acquisition than their nonacquiring counterparts—but *not significantly so.* The most strongly negative results are shown in the right-hand column, notably in the low percentage of the sample that offered a positive comparison. Commenting on the results for all seven countries, Mueller wrote:

> *No consistent pattern of either improved or deteriorated profitability can therefore be claimed across the seven countries. Mergers would appear to result in a slight improvement here, a slight worsening of performance there. If a generalization is to be drawn, it would have to be that mergers have but modest effects, up or down, on the profitability of the merging firms in the three to five years following merger. Any economic efficiency gains from the mergers would appear to be small, judging from these statistics, as would any market power increases. (Page 306)*

Ravenscraft and Scherer (1987) studied 471 acquirers between 1950 and 1977. The novelty in this study was the reliance of the researchers upon a special line-of-business database maintained by the Federal Trade Commission that would permit greater definition of control groups than in previous studies, and more careful assessment of asset values and the impact of accounting method choices. The drawback to the line-of-business focus is that acquisition synergies might occur in other areas of the acquiring firm, and therefore might be missed by this study. Also, the comparison in postmerger years is undermined by misalignment with the merger year.[9] The researchers considered the ratio of operating income to assets. Strengthening the analysis are controls for industry effects, accounting method choices, and market shares. Their principal finding is that profitability is one to two percentage points less for acquirers than for control firms—these differences are statistically significant. Purchase accounting and the entry into new (i.e., diversifying) lines of business are associated with material and significant decreases in profitability.

EXHIBIT 3.10 Excerpts of Findings about Change in U.S. Acquirers' Profitability Following Acquisition

	Acquirers: Three Years after versus Five Years before Compared to Two Control Group Companies (% Difference/% Positive)		Acquirers' Postmerger Performance Compared to Their Base Industry Peers (% Difference/% Positive)		Acquirer's Postmerger Performance Compared to a Projection of Performance Based on a Control Group and Industry Trends (% Difference/% Positive)	
What it means	Change in profitability of acquirers compared with a randomly selected nonacquiring firm.		Change in profitability of acquirers compared with a nonacquiring firm matched on size and industry.		Change in profitability of acquirers compared with what it would have been if they had followed industry trends.	
Pretax						
Return on equity	–0.084	53%	–0.128	48%	–0.065*	3%†
Return on assets	–0.038	53%	–0.049	34%	–0.045	3%†
Return on sales	–0.029	60%	–0.034	48%	–0.038	3%†
After tax						
Return on equity	0.011*	57%	–0.002	55%	–0.065†	4%†
Return on assets	0.003	57%	–0.001	31%	–0.002	17%†
Return on sales	0.003	70%‡	0.002	58%	–0.001	10%†

*Indicates significance at 2% level.
†Significance at 1% level.
‡Significance at 5% level.
Source: Mueller (1980).

Healy, Palepu, and Ruback (1992) studied the postacquisition accounting data for the 50 largest U.S. mergers between 1979 and mid-1984, and use industry performance as a benchmark against which acquirers' performance may be tested. Asset productivity improves significantly for these firms following acquisition, which contributes to higher operating cash flow returns relative to their nonacquiring peers. Acquirers maintain their rates of capital expenditure and R&D relative to their industries, suggesting that the improved performance is not at the expense of fundamental investment in the business. Most importantly, the announcement returns on stock for the merging firms is significantly associated with the improvement in postmerger operating performance, suggesting that anticipated gains drive the share prices at announcement.

FINDINGS ABOUT THE DRIVERS OF PROFITABILITY

The studies yield a number of interesting insights about the determinants of M&A profitability.

- ***Expected synergies are important drivers of the wealth creation through merger.*** Houston, James, and Ryngaert (2001) studied the association of forecasted cost savings and revenue enhancements in bank mergers and found a significant relationship between the present value of these benefits, and the announcement day returns. The market appears to discount the value of these benefits, however, and applies a greater discount to revenue-enhancing synergies, and a smaller discount to cost-reduction synergies. DeLong (2003) also studied bank mergers and found that investors responded positively to mergers where one partner was inefficient, and where the merger focuses geography, activity, and earnings: All are symptomatic of synergy gains. Chapter 11 discusses the valuation of synergies and its impact on share prices.
- ***Value acquiring pays, glamour acquiring does not.*** Rau and Vermaelen (1998) found that postacquisition underperformance by buyers was associated with "glamour" acquirers (companies with high book-to-market value ratios). Value-oriented buyers (low book-to-market ratios) outperform glamour buyers. Value acquirers earn significant abnormal returns of 8 percent in mergers and 16 percent in tender offers, while glamour acquirers earn a significant –17 percent in mergers and insignificant +4 percent in tender offers.
- ***Restructuring pays.*** Chapter 6 summarizes the research findings on restructurings, divestitures, spin-offs, carve-outs, and the debate over whether diversification pays better than a strategy of focus. The sale or redeployment of underperforming businesses is greeted positively by investors. But whether diversification helps or hurts is a matter of debate today. Informed wisdom these days probably sides with the antidiversification stance, though new findings suggest that it is not diversification or focus that matter. Rather it is continually reshaping the business to respond to the environment that matters.
- ***M&A to build market power does not pay.*** Studies by Ravenscraft and Scherer (1987), Mueller (1985), and Eckbo (1992) reveal that efforts to enhance mar-

ket position through M&A yield no better performance, and sometimes worse. Studies by Stillman (1983) and Eckbo (1983) find that share price movements of competitive rivals of the buyer do not conform to increases in market power by buyers. The studies suggest that the sources of gains from M&A do not derive from anticompetitive combination of firms.

- ***Paying with stock is costly; paying with cash is neutral.*** Chapter 20 reviews the research on how form of payment is associated with returns to investors. Asquith, Bruner, and Mullins (1987), Huang and Walkling (1987), Travlos (1987), Yook (2000), and Heron and Lie (2002) found that stock-based deals are associated with negative returns to the buyer's shareholders at deal announcements, whereas cash deals are zero or slightly positive. This finding is consistent with theories that managers time the issuance of shares of stock to occur at the high point in the cycle of the company's fortunes, or in the stock market cycle. Thus, the announcement of the payment with shares (like an announcement of an offering of seasoned stock) could be taken as a signal that managers believe the firm's shares are overpriced.
- ***Returns vary over time.*** The studies show a slight tendency for bidder returns to decline over time: Returns appear to be higher (more positive) in the 1960s and 1970s than in the 1980s and 1990s, except for deals in technology and banking, where returns to bidders increase in the 1990s.[10] Moeller et al. (2003) reported a dramatic decline in bidders' returns from 1997 to 2001. Fan and Goyal (2002) found that the average return to bidders and targets combined rises from 1962 to 1996.
- ***M&A regulation is costly to investors.*** Wier (1983) and Eckbo (1983) found evidence suggesting that Federal Trade Commission antitrust actions benefit competitive rivals of the buyer and target. Jarrell and Bradley (1980) and Asquith, Bruner, and Mullins (1983) found that returns to merging firms were significantly higher before than after implementation of the Williams Act of 1968. Schipper and Thompson (1983) considered four regulatory changes between 1968 and 1970, and found wealth-reducing effects associated with increased regulation.
- ***Rule of laws and property rights matter in cross-border deals.*** Chapters 5 and 12 discuss the impact of country risks on the success of cross-border mergers. Kuipers et al. (2003) found that "foreign acquirers earn significantly higher returns when the rule of law is strong in their country, and their associated U.S. targets earn significantly lower acquisition premiums." (Page 24)
- ***M&A to use excess cash generally destroys value except when redeployed profitably.*** Cash-rich firms have a choice of returning the cash to investors through dividends, or reinvesting it through such activities as M&A. Studies[11] report value destruction by the announcement of M&A transactions by firms with excess cash. However, Bruner (1988) reports that the pairing of slack-poor and slack-rich firms creates value. Before merger, buyers have more cash and lower debt ratios than nonacquirers. And the return to the buyers' shareholders increases with the change in the buyer's debt ratio due to the merger.
- ***Tender offers create value for bidders.*** Chapters 32 and 33 survey the tender offer process and research on returns. Mergers are typically friendly affairs, negotiated between the top management of buyer and target firms. Tender

offers are structured as take-it-or-leave-it proposals, directly to the target firm shareholders, often hostile in attitude. Some research summarized in Chapter 32 suggests that targets of hostile tender offers are underperformers with relatively low share prices. Thus, the better returns from tender offers may reflect bargain prices and/or the economic benefits of replacing management and redirecting the strategy of the firm. Several studies report larger announcement returns to bidders in tender offers, as compared with friendly negotiated transactions.[12]

- ***When managers have more at stake, more value is created.*** Studies suggest that returns to buyer firm shareholders are associated with larger equity interests by managers and employees.[13] In assessing the pattern of performance associated with deal characteristics, Healey, Palepu, and Ruback (1997) concluded, "While takeovers were usually break-even investments, the profitability of individual transactions varied widely . . . the transactions characteristics *that were under management control* substantially influenced the ultimate payoffs from takeovers."[14] A related finding is that leveraged buyouts (LBOs) create value for buyers. The sources of these returns are not only from tax savings due to debt and depreciation shields, but also significantly from efficiencies and greater operational improvements implemented after the LBO. In LBOs, managers tend to have a significant portion of their net worth committed to the success of the transaction. Exhibit 3.11 summarizes the findings of several studies about LBOs and reveals that cash flow increases and capital spending declines materially in the years following the transaction. Chapter 13 relates more research findings about LBOs and other highly levered transactions.
- ***The initiation of M&A programs is associated with creation of value for buyers.*** Asquith, Bruner, and Mullins (1983), Fuller, Netter, and Stegemoller (2002), Gregory (1997), and Schipper and Thompson (1983) report that when firms announce they are undertaking a series of acquisitions in pursuit of some strategic objectives, their share prices rise significantly. That these kinds of announcements should create value suggests that M&A generally creates value, and that the announcement is taken as a serious signal of value creation.

EXHIBIT 3.11 Summary of Performance Studies for M&A: LBO Results

Study	Change in Operating Cash Flow/Sales	Change in CapEx Sales	Sample Size	Sample Period	Event Window (Years)
Kaplan (1989)	11.9%	−31.6%	37	1980–1986	(−1,2)
Muscarella, Vetsuypens (1990)	23.5%	−11.4%	35	1976–1987	Various
Smith (1990)	18.0%	−25.0%	18	1976–1986	(−1,2)
Opler (1992)	16.5%	−42.2%	42	1985–1989	(−1,2)
Andrade, Kaplan (1998)	54.5%	−40.7%	124	1980–1989	(−1,1)

FINDINGS FROM SURVEYS OF EXECUTIVES

The findings of scholars in large-sample surveys are supplemented by studies by scholars and practitioners who focus on smaller samples and typically draw some or all of their findings from questions of managers directly. Ingham, Kran, and Lovestam (1992) surveyed chief executive officers in 146 large firms in the United Kingdom. Of them, 77 percent believed that profitability increased in the short run after merger; 68 percent believed that the improved profitability lasted for the long run.

Surveys by practitioners are often rather casually reported, limiting our ability to replicate the study and understand the methodological strengths and weaknesses. For this reason, scholars tend to give practitioner surveys rather less attention. Nevertheless, a sample of these surveys is reported here for the sake of comparison with the scholarly studies. It is interesting to consider whether managers tell us something different from the large-sample scientific studies.

The absence of statistical tests in these surveys limits the assertions one can make, but a qualitative review of results offers results surprisingly similar to the scientific studies. Exhibit 3.12 tabulates the results of 12 studies. Six of the 12 studies suggest negative results. The remainder seem neutral or positive. The similarity between these findings and the findings from the scholarly studies is striking. In the bulk of deals, it appears that investments in acquisitions at least pay their cost of capital.

To explore some of the problems of stability in executive surveys about M&A, I polled 50 business executives via the Internet. As with other surveys of this type, no effort was made to ensure representativeness or reduce bias, thus limiting our ability to generalize the results to all executives or all M&A deals. Nevertheless, the findings offer important insights about M&A profitability.

First, the survey considered all respondents, and asked their opinion about the percent of all M&A deals that create value and meet their strategic objectives. The resulting distributions of opinion were quite wide. But on average, the respondents said that only 37 percent of deals create value for the buyers. Even worse, the sample believes that only 21 percent of the deals achieve the buyers' strategic goals. These findings are similar to results of some other surveys of executives.

Next, the survey focused only on those respondents who had been personally involved in one or more M&A transactions, and asked them to comment on their own deals. In essence, this created a subsample of possibly better-informed respondents. For this subset, the results reversed themselves:

- Fully 58 percent of the informed respondents believe their own M&A deals created value; 51 percent believe their deals achieved their strategic goals. In contrast, only 23 percent believed their deals did not create value; 31 percent believed their deals did not achieve their strategic goals. The remaining respondents either did not know the results of their deals or concluded the results were mixed.

EXHIBIT 3.12 Sample of Practioner Studies and Their Key Findings

Source and Date	Sample Size	Sample Period	Findings
Johan Brjoksten, 1965 (cited in Lajoux and Weston, 1998)	5,409 manufacturing mergers	1955–1965	16% were a failure financially, strategically, technologically.
McKinsey & Co., 1987 (cited in Lajoux and Weston, 1998)	116 firms		61% failed to earn back the cost of equity.
PA Consulting (cited in Lajoux and Weston, 1998)	28 "major acquirers in banking"	1982–1988	80% of acquisitions had a negative effect on the acquirer's share price.
McKinsey & Co. (cited in Fisher, 1994)	N/A	A 10-year period	Only 23% of transactions recovered the costs incurred in the deal, much less any synergies.
Mercer Management and *Business Week*, October 1995 (cited in Lajoux and Weston, 1998)	150 deals of size $500 million or greater	1990–1995	Measured total returns to shareholders over a three-year period. 17% of the deals created substantial returns. 33% created marginal returns. 20% eroded some returns. 30% substantially eroded shareholder returns.
	248 acquirers purchasing a total of 1,045 targets, compared to 96 nonacquiring firms	1990–1995	69% of nonacquirers produced returns superior to their industries. 58% of the acquirers produced returns superior to their industries.
David Mitchell of Economists Intelligence Unit, 1996 (cited in Lajoux and Weston, 1998)	Survey of executives in 150 companies	1992–1996	30% called their mergers "successful, worth repeating." 53%, satisfactory, not worth repeating. 11% unsatisfactory. 5% disastrous.

Kenneth Smith in research for Mercer Consulting, 1997, and for Mitchell Madison Group 1998 (cited in Lajoux and Weston, 1998)	215 large transactions, valued at $500 million or more	Compared acquirers' performance in 1980s deals versus 1990s deals	52% of 1990s deals were outperforming their industry standards, compared to 37% of 1980s deals.
Michael Mayo, Lehman Bros. (cited in Lajoux and Weston, 1998)	Six banks	N/A	Acquirers' stock prices declined an average of 10% within one week of the announcement, but all recovered within two months.
Andersen Consulting (cited in Bahree, 1999)	Large mergers completed between 1994 and 1997	1994–1997	44% of all large mergers fell short of initial financial and strategic expectations. 70% of oil mergers fell short.
KPMG LLP (Kelly, Cook, and Spitzer, 1999)	700 "of the most expensive deals"	1996–1998	Interviews with 107 executives revealed that 82% believed their deals were "successful," yet analysis showed that "only 17% had added value to the combined company, 30% produced no discernible difference, and as many as 53% actually destroyed value. In other words, 83% of mergers were unsuccessful in producing any business benefit as regards shareholder value." (Page 2)
Chaudhuri, Tabrizi (1999)	53 acquisitions by 24 high-tech companies	N/A	Successful acquirers were differentiated from unsuccessful acquirers by a focus on capabilities. 11 were "considered successful by both sides." 9 were clear failures. 33 provided zero or slightly positive but disappointing returns on investment.
Booz-Allen & Hamilton 2001 (Adolph et al., 2001)	Sample size not reported	1997–1998	53% of all deals failed to deliver expected results. Of the part of the sample consisting of mergers aimed at exploiting scale economies, the failure rate was 45%. Of the part of the sample with "strategic motivations" (such as "add capabilities" or "new business model") the failure rate was 68%.

- The strength of the respondents' view about all M&A was inversely related to their view of their own deals: The better they felt about their own deals, the more they condemned M&A results in general. On the measure of value creation of deals (own deals vs. all deals), the responses were correlated –42 percent, a strongly negative degree of association for work in social science. But on the dimension of meeting strategic objectives, the correlation was even more negative, –72 percent.

This survey illustrates the important influence of one's frame of reference on survey responses. The effects of facts and impressions differ. Where the respondents were better informed (e.g., their own deals, with firsthand information), M&A seemed to pay. But for the broader judgment, the respondents fell back on a very different opinion. There is one other explanation for the disparate findings: For reasons of ego executives tell the world nicer things about their own deals than about the deals of others. Either way, one's frame of reference (informed by information or weighted by ego) shapes a very different and more optimistic view about M&A profitability.

The practitioner should evaluate critically the findings reported by consultants' surveys and discount those studies that hedge in answering the following kinds of questions:

- Is the study based on a large, representative sample?
- Were the survey questions framed in a way to avoid coaching the respondent to give a desired answer?
- Was this a survey of opinions or facts? Did the survey probe the respondent's factual knowledge of actual transactions?
- Was the response rate reported?
- Was the methodology rigorous and so clearly described that it would be possible to replicate?

FINDINGS FROM CLINICAL STUDIES

Clinical studies of M&A cases offer insights into the possible origins of the returns experience for outliers. Here are conclusions from some of these studies.

- *ATT/NCR.* Lys and Vincent (1995) examined the 1991 acquisition of NCR Corporation by AT&T. This acquisition decreased the wealth of AT&T shareholders by between $3.9 billion and $6.5 billion. The study offered three explanations for these results. The first was a set of managerial objectives that were not consistent with maximizing shareholder wealth. The second was managerial overconfidence, or hubris. And the third was "escalation of commitments," a psychological phenomenon that spurs decision makers to move forward despite information to the contrary.
- *Renault/Volvo.* Bruner (1999) examined the failed attempt to merge AB Volvo with Renault in 1993. The attempt temporarily erased 22 percent of Volvo's market value before Volvo's board of directors withdrew from the deal. The

study suggests that the value destruction was associated with disbelief in merger synergies and with the transfer of control to Renault.

- ***Leveraged buyout of Revco D.S.*** Bruner and Eades (1992) and Wruck (1991) studied the bankruptcy of one of the largest leveraged buyouts in the retailing industry, that of Revco Drug Stores. The failure was associated with overpayment, the use of extremely high debt financing, and the arguably self-serving behavior of management.
- **Cooper Industries' acquisition of Cameron Iron Works, and Premark's acquisition of Florida Tile.** Kaplan, Mitchell, and Wruck (1997) studied two acquisitions that experienced very different stock market reactions to their announcements (one positive, the other negative). Interviews after the fact revealed that neither acquisition succeeded in creating value. Causes were inappropriate incentives, incomplete knowledge of the target, and the imposition of inappropriate organizational designs on the target.
- ***Campeau's acquisition of Federated.*** Kaplan (1989) found that the value of Federated's assets *increased* under Campeau's ownership up to the point of bankruptcy filing. He does not identify the source of value creation, but suggests cost cuts, sale of underutilized assets, and tax benefits.
- ***Takeover fight for Paramount by Viacom and QVC.*** Hietala, Kaplan, and Robinson (2002) isolated the bidder overpayment and synergies implied in the stock price movements in this contest. They estimate that Viacom overpaid for Paramount by more than $2 billion despite the fact that Sumner Redstone, the CEO of Viacom, owned about three-quarters of the firm.
- ***DuPont's takeover of Conoco.*** Ruback (1982) assessed the net value creation to the shareholders of the buyer and target jointly. Whereas shareholders of the target (Conoco) received gains of $3.2 billion, shareholders of DuPont sustained losses of $800 million. Therefore, the net value created in the deal was $2.4 billion. Ruback explored various possible explanations for the net gain and was unable to identify a specific source. The study highlights the difficulty facing all researchers in explaining wealth creation or destruction in individual deals.

Clinical studies illuminate possible drivers of returns from acquisition. These and other studies have emphasized the role of strategic, financial, and organizational issues.

CONCLUSIONS OF REVIEWERS THROUGH TIME

Several scholars have considered the findings of scientific studies over the years, conducting an exercise much as here. How have they viewed the data?

- ***Dennis Mueller (1979).*** In testimony before the U.S. Senate, Mueller said, "And the predominant conclusion, what it comes to, from looking at this literature, is that the firms themselves are performing no better on average than they would have been in the absence of the mergers, and the stockholders who hold shares in those firms are doing no better than if they had shares in a firm that wasn't."[15]

- *Michael Jensen and Richard Ruback (1983).* Based on an analysis of 16 studies, the authors concluded that the return to bidders in successful mergers was zero, and in successful takeovers was +4.0 percent. They wrote, "The evidence indicates that corporate takeovers generate positive gains, that target firm shareholders benefit, and that bidding firm shareholders do not lose."[16]
- *Murray Weidenbaum and Stephen Vogt (1987).* Based on an analysis of 10 studies, the authors wrote, "We conclude that, based on historical data, negative returns to shareholders for acquisitions are more prevalent than the prevailing folklore on the subject admits. Clearly, there are winners and losers in the takeover game. Most studies confirm that, in general, target firm shareholders are winners. The evidence presented here indicates that, on average, acquiring firm shareholders are not as fortunate. At best, these shareholders are no worse off, but often they lose during acquisitions."[17]
- *Richard Caves (1989).* The author referenced 69 studies and considered the market-based share returns at the announcement of the deals and the performance in the years following merger. He concluded, "We have a conundrum. Ex ante, mergers appear to create value for bidder and target together that is substantial relative to the premerger worth of the target firm. That is, the financial markets appear to believe that bidders can wring a *lot* more value from the typical target's assets. Ex post, recent studies run exactly in the opposite direction, indicating that mergers not merely fail to warrant acquisition premia but actually reduce the real profitability of acquired business units, increase the intraindustry dispersion of plant productivity levels, and shrivel the acquiree's market share."[18]
- *Deepak Datta, George Pinches, and V. K. Narayanan (1992).* The authors considered 41 studies, and concluded that bidders earn a return of less than one-half of 1 percent. They wrote, "The synthesis of ex ante event studies presented in this paper provides robust evidence that, on average, shareholders of bidding or acquiring firms do not realize significant returns from mergers and acquisitions."[19]

VIEWING THE WHOLE MOSAIC: SOME CONCLUSIONS

What should a practical person conclude from this discussion? Arguably, the data support a range of views.

- *Does pay.* This answer is certainly justified for shareholders of target firms. Also, studies of targets and buyers *combined* suggest these transactions create joint value. Finally, for bidders alone, two-thirds of the studies conclude that value is conserved or created.
- *Doesn't pay.* This is true if you focus only on bidders, and define "pay" as creating material and significant abnormal value—this line of reasoning is behind statements that 60 to 70 percent of all M&A transactions "fail." But economics teaches that investors should be satisfied if they earn returns just equal to their cost of the lost opportunity (i.e., their required return). Therefore, the popular definition of failure is extreme. The reality is that 60 to 70 percent of all M&A transactions are associated with financial performance that at least compensates investors for their opportunity cost—against this standard it appears that buyers typically get at least what they deserve.

- ***It depends.*** This is true, from the perspective of the earlier section that describes determinants of higher and lower M&A profitability. Value is created by focus, relatedness, and adherence to strategy. Diversification (especially conglomerate), size maximization, empire building, and hubris destroy value. The implication of this is that good deals are not achieved by pricing alone: Strategy and skills of postmerger integration matter immensely. Some rich insights can be derived from an examination of types of deals. The key implication of these insights is that managers *can* make choices that materially influence the profitability of M&A. Cleverness gets its due. So does stupidity.
- ***We don't know.*** This is true from the perspective of the earlier section that discusses how research strictly rejects null hypotheses, and never confirms alternative hypotheses. One can only test for the association of M&A with profitability, never causation. Like intellectual tic-tac-toe, you prove anything only by eliminating all the alternatives. Even after many studies, we may not have exhausted the alternative explanations. It is hard to warm up to this view. While one admires its rigor and skepticism, surely the mass of tests tells us at least something about tendencies.
- ***All the above.*** This is apparently true. Each of the preceding positions has at least one leg (if not two) to stand on. While this position may be honest, this alternative gives equal weight to the various arguments, and is not very satisfying to the practical person who must decide. You must have a view.
- ***None of the above.*** Perhaps the cacophony of conflicting studies leads one to pure agnosticism. Such a conclusion is harsh, and hardly the foundation for an executive who must lead an enterprise in the hurly-burly of business life.

My reading of the studies leads me to choose "Does pay, but. . . ." I take the economists' perspective that an investment is deemed to "pay" if it earns at least the opportunity cost of capital. Abstracting from the studies, the majority of transactions meets this test for targets, bidders, and the combined firms. *But* the buyer in M&A transactions must prepare to be disappointed. The distribution of announcement returns is wide and the mean is close to zero. There is no free lunch. The negative performance postmerger (see Exhibit 3.6) is troubling, but absent a rigorous strong-form test, we must await further research to see whether the poor performance is tied to the mergers or to more general phenomena in markets. In the interim, shareholders of both target and buyer firms should be cautious. The outcomes of most transactions are hardly consistent with optimistic expectations. Synergies, efficiencies, and value-creating growth seem hard to obtain. It is in this sense that deal doers' reach exceeds their grasp.

Based on the mass of research, my advice to the business practitioner is to be coldly realistic about the benefits of acquisition. Structure your deals very carefully. Particularly avoid overpaying. Have the discipline to walk away from uneconomic deals. Work very hard to achieve the economic gains you hypothesized. Take nothing for granted. M&A is no money machine, and may well not offer the major career-building event you wanted. The only solace is that you could say the same about virtually any other form of corporate investment; on balance, your shareholders will earn a going rate of return on M&A activity. Given the uncertainties in M&A as elsewhere, one must remember the ancient advice, *caveat emptor* (buyer beware).

SPECIAL NOTE

This chapter is an expanded and updated version of an article by the same name and author (Bruner 2002) that appeared in the *Journal of Applied Finance*. It appears here by the kind permission of the editors, Ali Fatemi and Keith Howe.

NOTES

1. Grubb and Lamb (2000), pages 9, 10, 12, and 14.
2. In England, the village commons was a field jointly used by villagers to graze their animals. Because the field was, in effect, held by all, no one individually looked out for the welfare of the social good. The problem of the commons was to prevent behavior (such as overgrazing by selfish villagers) that would harm the welfare of all.
3. The story is rather different for the Time-Warner shareholders, who wound up cushioning the collapse of the Internet bubble for the AOL shareholders.
4. In a memorable comment, Caves (1989) wrote, "This technique was a genuine innovation—theoretically well grounded, cheap to execute, and able to evade the problem of holding constant other factors that plague *ex post* studies of mergers' effects. A better product, available at a lower price, naturally swept the intellectual marketplace." (Page 151)
5. Tests of significance also depend on sample size. The t values discussed here implicitly assume relatively large samples of observations, such as more than 100.
6. $[(1.01)^{52} - 1] = 0.678$.
7. See Dennis and McConnell (1986) and Billett, King, and Mauer (2003). Also, Maquieira, Megginson, and Nail (1998) report, "Apart from bidding firm stockholders in conglomerate mergers, all major classes of debt and equity securityholders of both bidders and targets either break even or experience significant wealth gains." (Page 30)
8. Meeks defines return on assets as pretax profits (after depreciation, but before tax) divided by the average of beginning and ending assets for the year. The key metric was $R_{Change} = R_{After} - R_{Before}$ where R_{After} and R_{Before} were measures of performance relative to the weighted average of returns of the buyer's and target's industries.
9. Ravenscraft and Scherer examine the performance between 1974 and 1977 of mergers that occurred from 1950 to 1977. In other words, the period under observation was not the same number of years after merger from one observation to the next.
10. Bradley, Desai, and Kim (1988) report that average announcement returns to bidders fell from 4.1 percent in the 1963 to 1968 period to –2.9 percent in the 1981–1984 period.
11. See Servaes, Lang, Stultz, and Walkling (1991), Harford (1999), and Jensen (1986).
12. Jensen and Ruback (1983) give a survey of returns in contested and friendly deals. Numerous studies report positive significant returns to bidders in hostile transactions: Asquith, Bruner, and Mullins (1987), Gregory (1997), Loughran

and Vijh (1997), Rau and Vermaelen (1998), Lang, Stultz, and Walkling (1989), and Jarrell and Poulsen (1989). On the other hand, Healey, Palepu, and Ruback (1997) found that hostile deals were associated with insignificant improvements in cash flow returns, owing possibly to the payment of higher acquisition premiums.

13. Agrawal and Mandelker (1987) found that lower equity investment by managers in their own firms was associated with higher propensity to undertake variance-reducing acquisitions. You et al. (1986) found that announcement returns to bidders were lower (i.e., more negative), the lower the managers' equity stake in the buyer firm.
14. Page 55, italics added.
15. Dennis Mueller (1979), page 307.
16. Jensen and Ruback (1983), page 5.
17. Weidenbaum and Vogt (1987), page 166.
18. Caves (1989), page 167.
19. Datta, Pinches, and Narayanan (1992), page 13.

PART Two

Strategy and the Origination of Transaction Proposals

CHAPTER 4

M&A Activity

INTRODUCTION

History is a tough instructor. Though its lessons are sometimes obscure, their ramifications can be severe. And, more often than not, they prove to be vital in charting a course for the future. This is why any serious student of M&A should reflect on the past century of activity. This chapter highlights some of the competing explanations for the activity we observe over time. Though these explanations are not mutually exclusive, one of them yields useful insights for the practitioner. This explanation argues that M&A activity is not a result of random behavior by managers, but rather is motivated by deep forces of change at work in an economy. Thus, to understand the influence of those forces is to be able to anticipate opportunities and challenges in the transaction development process. This chapter sketches some practical implications of this view.

M&A ACTIVITY APPEARS IN WAVES

The point of departure in a study of M&A activity is to look at the aggregate activity over the long term: the past 100 years. There are two ways to consider deal activity: in terms of the number of transactions, and in terms of their aggregate dollar value. A focus on the number of transactions, in effect, gives equal weight to all deals—this is an implicit measure of *breadth* of M&A activity in the United States. Conversely, a focus on the dollar value of all transactions helps to distinguish those episodes dominated by large deals—this might be regarded to be a measure of *depth* or materiality of sizable deals.

Exhibit 4.1 presents the history of M&A activity in terms of number of deals. Exhibit 4.2 gives M&A activity in terms of constant dollar value.[1] In both exhibits, the data are presented on natural and logarithmic scales—the log scales help to highlight those periods when M&A activity jumped sharply in percentage terms, such as 1895 to 1900 and 1965 to 1970. Exhibit 4.3 considers M&A activity relative to the size of the U.S. economy—this helps distinguish the materiality of successive periods of activity. Exhibit 4.4 presents some notes for the reader on the sources for the data in the graphs.

The first important insight from these graphs is that M&A activity reveals evidence of five periods of heightened merger activity; hereafter, I will call these "waves." The appearance of waves is not isolated to the United States. A study of

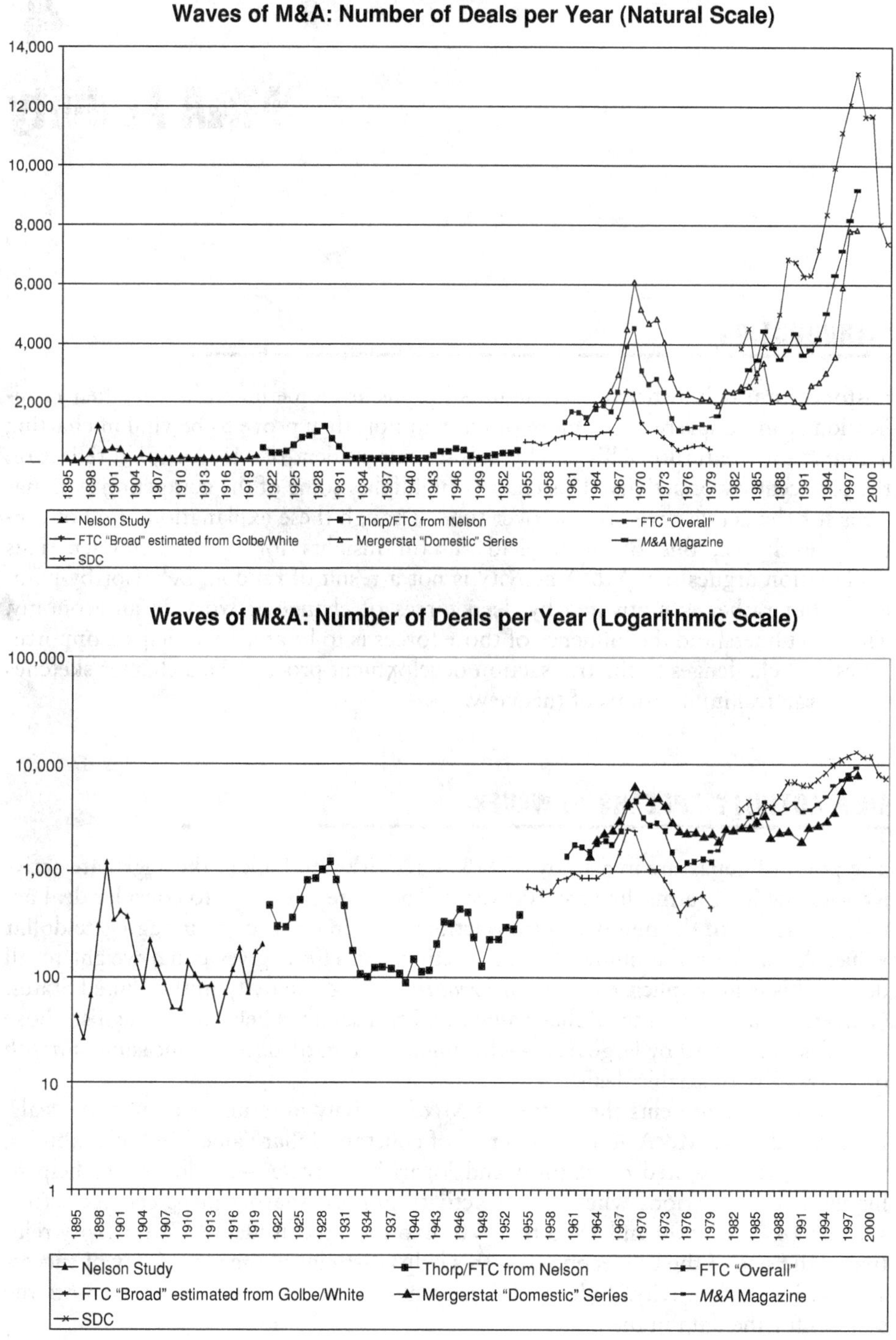

EXHIBIT 4.1 Number of U.S. M&A Transactions per Year on Natural Scale and Logarithmic Scale
See Exhibit 4.4 for sources.

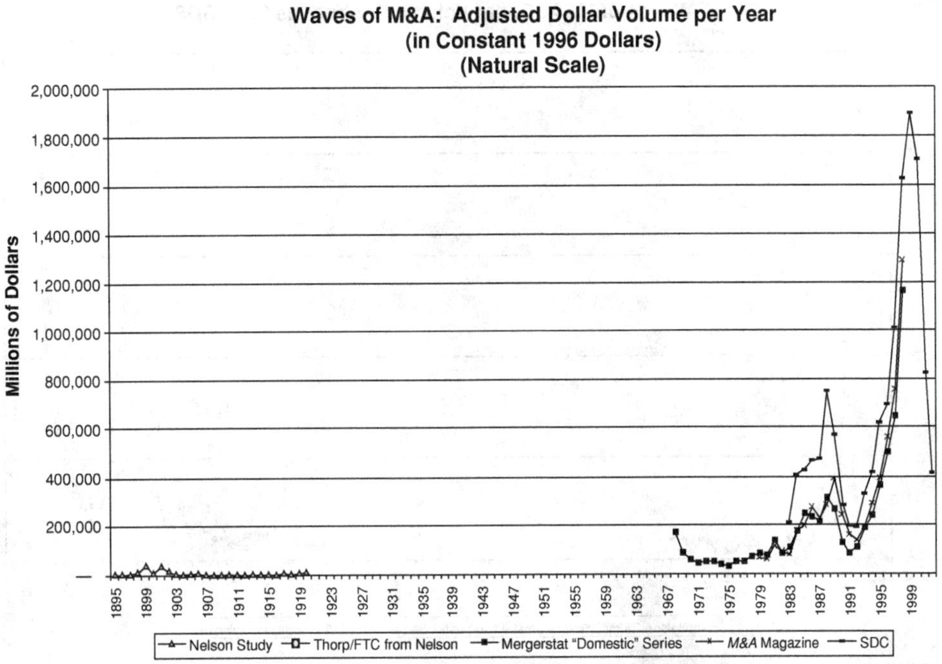

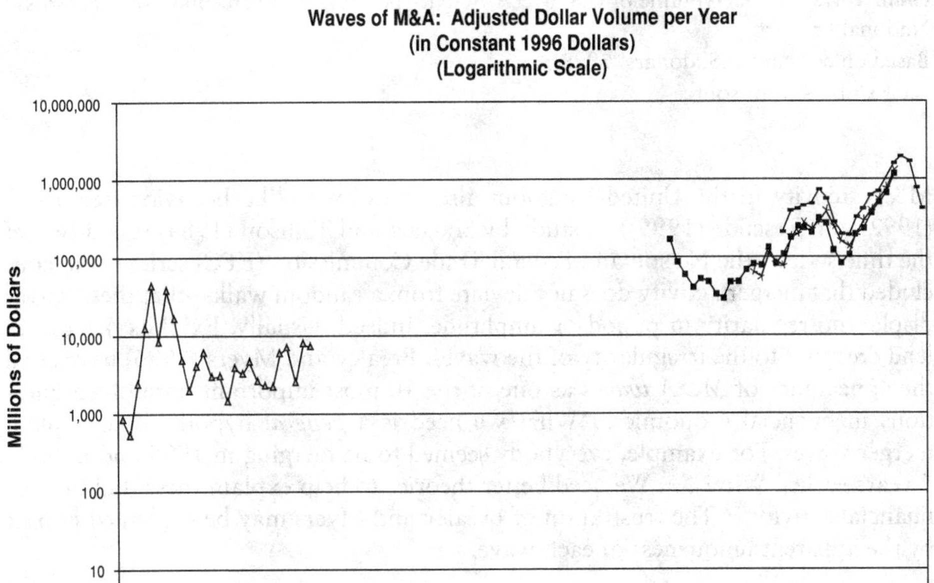

EXHIBIT 4.2 Dollar Volume of U.S. M&A Transactions per Year on Natural Scale and Logarithmic Scale
See Exhibit 4.4 for sources.

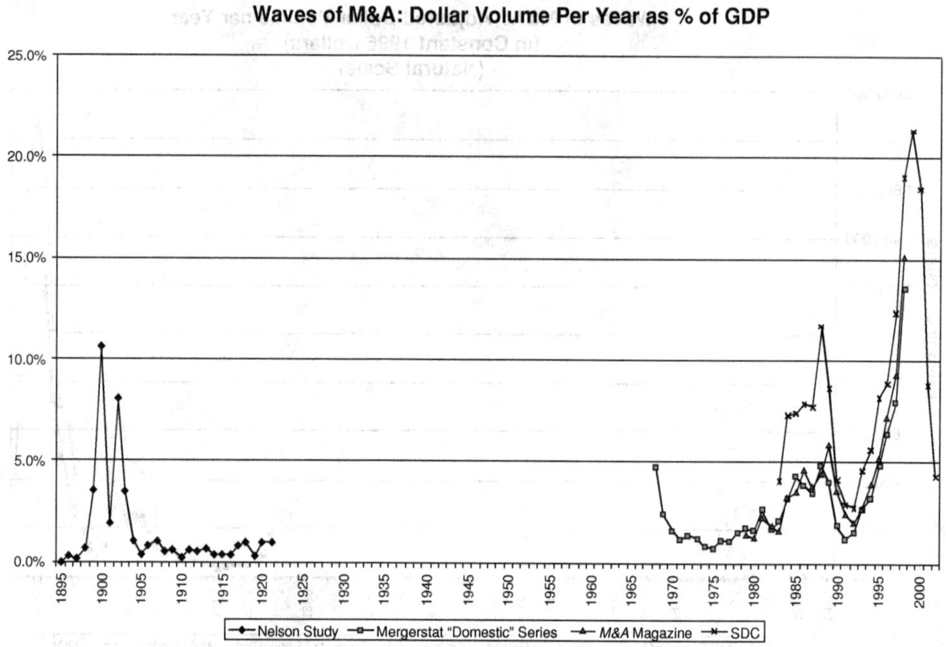

EXHIBIT 4.3 Dollar Volume of U.S. M&A Activity per Year as a Percentage of U.S. Gross National Product
Based on constant U.S. dollars, 1996.
See Exhibit 4.4 for sources.

M&A activity in the United Kingdom also shows wavelike behavior (see Town (1992) and Resende (1999)). A study by Shugart and Tollison (1984) tested two of the time series—the Nelson and Federal Trade Commission (FTC) series—and concluded that merger activity does not deviate from a random walk—that these waves display no regularity in period or amplitude. Indeed, visually, Exhibits 4.1 to 4.3 lend credence to the irregularity of the waves. Brealey and Myers (1996) have cited the appearance of *M&A waves* as one of the 10 most important unresolved questions in financial economics. "What we need is a *general* hypothesis to explain merger waves. For example, everybody seemed to be merging in 1995 and nobody 5 years earlier. Why? . . . We need better theories to help explain these 'bubbles' of financial activity."[2] The frustration of Brealey and Myers may be explained in part by the apparent uniqueness of each wave.

Wave 1: 1895–1904

Horizontal mergers characterized this wave. Beginning on the heels of the depression that ended in 1896, the wave coincided with a period of economic and capital market buoyancy. Firms sought to build market power in response to overcapacity induced by rapid technological innovation. The wave touched a wide variety of manufacturing industries. Examples of firms that originated in wave include DuPont, Standard Oil, General Electric, Eastman Kodak, and U.S. Steel. Stigler

EXHIBIT 4.4 Notes on the Sources of M&A Activity Series

Study	Time Period Available	Time Period Included	Notes
Nelson (1959)	1895 to 1920	1895 to 1920	Only manufacturing and mining included; bottom cutoff limit not clear; based on firm disappearances.
Thorp (1941) from Nelson	1921 to 1939	1921 to 1939	Only manufacturing and mining included; based on firm disappearances.
FTC Overall (1981)	1940 to 1979	1960 to 1979	All deals recorded by FTC; no value totals available.
FTC Broad—Estimated from Golbe/White (1988)	1940 to 1979	1940 to 1979	Only manufacturing and mining included; no acquisitions by individuals or groups included; no value totals available.
Mergerstat	1963 to present	1963 to 1998	Refer to announcements rather than completed deals; bottom cutoff limit is $500,000 in transaction value.
M&A Magazine	1967 to present	1979 to 1998	Lower cutoff limit through 1980 was $700,000 in transaction value; after 1980 lower limit value is $1 million; includes cross-border deals involving a U.S. buyer or target.
Thomson Securities Data Corp.	1983 to present	1983 to 1999	All completed deals of those announced; no lower cutoff limit; includes cross-border deals involving a U.S. buyer or target.

Series Citations:

Nelson, R. *Merger Movements in American Industry 1895–1956*. Princeton: Princeton University Press, 1959.

Thorp, W. "The Merger Movement." In Temporary National Economic Committee Monograph No. 27. Washington, D.C.: U.S. Government Printing Office, 1941.

Federal Trade Commission, Bureau of Economics. *Statistical Report on Mergers and Acquisitions*. Washington, D.C.: U.S. Government Printing Office, 1981.

Golbe, D., and L. White. "Mergers and Acquisitions in the U.S. Economy: An Aggregate and Historical Overview." In A. Auerbach, ed. *Mergers and Acquisitions*, 25–47, Chicago: University of Chicago Press, 1988.

W. T. Grimm & Co. and Houlihan Lokey Howard & Zukin, *Mergerstat Review*, Chicago and Los Angeles (various issues 1988–1999).

Mergers & Acquisitions (various issues 1989–1999).

Thomson Securities Data Corp., Mergers & Acquisitions Database.

(1950) characterized this wave as a period of "merger for monopoly." President Theodore Roosevelt's decision in 1902 to enforce the Sherman Act in the famous *Northern Securities* case was an important turning point of the first wave. The Supreme Court's decision in 1904 limited horizontal mergers among large competitors and took the momentum out of the trust-building trend.

Wave 2: 1925–1929

Vertical combinations characterized this wave as firms sought to integrate backward into supply and forward into distribution of their core businesses. Stigler (1950) called it a period of "merger for oligopoly." Large public utility holding companies emerged on the business landscape. The U.S. government increased its antitrust enforcement following the passage of the Clayton Act. The wave coincided with a boom in stock market prices and volume that began following the recession of 1923 and ended with stock market crash in 1929.

Wave 3: 1965–1970

In the context of heightened antitrust enforcement to limit horizontal combinations, firms turned to conglomerate or diversifying combinations in this wave. Activity was especially concentrated among a group of conglomerates and oil companies. The wave coincided with a strong economy and bull market in the 1960s. Antitrust enforcement against the rise of conglomerates marked the peak of this wave.

Wave 4a: 1981–1987

The popular hallmarks of this wave were larger deals involving more hostile takeovers, more leverage, and more going-private transactions than previous waves. However, the activity was very broad-based, touching virtually all sectors of the U.S. economy, and dominated by combinations among small and medium-sized firms. The Tax Reform Act of 1986 may have contributed to the boom in M&A activity as tax changes took effect. This wave featured the appearance of financial and international buyers as more significant players than ever before. The complexity of transactions increased in concert with growing capital market innovation and sophistication. This was a period of generally falling interest rates and rising stock prices.

Wave 4b: 1992–2000

Following the 1990–1991 recession, M&A activity increased briskly in all segments of the economy and all size categories. The announcement of a few large deals signaled to some observers a "paradigm shift"[3] in M&A where old rules about strategy, size, and deal design were being replaced by new rules. Of general note was the significance of "strategic buyers" who sought to combine with targets who were related along business lines, and with whom synergy value might be created. The superior economics of strategic combinations dampened somewhat the influence of financial buyers (i.e., LBO specialists). Of special note was the high M&A activity in banking, health care, defense, and technology. This sector-focused activity was a response to overcapacity as the industry was deregulated (banking), as national defense spending declined, and as the payment patterns by insurers changed (health care). In technology, the high rate of activity was stimulated by rapid invention and technological change. Finally, the high rate of M&A activity coincided with historically low rates of interest, and rising stock prices. As Exhibits 4.1, 4.2, and 4.3 reveal, the M&A activity in the most recent wave far exceeded any levels seen previously, with transaction values rising to about 15 percent of the U.S. gross national product (GNP) in 1999. Following the bursting of the Internet bubble in March 2000, M&A activity declined sharply, in tandem with the stock market and the U.S. economy, and in conjunction with the rise of global economic and security concerns.

This review of the four waves reveals much more about their differences than similarities. What they seem to bear in common is low or falling interest rates, a rising stock market, and an expanding economy. But they differ sharply in industry focus (e.g., oil, banking, utilities, Internet, conglomerate, etc.), in type of transaction (e.g., horizontal, vertical, conglomerate, strategic, or financial), in the presence or absence of hostile bids, in industry breadth, in breadth of deal size, and in the role of large blockbuster deals. Merger activity appears to slow down when the cost of capital increases, as measured by real interest rates. Studies[4] show that M&A activity is countercyclical to bond yields. More generally, merger activity increases with the level of overall economic activity, as measured by nominal GNP; see Golbe and White (1988).

On close examination, there appears to be an industry-based pattern to the waves of M&A activity. The Mergerstat database suggests that in 1998 and 1999 the most active 14 percent of industries accounted for 60 percent of all M&A deal value. In the period 1995 to 1998, financial services accounted for 22 percent of all M&A value. In 1981 to 1984, oil and gas accounted for 25 percent of all transaction value.

EXPLANATIONS OF M&A ACTIVITY

What drives these waves of M&A activity, creating "hot" and "cold" markets for firms? What causes some industries to grow hot and others remain cold? Research lends some speculative answers to these questions. The explanations should be approached with caution since they are not mutually exclusive and more research remains to be done. But these ideas can help the practitioner frame a view about M&A activity, and thus more ably interpret events and opportunities as they appear. While some of these explanations are stronger than others, they all offer a useful perspective on the activity we observe.

Hubris

The first explanation for M&A activity lies in managerial psychology. Richard Roll (1986) suggested that the urge to merge is driven by pride, or *hubris*, in the face of considerable evidence that earning supernormal returns from acquisitions is difficult. Roll notes that the negative returns following mergers are well known. Only an irrational belief that *your* deal will be different could prompt you to strive where others have failed. Popular accounts of particular deals or deal makers would seem to support this view (see, for instance, Bryan Burrough and John Helyar's classic 1990 account of the RJR Nabisco LBO, *Barbarians at the Gate*). The hubris of the rich and famous is a timeless theme, certain to sell books. And it is timeless for a very good reason: we benefit from the reminder that hubris undercuts rational analysis and self-discipline.

But the hubris hypothesis for M&A activity says too much and too little. It says too much in the sense that hubris could be used to explain most business failures. For instance, something like 70 percent of all new businesses fail within three years. Drug companies spend millions of dollars annually most of which hits dead ends. The revolution of digital computing has left countless failed firms in its wake. The odds of success are low in business start-ups, drug discovery, and technological innovation, and it takes an entrepreneur with at least a modicum of hubris to press ahead. We applaud hubris in these cases because it advances the welfare of society through the discovery of new products and markets. Isn't M&A a discovery process as well? If hubris were to be the dominant explanation for M&A activity, it would need to explain the appearance of merger waves and the clustering of merger activity by industry.

Hubris says too little in that one wishes it had more prescriptive content. It urges us to avoid managerial irrationality, and warns that if we fail to do so, markets will judge accordingly. Through the research work of Kahneman and Tversky (1979, 1984), Thaler (1992), and others, we are gaining a clearer view of the role of behavioral influences in financial decision making. But behavioral finance remains a young field; more research remains to be done. Questions for the analyst include these:

- ***Who are the decision maker and his or her advisers? What, in their background, might suggest a tendency to disregard rational analysis and disciplined thinking?*** M&A arbitrageurs often develop psychological profiles of the CEOs of companies they follow. Though imperfect, these give hints about the decision maker's ability or willingness to think critically about M&A proposals and to act in the interests of shareholders.
- ***Is the decision maker isolated or in touch with reality of the M&A situation?*** One hears about the imperial CEO. Like the fabled emperor who had no clothes, the CEO might have a culture of "yes people" who simply endorse what the CEO proposes.
- ***Does the decision maker operate under a governance system of monitoring and control?*** One of the benefits of good governance systems is to forestall problems of hubris. Chapter 26 discusses dimensions of governance.

Market Manias

A variant on the behavioral theme is the role of *mass behavior* that produces market bubbles, crashes, and fads. Kelly (1994) likened market movements to swarms of bees and flocks of geese. Others have sought to apply chaos theory to explaining the unpredictable movements in the market; see Gleick (1998). Robert Shiller (1998) discusses fads in financial markets as motive for takeover. He cites psychological literature on group behavior and gambling as parallels to merger fads. A variation on this point is the "I don't want to be left out" factor for companies who are surrounded by acquisitive competitors. Investment bankers tell interesting anecdotes about "deal frenzy," a kind of psychological momentum to get a deal done—

on almost any terms—after an executive has been working toward the deal for some period of time. Toxvaerd (2002) models merger waves as the result of the attempt by managers to improve the strategic positions of their firms through preemption in the competition for scarce targets. The competitors would prefer to delay and retain the option to acquire. But in constant reference to their competitors, they all snap into action as the result of an industry shock or the release of some decisive bit of information: this produces a stampede to acquire, a type of rational frenzy.

The practical person will find it hard to know what to do with the *mania* explanation. Chapters 30 and 31 emphasize the influence of psychological effects on M&A outcomes. Our understanding in this area is still in its infancy. Still, the practitioner seeking to understand M&A activity should ask at least two questions:

1. Does the market, my industry, or my firm seem in the grip of "deal frenzy"?
2. What is the tendency of the "herd" in my industry with respect to M&A? What is the "lead steer" doing?

Both of these questions invite, at best, qualitative answers. Generally, the size of acquisition premiums relative to historical averages will give some sense of whether the deal flow is hot or cold. A close following of speeches, interviews, scuttlebutt, and, above all, M&A actions is the grist from which answers to these questions will be made.

Overvaluation of Stocks and the Asymmetry of Information

Five studies associate the appearance of waves with buoyant capital market conditions: a rising stock market and low or falling interest rates. M&A waves are procyclical; they occur in line with increases in stock prices.[5] There is some disagreement about whether peaks in M&A lead or lag peaks in stock prices.[6] Nelson (1959) suggests that rapid development of a capital market (in countries where it had been previously undeveloped) may spur M&A activity. Golbe and White (1988) argued that merger activity increases when bargains are available, as measured by a low ratio of market value to replacement costs (Tobin's Q). Recent theories by Shleifer and Vishny (2001) and Rhodes-Kropf and Viswanathan (2003) consider an alternative explanation: that stock markets may overvalue stocks. Managers of firms have their own inside assessments of the intrinsic values of their firms. Because they know more than investors on the outside (economists call this "*information asymmetry*"), these better-informed assessments may vary from the prices in the market. When the prices in the market *exceed* the insider assessment of value, rational managers can enhance the wealth of their current shareholders by selling stock. Thus, equity issuance will tend to occur when stock prices are high, an idea advanced by Myers and Majluf (1984).

Recognizing that share-for-share deals were the equivalent of an equity issue by the buyer, Shleifer and Vishny (2001) modeled the behavior of buyer managers during "hot" and "cold" equity markets and found that merger activity (especially waves), form of payment, and who buys whom are driven by the relative valuations of the pairs of firms, synergies, and the time horizons of the managers. For instance, stock acquisitions are used by buyer managers who perceive that their shares are overvalued in the market—during buoyant stock markets, this would explain why we observe relatively more share-for-share deals; and it would explain the preponderance of cash deals in cold markets. They write, "Stock acquisitions are used specifically by overvalued bidders who expect to see negative long run returns on their shares, but are attempting to make these returns less negative than they would be otherwise. The examples of the acquisition of Time-Warner by AOL and of build-up of high valuation conglomerates with stock illustrate this phenomenon." (Page 19) This would also explain the periodic appearance of momentum-style acquisition strategies (see Chapter 17 for more on momentum acquiring). Shleifer and Vishny conclude:

> *We do not assume that markets are efficient, but rather that the stock market may misvalue potential acquirers, potential targets, and their combinations. In contrast, managers of firms are completely rational, understand stock market inefficiencies, and take advantage of them in part through merger decisions. This theory is in a way the opposite of Roll's (1986) hubris hypothesis of corporate takeovers, in which financial markets are rational, but corporate managers are not. In our theory, managers rationally respond to less than rational markets. (Page 2)*

Rhodes-Kropf and Viswanathan (2003) (RV) build on this framework. While Shleifer and Vishny offer a rationale for the behavior of buyers, why should targets accept stock offers from buyers whose shares are likely to be overvalued? RV suggest that targets are canny enough to assess the misvaluation of the buyer and target, but not canny enough to correctly assess the value of synergies—this is because of an information asymmetry between the buyer and target in which the buyer has a better idea of the possible economic gains between the two firms. They write, "Thus, when the market is overvalued then the target is more likely to overestimate the synergies *even though he can see that his own price is affected by the same overvaluation.*" (Page 2) Ang and Cheng (2003) give empirical evidence in support of the overvaluation/information asymmetry theory. Based on a sample of 9,000 observations from 1984 to 2001, they find:

> *Acquirers are much more overvalued than their targets. Successful acquirers are more overvalued than the unsuccessful ones. The probability of a firm becoming an acquiree significantly increases with its degree of overvaluation, after we control for other factors that may potentially affect the firm's acquiring decision. Since overvalued acquirers could only gain from their misvaluation by paying for the acquisitions with their stocks, we postulate and verify that stock-paying acquirers are substantially more overvalued than their cash-paying counterparts. . . . The probability of stocks being utilized as the payment method significantly increases with the acquirer's overvaluation. Long-term abnormal returns of the combined firms in stock mergers are negative. (Pages 3–4)*

The new theory of overvaluation and information asymmetry does little to explain the clustering of M&A activity in industries, but it advances our understanding of merger waves and lends a couple of practical implications. First, it helps explain the association between the buoyant stock markets of the 1960s, 1980s, and 1990s and the coincident large merger waves. Second, it presents a framework for thinking about the form of payment (about which more is said in Chapter 20). As a practical matter, then, this theory invites executives to consider three questions:

1. ***What is the level of the market today?*** Deal makers will be influenced by the relative levels of valuation. The practitioner can compare valuation multiples such as the price/earnings ratio or market/book ratio for the market averages today, with those prevailing in the past. During 1998–2000, such a comparison showed the market to be highly valued ("irrationally exuberant" in Robert Shiller's terms).
2. ***What is the valuation of my firm relative to the market?*** If you want to figure out where your firm is likely to be in the food chain, focus on its valuation relative to other firms. The new theory suggests that *more* overvalued firms will be buyers, and *less* overvalued firms will be targets.
3. ***What do I know that the market doesn't?*** This is one of the fundamental questions M&A practitioners should *always* ask. The new theory lends weight to it by suggesting that most practitioners ask it. The timing and form of payment of M&A activity is basically motivated by a disparity between one's own assessment of the intrinsic value of the firm and the market price. The theory suggests that the main basis for believing that your estimate of intrinsic value is better than the market price is because of an information advantage.

Agency Costs and the Correction of Governance Problems

The wave of M&A activity in the 1980s differed from others in two important ways: the relatively high volumes of hostile takeovers and of leveraged buyouts. Arguments prominently associated with Michael Jensen suggest that this was a decade of the disciplinary response of investors to the mounting agency costs of entrenched managements. *Agency costs* are inefficiencies arising from such things as self-interested risk management,[7] perquisites, and lax attention. These costs accumulate because of the failure of directors to monitor and control the management of the firm in the best interests of its shareholders. Shareholders bear the costs of agency problems in the form of depressed share prices. Taking over the firm and restoring it to more efficient operation rewards new management with profits in the form of dividends and capital gains.

A great deal of empirical evidence is consistent with this view. Chapter 6 summarizes findings that restructuring and redeployment of assets is profitable to investors. Chapter 20 surveys studies that report gains from leveraged buyouts and highly levered transactions. Holmstrom and Kaplan (2001) summarize findings that the 1980s were a wave of corrective M&A.

But did these corrective forces appear only in the 1980s and not in the other waves? The profit-seeking behavior should always be present. And what about the clustering of M&A activity within industries, or mergers between firms that are well governed? Still, the agency theory raises useful questions for the practitioner:

- ***How efficient are my firm and the potential buyers and targets in its arena?*** Efficiency is a fundamental gauge to explaining who will be buyers and targets. The more efficient take over the less efficient firms.
- ***To what extent do governance problems contribute to differences in efficiency?*** The quality of governance of a firm should be a telltale for the firm's efficiency. Chapter 26 summarizes research findings that good governance pays and summarizes dimensions on which one could assess the quality of governance.

Monopoly, Competitive Positioning, and "Rent-Seeking" Behavior

The long literature in Industrial Organization within economics studies the relation between returns on one hand, and firm size or market power on the other. Chapter 6 summarizes some of these relations and the uses of M&A to enhance the position and market power of the firm. The literature suggests that the creation of monopolies and collusive oligopolies permits producers to extract excessive returns from consumers—this is the so-called "rent-seeking" behavior condemned by public policy analysts. Active antitrust enforcement by governments is a brake on the creation of monopolies through M&A. The M&A waves of the 1890s and 1960s were seriously curtailed by antitrust enforcement action. Chapter 28 surveys the antitrust laws in the United States and their implications for deal development. Still, within the confines of antitrust law, firms have some latitude to exploit product market inefficiencies. A stream of literature, stimulated by Michael Porter (1980) sketches techniques by which firms may enhance their competitive position—this is surveyed in Chapter 6.

A contributor to the appearance of waves of M&A activity may be a kind of multiplier effect induced by the breaking up or rationalization of acquired firms. For instance, a buyer may want only the target's domestic operations, not foreign; or only certain product lines; or only specific assets. Thus, one acquisition triggers a cascade of other deals. Porter (1987) finds that 53 percent of acquisitions are sold within five years, evidence consistent with a process of asset rationalization.

The incentive to seek economic "rents" is always present. Theories of monopoly and competitive positioning have little to say about waves of M&A activity over time. But the theories help to rationalize tendencies toward industry consolidation. Exactly what triggers these consolidations is unclear in the theory. Still, the theory suggests two diagnostic questions useful to practitioners:

1. ***Does the structure of my industry provide opportunities for consolidation through M&A?*** Industries consisting of many small competitors may be ripe for consolidating mergers. Highly concentrated industries may pose barriers to entry through M&A.
2. ***What is the current antitrust policy in this country and toward this industry?*** Government policy changes with changes in administration and may be associated with different moods of constraint or buoyancy in M&A activity.

Industry Shocks

Nelson's (1959) classic study of M&A waves suggested that surprising changes in demand could trigger firms' acquisitions additional capacity through M&A. Acquisition is simply one branch of the "make or buy" decision. Gort (1969) suggested that the "economic disturbance" induced by industry surprises would trigger a wave of acquisition activity when it becomes cheaper to buy than to make. Gort's idea was that industry shocks alter the mean and variance of investors' assessments of intrinsic value for firms—such shocks could derive from unexpected changes in demand, changes in technology, movements in capital markets, and generally, changes in entry barriers within industries. Lambrecht (2002) extends the theory of industry shocks in a real options framework. He argues that firms always have the option to acquire instead of growing organically. Positive shocks increase the uncertainty or volatility of the firms' asset values, and therefore the value of the "merger option." This induces a rise in merger activity.

The theory of *industry shocks* is appealing, not only because it can rationalize merger waves (e.g., caused by large-scale shocks), but also the clustering of M&A activity within industries or regions (e.g., caused by more focused shocks). Finally, this theory can embrace a wide range of possible drivers, including globalization, trade liberalization, changes in tax, accounting, government regulation, and antitrust policy; see, for instance, Ravenscraft (1987). Several empirical studies support the notion that industry shocks drive M&A activity. Mitchell and Mulherin (1996) found that in the 1980s merger wave, industries with the greatest amount of takeover activity were those that experienced fundamental economic shocks like deregulation, technological innovation, demographic shifts, and input price shocks. They wrote:

> *Our work also has implications for interpreting the effect that a takeover announcement for one firm in an industry has on the equity value of other industry members. Because we find that takeover activity has industry-driven factors, our results imply that one firm's takeover announcement gives information about other industry members that may be tied to economic fundamentals rather than market power, as is often asserted by regulators. Some observers express concern that takeovers are too often followed by business failures. Because we find that takeovers are driven in part by industry shocks, it is not surprising that many firms exhibit volatile performance following takeovers, with actual failures following some negative shocks. Rather than being the actual source of performance changes, the takeovers are often merely messengers of the underlying economic changes taking place in the industry. (Pages 195–196)*

Schoenberg and Reeves (1999) identified the most important determinants of industry merger activity as being, in order: deregulation, industry growth rate (higher growth attracts more acquisitions), and industry concentration (lower concentration attracts more acquisitions). Jovanovic and Rousseau (2002) have argued that large technological change and M&A activity are associated. They studied the waves of the 1890–1930 and 1971–2001 and conclude that the former was significantly associated with the diffusion of electricity and the internal combustion engine and the latter with the diffusion of information technology. Mitchell and Mulherin (1996) offer a sample of industry shocks affecting M&A activity in the 1980s: banking and broadcasting by deregulation, textiles by liberalized trade policy, energy by petroleum price changes, food processing by a demographic shift/low population growth. Jensen (1988) noted that a slowdown in primary industry growth may spur firms to acquire as a means of reallocating resources into higher growth areas.

The theory of industry shocks also is relevant to the choice of diversifying or focusing the firm. Maksimovic and Phillips (2001, 2002) studied acquisitions of manufacturing plants. Their model suggests:

> *Firms become focused when their prospects in their main industry significantly improve. They may optimally choose to remain unfocused if their prospects in their main industry are not as good as other firms that choose to become focused. Firms sell assets in their less productive divisions following positive demand*

shocks for these divisions. . . . Industry shocks alter the value of the assets and create incentives for transfers to more productive uses. . . . Assets are more likely to be sold (1) when the economy is undergoing positive demand shocks, (2) when the assets are less productive than their industry benchmarks, (3) when the selling division is less productive, and (4) when the selling firm has more productive divisions in other industries. For mergers and acquisitions, we find evidence that the less productive firms stand to sell at times of industry expansion. Firms are more likely to be buyers when they are efficient and are more likely to purchase additional assets in industries that experience an increase in demand. (2001, pages 2020–2021)

As a practical matter, industry shocks yield a rich range of explanations for M&A activity, waves, and industry clusters of transactions. Detailed comments on implementing this perspective are given in the next two sections and in Appendixes 1–4 of this chapter. The tools and concepts in Chapter 6 further support an analytic understanding of the effect of industry shocks on M&A activity.

Summary Overview of the Drivers of M&A Activity

The primary inference from this research is that any explanation of the sources of M&A activity will tell a complicated multicause story. Consider a division of explanations for M&A activity based on the rationality of markets and buyers' managers. This creates a matrix of four camps of explanations for M&A activity, as shown in Exhibit 4.5.[8]

1. ***Rational managers and markets.*** In the northwest corner of the table is the "base case" of economics, which assumes that markets and the decision makers within those markets are rational. In this quadrant, share prices fairly reflect intrinsic value. Managers take effective action to maximize share prices. Economics offers the richest set of explanations for M&A activity here: Both waves and industry clustering can be rationalized. But assumptions of widespread rationality have become the piñata for business critics and reregulation advocates. Even the friends of M&A would have to admit, following the experience of 1995–2000, that bubbles happen.
2. ***Rational managers, irrational markets.*** The northeast corner accommodates the possibility of bubbles and assumes that individual managers can and will act rationally. This approach gains good traction on the explanation for why the form of payment in M&A varies with the market cycles. But it has less to say about industry clustering of M&A activity.
3. ***Irrational managers, rational markets.*** In the southwest corner is the world of managers who do stupid things for which the market reacts and penalizes them and their firms. Hubristic M&A is possible in a world with poor governance systems. But hubris says virtually nothing about M&A waves or industry clustering.
4. ***Irrational managers and markets.*** Economics has little to say about this world. When you assume away rationality, you sacrifice considerable traction from modeling and empirical research. Here, the best one can say is, "We don't know what's going on, but it's probably bad."

EXHIBIT 4.5 Explanations for M&A Activity Vary with Assumptions about Markets and Managers

	Markets Are:	
Buyer's Managers Are:	**Rational**	**Irrational**
Rational	Managers and firms pursue **competitive advantage** within constraints of antitrust. With **external shocks** markets, firms, and managers respond rationally. It is difficult to determine whether negative returns to buyers are due to merger or the shock. Firms conduct M&A to exploit profitable opportunities and avoid losses. This may include exerting capital market discipline to correct **agency problems** and improve **governance.**	With **overvaluation** markets express irrationality. With **information asymmetry** managers are able to respond rationally on behalf of shareholders. Firms conduct share-for-share M&A to exploit overvaluation of their shares. Explains why we see many share-for-share deals near market peaks, and cash deals in the troughs.
Irrational	Managers make decisions based on **hubris** and markets punish the managers' firms. Explains why firms do bad deals and why buyers' share prices fall after the deal is done.	Managers and markets exhibit **swarm behavior** and **market mania.** Market prices regularly overshoot or undershoot intrinsic values. Managers display deal frenzy. Buyers' shareholders approve acquisitions consistent with the prevailing mania, even though the deals may destroy value.

Where in this space would you position your view? It helps to reflect deliberately on this question because how you approach the tools and concepts in the rest of this book will be colored by your fundamental assumptions about what drives M&A.

My own view is that, on average and over time, markets and managers are rational (the operative phrase here is *on average and over time*). In the main, this encourages the use of tools and concepts founded on assumptions of rationality—these tools give a special benchmark for assessing deals *as if* markets and managers were rational. Periodically, markets and managers can lose their moorings. When they do, my practice is to cling to a value-style focus on intrinsic values and make decisions accordingly. This follows the philosophy that one must retain one's fundamental discipline regardless of market conditions (for more on this, see Chapter 9).

"CREATIVE DESTRUCTION" AS THE DRIVER OF M&A ACTIVITY

Rationality does not necessarily dictate stability of industrial markets. The catalog of industry shocks is long. But why is it rational for them to occur? The economist Joseph Schumpeter articulated some answers with his writing on the destructive quality of business cycles. Since waves of M&A activity are roughly associated with the ebb and flow of the economic cycle, Schumpeter's work has direct relevance to M&A activity. It is the fate of most economists to be remembered more for their path of reasoning than for their conclusions.[9] Schumpeter's important contribution to economics was to focus attention on the key figure in economic growth: the entrepreneur. All the important economic theorists who preceded Schumpeter either ignored (e.g., Adam Smith) or scorned (e.g., Karl Marx) what the entrepreneur *actually does*. Schumpeter argued that the entrepreneur seeks to create turmoil, and to profit from it. This bumptious actor[10] realizes that in any stable economic setting, profits will flow to established firms doing business in established ways. He wrote:

> *The function of entrepreneurs is to reform or revolutionize the pattern of production by exploiting an invention or, more generally, an untried technological possibility for producing a new commodity or producing an old or in a new way, by opening up a new source of supply of materials or a new outlet for products, by reorganizing an industry and so on. . . . This kind of activity is primarily responsible for the recurrent "prosperities" that are due to the disequilibrating impact of the new products or methods. To undertake such new things is difficult and constitutes a distinct economic function, first, because they lie outside of the routine tasks which everybody understands and, secondly, because the environment resists in many ways that vary, according to social conditions, from simple refusal either to finance or to buy a new thing, to physical attack on the man who tries to produce it. To act with confidence beyond the range of familiar beacons and to overcome that resistance requires aptitudes that are present in only a small fraction of the population and that define the entrepreneurial type as well as the entrepreneurial function. This function does not essentially consist in either inventing anything or otherwise creating the conditions that the enterprise exploits. It consists in getting things done.*[11]

Only by entering the competitive field with some new process or product can the entrepreneur hope to claim a cut of the profits of the industry. This describes an economy of *ceaseless and self-generated change*. Business cycles arise because entrepreneurs swarm or cluster around opportunities. Schumpeter wrote:

> *Why do entrepreneurs appear, not continuously, that is, singly in every appropriately chosen interval, but in clusters?* Exclusively because the appearance of one or a few entrepreneurs facilitates the appearance of others, and those the appearance of more in ever-increasing numbers. . . . *Hence the first leaders are effective beyond their immediate sphere of action and so the group of entrepreneurs increases still further and the economic system is drawn more rapidly and*

> *more completely than would otherwise be the case into the process of technological and commercial reorganization which constitutes the meaning of periods of boom.*[12] (Schumpeter's emphasis)

The swarming suggested by Schumpeter describes well the geographic attraction of technology entrepreneurs to places like Silicon Valley, northern Virginia, and the Boston beltway. But it also has relevance for observed clustering of M&A activity by industries. Like iron filings to a magnet, opportunity draws the M&A entrepreneur.

Why is it, then, that investment opportunities and M&A deals tend to cluster by industry? Schumpeter lays the foundation for answering this crucial question.

> *The essential point to grasp is that in dealing with capitalism we are dealing with an evolutionary process. . . . The fundamental impulse that sets and keeps the capitalist engine in motion comes from the new consumers' goods, the new methods of production or transportation, the new markets, the new forms of industrial organization, that capitalist enterprise creates. . . . The opening up of new markets, foreign or domestic, and the organizational development from the craft shop and factory to such concerns as U.S. Steel illustrate the same process of industrial mutation—if I may use that biological term—that incessantly revolutionizes the economic structure* from within, *incessantly destroying the old one, incessantly creating a new one. This process of Creative Destruction is the essential fact about capitalism. . . . Every piece of business strategy acquires its true significance only against the background of that process and within the situation created by it. It must be seen in its role in the perennial gale of creative destruction.*[13]

Schumpeter's foundation for our understanding of M&A activity might be distilled into the following points:

- Entrepreneurs who seek to create something new and profit by it drive waves of activity. If this is relevant to M&A, then we should observe at the center of individual transactions leaders who, as Schumpeter says, "get things done" against various forms of resistance in the environment. Schumpeter tells us that to understand waves of M&A activity, we should *find the leader/entrepreneurs at the center of this activity*.
- Profit-creating opportunities arise from new products and processes, new logistics, new markets (domestic and foreign), new forms of organization, and so on. If this is relevant to M&A, then we should observe at the center of individual transactions, and clusters of transactions within an industry, some kind of economic turbulence. Schumpeter implies that in order to understand waves of M&A activity, we should *listen for the turbulence at the level of firms and markets*, not at the level of the economy. The turbulence that is relevant is almost always industry-specific. This explains why deals cluster within industries, and why the attempt to explain M&A waves in the aggregate is fruitless: Each industry or market has its own rich story.
- M&A is a process of *creative destruction.* The destructive aspects of M&A are well documented in the press: plant closings, uprooting of managers and their

families, layoffs, transaction-related lawsuits, and so on. Schumpeter hastens to remind us that it is through these processes that the economy renews itself and makes itself more agile and resilient to macroeconomic shocks. To prevent the destruction is to prevent the renewal.

A case in point is presented in Naomi Lamoreaux' study of the M&A wave of 1894–1904. During that period, more than 1,800 firms disappeared into the formation of 93 consolidated firms with an important, if not dominant, share of market in their respective industries. Though most of these new firms quickly lost their position (because of Schumpeter's turbulence), a few still ranked among the important firms in the year 2000: U.S. Steel, General Electric, AT&T, DuPont, Eastman Kodak, and International Harvester. This merger wave created considerable alarm among editors, scholars, and public officials who weighed the possible benefits of increased efficiency against the evils of monopoly and predatory behavior.

Lamoreaux offers a different story. She found that the bulk of the M&A activity occurred within selected industries—those characterized by capital intensive and mass-production manufacturing processes in which new firms had recently entered with new and more devastating technology. With high fixed costs, these industries faced high operating leverage, and the resulting impulse to cut prices in an effort to maintain market share and, more importantly, volume. This triggered severe price competition during the depression of the mid-1890s.

M&A entrepreneurs entered this turbulent environment to remove older and less efficient excess capacity from the industry through a new form of organization, the trust. J. P. Morgan is a preeminent example of this entrepreneur. He personally led the reorganization of numerous industries, including steel and railroads. Though the newly structured firms successfully removed excess capacity, in the longer run, they proved to be no more efficient than their nontrust rivals, and therefore proved unable to maintain their dominance unless they erected entry barriers. Lamoreaux notes that federal antitrust policy should have been focused on minimizing the erection of barriers, in lieu of offering the "hodge-podge of policies that, as the example of the steel industry indicates, sometimes hindered the combines' efforts, sometimes helped them."[14] She concludes:

> *The consolidation movement was the product of a particular conjunction of historical events: the development of capital-intensive, mass-production manufacturing techniques in the late nineteenth century; the extraordinary rapid growth that many capital-intensive industries experienced after 1887; the deep depression that began in 1893. . . . This conjunction of events gave rise to serious price warfare during the depression of the nineties—price warfare that conventional types of collusion proved incapable of ending. After failing in repeated attempts to halt the decline in prices by means of gentlemen's agreements, selling agencies, and pools, manufacturers in these and many other industries finally organized consolidations.*[15]

Jensen (1993) applies a similar explanation for the wave of industrial restructuring of the 1980s and early 1990s. He argued that this wave had its roots in the turbulence of the 1970s, with the tenfold increase in energy prices, the emergence of the modern market for corporate control, and an explosion of innovation in the capital markets (specifically the emergence of a high-yield debt market). Most important, however, was the economic recovery that began in 1981 and triggered dramatic technological change, which included innovations that would improve the output of existing assets (e.g., from the rise of the personal computer), and changes that would create obsolescence of older products and processes (e.g., from the rise of Wal-Mart and wholesale clubs that introduced a new retailing model). He also cited the importance of deregulation, globalization of trade, organizational innovation (e.g., through the rise of "virtual firms") and dramatic political changes (e.g., the decline of the Soviet sphere) as forces of change. The aggregate impact of these changes was a rise in excess capacity in industries. Unfortunately, many firms were slow to adjust: General Motors remained the high-cost producer in the industry and removed its CEO in 1992; IBM was the high-cost producer in mainframe computers until it removed its CEO in 1991. Eastman Kodak changed slowly. General Electric successfully mounted a multiyear internal transformation effort that eliminated a quarter of its total workforce. Jensen called for innovation in organizational design, and applauded the rise of the LBO association as one example through which firms could transform themselves.

Bruce Wasserstein, a prominent M&A adviser, offers another Schumpeterian explanation for M&A activity:

> *The merger business reflects the hubbub of our society with all its bustling and pretense. It is at the edge of change and fashion, and yet a minefield for the unwary. Mistakes are common. Still, good, bad, or indifferent, mergers and acquisitions are an essential vehicle for corporate change, and the pace of change is increasing. The patterns of industrial development through mergers, like those of economic activity, are crude and imperfect. However, there do seem to be elemental forces, Five Pistons, which drive the merger process. They are regulatory and political reform, technological change, fluctuations in financial markets, the role of leadership, and the tension between scale and focus.*[16]

Wasserstein surveys several industries (energy, conglomerates, financial services, telecommunications, entertainment, and health care) to show that the boom in M&A activity in each of these industries during the 1990s could be traced to the turbulence induced by one or more of the five pistons. Each industry has its own story; one size does not fit all. He concludes:

> *The specifics driving each deal are different, but there is a common pattern to the process. Existing business strategies and structures ossify over time. These structures may survive for some period with the protection of systemic inertia. Eventually, however, external catalysts give a sharp jolt to the system. Outmoded practices become apparent. Mergers and acquisitions, a kind of roughhewn evolutionary mechanism, then occur as companies react to the new business realities.*[17]

Schumpeter, Lamoreaux, Jensen, and Wasserstein portray M&A activity as an instrument in the process of industrial renewal, of creative destruction. They present a rich framework for understanding M&A activity that leads to one very practical imperative: *Pay attention to economic turbulence, what form it takes, how and which firms it affects, and who exploits it.* Mastering an understanding of economic turbulence creates the foundation for many skills in this book: acquisition search, forecasting, valuation, deal design, and postmerger integration.

IMPLEMENTING THE "CREATIVE DESTRUCTION" VIEW: LISTEN TO MARKETS AND FIRMS

When one is conscious of the role of economic turbulence as a driver of M&A activity, one sees the world of M&A more richly. Just like fans follow baseball or music *aficionados* follow opera, the acute observer of M&A knows what information to look for, and where.

What to Look For: The Many Forms of Economic Turbulence

Interpreting M&A activity and anticipating and structuring deals depends on noticing the presence of the drivers of *economic turbulence* in a business setting. A consolidated list of such drivers (that expands on those identified by Schumpeter, Lamoreaux, Jensen, and Wasserstein) would include:

- *Deregulation.* The loosening of regulatory requirements in industries such as banking, airlines, trucking, and telecommunications has unleashed a wave of consolidation and rationalization of firms.
- *Trade liberalization.* The lifting of barriers to foreign trade has motivated inefficient protected firms to consolidate with more efficient domestic or foreign firms. The creation of the North American Free Trade Agreement (NAFTA) and the European Union are associated with M&A activity in trade-sensitive industries, such as textiles and agribusiness.
- *Geopolitical change.* The fall of the Iron Curtain triggered a wave of transactions in Central Europe as Western firms sought toehold acquisitions in that new market.
- *Demographic change.* Changes in the makeup of the population can affect competitive strategy and industry structure. Such changes include waves of immigration (in the United States, consumer products firms now compete explicitly for a share of the Hispanic-American market) and aging—for instance, the graying of the population in Japan affects the ability of firms to retain know-how.
- *Technological change.* Advances in all technology-linked industries have prompted firms to seek alliances, joint ventures, and acquisitions in order to stay abreast of change. Cisco Systems acquired 80 firms from 1994 to 2003 in its pursuit of technological leadership in the network systems industry. Generally, advances in information technology spur changes in the way firms compete.
- *Innovation in financial markets.* Since the early 1970s, capital markets have grown in sophistication and efficiency. The design of new financial instruments has permitted even small and privately held firms to access the capital they need to transform themselves. Jensen and Wasserstein mentioned the rise of the high-yield debt market as an example—this new instrument was highly influential in the rise of leveraged buyouts, and both private equity and debt financing.
- *Globalization.* As product and capital markets become more integrated across borders (thanks in large part to other contributing drivers mentioned here) the

competitive arena for any one firm will expand, with new adversaries, suppliers, and customers. Because of this linkage, turbulence abroad can resonate at home.

- ***Organizational invention.*** Each wave of M&A activity was accompanied by experimentation with a new form of enterprise structure: the horizontal trust, the vertically integrated firm, the conglomerate, the LBO specialist, and the venture capital portfolio.
- ***Changes in consumer demand and supply in product markets.*** In the past 20 years, industries as varied as toys, media and entertainment, bicycles, and automobiles encountered customers who demanded (and were given) products that were more tailored, more fadlike, more rapidly delivered (i.e., with shorter design and manufacturing cycles), and of higher quality. These requirements imposed on a number of marginal players the choice either to merge or to exit from the industry.
- ***Changes in capital market conditions.*** The cost of money must remain on any list of drivers of turbulence. Though this would seem to be a macroeconomic driver (and therefore a factor Schumpeter might have warned against) the reality is that capital markets distinguish carefully among industries and firms within industries, as any inter- and intra-industry comparison of valuation multiples will show.

Where to Look for Turbulence

The creative destruction view of M&A activity suggests that potential and actual M&A activity will occur in industries and company settings where forces of economic turbulence are particularly active. How one does this is straightforward to describe, and challenging to implement. First, one should *listen* to both markets and firms. *Listening to markets* is a "top down" approach of gathering insights. *Listening to firms* is a "bottom up" approach. The two approaches are complements, and are used by the best analysts in concert.

But where should one begin the listening process? Here, again, are two approaches, which complement each other. On one hand, it is useful to analyze the data that tells the story of the performance results of firms and industries: financial data, market share, cost information, and so on. This first approach could be considered "inside out" because it starts with the details and works toward generalizations. On the other hand, one could build an image of turbulence starting from qualitative information, opinions, and summaries of various sorts, and from these work toward more detailed M&A implications for industries and firms. This second approach would rely on newspaper and magazine articles, securities analyses, CEO speeches, opinion columns, and so on. This second approach might be thought of as "outside in" because it uses aggregative ideas to develop detailed implications.

Combining these two methods with the "what" and "where" approaches yields four styles of monitoring M&A activity and opportunities, as given in Exhibit 4.6. Ideally, no "listening" style should be used in isolation. But as a practical matter, the limitations of time and other resources may force the listener to follow one style. Each style is associated with a successful practitioner; there is no one right approach. The data-intensive "inside out" styles demand strong data-gathering and analytical abilities. Appendixes 4.1 to 4.4 offer some further guidance for ways of implementing an "inside out" approach. The more intuitive "outside in" styles

EXHIBIT 4.6 Styles of Listening for Turbulence, and the Resulting M&A Activity or Opportunities

	Listen to Markets ("Top Down")	**Listen to Firms ("Bottom Up")**
Start with Hard Data ("Inside Out") You can see a pattern of performance results and want to profile the source of turbulence and ultimately the M&A opportunity.	Dig into performance results for industry averages, and for individual players. Then step back and ask, "What turbulence is contributing to this industry's results?" and "Where is the M&A opportunity in this industry?" Practitioner: **J. P. Morgan.**	Dig into very detailed performance results for individual firms in the industry. Then step back and ask, "What turbulence is contributing to this firm's results?" and "Is there an M&A opportunity in this firm?" Practitioners: **Carl Icahn; Michael Price; Warren Buffett.**
Start with Ideas ("Outside In") You can identify the source of turbulence, and seek to determine its impact and ultimately an M&A opportunity.	Start with the *concept* of major change events and develop the implications for the aggregate industry and for the rivalry among players in the industry. Ask, "What is the impact of the turbulence on this industry?" and "Where is the M&A opportunity in this industry?" Practitioner: **Bruce Wasserstein.**	Start with the *concept* of major change events, and proceed immediately to develop implications for the target firm. Ask, "What is the impact of turbulence on this firm?" and "Is there an M&A opportunity in this firm?" Practitioners: risk arbitrageurs.

demand an unusual skill in seeing broad patterns and deducing the implications of those patterns.

CONCLUSION

M&A activity occurs in waves over time and hits industries differently. Research offers several explanations for this activity: managerial hubris, market mania, market overvaluation, information asymmetry, agency costs, and industry shocks—the thoughtful practitioner will find useful insights from all of these explanations. But underlying these perspectives are differing assumptions about the rationality of managers and markets. The M&A practitioner needs to have a view about this as a foundation to using effectively the tools and concepts in this book.

The notion that industry shocks drive M&A offers some traction for the analyst. The economic turbulence from industry shocks is always present, but it affects various industries, and the firms within them, differently. As a result, the M&A professional needs to develop an ability to tell industry-specific and company-specific stories about the impact of economic turbulence. This is an essential foundation for almost all of the professional skills surveyed in this book: transaction search, forecasting, valuation, due diligence research, negotiation, deal structuring, postmerger integration, and others.

APPENDIX 4.1
How to Listen to Customers of Firms

The most direct way to listen to customers is through the analysis of purchasing patterns and behavior. Four calculations could be done for all comparable products in an industry.

1. *Price elasticity of demand*, which is simply the percentage change in units sold for every percent change in price. Elasticity gives a measure of the sensitivity of the customer demand to changes in price.
2. Rates of *growth* on a unit basis, and their *sustainability*.
3. Sensitivity of demand to pricing and availability of *complements and substitutes*.
4. Demand *segmentation*, which focuses on pockets of demand based on geographic area, price, product features, and so on.

Careful demand analysis is challenging for at least two reasons. First, careful analysis requires specialized data that may need to be collected through primary research. Collection of primary data can be arduous and expensive. And second, buying behavior is influenced by numerous factors simultaneously. To isolate the influence of any one factor requires econometric techniques, and a fair amount of clean data. Barabba and Zaltman (1991) give an overview of the organizational and process requirements for successful demand analysis. This is a cautionary foundation for M&A professionals contemplating demand analysis.

APPENDIX 4.2
How to Listen to Macroeconomic and Sector Conditions

Though at first glance the macroeconomic perspective would seem to offer a uselessly high level of abstraction, in fact the themes identified in this chapter influence virtually everything else in an effort to understand M&A activity and conduct an acquisition search. A checklist of measures of the state of the economy would include these 12 measures:

1. ***Unemployment rate and factory capacity utilization rate.*** These signal activity levels in the economy, sector, and industry. High capacity utilization can signal increased capital spending. Low unemployment can signal upward pressure on wages.
2. ***Government fiscal policy:*** whether stimulative or not. Government spending should be scrutinized carefully for favored sectors and industries, and generally for political goals that would build up some segments of the economy at the expense of others. Sustained deficits over time are associated

with increased government borrowing, and the crowding out of corporate investment through higher interest rates.

3. *Central bank monetary policy:* expansionary or contractionist. The type of policy will influence interest rates, inflation expectations, exchange rates, business investment, and trading volumes in the capital markets.
4. *Inflation rate.* High rates can destabilize competition and increase uncertainty in business planning.
5. *Interest rates,* both for the government and corporations. These directly affect valuations of target firms.
6. *Exchange rates.* Volatility in these can destabilize competition and deeply affect prices and costs.
7. *Trade balance.* Sustained imbalances can affect the cost of funds, availability of capital, and prices and costs.
8. *Consumer optimism.* This is strongly correlated with demand for consumer goods and durables and should strongly influence forecast assumptions regarding corporate revenue growth.
9. *Gross domestic product,* especially its *growth rate.* The rate of macroeconomic expansion is perhaps the single most influential driver of corporate investment decisions. To the extent possible, one should try to disaggregate growth by sectors and/or industries.
10. *Current position in macroeconomic cycle.* Publications by the U.S. government afford a variety of indicators for tracking growth of the economy. Similar lists of economic indicators are followed in other countries, and by economic interest groups such as the Organization for Economic Cooperation and Development (OECD). In typical practice, each group of indicators (leading, coincident, and lagging) is combined to form an index of economic performance. Judgments about current and future growth are derived from an assessment of the index trends.

The analyst of macroeconomic themes uses data on these and other measures to identify current and prospective trends that because of their direction and magnitude are particularly relevant for the acquirer's acquisition strategy. The strategic force of strong consumer demand leads to the theme of increased capital spending. Heavy capital expenditures imply a large financing need. One way to finance capital expansion is by combining cash-rich and cash-poor firms. A second example would be a strengthening currency that triggers increases in imported goods leading to the theme of robust business revenues in shipping and transportation. The possibilities for identifying themes through macroeconomic analysis are numerous.

APPENDIX 4.3 Listening for Turbulence as Communicated through Capital Markets

If *markets tell stories* about the actual inner condition and prospects of firms, analysts should extend their attention to capital markets. In contrast to product markets, these markets are relatively more transparent about telling us what they see in firms. Moreover, listening to capital markets employs another precept, *stay close to investors*. By betting their wealth in tough-minded ways each day, investors impound news and expectations about firms into market prices. If, as the bulk of academic research suggests, markets are *efficient* on average and over time, then one can trust the market to distill what is known about firms and their outlooks into securities prices. Viewed broadly, capital markets offered three arenas from which to derive themes for top-down acquisition tracking: equity markets, debt markets, and the various markets for derivative securities.

DEBT MARKETS

Public and private corporations have trillions of dollars in debt securities outstanding. The prices and trading in these securities yield insights into economic conditions.

- ***Debt yields and their associated risk premiums.*** Debt yields[18] are excellent indicators of risk, and therefore may be useful sources of insights about strategic themes. The more risk one takes, the more one should get paid. This axiom is reflected daily in the pricing of debt securities. The acquisition search analyst should examine both the absolute yields in target businesses, and the risk premium in those yields. This premium is measured as the difference between the yield on a corporate debt instrument, and the yield on a contemporaneous government debt instrument. The premium increases as risk increases. The analyst should review the yields and premiums for candidates cross-sectionally in an industry and scrutinize outliers in risk. Also the analyst should consider trends and changes in risk over time. Divergence in yields among firms in an industry, or material changes in risk premiums are probably evidence of strategic themes.
- ***Credit ratings.*** Publicly traded debt issues are ordinarily rated for creditworthiness by rating agencies. Here, "creditworthiness" refers explicitly to risk of default in servicing the issue. The analyst should scrutinize the ratings of issuers in the target industry for consistency among the players. Outliers will have an interesting exposure to strategic forces. Also, rating changes are unusual and especially noteworthy—the acquisition analyst will find in these events one or more strategic themes. But it is also important to note that rating changes usually occur well after investors have recognized the need for a change. A better and more timely focus of attention would be the risk premiums for corporate debt over the yield on contemporaneous government debt issues.
- ***Maturity or duration for typical debt issues.*** The maturity structure of a firm's liabilities offers clues about the expectations of insiders and creditors about the firm's future cash flows, and about the nature of the assets standing behind those debts. The acquisition search analyst could compare the maturity structures for firms in a target industry, and check the extent to which those structures have changed over time. The classic advice to corporate borrowers is to set the life of their liabilities equal to the economic life of their assets. To mismatch these two lives is to expose the firm to financial risk.[19] While it is notable that most firms ignore this advice, it is a useful starting point for the analyst since the direction of the mismatch can help the search analyst reveal strategic themes. The main difficulty with maturity matching analysis is in determining the average maturity of a firm's assets; there is no rigorous way to do this.

- *Covenants or security pledges for typical debt issues.* Lenders and investment bankers who specialize in financing a given industry can offer insights into the practices of structuring corporate debt issues in those industries. The reasons for those practices often give fascinating insights into the risks and strategic themes faced in those businesses.

EQUITY MARKETS

Public corporations have several trillion dollars of equity securities outstanding on global markets. Equities offered three avenues of exploration for acquisition search analysts: multiples, betas, and charting/market sentiment.

Multiples

Pricing multiples are a commonly used tool of analysis in the global financial markets and give a convenient indication of the price of an asset relative to some benchmark, such as the earnings from that asset. Chapter 9, "Valuing Firms," gives a more detailed review and commentary on the varieties of multiples one could examine; that review will not be duplicated here. A hunt for strategic themes could examine multiples across the players in an industry, and over time.

Betas

This is a measure of the historical volatility of a firm's share price relative to the entire stock market. More precisely, it measures the degree to which investors in that firm's shares will assume systematic risk, or risk that cannot be diversified away through portfolio diversification. Ordinarily, betas for firms in the same industry will tend to cluster together around a similar value. Outliers should be studied for causes of their different risk. Also, using the Bloomberg financial data retrieval system, one can estimate betas for firms over different historical periods, and thereby determine the extent to which their systematic risk is changing. Betas have a statistical tendency to drift toward the value, 1.0, over long time periods. Bloomberg and other sources report raw betas, as well as betas that have been adjusted for their drift. Both betas should be studied. Sudden material changes in beta, especially away from 1.0, can be clues about strategic themes.

Charting and Measures of Market Sentiment

It is possible that examining the height, direction, and rate of change of stock prices will yield insights into strategic themes. Charting is a branch of securities analysis that seeks to derive insights about the future path of stock prices from their recent trends. Chartists presume that securities prices are driven largely by market psychology, rather than by economics. The discussion in this chapter, and throughout this book, presumes otherwise, for there is little scientific evidence that these techniques assist an investor in finding exceptional investments. But the task in this instance is to identify strategic themes of creative destruction, rather than to predict investment returns directly.

It may be possible that charting measures can reveal important themes not evident in the other approaches reviewed here. The acquisition analysts should consider classic charting measures as possible sources of themes. Indexes of *"odd lot" trading* show the relative presence of small-volume traders in the market—an "odd lot" trade has less than 100 shares. The belief is that odd-lotters are relatively unsophisticated traders who get sucked into purchasing shares near the end of a long run-up in prices, and into selling shares near the end of a long decline. In short, the conventional chartist point of view is that odd-lotters buy high and sell low. Some chartists follow statistics on *short sales*. In these transactions, the investor has sold shares that he does not own, in expectation of a stock price decline, after which the shares will be repurchased, and the position closed out at a profit. An increase in short-sale positions may indicate pessimism about a firm or industry.

Chartists follow various *confidence indexes*, one of the most common being the ratio of average corporate bond yields to average dividend yields. An increase in the confidence index is believed to signal optimism; a decrease, pessimism. *Relative strength* statistics measure the extent to which a firm's stock price moves faster or slower than the general market. Changes in relative strength would signal optimism or pessimism. *Volume of trading* data gives insights into the extent of action in a firm's shares. Sudden and material increases in trading volume may signal the arrival of new expectations about the firm. Finally, *moving average* analysis affords chartists a benchmark against which to assess daily price movements: a downward penetration of a moving average line suggests selling pressure; an upward penetration suggests buying pressure.

DERIVATIVES MARKETS

Open derivatives positions of all kinds on global markets carry an enormous notional value. Of most interest to the analyst would be standardized derivatives contracts on corporate securities, particularly in the options and futures market. Of greatest interest here will be the *implied volatility* embedded in the pricing of these derivatives. Volatility is a measure of the uncertainty or risk that derivatives traders and investors perceive in the price of the underlying security. These securities are said to "trade on risk" rather than on price since the investor must make a judgment about risk in assessing the price of the security. One source of possible themes would be a cross-industry comparison of volatilities of players in an industry. Another possible source would be to examine the time trend of volatilities for players in an industry for any changes in the direction and magnitude of their risk trends.

APPENDIX 4.4
Listening to Firms and Their Industries

The bottom-up approach is essentially a hunt for interesting anomalies. This can be surveyed in two ways: where to research and how. Research must be governed by the rule, "Stay close to facts." This means relying on one's primary research over that of secondary intermediaries who might predigest data, and seeking instead to absorb unrefined information. Business development analysts rely on sources as diverse as these: store visits, conferences and conventions, newspaper want ads, trade magazines and newsletters, focus group responses, and so on. Each industry segment has its special surveys and pools of interesting data. Rumors and word-of-mouth reports of the sort that your firm's field representatives will hear are valuable to the extent that they come directly from a credible source. Annual reports and SEC filings of peer firms, customers, and suppliers offer detailed financial insights.

The task of listening to firms and industries is to find valuable exceptions to the standard order of things. Graphs and frameworks of industry positioning, such as those outlined in Chapter 6, are useful ways of identifying gaps in markets and the firm's stance relative to other players. Focusing strictly on the firm, one can look for exceptions by functional area:

- ***Sales and marketing.*** Look for changes in the positioning of products in stores, specifically the number of "facings" of a product on store shelves, the use of coupons and discounts, and other special promotions. Significant changes in advertising content, placement, and amount may signal a change in strategy. A surge in want ads for field representatives or word of layoffs could also signal a change in the reliance on alternative channels of distribution. The word-of-mouth reputation of a product, particularly if it is new, might indicate promising growth opportunities for the company.
- ***R&D.*** Patent filings, solicitation of product test sites, and new product announcements convey information about a firm's research and development (R&D) capabilities, and may become the seed of an important economic anomaly.
- ***Manufacturing.*** Want ads or announcements of layoffs, major plant construction, plant closings, or land purchases may convey interesting anomalies relative to the general perception about a firm's ongoing volume of business. Collective bargaining agreements that vary markedly from standard industry practice may constitute interesting exceptions.
- ***Finance.*** Exceptional increases or decreases in earnings, dividends or cash flow, major new issues or repurchases of debt or equity, and major capital expenditures warrant closer scrutiny. Securities analysts may issue surprising revisions in their recommendations about the target's debt or equity. A comparative analysis of financial ratios and valuation multiples may suggest that a firm deviates from industry practice in important ways.

NOTES

1. It is useful to focus on constant dollar values in order to net out the possibly spurious effect of inflation or deflation. Over very long periods, even a slow rate of inflation can seriously distort the data. For instance, $100 of nominal purchasing power in 1996 could acquire the same basket of goods as $20 in 1895.
2. Brealey and Myers (1996), page 997.
3. Such "paradigm shift" deals would include Exxon/Mobil, AOL/Time Warner, WorldCom/MCI, Travelers/Citicorp, Daimler/Chrysler, Vodafone/Mannesmann. Characteristic of all of these was a redefinition of conventional thinking about size of transaction, industry focus, kinds of synergies, and antitrust regulation.
4. Melicher, Ledolter, and D'Antonio (1983) and Becketti (1986).

5. Weston (1953), Markham (1955), Nelson (1959), Melicher, Ledolter, and D'Antonio (1983), and Becketti (1986).
6. Nelson (1959 and 1966) concludes that peaks in M&A activity lead stock market peaks; Melicher, Ledolter, and D'Antonio (1983) conclude that M&A lags the market.
7. Self-interested risk management makes decisions based not on the welfare of shareholders, but on the welfare of management. Thus, management might choose to carry large balances of cash, inventory, and fixed assets; reduce the use of debt; and resist proposals to introduce new products or enter new markets—all out of a desire to reduce volatility in the life of managers even though such actions might impose an opportunity cost on shareholders.
8. This table follows the suggestion of Shleifer and Vishny (2002) quoted earlier.
9. With benefit of 60 years' hindsight, the echoing conclusions of Schumpeter's best-known book, *Capitalism, Socialism, and Democracy* (1947) are wrong. He wrote, "Can capitalism survive? No. I do not think it can. . . . Can socialism work? Of course it can." Perhaps in the fullness of time, history will reach his conclusion, though I doubt it. The basis for his conclusion was that capitalism creates so much internal turbulence in society that it will ultimately destroy the values and institutions that preserve it. He also believed that as the capitalist economy grows, ever-larger corporations will emerge—he argued that ultimately this would force the boisterous entrepreneur to adapt to working in a state bureaucracy, and that ultimately socialism could work. Any student of the collapse of the former Soviet Union and satellites, and of the economic rise of the West after World War II, however, would conclude otherwise.
10. With remarkable prescience, Schumpeter paints a profile of the entrepreneur that describes well many M&A professionals I have known: "First of all, there is the dream and the will to found a private kingdom, usually, though not necessarily, also a dynasty. . . . Then there is the will to conquer; the impulse to fight, to prove oneself superior to others, to succeed for the sake, not of the fruits of success, but of success itself. . . . Finally there is the joy of creating, of getting things done, or simply of exercising one's energy and ingenuity." (*Theory of Economic Development*, 1947, pages 93–94.)
11. Schumpeter (1950), page 132.
12. Schumpeter (1947), page 255.
13. Schumpeter (1950), pages 82–84.
14. Lamoreaux (1988), page 158.
15. Ibid., pages 187–188.
16. Wasserstein (1998), pages 2–3.
17. Ibid., page 163.
18. The discussion in this section focuses on "effective yields" (or the annualized internal rate of return on the debt instrument), not coupon yields (or the stated return on the face of the bond).
19. Firms assume *reinvestment risk* where the life of liabilities is greater than the life of assets. Conversely, firms assume *refinancing risk* where the life of liabilities is less than the life of assets.

CHAPTER 5

Cross-Border M&A

INTRODUCTION

This chapter explores the special M&A perspectives where the buyer and target firm are in different countries. This complements several chapters as the cross-border deal raises especially difficult questions about strategy, valuation, deal design, and implementation. The M&A practitioner should master the perspective of cross-border deals because they:

- ***Are significant.*** The volume of cross-border M&A activity is large, whether judged in terms of number of deals or value. The formation of trade blocs and regional associations hastens the growth in volume. And the volume of activity is likely to get bigger as country and regional markets integrate into the global market.
- ***Can be disruptive.*** In many countries and regions, cross-border M&A activity produces big surprises in the form of unanticipated entry by buyers, higher purchase prices, and changes in strategic assumptions about a local market.
- ***Can be motivated by a range of factors, different from domestic deals.*** These factors include growth by market expansion, extension of technology and brands, acquisition of special resources, tax and currency arbitrage, and the benefits of international diversification. This chapter will outline a number of these motives and summarize research on their effects.
- ***Entail a fundamental bet on countries.*** Countries differ in important ways that will affect the values of firms. Beneath every cross-border valuation analysis is some hidden assumption or bet about the future of a country market. Since 1945, local product and financial markets have trended toward greater integration with global markets. Integration brings with it economic benefits as well as costs to the local markets and institutions. One should have a view about the direction and pace of integration within home and foreign countries. This chapter will sketch some steps for country analysis.
- ***Affect analysis.*** It is a mistake to think that cross-border M&A is like domestic M&A, but with different-looking currency. In fact, going across borders requires adjustments in the valuation frameworks and analysis that one takes for granted in assessing domestic deals. Necessary adjustments in cash flows and discount rates can change the conclusions about a deal dramatically. Chapter 13 discusses the special adjustments for valuation across borders.

CROSS-BORDER M&A ACTIVITY

The volume of cross-border M&A transactions has risen to record levels in recent years. Exhibit 5.1 presents the trends of transactions involving a U.S.-based buyer or target:

- *Number of deals.* Columns 1, 2, and 3 show that the volume of transactions by number of deals more than doubled from 1991 to 2000—and then fell to half by 2002. Classifying by whether the deal was "inbound" (i.e., where a U.S. firm was the target) or "outbound" (i.e., where a U.S. firm was the buyer) reveals that the biggest growth in the 1990s occurred in the number of outbound deals.
- *Dollar value of deals.* Columns 4, 5, and 6 show huge increases in the dollar value of cross-border deals. In all years but two, the value of inbound deals has been greater than outbound deals (i.e., reversing the observation based on number of deals). Comparing the data on number of deals and value of deals, it appears that U.S. buyers have bought a larger number of smaller foreign targets, while foreign buyers have bought a smaller number of larger U.S. targets.
- *Cross-border volume relative to total M&A volume.* Columns 7 and 8 present the percentage of cross-border deals relative to total amounts for U.S.-based deal volume. The cross-border number of deals represents between 17.6 and 25 percent of the total. And comparing the dollar volumes with the total inbound and outbound foreign direct investment (FDI) in the United States, M&A volume accounts for the bulk of FDI.[1]

Looking beyond the confines of U.S.-related deals, the United Nations Conference on Trade and Development (UNCTAD) estimates that cross-border acquisition is the largest medium of foreign direct investment, accounting for 55 to 60 percent of the totals.[2] The volume of cross-border M&A is even larger if one considers other kinds of corporate transactions (e.g., joint ventures and project financings) possibly as partial or creeping acquisitions.[3] However, by any measure, cross-border M&A is sizable, and is a material element of all (i.e., domestic and cross-border) M&A activity.

Cross-border transactions have a different profile compared to domestic deals. Researchers have found that cross-border deals are:

- *More related.* Cross-border acquisitions tend not to represent diversification far beyond the buyer's core industry. Acquisitions into related businesses represent 60 to 75 percent of cross-border deals.[4]
- *Payment is mainly in cash.* Many cross-border buyers do not have shares listed for trading in the foreign market. Therefore, it is not surprising that buyers tend to pay with cash rather than stock.[5]
- *Targets are mainly manufacturing firms with low intangible assets.* Conn and Nielsen (1990) found that 97 percent of U.S. firms' targets and 74 percent of U.K. firms' targets were in manufacturing rather than finance or services.

EXHIBIT 5.1 Trends in Completed Cross-Border Mergers and Acquisitions Involving a U.S.-based Buyer or Target

Column	1	2	3	4	5	6	7	8	9	10
	Number of Cross-Border Deals			Value of Cross-Border Deals			Cross-Border Deals as a Percentage of All Transactions (Domestic and Cross-Border)		Value of All Foreign Direct Investment into and out from the United States	
	Total Number	Number of Inbound Deals	Number of Outbound Deals	Total Value (Billions)	Value of Inbound (Billions)	Value of Outbound (Billions)	% of Number of Deals	% of Total Value	Inbound U.S. FDI (Billions)	Outbound U.S. FDI (Billions)
2002	1,489	649	840	$107.0	$ 65.0	$ 42.0	17.6%	10.8%	$ 39.6	$137.8
2001	2,063	888	1,175	$216.0	$118.4	$ 97.6	20.3%	14.3%	$157.9	$156.0
2000	3,259	1,391	1,868	$433.8	$311.5	$122.3	24.0%	13.7%	$287.7	$152.4
1999	2,701	1,059	1,642	$349.9	$229.9	$120.0	25.0%	23.2%	$282.5	$155.2
1998	2,630	884	1,746	$320.3	$191.8	$128.6	21.9%	22.2%	$193.4	$132.8
1997	2,205	790	1,415	$143.8	$ 70.7	$ 73.1	20.7%	17.9%	$109.3	$109.8
1996	1,952	689	1,263	$121.2	$ 65.2	$ 56.0	19.8%	17.6%	$ 89.0	$ 92.7
1995	1,746	619	1,127	$ 83.2	$ 42.0	$ 41.1	19.9%	17.8%	$ 59.6	$ 99.5
1994	1,415	555	860	$ 60.6	$ 39.0	$ 21.6	19.7%	19.4%	$ 47.4	$ 80.7
1993	1,140	428	712	$ 33.2	$ 16.6	$ 16.6	19.5%	16.4%	$ 52.6	$ 84.4
1992	1,033	431	602	$ 28.3	$ 13.4	$ 14.9	19.5%	19.8%	$ 21.0	$ 48.7
1991	1,152	592	560	$ 42.1	$ 27.6	$ 14.5	23.0%	27.0%	$ 23.7	$ 38.2

Sources of data: Thomson Financial Securities Data and Bureau of Economic Analysis, U.S. Department of Commerce.

Notes:

- The foreign direct investment values in column 9 include only capital flows sourced from foreign markets. Funds sourced from the U.S. capital markets for acquisitions or investments made by foreign companies are not included. Hence, the comparison between column 5 and 9 is not perfect. Column 5 includes all sources of funding, domestic and abroad. Column 9 only includes foreign capital that "flowed in." A similar incomparability exists for columns 6 and 10.
- Despite the imperfect comparison between cross-border value and FDI, an analyst at the Bureau of Economic Analysis confirms that the majority of capital flowing into the United States for FDI in recent years has been for acquisitions. The analyst estimated the fraction to be between 60% and 80%.

M&A ACTIVITY WITHIN REGIONS AND TRADING BLOCS

Viewed from a global perspective, the most interesting laboratories for M&A today are the new *trading blocs* such as NAFTA and the European Monetary Union (EMU, or "Euroland").[6] The reason for this is that free trade changes the rules of competition by reducing entry barriers, making it easier to exploit economies of scale, increasing capital market integration (which improves capital flows and lowers the cost of capital), improving the transfer of technology and intellectual capital, and reducing the idiosyncrasies of government regulation and tax policies. These changes, in turn, will affect M&A activity. Most observers expect product market competition within trading blocs to increase thanks to greater transparency about product and factor prices within the blocs. For instance, with product prices denominated in the same units across Euroland, the more efficient producers are motivated to enter new markets and compete on price. In this context, M&A is used as both a defensive and an offensive tactic. The history of M&A in the United States offers abundant evidence that M&A waves are significantly driven by product market changes. Capital markets are likely to integrate more rapidly within trading blocs, making M&A financing cheaper, easier to obtain, and available in forms that are tailored more readily to the needs of M&A participants. We know that the level of capital costs and the availability of financing significantly influence M&A activity. Sleuwagen (1998) found that over the period 1994–1996, about 60 percent of all mergers and acquisitions in the EU involved firms located in the same member state. Pointing to the experience with NAFTA, many analysts believed that with the advent of the euro, the percentage of same-country mergers would decline and cross-border deals would rise.

Exhibit 5.2 shows the percentage change in cross-border acquisitions among the United States, Canada, and Mexico from 1991 to 1993, before NAFTA was formed, to 1994–1997, the three years following NAFTA. Within the United States, the number of U.S./U.S. acquisitions grew 60 percent, reflecting the onset of the largest acquisition wave in U.S. history; this domestic growth rate is a rough bench-

EXHIBIT 5.2 Percentage Rate of Growth in Transactions Domestically and Cross-Border among the United States, Mexico, and Canada, Comparing Deal Volumes from 1991–1993 to 1994–1996

	Country of Acquirer		
Country of Target	**United States**	**Canada**	**Mexico**
United States	60%	65%	38%
Canada	70%		
Mexico	44%	70%	

Note: The growth rate is calculated by dividing the number of all transactions 1991–1993 into the number of all transactions 1994–1996, and subtracting 1.0.

Source: Thomson Financial Securities Data Corporation, Mergers and Acquisitions Database.

mark for comparing cross-border M&A growth rates within NAFTA. The exhibit shows that acquisitions by U.S. firms into Canada and by Canadian firms into the United States outpaced the domestic U.S. acquisition growth rate. The results with respect to Mexico are significantly lower than the U.S. domestic deal growth, reflecting perhaps the massive devaluation of the peso in 1995 and offering a caution to executives.

Increasing capital market integration elevates the importance of the equity investor mind-set probably at the expense of other stakeholders. As the equity orientation grows, M&A practice changes. Overpayment is penalized; price becomes an object of greater attention. The volume of unsolicited acquisition attempts may rise. The product market scenario outlined earlier may place special importance on the advantage of the "first mover." To enter new markets rapidly, decisively, and first may dictate tactics that are at their core impatient. The unsolicited acquisition attempt is risky, but may be justified in managers' minds by the circumstances. Before the euro, the hostile tender offer was a rarity in Europe. But the weeks following the birth of the euro witnessed major hostile offers on the continent.[7] Deal structures following increased capital market integration may also reflect greater use of innovative terms including derivative securities, bridge loans, and "junk" debt. Growing sophistication in the capital markets will make this possible.

Acquisitions are inherently acts of optimism. Deteriorating economic conditions would likely impair that optimism, and the resulting volume of deals. Again, the experience of Mexico/U.S. cross-border deals is illustrative here. Exhibit 5.3 shows that Mexican acquirers virtually disappeared from the cross-border M&A market in the wake of the peso devaluation in late 1994. The financial crisis in East Asia in 1997 triggered a wave of M&A activity in that region. Precrisis in 1996, the regional volume of deals was $3 billion per year. In 1999, the volume had risen to $22 billion; this stemmed significantly from M&A activity in Korea and Thailand, two countries deeply affected by the "Asian flu" crisis. Especially strong activity was seen in real estate, financial services, retailing, and wholesaling. Mody and Negishi (2001) argued that driving the increased M&A was a general rise in inbound foreign direct investment associated with economic restructuring of the region after the crisis. Further, they argue that the M&A activity was driven by the creation of new opportunities due to government policy changes in the region than by the lure of bargain-basement asset prices.

EXHIBIT 5.3 Cross-Border Transactions between Mexico and the United States, 1994 and 1995

	1994	1995	% Change
Acquisitions by U.S. firms into Mexico			
Number of transactions	48	47	–2.1%
Value (US$ millions)	$496	$499	0.7%
Acquisitions by Mexican firms in the U.S.			
Number of transactions	14	1	–92.9%
Value (US$ millions)	$2,094	$0.1	–100.0%

Source of data: Thomson Financial Securities Data Corporation, Mergers and Acquisitions Database.

DRIVERS OF CROSS-BORDER M&A

A large body of research illuminates the forces behind cross-border M&A activity: exploiting market imperfections, intangible assets, risk reduction through diversification, exchange rates, financial market conditions, and tax rates.

Exploit Market Imperfections

A venerable stream of research in economics suggests that foreign direct investment through cross-border acquisition seeks to take advantage of market imperfections and failures[8] in foreign countries. The theory is that the buyer will recognize profitable opportunities to take advantage of cheap labor and raw materials, unmet consumer demand, deregulation, trade liberalization, and country integration of capital and product markets into global markets. Exhibit 5.4 presents a list of 17 large cross-border deals from 1997 to 2002. The forces of change are evident in the makeup of this list:

- *Telecommunications.* Seven of the 17 deals originate in the telecommunications industry and suggest these forces at work: rapid technological change and government deregulation. Vodafone/Mannesmann and Vodafone/AirTouch, both in the wireless segment of the industry, are notable for their size. Also, Vodafone initiated one of the few hostile offers ever to occur in Germany—and won.
- *Pharmaceuticals/chemicals.* Rising R&D expense and the desire to achieve distribution economies motivated the Astra/Zeneca and Hoechst/Rhône-Poulenc deals.
- *Consumer foods.* Two deals (acquisitions of BestFoods and BAT Industries) were driven by the desire for portfolio diversification across product categories, perceived benefits of global branding, perceived undervaluation of brands in the home capital markets, and an expectation of greater economies of scale in distribution.
- *Automobiles.* Rising new product development costs and the consequent consolidation in the industry motivated the combinations of Daimler/Chrysler, Ford/Volvo, and others.

In short, the surging volume in cross-border M&A is driven by the many of the same fundamental economic forces outlined in Chapter 4. From this perspective, cross-border M&A activity is not a curious sideshow to the large domestic U.S. volume, but is sizable and linked integrally with it.

Extend the Reach of the Buyer's or Target's Intangible Assets

Researchers[9] observe the heavier investment in manufacturing and speculate that cross-border M&A represents an effort of firms with significant intangible assets (such as brand names, patents, and managerial know-how) to broaden the scale of their use and preempt others who might be tempted to imitate or appropriate those intangible assets. Similarly, a foreign buyer may seek to acquire intangible assets of a foreign target with the intent of bringing the benefits of those assets back home. Eun et al. (1996) found that foreign acquirers benefit from targets' R&D. Morck and Yeung (1991) found that "the positive impact of spending for research and development

EXHIBIT 5.4 Seventeen Largest Cross-Border Deals, 1997–2002

Date Announced	Target Name	Target Nation	Acquirer Name	Acquirer Nation	Transaction Value ($ Millions)	Enterprise Value ($ Millions)	Equity Value ($ Millions)	Asset Value ($ Millions)
11/14/99	Mannesmann AG	Germany	Vodafone AirTouch PLC	U.K.	202,785	180,033	179,861	21,442
4/18/99	Telecom Italia SpA	Italy	Deutsche Telekom AG	Germany	81,528	74,613	66,801	52,744
1/18/99	AirTouch Communications	U.S.	Vodafone Group PLC	U.K.	60,287	65,770	60,212	17,262
8/11/98	Amoco Corp.	U.S.	British Petroleum Co. PLC	U.K.	48,174	54,768	47,902	32,274
5/30/00	Orange PLC (Mannesmann AG)	U.K.	France Telecom SA	France	45,967	N/A	N/A	2,901
5/17/99	US WEST Inc.	U.S.	Global Crossing Ltd.	Bermuda	41,105	51,097	41,098	18,709
5/7/98	Chrysler Corp.	U.S.	Daimler-Benz AG	Germany	40,467	49,377	40,467	64,256
6/20/00	Seagram Co. Ltd.	Canada	Vivendi SA	France	40,428	38,725	29,771	34,921
12/9/98	Astra AB	Sweden	Zeneca Group PLC	U.K.	34,637	31,787	34,637	7,841
10/21/99	Orange PLC	U.K.	Mannesmann AG	Germany	32,595	34,214	31,489	2,901
4/1/99	ARCO	U.S.	BP Amoco PLC	U.K.	27,224	33,702	27,224	25,199
5/2/00	Bestfoods	U.S.	Unilever PLC	U.K.	25,065	23,529	20,895	6,209
5/17/99	Hoechst AG	Germany	Rhone-Poulenc SA	France	21,918	28,526	21,917	33,338
11/16/98	Rhône-Poulenc SA—Life Sciences	France	Hoechst AG—Life Sciences Divs.	Germany	21,223	N/A	N/A	N/A
4/17/00	Allied Zurich PLC	U.K.	Zurich Allied AG	Switzerland	19,399	21,409	19,384	87,552
11/1/96	MCI Communications Corp.	U.S.	British Telecom PLC	U.K.	18,889	27,272	23,328	19,301
10/13/97	BAT Industries PLC-Financial	U.K.	Zurich Versicherungs GmbH	Switzerland	18,355	N/A	N/A	N/A

Note: Size judged on the basis of transaction value in millions of U.S. dollars.
Source: Thomson Securities Data Corporation, Mergers and Acquisitions Database.

and for advertising on market value increases with a firm's multinational scale, but that multinationality per se does not have any significant impact. . . . Intangible assets are necessary for direct foreign investment to make sense." (Page 185)

Reduce Tax Expense through Arbitrage across Different Tax Jurisdictions

Marginal corporate tax rates vary dramatically across the globe. In January 2002, they ranged from a low of 16 percent in Hong Kong and Chile to a high of 42 percent in Sri Lanka with a mean of 31.39 percent for OECD countries (see KMPG (2002)). Some have argued that this disparity permits multinational corporations to shift operations globally in ways that profitably arbitrages away from high-tax jurisdictions and toward lower-tax jurisdictions.[10] This is consistent with anecdotal evidence from practitioners (especially chief financial officers) about the importance of tax considerations in investment decisions. Nevertheless, empirical research at best gives mixed support for this motive.[11]

Reduce Risk through Diversification

If economic activity across countries is less than perfectly correlated, geographic diversification can reduce risk. This is a straightforward extension of modern portfolio theory. For instance, Adler and Dumas (1975) argued that international diversification pays when capital markets are not fully integrated. Whereas correlations among stock returns within a country can be high, correlations across countries are highly variable, and can be quite low or even negative. Exhibit 5.5 presents equity market correlations between the United States and various emerging markets countries. Rouwenhorst (1999) reported that from 1970 to 1998 the average correlation between index returns in Japan and the United States was 25 percent; between the United Kingdom and United States, it was 50 percent. Explanations for such variability across countries could be differing degrees of economic development and integration with global markets.[12]

Even though local market volatilities might be high, a low correlation with that market might make it attractive to invest there. This is the chief argument in favor

EXHIBIT 5.5 Emerging Market Correlations with U.S. Market

	1976–1985	1985–1992	1995–1999
Argentina	3%	10%	52%
Brazil	–7%	13%	48%
Chile	–11%	32%	46%
Mexico	13%	49%	60%
Thailand	–9%	43%	53%

Source of data: Standard & Poor's/International Finance Corporation, "The S&P Emerging Market Indices: Methodologies, Definitions, and Practices," February 2000, page 32.

of global diversification of equity investing. Madura and Whyte (1990) argued that "differences in characteristics between real assets and financial assets can cause different degrees of diversification benefits. For example, real sectors can cause different degrees of diversification than foreign financial sectors will offer greater potential diversification benefits *if* those sectors can be penetrated." (Page 75) But does this translate into benefits for shareholders at the level of corporate investing? Some evidence suggests that the share prices of multinational corporations (MNCs) reflect well the geographic diversification, while other studies suggest that MNCs do not provide all the benefits of direct investment in foreign securities.[13] Fatemi (1984) compared MNCs with purely domestic firms, and found that returns on MNCs fluctuate less than domestic firms, that the betas of MNCs are more stable than domestic firms. Thus, risk reduction through geographical diversification seems to work. Fatemi also reported that risk-adjusted abnormal returns for MNCs are similar to domestic firms. Mikhail and Shawky (1979) and Errunza and Senbet (1981) found that the degree of international presence has a positive effect on excess returns. Doukas and Travlos (1988) reported that investor reaction to news of entry into a new foreign market is positive and significant, and most pronounced when the entry is into an emerging market country.

Is risk reduced more effectively by diversifying across countries or across global industries?[14] Until the mid-1990s, low correlations among countries' stock markets led to the conventional wisdom that much of the variability in returns from global investing stemmed from country choice. Marber (1998, p. 172) reported the findings of Barr Rosenberg Associates and the International Finance Corporation (IFC), who studied the extent to which choices about country, industry, and specific firm explained cross-sectional variation in global equity returns. They estimated the percent of returns variance explained by country, industry, and *stock-specific factors* for investments in developed markets and emerging markets. The results of the study, summarized in Exhibit 5.6, are that *industry factors* are dominant in developed countries and *country factors* are dominant in emerging countries. Other studies[15] show that country choices are very important, if not the most important, drivers of returns performance. Solnik (1991, p. 360) reported a study by Frank Russell Company of investment activities of international managers, finding that on average the manager puts 50 percent of resources into country analysis, 15 percent into industry analysis, and 35 percent into company analysis. But recent research has suggested that growing integration of the global equity market and the rising

EXHIBIT 5.6 Factors Explaining Equity Returns in Emerging and Developed Markets

	Investments in Emerging Markets	Investments in Developed Markets
Stock-specific factors	16%	22%
Industry factors	38%	48%
Country factors	46%	30%
Total	100%	100%

Source of data: Marber (1998), page 172.

multinationality of companies elevate the importance of industry and firm-specific factors. However, other research suggests that country choice remains of preeminent importance. The relative significance of industry and country persists as a debate at the frontier of empirical finance. Either way, country choice will remain a material factor for some time to come. The global M&A analyst will seek to diversify across *both* countries and industries.[16]

Exploit Differences in Capital Market and Currency Conditions

One of the most reliable findings about M&A activity in the U.S. is the strong relationship between deal doing and high stock and bond prices. In the cross-border world, a strong relationship also exists though it is complicated by the fact that it is driven by comparative differences between *two* local financial markets. Feliciano and Lipsey (2002) found that acquisitions of U.S. firms by foreign firms decline with high U.S. stock prices, high industry profitability, and high industry growth, and increase with high U.S. interest rates, high U.S. growth rates, and high foreign currencies relative to the U.S. dollar. Vasconcellos et al. (1990) found that foreign firms increase their acquisitions in the United States when U.S. economic conditions are favorable compared to the foreign country, interest rates are high in the foreign country compared to the United States, and the dollar is weak relative to the foreign currency. Gonzalez, Vasconcellos, and Kish (1998) found that undervalued U.S. companies were more likely to be targets of acquisition by foreign companies.

Closely related to capital market conditions are currency market conditions. Variation in exchange rates can render one country's firms cheaper or dearer to buyers from another country. But conventional economic analysis would reject this, arguing that in an integrated global market, real rates of return on assets will be equal across countries, preventing profitable arbitrage on the basis of currency exchange rate variations. Froot and Stein (1991) linked currency changes to the relative wealth of buyers to argue, in effect, that countries with deep financial pockets because of strong currencies will tend to originate foreign direct investment. They find a strong relationship between exchange rate movements and FDI. Harris and Ravenscraft (1991) found a strong relationship between exchange rate movements and cross-border acquisition announcement effects. Vasconcellos and Kish (1998) reported a strong relationship between acquisition activity and exchange rate movements. Vasconcellos, Madura, and Kish (1990) concluded, "In the final analysis, the long-run outlook on the dollar is the critical factor in foreign acquisition of or by U.S. firms." (Page 184)

Improve Governance

Good governance pays, a point discussed in Chapter 26. Corporate governance practices vary significantly across countries. Researchers have examined whether M&A changes in investor protection stemming from these cross-border differences influence merger outcomes. Bris and Cabolis (2002) studied the change in investor protection arising from cross-country deals. They found that the valuation multiples (Tobin's Q[17]) in the home market rise when a foreign firm buys into that industry, coming from a country with greater investor protection. Rossi and

Volpin (2001) suggest that M&A is a means by which companies can exit from a poor governance environment. Companies from countries with poorer governance practices are more likely to be acquired; those with stronger governance are more likely to buy.

Other Drivers of M&A Activity

Biswas et al. (1997) list a range of other possible motives for cross border acquisitions. These include regulatory avoidance, financing, and the desire to maintain good relationships with customers who themselves may have a need for multinational delivery of goods or services.

RETURNS FROM CROSS-BORDER M&A

Does all of this activity pay? The following points highlight the findings of 17 studies regarding the abnormal returns to shareholders at the announcement of cross-border acquisitions.

- ***Returns to targets of foreign buyers.*** Exhibit 5.7 shows that returns to target shareholders are significantly positive. Two studies report that U.S. targets receive materially higher returns than do foreign targets. In five studies, returns of U.S. targets are higher with foreign buyers than domestic buyers. One study, by Dewenter (1995) yields the provocative suggestion that the difference in results between U.S. and foreign buyers could be due to differences in industrial profiles of the two groups of acquisitions—much more research is required here. Cross-sectional analyses suggest that returns to targets vary significantly by country, industry, and currency rates.
- ***Returns to buyers of foreign targets.*** Exhibit 5.8 shows that returns to buyer shareholders are essentially zero. In four studies, U.S. buyers of foreign targets earn returns insignificantly different from zero. In 12 studies of returns to foreign buyers, one reports significantly negative returns, two report significantly positive returns, and the rest report returns insignificantly different from zero.
- ***Joint wealth changes to buyers and targets.*** Exhibit 5.9 summarizes three studies that report positive joint wealth gains (two of them are significant) to shareholders of buyers and targets.

The total picture appears to be that cross-border M&A *does* pay. Consistent with the findings for U.S. domestic M&A reported in Chapter 3, targets earn large returns; buyers essentially break even; and on a combined basis, shareholders gain. We are left with the general impression that foreign bidders pay more than domestic bidders. Kohers and Kohers (2001) have argued that this premium represents payment for special local knowledge and market access that the target provides the foreign buyer.

EXHIBIT 5.7 Returns to Targets of Foreign Buyers

Study	Cumulative Abnormal Returns (% or avg$/acq)	Sample Size	Sample Period	Event Window (Days)	Notes
Conn, Connell (1990)	0.1822* non-U.S. (DMM)	73	1971–1980	–1,0	"Non-U.S." and "U.S." indicate country of target firm. "IMM" indicates returns estimated using a market model with an international market index. "DMM" uses a domestic market index.
	0.1984* non-U.S. (IMM)				
	0.3986* U.S. (DMM)				
	0.4331* U.S. (IMM)				
Biswas et al. (1997)	0.0623* all observations	81	1977–1987	–1,0	Focus is non-U.S. targets and financial sector deals.
	0.0350* non-U.S.	33			
	0.0752* U.S. only	48			
	0.1069* U.S. domestic	N/A			
Wansley et al. (1983)	0.3864* target of foreign buyer	39	1970–1978	–40,0	Focus is U.S. targets.
	0.2800* target of U.S. buyer	164			
	Difference is significant at 5% level.				
Shaked et al. (1991)	0.168* foreign buyer	29	1980–1983	–1,0	Focus is U.S. targets.
	0.148* domestic buyer	82			
	Difference is significant in oils, mining, and machinery.				
Harris, Ravenscraft (1991)	0.397* foreign buyers	1,273	1970–1987	–5,0	Focus is U.S. targets.
	0.263* U.S. buyers				
Marr et al. (1993)	0.1182* foreign buyers	96	1975–1987	–1,0	Focus is U.S. targets.
	0.0627* U.S. buyers				
	Difference is significant at 5% level.				
Kang (1993)	0.0907* Japanese buyers	102	1975–1988	–1,0	Focus is U.S. targets.
	0.0684 U.S. buyers				
	Difference is not significant.				

(Continued)

EXHIBIT 5.7 *(Continued)*

Study	Cumulative Abnormal Returns (% or avg$/acq)	Sample Size	Sample Period	Event Window (Days)	Notes
Pettway, Sicherman, Speiss, (1993)	0.3700†	10	1981–1991	–1,0	Focus is U.S. targets of Japanese buyers.
Servaes, Zenner (1994)	0.3802* 1979–1980 0.1520* 1981–1986 0.4161* 1987–1988	779	1979–1988	N/A	Focus is U.S. targets.
Dewenter (1995)	Domestic acquisition premium is not significantly different from foreign acquisition premium.	294	1978–1989	N/A	Focus is U.S. targets. Looked at premiums unique to two industries, chemicals and retailing. Argued that observed differences in other studies were due to industry composition of samples.
Eun, Kolodny, Scheraga (1996)	0.3702* all observations 0.3715* Canadian buyers 0.4855* Japanese buyers 0.3555* U.K. buyers 0.3530* all other buyers	213	1979–1990	–5,0	Focus is U.S. targets.
Kiymaz, Mukherjee (2000)	Strong effects of currency and relative GNP growth rates of two countries.	141	1982–1991	–1,0	Focus is U.S. targets.
Kuipers, Miller, Patel (2003)	+23.07%† $121.86 MM†	181	1982–1991	–1,0	Focus is U.S. targets.

*Significant at the 95 percent confidence level.
†Significant at the 99 percent confidence level.

EXHIBIT 5.8 Returns to Buyers of Foreign Targets

Study	Cumulative Abnormal Returns (% or avg$/acq)	Sample Size	Sample Period	Event Window (Days)	Notes
Conn, Connell (1990)	–0.0787* a non-U.S.(DMM) –0.0677* a non-U.S.(IMM) –0.025 U.S. (DMM) –0.026 U.S. (IMM)	73	1971–1980	–1,0	"Non-U.S." and "U.S." indicate country of buyer firm. "IMM" indicates returns estimated using a market model with an international market index. "DMM" uses a domestic market index.
Kang (1993)	0.0059 Japanese buyers –0.029. U.S. buyers Difference is significant at 5%.	119 102	1975–1988	–1,0	Focus is non-U.S. buyers of U.S. targets.
Mathur et al. (1994)	–0.0026	77	1984–1988	–1,+1	Focus is non-U.S. buyers of U.S. targets.
Servaes, Zenner (1994)	0.0044 takeovers 0.0005 units and minority interests	70	1979–1988	–1,0	Focus is non-U.S. buyers of U.S. targets.
Eun, Kolodny, Scheraga (1996)	–0.0120 all observations 0.0318 Canadian buyers 0.0362 Japanese buyers –0.0428 U.K. buyers –0.0046 all other buyers	117	1979–1990	–5,0	Focus is non-U.S. buyers of U.S. targets.
Cakici et al. (1996)	0.0046* foreign bidder 0.0000 U.S. bidder	195	1983–1992	–1,0	Focus is non-U.S. buyers of U.S. targets.
Doukas, Travlos (1988)	0.009 All observations –0.0003 operating in target's country 0.011 not operating in target's country 0.0199* going abroad first time	301	1975–1983	–1,0	Focus is U.S. buyers of foreign targets.

(Continued)

EXHIBIT 5.8 *(Continued)*

Study	Cumulative Abnormal Returns (% or avg$/acq)	Sample Size	Sample Period	Event Window (Days)	Notes
Pettway, Sicherman, Speiss, (1993)	0.0152†	16	1981–1991	–1,0	Focus is Japanese buyers of U.S. targets.
Markides, Ittner (1994)	0.0032 all observations 0.0055 related acquisitions –0.0087 unrelated	274	1975–1988	–1,0	Focus is U.S. buyers of foreign targets.
Yook, McCabe (1996)	0.0046 all observations 0.0085 large acquisitions	98	1979–1989	–1,0	Focus is U.S. buyers of foreign targets.
Biswas et al. (1997)	0.00126 all observations 0.00277 U.S. buyer, foreign target 0.00015 foreign buyers, foreign targets –0.00399* U.S. buyer and target	125	1977–1987	–1,0	Focus is buyers of foreign targets.
Kiymaz, Mukherjee (2000)	Strong effects of monthly stock returns and relative GNP growth rates of two countries.	112	1982–1991	–1,0	Focus is U.S. buyers of foreign targets.
Eckbo, Thorburn (2000)	–0.0030 U.S. buyers 0.0171 Canadian buyers	390 1,261	1964–1983	–1,0	Focus is U.S. and Canadian buyers of Canadian firms.
Kuipers, Miller, Patel (2003)	–0.92% –$31.26MM	138	1982–1991	–1,0	Focus is foreign acquirers of U.S. targets.

*Significant at the 95 percent confidence level.
†Significant at the 99 percent confidence level.

EXHIBIT 5.9 Summary of Shareholder Return Studies for M&A: Combined Returns to Shareholders of Acquiring Firm and Target Firm

Study	Cumulative Abnormal Returns	Sample Size	Sample Period	Event Window (Days)	Notes
Eun, Kolodny, Scheraga (1996)	$68 million, average combined wealth changes. $398 million.	117	1979–1990	−5,0	Focus is non-U.S. buyers and U.S. targets.
Biswas et al. (1997)	$135.4 million, average combined wealth changes, international acquisitions; 3.39% as percentage of size. $2.04 million, domestic acquisitions; 2.02% as percentage of size. Both are significant at 5%.	125	1977–1987	−5,+5	Focus is buyers of foreign targets.
Kuipers, Miller, Patel (2003)	+2.99%* $121.86 MM†	120	1982–1991	−1,0	Focus is U.S. targets and foreign acquirers.

*Significant at 95 percent confidence level.
†Significant at 99 percent confidence level.

STRATEGIC ANALYSIS OF COUNTRIES: GETTING A VIEW

The extensive research on foreign direct investment and on investor reaction to announcements of cross-border acquisitions underscores how important it is for the practitioner to have a view about a country in which an acquisition is contemplated. Such a view would inform the analysis of deals with insights about:

- Expected economic growth in the country and region. Exhibit 5.10 depicts the development curve of a country over time, commonly used by economists to convey the evolutionary process by which a country achieves developed status. The country progresses from entrepôt (distribution center), through stages of rising value-added manufacturing, to highly integrated operations. In seeking to gauge the attractiveness of a country market, the M&A analyst can use a framework such as the path of development to assess the current status and future outlook for a country.
- Foundations of special competitive advantage stemming from unique resources or capabilities. Porter (1990) highlighted the role of clusters of competition within countries that creates capabilities.
- Outlook for inflation, interest rates, and exchange rates.
- Relative valuation of assets.

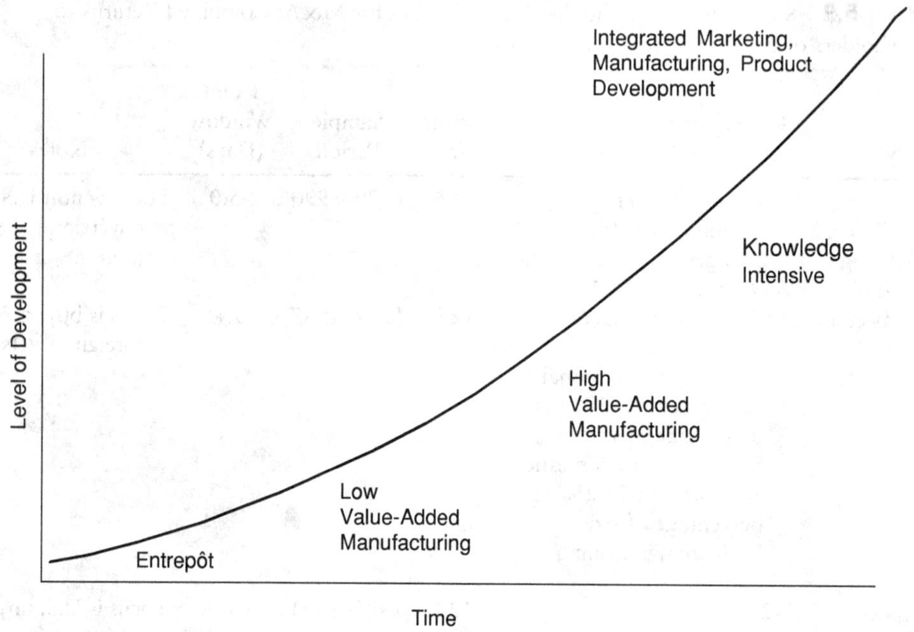

EXHIBIT 5.10 The Curve of Country Development

- Risks. Expectations about any of these elements are never certain. Country analysis should identify the sources of uncertainty and the size of their influence. A quick assessment of the risk in a country might be derived from its sovereign debt risk rating.

Most government issues are rated for default risk by major rating agencies. These form important assumptions that will underpin the cross-border deal evaluation outlined in Chapter 13. Four perspectives inform one's view: macroeconomic, microeconomic, institutional, and cultural.

Macroeconomic View

In the long run, national economic results are materially influenced by government policies in six areas:

1. *Fiscal policy.* This addresses the volume and priorities of government spending, as well as the means of financing that spending through taxes or the issuance of debt. Fiscal policy affects monetary, exchange rate, and employment policies. The key points of focus for an analyst are government surpluses or deficits, spending priorities, tax rates, and government indebtedness.
2. *Monetary policy.* Management of the national money supply through central bank and government activities is a major influence on inflation rates, interest rates, and currency exchange rates. Monetary policy affects fiscal policy, exchange rate policy, employment, and trade. Key points of focus for the analyst are interest rate levels and trends, inflation rates, the velocity of money, and government interventions that seek to influence these (e.g., open market transactions, bank reserve requirements, and discount window transactions).

3. ***Exchange rate policy.*** Governments may choose among a variety of alternatives from letting the national currency float against other currencies to fixing the rate of exchange (in terms of a commodity such as gold or other currencies). Exchange rates are closely linked to flows of capital and the national balance of payments. Exchange rate policy affects monetary, fiscal, trade, and employment policies. Key points of focus for the analyst are the trend and level of exchange rates, trade balances and capital flows (which indicate the relative supply and demand for the local currency), interventions in currency markets by the government or by supranational organizations such as the International Monetary Fund (IMF).
4. ***Intervention policy.*** Economies that are tightly centrally controlled by governments may be slow to adapt to innovations and changes in market conditions. On the other hand, intervention may dampen swings in economic activity. Governments intervene in business markets through industry regulations, state ownership of enterprises, the judicial system, and oversight of financial institutions. Key points of analysis are the severity of government regulations, the existence of centralized regulatory boards, policies on privatization or nationalization, the use of government subsidies to support private enterprise, the history of expropriation, and generally the development priorities indicated through government action in these areas.
5. ***Trade policy.*** Government policy can range from strong protectionism (through tariffs and other barriers) to free trade. Barriers may shelter the development of "national champions," but they restrict the inbound flow of goods and services to consumers in the country. In contrast, the theory of comparative advantage suggests that national welfare is maximized when goods trade freely across borders. Trade policy affects fiscal, monetary, and exchange rate policies. Key points of analysis are the size and distribution of tariffs across imported goods and services and the trend of flows of imports and exports.
6. ***Employment and welfare policy.*** Many countries seek to manage unemployment and stimulate the creation of jobs as the flip side of providing a social safety net of welfare and health care payments. Employment and welfare policy affect fiscal policy. The focus of analysis should be the trend and size of the unemployment rate, trend and size of social welfare payments in the economy, existence of labor unions, and laws and policies that affect union activity.

Microeconomic View

This second perspective on a country considers activity at the level of industries and firms. Of general interest to the analyst will be the demographic profile of the country's industrial base, the breadth of different industries, their maturity, and their prosperity. Central to microeconomic analysis is an understanding about average and marginal costs and revenues as indicators of the competitive advantage of individual firms, of entry barriers, and of the competitive makeup of industries. This view of a country is rooted in theory and research of industrial organization economics.

Porter (1990) argues that country performance is essentially a matter of microeconomic performance. Conventional thinking about national competitiveness, he says, is rooted in macroeconomics: trade balances, interest rates, exchange rates, labor costs, and economies of scale. Instead, he argues that national performance can be traced to processes of innovation and productivity improvement at the level of industries: "The only meaningful concept of competitiveness at the national level is *productivity*. . . . A nation's standard of living depends on the capacity of its companies to achieve high levels of productivity—and to increase productivity over time. Sustained productivity growth requires that an economy continually *upgrade itself*." (Page 76) Based on an analysis of competitive success in 10 trading nations, Porter concludes that the ability to innovate and to improve productivity resides in four interrelated factors. Exhibit 5.11 depicts these factors in the "diamond" of national competitive advantage:

- *Factor conditions.* These regard the inputs of production, such as labor, land, natural resources, physical facilities, and infrastructure. Human resources and intellectual capital are especially important in advanced national economies. Here the analyst should assess how specialized are a nation's factors, and how tailored they are to the needs of the acquisition target. Porter argues that "nations succeed in industries where they are particularly good at factor creation. Competitive advantage results from the presence of world-class institutions that first create specialized factors and then continually work to upgrade them." (Page 79)
- *Demand conditions.* The home-market demand for the goods or services of an industry will heavily influence the international success of that industry. Effective home demand can telegraph to domestic firms an earlier and clearer assessment of customer needs—the *guidance* from home demand is more important than its size. The best home demand arises from discerning and sophisticated customers. Here, the focus of the M&A analyst is less on aggregate demand than on segments and key customers (size, trends, and pressures within the customer group for cost, quality, and service). Thus, Porter says, "Sophisticated, demanding buyers provide a window into advanced customer needs; they pressure companies to meet high standards; they prod them to improve, to innovate, and to upgrade into more advanced segments." (Page 82)
- *Related or supporting industries.* No industry resides in a vacuum; instead, each depends on others for upstream or downstream assistance. The strength of these related industries will influence the success of an industry. Internation-

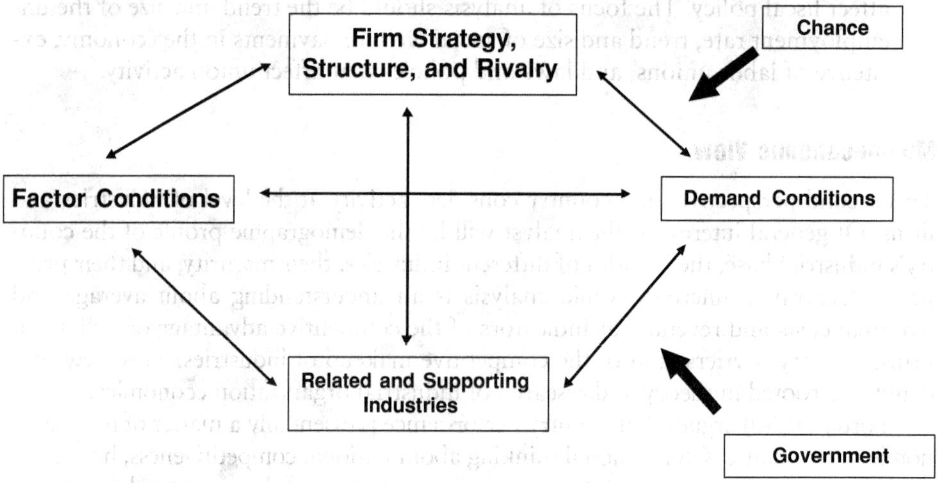

EXHIBIT 5.11 Porter's "Diamond" of National Competitive Advantage
Source: Porter (1990).

ally competitive suppliers "deliver the most cost-effective inputs in an efficient, early, rapid and sometimes preferential manner." (Pages 82–83) Close working relationships spur innovation and change through better information flow and technical exchange. Porter argues that this type of exchange within industrial "clusters" explains the dominance by countries of certain industries, such as leather footwear (Italy), chocolate confections (Switzerland, Belgium), machine tools (Italy), software (U.S.), and biotechnology (Denmark). The M&A analyst should consider the character of supplier industries: pressures for productivity improvement, internal competition, and key suppliers.

- ***Domestic rivalry and the strategy and structure of the competitors.*** Competition tends to strengthen the international competitiveness of local industries. The nature of that competition and the strategies adopted by individual rivals shapes the ability of that industry to withstand competition across borders. Cozy oligopolies created by high industry entry barriers will tend to stifle innovation and productivity improvement. Therefore, the analyst should assess the structure of competition in selected industries (e.g., by means of concentration ratios), evaluate the significance of entry barriers (especially barriers erected by governments), map the conduct of competition (e.g., familiar patterns such as leader-follower or territorial dominance by geographical area or industry subsegment), and look for the presence of "national champions." Porter writes, "Conventional wisdom argues that domestic competition is wasteful: it leads to duplication of effort and prevents companies from achieving economies of scale. The 'right solution' is to embrace one or two national champions, companies with the scale and strength to tackle foreign competitors, and to guarantee them the necessary resources, with the government's blessing. In fact, however, most national champions are uncompetitive." (Page 85)

These factors are self-reinforcing; they form a system. Dramatic improvement or deterioration in one factor will radiate through the others. This underscores the *cluster* nature of microeconomic strength in a country: the interlinkage of these factors amplifies industrial strengths (and weaknesses). Industrial clusters tend to arise in geographical proximity and from shared customers, technology, distribution channels, resources, and suppliers.

From the microeconomic vantage point, all national strength has local origins. Frameworks such as Porter's can help guide the analyst toward the identification of these sources.

Institutional View

The field of institutional economics emphasizes the important role played in national economic growth by a range of institutions that may not themselves be the direct producers of growth but that provide important economic infrastructure for development. In developed countries, these institutions are taken for granted. But in earlier stages of development (see Exhibit 5.10), the presence or absence of these institutions and the health of the institutions will affect the attractiveness of the country for foreign direct investment and acquisition. Institutions worth studying include these:

- ***Banking.*** In the 150 developing countries of the world, banks are practically the only means by which firms can acquire nonequity funds to grow. And within the developed world, the number and health of banks vary greatly. Measures of activity and soundness of banks (and thereby the banking system) include: loan growth, deposit growth, loan losses, capitalization (and especially in comparison with capital requirements imposed by country regulators and supranational organizations such as the IMF), return on equity, return on assets, and operating ratio (operating income divided by operating expenses).
- ***Stock market and investment regulations.*** The local stock market is a bellwether of integration from local markets to the global market. Indicators of stock market conditions are the number of listings, the daily trading volume, the number of initial public offerings, the height and trend of stock prices (especially the local stock market index), presence of sophisticated institutional investors, breadth of share ownership among households within the country, and concentration of share ownership of firms. Of vital importance to integration is the presence or absence of controls on the cross-border movement of capital, restrictions on share ownership by foreigners, and generally the adoption of market regulations in harmony with world market standards.
- ***Watchdogs: auditors, free press, opposition political parties.*** Transparency of financial reporting and the adoption of accounting principles by active professional auditors in the local country are foundations of strong banking and stock market systems. But the country analyst should broaden the assessment to include other institutions that also play a watchdog role such as journalists and opposition politicians. Issues of particular importance are the suppression of governmental and corporate corruption. Some international business organizations publish corruption indexes.
- ***Independent judiciary, rule of law, respect for contracts and property rights.*** Expropriation of wealth by government or by a private mafia is the nightmare of foreign direct investors. One measure of relief from these risks is the soundness of the system of justice in the local country. Failures of the judicial system often parallel failures in watchdog groups; therefore, information in the public domain may not give a clear indication of the strength of local justice. Here, interviews with local foreign investors will be indispensable. Respect for civil rights is another indicator of the integrity of the system of justice. Give careful attention to freedom of speech, freedom of religious observance, and respect for the rights of minorities and women.
- ***Educational system.*** Literacy rates, schooling requirements, and the number and health of educational institutions give demographic backing to conclusions about the likely strength of the workforce, of human capital, and of the possible generation of new intellectual property.

Cultural View

Economic growth may also be culturally determined by factors such as work ethic, leadership, and entrepreneurship. Great ingredients do not guarantee a tasty dinner—such an outcome depends importantly on the cook. The M&A country analyst needs to assess the ability of the local culture to nurture these important attributes. Any scientific effort to do so borders on organizational psychology and anthropology, disciplines well beyond the scope of this book. But one can start a rich process of observation by focusing on inflection points in the foreign culture: selection of leaders, treatment of upstarts, tolerance of risk and of failure, and appetite for profit.

Exhibit 5.12 summarizes these factors and graphically suggests that the four categories (macroeconomic, microeconomic, institutional, and cultural) jointly complete the mosaic of assessment. A view about the economic future of a country relies on a coherent assessment of all perspectives.

SUMMARY AND IMPLICATIONS FOR THE PRACTITIONER

This chapter has argued that the M&A practitioner should widen his or her frame of reference to embrace the global market. The volume of cross-border M&A is large, and, if present trends of market integration continue, will get larger. Research suggests that *foreign buyers pay more*, creating a natural incentive for target shareholders to entertain offers from across borders. Certainly, the drivers of M&A outlined in this chapter echo the drivers of domestic M&A: Chapter 4 portrayed market turbulence as the primary driver. If anything, the cross-border arena displays more turbulence.

Cross-border M&A activity and its drivers pose some important implications for the practitioner.

- ***Get a view about countries and regions.*** In the turbulent world arena, perhaps the worst stance is to be myopic, naive, and uninformed. This chapter gave a

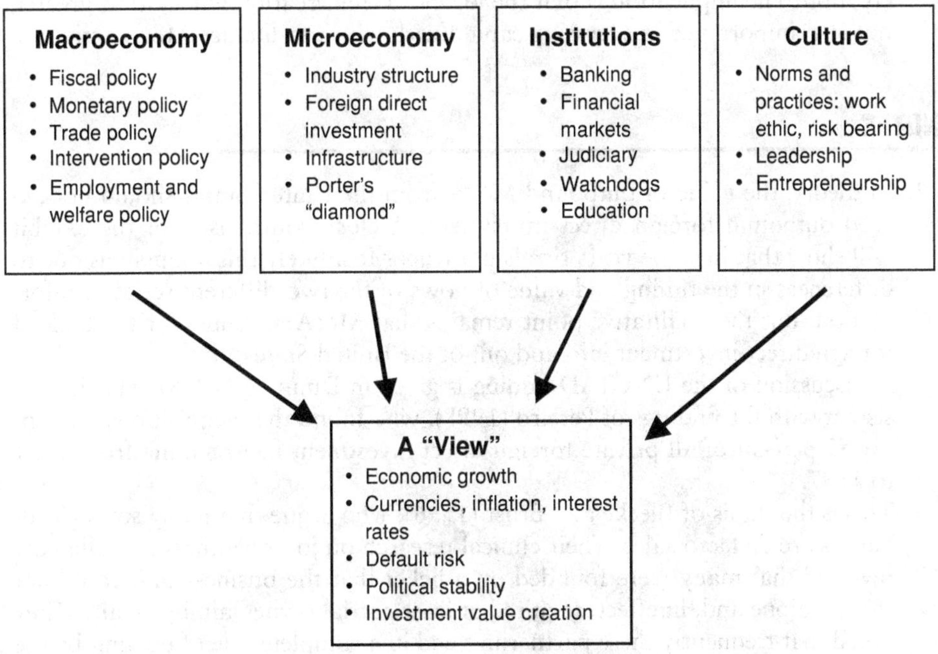

EXHIBIT 5.12 Country Analysis Based on Four Perspectives

rough sketch of four perspectives that can aggregate to a view: macroeconomic, microeconomic, institutional, and cultural. These perspectives are not easily given to a checklist of data to acquire or analysis to do. Country analysis is a process of diagnosis (like medicine) rather than design (like engineering). Skills of investigation and reflection are important foundations for cross-border M&A.

- ***Consider local and global turbulence and how it changes competition across borders.*** Attend to the sources of turbulence and its impacts—insights about these will spring from analysis of countries and regions. But one can also look to the well-known sources (technological innovation, deregulation, trade liberalization, demographic change, and market integration) and study their impacts on countries. Of special interest are "inflection points" or changes in economic or competitive conditions that may generate special investment opportunities. Also consider that turbulence usually has an asymmetric impact across countries—M&A can afford one form of arbitrage across these asymmetries.
- ***Anticipate the reaction of competitors.*** Global market integration will admit new competitors to country arenas. But to the extent that trade blocs may restrict the entry of outsiders into your market, it becomes extremely important to anticipate the competitive actions and reactions of competitors. It is reasonable to assume that competitors within, and outside of, the bloc recognize both the effects of turbulence and the associated asymmetries.
- ***Anticipate the reaction of investors.*** A mental trap of cross-border M&A is business imperialism, the view that your firm must "own" a place in a foreign market simply for its own sake. Under this view, the decision maker is distracted from a fundamental aim of capitalist enterprise, to create value for investors. The rise of sophisticated global financial intermediaries such as banks, mutual funds, and pension funds creates vocal investors who focus on value creation. The implication is that the logic of value creation will assume greater, not less, importance in accessing capital with which to finance M&A activities.

NOTES

1. In theory, the value of outbound M&A from the United States should not exceed outbound foreign direct investment. A close comparison of the exhibit will show that in some years this is not true. Most likely this anomaly is due to differences in the timing and value of flows of the two different series of information. But the qualitative point remains that M&A accounts for the bulk of foreign direct investment into and out of the United States.
2. A discussion of the UNCTAD finding is given in Dunning (1998). This is consistent with the findings of Pereiro (1998), who found that acquisitions account for 52 percent of all private foreign direct investment in Argentina from 1991 to 1997.
3. This is the thesis of Bleeke and Ernst (1996), who argue that many strategic alliances are de facto sales. Their clinical research on joint ventures and alliances revealed that many were founded on a belief that the business unit could not survive alone and, in effect, required at least partial ownership by an ally. They noted that frequently these partnerings end in a complete sale of the unit by the former parent.

4. Conn and Nielsen (1990) found that horizontal and vertical acquisitions represent 60 percent of deals for U.S. acquirers and 70 percent of deals for U.K. acquirers. Eun et al. (1996) found that 75 percent of foreign firms acquiring into the United States were buying into related businesses.
5. Conn and Nielsen (1990) found that 97 percent of U.S. acquirers and 93 percent of U.K. acquirers paid with cash. Ceneboyan et al. (1992) found that foreign buyers into the United States favored cash deals (85 percent), compared to 46 percent for domestic U.S. buyers.
6. Euroland includes 11 countries (Austria, Belgium, Finland, France, Germany, Ireland, Italy, Luxembourg, the Netherlands, Portugal, and Spain), which adopted the euro as a common currency on January 1, 1999. Within the European Community, other agreements commit members to open borders and to the alignment of tax and regulatory policies. The North American Free Trade Agreement (NAFTA) embraces Canada, Mexico, and the United States with reductions in trade barriers and tariffs.
7. Hostile bids contemporaneous with the formation of the EMU included:

   - Olivetti's hostile bid for the leading Italian telecommunications firm, Telecom Italia, the sixth-largest telephone company in the world. Olivetti's financial advisers were Italy's Mediobanca and three American firms: Donaldson, Lufkin & Jenrette; Lehman Brothers; and Chase Bank. Instituto Mobiliare Italiana and three American firms advised Telecom Italia: J. P. Morgan, CS First Boston, and Lazard. Olivetti's bid was denominated in euros and would be financed by the issuance of a "megabond" on the euro capital markets worth $15 billion.
   - Luxury-goods manufacturer LVMH Moet Hennessey Louis Vuitton's "creeping takeover" of Gucci. This contest featured a variety of legal maneuvers and antitakeover defenses.
   - Banque Nationale de Paris' hostile bid for *both* Societe Generale and Paribas, which would create the largest financial institution in the world, with assets of more than $1 trillion. In the outcome, BNP successfully acquired Paribas and a one-third interest in Societe Generale.

   North America witnessed hostile transactions across NAFTA members that might not have been possible before the formation of the trading bloc:

   - In 1999, Grupo Mexico successfully mounted an unsolicited offer for the U.S. copper producer Asarco, snatching the target from the U.S. bidder, Phelps Dodge.
   - American Airlines and Onex, a U.S. private equity investment firm, made an unsolicited offer for Air Canada.

8. See Vernon (1974), Kindleberger (1969), Caves (1971), Buckley and Casson (1976), Magee (1976), and Dunning (1988).
9. See Caves (1971) and Magee (1976).
10. For discussions about global tax arbitrage by corporations, see Lessard (1985), Lessard and Shapiro (1983), and Rutenberg (1985).
11. Harris and Ravenscraft (1991) found that changes in U.S. tax laws are not related to cross-border acquisition returns. Dewenter (1995) found no relationship between U.S. tax regime changes and cross-border M&A activity.

However, Servaes and Zenner (1994) did find significant variation in returns to investors based on changes in tax laws. Manzon, Sharp, and Travlos (1994) found that cross-border acquisition announcement returns are not related to tax differences between the buyer and target country.

12. The recent literature on emerging markets integration lends rich insight into the sources of variability in returns, volatilities, and correlations. See, for instance, Bekaert and Harvey (1995, 1997), Bekaert, Erb, Harvey, and Viskanta (1997), Bekaert, Harvey and Lumsdaine (2002), Wurgler (2000), and Errunza and Miller (2000).
13. Agmon and Lessard (1977) find evidence that MNC betas reflect international involvement well. In contrast, Jacquillat and Solnik (1978) and Senchak and Beedles (1980) conclude that the effect of international diversification on a firm's beta is less than direct, or at least nonlinear.
14. To diversify across global industries is to base portfolio allocations on industry choice *first* and then to pick the most attractive stocks within the industry, irrespective of country.
15. See, for instance, Lessard (1976), Solnik (1976), Solnik and de Freitas (1988), and Grinold, Rudd, and Stefek (1989).
16. Regarding findings about the rising influence of industry in explaining the cross section of global investing returns, see Diermeier and Solnik (2001), Cavaglia, Brightman, and Aked (2000), and Lombard, Roulet, and Solnik (1999). Studies that support the continued dominance of country choice include Heston and Rowenhorst (1994), Rowenhorst (1999), Kritzman and Page (2002), Gerard, Hillion, and de Roon (2002), and Isakov and Sonney (2002).
17. Tobin's Q is measured as the ratio of market value divided by book value.

CHAPTER 6

Strategy and the Uses of M&A to Grow or Restructure the Firm

INTRODUCTION

Strategy influences M&A outcomes. It should be the engine driving M&A search, analysis, deal design, negotiation, integration, and process management; this chapter explores this linkage and describes how M&A fits into the broad spectrum of transactions that can expand or restructure the firm. Lessons include these:

- To be strategic is to plan moves by looking ahead. A firm's strategy is part of the three-legged stool: *mission*, *objectives*, and *strategy*.
- Setting strategy begins with an assessment of the firm's resources and competitive position. The situation of the firm can be summarized in an analysis of its strengths, weaknesses, opportunities, and threats (SWOT). Numerous tools and frameworks help assess the firm's SWOT.
- Three successful strategies are (1) low cost leadership, (2) differentiation, and (3) focus. Many firms try to blend these, to be all things at once—but this can be dangerous. You must choose.
- The firm can grow organically (by internal investment) or inorganically by acquisitions, joint ventures, alliances, and contractual agreements. The right choice of the method of inorganic growth depends on the need for a business relationship, the need to be in control, and the need to manage risk exposure.
- The firm can restructure in a variety of ways to enhance its efficiency and create value. Key alternatives are divestiture, spin-off, carve-out, split-off, tracking stock, and liquidation. The choice of method of restructuring will depend on the relationship of the business to the core operations of the firm, the need for control, and whether the business or asset can operate as an independent entity.
- Whether diversification creates value for shareholders is a matter of sharp controversy. Conventional wisdom and some research hold that strategies of focus are better than strategies of diversification. Recent research raises the possibility that the diversification-versus-focus dichotomy may be false: Instead, the right stance may be to focus on relentless restructuring, through either diversification or focus, in response to changes in the firm's strategic environment. Continue to watch the evolving research on this question.

SETTING STRATEGY

The design of a firm's strategy springs from an understanding of the firm's mission, objectives, SWOT, and market position. This section describes these foundational elements in more detail.

Mission, Objectives, and Strategy

Setting strategy begins with the definition of a *mission* for the enterprise. A mission defines the business focus of the firm and implicitly what the enterprise will *not* do. Mission statements address a range of questions:

- Who are we?
- Whom do we serve?
- What do we do?
- What do we value? How do we measure ourselves?
- Why do we do this? What is our cause?

To draft succinct statements based on questions such as these is very challenging, and will absorb time of the CEO, senior executives, and directors. The best mission statements are short, and therefore easily communicated and repeated at all levels of the organization. Mission statements that are long and complicated sacrifice motive power. Furthermore, great mission statements express *strategic intent*—that is, what the firm aims to do or be. Exhibit 6.1 gives a sample of mission statements for some major U.S. corporations: notice their brevity and expression of intent.

Often accompanying the mission statement is a list of *strategic objectives*—these are overarching goals that flesh out the strategic intent and set the direction of the firm. In effect, they answer the question, "Where are we headed?" These are usually stated in the most general terms and mainly frame the effort for the organization: "To be the quality and cost leader . . ." "To be recognized as the premier service provider . . ." These objectives are expressed in terms of *market position.* "To be a Total Quality organization . . ." "We aim for zero defects." "To achieve a perfect safety record . . ." "To be responsible to our environment and community. . . ." These objectives are aspirations for the *operational management* of the firm. "To create value . . ." "To deliver shareholder returns greater than those of our peer group . . ." "To achieve average growth of 15 percent and shareholder returns of 15 percent for the next five years. . . ." These are examples of *financial objectives*. "To create the premium market franchise. . . ." Ultimately, firms often express the aim to "be the best" or "become the best." Expressions such as these litter the annual reports and press releases of corporations. Taken seriously, they can galvanize the organization into meaningful action.

The abstract tone of a mission statement and the many possible objectives for a firm may confuse rather than clarify aims for the executive. The key corporate objective (the "first among equals") observed in many firms and assumed as the baseline goal in this book is *to create value within ethical norms*. This should serve as the key test of reasonableness for individual proposal and for the priority among competing strategies. Shareholder wealth maximization pursued ethically promotes

EXHIBIT 6.1 Examples of Mission Statements

American Family Insurance Group	"The mission of the American Family Insurance Group is to provide financial protection for qualified individuals, families, and business enterprises. We will do so on a profitable basis in an expanding geographic territory. Our primary business focus will be to deliver personal lines insurance products through an exclusive agency force." (p. 59)
Anheuser-Busch Companies, Inc.	"The mission of Anheuser-Busch is to • Be the world's beer company • Enrich and entertain a global audience • Deliver superior returns to our shareholders." (p. 71)
Autodesk, Inc.	"To create quality software solutions and support services that foster innovation, creativity, and productivity for customers and partners around the world." (p. 78)
Blockbuster Inc.	"To be a global leader in rentable home entertainment by providing outstanding service, selection, convenience, and value." (p. 99)
Coca-Cola	"We exist to create value for our share owners on a long-term basis. We refresh the world. We do this by developing superior beverage products that create value for our Company, our bottling partners and our customers." (p. 132)
ConAgra	"Our mission is to increase stockholders' wealth. Our job is to feed people better." (p. 139)
Duke Power Company	"We produce and supply electricity, provide related products and services and pursue opportunities that complement our business. We will continually improve our products and services to better meet our customers' needs and expectations, helping our customers, employees, owners, and communities to prosper." (p. 169)
Hershey Foods Corporation	"Our mission is to be a focused food company in North America and selected international markets and a leader in every aspect of our business." (p. 226)
Merck & Co., Inc.	"The Mission of Merck is to provide society with superior products and services—innovations and solutions that improve the quality of life and satisfy customer needs—to provide employees with meaningful work and advancement opportunities and investors with a superior rate of return." (p. 300)
Pioneer Hi-Bred International, Inc.	"Our mission is to provide products and services which increase the efficiency and profitability of the world's farmers. Our core business is the broad application of the science of genetics. We will ensure the growth of our core business and develop new opportunities which enhance the core business." (p. 349)
Charles Schwab Corporation	"Our mission as a company is to serve the needs of investors. We have all kinds of customers. . . . We will focus our resources on the financial services that best meet our customers' needs, whether they are transactional, informational, custodial services, or something new." (p. 381)

Source: These examples (and page numbers) are drawn from Abrams (1999), a useful resource for developers and critics of mission statements.

the survival and prosperity of the firm. As Chapter 26 discusses, directors of a firm are obliged to make decisions in the shareholders' best interests.

The *strategy* is a plan for fulfilling the mission and achieving the strategic objectives. To be *strategic* is to behave like a chess player, looking several moves ahead and assessing the possible countermoves of the opponent to determine the next move. The opposite of "strategic" is *myopic*, looking ahead only one move at a time. Strategic chess players beat myopic players. The *Oxford English Dictionary* defines strategy as "a plan for successful action based on the rationality and interdependence of the moves of the opposing participants."[1] Major corporations typically prepare detailed strategy documents each year for each business unit. These begin with an assessment of the external environment and the internal condition of the unit; this results in an inventory of the strengths, weaknesses, opportunities, and threats for the unit. Then the document outlines actions to be taken in the next year (and possibly also over a longer time horizon) to address weaknesses and threats, and exploit strengths and opportunities. Specific attention is given to sources of growth, whether *organic* (i.e., by internal investment) or *inorganic* (i.e., externally, using acquisitions, joint ventures, alliances, etc.). The plan might also address restructuring steps (e.g., divestitures, spin-offs, plant closings, etc.). Usually the plan culminates in a financial forecast for the next year that becomes the benchmark against which the performance of managers is evaluated. A corporate strategy is the aggregation of strategies for the various business units. Properly developed, strategy follows mission and objectives.

Planning Strategy Starts with SWOT

Firms approach the planning process in a variety of ways. For instance, a bottom-up approach drives the development of business unit strategy beginning with the front-line managers of the unit: The strategy is reviewed by senior management who critique and approve the unit strategy. A top-down approach uses a central staff to cast the corporate mission and objectives into strategies, which are then imposed on the business units; this is sometimes called a "command-and-control" approach to setting strategy. The process chosen usually reflects the complexity of the firm, its culture and history, and the relative talents of operating managers. Current conventional wisdom probably favors a bottom-up approach in the belief that people closest to the front line see the strategic field most clearly. Jack Welch, the former CEO of General Electric, was a leading proponent of the bottom-up approach to strategic planning.

The strategic planning process begins with an assessment of the business unit. This focuses both inward on the condition and resources of the unit, and outward on the shape of its environment and the unit's position in the competitive field.

RESOURCES These may entail physical and financial assets, as well as talent and intellectual capital. Resources are like raw material; what matters is how the firm integrates resources to reach its objectives. *Capabilities* integrate resources to reach an objective. For instance, to produce custom-designed furniture, a firm must integrate across marketing, design, purchasing, manufacturing, and finance. *Core competencies* are strategic capabilities: those skills and activities that translate resources into special advantage for the firm. Home Depot, for instance, has a strategic capability in site location and store openings—design, construction, staffing, training, and marketing had to be coordinated to support the firm's strategic goal of 25 percent annual increase in store space *profitably*. Core competencies that are difficult for competitors to imitate create *sustainable competitive advantage* and are key drivers of superior investment returns. Examples of core competencies are Wal-Mart's logistics and inventory management, Honda's ability in new product innovation, Sony's skills at miniaturization, and Pixar's skills at computer-based animation. The competitive advantage that these core competencies create is generated from resources within the firm and does not rely on external resources; this *competitive advantage* is sustainable when current and potential competitors cannot or will not attempt to duplicate it.

COMPETITIVE POSITION Strength of position is also correlated with investment returns: the stronger the position, the higher the returns. For instance, a monopolist can extract higher returns than can a marginal player in a highly competitive industry. It is not only one's own share of market that matters, but also the distribution of shares among other players. In the abstract, a stronger *competitive position* should result in higher returns to investors. This is what Shoeffler, Buzzell, and Heaney (1974) found in their analysis of returns on investment by market position. Exhibit 6.2 gives their results: Return on investment rises with market share.

The relationship between a stronger market position and returns to investors has been the focus of considerable research. Shapiro (1999) summarized the sources of economic value as *barriers to entry*, *economies of scale*, *product differentiation*, access to special *distribution channels*, and advantageous government policy. He argues that "the essence of corporate strategy [is] creating and then taking advantage of imperfections in product and factor markets. . . . More important, a good understanding of corporate strategy should help uncover new and potentially profitable projects." (Pages 105, 106)

The aim of strategic assessment is to draw a profile of the strengths, weaknesses, opportunities, and threats of the business. Exhibit 6.3 presents a SWOT table such as confronted Chrysler Corporation and Daimler-Benz A.G. as they began merger negotiations in early 1998—this shows important areas of strategic fit of the two firms. Notice especially the complementary positions in products (luxury sedans versus SUVs, minivans, pickup trucks), cost leadership versus quality leadership, financial strength, and market presence. *SWOT analysis* is invaluable for preparing negotiators, deal designers, due diligence researchers, and integration planners.

EXHIBIT 6.2 Relationship between Market Share and Return on Investment

Market Share	Return on Investment
Over 36%	30.2%
22–36%	17.9%
14–22%	13.5%
7–14%	12.0%
0–7%	9.6%

Source of data: Schoeffler, Buzzell, and Heany (1974), page 141.

EXHIBIT 6.3 SWOT Analysis of Chrysler and Daimler-Benz Just before the Announcement of Their Merger in 1998

	Daimler-Benz A.G.	Chrysler Corporation
Strengths	Dominates "quality" niche; protected from trough of auto cycle. Strong international brand. New plant in Brazil, hot market. Strong new products: SLK, M-class, A-class, Smart Car. High share price; good acquisition currency. Good access to capital: Deutsche Bank is key stakeholder.	Strength in specific product segments such as minivans, trucks, SUVs. Manufacturing advantages: short product cycle; low supplier cost. Good position for Jeep worldwide and for Chrysler in Latin America. Cash and unused debt capacity. Engineering culture.
Weaknesses	High labor costs. High labor content: 60–80 hours/car (vs. 20 for Lexus). Declining unit volume in big luxury cars. Labor union on supervisory board may limit flexibility to change work practices. Losing large tax shields from operating loss carryforwards.	As third-largest North American player, very sensitive to economic cycle. Chronic financial weakness; near-demise in 1980. Products: not as much attention to detail and image. The least vertically integrated big manufacturer. Possibly undervalued in stock market.
Opportunities	Implement a shareholder value orientation (the so-called "Anglo-Saxon" perspective). Enter faster-growth product segments (e.g., SUVs) and geographic markets (e.g., Asia, Latin America). Distinguish the brand through distinct model platforms. Manufacture outside of Germany. Exploit synergies of $1.4–$3 billion.	"Long-term upside with no negative impact." A deal that is good for shareholders. Enter faster-growth product segments (e.g., SUVs) and geographic markets (e.g., Asia, Latin America). Get out from under the shadow of Ford and GM. Manufacture outside of United States. Exploit synergies of $1.4–$3 billion.
Threats	Industry overcapacity. Saturation of European market. Entry of other firms into key segments such as luxury sedans. European/North American trade war.	Industry overcapacity. Saturation of North American market. Entry of other firms into key segments such as minivans, SUVs, pickup trucks. Next recession.

Assessing Competitive Position

Determining the firm's position in its competitive environment and its internal resources and capabilities is the foundation for setting strategy. This assessment aims to profile the industry, and the firm's position in it, along several dimensions:

- Structure of the industry and intensity of rivalry.
- Sources of change and turbulence that may trigger a shift in industry structure. Chapter 4 highlights a number of the classic forces of change.
- Dimensions of relative strength and weakness among players in the industry.
- Propensity of individual players to take action, exploit change forces, and alter the industry structure.
- Drivers of competitive strength and weakness in the industry.
- Outlook for profitability of investment in the industry.

To prepare the executive for strategic planning, a number of analytic tools are worth noting because of their practical popularity and usefulness. As Exhibit 6.4 illustrates, none of these tools dictate strategy. But they lend insights useful in the effort to inventory the firm's SWOTs. This is the foundation for *strategic planning.*

GROWTH-SHARE MATRIX: WHO HAS AN ATTRACTIVE POSITION? This first tool seeks to identify the relative positions of firms in an industry or divisions within a firm along three dimensions: size, growth, and relative share of market. This was popularized by Boston Consulting Group (BCG) in the 1970s and is used to indicate positions of weakness and strength. The choice of the three criteria for comparison reveals an underlying view about competitive advantage: some economic research supports the view that large absolute size and large market share are associated with competitive power and higher returns. Relative market share is measured as the ratio of your own share of market to that of your largest competitor. Growth should be measured in real, not nominal, terms. High real growth and pricing power derived from strong competition position are important drivers of value creation. A stalemate where competitors grow rapidly but slug it out with heavy investment while failing to obtain the profits envisioned with growth can destroy value. In the parlance of BCG, this leads to four broad categories of positions, as sketched in Exhibit 6.5, and available to the reader on the CD-ROM in the spreadsheet model "Growth Share.xls."

1. A "*cash cow*" (lower left quadrant) is a business with high market share and low growth, and hence low ongoing investment to sustain the business; firms in this segment are net providers of cash. Within multibusiness firms, cash cows are often milked to support growth of other divisions.
2. A "*star*" (upper left quadrant) is a firm with high market share and high growth: It generates plenty of cash for its ongoing expansion. And because of its strong market position, the continued investment to grow that business is attractive.
3. A "*dog*" (lower right quadrant) is a business with low growth and low market share. This business has low competitive power in the marketplace and has low prospects for growing into a more attractive position. Unless the position is changed, a business in this quadrant will be a sump for cash.

EXHIBIT 6.4 Overview of Tools for Strategic Analysis

What It Is	How to Use It	Pros and Cons
Growth-share matrix Illustrates the relative competitive position of firms or divisions on three dimensions: growth rate, relative share of market, and size.	Load data into "Growth Share.xls" on the CD-ROM and interpret the resulting figure. • Cash cow generates cash with which to sustain other businesses. • Star generates cash and grows rapidly. A keeper. • Dog uses cash and grows slowly. Earmark for serious improvement or sale. • Problem child. Grows rapidly but has a disadvantageous market share. Earmark for improvement but watch closely.	+ A helpful graphic depiction of business units or competitors. + Highlights the different kinds of attention the various units might warrant. – Focused on market position, not directly on shareholder value. – Makes no clear action recommendation about the four categories—ultimately this remains a matter of judgment.
Porter model A diagram illustrating how the structure of competition in an industry drives conduct and outcomes.	Use the model as a general guide in assessing a firm's competitive position: 1. What are the barriers to entry? 2. What power do customers have? 3. What power do suppliers have? 4. Do substitutes affect pricing? 5. What are the patterns of competitive conduct in the industry?	+ A useful guide and discipline for industry and competitor analysis. + Adds the idea that *power* from barriers or outside players affects outcomes. – Focused on market position and only indirectly on shareholder value. – Prescriptions are a matter of judgment.
Learning curve A graph that depicts the decline in costs as cumulative volume grows.	Load the data into "Learning Curve.xls" on the CD-ROM and interpret the resulting figure. The curve lends a prediction for the future path of production costs for your firm and competitors. Think critically about what might cause the curve to change slope or kink.	+ A foundation for setting goals for internal transformation and cost management. – The curve smooths over the results of many observations. Inspect the specific points and inquire into sources of deviation from the curve.
Strategic map A generic figure for comparing the relative positions of competitors on three dimensions.	Load the data into "Strategic Map.xls" and interpret the resulting figure. Of particular interest will be the appearance of groups or "strategic clusters" as well as areas of the map that are unoccupied by any competitors.	+ A useful illustration of the relative positions of competitors. – Not guided by any theory that specifies which criteria matter.

(Continued)

EXHIBIT 6.4 *(Continued)*

What It Is	How to Use It	Pros and Cons
Strategic canvas A generic figure for comparing the strategies of competitors on a number of dimensions.	Load the data into "Strategic Canvas.xls" and interpret the resulting figure. Of particular interest are points of similarity and difference.	+ A useful illustration of the relative positions of competitors. – Not guided by any theory that specifies which criteria matter.
Attractiveness-strength matrix A grid for comparing business units of a diversified firm on the basis of industry attractiveness and the competitive strength of the unit within that industry.	Select a range of criteria for scoring industries for their attractiveness and business units for their competitive strength. Score the units and their industries. Position the unit in the nine-cell matrix. Interpret the resulting table.	+ A useful illustration of the relative positions of competitors. – Not guided by any theory that specifies which criteria matter.
Self-sustainable growth rate A formula for determining the rate at which the firm can grow its assets without issuing new equity or altering its capital structure.	Insert values into the formulas outlined in Appendix 6.1 and interpret the resulting estimates of self-sustainable growth rate (SSGR). Compare the SSGR to growth rates of competitors, industry, or internal goals as a test of feasibility of strategy.	+ An easy test of strategic feasibility and source of critical thinking about financial sustainability. – Not directly focused on value creation.

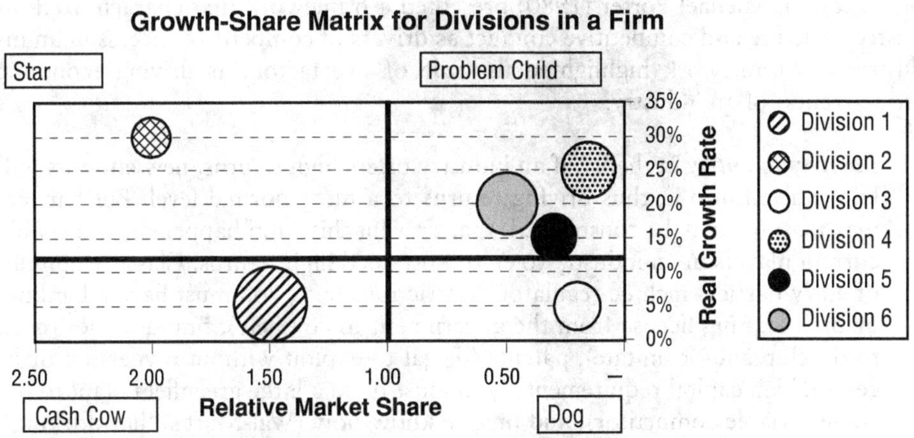

EXHIBIT 6.5 Illustration of Growth-Share Matrix

Note: The crosshairs separating the categories are to be placed as a matter of judgment by the analyst—the convention is to place the vertical line between 0.75 and 1.00, and the horizontal line at the average growth rate for the industry. Relative share of market is measured as the ratio of your share of market to that of your largest competitor. The rate of growth should be real (i.e., net of inflation) rather than nominal.

Source: Author's analysis.

4. A "*problem child*" or "question mark" (upper right quadrant) has a high growth rate and low market share—this business demands high rates of investment to grow the business but does not command the position in the market that might justify the investment.

A chart such as this can be used to depict the position of the units within a corporation for the purpose of assisting resource allocation decisions, as well as of competitors within an industry.[2] Also, one could prepare this chart based on current conditions and again based on expected performance over the next two- to five-year horizon—this before-and-after presentation would give a sense of competitive dynamics within the industry. The advantages of this chart are its strong graphic presentation and its appeal to marketers and strategists. On the other hand, the growth-share matrix relies heavily on historical data (rather than forecast data) and says nothing about the capabilities necessary for success in the various businesses. The model implies that market power matters most and that market power is driven by size, share of market, and growth. Yet theories of valuation and value creation indicate a broader set of drivers than market power alone. Stewart and Glassman (1999) criticized the growth-share matrix, writing, "A company's cash cows were supposed to fund the growth of promising businesses ('question marks') into highly performing 'stars.' By making a company self-funding and self-perpetuating, the BCG approach appealed to corporate managers because it circumvented the monitoring processes of the capital markets. In reality, the poorly performing "dogs" ate the cash while the "question marks" were either starved, overmanaged, or were acquired for obscene premiums." (Page 628)

DRIVERS OF INDUSTRY ATTRACTIVENESS (PORTER MODEL): HOW ATTRACTIVE WILL THIS INDUSTRY BE? Drawing on research in the subfield of economics, called industrial organization, Michael Porter (1980) presented a framework that characterized industry structure and competitive conduct as drivers of competitive success in an industry. His framework highlighted the role of five factors as driving economic attractiveness of an industry:

1. ***Barriers to entry.*** In theory, if an industry offers high returns, new entrants will be attracted into it, thus driving returns to a more normal level. But barriers may exist (or may be constructed) that prevent this from happening and enable current players in an industry to enjoy sustained high returns. Classic examples of entry barriers include regulatory restrictions (e.g., you must have a banking or broadcasting license from the government to compete), brand names (hard to develop and/or imitate), patents (illegal to exploit without ownership or license), high capital requirements (you must build a large greenfield plant to become a viable competitor), and unique know-how (Wal-Mart's "hot docking" technique of logistics management). Porter highlighted the role of accumulated experience as a potential barrier—this *learning curve* effect is illustrated in Exhibit 6.6 and consists in reducing one's cost of production as know-how accumulates. The effect of learning is apparent, for instance, in the substantial decline in the price of semiconductors over time: Unit costs decline by about 20 percent with each doubling of accumulated production. The learning curve gives a competitive advantage to the first or early mover. This benefit can be

achieved in either of two ways. First, one can accumulate experience faster than one's competitors can (e.g., through higher volume production or more rapid product changes) and thus get farther down the common learning curve faster. Second, one can try to steepen the slope of learning through larger leaps in internal development or the acquisition of know-how from outside the firm. Exhibit 6.6 shows the dramatic effects on unit cost of differing rates of cost reduction. Abernathy and Wayne (1974) discuss the impact of experience in various industries.

2. ***Customer power.*** Powerful customers can strongly influence prices and product quality in an industry. Examples are Wal-Mart and Federated Department Stores for consumer goods, and the U.S. government for the U.S. defense industry. Weak customers, on the other hand, are likely to be mere price-takers—examples would be consumers of filmed entertainment, cigarettes, and education. In those industries, the suppliers have been able to sustain prices increases well ahead of the rate of inflation.

	10% Cost Reduction	20% Cost Reduction	30% Cost Reduction
Slope	0.1	0.2	0.3
Base Cost	$100.00	$100.00	$100.00
Cumulative Unit Production			
0	$100.00	$100.00	$100.00
10	$ 90.00	$ 80.00	$ 70.00
20	$ 81.00	$ 64.00	$ 49.00
40	$ 72.90	$ 51.20	$ 34.30
80	$ 65.61	$ 40.96	$ 24.01
160	$ 59.05	$ 32.77	$ 16.81
320	$ 53.14	$ 26.21	$ 11.76

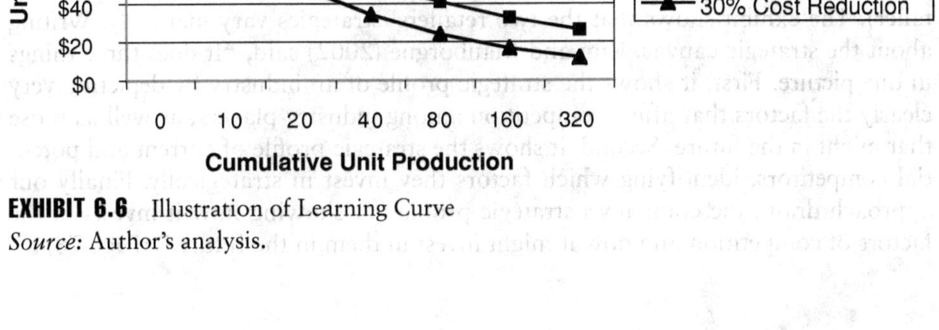

EXHIBIT 6.6 Illustration of Learning Curve
Source: Author's analysis.

3. ***Supplier power.*** Similarly, powerful suppliers (e.g., monopolists) can extract high prices from firms in an industry. Weak suppliers can be a source of positive value to an industry—through most of the 1990s, the U.S. auto industry extracted material price reductions and quality improvements from its suppliers.
4. ***Threat of substitutes.*** Substitutes limit the pricing power of competitors in an industry. For instance, the price of coal quoted to electric power generators is influenced by the prices of Btu (British thermal unit) substitutes such as oil and natural gas.
5. ***Rivalry conduct.*** This final force captures the effects of dynamic competition among players in an industry. Investment in new product or process innovation, opening new channels of distribution, and entry into new geographic markets can alter the balance of competitive advantage. Cartel agreements (banned under the antitrust regulations in most countries) create industries with few adverse surprises for its players. At the other extreme, predatory pricing aimed at driving peers out of business can produce sharp variations in profitability. Porter noted that rivalry may be sharper where the players are similar in size, the barriers to exit from an industry are high, fixed costs are high, growth is slow, and products or services are not differentiated.

STRATEGIC MAP AND STRATEGIC CANVAS: HOW DOES OUR STRATEGY COMPARE WITH OTHERS?

Assessing the industry and comparing the market shares of the players tells little about how they got there, and where they might be headed next. It is necessary to profile the strategies of competitors as a foundation for developing a strategy for your own business. Two tools are particularly useful here:

The first is a *strategic map* that, like a growth-share matrix, positions the players in an industry on the basis of size and two other dimensions that are strategically meaningful. Exhibit 6.7 gives an example of competing brands of sporty cars in the U.S. market, mapped on the basis of size, price/quality/image, and geographic market coverage. A map such as this helps to reveal niches of competition or *strategic groups* of competitors, as well as gaps in the competitive field where a firm might find unserved demand and/or a relatively safer haven from competition. In the example one observes two clusters: (1) high price/quality/image with small size and restricted geographic base and (2) medium price/quality/image with larger size and geographic base. Porter (1980) discusses the import of strategic group analysis at more length.

The second tool is a *strategic canvas* that illustrates in graphic form the similarity or difference among competitors' strategies. Exhibit 6.8 gives an example of a strategic canvas for two retailers, Brooks Brothers (a high-end primarily men's apparel retailer) and the Big & Tall Men's Shop (a mass-market men's apparel retailer). The exhibit shows that the two retailers' strategies vary markedly. Writing about the strategic canvas, Kim and Mauborgne (2002) said, "It does three things in one picture. First, it shows the strategic profile of an industry by depicting very clearly the factors that affect competition among industry players, as well as those that might in the future. Second, it shows the strategic profile of current and potential competitors, identifying which factors they invest in strategically. Finally our approach draws the company's strategic profile . . . showing how it invests in the factors of competition and how it might invest in them in the future." (Page 78)

	Price/ Quality/ Image (Max = 100)	Geographic Market Coverage (Max = 100)	Relative Size (Max = 100)
GM Corvette	75	100	100
Ford Thunderbird	40	95	95
Chrysler Prowler	50	85	80
BMW Z4	98	50	20
Porsche Boxster	100	30	5
Mazda Miata	60	70	30

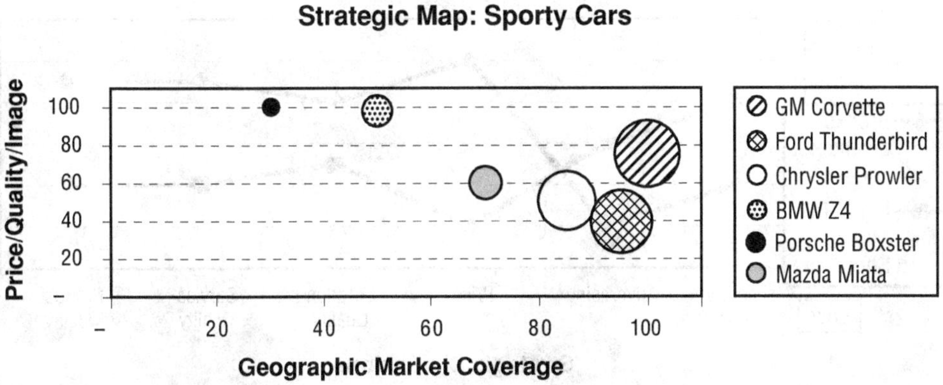

EXHIBIT 6.7 Illustration of Strategic Map
Source: Qualitative assessment based on author's analysis.

Excel templates for the strategic map and strategic canvas are given in two programs on the CD-ROM, "Strategic Map.xls," and "Strategic Canvas.xls."

ATTRACTIVENESS-STRENGTH MATRIX: HOW DO RETURNS VARY WITH INDUSTRY POSITION AND INDUSTRY ATTRACTIVENESS? General Electric sought to combine an assessment of the attractiveness of an industry (i.e., the ability of the industry to generate attractive investment returns) and the attractiveness of the *position* within the industry, drawing on the research that showed a direct correlation between market share and returns. Industry attractiveness would be assessed through a Porter-style analysis of growth and prospective returns based on structure and conduct of the industry, and the drivers of change. The firm's position would be assessed through measures such as market share and costs to produce, and qualitative assessments of resources, capabilities, and core competencies. The firm's business units and their industries are typically scored by means of a weighted average of ratings on various dimensions. These scores are used to place the various units in the nine-cell grid shown in Exhibit 6.9. The cells located toward the upper-left corner of the grid will be more attractive business/industry combinations—the grid implies that these should merit priority treatment for investment. Similarly, the lower right cells are

Strategic Criteria for Comparison	Brooks Brothers	Big & Tall Men's Shop
Product quality	4.5	2.0
Service quality	4.5	2.0
Location quality	4.0	2.5
Price	5.0	1.0
Advertising	1.0	3.0
Inventory turns	2.0	4.0

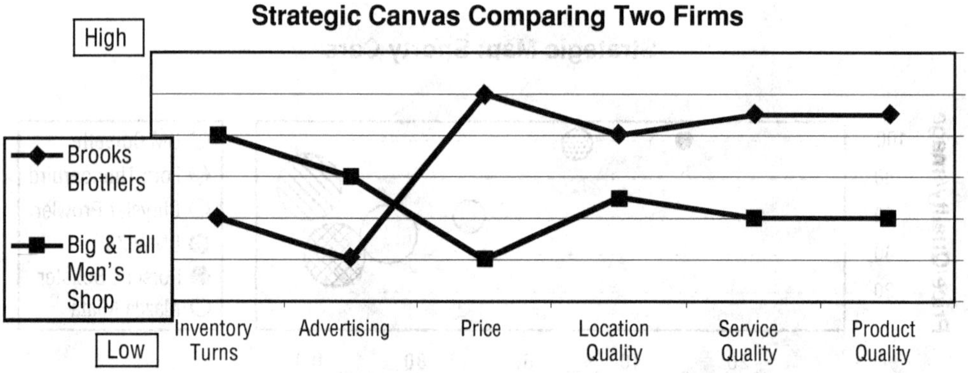

EXHIBIT 6.8 Illustration of Strategic Canvas
Source: Qualitative assessment based on author's analysis.

EXHIBIT 6.9 Illustration of Attractiveness-Strength Matrix

Industry Attractiveness	Competitive Position of the Unit: Strong	Average	Weak
High	Most attractive: Invest and build.		Question mark: Assess unit's profitability and prospects for improving position.
Medium		Moderate: restructure to improve.	
Low	Question mark: Analyze long-term profitability and prospects for endgame		Least attractive: Restructure or exit.

least attractive and would be candidates for divestment or at least a highly skeptical investment stance. Compared to the *BCG growth-share matrix*, this matrix admits a wider range of criteria on which to judge the attractiveness of a business and its industry. But the scoring system for producing the ratings for business and industry attractiveness is arbitrary and may not be linked to financial returns in an obvious way. This exposes the analyst and audience to possible abuses.

The resources of the firm will dictate the rate at which it can grow organically—this is the *self-sustainable growth rate (SSGR)* and is a test of fit between the firm's current capabilities and its aspirations. In its simplest form, SSGR is determined by the firm's return on equity (ROE) and dividend payout (DPO) ratio as follows:

$$g^{\text{Self-sustainable}}_{\text{book value assets}} = \text{ROE} \cdot (1 - \text{DPO})$$

This indicates that the maximum internally sustainable rate of asset growth will be a direct result of the firm's profitability (ROE) and retention rate—(1 − DPO) or one less the percentage of earnings paid out in dividends. This rate can be compared to projected asset growth rates for the firm, its competitors, and its industry as a test of financial feasibility. Appendix 6.1 discusses various models of the self-sustainable growth rate and illustrates their application.

Business Definitions Are Key

All of the analytic tools described in this chapter are judgment-intensive. They depend on proper definition of the business and the product being analyzed.

DEFINING THE BUSINESS The industry position of a multibusiness or multiproduct firm, such as General Motors (GM), is less useful to analyze in the aggregate than are the positions of its individual products or business units. GM has relatively stronger and weaker segments. To aggregate them into a single assessment for GM yields none of the richness of the strategy problem GM faces. Salter and Weinhold (1979, page 268) argue that the level at which to define the unit of analysis is typically driven by strategic considerations (are there well-defined strategic sectors?), resources (are there special capabilities, patents, know-how, etc. that would justify defining a business in a certain way?), and organizational factors (how does the organization chart define business units, divisions, and sectors?).

DEFINING THE PEER GROUP For instance, consider the example of the sporty cars segment (given in the strategic map of Exhibit 6.7). Is the relevant industry for the Porsche Boxster actually automobiles in general, or should it be two-seat European roadsters? Or transportation? Peers are those products or services that are reasonable substitutes in the customer's mind. For instance, most brands of ketchup are peers in narrow definition—but considered in terms of competition in "sauces," brands of ketchup, salsa, steak sauce, and gravy might be peers. One can aim to identify peer groups through competitive analysis, the use of focus groups, or the U.S. government's "SIC"[3] code. As discussed elsewhere in this book, the selection of a peer group for comparison will have a huge impact on the insights to be derived.

Classic Successful Strategies

To illustrate the importance of positioning, Porter (1985) described three classic strategies that seemed to yield special competitive advantage:

1. *Low-cost leadership.* This seeks to create a sustainable cost advantage over competitors and is often seen in industries where the product or service is a commodity. The attainment of this leadership position permeates the firm and is achieved through focusing on cost containment, strict asset management, an annual budgeting process characterized by great scrutiny, tough negotiation of union and raw materials agreements, and low-overhead central office operations. The advantage of this strategy is that the low-cost leader can't be undersold: This company will always win in a price war. A disadvantage of this strategy is that cost-minimization often requires a commitment to a particular product or process technology; such a commitment sacrifices flexibility. With technological innovation by competitors, this commitment can quickly turn from an advantage to a disadvantage.
2. *Differentiation.* This seeks to create a sustainable competitive advantage through distinguishing the firm or its products sufficiently to command a higher price and/or a strong customer franchise. It is seen in industries where customer demand is diverse and therefore unable to be satisfied with a commodity product. In pursuing this strategy, one must ask whether the pricing power achieved through differentiation is sufficient to compensate for the investment necessary to achieve it. Differentiation succeeds to the extent that it is hard to imitate and that it generates superior investment returns. Firms pursuing a differentiation strategy will focus on innovation, techniques of market segmentation, brand management, product quality, customer service, and warranties.
3. *Focus or specialization.* The focuser creates a competitive advantage by finding and dominating a market niche—there, the advantage springs from cost leadership or differentiation. This will be attractive where one can identify a niche of sufficient size to permit profitable and growing operations and where the firm has capabilities sufficient to serve demand. The disadvantage of a focus strategy is that the firm has all its eggs in one basket: Should the niche be successfully penetrated by a competitor, there will be no other market positions with which to mitigate the consequences.

In addition to defining these classic success strategies, Porter's analysis raises an equally important point: Don't get stuck in the middle. He argues that it is very difficult to establish a sustainable competitive advantage through hybrids of these approaches. By trying to be all things to all people, hybrids may become nothing to anyone. Skeptics of this point to Wal-Mart and Toyota, firms that successfully pursue cost leadership and the differentiation of products or services. Still, the difficulty of finding successful hybrids may justify them as the exception, rather than the rule.

EXPANSION BY INORGANIC GROWTH

M&A transactions should flow from the business strategy for the firm. Yet mergers and acquisitions are only part of the range of possible transactions a firm might contemplate in seeking to implement its strategy. Exhibit 6.10 charts the variety of tactics and shows that they extend from transactions that grow or *diversify* the firm to transactions that restructure or *focus* the firm.

In contemplating expansion of the business, executives first must decide upon the classic "make versus buy" decision: Should growth be *organic* (i.e., through internal investment) or *inorganic* (i.e., by investing or structuring an affiliation outside the firm)? A decision about make versus buy will typically follow from a strategic analysis and estimation of the prospective returns on investment from the alternatives.

Motives for Inorganic Growth

Strategists and scholars point to five main reasons why firms pursue *inorganic growth*:

1. Maturing product line.
2. Regulatory or antitrust limits.
3. Value creation through horizontal and vertical integration.
4. Acquisition of resources and capabilities.
5. Value creation through diversification.

GROWTH IN THE CONTEXT OF A MATURING PRODUCT LINE Many businesses experience a life cycle of growth, as depicted in Part A of Exhibit 6.11. The explosive growth rates of the start-up phase of the business are eventually replaced by more sedentary growth. This is to be expected: High growth tends to attract imitators, who may sap the growth of the leader. Also, all the forces of turbulence (see Chapter 4) such as technological innovation, demographic change, deregulation, and globalization render products (and industries) obsolete. This degradation of the business

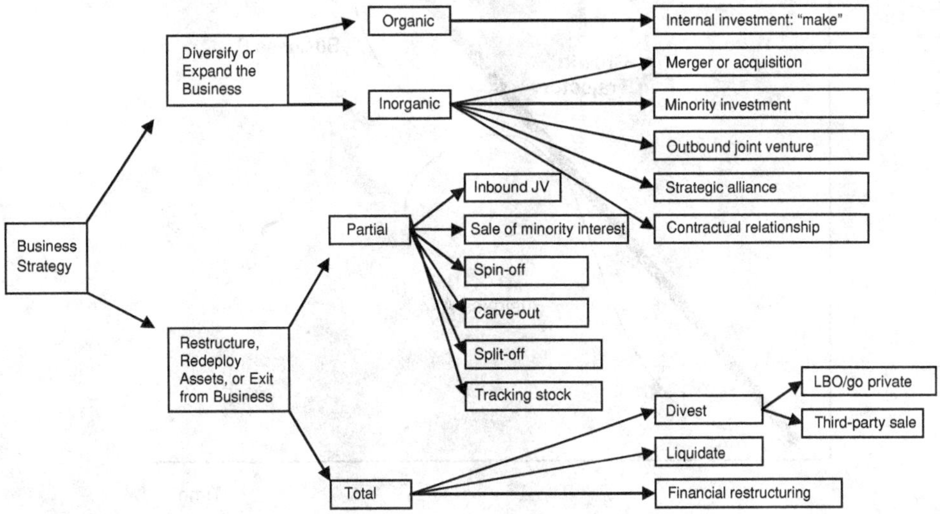

EXHIBIT 6.10 Range of Transactions in a Decision Framework

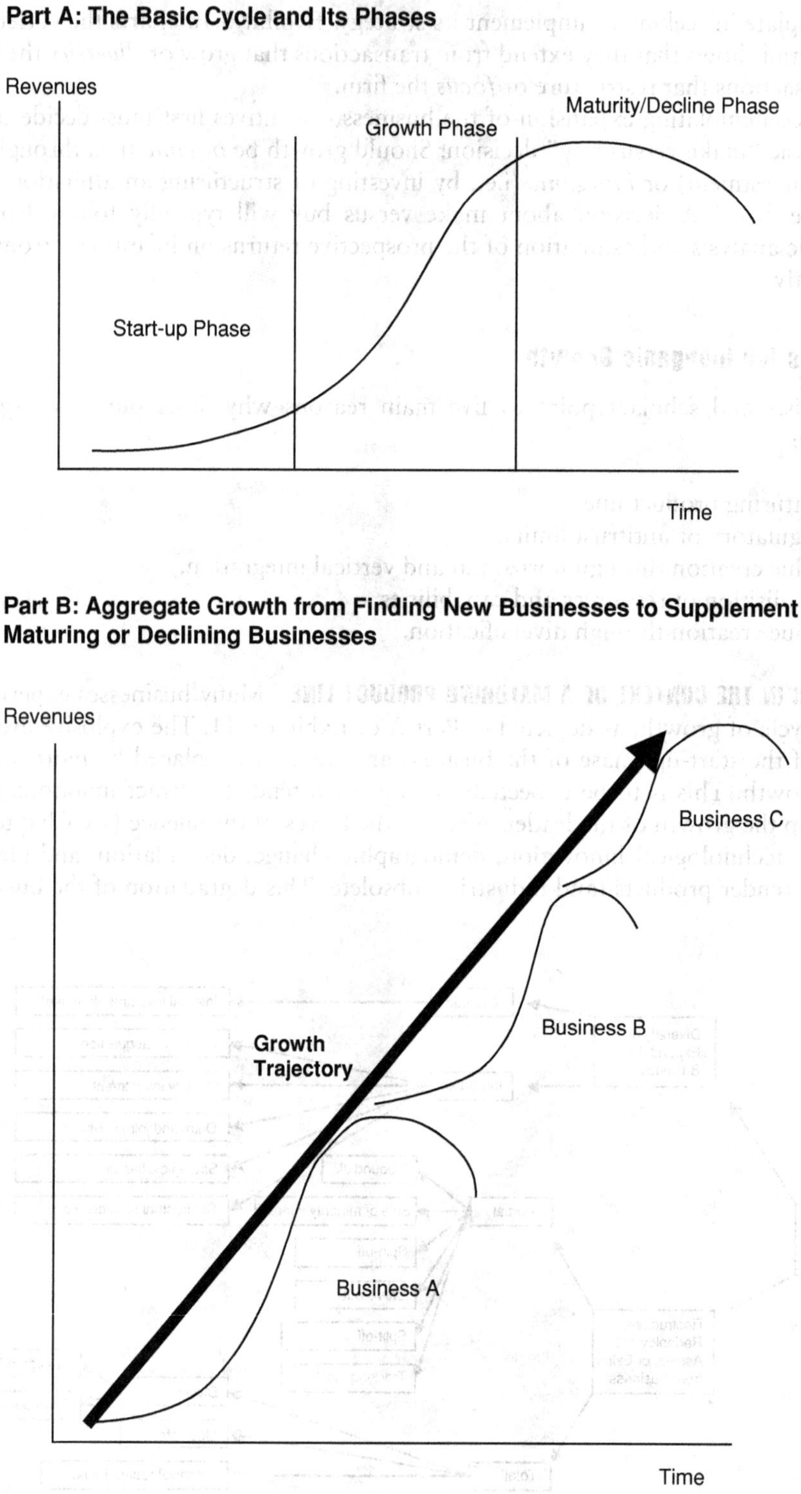

EXHIBIT 6.11 Life Cycle of the Firm

in its maturity years can produce headaches for CEOs. A common response is to acquire new businesses, still early in their life cycles, to create a total growth trajectory. This strategy of buying growth to sustain a growth curve is illustrated in Part B of Exhibit 6.11. The executive must retain two criticisms about this motive:

1. ***May harm shareholder value.*** This product life cycle perspective can create a frenzy for added revenue or earnings that ignores costs, investments, risks, and the time value of money. It is possible to achieve higher revenue growth and at the same time destroy shareholder value. See Chapters 9 and 17 for more about this.
2. ***Is it sustainable?*** In the limit, a trajectory of a high real growth rate (i.e., relative to the real growth rate of the economy) is bounded by the size of the economy. Growing at an excessive rate for a sufficiently long period of time, the firm will eventually own the entire economy.

GROWTH TO CIRCUMVENT REGULATORY OR ANTITRUST LIMITS Simply reinvesting in the core business may not be feasible if the firm operates under regulatory constraints. For instance, at various times broadcasters and banks have been limited in the scope of their operations. Inorganic growth through diversifying acquisition permits the maintenance of a growth trend. But like the previous point, one must critically assess the sustainability of growth and the impact on shareholder value of this kind of circumvention. The thoughtful CEO must relentlessly ask, "Is the shareholder better off if we return the cash through a dividend, and stop this growth program?"

VALUE CREATION THROUGH HORIZONTAL OR VERTICAL INTEGRATION Improving economic efficiency may be served by integration of the firm with peers, or with suppliers and customers. Chapter 4 described the first two large waves of M&A activity in the United States as waves of integration.

1. *Horizontal integration* entails combination with peer firms in an industry. This may exploit *economies of scale*, which will reduce costs, and *market power*, which may result in increased prices. Antitrust regulation seeks to forestall *monopoly power* in horizontal combinations (see Chapter 28).
2. *Vertical integration* combines firms along the value chain. For instance, a steel manufacturer might acquire upstream operations (such as iron ore mines) and downstream operations (such as fabricators of steel products). Harrigan (1985) noted that vertical integration can create value if it improves economic efficiency by cutting out intermediaries and reducing overhead expense and redundant assets. Improved coordination through inventory and purchasing business processes may create further efficiencies. And strategically it may guarantee a source of supply in a tight market, preempting competitors and preventing being locked out. But vertical integration also has potential disadvantages: Locking in suppliers and customers makes your firm an equity participant in their fortunes; if they fail to remain competitive, their problems can harm your core business. Furthermore, the creation of internal markets can lead to the loss of economic discipline and a distancing from the information conveyed by external markets.

ACQUISITION OF UNIQUE RESOURCES AND CAPABILITIES In some situations, it may be impossible to create internally those resources that are vital to the continued success of the firm. In fields such as biotechnology, computer software, defense electronics, and filmed entertainment, large corporations regularly reach beyond their internal operations to acquire intellectual property, patents, creative talent, and managerial know-how.

VALUE CREATION THROUGH DIVERSIFICATION The classic motive for diversification is to create a portfolio of businesses whose cash flows are imperfectly correlated, and therefore might be able to sustain one another through episodes of adversity—this is a straightforward application of the theory of portfolio diversification that Levy and Sarnat (1970) explored at the corporate level. It is not clear what value this kind of portfolio management adds to shareholders' wealth—couldn't shareholders build these portfolios on their own? If so, why should they pay managers to do this for them? Salter and Weinhold (1979) argued that corporate diversification could do things that shareholder portfolio formation cannot. Thus, diversification might pay if it:

- ***Promotes knowledge transfer across divisions.*** This might lift the productivity of weak divisions. For instance, General Electric practices Total Quality Management and extends its productivity-enhancing techniques to new businesses that it acquires.
- ***Reduces costs.*** Where the diversification is into related fields, it may be possible for the diversified firm to reduce costs through improved bargaining power with suppliers. Also, the cost of financing may be lower thanks to the portfolio diversification effect. Lewellen (1971) suggested that combining two unrelated businesses whose cash flows are imperfectly correlated can reduce the risk of default of the entire enterprise, and therefore expand debt capacity and reduce interest rates.[4]
- ***Creates critical mass for facing the competition.*** Diversification may bring an aggregation of resources that can be shaped into core competencies that create competitive advantage.
- ***Exploits better transparency and monitoring through internal capital markets.*** Internal markets might function better than external markets. First, there may be lower transaction costs: shifting funds from cash cows to cash users may not entail the contracting costs associated with loan agreements or equity underwritings. Coase (1932) argued that the chief explanation of why some firms internalize activities that could, in theory, be conducted among independent firms was that high transaction costs made it cheaper for the firm to do so. Weston (1970), Alchian (1969), and Williamson (1975) offered supporting arguments that internal markets may be more efficient in some circumstances than external markets; Stein (1997) highlights one of these circumstances to be where the corporate headquarters is competent in "winner-picking," the shifting of funds to the best projects. Second, disclosure is probably greater: within the confines of the diversified firm, senior executives can obtain sensitive information that might not be available to outside sources of funds. Chandler (1977) documented the rise of the modern corporation and showed that enhanced methods of monitoring and information transfer enabled senior executives to manage larger and more diverse operations effectively. But the evidence about the effectiveness of internal capital markets is mixed. For instance, Lam-

ont (1997) studied the behavior of oil companies during the oil price collapse of the mid-1980s and found evidence consistent with the story that "large diversified companies overinvest in and subsidize underperforming segments." (Page 106)

Transactions for Inorganic Growth

Executives enjoy a wide range of tactical alternatives for inorganic growth. Mergers and acquisitions are often the focus of financial advisers seeking to generate fee income by assisting firms on M&A. But the executive should consider at least four other avenues before embarking on an M&A effort. These include *contractual relationships*, *strategic alliances*, *joint ventures*, and *minority investments*.

CONTRACTUAL RELATIONSHIPS This is the simplest of all inorganic expansions; it may assume strategic significance if the relationship extends over the long term, if there is a two-way exchange of information; if the two firms are linked into each other's business processes (e.g., inventory management systems), and/or if it entails an exchange of managers. These relationships can take many forms. Several classic arrangements are these:

- ***Licensing agreements.*** Your firm simply "rents" the technology, brand name, or other assets that are the focus of your interest.
- ***Co-marketing agreements.*** Your firm and the partner each agree to sell the products of the other party. The owner of the product permits another firm to make and market the product under a different brand name in return for a fee and profits on ingredients sold to the partner.
- ***Co-development agreements.*** Your firm and the partner each agree to share the costs of R&D or creative work necessary to develop a new product or process.
- ***Joint purchasing agreements.*** Your firm and the partner each agree to combine purchase orders for raw materials or other resources, to exploit economies of scale in purchasing.
- ***Franchising.*** Your firm grants an exclusive market territory to the partner in return for a one-time payment or annual fee.
- ***Long-term supply or toll agreement.*** Your firm commits to a predictable volume of unit purchases over the long term, in return for advantageous pricing.

These kinds of agreements are widespread in business. For instance, Glaxo Holdings, a pharmaceutical company established a co-marketing agreement with Hoffmann–La Roche to market its best-selling product, Zantac, an antiulcer drug. Bruner et al. (1992) detail the economics of these agreements: The trade-off for Glaxo was between lost direct sales versus fee income, profits on ingredients, and faster time to market within a limited period of patent protection.

STRATEGIC ALLIANCE In comparison with a contractual relationship, an alliance is typically more complicated and expresses a more serious commitment between the parties. A contract may formalize the alliance. But it is the exchange of managerial talent, resources, capabilities, and possibly even equity investment that elevates the alliance beyond a mere contractual agreement. An equity investment under the alliance may be structured across a range of possible deals, including a joint venture or minority investment.

JOINT VENTURE A joint venture (JV) creates a separate entity in which your firm and the counterparty will invest. The JV agreement between the venture partners specifies investment rights, operational responsibilities, voting control, exit alternatives, and generally the allocation of risks and rewards. The entity could be a division carved out of one of the venture partners, or an entirely new business established for the venture. The agreement for large JVs may be as complicated as for an acquisition.

MINORITY INVESTMENT Here, your firm invests directly in the counterparty firm, rather than in an intermediate firm (like the joint venture). Sometimes firms take mutual *minority interests* in each other; this is called a *cross-shareholding arrangement* and is common among large Japanese and Continental European firms. Taking a direct equity interest in another firm is a strong signal of commitment and participation in the fortunes of that firm.

Research Findings about Joint Ventures, Alliances, and Minority Equity Investments

Continuing a trend of several decades, the formation of joint ventures and alliances grew dramatically during the 1990s, as shown in Exhibit 6.12. Robinson (2001) argued that the growth of JVs and alliances was due to their success as commitment devices between organizations—alliances bind the partners not to divert resources in inefficient ways. Also, he found that alliances are more likely than acquisitions where the risk of the venture is greater than the risk of the partner's core business.

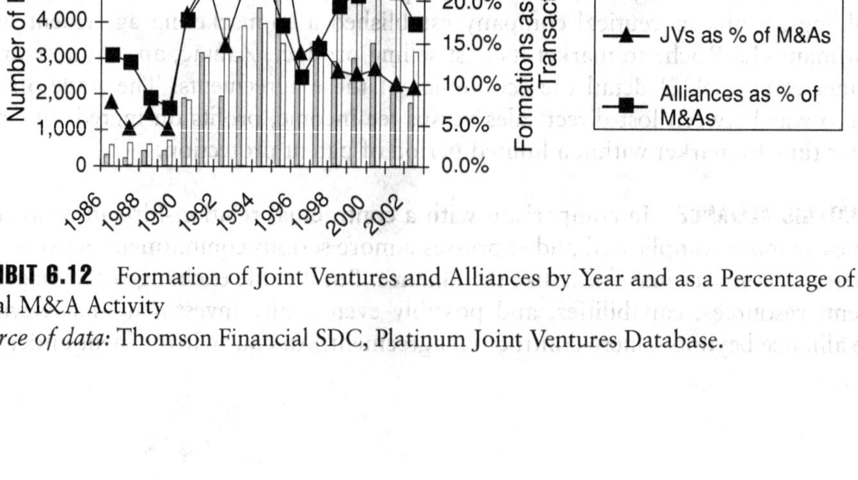

EXHIBIT 6.12 Formation of Joint Ventures and Alliances by Year and as a Percentage of Total M&A Activity
Source of data: Thomson Financial SDC, Platinum Joint Ventures Database.

Desai, Foley, and Hines (2002) studied the formation of international joint ventures and found a trend away from minority ownership and toward whole ownership. They speculated that this change might reflect relaxation of restrictions on whole ownership or changes in the geographic mix of investments. They found that "whole ownership is most common when firms coordinate integrated production activities across different locations, transfer technology, and benefit from world-wide tax planning" (page 1) and that this propensity toward global organization explained a declining tendency to organize foreign operations as joint ventures.

Lerner, Shane, and Tsai (2003) studied R&D ventures formed by small biotechnology firms. They found that when external equity financing is unavailable or limited in supply, these firms are more likely to fund their R&D by organizing research JVs with large corporations. And the agreements structured under these circumstances tend to assign the bulk of control to the large corporate partner. Such agreements are likely to be renegotiated and to be significantly less successful than others. Robinson and Stuart (2002) found that the staging of investment is ubiquitous between small biotechnology R&D firms and their partners. Staging releases investment funds as the R&D firm passes preset milestones—this is discussed in more detail in Chapter 14.

The overarching conclusion about the profitability of joint ventures, alliances, and minority equity investments is that, like M&A, it is profitable for targets, a break-even proposition for purchasers, and for both target and purchaser combined, an economically positive activity. Exhibit 6.13 summarizes findings across 12 studies and shows significantly positive abnormal returns of 0.5 to 1.0 percent to firms announcing investments in JVs. JVs seem to pay. The findings suggest that JV partners do better when:

- Buyers have good investment opportunities. Chen et al. (2000) find that where the buyer has a good record of investment returns, the announcement of a JV is associated with gains to shareholders. But where the buyer's record is weak, the JV announcement could be taken as a signal of pessimism about the buyer's internal opportunities.
- JV increases focus for the buyer. Ferris et al. (2002) find materially better returns for buyers where the JV increases the business focus of the firm.
- JV reduces agency costs. Allen and Phillips (2000) concluded that intercorporate equity investments in the form of JVs, alliances, and minority stakes reduced "the costs of creating, expanding, or monitoring the alliances or ventures between firms and their corporate block holders." (Page 2813) Robinson (2001) argued that JVs help to shelter "underdog" projects from the adverse behavior sometimes found in internal capital markets (e.g., winner-picking). Allen and Phillips (2000) found that the returns from JVs and alliances were greatest in the instance of R&D intensive industries. These gains may stem from alleviating the problems of information asymmetries arising from the development of new technology.
- JV is in a favorable foreign environment, in terms of laws and regulations. Returns from JVs vary by country and region, consistent with the discussion in Chapter 5 that variations in deregulation and rule of law will affect investment returns.

EXHIBIT 6.13 Summary of Studies of Market Returns to Parent Shareholders at Announcements about Joint Ventures, Alliances, and Minority Equity Investments

Study	Cumulative Abnormal Returns at the Event	Cumulative Abnormal Returns after the Event	Sample Size	Sample Period	Notes
Gleason, Mathur, Wiggins (2003)	+0.51%* full sample +0.45%* domestic +0.60%* international +0.61%* horizontal +0.47%* diversifying (days –1,0)	+7.94%† full sample +9.40%† domestic +4.05% international +14.79%† horizontal +5.10% diversifying (months +1,+18)	638 311 197 134 376	1985–1998	Sample of deals involving financial services institutions.
Ferris et al. (2002)	+0.52%* whole sample +0.71%* focus-increasing JVs 0.11% focus-decreasing JVs (all estimates are around days –1,0)	+5.31% whole sample +9.43%† focus-increasing –1.42% focus-decreasing (estimates around months 1,36)	325 200 125	1987–1996	Sample of international JVs by Singaporean firms.
Johnson, Houston (2000)	+1.67% horizontal JVs +5.0% suppliers in vertical JVs 0.0% buyers in vertical JVs	N/A	85 horizontal JVs 106 Vertical JVs	1991–1995	Compared returns to JV investors with returns to firms using simple contracts.
Schut, van Frederikslust (undated)	+0.40% (days –1,0) *		233	1987–1998	Sample of Dutch JVs.
Chen, Ho, Lee, Yeo (2000)	+0.96% (days –1,0) *		174	1979–1993	International JV announcements by Singaporean firms.

Allen, Phillips (2000)	+9.1% * alliance, JV target	150	1980–1991	
	+0.1% alliance, JV purchaser	150		
	+5.5%* no alliance, JV target	252		
	–1.1% no alliance, JV purchaser	252		
	+8.3% * alliance, JV with board representation, target	92		
	–0.4% alliance, JV with board representation, purchaser	92		
	(all estimates are around days –10,+10)			
Chan, Kensinger, Keown, Martin (1997)	+0.64%* whole sample, day 0	345	1983–1992	Sample of strategic alliances.
	+3.45%* horizontal alliance involving tech transfer			
	+1.00% horiz, nontech			
	+1.45%* nonhoriz, nontech			
	+0.27% nonhoriz, tech transfer			
Koh, Venkatraman (1991)	+0.87%* full sample	175	1972–1986	
	+0.80%* tech exchanges subsample			
	0.40% licensing agreements			
	0.01% marketing agreements			
	–0.13% supply agreements			
Chen, Hu, Shieh (1991)	+0.71%* full sample (days –1,0)	88	1979–1990	International JVs in China by U.S. firms.
Crutchley et al. (1991)	+1.05%† U.S. partner returns	82	1979–1987	Japanese-U.S. JVs.
	+1.08%† Japanese partner returns			
Lee, Wyatt (1990)	–0.466%† full sample	109	1974–1986	
McConnell, Nantel (1985)	+0.73% full sample (days –1,0)	210	1972–1979	
	+1.10% small firm subsample			
	+0.63% large firm subsample			

Unless otherwise noted, event date is announcement date of transaction.
*Significant at the 0.99 level or better.
†Significant at the 0.95 level.

RESTRUCTURING, REDEPLOYMENT, AND SALE

Restructuring is a lengthy process. Donaldson (1990) documented a restructuring program (consisting of many discrete transactions) at General Mills that spanned two decades. Kaiser and Stouraitis (2001) described the restructuring of Thorn-EMI that encompassed numerous transactions and lasted 13 years. Boone and Mulherin (2001, 2002) found that the median length of targeted restructuring events is 345 days and that the investor reactions to the initial and subsequent announcements are significantly positive. Their analysis of the auction processes in these restructurings finds the highest returns from asset sales to be associated with the entry of multiple publicly owned bidders.

Motives

The motives for exit mirror those for entry: the adverse effects of industry turbulence; the need to exit from unattractive businesses. As Chapter 3 reveals, not all acquisitions are successes. And even for good businesses, the forces of competition, turbulence, and the life cycle can bring an end to a period of good performance. Jensen (1999) noted that "Exit problems appear to be particularly severe in companies that for long periods enjoyed rapid growth, commanding market positions, and high cash flow and profits." (Page 583) He cited the reluctance of U.S. automobile tire manufacturers to close factories that produced the bias-ply tire when it became apparent that the radial tire product would displace it.

SHARPEN STRATEGIC FOCUS A portfolio of unrelated business activities requires senior management to master a wide variety of industrial concepts and to monitor disparate businesses. A portfolio organized around a focused strategy can exploit executive expertise in neighboring businesses. Weston (1989) argued that dismantling inefficient conglomerates was an important motive for divestitures and restructurings.

CORRECT "MISTAKES" AND HARVEST "LEARNING" Porter (1987) studied the acquisitions of diversified firms and found high rates of *divestiture* in the years following acquisition—on average, they divested 53 percent of their acquisitions within a few years. This implied to Porter a large failure rate in corporate acquisition. Weston (1989) replied that this rate of divestiture could be explained by a variety of effects such as antitrust enforcement and the harvesting of mature investments. He wrote, "Divestitures seem as likely to reflect past successes as mistaken attempts at diversification. Some are pre-planned for good business reasons. Some represent harvesting of sound investments. And some reflect organizational learning that contributes to improvements in future strategies. . . . Regardless of which version one accepts as the dominant explanation for divestitures—'mistakes' or 'learning'—the persistently high numbers and values of such transactions constitute reliable evidence that the market system is working, ensuring the mobility of resources essential to the effective operation of an enterprise economy." (Pages 75–76)

CORRECT THE MARKET VALUATION OF ASSETS Executives frequently complain that the stock market doesn't understand their firms and that it is worth more than the current price suggests. Restructuring can monetize undervalued assets. The firm may contain business units to which investors attribute little or no value. Restructuring can help to establish a monetary value for those assets. If certain business units would be worth more standing alone, a restructuring can exploit a pure-play premium (avoid a diversification discount). Investors may have an appetite for single-segment firms—the common argument is that these kinds of firms are easier to understand, and permit the investor more easily to construct efficient portfolios of securities. Finally, there may be a known buyer to whom the assets or business unit are worth significantly more than to your firm. A restructuring can redeploy assets to higher-valued uses. Your firm may be operating an asset effectively, but there may be alternative uses for the asset that create even more value.

IMPROVE THE INTERNAL CAPITAL MARKET Diversified firms can suffer from failures in the internal capital market to allocate resources effectively—the most prominent kind of failure is the subsidization of inefficient units by efficient units. By shedding the inefficient operations, a restructuring program can eliminate the cross-subsidies.

OPTIMIZE FINANCIAL LEVERAGE AND REDUCE TAX EXPENSE Many restructurings that entail a change in capital structure for the firm seek to create value for shareholders by reducing the risk of default to acceptable levels or exploiting the tax deductibility of interest expense. The valuation of debt tax shields is discussed in more detail in Chapter 13, and Chapter 34 gives a detailed discussion of leveraged restructuring.

STRENGTHEN MANAGERIAL INCENTIVES/ALIGN THEM WITH THE INTERESTS OF SHAREHOLDERS Financial restructurings and leveraged buyouts often result in management holding a meaningful investment in the equity of the firm. This tends to focus management attention on the efficiency of the business and align their interests more tightly with those of the other equity investors.

RESPOND TO CAPITAL MARKET DISCIPLINE Financial underperformance by firms can trigger a range of reactions from capital markets, from adverse comments by journalists and securities analysts to depressed share prices, higher interest rates, shareholder proxy contests to replace the board of directors, and hostile takeover attempts. A defensive restructuring is a prominent response to capital market discipline. Chapter 36 describes the case of American Standard's defensive restructuring.

GAIN FINANCING WHEN EXTERNAL FUNDS ARE LIMITED Firms with poor access to debt or equity markets may turn to the sale of assets to raise funds. Thus, divestiture may relax capital constraints. Consistent with this financing motive, Schlingemann et al. (2002) found that the liquidity of the market for the particular corporate assets is a significant determinant of *which* assets are likely to be divested. Kruse (2002) found that there is a greater probability of asset sales if the firm is performing poorly and suffers from low debt capacity.

Transactions to Restructure, Redeploy, or Sell

A strategic decision to focus or restructure the firm poses the choice about degree (partial deployment or outright exit) and method. Here, the possible transactions also span a wide range of alternatives.

SALE OF MINORITY INTEREST The sale of a block of shares to another firm gains the selling firm fresh capital and attracts a committed partner who might be induced to contribute know-how or other resources. This alternative should be compared to a public offering of shares (i.e., for pricing and costs). The investor may seek advantageous (i.e., low) pricing, arguing that it amounts to a private transaction. The trade-off for the issuer is whether the other resources the investor might contribute will compensate for any private transaction discount. An added consideration is political: How will the minority stake affect the balance of voting power in the firm, and how will other equity investors respond? Sometimes a minority stake is prelude to a takeover.

SALE OF JOINT VENTURE INTEREST The sale of a partial interest in a joint venture to a partner attracts fresh capital for the venture and the participation of a partner with know-how and other resources. Compared to the minority stake, this has the virtue of less political impact and affords more transparency about the contributions of the respective sides.

DIVESTITURE OR ASSET SALE The business unit, or certain assets in the unit (such as a factory), could be sold outright to an unrelated party. This raises funds for your firm and possibly frees it from a money-losing proposition. While divestitures account for a large proportion of M&A activity (26 to 35 percent of all deals are divestitures), two types of sales deserve special mention. In the *leveraged buyout/going private transaction*, the management of the unit will organize an investor group and debt financing with which to pay for the unit. Usually the ability to sell a unit into an LBO depends on its capacity to succeed as a stand-alone entity and on its capacity to bear debt used to finance the transaction. Chapter 13 discusses LBOs and other highly leveraged transactions in more detail. The *liquidation* is the extreme divestiture strategy: the firm sells *all* of its assets, pays any outstanding liabilities, dividends the net proceeds to shareholders, and then dissolves. Bruner et al. (1979) explored the liquidation of UV Industries, a Fortune 500–ranked firm, in 1979. Triggered by a hostile raid, the firm commenced a voluntary liquidation that yielded a return of 163 percent over its preraid value. Exhibit 6.14 illustrates the divestiture alternative.

CARVE-OUT This tactic organizes the business unit as a separate entity and sells to the public an interest in the equity of the unit through an initial public offering (IPO). This generates cash for the parent, monetizes the parent's interest in the subsidiary, and creates more transparency for investors to assess its value. Exhibit 6.14 presents the *carve-out* alternative.

SPIN-OFF Like the carve-out, the *spin-off* creates a separate entity for the business and results in public trading of its shares with majority ownership retained by the parent. But in the case of a spin-off, the shares are *given* to the parent's shareholders in the form of a dividend. No money is exchanged. Where one firm existed before, two firms exist after. At the point of spin-off, the same shareholder group owns both companies (though ownership will probably change once trading commences in the new firm's shares). Exhibit 6.14 diagrams the *spin-off* alternative.

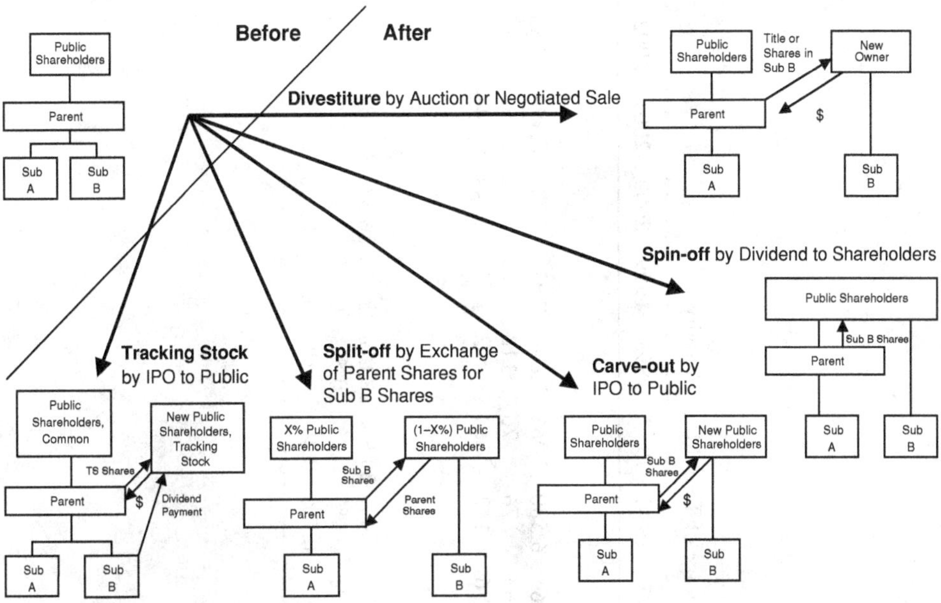

EXHIBIT 6.14 Comparison of Divestiture, Spin-off, Carve-out, Split-off, and Tracking Stock Where the Parent Considers Redeploying Subsidiary B

SPLIT-OFF, OR EXCHANGE In this instance, shares of the subsidiary business are swapped by shareholders of the parent for shares in the subsidiary. This results in a freestanding firm, no longer a subsidiary of the parent, owned initially by a subgroup of the former parent's shareholders. Exhibit 6.14 illustrates the *split-off* alternative.

TRACKING STOCK Here, there is no transfer of ownership of a business or its assets. But a special equity claim *on the subsidiary business* is created, the dividend of which is tied to the net earnings of the subsidiary. This results in monetization of the subsidiary and in greater transparency. Exhibit 6.14 illustrates the *tracking stock* alternative.

FINANCIAL RECAPITALIZATION This focuses on changes in the firm's capital structure.[5] The intent is usually to optimize the mix of debt or equity, or to adjust the equity interests in the business. Regarding the debt/equity mix, firms might undertake a *leveraged restructuring* in which the firm borrows debt to repurchase shares or pay an extraordinary dividend. Chapters 13, 20, and 34 explore the implications of capital structure altering transactions. Regarding changes in the equity base, firms could contemplate an *ESOP restructuring* in which the firm purchases its own shares (or issues them from its treasury) for sale to an employee stock ownership plan. Alteration of both the capital mix and equity ownership is seen in *reorganization in bankruptcy* in which the firm exchanges debt obligations for equity interests to reduce its debt burden under the protection of the court.

Exhibit 6.15 summarizes the activity in divestitures, spin-offs, and carve-outs from 1986 to 2002. The number of divestitures increased dramatically over this

EXHIBIT 6.15 Volume of Divestitures, Spin-offs, and Carve-outs by Year and as a Percentage of Total M&A Activity

	1986	1987	1988	1989	1990	1991	1992	1993	1994	1995	1996	1997	1998	1999	2000	2001	2002
Number of transactions																	
Divestitures	1,357	1,474	2,103	2,895	3,701	5,128	5,002	5,241	5,414	6,261	6,580	7,063	7,044	7,811	7,735	6,998	6,283
Spin-offs	34	28	38	37	48	31	42	46	39	63	76	76	118	81	102	63	35
Carve-outs	3	5	6	21	40	70	76	167	240	176	142	64	32	32	44	45	20
As a % of M&A deals																	
Divestitures	35.8%	30.8%	31.8%	31.5%	36.8%	37.2%	37.8%	37.8%	33.2%	31.8%	31.4%	30.9%	28.0%	28.5%	26.3%	31.3%	34.3%
Spin-offs	0.9%	0.6%	0.6%	0.4%	0.5%	0.2%	0.3%	0.3%	0.2%	0.3%	0.4%	0.3%	0.5%	0.3%	0.3%	0.3%	0.2%
Carve-outs	0.1%	0.1%	0.1%	0.2%	0.4%	0.5%	0.6%	1.2%	1.5%	0.9%	0.7%	0.3%	0.1%	0.1%	0.1%	0.2%	0.1%

Source of data: Thomson SDC Financial Services.

period, by almost five times. Also, relative to the total number of M&A transactions, divestitures account for about one-quarter to one-third of the total over time. The number of spin-offs and carve-outs is highly variable over this period and, relative to M&A activity, quite small.

Research on the Profitability of Unit Divestitures, Asset Sales, and Liquidation

Exhibit 6.16 summarizes studies of the shareholder wealth implications of divestiture: Announcements of divestitures uniformly create value for shareholders of sellers, on the order of a 1 to 3 percent significant abnormal return. The results for buyers are mixed: One study reports positive and significant returns (Hite et al. 1987); a second reports positive and insignificant returns (John and Ofek 1995); and a third reports negative and insignificant returns to buyers (Allen and Phillips 2000). The small absolute returns for buyers seen in the exhibit should be viewed with the same caution as discussed in Chapter 3. First, these returns occur over short time periods and should be annualized before being compared with other conventional returns to investors. Second, the divested assets are typically a fraction of the market value of the buyer or seller firm—this comparative size effect can make the profitability of divestiture seem inconsequential, when it may remain economically profitable in absolute terms.

Beneath the general results of Exhibit 6.16 are some interesting insights. First, the *redeployment of assets* seems to be what matters, not merely the sale. This is apparent in three sets of findings.

1. Lang et al. (1995) found an announcement return of almost 4 percent when the firm committed to returning the divestiture proceeds to investors (e.g., in the form of reducing the firm's debt). In comparison, the announcement return was insignificantly different from zero for cases where the firm planned to reinvest in the business.
2. Announcements of plant closings (Blackwell et al. 1990) are frequently the prelude to divestiture or *liquidation* and produce small but significantly negative returns to shareholders. Announcements of plant closings can be a surprising signal to investors of the failure of a strategy. The pattern of returns in the entire exhibit suggests that it is the redeployment of assets (e.g., through divestiture) that matters. The uncertainty about the future disposition of the investment in that plant is resolved only at the divestiture announcement.
3. Voluntary liquidations, the ultimate program of divestiture, deliver the highest returns to shareholders, in the range of 12 to 13 percent, market-adjusted. Liquidations completely disengage from business and return the funds to shareholders.

Second, the market seems to reward *divestitures that focus* the firm. John and Ofek (1995) document a significant relation between the announcement returns at divestiture and the degree of increase in strategic focus of the firm after divestiture. In his study of a 20-year restructuring program at General Mills, Donaldson (1990) found that announcements of the sale of noncore assets was associated with higher abnormal returns than was the sale of core-related assets (+2.03 versus –0.43 percent). Kaiser and Stouraitis (2001) studied the refocusing effort of Thorn-EMI and reported positive and significant abnormal returns.

EXHIBIT 6.16 Summary of Studies of Market Returns to Parent Shareholders at Unit Divestitures, Asset Sales, and Liquidations

Study	Cumulative Abnormal Returns at the Event	Cumulative Abnormal Returns after the Event	Sample Size	Sample Period	Notes
Boone, Mulherin (2001)	+6.40% * full sample +12.16%* possible sale +2.93% general restructuring (days –1,0)		298 97 75	1989–1998	Sample of announcements of corporate restructurings.
Allen, Phillips (2000)	+0.8% selling firm –1.1% purchaser firm (days –10,+10)		48	1982–1991	
Dittmar, Shivdasani (2002)	+2.6%* full sample sellers +3.0%* sellers who remain diversified +2.2%* sellers who become single-segment firms (days –1,0)	+12% full sample +14% remain diversified +17% become single (change in value estimated year t–1 to t+1)	188 91 97	1983–1994	Sample of asset sales. Finds significant negative correlation between event returns and change in the diversification discount.
Berger, Ofek (1999)	+3.0%* restructuring announcements +3.6%† first announcement +1.3%† second or later annc'ts. +7.3%† all sale related annc'ts. (days –1,0)		29 105 299 105	1984–1993	Sample of asset sales and spin-offs.
John, Ofek (1995)	+1.5%† full sample sellers +0.4% full sample buyers (days –2,0)		258 167	1986–1988	Sample of asset sales. Increasing focus is associated with larger returns.
Slovin, Sushka, Ferraro (1995)	+1.70%* full sample sellers (days –1,0)	–0.20% full sample (returns estimated days +2,+11)	179	1980–1991	Sample of asset sales.

Lang, Poulsen, Stulz (1995)	+1.41%* full sample +3.92%* proceeds used to pay dividend or reduce debt –0.48% proceeds to be reinvested (days –1,0)		93 40 53		Sample of asset sales. Difference between repay and reinvest subsamples is significant.*
Donaldson (1990)	+1.13%† full sample +2.03%* noncore sales –0.43% core sales		11 7 4	1966–1989	Divestitures by General Mills only.
Blackwell, Marr, Spivey (1990)	–0.55%* full sample –0.59%* operation not profitable –0.24% labor-management dispute		244 196 9	1980–1984	Sample of announcements of plant closings.
Sicherman, Pettway (1987)	Buyers returns +4.026%* related businesses 0.047% unrelated businesses (days –10,+10)		147	1983–1985	
Hite, Owers, Rogers (1987)	+1.66%* full sample, sellers in completed deals +0.83%‡ buyers in completed deals (returns estimated days –1,0)	+2.18% sellers in completed deals –1.72% buyers in completed deals (returns estimated days +1,+50)	55 41	1963–1978	Sample of asset sales.
Klein (1985)	+1.11%* sample of sellers (days –2,0)		215	1970–1979	Sample of asset sales.
Hearth, Zaima (1986)	1.42%* divesting firms 0.25% acquiring firms (days –1,0)		73	1975–1982	Sample of asset sales.
Jain (1985)	+0.07‡% sample of sellers +0.04% sample of buyers (days –5,–1) +0.34% sellers (day –1)		304	1976–1978	Sample of asset sales.
Rosenfeld (1984)	+2.33%* full sample		35	1963–1981	

(Continued)

EXHIBIT 6.16 *(Continued)*

Study	Cumulative Abnormal Returns at the Event	Cumulative Abnormal Returns after the Event	Sample Size	Sample Period	Notes
Alexander, Benson, Kampmeyer (1984)	+0.17% full sample (days –1,0)	–2.47% (days +1,+30)	53	1964–1973	
Hite, Owers, Rogers (1987)	+12.24%* at press date, full sample	–5.96% full sample	49	1963–1978	Sample of voluntary liquidations.
	+5.97%* liquidations with prior control bids	–4.79%* liquidations with prior control bids	24		
	+18.26%* liquidations with no prior control bids	–7.08%* liquidations with no prior control bids	25		
	(returns estimated days –1,0)	(returns est'd. months 1,12)			
Kim, Schatzberg (1987)	+13.53%* at announcement date		73	1963–1982	Sample of voluntary liquidations.
	+2.84%* at stockholder confirmation date				
	(returns estimated days –2,0)				

Unless otherwise noted, event date is announcement date of transaction.
*Significant at the 0.99 level or better.
†Significant at the 0.90 level.
‡Significant at the 0.95 level.

Third, firms selling assets tend to suffer from *lower profitability or high leverage*. Lang et al. (1995) concluded, "Management sells assets to obtain funds to pursue its objectives when alternative funding is either too expensive given its objectives or unavailable. . . . A successful sale means that the firm received enough money to make the sale worthwhile. . . . Firms selling assets typically are poor performers and they are more likely to pay out the proceeds when they find it difficult to service their debt." (Page 22)

Research on the Profitability of Carve-outs, Spin-offs, Split-offs, and Tracking Stock

The general finding is that carve-outs, spin-offs, and tracking stock are neutral to beneficial for shareholders. Exhibits 6.17 and 6.18 summarize studies of the event returns associated with spin-offs and carve-outs; these are generally profitable to investors. Exhibit 6.19 on page 164 shows that tracking stock is value neutral to slightly positive for investors.

Research amplifies some of the insights. First, the investment behavior and financial performance of spun-off units improves following the spin-off. Gernter, Powers, and Scharfstein (2002) found that spun-off units tended to cut investment in unprofitable businesses and increase investment in profitable industries. Chemmanur and Paeglis (2001) found material increases in the price-earnings and price-sales ratios for parents and subsidiaries as a result of the transactions. Cusatis, Miles, and Woolridge (1993) documented significant returns over the longer term following spin-offs. Hurlburt et al. (2002) found that sales, assets, and capital expenditures of carved-out subsidiaries grew significantly faster than industry peers in the first year after the transaction; but the parent firm shrank. Ahn and Denis (2001) reported that diversified firms improved their investment efficiency and eliminated the *diversification discount* following spin-offs. In contrast, Haushalter and Mikkelson (2001) found no material improvement in long-term performance following tracking stock or carve-outs.

Second, relatedness matters in the choice of transaction. Chemmanur and Paeglis (2001) found that carve-outs and spin-offs tend to involve business units that are less related to the core than do tracking stocks. McNeil and Moore (2001) reported that announcement returns are larger at the spin-off of unrelated businesses than related businesses.

Third, the findings are consistent with benefits of increased focus. Hite and Owers (1983), Schipper and Smith (1983), Daley, Mehrotra, and Sivakumjar (1997), and Desai and Jain (1998) argue that spin-offs resolve "information asymmetry" problems—these arise from the complexity of multidivisional firms and the lack of transparency for investors to monitor the managers. Krisnaswami and Subramaniam (1999) find that firms undertaking spin-offs have higher levels of information asymmetry and that these problems decrease after the spin-offs. Best, Best, and Agapos (1998) find that securities analysts significantly increase their short-term earnings forecasts after spin-offs. Daley, Mehrotra, and Sivakumar (1997) find significant value creation around cross-industry spin-offs (rather than same-industry spin-offs). Vijh (2000) reports higher carve-out returns when the subsidiary is in a different two-digit SIC code from the parent. Veld and Veld-Merkoulova (2002) report significantly higher returns at spin-offs that are focus-increasing.

EXHIBIT 6.17 Summary of Studies of Market Returns to Parent and Subsidiary Shareholders at Spin-Offs

Panel A: Returns to Shareholders of Parent

Study	Cumulative Abnormal Returns at the Event	Cumulative Abnormal Returns after the Event	Sample Size	Sample Periods
Davis, Leblond (2002)	+2.92%* full sample +2.14%* industrial +3.87%* high tech (days –1,0)		93	1980–1999
Veld, Veld-Meruklova (2002)	+2.66%* full sample +2.41% U.K. subsample +3.57% focus-increasing +0.76% not focus-increasing (days –1,+1)	–0.41% full sample +5.20% focus-increasing –12.96%* not focus-increasing (months 0,+36)	200	1987–2000
Chemmanur, Paeglis (2001)	+2.11%† (days –1,+1)		19	1984–1998
McNeil, Moore (2001)	+3.53%* full sample +4.05%* unrelated +2.39%‡ related (days –1,+1)		152 104 48	1980–1996
Desai, Jain (1999)	+3.8%	+25.4% (3 yrs.)	155	1975–1991
Krishnaswami, Subramaniam (1999)	+3.28%* full sample (days –1,+1)		118	1979–1993
Arbanell, Bushee, Raede (1998)		+3.23% return to parents –0.86% return to spin-off (days –1,+60)	245	1980–1996
Best, Best, Agapos (1998)	+3.41%*announcement date +2.94%* ex-date (day 0)		72 63	1979–1993

Daley, Mehrotra, Sivakumar (1997)	+3.4%* full sample +4.3%* focus-increasing +1.4% not focus-increasing		85	1975–1991
Parrino (1997) Clinical study of one spin-off by Marriott Corporation	+13.19% announcement date +41.12% five event dates		1	1993
Johnson, Klein, Thibodeaux (1996)	+3.96%* full sample +5.42%* "back to basic" subsample	N/A	104	1975–1988
Slovin, Sushka, Ferraro (1995)	+1.3%	N/A	37	1980–1991
Cusatis, Miles, Woolridge (1993)	N/A	+12.5%‡ (1 yr.) +26.7%‡ (2 yrs.) +18.1% (3 yrs.)	146	1965–1988
Vijh (1994)	+2.9%‡ annct. date +0.79% completion date +3.03%‡ ex-date		113	1964–1990
Rosenfeld (1984)	+5.56%* full sample		35	1963–1981
Schipper, Smith (1983)	+2.8%	N/A	93	1963–1981
Hite, Owers (1983)	+3.3%	+7.0% (5 mos.)	123	1963–1981
Miles, Rosenfeld (1983)	+3.34%* full sample (days –1,0)	22.9% (9 mos.)	55	1963–1980

(Continued)

EXHIBIT 6.17 *(Continued)*

Panel B: Returns to Shareholders of Subsidiary

Study	Cumulative Abnormal Returns at the Event	Cumulative Abnormal Returns after the Event	Sample Size	Sample Period
Desai, Jain (1999)	N/A	+15.7% (1 yr.) +36.2% (2 yrs.) +32.3% (3 yrs.)	155	1975–1991
Cusatis, Miles, Woolridge (1994)	N/A	+4.5% (1 yr.) +25.0% (2 yrs.) +33.6% (3 yrs.)	161	1965–1990

Unless otherwise noted, event date is announcement date of transaction.
*Significant at the 0.99 level or better.
†Significant at the 0.90 level.
‡Significant at the 0.95 level.

EXHIBIT 6.18 Summary of Studies of Market Returns to Parent and Subsidiary Shareholders at Carve-Outs

Panel A: Returns to Shareholders of Parent

Study	Cumulative Abnormal Returns at the Event	Cumulative Abnormal Returns after the Event	Sample Size	Sample Period	Notes
Vijh (2002)	+1.94%* full sample +4.92%* sub is large +1.19%* sub is small (days –1,+1)		336	1980–1997	Tests reject the asymmetric information hypothesis and support the divestiture gains hypothesis.
Hurlburt, Miles, Woolridge (2002)	+1.92%* full sample +2.10%* cross-industry –0.39% own industry		185 153 30	1981–1994	Finds negative effect of carve-out announcement on rival firms.
Hogan, Olsen (2002)	+11.42% carve-outs +16.53% IPOs matched (day 0)		219	1991–2000	Carve-out returns are lower than returns in a matched sample of IPOs at offering.
Schill, Zhou (2001)	+11.3%† (days –1,+1)		11	2000	Focus on carve-outs of Internet subsidiaries.
Haushalter, Mikkelson (2001)	+3.39%* full sample (days –2,+2)		13	1994–1996	
Hulburt, Miles, Woolridge (2000)	+1.9%* (days –1,0)		185	1981–1994	

(Continued)

EXHIBIT 6.18 *(Continued)*

Panel A: Returns to Shareholders of Parent

Study	Cumulative Abnormal Returns at the Event	Cumulative Abnormal Returns after the Event	Sample Size	Sample Period	Notes
Vijh (2000)	+1.94%* full sample +2.25%* sub not related industry +0.80% sub is related (days –1,+1)		336 221 100	1980–1997	
Prezas, Tarimcilar, Vasudevan (2000)	+5.83%* (day 0)	7.61%* (6 mos.) 11.75%* (1 yr.) 21.07%* (3 yrs.)	237	1986–1995	Carve-out returns are lower than returns in a matched sample of IPOs at offering and over the postoffering time periods.
Allen (1998)		+33.2% HPR (0,12 months) +229.3% HPR (0,60) Holding period returns adjusted for industry returns	1	1983–1995	Clinical study of 11 carve-outs by Thermo Electric
Allen, McConnell (1998)	+2.12%* full sample +6.63%* proceeds paid out –0.01% proceeds are retained (days –1,+1)		186 54 60	1978–1993	
Slovin, Sushka, Ferraro (1995)	+1.2%‡ (days –1,0)		32	1982–1991	

Klein, Rosenfeld, Beranek (1991)	+2.75%* full sample		52	1966–1980	
Schipper, Smith (1986)	+1.83%‡ subsidiary −3.5%* parent (days −4,0)	−0.5% subsidiary −1.40% parent (days +1,+40)	76	1965–1983	
Chemmanur, Paeglis (2001)	+1.96%‡ (days −1,+1)		19	1984–1998	

Panel B: Returns to Shareholders of Subsidiary in Carve-Out

Study	Cumulative Abnormal Returns at the Event	Cumulative Abnormal Returns after the Event	Sample Size	Sample Period	Notes
Hulburt, Miles, Woolridge (1994)	N/A	+12.5% (1 yr.) +14.4% (2 yrs.) +24.7% (3 yrs.)	80	1981–1989	

Unless otherwise noted, event date is announcement date of transaction.
*Significant at the 0.99 level or better.
†Significant at the 0.90 level.
‡Significant at the 0.95 level.

EXHIBIT 6.19 Summary of Studies of Market Returns to Parent Shareholders at Creation of Tracking Stocks

Study	Cumulative Abnormal Returns at the Event	Cumulative Abnormal Returns after the Event	Sample Size	Sample Period
Haushalter, Mikkelson (2001)	+3.00%* full sample (days –2,+2)		31	1994–1996
Billet, Vijh (2000)	+2.67%*	Parent company 1.07% (1 yr.) –5.77% (2 yrs.) –4.15% (3 yrs.) Tracking stock +9.74% (1 yr.) –15.26% (2 yrs.) –40.05%† (3 yrs.)	20	1984–1998
Elder, Westra (2000)	+3.1%* full sample (days –1,0)	N/A	35	1984–1999
D'Souza, Jacob (1999)	+3.61%* full sample (days –1,+1)		64	1984–1997
Logue, Seward, Walsh (1996)	+2.9%† (days –1,0)	N/A	8	1985–1994
Chemmanur, Paeglis (2001)	+3.09%* (days –1,+1)		19	1984–1998

Unless otherwise noted, event date is announcement date of transaction.
*Significant at the 0.99 level or better.
†Significant at the 0.95 level.

Fourth, the types of transactions do differ in their effects. Though the diagrams in Exhibit 6.14 suggest a strong similarity in their resulting structures, in fact the transaction types have materially different impacts: Tracking stocks do not result in increased focus, tax, or regulatory benefits, only increased transparency. Split-offs alter the ownership of the parent; carve-outs, like divestitures, change the ownership of the subsidiary. In a spin-off, no new funds flow to the parent—Anderson (2002) finds that the need to raise additional capital is significant in explaining the type of transaction chosen. Parrino (1997) documents a major transfer of wealth from bondholders to stockholders from a spin-off effected by Marriott Corporation. The variation in returns across transaction type could be explained by any of these factors: agency costs, internal capital markets, information, control, and so on. Notwithstanding the differences among the forms of these transactions, abnormal returns from these transactions are generally consistent: spin-offs return roughly 2 to 4 percent, compared to carve-outs of 2 to 3 percent, and tracking stocks of 3 percent.

Fifth, as with divestitures, deployment of funds raised in these transactions makes a difference. Allen and McConnell (1998) found a large difference in announcement day returns: Investors reacted positively to carve-outs that would generate cash to be paid to creditors; instances where the funds were to be reinvested in the business were met with zero response from investors.

Sixth, the restructuring has an impact on the rivals of the firm. Hurlburt et al. (2002) found that the effect of carve-out announcements on the returns of rival firms was significantly negative.

Seventh, the timing and type of the restructuring seems to be associated with the valuation of the parent and subsidiary in the capital markets. Nanda (1991) suggests that opportunistic behavior by managers will motivate them to favor carve-outs over divestitures when the parent's shares are relatively undervalued and the subsidiary's shares are relatively overvalued. Thus, a sale of equity in the subsidiary would become a signal to investors of the parent's undervaluation. The findings on carve-out announcement returns in Exhibit 6.18 generally support such a hypothesis. For instance, Schill and Zhou (2001) write, "Overall, the evidence can best be explained with models where clienteles of investors with optimistically biased expectations drive the prices of subsidiaries above parent valuations and arbitrage costs prohibit market forces from eliminating the disparity between parent-subsidiary valuations." (Page 27)

The hypotheses about the sources of gains from restructuring center predominantly on two: an agency cost argument that increased focus cures ills of internal capital markets; and hypotheses about exploiting misvaluations in the market. These hypotheses are not mutually exclusive. But the research supports the existence of both sources, giving, perhaps, more weight to the agency cost hypothesis on the grounds of the number of studies confirming the value of corporate focus.

FRAMEWORK FOR CHOOSING A PATH FOR INORGANIC GROWTH

The wide range of possible instruments for inorganic growth easily bewilders the senior executive. Yet the advantages and disadvantages of each alternative raise a number of considerations that can help the executive sort out the alternatives. These considerations help form a decision path:

1. ***Benefits from a relationship: learning and coordination gains.*** If one of the strategic objectives is knowledge transfer from the partner to your firm, a closer engagement would be warranted. Some targets of inorganic growth programs may be highly related to the main business activities of the buyer. In these instances, the demands of close integration necessary to realize benefits may dictate closer business ties. But other targets may have a weaker relationship to the core and thus may not require close ties.
2. ***Need for ownership and control.*** Control would be a priority in cases where the intentions of the partner are unclear and there is a risk that the partner will defect to a competitor, or worse, become a competitor. High control might also be dictated where the partner holds assets of strategic value to your firm, which would create a disadvantage if they fell into a competitor's hands. In many cases, total ownership is not required. Partial ownership may deliver a place on the board of directors and a say in management. But in other cases, simply doing business through a contractual agreement (i.e., with no ownership) may be sufficient to deliver the strategic needs.
3. ***Manage risk exposure.*** The risks of some target operations will be well known to the buyer, appear to be manageable, and may be at an acceptable level. But

for other targets, the risks will be uncertain, unmanageable, and potentially large—in these cases it may be desirable to isolate the target with legal "firewalls" that will contain the risk exposure to your firm. Another aspect of managing risk is in being able to intervene in the operations and financing of a weak partner with know-how and funds. As detailed in Chapter 19, a variety of acquisition structures permit the management of risks in a target. Nevertheless, the limited liability of minority investment or joint venture permits your firm to acquire a stake in the expansion business pending the resolution of uncertainty. Staged investing through these intermediate structures is a time-honored way to deal with uncertainty.

These three criteria convey the complexity of the choice. One could compound the complexity further with considerations of the desirability of a local identity (as in cross-border expansions) and size of the deal (i.e., large transaction costs for lawyers, due diligence, and financial advice may not be warranted for small transactions).

These considerations suggest a decision flowchart such as presented in Exhibit 6.20. First, one confronts the strategic perspective: How material are the benefits from a relationship in the expansion opportunity? Next is the need for control: Is this high or low? The third regards the risk exposure in the opportunity, and the possible need to isolate the risks: Are the risks and the need to isolate them high? Will the expansion opportunity need our capital? Is it financially weak? Tracing the branches of this decision tree over to the right-hand side one sees the array of transaction alternatives from merger or acquisition at the top extreme, to a simple contractual arrangement at the bottom. This tree was built from just these three considerations. Other considerations may dominate the thinking of senior executives, or they may bear influence in a different order of priority. But this decision

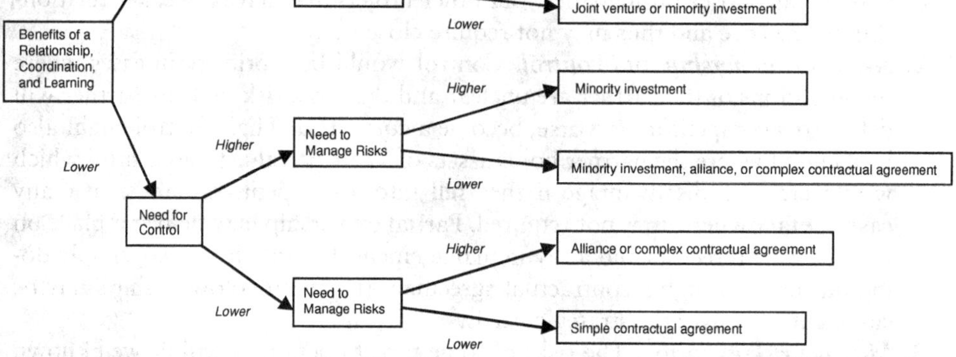

EXHIBIT 6.20 Decision Tree for Selecting among Inorganic Growth Opportunities

tree is sufficient to illustrate a few conclusions about the choice among inorganic growth alternatives:

- ***One kind of transaction does not fit all needs.*** Be skeptical of "one-trick ponies," those proposals by brokers and advisers that always amount to an acquisition. As the diagram suggests, you can achieve strategic aims of inorganic growth through a variety of alternatives.
- ***The choice among the alternatives is a logical result of balancing important considerations.*** Start the process by making a careful inventory of the decision criteria that are important to you. The three illustrated in Exhibit 6.20, relationship benefits, control, and risk management, will appear often in studies of inorganic growth alternatives. However, other considerations may be unique to a particular company or time, but no less important.
- ***Retain a bias for simplicity.*** Contractual arrangements are probably easier to structure than relationships based on an equity investment. Also, simple agreements may be a better foundation for getting to know a partner; with complexity come more opportunities for misunderstanding.
- ***Consider starting small.*** Staged investing will dominate lump-sum investing where risks are material. More is said about staged investing in Chapter 22.
- ***Remember value creation.*** The subtext for any comparison of alternatives should be their impacts on shareholder welfare.

FRAMEWORK FOR CHOOSING A PATH FOR RESTRUCTURING

The selection among alternatives for restructuring rests on the considerations illustrated in the decision tree of Exhibit 6.21.

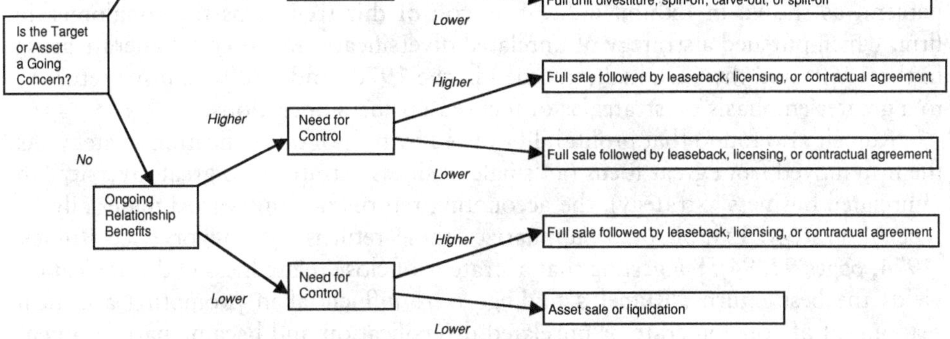

EXHIBIT 6.21 Decision Tree for Redeployment and Restructuring

- ***Relationship to the core business of the parent.*** If the target operation is unrelated to the core it might be sold outright with no adverse effect on the rest of the firm. But if the benefits of relationship are material, your firm might consider retaining a partial interest in the target either as a joint venture or as a minority investment.
- ***Need for control.*** Whether or not the asset or business remains strategically significant, your firm may want to retain some influence or control over the target if for no other reason than to assure that it does not fall into the hands of a competitor.
- ***Can the business or asset operate as an independent entity?*** Assets such as land, factories, or equipment may be too small or isolated to sustain an independent existence. Such assets might be earmarked for outright sale. On the other hand, disposing of an ongoing *business* in the form of a firm can capture for the seller a premium reflecting growth prospects and franchise value.

Here again, *to complete any strategic analysis of alternatives, one must assess the implications of each choice for shareholder value.* This is done by means of a valuation analysis. No choice should be final until its implications for your firm's share price are estimated and understood. The capital markets perspective embedded in valuation analysis may presuppose very different outlooks than the product markets perspective of the strategist. Also, there may be an information asymmetry reflected in the perspectives of the insiders and capital market outsiders (e.g., perhaps the discount rate derived from the capital markets is inconsistent with the inside strategic perspective).

DOES IT PAY TO DIVERSIFY OR FOCUS THE FIRM?

One of the robust debates today deals with whether and how the strategic efforts to diversify or focus the firm pay. The question is significant because of the prevalence of diversification-based business strategies among large firms today, and because of the relatively high volume of transactions motivated in part by a theory of the need to diversify or focus. Villalonga (2003) noted that between 1990 and 1996, diversified firms accounted for half of the employment in the United States, and 60 percent of the assets of traded firms. Following World War II, the U.S., European, and Japanese economies witnessed a dramatic increase in diversification and divisionalization.[6] Rumelt (1974) found that 70 percent of the Fortune 500 firms were heavily or exclusively focused on one segment. By 1969, that group had fallen to 35 percent, as shown in Exhibit 6.22. The icon of this trend was the conglomerate firm, which pursued a strategy of unrelated diversification. The conglomerate arose in the 1960s and then gradually receded in the 1970s and 1980s as firms returned to a greater emphasis on strategies of focused business operations.

Rumelt also found that profitability varied by type of diversification strategy: As the firm moved from great focus (a "single business" strategy) to great diversity (an "unrelated business" strategy), the accounting returns of firms varied materially by type of strategy. Exhibit 6.23 summarizes these returns by category; see Rumelt (1974, pages 92, 94). Suggesting that a strategy of close relatedness in diversification yields the best returns, Rumelt's findings were influential in prompting a critical reappraisal of conglomerate or unrelated diversification and became part of a general trend in the 1970s and 1980s toward increasing emphasis on strategic focus.

EXHIBIT 6.22 Changing Mix of Diversification Strategies for the Fortune 500 Firms

	Percentage of Firms in Each Strategic Category		
Strategic Category	1949	1959	1969
Single business	34.5%	16.2%	6.2%
Dominant business	35.4%	37.3%	29.2%
Related business	26.7%	40.0%	45.2%
Unrelated business	3.4%	6.5%	19.4%

Note: "Single business" indicates firms focused entirely on one industry segment—not multibusiness firms.
"Dominant business" indicates firms deriving between 70 and 95 percent of their revenues from one segment and 70 to 100 percent from the largest related group of businesses.
"Related business" indicates firms deriving up to 70 percent of revenues from one segment *and* 70 to 100 percent from the largest related group of businesses.
"Unrelated business" indicates firms with relatively low influence from one single segment or group of related segments.
Source of data: Rumelt (1974), page 51.

EXHIBIT 6.23 Returns by Diversification Strategy

Category	Return on Capital	Return on Equity
Single business	10.81%	13.20%
Dominant business	9.64%	11.64%
Related business	11.49%	13.55%
Unrelated business	9.49%	11.92%

Note: "Single business" indicates firms focused entirely on one industry segment—not multibusiness firms.
"Dominant business" indicates firms deriving between 70 and 95 percent of their revenues from one segment and 70 to 100 percent from the largest related group of businesses.
"Related business" indicates firms deriving up to 70 percent of revenues from one segment *and* 70 to 100 percent from the largest related group of businesses.
"Unrelated business" indicates firms with relatively low influence from one single segment or group of related segments.
Source of data: Rumelt (1974), page 91.

Value Drivers in Diversification and Focus

Numerous hypotheses about the profitability of diversification and focus boil down to two lines of argument:

EFFICIENCY (OR INEFFICIENCY) OF INTERNAL CAPITAL MARKETS The diversified firm internalizes the capital market by acting as an allocator of resources among businesses in the portfolio. Advocates of diversification claim that the closer proximity to the companies and access to better information about them permits the internal capital market to operate more efficiently than external markets. Advocates of focus argue that behavioral and agency considerations intervene to make the internal capital markets less efficient; people avoid unpleasant decisions about starving or selling unprofitable businesses and therefore tend to subsidize poorly performing units from the resources of high-performing units. Four papers[7] make the basic argument for efficiency of internal capital markets. Also, Matsusaka and Nanda (1996) have argued that the internal capital market creates real option value for the firm by virtue of the strategic investment flexibility it affords.

COSTS OF INFORMATION AND AGENCY Multidivisional firms are complicated to understand; investors require considerable information to value these firms. Yet most diversified firms provide no more information about their operations than do more focused firms. This opacity creates an asymmetry of information that might cause investors to discount the value of diversified firms more than focused firms. Also, the opacity shelters managers of diversified firms from the scrutiny and discipline of capital markets, creating the threat of agency costs and the manager's expropriation of private benefits. This, too, leads to lower profitability. Scharfstein and Stein (2000) and Rajan, Servaes, and Zingales (2000) argued that unrelated diversification is inefficient and is a result of agency costs. Cross subsidization of business units within the firm is inefficient. Agency costs appear principally in efforts by managers to reduce risk of the firm out of self-interest only, and extract private benefits of control.

Summary of Research Findings

Studies of the economic impact of diversification or focus approach the question from among six methodologies. Each approach lends a different perspective and has its peculiar strengths and weaknesses. As with the general summary of the profitability of M&A (see Chapter 3), the findings lend no ironclad conclusions. Rather, one needs to look for tendencies. In general terms, here is a breakdown of the research approaches and their findings.

EVENT STUDIES A number of papers consider the differences in return associated with the announcement of diversifying or focusing acquisitions, divestitures, spin-offs, and carve-outs. If diversification pays, it should be reflected in higher returns for acquisitions and disposals that result in a more diverse business portfolio for the firm. If focusing pays, announcements that herald acquisitions or disposals that will focus the firm should result in higher returns. The event study approach has the strength of focusing on investor reactions and on market prices. The weaknesses stem from possible noise in the market from conflicting events and questions about market efficiency.

- *Acquisitions.* Seven studies[8] find cumulative average residuals (CARs) at the announcements of transactions are significantly more negative for diversifying deals than for focusing deals. These studies suggest that mergers that focus the firm enhance the buyer's share value by 1 to 3 percent more than diversifying deals. Yet six other studies[9] show significantly positive CARs for diversifying acquisitions. Most of these, however, are studies of conglomerate acquisitions in the 1960s (e.g., Hubbard and Palia 1999) or are associated with the relaxation of regulatory constraints on diversifying acquisitions (e.g., Carow 2001). On balance, the event studies of acquisition announcements suggest that focus pays more than diversification.

- ***Joint ventures and alliances.*** Three studies consider the effect of focusing or diversifying JVs. Ferris et al. (2002) find focus-increasing JVs show materially larger CARs than diversifying JVs. Chan et al. (1997) report that horizontal alliances involving technology transfer have a materially higher CAR. And Gleason et al. (2003) find that horizontal deals in the financial services industry have materially higher CARs than diversifying deals. The event studies of JV and alliance announcements suggest that focus pays more than diversification.
- ***Divestitures, spin-offs, and carve-outs.*** Generally, divestitures, spin-offs, and carve-outs are good news for investors: Since these deals shed assets, the results would seem to be roughly supportive of focusing. But what matters is the nature of the assets being disposed. Two studies of carve-outs reported in Exhibit 6.18 suggest a materially larger announcement CAR when the carved-out unit is not from an industry related to the parent's core business (Hurlburt et al. 2002; Vijh 2000). Three studies of spin-offs in Exhibit 6.17 show a materially larger announcement CAR when the transaction is focus-increasing (Veld and Veld-Meruklova 2002; McNeil and Moore 2001; Johnson et al. 1996). Regarding divestitures, Donaldson (1990) reports materially larger positive CARs at the announcement of sale of noncore assets compared to core asset sales. Dittmar and Shivdasani (undated) report that over the year following the divestiture, firms that became single-business firms had a 3 percent higher return than those that remained diversified. In short, the event studies of divestitures, spin-offs, and carve-outs are consistent with benefits from focusing and penalties from diversification.

Q TESTS *Tobin's Q* is a measure of economic efficiency estimated as the ratio of the market value of assets divided by book value. The higher the Q, the higher is efficiency. Typically, these studies regress Q against a variety of independent variables, including measures of diversification and focus. Four studies give findings consistent with the benefits of focus. Lang and Stulz (1994) find that diversified firms have lower Qs than single-business firms. Morck and Yeung (1998) find that diversification is associated with lower Q except where the industry is information-intensive. Aggarwal and Samwick (2003) report that diversification has a significantly negative effect on Q.

EXCESS VALUE STUDIES: TESTS FOR A DIVERSIFICATION DISCOUNT A logical test of the impact of diversification on value is to compare the actual market value of the firm with its "sum of the parts" value, where each part of the firm is valued at multiples consistent with industry peers. The "excess value" of a diversified firm is simply the difference between actual and imputed values. Nine studies[10] find negative excess values for diversified firms, in the range of 8 to 15 percent—this is the famous "diversification discount"[11] that is often cited in debates over the unprofitability of diversification. On the basis of these findings Lamont and Polk (2002, page 75) asserted, "Diversification destroys value." Yet, more recent studies have challenged the size and even the existence of the diversification discount. The line of attack is that certain data sources contain an inadvertent bias in favor or the diversification discount and that many of the units acquired by diversified firms were already discounted *before* their acquisition—this means that the existence of a discount has little to do with a strategy of diversification. Finally, some studies use more granular data arguing that business segments are too large to capture the costs or benefits of diversification. Nine studies[12] report *no* discount, or even a diversification premium using these revised research approaches. If one believes in the power of the newer techniques, the excess value studies would suggest that diversification has a neutral or positive effect on value.

PRODUCTIVITY STUDIES Another line of research is to consider the impact of diversification or focus on the productivity of business units and plants. Lichtenberg (1992) found lower total factor productivity with increases in diversification. But Schoar (2002) reported that plants in diversified firms were 7 percent *more* productive than plants in single-business firms. Nevertheless, increases in diversification are associated with a net decrease in productivity. Plants that had been acquired actually increased their productivity, whereas incumbent plants decreased in productivity—but since there were fewer acquired than incumbent plants, the total effect on productivity was negative. Schoar wrote, "Diversified firms experience a 'new toy' effect, whereby management focus shifts towards new segments at the expense of existing divisions. As a whole, these results indicate that diversified firms have a productivity advantage over their stand-alone counterparts. They even increase the productivity of their acquired assets. With each diversifying move, however, these firms lose some of their productivity advantage." (Page 2380)

PROPENSITY TOWARD DIVESTITURES Scholars have studied the characteristics of those firms that undertake divestment. Porter (1987) and Ravenscraft (1987) found that divestiture follows acquisition: Firms may buy, but are not assured of *retaining* their purchases. Their reading was that growth through acquisition was not a stable growth strategy. Weston (1989) offered the rebuttal noted earlier. Kaplan and Weisbach (1992) found that firms were more likely to divest unrelated acquisitions than related acquisitions, suggesting that unrelated acquisitions don't pay.

STUDIES OF LONG-TERM REPORTED FINANCIAL RESULTS Though accounting results are easily "managed" by executives and are vulnerable to exogenous effects unrelated to diversification, they are an ongoing focus of investigation. Four studies[13] showed that firms following strategies of unrelated diversification underperform those firms who focus more. Yet four other studies[14] found *improvements* in operating performance following diversifying acquisitions. In addition, Anslinger and Copeland (1996) found that firms pursuing a conscious strategy of unrelated diversification have realized high abnormal returns for sustained periods. Baker and Smith (1998) documented high absolute returns to Kohlberg, Kravis, and Roberts, a well-known leveraged buyout firm and owner of a diversified portfolio of industrial interests. Fluck and Lynch (1999) presented a model of corporate strategy in which *both* diversifying acquisition and then focusing divestiture create value: This relies on the existence of positive net present value (NPV) projects that are unable to obtain financing in public markets. The large firm acquires, finances, grows, and then divests these businesses profitably. In sum, it seems that diversification or focus may not help to discriminate among firms on the basis of long-term performance.

Anslinger and Copeland (1996) argued that it is the postacquisition management strategy and structure, rather than the strategy of diversification or focus, that matters in producing long-term performance.

Practical Implications of the Research Debate over Diversification versus Focus

How are we to make sense of these disparate and contradictory findings? Villalonga (2003b) argues that the debate revolves around three categories of tests, of differing strength. Like the old research on capital market efficiency, there are three forms of assertions about whether diversification destroys value:

1. *Weak form.* Does the diversified firm trade at a discount relative to stand-alone businesses in the same industry? The evidence is mixed here, and the more recent studies favor "no" as an answer.
2. *Semistrong form.* Does the diversified firm trade at a discount relative to its "bust-up" value? A positive answer here asserts that the diversified firm destroys value by staying diversified, and is supported by the numerous studies finding that value is created when firms divest, spin off, or carve out their businesses. Villalonga (2003b) writes, "When firms are outperformed by their competitors, any change in their current strategy is welcomed by the stock market. There is as much evidence that firms are destroying value by staying diversified as there is evidence that single-segment firms are destroying value by not diversifying." (Page 4)
3. *Strong form.* Does the diversified firm trade at a discount relative to what it would be worth *if it had not diversified?* A positive answer here asserts that the act of diversification destroys value. Unfortunately, this "had not diversified" value is unobservable and efforts to find an implied value are challenged by a strong selection bias: Firms that diversify are found to be significantly different from those that don't.

The conclusion from this survey is that one cannot confidently condemn diversification or endorse focus. Still, the research holds some useful implications for the practitioner.

DIVERSIFY ONLY WITH A SOUND ECONOMIC RATIONALE Even if there is no diversification discount, the distribution of outcomes is large, meaning that a nontrivial portion of diversifiers destroy value. The solution is to use an economics perspective to guide your strategic planning and transaction design. The research shows that diversification may be successful under certain circumstances.

- ***Where there is high relatedness in terms of industry focus between the target and buyer.*** Richard Rumelt (1974, 1982) found that returns on equity were higher for strategies of related diversification than for strategies of unrelated diversification or for single-business focus.
- ***Where the internal markets for talent and capital are truly disciplined, and managers are properly rewarded.*** Studies by Amihud and Lev (1981) and Denis et al. (1997) suggest that diversification imposes a kind of agency cost: Manager-controlled firms do more diversifying deals than shareholder-controlled firms.[15]

Anslinger and Copeland (1996) studied 21 firms with little or no internal relatedness, and found that they produced returns of 18 to 35 percent per year by making nonsynergistic acquisitions. They explained the superior performance of these firms as due to seven principles: "Insist on innovating operating strategies. Don't do the deal if you can't find the leader. Offer big incentives to top-level executives. Link compensation to changes in cash flow. Push the pace of change. Foster dynamic relationships among owners, managers, and the board. Hire the best acquirers." (Page 127)

- *Where the public capital market is less effective.* Hubbard and Palia (1999) found that returns from conglomeration were positive and significant during the 1960s, a time when the authors believed the U.S. capital markets were less efficient in allocating capital than they are today. Khanna and Palepu (1997, 2000) made a similar argument in studying conglomerates in India. The authors concluded that these industrial groups enjoyed greater efficiency because of their ability to allocate resources better than the capital market there. And Fauver, Houston, and Naranjo (2002) studied 8,000 companies in 35 countries, concluding, "Internal capital markets generated through corporate diversification are more valuable (or less costly) in countries where there is less shareholder protection and where firms find it more difficult to raise external capital." (Page 1) The distinction between developed and developing countries is therefore interesting as a possible focus for diversification strategies. The research of Lins and Servaes (1999, 2002) lends such a comparison. They found a diversification discount of zero percent in Germany, 10 percent in Japan, and 15 percent in the United Kingdom. But in seven emerging markets, they found a diversification discount of about 7 percent, and concluded that the discount was concentrated among firms that are members of industrial groups. This contradicts the idea that diversification pays where public markets are less efficient, and suggests that differences in corporate governance and/or rule of law across countries may have a material impact on the benefits of a diversification strategy.
- *Where product markets are experiencing an episode of deregulation or other turbulence.* Deregulation of markets invites entry by firms in related industries. The merger of Citicorp and Travelers insurance (see Carow 2002) reflected the deregulation of commercial banking in the United States permitting "bancassurance," the convergence of commercial banking and insurance industries. Also, during periods of product market uncertainty, a disciplined and patient investor may be better at allocating capital into that industry than would a more volatile public capital market.
- *Where one or both firms have significant information-based assets.* There is evidence that diversified firms transfer knowledge and intellectual capital more efficiently than do public markets. Thus, Morck and Yeung (1997) find that diversification pays when the parent and target are in information-intensive industries.

VALUE CREATION DISCIPLINE IS VITAL; AVOID MOMENTUM LOGIC Growth can become a narcotic, such that growing well matters less than growing by any means. Chapter 17 describes the economics of momentum strategies in detail. If strong discipline is maintained, it is possible to grow in a way that creates value for shareholders. Indeed, one of the best-performing stocks of the past 40 years has been Berkshire Hathaway, nominally an insurance company but actually a quirky conglomerate run by Warren Buffett, with interests in furniture retailing, razor blades, airlines, paper, broadcasting, soft drinks, and publishing. Buffett's success seems to say that instead of debating diversification and focus, one should simply concentrate on sound investing and value-oriented management. Study Warren Buffett not as a stock investor but as a CEO of a conglomerate. While we know a lot about his philosophy of value-oriented investing, we know much less about how he finds and manages his diversifying acquisitions.

PERHAPS DIVERSIFICATION AND FOCUS ARE PROXIES FOR SOMETHING ELSE If the choice of strategy (diversification or focus) does not help us discriminate well across outcomes, then perhaps we should look elsewhere for explanations of where strategy has an impact. One could look more deeply to the drivers of the returns in these transactions, such as governance systems, financial discipline, transparency of results, managerial talent, incentive compensation, and so on. Research on these is discussed elsewhere in this book and finds that the drivers are significant in explaining outcomes.

PRESUPPOSE RATIONALITY, BUT GUARD AGAINST STUPIDITY Pay attention as future research unfolds. Growth by diversification is one of the strategic staples for corporations, easily abused and misused. If, as Nobel laureate George Stigler once argued, rational people don't do stupid things repeatedly, firms must be diversifying because there is something in it. One wants to understand the economic consequences of diversification. The evolution from one view to another evokes similar shifts in other areas of M&A, such as poison pills and the perennial question of whether M&A destroys value for bidders.

CONCLUSIONS

The design of good M&A transactions takes root in good strategy. This chapter explores the role of strategy in deciding to grow by acquisition or restructure the firm. Strategy picks positions and capabilities. Analysis of positions and capabilities using a variety of tools outlined here should underpin the effort to profile your firm's strengths, weaknesses, opportunities, and threats (SWOT).

M&A is one of the tactical instruments of strategy. This chapter outlines the variety of alternatives by which the firm could grow inorganically, ranging across contractual agreements, alliances, joint ventures, minority investments, acquisitions, and mergers. The choice among these alternatives is driven by at least three considerations: the benefits from relatedness of the target business to the core of the acquirer, the need for control, and the need to manage risk.

Restructuring activity is a significant source of M&A activity: one-quarter to one-third of all deals annually are divestitures by other firms. But divestiture is only one of the tactical instruments of a strategy of restructuring. This chapter outlines other alternatives, including liquidations, minority investments, spin-offs, carve-outs, split-offs, and tracking stock. (Financial restructurings are reserved for discussion in Chapter 13.) The selection among the various tactical alternatives will be driven by the relatedness of the unit to the core of the parent, the need for control, and whether the unit can survive as an independent entity.

The survey of research in this chapter suggests that restructuring creates value: Divestiture, spin-offs, carve-outs, and tracking stock are associated with significant positive returns at the announcement of those transactions.

However, the costs and benefits of a strategy of diversification remain unsettled. That diversification destroys value is the conventional wisdom in 2003, but the latest research challenges its certainty. This suggests that the practitioner should think critically about blanket assertions about the value of a strategy of diversification or focus. Future research will likely give a more contingent explanation, such as "diversification pays in these circumstances." In the interim, it is too early to tell.

APPENDIX 6.1
A Critical Look at the Self-Sustainable Rate of Growth Concept and Formulas

The self-sustainable growth rate (SSGR) is the maximum rate at which a firm can grow without sales of new common equity. A firm that has a high SSGR relative to its targeted growth rate can execute its business strategy without having to dilute the interests of existing shareholders, submit its plans and intentions to the scrutiny of a stock offering, and incur the relatively high costs of stock issuance. Also, a firm that has a high SSGR relative to its competitors is bound to have some strategic advantage in exploiting the random flow of growth opportunities that come to every industry. Regardless of the popularity of this concept, the financial adviser and analyst must understand its possible application and limitations in order to put it to best use.

BEGINNINGS: A FOCUS ON VALUE

The interest in self-sustainable growth had its origins in the work of two academicians, Merton Miller and Franco Modigliani (1961) (M&M), who asked the question: At what rate will the market value of the firm grow? They argued that the only kind of growth on which operating managers should focus is growth of *value* because any of the other bases of growth (e.g., sales or assets) are flawed guides[16] for corporate policy; only growth of market value was consistent with an interest in *value creation.* M&M showed that the growth rate in market value is simply the product of two variables: the internal rate of return (IRR) of expected future cash flows, and the rate of reinvestment of that cash flow back into the firm.

$$g_{\text{market value}}^{\text{Self-sustainable}} = \rho \cdot K \tag{1}$$

Here K is the reinvestment rate of the cash flows, and ρ (or "rho," a Greek letter) is the IRR of cash flows. The virtue of the M&M growth rate model is that it is economically correct: (1) it focuses on cash flow; and (2) it takes into account the time value of an entire stream of cash. The formula is deceptively simple: Whether the firm can reinvest in the same activities that produce a given IRR depends on a wide range of strategic assumptions such as the rate of technological change, the length of a product life cycle, or the persistence of competitive advantage. In short, the application of this model takes careful thought.

THE POPULAR MODEL FOR ASSET GROWTH

As a shorthand for estimating the self-sustainable growth rate, many analysts use the model shown in equation (2) and its variants, equations (3 and 4):

$$g_{\text{book value assets}}^{\text{Self-sustainable}} = \text{ROE} \cdot (1 - \text{DPO}) \tag{2}$$

$$g_{\text{book value assets}}^{\text{Self-sustainable}} = \left[\text{ROTC} + \left(\text{ROTC} - K_d\right)\frac{\text{Debt}}{\text{Equity}}\right] \cdot (1 - \text{DPO}) \tag{3}$$

$$g_{\text{book value assets}}^{\text{Self-sustainable}} = \left(\frac{\text{New income}}{\text{Sales}} \cdot \frac{\text{Sales}}{\text{Assets}} \cdot \frac{\text{Assets}}{\text{Equity}}\right) \cdot (1 - \text{DPO}) \tag{4}$$

In the formulas, ROE is the accounting return on equity, ROTC is return on total capital[17], K_d is the after-tax cost of debt, and DPO is the dividend payout ratio.[18] Equation (2) is simply an accrual-accounting version of M&M's formula: (1 – DPO) is equivalent to M&M's *K*. For ROE, many analysts use the expected return for the next few years. A less sensible assumption is to use the past few years' average ROE.

Equation (3) expands the preceding equation by inserting a well-known formula for the ROE of a levered firm. The virtue of this form of the model is that it allows the analyst to tinker with a possible interdependence between the firm's mix of capital and its cost of debt. For instance, the firm's cost of debt might be supposed to rise as the firm increased its debt/equity ratio past some moderate level.

Equation (4) also expands equation (2) by inserting the well-known DuPont system of ratios for ROE. This version is appealing to operating managers since it decomposes ROE into a measure of margin profitability (net income/sales), a measure of asset turnover (sales/assets), and a measure of leverage (assets/equity). With the aid of this model, one can see more directly the effects of price or cost improvements and better asset utilization.

INSIGHTS TO BE GAINED FROM THE POPULAR ASSET GROWTH MODEL

Comparisons across Firms

The popular self-sustainable growth model can yield insights into the comparative strategic robustness of competitors within an industry. For instance, Exhibit 6A.1 gives the calculations for the self-sustainable growth rates for five retailers competing in selling women's apparel. The data, drawn from Value Line,[19] are *forecasts* of

EXHIBIT 6A.1 Self-Sustainable Growth Rates for Five Retailers

Name	Self-Sustainable Growth Rate	Dividend Payout Ratio	Return on Total Capital	Hypothetical Bond Rating and After-Tax Cost of Debt	Debt-to-Equity Ratio
Charming Shoppes, Inc.	13.2%	15%	14.5%	A 6.1%	12.6%
Deb Shops, Inc.	11.3%	20%	14.0%	Baa 6.6%	2.0%
The Dress Barn	17.5%	0%	17.5%	Baa 6.6%	0.0%
Petrie Stores Corporation	8.0%	25%	10.0%	Baa 6.6%	19.0%
The Limited, Inc.	27.6%	22%	23.0%	A 6.1%	53.8%

the variables for each firm in early 1991 for the period through 1995. Consider each firm's strategic ability to grow and the sources of that strength.

The exhibit reveals dramatic strategic disparities among these competitors. The Limited enjoys an unusually robust self-sustainable growth rate of 27.6 percent, stemming in large part from its high internal profitability and its relatively more aggressive use of debt capital. At the other end of the spectrum, Petrie Stores Corporation appears to be able to self-sustain only an 8 percent annual growth rate; this is due largely to its relatively low internal profitability. The Dress Barn stands out for its unusual set of financial policies: no debt and no dividends. Given that this firm has the second-highest internal profitability in the competitive group, The Dress Barn could probably boost its self-sustainable growth rate materially by even modest use of leverage.

Analysis of Policies within a Firm

The popular self-sustainable growth model may be solved in reverse to show what policy (or policies) can be changed, and with what effect, in order to achieve a *targeted* growth rate. Used in this way, the model can help an analyst prepare policy recommendations. As an illustration, suppose that the CEO of Acme Corporation, a privately held manufacturer of specialized machine tools, feels compelled by competitive conditions to set a target for the firm to grow at a 15 percent annual rate in order to survive and prosper in its market niche. Can this rate of growth be sustained? Exhibit 6A.2 summarizes the modeling assumptions and the results.

Because Acme Corporation can self-sustain a growth rate of only 6.5 percent and needs to grow at 15 percent, management has a problem: how to increase the firm's self-sustainable rate of growth. The CEO continues to analyze the operations of the firm and determines that any of the policy changes presented in Exhibit 6A.3 would raise the self-sustainable growth rate to 15 percent.

EXHIBIT 6A.2 Summary of Modeling Assumptions

Acme Corporation Self-Sustainable Growth Rate Analysis	Assumptions and Result
Dividend payout ratio	50%
Target debt/equity ratio	25%
Expected return on equity	13%
Expected return on total capital	11.4%
Expected after-tax cost of debt	5%
New issues of common equity	Nil
Self-sustainable growth rate	**6.5%**

EXHIBIT 6A.3 Policy Changes to Raise Self-Sustainable Growth Rate

Change in Policy	New Policy Target	Existing Policy	Required Change
1. Increase debt/equity ratio. Finance the growth with debt.	D/E = 2.9	D/E = .25	Tenfold relevering.
2. Sell equity.	DPO = –115% (i.e., sell about as much equity each year as you generate internally)	DPO = 50% (i.e., no equity sales)	Drop the dividend. Sell equity.
3. Improve internal profitability.	ROE = 30% ROTC = 25%	ROE = 13% ROTC = 11.4%	More than double the margins.
4. Improve internal profitability *and* increase debt/equity ratio.	ROTC = 18% D/E = .667	ROTC = 11.4% D/E = .25	Increase margins and leverage a lot.
5. Cut dividend payout ratio and improve internal profitability and increase debt/equity ratio.	DPO = 11.8% ROTC = 13% D/E = .50	DPO = 25% ROTC = 11.4% D/E = .25	Cut dividend in half. Double the leverage. Increase margins.

Considering the various advantages and disadvantages, the fifth alternative, which involves a blend of changes in all policy areas, seems most attractive. A higher debt/equity ratio could still be consistent with average ratios in the industry and with the firm's internal debt rating preferences. While the owners of the firm would feel the cut in dividend payments, the improvement in competitive standing might translate into capital gains later. Of all the policy changes, an increase in ROTC from 11.4 percent to 13 percent would be the hardest to implement, though management believes it is obtainable.

Analysis like this can be performed at a more detailed level, using spreadsheet forecasts. Churchill and Mullins (2001) illustrate the spreadsheet approach and show that, to avoid running out of cash, the firm can consider speeding up the cycle of operating cash within the firm, reducing costs, or raising prices.

SOME CAVEATS ABOUT THE POPULAR SELF-SUSTAINABLE GROWTH MODEL OF ASSETS

In the hands of an artful analyst, the popular model can yield valuable insights. But it can be abused and misused easily. Financial executives and their advisers should beware of six potential problems:

1. ***The model says nothing about value creation.*** The popular model describes the maximum growth rate in *assets*, not *market value*. All too often, financial advisers take for granted the wisdom of stated growth targets—but such growth targets are usually stated in terms of sales or assets and may be realizable only with the destruction of market value of equity and/or debt. The model should not be used without some complementary analysis proving the economic attractiveness of the growth goals. A much more detailed analysis of self-sustainable growth and its sources may be gained from a forecast of financial statements, or cash receipts and disbursements. The self-sustainable growth model is nothing more than a summary of such a forecast. This detailed model could be prepared as a computer spreadsheet with various operating and financial policy variables as assumptions or outputs, depending on whether the objective is to determine growth-sustaining policies or merely to compute the cash flow and time-value-adjusted self-sustainable growth rate.
2. ***The popular model is an accrual-accounting-based, one-year measure.*** ROE and ROTC are measured over one year, typically from historical performance. Can this performance be sustained over the long term into the future? Moreover, by focusing on reported earnings, the model ignores cash flow items such as deferred taxes, which might be the basis for much higher self-sustainable growth.
3. ***The popular model assumes fixed assets grow at the rate of sales.*** This would be inappropriate for firms whose fixed asset additions are large, lumpy, and intermittent. Also, firms that have spare productive capacity may not need to add assets in a particular year.
4. ***The popular model estimates the* nominal *self-sustainable growth rate; yet it is the* real *self-sustainable growth rate that is of strategic interest.*** Under inflation, the real growth rate will be smaller than the nominal rate, and indeed, could even be negative even though the nominal rate is large and positive. Roughly speaking, the real self-sustainable rate will be equal to the difference between the nominal self-sustainable rate and the rate of inflation.
5. ***The self-sustainable growth rate is no panacea.*** Rarely are the remedies indicated by the model easy to implement. This is because many of the variables in the model are exogenous to the firm: (1) interest rates are set in the capital markets; (2) product and factor prices are determined by competitive conditions; (3) internal programs to cut costs may be limited by managerial talent; and so on.

6. ***The assumption of only internal equity financing violates a basic premise of modern finance theory.*** The premise is that capital is always accessible to firms having profitable investment opportunities. Indeed, from a macroeconomic point of view, society should want managers to fund all profitable opportunities. Why managers choose to constrain their own growth is not well understood, though many of the reasons suggested at the opening of this note probably explain why: concerns about control, confidentiality, transaction costs, and so on. In any event, the fact is that the American business economy relies very little on equity financing: From 1950 to 1990, only 4 percent of all capital investment was financed by the sales of new equity. In short, even though equity capital is always accessible, most executives make little use of it.

NOTES

1. *Oxford English Dictionary*, 2nd ed., Oxford: Oxford University Press, 1998, Vol. 16, page 852.
2. For a more detailed discussion of the growth-share matrix in strategic planning, see Hax and Majluf (1984), Chapter 7.
3. SIC stands for "Standard Industrial Classification." The U.S. Commerce Department's classification of firms in an industry should be checked for reasonableness.
4. This financial rationale for conglomerate mergers presupposes that shareholders are unable to replicate this through their own investing and homemade leverage. Taxes, transaction costs, margin requirements, and high consumer loan rates can frustrate the individual investor's attempt to synthesis this benefit.
5. Financial recapitalizations may also affect the operations and asset mix of the firm. These deals are often predicated on asset sales, plant closings, spin-offs, and so on.
6. To "divisionalize" is to adopt an organizational structure for the firm that shapes major segments or divisions around product groups.
7. See Weston (1970), Chandler (1977), Alchian (1969), and Williamson (1975).
8. See Morck, Schleifer, and Vishny (1990), Sicherman and Pettway (1987), Morck (1990), Maqueira et al. (1998), Nail, Megginson, and Maqueira (1998), Delong (2001), and Megginson, Morgan, and Nail (2002).
9. See Carow (2001), Hubbard and Palia (1999), Schipper and Thompson (1983), Elgers and Clark (1980), Matsusaka (1993), and Ferris et al. (2002).
10. See Berger and Ofek (1995, 1999), Lang and Stulz (1994), Servaes (1996), Comment and Jarrell (1995), Lins and Servaes (1999), Mansi and Reeb (2002), Denis, Denis, and Yost (2002), and Lamont and Polk (2002).
11. Berger and Ofek (1995) compute the diversification discount as excess value divided by the imputed value of the firm. The actual value is the market value of equity plus the book value of liabilities. The imputed value is the sum of segment values estimated by the product of a valuation multiple for single-business peers (total capital divided by assets, sales, or operating earnings) times the accounting value for the segment.

12. See Chevalier (2000), Hyland and Diltz (2002), Klein (2001), Graham, Lemmon, and Wolf (1998), Campa and Kedia (1999), Villalonga (1999, 2003a), Mansi and Reeb (2002), and Whited (2001).
13. See Rumelt (1974, 1982), Ravenscraft and Scherer (1987), and Kaplan and Weisbach (1992).
14. See Kruse (2002), Healey, Palepu, and Ruback (1992), Parrino and Harris (1999), and Cornett and Tehranian (1992).
15. Amihud and Lev (1991) concluded, "Risk reduction through conglomerate merger may be convincingly rejected on *a priori* grounds as a merger motive from the stockholders' point of view." (Page 615)
16. It is easy to grow sales or assets by investing willy-nilly, without attention to value creation. For instance, it is possible for many firms to expand sales by relaxing credit standards and investing in more accounts receivable. But doing so without giving attention to the pricing of that credit or the probability of being repaid can, in the long run, destroy firm value.
17. Return on total capital is computed by dividing earnings before interest and after taxes (EBIAT) by the total capital of the firm (i.e., debt plus equity). This is also sometimes called "return on net assets" and is computed as EBIAT divided by net assets (i.e., total assets less current liabilities).
18. The dividend payout ratio is computed as dividends divided by earnings.
19. The hypothetical bond rating is inferred from Value Line's rating of financial stability. The after-tax cost of debt is associated with that bond rating as of early 1991.

CHAPTER 7

Acquisition Search and Deal Origination: Some Guiding Principles

INTRODUCTION

Compared to other phases of M&A transaction development, *acquisition search* is nonlinear and even unruly: One hits many dead ends and must refine a lot of ore to get the valuable metal. AlliedSignal Corporation surfaced 550 attractive potential businesses to acquire in 1996–1997. Of these, 190 targets were selected. Further screening reduced the sample to 52 firms, for which the firm initiated negotiations on 28. Detailed due diligence research was conducted on 17; AlliedSignal consummated 10 of these deals.[1] Perhaps the all-time record for acquisition search was Ciba-Geigy's acquisition of Airwick Industries in 1974, which was preceded by a review of more than 18,000 companies, a more detailed review of 100 firms, and ultimately the acquisition of one.[2] Against these small ratios of "done deals" to firms reviewed, even modest improvements in the efficiency of search could yield major improvements in results.

M&A transactions may spring from a search process by a buyer or from an origination process by an intermediary (hereafter called "the banker") who stands to gain from the consummation of a deal. Search and origination draw on the same principles. Thus, this chapter uses the terms "search" and "origination" interchangeably.

Search skills entail a large amount of tacit knowledge best learned at the side of a seasoned professional. The aim of this chapter is not to displace that kind of learning, but rather to offer a few insights that will help the reader get started down the right path. This path begins with the insight that acquisition searches are essentially intelligence-gathering operations, and therefore the search effort needs to be structured in a way to enhance the acquisition of *information*, and the right kind. The path begins at the intersection of four crucial perspectives:

1. ***Economics of information.*** Searches should be focused on gathering high-quality information about prospective targets. Research on the economics of information lends a succinct profile of what "quality" means in the M&A search world. Deal-rich information is private and clear—it is also likely to be costly. Develop *private information* and private insights.
2. ***Networks.***[3] Connectivity with others helps the deal searcher get high quality information. Research on networks suggests that through the short cuts that participating in a network affords, you may be closer than you think to your targets.

3. *Options.* Investment to build a search network is like investing in options. While the payoff on those options remains uncertain to the researcher, the very uncertainty of the search makes that network valuable.
4. *Contagion.* The *diffusion* of information about deal opportunities through a market resembles the spread of rumors in a financial crisis, or of disease in an epidemic. Research on diffusion suggests that your awareness of other buyers and sellers depends on the setting, on the clarity of your message, and on the existence of key people who can help carry the message.

The virtue of thinking about acquisition search in these terms is that they afford a framework for strategy, management, and evaluation of an acquisition search. Knowing how a search is going and how effectively the searchers are performing is of serious concern to investors, observers, and the searchers themselves.

SOME PRINCIPLES OF ACQUISITION SEARCH

To most practitioners, the search process feels pretty haphazard. It is neither possible nor desirable to eliminate the role of chance. However, a healthy observance of a few principles can enhance one's odds of success.

The Currency of Acquisition Search Is *Information*

Acquisition search is an information-gathering process. While this may seem obvious, many searchers assume that it is merely a deal-gathering process or a contact-building process. A good search process begins with building a network of information-generating contacts and results in a stream of deal opportunities. But the path from contacts to deals is paved with *information*. As Exhibit 7.1 suggests, contacts generate information; information generates insights; and insights generate deals. Information and insights also feed backward through the chain: a flexible

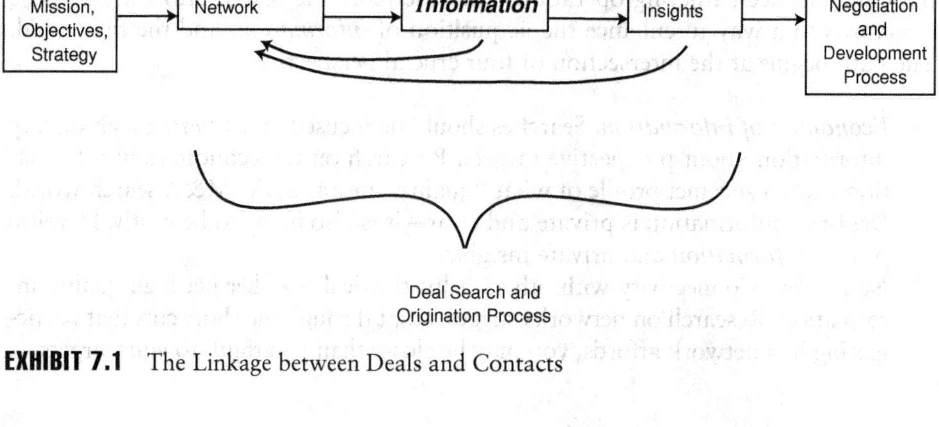

EXHIBIT 7.1 The Linkage between Deals and Contacts

system adapts to news. One needs to build a search effort that generates a flow of high quality, credible, usable information.

Some M&A professionals think of the transaction itself as the basic unit of the search. While the virtue of focusing on outcomes should not be ignored, to focus solely on transactions will not yield insights about how or from where a transaction originated, and where the search might go to his or her best advantage. When one is in search mode, it is better to focus on interesting facts because they tend to lead to interesting transactions. Focusing on information, rather than transactions, implies a very different perspective on acquisition search: a focus on *process* rather than outcomes. This is an insight known to many golfers; focusing on how you swing the club results in a better game than focusing on driving the ball a long way.

Clarity, Privacy, and Cost: What the Market Knows Clearly Is Fully Priced

Not all information is created equal. Two key dimensions explain a great deal of the impact that information can have on asset prices: *ambiguity* and privacy. High quality information is clear and costly. Think of your options receiving television broadcasts; you can use a rabbit-ears antenna and get a grainy picture; but such a picture is much less expensive than the picture you get by cable or satellite. Markets discount ambiguous signals and mark up clear signals, a core idea of the budding field of information economics.[4] For instance, Michael Spence (1973) and Stephen Ross (1977) considered markets of employers and investors in a world of *adverse selection* (i.e., where the seller has an incentive to misrepresent the item to be sold). They found that *costly attributes* (such as academic degrees or promises to pay dividends or interest) would tell buyers things that mere words would not. Sirri and Tufano (1998) report that investors choose mutual funds that are less costly to find.

Clarity is not the only driver of quality. Another is how widely it is known. Capital markets are reasonably efficient. Academic research on security prices confirms that *public information* gets impounded into security prices rapidly and without bias. This is the so-called "*efficient markets hypothesis*," first advanced by Eugene Fama in 1965. Efficiency in pricing is produced by competition among investors, who, through their buying and selling in the market, reflect in their settlement prices the information they know. This implies that if you want to beat the market you must know something that the market doesn't. *Information asymmetry* is the telltale for profitable arbitrage. Efficiency and competition eliminate profitable arbitrage.[5]

To extend one's understanding of the deal development implications of the privacy of information, consider a range of publicity across three situations in time: (1) At the start, an acquisition opportunity is privately known; there has been no public announcement. (2) A public announcement has just been made that the target firm is available for sale, but diffusion of the news through the market is slow and incomplete—at best, the information is "semipublic." (3) A public announcement was made, followed by active marketing of the target and even possibly an auction; as a result, diffusion of the news is complete. Exhibit 7.2 gives some implications of each scenario: It suggests that public information is fully priced; private information is not. The buyer's "sweet spot" is the world of private information. There, the buyer is likely to find lower competition, more advantageous pricing,

EXHIBIT 7.2 Three Information Scenarios and Their Impact on Competition, Pricing, and Tailoring

	Information about the Acquisition Opportunity Is:		
	Private	Semipublic	Fully Public
Degree of competition among potential buyers	Low	Medium	High
Likelihood that the opportunity is fully priced	Low	Medium	High
Likelihood that a buyer can intervene in ways to tailor the pricing and terms to greater advantage	High	Medium	Low

and better opportunities for deal tailoring. There, too, the banker is likely to provide greater service, build a stronger reputation, and earn higher fees. Quite simply, private knowledge of high return investment opportunities is a crucial ingredient for creating value through M&A. Exhibit 7.3 depicts this "sweet spot."

The significance of private information implies that the deal search should be structured to generate private information and transactions before they become widely known. The potential asymmetry of information in the market implies the existence of a *first-mover advantage.* Specialists (i.e., bankers) who focus their expertise will thrive in the context of information asymmetries because they can get paid to help buyers exploit a first-mover advantage.

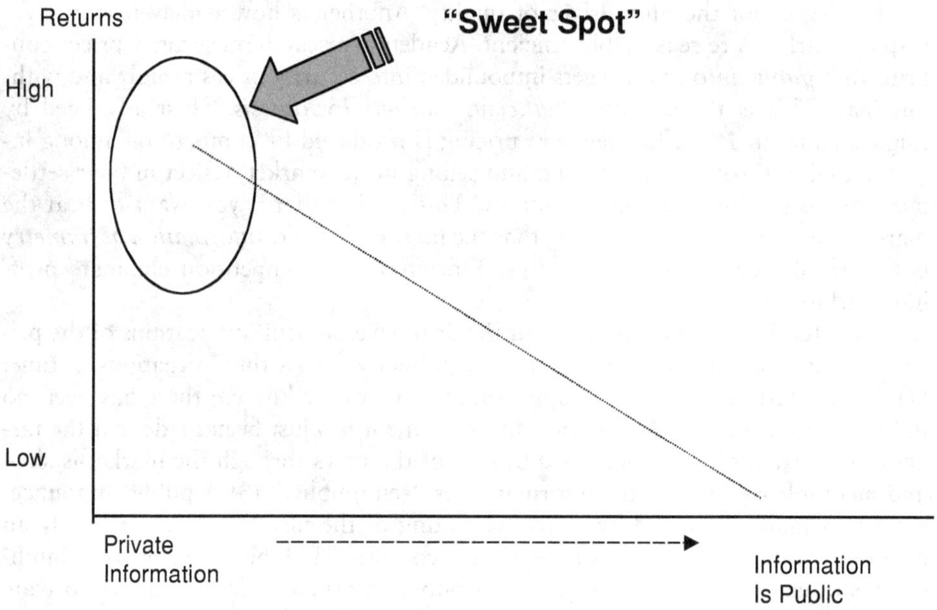

EXHIBIT 7.3 Locating the Sweet Spot

Information Arrives Sequentially and Must Be Filtered

This third principle underscores the crucial importance of *screening criteria.* News over a *network* arrives randomly; as information accumulates, deal opportunities begin to take shape. But they rarely gel in a way that permits pairwise comparison of comparable opportunities. Thus, the searcher is faced with the need to make "yes/no" decisions sequentially, rather than the vastly preferable "either/or" kind of decision. One of the large lessons of the field of economics is that "either/or" decisions are better because they permit an assessment of the *opportunity cost* associated with taking one path over the other. In the absence of a peer comparison, how is one to assess the cost of the lost opportunity?

Discounted cash flow (DCF) valuation analysis explicitly tests the cost of the lost opportunity through the choice of a discount rate that presumes the existence of other assets with comparable risk. But valuing *every* possible deal that the searcher encounters is impractical: Valuation is so time-consuming that the searcher can value only a few firms in a brief period. One needs to prequalify the deal opportunities worth valuing. Screening criteria enable the searcher to reject unattractive opportunities.

Popular screening criteria would include the following:

- ***Industry and position in it.*** Strategic searches will give great attention to industry and even segments within an industry. This criterion is the predominant screen for one's thinking about strategic "themes" or "big bets." Frameworks such as Michael Porter's (1980) industry and competitor analysis can help illuminate the attractiveness of a firm's position in the industry—but it is also time-consuming to do well. One should do this analysis later in the screening process. Chapter 6 describes various frameworks for industry and competitor analysis.
- ***Resources and strategic capabilities.*** Some searchers look for unusual resources or capabilities, rather than market positions. Hamel and Pralahad (1994) argue that it is capabilities, rather than current market positions, that better predict future performance of firms. Examples of strategic capabilities are animated film production at Walt Disney, know-how in the production of computer chips at Intel, logistics management at Wal-Mart, and naval architecture skills at Johnson Boats. Strategic capabilities favorably position a firm to be the leader even as its industry continues to evolve. A strategic capability creates high rates of return, enhances agility, and promotes the survival of the firm.
- ***Size of the business: sales or assets.*** Searchers usually have a target range of firm size. This typically reflects both a strategic view (e.g., how large a firm must be to survive and prosper in the field), and the searcher's own resources or investment budget.
- ***Profitability.*** This is a test of financial health: while the target may have passed the size test, it might not be generating enough earnings to justify acquisition. At the very least, searchers must have a view on the desirability of buying assets or a firm in bankruptcy or financial distress. While there is a well-known search strategy of focusing on distressed targets, "vulture acquiring" requires a special expertise and thus remains a very small portion of all transactions. More often than not, searchers dictate a desire to buy a stream of profits expressed in absolute terms (e.g., earnings before interest and taxes of at least $5 million) or in percentage terms (e.g., a net profit margin of at least 5 percent).

- *Risk exposure.* Searchers often have strong aversions to some risks, and a willingness to accept others. Potent risks for many firms are environmental liabilities, inflation exposure, and uncertainties about health care expenses for employees and retirees. Classic concerns for operating managers are technological change, supply chain disruptions, and union activism in the form of strikes. Marketers justifiably worry about undue concentration of sales with one major customer—the risks of the customer thereby become the risks of the supplier. "Key person" risks arise when one employee is crucial to the survival and prosperity of the firm—illness, accident, or disgruntlement could destabilize that firm. Chapter 8 ("Due Diligence") describes in more detail how one would search for risks.
- *Asset type.* Some searchers will screen away firms for whom a large part of its market value resides in intangible assets that are difficult to audit and value. Such intangibles may include patents, brand names, and human capital. For instance, at many service businesses, it is said that the most important asset walks out the door each night. For many retailers, a crucial asset is *location.* Technology firms depend not only on existing patent positions, but also on R&D-in-process that will determine the competitiveness of the firm in the future.
- *Management quality.* Searchers should have a view on the quality of management currently in place and likely to transfer to Newco after a transaction. Large corporate buyers with depth of management may be indifferent to the quality of target management because they can fill the target's ranks from their own. But smaller buyers may depend crucially on the quality of management in place.
- *Prospective control.* Not all transactions are for sale of 100 percent control. The searcher must have a view on the desirability of total versus partial or minority control in the target.
- *Organizational fit.* This is the most difficult screening criterion to test in a short period of time, but probably accounts for the failure of a large number of acquisition discussions. Searchers who are intimately familiar with the players in an industry will know by direct experience or hearsay about the culture and values of the target firm. The less familiar searcher will learn in due course about these.

Specialized searches will generate additional screening criteria. A relatively short list of criteria, however, can serve effectively to eliminate the bulk of the uninteresting deals and information, preserving the searcher's time for the more promising subset.

The reality is that your search experience feeds back upon the criteria and tends to shape them as you learn more. Haspeslagh and Jemison (1991) wrote, "Most acquisitions involve an iteration between a strategy that is clarified over time and the opportunistic consideration of acquisition possibilities." (Page 45) Acquisition search involves *dynamic learning by doing.* One must allow for a certain degree of opportunism, since opportunities help clarify strategy.

Invest in Social Networks: They Make Search More Efficient and Effective

The nature of a search is that one seeks to acquire information held by others. Successful searches are almost never conducted simply by reading one-way communications, such as want-ad listings of businesses for sale. High quality information is obtained through a social contact and exchange, such as payment to attend an industry trade show, payment for a research report, or subscription to a directory of players in an industry. The relationships between a searcher and other players in the environment form a network that can reduce the cost of search. The alternative to a network would be a sequence of one-off exchanges of information—but this alternative is a costly way to acquire information. Networks afford economies of scale and scope in search.

Two ideas from research on social networks are especially relevant to the problem of searching for firms to buy. The first is your *degree of separation* from those people who know about attractive acquisition opportunities. The second is the *rate of diffusion* by which knowledge spreads through a network.

In 1967, Stanley Milgram undertook a study of the "small world" phenomenon: You meet a stranger and discover that you have a friend in common. In unison, you and your new acquaintance say, "It's a small world." He tested the linkage of acquaintances in the United States by asking a sample of people in Omaha, Nebraska, to send a letter to a stockbroker in Massachusetts only by passing the letter through a chain of people they knew by first name. Travers and Milgram (1969) reported that the average length of the chain was 5.2 people; this is the origin of the phrase "six degrees of separation."[6] Subsequent studies have replicated the finding across racial lines giving the six degrees of separation more universal status. This is a surprising finding. Most of us would guess that the chain would run into the hundreds or thousands. The variance was large, ranging from as few as one link to as many as 11. About a quarter of the letters never made it. Travers and Milgram speculated that the people at the dead ends were either not sufficiently motivated or did not know someone to forward the letter on to. Equally surprising was a second finding: About half the letters that did get to the target passed through three key people. Travers and Milgram called these "stars." Stars are very rich *nodes* in a network.

The way networks function was the focus of a stream of research[7] on *diffusion* of innovations, influence, fashions, diseases, and new drug adoptions. Research on word-of-mouth advertising reveals that news travels unevenly: At first it disseminates slowly; then it spreads explosively. Malcolm Gladwell (2000) has written, "The best way to understand the emergence of fashion trends . . . [and] the transformation of unknown books into bestsellers . . . is to think of them as epidemics. Ideas and products and messages and behaviors spread just like viruses do." (Page 7) The *tipping point* is the dramatic moment of explosive growth.

But diffusion occurs at different speeds through networks. Davis and Greve (1997) studied the diffusion of the golden parachute and poison pill antitakeover defenses[8] through a sample of large U.S. corporations. The presence of interlocking directors[9] proved to be a major predictor of whether a corporation would adopt these defenses: having an authoritative voice from an estimable corporation lent legitimacy to the spread of these defenses. But the two defenses diffused at different rates. It took the pill just three years to be adopted by 50 percent of the corporations, while it took seven years for the golden parachute to reach that mark. The existence of a network of interlocking directors proved to be decisive in the spread of the poison pill. In the case of the parachute, what mattered more was geographic proximity. The authors argued that the rate of diffusion is affected by three factors: "Complex innovations spread slower than simple ones. . . . Practices that are observable spread faster than those that are not. . . . Innovations that are compatible with the norms of a social system spread faster than those that are not." (Page 30) They argued that the pill was more observable and more compatible with social norms.

The "small world" and diffusion research streams offer insights that are highly relevant for acquisition search:

WHAT YOU SEEK MAY BE CLOSER THAN YOU THINK Close proximity is surprising. The party game, "Six Degrees of Kevin Bacon," challenges the players to find an actor separated by a chain of six links (movies) or less to the actor Kevin Bacon. You can play this game on the Internet through a program devised by the computer science department at the University of Virginia.[10] It is challenging to find an actor separated by more than *four* degrees from Kevin Bacon.

YOUR SOCIAL NETWORK GIVES YOU PROXIMITY TO YOUR GOAL Watts (1999) argues that the essence of the network's value lies in its shortcuts to the goal. You don't have to be everywhere and know everything. You just have to be connected. The small world research adds a new phrase to the M&A lexicon: social capital. One's connectivity to others is an asset that M&A professionals should cultivate as carefully as other categories of assets such as talent, financial capital, and physical property. It helps to be visible in the network. Achieving search economies through a network may require an initial investment for letter or brochure that describes the searcher and the search, mailings and telephone calls that introduce the searcher, attending industry conferences and conventions, fees to gatekeepers, retainers to river guides.

THERE IS STRENGTH IN WEAK TIES: DIVERSITY AND BREADTH OF THE NETWORK MATTER Mark Granovetter (1973, 1974) studied how people find jobs. He discovered that personal connections were decisive. But the surprise was that three-quarters of the successful connections to a job offer were through "weak ties," people whom the job seeker saw "occasionally" or "rarely." Commenting on this, Malcolm Gladwell (1999) wrote, "*Weak ties* tend to be more important than strong ties. Your friends, after all, occupy the same world that you do. They work with you, or live near you, and go the same churches, schools, or parties. How much, then, do they know that you don't know? Mere acquaintances, on the other hand, are much more likely to know something that you don't. . . . The most important people in your life are, in certain critical realms, the people who aren't closest to you, and the more people you know who aren't close to you the stronger your position becomes. . . . Granovetter, by contrast, argues that what matters in getting ahead is not the quality of your relationships but the quantity—not how close you are to those you know but, paradoxically, how many people you know whom you aren't particularly close to." (Pages 12–13) The "weak tie" phenomenon emphasizes the virtues of diversity and breadth in a network. It turns out that networks are more valuable the more "nodes" there are. A node is one point of connection (such as a person) in a network. The relationship between nodes and networks is well illustrated by the fax machine. In a world of only one fax machine, the machine is useless and without value. But the value turns positive and increases as the number of other fax machines to communicate with rises. This is Metcalfe's Law: The value of a network is proportional to the number of working nodes in it.[11]

SIMPLE SEARCHES BASED ON OBSERVABLE CRITERIA GO FASTER The diffusion research suggests that the kind of information the network is asked to channel will affect the speed with which the network delivers. This would argue for using simple and clear search criteria. But it also points to network capacity (the richness of the network's nodes, and the bandwidth of its links) as determinants of *speed*. Evans and Wurster (2000) argue that "richness" of a node determines its effectiveness. Richness consists of credibility, contacts, information, interpretive insights, and resources for generating more insights. As a search adviser, becoming a rich node is the most powerful way to compete in a world where former economic relationships are getting "blown to bits" by the Internet. Very substantive, useful, helpful nodes gain the attention of users, and possibly even acquire their loyalty. "*Bandwidth*" is a term used by information technologists to indicate the information carrying capacity of a channel, such as a fiber-optic cable. High bandwidth channels are more valuable because they are more flexible to surges in demand. Moore's Law suggests that hardware capacity increases at an accelerating rate.[12]

The Best Information Is Firsthand

As argued earlier, the extent to which information is public affects the potential returns on an investment—the existence of *tipping points* lends urgency to the question of *where* the searcher should position himself/herself in the stream of news. Tippy news (an event or new information that triggers a tipping point in the diffusion of an idea) suggests that the searcher should seek an early or "*upstream*" *position* in the flow of news about investment opportunities. Market positioning is always an important consideration for business people, but it becomes crucial in tippy markets because they tend to give winner-take-all outcomes.

In studying new product introductions, Geoffrey Moore (1991) illuminated the variety of positions in the stream of dissemination: innovators, early adopters, early majority, and so on. Moore argues that there are large differences among the groups, and that they tend not to communicate well from group to group. The implication of this research for acquisition search is that there may be no substitute for *being upstream* in the flow of news about deal opportunities. Simply looking (as opposed to being) upstream is probably insufficient for identifying emerging *sweet spots*—the way to get upstream is with the help of *navigators*.

Primary research is the best and safest source of insights about investment sweet spots. Such research includes field interviews with managers and industry observers, attendance at trade shows and product demonstrations, and direct surveys of public information on firms and industries. *Secondary* research, though less rich, is also less costly; one must examine the trade-off on cost and richness. A great deal of information about companies is in the public domain. Exhibit 7.4 offers a synopsis of sources of public information that have proved useful to M&A searchers.

Navigators Affect Dissemination and Search: Gatekeepers and River Guides

The speed of dissemination is affected by the setting or context, by the impact of the message, and by the involvement of people with special gifts. Gladwell (1999) describes three types. First, *connectors* know lots of people, and the right kinds of

EXHIBIT 7.4 Annotated List of Recommended Sources of Public Information about Companies

The Directory of Corporate Affiliations
The Directory of Corporate Affiliations (DCA) provides insight into more than 174,000 parent companies, affiliates, subsidiaries, and divisions—all the way down to the seventh level of reporting relationships. The DCA is available in print, CD-ROM, and on the Web. Information includes type of business, net worth, sales data, and contact information of key personnel and outside firms. *The Directory of Corporate Affiliations* is published by Lexis-Nexis Group.

Dun & Bradstreet's Million Dollar Database
D&B's North American Million Dollar Database provides information on approximately 1,600,000 U.S. and Canadian leading public and private businesses. Company information includes industry information with up to 24 individual 8-digit SICs, size criteria (employees and annual sales), type of ownership, principal executives, and biographies.

D&B's International Million Dollar Database (IMDD) provides information on over 1,600,000 international companies. Find SIC, total employees, legal status, annual U.S. sales dollar equivalent, and more, plus identify up to four executives on the world's largest entities.

Factiva
A journal and news database created by Dow Jones and Reuters, Factiva includes a "Company Quick Search" module, which allows researchers to gather contact information, list of competitors, business description, corporate performance information, and the latest news on public and private companies. A "Company Screening" feature is also available.

Hoover's Online
A company and industry database that provides company profiles for public and private companies. Company profiles include contact information, history, news and analysis, financial data, locations and subsidiaries, products and operations information. An "Advanced Search" feature allows users to screen for companies by location, industry, size, exchange, number of employees, assets, annual sales, and sales growth. The "StockScreener" feature allows users to screen by other financial and performance data.

Lexis-Nexis
Lexis-Nexis is primarily a journal and news database that also includes various domestic and international public and private company directories. The directories include Disclosure, Hoover's Online, Nelson's Public Company Profiles, Standard & Poor's Register of Corporations, U.S. Business Directory, and many other international company directories.

InfoUSA
InfoUSA.com is a provider of sales and marketing support for products for all types of businesses, from small businesses to large corporations. The company compiles a database of 14 million U.S. businesses and 300 million U.S. consumers, and 1.2 million Canadian businesses and 12 million Canadian consumers.

(Continued)

EXHIBIT 7.4 *(Continued)*

Standard & Poor's Stock Reports
Standard & Poor's Stock Reports cover approximately 5,000 publicly traded companies listed on the New York, American, Nasdaq, and regional stock exchanges. Each report provides a concise picture of a company's health, along with Standard & Poor's estimates of the stock's worth, whether it's overvalued or undervalued, and analyst opinions on investment potential and earnings estimates. Features includes analysis, commentary, and quantitative data on about 5,000 publicly held U.S. corporations, STARS rankings that provide the buy/hold/sell recommendations of Standard & Poor's analysts, more than 200 data elements used to screen stocks, and Wall Street consensus data from I/B/E/S, current and historical financial performance, comparative peer company statistics, and earnings and dividends news. The stock reports are available in print, on the Web, or via fax.

Value Line Investment Survey
The *Value Line Investment Survey* is a source of information and advice on approximately 1,700 stocks, more than 90 industries, the stock market, and the economy. It has three parts. The *Ratings & Reports* section contains one-page reports on approximately 1,700 companies and more than 90 industries. Each company report contains, among other things, Value Line's Timeliness, Safety, and Technical ranks, financial and stock price forecasts for the coming three to five years, an analyst's written commentary, and much more. The *Summary & Index* contains an index of all stocks in the publication as well as many up-to-date statistics to keep investors informed about the latest company results. It also contains a variety of stock "screens" designed to help investors identify companies with various characteristics. The *Selection & Opinion* section contains Value Line's latest economic and stock market forecasts, one-page write-ups of interesting and attractive stocks, model portfolios, and financial and stock market statistics. This publication is backed by an independent research staff of more than 70 independent professional security analysts.

Ward's Business Directory of U.S. Public and Private Companies
Ward's lists approximately 100,000 companies, 90 percent of which are private. The first three volumes are arranged alphabetically and offer data on small and mid-sized companies as well as complete profiles of large corporations. The fourth volume lists companies geographically by ZIP code within state and offers evaluations of industry activity through rankings and analyses. The fifth volume ranks companies nationally within SIC codes. The sixth and seventh volumes rank companies in each state by sales within SIC codes. The eighth volume sorts companies by NAICS codes.

Source: This annotated list was prepared by Frank Wilmot, research librarian.

people. Second, *mavens* accumulate knowledge, and use it in potentially helpful ways. Gladwell writes, "Mavens have the knowledge and social skills to start word-of-mouth epidemics."[13] Third, *salespersons* convince people downstream of the importance of what they are hearing. One can imagine other categories as well; but the three categories convey a useful mosaic of the attributes of people who are upstream in the flow of information about acquisition opportunities. For shorthand, we can call these critical intermediaries *navigators*. They are especially important in turbulent industries and business climates. For instance, Evans and Wurster (2000) argued that in industries being affected by disruptions of the Internet, these two kinds of navigators become important:

Deconstruction implies choice. Choice, beyond a certain point, implies bewilderment. Hence, . . . the rise of navigators as independent businesses is destined to be one of the most dramatic aspects of deconstruction. It is also destined . . . to drive fundamental power shifts among the other players.[14]

In the acquisition search, field navigators appear in various guises such as consultants, lawyers, accountants, venture capitalists, business brokers, and investment bankers. Many of these are highly professional and effective players, but the searcher should remain cautious until a skill is proved. Moreover, other useful upstream players may defy any discrete professional label. It is perhaps more useful to group the upstream specialists into two categories:[15]

1. ***Gatekeepers*** give access to information and deals. The starkest example of a *gatekeeper* is a broker or investment banker who has an exclusive engagement to sell a firm. Other gatekeepers may control proprietary data that could greatly influence a search.
2. ***River guides*** explain existing conditions in an industry or region, and highlight emerging trends that might affect the availability of investment opportunities.

Gatekeepers and river guides are important, because as conduits for information, they make decisions about who hears news, what they hear, and how soon they hear it. Cultivating strong relationships with players such as these effectively moves the searcher farther upstream.

Plainly, not all navigators are equally attractive. How should one choose? Shapiro and Varian[16] offer some insights into the attributes of the best navigators:

- ***Control over an existing base of customers or suppliers.*** Firms with proprietary information and/or exclusive rights to represent a seller will carry an advantage in the market.
- ***Intellectual property rights.*** In the search field, these may appear in the form of patents over specialized search software, or unpatented but proprietary know-how.
- ***Ability to innovate*** better than other navigators.
- ***First-mover advantages.*** Good navigators discover trends and sweet spots before others. Through research or direct inquiry, one can ask whether the navigator has a record of successful discovery.
- ***Low-cost provider of search services.*** The best navigators enjoy a cost advantage over competitors, owing perhaps to economies deriving from large scale, or specialization. Strictly speaking, costs should never be weighed alone, but always be weighed relative to benefits. Thus, one should determine how costly is the navigator relative to deal concepts or proposals that have been delivered in the past.
- ***Reputation and brand name.*** Good navigators benefit from a positive reputation in the field, and seek to conduct business in a way that maintains or enhances that reputation.[17]

Organize Consistently with the Search Environment

One of the leading principles in cybernetics, Ashby's Law of Requisite Variety, states, "Any system must encourage and incorporate variety internally if it is to cope with variety externally" (Ashby 1956). This implies that the searcher that is most flexible and has prepared the best will have the highest probability of succeeding. The practical implication is that the search or origination team needs to be organized in ways consistent with the complexity of the external environment. Adopt a flexible organizational structure where the environment is changing rapidly.

Persistence and Repeated Effort Pay

Investing in an acquisition search or deal development effort is like investing in an option. Option pricing theory suggests that a search will be more valuable the greater the probability of a positive payoff. The searcher can influence this probability through:

- Choosing *promising arenas*. Option theory says that options are more valuable the greater the uncertainty. As described earlier, an important driver of uncertainty is information asymmetry. Thus, a promising arena for transaction development is one where there is uncertainty about who knows what information.
- Increasing the *total number* of deal opportunities reviewed. To the extent that search is a learning process, the search will improve as one gains experience. An improved search should help skew the probability of doing a good deal in the favorable direction.
- Increasing the *frequency* of reviews. Frequency will rise as one shortens the cycle time to absorb information and do a deal. This presumes, of course, that the quality of the analysis and decision making does not deteriorate as cycle time declines.
- Optimizing the network infrastructure so that it sends to the searcher valuable information and high-quality deal opportunities.

Searches require pro-activity. Passivity is costly. Activity pays. As Thomas Jefferson said, "I am a great believer in luck, and I find that the harder I work, the more I have of it."

CASE STUDY: KESTREL VENTURES LLC

Kestrel Ventures[18] was a partnership organized in the fall of 1998 by three young entrepreneurs (Bart Crawford, Dave Edinger, and Jim Kingdon, henceforth the "Managers"), who raised $750,000 from private investors for the purpose of searching for a company to acquire. This type of enterprise was called a "search fund," and was an investment vehicle by which an entrepreneur could finance the expense of a one- to three-year search for a business to acquire. Typically, the entrepreneur would organize a company in which equity shares would be sold to 10 to 20 investors. The shares would carry the right of first refusal (without an obligation) to invest in the ultimate acquisition. Targeted acquisition size and search criteria would be stated in the offering memorandum, suggesting the likely attributes of the ultimate acquisition. Once the acquisition was completed, the entrepreneur would assume general management of the firm. Typically an interest in the search fund would carry over into a share in the equity of the firm acquired. Some observers believed that the search fund was developed in 1984, but the concept had existed for some time.

Typically, the search fund offered wealthy individual investors access to investment in a class of firms that were too small for leveraged buyout funds, too mature for venture capital groups, and too large for outright acquisition by an individual. One study[19] of 16 search funds established between 1984 and 1996 concluded that they provided investment returns (IRRs) in the range of 32 to 40 percent. Another study[20] of nine search funds found a 32 percent median IRR to investors.

In their promotional materials and conversations with investors, the Managers expressed the intention to focus their acquisition search on three fields:

1. Animal health and companion animal products and services.
2. Postsecondary education products and services (including business-to-business training).
3. Geriatric ancillary services (health care and otherwise).

These had been chosen after a complex process of analysis and reflection by the three. Large players did not dominate the fields; competition was fragmented and seemed to offer entry opportunities for energetic Managers. None of the three fields was technology-intensive or subject to rapid technological change of the sort that might surprise new entrants or extend beyond the technical familiarity of the three. Demand for goods and services in these fields seemed stable; yet expected changes seemed to offer opportunities for growth in the future. Within these industries, the managers focused on finding companies for sale with:

- Revenues in excess of $5 million.
- Operating cash flow in excess of $1 million.
- A low- to medium-tech business process or product.

They sought to place at least one Manager in an active day-to-day position in the company acquired. Also, they required a majority-stake ownership position, and the opportunity to offer substantial returns to Kestrel's investors.

In describing their search approach, the Managers wrote:

The viable transaction opportunities we see at KV come from several sources. First, we utilize a traditional "outside-in" approach relying on our ever-growing network of contacts . . . in the investment banking, private equity, professional services, and business brokerage sectors. Regular contact . . . ensures that we see a higher percentage of deals fitting KV's profile. The maintenance of this growing contact base is equally important as our grass-roots industry efforts.

We detailed the "inside-out" approach in our brochure as a strategy unique to the search fund concept. By initiating direct contact with companies, industry consultants and other professionals not directly related to the transaction process, we hope to uncover transactions before they are formally represented by an intermediary. Through this approach, we endeavor to avoid auctions and to negotiate a favorable transaction price and structure. Our primary selling points when approaching companies are the quality of the KV team—Managers, Advisory Board and investors, our day-to-day management focus versus installing separate management, and our growth strategy.

We borrowed the term "River Guide" to indicate an industry expert interested in leading us to viable acquisition candidates. These guides may be industry consultants, retirees or another form of expert. River Guides bring years of focused industry experience and contacts to KV. We intend to build relationships with River Guides in each of our target industries.[21]

The Managers planned to focus on inside-out industry coverage through the use of River Guides. They believed that this route would provide the best opportunities to find transactions that would leverage the Managers' skills in day-to-day positions with the acquired company.

In the first three months of their search, the Managers focused on developing a network of useful contacts, both the outside-in business brokers and the inside-out River Guides. They estimated that there were more than 2,000 intermediaries in the United States, but that most of these were inappropriate for various reasons. It was necessary, therefore, to screen the intermediaries, and thereby reduce the number to 450, whom they would contact regularly. Each of the three Managers assumed responsibility for developing a geographic segment of a network of contacts.

In addition to developing their network of deal intermediaries, the Managers evaluated opportunities that began flowing in almost immediately. Some of these opportunities arrived in the form of professionally developed business investment proposals. Others were rather crude "spec sheets" of the sort that might be mass distributed by business brokers. Still others were oral descriptions of an opportunity without written documentation—in these cases the Managers would need to develop their own research on the opportunity. The research and deal development process would entail several phases:

- ***Preliminary evaluation.*** One of the three Managers would screen an opportunity to determine its fit with the search objectives of Kestrel. Of the approximately 360 deals Kestrel had identified as of the advisory board meeting, only 170 survived the preliminary evaluation phase. Rejection of an opportunity at this stage was due typically to a mismatch on size, industry, or control criteria, absence of information, and/or low expected returns. About 55 percent of all investment opportunities were rejected at this stage. In other words, the Managers proceeded with more thorough company and industry research on approximately 45 percent of transaction opportunities.
- ***Company and industry research.*** If an opportunity met the basic criteria, one of the Managers would assume responsibility for building the base of information on the target firm and its industry, interviewing customers, suppliers and competitors, and ultimately visiting the company itself. Most private firms were reluctant to release a great deal of information without a signed letter of

intent and/or confidentiality agreement, so much of the research derived from public or semipublic information. The Manager responsible for a specific opportunity would begin to build a written case describing the opportunity, its fit with Kestrel's criteria, and its potential investment returns. Many opportunities were rejected at this stage on the basis of the discovery of company- or industry-specific risks, or unusual requirements of the sellers. Kestrel had analyzed 75 opportunities at this level by late August, implying survival rates of 45 percent of the preliminary evaluation stage and 20 percent of total deals seen.

- ***Company visit(s) and meetings with management.*** If the research warranted it, Managers visited companies exhibiting potential. This phase represented both an additional deal evaluation step, to evaluate company management and post-transaction Manager integration, and a chance to describe the unique features of Kestrel's structure and philosophy. The Managers had visited 31 companies by the end of Kestrel's third quarter. Work at this stage was the foundation for a decision to sign a letter of intent, with a preliminary offering price. As the letter of intent approached, the investment opportunity would demand an intense commitment of time.
- ***Letter of intent and in-depth due diligence research.*** Kestrel would submit a letter indicating a serious interest in acquiring the target firm at a likely price or price range. The contents of the letter and the price might be the source of ongoing negotiations, with a revised draft submitted to the seller. As of August 1999, six preliminary term sheets or letters of intent had been submitted, but none were accepted. Rejection typically followed from differences in valuation or seller withdrawal from the process. The Managers expected that with the acceptance of a letter of intent, they would embark on an intensive, time-sensitive due diligence research process to be followed by the negotiation of definitive agreements, including a purchase-and-sale agreement, and ultimately, closing of the sale.

Over the first three quarters of 1999, of the universe of 2,000 intermediaries, the Managers had screened 1,429, and established continuing relationships with 437. Furthermore, the rates of change in various categories suggested that in recent months the Managers were shifting their time and attention away from network building and toward research on companies.

Acquisition Guidelines

Industries were reviewed and prioritized based on macroeconomic dynamics and trends. Companies within selected industries will be evaluated on the basis of transaction completion and return potential. All search and return objectives were based on a mid- to long-term view as opposed to short-term strategies. The Managers did not consider turnaround or workout investing. Kestrel Ventures believed that disciplined adherence to the following industry screening criteria would support the identification of acquisition candidates with above-average return potential. A summary of the acquisition guidelines used by the Managers is given in Exhibit 7.5.

EXHIBIT 7.5 Acquisition Guidelines, Kestrel Ventures LLC

Industry Criteria	Description
Fragmented Industry Structure	A highly fragmented or newly consolidating industry offers advantages to Kestrel Ventures across the entire search and acquisition timeline. • Numerous companies within the $10 to 50 million revenue range will support an efficient search. Intensive up-front industry research may be spread over a broader field of potential acquisition candidates. • Industry fragmentation supports incremental growth postacquisition through niche identification and avoidance of dominant industry players. • Fragmentation encourages postacquisition growth through follow-on acquisitions. • Industry consolidation trends enhance exit opportunities.
Favorable Growth Potential	Because top-line growth generally improves investment return, Kestrel Ventures will participate in industries that exhibit favorable future growth trends. While historical growth trends are a well-correlated indicator of future potential, multiyear historical growth trends will not serve as a prerequisite to industry selection. Kestrel Ventures will target newly developing industry segments exhibiting multiple sources of growth in an effort to improve the fundamentals for company growth.
Reasonable Valuations	While numerous industries show fragmentation, consolidation, and favorable growth potential, not all such industries will be appropriate for Kestrel Ventures' consideration. Kestrel Ventures anticipates competitive pressure in the industries it reviews and expects that its screening criteria will be sought by other investors, thereby driving up company valuations within commonly identified industries. Kestrel Ventures will generally avoid "popular" industries and focus on dormant, emerging, or otherwise unidentified opportunities.
Basic Operations	Kestrel Ventures will target industries with basic operations. A simple product or process will facilitate acquisition financing, management integration, and incremental operating improvement. Long product life cycles and low product obsolescence may provide stability and should allow the Managers and existing management to focus on revenue growth. Kestrel Ventures intends to develop competitive advantages by employing sophisticated financing, management, and operational improvement tools and techniques.

(Continued)

EXHIBIT 7.5 *(Continued)*

Industry Criteria	Description
RECURRING REVENUE STREAMS	Kestrel Ventures is interested in industries where a major portion of ongoing revenue comes from regular, periodic payments by customers (e.g., cable TV, alarm systems monitoring), or from business-to-business outsourcing relationships (e.g., janitorial services, document management). Recurring revenues, which "lock in" customers and revenues for a defined period, are highly desirable because they: • Contribute to the stability of cash flows and support cash flow based financing. • Enable concentrated selling efforts on new accounts and provide sales leverage. • Provide the opportunity to strengthen relationships with "captive" customers, building loyalty and increasing switching costs. • Permit time and resources to be focused on service efficiency and operating margins.
LIMITED REGULATION	Kestrel Ventures will target industries with minimal government or other regulation. Regulatory constraints may cap investor return potential and can often become a corporate resource drain. Kestrel Ventures believes that a low-regulation criterion substantially improves industry financing opportunities, management focus, and strategic planning by mitigating the chance of uncontrollable externalities limiting growth prospects.

Source: Used with permission of the company.

Company Screening Criteria

Kestrel Ventures sought opportunities where the seller would like the company placed in approved hands. The seller's careful consideration given to succession may stem from:

- Lack of a logical successor within the company.
- Emotional ties to the company and reluctance to relinquish them.
- Strong relationships with company employees.

Because of the long-term, nondisruptive strategy taken by the Kestrel Ventures management team, sellers may view the transaction differently from alternatives with other strategic or financial buyers. A summary of the screening criteria used by the Managers is given in Exhibit 7.6.

Kestrel Ventures' search was ultimately successful, resulting in an acquisition of a firm 17 months after the partnership had been organized. The case study of Kestrel Ventures illustrates:

- The use of industry and company screening criteria.
- The use of navigators.
- Organization for flexibility.
- Investment in a network and in becoming a valuable node.
- The value of information and the development of primary research.

EXHIBIT 7.6 Screening Criteria, Kestrel Ventures LLC

Company Criteria	Description
ESTABLISHED MARKET POSITION	Kestrel Ventures will target companies with geographic and/or product/service niche potential. The Investment Opportunity's established market position could serve as a low-risk platform for niche development through incremental growth and/or acquisitions.
GROWTH POTENTIAL	Although related to industry growth potential, corporate growth potential will also serve as a screening prerequisite. Company growth may be achieved through optimization programs including but not limited to human resource reallocation, enhanced capital spending programs, and internal incentive programs. Expansion of a company's core capabilities, geographically or through products and services, may serve as an effective means of gaining incremental growth. Expansion potential may be limited without significant capital spending; therefore Kestrel Ventures will conduct thorough due diligence of asset leverage capabilities for all candidates.
STRONG CASH FLOW POTENTIAL	Stable, positive cash flows will service acquisition debt; therefore, Kestrel Ventures will target companies exhibiting suitable cash flow performance. Companies with varied historical performance may be considered but identified improvements must be feasible.
	Cash flow stability will mitigate risk by creating cash cushions against early-stage and unforeseen problems. Therefore, seasonal companies and turnaround opportunities with unstable cash flows will be avoided.
FINANCING POTENTIAL	Targeted companies will exhibit cash flows or assets suitable to support acquisition leverage. Additionally, Kestrel Ventures will seek companies with seller financing potential.
MANAGEMENT PLATFORM	The Managers and Investors will determine the best fit for existing management at the time of acquisition, and will seek to rely on existing management for information and expertise where applicable. Kestrel Ventures will retain existing Managers who will maintain stability and successfully implement key programs.

Source: Used with permission of the company.

In these various ways, the experience of this firm shows the usefulness of the principles offered in this chapter.

SUMMARY

This chapter introduces the reader to some guiding ideas about acquisition search and illustrates them with a case study of a successful search. Exhibit 7.7 summarizes the principles described here. Central to all of these is the use of an

EXHIBIT 7.7 Summary of Search Principles

Principle	Implication
1. The currency of acquisition search is *information*.	Build a search effort that generates a flow of high-quality, credible, usable information.
2. Clarity, privacy, and cost: What the market knows is fully priced.	The deal search should be structured to generate credible private information and transactions before they become widely known.
3. Information arrives sequentially and must be filtered.	Acquisition searches require a screen, a set of criteria that afford the basis for a go/no-go decision on any particular opportunity without seeing the entire potential set of opportunities.
4. Invest in social networks. They make search more efficient and effective.	The opportunity may be closer than you think. The network provides shortcuts to the opportunity. Social capital is valuable. Weak links are the source of strength. Build a search network. Search networks are more valuable the more the "nodes"; the higher the bandwidth; and the higher the speed. Search nodes in a network are more valuable the higher the content.
5. The best information is firsthand.	Firsthand information is valuable because it helps the searcher find the sweet spot in a particular situation. Try to beat the news to the market. Intercept it before it disseminates explosively. The way to do this is to move upstream in the news flow.
6. Navigators affect dissemination and search: gatekeepers and river guides.	Navigators help one move upstream. Look for navigators who control access, and who provide counsel.
7. Organize consistently with the search environment.	Design the search team in ways to match the complexity of the environment. Adopt an adaptable organization.
8. Persistence and repeated effort pay.	Focus on increasing the total number of deal opportunities reviewed, increasing the frequency of reviews, and optimizing the network infrastructure.

information-gathering network as the foundation for critical ideas. As a foundation for due diligence research (see Chapter 8), the gathering of information-rich ideas is key.

NOTES

1. "The Acquisition Search Process," public presentation by AlliedSignal Corporation, April 14, 1998.
2. Reported in Salter and Weinhold (1981), page 162.
3. As used in this chapter, "network" describes one's social connections to others. The *Oxford English Dictionary* defines "network" as "an interconnected chain or system of immaterial things."
4. As another mark of importance of the economics of signaling, the Nobel Prize in Economics in 2002 went to three scholars who explored the problem of signaling quality: George Akerlof, Michael Spence, and Joseph Stiglitz.
5. Assuming that the pricing of a firm's shares is efficient is probably a reasonable default. However, it is healthy to retain a sense of irony about the efficiency assumption. First, research indicates that the market is not "strong form" efficient; that is, the market does not know *all* information, both public and private. Second, there remain numerous anomalies not consistent with efficiency such as panics and crashes, January effects, and firm size effects.
6. This was later the premise for a play and movie *Six Degrees of Separation* (Guare 1990).
7. Rogers (1995) notes that there are over 4,000 studies on diffusion.
8. Antitakeover defenses are discussed in Chapter 35.
9. Persons who sit on more than one corporate board of directors are said to *interlock* the boards by creating a social connection between them; as generally used, *interlocking* is a social, rather than legal or economic phenomenon.
10. See www.cs.virginia.edu/oracle/.
11. Robert Metcalfe, who founded 3Com Corporation and invented the Ethernet protocol for networks of computers, asserted that the usefulness of a network rises with the square of the number of users in the network.
12. Specifically, Moore's Law pertains to the number of transistors capable of being embedded in a semiconductor: the number will double every 18 months. Gordon Moore is one of the inventors of the semiconductor.
13. Gladwell (2000), page 67.
14. Evans and Wurster (2000), page 64.
15. These categories were named by Bart Crawford, Dave Edinger, and Jim Kingdon.
16. See Shapiro and Varian (1999), pages 270–272.
17. Reprinted by permission of Harvard Business School Press. From *Information Rules: A Strategic Guide to the Network Economy*, by Carl Shapiro and Hal R. Varian. Boston, MA, 1998, pages 270–272. Copyright © 1998 by Carl Shapiro and Hal R. Varian; all rights reserved.
18. This description is based on Bruner (2000).
19. Reported in James C. Collins, "Keystone Management Corporation (A)" undated case.
20. The study was conducted by Douglas A. Wells, MBA student at Stanford Uni-

versity, June 28, 1996, and reported in an unpublished manuscript. The IRR was based on a blended return across classes of securities within each fund, and assumed the same start date across all observations. Wells noted that "For the purpose of this study, search funds are defined as those individuals who had recently graduated from business school prior to beginning their search. Three of the nine respondents had already sold their companies and the returns on these funds were straightforward to calculate. In the cases of companies still under search fund management, several assumptions had to be made to determine investor returns. To calculate the value [of] the company, presidents were asked to assume they sold their company at their purchase multiple. In at least one case, the original purchase multiple was considered to be above the current fair market multiple. To remain conservative, the study used the fair market multiple for this company. In all cases, the study then assumed that all debt was repaid and that funds were disbursed to investors in proportion to the equity owned by them. All returns are calculated on a pre-tax basis to investors. Finally, to eliminate skew based on deal size, it was assumed that individuals invested equal amounts in each search fund and subsequent acquisition. In addition, all search funds were assumed to start on the same date. However, the actual search period was used for each fund. If one fund finalized their acquisition in 12 months and another in 24 months, that is the time period that was used. Utilizing the same start date had the effect of lowering the blended IRR. Results are based on fiscal year 1995 performance for the companies, or their last 12 months of operating history for those that had recently completed their acquisition."

21. "First Quarter Highlights" newsletter from Kestrel Ventures LLC, to investors, March 31, 1999.

PART Three

Diligence, Valuation, and Accounting

CHAPTER 8

Due Diligence

INTRODUCTION

Know what you are buying. Research suggests that ignorance of potential problems in an acquisition is one of the more common causes of failure in M&A.[1] But learning about the target, the task of due diligence, is very challenging, harder than the novice can imagine. Relatively little has been written about due diligence. This chapter aims to fill the gap by surveying the subject, introducing the reader to elements of good practice, and highlighting aspects demanding care and expertise. In the context of designing a particular deal, one should explore these issues with the assistance of professionals in the various fields mentioned here. But excellence in due diligence begins with the *right mind-set* for both novices and experienced professionals including these points:

- ***Think like an investor, not like a compliance officer.*** An underlying theme of this book is that M&A success is founded on an investor mentality. *Due diligence* easily degrades into checking things without necessarily thinking about its import for the big questions: Is this target an attractive acquisition? What will it take for this acquisition to really succeed? While risk assessment is very important, it is only half of the shareholder's focus on risk *and return.*
- ***Due diligence is part of the buyer's risk management tool set.*** *Risk management* seeks to mitigate the uncertainty of returns. Techniques of good process and deal design offer a spectrum of tactics for managing risk: Due diligence is one of the process techniques. One gains the right to learn things that are not fully revealed to the outsider—thus, investing in due diligence is like acquiring a call option on unknown discoveries. As option valuation suggests, the value of due diligence research will be greater, the more the uncertainty surrounding the target.
- ***Narrow- versus broad-scope due diligence: The buyer always pays.*** The pressures of time, reluctance to offend the target, and cost all argue for a due diligence review that is brief, focused on just the basics, and not invasive—all without further adjustment in the deal terms. But this is like giving away option value to the target. *Thinking like an investor*, the proper comparison to the broad due diligence review would be a narrow review plus the cost of an insurance policy[2]—either way, the buyer pays. A strategy of *"surprises now"* will serve one's shareholders, management team, and career better than will *"surprises later."* But in competitive situations, such as an auction, you may not have the luxury of time or access with which to conduct a broad due diligence review. In such cases, look for other tactics to help mitigate your risk.

- ***Be fact-based but knowledge-oriented.*** Due diligence is necessarily a bottom-up research process: One gathers data, ascertains facts, analyzes trends and patterns, and produces actionable knowledge. This is easy to describe, but hard to implement. There are many opportunities to cut corners, the shortest of which is to simply check facts rather than look for patterns or develop implications for managers. Mere fact checking is consistent with a compliance mentality. Seeking to develop real knowledge and insights is consistent with an investor mentality.
- ***Output: plain-language briefings for managers, but leave a detailed paper trail.*** Even if one does generate good knowledge, communicating it in a meaningful way to executives can be a challenge. The diligence research findings need to be packaged in a form that is usable by negotiators and executives. It matters not only what you concluded, but also how you got there. Due diligence is ultimately an educative process that informs integration managers, and perhaps protects your firm in the event of postmerger litigation. Having the notes to back up your work is essential.
- ***Leadership matters.*** The research process is demanding. Negotiators and executives always want more insight, sooner, and of higher quality. The due diligence process requires strong skills of leadership and process management. Begin the due diligence research process early, and link the process and conclusions to the valuation, negotiation, and postmerger integration processes.

THE CONCEPT OF DUE DILIGENCE

"Due diligence" is research. Its purpose in M&A is to support the valuation process, arm negotiators, test the accuracy of representations and warranties contained in the merger agreement, fulfill disclosure requirements to investors, and inform the planners of postmerger integration. Due diligence is conducted in a wide variety of corporate finance settings, and is usually connected with the performance of a professional or fiduciary duty. It is the opposite of negligence. One dictionary declared that "due diligence" is:

> *Such a measure of prudence, activity, or assiduity, as is properly to be expected from, and ordinarily exercised by, a reasonable and prudent man under the particular circumstances; not measured by any absolute standard, but depending on the relative facts of the special case.*[3]

In a classic definition, a court defined diligence as:

> *Vigilant activity; attentiveness; or care, of which there are infinite shades, from the slightest momentary thought to the most vigilant anxiety. Attentive and persistent in doing a thing; steadily applied; active; sedulous; laborious; unremitting; untiring.*[4]

In corporate finance, due diligence research is the hunt for risks to be disclosed to the potential investor in an issuance of securities. Under the Securities Act of 1933 and the Securities Exchange Act of 1934, underwriters and other professionals can be held liable for the failure to know and disclose risks, which a "duly diligent" researcher should have been able to uncover. And in M&A, buyers will find ignorance of knowable risks to be a weak basis for a lawsuit seeking damages from sellers.

DUE DILIGENCE PRINCIPLES AND STRATEGIES

To *think like an investor* is to lay the foundation for M&A success. Its relevance to due diligence is to inspire an attention not only to risks, but also to returns, especially their drivers, uncertainties, and constraints. To focus narrowly on risks is to adopt a *compliance mentality* that easily reduces to data-fetching and checking lists. On the other hand, an *investor mentality* goes farther: it seeks to gauge the risk exposure *and* the investment attractiveness of the target. To think like an investor during a due diligence review is to assess critically both risks and returns; to understand opportunities as well as threats (strengths as well as weaknesses); lay the foundation for sound bargaining and integration; and generally help senior executives answer the question, "Does this target present an attractive risk-return trade-off?" The first principle of due diligence work should be to *avoid a compliance mentality and adopt an investor mentality.*

The second principle is that *due diligence is a risk management device.* Investing in due diligence is like investing in R&D: you're not sure what the payoff will be, but the right to find out is worth enough to buy. Due diligence is like buying an option that will be more valuable the greater the uncertainty about the target firm.[5] The virtue of thinking about due diligence this way is that it immediately raises the fact that the buyer actually has a spectrum of risk management tools available, categorized into areas of process and deal design. The use of best practice valuation techniques (outlined in Chapters 9 through 15), sound infrastructure and deal management processes (Chapter 37), and effective integration approaches (Chapter 36) would be examples of mitigating risk through good process. The drafting of documents (Chapter 29), the use of escrow accounts, claw-back provisions, staged investments, earnouts, caps, collars, and floors (Chapters 22 and 23), the careful choice of form of payment and financing terms (Chapters 19, 20, and 21) and generally the design of the deal (Chapter 19) are examples of mitigating risk through deal design. The point of this is that due diligence is part of a spectrum of risk management devices. Thus your approach to due diligence should be tailored to fit with your total strategy for risk management in the deal.

The third principle is that *risk bearing is always costly.* There is no free lunch. Making a fair comparison, broad and narrow reviews are equally costly (your acquisition target will try to make you think otherwise). To take an absurd example, it would seem to be cheapest to go without any due diligence review. But this judgment of expense ignores that in doing so you bear the risk entirely, like self-insuring your car or health, which can be dangerous (though it might have cash flow benefits in the short term). To illustrate this more practically, consider two classic strategies for due diligence:

1. ***Broad review.*** This review looks everywhere, takes the time it needs, and makes large demands on the target. It yields the basis for thinking like an investor that due diligence is less about avoiding future legal proceedings and more about wise acquiring. One writer noted:

> *Due diligence is the act of critical analysis that informs the entire acquisition process. This, of course, includes the detailed assessment of the acquisition prospect's historical sales and financial experience, as well as an evaluation of that prospect's management team and physical assets. However, limiting the process to an evaluation of financial statements, management, and physical assets leaves the acquisition process—and more importantly, the acquirer—with serious vulnerabilities. It is absolutely essential that due diligence go beyond the obvious analyses and also include a detailed self-analysis and thorough review of the markets and competitive environment of prospective acquisitions.*[6]

2. ***Narrow review plus other insurance.*** With this strategy the due diligence review is brief, contained, and focused. In a competitive setting, this may be the only feasible strategy. The disadvantage is that it does not serve the investor mentality; it focuses mainly on the legal and accounting issues necessary to get the deal done. The thrust of the research is disaster avoidance. Buyers eager to do a deal will avoid making an issue out of seemingly innocuous issues, or hypothetical concerns. A *narrow review* might be justified by lower risk, as in the case of asset acquisitions, which do not carry the fatal liability tail of entity acquisitions. Bing (1996) describes a number of considerations that might justify reducing the scope of due diligence: stable and experienced management team, audited financial statements with simple notes, consistent earnings, simple corporate organization (few subsidiaries), strong competitive position, no litigation, no intangible assets, strong financial controls, few locations—these have to do mainly with conditions of lower risk or uncertainty about the target. And sometimes, the decision to acquire is a foregone conclusion, leaving the diligence researchers the unpalatable task of an investigation that is merely pro forma—this is low uncertainty of a different sort.

To compare the broad and narrow reviews on an apples-to-apples basis, the narrow review would need to be bundled with other risk management devices to (hopefully) achieve the same economic impact. Such a comparison will show the narrow review strategy to be as costly as the *broad review*. The differences have to do with timing of cash flows and how you bear risk. Think of the comparison this way: The buyer confronts a trade-off as shown in Exhibit 8.1, a choice between "surprises now" versus "surprises later." In this graph, the vertical axis describes the depth of the research process; the horizontal axis describes the breadth. In all cases, the buyer eventually discovers the true condition of the target. The difference is a matter of timing.

- ***"Surprises now"*** entails higher expenditure for due diligence measured in cash outlay, time, human resources, goodwill of the target. It also yields greater insight for deal structuring and integration. To get the surprises sooner is costly but affords more managerial flexibility (and probably a better deal structure for the buyer).
- ***"Surprises later"*** entails lower expenditure for due diligence, but yields lower immediate insight for structuring and integration. Over time, the buyer learns the true nature of the target.

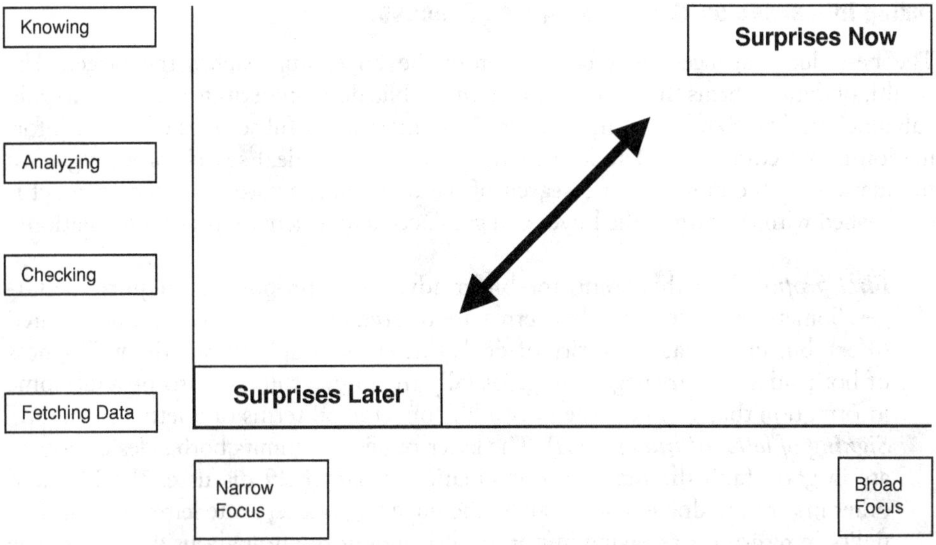

EXHIBIT 8.1 Fundamental Trade-off in Due Diligence Approach

Economics would suggest that where along this trade-off a manager will choose to settle depends on a trade-off between risk and return—that is, the risk exposure of the buyer versus the expected benefits of the diligence research (net of the costs of the research).

Conclusion: Broad Is Good

Given the virtue of the investor mentality and the career-limiting consequences of uncertainty in M&A, the option value of a broad due diligence review would seem to be quite high. Surprises now are inevitably better than surprises later. Due diligence research should go beyond a narrow focus on risk (e.g., on law and accounting) to include the mate of risk (i.e., return). In other words, due diligence research should be viewed as the foundation for valuation analysis, deal negotiation, and the organization of postmerger integration processes. Simply searching for risks is too narrow a definition for the research required in an acquisition. Instead, one should want to know about:

- Risks *and* opportunities.
- The past, present, *and* future.
- The firm *and* its partners such as key customers and suppliers.
- The financial condition *and* the business that generated it.
- Internal conditions of the firm *and* external conditions of the firm's environment.
- The basic data of the target *and* the refined opinions of the experts.

PROCESS: TIMING, TEAM, AND OUTPUTS

Where does due diligence occur in the deal development process? And how is due diligence conducted? This section describes the overall process considerations.

Timing Influences on the Due Diligence Process

The best due diligence effort begins before the buyer approaches the target. The wealth of data on firms that is available in the public domain permits the buyer to gain valuable insights. Exhibit 7.4 in Chapter 7 summarizes useful sources of public information about companies. The information gained in the deal search process gives a foundation for the more direct research of the due diligence process. Once contact is established with the target, the buyer can gain access to a richer kind of information:

- *First proposal.* At this point, the buyer advances a proposal to acquire the target. Sometimes price and other terms are offered (as in the case of an unsolicited offer), but in the vast majority of deals this event simply marks the willingness of both sides to start negotiating. Usually the target will agree to provide some information that will help the two sides converge on terms of a letter of intent.
- *Signing of letter of intent (LOI).* The letter publicly commits both sides to negotiate in good faith the terms of combination. Chapter 29 discusses the LOI and other first-round documents. Usually the buyer signs a separate letter of confidentiality in return for receiving important private information about the target. The LOI often specifies a deadline for reaching agreement, the coverage of expenses related to due diligence and drafting, and any break-up or topping fees (which are discussed in Chapters 23 and 29). Signing the LOI commences a period of deeper due diligence research, oriented toward informing the deal negotiators, and contributing to the postintegration planning. The buyer typically delivers a formal request for information that may run into thousands of pages of documents, and expands the due diligence team with a number of outside experts. The seller may organize a "data room" in which the due diligence materials can be accessed. Also following the LOI, the postmerger integration analysis begins in earnest.
- *Signing the merger or acquisition agreement.* Upon reaching formal agreement, the due diligence research effort turns toward testing the accuracy of representations and warranties in the agreement, preparing a statement of the target's risks and condition to the buyer and its investors, and significantly preparing the postmerger integration. Between the LOI and merger agreement, the diligence team will reach maximum size.
- *Closing the deal.* At the closing, conditions of the contract are affirmed, and consideration is exchanged. Postmerger integration begins. After closing, the new owner completes a careful audit and makes adjustments to any escrow or claw-back accounts that may have been included in the deal.

In short, these events mark phases in the due diligence process that affect the character of the research, size of due diligence team, and objectives of the research. Exhibit 8.2 summarizes these changes over the life cycle of a deal.

Due Diligence Team

Exhibit 8.3 gives a listing of possible participants on a due diligence team—the size of this team will vary across the life cycle of the deal, and with the size of the target. In large transactions, the team size could grow to hundreds of people. In the case of

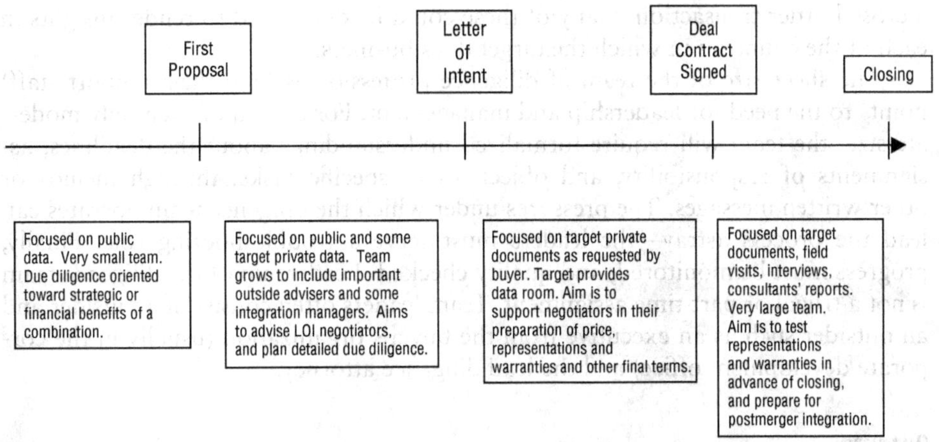

EXHIBIT 8.2 Due Diligence over the Life Cycle of a Deal

EXHIBIT 8.3 Participants in a Hypothetical Due Diligence Review

- Attorney, general corporate review.
- Attorney, tax specialist.
- Attorney, regulation specialist.
- Attorney, risk management specialist.
- Attorney, environment specialist.
- Attorney, intellectual property specialist (especially patents).
- Attorney, pension and benefits specialist.
- Accountant, general audit.
- Accountant, tax specialist.
- Accountant, MIS and internal reporting.
- Consultant, information technology specialist.
- Buyer employee, information technology specialist.
- Actuary.
- Buyer employee(s), human resources, compensation, pension, benefits, and training.
- Consultant, human resources, compensation, pension, benefits, and training.
- Buyer employee, risk management specialist.
- Consultant, environment risk assessment specialist.
- Buyer employee, environment risk management specialist.
- Buyer employee(s), marketing and sales.
- Buyer employee(s), operations.
- Buyer employee(s), postmerger integration specialist.
- Buyer employee, cash management.
- Buyer employee, finance and valuation.
- Consultant, solvency analysis and credit analysis.
- Consultants, business forecasts and operations.
- Consultant, real and personal property appraisal.
- Consultant, valuation specialist.

a cross-border transaction, many of these could be duplicated to render insights in each of the countries in which the target does business.

The sheer size of the team of diligence professionals (and their support staff) points to the need for leadership and management. For a team of even only moderate size, the team will require formalized understandings about the deadlines, assignments of responsibility, and objectives of specific tasks, through memos or other written messages. The pressures under which the diligence team operates can lead the process astray—the leaders must serve a troubleshooting role. Finally, progress must be monitored, and quality checked. Leadership of the diligence team is not a trivial or part-time assignment. Team leaders often consist of an insider and an outsider such as an executive from the buyer's organization (usually in the corporate development office) and the lead diligence attorney.

Outputs

The due diligence effort supports negotiators and creates a record that can protect the buyer in case of the need for postmerger adjustments or litigation. Therefore, it is vital that the diligence effort leave a well-documented paper trail through the research. The form of this record would consist of five types of documents:

1. ***Primary work papers and other resources.*** These are the raw material of the diligence effort, and would consist of lists of records checked, *work papers* and notes from the checking process, transcripts and audiotapes from interviews, videotapes from field visits and inspections, photographs, soil samples, and the like. They must be stored in a manner that will permit retrieval.
2. ***Summaries by specialists.*** In each of the areas of focus (i.e., those indicated in Appendix 8.1), a specialist should be tasked with preparing a summary of findings. The summary should refer to any of the primary resources as supporting items.
3. ***Diligence synthesis.*** This is a technical overview of the entire due diligence effort usually written for the benefit of negotiators, and to combine the specialists' findings for possible future reference. This should cross-reference reports, and provide a master index to all diligence materials.
4. ***Integration recommendations.*** Due diligence is the foundation for postmerger integration. Integration planners begin their work after the signing of the definitive agreement and draw on the findings from the diligence review. The diligence team should highlight recommendations for integration (see Chapter 36 for discussion of integration strategy).
5. ***Executive summaries.*** None of the foregoing documents is necessarily prepared for senior executive consumption. But, the diligence and integration leaders should produce summaries suitable for informing and guiding executives at several points along the way (certainly no less frequently than each of the milestones outlined earlier in the section on timing influences on the due diligence process).

TARGET'S VIEW: PRESSURE AND THE DATA ROOM

The discussion so far suggests a big effort on the part of the buyer. On the other side of the transaction, the pressures are different but no less intense. Upon conclusion of the LOI, the target receives a lengthy request for materials. Collecting these will require a document retrieval effort. Executives and specialists respond to requests for interviews, sometimes taped and transcribed. Because of their potential appearance in postmerger litigation, the interviews require preparation and the careful choice of words. Facilities visits must be scheduled, often under the cloak of secrecy. The process feels invasive to the target's employees. To compound matters, the work must be done under pressure of time. The diligence process is seen as interfering with the ordinary conduct of business. And hovering over everything are anxieties stemming from the prospective change in control, and the loss or reassignment of jobs.

The stresses on the target may generate resistance. Each deal has an advocate within the buyer firm—this person's incentive compensation may depend on the completion of the deal. The target may appeal to the advocate to relent on information demands, or later, to influence the results and interpretations of the review. Senior leadership within the buyer company should anticipate this essentially political process, and manage it carefully.

Handling the diligence process from the target's side requires strong leadership and management skills. Important here is winning the commitment of management and employees, especially key persons on whose future contributions the merger synergies depend. The challenge is to organize, plan, and control the process to satisfy the buyer's due diligence needs with least disruption to the target's operations. An important means for this is the "data room," a location (perhaps away from the target's facilities) where the requested documents are placed for inspection by the buyer's diligence team. The data room reduces somewhat the interaction between the buyer's diligence team and the target's employees, and affords a logical gatekeeping function: requests for more data, interviews, visits, and so on should be directed through the target's diligence leader, who can then manage their impact on the target. In the case of small and midsize targets (who constitute the bulk of M&A activity), the firm may have little of the expertise or staff support to establish a data room—in this instance, the diligence team has to spell out what they need and perhaps retrieve materials themselves. In any event, due diligence should reach beyond the information contained in a data room. The use of the data room, gatekeeping rules, and other rules of conduct should be established in a preliminary meeting between the diligence leaders of the buyer and target.

WHAT TO LOOK FOR: FOCUS ON KNOWLEDGE

An insightful due diligence research process will have many facets. The following 15 elements (legal, accounting, tax, information technology, risk and insurance, environmental, sales, operations, property, intellectual assets, finance, cross-border issues, human resources, culture, and ethics) broadly cover the most often mentioned areas of research, though it should be emphasized that every research process should be tailored to the attributes of the target in consultation with qualified diligence experts. The issues discussed here are summarized in Appendix 8.1. Due diligence builds from the bottom up—from data to information to knowledge. Data are raw facts, such as entries in a ledger or characters on a magnetic tape—for instance in business data would be market shares by product line. Information consists of data that is concentrated and improved, for instance, through the calculation of historical trends in market share or comparisons of those shares to peers. Knowledge suggests *understanding*—to extend the example, knowledge would be a conclusion about the competitive strength of a target firm derived from the information about market share trends and standings. The spirit of this chapter is that a focus on knowledgeable insights supports the investor mentality; the compliance mentality is more consistent with a focus on data. The best due diligence requires an inquisitive frame of mind. Thus, the questions and issues mentioned here and expanded in Appendix 8.1 are intended to serve mainly as the point of departure, rather than the destination.

Legal Issues

Due diligence in the legal area must assess the condition of the target in four dimensions:

1. ***Corporate organization.*** A prime aim is to ensure the accuracy and viability of the warranties and representations contained within the agreement and the proper disclosure of company documents. The buyer must seek to determine that the target is properly organized as a business and therefore enjoys proper legal standing as a counterparty in the transaction. Officers of the target should have the power to consummate a transaction with the buyer. The target's bylaws will indicate the procedures for electing directors and appointing officers—elections and appointments should have been made in conformance with the bylaws. Relevant here are the authorization of stock, voting rules, and anti-takeover defenses. The target should have been incorporated in conformance with the relevant state corporation laws.
2. ***Ownership of assets and exposure to associated liabilities.*** The buyer must be assured that the target (or seller) actually owns the assets to be conveyed. This is accomplished by inspecting titles, deeds, patents, proofs of purchase, and so on. Past transactions by the target (e.g., acquisitions, joint ventures, divestitures) could carry with them liabilities stemming from representations and warranties made at the time of the transaction.
3. ***Litigation, actual and potential.*** The buyer must understand the potential for adverse (or favorable) judgments in pending litigation at the target firm. This should extend to issues on which litigation is not currently pending, but which may ultimately result in litigation.
4. ***Regulation.*** Conformity with government regulations is of vital importance to a buyer. The failure to conform could result in the loss of a license to operate (e.g., in trucking and broadcasting) or fines and penalties.

Various special subjects should attract special attention of the diligence research team, including environmental compliance, intellectual property (both discussed later in this chapter), antitrust (discussed in Chapter 28), and disabilities. The Americans with Disabilities Act (ADA) motivates the buyer to determine whether the target's facilities are accessible to the disabled, and that its employment policies are not discriminatory. Bringing properties and operations into compliance can be costly.

Accounting Issues

The work of the diligence accountants covers a broad range of issues, including:

- Adequacy of accounting procedures and acceptability of audited or unaudited financial statements in terms of compliance with generally accepted accounting principles (GAAP). The first and most important task is to judge the financial reporting of the target. A full audit of the target may be required if the target is small, privately held, foreign, or any firm in whose financial statements the buyer is not confident. Payment for the audit is negotiated between buyer and seller, often stipulated in the LOI.
- Identification of good and bad trends in reported financial results, and good and bad comparisons with peers in the industry.
- Identification of managerial issues in the areas of cash balances, backlogs, inventory management, obsolescence, bad debts, costs, obligations to suppliers, contingent liabilities such as unfounded pension obligations and guaranties, forecasts, and so on.
- Effectiveness of internal auditing procedures.
- Exposure to fraud. In health care, for instance, the buyer can be held liable for undiscovered billing problems that result in penalties.

These tasks, and the issues they raise, can undermine the delicate dance toward closing a deal. In the context of a merger of equals, accounting due diligence has seemed in decline altogether:

> *In part, that's about trust, but at base, it's about power: since no one dominates, a demand to see the other's books can kill a deal. "There is less official due diligence," confirms a senior partner at one Big Five accountancy. "Companies are in the same markets; the executives know each other and how they behave reputationally. They believe that is their due diligence."*[7]

Tax Issues

Attorneys and CPAs with expertise in taxes should be retained to opine on the target's compliance with tax laws and regulations. Whereas tax avoidance is legal, tax evasion is not. Even tax avoidance can be practiced so aggressively as to create the risk of future liabilities. Thus, the primary concern here is to determine the buyer's exposure to possible unpaid taxes of the target and to tax fraud. Additionally the tax diligence review should seek to identify alternative ways of doing business that might reduce taxes.

Information Technology

Accountants and information technology (IT) consultants must address four tasks:

1. Establish the adequacy of management information systems (MIS). Adequacy could be measured in a variety of ways, though the concept is to compare system capacity to the needs of the firm and to best practices in the industry.

2. Evaluate effectiveness of target's IT department. An assessment of budgets, staffing, access and security, and user service levels will begin to yield insights into the target's IT effectiveness.
3. Assess the IT compatibility between target and buyer.
4. Plan for the postmerger integration of target with buyer IT. Capturing data after the deal closes is critical and often the first source of nightmares. Any system integration effort should be motivated by a long-range strategy for the buyer.

Due diligence in IT should encompass hardware, software, communications and networks, technical support, end-user computing, and human resources, including training. Technical infrastructure is the most well defined aspect of IT, but also the arena in which ownership and turf considerations are likely to be sharpest. Some buyers may conclude that autonomy for the target and coexistence of separate systems is the more prudent solution, at least in the near term. But this will not be an option in industries, such as banking, in which systems integration is one foundation for achieving synergies.

Reed (1998) argues that differences in IT *culture* can be a more significant barrier to integration than technical infrastructure. He cites 10 critical dimensions along which buyer and target need to reach cultural alignment:

1. Best-of-breed versus sole-source solutions.
2. Interfaced versus integrated data and applications.
3. Professionals as generalists versus specialists.
4. IT accountability versus user accountability.
5. Team versus individual alignment.
6. Cost versus value-focus.
7. Bottom-up versus top-down planning.
8. Direct versus consensus issue resolution.
9. Utility versus control orientation.
10. In-house versus outsourced.

Eckhouse (1998) reported the results of a survey of IT managers regarding their activities before and after an M&A transaction, as shown in Exhibit 8.4. The comparison reveals that focus of due diligence and integration, at least in respect to IT, vary significantly.

Risk and Insurance Issues

The exposure to insurable risks, and the extent and method by which the target has insured against them is of serious concern to diligence teams. Diligence in the area of insurance and risk management is necessarily the province of specialists, notably attorneys and risk management consultants. Their report should opine on the adequacy of insurance coverage by the target, and offer recommendations for optimizing this coverage. Integration planners should assess the compatibility of the target's insurance strategy with that of the buyer. Specific areas of focus should be:

- Review of claims experience by the target.
- Exposure to catastrophic loss from personal injury, property loss, and business interruption.

EXHIBIT 8.4 Priorities in Information Technology Diligence and Integration

Focus of IT Diligence before the Deal Closes (With % that researched; multiple responses allowed.)	Focus of IT Integration after the Deal Closes (With % that researched; multiple responses allowed.)
1. Financial systems (72%).	1. Streamlining operations (44%).
2. Core business applications (70%).	2. Unifying or consolidating data centers (38%).
3. Networked operating environments (59%).	3. Retaining key IT employees (31%).
4. Legacy systems compatibility (57%).	4. Centralizing operations (24%).
5. Operating systems (53%).	5. Prioritizing IT projects (23%).
6. Database or data warehouse applications (46%).	6. Forming partnerships with the new team (23%).
7. Year 2000 compliance (45%).	7. Choosing the transition team (20%).
8. Telephony strategies (43%).	8. New IT budget (18%).
9. Corporate messaging systems (39%).	9. Establishing corporate culture (15%).
10. Electronic commerce systems (37%).	10. Determining head count (12%).
11. No diligence (15%).	

Source: Eckhouse (1998).

- Reserves for product liability claims.
- Property insurance.
- Directors and officers liability insurance.
- Workers' compensation program.
- Umbrella liability coverage.
- Adequacy of insurers, with indication of their ratings by A. M. Best.
- Recommendation of adjustments in insurance coverage, and estimation of pro forma cost of that coverage.
- Review of proposed purchase and sale agreement, with recommendation for revisions.

Environmental Issues

Under six federal environmental laws[8] in the United States, the buyer and target firms can be held liable for cleaning up a polluted site. For instance, the Superfund Law creates joint and several liability for current and prior owners and operators. The buyer's nightmare is the inheritance of a legacy of pollution from prior owners of the site, leading to great expense, and years of dispute with former owners. With a "base line" audit of the extent of pollution at a site, the buyer can take the first step in allocating responsibility for cleanup in the definitive agreement. This is equivalent to determining who polluted what, and when. Understanding the extent of liabilities permits the negotiators to allocate the costs of remediation through the purchase price, or through some other kind of risk-sharing mechanism after the closing of the deal.

Best practice dictates that the due diligence team should walk all of the properties of the target giving careful scrutiny to signs of environmental damage. Risk exposure is large enough in the environmental realm that the buyer should not rely strictly on the findings of environmental consultants: a firsthand inspection is important. Environmental due diligence is oriented toward reviewing:

- Compliance with laws and regulations.
- Exposure to environmental liabilities, and estimate of costs to remediate.
- Compatibility with buyer's environmental strategy (which might range from benign neglect to mere compliance to proactive remediation).
- Inefficiencies in recycling or the disposal of waste, which, if improved, might reduce costs.

The first two tasks are accomplished through three possible phases of research. In Phase I, an environmental professional reviews the property's historical uses and any Freedom of Information requests about the property, and visually inspects each site of operation. If warranted, the research enters Phase II, which involves taking samples of soil, air, and water (both surface and in the ground). In the event that significant exposures are determined, it may be necessary to enter Phase III, which is a comprehensive and more intrusive testing of the property.

Market Presence and Sales Issues

A broad due diligence review in the marketing area will focus on a number of aspects:

- Strength of brand, franchise, or goodwill with customers.
- Strength of marketing and sales organization.
- Perception of product or service quality and variety in the marketplace.
- Effectiveness of sales and marketing efforts, in terms of coverage, cost, profitability, and so on.
- Competitive marketing and sales advantages (or disadvantages) versus peers.
- Opportunities for improvement and potential revenue enhancement synergies.
- Exposure to product or service warranty claims.
- Compatibility of sales and marketing policies with buyer.
- Outlook for future performance: customer base, units sold, revenues, and collections.

Marketing due diligence considers the target's products and their marketing, sales, and distribution. In this process, the characteristics and attributes of acquirer's and target's business development systems and capabilities are examined in light of the promotional success and failures of product lines. Marketing due diligence is designed to uncover revenue enhancement synergies that will aid the long-term vitality of the combined firm.

Customer bases should be examined so as to determine if the transaction would diversify or focus the customer base and market position. Suppliers need to be considered for their performance and potential to handle the demands of the new firm. Product-focused due diligence should permit the acquirer to forecast the performance of old and new products in the marketplace.

Operations

Broad due diligence should seek insights on various aspects of the target's manufacturing or service operations:

- Strength of operations, judged in light of asset efficiency, cost, flexibility, quality, innovation, condition (of property, plant, and equipment), and other means of differentiation.
- Opportunities for improvement, and potential cost-reduction and asset-reduction synergies.
- Exposure to unions or other workforce-related risks.
- Exposure to technological change risks.
- Compatibility of operational policies with buyer (e.g., regarding technology, innovation, workforce, capital spending, producing to order vs. to stock, inventory practices, etc.).
- Outlook for future performance: operating cost trends, efficiency trends, inventory management, and so on.

Necessarily, this assessment of a firm's operations must be based on an understanding of *processes or the flow of work.* Visits to sites of operations, interviews with operations managers (and perhaps even front-line employees), development of process flowcharts, identification of bottlenecks, and so forth are means of understanding the operating processes of the firm.

Plant tours can be helpful if structured effectively. A useful visit begins with an understanding of your firm's strategy in buying the target and then focusing on those operational dimensions of the plant that are critical to a successful strategy. Advance preparation is important to building a critical frame of reference to what you see—this might include studying the operational strategy of your firm's plants and of the target's peers. Also, bringing a seasoned plant manager from your firm affords an important frame of reference. Best practitioners in due diligence seek to meet not only with the plant manager but also with front-line supervisors and skilled employees—their comments yield an opportunity to check the assertions of senior management. A general point of review is to look for congruence or fit between the products the plant makes and the processes by which it makes them. Hayes and Wheelwright (1979) note that a plant with a continuous flow production process that produces many different products will sustain relatively high costs for setup and changeover of equipment. On the other hand, a job shop that produces one standardized product in steady production loses the opportunity to exploit cost savings that naturally derive from more standardized and continuous forms of production. Other specific points of observation could include the presence and use of buffer stocks, generation of scrap, defect rates, quality levels, plant conditions, workforce profile, disposal of waste, use of improvement programs (such as Total Quality Management), visible indications of achievement, and plant culture. Upton and McAfee (1997) give a detailed approach to taking a plant tour.

Real and Personal Property Issues

The purchase and sale of companies usually entails listing and transferring title to specific properties and assets. Broad due diligence should go further, to offer insights on a range of issues:

- Condition of the properties being acquired.
- Opportunities to create value.

- Implications for integration with the buyer.
- Ownership of assets.
- Exposure to encumbrances by other existing or potential claimants, including taxes and claims from injured persons.
- Compatibility of property policies with buyer.

Specialist attorneys and property valuation consultants are often employed to perform diligence in this area. However, employees from the buyer's organization, specifically the integration team, should be included as well.

Intellectual and Intangible Assets

The focus of most due diligence is on intellectual and intangible assets that can be owned in a legal sense, such as patents, copyrights, trademarks, trade secrets, software, and recipes. But within some firms, great value is generated from intangible assets such as business relationships, know-how, skills, and reputation. Broad due diligence should encompass both classes. Those intangible assets that can be owned must be evaluated in terms of three concerns:

1. Adequacy of intellectual property protection. This addresses the validity and ownership of these assets. In the United States, holding a patent is a presumption of its validity. But a competitor who can point to weaknesses in the patent may succeed in getting the patent invalidated. Patent law sets standards for subject matter, novelty, utility, and nonobviousness. Diligence should assess whether these standards are still met by the patent. Similarly, the scope of claims under the patent will determine its strength: Courts tend to interpret claims narrowly. Therefore, a narrowly specified patent claim may not provide much exclusivity in the face of a competitor. The term of a patent is either 20 years from the date of application or 17 years from the date of issue.
2. Exposure of the target to infringement claims by others.
3. Postmerger integration and strengthening of intellectual property protection. The buyer should assess the compatibility of the target's protection policies with buyer.

Interviews of employees regarding their prior employers should ensure that those employers have no grounds for claiming theft of proprietary information or trade secrets.

Finance

In most cases, the buyer will assume responsibility for the financial management of the target. Nevertheless, preclosing diligence should gauge the condition of the target in four important areas:

1. Adequacy of cash management system.
2. Exposure to covenants and guarantees (e.g., in debt contracts, other acquisitions, etc.).

3. Creditworthiness and solvency. If the financing for the acquisition is to be guaranteed by the cash flow of the target, creditors may require obtaining a solvency letter from a consultant or financial adviser.
4. Compatibility of financial policies with buyer.

Cross-Border Issues

When deals cross borders, diligence will be complicated by differences in laws, accounting, business practices, and culture. Legal differences are most obvious in the gulf between Anglo-Saxon legal systems in the United Kingdom, Canada, Australia, New Zealand, and the United States, and the civil law systems dominant in the rest of the world. Anglo-Saxon practice imposes the doctrine of *caveat emptor*, or "buyer beware," in which the burden of research is carried by the buyer. As a consequence, buyers from countries with Anglo-Saxon legal traditions will tend to organize thorough due diligence efforts in advance of the closing of the deal. In civil code countries, the diligence research may be foreshortened or somewhat more relaxed. In short, the expectations about the timing and depth of due diligence can vary dramatically between buyers and targets in the two legal systems. This can be a source of serious friction.

Due diligence in the setting of a cross-border deal should address:

- Exposure to foreign currencies.
- Exposure to foreign laws and regulations.
- Impact of cultural differences between buyer and target organizations.
- Business practices: hours of operations, vacations, compensation and benefits, relations with customers, suppliers, and governments.
- Adequacy of management and monitoring of foreign operations.

Organization and Human Resources

Due diligence in the area of organization and human resources (HR) should address:

- Adequacy of talent and leadership. Measures of this would include tenure, training, and work experience of managers and supervisors. Interviews and an inspection of resumes can yield insights here.
- Exposure to workforce problems, especially union issues. What are the levels of turnover and employee satisfaction? What is the degree of employee affiliation with the company? The diligence research should examine the current labor contract and the previous two contracts, in order to determine trends in bargaining. Other telltales to be studied are current grievances, recent arbitration decisions, unfair labor charges, labor and employment litigation, and the history of union representation.
- Inefficiencies in compensation and benefits. Which key employees should be retained? What package of compensation and benefits will be necessary to keep them?
- Exposure to benefits claims.
- Compatibility of organization and HR policies with buyer. Is there a proactive HR function within the target?

The adequacy of compensation and benefits plans, audits of managerial leadership and talent, and mapping the culture of the target are essential foundations for the postmerger integration effort. Human resources due diligence will often have great impact on the long-term success of an M&A transaction. Research shows that the factors that are most poorly handled during the M&A process and do most to undermine the success of the deal are those that affect the employees of both parties involved. The leadership of both companies needs to be examined, because it is from the leaders of the companies that the company policies come and thus the culture is derived. It is essential to determine the organizational structure of the firms from a leadership standpoint and also examine the structure of the new organization. Burrows (2000) identified six "red flags" for diligence researchers in the area of HR: difficulty of gaining access to one-on-one meetings with employees; employee fears about talking openly; lack of employee affiliation or affection for the company; absence of trust between management and employees; absence of an HR function within the company; and high employee turnover.

Culture

Cultural differences between the buyer and target organizations are believed by many to be a major source of M&A failure. For purposes of discussion here, culture includes a wide range of social qualities such as beliefs, sense of mission, values, norms, traditions, how victories are celebrated, physical layout (e.g., open plan vs. closed offices), how conflicts get resolved (e.g., consensus vs. command-and-control), leadership style (e.g., team-based vs. "Lone Ranger"), communication style (e.g., candor vs. diplomacy; speed vs. deliberation), and interpersonal practices (e.g., formality/informality). The combination of breadth and looseness make due diligence experts such as auditors and attorneys uncomfortable. Edgar Schein, one of the foremost scholars of organizational behavior, wrote,

> *Culture may be loosely thought about, but it is only after the merger that it is taken seriously, suggesting that most leaders make the assumption that they can fix cultural problems after the fact. I would argue that leaders must make cultural analysis as central to the initial merger/acquisition decision as is the financial, product, or market analysis.*[9]

Due diligence research on the target's culture should aim to assess *congruence* on three dimensions:

1. ***Between actions and aspirations*** (i.e., as expressed in statements about mission and values). In discussing cultural due diligence, Bouchard and Pellet (2000) argue that the health of an organization is determined by the alignment of people, organizational structure, and operational processes. Incongruence breeds low morale, low productivity, and ultimately, poor financial performance.
2. ***Between the cultures of buyer and target.*** In our study of the failed joint venture and merger attempt between Volvo and Renault, Robert Spekman and I[10] noted sharp disparities between the two firms. Volvo was investor-owned, Swedish, and valued safety and engineering. Renault was state-owned, French, and valued styling and economy. The partners clashed over product designs

and capital spending where the strategic alternatives represented trade-offs between safety and cost, and engineering and economy.

3. ***Between the target's culture and its strategic threats and opportunities.*** Luis (1999) argues that cultures arise in response to demands in the market environment: "Each market environment demands certain organizational behaviors in order for a company to be successful in capitalizing on its primary source of competitive advantage. These organizational behaviors also may be defined as strategic cultures. They are enmeshed in beliefs, values, compensation systems that the finance department measures, conversations, meetings, budget reports, 'how to grow the business,' how strategic plans are prepared, how risk is assessed, the philosophy on product introduction, who invokes it to senior management, and so on."[11]

Luis (1999) argues that strategic cultures tend to cluster around any of four models:

1. ***Customer service cultures*** focus on loyalty, service collaboration, and consensus.
2. ***Product uniqueness cultures*** focus on innovation, distinctiveness, and problem solving.
3. ***Cost orientation cultures*** focus on control, reliability, analysis, accuracy, and predictability.
4. ***Preeminence cultures*** focus on growth, competition, size, and aggressiveness, and strength, speed.

He concludes that acquisitions fail when the buyer makes demands on the target inconsistent with the target's culture. In other words, integration must be tailored to the culture of the target. While there may be many types of corporate cultures, cultural differences can torpedo a deal. One must identify the thought leaders in the culture, and how the culture must evolve to (1) fit with the target's opportunities or threats in its markets, and/or (2) complement or align with the buyer.

Ethics

Diligence with respect to ethics should focus on:

- Compliance with existing policies and laws related to ethics.
- Exposure to liabilities arising from ethics issues. These could include actions such as price fixing, bogus accounting, discriminatory hiring, false advertising, slipshod product safety testing, product misrepresentation, or copyright violation.
- Ethics policy and training.
- Compatibility of ethics policies with buyer.

The placement of business ethics in this discussion (last) is not meant to indicate its lack of importance, but rather to suggest that it affords a special lens to examine all the other aspects of the diligence effort. Ethical abuses can occur at all levels of an organization and in many areas of the company from misleading marketing practices to employee discrimination. Cross-border M&A offers special concerns about ethical business conduct. In some countries, bribery and child labor are acceptable business practices, for example. Investigating the target's business ethics can be a very sensitive task, potentially destabilizing a harmonious deal—the very act of asking may imply to some target managers that their business ethics are in doubt. Yet, the Federal Sentencing Guidelines of 1991 place the responsibility for controlling illegal activity on top management—the main defense must be the demonstration of diligence in preventing misconduct. Evidence of diligence is an ethics awareness policy, training, and a monitoring program. Ferrell, LeClair, and Ferrell (1998) conclude that:

> *Most crimes and unethical actions are not committed by individuals who want to advance themselves and destroy their organizations. Instead they occur because of two organizational factors: opportunity and the actions of peers and supervisors. . . . A corporate culture that provides incentives and opportunities for unethical activity creates a climate in which infractions are possible and even encouraged. (Page 353)*

SOURCING INFORMATION

The premise of much of the professional discussion of due diligence is that the researcher has access to the target's internal information. That may be true after a letter of intent is signed, but research is vital to support decisions *before* the LOI. In addition, there is a wealth of information in the public domain about targets that can provide a valuable check on what one learns inside. For that reason, excellent due diligence taps information sources beyond the target.[12] The objectives of consulting public sources include:

- Obtaining basic financial information about a target. Assessing the target's industry and peer firms.
- Identifying economic forces affecting the target, such as deregulation, technological change, demographic change, and trade liberalization.
- Gauging the view of peers and investors about the target.
- Developing a basic factual foundation about the target.

A list of useful sources of public information on companies is available in Exhibit 7.4 of Chapter 7. Data from sources such as these can build at least a partial foundation for valuation, and the expression of interest necessary to negotiate a letter of intent.

EXCELLENCE IN DUE DILIGENCE

This chapter has emphasized taking a broad research approach to due diligence. This requires qualities of leadership and management at many levels of the due diligence team. At the core of excellent diligence is a research mind-set that includes these qualities:

- *Fact-based.* Opinions are relatively easy to obtain, and usually comforting when they come from people with credentials. But opinions that have no basis in fact are dangerous. Be an empiricist. Focus on getting facts. Facts, or data, are the building blocks of important due diligence insights. W. Edwards Deming said, "In God we trust. Everyone else must bring data."

- ***Inquisitive.*** The vast body of writing on due diligence is oriented toward checklists of data to obtain. Appendix 8.1 provides such a checklist. But checklists are useful mainly for organizing the acquisition of facts, not the development of knowledge. To produce really useful research requires an inquisitive mind-set to move from acquisition to comprehension, and then to evaluation.
- ***Knowledge focused.*** There are immense differences between mere data, information, and knowledge. The best due diligence efforts focus on acquiring knowledge rather than just amassing information or data. To illustrate the difference, consider the following distinctions gleaned from a target's financial statements:
  - *Data.* The target has audited financial statements. The target's competitors also have audited financial statements.
  - *Information.* Footnotes reveal an aggressive policy of revenue recognition wherein a sale is booked when the product has been shipped for customer trials, and before a firm purchase contract or payment has been received. Checking the target's peers reveals that the target's revenue recognition policy is not typical of the industry.
  - *Knowledge.* If the target's financials were restated to reflect the typical revenue recognition of its peers, the target would report a sizable loss, as opposed to the profits it is currently reporting.
- ***System-focused: sees the links to valuation, negotiation, and closing.*** Due diligence research should not be an afterthought in the valuation and deal-design process, but rather should be linked closely to it.
- ***Initiative.*** The timing of the research is crucial, and should begin as soon as the possibility of a transaction arises. Research suggests that the earlier a due diligence research effort begins, the more effective will be the acquirer in the deal-making process, and the less will be the unexpected legal problems.[13]
- ***Takes enough time.*** Many M&A transactions are rushed. Unfortunately, the development of knowledge is difficult to accelerate.
- ***Diversity.*** A broad due diligence review draws on a diverse range of expertise (technical, legal, accounting, HR, IT, marketing, and general management) and experience—often the research is delegated to relatively junior employees when a more seasoned reviewer can bring a more insightful perspective. Because employees of the acquirer can become psychologically invested in the deal, it is healthy to have outside consultants on the team as well, who can judge objectively the effectiveness of the process and conclusions. To some extent, greater team size can offset the limitations of time.
- ***Avoids surprises,*** reduces or manages downside risks, provides a solid foundation for valuation, negotiation, postmerger integration, and business planning.
- ***Writes it all down: due diligence books.*** These should be binders containing the diligence reports of all experts. Material and working papers that back up the reports should be contained in files that may be accessed if

necessary. Copies of the books should be available to negotiators, valuation advisers, business-planning advisers, and postmerger integration advisers. A due diligence process generates a mass of information. But if it is to be effective, the process should:

- *Focus on usable knowledge.* The key consumers of the research really only want to know the conclusions. Thus, the process should aim to create a briefing book that contains summary memos and key conclusions from the various experts. This is often a three-ring binder of which numbered copies are made for the limited users.
- *Keep a paper trail.* The work papers and source materials that underlie the summary memos should be kept accessible in files during the negotiations or afterward.
- *Prepare for the closing.* Lawyers drafting the purchase agreement may require access to information about the condition of the target.

Due diligence is an inherently messy process. Combined with the stresses induced by limited time, and a large team, the buyer's demands for information can strain a business relationship between two companies at the most delicate points in the process of merging. Demands for information that are frivolous, heavy, or abrupt could sour the seller's interest. Each due diligence team needs a leader to coordinate the demands of the team.

APPENDIX 8.1
Comprehensive Overview of Due Diligence: Knowledge, Information, Data

Data, information, and knowledge serve the investor mentality of due diligence in ascending priority. This overview is an abstraction drawn from the author's experience, interviews of M&A professionals, and published sources, including Bing (1996), Lajoux and Elson (2000), and Lawrence (1999). Much of this is common knowledge, though the cited books give helpful detailed discussions of the analytic points. To my knowledge this is the first presentation of the due diligence task in the data/information/knowledge format.

LEGAL ISSUES

Knowledge

- Corporate organization and ownership.
- Litigation risk: existing and potential.
- Compliance with laws and regulations.

Information

- Obtain and opinion from legal counsel that the target's stock is validly issued, fully paid, and nonassessable, and that the corporation is in good standing in the state of its incorporation.
- Identify any outstanding legal matters that should be dealt with in the M&A agreement.
- See section on real and personal property.
- See section on environmental issues.
- See section on intellectual and intangible assets.
- Through inspection, determine extent to which target's facilities are accessible to disabled persons on a nondiscriminatory basis.

Data

- List of charges pending against the target by federal, state, or local courts or agencies.
- Summary of disputes with suppliers, competitors, or customers.
- Correspondence with auditor or accountant regarding threatened or pending litigation, assessment, or claims.
- List of decrees, orders, or judgments of courts or governmental agencies.
- Copies of pleadings or correspondence for pending or prior lawsuits involving the company or the founders.
- Copies of material contracts, for legal review.
- List of pending and previous OSHA citations.
- Record of target's relationship with OSHA (inspections, complaints, etc.).
- Target's written safety and health program and training.
- Summaries of past health and safety audits.
- OSHA Forms 200 and 101.
- Employee health and safety complaints filed with the company and OSHA.
- Frequency of disabled persons employed in the target, and kinds of disabilities.
- Complaints or citations of the target under the American with Disabilities Act (ADA).

ACCOUNTING ISSUES

Knowledge

- Adequacy of accounting procedures.
- Acceptability of audited or unaudited financial statements.
- Compliance with generally accepted accounting principles (GAAP).
- Identification of good and bad trends in reported financial results, and good and bad comparisons with peers in the industry.
- Identification of financial management issues in the areas of cash balances, backlogs, inventory management, obsolescence, bad debts, costs, obligations to

suppliers, contingent liabilities such as unfounded pension obligations and guaranties, forecasts, etc.
- Effectiveness of internal auditing procedures.
- Exposure to fraud.

Information

- Assess trends in sales, net income, wage expense.
- Determine compound growth rate.
- Review commissions, selling expenses, and general and administrative expenses for significant trends, especially in controllable costs, such as advertising, management, and support labor.
- Examine extraordinary and nonrecurring expenses.
- Perform a detailed ratio analysis of the target, focusing on measures of profitability, asset activity, leverage, and liquidity. Compare the target to peer firms.
- Prepare common-sized income statements and balance sheets, and compare to industry standards and peers.
- Assess cash management practices: need for seasonal balances; speed with which idle balances are invested; collection practices.
- Evaluate accounts receivable, especially for credit policy (compared to peers in the industry) collectability, provision for bad debts.
- Evaluate the firm's efforts to collect overdue receivables.
- If necessary, obtain an audit opinion from a certified public accountant.
- Assess the effectiveness of the target's internal management reporting system. Focus particularly on the timeliness, and substance of these reports, and whether they are related to forecasts or budgets.

Data

- Monthly, quarterly, and annual financial statements for prior three years (SEC reports, ideally).
- Comparative financial results by division.
- Current year projected financial statements.
- Chart of accounts and description of accounting practices.
- List of banks where the target maintains accounts and related balances at balance sheet date.
- List of total receivable balances due from customers, officers, employees, and others, along with "aging" of the receivables, using measures of days' sales outstanding, and percent of receivables outstanding 30, 60, and 90 or more days.
- Description of amortization policy for prepaid expenses, deferred charges, goodwill, or other intangibles, along with the history of these accounts.
- List of accounts payable, the type, and payment practices for each. Note all delinquencies in settlement of payables.
- List of principal suppliers, together with the approximate annual amounts purchased.

- List of contingent liabilities, and their history.
- List of contracts and agreements to which the target is a party, and any indication of price renegotiation or redetermination.

TAX ISSUES

Knowledge

- Compliance with tax laws and regulations.
- Exposure of buyer to target's unpaid taxes.
- Indemnification.
- Exposure to fraud.
- Tax policy inefficiencies.

Information

- Reconcile tax returns to financial statements.
- Compare tax and GAAP basis in assets and/or stock, including subsidiaries.
- Estimate net operating loss carryovers and investment tax credits. Determine how the M&A transaction will affect these carryovers.
- Review implications of target's transfer pricing practices.
- Identify opportunities for tax savings or planning.
- If necessary, obtain an opinion from a qualified tax expert (CPA or tax attorney) regarding the conformity of the target to past and current tax obligations.

Data

- Domestic and foreign, local, state, and federal tax returns for prior five years, IRS letters, schedule of unused loss carryovers.
- List all taxes to which the target is subject.
- Date of latest federal and state tax audit, and result of that audit.
- Record of payroll tax deposits and compliance with withholding requirements.

INFORMATION TECHNOLOGY ISSUES

Knowledge

- Adequacy of MIS systems.
- Evaluate effectiveness of target's IT department.
- Compatibility between target and buyer.

Information

- Through interviews, assess the current needs of individual departments. Focus on ability of the target's current technology to permit employees to complete job tasks efficiently and effectively. Evaluate ways in which employee work could be improved through added technology.
- Through interviews, profile the IT policy of the target, especially regarding package vs. development orientation; best-of-breed vs. sole-source solutions; interfaced vs. integrated data and applications; professionals as generalists vs. professionals as specialists; IT accountability vs. user accountability; team vs. individual alignment; cost vs. value focused; bottom-up vs. top-down planning; manager vs. consensus issue resolution; utility vs. control orientation; in-house vs. outsource orientation.
- Assess the ability of the IT department to fulfill needs within the target firm.
- Assess the dependence of the target on (or the opportunities created by) the emergence of new MIS technology.
- Estimate the cost of bringing all departments up to the current level of technology that is available.
- Develop an MIS integration plan. Assess the costs in cash, human resources, and time, necessary to integrate the target's IT system with the buyer's.

Data

- List of current IT hardware and software, along with dates of purchase and integration.
- List of current IT projects, along with workflows and current status reports.
- List of unfilled IT requests.
- Operating budget for IT department.

RISK MANAGEMENT ISSUES

Knowledge

- Adequacy of insurance.
- Compatibility with buyer.

Information

- Assess terms and adequacy of policies currently in force. Focus on director and officer policies.
- Evaluate target's risk management strategy, giving particular attention to self-insurance practices, use of deductibles and retentions.
- Identify uninsurable activities or risks.

- Through interviews, assess the knowledge and effectiveness of the risk management staff.
- Highlight opportunities to reduce costs through revision of insurance policies.

Data

- List of all material insurance policies of the company covering property, liabilities, and operations, including product liabilities.
- List of "key man" or director indemnification policies.
- List of claims made, and payments received. Loss experience by category.
- List of historical acquisitions and divestitures, and extent of retained or trailing liabilities.
- Exhaustion of coverage limits.
- Credit reports and ratings (A. M. Best) on current insurers and underwriters.

ENVIRONMENTAL ISSUES

Knowledge

- Compliance with laws and regulations.
- Exposure to environmental liabilities, and estimate of costs to remediate.
- Compatibility with buyer's environmental strategy.
- Inefficiencies in recycling and/or sale of scrap and waste.

Information

- Review disposal practices, both in-house and with outsourced providers.
- Study activities conducted on nearby premises for possible migration of pollutants.
- Profile the results of the Phase I review (i.e., based on the public information obtained).
- If necessary, obtain a Phase II report from a qualified consulting expert in environmental assessment.
- If necessary, obtain a Phase III report from a qualified consulting expert in environmental assessment.

Data

- List of pending environmental claims and litigation, along with historical cases previously settled, and memoranda on any suspected potential environmental claims.
- List of penalties imposed for noncompliance with regulations.
- Files referring to the storage, transportation, and disposal of hazardous and nonhazardous materials.

- Geological or other technical reports, diagrams, photos, and maps of known or suspected sites of environmental claims.
- List of operating permits, compliance files, registrations, regulations, and requirements (local, state, and federal).
- Copies of pollution control capital expenditure reports as required by the Clean Air Act.
- List of citizen complaints related to air, soil, water, and noise pollution.
- List of hazardous materials or regulated pollutants used or produced on-site.
- Prior environmental assessments, technical reports, studies.
- Public records (local building department, historical documentation, state, federal etc.).
- Disclosures to SEC or other regulatory agencies regarding environmental liabilities.
- Coordinates and organizational role for persons responsible for environmental monitoring and remediation.
- Summaries of previous ownership of assets, including current coordinates of those parties.
- Copy of response plans for environmental emergencies. Information regarding compliance with EPCRA (Emergency Planning and Community Right-to-Know Act). Evidence of communication with public about environmental emergency planning.
- Notices of potential liability under Superfund Law (CERCLA or Comprehensive Environmental Response, Compensation, and Liability Act). Documents relating to prior or present litigation regarding CERCLA. List of sites that have been nominated for National Priorities List.
- List of wastewater and storm water discharges from all facilities subject to NPDES (National Pollution Discharge Elimination System) or other aspect of CWA (Clean Water Act).
- Documentation of groundwater monitoring efforts. Results of hydrological tests conducted in recent years.

MARKET PRESENCE AND SALES ISSUES

Knowledge

- General image of the firm.
- Strength of brand, franchise, or goodwill with customers.
- Strength of marketing and sales organization.
- Perception of product or service quality and variety in the marketplace.
- Effectiveness of sales and marketing efforts, in terms of coverage, cost, profitability, etc.
- Competitive advantages (or disadvantages) vs. peers.
- Opportunities for improvement, and potential synergies.
- Exposure to product or service warranties.
- Compatibility of sales and marketing policies with buyer.

- Outlook for future performance: customer base, units sold, revenues, and collections.

Information

- Trend of market share.
- Identify market segments in which the target competes, and competitive position in each.
- Analyze current and expected pricing policies for product lines (target vs. peers). Existence of a price leader. Excess capacity, which might depress prices. Ability of target to pass along cost increases to customers.
- Assess profitability of major customer relationships.
- Evaluate cost and effectiveness of sales promotion programs.
- Assess trends in sales cancellations, costs, variances from forecasts, customer complaints, lost customers, discount patterns.
- Through field interviews and focus groups, assess the customer perception of the target and its peers in terms of service performance, delivery history, technological advantage, pricing, quality, and product breadth.
- Through interviews and focus groups with the field sales force, assess the effectiveness of the sales organization in terms of knowledge, frequency of contact with customers and prospects, responsiveness to inquiries, consistency of message, form of representation (directly, distributor, representative), cost of attracting new customers/keeping old customers, and the profitability of marketing campaigns.
- Profile the product lines, marketing policies, profitability, and ownership structures of competitors.

Data

- Press releases from the target for recent years.
- Articles and marketing studies relating to the company or industry.
- Current brochures and sales materials.
- Printout of current web site.
- New product announcements.
- Comments from customers by interview or questionnaire.
- Recent advertising budget, including placements and timing of ads. Advertising and sales promotion practices in the industry.
- Major customer relationships. List along with percentage of overall business. Information regarding trends of major customers toward backward integration, or purchasing substitutes (i.e., departing from purchasing from the target firm).
- Channels of distribution for target and peers, and their relative importance.
- Organization and budget for field sales organization.
- Actual sales and forecasts for recent years, by department or product line.
- Forecasts of sales for future years, from target organization, and any outside knowledgeable sources (such as securities analysts).
- History of sales cancellations, and their reasons.

- Sales and expenses per salesperson.
- Information on customer complains and lost customers.
- Policy on product or service warranties, and outstanding exposure. History of claims under warranties.

OPERATIONS ISSUES

Knowledge

- Strength of manufacturing or service operations.
- Opportunities for improvement, and potential synergies.
- Innovativeness.
- Exposure to unions or other workforce-related risks.
- Exposure to technological change risks.
- Congruence of operational policies with buyer, and with customer demand or competitive positioning.
- Outlook for future performance: operating cost trends, efficiency trends, inventory management, etc.

Information

- Appropriateness of process flow of operations.
- Quality of operations based on external measures such as customer satisfaction.
- Quality of operations based on internal measures such as product cost, response time, variety, and quality.
- Adequacy of management of R&D program, and assessment of effectiveness of R&D efforts.
- Visual assessment of operations by plant tour.
- Inspection of equipment to determine wear, maintenance, and/or obsolescence.
- Inspection of inventory to determine obsolescence or spoilage.
- Appropriateness of subcontracted operations.
- Interviews with suppliers to determine problems.
- Calculation of production break-even volume.
- Assessment of adequacy of controls over purchasing activities.
- Assessment of adequacy of distribution and logistical policies.

Data

- Process architecture and flowchart: inputs, outputs, flow units, network of activities and buffers, resources required, and information structure.
- Product attributes necessary to satisfy customers: cost, response time, variety, quality, etc.
- Process attributes necessary to deliver desired products: cost, flow time, flexibility, quality.

- Description and rationale for R&D projects currently in process.
- Forecast of completion dates, and costs to complete current R&D projects.
- Historical cost of R&D projects, and success rate.
- Data on utilization rates of manufacturing or service operations.
- List of order backlogs.
- List of assets in raw materials, work-in-process, and finished good inventories.
- Copy of quality control procedures.
- Records on defective products.
- Records on scrap and unshipped and rejected products.
- Records on subcontracted labor, parts, or products.
- List of suppliers, with dollar and unit volumes of business. Copies of supply contracts and commitments. Highlight of sole-source-of-supply situations.
- Terms of payment to suppliers and/or vendor financing.
- Historical percentage of sales represented by purchased goods and services.
- Use of commodity price agreements or other risk-management devices to hedge price uncertainties in supply.
- Copies of distribution or logistical contracts.
- Records of labor strikes, grievances, etc.

REAL AND PERSONAL PROPERTY ISSUES

Knowledge

- Condition of the properties being acquired.
- Opportunities to create value.
- Implications for integration with the buyer.
- Ownership of assets.
- Exposure to encumbrances by other existing or potential claimants.
- Compatibility of property policies with buyer.

Information

- Through tours and direct inspection, assess the condition of plants and equipment, real estate, and other property.
- Identify possible exposures to climate, natural hazards, technological change, change in government policy, misuse, or abuse.
- Obtain a valuation analysis of real property from a valuation expert.

Data

- List and description of real and personal property assets, along with their location, and departmental use. Current, prior, and anticipated uses for each property. Indicate proximity to transportation.
- Identify any assets excluded from sale.

- Maintenance and repair records.
- List of liens, mortgages, or security pledges on the assets.
- Appraisals and tax records on each property.
- Zoning and other land use restrictions.
- List of all property titles.
- Target's current estimated value of each property. Details of recent market transactions for comparable properties.

INTELLECTUAL AND INTANGIBLE ASSETS ISSUES

Knowledge

- Ownership or rights to use.
- Exposure to infringement.
- Compatibility of protection policies with strategy of buyer.

Information

- Evaluate the rights of competitors or partners to use the target's patented technology, copyrighted material, service marks, trademarks, and know-how.
- Assess the economic significance and impact of comparable or new technology, copyrights, etc., if deployed by competitors.
- Profile the target's emerging technology, patents, copyrights, etc.
- Identify the potential benefits and costs of transfer of the intellectual and intangible assets from the target to the buyer. Of special interest here is technology transfer, and its limitations.

Data

- List all patents granted, pending, or to be pursued by the target. Identify how these were acquired, and claims of employees or outsiders in these assets.
- List all copyrights, trademarks, service marks claimed by the target. Identify how these were acquired, and claims of employees or outsiders in these assets.
- List all disputes over patents, copyrights, etc.
- Identify comparable technology, patents, copyrights, etc., not held by the target, and held by competitors, or potentially available to them.
- Target's policies and procedures for documenting and protecting inventions or creations.
- History of royalties or indemnifications.
- Contracts regarding the use or protection of intellectual and intangible assets.

FINANCE ISSUES

Knowledge

- Adequacy of cash management system.
- Exposure to covenants and guarantees (e.g., in debt contracts, other acquisitions, etc.).
- Compatibility of financial policies with strategy of buyer.

Information

- Evaluate the mix of the target's debt and equity capital, versus industry peers and the buyer's practice (for instance, compare debt/equity, and interest coverage ratios).
- Assess opportunities for increasing the leverage of the target firm (i.e., the reasonableness of target leverage compared to the target's cash flows).
- Through interviews with principal banks and other creditors, assess their view of the target's creditworthiness.
- Assess the ability of the target to meet interest and principal payments through forecasted flows of cash. Test the effect of interest rate fluctuations on the firm's debt service capacity.
- If necessary, obtain a solvency opinion from a qualified financial consultant.

Data

- List of the amounts of all commitments, guarantees, "keep well" agreements, and financial liabilities, along with details on their specific terms, especially covenants and guarantees.
- List of assets pledged as collateral, noting the nature of the pledge and the estimated amount of collateral value.
- Record of compliance with loan covenants.
- List of payments due to officers or stockholders, along with advances and repayment terms.
- Dun & Bradstreet credit report on the target.
- List of capitalized and operating leases, and their terms. Property leased should be identified.
- List of any established lines of credit, terms, covenants, and unused amounts available.
- List of shareholders.
- Rights of different classes of stockholders (if more than one).
- Details of any preferred stock.
- Capital expenditure budgets for recent years, along with actual expenditures.

CROSS-BORDER ISSUES

Knowledge

- Exposure to foreign currencies.
- Exposure to foreign laws and regulations.
- Adequacy of management and monitoring of foreign operations.

Information

- Analysis of cross-border exposures will entail the same tasks as indicated in the other areas of this guide. Overlaid on these other tasks must be considerations of exposure to currency fluctuations, country risk, local and regional growth and economic conditions, etc.

Data

- List of countries in which the target has operations, conducts business, holds investments, and/or has shareholders or creditors. These should be broken down by country.
- Breakdown of revenues, costs, investments, and financial obligations by currency.
- List of outstanding contracts used to hedge foreign currency exposures.
- Organization chart for target indicating managerial reporting relationships for cross-border operations.
- For all relevant countries, obtain country risk ratings from Euromoney, EIU, OPIC, and/or sovereign debt rating agencies.

ORGANIZATION AND HUMAN RESOURCES ISSUES

Knowledge

- Adequacy of talent and leadership.
- Exposure to workforce problems, especially union issues.
- Adequacy of compensation and benefits.
- Exposure to benefits claims.
- Compatibility of organization and HR policies with buyer.

Information

- Assess adequacy of employee benefit and incentive plans. Compare to peers, industry practice, and buyer. Estimate cost of upgrading plans to industry or buyer practice.
- Review general labor pool in the target's geographic markets.

- Estimate extent of over- or underfunding of health and retirement plans, both for active employees and retirees.
- Evaluate working conditions, attrition statistics, and reasons for attrition.
- Assess medical problems and sick leave frequency.
- Through interviews, assess target's managers for possible retention post-acquisition. These interviews could be formalized into a "talent and leadership" survey.
- Obtain opinions regarding the qualification of benefit plans and the adequacy of coverage from an actuary and an attorney specializing in employee benefits.
- Obtain opinions regarding the compliance of the target with government regulations, including those issued by federal and state labor agencies.

Data

- Number of employees, broken down by hourly and salaried, and into finer groups based on job descriptions.
- Wages, commissions, benefits, and perquisites for employee groups.
- Organization chart.
- Biographical information on managers.
- Summary information on employee incentive plans, retirement and health benefits. Annual cost of premiums, and percentage of premiums paid by employees for recent years.
- List of unfilled positions.
- Collective bargaining or union contracts and material employment contracts.
- Histories of compensation disputes, and their outcomes.
- Description of medical, vacation, transportation, tuition assistance, and other programs.
- Latest IRS determination letter for any retirement, profit sharing, or pension plan for any Section 501c(9) trust. Form 5500 annual reports for employee benefit plans. Forms 990 for any 501c(9) trust.
- Copy of all audit or actuarial reports concerning pension and retirement plans for recent years.
- Standard COBRA forms and disclosure notices, with a list of employees and qualified beneficiaries.
- Description of stock option and phantom stock incentive programs.
- A list of promises of employee benefits not elsewhere mentioned.
- A list of any "reportable events" or "prohibited transactions" with respect to all pension plans for recent years.
- Copies of written inquires or complaints as to ERISA compliance, or compliance with trust instruments.
- Copies of information related to IRS or DOL employee benefit audits.
- For multiemployer pension plan, information on the target's withdrawal liability.
- Forms PBGC-1 relating to Pension Benefit Guarantee Corp premium payments for defined benefit pension plans.
- Fidelity bond and fiduciary liability insurance policies.
- Investment management contracts and group annuity/guaranteed investment contracts (GICs) for pension benefit plans.
- Administrative service contracts for all employee benefit plans.

- A list of vacation plans/policies and employee fringe benefits, including moving expense policy, travel/entertainment policy, and company auto and car allowances.
- Schedule of compensation paid to officers, directors, and key employees, showing separately salary, bonuses, and noncash compensation.
- List of employment agreements and/or unwritten understandings.
- Key employee losses to (or gains from) competitors or other firms.
- Summary of labor disputes, including correspondence, memoranda, or notes concerning pending or threatened labor stoppage.
- List of negotiations with any group seeking to become the bargaining unit for any employees.
- Copy of all collective bargaining agreements to which the target company or any subsidiary is a party, and the number of employees covered by each agreement.
- Employment and consulting agreements, loan commitments, and documents relating to other transactions with officers, directors, key employees, former employees, and related parties.
- Noncompete agreements with current and former employees.

CULTURE ISSUES

Knowledge

- Congruence of target culture with beliefs and vision.
- Congruence of buyer and target cultures.
- Congruence of target culture with its strategic threats and opportunities.

Information

Much of cultural due diligence cannot be adequately investigated with checklists. Executive interviews and employee focus groups are superior means of profiling the target's culture. The focus here should be on:

- Communication style (formal vs. informal)
- Decision making (top-down vs. decentralized; unilateral vs. team-based).
- Importance of "silos" of expertise (vs. multifunctional attitude).
- Innovation (reliance on traditional approaches vs. experimentation with new methods).
- Solutions sharing (extent of transfer of best practices within the firm).
- Training (how much required; focused on functional silos vs. cross-firm).
- Work orientation (emphasis on processes and roles vs. getting results).

Data

- Copy of the corporate mission statement, vision statement, and values statement.
- Copies of departmental goals and objectives.

- Stories about internal conflicts and how they were resolved.
- Stories about traditions, celebrations.
- Sketches of layouts of offices, service areas, manufacturing areas.
- Observations about telephone and e-mail etiquette.
- Observations about in-person interactions: between employees, and between employees and customers.
- Observations of bulletin boards, cafeteria, and reception areas.
- Copy of organization chart.
- Copy of corporate capital expenditures procedures.
- Copy of corporate training offerings and the attendance rates.
- Copy of agenda of recent senior management meetings with details on structure and content.
- Biographical sketches of managers and supervisors.
- Stories of conflict or harmony on the basis of race, gender, religion, ethnic origin, or sexual orientation.
- Records of charitable and political contributions of cash or in-kind resources.
- Copy of written code of conduct.

ETHICS ISSUES

Knowledge

- Compliance with existing policies and laws related to ethics.
- Exposure to liabilities arising from ethics issues.
- Compatibility of ethics policies with buyer.

Information

- Analyze patterns in code infractions to determine problems, departmentally or managerially.
- Examine company's business practices for the following:
  - Off-the-books accounts where payment is made to a company executive who then diverts part of the proceeds to a separate account for unexplained reasons.
  - A company executive requests over-invoicing requests checks be made out to "bearer" or "cash," or seeks payments by some other anonymous means.
  - A company executive requests an unusually large credit line for a new customer, unusually large bonuses, or similar payments.
  - A company executive has family or business ties with government officials, or has a bad reputation in the business community.
- Through focus groups of company employees from various departments and managerial levels consider:
  - Ethics abuses at the target.
  - Procedures for reporting ethical abuses.

  - Climate for reporting wrongdoing within the company.
  - Trust of management.
  - Comprehensive ethics training programs.
  - Punishment of corporate wrongdoing and reward for ethical behavior.
  - Fair and respectful treatment.
  - Sources of advice on ethics problems within the company.
  - The extent to which management and employees follow corporate policies and ethics standards.
  - Seriousness of the target's ethics program.
  - Belief that the target has integrity and values that they can support.
  - Respect for the CEO.

- Conduct focus group interviews of customers, suppliers, community business leaders, and other sources with the following topics:
  - Customer and supplier satisfaction, giving attention to fair dealing.
  - Reputation of the target, and comparison with peers.
  - Views of other businesses and associations in the community or the industry.
  - Views of other CEOs about the target's CEO.

- When investigating a company from another country, include the following:
  - Determine whether participants in the potential deal are foreign officials, members of a foreign political party, or candidates for office.
  - Conduct a thorough background check of key participants in the deal, including their reputations within the financial, legal, and government communities.
  - Check with U.S. government sources, including those in the State and Commerce Departments and at the U.S. embassy in that country.
  - Conduct a complete study of the prospective target's executive and management structure, including the identities and relationships to government, candidates for office, and political parties of all stockholders, partners, directors, officers, and other members of the firm.

Data

- Target's written code of conduct or ethics.
- Target's guidelines for handling infractions.
- Records of infractions.
- Ethics training course offerings—descriptive materials, timing, and attendance. Criteria for attending—mandatory or voluntary. Goals and objectives. Follow-up assessments of effectiveness. Nature of curriculum.
- Coordinates for ethics hotline, ethics office, or ombudsperson. Records on items handled.
- Written ethical review procedure regarding research and development. Names of managers charged with conducting the ethical reviews.
- Community or consumer complaints to outside agencies (government, Better Business Bureau, etc.).

- Employee interviews regarding bogus accounting, price fixing, discriminatory hiring, environmental infractions, false advertising, bribery, and product safety testing.
- List of criminal proceedings, regulatory violations, or significant civil court litigation.

NOTES

1. See, for instance, a summary of a report by KPMG described in Millman and Gray (2000). This is supplemented by the research of Sirower (1997), who argues that unrealistic assumptions about synergy benefits causes buyers to overpay—in a rational world, unrealistic assumptions are an indicator of the failure to do one's homework.
2. Escrow accounts, claw-back provisions, staged investment, and earnouts are examples of such an insurance policy. In all of these cases, the buyer is the insured, and the seller is the insurer. It may seem that the target pays for the insurance. In fact, the insured *always* pays for insurance; in the case of M&A, the payment would take the form of a higher purchase price, higher payments for social issues, favorable tax treatment for the seller, or countervailing commitments on the buyer's part that in some way insure against the seller's risks.
3. From page 457, *Black's Law Dictionary*, 6th ed., 1990, Henry Campbell Black, ed., St. Paul, MN: West Publishing Company.
4. *National Steel & Shipbuilding Co., v. U.S.*, 190 Ct.Cl.247, 419 F.2nd 863, 875. Quoted in ibid., p. 457.
5. For more on options and the value drivers of R&D investments, see Chapters 10 and 14.
6. From Aaron L. Lebedow, "Due Diligence: More than a Financial Exercise," *Journal of Business Strategy*, Jan./Feb. 1999, page 12.
7. Reprinted from the August 17, 1998, issue of *BusinessWeek* by special permission. © 1998 by The McGraw-Hill Companies.
8. These laws include the Comprehensive Environmental Response, Compensation, and Liability Act (CERCLA or Superfund Law), Resource Conservation and Recovery Act (RCRA), Emergency Planning and Community Right-to-Know Act (EPCRA), Occupational Safety and Health Act (OSHA), Clean Water Act (CWA), and Clean Air Act (CAA).
9. Edgar H. Schein, *Organizational Culture and Leadership*, San Francisco: Jossey-Bass Inc., 1985, page 384.
10. Robert Bruner and Robert Spekman, "The Dark Side of Strategic Alliances: Lessons from Volvo-Renault," *European Management Journal*, April 1998.
11. Luis (1999), page 19.

12. Information gathering can easily morph into activities that are unethical, unprofessional, and illegal. The pressures to do a deal can motivate spying, bribery, combing through garbage, the use of "Trojan horse employees," and other invasions of privacy. The diligence manager must reject these and insist on the highest professional conduct at all times.
13. Harvey and Lusch (1995) and McCurry (2000).

CHAPTER 9

Valuing Firms

INTRODUCTION

Valuation is one of the key business skills, not just because it is a primary concern in mergers and acquisitions, but also because an understanding of valuation can guide managerial action in a wide variety of business dilemmas. Unfortunately, valuation is not easy, for reasons this chapter illuminates. Entire industries (investment banking, consulting, and securities analysis) have grown prosperous providing valuation services to managers and investors. Today, leading corporations are internalizing these valuation skills in recognition of the importance of valuation to daily management, and out of a desire to be more knowledgeable consumers of the more advanced valuation advisory work provided by outsiders. Forward-thinking managers and analysts should have a good understanding of valuation techniques and processes.

The aim of this chapter is to give a general grounding in valuation, but in sufficient detail as to help the reader recognize important nuances, limitations, and opportunities to improve valuation estimates. This survey assumes some modest grounding in finance concepts. Also, this chapter offers a recommended *process* for valuing the firm. It surveys a number of valuation approaches, highlighting their relative strengths and weaknesses. In addition, the chapter discusses eight practical rules or tips for excellent valuation work.

In truth, this chapter tells only part of the valuation story. It surveys techniques for valuing the firm on a *stand-alone* basis only. It leaves the valuation of jointly created gains, or synergies, for Chapter 11, "Valuing Synergies." Also, it leaves for later chapters important valuation problems regarding options (Chapters 10 and 14), cross-border considerations (Chapter 12), financing choices (Chapter 13), and liquidity and control issues (Chapter 15). This chapter is a foundation for all of those elaborations. Valuation is a huge topic. But as the Chinese proverb says, "A walk of a thousand miles begins with a single step." The first step for the mastery of valuation begins with the following extremely important admonition, or rule:

RULE #1: THINK LIKE AN INVESTOR

To implement the rule to *think like an investor* means merely to ask whether one will be wealthier or not as a result of a transaction, or after adopting a strategy or managerial policy. Rational investors participate in transactions that they believe will make them better off. They want to *create value*. If valuation analysis is careful and comprehensive, it can shed light on the reasonable course of action for participants in M&A transactions. But successful investors go further: They think about *intrinsic value* very carefully. Here are the most important elements of their view of value.

Look to the Future, Not the Past

Investors make decisions based on expectations of future performance. Obviously, the past might be a fair indicator of the future, though many sadder but wiser investors have been burned by simply extrapolating from the past. The most important implication of this for valuation is that the analyst should base estimates on forecasts of the future, rather than on past results.

Focus on *Economic* Reality

Seasoned investors pay attention to the *flows of cash*, rather than accounting profits. The reason for this is that financial performance described under a system of generally accepted accounting principles (GAAP) is, in the words of one textbook, "not the result of natural laws, but, instead, is the result of ongoing research, experimentation, debate, and compromise."[1] Another text described GAAP as "a humanly devised arbitrary system of measurement and presentation."[2] Warren Buffett, who has perhaps the best investment record of any living corporate manager, wrote:

> *Because of the limitations of conventional accounting, consolidated reported earnings may reveal relatively little about our true economic performance. Charlie and I, both as owners and managers, virtually ignore such consolidated numbers. . . . Accounting consequences do not influence our operating or capital-allocation process.*[3]

Buffett and others rely instead on cash flow as an estimate of the economically realistic performance of a firm. Cash flow may be measured from several perspectives, including all providers of capital (this is "free cash flow") or only the common stockholders ("residual cash flow"). But the generic definition of cash flow is:

$$\text{Cash flow} = \text{Earnings} + \text{Noncash charges} - \text{Investments}$$

Get Paid for the Risks You Take

The more risk you accept, the more return you should require from an investment. Each day, investors in the capital markets demonstrate this simple but profound idea. This is seen in Exhibit 9.1 in the yields available on corporate bonds: As you go from the least risky (U.S. Treasuries and AAA bonds) to the more risky (B bonds), yields rise unerringly. In results like these, the market tells us that investors require more return for more risk.

EXHIBIT 9.1 Yields on Five-Year Corporate and U.S. Government Bonds by Credit Ratings, May 28, 2002

Bond Quality Grade	Annual Yield to Maturity
U.S. Treasuries	4.45%
Commonly regarded as the least-risky bond investment.	
AAA	5.40%
"Capacity to pay interest and repay principal is extremely strong."	
AA	5.52%
". . . very strong capacity . . ."	
A	5.87%
". . . strong capacity . . . somewhat more susceptible to the adverse effects of changes in circumstances and economic conditions."	
BBB	6.79%
". . . adequate capacity . . . adverse economic conditions or changing circumstances are more likely to lead to a weakened capacity."	
BB+	8.40%
BB/BB–	8.67%
B	10.82%
". . . regarded as predominantly speculative with respect to capacity to pay . . . outweighed by large uncertainties or major risk exposures to adverse conditions."	

Source: Standard & Poor's *Current Statistics*, June 2003. Rating definitions are quoted from Standard & Poor's *Ratings Guide*, New York: McGraw-Hill, 1979, pages 327–328. Reprinted by permission of Standard & Poor's, a division of the McGraw-Hill Companies.

Value Creation: Time Is Money

To think like an investor is to recognize the *time value of money*—that a dollar you will receive in a year is worth less to you now than a dollar received today. This implies that one should make business decisions based on *present values* of future expectations, rather than on undiscounted future values. Warren Buffett assesses intrinsic value as the present value of future expected performance and argues that it is the best method for determining whether

> *an investor is indeed buying something for what it is worth and is therefore truly operating on the principle of obtaining value for his investments. . . . Irrespective of whether a business grows or doesn't, displays volatility or smoothness in earnings, or carries a high price or low in relation to its current earnings and book value, the investment shown by the discounted-flows-of-cash calculation to be the cheapest is the one that the investor should purchase.*[4]

Remember "Opportunity Cost"

One of the most important lessons of the field of economics is that the best decision making takes into account alternative courses of action. That is, one should avoid go/no-go decisions, and instead try to frame acquisition analyses as either/or decisions.

Doing so accounts for alternative opportunities the decision maker should face. The concept of *opportunity cost* has at least two important implications for M&A analysis.

First, opportunity cost is helpful for defining the kinds of deals a firm will or will not do. Exhibit 9.2 reproduces the statement of acquisition goals of Berkshire Hathaway written by Warren Buffett. What motivates this list is an understanding of Berkshire's own competencies; it is prepared to do on its own the kinds of deals that are not generally available in the stock market. Then the statement bluntly concludes with, "*We are not interested, however, in receiving suggestions about purchases we might make in the general stock market.*" Buffett understands oppor-

EXHIBIT 9.2 Berkshire Hathaway Acquisition Criteria

We are eager to hear about businesses that meet all of the following criteria:

1. Large purchases (at least $10 million of after-tax earnings),
2. Demonstrated consistent earning power (future projections are of no interest to us, nor are "turnaround" situations),
3. Businesses earning good returns on equity while employing little or no debt,
4. Management in place (we can't supply it),
5. Simple businesses (if there's lots of technology, we won't understand it),
6. An offering price (we don't want to waste our time or that of the seller by talking, even preliminarily, about a transaction when the price is unknown).

The larger the company, the greater will be our interest: we would like to make an acquisition in the $2–3 billion range.

We will not engage in unfriendly takeovers. We can promise complete confidentiality and a very fast answer customarily within five minutes as to whether we're interested. We prefer to buy for cash, but will consider issuing stock when we receive as much in intrinsic business value as we give.

Our favorite form of purchase is one fitting the pattern through which we acquired Nebraska Furniture Mart, Fechheimer's, Borsheim's, and Central States Indemnity. In cases like these, the company's owner-managers wish to generate significant amounts of cash, sometimes for themselves, but often for their families or inactive shareholders. At the same time, these managers wish to remain significant owners who continue to run their companies just as they have in the past. We think we offer a particularly good fit for owners with such objectives and we invite potential sellers to check us out by contacting people with whom we have done business in the past.

Charlie and I frequently get approached about acquisitions that don't come close to meeting our tests: We've found that if you advertise an interest in buying collies, a lot of people will call hoping to sell you their cocker spaniels. A line from a country song expresses our feeling about new ventures, turnarounds, or auction-like sales: "When the phone don't ring, you'll know it's me."

Besides being interested in the purchase of businesses as described above, we are also interested in the negotiated purchase of large, but not controlling, blocks of stock comparable to those we hold in Capital Cities, Salomon, Gillette, USAir, and Champion. *We are not interested, however, in receiving suggestions about purchases we might make in the general stock market.*

Source: Berkshire Hathaway Annual Report, 1994, page 21.

tunity cost: By simply making random purchases in the stock market, he would be doing nothing for shareholders that they cannot do themselves.

Second, in an M&A setting, the concept of opportunity cost should direct the analyst to consider alternative strategies for the buyer and seller, including the use of alternative assets and the development of alternative transactions. For instance, the value of a target to the *buyer* should reflect the buyer's plans for operating the target (i.e., not the seller's plans), as well as the possibility that the buyer may be able to obtain the same economic benefits more cheaply from another firm or in a different kind of deal (joint venture, strategic alliance, etc.). An example would be that a buyer might seek to obtain manufacturing capacity. The value of that capacity to the buyer should be worth no more than the maximum of cost of alternatives such as leasing other facilities, establishing a joint venture, or outsourcing production. All of these alternatives can be valued using the techniques summarized in this chapter.

For simplicity, the balance of this chapter will assume that acquisition is the cheapest course of action for the buyer—but every analyst should test this assumption early in any acquisition analysis process. The value of the target to the *seller* should be the target's value in its highest alternative deployment. This should include possible payments by other bidders, liquidation of the firm, and simply continuing to operate it as is. Both the seller and buyer should consider synergies realized in an acquisition by the buyer—though, as discussed in Chapters 11 and 21, the division of these joint benefits is always uncertain, and determined largely by the relative bargaining power of the buyer and seller.

Information Is the Core Source of Advantage in Identifying Value-Creating Investments

A great deal of research suggests that on average and over time security prices reflect what is known about a company—this supports the hypothesis of efficient capital markets. The phrase "on average and over time" is intentionally ambiguous, to allow for the fact that there have been exceptions[5] that make it profitable for professional money managers to do what they do. The general point is, *focus on what you know about a target company that the market does not already know*—this was a key point emphasized in Chapter 8. Warren Buffett has said, "Anyone not aware of the fool in the market probably is the fool in the market."[6] Buffett was fond of repeating a parable told him by Benjamin Graham:

> *There was a small private business and one of the owners was a man named Market. Every day Mr. Market had a new opinion of what the business was worth, and at that price stood ready to buy your interest or sell you his. As excitable as he was opinionated, Mr. Market presented a constant distraction to his fellow owners. "What does he know?" they would wonder, as he bid them an extraordinarily high price or a depressingly low one. Actually, the gentleman knew little or nothing. You may be happy to sell out to him when he quotes you a ridiculously high price, and equally happy to buy from him when his price is low. But the rest of the time you will be wiser to form your own ideas of the value of your holdings, based on full reports from the company about its operations and financial position.*[7]

Diversification Is Good

The Nobel prize in economics for 1990 went to Harry Markowitz for his theoretical work on portfolio optimization, which founded the theory of diversification. The core idea is that spreading wealth across a number of assets reduces the risk of loss—as long as the returns on those assets are less than perfectly correlated. An extreme example of negatively correlated investments would be shares in an umbrella manufacturer and a suntan lotion manufacturer: No matter whether the climate is sunny or rainy, the portfolio of the two kinds of shares can be constructed in a way to yield an expected return at much less risk than could be obtained by concentrating one's wealth in either company alone. Buying the shares of two steel companies does not provide much risk reduction because both companies are likely to be affected by the same economic forces. But diversifying across industries reduces the correlation of possible investment outcomes, and increases the benefits of diversification. Risk reduction through diversification is the principle underlying the insurance industry. A very important implication of diversification for M&A deal doers is that investments should be evaluated in terms of the risk they add to your existing portfolio, rather than the total risk the investment offers on a stand-alone basis.

These seven points summarize what it means to think like an investor and can help the decision maker work through fairly knotty problems by going back to basics. Sensible analysis and action almost always arise from considering a merger or acquisition proposal in light of these issues.

RULE #2: INTRINSIC VALUE IS UNOBSERVABLE; WE CAN ONLY ESTIMATE IT

An important point of departure in all valuation analysis appears at first to be an exercise in semantics, a mincing of definitions of "value." The analyst has, after all, numerous points of reference, such as *book value*, *liquidation value*, replacement value, present value, and multiples value. These many approaches to value generate confusion or false confidence, the rock and the hard place of M&A. The novice may well wonder which value is "right." Conversely, with an abundance of definitions, the novice may conclude that valuation is really a very straightforward process of generating numbers. It is only the concept of intrinsic value that can help steer between these twin threats of confusion and false confidence.

The aim of all valuation analysis is to assess the true or intrinsic value of an asset. Unfortunately, intrinsic value is unobservable. All of the "values" listed here are merely vantage points from which to assess intrinsic value: These values are not necessarily "intrinsic." Virtually every number you use in valuation is *measured with error*, either because of flawed methods to describe the past or because of uncertainty about the future. This simple fact has several important implications for valuation analysis:

- The results of valuation analysis are *estimates*. To label the valuation results this way is gently to remind the user of these results that intrinsic value is unobservable, a subtle kind of "truth in valuation" disclaimer.

- The entire process of valuation analysis should be structured as a *triangulation* from several vantage points. To triangulate is to measure something indirectly based on different points of observation. As a general matter this would suggest that more points of observation are better in valuation analysis (up to a limit imposed by one's time and budget). The larger implication is that one should work with many estimates and *estimators*.
- Do not work with point estimates of value; work with ranges. If intrinsic value is unobservable, then producing point estimates of value creates false precision. Professionalism lies in identifying the range within which intrinsic value reasonably resides. Through careful analysis, one should aim to narrow the range, but not eliminate it.

RULE #3: AN OPPORTUNITY TO CREATE VALUE EXISTS WHERE PRICE AND INTRINSIC VALUE DIFFER

The whole aim of valuation is to find, and exploit, profit-making opportunities. Value is created (profit is "made") where you sell something for more than it is worth to you, or buy something for less than it is worth—in these two instances, price and intrinsic value differ. Cast in the context of M&A, the *rules for creating value* may be summarized as:

Rules for Creating Value and Avoiding Value Destruction

Buyer's view: Accept the proposed deal if: Intrinsic value of target to the buyer > Payment.

Seller's view: Accept the proposed deal if: Payment > Intrinsic value of target to the seller.

These rules embody the simple logic that *rational businesspeople do not want to be worse off after the deal than they were before.* In simple terms, investors want to create value, or at the very least, conserve it; this is the fundamental quality of thinking like an investor.

Why intrinsic value and price may differ is in a sense the focus of this book, and a subject worth very lengthy discussion. Virtually all strategic buyers illustrate this rule at work: The target company has an intrinsic worth to them that is higher than acquisition price because of possible economies of scale and scope, various synergies, and opportunities for cost cutting.

A very important offshoot of this rule is the concept of *value additivity.* This concept says that in perfect circumstances, the value of the whole should equal the sum of the values of the parts.

$$\text{Value}_{\text{Enterprise}} = \Sigma(\text{Value of business units}) = \text{Equity} + \text{Debt} \qquad (1)$$

The radical idea here is the notion that these three quantities should be equal. This follows intuition: If markets work well, one will not be willing to pay more for a basket of 10 apples than one could pay for 10 individually. In addition, the idea that the enterprise value should be equal to the value of all the firm's securities is just another expression of the basic idea that the whole should equal the sum of the parts. Also, this equality is reflected in the basic accounting identity that Assets = Debt + Equity.

Our interest, however, is not in the theory premised on perfect conditions, but rather in departures from it. In other words, value additivity gives us a framework for testing for deviations of price from intrinsic value: Simply value the parts, and see whether the sum differs from the value of the whole. This is a steady practice among securities analysts, and was the underlying analysis of the "bust-up" acquisitions of the 1980s and 1990s.

The idea of value additivity highlights one final important detail: When we talk about value, we must be clear about *what* it is we are valuing. Specifically, in valuation work one finds two sorts of valuations:

1. ***Enterprise value.*** This is the value of the whole firm, the intrinsic value of the firm's net assets. The convention of most M&A analysts is to work with net assets (which equals total assets less current liabilities) in recognition of the fact that accounts payable and accruals arise in the ordinary course of generating current assets.
2. ***Equity value.*** This is the value of the residual claim on the firm's assets, typically the intrinsic value of the firm's common stock.

These two types of value are related by the economic identity that:

$$\text{Enterprise value} = \text{Value of debt} + \text{Value of equity} \tag{2}$$

RULE #4: SO MANY ESTIMATORS, SO LITTLE TIME—IT HELPS TO HAVE A VIEW

There are, by conservative count, nine approaches to valuing a firm:

1. Book value of the target firm.
2. Liquidation value of the target firm.
3. *Replacement cost* of the target firm.
4. *Current market value* of the target firm.
5. *Trading multiples* of comparable firms applied to the target.
6. *Transaction multiples* of comparable acquisitions applied to the target.
7. *Discounted cash flow* of the target firm.
8. Venture capital/private equity approach.
9. Option theory valuation of the target firm.

Not all these estimators carry equal influence in the field of M&A valuation. To some extent, the problem of many estimators can be mitigated by understanding their relative strengths and weaknesses, and weighting the estimates according to your view of the method. To appreciate the importance of Rule #4 requires a survey of the essential points of these various methods.

Estimates Based on Accounting Book Value

Book values are estimated by auditors based on GAAP and techniques of sampling and transaction analysis that auditors use. This approach is dominated by the principle of conservatism that tends to reflect only what has already happened, and ignore most assets or values that are not tangible. This is one of the easiest approaches available to any analyst of a company with audited financial statements. These estimates carry the imprimatur of the certified public accountant, which lends an aura of certitude and is influential with some segments of the public who have no familiarity with financial ideas.

The important defects of this approach stem from its reliance on accounting practices. Book values ignore intangible assets like brand names, patents, technical know-how, and managerial competence. The method ignores price appreciation due, for instance, to inflation. It invites disputes about types of liabilities. For instance, are deferred taxes equity or debt? Most importantly, the book value method is *backward looking*. It ignores the positive or negative operating prospects of the firm. If "think like an investor" means anything, it surely means that one should make financial decisions based on expectations about the future rather than knowledge about the past.

Book value has rather limited significance as an estimator of the value of healthy, growing firms. These estimates may be appropriate for firms with no intangible assets, commodity-type assets valued at market, and stable operations.

Liquidation Value of the Target Firm

This is perhaps the most conservative valuation approach, as it simply sums the values that might be realized in a liquidation of the firm today. Estimates of these values are developed from a blend of the methods surveyed in this chapter. But the fundamental question asked in valuing the various assets always is, "What will this asset fetch in an auction?" Experienced liquidation analysts typically assess these values as a percentage of the book value of the asset.

Exhibit 9.3 gives an example in which an analyst assumes that the liquidation of ABC Corp. would result in realization of all of its cash, 80 percent of its receivables, 60 percent of its inventory, and 40 percent of the book value of its plant and equipment. Note that in this example, liquidation value is considerably smaller than book value. This is usually the case, since the accounting conventions that produce book value assume that the firm is a *going concern* that will live indefinitely. In contrast, a liquidating firm has a short life remaining. Receivables thought to be collectible in the fullness of time may be uncollectible at liquidation; some kinds of inventory like intermediate manufacturing products may be valuable only if converted to a finished product; finished goods inventory may be worth much less to the customer if there will be no company to stand behind product warranties. Plant and equipment may be so specialized that they have little value to other firms.

The weaknesses of this approach are manifest in the methodology just illustrated. First, liquidation values tend to be highly appraiser-specific. One should look for reasonable rules of thumb or recovery ratios based on comparable liquidations as foundations for the analyst's work. Second, estimates under this method are highly influenced by judgments about how finely one might break up the company: Will one

EXHIBIT 9.3 Liquidation Estimate of Value of ABC Corp.

	Book Value	Assumed Percentage of Book Value Collected in Liquidation	Liquidation Value
Cash	$ 10	100%	$10
Receivables	$ 30	80%	$24
Inventory	$ 25	60%	$15
Plant and equipment	$ 35	40%	$14
Total	$100		$63
Debt	$ 50	100%	$50
Equity	$ 50		$13

sell a fully stocked plant, or sell the assets individually down to the nails? Third, physical condition of the assets will affect values significantly; the auditor's estimate of remaining book value in an asset category may not reflect real economic wear on machinery, the longevity of products, or the obsolescence of inventory. There can be no substitute for an on-site assessment of a company's assets. Fourth, this method easily ignores the value of hidden rights (or "options," as discussed later), growth opportunities, and valuable intangible assets such as patents and brand names.

Practiced at its most conservative level, this method probably is not useful for analysts in an M&A setting. However, it will be appropriate for firms in financial distress, or more generally, for firms whose operating prospects are very cloudy. This method of valuation requires the skills of an experienced asset valuation expert rather than an operating manager.

A variation of liquidation value, commonly known as *bust-up value*, is estimated in M&A by opportunistic investors (commonly called "hostile raiders"), by financial investors seeking to take firms private, and by industry consolidators. One classic example of this valuation approach was UV Industries in which the raider, Victor Posner, took an unsolicited investment position in 1978. The company's market value of equity was trading near its book value of equity, $266 million. UV Industries was a conglomerate consisting of business units in electrical equipment manufacturing, railroad transportation, extraction of coal, copper, gold, oil and gas, steel manufacturing, and copper and brass fabrication. Valuing these pieces independently and then summing the pieces, UV's common equity was estimated conservatively to be worth $470 million.[8] This disparity between price and estimated intrinsic value constituted a value-creating opportunity (see Rule #3). The board of UV ordered the firm to be liquidated rather than permit a takeover by Posner. Within 18 months the pieces had been sold and the shareholders had received total liquidating dividends of $806 million.

Replacement Cost Valuation

Replacement cost values of firms are estimated by determining the cost to replace the assets of the firm piecemeal today. In the 1970s and early 1980s, during the era of high inflation in the United States, the Securities and Exchange Commission required public corporations to estimate replacement values and report them annually. This method has been less useful in recent years. But generally, replacement cost valuation will give valuable insights in any high-inflation setting, and would be of particular value today in some developing countries.

This valuation approach has one important virtue over the ordinary accounting book value approach: It reflects current conditions rather than past experience. A convention in accounting is to carry assets at a value that is the lower of cost or market. Fixed asset values in healthy firms reflect original investment outlays rather than current replacement values. In an inflationary environment, historical cost will be a poor indication of current value.

But replacement cost valuation has several potential weaknesses. First, it is often unclear what is to be replaced. Realistically, many managers would not replace an old and inefficient plant with the same design. Instead they would use the replacement opportunity to streamline the manufacturing process and incorporate advances in technology and manufacturing concepts. Analysts and decision makers should determine *which* replacement value is to be estimated: old plant or new plant? Second, replacement cost estimation is relatively highly subjective, often relying on rules of thumb. Third, these estimates ignore the uses to which the assets will be applied, and the resulting expectations of future performance. Fourth, some intangible assets may be difficult if not impossible to value under this method—some replacement cost valuations ignore them altogether.

In short, this method may have limited usefulness in low-inflation environments. But it remains a potentially useful tool for special circumstances.

Current Trading Value or Market Value

The current market value of an enterprise is simply the sum of the market values of its debt and equity. The value of equity is simply share price times the number of shares. The value of debt can be estimated by literally estimating the present value of debt cash flows, though ordinarily book value will be close to market value unless the firm's credit rating has changed or the general level of interest rates has moved since the debt was issued.

In estimating the market value of "debt," two kinds of liabilities are ignored. First, deferred taxes are viewed as a government subsidy (these taxes will not be paid by a growing firm), and thus are captured in the market value of equity. Second, current liabilities are seen as a claim against current assets: Positive or negative working capital is reflected in the market value of equity.

The current market value of the firm's securities is an extremely important reference point to the valuation of the public corporation, because we can reasonably assume that *market prices reflect what is known about a firm.* To think like an investor is to know that information is a key source of economic advantage; one must concentrate on identifying what one knows relative to what is known broadly in the market. Current market value can help the analyst focus attention on possible information asymmetries, on private information known only to insiders or acquirers who may see a special economic opportunity in the target company.

These prices will be relatively more useful if the target firm's securities are actively traded, followed by professional securities analysts, and if the market efficiently impounds all public information about the company and its industry. This approach is less helpful for less well-known companies with thinly or intermittently traded stock. It is simply not applicable to privately held companies—see Chapter 15 for more on the impact of illiquidity on valuation.

Current market value is a useful reference in merger negotiations. Very rarely do merger terms settle at prices below current market value. One recent exception was Bell Atlantic's merger with GTE announced in July 1998. The terms called for an exchange of shares that valued GTE at 6 percent less than the price prevailing before the announcement. One investor said, "It unnerves me that they offered a below-market price."[9] In this case, as in the few other memorable instances, observers point to the overriding influence of "social issues" such as the distribution of power between the bidder and target CEOs and/or the possibility that the *ex ante* target price was unduly inflated by market rumors that did not reflect the reality of the impending deal.

Trading Multiples of Peer Firms

This approach estimates a target's value by applying the valuation multiples of peer firms to the target. The assumption is that these multiples reflect the general outlook for an industry or a group of firms. Exhibit 9.4 lists multiples one may encounter in practice. As this exhibit shows, *the analyst must remember that some multiples estimate the value of the whole enterprise, while others estimate the value of equity only.*

Valuation by multiples is widely used in the financial community. The artistry of this method lies in selecting the sample of peer firms on which to base the valuation of the target. Ideally, one would use only those firms that matched the target on the basis of current lines of business, outlook for the future, financial policy, and size. Finance theory suggests that the size of a multiple is driven by two main factors: risk and expected growth. For instance, the widely used price/earnings (P/E) multiple can be decomposed into two factors:

$$\frac{\text{Stock price}}{\text{E(EPS)}} = \frac{1}{r} + \frac{\text{PVGO}}{\text{E(EPS)}} \tag{3}$$

EXHIBIT 9.4 Classic Valuation Multiples

Multiples That Value the Enterprise	Multiples That Value Equity
Enterprise value/EBIT	Stock price/earnings per share
Enterprise value/EBITDA	Stock price/book value of equity per share
Enterprise value/sales	
Enterprise value/book value of assets	

Note: Enterprise value equals the market value of equity (calculated as share price times number of shares) plus market value of debt (for which book value is usually a reasonable approximation). EBIT stands for earnings before interest and taxes. EBITDA stands for earnings before interest, taxes, depreciation, and amortization.

E(EPS) is the earnings per share expected to be reported next year. The factor "r" is the required return on equity, which is determined by risk. And PVGO is the present value of growth opportunities per share, an estimate of today's value of investments expected to be made in the future.[10] The term "growth company" is not defined by the growth rate of sales, earnings, or assets, but by the size of PVGO relative to the market value of equity. In other words, the P/E ratios of growth firms are typically sizable and driven significantly by attractive future growth opportunities. One can decompose other ratios in a similar fashion. But the key idea is that multiples reflect important economic phenomena. To judge whether a multiple is appropriate, one should look into the underlying economic fundamentals.

Although widely used and simple to use, valuation by the multiples approach is vulnerable to several potential problems. First, rarely does one find a "pure play" peer on which to base a valuation. How far to stray from the narrow profile of the target company in choosing peers is a major point of judgment.

A second possible weakness is the dependence of this method on accounting practices. Generally accepted accounting principles (GAAP) afford managers rather wide latitude in reporting the financial results of the firm. In using this method, the analyst must scrutinize the accounting practices of the target and peer firms to determine the comparability of their reporting policies and their results.

A third caveat concerns when the multiple is computed: Multiples are often based on the financial performance for the fiscal year just completed. But some analysts quote multiples based on *expected* performance for the year ahead. Lagging multiples (based on the prior calendar year's, fiscal year's, or 12 months' financial performance) will usually be larger than leading multiples (based on a forecast of the next year's performance). For growing firms, the difference in financial performance between the year just past and the year ahead will be material. Another manifestation of this timing problem is that fiscal year-ends may vary among the target firm and the peers. In industries experiencing some volatility, a difference of one or two quarters in the reporting of year-end results may result in rather different multiples. Further, firms in the same peer group may end their fiscal years at different times. If an industry has any cyclicality or business surprises, these different fiscal year-ends could create large variances in the resulting P/Es.

Fourth, this method focuses on proxies for cash flow, rather than cash flow itself. Thus, it ignores important effects of capital investment, investment in working capital, and depreciation. Also, it may naively discriminate against targets currently losing money or with negative equity—for instance, in the 1990s many cable television companies fell into this category. The ignorance of factors such as taxes, depreciation, and investment has led some analysts to reject the use of multiples. Others look toward specialized multiples such as revenues/enterprise value, price/cash flow, or price/EBITDA (earnings before interest, taxes, depreciation, and amortization)—but these alternatives suffer many of the same flaws as P/E. One money manager said, "EBITDA is like Alice in Fantasyland. It should be outlawed from securities analysis."[11]

Finally, multiples are "opaque boxes," abstractions of investment value. It is challenging under this method to conduct a meaningful sensitivity analysis, for instance to test the impact of different future expectations and scenarios on the value of the firm.

Transaction Multiples for Peer Firms

In an M&A setting, valuation analysts will look to comparable transactions as an additional benchmark against which to assess the target firm. This approach harnesses many of the same multiples mentioned earlier, adapted to the *actual prices* paid for the firms. The caveats for this approach are the same as those discussed in the preceding section. The chief difference between transaction multiples and peer multiples is that the former will reflect a *control premium*, typically of 30 to 50 percent, that is not present in the ordinary trading multiples of firms' securities. The premium for control is discussed further in Chapter 15.

Discounted Cash Flow Values

This approach calculates the present value of cash flows using an estimated cost of capital. The result will be the present value of the enterprise. Finding the present value of a stream of cash (or "discounting") is arithmetically the opposite process of compounding. One divides an individual flow of cash (CF) by a factor $(1 + K)^N$, reflecting the number of years into the future (N) and one's impatience for receiving the cash (reflected by K, called "cost of capital"). The formula for valuing a stream with an infinite life is:

$$\text{DCF value} = \frac{CF_1}{(1+K)} + \frac{CF_2}{(1+K)^2} + \frac{CF_3}{(1+K)^3} + \ldots + \frac{CF_\infty}{(1+K)^\infty} \quad (4)$$

While most firms have infinite lives, actually valuing such a stream would be impossible. Therefore, analysts typically forecast cash flows out to a reasonable horizon such as five or at most 10 years, and then add a *terminal value* or *continuing value* to the final flow, reflecting the firm's value at that date of all the cash flows occurring thereafter. This simplifies the formula considerably; here is an example of the formula for a five-year forecast. Note that the last term values the cash flows in the fifth year plus the value of the firm as of the end of that year (TV_5).

$$\text{DCF value} = \frac{CF_1}{(1+K)} + \frac{CF_2}{(1+K)^2} + \frac{CF_3}{(1+K)^3} + \frac{CF_4}{(1+K)^4} + \frac{CF_5 + TV_5}{(1+K)^5} \quad (5)$$

KEY PRINCIPLE: USE A DISCOUNT RATE CONSISTENT WITH THE RISK OF THE CASH FLOW BEING VALUED Remember that one can value the enterprise or equity. Discounted cash flow (DCF) can value both. A common mistake of novices is to mix the two in estimating DCFs. Instead, one needs to be consistent throughout the analysis, discounting cash flows to all providers of capital (also known as free cash flows) at a blended cost of capital reflecting the required returns of all providers of capital, also known as *weighted average cost of capital* (WACC). This approach values the enterprise. Alternatively, one can value equity by discounting cash flows to equity (also known as residual cash flows) at the cost of equity. These are the correct pairings of discount rates and cash flows. *Do not mix the pairings.*

The large implication of this is that we need to be careful about how we define "cash flow" and "cost of capital." Generally, cash flow will be the sum of after-tax earnings, plus depreciation and noncash charges, less investment. But from an enterprise valuation standpoint, "earnings" must be earnings after taxes available to *all* providers of capital or EBIAT (earnings before interest and after taxes). From an equity standpoint, earnings must be net income. A useful acid test in determining where one is working with equity or enterprise cash flows is to ask, "Are the cash flows net of interest and principal payments?" If so, they are equity flows; if not, they are enterprise flows. A similar careful distinction must be drawn with respect to discount rate and terminal value. The distinctions are summarized in Exhibit 9.5.

CAVEATS ABOUT TERMINAL VALUE Terminal value is typically a large component of the present value of a company. Exhibit 9.6 shows that for a dart-selected sample of stocks on the New York Stock Exchange, terminal value accounts for about 90 percent of the share price. The overwhelming influence of terminal value is troublesome to many executives, who ask why something so far off in the future should have such a big impact today. Intuitively, the answer is that terminal value matters so much because it capitalizes the long-term growth prospects of the firm. Growth is the "big enchilada" of valuation. Thus, in view of its importance, the first caveat here is: *Pay careful attention to terminal value.*

A range of residual values can be estimated using the various estimation

EXHIBIT 9.5 Properly Match Discount Rates and Cash Flows

Value of:	Cash Flow	Terminal Value	Discount Rate
Firm or assets	Free cash flow (FCF) (i.e., before servicing debt, preferred, or common equity) FCF = [EBIT × (1 – t)] + Depreciation – Capex – ΔNWC + ΔDefTax	Firm or asset value $TV_{Firm} \dfrac{FCF \cdot (1+g_{FCF})}{WACC - g_{FCF}}$	Weighted average cost of capital
Equity	Dividends or residual cash flow (RCF) (i.e., after servicing debt): RCF = Net Income + Depreciation – Capex – ΔNWC + ΔDefTax + ΔDebt	Value of equity $TV_{Equity} = \dfrac{RCF \cdot (1+g_{RCF})}{K_e - g_{RCF}}$	Cost of equity
Debt	Interest, fees, principal	Principal outstanding at maturity	Cost of debt

Capex—Capital expenditures
NWC—Net working capital
DefTax—Deferred taxes

EXHIBIT 9.6 Dart-Selected Sample of Firms with Analysis of Five-Year Dividends as a Percent of Stock Price, 1996

Company	Recent Price	Annual Dividend	Five-Year Dividend Growth	Beta	Equity Cost	Present Value of Five Years' Dividends	Percent of Market Price Not Attributable to Dividends
AlliedSignal	$42.00	$0.78	14.5%	1.15	12.3%	$4.14	90%
Burlington Northern	78.00	1.20	0.0	1.15	12.3	4.30	94
Caterpillar	57.00	1.20	30.0	1.25	12.8	9.37	84
Cooper Industies	34.00	1.32	2.5	1.15	12.3	5.06	85
Cummins Engine	35.00	1.00	26.0	1.10	12.0	7.22	79
Delux Corp.	28.00	1.48	1.5	0.90	10.9	5.71	80
R.R. Donnelley	39.00	0.68	16.0	1.05	11.7	3.81	90
Dun & Bradstreet	62.00	2.63	4.0	1.00	11.5	10.73	83
Eaton Corp.	51.00	1.50	6.5	1.05	11.7	6.51	87
Emerson Electric	71.00	1.75	9.5	1.05	11.7	8.24	88
Equifax	20.00	0.32	6.5	1.25	12.8	1.35	93
Federal Express	82.00	0.00	0.0	1.35	13.4	0.00	100
Fluor Corp.	58.00	0.60	11.5	1.25	12.8	2.90	95
Honeywell	44.00	1.01	11.5	1.10	12.0	4.98	89
Illinois Tool Works	59.00	0.62	10.5	1.10	12.0	2.98	95
Kelly Services	28.00	0.78	11.0	1.10	12.0	3.80	86
Owens-Corning	44.00	0.00	0.0	1.50	14.2	0.00	100
Raychem	57.00	0.32	4.5	1.30	13.1	1.27	98
ServiceMaster	30.00	0.95	2.5	0.80	10.4	3.82	87
Sherwin-Williams	40.00	0.64	6.5	1.10	12.0	2.76	93
Stone Container	18.00	0.15	7.0	2.25	18.2	0.56	97
Tenneco	47.00	1.60	6.0	1.15	12.3	6.75	86
WMX Technologies	30.00	0.60	5.5	1.20	12.6	2.48	92
Westinghouse	16.00	0.20	0.0	1.15	12.3	0.72	96
							Average 90%

Note: To illustrate the estimate of 90% for AlliedSignal, the annual dividend of $0.78 was projected to grow at 14.5% per year to $0.89 in 1997, $1.02 in 1998, $1.17 in 1999, $1.34 in 2000, and $1.54 in 2001. The present value of these dividends discounted at 12.3% is $4.14. This equals about 10% of AlliedSignal's stock price, $42.00. The complement, 90%, is the portion of market price not attributable to dividends.

Source of data: Value Line *Investment Survey* for prices, dividends, growth rates, and betas. Other items calculated by the author.

procedures summarized in this chapter. A standard estimator of terminal value is the constant growth valuation formula:

$$\text{Terminal value} = \frac{CF \cdot (1 + g^{\infty})}{K - g^{\infty}} \qquad (6)$$

Two of the variables in this model are relatively straightforward. Cash flow (CF) is taken from the final year of the financial forecast. The cost of capital (K) is estimated using the techniques described in the following section. The third item, g^{∞}, is the compound average growth rate of the cash flows to infinity, and is the "tail that wags the dog"—typically small changes in g^{∞} will produce relatively large changes in terminal value and DCF value. This motivates the second caveat: *Take care in estimating* g^{∞}.

There are two classic approaches for estimating a growth rate to use in the constant growth formula. The first is to use the self-sustainable growth rate formula:

$$g^{\infty} = \text{ROE} \times (1 - \text{DPO}) \tag{7}$$

This assumes that the firm can grow only as fast as it adds to its equity capital base through the return on equity (ROE) less any dividends paid out, indicated through the dividend payout (DPO) ratio. Novices may simply extrapolate *past* ROE and DPO without really thinking about the future. Also, it relies on accounting ROE and can give some unusual results. For a full discussion and critique of the self-sustainable growth model, see Appendix 6.1 in Chapter 6.

The second approach assumes that nominal growth of a business is the product of *real growth* and *inflation*. In more proper mathematical notation the formula is:

$$g^{\infty}_{\text{Nominal}} = [(1 + g^{\infty}_{\text{Units}}) \times (1 + g^{\infty}_{\text{Inflation}})] - 1 \tag{8}$$

This formula uses the economist's notion[12] that the nominal rate of growth is the product of the rate of inflation and the "real" rate of growth. We commonly think of real growth as a percentage increase in units shipped. But in rare instances, real growth could come from price increases due, for instance, to a monopolist's power over the market. For simplicity, many analysts just use a short version of the model (less precise, though the difference in precision is usually not material):

$$g^{\infty}_{\text{Nominal}} = g^{\infty}_{\text{Units}} + g^{\infty}_{\text{Inflation}} \tag{9}$$

Both variations of the equation focus on two interesting issues: the real growth rate (that is, the growth rate in units shipped) in the business, and the ability of the business to pass along the effects of inflation. The consensus inflation outlook in the United States today calls for an inflation rate between 1 and 3 percent indefinitely. The real growth rate is bound to vary by industry. Growth in U.S. unit demand of consumer staple products (like Band-Aids) is probably determined by growth rate of the population—less than 1 percent in the United States. Growth in demand for industrial commodities like steel is probably about equal to the real rate of growth of gross national product (GNP)—about 2.5 percent on average through time. In any event, all of these are small numbers.

The sum of the real growth rate and the expected inflation rate today yields a small number; this is intuitively appealing since over the very long run, the increasing maturity of a company will tend to drive its growth rate toward the average for the economy. This leads to the third caveat: *Growth to infinity is likely to be a small number; avoid "irrational exuberance" in estimating these growth rates.*

The fourth caveat addresses a final issue about growth: *Assuming a growth rate greater than WACC gives a negative terminal value.* This is an instance in which you cannot use the constant growth model. However, WACC less than g cannot happen; a company cannot grow to infinity at a rate greater than its cost of capital. To illustrate why, let's rearrange the constant growth formula to solve for WACC:

$$\text{WACC} = \frac{\text{FCF}_{\text{Next period}}}{\text{Value of firm}_{\text{Current period}}} + g^{\infty}_{\text{FCF}} \tag{10}$$

If WACC were less than g, then the ratio of FCF divided by value of the firm would have to be *negative*. Since the value of the healthy firm to the investors cannot be less than zero,[13] the source of negativity must be FCF—that means the firm is absorbing rather than throwing off cash. Recall that in the familiar constant growth terminal value formula, FCF is the flow that compounds to infinity at the rate g. Thus, if FCF is negative, then the entire stream of FCFs must be negative—such a company is like Peter Pan: *It never grows up*; it never matures to the point where it throws off positive cash flow. This makes no sense, for investors would not buy securities in a firm that never paid a cash return. In short, you cannot use the constant growth model where WACC is less than g, because of the unbelievable implications of that assumption.

WHERE DISCOUNT RATES COME FROM The discount rate should reflect the investor's opportunity cost, the rate of return required on assets of comparable risk. For free cash flows (that is, flows to all providers of capital), the appropriate rate will be a blend of the required rates of return on debt and equity, weighted by the proportion of those sources of capital in the firm's market value capital structure. The result is the weighted average cost of capital, or WACC. The equation for this is:

$$\text{WACC} = i_d(1 - t)\, W_d + K_e W_e \tag{11}$$

where i_d = expected yield (internal rate of return—IRR) on target's new debt after merger.

K_e = Current cost of target's equity capital (see below).

W_d, W_e = Debt and equity as percentages of the target firm's *market value* capital structure after merger. The market values should be estimated from current market prices of the debt and equity. For private firms, estimates by DCF or other methods must suffice.

t = Marginal (not average) tax rate of the target firm.

Bradley and Jarrell (2003) have argued that this standard WACC formula understates the true nominal WACC in the presence of taxes and inflation. They show that an alternative formulation of WACC by Miles and Ezzell (1980) (M&E) correctly adjusts for taxes and inflation. The M&E WACC model is:

$$\text{WACC} = K_U - \frac{t i_d \dfrac{D}{V_L}(1 + K_U)}{(1 + i_d)} \tag{12}$$

where i_d = Expected yield (IRR) on target's new debt after merger.
K_U = Cost of target's equity capital *as if unlevered* (i.e., computed using an unlevered beta).
D = Market value of the target's debt.
V_L = Enterprise value of the target, levered. The market value should be estimated from current market prices of the debt and equity. For private firms, estimates by DCF or other methods must suffice.
t = Marginal (not average) tax rate of the target firm.

Bradley and Jarrell find that at higher levels of inflation the traditional WACC model produces material (greater than 15 percent) valuation errors. At low levels of inflation (such as 1 to 3 percent during the 1998–2003 period in the United States) and conventional levels of debt, the difference in WACC estimates is small and within what a practical analyst would call the "noise level" of valuation. Given widespread familiarity with the traditional model and low prevailing inflation rates, this book applies the traditional WACC model rather than the M&E model. Nevertheless, the careful analyst should apply the M&E model under conditions of higher inflation.

There are two general approaches to estimating the cost of equity: the *dividend growth model* and the *capital asset pricing model* (*CAPM*).

Dividend Growth Model of the Cost of Equity

$$K_e = \frac{\text{DIV}_1}{P_0} + g^{\infty} \tag{13}$$

where DIV_1/P_0 = Current dividend yield.
g^{∞} = Constant expected growth rate of dividends to infinity.

This model is best used in estimating the equity costs for firms in stable industries, such as public utilities. The caveat in using this model is that it implies that growth drives the cost of equity, when there is no obvious reason why this should be so. Some analysts will argue that rapidly growing firms are riskier, thus necessitating higher cost of equity. If this is so, then the capital asset pricing model (CAPM) is better to use since it explicitly models the risk-return relationship.

Capital Asset Pricing Model of Cost of Equity

$$K_e = R_f + \beta(R_m - R_f) \tag{14}$$

where R_f = The expected return on risk-free securities over a time horizon consistent with your investment in the target. Generally use long-term government bond rates.
$R_m - R_f$ = The risk premium for common stocks. From 1926 to 2000, the risk premium for common stocks has averaged about 6 percent when measured geometrically, and about 7.5 percent when measured arithmetically.[14]
β = *Beta*, a measure of the systematic risk of a firm's common stock. Estimates of beta are available from Bloomberg, Value Line, and

Merrill Lynch. Alternatively, it can be estimated by regression; most analysts use at least 60 observations of prices. If beta is greater than 1.0, the target's stock is more volatile than the market; if less than 1.0, the stock is less volatile.

If the acquirer intends to change the financial leverage of the target significantly, beta should be adjusted.

Step 1: Unlever the beta. This *unlevered beta* captures the degree of risk in the firm's operations, before financing:

$$\beta_{\text{Unlevered}} = \frac{\beta_{\text{Levered}}}{1+(1-t)\text{D/E}} \tag{15}$$

where D/E is the target's market value debt-equity ratio *before* acquisition, and t is the marginal tax rate of the firm.

Step 2: Relever the beta:

$$\beta_{\text{Levered}} = \beta_{\text{Unlevered}}[1 + (1 - t)\ \text{D/E}] \tag{16}$$

where D/E is the target's debt-equity ratio *after* relevering, and t is the target's marginal tax rate.

An alternative formula for the unlevered or *asset beta* of a firm holds that the unlevered beta is a weighted average of the firm's debt and equity betas. This unlevered beta is also called the enterprise beta or asset beta:

$$\beta_{\text{Unlevered}} = \beta_{\text{Debt}}\left(\frac{\text{Debt}}{\text{Debt}+\text{Equity}}\right)+\beta_{\text{Equity}}\left(\frac{\text{Equity}}{\text{Debt}+\text{Equity}}\right) \tag{17}$$

Note that in this alternative model of the unlevered beta, there is no provision for the impact of taxes. This model assumes that through homemade leverage, investors can appropriate for themselves the benefits of debt tax shields and that the tax impact of leverage is neutralized.[15] This implies that the levered beta (that is, equity beta) formula will be:

$$\beta_{\text{Levered}} = \beta_{\text{Asset}} + (\beta_{\text{Asset}} - \beta_{\text{Debt}})\frac{\text{Debt}}{\text{Equity}} \tag{18}$$

This alternative version of the levered beta formula is useful because it permits the analyst to assume that the firm has risky debt outstanding, meaning that the debt bears some degree of default risk of the enterprise. The debt betas of corporate bonds are typically in the range of 0.15 to 0.25 for investment grade issues. But for non–investment grade debt (so-called "junk" debt) the betas will be materially higher. By subtracting the debt beta, this formula recognizes that the creditors bear some of the risk of the enterprise.

If, in this second formula, you assume debt free of default risk (i.e., the debt beta has a value of zero) and a world in which corporate taxes do matter—that is, (1 – *t*) is reinserted into the formula—then it boils down to the same formula as the first:

$$\beta_{\text{Levered}} = \beta_{\text{Asset}} + (\beta_{\text{Asset}} - \beta_{\text{Debt}})(1 - t)\frac{\text{Debt}}{\text{Equity}} \tag{19}$$

This formula reduces to:

$$\beta_{\text{Levered}} = \beta_{\text{Unlevered}}[1 + (1 - t)\text{D/E}] \tag{20}$$

DEBATE OVER CAPITAL ASSET PRICING MODEL Since its founding in 1963, CAPM has provoked considerable debate within the financial community. The chief lines of attack are these:

- Nothing in the theory of CAPM says how the inputs are to be derived. Thus, the model is applied in a plethora of ways, none of which is certifiably "right."
- R_m, the return on the market of all assets, is simply unobservable. This means that there exists no pure test of the adequacy of CAPM.
- Beta is an objectionable measure of risk. It is unstable over time, though it tends to drift to the overall average of 1.0. Some practitioners will argue that beta's focus, undiversifiable risk, is inappropriate since it implies that the market compensates investors only for systematic risk. These practitioners will claim that investors bear unsystematic, diversifiable risks, too. This may be true for targets whose common stock is thinly traded or closely held—in these cases one must rely on a beta estimated from a sample of comparable companies.
- CAPM really is not that powerful; R-squares are typically low, suggesting that beta does not explain much of the variation in returns from one stock to the next.
- Other, more recent, models are better; CAPM simply does not explain much.[16] More recent studies[17] suggest that size and growth opportunities should be added to CAPM as worthwhile predictors of required returns. For instance, some large asset managers use multifactor arbitrage pricing models to generate benchmarks for investment decision making. These enhanced models rely on specialized data sets for which the estimated coefficients are usually not publicly available.

These objections notwithstanding, the actual practices of leading-edge firms suggest that CAPM has strong intuitive appeal: It embodies the risk-return logic at the heart of investment decision making. Surveys[18] of practitioners find that CAPM is the dominant method of estimating equity capital costs.

PROS AND CONS OF DISCOUNTED CASH FLOW VALUATION APPROACH The DCF method of valuation has several strengths. It is not tied to historical accounting values and is forward-looking. It focuses on cash flow, not profits, and therefore reflects noncash charges and investment inflows and outflows. It recognizes the time value of money and explicitly models the outlook for the firm. It probably values the effect of intangible assets better than other methods.

The chief weaknesses of this method are its complexity and the possible tendency for naive analysts to get entangled in the details at the expense of larger insights from the analysis. It is challenging to explain this method to judges and juries, and to the general public. Finally, it is easy to lose sight of a basic point with DCF: It can be used to value the enterprise or the equity, and not infrequently analysts mix the two valuation approaches.

Valuation by Another DCF Method, Adjusted Present Value

Thus far we have considered two DCF valuation approaches: the free cash flow (FCF) approach and the residual cash flow (RCF) approach. There is, however, a third DCF approach, *adjusted present value* (*APV*). This approach grew out of the pathbreaking work by Franco Modigliani and Merton Miller, for which they won Nobel prizes in economics. They looked at the firm as a bundle of operating assets, and tax benefits for shielding the profits of the operating assets. The most interesting type of tax shield is the deductibility of corporate interest expense. Modigliani and Miller showed that in well-functioning capital markets, the value of the enterprise must equal the sum of the values of these operating assets, plus the present value of debt tax shields. This yields the third classic DCF method for valuing the firm:

$$\text{Value}_{\text{Enterprise}} = \text{Value}_{\text{Enterprise, no debt}} + \text{Present value of debt tax shields} \quad (21)$$

$$\text{Value}_{\text{Enterprise}} = \sum \frac{\text{Free cash flow}}{(1+\text{WACC}_{\text{Unlevered}})} + \sum \frac{\text{Interest expense} \cdot \text{Tax rate}}{(1+K_{\text{Tax shields}})} \quad (22)$$

By isolating the effects of financing into the second term, APV can simplify the valuation analysis of certain acquisitions where the financing is expected to change materially through time—as in leveraged buyouts, leveraged restructurings, real estate deals, project financings, and so on. The FCF and RCF approaches must explicitly model how the cost of capital changes over time as the firm's financing changes, which can get to be complicated.[19] APV skirts this.

An ambiguity of APV is in the choice of discount rate for the debt tax shields. Nothing in the theory dictates exactly what this rate should be. The leading contender, based on a survey of finance textbooks and conversations with practitioners, is to use the pretax cost of debt. But in a series of papers, Fernandez (2001, 2002a,b,c,d) argues that the correct discount rate for the second term is the cost of capital of the unlevered firm. The difference in discount rates could amount to 200 to 400 basis points, nontrivial to most finance professionals. Using the lower discount rate (pretax cost of debt) will give a higher estimate of the present value of debt tax shields than will using the $\text{WACC}_{\text{Unlevered}}$. For firms with low or moderate leverage, the resulting difference in value may not be material. The analyst should consider the competing approaches and take a view.

DOES IT MATTER WHICH DCF MODEL IS USED? In theory, the three DCF approaches should give identical estimates of value. Therefore, choosing the DCF approach is a matter of taste, convenience, and data availability.

Exhibit 9.7 gives an illustration of the equivalence of the three approaches. Assume that you are planning to acquire a company for $2,000. You will finance the purchase half with debt (at an interest rate of 10 percent, reflecting a debt beta of 0.75), and half with equity (at a cost of equity of 14.8 percent, and an equity beta of 1.3). You intend to maintain the present mix of capital in perpetuity. The debt is rolled over to infinity. The firm does not grow. Depreciation equals $500 per year, as does replacement investment. The pretax net operating income is $2,000 per year. The tax rate equals 35 percent. Given these assumptions, what is the net present value of the investment?

EXHIBIT 9.7 Example of the Equivalence of Results from the Three DCF Valuation Approaches

	Residual Cash Flow	Free Cash Flow	Adjusted Present Value
1 Net operating income	2,000	2,000	2,000
2 Depreciation	500	500	500
3 Interest	100	—	—
4 Subtotal	1,400	EBIT 1,500	EBIT 1,500
5 Tax (@ .35)	(490)	(525)	(525)
6 Net income	910	EBIAT 975	EBIAT 975
7 + Depreciation	500	500	500
8 – Investment	(500)	(500)	(500)
9 Cash flow	RCF 910	FCF 975	FCF 975
10 Discount rate	K_e 14.8%	WACC 13.6%	WACC (Unlevered) 14.3%
11 Value of unlevered firm			6,799
12 PV debt tax shields			350
13 Value of levered firm		7,149	7,149
14 – Value of debt		(1,000)	(1,000)
15 Value of equity	6,149	6,149	6,149
16 – Equity investment	(1,000)	(1,000)	(1,000)
17 Net present value	5,149	5,149	5,149
18 Risk-free rate	7.0%	7.0%	7.0%
19 Equity beta	1.3	1.3	1.3
20 Debt beta			0.752
21 Asset beta ("unlevered beta")			1.223
22 Equity market premium	6.0%	6.0%	6.0%
23 Cost of equity, levered firm	14.8%	14.8%	14.8%
24 Cost of equity, unlevered firm			14.3%
25 Market yield on debt	10.0%	10.0%	10.0%
26 Tax rate	35.0%	35.0%	35.0%
27 After-tax cost of debt	6.5%	6.5%	6.5%
28 Weight of market value debt	14.0%	14.0%	14.0%
29 Weight of market value equity	86.0%	86.0%	86.0%
30 Weighted average cost of capital	13.6%	13.6%	13.6%

First, the exhibit shows that the NPV (line 17) is the same regardless of valuation approach. Second, the exhibit shows the distinctive features of each approach. RCF is characterized by discounting residual flows at the cost of equity, and yielding the value of equity. FCF is characterized by discounting flows before interest expense at the weighted average cost of capital. Under the FCF approach, the impact of debt financing is reflected in the discount rate (WACC) rather than in the cash flows. APV is distinguished by isolating the debt tax shield effect entirely into a separate term (seen in line 12), for neither the free cash flows nor the discount rate for those flows reflects the tax shield.

Intuitively, we should not be surprised by the equivalence result. All APV does is slice the firm along different lines. But if in well-functioning capital markets the whole should equal the sum of the parts, then no matter how we slice up the enterprise, we should always arrive back at the same aggregate value. This argument implies the equivalence of the three approaches:[20]

$$\text{Value}_{\text{Enterprise}} = (\text{Value}_{\text{Equity}} + \text{Value}_{\text{Debt}}) = (\text{Value}_{\text{Unlevered Ent.}} + \text{PV}_{\text{Tax shields}}) \quad (23)$$

$$\begin{aligned}[\text{FCF @ WACC} &= [(\text{RCF @ } K_e + (\text{Interest @ } K_d)] \\ &= [(\text{FCF @ WACC}_{\text{Unlevered}}) + (\text{Tax savings @ } K_d)] \end{aligned} \quad (24)$$

DO YOU *REALLY* GET THE SAME ANSWER UNDER ALL THREE APPROACHES? In practice one rarely obtains the same exact answer under all three approaches. But done carefully, the three approaches will yield estimates that are close to each other. The illustration just given is premised on well-functioning capital markets and very simple assumptions about the growth and future financing of the firm. Departures from these require nettlesome variations in the approaches, which may not be worth the analyst's time. Professionalism in the use of DCF approaches requires choosing the approach best suited for the problem—and applying that approach carefully, rather than producing estimates under all three approaches and then hunting for causes of variation among the estimates.

Venture Capital/Private Equity Approach

Analysts in the world of private equity investment avoid the detailed DCF valuation analyses described in the preceding section in favor of an approach that focuses on the practicalities of risk capital investing, especially entry, exit, and interim rounds of financing. Analysis for second and later round valuations can be complicated.[21] In its simplest terms, the *venture capital approach* is a stripped-down variant of the DCF methods. First, the analyst projects the performance of the firm into the future, and assumes that the private equity investor will exit typically in three to five years. Second, the exit value at that horizon is estimated using an exit multiple. Third, that exit value is discounted to the present, using a discount rate in a range from 30 to 75 percent. Alternatively, the analyst would calculate the internal rate of return of these flows and compare them to a targeted rate of return.

The virtue of this approach is its simplicity and focus. The analyst assumes that interim cash flows (i.e., before the exit date) will be nil, which is not unreasonable for investments of the venture capital/private equity type. The venture analyst typically uses an arbitrarily high discount rate rather than an estimate derived from capital market models—the analyst will defend this practice on the ground that capital market expectations are simply unobservable for this class of (private) investment: The typical venture capital target is on the fringe of its industry, without peers, without a public market for its securities, and working under significant capital market information asymmetries. Finally, this approach rivets the analyst's attention on *exit value* and *timing*, the two crucial drivers of the venture capitalist's returns.

To the sophisticated analyst, this technique will appear to assume away a great deal of detail. The venture capitalist's discount rates will appear to be arbitrary and too high relative to returns on other mainstream investments. Interim cash flows may be positive and large enough to drive present values significantly. At its most simplistic, the venture capital approach seems to ignore debt financing, and supposes that the firm will be financed entirely with equity; more mature firms will draw on debt financing. More mature firms will have growth trajectories that are easy to model over long periods. Patient investors will remain with the company for the long run. Mature firms often have securities traded in the capital markets and are followed by securities analysts, which suggests that those prices might in some sense be trusted.

Option Valuation Approach

The final approach in this survey draws on what is perhaps the most important theoretical development in finance of the past 30 years, option pricing theory. A deeper presentation of this theory is given in Chapter 10 ("Valuing Options"), and therefore will only be sketched here for the sake of comparison with other methods.

In essence, the *option valuation approach* views the equity in a levered firm as equivalent to a call option on the asset value of the firm. This recognizes the logic of most owners of a mortgaged home who claim that they don't own the house, the creditor does. But the equity holder (homeowner) retains the right (the option) to reclaim the ownership of the asset (the home) by repaying the firm's debt (the home mortgage).

If the equity in a firm is like a call option, then techniques for valuing call options can be applied to the valuation of equity stakes. Valuing a call option requires knowing at least five parameters:

1. The value of the underlying asset. In the case of firms, this is enterprise value.
2. The exercise price of the call option. In the case of firms, this is the par value of debt outstanding.
3. The term of the option. In the case of firms, this is the duration (or roughly average expected life) of the debt outstanding.
4. The risk-free rate. In the case of firms, this is yield to maturity on government securities with a life equal to the duration of the firm's debt outstanding.
5. The volatility of returns on the underlying asset. Volatility is measured as the standard deviation of the price changes on the underlying asset. For firms, this can be approximated by a weighted average of the volatilities of the firm's debt and equity.

To illustrate this, consider the problem of valuing Chrysler Corporation's equity in May of 1980, at the nadir of its fortunes when it required a loan guarantee by the U.S. government. Many observers claimed that the firm was bankrupt, since its asset value was at most equal to the value of debt outstanding.

- Let us assume that the enterprise value of Chrysler was \$1.5 billion, equal to the par value of debt outstanding (and to be guaranteed).
- Exercise price equaled par value or \$1.5 billion.
- The duration of this debt (assuming rollovers) was 10 years.
- The risk-free rate was 10.52 percent, the yield of 10-year U.S. Treasury bonds.
- The volatility, a weighted average of Chrysler's debt and equity volatilities, was 100.5 percent.

The resulting option value estimate of Chrysler's equity value is \$1.4 billion.[22] This is large in absolute terms, owing particularly to the long term and very high volatility of the underlying asset. The option pricing approach tells us that the equity of firms—even those that are highly levered and in financial distress—may be valuable because of the probability (even small) of a large payoff in the future.

This example illustrates important advantages and disadvantages of the option pricing approach. First, the approach is especially useful where the firm is highly levered and the equity is of doubtful value. In short, this approach helps us value "out of the money" firms. However, the approach is broadly applicable to firms carrying *any* debt. Second, the main disadvantage of this approach is that one must have a view about the enterprise value of the firm to begin with—isn't this where one wants to end up?

But the theory of option pricing is important beyond its usefulness in valuing the firm. It is doubtful that the DCF estimators of intrinsic value reflect hidden "rights" embedded in the firm. The implication of this is that in estimating the value of a firm, the DCF value should be adjusted upward for any long option positions, and adjusted downward for any short option positions:

$$V_{\text{Enterprise, option-adjusted}} = V_{\text{DCF of enterprise}} + V_{\text{Long options}} - V_{\text{Short options}} \tag{25}$$

This implies a four-step approach to valuing the firm:

1. Estimate the DCF value of the firm using the techniques outlined earlier.
2. Identify *significant* option positions of the firm: long versus short, put versus call. A moment's reflection will suggest that the firm contains a very large number of rights. The analyst will not be rewarded for valuing the vast majority of these rights. The option positions of a firm should be screened for materiality.
3. The option positions should be valued. This is accomplished either by building a specially tailored option valuation model or by mapping the option position onto the parameters of a simple model, such as the Black-Scholes option pricing model. The specially tailored approach is more precise, but quite a bit more expensive and time-consuming to implement—there exist no off-the-rack models for common situations such as sequential investment over time, nonnormal distribution of outcomes, and changing uncertainty. The simple approach assumes that the standard Black-Scholes model gets one close enough to what will be an imprecise estimate of value, anyway. Some practitioners will use the

simple approach first, as a way of determining the materiality of the size of the option position, and then try a specially tailored solution if warranted.

4. Sum the DCF value and the estimated option values.

Forward-thinking firms are applying option pricing techniques with greater frequency. It would not be unreasonable to expect that in the course of time, option pricing-adjusted estimates of intrinsic value will become the norm. See Chapter 14 for more detailed discussion of real options.

RULE #5: EXERCISE ESTIMATORS OF INTRINSIC VALUE TO FIND KEY VALUE DRIVERS AND BETS

Novices assume that point estimates of value are sufficient to drive M&A decision making. As stated earlier, these estimates ignore uncertainty. Consistent with the earlier advice to work with ranges of value instead of point estimates, analysts should exercise the estimators to define the reasonable range of value and to identify the key value drivers or assumptions to which the estimates are most sensitive. There are four classic approaches:

1. ***Univariate and bivariate sensitivity analysis.*** *Sensitivity analysis* is based on one-way and two-way tables that give the estimate of firm value as it changes with key assumptions. Spreadsheet programs, such as Microsoft Excel, contain features that easily generate one-way and two-way data tables. These kinds of tables are the basis for sensitivity analysis.
2. ***Scenario analysis.*** *Scenario analysis* recognizes that assumptions tend to vary together to create scenarios. A classic example would be macroeconomic scenarios in which profit margins and unit volumes increase in buoyant times, and fall in recessions. Setting a number of assumptions at levels consistent with that possible future state of the world creates a scenario estimate of value.
3. ***Breakeven analysis.*** This is an agnostic approach to sensitivity analysis: *Breakeven analysis* seeks the levels of certain assumptions at which the estimated intrinsic value falls below a certain target (such as the current stock price). In Microsoft Excel, the "Goal Seek" feature automates the determination of breakeven assumptions.
4. ***Monte Carlo simulation.*** This is the most advanced (and analytically complex) of the sensitivity analysis alternatives. It explicitly models the uncertainty around assumptions and can be used to estimate the probability distribution of value. The software found on the CD-ROM, "Crystal Ball," can be used to automate a simulation analysis.

RULE #6: THINK CRITICALLY; TRIANGULATE CAREFULLY

Done right, valuation analysis could generate a blizzard of value estimates. These need to be boiled down to a point estimate, or, better yet, a *range of value* that could form the basis for negotiation strategy. These summary figures are achieved through a process of *triangulation*. This is a term borrowed from trigonometry and surveying: A surveyor measures the height of a mountain not by direct measurement, but from indirect data and perhaps several observation points. Deriving summary valuation figures employs a similar approach. Triangulation in valuing a firm would entail the following kinds of steps:

Scrutinize Estimators

Develop a view about the appropriateness of the different valuation approaches in the particular valuation problem you face. Exhibit 9.8 gives a summary of the chief virtues and defects of each of the main approaches. The point of this survey of valuation methods is not to belabor the reader with analytical approaches that are better presented elsewhere, but rather to make several points:

- There are many valuation approaches.
- No approach is flawless. At best, each *estimates* intrinsic value.
- The professional analyst understands these approaches sufficiently to be able to apply them when reasonable, and tailor them as necessary.
- Not all approaches warrant equal weight in the thinking of decision makers. To decide how much weight any approach should have is to have a view. Discounted cash flow approximates best what it means to think like an investor, and therefore may deserve more weight than other approaches. Book value poorly applies the investor's point of view, and therefore deserves little weight.
- Be flexible, not doctrinaire. Adapt your view to the circumstances of the firm you are valuing. While DCF generally does the best job, it can be quite awkward if not impossible to apply to some types of businesses like trading operations, to firms in financial distress, to assets that are to be liquidated, and in instances of high inflation.[23]

Scrutinize Data

Remember that virtually all of the approaches summarized here rely on information about the target firm and/or its peers. A good due diligence research process should help one assess the reasonableness of financial data supplied by the firm; but recall that generally accepted accounting principles permit relatively wide latitude in the recognition of economic events. These latitudes can be considerably wider outside the United States. Regarding information about peers, remember that *the choice of firms to include in the peer sample is of crucial importance*. Therefore, one should review the peer sample in the triangulation process as a step in developing a level of confidence in the valuation estimates.

Scrutinize the Spreadsheet Model

In practice, spreadsheet models are often passed among professionals and tailored to meet the needs of particular situations. Errors creep in undetected and cause em-

EXHIBIT 9.8 Overview of Classic Measures of Value

Approach	Advantages	Disadvantages
Book value	• Simple • "Authoritative"	• Ignores some assets and liabilities. • Historical costs: backward-looking. • Subject to accounting manipulation.
Liquidation value	• Conservative	• Ignores "going concern" value. • (Dis)orderly sale?
Replacement value	• "Current"	• Replace *what*? • Subjective estimates.
Multiples, earnings capitalization • Price/earnings • Value/EBIT • Price/book	• Simple • Widely used	• "Earnings" subject to accounting manipulation. • "Snapshot" estimate: may ignore cyclical, secular changes. • Depends on comparable firms: ultimately just a measure of relative, not absolute value.
Discounted cash flow • FCF @ WACC • RCF @ K_e • APV	• Theoretically based • Rigorous • Affords many analytical insights • Cash focus • Multiperiod • Reflects time value of money	• Time-consuming. • Risks "analysis paralysis." • Easy to abuse, misuse. • Tough to explain to novices.
Venture capital/private equity approach	• Simpler than standard DCF approaches. • Focuses on timing and exit values. •Avoids heavy theoretical assumptions.	• Discount rates may appear to be arbitrary and too high. • Interim cash flows may be material.
Option-adjusted valuation	• Augments DCF for hidden option value. • Permits explicit modeling of important rights.	• Difficult to estimate parameters, especially volatility. • Some hidden options do not map easily onto the simple models. • Complex modeling may be required.

barrassment (or worse) later. Here's a general approach for checking out a spreadsheet model:

- ***Look for obvious errors.*** Does the balance sheet balance? Are earnings from the income statement posted correctly to retained earnings? Are subtotals correct? Is interest expense linked to the balance of debt outstanding? Are there any discontinuities in the assumed growth rate, tax rate, and interest rate over time?

- ***Take it for a test drive.*** It is very hard to detect some errors without exercising the model. First, insert some extreme assumptions in growth or profit margins to see what happens to the results. Then, vary a number of assumptions simultaneously, perhaps using a data table to capture the results. Do the results change according to your intuition?
- ***Screen it with common sense.*** Ravindran, Phillips, and Solberg (1987) offer 10 questions against which an analyst should benchmark a computer model. These are especially relevant for M&A work:

 1. How much complexity and precision are necessary? Don't build a complicated model when a simple one will suffice.
 2. What is the problem? Beware of molding the problem to fit the technique.
 3. Have you fully specified the major drivers of the model? The deduction phase of modeling must be conducted rigorously.
 4. Have you checked the model for programming errors and reasonableness? Models should be validated before implementation.
 5. Where is your sense of irony? A model should never be taken too literally.
 6. What is the intended purpose of the model? A model should neither be pressed to do nor be criticized for failing to do that for which it was never intended.
 7. What promises are made about the model? Beware of overselling it.
 8. What have you learned from the modeling process? Some of the primary benefits from modeling are associated with the *process* of development.
 9. What is the foundation for your modeling assumptions? Garbage in, garbage out. A model cannot be any better than its parameters.
 10. Who will use the model? Models cannot replace decision makers. Is this model accessible to them?

The spreadsheet model "Value Merge.xls," available on the CD-ROM, is one example of a built-out spreadsheet valuation model for general M&A application. This model is described in Appendix 9.1 later in this chapter.

Scrutinize Sensitivity Assumptions

The sensitivity analysis outlined in the preceding section depends crucially on choosing sensible ranges over which to vary valuation assumptions. Uncertainty accumulates rapidly in this kind of analysis. Choosing an arbitrarily wide range on a few forecast assumptions can easily generate a resulting range of value in which you would have relatively little confidence. Wherever possible, one should seek to tighten sensitivity ranges, based on an *informed view* about the target's business (that is, not based on arbitrary guesswork).

Eliminate Estimates in Which You Have Little Confidence

This is a process of eliminating "noise" in order to find the "signal" about intrinsic value. An obvious example regards the use of the liquidation value approach—this is rarely useful for healthy firms considered to be going concerns. Your analyst may have calculated a liquidation value for the sake of completeness, but its use for negotiation purposes may be nil.

Compare the Finalist Estimates of Value

This comparison can be offered in several ways, though one that has helped executives is a graphic comparison, using a bar chart such as the one shown in Exhibit 9.9. A chart such as this summarizes visually the various valuation ranges, and permits the decision maker to absorb data more readily. This chart is also available in a template program, "Triangulation Graph.xls," found on the CD-ROM.

Choose

Realistically, this is the hardest step of all. One cannot automate judgment of this sort; there is no formula or heuristic to lead to a final decision. But judgment is accelerated to the extent that you follow the preceding steps. Referring again to Exhibit 9.9, suppose that the decision maker is a buyer, and that he or she must choose a negotiation range of values, varying between an opening bid and a walk-away bid.

- ***The opening bid*** will be bounded on the low side by the recent market price range of $82 to $88 per share. It is extremely rare for a target to be acquired at a price less than its recent share value in the market. How much higher to open above this floor is determined by synergies (see Chapter 11), negotiation tactics (see Chapter 30), and competition with other potential bidders (see Chapters 31 through 33).
- ***The walk-away bid*** will be bounded on the high side by the intrinsic value of the target. As the example in Exhibit 9.9 reveals, the DCF approach estimates

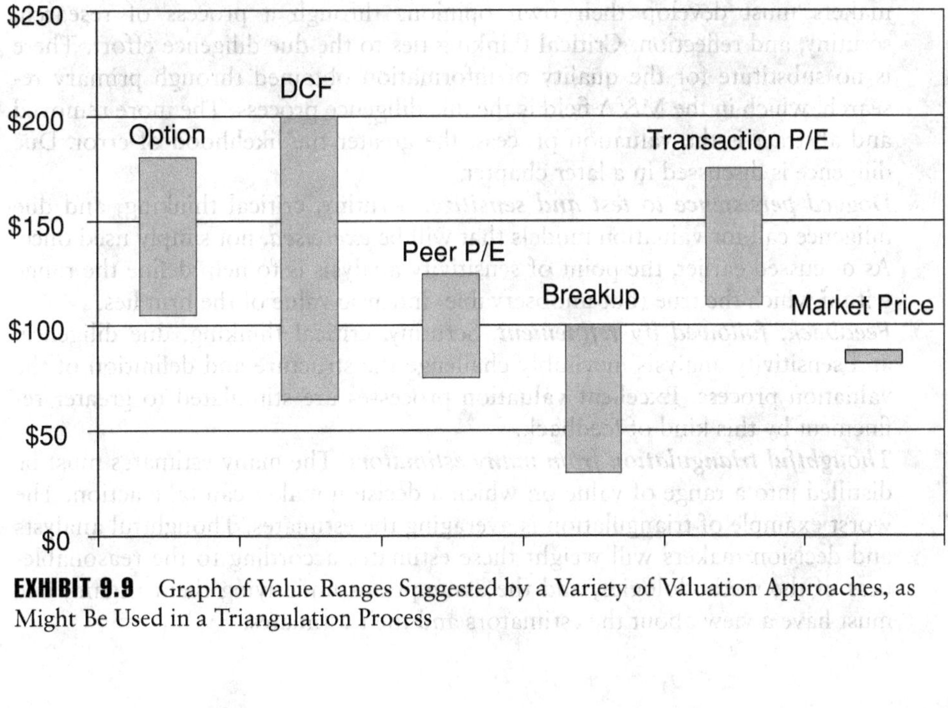

EXHIBIT 9.9 Graph of Value Ranges Suggested by a Variety of Valuation Approaches, as Might Be Used in a Triangulation Process

the maximum intrinsic value to be $200 per share (this includes the impact of synergies and optimistic forecast assumptions). But none of the other approaches support as high a maximum. While you may like the DCF approach better than all others, you may decide to reduce your walk-away bid slightly to reflect the information contained in the other estimates. A value of $175 per share would be at the high end of the ranges estimated by the option approach and the transaction multiples approach.

As a buyer, you might choose an opening bid of $100 and a walk-away bid of $175. The triangulation process is finished. (As will be explained in later chapters, whether you actually quote these values to the seller will depend on your other choices about form of payment, other deal terms, and your bargaining strategy.)

RULE #7: FOCUS ON PROCESS, NOT PRODUCT

Some of the key conclusions of this chapter are that the valuation of firms is riddled with judgments, and that excellence here depends rather more on wisdom than on computing power. Simply asking a staff member to run the numbers and tell you what a target firm is worth may be starting down the easy road to M&A hell. Instead, there is no substitute for the following virtues of M&A valuation:

- ***Scrutiny of assumptions and critical thinking.*** "Garbage in, garbage out" goes the saying. Financial forecasts are only as good as their assumptions. The aggregate effect of many small, inadvertent forecasting biases can be huge. *The only solution is to "have a view."* This means that instead of passively accepting historical trends or industry consensus outlooks, the analysts and decision makers must develop their own opinions through a process of research, scrutiny, and reflection. Critical thinking ties to the due diligence effort. There is no substitute for the quality of information obtained through primary research, which in the M&A field is the due diligence process. The more removed and abstract is the valuation process, the greater the likelihood of error. Due diligence is discussed in a later chapter.
- ***Dogged persistence to test and sensitize.*** Scrutiny, critical thinking, and due diligence call for valuation models that will be *exercised*, not simply used once. As discussed earlier, the point of sensitivity analysis is to help define the range within which the true (but unobservable) intrinsic value of the firm lies.
- ***Feedback, followed by refinement.*** Scrutiny, critical thinking, due diligence, and sensitivity analysis inevitably challenge the structure and definition of the valuation process. Excellent valuation processes are stimulated to greater refinement by this kind of feedback.
- ***Thoughtful triangulation from many estimators.*** The many estimates must be distilled into a range of value on which a decision maker can take action. The worst example of triangulation is averaging the estimates. Thoughtful analysts and decision makers will weight these estimates according to the reasonableness of the methodologies, and the assumptions underlying them. Again, one must have a view about the estimators and their estimates.

- ***Acceptance of estimates, not certainty.*** M&A professionals view the resulting estimates with neither belief, nor disbelief but rather with a sense of *irony* that acknowledges there are no "right" answers in valuing firms (though there may be many wrong ones).

Many of these virtues are reflected in Exhibit 9.10, which offers a summary of the analytic flow described in this chapter.

Excellence in valuation arises from careful attention to process, in the belief that if the valuation process is well executed, good results will follow. Excellent process management draws on skills that go beyond the scope of this book, though in my experience it includes these features:

- ***Positive team dynamics.*** A team is formed consisting of a sponsor, a project leader, one or two analysts, due diligence researchers, and possibly specialists who know the target company and/or its industry. The mission of the team is clear. The commitment of team members to that mission is strong and positive. Team members respect each other's contributions. Energy level and spirit of collaboration are high. Members take initiative, rather than wait to be told what to do. Responsibilities are backstopped, so that a temporary absence by any member does not stall the process.
- ***Learning mind-set.*** The team members are in a search for the truth, and enjoy the process. They challenge the assumptions and thinking of one another.

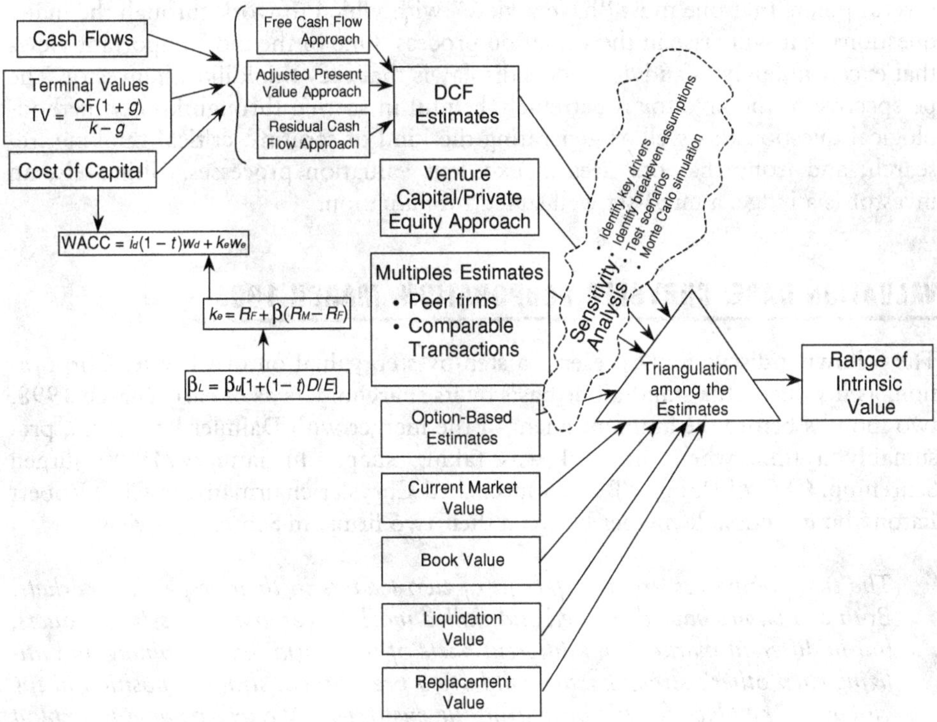

EXHIBIT 9.10 Summary Flowchart of the Valuation Process

Fact-based judgments are valued; but dogmatic assertions are discounted. Tough-mindedness dominates, but is tempered with an openness to new ideas and creative thinking.

- ***Resource commitment.*** The team has enough money, information, and time to do the job. Target expectations, particularly about time, are tight enough to be motivating. The team sponsor helps obtain the resources as needs arise.
- ***Culture of excellence.*** Great project processes seem to have at their core a desire to excel, defined in terms of the quality of the work itself. Excellent teams avoid the trap of believing that a deal has to get done to justify their work. Viewing their work as an end in itself empowers them to walk away from bad deals.

Ultimately, these qualities emerge from good organization, culture, and leadership.

RULE #8: WHEN IN DOUBT, SEE RULE #1

The aim of this chapter has been to survey techniques for valuing the firm and to draw some implications for managing the valuation process. The chapter shows that there are numerous valuation techniques and that these can be fashioned into an analytic process. Good work in this area depends heavily on wise judgment, not only careful analytics. Therefore, the valuation process should be managed in ways that broaden and deepen the quality of judgment in the process. I have argued at several points that one must "have a view" with which to work through the many questions that will arise in the valuation process. One of the most important views that excellent analysts and deal doers display is that they think like an investor. The perspective of the investor is extremely helpful in sorting through knotty methodological questions, as well as generating the kind of scrutiny, critical thinking, research, and irony that one sees in excellent valuation processes. Ultimately, an investor is a judge, a mind-set well suited for valuation.

VALUATION CASE: CHRYSLER CORPORATION, MARCH 1998

The following discussion[24] presents a step-by-step valuation of Chrysler Corporation, as if valued on a stand-alone basis by its shareholders as of early March 1998, two months before the announcement of the merger with Daimler-Benz A.G., presumably a time when the deal was taking shape. In January 1998, Jürgen Schrempp, CEO of Daimler-Benz, approached Chrysler chairman and CEO Robert Eaton about a possible merger between their two firms. In Schrempp's view,

> *The two companies are a perfect fit of two leaders in their respective markets. Both companies have dedicated and skilled work forces and successful products, but in different markets and different parts of the world. By combining and utilizing each other's strengths, we will have a pre-eminent strategic position in the global marketplace for the benefit of our customers. We will be able to exploit new markets, and we will improve return and value for our shareholders.*[25]

Independently Eaton had concluded that some type of combination of Chrysler with another major automobile firm was needed: The firm was currently financially healthy, but industry overcapacity and huge prospective investment outlays called for an even larger type of global competitor. Before seeing Schrempp, Eaton had polled investment bankers for their ideas about a major automotive merger, and had spoken with executives from BMW on this topic.

Eaton replied positively to Schrempp's idea of an industrial combination. Now lay ahead the task of forging the details of the agreement to combine. Eaton appointed a small task force of business executives and lawyers to represent Chrysler in the detailed negotiations. He challenged this team on several counts: exploit the benefits of combination; preserve and strengthen the Chrysler brands; minimize the adverse effects of combination on employees and executives; and maximize shareholder value. Eaton reflected on the varieties of terms the Chrysler team might seek, and immediately convened a meeting to begin planning the team's negotiation strategy. Eaton said,

> *My number one criterion is that [any deal] has got to be a long-term upside with no negative short-term impact. It's got to be good for the shareholders. That's my—and my board's—fiduciary responsibility.*[26]

One can apply the valuation process to Chrysler using the steps outlined previously in this chapter:

Think Like an Investor

Robert Eaton seemed to be in this mode when he acknowledged that "it's got to be good for the shareholders." This emphasizes that one should think in terms of rational economic value.

Estimate Values

Recall that the emphasis is on the word "estimate," and that one should seek as many vantage points as possible about true intrinsic value. An important practical tip is that all estimates should be put on the same basis, such as total value versus value per share of stock, or enterprise value versus equity value. In the illustration that follows, all values will be expressed in equity value per share of Chrysler stock outstanding.

ACCOUNTING BOOK VALUE This is obtained by dividing the total shareholders' equity reported by Chrysler on its most recent balance sheet by the number of shares outstanding, plus any shares under option that might be exercised as a result of the transaction.[27] It is a common error to use authorized shares, or average shares over the past year. Instead one wants to use the number of shares actually outstanding at the end of the most recent reporting period. Chrysler's shareholders' equity was $11.362 billion; the number of shares outstanding was 648.4 million. The accounting book value per share was $17.52—this is a value far below all other values estimated, a real outlier. For the reasons outlined earlier, this value will be dropped from further discussion in our valuation analysis.

LIQUIDATION VALUE One could estimate the liquidation value of each asset item on the latest balance sheet, subtract the liabilities outstanding, and divide by the number of shares outstanding. But as described earlier, liquidation value ignores the franchise value of Chrysler as a going concern. This is not an instance of bankruptcy or liquidation. Chrysler is healthy. It would be inappropriate to give this any weight in the valuation process. Therefore, liquidation value will be ignored here.

REPLACEMENT VALUE Because of annual styling changes and tooling, a significant part of Chrysler's physical plant was probably close to replacement value; therefore one might simply settle for book value as a proxy for replacement value. Generally, replacement value estimates are important where, because of old age and inflation, the book and replacement values are likely to differ. But during much of the 1990s the United States experienced a very low rate of inflation. The replacement value estimate will be ignored in this analysis.

CURRENT VALUE IN THE MARKET This is an extremely important estimator, because it represents an economic floor below which it would be irrational for the target to sell. Exhibit 9.11 gives the recent stock price history of both firms, as well as estimates of their betas, based on trading on the New York Stock Exchange. In February 1998, Chrysler's stock price per share closed at $38.75. In 1996, Chrysler's share price varied between a high of $36.375 and a low of $25.75. In 1997, the high and low were $38.75 and $25.125.

VALUE BASED ON TRADING MULTIPLES OF PEERS The data in Exhibit 9.12 show that Chrysler's trailing price/earnings multiple of 9.8 was the highest of the "big three" American automobile manufacturers. The other very interesting insight from that exhibit is that the American car firms had the lowest P/E multiples of all the global car manufacturers. The existence of differing industry multiples is inconsistent with the existence of a global capital market. But this difference could be explained by differing growth outlooks among car firms just as easily as by capital market imperfections. A crucial question then is, "Who are Chrysler's peers?" The answer lies in a comparison of product and market positions of Chrysler and the other car firms. In essence, one could argue that Chrysler was the most American of the "big three," and that therefore its proper peer group included only the four North American manufactureres. Choosing the average of the four North American firms (10.67) one might lower the weight given to Navistar, yielding an adjusted average of 10.1. This suggests a multiple for Chrysler in the range of 9.8 to 10.1, implying a stock price of $40.75 to $41.92.

VALUE BASED ON ACQUISITION PREMIUMS The valuation based on peer multiples ignores the fact that buyers must pay some premium to acquire a target. There were relatively few comparable acquisitions in the automobile industry, so one could turn to a sample of acquisition premiums in very large deals[28] to gain some insight. It would be better if this sample could be restricted to only the car firms. But since that would not yield a feasible sample, Exhibit 9.13 offers a sample that crosses several industries. Exhibit 9.14 shows average premiums across major acquisitions—these display a great deal of variation. From the data of these two exhibits, one must make a judgment about the reasonable range of acquisition premiums. No calculation, such as an average, can easily substitute for judgment. For pur-

EXHIBIT 9.11 Recent Stock Price Information Chrysler Corporation and Daimler-Benze A.G.

Chrysler Corporation		Daimler-Benz (ADR in US$)		
Month	Month-End Stock Price	Month	Month-End Stock Price	Ratio of Chrysler to Daimler
May 1996	$33.31	May 1996	$53.50	0.6227
June 1996	$31.25	June 1996	$53.00	0.5896
July 1996	$28.38	July 1996	$53.13	0.5341
August 1996	$29.25	August 1996	$54.25	0.5392
September 1996	$28.63	September 1996	$58.25	0.4914
October 1996	$33.63	October 1996	$64.50	0.5213
November 1996	$35.50	November 1996	$67.31	0.5274
December 1996	$33.00	December 1996	$71.00	0.4648
January 1997	$34.88	January 1997	$71.13	0.4903
February 1997	$34.00	February 1997	$76.00	0.4474
March 1997	$30.00	March 1997	$73.13	0.4103
April 1997	$30.00	April 1997	$78.00	0.3846
May 1997	$31.88	May 1997	$80.13	0.3978
June 1997	$32.88	June 1997	$82.13	0.4003
July 1997	$37.19	July 1997	$73.50	0.5060
August 1997	$35.13	August 1997	$80.75	0.4350
September 1997	$36.81	September 1997	$67.31	0.5469
October 1997	$35.25	October 1997	$69.44	0.5077
November 1997	$34.31	November 1997	$71.00	0.4833
December 1997	$35.19	December 1997	$68.75	0.5118
January 1998	$34.81	January 1998	$79.75	0.4365
February 1998	$38.75	February 1998	$99.63	0.3890
High	$38.75	High	$99.63	0.6227
Low	$28.38	Low	$53.00	0.3846
Average	$33.36	Average	$70.25	0.4835
Adjusted beta*:	0.85	Adjusted beta*:	0.97	
Volatility†:	25.83%	Volatility†:	29.39%	

*Beta was calculated with respect to the S&P 500 index from weekly data over the period May 3, 1996, to March 1, 1998, and adjusted for beta's tendency to converge to 1.0 according to the formula: Adjusted beta = .67 · Raw beta + .33 · 1.00.
†Volatility was calculated from daily data for the 260 most recent trading days.
Source of data: Bloomberg Financial Service.

poses of this illustration, one could assume that the going premium to acquire a very large firm was in the neighborhood of 31 to 39 percent, which would suggest a value in the range of $50.76 and $53.86.

DISCOUNTED CASH FLOW VALUATION

- *Cost of equity.* Using the capital asset pricing model, Chrysler's cost of equity can be estimated directly. Chrysler's beta was 0.85. The risk-free rate (the yield on 30-year U.S. government debt) was 5.97 percent. The equity market risk premium had averaged (geometrically) about 5.6 percent over the previous 70

EXHIBIT 9.12 Comparable Automobile Manufacturers (in US$ Millions, Except Where Otherwise Noted)

	Price Feb. 1998	1997 Revenues	1997 Profits	1997 EPS	1998E EPS*	1997 CF/ Share	Trailing P/E	Forward P/E	Price/ Cash Flow	Shares Outstanding	Long-Term Debt	Debt/ Total Cap	Market/ Book Value	Beta†
U.S.														
Ford Motor	37 9/16	$153,627	$6,920	$ 5.75	$ 5.38	$ 11.97	6.5	7.0	3.1	1,194	$80,245	64%	1.51	0.86
General Motors	68 15/16	166,445	6,276	8.70	7.97	22.82	7.9	8.6	3.0	721	41,972	46%	2.67	0.96
Chrysler	40 3/4	61,147	2,804	4.15	5.01	8.43	9.8	8.1	4.8	648	9,006	25%	2.33	0.85
Navistar	30 3/8	6,321	150	1.65	2.60	3.33	18.4	11.7	9.1	72	1,316	37%	2.83	1.03
Average, U.S.						*11.64*	*10.67*	*8.86*	*5.03*			*43%*	*2.33*	*0.93*
Japan														
Honda Motor	70 3/8	45,111	1,960	4.02	4.40	6.39	17.5	16.0	11.0	487	5,096	13%	4.55	0.80
Nissan Motor	8 7/8	49,358	382	0.30	0.55	3.34	29.6	16.1	2.7	1,257	12,554	53%	0.92	0.66
Toyota Motor	54 7/8	87,807	3,416	1.79	2.35	3.81	30.7	23.4	14.4	1,902	16,006	13%	2.70	0.63
Average, Japan						*4.51*	*25.92*	*18.49*	*9.36*			*26%*	*2.72*	*0.70*
Europe														
Daimler-Benz	99 5/8	68,951	1,764	3.38	3.75	11.50	29.5	26.6	8.7	517	9,564	16%	2.69	0.86
Volvo	27 1/8	23,118	400	0.88	2.20	2.99	30.8	12.3	9.1	442	2,913	20%	1.59	0.71
BMW DM	1,475	60,137	1,246	50.63	59.50	412.99	29.1	24.8	3.6	25	10,516	22%	3.59	0.88
Peugeot-C FFr	867	186,785	(2,768)	(55.24)	48.20	336.97	NM	18.0	2.6	50	17,004	28%	0.82	0.88
Fiat Lira	6,292	89,658	2,417	459.90	379.60	2,141.76	13.7	16.6	2.9	5	10,938	25%	1.35	0.73
Audi DM	1,450	22,410	367	85.35	125.00	536.28	17.0	11.6	2.7	4	—	0%	2.93	0.68
Renault FFr	212	207,912	5,427	22.79	16.00	48.88	9.3	13.3	4.3	238	30,760	38%	1.16	0.78
Average, Europe						*NM*	*21.57*	*17.59*	*4.84*			*21%*	*2.02*	*0.79*
Average, all firms							*19.22*	*15.29*	*5.86*			*29%*	*2.26*	*0.81*

NM = Not meaningful.

Note: Data is taken from Value Line Investment Survey and Bloomberg.

*Domestic EPS estimates are taken from Nelson's. International EPS estimates are taken from Value Line and IBES.

†Beta is calculated against the S&P in all cases and is based on weekly observations between Mar-96 and Feb-98.

EXHIBIT 9.13 Twelve-Month Moving Average Stock Premiums

One Month before Announcement		One Week before Announcement	
2Q97	35.31%	2Q97	29.53%
3Q97	47.97%	3Q97	39.61%
4Q97	36.51%	4Q97	28.34%
1Q98	37.11%	1Q98	31.61%

Source: Mergers and Acquisitions, July/August 1998.

years. Inserting these values into the capital asset pricing model yields an estimated cost of equity of 10.7 percent.

- ***Weighted average cost of capital.*** Chrysler's pretax cost of debt derived from market yields on outstanding debt was about 6.3 percent, the average yield on debt rated "A." The market value of debt could be assumed to be similar to the book value, since the coupon rates and market yields on Chrysler's debt were similar. If this were not true, it would be desirable to actually estimate the market value of Chrysler's debt. The amount of debt used in the calculation was \$15.485 billion. The market value of Chrysler's equity was estimated by multiplying the most recent price per share for Chrysler (\$38.75) times the number of shares outstanding plus shares under option (648.4 million). This gave a market value of equity of \$25.126 billion. Thus, the percentage weights of debt and equity in Chrysler's capital structure were 38 and 62 percent. Including a marginal assumed tax rate of 38 percent on Chrysler's income and the cost of equity estimated in the previous section gives an estimated weighted average cost of capital of 8.1 percent, computed as follows:

$$\text{WACC} = [.063(1 - .38)0.38] + (0.107 \cdot 0.62) = 0.081 \qquad (26)$$

  For greater accuracy, the WACC is recalculated each year in the spreadsheets prepared for this analysis.
- ***Forecast of cash flows.*** A forecast of free cash flows and equity cash flows is given in Exhibits 9.15 and 9.16. These use the forecast template given in the spreadsheet, "Value Merge.xls," on the CD-ROM. The assumptions for growth, margins, and asset investments are drawn from the expectations of securities analysts or, where specific outlooks are lacking, from historical experience.
- ***Terminal values.*** A forecast of continuing value at the end of the forecast period is drawn from the constant growth valuation model. For enterprise terminal values, the numerator was the free cash flow in the final year times 1 plus a perpetual growth rate of 3 percent, all divided by the WACC less the perpetual growth rate. For equity valuation, the numerator was the residual cash flow in the final year times 1 plus the perpetual growth rate for RCF (also assumed to be 3 percent), divided by the cost of equity minus the equity growth rate. The long-term growth rate was estimated from the Fisher formula, which accounts for long-term real growth (assumed to be similar to the U.S. GNP growth rate for the past decade of about 1 percent) and the long-term inflation rate (derived from the U.S. Treasury yield curve, and suggesting a rate of 2.0 percent).

EXHIBIT 9.14 Recent Jumbo M&A Activity (Greater than US$ 10 Billion) (in Millions, Except Where Otherwise Noted)

Acquirer	Target	Date	Value	P/E	Premium to Stock Price One Week Prior	Outcome
Nonfinancial Companies						
Tracinda Corp.	Chrysler	April 1995	$21,618	5.40	37.50%	Withdrawn
Walt Disney	Capital Cities/ABC	July 1995	$18,837	25.40	25.20%	Completed
SBC Communications	Pacific-Telesis	April 1996	$16,490	15.50	36.20%	Completed
WorldCom	MFS Communications	January 1997	$13,596	NM	60.00%	Completed
CSX Corp.	Conrail	June 1997	$10,436	58.40	60.30%	Withdrawn
Bell Atlantic	NYNEX Corp.	August 1997	$21,346	19.50	–0.40%	Completed
Boeing Corp.	McDonnell Douglas	August 1997	$13,359	NM	22.70%	Completed
CUC International	HFS Incorporated	December 1997	$11,343	40.30	3.00%	Completed
Lockheed Martin	Northrup Grumman	February 1998	$11,831	28.00	41.20%	Withdrawn
Starwood Lodging	ITT Corp.	February 1998	$13,748	24.70	98.30%	Completed
Financial Companies						
Chemical Banking Corp.	Chase Manhattan Corp.	March 1996	$10,446	10.70	7.50%	Completed
Wells Fargo	First Interstate Corp.	April 1996	$10,930	13.10	36.30%	Completed
Dean Witter Discover	Morgan Stanley	February 1997	$10,573	10.70	12.80%	Completed
Nationsbank	Barnett	January 1998	$14,822	25.00	43.90%	Completed

NM = Not meaningful.
Sources: Thomson Financial Securities Data Company; Bloomberg Financial Services.

- ***Deriving the DCF estimates.*** Exhibits 9.15 and 9.16 give the resulting worksheets for Chrysler and suggest base-case values of $64.53 using the WACC method, and $60.71 per share using the equity residual method.
- ***Sensitivity analysis.*** One could exercise the valuation model to demonstrate the sensitivity of Chrysler's share value to variations in revenue growth and profit margins. Interpretation of these tables requires one to have a view about what levels of assumptions are reasonable. The outlook of securities analysts is

EXHIBIT 9.15 Valuation of Chrysler Corporation Shares Discounting Free Cash Flows at WACC

	Projected				
Discounted Cash Flow Analysis: WACC Method	**1998**	**1999**	**2000**	**2001**	**2002**
Net income	3,037.0	3,291.1	3,582.1	3,883.8	4,201.1
Interest expense	1,002.7	929.1	815.9	706.8	595.2
Tax effect of interest expense	(385.0)	(356.8)	(313.3)	(271.4)	(228.6)
After-tax interest expense	617.6	572.3	502.6	435.4	366.7
NOPAT	3,654.6	3,863.4	4,084.7	4,319.2	4,567.7
Depreciation	3,194.7	3,406.7	3,631.4	3,869.7	4,122.2
Amortization	39.3	38.3	37.4	36.4	35.5
Deferred taxes	1,537.2	1029.0	702.2	492.9	359.4
Minority interest	0.0	0.0	0.0	0.0	0.0
Income from affiliates	0.0	0.0	0.0	0.0	0.0
Other noncash items	0.0	0.0	0.0	0.0	0.0
Changes in net working capital	2,676.0	(182.3)	(193.2)	(204.8)	(217.1)
Cash flow from operations	11,101.8	8,155.1	8,262.5	8,513.4	8,867.8
Capital expenditures	(4,000.3)	(4,240.3)	(4,494.7)	(4,764.4)	(5,050.3)
Other	0.0	0.0	0.0	0.0	0.0
Free cash flow	7,101.6	3,914.8	3,767.8	3,749.0	3,817.5
Terminal value (perpetuity)	0.0	0.0	0.0	0.0	59,696.5
Total free cash flows to capital providers	7,101.6	3,914.8	3,767.8	3,749.0	63,514.0
Valuation					
Firm value	56,227.4	54,297.2	55,178.6	56,432.3	57,957.7
Plus: excess cash	2,848.0	3,318.9	3,818.0	4,347.1	4,907.9
Less: debt outstanding	15,485.0	15,107.1	13,270.6	11,561.5	9,856.3
Less: minority interest	0.0	0.0	0.0	0.0	0.0
Less: preferred stock	0.0	0.0	0.0	0.0	0.0
Equity value	43,590.4	42,508.9	45,726.0	49,217.9	53,009.4
Value per share, beginning of year	**$64.53**	**$70.28**	**$75.60**	**$81.37**	**$87.64**
Memo: WACC Calculation					
Debt market equity	35.5%	35.5%	29.0%	23.5%	18.6%
Relevered beta	0.91	0.91	0.88	0.86	0.84
K_e	11.1%	11.1%	10.9%	10.8%	10.6%
WACC	9.2%	9.2%	9.3%	9.5%	9.6%

EXHIBIT 9.16 Valuation of Chrysler Corporation Shares Discounting Residual Cash Flows at the Cost of Equity

Discounted Cash Flow Analysis: Equity Residual Method	Projected 1998	1999	2000	2001	2002
Net income	3,037.0	3,291.1	3,582.1	3,883.8	4,201.1
Depreciation	3,194.7	3,406.7	3,631.4	3,869.7	4,122.2
Amortization	39.3	38.3	37.4	36.4	35.5
Deferred taxes	1,537.2	1,029.0	702.2	492.9	359.4
Minority interest	0.0	0.0	0.0	0.0	0.0
Income from affiliates	0.0	0.0	0.0	0.0	0.0
Other noncash items	0.0	0.0	0.0	0.0	0.0
Changes in net working capital	2,676.0	(182.3)	(193.2)	(204.8)	(217.1)
Equity cash flow from operations	10,484.2	7,582.8	7,759.9	8,078.1	8,501.1
Capital expenditures	(4,000.3)	(4,240.3)	(4,494.7)	(4,764.4)	(5,050.3)
Change in debt	(377.9)	(1,836.5)	(1,709.1)	(1,705.2)	(1,787.8)
Change in preferred	0.0	0.0	0.0	0.0	0.0
Preferred dividends (includes convertible)	0.0	0.0	0.0	0.0	0.0
Other	0.0	0.0	0.0	0.0	0.0
Residual cash flow	6,106.0	1,506.0	1,556.1	1,608.4	1,663.0
Terminal value (perpetuity)	0.0	0.0	0.0	0.0	45,790.8
Cash flows to common equity holders	6,106.0	1,506.0	1,556.1	1,608.4	47,453.8
Valuation					
Equity value	36,722.0	34,708.5	37,321.1	40,024.4	42,843.0
Value per share at beginning of year	**$60.71**	**$57.38**	**$61.70**	**$66.17**	**$70.83**
Plus: debt outstanding	15,485.0	15,107.1	13,270.6	11,561.5	9,856.3
Plus: minority interest	0.0	0.0	0.0	0.0	0.0
Plus: preferred stock	0.0	0.0	0.0	0.0	0.0
Less: excess cash	2,848.0	3,318.9	3,818.0	4,347.1	4,907.9
Firm value	49,359.0	46,496.8	46,773.7	47,238.9	47,791.4
Memo: Cost of Equity Calculation					
Debt/market equity	42.2%	43.5%	35.6%	28.9%	23.0%
Relevered beta	0.94	0.95	0.91	0.88	0.86
K_e	11.3%	11.3%	11.1%	10.9%	10.8%

helpful in benchmarking one's own views about the future. For the purposes of this case, the DCF values were sensitized around medium- and long-term growth rates of revenues. The sensitivity analysis yielded a range in share value between $48 and $75 per share.

ADJUSTED PRESENT VALUE Under this valuation approach, one discounts the free cash flow forecast at the unlevered cost of capital for Chrysler and then adds the present value of debt tax shields. To derive the unlevered cost of capital, one simply uses the *asset or unlevered beta* for Chrysler in the capital asset pricing model. The observed beta for Chrysler was 0.85. The tax rate was assumed to be 38 percent. The market value debt-to-equity ratio was 58.6 percent. Inserting these into the formula for the unlevered beta yields 0.75. Using this unlevered beta in the capital asset pricing model along with the other assumptions cited previously yields an estimated unlevered cost of capital of 10.2 percent. The terminal value for the APV approach simply uses the free cash flow for the final year times 1 plus the long-term growth rate, all divided by the unlevered cost of capital less the long-term growth rate. To this DCF value we must add the present value of Chrysler's debt tax shields, assumed to be equal to the marginal tax rate times the market value of Chrysler debt outstanding (assumed to be equal to the book value). As shown in Exhibit 9.17, the sum of the unlevered value of the firm and the present value of debt tax shields, less net debt yields a value of equity of $70.34 per share.

VENTURE CAPITAL VALUATION Chrysler is a firm with sustainable moderately growing cash flows. The venture capital approach is inappropriate here, because we have better and more information than merely a value at entry and a potential value at exit. For this reason, the venture capital approach was not applied in this case.

OPTION VALUATION APPROACH Chrysler arguably consists of a bundle of assets in place, and growth options. But given the dynamics of overcapacity in the auto industry, it seemed that the valuation based on the assets in place would represent the bulk of Chrysler's value. While the option approach might yield more insight, this did not seem to be a suitable instance for applying it.

Triangulate toward a Negotiation Range

The valuation analyses yielded a variety of estimates of value for Chrysler. These are summarized in a triangulation graph in Exhibit 9.18. This is where one must exercise significant judgment. The logic begins by recognizing a *floor* for the range:

- The market value of the firm just before negotiations began ($38.75 per share).
- Market value plus a typical acquisition premium of 30 percent, to raise the floor to $42.55 per share.
- Restructuring value. There may be actions that Chrysler management could take on its own to lift the value of the firm. One can estimate the benefits of any restructuring actions (i.e., through DCF valuation), and add them to the existing market value of the firm. Also, one could estimate the value of a firm under a leveraged buyout or other kind of capital restructuring (see Chapters 20 and 34 for more discussion on this). Since the data necessary to support either of these kinds of estimates was not publicly available, they will not be pursued further in this discussion.

The logic for recognizing a *ceiling* for the range will be specific to the buyer and seller. The buyer will not want to pay more for the target than the stand-alone value of the target, plus the value of any synergies (see Chapter 11 for more on the valuation of

EXHIBIT 9.17 Valuation of Chrysler Corp. Shares Adjusted Present Value Approach

	Projected				
Discounted Cash Flow Analysis: Adjusted Present Value	**1998**	**1999**	**2000**	**2001**	**2002**
Net income	3,037.0	3,291.1	3,582.1	3,883.8	4,201.1
Interest expense	1,002.7	929.1	815.9	706.8	595.2
Tax effect of interest expense	(385.0)	(356.8)	(313.3)	(271.4)	(228.6)
After-tax interest expense	617.6	572.3	502.6	435.4	366.7
NOPAT	3,654.6	3,863.4	4,084.7	4,319.2	4,567.7
Depreciation	3,194.7	3,406.7	3,631.4	3,869.7	4,122.2
Amortization	39.3	38.3	37.4	36.4	35.5
Deferred taxes	1,537.2	1,029.0	702.2	492.9	359.4
Minority interest	0.0	0.0	0.0	0.0	0.0
Income from affiliates	0.0	0.0	0.0	0.0	0.0
Other noncash items	0.0	0.0	0.0	0.0	0.0
Changes in net working capital	2,676.0	(182.3)	(193.2)	(204.8)	(217.1)
Cash flow from operations	11,101.8	8,155.1	8,262.5	8,513.4	8,867.8
Capital expenditures	(4,000.3)	(4,240.3)	(4,494.7)	(4,764.4)	(5,050.3)
Other	0.0	0.0	0.0	0.0	0.0
Unlevered free cash flow	7,101.6	3,914.8	3,767.8	3,749.0	3,817.5
Terminal value (perpetuity)	0.0	0.0	0.0	0.0	54,857.3
Cash flows to capital providers	7,101.6	3,914.8	3,767.8	3,749.0	58,674.8
Valuation					
Unlevered free cash flows	51,190.6	49,294.0	50,391.2	51,747.1	53,259.5
Debt tax shield	3,992.8	3,859.4	3,745.7	3,688.4	3,628.1
Firm value	55,183.5	53,153.4	54,137.0	55,415.5	56,887.6
Plus: excess cash	2,848.0	3,318.9	3,818.0	4,347.1	4,907.9
Less: debt outstanding	15,485.0	15,107.1	13,270.6	11,561.5	9,856.3
Less: minority interest	0.0	0.0	0.0	0.0	0.0
Less: preferred stock	0.0	0.0	0.0	0.0	0.0
Equity value	42,546.5	41,365.1	44,684.3	48,201.0	51,939.2
Value per share at beginning of year	**$70.34**	**$68.39**	**$73.87**	**$79.69**	**$85.87**

synergies). The target will not want to drive the buyer away with an unreasonably high asking price. On the other hand, the target will feel a legitimate claim to at least some of the synergies to be created in the deal. Compounding the challenge is the fact that the buyer and seller will view the target from different vantage points, perhaps reflecting differing degrees of optimism. The buyer would be ill served by a ceiling that offered more than the value of the firm on a stand-alone basis, plus the value of synergies. Since a discussion of synergies is deferred to Chapter 11, the story will end here with a judgment that on a stand-alone basis (that is, without synergies) the intrinsic value of Chrysler might be in a range of $50 to $65 per share.

The level of analysis represented in this example is perhaps a reasonable "first cut" at valuing a firm. One could easily extend it by deepening levels of scrutiny of as-

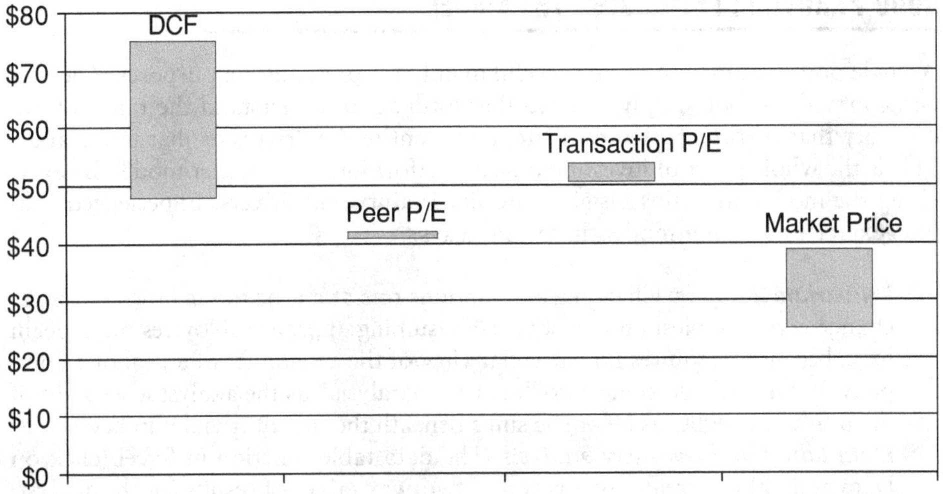

EXHIBIT 9.18 Triangulation Graph, Chrysler Corporation Shares

sumptions, richer sensitivity analysis, the use of scenarios and breakeven analyses, and greater detail in modeling. Where one stops is inevitably dictated by practical limits on energy, time, and money. Negotiators and managers will often request refinements as the deal matures. Therefore, it always makes sense to offer interim reports on the analysis, rather than drill deeply from the start and discover that one is drilling in the wrong area.

APPENDIX 9.1
Value Merge.xls: When and How to Use the Model

WHEN TO USE THE MODEL

"Value Merge.xls" is a multipurpose model[29] on the CD-ROM that enables users to forecast a company's financial data, value the company, and assess the earnings impact of merger scenarios. The most common application for the model will be in M&A analyses performed from the acquirer's point of view. On a macro level, key issues weighing on any acquirer's mind will be:

- What is the target company worth?
- What critical assumptions are built into the valuation?
- How much should we pay?
- What mix of acquisition currencies (cash, stock, 50–50) will we offer?
- What will be the earnings impact under various deal structures?

The model is designed as a tool for managers to address these questions. It is not designed to give a single point estimate answer. Therefore, multiple analysts of the same deal may well arrive at different estimates.

GOOD PRACTICE: EXERCISING THE MODEL

A single point estimate of value is useful mainly for presentation purposes. The best decision makers look deeply beneath that estimate to understand the range of uncertainty that surrounds that estimate, and identify the drivers of that uncertainty. This is the whole point of investing time and effort into a computer model: By exercising the model one gains insights into uncertainty and drivers. Experienced analysts exercise computer models in several ways:

- *Univariate analysis:* Changing assumptions one at a time to see how the results change is the simplest and most time-consuming approach. Novices often begin here, because it requires no particular view of the economics of a deal or a company. But it easily descends into "analysis paralysis" as the analyst loses sight of the ultimate insights as he or she sinks beneath the tide of trivial numbers.
- *Data tables and two-way analysis.* The data table function in Excel (click on Data and Tables) creates one-way and two-way tables of results for the analyst. These are highly useful in giving the decision maker some feel for how the key result (e.g., value of a firm) varies as key assumptions vary. As with the univariate analysis, it is useful to start with some idea of what are likely to be the key drivers and work with those rather than simply generating numerous tables.
- *Scenario analysis.* Experienced practitioners often work with scenarios of the future, typically an upside and downside scenario that might roughly correspond to macroeconomic views of the future such as "expansion" and "recession." With each new scenario, the analyst possibly varies *many* assumptions at the same time—this reflects the reality that assumptions tend to move together (that is, they "covary" rather than remain independent). Successful scenario forecasting requires careful reflection to assess possible states of the future.
- *Breakeven analysis.* When experienced practitioners have no particular view of the future, models such as this one can be used to "backsolve" for those assumptions (such as growth rate or margins) that produce a key result (such as a minimum acceptable rate of return). With knowledge of these breakevens, the decision maker can ask whether the firm's performance is likely to exceed the breakeven.
- *Monte Carlo simulation.* Simulation can be used to look at many possible future scenarios in order to build a probability distribution of outcomes such as value. Usually, add-on software is required to supplement the capabilities of Excel in order to produce a simulation analysis. "Value Merge.xls," on the CD-ROM, could be adapted for use with simulation software.

LAYOUT AND CONTENTS

Worksheets or tabs are used to break up the analysis. Upon opening the model, you will notice these in the lower left-hand corner of the computer screen. These tabs and their contents are:

- Tab 1: "Financials" (7 pages). Allows the user to perform income statement, balance sheet, and cash flow forecasting over a five-year time horizon. Historical data is also required. Schedules for debt issuance/amortization and capital expenditure requirements are included. The final page contains calculations of profitability, leverage, and interest coverage ratios.

- Tab 2: "Valuation" (4 pages). The first page requires users to input cost of capital and terminal value (both perpetuity and terminal multiple) assumptions. Free cash flow forecasting for the valuation analyses is based on the statement of cash flows built in Tab 1. The WACC, equity residual, and adjusted present value methodologies are presented.
- Tab 3: "Merger Scenario" (2 pages). Enables users to combine the target and acquirer's financial data. Target data is based on the inputs from Tab 1, while summary income statement and balance sheet data is required for the acquirer. Potential scenarios include cash and stock combinations and the impact of deal synergies. Under these scenarios, the model calculates the earnings accretion or dilution to the acquirer.

MODELING RULES

- Blue cells are your only inputs to the model. All inputs should be in millions, except share data (weighted average shares outstanding, options, stock appreciation rights, convertible share equivalents).
- Red cells are toggle cells, which allow you to run different scenarios based on the number entered. An example is the option to Build Cash (1) or Repay Debt (2) in cell G37 of the Financials tab.
- Black cells are calculations and should not be altered by the user under any circumstances.

NOTES

1. E. Richard Brownlee, Kenneth R. Ferris, and Mark E. Haskins, *Corporate Financial Reporting: Text and Cases*, 3d ed., Burr Ridge: Irwin/McGraw-Hill, 1996, page 6.
2. R. Kay and G. Searfoss, *Handbook of Accounting and Auditing*, 2d ed., New York: Warren, Gorham & Lamont, 1989.
3. Berkshire Hathaway Annual Report, 1994, page 2. "Charlie" is Charles Munger, vice chairman of Berkshire Hathaway.
4. Berkshire Hathaway Annual Report, 1992, page 14.
5. Some of these exceptions are manias and panics, the January effect, and the usually temporary inefficiencies that hedge funds exploit.
6. Quoted in Michael Lewis, *Liar's Poker*, New York: Norton, 1989, page 35.
7. Originally published in Berkshire Hathaway Annual Report, 1987. This quotation was paraphrased from James Grant, *Minding Mr. Market*, New York: Times Books, 1993, page xxi.
8. See "UV Industries Inc." Case Study 9-280-072, Harvard Business School, Copyright © 1979, and associated teaching note by Robert F. Bruner, under the direction of R. R. Glauber and D. W. Mullins Jr.

9. Quoted in Steven Lipin, "Lack of Premium May Irk GTE Holders, but It's a Feature of Some 1998 Megadeals," *Wall Street Journal*, July 29, 1998, page A3.
10. Stewart Myers originally suggested the important role of growth options in the valuation of the firm. See his paper, "Determinants of Corporate Borrowing," *Journal of Financial Economics*, 5:146–175 (1977). The decomposition of P/E presented here is discussed more fully by Myers in his book with Richard Brealey, *Principles of Corporate Finance*, 6th ed. (Burr Ridge: McGraw-Hill/Irwin, 2000), page 73.
11. A quotation of Robert Olstein in "Ebitda: Never Trust Anything That You Can't Pronounce," by Herb Greenberg, *Fortune*, June 22, 1998, page 192.
12. The economist Irving Fisher derived this model of economic growth. Its common name is the Fisher Equation.
13. This is a sensible assumption under the axiom of the limited liability for investors in corporations: Investors cannot be held liable for claims against the firm beyond the amount of their investment in it.
14. The arithmetic average is calculated by adding the annual returns over the period, and dividing by the number of observations. The geometric average is calculated as the *compound* average of the returns. Which should one use? There are arguments for both. If one foresees a normal probability distribution of *expected* annual returns, then the arithmetic average is the correct summary of the expected value of that distribution. But if, like most people, one extrapolates from past history into the future, then one should use the geometric average of past returns, since that correctly describes historical experience. As proof of this, consider the average return over two years, having earned +100 percent in the first year and –50 percent in the second. The arithmetic average is +25 percent, which is a flawed view of historical performance since you are no wealthier at the end of the second year than when you started. Only the geometric average captures this with a mean return of zero percent. Bruner, Eades, Harris, and Higgins (1998) surveyed the financial offices of 27 firms that were judged to be "best practitioners" in corporate finance by a finance magazine. They found great variation in the figure used for the equity risk premium; the largest cluster (37 percent) of practice in the sample was in the range of 5 to 6 percent. Another 11 percent used even lower assumptions. This book generally assumes a risk premium in the neighborhood of 6 percent.
15. The case for this assumption was originally advanced by Miller (1977).
16. In technical terms, the ability of CAPM to explain investor returns is measured by R-squared, a statistic that measures the percent of variation explained by the CAPM equation. This statistic can vary from 100 percent (indicating that the model explains *all* variation) to 0 percent (the model explains *nothing*). Typically, the R-squared for CAPM is low, between 10 and 20 percent.
17. See, for instance, Fama and French (1992 and 1993).
18. See Bruner, Eades, Harris, and Higgins (1998) and Graham and Harvey (2001).
19. Chapter 13 illustrates the construction of a model with these complications, in valuing a firm in a highly levered transaction.
20. In the second equation, the "at" symbol, @, is used to show clearly that each cash flow is discounted at (@) a specific discount rate. For instance, "FCF @

WACC" indicates that the value of the enterprise is obtained by discounting free cash flow (FCF) at the weighted average cost of capital (WACC).

21. For further discussion see Lerner (1999).
22. This estimate is derived using the Black-Scholes option pricing model, "Option Valuation.xls," available on the CD-ROM.
23. DCF is perhaps the *only* feasible valuation approach under conditions of high inflation. Nevertheless, effective application of DCF takes extremely careful work largely because inflation is very subtle in the way it distorts cash flows, discount rates, tax rates, and so on.
24. This section draws from the case studies of the merger of Daimler and Chrysler by Bruner, Christmann, and Spekman (1998); this book defers until Chapter 11 ("Valuing Synergies") a discussion of the synergies anticipated in the merger of Daimler-Benz and Chrysler.
25. Press release, Daimler-Benz A.G., May 6, 1998.
26. John Pepper, "Why Eaton Cut the Deal," *Detroit News*, May 7, 1998, www.detnews.com.
27. Shares under option may be found in the firm's annual report. The exercise price on such options is typically not reported in detail. But common (and conservative) assumptions are that the exercise price is probably below the consummation price in the merger agreement and that all the options will be exercised. Therefore, a simple approach would be to count all outstanding shares under option. However, due diligence research at the target company should permit a more refined assumption about the exercise of shares under option.
28. Many practitioners prefer to base peer analysis on size as well as industry. Some research (e.g., on takeover defenses) finds that size helps to explain variations in returns. Intuitively, size matters in choosing a sample of peers if large firms are harder to take over than smaller firms.
29. This appendix and the associated model were prepared by Mark Miles and modified by Baocheng Yang, both under the direction of Professor Robert F. Bruner.

CHAPTER 10

Valuing Options

OVERVIEW

The world of M&A has been influenced greatly by *options* concepts; in addition, these concepts help explain behavior and deal features that were previously difficult to understand. Options concepts surface in many chapters in this book simply because of their explanatory force. This chapter provides a conceptual foundation for the discussions in other chapters as it:

- Surveys the determinants of an option's value.
- Considers models of an option's value.
- Illustrates the practical valuation of financial options.
- Suggests how option pricing theory may be used to value securities as different as loan guarantees, bonds, and common stock.
- Points you toward further study in this area. This chapter is intended to be a summary rather than a detailed exposition of theories.

Option pricing theory is highly relevant to the field of mergers and acquisitions for three main reasons:

1. ***Valuation of firms.*** As discussed in Chapter 9, DCF and other estimation approaches probably do not capture the option value present in assets and enterprises. Option valuation may be an important supplement, therefore, to these other approaches.
2. ***Options' value, even if deep out of the money.*** Options are more valuable the longer the life of the option and the greater the uncertainty about future value. The implication of this is that the valuation approaches discussed earlier may *under- or overestimate* the value of a target firm. One of the limitations of discounted cash flow is that it does not capture well the strategic aspects of capital investment. Such strategic elements include the right to make future investments, the right to sell or liquidate in the future, the right to abandon, and the right to switch investments.
3. ***Pervasiveness of options.*** Options permeate M&A deals and, more generally, the economic environment. Presented in this chapter are some examples of both obvious and hidden options. Also discussed here are simple questions to help you determine whether an option exists in a given situation, and if so what

type of option it is. Later chapters will address how to value options represented by earnouts, staged investments, and other deal terms.

The *Black-Scholes option pricing model*, the first formula developed for use in valuing call options, was published in 1973, a year before the Chicago Board Options Exchange (CBOE) opened for trading. Before that time, a modest over-the-counter market existed in corporate warrants and some options. In the years since then, the volume of options trading has risen dramatically across the exchanges around the world that make markets in equity options. Optionlike securities are traded on many other exchanges. The options markets have been the sector with highest growth among worldwide capital markets in recent years.

The trading in the form of options also greatly exceeds the value of underlying assets traded. In mid-2000, the notional amount of derivatives contracts outstanding was about $94 trillion. This exceeded the global stock of financial assets (shares, bonds, bank deposits, and cash), which stood at around $80 trillion.[1]

OPTION BASICS

This section reviews some of the terms and investment positions of the options realm and highlights some of the settings in which options are present.

Some Terminology

Before proceeding, it is useful to survey some definitions:

- An *option* is the right, not the obligation, to do something. The term "right" is virtually synonymous with "option." Rights are everywhere. Options are contracts between two parties.
- A *call option* is the right to *buy* an asset (e.g., a share of stock) at a stated price within a certain time period. A *put option* is the right to *sell* an asset at a stated price within a certain time period.
- In contrast, a *warrant* is a call option contract between an investor and *the same* company that owns or issues the underlying asset. (An equity option traded on the CBOE is a contract between any two parties, not the issuer of the underlying equity.) Warrants are often issued as sweeteners (i.e., yield enhancements) in connection with securities offerings.
- A call (put) option is *in the money* if the current stock price is higher (lower) than the *exercise price*. It is *out of the money* if the stock price is lower (higher) than the exercise price. It is *at the money* if the stock price is the same as the exercise price.
- An *American option* may be exercised at any moment up until expiration. In contrast, a *European option* may be exercised *only* at expiration.
- For you to *sell short* a share of stock is to sell stock that you have borrowed. Eventually you will have to cover your short position by buying a share of stock to give back to the broker who lent it to you. You will make a profit on your transaction if the stock price falls below what you sold the share of stock for. You will lose money if the stock price rises above your sale price.

Options Are Pervasive

The business environment is permeated with "rights." A right is an option, not an obligation, to take some action. All forms of insurance, for instance, are options. Examples of relevance to M&A executives would include:

- Option to buy or reinvest.
- Option to extend.
- Option to abandon.
- Option to force a sale.

All of these rights are examples of *managerial flexibility*. Another class of strategic elements appears when managers promise to do certain things in response to others—for example, invest more heavily if a competitor enters a market or acquires a new technology, buy if others choose to sell, sell if others choose to buy, and so on. These promises amount to *managerial commitment*. One should define the corporate investment decision broadly to include flexibility and commitment, and then value the strategic element of the investment. In other words, one must see that *the value of an investment is the sum of its discounted cash flow and the value of its flexibility or commitment*. The challenge in thinking about capital investments this way lies in placing a value on flexibility and commitment. Fortunately, option pricing theory can help with this challenge.

Four Simple Option Positions

The key task is to define elements of flexibility or commitment in terms of options, and then use the theory to estimate a value. As a general rule, flexibility is analogous to a *long* position in call or put options. Conversely, commitment is analogous to a *short* position in call or put options. Here is a brief taxonomy of options latent in capital investments:

Long Call

- Right to invest at some future date, at a certain price.
- Right to harvest[2] at some future date.
- Generally, any flexibility to invest, to enter a business, or to delay harvesting.

Long Put

- Right to sell at some future date at a certain price.
- Right to abandon at some future date at zero or some certain price.
- Right to force someone else to harvest.
- Generally, any flexibility to disinvest, to exit from a business, or to accelerate harvesting.

Short Call

- Promise to sell if the counterparty wants to buy.
- Generally, any commitment to disinvest or accelerate harvesting upon the action of another party.

Short Put

- Promise to buy if the counterparty wants to sell.
- Generally, any commitment to invest or delay harvesting upon the action of another party.

Identifying and Mapping a Firm's Hidden Options

As argued in Chapter 9, the value of a firm will equal the present value of its predictable cash flows, plus the value of rights or options embedded in the firm. Usually these options are not plainly obvious; they are hidden; you must look for them. The identification and mapping of hidden options are the novelties in this approach and the critical skills to master if one is to become competent in it. Consider this simple problem from an M&A point of view. Suppose that your DCF valuation of a target company yields a value that is $10 million. But your financial forecast of the target ignores an R&D program ongoing within the target firm. You estimate that it will take three years for the program to either produce a commercializable product or admit defeat. You believe the product line has an expected value of $20 million. To gear up production and introduce the product will cost $20 million in the future. Because the cost to gear up equals the value of the product to the firm, the benefit of the R&D program appears to be nil. But your staff tells you the success of the program is quite uncertain: the expected value of the product line has a standard deviation of 80 percent. The government bond yield today is 6 percent.

The analyst's first task is to identify the option hidden in the R&D program. Recall the two key dimensions: long versus short and put versus call. Does the firm "get" (call) or "give" (put) under this program? It gets a new product if the program pays off; therefore, the program must be a call option. Does this program represent flexibility (a long position) or commitment (a short position)? The program gives the firm flexibility in its product offerings. The R&D program is a long call option on the uncertain new product; characterizing it correctly helps us know how to value the option. Long calls are easily valued using the Black-Scholes option pricing model.

The analyst's second task is to "map" the information about the R&D program onto the standard parameters of a call option's value. The asset value is what we believe the value of the asset underlying the option is worth today. The exercise price is what it will cost to "get" that asset in the future. Time is the life of the option. Volatility is the standard deviation of the asset value expressed in annualized percentage terms. The risk-free rate is the yield on U.S. Treasury securities having a life equal to the life of the option. Exhibit 10.1 gives the data for the R&D program. The resulting option value estimated is $11.1 million, a value that dominates the DCF value of the assets in place. In this case, option valuation significantly affects our outlook on the value of the firm.

Caveats about the Option Pricing Approach

While intuitively appealing, applying the option pricing approach can be extremely challenging. The first reason is the asymmetry of information; to identify an option you must know about it. Many analysts outside a firm will not have the information

EXHIBIT 10.1 Estimating the Hidden Value of an R&D Program

Investment in an R&D program could be modeled as a call option on an uncertain new discovery. The parameters are:

Time = 3 years
Value of the underlying asset = $20 million
Exercise price = $20 million
Volatility = 0.80
Risk-free rate of return = 6%

Hidden value of the R&D program	$11.105 million
DCF value of the assets in place	$10.0 million
Total value of the firm	**$21.105 million**

necessary to identify the hidden options. Second, some options will defy valuation by the standard option valuation models. While specially tailored option valuation models can be developed, these require the skills of a specialist. Third, the modeling requires assumptions about the parameters that can be challenging to derive.

These objections notwithstanding, forward-thinking firms are applying option pricing techniques with greater frequency. It would not be unreasonable to expect that in the course of time, option pricing-adjusted estimates of intrinsic value will become the norm.

OPTION PRICING THEORY

The Drivers of an Option's Value

Any day in the financial pages of a major newspaper, one can observe the prevailing prices on quoted options, such as those contained in Exhibit 10.2. The tables give prices as of closing the day before for puts and calls on each contract that traded the day before. Next to each company name is the closing stock price of the preceding day. Moving right, the next two columns give the terms of specific option contracts: the strike price and the expiration month. Then the columns give the number of contracts traded ("Vol.") and price[3] ("Last") for calls and puts.

This exhibit illustrates the major drivers of an option's value:

- Spread between market price of asset and exercise price of option.
- *Time to expiration.*
- *Risk (volatility).*

SPREAD BETWEEN MARKET PRICE OF UNDERLYING ASSET AND EXERCISE PRICE OF OPTION

In Exhibit 10.2, consider the call option prices of Cisco Systems ("Cisco"). Observe how prices differ for the:

- **Cisco April 20s versus Cisco April 50s** The April 20s call price is $4.25, in comparison to the April 50s call price of $0.13. Holding all else constant, the

EXHIBIT 10.2 Excerpt from Options Quotations Page, *Wall Street Journal*, March 9, 2001, page C15

Company, Price	Option Strike	Exp.	Call Vol.	Call Last	Put Vol.	Put Last
Cisco $22.81	20	Apr	458	4.25	987	1.13
Cisco $22.81	25	Mar	6,224	0.31	1,509	2.56
Cisco $22.81	25	Oct	798	4.00	651	5.75
Cisco $22.81	50	Apr	24	0.13	402	27.13
Citigroup $50.75	50	Mar	2,186	1.55	1,154	1.00
Costco $40.19	45	Apr	337	1.13	—	—
eBay $39.13	45	Apr	381	3.38	300	7.88
JPMorgCh $50.24	50	Mar	1,130	1.50	473	1.35

higher the exercise price relative to the price of the underlying asset, the lower will be the value of the call option. Similarly, compare the put prices for these two options: $1.13 versus $27.13. Holding all else constant, the higher the exercise price relative to the price of the underlying asset, the higher will be the value of the put option. These relationships are true for other pairwise comparisons throughout the tables. *The spread of price minus exercise price is directly related to the value of a call option, and inversely related to the value of a put option.*

TIME TO EXPIRATION As the life of the option contract lengthens, the put and call prices grow larger. In Exhibit 10.2, consider this comparison:

- **Cisco March 25s versus October 25s** The call option price for the March 25s is $0.31, compared to $4.00 for the October 25s. The put option price for the March 25s is $2.56 versus $5.75 for the October 25s. This relationship is true for other pairwise comparisons where the only dimension that varies is time. *The longer the time remaining in the option, the greater the price of the option.*

RISK All else constant, the riskier the underlying asset, the more valuable the call or put option. In the table, consider an imperfect[4] comparison between these pairs:

- **Costco April 45s versus eBay April 45s** In this comparison, time and exercise price are the same, and the price of the underlying stock is similar. Notice that the Costco calls are priced at $1.13, while the eBay calls are priced at $3.38. Costco is a discount bricks-and-mortar retailer, a reasonably steady producer of earnings and cash flow; eBay runs an Internet-based auction service, and is subject to the tribulations of the tech sector.
- **Citigroup March 50s versus JP Morgan Chase March 50s** In this comparison, Citigroup's calls are priced at $1.55, while JP Morgan Chase's calls are priced at $1.50. The similarity of these call prices might be explained by the similarity of option terms, and the fact that both firms are in the same industry (financial services) and occupy leading positions within that industry.

These and other pairwise comparisons suggest that risk is a major driver of option values. *The higher the volatility of price of the underlying asset, the higher will be the price of the put and call options.*

For the sake of completeness, two other factors drive the value of an option, though their effect is not apparent through the quotations in the options tables of a newspaper.

DIVIDENDS PAID ON UNDERLYING ASSET As the dividend payout rises, the value of a call option declines, and the value of a put option rises. The reason for this is that the dividends are paid to whoever holds the underlying asset; the dividends do not accrue to the option holder. As dividends are paid, the value of the underlying asset declines, a well-observed fact in the stock pages of a newspaper. As the price of the underlying asset gets smaller, relative to the exercise price, the call option value will decline, and the put option value will rise.

INTEREST RATE As the mathematical presentation later in this chapter will show, at the heart of option valuation is a present value calculation. As the discount rate rises, the present value of a future payment of exercise price gets smaller. Thus, as interest rates rise, the value of a call option gets larger and the value of a put option gets smaller.

To summarize, six factors drive the value of options: price of the underlying asset, exercise price, time, risk, dividends, and interest rates.

Payoff Structure of Options

In options terminology, *payoff* is the flow of cash to the parties to an option contract at the time of exercise of the option. Profit differs from payoff by recognizing the outlay necessary to establish the option position. The discussion here focuses on payoff instead of profit in order to simplify the explanation. Option payoffs have a kinked aspect.

- The minimum payoff of an option is zero. The owner of an option would never choose to exercise the option if doing so resulted in a loss. An option has a zero payoff when the option is out of the money.
- When an option is in the money, its payoff is determined by the difference between the exercise price and the price of the underlying asset.
- The pivotal point where the payoff turns from zero to something other than zero will always be the *exercise price* of the option. At the pivot point, the option is said to be "at the money."
- Option positions can be long or short. A "long" position means that the investor holds the right to exercise. A "short" position is the counterpart to the long position: In a short position, the investor has a commitment to perform in the event that the long investor does exercise.

This structure of payoffs leads to a kinked, or "hockey stick" shape to payoffs. In mathematical terms, the payoffs on long positions are:

Payoff on a long call position = Maximum of zero or (price minus exercise price) (1)

Payoff on a long put position = Maximum of zero or (exercise price minus price) (2)

Mathematically, the payoffs on short positions are just the arithmetic complement of the long position (notice the negative signs):

Payoff on a short call position = – Maximum of zero or (price minus exercise price) (3)

Payoff on a short put position = – Maximum of zero or (exercise price minus price) (4)

In order to see the hockey stick shape, consider the payoff on four option positions on Cisco Systems stock with an exercise price (or strike price) of $25 and an expiration date at the third Saturday in April 2001. The payoff on the expiration date depends on the stock price on that date. Exhibit 10.3 shows the payoff that results at the expiration date, given the stock price.

- ***Long call position.*** If the stock price is less than the exercise price of $25, then the long option value is zero. If, on the other hand, the stock price is above $25, it is in our best interest to exercise the option. In this case, we get to buy the stock at $25, a price that is less than the current market price. The payoff of the long call option position here is the difference between the option exercise price and the market price on the stock on the expiration date of the option. One way to view the purchase of a call option is as the purchase of the upper end of the stock price distribution; that is, we gain if the stock price goes up but do not lose if the stock price goes down. It is important to note, however, that this exhibit does not include the original purchase price of the call option.
- ***Short call position.*** Assuming that we "wrote" the call option (that is, we took on the obligation of selling the stock at $25 if the buyer decides to exercise the option), the payoff is the mirror image of the long position. As the stock price rises, the owner of the call (the long position) exercises the option to the disadvantage of the writer. It is a zero-sum game!
- ***Long put position.*** Assume you bought a Cisco Systems April 25 put option,[5] in which the payoff would be zero at stock prices equal to or greater than $25. As the stock price declines below $25, the payoff increases dollar-for-dollar to a maximum of $25 (if the stock price falls to zero). Buying a put (that is, buying the right to sell the stock at the exercise price) is not the same as writing a call option. In the first case, you have a right to do something, that is, sell the stock when it is to *your* advantage, while in the second, you are assuming an obligation, that is, you will buy the stock when it is to *someone else's* advantage.
- ***Short put position.*** The short put position is the mirror complement of the long put. At prices above $25, the payoff is zero. As the stock price falls below $25,

EXHIBIT 10.3 Classic Hockey Stick Diagrams

Stock Price	Long Call	Short Call	Long Put	Short Put
$ 0.00	$ 0.00	$ 0.00	$25.00	($25.00)
$ 5.00	$ 0.00	$ 0.00	$20.00	($20.00)
$10.00	$ 0.00	$ 0.00	$15.00	($15.00)
$15.00	$ 0.00	$ 0.00	$10.00	($10.00)
$20.00	$ 0.00	$ 0.00	$ 5.00	($ 5.00)
$25.00	$ 0.00	$ 0.00	$ 0.00	$ 0.00
$30.00	$ 5.00	($ 5.00)	$ 0.00	$ 0.00
$35.00	$10.00	($10.00)	$ 0.00	$ 0.00
$40.00	$15.00	($15.00)	$ 0.00	$ 0.00
$45.00	$20.00	($20.00)	$ 0.00	$ 0.00
$50.00	$25.00	($25.00)	$ 0.00	$ 0.00

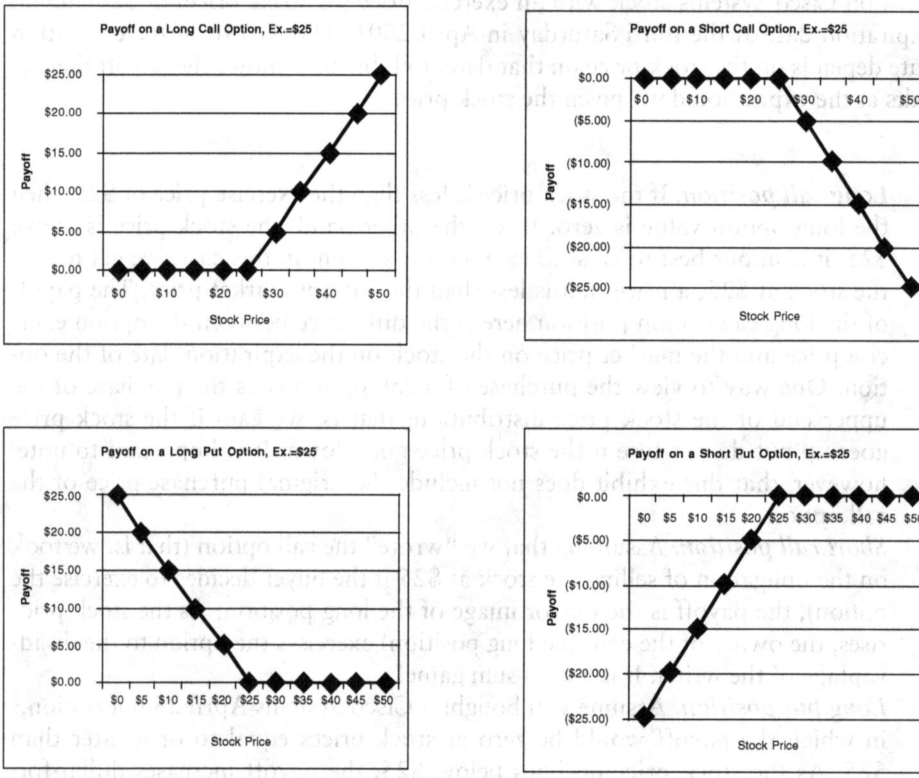

the writer of the put must purchase the stock from the long option holder—in these cases, the writer pays $25 for a share that is worth less. The writer presumably sells the share in the market, and suffers the loss between market price and exercise price.

These examples illustrate the mathematics of option payoffs: At expiration, the value of a call option is the maximum of either zero or the stock price minus the exercise price. The value of a put option is the maximum of zero or the exercise price minus the stock price.

Payoff Structure of Combining Positions

One of the most interesting things about options is the ability to combine option positions to achieve more complex payoff diagrams. Exhibit 10.4 gives an illustration of *bull/bear spreads*, two classic option positions that are important for M&A deal designers:

1. ***Bull spread.*** Suppose you buy a Cisco call option exercisable at $25 and write a Cisco call option exercisable at $30. The payoff shows a middle range in which you might experience a positive gain *if the stock price rises.* A floor and a cap otherwise bound the payoff opportunity.
2. ***Bear spread.*** Suppose you buy a Cisco put option exercisable at $25 and write a Cisco put option exercisable at $20. The payoff shows a middle range in which you might experience a positive gain *if the stock price declines.* Otherwise, a floor and a cap bound the gain.

EXHIBIT 10.4 Classic Bull and Bear Spread Payoff Diagrams

Stock Price	Long Call	Short Call	Bull Spread	Stock Price	Long Put	Short Put	Bear Spread
$ 0.00	$ 0.00	$ 0.00	$ 0.00	$ 0.00	$25.00	($10.00)	$15.00
$ 5.00	$ 0.00	$ 0.00	$ 0.00	$ 5.00	$20.00	($ 5.00)	$15.00
$10.00	$ 0.00	$ 0.00	$ 0.00	$10.00	$15.00	$ 0.00	$15.00
$15.00	$ 0.00	$ 0.00	$ 0.00	$15.00	$10.00	$ 0.00	$10.00
$20.00	$ 0.00	$ 0.00	$ 0.00	$20.00	$ 5.00	$ 0.00	$ 5.00
$25.00	$ 0.00	$ 0.00	$ 0.00	$25.00	$ 0.00	$ 0.00	$ 0.00
$30.00	$ 5.00	$ 0.00	$ 5.00	$30.00	$ 0.00	$ 0.00	$ 0.00
$35.00	$10.00	$ 0.00	$10.00	$35.00	$ 0.00	$ 0.00	$ 0.00
$40.00	$15.00	$ 0.00	$15.00	$40.00	$ 0.00	$ 0.00	$ 0.00
$45.00	$20.00	($ 5.00)	$15.00	$45.00	$ 0.00	$ 0.00	$ 0.00
$50.00	$25.00	($10.00)	$15.00	$50.00	$ 0.00	$ 0.00	$ 0.00

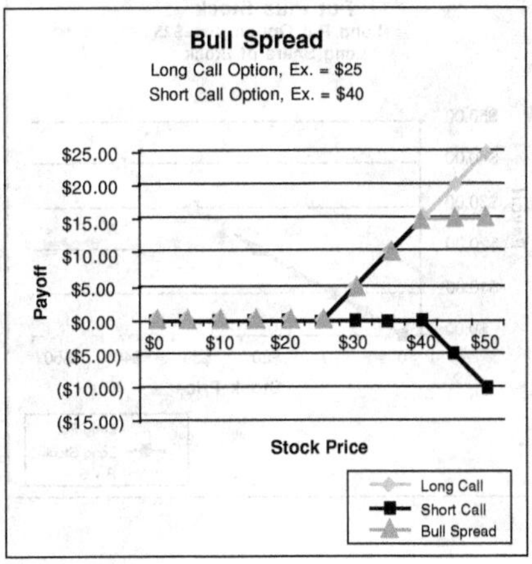

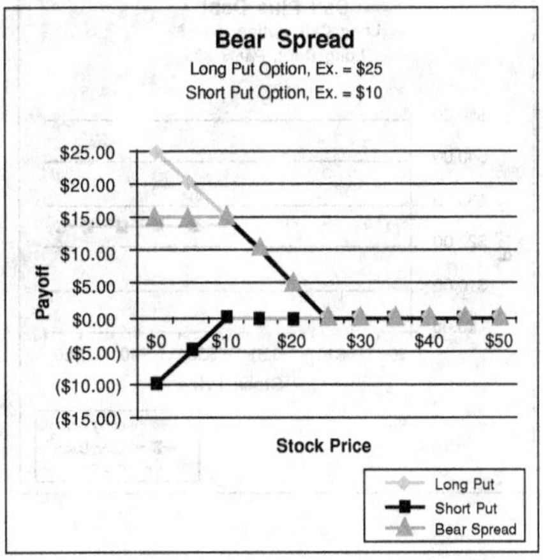

These positions are attractive to options traders because the cash inflows from writing the respective calls can be used to help finance the purchase of the respective long options.

Put-Call Parity

We can use the combination of positions in options and the underlying security to examine an important pricing relationship for options. One of the major contributions of Fischer Black and Myron Scholes was to suggest a relationship among the put and call options markets, the debt market, and the stock market. The relationship is called *put-call parity*. Its practical significance is that it acts as a kind of grand unification theory about the relationships among major financial markets.

The simplest introduction to put-call parity is visible in Exhibit 10.5, where

EXHIBIT 10.5 Put-Call Parity: The Equivalent Payoffs of Two Different Portfolios

Stock Price	Long Call	Long Debt	C+D	Stock Price	Long Put	Share of Stock	S+P
$ 0.00	$ 0.00	$25.00	$25.00	$ 0.00	$25.00	$ 0.00	$25.00
$ 5.00	$ 0.00	$25.00	$25.00	$ 5.00	$20.00	$ 5.00	$25.00
$10.00	$ 0.00	$25.00	$25.00	$10.00	$15.00	$10.00	$25.00
$15.00	$ 0.00	$25.00	$25.00	$15.00	$10.00	$15.00	$25.00
$20.00	$ 0.00	$25.00	$25.00	$20.00	$ 5.00	$20.00	$25.00
$25.00	$ 0.00	$25.00	$25.00	$25.00	$ 0.00	$25.00	$25.00
$30.00	$ 5.00	$25.00	$30.00	$30.00	$ 0.00	$30.00	$30.00
$35.00	$10.00	$25.00	$35.00	$35.00	$ 0.00	$35.00	$35.00
$40.00	$15.00	$25.00	$40.00	$40.00	$ 0.00	$40.00	$40.00
$45.00	$20.00	$25.00	$45.00	$45.00	$ 0.00	$45.00	$45.00
$50.00	$25.00	$25.00	$50.00	$50.00	$ 0.00	$50.00	$50.00

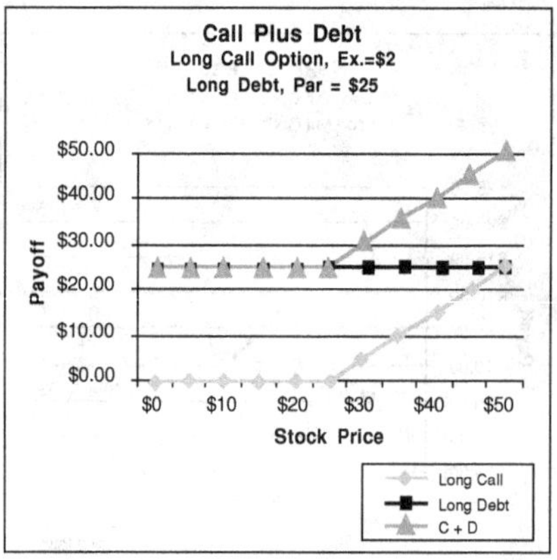

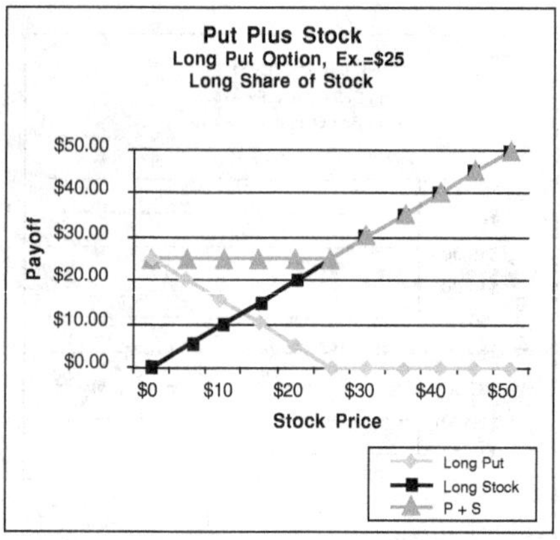

you can see the construction of two identical payoff diagrams through the composition of different portfolios:

1. Share of stock, plus a long put option exercisable at $25.
2. Debt with a face value at maturity of $25, plus a long call option exercisable at $25.

It must be true that these two alternatives have the same value in competitive financial markets. This equivalence of value is "parity." The cost of taking this combined position (i.e., buying the stock, S_t, buying the put option, P_t, and writing the call option, C_t) must be equal to the present value of the payoff at expiration, which is the exercise price of the options, E. Since the payoff is riskless, the appropriate discount rate is the risk-free rate of return. Thus, the relationship between put and call prices at time t given expiration at time T is:

$$S_t + P_t - C_t = E/(1 + R_f)^{T-t} \tag{5}$$

or

$$P_t - C_t = E/(1 + R_f)^{T-t} - S_t \tag{6}$$

where R_f is the risk-free rate of return and $T - t$ is the time to the expiration date. Based on this arbitrage relationship, if we know the current stock price, S_t, and the price of a put option, P_t, we can easily calculate the value of a call option with the same exercise price and maturity as the put option. It is the arbitrage relationship of put-call parity that forms the foundation of option pricing theory.

Value of Options at Times Other Than Maturity

The payoff diagrams look at the value of an option an instant before its expiration. Option theory and applications get interesting when we relax the assumption about time. In fact, this is the reality for most options: Time remains until expiration. These diagrams help us understand one of the two components of an option's value, *intrinsic value*. Black and Scholes made their signal contribution in modeling the other component, *time value*. Exhibit 10.6 depicts a hypothetical value function for a call option, and shows that at any stock price, the option value consists of the sum of intrinsic value and time value:

$$\text{Option value} = \text{Intrinsic value} + \text{Time value} \tag{7}$$

As the diagram suggests, even an out-of-the-money option will be valuable because of its time value (i.e., there remains some chance that, in the remaining life of the option, it will pay off).

The logic of Black and Scholes was remarkably simple, and derived from the same kind of arbitrage logic seen in the put-call parity argument: With options, it is possible to construct a riskless hedge, which by definition must earn a riskless return. If we know the return on the option position, it must be possible to solve for the value of the call option.

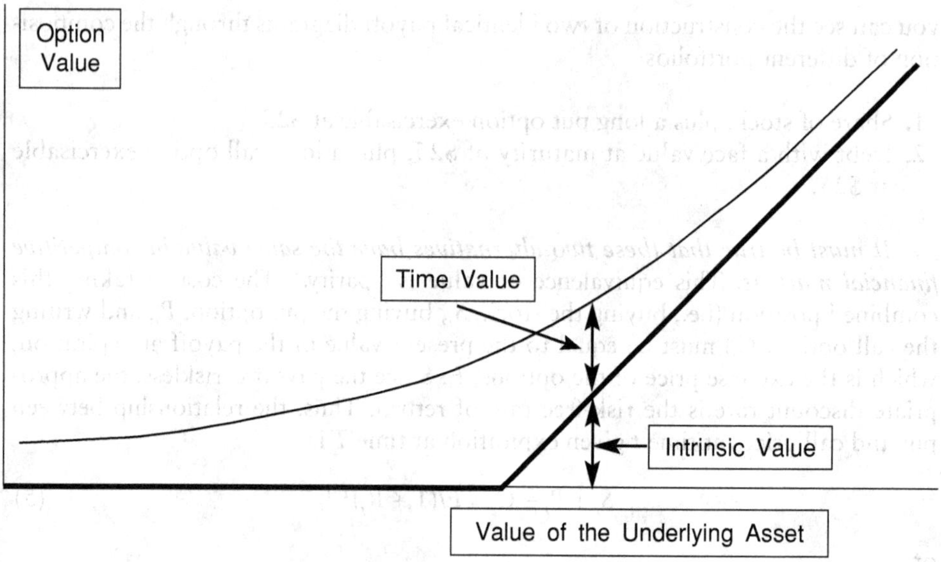

EXHIBIT 10.6 Time and Intrinsic Value in an Option

To illustrate, consider this call option: The exercise price is $32; the time to expiration is one year; the price of the underlying stock is now $30; and the risk-free rate of return on one-year instruments is 6 percent. You believe that there are two equally likely outcomes for the stock at the end of the year: that the stock has risen to $40 per share or that it has fallen to $20 per share. What is a call option such as this worth?

The solution is to find the riskless hedge formed with this option and solve for the cost of the option that equates the present value of the payoff with the cost of the riskless portfolio. Take these two simple steps:

1. Find the riskless portfolio. This will contain Δ ("delta") shares of stock and a short call. By definition, the riskless portfolio yields the same payoff regardless of variations in stock price. Thus, we must find Δ. To do this, identify the cost of the position if the stock is at $40 or $20:

   $(40 \cdot \Delta) - (40 - 32)$ is the payoff if the stock rises to $40.
   $(20 \cdot \Delta) - (0)$ is the payoff if the stock falls to $20.
   Solve for Δ by setting these two outcomes equal:

$$(40 \cdot \Delta) - (40 - 32) = 20 \cdot \Delta$$
$$\Delta = 8/20 = 0.40$$

   Thus, at $\Delta = 0.40$, the constant payoff is $8; 0.40 shares and one short call equal the riskless portfolio.

2. Solve for the cost of the option that equates the cost of the riskless portfolio with the present value of the payoff.

$$\text{(Stock price} \cdot 0.40) - \text{Call price} = \text{PV(Payoff)} \text{ ["PV" means "present value of."]}$$
$$(\$30 \cdot 0.40) - \text{Call price} = \$8/1.06$$
$$\$12.00 - \text{Call price} = \$7.55$$
$$\text{Call price} = \$4.45$$

The basic arbitrage relationship suggests that this out-of-the-money call option is worth $4.45 per underlying share of stock.

Dividing up the one period into smaller time periods can expand this two-state model, but the basic approach would still be the same. We would set up a risk-free hedge by buying the stock and writing (selling) the appropriate number of call options. Then taking the payoff from the risk-free hedge, we set the discounted value of the payoff equal to the cost of taking the position. Based on the current stock price we can then estimate the call option price. Note that we can use the put-call parity to estimate the put price once we have the call option value.

How Volatility Affects Option Values

The simple example in the previous section can be extended to show that *the higher the volatility in the price of the underlying asset, the higher the value of the option.* The intuition behind this effect is that with more volatility, the option stands a greater chance of being in the money.

To illustrate, consider the same problem, with the only difference that the stock prices you envision at the end of the year are either $50 or $10.

1. The Δ will equal 0.45 shares of stock, estimated as follows:

$$(50 \cdot \Delta) - (50 - 32) = (10 \cdot \Delta) - 0$$
$$\Delta = 0.45$$

The constant payoff will be $4.50.[6]

2. Inserting the Δ into the valuation model yields a value of the call of $9.25.

$$(\$30 \cdot 0.45) - \text{Call price} = \$4.50/1.06$$
$$\text{Call price} = \$9.25$$

The call value has about doubled from the previous example. The reason is that the possibility of payoff under the call has increased. As risk increases, options become more valuable. Exhibit 10.7 offers a graphic illustration of this by comparing the expected value of the payoff on a call option exercisable at $50 under two cases, low and high uncertainty. In the first case where the probability distribution is relatively narrow, the expected value of the payoff under the call option is only $3; but where the probability distribution is wide as in the second case, the payoff is $8.20. The difference between the two expected values is wholly due to differences in probability distributions. The higher expected payoff is associated with a greater probability of the option expiring in the money.

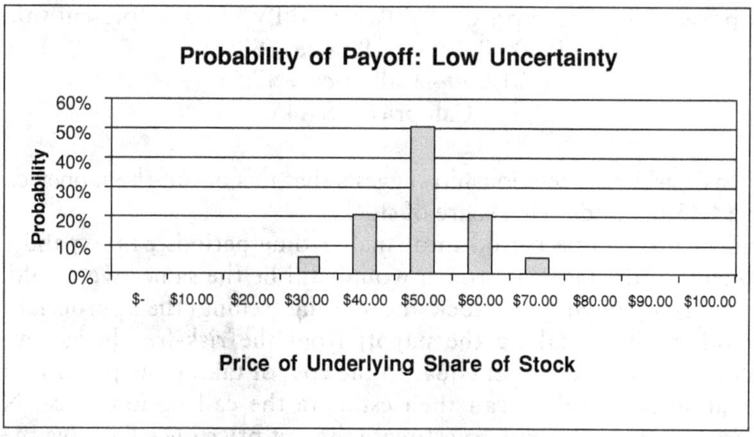

Stock Price	$ —	$10.00	$20.00	$30.00	$40.00	$50.00	$60.00	$70.00	$80.00	$90.00	$100.00
Probability	0%	0%	0%	5%	20%	50%	20%	5%	0%	0%	0%
Payoff (Ex = $50)	$ —	$ —	$ —	$ —	$ —	$ —	$10.00	$20.00	$30.00	$40.00	$50.00
Payoff Probability	$ —	$ —	$ —	$ —	$ —	$ —	$ 2.00	$ 1.00	$ —	$ —	$ —

Expected Value of Payoff = $ 3.00

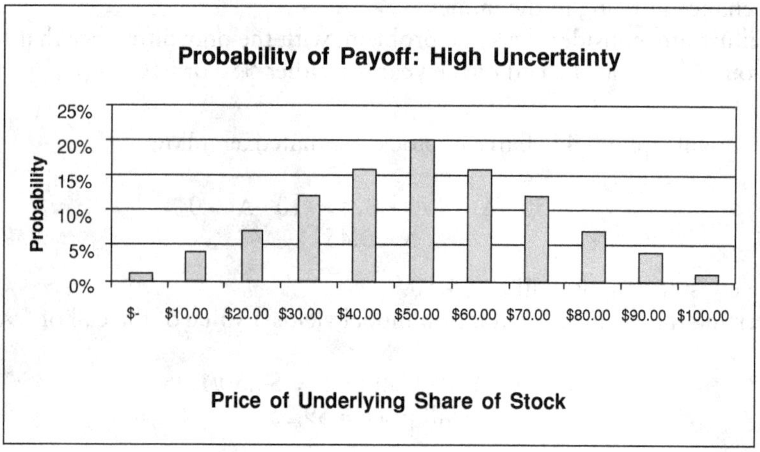

Stock Price	$ —	$10.00	$20.00	$30.00	$40.00	$50.00	$60.00	$70.00	$80.00	$90.00	$100.00
Probability	1%	4%	7%	12%	16%	20%	16%	12%	7%	4%	1%
Payoff (Ex = $50)	$ —	$ —	$ —	$ —	$ —	$ —	$10.00	$20.00	$30.00	$40.00	$50.00
Payoff Probability	$ —	$ —	$ —	$ —	$ —	$ —	$ 1.60	$ 2.40	$ 2.10	$ 1.60	$ 0.50

Expected Value of Payoff = $ 8.20

EXHIBIT 10.7 Comparison of the Expected Value of Payoffs under Scenarios of Low and High Uncertainty

Valuation of Call Options: The Black-Scholes Model

The single-period, two-outcome examples do not correspond well to reality. Black and Scholes relaxed these assumptions to an infinite number of infinitesimally small periods and a continuous probability distribution of outcomes. The result is the famous Black-Scholes option pricing model. The basis of the model is exactly the same as that developed earlier where a riskless hedge is created. Once the riskless hedge is created, we can then set the cost of the hedge equal to the present value of the hedge payoff discounted at the risk-free rate. The exact formula is:

$$C_t = [S_t \cdot N(d_1)] - [\text{Ex}(e^{-r(T-t)})] \cdot N(d_2) \tag{8}$$

where $$d_1 = \ln[S/\text{PV}(\text{Ex})]/\sigma\sqrt{t} + \sigma\sqrt{t}/2 \tag{9}$$

$$d_2 = d_1 - \sigma\sqrt{t} \tag{10}$$

S_t = Current price per share of the underlying stock.
Ex = Exercise price per share in the option contract.
r = Risk-free rate of return per period (i.e., daily, weekly, monthly, or annually).
$T - t$ = Time to expiration of the option expressed in the same terms as the risk-free rate (i.e., days, months, weeks, or years).
$N(\cdot)$ = Cumulative standard normal distribution function; $N(x)$ is the probability that a random variable will be less than or equal to x.
σ = Standard deviation of price relatives for the underlying asset.
$\ln(\cdot)$ = Natural logarithm.

The Black-Scholes model tells us that a call option is more/less valuable as:

	More Valuable	*Less Valuable*
Risk (σ)	Increases	Decreases
Time to expiration ($T - t$)	Increases	Decreases
Exercise price (Ex)	Decreases	Increases
Stock price (S)	Increases	Decreases
Risk-free rate (r)	Increases	Decreases

These are the same drivers of option value as illustrated in the earlier section on option price theory using the options quotations from the financial pages of a newspaper.

The reason option values increase with risk is that higher variability increases the probability that the option will be in the money at some point in the future. At first, this effect may seem counterintuitive, because for most bonds and stocks, as risk increases the value of the security *decreases* (thus increasing the potential rate of return to the security holder to compensate for the higher risk). As stated previously, however, options are explicit plays on risk; it is *because* of variability that options have value.

Why must the option pricing model be so complicated? Because we are attempting to distill into one formula the calculation of present values of all the potential payoffs (weighted by their probabilities). What the model says, in intuitive terms, is that the value of an option is the difference between revenues and costs of the option—the first term in the Black-Scholes model is the expected price of the underlying stock. The second term is the present value of the probable exercise price. To take one "best guess" case and determine the present value of the payoff is not sufficient, because the whole point of an option is to exploit the variability around some best guess.

OPTION APPLICATIONS

The impact of option pricing theory stretches well beyond the valuation of the equity options traded on major exchanges. Almost all financial securities can be thought of as bundles of options and long (or short) positions in the underlying assets. This rather abstract way of thinking about securities has very practical implications for the practice of valuation and the design of financial securities. Indeed, this way of viewing financing leads to solutions of problems that were heretofore imponderable. The objective of this section is to summarize several of these applications.

Valuing Equity

In their seminal article, Black and Scholes suggested that option pricing theory could be applied to the problem of valuing the residual claim on the firm's assets. Equity, they said, is analogous to an option on the assets of the firm, with the exercise price equal to the par value of the debt, and expiration equal to the maturity of the debt. This application is very useful in situations where:

- A company is privately held or the "float" on a firm's shares is very thin. In either case, the analyst would not have a price quotation available in which he or she could have much confidence.
- Cash-flow forecasts are unavailable, or if they are available, the forecasts offer no basis for a positive discounted cash flow valuation. Firms in deep financial distress, such as Wheeling-Pittsburgh Steel in 2000, may offer little hope of a positive return on a DCF basis yet have shares trading at a positive (if small) value. Shares of firms in financial distress illustrate the optionlike qualities of common equity.
- The analyst simply wants another opinion. Option pricing–based estimates can be used to check valuations based on DCF, price/earnings ratios, asset values, and so on.

The reader should be aware of two potential complications of applying option pricing theory to value common equity. The first is that the measure of volatility used should be the volatility of the *assets*, not the common shares. Only if the firm has no debt in its capital structure will these two measures be the same. Econometric data may be used to estimate asset volatility for some single-industry firms (e.g., agriculture, mining, savings and loans), but diversified firms present a serious challenge. The second complication is that the option-pricing computation must be adjusted for any payments to providers of capital over the life of the option.

Valuing Bonds

The option analogy can be extended to debt securities also. The basic assumption in this regard is that the market value of a firm's debt must be equal to the market value of the firm's assets, less the market value of its equity—a simple economic accounting identity:

$$V_{Bond} = V_{Assets} - V_{Equity} \tag{11}$$

If we express the put-call parity equation in terms of debt and equity of the firm, we have

$$V_{Asset} - V_{Equity} = Exe^{-rt} - V_{Put} \tag{12}$$

Recognizing that the left-hand side of equation (12) is equal to the right-hand side of equation (11), we have an option-pricing formula for the value of debt:

$$V_{Bond} = Exe^{-rt} - V_{Put} \tag{13}$$

In simple terms, this equation suggests that the market value of a firm's debt will equal the present value of a riskless zero-coupon bond (with the same term and yield to maturity as the firm's debt) less the value of a put option written on the firm's assets. This put option can be thought of as a *default risk discount*, which in itself is a very useful concept, because bond analysts have few other tools than simple judgment with which to determine these discounts—a task that in some markets, such as junk bonds, is difficult. Equation (13) is a simple and practical alternative for determining the value of debt.

Valuing Loan Guarantees

Loan guarantees in various forms (credit enhancement, letters of credit, insurance, government loan guarantees of distressed firms) permeate the world financial economy. Option pricing theory provides the first rigorous approach to valuing these guarantees. The value of the put or default risk discount presented in equation (13) will be equal to the value of a loan guarantee necessary to convert the debt from risky to default-risk free. The lender receives a put option for which the borrower pays. The guarantor assumes the contingent liability (i.e., writes a put option) and receives payment in return. Under put-call parity and equation (13), the value of the contingent liability the guarantor assumes will equal the value of a put option on the firm's assets.

Like many other kinds of insurance, the value of a loan guarantee can be material. At the bottom of its financial distress in 1980, Chrysler Corporation arranged with the U.S. government for guarantees of Chrysler's debt up to $1.5 billion. The estimated value of the loan guarantee was $440 million, almost a third of the value of the debt being guaranteed. The relatively large value of the loan guarantee derived from the very high uncertainty about the value of Chrysler's assets and the long (10-year) life of the guarantee.[7]

Valuing Subordinated Debt

Option pricing theory affords some useful insights into the nature of *subordinated debt*. Corporate financial managers often question whether it is debt or actually equity; it seems to fall in a gray area between the two. Understanding how the value of subordinated debt is determined can help predict the behavior of these investors as the fortunes of the firm wax and wane.

Exhibit 10.8 plots the value of senior debt, subordinated debt, and equity as a function of the total value of the firm. Recall the suggestion that equity is equivalent to a call option on the assets of the firm: It is worth something at exercise so long as the value of the assets exceeds the exercise price. Senior debt is worth its face value or the value of the assets underlying the debt—whichever is smaller. As Exhibit 10.8 shows, a positive payoff on subordinated debt begins when the asset value exceeds the obligation to senior creditors, and then the subordinated debt payoff behaves like a bond when asset value exceeds the combined obligations to senior and subordinated creditors. Note that the sloping portions of the senior and junior debt functions in Exhibit 10.8 suggest that, over some range, the creditors will feel like equity holders: The size of their payoff is *directly* affected by modest changes in the value of the assets.

Researchers have explicitly modeled the value of subordinated debt and revealed the "dual personality" of this type of security.[8] When the value of the firm's assets is low, the junior-debt price will behave more like equity than debt; when it is high, the junior-debt price will behave more like debt than equity. This phenomenon may explain the reluctance of subordinated bondholders to throw distressed firms into bankruptcy: By definition, if a firm is in distress the bondholders are economically equivalent to equity holders and may benefit from continued freedom for the firm to operate.

Valuing Equity-Linked Debt

Option pricing theory is also relevant for valuing hybrids of securities, such as those that combine debt and equity in a package. What used to be a difficult and subjective valuation problem may now, by decomposition of the securities into debt and options, be addressed straightforwardly. Examples of equity-linked debt are:

- *Convertible debt:* debt that may be converted into the common stock of the issuer. This conversion feature is actually a call option, which may be valued using option pricing formulas. This call option is virtually never separable from the underlying debt.
- *Units of debt with warrants:* like convertible debt except that the options (i.e., the warrants) may be traded separately from the debt after they are issued.
- *Exchangeable debt:* like convertible debt except that the debt is exercisable into the common stock of a company other than the issuer. The option to exchange is not separable from the debt security.
- *Exchangeable units of debt with warrants:* like exchangeable debt except that the options (i.e., the warrants) may be traded separately from the debt after they are issued.

EXHIBIT 10.8 Payoffs on Senior and Subordinated Debt

Asset Value	Senior Debt Par = 50	Sub Debt Par = 25	Total
$ 0.00	$ 0.00	$ 0.00	$ 0.00
$10.00	$10.00	$ 0.00	$10.00
$20.00	$20.00	$ 0.00	$20.00
$30.00	$30.00	$ 0.00	$30.00
$40.00	$40.00	$ 0.00	$40.00
$50.00	$50.00	$ 0.00	$50.00
$60.00	$50.00	$10.00	$60.00
$70.00	$50.00	$20.00	$70.00
$80.00	$50.00	$25.00	$75.00
$90.00	$50.00	$25.00	$75.00
$100.00	$50.00	$25.00	$75.00

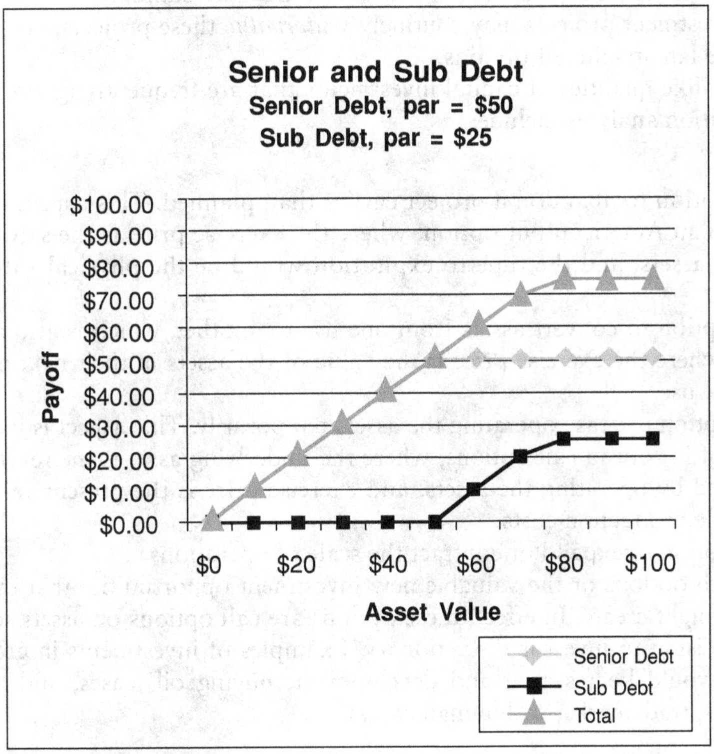

Designing Securities

As the previous section showed, we can view a security as a bundle of options and long positions. For instance, consider that a standard long-term bond may have a current coupon, a sinking-fund payment, a call provision, and/or provisions allowing the issuer to extend or retract the term of the bond. *All* these features are options added onto the "chassis" of a zero-coupon bond.

- *Payments (coupon and sinking fund).* Making a required payment may be considered the purchase of an option by the equity holders of the firm on the firm's assets until the next interest payment is due. The failure to pay a coupon or sinking fund would entitle the creditors to terminate the equity holders' claim to the assets.[9]
- *Call provisions.* A call provision simply gives the equity holders the option to call in (i.e., buy back) the bond at some point in the future.
- *Retraction/extension provisions.* A retractable bond can be redeemed prior to maturity at the option of the bondholder. An extendible bond is often a short-term instrument on which the maturity can be lengthened at the option of the bondholder.[10]

Assessing Capital Investments

Even opportunities to invest in real assets can be viewed as bundles of long positions and options. To take this view suggests that the standard DCF analysis of capital-investment projects may routinely *undervalue* these projects, because DCF ignores the latent value of options.

Optionlike qualities of capital investments that are frequently ignored in standard valuation analyses include:

- The option to abandon a project earlier than planned. This aspect is equivalent to an American put option, where the exercise price is the salvage value of the assets, and the time to expiration would be the physical value of the assets.
- The option to convert assets from one use to another, which is also a put option, where the exercise price is the value of the assets in their next most productive use.
- The option to cease operating the assets temporarily. This aspect is like a portfolio of European call options, where the underlying asset is the revenue to be received by operating the assets, and exercise price is the present value of the variable production costs.
- The option to expand or contract the scale of operations.
- Growth options or the valuable new investment opportunities that the investment might create. In effect, these options are call options on assets so long as the decision to invest is discretionary. Examples of investments in growth options would be research and development, buying oil leases, and acquiring patents, trademarks, and human capital.

Practicing managers often indicate the value of these optionlike features when they discuss "strategic flexibility" or "operational flexibility." In theory, all these features of capital investments can and should be valued as part of the standard analysis of the attractiveness of project proposals. In practice, the standard option pricing formulas may need to be modified to conform to the features of these opportunities.

A PRACTICAL GUIDE TO VALUING FINANCIAL OPTIONS

Understanding the formula for valuing options is relatively easy. Using the formula well is hard. This section of the chapter turns to the sources of inputs and ways in which the model might not conform to your task.

Finding Parameters

The software supplementary to this book includes a program for estimating option values using the Black-Scholes option pricing model. This is the model "Option Valuation.xls" contained on the CD-ROM. With the assistance of a program such as this, the chief task is to determine the parameters: stock price, time to expiration (expressed in years), exercise price, volatility, and interest rate. The first three of these are usually given as terms of the option contract. Where, then, do interest rate and volatility come from?

INTEREST RATE The interest rate to be used should be the yield to maturity of a default-risk-free bond maturing at the same time as the option. For analysts in the United States, the usual instrument would be U.S. Treasury debt, yields on which are available daily on the Internet or in a financial newspaper such as the *Wall Street Journal* in a section titled "Treasury Bonds, Notes, and Bills." The yield quoted with each instrument is the annualized yield to maturity and can be used in option-pricing calculations.

VOLATILITY The degree of volatility of a stock (or other asset) is measured by the standard deviation of price movements. However, the Black-Scholes model requires some special adjustments in making this calculation. Exhibit 10.9 illustrates calculating the standard deviation for General Mills Corporation common stock.

Step 1 Draw a sample of the 50 to 60 observations, such as the *most recent* daily closing prices.

Large, active options traders use minute-by-minute trading data as a basis for calculating standard deviation, although minute data are unnecessary for most corporate financial purposes. The most important quality of the data is that it be recent.

Some judgment may be required here in making a trade-off between representativeness and safety. If General Mills announced 15 days ago that it would sell its flour manufacturing operations and invest in Treasury bills, then only the most recent 15 days' closing prices would be representative of the company as now known. As the number of observations shrinks, however, you run the risk that one unusual observation could affect the standard deviation. There is safety in more observations.

Step 2 Base the standard deviation on the lognormalized price relatives, not the absolute changes in stock price.

A "price relative" is simply calculated as today's stock price divided by yesterday's stock price. We use this price because theorists and professional traders alike believe that percentage-based changes in stock price are more meaningful measures of movement than are absolute measures.

EXHIBIT 10.9 Calculation of the Volatility on General Mills Stock

Estimation of General Mills Stock Price Volatility across 53 Weeks, November 29, 1999 to November 27, 2000

Date	Weekly Closing Prices	Price Relative	Log of Price Relative	Squared Error of Price Relative
29-Nov-99	$36.56			
6-Dec-99	$33.55	0.918	–0.086	0.007731
13-Dec-99	$32.47	0.968	–0.033	0.001212
20-Dec-99	$32.65	1.006	0.006	0.000013
27-Dec-99	$34.45	1.055	0.054	0.002695
3-Jan-00	$32.67	0.948	–0.053	0.003028
10-Jan-00	$31.76	0.972	–0.028	0.000914
17-Jan-00	$30.61	0.964	–0.037	0.001518
24-Jan-00	$29.39	0.960	–0.040	0.001802
31-Jan-00	$29.51	1.004	0.004	0.000005
7-Feb-00	$29.58	1.002	0.002	0.000000
14-Feb-00	$31.15	1.053	0.052	0.002505
21-Feb-00	$32.07	1.029	0.029	0.000721
28-Feb-00	$31.46	0.981	–0.019	0.000444
6-Mar-00	$30.49	0.969	–0.031	0.001111
13-Mar-00	$33.52	1.100	0.095	0.008646
20-Mar-00	$33.28	0.993	–0.007	0.000085
27-Mar-00	$35.16	1.057	0.055	0.002816
3-Apr-00	$34.63	0.985	–0.015	0.000293
10-Apr-00	$35.43	1.023	0.023	0.000430
17-Apr-00	$35.43	1.000	0.000	0.000004
24-Apr-00	$35.61	1.005	0.005	0.000010
1-May-00	$37.27	1.046	0.045	0.001882
8-May-00	$37.63	1.010	0.010	0.000062
15-May-00	$38.98	1.036	0.035	0.001101
22-May-00	$40.14	1.030	0.029	0.000752
29-May-00	$38.73	0.965	–0.036	0.001418
5-Jun-00	$38.12	0.984	–0.016	0.000320
12-Jun-00	$37.88	0.994	–0.006	0.000071
19-Jun-00	$37.08	0.979	–0.021	0.000538
26-Jun-00	$37.45	1.010	0.010	0.000062
3-Jul-00	$37.41	0.999	–0.001	0.000009
10-Jul-00	$35.81	0.957	–0.044	0.002092
17-Jul-00	$34.82	0.972	–0.028	0.000893
24-Jul-00	$34.33	0.986	–0.014	0.000263
31-Jul-00	$34.27	0.998	–0.002	0.000014
7-Aug-00	$34.33	1.002	0.002	0.000000
14-Aug-00	$32.73	0.953	–0.048	0.002477
21-Aug-00	$31.86	0.974	–0.027	0.000823
28-Aug-00	$31.43	0.986	–0.014	0.000243
4-Sep-00	$31.74	1.010	0.010	0.000061
11-Sep-00	$32.36	1.019	0.019	0.000298
18-Sep-00	$33.96	1.050	0.048	0.002150

(Continued)

EXHIBIT 10.9 *(Continued)*

Estimation of General Mills Stock Price Volatility
across 53 Weeks, November 29, 1999 to November 27, 2000

Date	Weekly Closing Prices	Price Relative	Log of Price Relative	Squared Error of Price Relative
25-Sep-00	$35.01	1.031	0.030	0.000808
2-Oct-00	$37.20	1.063	0.061	0.003454
9-Oct-00	$37.07	0.997	–0.003	0.000028
16-Oct-00	$37.45	1.010	0.010	0.000065
23-Oct-00	$39.37	1.051	0.050	0.002320
30-Oct-00	$40.05	1.017	0.017	0.000232
6-Nov-00	$40.74	1.017	0.017	0.000223
13-Nov-00	$39.81	0.977	–0.023	0.000630
20-Nov-00	$40.99	1.030	0.029	0.000742
27-Nov-00	$40.49	0.988	–0.012	0.000200
Sum		52.132	0.102	0.060218
Average	35.0548	1.003	0.002	0.001158

Number of price relatives:	52
Number of stock prices:	53
Adjusted weekly variance:	0.001181
Annual variance:	0.061
Annual standard deviation or sigma:	0.248

Source of data: Bloomberg Financial Services.

Next, calculate the natural log of the price relative. Standard deviation is most meaningful for a *normal* distribution of price relatives, but simple price relatives are not normally distributed: They never fall below zero, and they have a long tail on the right. Using the natural logs of the price relatives in effect transforms that distribution into a normal curve.

Step 3 Calculate the variance of the lognormalized price relatives.

Step 4 Correct for possible bias in the estimated variance. Then annualize the variance (so far, you have calculated *daily* variance). Then find the square root of the annualized variance, which gives you the standard deviation, or volatility, of the underlying stock.

$$\text{Adjustment for bias} = \frac{\text{Number of observations}}{\text{Observations} - 1}$$

$$\text{Annualized variance} = \text{Daily variance} \cdot 365$$

$$\text{Standard deviation} = (\text{Annualized variance})^{.5}$$

There are at least two other ways to estimate a standard deviation.

1. If options on the common stock already exist, then the Black-Scholes model can be solved by trial and error for the standard deviation that explains the current option value, which is called the *implied volatility* of the asset. It is the value that equates the market and theoretical prices of the option. One warning is in order: Different options on the same stock may result in different implied volatilities because of an interaction between maturity and volatility and because the measurement of stock and option prices may contain some error.
2. Volatilities on stocks of comparable companies may be melded into an estimate for a particular company. Some investment banks and statistical services publish their estimates of *historical volatility* for a range of companies. This method is relatively crude, however, and should be used only when the preceding two methods are not available (e.g., in valuing the option to buy a private company).

To give the reader a sense of the magnitude of volatility estimates, Exhibit 10.10 presents data on the range and distribution of volatilities. This exhibit reveals that equity volatilities are clustered between .20 and .40 and that they cluster somewhat by industry (e.g., public utilities, electronics), although even within an industry, sizable differences in volatility remain, probably because of differences in leverage and product/market circumstances.

Using the stated parameters in the option pricing models gives a value for the call option on a *per-share basis*. To calculate the price of a contract (based on 100 shares), you must multiply the resulting option value by 100.

How to Compute Put Option Values

The value of a put option cannot be computed directly because no model exists to do this (the Black-Scholes model is specifically for call options). One can rely on the put-call parity equation to determine the value of a put. Put-call parity says that:

$$\text{Value of put option} + \text{Value of share of stock} = \text{Value of call option} + \text{Present value of call option exercise price} \qquad (14)$$

Simply by rearranging this equation, we have a formula for the value of a put option:

$$\text{Value of put option} = \text{Value of call option} - \text{Value of share of stock} + \text{Present value of call option exercise price} \qquad (14)$$

Some Caveats

The Black-Scholes formula will be appropriate in many situations, but in many others it will not, mainly because in the latter situations the assumptions on which the model was developed are violated. These assumptions are:

- The underlying stock pays *no dividends* during the life of the option. The alternate binomial option pricing model provides a way to overcome this

EXHIBIT 10.10 Historical Price Volatility 60-Day Volatility Ending September 30, 1997 and March 1, 2001

		9/30/97	3/1/01
U.S. Treasuries			
6-Month T-bill		9.53%	12.65%
30-Year bond		13.01%	14.73%
Foreign Exchange			
Canadian dollar		3.10%	4.42%
Italian lira		10.82%	4.30%
Mexican peso		5.34%	2.51%
Brazilian real		1.17%	3.97%
Deutsche mark		11.54%	4.17%
Japanese yen		13.40%	6.08%
Venezuelan		3.64%	0.38%
Peruvian		3.55%	3.71%
South Korean won		7.42%	2.58%
Metals			
Gold		11.13%	10.96%
Silver		24.01%	12.44%
Preferred Stock			
Fleet Boston	7 7/8%	8.50%	7.24%
Pacific Gas & Electric	7.44%	7.72%	14.02%
New England Electric	6.84%	22.97%	N/A

		9/30/97	3/1/01
Common Stock			
S&P 500 Index		7.64%	10.61%
Apple Computer		91.31%	32.78%
Fleet Boston		25.60%	17.12%
Consolidated Edison		14.60%	12.16%
General Motors		28.12%	17.22%
Iomega		50.20%	38.25%
Pacific Gas & Electric		26.02%	57.22%
Philip Morris		30.63%	18.65%
Telmex		33.28%	35.42%
Staples		30.65%	33.57%
Microsoft		37.95%	29.36%
Corporate Bonds			
Fleet Boston	2009	5.85%	3.22%
Pacific Gas & Electric	2023	8.99%	27.56%
Philip Morris	2015	14.05%	2.78%
Staples	2007	4.24%	5.20%
General Motors	2025	9.84%	6.34%
New England Electric	2023	8.75%	N/A
High-Yield Bonds			
Weirton Steel		5.25%	39.29%
Geneva Steel		12.96%	N/A
Nextel Communications		6.58%	5.74%
Bally		8.12%	8.48%
Grand Union		66.43%	N/A
Apple Computer		22.56%	1.64%
Family Restaurants		19.54%	N/A

Source of data: Bloomberg Financial Services.

limitation.[11] It may be adapted easily to correct for many of the Black-Scholes assumptions that are typically violated. On the other hand, solving it may require more time for modeling the problem by the analyst. An easier, but less accurate, way to resolve this problem is to reduce the stock price used in the Black-Scholes model by the present value of expected dividends.

- The option is *European*: It can be exercised only on expiration date. For many options, however, rational early exercise cannot be foreclosed. The binomial model provides a way to correct for this situation also.
- There are no costly *frictions* such as margin requirements, taxes, and transaction costs. So long as the following assumptions hold, no change is needed in the Black-Scholes formula:

  - Ordinary income and capital gains are taxed at the same rate.
  - Taxes are instantly collected based on realized and accrued gains.
  - Trading losses, interest paid, and dividends paid to cover short sales of stock are taken as full offsets against gains.

  These conditions are realistic for full-time traders and arbitrageurs, and because these individuals tend to be the price setters at the margin, the assumptions do not seriously invalidate the model.
- The interest rate and volatility are *constant*. Although the Black-Scholes model provides estimated values that are robust to moderate changes in interest rates and volatility, the authors assumed away random jumps or discontinuities in the time series of interest rates and volatility. The movement and unpredictability of future interest rates are not, however, trivial exceptions to the Black-Scholes model. Explicit models that correct exactly for changing volatility have been developed, and the Black-Scholes model can be modified in certain ways to accommodate this factor.[12] The practical approach is to adjust the historical volatility for (1) the change in volatility of all stocks, (2) the tendencies of volatility to revert slowly toward a mean level, and (3) the historical volatility implied in the option.[13]

Perhaps for these and other reasons, Myron Scholes said of the Black-Scholes model:

> *Black-Scholes gives me a better method of valuation than I would otherwise have, but it's not God's truth. If we tried to use the model as bookies, we'd go broke. It's like saying that because you have just learned in high school physics that the angle of incidence equals the angle of reflection, you're ready to go to the pool hall and challenge Lenny the local hustler. Lenny will clean you out, even though he doesn't know what physics is.*[14]

CONCLUSION: FIVE GENERAL LESSONS FOR THE M&A DEAL DESIGNER

Option pricing theory is one of the most important contributions to financial practice. This chapter has reviewed the terms, concepts, and valuation techniques in this important area. The discussion here is merely an introduction. Students and practitioners who wish to solidify their mastery of this important subject are urged to explore it further through Chapters 14, 15, 22, and 23 in this book and the readings and textbooks listed in the references. Option pricing theory will continue to spur the development of innovations in financial practice, design of securities, and changes in institutions. *Over the coming decade, there can be few higher-payoff priorities in the development of practitioners than to gain mastery of option pricing theory and practice.*

To reemphasize the importance to option pricing theory to the practice of M&A, consider these five general implications of option pricing theory:

1. ***Rights are options.*** Traditionally, a "right" was viewed as a concept from the domain of philosophy or law. Option pricing theory now permits rights to be viewed through the lens of economics and finance. *Rights can be valued. Rights are valuable.*
2. ***Rights permeate M&A transactions.*** Rights are literally everywhere in the business environment. They are manifest in a merger agreement, in the form of warranties, commitments, pledges, contingencies, various forms of payment, and so on. *It is imperative that due diligence research should look for the presence of hidden options, and that the deal designer should be aware of the presence or absence of rights in an agreement.*
3. ***Rights affect the attractiveness of a deal.*** If, as the first point asserts, rights are valuable, then including or excluding certain rights can affect the estimated value of the transaction to both the buyer and the seller. As will be argued in several chapters of this book, *rights (derivative securities) are a useful way to bridge differences of opinion between buyers and sellers.*
4. ***Rights can be valued.*** The techniques discussed in this and other chapters illustrate how contingent claims can be valued. Though the techniques have their limitations, *more rigor is better than less.*
5. ***Good analysis drives good deal design.*** As Myron Scholes said, option pricing theory does not necessarily summon forth truth. Nevertheless, it certainly gets one closer to truth, if the theory is harnessed sensibly. The theory and techniques are especially valuable if used in these ways:
   - *As illustrative estimates of downside or upside deal values.* As asserted in Chapter 9, we cannot observe intrinsic value; we can only *estimate* it. These estimates must be used for what they are. Nevertheless, they can help frame a range of valuation or negotiation, and therefore help buyers and sellers converge toward better deals faster.
   - *As drivers of inquiry.* One must have a view about the parameters inserted into the option pricing models. The process of option valuation will trigger questions about the reasonableness of different assumptions, a healthy intellectual process that could be married with due diligence research to produce improved estimates of value.
   - *As a source of sensitivity testing.* Deal design entails a relentless testing of what-if alternatives. Option pricing techniques can help place monetary values on alternatives, thus helping illuminate the size of value changes across the alternatives.

NOTES

1. The value of the notional amount of derivatives is quoted from Bank for International Settlements, press release, November 13, 2000. The value of financial assets was reported in "Finance: Trick or Treat?," *The Economist*, October 21, 1999.
2. The word "harvest" is meant both literally and to stimulate the reader's thinking. For instance, consider that you have an option on a tree farm. The trees are immature now but will certainly grow to have commercial value. The right to delay harvesting the trees is a call option. Analyzing the trees' value is quite similar to analyzing the investment in an R&D program, where each year's investment extends the "harvesting" horizon by one year.
3. The options contracts are traded in claims on 100 shares of underlying stock, but the options prices as quoted are in terms of *per individual share*. Thus, though the Cisco April 20s are priced at $4.25, you will actually pay $425.00 for a contract (plus any fees and commissions). This method of quotation makes it easy to compare option prices to the underlying stock price.
4. Imperfect because the prices of the underlying stock are not exactly the same in either of these pairs. But the prices are close enough to illustrate the basic points.
5. This is a shorthand way of saying a put option on Cisco Systems stock with an exercise price of $25, which expires in April.
6. If the stock price rises to $50, the payoff will be ($50 · 0.45) – $18. If the stock price falls to $10, the payoff will equal .45 · $10.
7. The process of estimating the value of the loan guarantee begins by estimating the value of a call on the assets and then applying put-call parity to estimating the value of the put, or loan guarantee. The call value was $1.42 billion, based on assumed value of assets of $1.5 billion, exercise price (value of debt) of $1.5 billion, volatility of 104.6 percent, life of 10 years, and risk-free rate of 10.52 percent. Inserting into equation (7) the call value ($1.42), asset value ($1.5), and present value of debt ($0.524) yields a value of $0.44 billion. For more on this case, see Bruner (1986b).
8. See, for example, Black and Cox (1976).
9. Two articles by Robert Merton (1973, 1976) incorporate coupons and sinking-fund payments into the option pricing formula.
10. Brennan and Schwartz (1977) modeled the value of retractable and extendible bonds using the option pricing framework.
11. The texts by Hull, Ritchken, and Cox and Rubinstein discuss this model in more detail.
12. See Chapter 7 of Cox and Rubinstein's book for a discussion of these methods; they are beyond the scope of this discussion.
13. For a more extensive discussion of this procedure, see pages 280–285 in Cox-Rubinstein or *Fischer Black on Options*, Vol. 1, No. 8, May 1976.
14. Allan Sloan and Richard L. Stern, "How $V_o = V_s N(d_1) - E(e^{-rt})N(d_2)$ Led to Black Monday," *Forbes*, January 25, 1988, page 59.

CHAPTER 11

Valuing Synergies

THE CONCEPT OF SYNERGY WHEN ONE THINKS LIKE AN INVESTOR

The word *synergy* derives from an ancient Greek word meaning to cooperate or to work together. Where synergy happens, the whole is greater than the sum of the parts, the so-called 2 + 2 = 5 effect. The concept is demonstrated in numerous fields. For instance, in medicine, synergy results when two drugs taken in concert produce an effect greater than the sum of effects of each one taken alone. In sports and the performing arts, synergy can be observed in superior teamwork.

In business, the opportunities for synergy are legion. Often, the synergies are expressed in vague strategic or organizational terms. The inability to express the benefits in measurable terms is the telltale of future difficulties. Mark Sirower, a vice president at Boston Consulting Group, noted that "The easiest way to lose the acquisition game is by failing to define synergy in terms of real, measurable improvements in competitive advantage,"[1] such as cash flows. This chapter defines synergies in economic terms and illustrates how you can value them.

Some benefits of a merger merely duplicate what shareholders can do on their own. These can hardly be expected to lift the buyer's stock price. Value creation is the toughest, and best, gauge of synergies. The key idea in this chapter is that *true synergies create value for shareholders by harvesting benefits from merger that they would be unable to gain on their own.* Shareholders can combine shares of publicly traded firms in their own portfolios. Why should they pay managers to do this for them if they can easily do it themselves?

Some will point out that the vast bulk of M&A transactions occur among privately held firms in whom ordinary investors cannot take positions through the public equity market. Others will point to the growing tide of cross-border deals, which present estimable barriers of information and trading to the ordinary investor. In arenas such as these, it may be true that investors cannot do these deals on their own. But even here, the investor's point of view gives extremely valuable guidance: One can still apply it *as if* public investors could take positions in the combining firms.

Synergy defined from the perspective of the investor is the toughest definition since it controls for so many potentially false sources of benefit. Recall the seven criteria for thinking like an investor that were outlined in Chapter 9: look to the future, focus on cash flow, get paid for risks, account for the time value of money and opportunity cost, consider any information advantages, and diversify efficiently.

While controlling for all of these elements still may not guarantee the correct decision about a deal, failing to control for them increases the odds of a bad decision.

SYNERGY ESTIMATES MUST BE A CENTRAL FOCUS OF M&A ANALYSIS

Synergy assessment should be the centerpiece of M&A analysis for four reasons. First, value creation should be a fundamental aim of M&A transaction design. Managers, as agents of investors, should think like investors. While there is no guarantee that even the best-designed deal will ultimately create value (see, for instance, the challenges of postmerger integration discussed in Chapter 36) the odds are that a deal having no foreseeable synergies at closing will destroy value in the long run—certainly such a deal will do nothing for investors that they cannot do for themselves.

Second, assessing synergies addresses an extremely important tactical problem for the deal designer: anticipating the likely investor reaction to the announcement of the deal. If the buyer is perceived to have overpaid for the target, the buyer's share price will fall at the announcement of the deal. But in the presence of true synergies, as defined in this chapter, the buyer's share price might rise, depending on the relationship between price and value of the target (V_{Target}) plus value of synergies ($V_{Synergies}$).

Buyer's Share Price Will:	*If This Equation Is Satisfied*
Rise	$\text{Price} < V_{\text{Target, stand-alone}} + V_{\text{Synergies}}$
Not change	$\text{Price} = V_{\text{Target, stand-alone}} + V_{\text{Synergies}}$
Fall	$\text{Price} > V_{\text{Target, stand-alone}} + V_{\text{Synergies}}$

Two of the three variables in this equation are easily observable. The deal announcement will reveal the deal price. The value of a publicly owned target before the offer can be observed and is easily assumed to be the *stand-alone value*. By valuing the synergies expected to be created in the deal, the analyst can anticipate the reaction of investors to the announcement (i.e., buy, sell, hold). Anticipating their reaction is important to deciding about the use of collars, caps, floors, and other transaction risk management tactics.

Here's a case in point: in 1978, Brown-Forman Distillers Corporation announced the acquisition of Southern Comfort Corporation for $94.6 million—my own analysis suggested that this was a full price for the target on a stand-alone basis. The target was the producer of a sweet liqueur by the same name. The buyer was (and is) a leading producer of distilled spirits, notably "Jack Daniel's," a rapidly growing brand and the highest-priced American whiskey of any notable volume. Analysts and investors believed that Brown-Forman would carry its brand-management expertise to an undermanaged brand that had high growth potential and that the acquisition would use Brown-Forman's financial slack: in short, the deal would create revenue and financial synergies. In response to the announcement, investors bid up the *price of Brown-Forman shares by 14.1 percent over the return on the S&P 500 Index (in dollar terms, $61.5 million)—this gain lasted. Using the framework on the preceding page, given that price and stand-alone value were roughly equal, Brown-Forman's share price must have risen because the synergies were worth $61.5 million.*[2]

Third, valuing the synergies in a deal can help the analyst develop a strategy for disclosing those synergies to the investors and shaping their understanding of them. Investors will want to know about the possible sources of synergy value, their relative certainty of realization, their duration, and their magnitude. Some executives choose to disclose only the most certain synergies in any detail. Others will choose to offer guidance to analysts and investors about the less certain synergies, too. But any disclosure strategy should be informed by an understanding of the possible value attached to deal synergies.

Finally, valuing synergies should be a foundation for developing a strategy for postmerger integration. Managers should tailor integration plans to deal with the points of greatest impact and leverage in realizing synergy value. Valuation analysis can illuminate the path.

A FRAMEWORK FOR SYNERGY ANALYSIS

The rigorous analysis of synergy value must begin with a careful inventory of its sources. The valuation framework outlined in Chapters 9 and 10 affords an organizing scheme: synergies as a bundle of two types—*synergies "in place"* and *real option synergies*:

$$V_{\text{Synergies}} = V_{\text{synergies}}^{\text{In place}} + V_{\text{synergies}}^{\text{Real options}} \tag{1}$$

This approach follows the work of Stewart C. Myers,[3] who decomposed firm value into the value of "assets-in-place" and "growth options." Valuation approaches illuminate each of the terms on the right-hand side of the equation.

Synergies from Assets or Activities That Are In Place

The first class of synergies derives from assets or activities whose payoffs are reasonably predictable. Discounted cash flow valuation is the best approach for valuing streams of cash generated from these synergies. The framework of DCF valuation casts the drivers of synergy value into useful form. Recalling the discussion in Chapter 9, a standard formula for DCF valuation of synergies is:

$$V_{\text{Synergies in place}} = \sum_{t=0}^{n} \frac{\text{FCF}_t}{(1+\text{WACC})^t} \tag{2}$$

Free cash flow (FCF) is the after-tax operating profit, plus noncash deductions, less investments in net working capital and capital projects. The weighted average cost of capital (WACC) is the blended opportunity cost of all investors.

The DCF formula implies that synergies in place can arise from improvements in any of the FCF components or in WACC. Implied in FCF or WACC are *improvements in timing*, shown by the "t" in the formula. These improvements, however, need to be scrutinized. They include:

REVENUE ENHANCEMENT SYNERGIES Newco sells more product than either of the two firms would have sold independently. Typically, these *revenue enhancements* are envisioned to arise from cross-selling by the two firms' sales forces, or cross-branding (or rebranding) between the target's and buyer's products. For instance, when Eli Lilly, a large pharmaceuticals firm, acquired Hybritech Inc., a small biotech boutique, in 1986, it foresaw the ability to channel Hybritech's pathbreaking products through Lilly's large and efficient marketing force. The increase in product sales resulting from this combination was a classic synergy.

COST REDUCTION SYNERGIES Newco's unit costs decline as a result of the transaction. Sources of *cost reductions* include economies of scale arising from higher capacity utilization of existing plant and equipment, greater purchasing power vis-à-vis suppliers, the elimination of intermediaries in a supply chain, the improvement in logistics and distribution, closing the target's headquarters and managing Newco without an offsetting increase at the buyer's headquarters, and the transfer of technology or know-how from one firm to the other. Of all the sources of synergy, this appears to be the most credible. A study of bank mergers by Houston and Ryngaert yielded the conclusion that "the market is readily persuaded by the cost-cutting motive for mergers, while subjecting other rationales to considerable skepticism."[4]

ASSET REDUCTION SYNERGIES Combining two firms may permit the disposal of idle assets, such as vacant real estate, a redundant headquarters building, unused plant capacity, and excess inventories, receivables, or cash balances. These *asset reductions* represent real economic benefits, though the analyst should be reminded that these are typically one-shot events, not recurring through time.

TAX REDUCTION SYNERGIES Acquisitions can unlock two kinds of *tax reduction* synergies that investors would not have been able to achieve on their own. The first is the exploitation of an increase in depreciation tax shields deriving from the step-up in basis following a purchase transaction. The second is the de facto transfer of net operating losses (NOLs) from a target to a buyer through merger or acquisition. This is a "2 + 2 = 5" transaction if the target were unable to fully use these losses to reduce tax expense before the expiration of those tax losses. The carryforward of operating losses to apply against future earnings usually has a finite life. By combining with a profitable firm, it may be possible for the target's NOLs to be fully used, or used more quickly than on a stand-alone basis. The step-up in basis with purchase transactions may permit the buyer to exploit depreciation tax shields that would not otherwise exist. The full and/or faster use of tax shields that investors cannot replicate is a genuine synergy. In contrast, a tax reduction that may not be a synergy involves the exploitation of debt tax shields through financing the transaction, discussed next.

FINANCIAL SYNERGIES One must exercise caution in evaluating synergies that are claimed to reduce Newco's weighted average cost of capital. The key idea is that if financing creates value for investors that they cannot create for themselves, then it is a synergy; otherwise not. There are two classic *WACC reduction* arguments, one of which probably meets this synergy definition, and the other of which probably does not.

Reducing WACC by Optimizing the Use of Debt Tax Shields As discussed in Chapter 9, the use of interest-bearing debt to finance the firm reduces the firm's tax expense. But if investors can borrow on their own, simply financing a deal with debt doesn't do anything for investors that they cannot do themselves. The operative word here is "if"—individual investors may find it difficult to borrow in sufficient amounts, and at rates as advantageous as those received by the larger corporations. The difference between corporate and individual borrowing terms may not be trivial, but if the attractiveness of a deal hinges on this difference, it may not be worth doing. One must remember that beyond some reasonable amount of leverage, adding more debt does not create more value, and indeed, may destroy it. Helping an overlevered target return to more moderate use of debt financing might create value.

In 1995 Craig McCaw sold McCaw Cellular Communications to AT&T. At the time, McCaw's debt carried a CCC rating, while AT&T's carried AA. McCaw was constrained in the amount of financing it could obtain to build out its national wireless telecommunications business; AT&T was virtually unconstrained. A naive analyst might have looked at this deal as an opportunity to exploit AT&T's creditworthiness in pursuit of the expansion of McCaw. But AT&T shareholders would almost certainly want to be compensated for the deterioration in their credit rating that would ensue from financing McCaw, so it looked like a dubious synergy. Also, there may be an adverse interaction between operating synergies (revenues, costs, assets) and default risk reduction that reduces Newco's WACC.

In theory, managers should strive to finance their firms with an optimal mix of debt and equity—a "Goldilocks" blend of not too much or too little debt. But some managers choose not to do so, perhaps out of ignorance or a failure to be faithful agents to the interests of investors. Some raiders take this as a cue to take over the target and leverage it more optimally. Kirk Kerkorian's two attempts to gain control of Chrysler are examples of the effort to optimize the financing of the firm. But this is an action that investors may be able to accomplish on their own through homemade leverage. In short, *WACC optimization* usually will not meet the economic definition of synergy.

Coinsurance Effects: Shifting the Curve The theory of portfolio diversification suggests that combining two cash flow streams that are less than perfectly correlated can produce a joint stream that is less risky than a simple sum of the streams would imply.

Wilbur Lewellen (1971) used this argument to show that the joint probability of financial distress would be lower for Newco than would be the simple average of the probabilities (assuming that the returns of the two firms have a correlation of less than 1.00). This reduction of risk lowers the risk per unit of cash flow (again assuming no change in the earnings stream of the firms), which makes the surviving firm more attractive to creditors and equity investors; in effect, the merging firms *coinsure* the obligations of Newco, making them less risky to lenders. Lewellen argued that coinsurance cannot create value for shareholders by reducing the cost of capital (remember that shareholders can already do this on their own) but it *could create additional borrowing capacity* for Newco. By using this capacity (borrowing more) one exploits debt tax shields more and creates value for shareholders.

Robert Merton and Andre Perold[5] note that the covariability of returns among different business activities can be exceedingly complex to track, rendering the rigorous estimation of *coinsurance effects* quite difficult.

In summary, the story on financial synergies is that they are reflected best in *access to capital*, in shifting the WACC curve in advantageous ways—of changing the rules of the game, so to speak. See Exhibit 11.1 for a graphic depiction of how WACC curves may shift. More debatable WACC synergies arise from optimizing the WACC curve as it is—here the investors' abilities to "homemake" their own financing for firms must be given some consideration. Even though investors may not enjoy the same financing terms as corporations, the fact that they can partially exploit the benefits on their own should prompt the analyst to scrutinize skeptically claims of genuine WACC synergies. Best practice should place a high burden of proof on analysts claiming the existence of financial synergies.

Real Option Synergies

The other class of synergies depends on some triggering event to produce a payoff. These are *real option* synergies. In essence, options that create flexibility for managers or extract commitments from others will convey positive value. Consider these possibilities:

- ***Growth option synergies.*** These would arise from the combination of resources in a transaction that create the right but not the obligation to grow. Examples of this would include R&D or creative capabilities, the matching of licenses to enter new markets with the resources to do so, leases on land or mineral reserves, and access to an information base or network.
- ***Exit option synergies.*** A merger might make Newco less *path dependent*, giving the firm more alternatives to respond to market conditions as they change or to alter investment strategies.
- ***Options to defer.*** A combination of two firms could grant the flexibility to wait on developing a new technology, entering a new market, or undertaking some other risky action.
- ***Options to alter operating scale (i.e., expand, contract, shut down, and restart).*** A combination of two firms could help the buyer to exit or enter a business more readily.
- ***Options to switch.*** These would include the ability to change the mix of inputs or outputs of the firm, or its processes. The acquisition of Maxus Energy by Yacimientos Petroliferos Fiscales S.A. (YPF) in 1995 permitted YPF to source oil from a wider range of reserves, permitting it greater flexibility in supply.

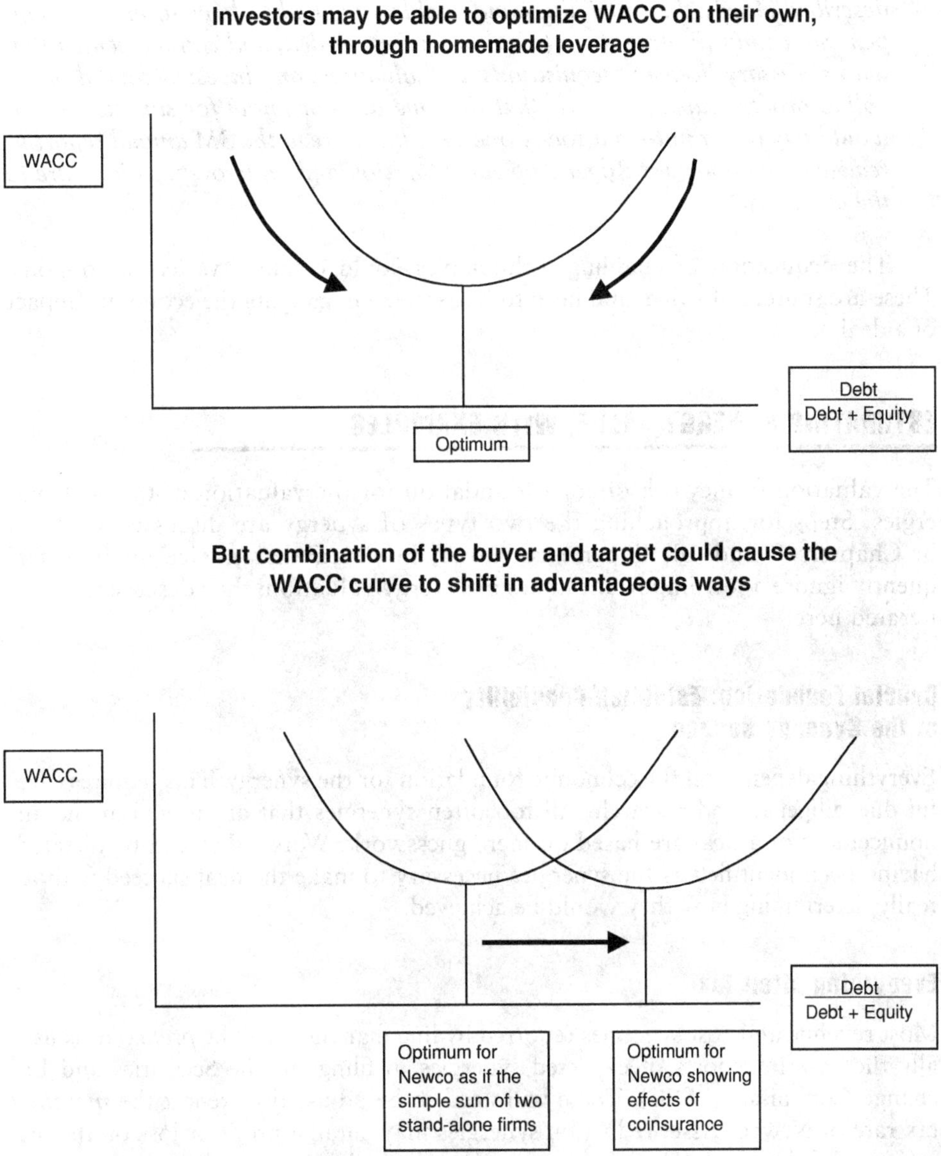

EXHIBIT 11.1 How WACC Curves May Shift

To illustrate the effect of these synergies, Ron Mitsch, former vice chairman of 3M Corporation, told me about 3M's acquisition of "enabling technologies." He said,

In the 1960s Roger Appledorn invented the Fresnel lens for use in overhead projectors. In the early 1980s he expressed his vision and foresight that "microreplication" represented a broad-based technology platform that could lead to hundreds of millions of dollars of growth in several market areas. He also described clearly the capabilities and enablers we had to have to make it happen. So we put in place the internal programs needed, and complemented that with necessary licenses, acquisitions, and alliances, and invested capital in enabling process capabilities. At that time we did not know for sure whether it would pay off or not—but today one only has to read the 3M annual report to realize how important Roger Appledorn's vision and "microreplication" are to the company.[6]

The acquisition of enabling technologies could create a variety of options. These are sources of value, and need to be assessed in gauging the economic impact of a deal.

ESTIMATING SYNERGY VALUE, WITH EXAMPLES

The valuation framework offers a foundation for the valuation of the deal synergies. Steps for approaching the two types of synergy are discussed in detail in Chapters 9 and 10. Experience shows, however, that novice analysts frequently ignore a few important issues in synergy valuation; they deserve to be reiterated here.

Crucial Foundation: Establish Credibility of the Synergy Source

Everything depends on the economic foundation for the synergy. This requires careful due diligence and research. All too often synergies that are touted at the announcement of a deal are based on mere guesswork. Worse, they can be dictated, having been identified as the synergies necessary to make the deal succeed without really determining how they would be achieved.

Everything after Tax

Most revenue and cost synergies reported by line managers will be *pretax*, as is usually the case in reports of expected synergies in filings to the Securities and Exchange Commission (SEC). These will need to be adjusted to reflect the *marginal* tax rate of Newco. Asset reduction synergies may entail a profit or loss on the disposition of the asset—these, too, must be adjusted for the marginal tax rate of Newco. WACC-related synergies must reflect the marginal tax rate also.

Choose a Discount Rate Consistent with the Risk of the Synergy

The synergies outlined in this chapter differ in risk. Operating managers typically will assert that cost synergies are most certain and revenue synergies least certain. Tax reduction and asset reduction synergies are probably even more certain than others. WACC synergies are probably in between. The difference in risk may be material enough to warrant using different discount rates to evaluate the synergy benefits. After all, one of the most important tenets of financial economics is that one should value a stream of cash using a discount rate consistent with the risk of that stream. If, as practitioners tell us, the different synergies have different degrees of risk, then using different discount rates seems sensible.

Theory offers no detailed suggestions for which discount rate to use in valuing different kinds of synergy cash flows. The analyst must rely on judgment and intuition instead. Here are a range of possibilities:

- "Sure things" should be discounted at the risk-free rate. For instance, the cash flow from selling redundant raw material inventory into a liquid market with quotable prices (such as steel) might fall in this category.
- Cash flows that are as variable as EBIT could be discounted at the cost of debt. The interest expense charged by lenders in effect prices the uncertainty impounded in EBIT.
- Cash flows that are as risky as the free cash flows of the enterprise should be discounted at the firm's weighted average cost of capital (WACC).
- Cash flows that are as risky as the residual cash flows of the firm (such as dividends and share repurchase flows) should be discounted at the firm's cost of equity.
- Cash flows that are as speculative as a venture capital investment should be discounted at the venture capitalists' required rate of return (e.g., 30 percent or higher).

Exhibit 11.2 gives a graphical representation of the spectrum of synergies and the discount rates consistent with their risks.

The whole point of tailoring the discount rate to the type of synergy is to *adjust for risk*. An alternative approach is to use a prescribed discount rate like the WACC, and to give the synergy cash flows a "haircut" if they seem riskier than the WACC would imply—but doing so is even *more* arbitrary than selecting a discount rate. How large a haircut should you give? The haircut method is vulnerable to the analyst's biases. It is better to work within a range of discount rates suggested by the capital markets. Here, for instance, is an excerpt of Merrill Lynch's valuation of synergies produced in the acquisition of Quaker Oats by PepsiCo.

> *Merrill Lynch performed a discounted cash flow analysis of the expected synergies based upon the estimates provided by PepsiCo. The discounted cash flow valuation was calculated assuming discount rates ranging from 10.0% to 12.0% and was comprised of the sum of the present values of: (1) the projected after-tax synergies for the years 2001 through 2012; and (2) the terminal value of the expected synergies in 2012, utilizing a range of perpetuity growth rates of 1.0% to 3.0%. Based upon this discounted cash flow analysis, Merrill Lynch valued the expected synergies at a range of \$11.35 to \$16.85 per Quaker share.*[7]

The use of a *range* of discount rates at least expresses professional honesty: When you don't have a strong basis for asserting the relevance of a given rate, then it is appropriate to disclose your uncertainty and use a range of rates consistent with capital market information. No matter what, choose discount rates with caution.

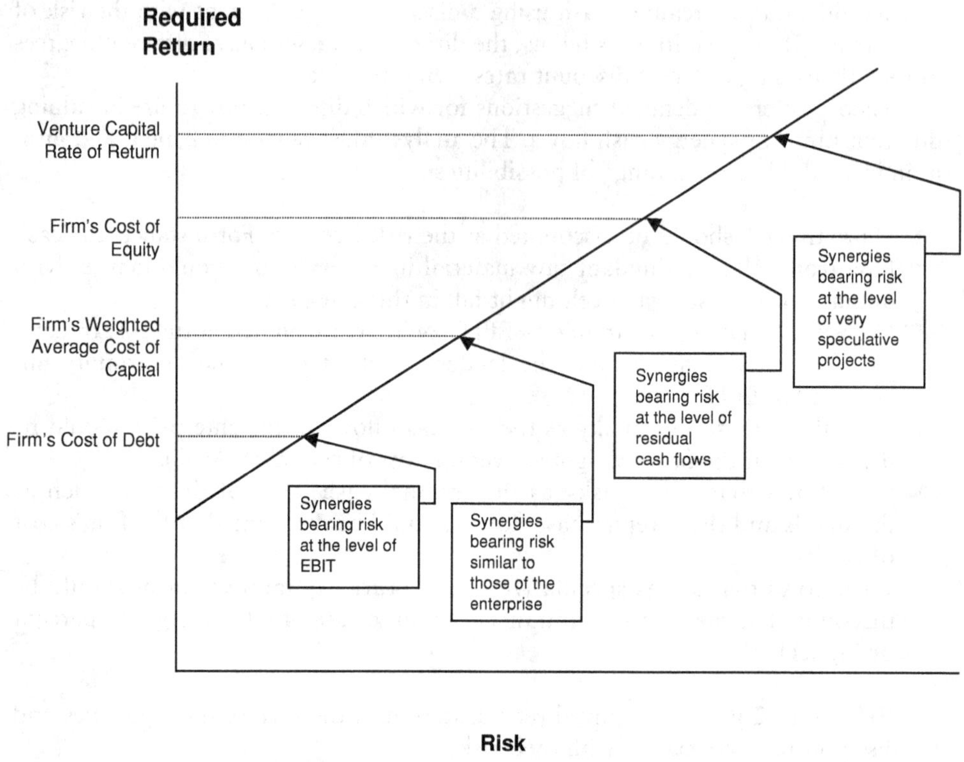

EXHIBIT 11.2 Tailor the Discount Rate for Synergies to Their Risk

The practical conclusion of all this is that the professional M&A analyst should start from the WACC (if valuing the target as an enterprise) or cost of equity (if valuing the target's equity) and then prepare to adjust the discount rate for synergies upward or downward to reflect the analyst's judgment about the degree of risk in those synergies.

Reflect Inflation, Real Growth, and a Reasonable Life

Most synergy estimates are at best one-year forecasts. Yet the reality is that synergies in costs, taxes, WACC, and revenues could continue for a long time. One must capture the entire expected life of the synergies. The discounted cash flow framework can give a means of valuing these synergies. The venerable constant growth model can capitalize a perpetually growing synergy stream.

Growth of synergy begs scrutiny of the rate. As Chapter 9 suggests, this growth rate can be modeled as the product of inflation and real growth, in a Fisher Equation. One must weigh the prospect for both sources of growth. Revenue synergies are almost certainly subject to both forms of growth. But cost synergies may or may not be. Tax and WACC synergies are probably unaffected by real growth, and maybe even inflation. Asset reduction synergies, largely being one-time or short-term benefits, are also unaffected.

Use a Terminal Value to Reflect Extended Life of Synergies

Terminal value is frequently overlooked or assumed to be nil out of an arbitrary sense of conservatism. Of course, one should always scrutinize the assumption that cost savings can be sustained indefinitely. But if they can, then including a terminal value is essential. This terminal value can be estimated using the approaches described in Chapter 9—the constant growth valuation model is perhaps the best to use because it permits closer scrutiny of the effect of variations in basic assumptions.

Be Flexible: $X(A + B) = XA + XB$

Adapt the assessment of synergies to the problem at hand. Some analysts prefer to enter the synergy effects into the valuation of the entire firm, thus producing different case results. Other analysts prefer to estimate separately the stand-alone value of the firm and synergy values. *These two approaches should yield the same estimate of the value of the firm with synergies*, under the basic principle of algebra: $X(A + B) = XA + XB$.

$$PV(CF_{\text{Alone}} + CF_{\text{Synergies}}) = PV(CF_{\text{Alone}}) + PV(CF_{\text{Synergies}}) \quad (3)$$

"PV" stands for "present value of . . ." and is the discounting operator. "CF" stands for cash flow.

The equivalence of these two approaches permits the analyst to tailor the approach to the requirements of the situation. The disaggregated approach will be useful where one needs to isolate the synergy effects for clarity. The aggregated approach will be useful where one wishes to show the impact of synergies on the total financial results of Newco.

Example: Valuing Cost Saving and Asset Reduction Synergies

Suppose that managers anticipate cost savings pretax of $50 million in the first year of the deal, and $100 million the next, and that thereafter the savings would grow at the rate of inflation, 2 percent. The marginal tax rate is 40 percent. The firm must invest $1 billion to achieve these savings, and starting in the third year, must spend 5 percent of the pretax savings to sustain the rate of savings. As part of the rationalization of operations, some assets will be sold, generating a positive cash flow of $20 million net of tax in years 1 and 2, and $10 million in year 3. The analyst judges that these cost savings are *rather certain*, reflecting a degree of risk consistent with the variability in the firm's EBIT. Accordingly, the analyst decides to discount the cash flows at the firm's cost of debt of 6 percent.

Exhibit 11.3 lays out the flows of cash associated with the cost savings and asset reduction. Discounted at the rate of 6 percent, the present value of these flows is $428 million. The internal rate of return on the outlays associated with the restructuring is 15 percent. Note that the bulk of this synergy value derives from the terminal value.

Example: Valuing Revenue Enhancement Synergies

In this example, managers conclude that the combination of two firms will expand revenues through cross-selling of products, efficient exploitation of brands,

EXHIBIT 11.3 Example: Valuing Cost Savings and Asset Reduction Synergies

	Year					
	0	1	2	3	4	5
1 Pretax cost savings, constant dollars		$50	$100	$100	$100	$100
2 Expected inflation rate		2%	2%	2%	2%	2%
3 Growth rate of FCF (nominal), in perpetuity	2%					
4 Discount rate	6%					
5 Ongoing investment/savings (year 3+)	5%					
6 Pretax cost savings, current dollars		$51	$104	$106	$108	$110
7 Tax expense (@ .40)		(20)	(42)	(42)	(43)	(44)
8 After-tax cost savings		31	62	64	65	66
9 Less: investment necessary to realize the savings	$(1,000)			(5)	(5)	(6)
10 Plus: disinvestment associated with the savings		20	20	10	—	—
11 Subtotal	(1,000)	51	82	68	60	61
12 Terminal value						1,548
13 Free cash flow	$(1,000)	$51	$82	$68	$60	$1,609
14 Net present value of cost savings	$428					
15 Internal rate of return of synergy investment	15%					

and geographic and product line extension. They forecast revenue growth of $100 million in the first year and $200 million in year 2 and thereafter. The cost of goods underlying these new revenues is 45 percent of the revenues. This forecast is in constant dollar terms and needs to reflect expected inflation of 2 percent per year. To achieve these synergies will require an investment of $400 million initially, and 5 percent of the added revenue each year, to fund working capital growth.

Exhibit 11.4 gives the cash flows associated with the revenue enhancements (assuming a higher degree of risk on the new revenue-generating activities). Discounted at the firm's cost of equity, the present value of these flows is $50 million, with an internal rate of return (IRR) of 18 percent.

Example: Valuing Financial Synergies

The simplest financial synergy to value is an expansion of Newco's debt capacity beyond the simple sum of the buyer and target firms. This arises from Lewellen's coinsurance effect. Assuming Newco increases its borrowings to the new, higher optimum, then the gain in value is simply the present value of additional debt tax shields. Under assumptions outlined in Chapters 9 and 13, this could be estimated simply as the marginal tax rate times the increased perpetual debt outstanding.

As noted earlier, the other form of financial synergy, WACC reduction, should be valued cautiously and skeptically, for it assumes that financial securities of the

EXHIBIT 11.4 Example: Valuing Revenue Enhancement Synergies

		Year					
		0	1	2	3	4	5
1 Revenue enhancements, constant dollars			$100	$200	$200	$200	$200
2 Expected inflation rate			2%	2%	2%	2%	2%
3 Growth rate of FCF (nominal), in perpetuity	*3%*						
4 Discount rate	*15%*						
5 Ongoing investment/revenue (year 1+)	*5%*						
6 Operating cost/revenues	*45%*						
7 Revenue enhancements, current dollars			$102	$208	$212	$216	$221
8 Operating costs to support revenue enhancements			(46)	(94)	(96)	(97)	(99)
9 Tax expense (@ .40)			(22)	(46)	(47)	(48)	(49)
10 After-tax cost savings			34	69	70	71	73
11 Less: investment necessary to realize the added revenue		$(400)	(5)	(10)	(11)	(11)	(11)
12 Plus: disinvestment associated with the revenue			10	5	—	—	—
13 Subtotal		(400)	39	63	59	61	62
14 Terminal value							$531
15 Free cash flow		$(400)	$ 39	$ 63	$ 59	$61	$593
16 Net present value of cost savings		$50					
17 Internal rate of return of synergy investment		18%					

buyer and target are inefficiently priced. To illustrate where the inefficiency occurs, consider the following case. Suppose that managers believe that a combination of the two firms will reduce the risk of the combined enterprise more than investors could achieve through simple portfolio diversification. This belief springs from the fact that one of the firms holds secret proprietary processes that are unknown by public investors. These processes will dampen the volatility of earnings. Analysts believe that this volatility reduction equates to a reduction in the asset beta of Newco of –0.10 from a simple weighted average of the asset betas of the two firms. The key assumption here is that the equity market does not anticipate this reduction.

Exhibit 11.5 shows the calculations associated with this asset beta reduction. Line 4 of the exhibit calculates the dollar cost of capital of Newco with and without the asset beta reduction. Line 5 shows the annuity value of this saving. In the exhibit, the unexpected reduction of asset beta yields a decrease in WACC by 60 basis points, worth $77 million if Newco's market value of capital is $12 billion. The present value of this annual saving is $760 million. As the example suggests, it does not require much of a reduction in asset beta to produce a material financial synergy. But the analyst should always approach projections of such synergies very cautiously. Although, as Chapters

EXHIBIT 11.5 Valuing Financial Synergies

	Buyer (Before)	Target (Before)	Sum of Buyer and Target (Before)	Newco	Value Impact
1 Weighted average cost of capital, before the acquisition	10.2%	11.2%	10.7%		
2 Newco's weighted average cost of capital, after the acquisition				10.1%	
3 Total capital of buyer and target, before the acquisition	$6,000	$6,000		$12,000	
4 Dollar cost of capital	$612	$674	$1,286	$1,209	$77
5 Implied present value of financial synergies from acquisition					$760
Calculation of Newco's Cost of Capital after Acquisition					
6 ***Cost of equity estimate***	**12.0%**	**15.5%**		**12.6%**	
7 Beta of buyer, before the acquisition	1.00				
8 Beta of target, before the acquisition		1.50			
9 Unlevered beta	0.83	1.01		0.92	
10 Adjustment in Newco asset beta because of covariance unanticipated by market				–0.10	
11 Market value weight of buyer in Newco (%)	50%				
12 Market value weight of target in Newco (%)		50%			
13 Beta of Newco				1.08	
14 Risk-free rate of return	0.05	0.05		0.05	
15 Equity market risk premium	0.07	0.07		0.07	
16 Cost of equity from CAPM	12.0%	15.5%		12.6%	
17 ***Cost of debt estimate***	**4.8%**	**6.0%**		**5.4%**	
18 New rating associated with Newco's target capital structure	AA	BBB		A	
19 Average maturity of debt associated with target capital structure (in years)	7	7		7	
20 Current *pretax* yields on debt, at rating and tenor or Newco	8.0%	10.0%		9.0%	
21 Marginal tax rate for Newco	40.0%	40.0%		40.0%	
22 After-tax cost of debt for Newco	4.8%	6.0%		5.4%	
Weights in target capital structure for Newco					
23 Targeted weight of debt (%)	25%	45%		35%	
24 Targeted weight of equity (%)	75%	55%		65%	

4 and 20 show, inefficient valuation of securities can occur at peaks of the M&A cycle, and claims of inefficiency are easily abused. Best practice imposes a high burden of proof on analysts who place much emphasis on likely WACC reduction synergies.

Example: Valuing Real Option Synergies

Options values are driven by six parameters: price of the underlying asset, exercise price, term of the option, volatility of returns on the underlying asset, the risk-free rate of return, and dividends, if any. Here's an illustration. Suppose you are considering acquiring a small, profitable technology firm, which has just obtained patents on a new process that *might* be applicable to your business. You won't know how useful these processes will be until you buy the firm and invest in a little more development research. Your estimate of the intrinsic value of the target, based on its *predictable, expected* cash flows, is $100 million. The seller won't settle for less than $120 million. On the basis of what is known right now, the deal looks like a loser if there are no real option synergies:

$$\text{Price} > V_{\text{cash flows}}^{\text{Expected}} + V_{\text{synergies}}^{\text{Contingent}} \tag{4}$$

$$\$120 \text{ mm} > \$100 \text{ mm} + ? \tag{5}$$

But it is possible that the acquisition of the new process technology might create an opportunity to extract more synergy value from the combination of the two firms. What is the real option synergy value worth?

The acquisition grants the buyer a right to apply the new process technology. Casting the acquisition of enabling technologies into this framework yields the drivers shown in Exhibit 11.6. Suppose that for the sake of simplicity,[8] you decide to model this synergy value as a simple call option. Inserting the parameters into the Black-Scholes option pricing model ("Option Valuation.xls," found on the CD-ROM) yields a relatively large real option synergy value, $28.06 million. This may seem counterintuitive, since the option is deeply out of the money. A little sensitivity analysis reveals that the high option value derives from the relatively long term and very high volatility of the technology. In other words, what makes the synergy value from acquiring the enabling technology so large is the good chance that the option will be in the money someday (i.e., the good chance derives from the option's long life and high volatility).

The real option synergy value turns the acquisition into a winner. Your estimated value of the target is now higher than the asking price:

$$\text{Price} < V_{\text{cash flows}}^{\text{Expected}} + V_{\text{synergies}}^{\text{Contingent}} \tag{6}$$

$$\$120 \text{ mm} < \$100 \text{ mm} + \$28.06 \text{ mm} \tag{7}$$

Example: Backsolving for the Required Synergies from the Acquisition Premium

The uncertainty surrounding most synergy estimates will make decision makers uncomfortable and even cynical about these estimates. Skepticism is a useful attitude when assessing synergies, but it can also blind decision makers to the possibilities in

EXHIBIT 11.6 Illustration of Valuing an Enabling Technology as a Call Option

Option Value Driver	Application to Acquisition of Enabling Technology	Parameter
Price of underlying asset	This is the present value of expected future cash flows from the new technology. Suppose your analysts say that this product line could yield cash flows of as much as $2 billion per year. But you are a realist, and make decisions on present expected values. You ascribe a present expected value of $50 million to the new technology, based on what you know today.	$50 million
Exercise price	To actually commercialize the new technology, if and when you choose to do it, will take an investment of $500 million.	$500 million
Dividends	If you were to exercise this option immediately, it would start throwing off some cash. By waiting, you forgo the cash flow. Incorporating the forgone dividend from this technology into your assessment is important. The dividends reflect your impatience to exercise the option out of a concern for being first, not getting scooped, or defining the market. You guess that the cash flow would be $3 million per year initially, and that it would vary with the volatility of returns.	$3 million
Term	Patent protection gives you an exclusive right to exploit this synergy. If you add in the nonexclusive period thereafter, this is a potentially very long-lived option. Offsetting this is the rate of technological innovation in the field. Your best guess is that this technology will dominate others for a shorter period, such as 10 years.	10 years
Volatility	The uncertainty about the returns from this project is huge as the discussion of price of the underlying asset implies. Your staff runs a Monte Carlo simulation of IRRs on the enabling technology, and concludes that the standard deviation of returns is about 80%. You choose 80% because it is very much higher than the volatilities for more stable investments.	80%
Risk-free rate	The yield on the 10-year U.S. Treasury bond is 7 percent. You choose a bond whose life is contemporaneous with the life of the option.	7%
Real option synergy value from acquiring the enabling technology		**$28.06 million**

a deal. One way to address the problem is to reverse the inquiry and ask, *what synergies are necessary to make this an economically attractive deal given the price necessary to do the deal?* This synergy value can then be backsolved for the pretax cost savings, asset reductions, revenue enhancements, financial synergies, and contingencies necessary to produce that value. Operating managers and chief executives generally find it easy to assess the likelihood of achieving annual improvements in costs, revenues, and reductions in assets. In other words, the backsolving approach helps managers test the feasibility of synergies required to justify the deal.

The personal computer and a spreadsheet program make backsolving relatively easy. The program "Valuing Synergies.xls," found on the CD-ROM, contains the basic examples given in the preceding sections. Excel spreadsheet software contains two tools that are useful in the backsolving exercise. The first is "Goal Seek," which varies the value in an assumption cell until a formula that depends on that cell yields the result you want. The second is "Solver," which varies more than one cell used in a formula to produce the result you want.

To illustrate the backsolving process using the "Goal Seek" feature, reconsider the cost saving synergy example given earlier in this chapter. Suppose that the deal designer needs a present value of synergies of at least $1 billion in order to justify a deal. The analyst should click on "Tools" and "Goal Seek," and then at the prompt indicate the cell address for the NPV of synergies, the target amount ($1,000), and the cell to be varied (pretax cost savings starting in year 2). The result is that constant dollar pretax cost savings of $142 million are needed starting in year 2 in order to generate NPV of synergies equal to $1 billion. The resulting analysis is given in Exhibit 11.7. An analysis like this is easily replicated for asset reductions, revenue enhancements, and WACC reductions.

Knowing that he or she must generate constant dollar pretax savings of $142 million in order to justify the deal, the executive can research possible sources, and interview the operating managers about the likelihood of attaining those savings. This kind of research must be conducted carefully, as CEOs might simply be told the answers they want to hear. Furthermore, if the entire organization is in the grip of deal frenzy, there may be a tendency to bless any synergy assumptions simply to consummate the deal. In short, backsolving with the aid of a computer appears to be rigorous, but is no guarantee of rationality. As argued repeatedly in this volume, discipline is an indispensable virtue.

SYNERGIES IN THE DAIMLER/CHRYSLER MERGER

In the spring of 1998, the CEOs of Chrysler Corporation and Daimler-Benz A.G. sought to structure the terms of merger. More details of this situation are given in Chapter 9 ("Valuing Firms"). The executives rationalized the merger in terms of the economic benefits to be created. Thus, an estimate of the size of these joint gains would be influential, and perhaps decisive, in the shareholders' conclusions about the deal. How much value would the merger create?

The analysis of synergies should follow this range of steps:

1. ***Identify.*** Many CEOs will simply set targets for synergies, based on the belief that it will be possible to wring savings out of the two companies in a merger—

EXHIBIT 11.7 Illustration of Backsolving to Find the Required Constant Dollar Pretax Cost Savings in Years 2 and Beyond Necessary to Yield Present Value of Synergies of $1 Billion

	Year					
	0	1	2	3	4	5
1 Pretax cost savings, constant dollars		$50	$142	$142	$142	$142
2 Expected inflation rate		2%	2%	2%	2%	2%
3 Growth rate of FCF (nominal), in perpetuity	2%					
4 Discount rate	6%					
5 Ongoing investment/savings (year 3+)	5%					
6 Pretax cost savings, current dollars		$51	$148	$151	$154	$157
7 Tax expense (@ .40)		(20)	(59)	(60)	(62)	(63)
8 After-tax cost savings		31	89	91	92	94
9 Less: investment necessary to realize the savings	$(1,000)			(8)	(8)	(8)
10 Plus: disinvestment associated with the savings		20	20	10	—	—
11 Subtotal	(1,000)	51	109	93	85	86
12 Terminal value						2,202
13 Free cash flow	$(1,000)	$51	$109	$93	$85	$2,289
14 Net present value of cost savings	$1,000					
15 Internal rate of return of synergy investment	23%					

this casual approach to synergy planning is surely the route to disappointment. Instead, analysts should consider carefully where the savings might come from, their timing, and their size. The list of synergy sources given earlier in this chapter affords a framework for identifying the possible range of savings. Exhibit 11.8 gives a hypothetical listing of the synergies the two CEOs considered in the deal between Daimler-Benz and Chrysler.

2. ***Scrutinize.*** After identifying all possible synergies, one must judge them with cold realism. All synergies are not created equal: Some are more likely than others; some can be realized speedily, others only after great exertion. The step of scrutinizing the potential synergies is essentially the step of thinking like an investor (see Chapter 9). Synergies that are far-fetched or have a complicated story simply will not be credible, and might endanger shareholder approval of the deal. Exhibit 11.8 gives a critique of the hypothesized synergies in the deal.
3. ***Value.*** The cost savings synergies survived the test of scrutiny. Exhibit 11.9 enters them into the model, "Valuing Synergies.xls," on the CD-ROM.

- *Base case.* The pretax savings are projected to grow in a straight line from $1.4 billion to $3.0 billion from 1999 to 2001, and thereafter to grow at the rate of inflation, about 2.5 percent. The investment necessary to generate this

EXHIBIT 11.8 Identification of Potential Synergies, Merger of Daimler-Benz and Chrysler

Synergy Category	Hypothesized Synergies	Comments upon Scrutiny
Cost savings	Savings in purchasing (from greater power over suppliers) and in new product design and development. As subsequently reported, these savings were expected to amount to $1.4 billion in 1999 and $3.0 billion by 2001.	Because the product lines of the two firms did not overlap materially, it seemed unlikely that savings would accrue from consolidating plants or distribution channels. But savings from purchasing and development were fairly credible estimates, compared to the experience from other mergers in the automotive industry. Unclear in the case of this merger would be the size of any outlays necessary to realize these savings.
Asset reductions	Savings from closing redundant offices and plants.	Given the complementary nature of the two firm's automotive businesses, it was unclear what redundancies might be created in the merger. Chrysler's headquarters in Bloomfield Hills, Michigan, might be necessary to house the management of the North American business of the new firm.
Revenue enhancements	Sell more units at higher prices.	Neither sources of enhancement seemed likely in the case of the Daimler/Chrysler merger. The plan of the two CEOs was to preserve the separate brand names and dealership structures for Chrysler and Daimler. Therefore, it seemed unlikely that Chrysler would benefit from a rebranding effect from its association with Mercedes-Benz.
Financing synergies	Reduction of WACC from cross-border combination.	WACC reduction assumed failure of arbitrage between U.S. and Germany, which is not realistic. Anyway, Daimler-Benz was listed on the NYSE for trading.
Real option synergies	The merger might give Chrysler an entrée into Europe, a continent that it had not penetrated as successfully as the other two major American auto firms. Chrysler's Jeep brand and its minivans were appealing to European consumers. Technology transfer was also an important real option benefit.	On the other hand, Europe had serious overcapacity in its automotive industry, and other manufacturers were offering competing models. The benefit of this entry option might not be material. The cultural gulf between the two firms might impede the rate and timing of transfers of know-how.

(Continued)

EXHIBIT 11.8 *(Continued)*

Synergy Category	Hypothesized Synergies	Comments upon Scrutiny
	Chrysler was a champion at rapid model design and production. Mercedes was known for its production quality and engineering. The option to transfer this firm-specific know-how might create value	

EXHIBIT 11.9 Base-Case Estimate of Synergy Value, Merger of Daimler-Benz and Chrysler (Values in Millions of Dollars, Except for per-Share Amounts)

		Year					
		0 1998	1 1999	2 2000	3 2001	4 2002	5 2003
1 Pretax cost savings, constant dollars			$1,400	$2,200	$3,000	$3,000	$3,000
2 Expected inflation rate			2.5%	2.5%	2.5%	2.5%	2.5%
3 Growth rate of FCF (nominal), in perpetuity	2.5%						
4 Discount rate	8.1%						
5 Ongoing investment/ savings (year 3+)	2%						
6 Tax rate	38.5%						
7 Pretax cost savings, current dollars			$1,435	$2,311	$3,231	$3,311	$3,394
8 Tax expense			(552)	(890)	(1,244)	(1,275)	(1,307)
9 After-tax cost savings			883	1,421	1,987	2,037	2,087
10 Less: investment necessary to realize the savings		$(1,000)			(65)	(66)	(68)
11 Plus: disinvestment associated with the savings			—	—	—	—	—
12 Subtotal		(1,000)	883	1,421	1,922	1,970	2,020
13 Terminal value							36,965
14 Free cash flow		$(1,000)	$883	$1,421	$1,922	$1,970	$38,985
15 Net present value of cost savings	**$34,986**						
16 Internal rate of return of synergy investment	**163%**						
17 Number of Chrysler Corporation shares	648.4						
18 Value of synergy per Chrysler share	**$53.96**						

savings is assumed to be 2 percent. The WACC and tax rate are 8.1 and 38.5 percent respectively, consistent with the discussion in Chapter 9. An initial investment of $1 billion for tooling, technology transfer, and other costs is also assumed. The base-case estimate of the present value of this stream of cost savings is $34.9 billion, which translates to $53.96 per share of Chrysler stock. This is a huge creation of joint value, especially when measured against the intrinsic value of Chrysler shares, estimated in Chapter 9 as between $50 and $65 per share. Remember that the estimate of synergy value is over and above the estimate of intrinsic value of the target firm on a stand-alone basis.

- *Sensitivity analysis.* Perhaps the savings estimate has been irrationally exuberant. Exhibit 11.10 tests the sensitivity of the synergy value to variations in growth rate and investment. Under sensitivity tests, the values of synergy per Chrysler share remain large. Even assuming that the cash flows experience zero growth per year and that the initial outlay to realize these savings is $1.4 billion, the synergy value per Chrysler share is $34.46, still sizable compared to Chrysler's intrinsic value.
- *Backsolving analysis.* One can exercise the model in reverse to determine a range of breakeven assumptions necessary to generate acceptable outcomes. For instance, the constant dollar cost savings in the third year and thereafter necessary to generate synergies that will yield only a 15 percent IRR despite a $1 billion investment is negative. In other words, simply to reach a rate of return that would merely be acceptable in most large industrial corporations would require a dramatic erosion of actual performance from projected, on the order of half.
- *Extensions.* The analyst should anticipate possible extensions of the valuation analysis, which might not be reported in a first-cut assessment. Premier among these would be the effect of a *cyclical downturn* on the synergy benefits. After all, the automotive industry is highly cyclical, and by 1998 the U.S. economy was already in the late stages of an economic expansion. Further modeling work could shed light on synergy values in various economic scenarios, as well as sensitivities and breakevens within those scenarios.
- *Triangulate toward a range of estimates of synergy value.* Many of the assumptions in the base-case estimate are conservative: any growth in the synergy savings is merely at the rate of inflation. Unknown is how liberal are the projections of $1.4 billion rising to $3.0 billion in two years. Ideally the analyst would be within, or close to, the merging firms, and be able to gauge the realism of the savings. Lacking inside information, the sheer size of the $53.96 synergy value per share seems optimistic—this could form the high end of one's triangulation range. A skeptical analyst might favor a scenario of eroding benefits and higher investments, which would be consistent with synergy values of around $25 per share (from Exhibit 11.10).

EXHIBIT 11.10 Sensitivity Analysis of Synergy Values per Chrysler Share in the Merger of Daimler-Benz and Chrysler (Values in Dollars per Share)

Initial Investment Outlay Necessary to Realize Savings	Growth Rate of Savings			
	–2.5%	0.0%	2.5%	5.0%
$ —	$26.69	$36.62	$55.50	$105.01
$ (250)	$26.30	$36.23	$55.11	$104.62
$ (500)	$25.91	$35.84	$54.73	$104.24
$(1,000)	$25.14	$35.07	$53.96	$103.46
$(1,400)	$24.53	$34.46	$53.34	$102.85

4. *Prepare implications for deal designers and negotiators.* The main insight from this analysis is that the merger will create significant value; the CEOs of the two firms should develop a communication effort to the shareholders that builds credibility in these savings. Second, synergies of approximately $25 to $54 per share are a joint surplus that remains to be divided in structuring a deal. Obviously, Daimler-Benz would not want to pay more for Chrysler than Chrysler's stand-alone value plus value of synergies. Choice of the form of payment can affect how the synergy value gets allocated between the shareholders of Daimler-Benz and Chrysler. Third, the CEOs will need to give careful thought to structuring the postmerger integration plan in order to achieve these savings. It may be necessary to motivate managers with special plans and compensation targeted toward the achievement of these savings.

RULES OF THUMB

One of the most important reasons to exercise caution and discipline in M&A analysis is that there are almost no respectable benchmarks against which to test the reasonableness of synergy assumptions. The problem arises from the uniqueness of companies, and the economic forces in different industries. But in a few industries experiencing a high volume of deals, it is possible to derive some expectations about where synergies should be relatively higher and lower:

- Highest in horizontal deals; middling in vertical combinations; lowest in conglomerate deals. Generally, the work of Rumelt (1986) suggests that returns on investment depend on the strategic relatedness of the buyer and target firms. Unrelated firms will have fewer opportunities for cost savings, revenue enhancements, and the like.
- Highest in *in-market deals*; lower in *market extension deals*.[9] Rhoades[10] reports that in-market bank mergers show cost savings equal to 30 to 40 percent of the target bank's noninterest expense. Gilson and Escalle[11] report research by the Mitchell Madison Group that affords an interesting comparison: The market-extension merger of First Union and First Fidelity banks in 1995 produced synergies of only 5 percent of the target's noninterest expense. This disparity is even sharper in functional areas of banks. For instance, for in-market mergers, the savings are 35 percent for branch networks and 40 percent for staff, systems, and operations. In contrast, for market extension deals, the savings are 5 percent for branch networks and 20 percent for systems and operations.

CONCLUSION: OBJECTIVITY ABOVE ALL ELSE

The examples and discussion in this chapter validate an important insight: "Synergy" can be a fluffy concept; its value implications are easily overblown. Michael Goold and Andrew Campbell wrote, "Most corporate executives, whether or not they have any special insight into synergy opportunities or aptitude for nurturing collaboration, feel they *ought* to be creating synergy. . . . The synergy bias becomes an obsession for some executives. Desperately seeking synergy, they make unwise decisions and investments."[12]

The first defense against this is to apply tools of rigorous analysis to gain clarity about the size and variability of synergy values. The second defense is skepticism: in competitive markets it is difficult to win sustained, supernormal rates of return for very long. One must always scrutinize the source of synergy, and ultimately ask why someone else hasn't tried it before, or how long it will be until a competitor imitates the source of synergy. In addition, one must ask, "Does this reputed 'synergy' do something for shareholders that they cannot do for themselves?" It was in this spirit of skepticism that Warren Buffett offered the following comment:

> *Many managers were apparently over-exposed in impressionable childhood years to the story in which the imprisoned, handsome prince is released from the toad's body by a kiss from the beautiful princess. Consequently they are certain that the managerial kiss will do wonders for the profitability of the target company. Such optimism is essential. Absent that rosy view, why else should the shareholders of company A want to own an interest in B at a takeover cost that is two times the market price they'd pay if they made direct purchases on their own? In other words investors can always buy toads at the going price for toads. If investors instead bankroll princesses who wish to pay double for the right to kiss the toad, those kisses better pack some real dynamite. We've observed many kisses, but very few miracles. Nevertheless, many managerial princesses remain serenely confident about the future potency of their kisses, even after their corporate backyards are knee-deep in unresponsive toads.*[13]

NOTES

1. Sirower (1997), page 5.
2. For more on this case, see Bruner (1983).
3. Myers (1977).
4. Quoted from Houston and Ryngaert (1996), page 76.
5. See Merton and Perold (1993).
6. Interview with Ron Mitsch, January 27, 2000.
7. S-4 Registration Statement filed with the Securities and Exchange Commission, December 2000, by Quaker Oats and PepsiCo, page I-67.
8. Chapter 14 surveys the range of real option valuation methods, most of which are more flexible to the nuances of valuing an R&D program than is the Black-Scholes option pricing model used in the illustration here. Black-Scholes is applied here only for simplicity of illustration.
9. In-market deals combine two firms in the same geographical market. Market-extension deals combine two firms in differing geographical markets.
10. Reported in Rhoades (1998), page 285.
11. See Gilson and Escalle (1998).
12. Quoted from Goold and Campbell (1998), page 132.
13. Quoted from the Chairman's Letter to Shareholders (written by Warren Buffett), Berkshire Hathaway Annual Report, 1981. Copyright © 1981 by Berkshire Hathaway. Reprinted by permission of Warren E. Buffett.

CHAPTER 12

Valuing the Firm across Borders

INTRODUCTION

When the buyer and target firm are in different countries, special challenges arise for valuation. This chapter explores ways in which borders are disruptive to the analyst and how to deal with them. Even practitioners with a purely domestic focus should consider these issues. As Chapter 5 argued, cross-border M&A activity is sizable and likely to grow. The foreign buyer or target influences domestic prices, M&A practices, and deal structures. It is a mistake to think that cross-border M&A is like domestic M&A but in different currency. In fact, going across borders affects many of the valuation assumptions outlined in various chapters of this book. Thus, this chapter enlarges upon the valuation story. The chief lessons include these:

- *Cross-border M&A is different.* The tools and concepts of valuation and strategy, as outlined in previous chapters, remain relevant for deals done across borders. But one needs to factor in differences in inflation, currency, taxes, accounting, law, and culture and the possibility that the foreign country may not be very well integrated into the global capital markets.
- *There are two ways to value.* Under conventional assumptions, you can value a target in foreign local terms or in home terms—and adjusting for the differences in currency, the investment attractiveness of the deal should be the same. This equivalence grants you some flexibility in how you approach valuation, thanks to a concept called *interest rate parity*, and assuming no political or segmentation risk.
- *Adjustments in cash flows or discount rates.* The way to accommodate the cross-border differences in valuation is by adjusting either the cash flows or the rate at which you discount them. Adjusting the cash flows will be arbitrary and vulnerable to the analyst's biases. Adjusting the discount rates relies on capital market information. Three models are highlighted in this chapter.

HOW BORDERS AFFECT M&A VALUATION

Any mastery of cross-border valuation must be founded upon an understanding of the peculiar challenges raised by variations in business across countries. In particular, one should regard nice sources of variation: inflation, *foreign currency ex-*

change rates, tax rates, the timing of cash remittance, political risk, market segmentation, governance, accounting principles, and social/cultural issues.

Inflation

As outlined in Chapter 5, entry into a foreign country entails a "bet" on the macroeconomic policies of that country—these policies can vary dramatically and produce widely differing inflation rates and exchange rate uncertainty. Exhibit 12.1 identifies the countries with the highest and lowest consumer price inflation rates during the 1990s. Plainly, it is inappropriate to apply the inflation rate of either the United States or Organization for Economic Cooperation and Development (OECD) countries or the world economy to all individual countries. The differences matter because inflation affects forecasted local cash flows and local discount rates. A challenge for the analyst is to ensure that inflation assumptions are handled consistently throughout the valuation analysis. A challenge for the practitioner is to understand that analysts debate the relative merits of valuing real cash flows or nominal cash flows and that therefore he or she must develop an individual view on how to adjust for inflation. (Adjustments for inflation are discussed further in the section on valuing real versus nominal cash flows and translating foreign currency cash flows into home currency later in this chapter.)

EXHIBIT 12.1 Inflation by Country

Country	Inflation Rate
Highest inflation, 1996–2001	
Angola	235.8%
Belarus	117.1%
Bulgaria	75.7%
Turkey	68.4%
Romania	63.2%
Laos	49.6%
Ecuador	48.8%
Zimbabwe	40.5%
Suriname	36.4%
Russia	31.9%
Lowest inflation, 1990–2000	
China	0.3%
Japan	0.1%
Bahrain	0.0%
Hong Kong	–0.2%
Syria	–0.3%
Argentina	–0.4%
Saudi Arabia	–0.6%
Central African Republic	–0.6%
Azerbaijan	–0.6%
Lesotho	–0.9%

Source of data: Pocket World in Figures, 2003 Edition, London: *The Economist* and Profile Books Ltd., 2002.

Foreign Currency Exchange Rates

Inflation also affects currency exchange rates, which, as Chapter 5 discusses, can be major influences on M&A activity and valuation. Drawing upon the theories of interest rate parity and the Fisher Equation, economists hypothesize a relationship between the inflation rate differences between two countries, and the foreign exchange rate between the two currencies. If there were one worldwide currency in which to estimate values, the valuation task would be simple. But given the presence of a multitude of currencies, the analyst is confronted with the need to reconcile the differences between a foreign (or "local") currency and the home currency. What makes this particularly challenging is that the differences vary over time and across pairs of currencies. Exhibit 12.2 shows the movement in exchange rates between the U.S. dollars and the Japanese Yen, euro, Thai baht, and New Zealand dollar. Plainly, exchange rates do not sit still, as they demonstrate drift over time. Even worse, during crises, exchange rates may display *contagion*, "the propagation of shocks among markets in excess of the transmission explained by fundamentals." (Rigobon 2002, page 5) If and when markets act rationally, however, the economic theories of purchasing power parity (PPP)[1] and interest rate parity (IRP) suggest that there is a relationship between average investment returns in a country and that country's spot and forward foreign exchange rates such that exchange rates will always adjust to reflect the inflation outlook in a country. Inflation rate changes and foreign currency exchange rates tend to compensate for one another: Though you might feel richer because of a foreign exchange rate movement, such a feeling is just a "money illusion" because your sense of wealth comes from inflation, not real returns.

To show how this trading across borders might work, consider two possible investment alternatives for a U.S. investor with U.S. dollars to invest either domestically or in Mexico, and a desire to invest in the same asset (i.e., with the same risk in either country), wherever it might be:

1. Invest the U.S. dollars in the United States, and earn a dollar return appropriate for the risk of the asset.

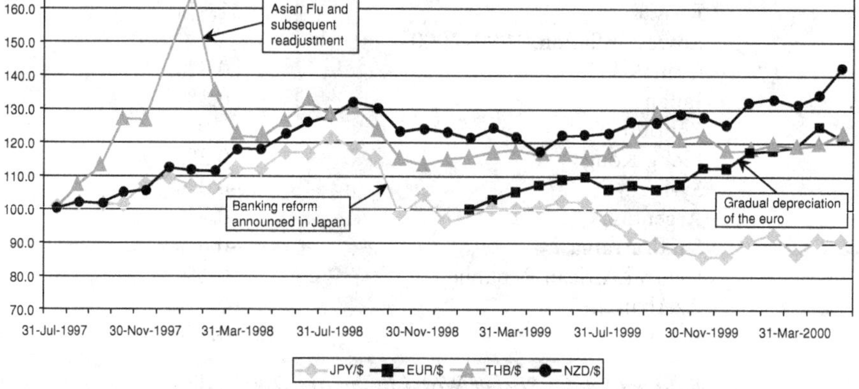

EXHIBIT 12.2 Exchange Rate Movements (7/31/97 Spot Rate as Baseline = 100)

2. Convert the U.S. dollars to Mexican pesos at the "spot" exchange rate (i.e., today's rate), and invest the pesos in Mexico to earn a return there appropriate for the risk of the same asset. Then, at the end of the holding period (say, one year) translate the value of that investment back into dollars at the exchange rate prevailing at that time. The "forward" (FWD) rate may be regarded as a reasonable estimate today of the rate expected to prevail in the future.[2]

If investors are allowed to "arbitrage" (i.e., move freely into and out of markets in order to make a profit upon differences across markets) between these two identical investments, then it is reasonable to assume that one's wealth under these two alternatives would be equal. In equilibrium, there should be no arbitrage opportunities, so the investor should be indifferent between the two alternatives. This is expressed in the following formula:

$$\$1 \cdot (1+R_{\text{Dollar}}) = \$1 \cdot SPOT_{\frac{\text{Peso}}{\text{Dollar}}} \cdot (1+R_{\text{Peso}}) \cdot \frac{1}{FWD_{\frac{\text{Peso}}{\text{Dollar}}}} \tag{1}$$

It is straightforward to rearrange the covered interest arbitrage model into the important model of interest rate parity:

$$\frac{SPOT_{\frac{\text{Peso}}{\text{Dollar}}}}{FWD_{\frac{\text{Peso}}{\text{Dollar}}}} = \frac{(1+R_{\text{Dollar}})}{(1+R_{\text{Peso}})} \tag{2}$$

In words, interest rate parity suggests that the ratio of spot and forward currency exchange rates will equal the ratio of returns in the two currencies. This is a provocative description of markets, for it suggests that currency and capital markets are linked.[3] This relationship offers a simple and practical solution to a nagging problem in cross-border valuation: forecasting exchange rates.

Tax Rates

The corporate tax rate affects both the forecasted cash flows and the discount rate—this challenges the analyst to ensure consistency of assumption throughout the valuation process. As Exhibit 12.3 shows, the marginal corporate tax rate varies substantially across countries. While the trend over the past 25 years has been toward increasing harmonization of tax rates, the exhibit suggests that it is still inappropriate to make a single tax rate assumption across all countries. This leads to the first rule of cross-border valuation: Choose a marginal tax rate appropriate to the country in which the cash flows are generated.

The question of what is truly "marginal taxation" can best be settled in consultation with expert tax counsel, but the answer will depend at least in part on the buyer country's tax system. Security/equity analysts (or tax experts) have differing opinions:

- Some analysts argue that one should use the marginal tax rate of the foreign country only. This makes sense only if the buyer resides in a country that is

EXHIBIT 12.3 Marginal Corporate Tax Rates for Selected Countries

Country	Tax Rate, January 1, 2003	Comments
Austria	34.00%	
Bangladesh	30.00%	Foreign companies are taxed at 40%.
Belgium	33.99%	Lower tax rate applies to corporations more than 50% owned by individuals.
Canada	36.60%	Federal tax plus provincial tax.
Chile	16.50%	If profits are distributed abroad, a withholding tax rate of 35% is applied, with a credit for the 16% taxes paid.
France	34.33%	Does not include a 3.3% "social contribution."
Germany	39.58%	Includes corporate tax, "solidarity surcharge," and trade tax.
Hong Kong	17.00%	
Italy	38.25%	Includes corporate and regional taxes.
Japan	42.00%	Includes corporate, prefectural, and municipal taxes.
Mexico	34.00%	Some corporate income tax liability may be deferred if earnings are reinvested.
New Zealand	33.00%	
Singapore	22.00%	
South Africa	37.80%	Includes corporate tax rate plus "Secondary Tax on Companies."
United Kingdom	30.00%	Rates vary in dependent territories.
United States	40.00%	Includes federal, state, and local taxes.

Source of data: "KPMG's Corporate Tax Rate Survey—January 2003," KPMG International.

part of a *territorial tax system* in which the buyer's country exempts foreign income from further taxation. About half of the OECD countries use a territorial tax system.

- Other analysts argue that one should use the higher of the buyer's or target's country tax rate. However, this only makes sense if the buyer resides in a country that is part of a *worldwide tax credit system*. Under such a system, the buyer's country recognizes taxes paid in a foreign country as a credit against tax liability at home. Thus, if the buyer's country tax rate is higher than the target's, the buyer will receive a credit and still be liable at home for the balance. The United States has adopted a worldwide tax credit system. The desire to reduce tax expense may motivate some companies to move their headquarters from countries with worldwide tax credit systems to countries with territorial tax systems—the wisdom of such proposals merits sharp scrutiny.

Correct analysis would dictate determining the type of tax system to which the shareholders of the parent are subject, and using the actual rate of taxation consistent with that system in your valuation analysis.

Timing of Remittance of Cash

Some countries limit the outbound movement of cash and capital. This is a particular concern in three areas. The first is financial management: Where costs to manufacture are incurred in one country but revenues are received in another country that limits the outflow of cash, it would be difficult for the manufacturer to cover the costs of production. Second, such limitations sacrifice capital mobility of corporations and expose them to risks of low or negative returns, expropriation, punitive taxation, and so on. And finally, it may affect the timing of taxes paid. Thus, the timing of remittances would seem to impose upon the analyst the responsibility not merely to forecast operating cash flows, but also to model the timing of their return to the parent—this will be especially important in investments in emerging markets with large-scale project financings and joint ventures.

Remittance controls are not an issue among developed countries. And even with developing countries, the long-term trend is toward the relaxation of capital controls. Other things equal, as long as the nonrepatriated foreign cash flow is invested to yield a zero net present value, shareholders of the parent company in the home country will benefit no more or less economically than if the funds had been repatriated and invested in zero NPV projects at home. Ultimately, parent corporations can use financial intermediaries to synthesize a repatriation of cash even though a formal transfer has not occurred.[4] For these reasons, a base-case assumption of many valuation analysts is to ignore the timing of repatriating cash.

Accounting Principles

Accounting principles used in preparing financial statements can vary materially across countries. Mueller, Gernon, and Meek (1994) identified several distinct regional profiles of principles:

- ***Anglo-American-Dutch.*** The mission of the financial reporting system in this sphere is to address the needs of investors and creditors. In comparison to other systems, it limits the use of accounting reserves[5] and affords relatively high flexibility in application of the principles to the situation of the individual company.
- ***Continental Europe.*** This financial reporting system addresses first and foremost the needs of government, especially regarding tax accounting and compliance with government planning. Financial reporting principles are less flexible and more codified; accounting practices are distinguished by the active use of reserves and in that sense more conservative.
- ***South American.*** Here also the accounting system is government-focused, with financial reporting driven by tax-basis accounting. Another distinguishing feature is the use of accounting adjustments for inflation, with which the region has had extensive experience.
- ***Mixed economies.*** Countries of Eastern Europe slowly abandoned command economy accounting and adopted market economy accounting. Accordingly, enterprises often produced two sets of financial reports. One set (e.g., still in use in Cuba) is a uniform set of financial reports prepared for government planners; the focus is on production quotas rather than on income, and balance

sheet items are dictated by a government agency, rather than drawn from market costs or values. (That is, "the lower of cost or market" has no meaning in a planned economy without free market prices.) The other set of reports is oriented toward investors and creditors along the lines of the Anglo-American-Dutch model.

- *Islamic.* Islamic finance prohibits the recognition of interest on money. Assets and liabilities are measured by current market values.
- *International Accounting Standards Committee (IASC).* Focused on the harmonization of worldwide accounting standards since its founding in 1973, the IASC has issued international accounting standards that seek to eliminate idiosyncratic differences in financial reporting practices. Adoption of these practices by corporations is voluntary. The IASC is an association of professional accounting organizations worldwide, and has no governmental authority to impose standards.

Given this global diversity, the M&A analyst should be familiar with local accounting principles. Mueller, Gernon, and Meek (1994) offer some examples:

- *Cash.* In the United States, this includes demand deposits and highly liquid investments held for short periods. In New Zealand, the balance of cash deducts short-term borrowings.
- *Expense and investment recognition.* In some countries, merger premiums, unusual gains and losses, and some financing transactions skirt the income statement entirely and are posted to shareholders' equity. Accounting rules in some nations permit the creation of secret reserves, assets held off-balance sheet and overstated liabilities, in the spirit of conservatism and to manage reported earnings. Some accruals are dictated by legal formulas rather than economics.
- *Pension accounting.* Few countries require annual revaluation of pension plan obligations. Principles for reporting pension expense and obligations vary significantly across countries.
- *Inflation accounting.* A few countries require that companies report the effects of changing prices on the financial statements.

Are these differences in accounting principles relevant? Since DCF focuses on flows of *cash* rather than accrued earnings, these national differences in accounting principles are not meaningful: Cash flow is cash flow in all countries. But the process of deriving cash flows from financial statements requires careful familiarity of accounting principles in the foreign country.

Political Risk

The extent to which local governments intervene in the working of markets and firms can have a material effect on the value of corporate assets. Such intervention could occur through regulation, punitive tax policies, restrictions on cash transfers, employment policies, and so on. Governments can also intrude through outright expropriation of assets of foreign firms, or at the extreme opposite, through the breakdown of civil order as in insurrections and civil wars. Finally, official corruption[6] may be, in effect, an alternative form of taxation. Exhibit 12.4 shows political

EXHIBIT 12.4 Country Risk Measures, at Late October 1999

Country	Sovereign Debt Ratings		Euromoney		Economist Intelligence Unit		Institutional Investor		International Country Risk Guide		
	S&P/Moody's	Fitch IBCA	Rank	Score	Rating	Score	Rank	Score	Political	Financial	Economic
Highest Ratings											
Luxembourg	AAA/Aaa	AAA	1	98.7	A	10	6	90.3	90	42.0	45.5
Switzerland	AAA/Aaa	AAA	2	97.8	A	0	1	93.0	85	45.5	44.0
United States	AAA/Aaa	AAA	3	94.5	A	15	5	90.9	88	36.0	42.0
Norway	AAA/Aaa	AAA	4	94.1	A	20	9	87.7	86	44.5	43.5
Germany	AAA/Aaa	AAA	5	93.4	A	10	2	92.0	87	39.5	40.5
Netherlands	AAA/Aaa	AAA	6	92.4	A	10	4	91.2	93	36.5	43.0
France	AAA/Aaa	AAA	7	92.3	A	5	3	91.4	79	38.5	41.0
Denmark	AA+/Aaa	AA+	8	92.3	A	10	11	85.1	89	38.5	42.0
Austria	AAA/Aaa	AAA	9	91.8	*	*	8	89.4	85	42.0	39.5
United Kingdom	AAA/Aaa	AAA	10	91.2	A	20	7	90.2	86	37.0	39.5
Japan	AAA/Aa1	AA+	11	90.9	A	10	10	86.5	78	46.0	39.5
Finland	AA+/Aaa	AAA	12	90.3	B	35	13	83.6	93	36.5	45.5
Ireland	AA+/Aaa	AAA	13	90.0	B	30	15	83.4	88	40.0	46.0
Sweden	AA+/Aa1	AA	14	89.8	A	20	19	81.2	86	35.0	44.0
Belgium	AA+/Aa1	AA	15	89.5	B	25	12	84.9	78	38.0	42.5
Canada	AA+/Aa2	AA	16	88.8	A	20	14	83.5	86	39.0	42.5
Singapore	AAA/Aa1	AA+	17	88.5	A	18	16	81.9	84	46.0	47.5
Australia	AA+/Aa2	AA	18	88.1	B	30	21	75.8	89	35.0	39.5

(Continued)

EXHIBIT 12.4 *(Continued)*

	Sovereign Debt Ratings		Euromoney		Economist Intelligence Unit		Institutional Investor		International Country Risk Guide		
Country	S&P/Moody's	Fitch IBCA	Rank	Score	Rating	Score	Rank	Score	Political	Financial	Economic
Italy	AA/Aa3	AA–	19	87.1	A	20	18	81.3	71	39.5	41.0
Spain	AA+/Aa2	AA+	20	86.6	A	20	17	81.7	74	39.0	40.5
New Zealand	AA+/Aa2	*	21	85.4	B	32	23	74.0	88	31.5	38.0
Iceland	A+/Aa3	*	22	84.4	B	30	24	67.8	88	36.5	42.0
Portugal	AA/Aa2	AA	23	82.8	A	20	20	78.4	90	34.5	39.0
Taiwan	AA+/Aa3	*	24	80.7	B	23	22	75.3	79	44.0	43.5
Bermuda	AA/Aa1	AA	25	78.0	*	*	*	*	*	*	*
Hong Kong	A/A3	A+	26	77.1	B	34	27	61.3	67	44.0	38.5
Greece	BBB/A2	BBB	27	76.8	B	39	31	59.1	76	35.0	38.5
United Arab Emirates	*/A2	*	28	75.0	B	36	25	63.2	72	42.0	39.5
Cypress	A+/A2	*	29	73.5	C	45	33	57.5	71	42.0	37.0
Malta	A/A3	A	30	71.1	*	*	26	61.6	87	37.0	37.5
Lowest Ratings											
Guinea	*	*	151	25.7	*	*	118	16.3	57	31.5	33.5
Central African Republic	*	*	152	25.6	*	*	*	*	*	*	*
Nicaragua	*/B2	*	153	25.4	D	65	123	12.1	61	20.0	24.0
Congo	*	*	154	25.0	*	*	128	9.3	40	25.0	32.5
Mozambique	*	*	155	24.5	*	*	107	19.3	60	28.5	26.5
Ethiopia	*	*	156	24.5	*	*	117	16.6	58	25.5	31.0
Angola	*	*	157	24.4	E	92	125	11.6	39	18.5	21.0

Nambia	*	*	158	23.3	B	40	67	38.0	75	41.5	37.5
Russia	SD/B3	CCC	159	23.0	D	78	105	19.3	49	33.0	24.0
FYR Macedonia	*	*	160	23.0	C	63	*	*	*	*	*
Madagascar	*	*	161	22.3	*	*	*	*	64	29.5	34.5
Rwanda	*	*	162	20.9	*	*	*	*	*	*	*
New Caledonia	*	*	163	20.2	*	*	*	*	*	*	*
Democratic Republic of Congo	*	*	164	20.0	*	*	*	*	28	27.0	23.5
Sudan	*	*	165	19.0	E	88	133	7.10	36	15.0	29.0
Myanmar (Burma)	*	*	166	18.7	E	86	112	17.9	46	40.0	32.0
Albania	*	*	167	18.6	*	*	122	12.4	58	34.5	32.5
Sao Tome & Princi	*	*	168	17.8	*	*	*	*	*	*	*
Sierra Leone	*	*	169	17.6	*	*	135	6.10	40	15.0	20.0
Guinea-Bissau	*	*	170	17.4	*	*	*	*	47	23.0	25.5
Antigua & Barbados	*	*	171	16.6	*	*	*	*	*	*	*
Libya	*	*	172	16.1	D	68	83	29.1	57	37.0	30.0
Somalia	*	*	173	16.0	*	*	*	*	26	22.0	28.5
Yugoslavia	*	*	174	14.8	E	95	130	8.2	38	25.0	25.5
Liberia	*	*	175	14.4	*	*	129	9.0	43	20.0	23.0
Suriname	*	*	176	12.2	*	*	*	*	60	30	25.5
Cuba	*/Caa1	*	177	7.4	D	65	124	12.1	58	30.5	31.5
Afghanistan	*	*	178	5.1	*	*	136	5.8	*	*	*
Iraq	*	*	179	4.0	E	96	131	7.7	32	25.0	23.5
North Korea	*	*	180	1.0	*	*	134	6.7	56	18.0	7.0

(Continued)

EXHIBIT 12.4 *(Continued)*

	Sovereign Debt Ratings		Euromoney		Economist Intelligence Unit		Institutional Investor		International Country Risk Guide		
Country	S&P/Moody's	Fitch IBCA	Rank	Score	Rating	Score	Rank	Score	Political	Financial	Economic
Bosnia & Herzegovina	*	*	*	*	*	*	*	*	*	*	*

*Not available.

Sources:

Standard & Poor's (S&P)—Assigns credit ratings to sovereign debt. S&P uses the same rating scale for sovereigns as it does for private sector companies, ranging from AAA (most creditworthy) to C (least creditworthy). In September 1999, the United States was rated AAA. More information is available at www.standardandpoors.com/ratings/sovereigns/index.htm or by calling 212-438-2400.

Moody's—Assigns credit ratings to sovereign debt. Moody's, like S&P, uses the same scale for sovereigns as it does for private sector companies. Moody's scale ranges from Aaa (least risky) to C (most risky). As of July 2000, the United States was rated Aaa. The latest ratings are available at www.moodys.com/repldata/ratings/ratsov.htm.

Fitch IBCA—Assigns credit ratings to sovereign debt. Fitch uses a rating scale similar to S&P, ranging from AAA (least risky) to C (most risky). As of July 2000, the United States was rated AAA. The latest ratings are available at www.fitchibca.com/sovereigns/sovereign_ratings/.

Euromoney—Assigns an overall risk rating to a country. *Euromoney* provides both a worldwide rank and a scaled score from 100 (least risky) to 0 (most risky). As of September 1999, the United States was ranked #3 and scored 94.5. Semiannual results are available in the March and September issues of *Euromoney* magazine.

Economist Intelligence Unit (EIU)—Assigns an overall risk rating to a country, ranging from A (least risky) to E (most risky). EIU also provides a numerical score ranging from 0 (least risky) to 100 (most risky). As of June 1999, the United States was rated an A risk with a score of 15. More information is available at www.eiu.com or by calling 212-586-0248.

Institutional Investor (II)—Assigns a creditworthiness rating to a country based on surveys of international bankers and economists. Each country is given both a score from 100 (least risky) to 0 (most risky) and a worldwide rank. As of September 1999, the United States was ranked #5 with a score of 90.9. Results are published semiannually in March and September. The latest ratings are available at www.iimagazine.com/research/interface.html.

***International Country Risk Guide (ICRG)**, published by the Political Risk Services Group*—Assigns an overall risk rating to a country, as well as separate ratings for political, financial, and economic risks. Overall ratings range from 100 (least risky) to 0 (most risky). As of June 1999, the United States was rated at 83.3, the ninth highest score. Additional information and sample data are available at www.prsgroup.com/icrg.html or by calling 315-431-0511.

and default risk measures for a subsample of the countries in the world, drawing on various independent sources:

- ***Bond ratings*** of sovereign debt, as judged by ratings agencies such as Standard & Poor's (S&P), Moody's Investors Service, and Fitch's Ratings. Assigns credit ratings to sovereign debt. S&P uses the same rating scale for sovereigns as it does for private sector companies, ranging from AAA (most creditworthy) to C (least creditworthy). Moody's scale ranges from Aaa (least risky) to C (most risky). Fitch uses a rating scale similar to S&P, ranging from AAA (least risky) to C (most risky). As of year 2000, the United States sovereign debt carried a risk rating of AAA. Thirteen out of 181 countries carried the AAA rating from at least one rating service, as of October 1999. Another 11 countries carried an AA rating. In total, 55 countries out of 181 carried an investment rating that was nominally "investment grade" (BBB or better from at least one rating agency). Given that the remaining 126 countries fell below investment grade, high default risk characterizes the majority of countries in the world.
- **Euromoney *Country Risk Rating.*** *Euromoney* magazine provides both a worldwide rank and a scaled score from 100 (least risky) to 0 (most risky). As of September 1999, the U.S. scored 94.5 and was ranked third among 181 countries, after Luxembourg and Switzerland.
- ***Economist Intelligence Unit (EIU).*** EIU, an affiliate of *Economist* magazine, assigns an overall risk rating to a country ranging from A (least risky) to E (most risky). EIU also provides a numerical score ranging from 0 (least risky) to 100 (most risky). As of June 1999, the United States was rated an A risk with a score of 15.
- **Institutional Investor *Country Risk Rating.*** *Institutional Investor* magazine assigns a creditworthiness rating to a country based on surveys of international bankers and economists. Each country is given both a score from 100 (least risky) to 0 (most risky) and a worldwide rank. As of September 1999, the United States was ranked fifth with a score of 90.9.
- **International Country Risk Guide (ICRG)** published by the Political Risk Services Group of the World Bank. This source gives individual ratings for political, financial, and economic conditions, as well as a composite of these three ratings. ICRG assigns an overall risk rating to a country, as well as separate ratings for political, financial, and economic risks. Overall ratings range from 100 (least risky) to 0 (most risky). As of June 1999, the United States was rated at 83.3, the ninth highest score.

A quick scan of Exhibit 12.4 yields some important insights. These various estimates of political risk do not agree perfectly. The subtle differences in how the sources look at countries is beyond the scope of this chapter.[7] But the signal here is that political risk is an intangible quality, measured imperfectly. An acquirer's political risk exposure varies greatly across these countries. Buyer beware.

There are two ways to adjust the DCF valuation approach for political risk. These must be mutually exclusive in order to avoid double-counting risk:

1. ***Adjust the cash flows of the target firm.*** In Wall Street parlance, one could "give a haircut" to the target firm's expected cash flows, reflecting added risk

of the foreign country relative to the home country. Marriott Corporation adjusts for political risk in this way, based on a proprietary political risk index.[8] One needs a rule or framework in order to be consistent from one country to the next. Unfortunately, no formal theory for such a framework exists. The analyst's adjustment may be arbitrary and risks tainting the valuation through personal biases.

2. ***Adjust the discount rate for the target firm's cash flows.*** One could boost the discount rate for cash flows from a riskier foreign country. Practitioners point toward two sources for these *political risk premiums*: the OPIC[9] risk insurance spreads, and differences in government bond yields or yields on corporate bonds of similar risk in the home and foreign markets. This approach has the virtue of drawing on market rates for the adjustment; it is less arbitrary than the first approach. To use the bond premium approach, both bonds must be denominated in the same currency (preferably dollars) and must be a similar class of asset (e.g., both must be sovereign bonds of the respective governments, or both must have the same corporate bond rating).

Any resulting estimates must be subjected to an intuitive test of reasonableness, giving special attention to the possibility of double-counting or overcorrecting for risk.

Segmented Markets

Interest rates and equity market multiples can vary substantially across countries, owing in part to inflation and currency effects and also to the degree of integration of the local financial markets with the global financial markets. Only a small percentage of analysts believe that markets are integrated (see Keck et al. 1998). Bekaert and Harvey (1995) and others have found that the lack of integration (or the "segmentation" as economists term it) explains some of the variation in returns across countries. A local market is segmented when financial assets command a different price there than in global markets. Segmentation arises from barriers to trade that prevent arbitrage from driving local and global prices into parity. The degree of segmentation is important because it affects one of the fundamental assumptions in valuation: that investors can arbitrage across markets and that arbitrage will therefore drive returns toward a global equilibrium. If arbitrage is not possible, the reference point for investors will be the local, rather than the global, cost of capital. Thus, segmentation affects the discount rate the M&A analyst will choose. Approaches to estimating discount rates under segmentation and integration are discussed later in this chapter.

Rule of Law, Corruption, Corporate Governance, and Protection of Minority Shareholders

Weak systems of fairness and justice in a foreign country can impose unanticipated costs on investors. Markets already recognize this. For instance, La Porta et al. (1998, 1999, 2000) find that variations in corporate law and governance help to explain the valuation differences among countries. M&A valuation analysis logically should reflect the impact of these hidden costs, though procedures for doing so are not well developed. A starting point is to consult country rankings of corruption and justice.[10]

Social Issues and Culture

Some business cultures endorse practices such as nepotism (employment of family members); paternalism (welfarelike support for employees' families); discrimination (religious, ethnic, racial, etc.); tax evasion; official corruption; and reliance on government assistance. These practices should trigger careful reflection on their consistency with the values and business ethics code of the buyer firm. The M&A analyst must also recognize that they impose (perhaps hidden) costs on investors. Changing such practices to conform to the buyer's culture can be difficult and costly. Either way, the valuation analyst and executive must consider such costs in their assessment of the target firm's value.

STRATEGY FOR DCF APPROACH: HOME VERSUS FOREIGN VALUATION

In valuing firms across borders, the analyst could draw on a range of methods, such as those outlined in Chapter 9. Most of these approaches are relevant to cross-border valuation, though the analyst should be vigilant for effects such as those outlined in the preceding section. Of all the methods, DCF remains the most useful in the cross-border setting because of its transparency and versatility in adapting to the special cross-border challenges. Leading practitioners in large firms rely on DCF.[11] For these reasons, the balance of this chapter focuses on the application of DCF to the cross-border valuation task.

A strategic question for the valuation process is whether to conduct the DCF analysis in home or foreign currencies. As a practical matter, most corporations cast all investment decisions in terms of a common home currency—this permits direct comparison among investment proposals by directors and also facilitates financial planning and reporting. If markets are truly in parity, the DCF valuation conducted in either home or foreign currencies should produce the same economic conclusion. Exhibit 12.5 illustrates the two alternative routes by which the analyst might derive a U.S. dollar net present value from Argentine peso free cash flows.

1. *Approach A.* The analyst could convert the peso flows to dollars, using the forecast of forward peso/U.S. dollar exchange rates. The dollar cash flows should be discounted using a dollar WACC. Estimation of the dollar WACC must reflect not only the systematic risk of the target industry, but also the local equity market risk and political risk of the country.[12] Where the home and foreign countries are very similar in risks (such as between two developed countries like the United States and Canada), no particular adjustment may be required. But where the home and foreign countries are materially different in risks (such as between a developed country like the United States and a developing country like Argentina) the home country WACC will not adequately reflect the foreign country risk. Thus, the U.S. dollar WACC for discounting cash flows from an investment in Argentina must be adjusted to reflect the foreign

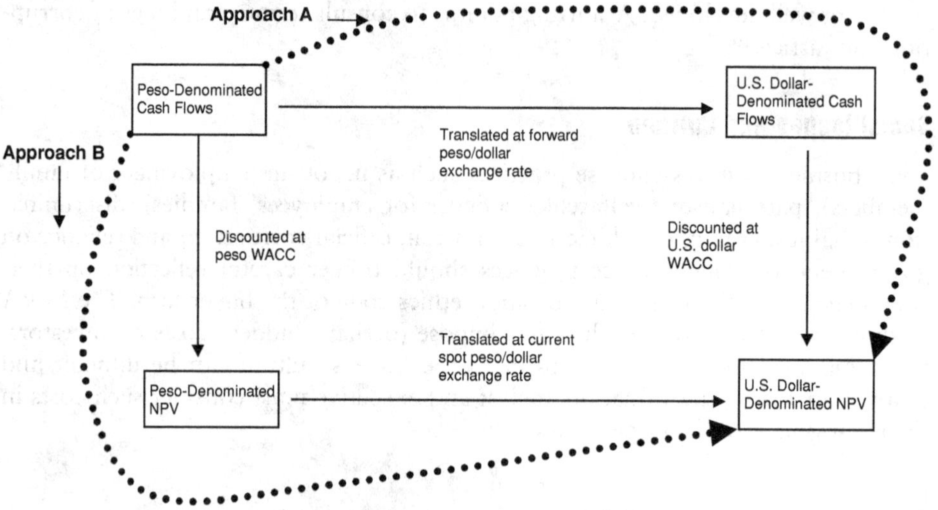

EXHIBIT 12.5 Comparison of Alternative Approaches (A and B) for Estimating a U.S. Dollar Net Present Value from Argentine Pesos

local risks. The business risk could be priced from the CAPM and cost of debt for comparable firms in the United States. The country risk could be estimated as the yield difference between U.S. Treasuries and yields on dollar-denominated foreign government bonds. The end result is a DCF value denominated in U.S. dollars.

2. *Approach B.* The analyst could discount foreign cash flows using a foreign WACC, and then translate the foreign DCF into a dollar DCF using the spot exchange rate.

One can debate at length the merits of the two approaches. To focus the debate, it is useful to note that each approach has one or more embedded key bets,[13] as well as various strengths and weaknesses as summarized in Exhibit 12.6. If assumptions are consistent between the two approaches, they should produce identical estimates of NPV; if the inflation rate is the only difference between the two countries, then interest rate parity assures this result. But if the two countries differ in political and segmentation risks, then the challenges of estimating and adjusting for these two effects may cause the two approaches to differ. Specifically, the U.S. dollar WACC needs to reflect the same premium for segmentation and political risks that are embedded in the foreign WACC—as a practical matter, the analyst cannot actually observe the embedded risk premium, only estimate it. Therefore, in practice the two methods may differ in their resulting NPVs. The choice between the two depends on one's relative confidence in local capital market data versus one's relative confidence in the existence of a theoretical equilibrium within and between international currency and capital markets.

Does the choice really matter? In terms of economics, no: If interest rate parity holds and political and segmentation risks are treated consistently, an NPV expressed in dollars or pesos should lead to the same investment decision. It may be more convenient to value cash flows in the foreign currency if it is easy to obtain

EXHIBIT 12.6 Comparison of Two DCF Valuation Approaches

	Approach A: Converting Foreign Cash Flows into Home Currency and Discounting at a Home WACC	Approach B: Forecasting in Foreign Currency and Discounting at a Foreign WACC
Key features/ Key bets	• Purchasing power parity (PPP) and interest rate parity (IRP) hold. • Inflation forecasts in foreign and home currencies are appropriate. • Foreign country political risk premium estimate is appropriate.	• Quality of foreign capital market data is good. • Local capital costs are free market yields.
Strengths	• Information environment. • Can use high-quality capital market information from developed countries.	• Simplicity. • Translation at spot foreign exchange rates.
Weaknesses	• Purchasing power parity and interest rate parity do not hold in all markets at all times. Implicitly assumes home interest rates are consistent with forward currency exchange rates. • Long-term inflation forecasts are unreliable.	• Information environment in developing countries may not be strong. • Availability and quality of foreign capital market data may be poor. • Betas are not estimated for many stocks in emerging markets, so must estimate betas yourself. Many interest rates are heavily administered by central banks, and do not reasonably reflect inflation expectations or required real rates of return.

the foreign discount rate.[14] Other things equal,[15] translating the NPV from pesos into U.S. dollars is a matter of *consistency* of global financial reporting and the *convenience* of decision makers. For these reasons, Approach A is the dominant method of valuation across borders used by large multinational corporations and foreign acquirers from developed countries.

ADJUSTING CASH FLOWS

The domestic, or "home," cash flow forecasting model will likely need to be adapted to a foreign setting in ways that reflect all of the considerations discussed in the preceding section. Of these, three details are worth further discussion.

Need for Internal Consistency

Discounted cash flow is highly adaptable to special conditions that the analyst may perceive and wish to incorporate into the valuation. But almost unknowingly, the analyst may insert internal contradictions between cash flows and discount rates. These are to be avoided: Required rates of return and cash flows must be consistent with one another. Unless you have an explicit (and sound) reason for deviating, you should build an internally consistent valuation model. In particular, look for consistency in the use of:

- ***Tax rate assumptions.*** The same tax rate should be assumed in estimating after-tax cash flows, a levered beta (in the presence of tax-deductible interest expense), the weighted average cost of capital, and the value of debt tax shields.
- ***Inflation rate assumptions.*** The same inflation rate should be assumed in forecasting revenues, costs, additions to working capital, investment outlays, the risk-free rate of return, interest rates, and foreign currency exchange rates.

Valuing Real versus Nominal Cash Flows

Analysts have two polar choices in valuation procedure:

1. ***Value nominal cash flows at nominal discount rates.*** A nominal cash flow grows at the compound product of the actual rate of inflation and the real rate of growth. Nominal discount rates *are* the compounded product of inflation and real return, as is summarized in the Fisher Equation, discussed in the next section. This *nominal/nominal valuation* approach is the prevalent valuation method within global corporations.
2. ***Value real cash flows at real discount rates.*** Real flows and rates reflect actual economic activity, apart from illusions created by price changes. One can think of this as the "zero inflation" approach. This *real/real valuation* method is sometimes used by practitioners in high inflation environments where the illusions become large.

In theory, if cash flows and discount rates are internally consistent, markets will value an asset the same under either approach. The equality of results is realized if compounding and discounting are done at the same rate. For instance, suppose you contemplate making an investment that offers cash flows growing at 8 percent in real terms and is exposed to a 3 percent inflation rate. You believe a 10 percent real discount rate is appropriate—with the 3 percent inflation rate accounted for, you believe the project should have a 13.33 percent nominal required rate of return. The nominal annual cash flows compound at 11.24 percent from a base of $1,000 over five years and then slow down to 8.2 percent in year 6. The real annual cash flows compound at 8 percent from a base of $1,000, and then slow down to 5 percent starting in year 6. Exhibit 12.7 shows that the present value of cash flows under both approaches is the same with a terminal value (lines 13 and 18) or without (lines 10 and 15).

The problem is that cash flows rarely compound at the same rate as that with which one discounts. For instance, depreciation is a deductible expense for tax purposes, but depreciation expense is typically tied to the historical cost of the firm's assets, not the current (inflation-adjusted) value. As inflation rises, firms will not

EXHIBIT 12.7 Demonstration of the Equality of Real and Nominal Discounting in the Absence of Fixed Costs

	Assumptions
1 Inflation rate for target company cash flows	3.0%
2 Real growth rate for target company cash flows	8.0%
3 Nominal growth rate for target company cash flows	11.24%
4 Current year cash flows	1,000.00
5 Nominal discount rate	13.30%
6 Real discount rate	10.00%
7 Long-term real growth rate	5.00%
8 Long-term nominal growth rate	8.2%

	Year						
	0	1	2	3	4	5	6
A: Nominal Cash Flows Discounted at Nominal Discount Rate							
9 Nominal cash flows		$1,112.40	$1,237.43	$1,376.52	$1,531.24	$1,703.35	$1,842.18
10 Present value of nominal cash flows at nominal discount rate	$4,733.79						
11 Terminal value						$35,770.43*	
12 Cash flows plus terminal value		$1,112.40	$1,237.43	$1,376.52	$1,531.24	$37,473.79	
13 Present value of cash flows and terminal value at nominal discount rate	$23,892.87						
B: Real Cash Flows Discounted at Real Discount Rate							
14 Real cash flows		$1,080.00	$1,166.40	$1,259.71	$1,360.49	$1,469.33	$1,542.79
15 Present value of real cash flows at real discount rate	$4,733.79						
16 Terminal vale						$30,855.89†	
17 Cash flows plus terminal value		$1,080.00	$1,166.40	$1,259.71	$1,360.49	$32,325.22	
18 Present value of cash flows and terminal value at real discount rate	$23,892.87						

*The terminal value in the nominal/nominal case assumes growth after year 5 at the long-term nominal growth rate.
†The terminal value in the real/real case assumes growth after year 5 at the long-term real growth rate.
Source: Detail underlying this calculation may be found in the spreadsheet file "Real versus Nominal.xls," on the CD-ROM.

deduct enough depreciation expense to replace assets as they age even though investment outlays do rise with inflation. As a result, firms will overpay taxes. In short, under the nominal cash flow/nominal discount rate approach, the distortion of historical cost assets causes cash flows to be less than they would be with current cost assets—this is an actual economic cost imposed on investors. The real/real approach ignores this distortion, unless the analyst specifically models it. Exhibit 12.8 gives an example illustrating that the results under the two approaches differ because of the distortion—in this example, the "real/real" approach gives a dramatically higher estimate of value because it ignores the failure of depreciation to keep up with rising investment outlays. Some countries have permitted inflation-indexing of asset values, which ameliorates this distortion. In those settings, the real/real approach is reasonable, and will yield valuation estimates similar to the nominal/nominal approach.

The M&A analyst should be encouraged to research principles of inflation accounting in the foreign country. In the absence of accounting practices, however, that would eliminate distortions from inflation. Thus, the nominal/nominal approach better serves the goal of realistic estimates of value.

Translating Foreign Currency Cash Flows into Home Currency

Approach A requires that future cash flows be converted from foreign to home currency before discounting them. Markets for most currencies rarely offer forward exchange rates beyond three years out. Since the valuation of most firms requires discounting future cash flows over a longer period, the analyst must rely on exchange rate forecasts. Financial advisers and institutions routinely offer only one or two-year forecasts, and beyond that, a qualitative outlook for the strength of one currency versus another. The only practical alternative on which the valuation analyst can rely is the interest rate parity formula described earlier.

A useful application of the parity formula is in estimating forward currency exchange ratios. These forward rates are important in translating local currency cash flows into home currency cash flows. Banks and capital markets typically quote forward rates out to a maximum of two or three years. A variant of the interest rate parity formula can extend the forward rate forecast considerably further. The key requisite for this application is a view about the long-term future inflation rates in the two currencies. For instance, we know from the work of Irving Fisher that observed nominal rates of returns on assets can be decomposed into the real rate of return (R_{Real}), and the inflation rate (Inf); this is the famous Fisher Equation:

$$(1+R_{Nom})^n = (1+R_{Real})^n(1+Inf)^n \qquad (3)$$

The superscripts, "n," indicate the number of years from today at which inflation and returns will compound. Drawing on Fisher's insight, if real rates of return are constant across countries, then the interest rate parity formula can be recast to show the relation between spot and forward currency exchange rates and the *inflation rates* in the two countries:

EXHIBIT 12.8 Comparison of "Nominal/Nominal" and "Real/Real" Valuation Approaches in the Presence of Fixed Depreciation

	Assumptions
Inflation rate for target company costs, revenues, and investment	5.0%
Real growth rate for target company costs, revenues, and investment	4.8%
Nominal growth rate for target company costs, revenues, and investment	10.04%
Current year revenues	2,000.00
Current year cost of labor and raw materials	1,000.00
Depreciation expense (fixed over time)	500.00
Current year investment	500.00
Marginal tax rate	35.0%
Nominal discount rate	10.0%
Real discount rate	4.8%

	Year					
	0	1	2	3	4	5
Nominal/Nominal Valuation Approach						
Nominal revenues		$ 2,200.80	$ 2,421.76	$ 2,664.91	$ 2,932.46	$ 3,226.88
Nominal cost of labor and raw material		$(1,100.40)	$(1,210.88)	$(1,332.45)	$(1,466.23)	$(1,613.44)
Depreciation expense		$ (500.00)	$ (500.00)	$ (500.00)	$ (500.00)	$ (500.00)
Pretax income		$ 600.40	$ 710.88	$ 832.45	$ 966.23	$ 1,113.44
Tax expense		$ (210.14)	$ (248.81)	$ (291.36)	$ (338.18)	$ (389.70)
After-tax income		$ 390.26	$ 462.07	$ 541.09	$ 628.05	$ 723.74
Plus depreciation		$ 500.00	$ 500.00	$ 500.00	$ 500.00	$ 500.00
Less nominal investment		$ (550.20)	$ (605.44)	$ (666.23)	$ (733.12)	$ (806.72)
Terminal value (final FCF/k)						$ 4,170.16
Nominal free cash flows		$ 340.06	$ 356.63	$ 374.87	$ 394.43	$ 4,587.18
Present value of nominal cash flows at nominal discount rate	$4,003.55					

(Continued)

EXHIBIT 12.8 *(Continued)*

	Year					
	0	1	2	3	4	5
Real/Real Valuation Approach						
Real revenues		$ 2,096.00	$ 2,196.61	$ 2,302.05	$ 2,412.54	$ 2,528.35
Real cost of labor and raw materials		$(1,048.00)	$(1,098.30)	$(1,151.02)	$(1,206.27)	$(1,264.17)
Depreciation expense		$ (500.00)	$ (500.00)	$ (500.00)	$ (500.00)	$ (500.00)
Pretax income		$ 548.00	$ 598.30	$ 651.02	$ 706.27	$ 764.17
Tax expense		$ (191.80)	$ (209.41)	$ (227.86)	$ (247.20)	$ (267.46)
After-tax income		$ 356.20	$ 388.90	$ 423.16	$ 459.08	$ 496.71
Plus depreciation		$ (500.00)	$ (500.00)	$ (500.00)	$ (500.00)	$ (500.00)
Less real investment		$ (524.00)	$ (549.15)	$ (575.51)	$ (603.14)	$ (632.09)
Terminal value (final FCF/*k*)						$ 7,657.14
Real free cash flows		$ 332.20	$ 339.75	$ 347.65	$ 355.94	$ 8,021.77
Present value of real cash flows at real discount rate	$7,581.55					

Source: Detail underlying this calculation may be found in the spreadsheet file "Real versus Nominal.xls," on the CD-ROM.

$$\frac{SPOT_{\frac{Peso}{Dollar}}}{FWD_{\frac{Peso}{Dollar}}} = \frac{(1+Inf_{Dollar})^n}{(1+Inf_{Peso})^n} \quad (4)$$

Rearranging this formula by solving for the forward rate yields a basic workhorse of cross-border valuation: a robust formula that one can use to estimate exchange rates for translating foreign-denominated cash flows into the home currency:

$$FWD_{\frac{Peso}{Dollar}} = SPOT_{\frac{Peso}{Dollar}} \left[\frac{(1+Inf_{Peso})^n}{(1+Inf_{Dollar})^n} \right] \quad (5)$$

An application of this formula is given in the example of Westmoreland Energy's power project at Zhangzhe, China, later in this chapter.

Exhibit 12.9 gives an illustration of the conversion of future peso cash flows into dollars, based on the spreadsheet template, "Country IRP.xls" (which can be found on the CD-ROM). Because the foreign currency inflates faster than the home currency in this example, it depreciates against the home currency.

The use of IRP to translate foreign flows depends on two assumptions worth examining critically. First is strong confidence in one's forecast of the inflation rate for home and foreign currencies. As a practical matter, our forecasts of inflation beyond a year ahead are highly uncertain. This means that your valuation analysis is heavily dependent on your view of the home and foreign countries. As Chapter 5 argues, you must have a view of countries.

The second key assumption is that parity prevails in global currency and capital markets. The research evidence is that markets on average tend toward parity, but that variance from parity is the standard condition. Over the course of 10 or more years, parity may not be an unreasonable assumption. Over a shorter period, you must have a view on parity and attempt to model it into your valuation.

ESTIMATING THE DISCOUNT RATE FOR FOREIGN CASH FLOWS

In this section, the focus turns to issues in the practical application of Approach A, given its prominence in cross-border M&A. Here, we seek to estimate a U.S. dollar (or "home currency"[16]) NPV based on the translation of foreign cash flows into dollars and a dollar-based WACC.

Some Basic Principles

Asset pricing theory, a subfield of financial economics that bears on investors' required rates of return, is amassing a body of research notable for mathematical density, econometric complexity, numerous competing approaches and models, and spirited debate. The discussion that follows offers a few highlights and practical implications,

EXHIBIT 12.9 Illustration of the Use of the Interest Rate Parity Relationship to Translate Foreign Currency Cash Flows into Home Currency Cash Flows

	Assumptions
Inflation rate in home currency	2.0%
Inflation rate in foreign currency	6.0%
Spot exchange rate (foreign/home)	1.00

	Year					
	0	1	2	3	4	5
Cash flows in foreign currency		$10,000.00	$10,000.00	$10,000.00	$10,000.00	$10,000.00
Forward exchange rate		1.039	1.080	1.122	1.166	1.212
Cash flows translated into home currency		$9,622.64	$9,259.52	$8,910.11	$8,573.88	$8,250.33

Note: For more background on the calculations underlying this exhibit, please see the spreadsheet model "Country IRP.xls" on the CD-ROM.

and directs the interested reader to more examples and detailed discussions. It is important to bear in mind that the convention in this discussion is that the "discount rate" refers to the weighted average cost of capital. But since the cost of debt, tax rate, and capital structure are easily identified, all of the discount rate discussion will focus on one component, the cost of equity.

ESTIMATE A COST OF EQUITY CONSISTENT WITH THE RISK OF THE FOREIGN TARGET Use a discount rate for a stream of cash consistent with the risk of that stream. The foreign target is almost inevitably very different from the buyer. As the section on strategy for DCF approach outlines, the foreign investment is victim to a host of uncertainties to which the buyer at home may not be exposed. The large volume of research in asset pricing deals with how to adjust for the risks of cross-border investment. The more risk, the greater the return.

ESTIMATE RISK (AND COST OF EQUITY) BASED ON THE TARGET'S STOCK PRICES, OR PRICES OF COMPARABLE FIRMS This steers the analyst in the direction of the venerable capital asset pricing model or its younger peers—the reason for this is that stock prices tell us what investors think, and those are the same people whom the M&A professional is trying to serve. Also, recent stock prices tell us what the investors are thinking based on the latest news. Obviously, this imposes a data requirement on the analyst that is not trivial. Not all foreign companies are publicly listed for trading; not all publicly listed companies trade with regularity. To focus only on those firms where one can get data is to exclude from consideration target firms that may be in highly profitable niches of investment. For this reason, a great deal of asset pricing analysis is based on firms *comparable* to the target.

CHECK FOR MARKET SEGMENTATION, AND REQUIRE COMPENSATION FOR IT A simple test for segmentation is to see if the beta of a foreign country equity index versus the global equity market index is materially different from 1.0. Segments exist where identical assets command different prices in different geographical areas. In theory, arbitrage should drive different local markets into equilibrium. At the end of this process of arbitrage, capital markets should be globally integrated—not an unreasonable or unattainable possibility in a world of continuous trading, advanced information and communication technology, and the participation of very large banks, corporations, and investors. But because of the less-than-perfect correlation in returns between foreign and home equity markets, and of differences in volatility, it is not possible simply to apply home market betas to foreign cash flows. The reality is that capital markets display some degree of segmentation. Bekaert (1995, page 75) finds that segmentation is driven, in turn, by a variety of factors, such as:

- Foreign exchange controls.
- Controls on investment by foreigners.
- High and variable inflation.
- Lack of a high-quality regulatory and accounting framework.
- Lack of country funds or cross-listed securities that provide benchmarks for arbitrage.
- Small size of market.
- Poor credit ratings or absence of credit ratings.

Research suggests that local capital markets progress toward integration by surmounting these factors. This progress affects local equity market volatility and the correlation of local equity market returns with world returns. Therefore, both correlation and volatility drive the betas that determine the cost of capital.

One can think of the drivers of segmentation in terms of the formula for the equity beta. The following describes beta in terms of the volatility (or standard deviation of returns) on a particular stock or on the local market index (indicated by the Greek letter "sigma," σ) and the correlation of returns between the stock and the market (indicated by the Greek letter "rho," $\rho_{i,M}$).[17]

$$\beta_i = \rho_{i,M} \frac{\sigma_i}{\sigma_M} \tag{6}$$

Betas reflect segmentation in two ways. First, volatilities may be different for each segment (i.e., national equity market). Second, correlation of local equity markets with the global equity market could differ from country to country. In *integrated markets*, assets with the same risk have identical expected returns irrespective of the market, holding constant the currency (IRP) effect. In the ideal world of perfect capital market integration, efficiency, and competition, global securities would be priced to lie on the capital market line, indicating that a firm's beta versus the global market index explains its returns. Persistent deviations from the capital market line suggest the existence of segments. In *segmented markets*, a beta versus the global equity market index will poorly explain returns. The particular beta definition to be used for cross-border investing when there is segmentation will be different from the definition when there is integration.[18]

One example of relative segmentation can be found in developing countries. Bekaert and Harvey (1997) find that the volatilities and returns in the equity markets of emerging countries are different from those in the United States and other developed markets in several ways. They find that stock returns in emerging markets are higher and have higher volatility. Exhibit 12.10 gives the returns of a range of foreign country stock market indexes, and shows that the nine-year returns exceed nine-year returns of the U.S. stock market indexes. The exhibit also gives the standard deviations of return (the volatilities) for selected countries and the United States. They find that the greater the development of the stock market and degree of integration, the lower the volatility. The greater the trading liquidity, the lower the volatility. The lower the rate of inflation, the lower the volatility. Generally, emerging markets returns have lower correlations with the United States than do those of developed market returns.[19] And finally, market liberalization is associated with differences in volatility and correlation. Volatility decreases in most countries that experience liberalization. The cost of capital declines following liberalization. The proportion of volatility due to world factors rises after liberalization and returns become more predictable.

An Overview of Cost of Equity Models for Cross-Border Investing

Research offers numerous models on which the analyst can draw. They make differing assumptions about the pricing of securities and place varying demands on

EXHIBIT 12.10 U.S. Dollar Returns (in Percent) on Emerging Markets, 1991–1999

	Mean	Standard Deviation	Mean/Standard Deviation
Latin America			
Argentina	55.03	149.13	0.37
Brazil	49.00	93.96	0.52
Chile	26.81	34.70	0.77
Colombia	14.93	29.32	0.51
Mexico	30.77	47.03	0.65
Peru	18.48	16.10	1.15
Venezuela	12.54	54.26	0.23
Asia			
China	14.15	58.07	0.24
India	13.37	38.40	0.35
Indonesia	12.75	63.47	0.20
Korea	4.53	60.32	0.08
Malaysia	11.01	49.14	0.22
Thailand	3.72	54.42	0.07
Europe			
Hungary	32.97	51.09	0.65
Poland	123.62	293.80	0.42
Mideast/Africa			
Jordan	9.62	15.81	0.61
South Africa	23.62	37.86	0.62
Other Indexes			
S&P 500	18.65	12.46	1.48
S&P/IFCG Composite	12.43	48.99	0.25

Sources: Standard & Poor's/International Finance Corporation, *The S&P Emerging Market Indices: Methodologies, Definitions, and Practices*, February 2000, page 34. Reprinted by permission of Standard & Poor's, a division of the McGraw-Hill Companies. Bridge Information Systems provided the data for the S&P 500 index in the United States.

the analyst for quality data and computational sophistication. Exhibit 12.11 gives an overview of the field of some possible models, divided according to the information environment and beliefs about market segmentation. A strong information environment offers data that are high in quality but insufficient in quantity (at reasonable cost). The quality of information refers to the credibility of reported financial results, the efficiency of market prices set in liquid trading, the absence of government intervention in market pricing, and the representativeness of market indexes. Exhibit 12.11 suggests four general groups of models:

1. ***Asset pricing is*** **globally integrated** ***and the information environment is*** **strong.** This northwest quadrant of the table perhaps characterizes large, multinational companies that are actively traded and listed for trading in developed country exchanges. These companies give reasonably transparent financial reports to shareholders and disclose corporate news in ways consistent with developed-country standards. One could logically assume that the securities of these companies are priced without segmentation. For instance, the Swiss pharmaceuticals

EXHIBIT 12.11 Suggested Application of Cost of Equity Models by Country Segmentation and Information Environment (Assuming Foreign Cash Flows Are Translated into Home Currency Cash Flows Using Interest Rate Parity)

	Target Country Is Integrated	Target Country Is Segmented
Foreign capital market information environment is *strong*.	• CAPM, ICAPM • Multifactor model	• Multifactor model • Credit model • Adjusted CAPM
Foreign capital market information environment is *weak*.	• CAPM	• Adjusted CAPM • Credit model

firm Novartis is probably priced on this basis. Furthermore, the security prices of Novartis are readily available from major data providers. It is relatively easy to estimate parameters for asset pricing models.

2. ***Asset pricing is* segmented *and the information environment is* strong.** In the northeast quadrant might be large firms actively traded in country exchanges where one expects segmentation effects. An example would be the large oil company Petrobras (Brazil), a firm well integrated into global product markets, followed by numerous securities analysts, and traded regularly in local markets. But there may be questions as to the liquidity of trading in these securities or fears of local government intervention in trading. Also, the Brazilian equity market index is heavily concentrated in the market capitalization of Petrobras and a handful of other firms.
3. ***Asset pricing is assumed to be* globally integrated *though the information environment is* weak.** In the southwest quadrant of the table, the analyst chooses to make the assumption that the target is globally integrated, even though the analyst cannot obtain data believed to be reliable for econometric purposes. A large privately owned firm in Germany or the United Kingdom, for instance, would appear in this quadrant. Generally one should ask whether it is possible for a firm's securities to be integrated into global capital markets without strong information—in other words, this quadrant contains a hypothetical basis for valuing a class of firms outside the realm where mainstream valuation assumptions of this chapter can be applied. The models offered in this quadrant estimate required returns based on benchmarks from outside the foreign country and company.
4. ***Asset pricing is* segmented *and the information environment is* weak.** This southeast quadrant would characterize foreign firms outside the global capital market mainstream: Firms that are in emerging markets far from developed status would fall in this quadrant, as would foreign new enterprises, joint ventures, project financings, and generally foreign direct investment in physical assets in segmented markets. The data problems here are severe.

The key point of Exhibit 12.11 is that the pragmatic analyst will adopt different models in different settings. Generally, the best practice alternative is the multifactor asset pricing model—but this is the most data-hungry and time-intensive approach. In situations where there is less available time, data, or computing capacity, some variant of the CAPM is recommended. The credit-based model is easy to use and well adapted to estimating *country-level* discount rates in emerging markets. You should be aware of all three classes of models, and use the best possible under your circumstances. The next three subsections describe the models that are mentioned in Exhibit 12.11.

Multifactor Model

Various researchers have argued that the risks in international investing are best captured through more fully specified econometric models.[20] Under this approach, the required return on a security is equal to a risk-free rate plus the exposure of the stock to various factors—nothing in asset pricing theory dictates *which* factors to insert in the *multifactor model,* though the thoughtful analyst can pick likely drivers. For instance, Bodnar, Dumas, and Marston (2003) highlight several factors:

- ***World stock-market price risk.*** This is the risk arising from the volatility of returns on the global equity market portfolio. Stocks will be affected by this risk exposure to different degrees. Morgan Stanley Capital International (MSCI) reports the value of the global equity market portfolio each day (this is actually a subset of the true universe of global stocks).
- ***Country stock-market price risk.*** This arises from variations in the price of a country's equity market portfolio. Logically, this would capture all risk exposure in a country's business sector. MSCI reports the daily performance of various country indexes each day.
- ***Industry price risk.*** This arises from variations in the price of the industry's global equity market portfolio. For instance, the global automobile portfolio would consist of the equities of all automobile manufacturers, regardless of their location. This factor captures risks unique to an industry. MSCI reports the returns on numerous industry and sector portfolios each day.
- ***Exchange rate risk.*** This captures the risk exposure of returns to variations in exchange rates. It is measured by variations in returns on foreign-currency deposits.
- ***Political risk.*** This embraces the risks of expropriation, turmoil, and sovereign default. This could be measured by the return differentials on various credit classes of bonds. Unfortunately, looking at *realized* spreads sometimes yields negative values. What is needed is an *expected* spread, which can be hard to estimate. But J.P. Morgan Chase, for example, produces estimates of the expected returns on sovereign debt based on a scoring system for country risk factors.
- ***Liquidity risk.*** This risk is clearest and most relevant in emerging markets, where the need to sell quickly might sharply depress the price of securities. This might be measured as the difference in returns between more liquid and less liquid securities.

Other risk factors could be relevant in specific cases, but these six factors appear most commonly in discussions with investment professionals. The multifactor approach incorporates explanatory variables such as these six into a multiple regression model and estimates the coefficients. The general form of the model is:

$$(R_i - R_f) = \alpha_i + \beta_{i/W}(R_W - R_f) + \beta_{i/C}(R_C - R_f) + \beta_{i/I}(R_I - R_f) + \beta_{Ex}(R_{Ex} - R_f) + \beta_D(R_C^D - R_{AAA}) + \beta_L(R_L^{Lo} - R_L^{Hi}) + \varepsilon \quad (7)$$

where R = Return.
β = Regression coefficient.
i = Specific company.
f = Risk-free.
W = Global equity market portfolio.
C = Country equity market portfolio.
I = Industry equity portfolio.
Ex = Portfolio of foreign currency deposits.
D = Sovereign debt instrument of the company's home country (C).
AAA = Highest-rated sovereign debt instrument.
L = Portfolio of low or high liquidity bonds.
ε = Regression residual indicating company-specific variability of returns (unsystematic risk).

Clearly, this is a data-intensive model. Because of its multiple factors, it has much higher explanatory power than the conventional one-factor CAPM.

Credit Model

Given market imperfections, beta may have little meaning in an emerging market setting. Furthermore, beta may not be applicable in some local market settings if there is no stock market. Erb, Harvey, and Viskanta (1995) offer a country credit risk rating–based model:

$$K_{i(t+1)} = \gamma_0 + \gamma_1 \cdot \ln(\text{Country credit risk rating}_{it}) + \varepsilon_{it+1} \quad (8)$$

where $K_{i\,(t+1)}$ = Expected return on the country's equity market portfolio.
γ_0 = Intercept in a regression of leading returns on country credit risk rating.
γ_1 = Slope coefficient in a regression of leading returns on country credit risk rating.

The country credit risk rating for the current period is derived from *Institutional Investor*'s semiannual survey of bankers. By relying on nonequity market measures, the model skirts estimation difficulties arising from the definition of local and global equity market portfolios, returns measurement, data gathering, and so on. At the same time, measures of country risk impound assessments of political, currency, segmentation, and other types of risk to which an enterprise in that country might be subject. Erb, Harvey, and Viskanta find that the country credit risk rating explains 30 to 50 percent of the variation in returns, and a similar magnitude of the variation in equity market volatility. They note that the resulting estimates are consistent with intuition that investments in riskier emerging markets should require higher rates of return than those in less risky developed markets. In contrast, the international CAPM generates lower required rates of return for emerging markets, largely because of low correlations of returns between those markets and the returns on the global portfolio. Thus, they argue that the *credit risk model* will be superior for estimating required rates of return in emerging markets (and all countries, generally).

Since this model estimates an average required equity return for a country, it will be necessary to adjust the estimate for firm-specific risk. The virtue of this approach is that it allows the analyst to estimate cost of capital from publicly available sovereign risk ratings.[21]

Capital Asset Pricing Model (CAPM) and Its Variants

The starting point for asset pricing across borders is to use the CAPM, the method outlined for domestic transactions in Chapter 9. In the cross-border setting, however, the parameters of the model require careful reflection. Equation (9) gives the CAPM in simple form—this would be appropriate for valuing dollar-denominated cash flows from a foreign target subject to *no greater* segmentation or political risk than the acquirer faces (as would be the case with a U.S. firm acquiring a Canadian firm):

$$k_e = R_f + \beta_i \cdot (R_{\text{Market}} - R_f) \quad (9)$$

where $R_f =$ Risk-free rate, such as the U.S. Treasury long-term bond yield. This yield is assumed to be a reasonable proxy for political risk in the foreign country (such as Canada).

$\beta_i = \sigma_{i,\text{Market}} / \sigma^2_{\text{Market}} =$ Covariance between the stock's returns and the market returns divided by the variance of returns on the market. Assuming a high degree of integration, it is immaterial whether the beta is estimated against the foreign country's (Canada's) equity market returns, or against the U.S. market. The simplest would be to use the company's foreign (Canadian) beta. If the foreign company is privately owned, one could easily use an average from a sample of Canadian or U.S. firms, again, on the assumption of a high level of integration between the two countries.

$R_{Market} - R_f =$ Equity market risk premium. As Chapter 9 suggested, a premium of 6 percent would be appropriate for domestic U.S. valuations. Under the assumption of high capital market integration between foreign (Canadian) and domestic (U.S.) markets, one could use the domestic equity market risk premium.

A variant of the basic model is the *international CAPM (ICAPM)*. Several authors[22] have argued that as the world becomes more integrated and investors hold globally diversified portfolios, the relevant measure of a stock's risk is its covariance relative to the variance of returns on the global market portfolio. Accordingly, the formula for the global CAPM is given in equation (10):

$$k_e = R_f + \beta_i^w \cdot \left(R_m^w - R_f\right) \quad (10)$$

where R_f = Risk-free rate consistent with the currency denomination of the cash flows being valued. As noted earlier, our discussion assumes that cash flows have been translated into U.S. dollars; thus, the appropriate risk-free rate to use would be the long-term U.S. Treasury bond yield.

β_i^w = World beta of asset *i*, that is, the covariance of returns on asset *i* relative to the global equity portfolio such as the Morgan Stanley Capital International (MSCI) Index, divided by the variance of the MSCI Index. This beta may be available from commercial vendors, or else it must be estimated using linear regression.

$R_m^w - R_f$ = Equity market risk premium on the global portfolio. Because the U.S. equity market accounts for over half of the market value of the global portfolio, it would not be unreasonable to use the U.S. equity market risk premium[23] as a starting assumption.

The second variant of CAPM accounts for adjustments that are necessary in order to use the model in settings where markets are segmented and where political risk is different from that of the home market. This is called *adjusted CAPM* (i.e., CAPM adjusted for segmentation and political risk). Lessard (1996) has argued that a U.S. firm's beta in an investment in an offshore project would be the product of a domestic beta for the project and a "country beta" reflecting the volatility of the U.S. equity market relative to the volatility of the offshore equity market, as shown in equation (11).[24]

$$\beta_{\text{Offshore project}} = \beta_{\text{US project}} \cdot \beta_{\text{Offshore equities vs US equities}} \tag{11}$$

For example, the country beta of the Argentine equity market relative to the U.S. is estimated as:

$$\beta_{\text{Argentina vs. US}} = \rho_{\text{Argentina/US}} \cdot \frac{\sigma_{\text{Argentina}}}{\sigma_{\text{US}}} \tag{12}$$

Here, ρ is the correlation in returns between Argentina and the U.S. equities, and σ measures standard deviations of equity returns in the two markets. The country betas of the Argentine, Brazilian, and Chilean equity markets versus the United States in 1996 were 1.96, 2.42, and 0.65, respectively. Exhibit 12.12 gives country betas estimated from data provided by the International Finance Corporation (IFC):[25] Plainly, country betas can vary dramatically with differences in local volatility and correlation. Currently, the notion of adjusting for country betas in estimating local WACCs in emerging markets is starting to be practiced. The country beta adjustment may be warranted if there is capital market segmentation based on (or across) geographic or currency lines. Some might argue that the extent of segmentation may not be large enough to justify the adjustment. Others will oppose making adjustments by arguing that over the life of the investment capital markets will integrate substantially.

Lessard (1996) and Godfrey and Espinosa (1996) describe the country risk premium method of calculating the cost of equity. This method adjusts the CAPM to account for segmentation and political risk.[26]

EXHIBIT 12.12 Example of Country Betas and Their Components

	Country Beta	Local Volatility	U.S. Volatility	Correlation, Local with U.S.
Argentina	1.96	61.93%	10.08%	0.32
Brazil	2.42	60.86%	10.08%	0.40
Chile	0.65	28.54%	10.08%	0.23

Source: Lessard (1996) and International Finance Corporation.

$$k_e = R_f^{US} + \pi + \left(\beta_i^{Foreign} \cdot \beta_{Foreign}^{US}\right) \cdot \left(R_m^{US} - R_f^{US}\right) \qquad (13)$$

where π = Country credit spread (also known as the "political risk premium"), measured by rate-of-return differentials between U.S. government bonds and U.S. dollar denominated sovereign bonds of the same tenor. Bond yields are an approximation of the *ex ante* rates of return that one should ideally use in this estimation. Since the country credit spread is calculated directly from rates of return on dollar denominated bonds rather than those (or return rates) from local currency bonds, it does not incorporate any currency effects.[27] What results from adding π to the U.S.-based risk-free rate is a foreign risk-free rate, denominated in U.S. dollars.

$\beta_i^{Foreign}$ = Beta of asset *i* estimated against the foreign country equity market index (M_{dom}).

$\beta_{Foreign}^{US}$ = Country beta of the foreign country equity market index (M_{dom}). relative to the home (U.S.) equity market index.

This model imposes an important assumption to be aware of: Transposing required rates of return from one country to another through the use of the country beta assumes independence between the country-specific return and the global equity market risk premium. Rarely will this be true. Bodnar, Dumas, and Marston (2002) estimate an example for Thales, the French manufacturer, and find that the transformation described earlier materially overstates the exposure to country and world risk. In the final analysis, the multifactor model is superior to the adjusted CAPM and should be used wherever the analyst can obtain data and computing expertise to estimate the regression coefficients. But as a practical matter, the data requirement is a serious constraint on using the multifactor model in weak information environments. In conclusion, the recommendation would be to follow what Exhibit 12.11 suggests: Use the superior multifactor model in those environments that can support it. For other cross-border situations, we must settle for using Lessard's country beta transformation or the country credit risk model.

How Much Difference Does the Choice of Model Make? Why?

Exhibit 12.13 summarizes the differences among the models and offers considerations for the analyst in selecting which model to use. The range of models invites the question of whether the resulting estimates differ by much. For investments

EXHIBIT 12.13 Summary Comparison of Cost of Equity Models

	Advantages	Other Considerations
Multifactor Model • Usually estimated in a benchmark currency like the dollar or euro.	• "Best practice" approach. • Most flexible. Permits inclusion of any suspected sources of risk. • Probably carries the highest explanatory power of any class of model.	• Coefficients must be estimated by the analyst. • Requires data and computational skill. • Theory does not dictate which factors should be included in the model.
Credit Model • Usually estimated in a benchmark currency like the dollar or euro.	• Intuitively appealing focus on country; permits assessment of segmentation. • Based on analyst estimates of country risk. • Lower requirement for data. • Coefficients are commercially available.	• Gives cost of equity estimates for equity market index of a country. • Must be adjusted further for firm-specific risks.
CAPM • Can estimate in home currency (adjust for industry beta only). • Can estimate in foreign currency (adjust for beta and inflation).	• Simple to use. Parameters readily obtained. • Domestic CAPM is easily extended to cross-border setting through strong assumptions of capital market integration and similar political risk. • Method of estimating discount rate in foreign currency without relying on foreign data.	• Supposes no segmentation or political risk difference. • Requires a "view" about expected inflation in home and foreign currencies. • CAPM has relatively low explanatory power (R^2).
International CAPM (ICAPM) • Usually estimated in a benchmark currency like the dollar or euro.	• Expression of integrated world markets. • Permits comparison of all equities against a common benchmark, the global equity market portfolio. • Simple model.	• Supposes no segmentation or political risk difference. • Betas for ICAPM must be purchased or estimated by the analyst. Requires data and computational skill. • CAPM has relatively low explanatory power (R^2).
Adjusted CAPM • Estimated in home currency as presented in text.	• Transparency: enables assessment of segmentation and political risk.	• Criticized by some researchers for its ad hoc adjustments. • Returns may not be linear in cross-product of country and firm betas. • Requires country beta, which may need to be estimated by the analyst. • Country risk premium estimation may require analyst judgment.

among developed countries, the benefits may be less significant; between developed and developing countries, however, the choice of model will make a sizable difference. Five studies lend some insight into the size and causes of differences.

1. ***Local versus global CAPM estimates for U.S. firms.*** Mishra and O'Brien (2001) estimated the cost of equity for 2,989 U.S. stocks, using the traditional local CAPM, a single-factor global CAPM (such as outlined in this chapter), and a two-factor global CAPM containing both market and currency index factors. The average spread between the local and single-factor global estimates was 48 basis points, a small difference compared to the average standard error of 190 basis points. The spread is smaller for large firms: 41 basis points. The difference in estimates between the single and two-factor global CAPMs is about 61 basis points. The authors concluded, "The models do not make substantial difference in cost of equity estimates, on average." (Page 46)
2. ***Local versus two-factor global CAPM estimates for firms from nine countries.*** Koedijk et al. (2001) estimated the cost of equity for 3,293 firms from nine countries,[28] using the traditional local CAPM and a two-factor global CAPM that contained both market and currency index factors. They found that the difference in estimates was insignificant for all but 3 percent of the sample. They concluded, "For virtually every firm in our sample, the risk that is diversifiable locally is also fully diversifiable in the global market. . . . The marginal contribution of global factors is very limited, which indicates strong country factors in our data. Firms within a country demonstrate a joint exposure to the global factors, which is captured in the international pricing of the domestic market index." (Page 13)
3. ***Local versus two-factor global CAPM estimates for cross-listed firms.*** Koedijk and Van Dijk (2000) estimated the cost of equity for 336 firms whose shares were traded on stock exchanges of more than one country. They used the traditional local CAPM and two-factor global CAPM that contained both market and currency index factors. The estimates yielded significant differences for only 7 percent of the sample. The cost of capital differential was 50 basis points for securities traded in the United States, 75 basis points for the United Kingdom, and 100 basis points for France. They concluded that "most companies can therefore rely on the domestic CAPM for the computation of their cost of capital." (Page 13)
4. ***Global CAPM versus adjusted CAPM.*** Bodnar, Dumas, and Marston (2002) compared the global beta versus the beta created in the adjusted CAPM by the product of company and country betas, for firms in four countries. Across 20 French firms, the mean difference[29] was 4.4 percent; for 20 U.S. firms, the mean difference was 0.2 percent; for 13 Belgian firms the mean difference was –4.7 percent; for 13 Polish firms the mean difference was –8.2 percent. Assuming an equity market premium in the neighborhood of 5 percent, these differences in beta amount to differences in cost of equity ranging from 1 to 40 basis points.
5. ***Differences across models in emerging markets.*** The first four studies focused principally on developed countries. In contrast, Bruner and Chan (2002) focused on five countries classified by the World Bank as "developing": Brazil, South Africa, Thailand, Malaysia, and Poland. In each country, they selected two of the five largest companies in terms of market capitalization and estimated costs of

equity for each company using four different methods, namely, the CAPM, the ICAPM, the CAPM adjusted for political risk and market segmentation, and the multifactor model. Within this small sample, they found material differences in estimates across the models, on the order of 300 to 1,000 basis points. These differences were attributed to alternative beta estimates, inflation, political risk, and equity market returns.

The bottom line seems to be that among developed countries, the differences in the cost of equity are relatively small. But those differences become larger in developing countries. Of course, the definition of "large" and "small" are often relative to the requirements of the decision maker. In this context, it is important to bear in mind that global portfolio managers often live or die by a few basis points of return. In general, for large industrial corporations—which invest much less frequently, whose target assets are much less liquid, and which face sizable operating uncertainties and suffer so much noise in valuation analysis—it may be sufficient to obtain an imprecise estimate of capital cost that is nevertheless approximately right.

RECAPITULATION: VALUATION PROCESS WITH ADJUSTED CAPM

One of the hardest models to use well is the CAPM adjusted for political risk and market segmentation. The difficulties arise because of the analyst is required to make many judgment calls. To illustrate its application, this section summarizes the valuation process using the adjusted CAPM in an emerging market context. The following two sections apply the model to actual cross-border investments.

1. *Use DCF.* See Chapter 9 for a more detailed discussion of this method as applied in a domestic acquisition setting. One can also use the other valuation methods if the target is located in a developed country where the domestic capital markets are well integrated into the global market, and where accounting practices are rigorous and approximate the international standards. But DCF, practiced rigorously, is the one approach that affords the acquirer any comparability among acquisition opportunities in countries as diverse as Germany, Argentina, and Mali.
2. *Estimate cash flows* of the target firm in its local currency.
3. *Translate those local cash flows* to the home currency at forward exchange rates as estimated from the interest rate parity formula.

$$FWD_{\frac{Peso}{Dollar}} = SPOT_{\frac{Peso}{Dollar}} \left[\frac{\left(1 + Inf_{Peso}\right)}{\left(1 + Inf_{Dollar}\right)} \right] \tag{14}$$

To use this formula, you will need a view about the long-term inflation rates in the foreign and home currencies.

4. *Discount* the converted cash flows at a rate consistent with a *dollar-based* estimate of the foreign country inflation, country political risk, country beta, and industry beta. WACC is estimated using after-tax costs of debt.

$$WACC = \left(W_{\text{Debt}} \cdot K_{\text{Debt}}\right) + \left(W_{\text{Equity}} \cdot K_{\text{Equity}}\right)$$

$$K_{\text{Debt}} = K_{\text{debt}}^{\text{Local}} = \Pi_{\text{Country risk}} + K_{\text{debt}}^{\text{Home}} \quad (15)$$

$$K_{\text{Equity}} = \Pi_{\text{Country risk}} + R_{\text{Risk-free}} + [(\beta_{\text{Country}} \cdot \beta_{\text{Firm}}) \cdot (R_{\text{Market}} - R_{\text{Risk-free}})]$$

In short, the novelties required for cross-border DCF valuation include the country risk premium, country beta, and the use of the interest rate parity condition to estimate forward exchange rates.

VALUATION CASES ACROSS BORDERS

Example: Westmoreland Energy Inc., Power Project at Zhangzhe, China[30]

In 1994, senior executives at Westmoreland Energy, Inc. (WEI—a subsidiary of Westmoreland Coal, a U.S. corporation) contemplated a \$540 million equity investment in an electric power-generating project at Zhangzhe, China. This investment would grant the executives a 50 percent equity interest in the venture. Analysts for Westmoreland Energy projected equity cash flows from the venture in renminbi (RMB), the Chinese currency. They sought to estimate an RMB IRR for the investment from these flows, and wanted to determine the appropriate "hurdle rate" for the investment. They adopted Approach B. Key elements in their analysis included:

- The dollar would inflate at between 2.5 and 4.0 percent over the life of the project. RMB would inflate at 10 percent.
- The tax rate would escalate from zero percent in the first two years of the project to 30 percent in years 6 onward.
- China's country beta relative to that of the United States was 1.08.
- China's sovereign debt premium relative to U.S. Treasuries was about 100 basis points.
- Since there were no comparable publicly traded power projects in China from which to gain a local beta, the analysts estimated a cost of equity by incorporating the country premium and country beta with U.S. data and then translated it to RMB using the Fisher formula:

$$K_{\text{China}} = \left[\left(1 + K_{\text{US}}\right) \cdot \left(\frac{1 + Inf_{\text{China}}}{1 + Inf_{\text{US}}}\right)\right] - 1 \quad (16)$$

Exhibits 12.14 and 12.15 give the calculations used to determine the project IRR of 23 percent and the hurdle rate of 21.6 percent. Sensitivity analysis revealed

EXHIBIT 12.14 WACC Estimation, WEI Investment in Project at Zhangzhe, China, 1995

Debt equity ratio	0.54
Unlevered beta	0.45
Tax rate	30%
Levered beta	0.62
Equity market risk premium	5.50%
Risk-free rate	8.09%
Political risk premium	1.55%
Country beta	1.08
Cost of equity, US$, power project in China	13.3%
Inflation, U.S.	2.5%
Inflation, China	10.0%
Cost of equity, RMB, power project in China	**21.6%**

Source: Author's analysis.

that higher project IRRs would be available if the plant operated at higher rates and was brought into production sooner.

WEI decided not to pursue the project further. The decision reflected two major factors: the slow decision making in the Chinese bureaucracy and the fear of high inflation—WEI's implicit bet was that China would not integrate as rapidly into the global economy as it had initially thought, preventing the benefits of trade and technology transfer that would have justified a lower capital cost.

Example: Continental Cablevision's Investment in Fintelco[31]

In 1994, the senior management of Continental Cablevision contemplated acquiring a 50 percent interest in the largest Argentine television cable company, Fintelco, for $80 million up front, and an additional $70 million over the next few years. Continental was facing a maturing market in the United States, and sought new avenues for growth and outlets for its strong positive cash flow. Meanwhile, Fintelco needed cash for the aggressive build-out of its cable system.

Strategically and organizationally, the investment seemed to make sense. But was the price right? Analysts for Continental followed Approach A. They forecasted cash flows in Argentine pesos. As a matter of government policy, the peso was pegged to the dollar at a 1:1 exchange rate. But observers wondered whether this was sustainable: the Economist Intelligence Unit projected inflation in the dollar at 2.5 percent for the next five years and inflation in the peso at 6 to 12 percent over the same period. There were no firms comparable to Fintelco listed for trading on the Argentine equity market.

Continental's analysts took a sample of betas for cable firms in the United States, unlevered and averaged them, and then relevered the average to derive a firm beta for Fintelco. The country beta for Argentina currently was 1.96. The country risk yield premium was 350 basis points over U.S. Treasuries at the time. Continental was uncertain about the government's commitment to maintaining a

EXHIBIT 12.15 IRR Estimation, WEI Investment in Project at Zhangzhe, China

	Calendar Year																		
	1995	1996	1997	1998	1999	2000	2001	2002	2003	2004	2005	2006	2007	2008	2009	2010	2011	2012	2013
Profit after tax				35	157	178	226	277	273	320	371	425	483	545	568	592	616	640	664
(+) Depreciation				279	279	279	279	279	279	279	279	279	279	279	279	279	279	279	280
(–) Debt amortization				(226)	(250)	(275)	(303)	(335)	(369)	(407)	(449)	(495)	(546)	—	—	—	—	—	—
(–) Equity investment	(317)	(454)	(366)																
Residual cash flow (Total project)	(317)	(454)	(366)	88	186	182	202	221	183	192	201	209	216	824	847	871	895	919	944
IRR (of total equity cash flows)	18.79%																		
WEI's Perspective																			
WEI economic interest	49.00%																		
WEI equity investment %	40.00%																		
RCF, WEI portion only	(117)	(161)	(125)	43	91	89	99	108	90	94	99	103	106	404	415	427	438	450	462
IRR (WEI equity in project)	**23%**																		

1:1 convertibility between the Argentine peso and the U.S. dollar, so the analysts modeled the cost of capital estimate under both scenarios. Under the 1:1 convertibility and devaluation scenarios, the resulting estimates of cost of capital were 17.1 and 16.6 percent respectively.

Exhibits 12.16 and 12.17 give the calculations of the WACC and NPV for the investment. The results present two exchange rate scenarios: 1:1 and depreciating peso. Under the stable scenario, the NPV would be $117 million and the IRR would be 22.7 percent. Under the depreciating peso scenario, the NPV would be $13 million and the IRR would be 17.8 percent.

Continental consummated the deal in October 1994, shortly before the "Tequila Crisis" associated with the Mexican peso devaluation in December 1994.

EXHIBIT 12.16 WACC Estimation, Continental Cablevision Investment in Fintelco, 1994

	Calculations Consistent with Exchange Rate Scenarios	
Estimation of WACC for Fintelco	**1:1 Convertibility**	**Devaluation**
Estimate of Levered Beta		
Book value of debt at closing (millions)	$133	$133
Market value of equity (DCF estimate)	$277	$173
MV debt equity	0.480	0.768
Mix assumed in analysis: % Debt	32%	43%
%Equity	68%	57%
Tax rate assumed (from forecast, average 1994 to 2002)	27.3%	27.3%
Unlevered beta (average of Viacom, TCI)	0.854	0.854
Equity (levered) beta:	**1.15**	**1.33**
Cost of Equity		
Risk-free rate (20 years)	6.4%	6.4%
Equity market risk premium	6.0%	6.0%
Levered firm beta	1.15	1.33
Argentine country beta relative to U.S.	1.96	1.96
Beta for Fintelco adjusted for country beta	2.26	2.61
Plus country risk premium	3.5%	3.5%
U.S.-based cost of Argentine equity	**23.4%**	**25.5%**
Cost of Debt		
Pretax cost of U.S. debt (at average BBB, BB yields)	8.6%	8.6%
Plus country risk premium	3.5%	3.5%
Pretax U.S. dollar cost of Argentine debt	12.1%	12.1%
Tax rate	27.3%	27.3%
After-tax cost	**6.3%**	**6.3%**
Weights of Debt and Equity		
Debt	32%	43%
Equity	68%	57%
WACC for Continental Investment in Fintelco	**17.9%**	**17.2%**

EXHIBIT 12.17 Discounted Cash Flow Valuation of Continental Cablevision's Investment in Fentelco

	Actual	Forecast								
	1993	1994	1995	1996	1997	1998	1999	2000	2001	2002
Revenues (Peso 000)	136,604	190,529	329,478	360,878	384,951	413,585	440,706	470,289	502,014	536,414
Expenses										
Operating	10,923	17,567	32,091	32,876	33,876	34,824	35,873	37,106	38,404	40,070
Local origination	4,858	7,031	12,059	11,259	11,279	11,456	11,899	12,463	13,153	13,893
Programming	42,163	73,773	100,425	103,464	107,786	113,074	118,991	125,802	133,686	142,740
G&A	19,878	35,305	86,158	80,873	80,185	80,856	82,632	86,439	90,764	95,911
Marketing	25,022	31,666	29,620	31,180	32,259	33,707	35,565	37,576	39,810	42,323
Total expenses	102,844	165,341	260,353	259,652	265,385	273,918	284,960	299,386	315,817	334,937
Operating Income	33,760	25,188	69,124	101,226	119,566	139,668	155,745	170,903	186,197	201,477
Less depreciation	5,101	9,004	17,317	20,259	24,642	28,193	30,770	33,305	35,270	37,359
Less amortization	—	—	16,195	17,280	17,243	17,243	17,243	17,243	17,243	17,243
Less financial and other expenses	4,498	2,296	—	—	—	—	—	—	—	—
EBIT	24,161	13,888	35,612	63,687	77,681	94,232	107,732	120,355	133,684	146,875
Less taxes	7,236	8,617	10,791	11,432	14,045	17,678	21,439	31,340	33,528	40,552
EBIAT	16,925	5,270	24,822	52,255	63,636	76,554	86,294	89,015	100,156	106,323
Plus amortization	—	—	16,195	17,280	17,243	17,243	17,243	17,243	17,243	17,243
Plus depreciation	5,101	9,004	17,317	20,259	24,642	28,193	30,770	33,305	35,270	37,359
Less capital expenditures	13,320	22,762	84,500	71,500	58,500	45,500	32,500	32,500	26,000	26,000
Less additions to net working capital	—	—	16,243	1,949	1,694	1,282	1,278	1,693	1,556	1,824
Free cash flow	8,706	(8,488)	(42,409)	16,346	45,327	75,208	100,529	105,370	125,113	133,101

(Continued)

EXHIBIT 12.17 *(Continued)*

Panel 1: Valuation Assuming No Devaluation: Fixed Exchange Rate Prevails: 1:1 (Peso/Dollar)

	BOY 1993	1994	1995	1996	1997	1998	1999	2000	2001	2002
TV WACC = 17.9%										
TV growth rate = 5.0%										
Debt of Fintelco	–133,000									
Equity invested in Fintelco (implied)	–160,000									
Dollar cash flow		–8,488	–42,409	16,346	45,327	75,208	100,529	105,370	125,113	133,101
Terminal value										1,085,091
Final free cash flow	–$293,000	–$8,488	–$42,409	$16,346	$45,327	$75,208	$100,529	$105,370	$125,113	$1,218,192
Net present value WACC = 17.9%	$117,299									
Internal rate of return	22.70%									

Panel 2: Valuation Assuming Devaluation: Parity-Implied Exchange Rates Prevail

	BOY 1993	1994	1995	1996	1997	1998	1999	2000	2001	2002
TV WACC = 17.2%										
TV growth rate = 5.0%										
Peso cash flow		(8,488)	(42,409)	16,346	45,327	75,208	100,529	105,370	125,113	133,101
Exchange rate (peso/dollar)*		1.124	1.184	1.294	1.389	1.436	1.436	1.436	1.436	1.436
Dollar cash flow		$(7,551)	$(35,819)	$12,632	$32,633	$52,373	$70,006	$73,377	$87,126	$92,689
Debt of Fintelco	–133,000									
Equity invested in Fintelco (implied)	–160,000									
Terminal value (in dollars)										799,072
Final free cash flow (in dollars)	–$293,000	–$7,551	–$35,819	$12,632	$32,633	$52,373	$70,006	$73,377	$87,126	$891,761
Net present value WACC = 17.2%	$13,156									
Internal rate of return	17.79%									

*Parity-implied exchange rates assume U.S. inflation at 2.5% over the entire forecast period, and Argentine inflation of 7%, 8%, 12%, 10%, 6%, 2.5%, 2.5%, 2.5%, and 2.5% for the years 1994 to 2002 respectively.

Notwithstanding the poor environmental conditions, Fintelco continued with the build-out of its system, and seized an important first-mover advantage in the Argentine market. In 1997, U.S. West bought Continental Cablevision and liquidated its interest in Fintelco at a price that yielded an IRR to Continental of between 32 and 56 percent.

SUMMARY

This chapter has given an overview of the challenges and solutions relative to valuing firms across borders. This is important since cross-border deals account for a material fraction of the total M&A activity in the United States (between 20 and 25 percent). In addition, country choice has a large influence on investment returns; carefully adjusting for the impact of crossing country borders should be an important goal for analysts.

The chapter has reviewed three adjustments to be made in the cross-border DCF valuation process:

1. ***Currency and inflation.*** Many executives prefer to see DCF analysis completed in the currency of the home country. The chapter showed that for long-lived projects, the interest rate parity formula can be used to generate forward currency exchange rates by which foreign cash flows can be translated to home cash flows. The use of the interest rate parity formula, however, requires a view about future inflation in both the local and home currencies.
2. ***Taxes.*** Tax rates differ across countries. While corporate tax rates are moving toward similar levels, the analyst should scrutinize the foreign tax rate and tax regime (territorial or worldwide). The tax assumption should be used consistently throughout the DCF valuation process.
3. ***Discount rate.*** Among developed countries whose economies are highly integrated, using a home market cost of equity to value a foreign company may be reasonable. But where cross-border differences are material, the analyst should use a discount rate that adequately reflects the risks of the foreign investment. The analyst should consider two factors of special concern in the cross-border setting: political risk and the impact of capital market segmentation. The multifactor model is the best practice approach to adjusting for these effects, but it is also the most costly in terms of time, data, and estimation skill. The credit model is easiest to use, but grants required returns at the country, not firm, level. The CAPM and its variants fall in the middle. The chapter illustrates the application of the CAPM adjusted for political risk and market segmentation.

Fundamentally, a review of cross-border valuation techniques must reemphasize to the reader the importance of having a view not merely about the forecast assumptions for the target firm, but as importantly, about the country and local market in which the target firm competes. Simple numerical analysis is relatively easy. It is more difficult to underpin that analysis with an appreciation for the strategic drivers of cross-border investment success or failure.

NOTES

1. Purchasing power parity is a theoretical concept of equilibrium in international markets whereby a commodity costs the same across different currencies. In equilbrium, the exchange rate between two currencies should equal the ratio of commodity prices. The classic test of parity is the "Big Mac" index published semiannually by the *Economist* magazine—the routine finding is of a few sizable departures from parity, and of broad but modest departure for most countries. Perhaps the academic consensus about PPP and IRP is that markets tend toward parity over time, though they virtually never actually achieve it. Macroeconomic shocks from commodity price changes (e.g., the oil embargo of 1974) and government policy changes are two possible causes of deviation from PPP and IRP.
2. The forward rate is observable daily in foreign exchange markets where forward foreign exchange contracts are struck by investors who require exchange at some future date of a quantity of one currency for a quantity of another. The rate of exchange embedded in this contract is the forward rate. Research suggests that forward rates are an unbiased (though imprecise) predictor of the exchange rate that actually prevails on that future date. For more on this, see the research by Meese and Rogoff (1983) and Goodman (1979).
3. Indeed, interest rate parity, combined with the theory of put-call parity (described in Chapter 10, "Valuing Options") affords a notion of the fundamental interrelatedness of all financial markets.
4. For instance, suppose a U.S. buyer wants to acquire a target company in Malaysia, which, for a while, imposed capital controls that would limit remittance of cash dividends from the Malaysian subsidiary. The U.S. firm could annually borrow an amount from a multinational bank equal to the remittance, and pledge the subsidiary to repay the loan. Except for the burden of interest expense and transaction costs, this synthesizes a flow of cash despite the limitation on remittances. Some countries are familiar with this tactic and limit its use.
5. In financial accounting, reserves may be established in anticipation of possible losses, such as write-offs stemming from the inability to collect debts or receivables. Reserves can be abused, creating "cookie jars" on which management can draw to smooth the earnings of the firm over time. The abuse of reserve accounting is a form of earnings management, the adverse consequences of which are discussed in Chapters 16 and 17.
6. Bribes and other forms of corrupt payments are condemned in the ethics statements of many companies and are forbidden to U.S. firms under the Foreign Corrupt Practices Act.
7. To hint at these differences, consider the fact that bond ratings reflect simply the estimated risk of default of the country on its sovereign debt—the risk of default depends only in part on political risk. The *Economist* ratings give meaningful weight to estimated levels of official corruption. For a helpful discussion of these risk rating sources, see Bekaert, Erb, Harvey, and Viskanta (1997).
8. For more on Marriott's use of this method, see Bruner and Humphries (1989).
9. OPIC is the acronym of the Overseas Private Investment Corporation of the U.S. Department of Commerce, which provides political risk insurance for U.S. firms on certain kinds of foreign investments.

10. For an example of a rating of countries on the basis of corruption, see the survey by Transparency International at www.transparency.org/cpi/2002/cpi2002.en.html. The ranking of selected countries in 2002 was Finland (#1), United Kingdom (#10), United States of America (#16), Germany (#18), Japan (#20), France (#25), Italy (#31), and Bangladesh (#102). The Economist Intelligence Unit has a database of over 3,000 publications that provide economic and political analysis and forecasts for 200 countries and regions. The country risk service assesses sovereign risk (www.eiu.com). The Institute for Management Development (IMD) publishes yearly a World Competitiveness Scoreboard that ranks 59 countries and regional economies (www01.imd.ch/wcy/ranking). The economies are ranked from the most to the least competitive, and past rankings can be seen for the last five years. The PRS Group, Inc., publishes two systems for evaluating the risks faced by business in countries around the globe. The Political Risk Services system forecasts the risks related to the general business concerns of regime stability, turmoil, financial transfer, direct investment, and export markets. The ICRG system rates political, economic, and financial risks, breaking each down into its key components, as well as compiling composite ratings and forecasts (www.prsgroup.com/commonhtml/methods.html). The World Economic Forum's Global Competitiveness Programme publishes yearly competitiveness reports covering the major economies of the world (www.weforum.org/site/homepublic.nsf/Content/Global+Competitiveness+Programme). Freedom House is a nonprofit, nonpartisan organization that seeks to promote political and economic freedom around the world. Since 1972, Freedom House has published an annual assessment of state of freedom by assigning each country and territory the status of "Free," "Partly Free," or "Not Free" by averaging their political rights and civil liberties ratings. The link to FH's country rankings is: www.freedomhouse.org/ratings/index.htm.
11. Field research finds that DCF is the dominant corporate valuation method used by financial executives. See Bruner et al. (1998), Graham and Harvey (2001), and Pereiro and Galli (2000).
12. Lessard (1996) gives an excellent presentation of the difference between these two types of risk, and the need to adjust for both of them.
13. As used throughout this book, "key bets" are major assumptions that require careful reflection and a view about how the world works.
14. For instance, a U.S. firm acquiring a European firm should be able to estimate a euro-based discount rate easily from European capital market information.
15. Of course, other things may not be equal. At any moment in time interest rate parity and purchasing power parity are violated somewhere on Earth. In some countries, various frictions such as taxes, transaction costs, regulations, and the host of other barriers that prevent integration with global capital markets may have differing effects on Approaches A and B. Still, the methods outlined here give a good framework for approaching the problem of cross-border valuation. The analyst should adapt the framework to meet the challenges of a particular situation.
16. The discussion here focuses on U.S. dollars, though one could easily substitute euros, yen, or pounds in place of dollars as the "home currency" and still describe the same analysis. This streamlines the discussion and spares the reader tedious references to multiple currencies.

17. The more familiar beta formula is equivalent to the version described earlier in equation 6 if one remembers that the numerator, the covariance between returns on the stock and returns on the market, equals the correlation times the standard deviations of each of those two returns: $COV_{i,M} = \rho_{i,M}\sigma_i\sigma_M$.
18. Under integration, the beta is estimated with respect to the home market, foreign market, or global market—under integration the beta will be the same estimated against all three. But under segmentation, the three betas will differ. As a cross-border investor, you want to be compensated for the risk of the foreign investment against the risk of your home market. Therefore, the appropriate beta under segmentation is estimated against your home market.
19. Bekaert and Harvey (1995), page 403.
20. See, for instance, Bodnar, Dumas, and Marston (2003), Errunza and Losq (1985, 1987), Solnik (1976, 1996), Diermeier and Solnik (2001), and Cavaglia, Hodrick, Vadim, and Zhang (2002).
21. One of the co-authors of the credit model, Professor Campbell Harvey, makes the estimation program available for purchase. See www.duke.edu/~charvey/applets/iccrc.html.
22. For a discussion of ICAPM, see O'Brien (1999), Schramm and Wang (1999), and Stulz (1995, 1999).
23. As suggested in Chapter 9, the long-term geometric mean equity market risk premium is about 6 percent. This is the *mean* premium. At any given point in time, the observed premium may differ substantially from the long-term average. Still, the long-term average may be the best guess if one's view about markets is that the premium will be mean-reverting.
24. This is an application of a more general way of approximating the beta of *any* asset with respect to the market. It is useful wherever one faces limited information in the particular financial market segment within which one is performing the valuation. It uses an approximation based on some relationship (i.e., beta) observed in some other market segment.
25. International Finance Corporation, *Emerging Stock Markets Factbook*, 1996.
26. Lessard suggests that other sources of overseas investment risk, such as those of operating risk, demand risk, and domestic market price risk, among others, may be modeled directly into the cash flows.
27. Lessard (1996) argues that currency effects may have a significant impact on cash flows, but not on market covariance risk. He says of currency risks that "since they are the relative prices of different currencies, by definition they cannot affect all assets in the same way." As such, they do not require a premium.
28. The nine countries were Australia, Canada, France, Germany, Japan, the Netherlands, Switzerland, the United Kingdom, and the United States.
29. The author's calculation from estimates presented in Bodnar, Dumas, and Marston (2002). The difference was calculated as the product of country and industry betas minus the beta of the company to the global index.
30. This illustration is based on research for the case study by the same name. See Bruner, Meiman, and Menefee (1996).
31. This illustration is based on research for the case study by the same name. See Bruner and Paddack (1997).

CHAPTER 13

Valuing the Highly Levered Firm, Assessing the Highly Levered Transaction

INTRODUCTION

High leverage presents special challenges for the M&A analyst. With high leverage, one enters the terra incognita of corporate finance, where neither theory nor empirical research is very prescriptive. Anecdotal evidence about this region suggests that investors behave as if the old linear assumptions turn nonlinear in the realm of high leverage, as attested by the high rates of return required by *leveraged buyout* funds and "vulture capitalists" (investors in bankrupt firms). Because of the complexity and relatively low volume of *highly leveraged transactions (HLTs)*, this is an area of M&A in which sound judgment comes at a superpremium. At high leverage, failure means financial distress, bankruptcy, and management change; thus, the HLT is not for the faint of heart. And HLTs present opportunities for *wealth transfers* among participants in the deal, making it vital that you negotiate your participation from a clear understanding about the division of returns. Having a rigorous view of the way to analyze these deals and their wealth-transfer possibilities is vital. In addition to helping you build such a view, this chapter aims to:

- ***Illustrate the application of classic DCF techniques to HLTs.*** Methods outlined in Chapter 9 are applied to actual deals: one *leveraged recapitalization* and two leveraged buyouts. Also shown are the adjusted present value method and the free cash flow approach.
- ***Highlight assumptions warranting special scrutiny.*** Adherence to the linear assumptions of risk and return or between levered and unlevered beta merits reflection. The convention in standard DCF analysis is to use one discount rate applicable to all years into the future. In the world of HLTs, the firm's capital structure will vary so materially as to warrant explicit modeling of the time-varying cost of capital. This creates an even greater-than-usual need for internal consistency in modeling—if done correctly, it creates circularities in modeling among the debt/equity ratio, cost of capital, and DCF value.
- ***Outline an analytic approach to the HLT.*** The main argument in this chapter is that the proper assessment of an HLT is grounded in an understanding of the risks and returns to all players. Thus, one must value not only the equity, but

also the various layers of debt and then critically assess the risk exposure and returns to each of the players.

- *Emphasize the role of judgment.* Whether the various players who invest at each level of capital in the HLT receive an adequate return for the risk they bear is a matter of judgment—in the terra incognita of corporate finance, there are no theories and few practical benchmarks against which to judge the fairness of returns. You must have a view about what is appropriate and then be prepared to abandon a deal in the face of an unattractive risk-return proposal.

THE WORLD OF HIGHLY LEVERED FIRMS

Forms of Highly Levered Transactions

While highly levered transactions appear in corporate finance in many guises, the practitioner should be familiar with the three classic forms.

LEVERAGED BUYOUT (LBO) In this transaction a private group of investors acquires a company (or division) financing it with a mixture of debt and equity that Shleifer and Vishny (1988) say ranges from 6:1 to 12:1. The major[1] source of equity for the LBO is typically a private investment company that specializes in organizing and investing in LBOs: the *buyout specialist.* Kohlberg, Kravis, and Roberts (KKR) is the largest and best known of these independent firms, though private equity affiliates of financial institutions, family groups (the Bass brothers, the Pritzkers, and the Bronfmans) and corporations (Berkshire Hathaway) have functioned in similar roles as *merchant bankers*, committing their own capital in support of transactions. Studies by Baker and Smith (1998) and others reveal that LBO firms seek returns on their equity investment in the range of 25 to 40 percent. Jensen (1989b) indicates that realized returns to equity investors in LBOs are in the range of 40 to 50 percent. This may be the case for successful deals, for Baker and Smith (1998) find that returns on portfolios of LBO investments are in the high 20 percent range. Cotter and Peck (2001) find that deals controlled by buyout specialists were less likely to experience financial distress and argued that the participation of a buyout specialist is associated with less stringent debt covenants and terms of repayment.

In the LBO, the management of the target is usually retained and often takes an equity interest in Newco—hence the alternative name for this transaction, *management buyout.* Often the terms for management participation require the managers to raise significant personal funds, thus giving them a personal stake in the success or failure of the transaction.[2] Whereas the firm may have been a public company before the transaction, it is a private company after; thus, the transaction acquired its third name, *going-private transaction.*

One of the hallmarks of LBO targets is their stability of cash flows. This is necessary to enable the assumption of a high ratio of debt to equity. A typical LBO candidate would have most of the following features: (1) strong cash flows, (2) low level of capital expenditures, (3) strong market position, (4) stable industry, (5) low rate of technological change (and low R&D expense),[3] (6) proven management with no anticipated changes, (7) relatively low (or under-) valuation in the stock market,[4] and (8) no major change in strategy. The impact of the LBO is to subject the firm to rigors usually associated with financial distress: a keen focus on improving efficiency, selling unnecessary assets, and repaying the debt. Lehn and Poulsen (1989) found a strong relationship between a firm's undistributed profits and the decision to go private. Hall (1991) reported that LBOs do not tend to occur in research-intensive industries, and that R&D spending declines after a major increase in leverage. Kaplan (1992) noted that the average life of the LBO is 6.7 years, at the end of which is an exit whereby the LBO firm and its investors either take the firm public through an IPO or sell it to another firm.

LEVERAGED RECAPITALIZATION In a "recap," the company dramatically levers itself and uses the proceeds of the financing to pay an extraordinary dividend or to repurchase shares. The chief differences between this and an LBO are that the target remains a public company and that therefore the public investors may participate in the post-transaction performance of the firm. There is no change of control and no participation by an LBO boutique. Management often does not take a significant stake in the equity of the firm. Recapitalizations are a defensive tactic in response to rumored or actual hostile takeovers. But in broad outline, the effects of the recap are similar to those of the LBO: self-imposed financial distress with pressure to improve operating efficiency and sell unnecessary assets. Chapter 34 describes the recap of American Standard.

REORGANIZATION IN DISTRESS OR BANKRUPTCY Whereas LBOs and recaps are voluntary, a transaction that recapitalizes a firm in distress or bankruptcy is involuntary.[5] In addition, a judgment by a court of law is usually necessary to discharge or reorganize contractual obligations of the firm. Ultimately, the aim of these reorganizations is to reduce, rather than increase, the firm's financial leverage. Bankruptcy is beyond the scope of this book and will not be discussed in more detail. However, the principles of valuation, assessment, and financing described in this chapter and in Chapter 20 are relevant to reorganizations in distress and bankruptcy.

LBO Activity

Exhibit 13.1 gives a perspective on the volume of LBOs and recaps in recent years. The buyout boom gained momentum in the early 1980s owing in no small part to economic recovery, declining interest rates, and a rising stock market. LBO activity peaked in the late 1980s, accounting for 5 to 7 percent of the number of all M&A deals, and 9 to 20 percent of the value of all M&A deals. The massive buyout of RJR Nabisco occurred in 1988. From 1999 to 2002, another wave of LBO activity appeared to be taking shape. Jensen (1989a) argued that the wave of LBOs and takeovers in the 1980s was a response to failures in corporate governance. Holmstrom and Kaplan (2001) summarized this view:

> *Ever since the 1930s management incentives had become weaker as corporations had become larger, management ownership had shrunk and shareholders had become more widely dispersed. No one watched management the way J.P. Morgan and other large investors did in the early part of the 20th Century. Boards, who were supposed to be the guardians of shareholder rights, mostly sided with management and were ineffective in carrying out their duties. One of*

EXHIBIT 13.1 Highly Levered Transaction Activity over Time and as a Percentage of All M&A Activity

	Leveraged Buyouts				Leveraged Recaps			
Year	Number	% of All M&A	Dollar Value	% of All M&A	Number	% of All M&A	Dollar Value	% of All M&A
1981	14	1.3%	$ 819	0.9%	—	0.0%	$ —	0.0%
1982	21	1.2%	$ 2,344	4.0%	—	0.0%	$ —	0.0%
1983	62	2.1%	$ 9,107	8.7%	—	0.0%	$ —	0.0%
1984	120	3.3%	$ 13,066	6.7%	—	0.0%	$ —	0.0%
1985	165	7.0%	$ 24,861	11.1%	6	0.3%	$ 109	0.0%
1986	277	7.3%	$ 38,740	14.1%	8	0.2%	$ 9,010	3.3%
1987	302	6.3%	$ 51,234	15.6%	6	0.1%	$16,828	5.1%
1988	439	6.6%	$101,163	20.5%	18	0.3%	$15,403	3.1%
1989	478	5.2%	$ 49,081	9.1%	26	0.3%	$ 8,699	1.6%
1990	402	4.1%	$ 18,654	4.7%	2	0.0%	$ 148	0.0%
1991	627	4.6%	$ 12,843	4.1%	3	0.0%	$ 794	0.3%
1992	673	5.2%	$ 14,358	4.3%	2	0.0%	$ 3	0.0%
1993	547	4.0%	$ 12,330	2.9%	1	0.0%	$ 111	0.0%
1994	563	3.6%	$ 16,476	3.1%	2	0.0%	$ 488	0.1%
1995	660	3.4%	$ 23,885	2.7%	3	0.0%	$ 1,334	0.1%
1996	635	3.1%	$ 23,549	2.3%	—	0.0%	$ —	0.0%
1997	737	3.3%	$ 36,943	2.4%	—	0.0%	$ —	0.0%
1998	784	3.2%	$ 42,309	1.8%	—	0.0%	$ —	0.0%
1999	1,102	4.1%	$ 73,991	2.4%	—	0.0%	$ —	0.0%
2000	1,116	3.8%	$ 78,467	2.5%	—	0.0%	$ —	0.0%
2001	880	3.9%	$ 55,059	3.7%	—	0.0%	$ —	0.0%
2002	768	4.2%	$ 71,232	7.2%	—	0.0%	$ —	0.0%

Source of data: Thomson Financial SDC Platinum database.

> *the big drawbacks of the corporation, according to Jensen, was that it could and did subsidize poorly performing divisions using the cash generated from successful ones instead of returning the "free cash flow" to the investors. (Page 10)*

Holmstrom and Kaplan (2001) argue that changes in the LBO business could be attributed to several factors. New entrants seeking a part of high LBO returns and new financing (the "junk bond" financing introduced by Michael Milken and others) produced a flood of new money that led to more aggressive deals, more defaults, lower returns, and falling interest. Kaplan and Stein (1992) documented that (1) buyout prices rose in the late 1980s, (2) LBO prices were particularly high in deals financed by junk bonds, (3) as prices rose capital structures became more aggressive, (4) targets came from increasingly risky industries—all of which led them to conclude that the LBO market had become overheated and that many of the deals of the late 1980s were "bad ideas" that should have been unattractive to smart investors. In the 1990s, the boom in strategic M&A meant that strategic buyers competed to acquire firms and divisions against the LBO firms. Given the synergy possibilities, strategic buyers were often able to outbid the LBO firms.

Effects of LBOs

The effects of the LBO wave have been the subject of research interest. Shareholders of target companies earn sizable abnormal returns, roughly in line with the target returns detailed in Chapter 3. DeAngelo, DeAngelo, and Rice (1984) find a 25 percent abnormal return over a period from 40 days before to 40 days after the announcement. At the announcement, Marais, Schipper, and Smith (1989) report a 13 percent abnormal return, and Lee (1992) finds a 14.9 percent abnormal return.

The shareholders of the buyer group fare even better. Jensen (1989a) cites findings of Steven Kaplan that the total net-of-market return to buyers over the life of their equity investment is 785 percent. Estimated on the entire capital base used to purchase the target firm, the net-of-market returns are 42 percent.

The large returns to target and buyer shareholders presage significant improvements in operating efficiency. Exhibit 3.8 of Chapter 3 reveals that LBO transactions are followed by sizable increases of operating cash flow relative to sales and by large decreases in capital expenditures. Lee (1992) and Amess (2002) report significant gains in efficiency. Smith (1990) found sustained increases in operating returns following buyouts owing to tighter management of working capital rather than to layoffs or cuts in advertising, R&D, maintenance, or capital spending. Opler (1992) examined LBOs in the late 1980s, a time when LBO profitability was believed to have declined: He found that even during this period operating margins in LBOs increased on a par with increases in earlier deals. Lichtenberg (1991) and Jensen (1989a) report significant gains in productivity. Some of these gains in efficiency may have come from concessions in employee compensation, as illustrated by Gilson (2000) in the case of the employee buyout of United Airlines.

Critics believed that LBOs were primarily motivated by tax considerations (e.g., the deductibility of interest expense) and that therefore the LBO wave triggered a large wealth transfer from the public sector to the private sector. Jensen, Kaplan, and Stiglin (1989) examined the tax revenue implications to the U.S. government and concluded that the Treasury's revenues actually increased as a result of

LBOs. They pointed to five sources of increased tax revenue: increased capital gains taxes paid by target firm shareholders, taxes on increased operating earnings, taxes on added interest income earned by creditors, taxes on the capital gains from asset sales, and additional taxes arising from more efficient use of capital. The increased interest *tax shield* and lost taxes on dividends forgone were offsetting factors.

Critics also noted several prominent defaults[6] by LBO targets, challenging the existence of improved efficiency in LBOs. Kaplan (1989a) and Kaplan and Stein (1993) found that in the early stage of the LBO wave, defaults were infrequent, about 2 percent. But in the late 1980s, almost 27 percent of LBOs defaulted on loans. Jensen (1989a) said, "LBOs frequently get in trouble, but they seldom enter formal bankruptcy. Instead they are reorganized in a short time (several months is common), often under new management, and at apparently lower cost than would occur in the courts." (Page 43) He called this the "privatization of bankruptcy." Kaplan and Andrade (1997) studied financially distressed HLTs and found that they had viable businesses with operating margins greater than the median for their industries—these firms were financially distressed, not economically distressed. Also, they found that from before the HLT transaction to after the resolution of distress, the value of the target firm actually *increased*.

EFFECT OF LEVERAGE ON VALUE OF THE FIRM

At the core of many discussions about the motives of HLTs is a set of notions about the impact of leverage on the value of the firm. It is necessary to understand both the financial and operating effects of leverage.

Leverage has two offsetting effects on firm value. The first is the benefit of debt tax shields, literally, the savings in free cash flow owing to a lower tax bill. This savings derives from the deductibility of interest expense from the firm's taxable income. In the modeling of Nobel laureates Franco Modigliani and Merton Miller (M&M), the impact of these tax savings is seen in the second term of this equation:

$$V_{\text{Levered}} = V_{\text{Unlevered}} + tD \tag{1}$$

This equation says that the value of the levered firm equals the value of the firm as if it were unlevered, plus the *present value of debt tax shields*, which M&M show is equal to the tax rate, t, times the amount of debt outstanding, D. The first term of the equation is the present value of operating cash flows. The second term of the equation, tD, can be viewed as the value effect of the firm's financing, the present value of debt tax shields. Chapter 9 presents this equation as the adjusted present value method of valuation.

The M&M model was controversial in large part because it implied that to maximize shareholder value, managers should lever the firm extremely and that to do so would expose the firm to the risk of bankruptcy, which the M&M model did not capture—M&M's debt was free of *default risk*. M&M's model was relevant over "reasonable" levels of debt (which is why it remains relevant today). But with higher levels of debt, one needed to impose costs of bankruptcy. This would be like subtracting a third term, C, from equation (1), to reflect the present value of expected bankruptcy and costs of financial distress.

$$V_{\text{Levered}} = V_{\text{Unlevered}} + tD - C_{\text{Bankruptcy and distress}} \tag{2}$$

As the borrowing of the firm increases, the effect of default risk will *offset* the value created by borrowing. At some point in the range between all equity and all debt financing of the firm, the impact of default risk will begin to more than offset the benefits of debt tax shields. That point is the optimum mix of debt and equity financing for the firm. Cast in graphical terms, Exhibit 13.2 illustrates this effect. The value of the firm rises as the firm goes from no debt to a moderate amount; this is because of the beneficial effects of the debt tax shields. Then the effect of default risk begins to be felt: As leverage increases beyond the optimum, the value of the firm begins to decline. Increasing the mix of debt beyond the optimum destroys value—it is equivalent to accepting financing whose cash received is less than the present value of future debt payments.

The large problem with valuing highly levered firms is that *costs of distress and bankruptcy* are unobservable. There is no fluid market in which these costs are isolated, priced, and may be observed from one day to the next. The analyst can look for some guidance about the size of C in equation (2) from two sources:

1. ***Debt markets.*** Costs of distress and bankruptcy are embedded in the interest rates charged by lenders: Interest rates rise as the risk of default increases. Exhibit 13.3 presents the yields to maturity on bonds of different risk ratings. As credit quality worsens, the cost of debt rises, at an increasing rate—this is the effect of increased default risk.[7] One could value the interest rate differential between default-risk-free debt (e.g., AAA-rated) and risky debt to determine the value of C. Unfortunately, theory offers no guidance on what should be the discount rate for determining the present value.
2. ***Put option valuation.*** In concept, C should be equal to the cost of an insurance policy necessary to convert risky debt into riskless debt. This is like a put option with a strike price equal to the face value of the debt and a value of the underlying asset equal to the market value of assets of the firm. Chapters 10 and

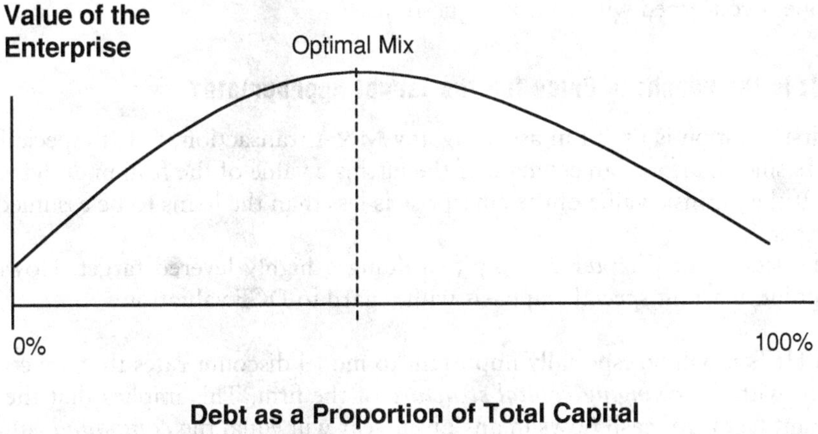

EXHIBIT 13.2 Finding the Optimal Mix of Debt and Equity: The Optimal Capital Structure Maximizes the Value of the Enterprise

EXHIBIT 13.3 Yields to Maturity by Risk Rating, August 1995

	AAA	AA	A	BBB	BB	B
Cost of debt (pretax)	6.70%	6.90%	7.00%	7.40%	9.00%	10.60%
Cost of equity	10.25%	10.3%	10.4%	10.5%	11.75%	13.00%

Source: Polaroid Corporation documents and analysis, August 1995, data calculated for 314 publicly rated industrial firms. Presented in Bruner and Chaplinsky (1998).

14 discuss aspects of this approach in more detail, though the answer you obtain will depend highly on the volatility assumption you adopt. There exists currently a market in credit derivatives from which such an insurance policy might be priced.

The difficulty of estimating the value of the highly levered firm has two main implications for the M&A practitioner. First, analytic rigor is even *more* important in the instance of HLTs, not less. Consistent with the messages of Chapter 9, the analytic rigor surrounding HLTs must seek to map the uncertainties about value and the risk of default. It remains that we cannot observe intrinsic value, we can only *estimate* it.

Second, the ambiguities about valuing the highly levered firm mean that there will be many opportunities to transfer value from some players (e.g., creditors) to others (e.g., equity holders) in the design of the transaction. Because of this risk of wealth transfers, the right approach is to assess the deal from the perspectives of all the providers of capital in the deal. This is the *"whole deal" approach*.

"WHOLE DEAL" APPROACH TO EVALUATING THE HIGHLY LEVERED FIRM AND TRANSACTION

In assessing a proposal to acquire or recapitalize a firm in a highly levered transaction, one is concerned with four key questions.

Step 1: Is the Purchase Price for the Target Appropriate?

This first question is useful in assessing any M&A transaction, but is especially so in HLTs since it affords an estimate of the intrinsic value of the firm underlying the loans. If the intrinsic value of the enterprise is less than the loans to be assumed, go no further.

The lessons of Chapter 9 apply to valuing a highly levered target. However, three points warrant special emphasis with regard to DCF valuation:

1. In HLTs it will be especially important to model discount rates that are consistent with the *changing capital structure* of the firm. This implies that the discount factor for cash flows in any given year will equal the *compound* value of the differing discount rates through time.[8] Strive to model precisely the time pattern of discount rates.

2. In HLTs the changing mix of debt and equity must be modeled so that they are consistent with the interest payments and changing quantities. For instance, the convention among practitioners is to reflect the debt balance as equal to the book value[9] of debt after principal payments, and to reflect interest expense consistent with that changing debt balance. The value of equity should be equal to the DCF value *each year* in order to reflect the changing value over time. This creates a *circularity* in a computer spreadsheet model that should be resolved by instructing the program to iterate several times to bring the cash flows, weights, and discount rates into consistent alignment. The circularity is shown in Exhibit 13.4. An example of this circularity is given in the MediMedia case that follows.
3. In HLTs the equity betas estimated using the levered beta formula could vary from those a reasonable investor might require. Recall that the formula in equation (3) is a *linear expression*, while in the terra incognita of high leverage, risk and return might not vary linearly.

$$\beta_{\text{Levered}} = \beta_{\text{Unlevered}}[1 + (1 - t)\ D/E] \qquad (3)$$

There is no theory and little empirical foundation for adjusting the levered beta formula for possible *nonlinearities*. As a test of reality, one could estimate betas for a sample of high yield bonds (i.e., debt of highly levered firms) in a similar industry; logic would suggest that the equity beta for a highly levered firm should be *no less* than the beta for its debt. As a matter of best practice, one should use the beta of a highly levered firm as an uncertain variable in estimating the valuation range and generally in doing sensitivity analysis.

Step 2: What Are the Sources of Positive Net Present Value?

In competitive markets, returns to investors should tend toward the level of investors' required rates of return, rendering NPVs to be zero. When one encounters a positive NPV, it makes sense to determine its sources. A simple valuation of the debt tax shields is a useful point of departure. But ordinarily, an HLT will also presume asset redeployments and improvements in operating efficiency. Sensitivity analysis of assumptions, scenario analysis, and estimation of breakeven assumptions (i.e., necessary to produce a zero NPV) can illuminate the key bets that undergird the positive NPV.

Step 3: Can the Firm Sustain the Debt It Will Assume?

This is of basic concern to all creditors. This question turns to the likelihood that the firm will default on its covenants or interest payments over the life of the loan. If default seems likely, you should either restructure the terms of the debt to reduce the probability or go no further.

How creditors evaluate default risk is discussed in more detail in Chapter 20 (see, especially, the "Six C's of Credit"). Fundamentally, credit analysis focuses on three tests worthy of careful scrutiny by the analyst in the setting of an HLT:

1. ***Asset coverage test.*** This seeks to determine whether over time sufficient collateral value exists with which to liquidate the loan. The first question answers

EXHIBIT 13.4 Circularity in Valuation

Line		Year				Notes
		Dec. 31, 2003	Dec. 31, 2004	Dec. 31, 2005	Dec. 31, 2006	
1	Revenues		1,000	1,050	1,102.5	Revenues grow at 5% annually.
2	Operating costs		–350.0	–367.5	–385.9	Operating costs are 35% of revenues.
3	Interest expense		–90.0	–60.3	–30.6	Interest expense is 9% of debt balance, prior year-end.
4	Taxes		–196	–217.8	–240.1	Taxes are at 35% of pretax profit.
5	Profit		364	404.4	445.9	Sum of revenues and costs.
6	Investments		–60	–63.0	–66.2	Equal to annual growth in assets.
7	Depreciation		30	31.5	33.1	Equal to half of annual asset growth.
8	Principal payments		–330	–330	–330	Starting debt amortizes one-third each year.
9	Residual cash flows		4	42.9	82.8	Sum of profits, investments, depreciation, and principal payments.
10	Terminal value (g = .05)				1,805.9	Constant growth model assuming 5% perpetual growth and cost of equity.
11	Total residual cash flows		4	42.9	1,888.8	Sum.
12	Assets	1,200.0	1,260.0	1,323.0	1,389.2	Assets grow at 5% annually.
13	Debt	1,000.0	670.0	340.0	10.0	Starting debt repaid one-third each year.
14	Equity	200.0	564.0	968.4	1,414.3	Equity grows as profit is retained (no dividends).
15	Liabilities & equity	1,200.0	1,234.0	1,308.4	1,424.3	Sum.
16	Risk-free rate	0.05	0.05	0.05	0.05	Constant risk-free rate assumed.
17	Equity market premium	0.06	0.06	0.06	0.06	Constant equity market premium assumed.
18	Unlevered beta	0.8	0.8	0.8	0.8	Constant unlevered beta assumed.
19	Book value of debt	1,000.0	670.0	340.0	10.0	Same as Line 13.
20	DCF value of equity	1,440.8	1,600.8	1,762.9	1,888.8	Sum of current year RCF and discounted value of prior year's DCF value of equity.
21	Debt/equity (DCF)	0.69	0.42	0.19	0.01	Line 19 divided by Line 20.
22	Levered beta	1.16	1.02	0.90	0.80	Equal to Line 18 times [1 + (1 – 0.35) Line 21].
23	Cost of equity	12.0%	11.1%	10.4%	9.8%	Equal to Line 16 plus Line 17 times Line 22.

this at time zero (i.e., whether the value of the firm exceeds the value of the debt). But the *asset coverage test* should be repeated for each year during the life of the debt. Using a model with circular reference that estimates equity value each year, this test is easily performed.

2. ***Interest coverage test.*** In its simplest form, the *interest coverage test* asks whether there is sufficient operating income to cover the pretax interest expense each year. This is the so-called EBIT/interest coverage ratio.

$$\text{EBIT/interest coverage ratio} = \frac{\text{Earnings before interest and taxes}}{\text{Interest expense}} \quad (4)$$

This ratio could be modified to use earnings before interest, taxes, depreciation, and amortization (EBITDA) or even free cash flow as the numerator. One could enlarge the denominator to include interest, principal payments, and debt-related fees (e.g., loan administration expenses). An EBIT/interest coverage ratio less than 1 suggests default. High yield debt carries coverage ratios in the range of 2.5 to 3.5 times. Exhibit 13.5 gives coverage ratios and other indicators of financial health by debt rating category.

3. ***Covenant coverage test.*** The loan agreement will specify that the borrower must maintain asset values (the asset coverage test), make timely interest and principal payments (the interest coverage test), and operate the firm so as to maintain certain financial ratios at acceptable levels (the *covenant coverage*

EXHIBIT 13.5 Key Industrial Financial Ratios by Rating Categories Median Values for 1993–1995

	AAA	AA	A	BBB	BB	B
Pretax interest coverage (×)	13.50	9.67	5.76	3.94	2.14	1.17
EBITDA interest coverage (×)	17.08	12.80	8.18	6.00	3.49	2.16
Funds from operations/ total debt (%)	98.20%	69.10%	45.50%	33.30%	17.70%	12.80%
Free operating cash flow/ total debt (%)	60.00%	26.80%	20.90%	7.20%	1.40%	–0.90%
Pretax return on permanent capital (%)	29.30%	21.40%	19.10%	13.90%	12.00%	9.00%
Operating income/sales (%)	22.60%	17.80%	15.70%	13.50%	13.50%	12.30%
Long-term debt/capital (%)	13.30%	21.10%	31.60%	42.70%	55.60%	65.50%
Total debt/capitalization including short-term debt (%)	25.90%	33.60%	39.70%	47.80%	59.40%	69.50%

Standard and Poor's defined these ratios based on the book value of these items as follows:
Pretax interest coverage is EBIT/interest expense.
EBITDA interest coverage is EBIT plus depreciation and amortization/interest expense.
Long-term debt/capital = Long-term debt/(Long-term debt + Stockholders' equity).
Total debt/capitalization including Short-term debt = (Short-term debt + Long-term debt)/(Short-term debt + Long-term debt + Stockholders' equity).
Source: Standard & Poor's *CreditWeek*, October 30, 1996, page 26. Reprinted by permission of Standard & Poor's, a division of the McGraw-Hill Companies.

test). For instance, covenants in the loan agreement might require the borrower to maintain the current ratio or quick ratio above specified levels. The ability to clear these covenants each year should be tested by examining a forecast of financial statements under various adverse scenarios.

Perhaps the ultimate exercise of any of these coverage tests is to estimate the probability of failure using Monte Carlo simulation; this is discussed further in the section on leveraged buyout later in the chapter.

Step 4: What Are the Prospective Returns to the Various Providers of Funds in This Deal?

This final question raises the issue of *fairness* to the various players. For instance, creditors in HLTs provide most of the funds and yet enjoy lower rates of return than equity holders; whether the return difference is appropriate is a matter of judgment. But estimating the payoffs for all players at least brings them into daylight and gives the basis for an objective assessment of whether to accept or renegotiate the terms.

A LEVERAGED RECAPITALIZATION: KOPPERS COMPANY

On March 3, 1988, Beazer Plc. (a British construction company) and Shearson Lehman Hutton, Inc. (an investment banking firm) commenced a hostile tender offer to purchase all the outstanding stock of Koppers Company, Inc., a producer of construction materials, chemicals, and building products. Originally the raiders offered $45 per share; subsequently the offer was raised to $56, and then finally $61 per share. The Koppers board asserted that the offers were inadequate and its management was reviewing the possibility of a leveraged recapitalization in which the firm would borrow and dividend the proceeds to its shareholders. If Beazer proceeded to acquire Koppers it would be assuming a large debt burden and acquiring a firm with shrunken equity value. Analysts and investors wondered how the leveraged recapitalization would affect Koppers' equity value.

To test the valuation effects of the recapitalization alternative, assume that Koppers could borrow a maximum of $1,738,095,000 at a pretax cost of debt of 10.5 percent and that the aggregate amount of debt would remain constant in perpetuity. Thus, Koppers would take on additional debt of $1,565,686,000 (i.e., $1,738,095,000 minus $172,409,000 already outstanding in 1988). Also assume that the proceeds of the loan would be paid as an extraordinary dividend to shareholders.

Exhibit 13.6 presents Koppers' book- and market-value balance sheets assuming the capital structure before and after recapitalization. Note the changes from before to after. Book value of debt rises and book value of equity falls by $1,565,686,000. This produces a *negative* book value of equity for Koppers, suggesting bankruptcy—but no: Business and financial decisions are based on market value, not book value. The lower half of Exhibit 13.6 reveals that the market value of equity is *positive* $668,391,000. The difference between book and market values of equity after the recapitalization is due to two effects. First, Koppers' market value of equity was greater than its book value before the recap. Second, the additional debt created valuable tax shields that benefited shareholders. The example

EXHIBIT 13.6 Estimate of Gains from Restructuring Defense of Koppers Company

	Before Recapitalization	Changes	After Recapitalization
Book Value Balance Sheets			
Net working capital	$ 212,453		$ 212,453
Fixed assets	601,446		601,446
Total assets	$ 813,899		$ 813,899
Long-term debt	172,409	1,565,686	$1,738,095
Deferred taxes, etc.	195,616		195,616
Preferred stock	15,000		15,000
Common equity	430,874	(1,565,686)	(1,134,812)
Total capital	$ 813,899		$ 813,899
Market-Value Balance Sheets			
Net working capital	$ 212,453		$ 212,453
Fixed assets	1,618,081		1,618,081
PV debt tax shield (equals .34 times debt balance)	58,619	532,333	590,952
Total assets	$1,889,153		$2,421,486
Long-term debt	$ 172,409	1,565,686	$1,738,095
Deferred taxes, etc.	0		0
Preferred stock	15,000		15,000
Common equity	1,701,744	(1,033,353)	$ 668,391
Total capital	$1,889,153		$2,421,486
Number of shares	28,128		28,128
Price per share	$ 60.50		$ 23.76
Value to Public Shareholders			
Cash received	0		$1,565,686
Value of shares	$1,701,744		$ 668,391
Total	1,701,744		2,234,077
Total per share	$ 60.50		$ 79.43

assumes that the present value of the debt tax shield is equal to the product of the marginal tax rate (t) and the amount of debt (D).[10]

At the bottom of Exhibit 13.6, one sees that the share price of Koppers will shrink from $60.50 per share to $23.76 per share. But accounting for the extraordinary dividend, the recapitalization will deliver a total of $79.43 per share to equity holders, a 31 percent increase in value over the pre-recapitalization value and Beazer's bid price.

Exhibit 13.6 illustrates the fundamental logic of the adjusted present value approach to valuation. To replicate this analysis on another transaction, follow these steps:

1. Project the book value balance sheets before and after the transaction. This creates the top half of Exhibit 13.6.

2. Estimate the market value of the enterprise before the transaction by adding together the book value of liabilities and the market value of equity of the firm. Using the book value of liabilities is reasonable in situations where obligations have floating interest rates or where the fixed interest rates on a firm's debt are reasonably close to yields on similarly-rated debt in the open market. Many analysts attribute no liability value to deferred taxes: In most jurisdictions a growing firm will never pay these; they are a subsidy from the government.
3. Estimate the present value of the firm's debt tax shields before the HLT. Fernandez (2002a,b,c,d) argues that these should be valued using the cost of equity of the unlevered firm.
4. Solve for the implied market value of the firm's long-term business assets before the HLT. This will be equal to the book value of liabilities plus the market value of equity less the book value of current assets and less the present value of debt tax shields.
5. Now solve for the market value of equity of the firm after the HLT. First, estimate the market value of the enterprise *after* the transaction; this equals the value of current and fixed assets that existed before, plus the *new* present value of debt tax shields. Now, subtract the *new* value of liabilities. This yields the new market value of equity.
6. Estimate the new price per share as equal to the new market value of equity, plus any extraordinary dividend to be received, divided by the number of shares.

A LEVERAGED BUYOUT: MEDIMEDIA INTERNATIONAL, LTD.

In February 1991, MediMedia sought to raise $70.13 million to finance an LBO by management who would purchase it from its parent, Dun and Bradstreet (D&B).[11] MediMedia had four principal medical product groups: medical journals, drug directories, office media (such as prescription pads and other medical stationery), and custom media (such as single-sponsored publications, educational videos, and training services). D&B was refocusing its business operations and sought to shed the MediMedia unit. Management proposed to raise funds from various sources for the buyout: senior debt, mezzanine debt, a vendor note, and equity—these are summarized in Exhibit 13.7.

Management had forecasted the financial results for the period 1991–1998 (see Exhibits 13.8 and 13.9), which suggested that the outstanding debt under the senior term loan facility could be repaid in full within six years. An important feature of the projections was that they assumed no asset sales, acquisitions, capital expenditure cutbacks, or cost-reduction programs.

Revenue in 1991 was expected to grow at 21 percent; this forecast was significantly influenced by the weakening of the U.S. dollar against those European currencies that accounted for over two-thirds of the group's revenues. At constant rates, revenue growth would be 11 percent. Growth in 1991 was expected to be achieved through a combination of price increases (to keep pace with inflation), new products, increased publication frequency, and the publication of certain biannual products.

EXHIBIT 13.7 MediMedia International, Ltd.: Deal Structure

Revolver and Senior Term Debt	$32.00 million
Term: 7 years	
Rate: LIBOR + 2.25 percent	
Secured	
Restrictive covenants	
Mezzanine Debt	$15.00 million
Term: 8 years	
Rate: LIBOR + 3.25 percent	
Warrants: 15 percent of fully diluted shares	
Nominal exercise price	
Put option on warrant shares	
Vendor Note	$11.00 million
Term: 10 years	
Rate: Contemporaneous U.S. Treasury + 0.52 percent	
Pay-in-kind, first two years	
Profit participation on asset sales	
Equity	$11.00 million
No dividends permitted	
Fully owned by management (before warrants)	
Existing liabilities	$ 1.13 million
Total sources of funds	$70.13 million

Proposed Terms, Senior Revolving and Term Debt

Borrowers: New holding companies in the Netherlands, Hong Kong, Switzerland, Germany, and France, as well as Les Editions du Médecin Généraliste S.A.

Guarantors: MediMedia (the ultimate parent), the regional holding companies, and Les Editions du Médecin Généraliste S.A., jointly and severally.

Purpose: To finance the acquisition, and pay the fees, costs, and expenses relating thereto.

Currency: The senior term loan facility will be divided into two tranches, A and B. Tranche A drawings will be denominated in ECUs, and tranche B drawings will be denominated in U.S. dollars. Advances under the revolving loan facility may be in U.S. dollars and other freely convertible foreign currencies.

Amounts: The senior term loan facility aggregate drawings under tranche A: ECU 10,090,000. Aggregate drawings under tranche B: US$18,000,000. Revolving loan facility amount is US$4,000,000, or the equivalent in other currencies.

Agent: BHF-Bank, Frankfurt.

Lead Managers: Kleinwort Benson, Ltd., and BHF-Bank.

Repayment: Revolving loan facility must be repaid in full no later than the seventh anniversary of the senior facilities agreement.

Senior term loan installments:

	Tranche A	Tranche B
November 30, 1991	0	US$2,000,000
November 30, 1992	0	US$4,000,000
November 30, 1993	ECU 1,550,000	US$1,850,000
November 30, 1994	ECU 1,800,000	US$2,000,000
November 30, 1995	ECU 2,150,000	US$2,500,000
November 30, 1996	ECU 2,525,000	US$3,000,000
November 30, 1997	**The balance**	**The balance**

EXHIBIT 13.8 Financial Forecast, MediMedia International, Ltd.: Forecasted Profits and Cash Flows, 1991–1998, Fiscal Years Ending November 30 (US$ Millions)

	Historical			Projected							
	1988	1989	1990	1991	1992	1993	1994	1995	1996	1997	1998
EBIT	7.60	9.50	8.90	11.42	14.60	16.89	18.25	19.71	21.29	23.00	24.85
Less interest on:											
Existing debt	N/A	N/A	N/A	1.00	0.03	0.03	0.03	0.03	0.03	0.03	0.04
Working capital revolver	N/A	N/A	N/A	0.17	0.17	0.17	0.17	0.17	0.17	0.17	0.17
Senior term loan	N/A	N/A	N/A	1.69	3.20	2.83	2.83	1.87	1.25	0.52	0.00
Mezzanine loan	N/A	N/A	N/A	0.99	1.99	1.99	1.99	1.99	1.99	1.99	1.99
Junior subordinated debt	N/A	N/A	N/A	0.47	0.94	0.94	0.94	0.94	0.94	0.94	0.94
Total interest expense	N/A	N/A	N/A	(4.32)	(6.33)	(5.96)	(5.51)	(5.00)	(4.38)	(3.65)	(3.14)
Interest income	N/A	N/A	N/A	0.32	0	0.13	0.25	0.38	0.55	0.74	1.06
Tax expense	N/A	N/A	N/A	(1.82)	(2.53)	(3.38)	(3.95)	(4.58)	(5.29)	(6.08)	(6.89)
Net income	N/A	N/A	N/A	5.60	5.74	7.68	9.04	10.51	12.17	14.01	15.88
Depreciation	0	1.30	2.00	1.90	1.98	2.01	2.11	2.22	2.22	2.22	2.22
Increase in deferred taxes	(0.10)	0	0.70	(0.25)	(0.19)	(0.20)	(0.20)	0	0	0	0
Capital expenditures	0	0	0	(2.69)	(1.40)	(2.64)	(2.77)	(2.91)	(2.91)	(2.91)	(2.91)
Decrease in accounts receivable	1.80	0.70	(6.40)	(0.02)	(2.24)	(2.73)	(2.95)	(3.19)	(3.44)	(3.72)	(4.02)
Decrease inventories	0.30	0	(1.20)	0.17	(0.23)	(0.32)	(0.40)	(0.43)	(0.46)	(0.50)	(0.54)
Decrease prepaid expense	0	(1.20)	(0.80)	0.40	(0.12)	(0.14)	(0.15)	(0.16)	(0.18)	(0.19)	(0.21)
Increase accounts payable	0.50	0.80	(10.80)	0.18	0.80	1.15	1.41	1.52	1.64	1.77	1.91
Increase taxes payable	0	0	1.30	0.45	0.57	0	0	0	0	0	0
Increase accrued liabilities	0	0	11.30	(1.33)	0.70	0.85	0.92	0.99	1.07	1.16	1.25
Noncash interest expense	0	0	0	0.47	0.94	0.47	0	0	0	0	0
Cash available for debt repayment	N/A	N/A	N/A	4.88	6.55	6.13	7.01	8.55	10.11	11.84	13.58
Scheduled debt repayments											
Senior term	N/A	N/A	N/A	2.00	4.00	4.00	4.50	5.50	6.50	5.50	0
Mezzanine	N/A	N/A	N/A	0	0	0	0	0	0	0	15.00
Junior subordinated debt	N/A	N/A	N/A	0	0	0	0	0	0	0	0
Total	N/A	N/A	N/A	2.00	4.00	4.00	4.50	5.50	6.50	5.50	15.00
Revolver repayment	N/A	N/A	N/A	(1.70)	0	0	0	0	0	0	0
Residual cash flow (Addition to cash balance)	10.10	11.10	5.00	4.58	2.55	2.13	2.51	3.05	3.61	6.34	(1.42)

Source: Offering memorandum.

EXHIBIT 13.9 MediMedia International, Ltd.: Historical and Forecasted Net Assets and Capital Structure, 1991–1998 (US$ Millions)

	Preclosing Nov. 1990	Changes	Pro Forma Nov. 1990	1991	1992	1993	1994	1995	1996	1997	1998
Net assets											
Net working capital	$11.04	$ (4.47)	$ 6.57	$11.30	$14.37	$17.69	$21.37	$25.69	$30.67	$ 38.49	$ 38.68
Gross PPE	7.71		7.71	10.40	11.80	14.44	17.21	20.12	23.03	25.94	28.85
Accumulated depreciation	0		0	1.90	3.88	5.89	8.00	10.22	12.44	14.66	16.88
Net PP&E	7.71		7.71	8.50	7.92	8.55	9.21	9.90	10.59	11.28	11.97
Other LTA	2.42		2.42	2.42	2.42	2.42	2.42	2.42	2.42	2.42	2.42
Goodwill	0	45.93	45.93	45.93	45.93	45.93	45.93	45.93	45.93	45.93	45.93
Transaction costs	0	7.50	7.50	7.50	7.50	7.50	7.50	7.50	7.50	7.50	7.50
Total net asset	21.17	48.96	70.13	75.65	78.14	82.09	86.43	91.44	97.11	105.62	106.50
Capital structure:											
Existing debt	0.29		0.29	0.29	0.29	0.29	0.29	0.29	0.29	0.29	0.29
Revolver	0	0	0	1.70	1.70	1.70	1.70	1.70	1.70	1.70	1.70
Senior term debt	0	32.00	32.00	30	26.00	22.00	17.50	12.00	5.50	0	0
Mezzanine debt	0	15.00	15.00	15.00	15.00	15.00	15.00	15.00	15.00	15.00	0
Junior subordinated debt	0	11.00	11.00	11.47	12.41	12.88	12.88	12.88	12.88	12.88	12.88
Total debt	0.29	58.00	58.29	58.46	55.40	51.87	47.37	41.87	35.37	29.87	14.87
Deferred tax	0.84		0.84	0.59	0.40	0.20	0	0	0	0	0
Equity	32.33	(21.33)	11.00	16.60	22.34	30.02	39.06	49.57	61.74	75.75	91.63
Total capital	33.46	48.96	70.13	75.65	78.14	82.09	86.43	91.44	97.11	105.62	106.50
Ending debt/equity (×)	0.01	36.67	4.92	3.40	2.44	1.72	1.21	0.84	0.57	0.39	0.16
Average debt/equity (×)				4.16	2.92	2.08	1.46	1.03	0.71	0.48	0.28
EBIT/interest (×)				2.6	2.3	2.8	3.3	3.9	4.9	6.3	7.9
EBIT/interest & principal (×)				2.5	1.4	1.7	1.8	1.9	2.0	2.5	1.4

Source: Offering memorandum.

The modest improvement in gross margins projected for 1991 was believed to be conservative, because of the absence of substantial one-time costs for restructuring, product relaunches, and redundancies taken to direct costs during 1990. Management forecasted no other significant margin improvements, although it expected improved performance from several products.

Management assumed no improvement in working-capital control in 1991 and only a modest improvement in 1992. Historically, there had been little incentive to speed cash collection, although management believed there was considerable room for improvement.

The projections assumed a 30 percent effective tax rate, even though the marginal corporate tax rate throughout most of the European Community and the United States was about 35 percent. This lower rate reflected efforts to create a tax-efficient corporate structure by channeling earnings away from high-tax jurisdictions and debt toward low-tax jurisdictions.

As MediMedia was a division, it had no beta or other basis for directly estimating a cost of equity. A sample of peer companies' unlevered betas were averaged and relevered to reflect the prospective capital mix of MediMedia. The new firm's debt was priced off of the London interbank offered rate (LIBOR), then at 6.75 percent.

Equity Holder's Perspective: Residual Cash Flow Valuation Approach

The equity investors' discounted cash flow (DCF) analysis of the buyout is relatively straightforward. Exhibit 13.10 presents the cash flows to equity holders, estimated from the financial forecasts for the firm, and the completed DCF value. To estimate a discount rate, one should look for companies concentrated in professional journals, and with a multinational business base. Three companies that fit this profile were Commerce Clearing House, Elsevier N.V., and Euromoney Publications PLC. The top panel in Exhibit 13.10 presents a calculation of the average unlevered beta for the three comparable companies. The cost of equity is based on the DCF value of equity, estimated recursively year by year. As Exhibit 13.10 reveals, MediMedia's debt/equity ratio will vary in a determinate way (i.e., downward) over the forecast period. This trend will cause the levered beta and the cost of equity to fall over time. A careful analyst would relever each year's beta using the average debt/equity ratios given in the financial forecasts. The analyst can estimate the exact discount factor for each year by compounding the costs over time, then discounting the cash flows. The estimate of terminal value uses the constant growth valuation model discussed in Chapter 9. The estimated internal rate of return (IRR) is 54.2 percent; the net present value (NPV) is about $57 million. This investment appears to be very attractive from the equity investor's standpoint.

Sources of Positive Net Present Value

An NPV of $57 million represents significant value created, especially relative to the initial equity outlay of $11 million. This should motivate a discussion of the sources of new value:

- *Operating economies.* Management planned to run a leaner and more aggressive operation than before the LBO. For instance, it proposed to reduce working

EXHIBIT 13.10 Valuation Analysis of LBO: MediMedia International, Ltd.; DCF Analysis of Equity Cash Flows (in Millions of US$)

	Leveraged Beta	Market D/E	Asset Beta
Estimate of Unlevered Beta			
Commerce Clearing House	0.7	0.028	0.69
Elsevier N.V.	1.05	0.005	1.05
Euromoney Publications PLC	1.05	0.01	1.04
Averaged unlevered beta			0.93

	At Closing	1991	1992	1993	1994	1995	1996	1997	1998
Estimate of Annual Discount Factors									
Book value of debt at end of year	58.29	58.46	55.40	51.87	47.37	41.87	35.37	29.87	14.87
DCF value of equity at end of year	57.41	79.17	86.06	96.05	107.67	120.21	133.58	147.89	160.50
Debt/equity ratio (using DCF value of equity)	1.02	0.74	0.64	0.54	0.44	0.35	0.26	0.20	0.09
Relevered beta using DCF value D/E	1.58	1.40	1.34	1.27	1.21	1.15	1.10	1.06	0.99
Cost of equity		15.7%	15.4%	15.0%	14.6%	14.3%	14.0%	13.8%	13.4%
Annual discount factor		0.86	0.75	0.65	0.57	0.50	0.44	0.38	0.34
Estimate of Cash Flows to Equity Holders									
Residual									
Cash flow	($11.00)	$4.58	$2.55	$2.13	$2.51	$3.05	$3.61	$6.34	($1.42)
Terminal value									$161.92*
Assumed perpetual growth rate 5.00%									
Total residual cash flow	($11.00)	$4.58	$2.55	$2.13	$2.51	$3.05	$3.61	$6.34	$160.50
DCF Estimates									
DCF =	($11.00)	$3.96	$1.91	$1.39	$1.43	$1.52	$1.57	$2.43	$54.21

IRR = 54.2%

NPV = $57.41 ⇐ **This estimate uses the time-varying discount factors estimated above.**

*The terminal value is estimated by dividing cash flow *before* debt amortization in 1998 by the cost of capital (14% in 1998), less a reasonable growth rate to infinity, 5.0% (approximately the rate of inflation in Western Europe in 1992). The use of cash flow *after* amortization is to be avoided in this instance because it reflects an extraordinary debt-amortization payment in 1998, which will not be repeated thereafter.

capital by $4.47 million to help fund the buyout. The earnings before interest and taxes (EBIT) were forecasted to grow at an aggressive growth rate (11.7 percent compounded) compared to the EBIT stream under D&B's ownership or compared to the expected growth rates of comparable companies.

- ***Debt tax shields.*** The aggressive use of debt could create value by reducing the firm's tax expense. Separate valuation reveals that the present value of this tax savings would be $6.99 million—these are relatively small in comparison to the total value created.
- ***Structuring and wealth transfers.*** A skeptic might assert that the value created for equity holders represents wealth extracted from other participants in the deal. This hypothesis has foundation. For instance, the true value of the vendor note is probably not $11 million, but rather something less—the true value reflects the extraordinarily low coupon. If one discounts the vendor note cash flows at 14 percent (the internal rate of return of the mezzanine debt), the market value of the note is only $6.6 million, or $4.4 million less than par value. Of course, if one suspects that the required rate of return for the mezzanine debt and vendor note should be higher than $6.6 million, the discount from par value would rise. The point of this analysis is to suggest that the equity holders may gain at the creditors' expense. More is said later about the interesting structural aspects of this deal.

Banker's Perspective

The two classic questions that the bankers should weigh are (1) the *probability of default* and (2) the adequacy of returns. Regarding default risk, one could perform a sensitivity analysis of the forecast results. At the minimum, one should compare the forecast EBIT coverage ratios to the minimum acceptable ratios in the terms. This simple comparison reveals that MediMedia was forecasted to cover its minimum ratio, although the coverage is rather thin in 1992 (2.3 times versus a typical minimum of 2.0 times).

Regarding the adequacy of returns, one could generate two different kinds of measures. The first is the traditional estimate of IRR on assets, which is computed on cash flows to the banks after taxes and after funding costs. This measure makes a straightforward comparison to the typical benchmark, one percent IRR on assets for banks. As calculated in Exhibit 13.11, the IRR on assets is a relatively attractive 2.79 percent. The main problem with this measure is that it is not directly comparable to the IRRs estimated for either the equity holders or mezzanine investors. IRRs for mezzanine investors reflect neither funding costs nor the investors' taxes.

To compare returns across participants in the buyout, one could calculate a second measure, the IRR of cash flows before bank taxes and funding costs. As calculated in Exhibit 13.11, this IRR is 9.04 percent, or 1.17 percent greater than the contemporaneous long-term risk-free rate of 7.87 percent.

Is the risk premium enough compensation? On one hand, the bank lenders are the *senior* claimants on the firm's cash flows and assets; also, the terms of the loan agreement seem to have anticipated possible adversities (see the discussion on structuring that follows). On the other hand, this loan is big for the relatively few tangible

EXHIBIT 13.11 MediMedia International, Ltd.: Estimation of Bankers' IRRs (Flows in Millions of US$)

	At Closing	1991	1992	1993	1994	1995	1996	1997	1998
Basic Assumptions									
LIBOR = 6.75%									
Spread: LIBOR – Cost of funds = 200 basis points									
Revolver balance	0.00	1.70	1.70	1.70	1.70	1.70	1.70	1.70	0.00
Senior term balance	32.00	30.00	26.00	22.00	17.50	12.00	5.50	0.00	0.00
IRR of After-Tax Cash Flows Net of Funding Costs									
Net interest income									
Revolver		0.00	0.07	0.07	0.07	0.07	0.07	0.07	0.07
Senior term		1.36	1.28	1.11	0.93	0.74	0.51	0.23	0.00
Commitment fee		0.00	0.01	0.01	0.01	0.01	0.01	0.01	0.01
Income tax		–0.48	–0.48	–0.42	–0.36	–0.29	–0.21	–0.11	–0.03
Debt amortization									
Revolver	0.00	–1.70	0.00	0.00	0.00	0.00	0.00	0.00	1.70
Senior term	–32.00	2.00	4.00	4.00	4.50	5.50	6.50	5.50	0.00
Total cash flow	–$32.00	$1.18	$4.88	$4.77	$5.16	$6.04	$6.89	$5.71	$1.75
IRR (ROA) =	2.79%	Traditional measure of loan profitability							
IRR of Cash Flows before Funding Costs and Bank Taxes									
Gross pretax cash flow =	–$32.00	$3.18	$6.86	$6.50	$6.64	$7.24	$7.74	$6.16	$1.86
Gross pretax IRR (ROA) =	9.04%	A comparable measure to the IRRs computed for equity holders and mezzanine investor							

EXHIBIT 13.12 MediMedia International, Ltd.: Estimation of Mezzanine Investor's IRR (Flows in Millions of US$)

	At Closing	1991	1992	1993	1994	1995	1996	1997	1998
IRR Estimate, Assuming Value of Equity Is $11 million									
Interest income		0.99	1.99	1.99	1.99	1.99	1.99	1.99	1.99
Principal payments	–15.00	0	0	0	0	0	0	0	15
Option value*	1.40								
Total cash flow	–13.6	0.99	1.99	1.99	1.99	1.99	1.99	1.99	16.99
IRR =	**14.02%**								
IRR Estimate, Assuming Value of Equity Is $50 Million									
Interest income		0.99	1.99	1.99	1.99	1.99	1.99	1.99	1.99
Principal payments	–15.00	0	0	0	0	0	0	0	15
Option value†	6.37								
Total cash flow	–8.63	0.99	1.99	1.99	1.99	1.99	1.99	1.99	16.99
IRR =	**24.16%**								

*The value of the warrants to be given to the mezzanine investors is estimated using the Black-Scholes option pricing model and these parameters:
Time = 8 years
Risk-free rate = 7.87%
Exercise price = $0.01 million
Current value of stock = $1.4 million (equal to 15 percent of $11 million, the outlay of equity investors at closing, less 15 percent warrant dilution)
Volatility = 0.29 (the average of volatilities for Commerce Clearing House, Elsevier, and Euromoney; see case Exhibit 13.10)
†The value of the warrants to be given to the mezzanine investors is estimated using the Black-Scholes option pricing model and these parameters:
Time = 8 years
Risk-free rate = 7.87%
Exercise price = $0.01 million
Current value of stock = $6.38 million (equal to 15 percent of $50 million, the rough DCF value of equity at closing, less 15 percent warrant dilution)
Volatility = 0.29 (the average of volatilities for Commerce Clearing House, Elsevier, and Euromoney; see case Exhibit 13.10)

assets. The trademarks and titles have value, although, after a period of financial distress, their value could have deteriorated. Though a market for medical journals exists, it is not very liquid. Also, the loan agreement was structured so that the principal intellectual property was transferred to the borrowing companies, permitting the lenders to take direct security interests. The most significant assets of the firm walk out of the door every evening: a loan to this company is first and foremost a loan against its human capital. At this point seasoned lenders become nervous. The IRR on assets of 2.79 percent is high for a reason: risk.

Mezzanine Investors' Perspective

The mezzanine investors' credit concerns are analogous to those of the senior creditor. As subordinated lenders, however, the mezzanine investors receive a higher interest rate (LIBOR plus 3.25 percent rather than 2.75 percent) and an equity "kicker" to compensate for the absence of a senior claim. Mezzanine investors aim for all-in returns in the region of 20 to 30 percent. Does the mezzanine loan to MediMedia as currently structured provide such a return?

Exhibit 13.12 estimates an all-in return, taking into account the cash flows on the debt (i.e., interest and principal payments), as well as the value of the warrants at date of closing. This treatment of the warrants assumes that they are liquid securities (i.e., can be sold a moment after the closing) and thus represent a discount against the total principal invested. The exhibit shows the IRR to mezzanine investors calculated two ways: assuming the value of the equity is $11 million at closing, and assuming it is $50 million. Assuming $11 million (an approach many students will adopt), the IRR to the mezzanine investors is 14 percent. Assuming $50 million, the IRR is 24 percent. The latter estimate is correct in that it reflects intrinsic value, as opposed to book value reflected in the $11 million estimate of the first approach. An axiom of finance is to make decisions based on market, rather than book, values.

Numerous practitioners take issue with this treatment of the warrants and treat the warrants as a *certain flow*—that is, they assume that equity flows will materialize as forecast and that the equity will be worth about $149 million in 1998. Thus, in the option value line of Exhibit 13.12, they propose to insert $22.25 million (.15 times 149, less an exercise price of $0.1 million) as an inflow in 1998 and project no inflow at closing. This calculation yields an IRR of 15.4 percent. This approach is inappropriate, because it assumes the flows of funds under the option are as certain as the flows under the bond; the flows are not equally certain. All we know about the option value takes place at closing; its payoff in 1998 is uncertain, and we need to take this uncertainty into account. The option treatment as in Exhibit 13.12 does so.

Some students may point out that the IRR to the mezzanine investors will change if management exits sooner than 1998. This argument is true. All else equal, early exit will increase the IRR. Typically, leveraged buyout deals flip within three to five years of going private.[12]

The buyout was consummated in June 1991 largely along the lines described in the case. MediMedia performed ahead of plan, delivering substantial value to its investors (the details of its subsequent disposition remain private). To some extent, the investors could thank Dun & Bradstreet: The businesses constituting

MediMedia had gone through two substantial restructurings (in 1988 and 1990) in an effort to prepare for sale. Apparently, D&B's selling price did not adequately capture the value of these improvements; instead, the value accrued to the management/investor group.

"Whole Deal" Summary

Exhibit 13.13 summarizes the perspective of the various players in the transaction. There are various possible reasons for the pattern of wealth distribution here, including institutional factors (such as the banks wanting to take rather limited risk, and therefore receiving fixed return) and bargaining power—wealth flows to those players who have the capacity to extract it from other parties or seize it from the commons. The source of the equity holders' bargaining power may be inferred from three facts. First, the management of MediMedia had the financial capacity to provide all the equity for the deal. Second, the volume of leveraged buyouts was declining at the time. This meant that banks and mezzanine funds had fewer competing demands on their capacity, and less choice. Third, the management team emerged as the only bidder for the firm; the seller had no alternatives.

A LEVERAGED BUYOUT: REVCO DRUG STORES

On December 29, 1986, an investor group purchased the stock of Revco Drug Stores[13] at a 48 percent premium to the firm's stock price 12 months earlier, and 71 percent premium over the price at which Revco repurchased shares in July 1985. The proxy statement issued the previous month cited several reasons why the buy-

EXHIBIT 13.13 "Whole Deal" Summary of Returns to Players in the Leveraged Buyout MediMedia International, Ltd.

Participant	Expected Returns	Issues
Senior creditors	• IRR (gross) = 9% and IRR = 2.8% (ROA after taxes and cost of funds) • Benchmark IRR = 1–2%	• IRR (ROA) good by bank standards. • Secured, but on intangible assets. • How easy to monitor the business? • Managers = Owners: What are the implications for agency conflict?
Mezzanine investors	• IRR = 24% • Target IRR = 20–30%	• Meets target return. • Kicker provides upside payoff.
Vendor (D&B)	• IRR = 8.4%	• Subnormal return. • Appearances important. • Participation if gains on asset sales. • Only way to get the deal done?
Equity investors (management)	• IRR = 54.2% • Target IRR = 40%+	• Equity control. • IRR consistent with targets. • Large NPV in absolute terms.

ing group regarded the purchase of Revco as "an attractive investment opportunity": (1) favorable business prospects, (2) being private would permit Revco to have a higher debt-to-equity ratio and thus realize higher return on equity and higher growth in net worth; and (3) the value of Revco depended on long-term expansion of the business, rather than on quarterly results to which the public investors give undue attention. The buyout consummated a long episode of anxiety for Sidney Dworkin, the CEO of Revco, about possible takeover threats, internal fighting over control of the firm, and declining financial performance.

The financial structure of the LBO is summarized in Exhibit 13.14. This was one of the most complicated financial structures ever seen for an LBO.

EXHIBIT 13.14 Financial Structure for the Leveraged Buyout of Revco Drug Stores

As of November 5, 1986, Revco had a total of 32,450,442 shares of outstanding common stock. The price of the buyout would total $1,253,315,000 for the repurchase of these outstanding shares and the cancellation of employee stock options. In addition, Revco would need to repay $117,484,000 of Revco's present debt obligations and would incur a charge of approximately $78,000,000 in investment banking fees.* The sources and uses of funds in this transaction were as follows:

	Dollars (Thousands)
Sources	
Bank term loan	$ 455,000
Senior subordinated notes	400,000
Subordinated notes	210,000
Units:	
Junior subordinated notes	$ 91,145
Common stock (375,000 shares) and common stock puts (on 375,000 shares)	93,750
Exchangeable preferred stock	130,020
Convertible preferred stock	85,000
Junior preferred stock	30,098
Common stock (the investor group)	34,276
Cash of Revco	10,655
Total sources	$1,448,799
Uses	
Purchase of Revco common stock and cancellation of employee stock options	$1,253,315
Repayment of debt	117,484
Fees and expenses	78,000
Total uses	$1,448,799

*The fees included underwriting commissions of $31,150,000, investment banking advisory fees of $16,100,000, bank commitment fees of $14,800,000, and legal and accounting fees of $10,300,000.

Source: Company filings with SEC.

- *Common stock.* This accounted for about 2.4 percent of the total sources of financing, much lower than rules of thumb for equity financing of LBOs.
- *Preferred stock,* like common stock, served to cushion the potential asset claims of creditors. The amount of cushion the firm needs is probably dictated by expectations about the firm's asset values and cash flows. Preferred holders cannot initiate a bankruptcy proceeding in the event a dividend is passed. At the same time, preferred stock is probably cheaper than common stock: Dividends on preferred stock are not tax deductible, although corporate investors do enjoy an 80 percent preferred-dividend exclusion that creates a tax savings that investors and issuers frequently share (via a lower dividend).
- ***Bundling the subordinated notes into units*** with common stock shares and common stock puts essentially kicks the expected return on the notes upward (if one is optimistic). The natural question to ask is, "Why, then, didn't Revco simply issue the notes with a coupon of 15 or 20 percent?" Again, the answer must be that the financial engineers did not anticipate sufficient strength of cash flow. The strategic role of the equity kick is also applicable to the convertible preferred stock.
- ***The exchangeable preferred*** is perhaps the most interesting layer in the deal structure. In essence, it was to be a "pay-in-kind" (PIK) preferred for the first five years, thereafter reverting to an ordinary current cash dividend preferred. In addition, the company retained the option to exchange the preferred for subordinated debt carrying the same yield, 15.25 percent. Upon exchange, investors would lose the 80 percent dividend exclusion but would gain modestly higher seniority in the event of liquidation. The company, on the other hand, would gain a new tax deduction with which to shelter its cash flow. The closing section of the case raises the question of whether the exchangeable preferred issue is really debt instead of equity. The answer must be found in the anticipated economic behavior of management, and in the economic role this issue plays. One should anticipate that Revco would exercise its right of exchange as soon as the firm gets a whiff of tax expense in 1992. Over the 1987–1989 period, this issue could just as easily have been carried as a debt issue; either way, additions to retained earnings would have been the same. It is a preferred stock in name only, so named in order to exploit a curious feature of the tax code.
- ***The junior preferred*** was to be purchased entirely by Salomon Brothers and TSG, another investor group. These investors could just as easily have committed the capital in the form of common equity; they probably chose to take a portion of their return in the form of PIK preferred to exploit the dividend exclusion. Economically speaking, one could view the junior preferred as common equity.

To summarize, Revco's ornate capital structure could be explained as a sophisticated solution to a complex financial problem: (1) raise a lot of money to pay the buyout premium; (2) get as much as possible from the senior lenders (it's the cheapest capital); (3) get as little as possible from the equity investors (they want to maximize returns); (4) tailor the terms of the capital in the "mezzanine" to be serviceable by the expected flow of cash and yet to be attractive to the providers of that capital (i.e., where necessary use contingent forms of payment).

Assessment of Probability of Default

Revco seemed aggressively levered from the start. The financial forecast projected material earnings losses in the years 1987–1989. The combination of losses and investment necessary to sustain the firm's growth strategy results in a significant upward leveraging of the company over the same period. If one doubted the ability of the firm to sell $230 million of assets in 1987, then the leveraging would only be greater. Ultimately, the company must continue to borrow—it cannot meet all of these demands out of cash from internal operations. "Working capital loans" rise dramatically from 1989 onward.

A sensitivity analysis of the financial forecast revealed that increasing growth is no way to provide cash for coverage of financial obligations. Indeed, lowering the growth rate will help. Instead of growth, the major key drivers appear to be operational: Margins and net working capital assumptions prove to produce major swings in the firm's ability to generate positive earnings and reduce debt. Also, the forecast showed that in none of the forecast years would the EBIT coverage ratio be greater than 1.0.

A vivid indicator of Revco's prospective difficulties is a Monte Carlo simulation analysis of the EBIT and cash flow coverage ratios as conducted by Bruner and Eades (1992). Exhibit 13.15 presents the probability histograms of cash flow coverage[14] resulting from 200 trials of the simulation model. These figures illustrate that the average coverage ratio is in the 90 percent decile and the bulk of each of the probability distributions lies below the minimum cutoff of 1.0 coverage. In each of

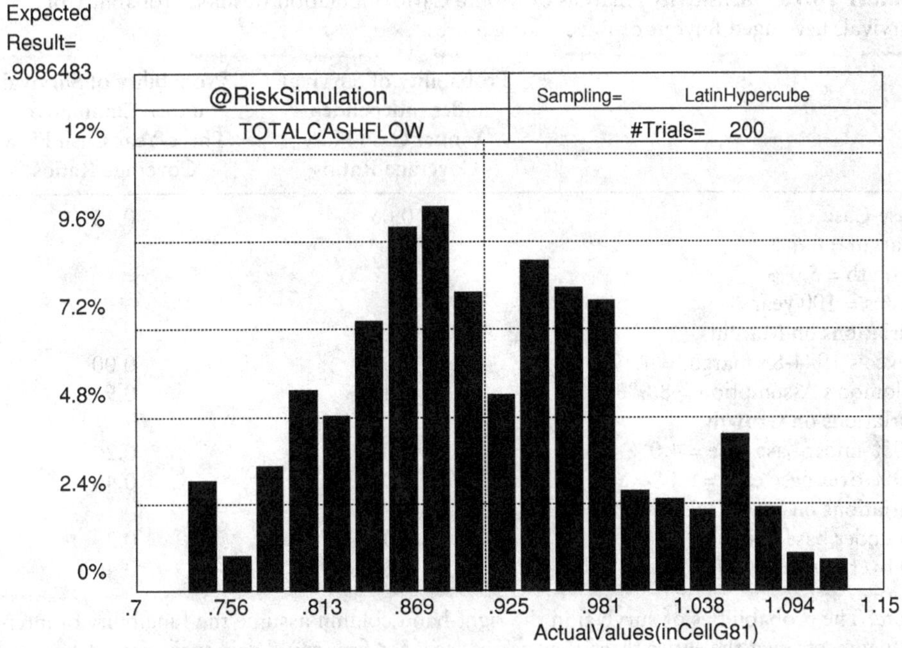

EXHIBIT 13.15 Probability Histograms Cash Flow Coverage Ratio for Years 1987–1989, Cumulatively
Source of figure: Bruner and Eades (1992).

the first three years, the probability of surviving is 0.43, 0.45, and 0.27, and the cumulative probability of survival is 0.052 (0.43 · 0.45 · 0.27). Exhibit 13.15 shows the histogram for the cash flow coverage ratio based on cumulative cash flows and debt service over the first three years *combined.* This figure assumes that the past and future cash flows are available to service the financial obligations for any year. Thus, the ratio represents a best-case measure of Revco's ability to pay. The resulting probability of survival is about 15 percent.

Applying different assumptions to the Monte Carlo simulation reveals that the assumed EBIT margin was a source of difficulty. The pitch book for the deal assumed a base case EBIT margin of 6.6 percent. Yet Revco's historical average EBIT margin was 4.17 percent. And the estimate of Revco's adviser, Salomon Brothers, was a more optimistic assumption of 8.0 percent. Exhibit 13.16 presents the resulting estimates of probability of survival under the alternative assumptions and shows that the probability of survival is low for all cases except where EBIT/sales is 8.0 percent and coverage is measured cumulatively over the three years. If Salomon really believed in its EBIT margin assumption of 8.0 percent, then it was probably justified in thinking that Revco had a high probability of survival. There was, however, plenty of historical data on Revco and data on other discount drug retailers to suggest that an EBIT margin of 8.0 percent was optimistic.

In conclusion, a risk analysis of Revco based on information publicly available at the time of going private suggests a very low probability of survival.

EXHIBIT 13.16 Sensitivity Analysis of Monte Carlo Simulation Results, Probability of Survival, Leveraged Buyout of Revco Drug Stores

	Probability of Survival under Independent Annual Cash Flow Coverage Ratios	Probability of Survival under Cumulative Three-Year Cash Flow Coverage Ratios
Base Case	0.05	0.15
Margin = 6.6%		
Growth = 5.0%		
Stores = 100/year		
Variations on Margin		
Revco's 1984-85 margin = 4.17%	0.00	0.00
Salomon's Assumption = 8.0%	0.48	0.94
Variations on Growth		
1.0% under base case = 4.0%	0.02	0.20
1.0% over base case = 6.0%	0.06	0.40
Variations on Store Openings/Year		
50 under base case = 50	0.02	0.23
50 over base case = 150	0.10	0.40

Note: The probabilities of survival in the right-hand column assume the fungibility of interest payments over the entire three-year period, as if the firm could gain waivers to delay payments from bad years to good years. The middle column probabilities assume complete independence of payments, as if no waivers would be available.
Source of sensitivity analysis results: Bruner and Eades (1992).

Some Insights about Debt Capacity

The methodology and results of the risk analysis offer some important lessons about debt capacity and capital adequacy.

- Capital adequacy should be measured by the ability of expected cash flows to cover debt service requirements. This argues against relying simply on peer comparisons or historical ratios to set target debt/equity mixes for HLTs.
- In setting capitalization targets, point estimates of coverage are of limited value. What matters is the probability of default. This implies that capitalization policy should be stated in probabilistic rather than deterministic terms—for example, "We are comfortable with a debt capitalization target that is consistent with at least a 95 percent probability of successfully covering principal and interest."
- Default risk is visible in the shape of the coverage histogram, especially in its spread and peakedness. Comparing the histogram to the familiar bell-shaped normal curve draws the analogy to the concept of risk in the risk-return paradigm of finance. It also helps draw the analyst's attention to risk as characterized by option pricing theory. Loan guarantees will be priced off of the risk of default—so will the equity of a levered firm.

Financial problems at Revco appeared shortly following the buyout. The firm declared bankruptcy 19 months after going private, a victim of an overly aggressive capital structure.

SUMMARY

Highly levered transactions are a prominent fixture on the M&A landscape. Though a small percentage of the number and dollar volume of all M&A transactions, they have played an important role in the industrial restructuring of mature firms. Their spectacular successes (and failures) merit the attention of M&A professionals. They are among the most complex transactions to analyze and bring the firm closer to the edge of financial distress. These transactions therefore require extra scrutiny in analysis for the probability of default, for nonlinearities in the estimation of beta, for circularities in respect to capital structure assumptions, and for changing capital structures. This chapter has outlined stages of an analytic approach that builds on the same methods of valuation as advocated for ordinary transactions: discounted cash flow based on rates reflecting the classic risk-and-return relationship of modern financial theory. The approach outlined in this chapter culminates in a "whole deal" view of the division of returns to various participants and thus prepares the deal designer for more thoughtful negotiation and deal structuring.

NOTES

1. Jensen (1989a) notes that buyout specialists own or represent an average of 60 percent of the firm's equity. Presumably the balance is held by management or affiliates. Kaplan (1989b) finds that the CEO of the target firm increases his

or her equity stake in the firm from an average of 1.4 percent to 6.4 percent, postbuyout.

2. Jensen (1989a) cited a study by Steven Kaplan finding that the pay-to-performance ratio for a CEO of an LBO target was 20 times higher than for the CEO of a public corporation.
3. Opler and Titman (1993) and Hall (1991) find that firms with higher R&D expenditures were less likely to undertake LBOs.
4. Undervaluation creates an interesting dilemma for managers of LBO targets. Shleifer and Vishny (1988) argue that MBOs are a response to undervaluation owing to poor performance. Frydman, Frydman, and Trimbath (2002) report that targets of financial buyers have significantly lower profits and higher costs than other firms. In a survey of CFOs of firms that went private, Maupin, Bidwell, and Ortegren (1984) note, "The below book value selling price of the publicly traded shares did not reflect the higher 'real' value of the company." They contend that the primary reason for the buyout transaction was that "the stock had been selling so far below its real value that the best way to enable shareholders to realize the maximum amount on their investment was through a management buyout." (Pages 441–442) Lee (1992) studies the possible effect of "inside information" by looking at the impact of withdrawn LBO proposals. His findings dispute the information argument and are consistent with value-increasing changes expected after the LBO. Bruner and Paine (1988) explore the ethical implications of the conflict of interest arising from CEOs having inside information in advance of an LBO proposal, and argue that directors should compare the benefits of the LBO against the benefits of a recap.
5. Some firms might actively arrange a reorganization plan with their creditors in advance of filing for bankruptcy. The aim is to minimize the time spent in bankruptcy and possibly to thwart efforts by hostile parties to gain control of the firm through the bankruptcy process. This is called a prepackaged bankruptcy, or "prepack."
6. See studies of the failures of Revco Drug Stores (Bruner and Eades 1992; Wruck 1991) and of Federated Department Stores (Kaplan 1994).
7. Note also that the cost of equity rises at an increasing rate, which hints at the nonlinearity of cost of equity with respect to default risk. These equity cost estimates were not obtained from CAPM, but from a leading investment bank based on their qualitative assessment of capital market conditions and surveys of institutional investors. In short, there is no quantitative model based on theory and tested in practice that can estimate the cost of equity as a function of credit rating or default risk. This is terra incognita.
8. If annual capital costs are 30, 15, and 7 percent in three successive years, the discount factor for the first year will be $1/(1.30)$. For the second year, it will be $1/(1.30 \cdot 1.15)$. For the third year, it will be $1/(1.30 \cdot 1.15 \cdot 1.07)$. And so on.
9. It would be possible to revalue the debt each year to reflect the changing probability of default. This will add a great deal more complexity to the valuation model. As noted earlier, estimating the changing default risk discount is difficult. And where the creditor's assessment of default risk is reflected in the interest rate, book value would be a close approximation of market value. For these reasons, most practitioners use the book value of debt as a simplifying assumption.

10. In a series of papers, Fernandez (2001, 2002a,b,c,d) directs practitioners not to use *tD* as an estimate of the present value of tax shields in general circumstances. *tD* is appropriate only for cases where the debt balance remains constant, as assumed in this illustration.
11. The mini-case is based on Bruner (1992a,b).
12. A leveraged buyout flips when the buyout investors liquidate partially or completely by taking the company public or by selling to another investor.
13. The section on Revco Drug Stores draws on the research in Bruner and Eades (1992).
14. For parsimony, a report of the results of EBIT coverage is excluded here. In general, they show even more dramatic shortfalls in the probability of covering debt service.

CHAPTER 14

Real Options and Their Impact on M&A

INTRODUCTION

This chapter explores one of the important frontiers of valuation: *real options.* Chapter 9 ("Valuing Firms") argues that the value of the firm is the sum of the present values of predictable cash flows and option value. Chapter 10 ("Valuing Options") explores the logic of simple financial options and their valuation using the Black-Scholes option pricing model. But in the broader perspective of M&A, finance, and business administration, financial options are a relatively small subset of the options a decision maker encounters. Financial options are distinct in that they are standardized, derived from an underlying financial asset, exchange traded, and therefore relatively easy to value. Real options are often unique, derived from nonfinancial (or "real") assets such as land, plant and machinery, patents, artistic property—these assets tend to be illiquid, and real options on these assets tend to be complex. Therefore, real options tend to be relatively hard to value. Real options remain a young subject; Stewart Myers introduced the term in 1977. Since then, real options thinking has emerged as a powerful influence on analysis in M&A. Today analysts and executives should strive to master real options thinking for at least four reasons:

1. Real options are *pervasive.* Whenever you hear a manager discuss notions such as "rights," "*flexibility,*" or "commitments," that manager is describing a real option.
2. Real options will probably have a *big influence on firm value* where the firm is growing, has the ability to do things other firms cannot, and/or has unique assets. Given the pervasiveness of real options in some industries such as high technology, pharmaceuticals, defense, aerospace, and entertainment, the ratio of real option value to the total value of the firm could easily exceed 50 percent.
3. Executives and M&A deal designers *easily create and destroy real option value,* with a potentially large impact on careers.
4. Ultimately, real options analysis *captures effects that DCF doesn't* as managers' and investors' behavior seems to show.[1] The common complaint about discounted cash flow valuation is that it fails to capture qualities about an asset

that are not reflected in the projected cash flows. Therefore, DCF alone misestimates the value of an asset. Managers' intuition tells them that there is more to many assets than meets the DCF analyst's eye. Real options treat the missing qualities. In addition, options thinking focuses on total risk (i.e., not just systematic risk), which most managers worry about.

The bad news about real options is that they can be complicated to value rigorously. This is because the kinds of contingent rights that businesspeople face may have these features:

- Exercise price may be contingent rather than fixed. It may be driven by a complicated formula, may vary over time, and/or may be subject to future negotiation.
- Expiration date may be contingent, rather than fixed. Many real options expire in stages.
- The value of the underlying asset may not be clear. Trading in the underlying asset may be limited or nonexistent, preventing the ability to observe the asset value. This implies that one must rely on imperfect estimates of value and volatility.
- Transaction costs may be high and/or contingent.
- The option may actually consist of a cluster of options, or a time-series of options, or options on options.

There are no simple approaches to modeling option value in these cases. Unless the problem can be broken down into simple pieces and analyzed using a familiar option pricing model, one must resort to using numerical methods that must be custom-tailored to each new valuation problem.

These difficulties notwithstanding, best practice in M&A draws on real options theory to:

- ***Estimate the value of optionality*** where the problem can be structured clearly and reasonable assumptions applied.
- ***Structure critical thinking*** about company values and/or deal design. Even if one cannot derive estimates of value in which one might have some confidence, real options thinking can lend discipline to a qualitative assessment of an M&A transaction, and help anticipate how options will affect value.
- ***Guide negotiation and problem solving.*** An understanding of real options can prepare one to adjust to proposals and arguments in the midst of a deal negotiation and to look for solutions when parties are at an impasse.

The aim of this chapter is to present an introduction to the subject of real options as applied to the M&A context. Specifically, it illustrates the kinds of situations where real option valuation may be warranted, as well as the kind of analytical work that a businessperson might strive to perform. More detailed presentation of analytic techniques is given in a number of resources recommended at the end of this chapter.

Some Generic Types of Real Options

Real options cluster into four common categories. This section describes these and considers their impact on shareholders and managers.

Entry or Growth Options

In 1977, Stewart Myers suggested that the value of the firm could be decomposed into two components: the value of assets in place and the value of growth options—rights to undertake new investments. Options to grow are like call options on new and uncertain businesses.[2] Perhaps the most prominent example of *entry or growth options* is investing in R&D projects. To invest in R&D is to buy an option on an uncertain, yet-to-be-discovered business.[3] Consistent with the concept, Chan, Martin, and Kensinger (1990) found that announcements of increased R&D spending are associated with a significant 1.38 percent gain in share value. Pharmaceutical companies face the opportunity to invest in these options every time a research scientist proposes a new product development project. A second example would be purchasing a territorial franchise for restaurants—this is the right to expand a business geographically. A third example would be purchasing drilling rights for oil or gas over a geographical range.[4] It would be rational to exercise these options when the present value of uncertain expected future cash flows exceeds the exercise price (i.e., the investment to commercialize the drug discovery, the cost of building the restaurant, or the cost to drill). Growth options, or options to enter a business, are *call options* on the underlying business activity. They are more valuable the longer the life of the option, and the greater the uncertainty about the value of the underlying asset.

Here's a simplistic example of how one might value an entry option. Suppose it costs $1 million to conduct the R&D necessary to prepare a prototype for market testing. Given the R&D efforts of competitors and the fickleness of consumers, you believe there will be a 20 percent chance that the product will succeed in the market, and that, if it does, it would be a business worth $10 million in present value terms. If the product fails, you would not proceed to bring it to market but rather write off the investment, at which point the value of the business will be zero. Should you proceed?

Exhibit 14.1 gives the problem expressed as a decision tree: "go/no-go." The calculation reveals that the decision to invest in the R&D creates more value than the decision not to invest. How can this be? The project is costly, and the odds of success are low. The answer lies in the asymmetry of outcomes: You have a right, not an obligation, to proceed once the R&D and product testing are complete. You will choose to exercise the option if it is in the money, and otherwise won't exercise it. Investing in the R&D gives you the right to invest later in a new research breakthrough if such an investment appears to be in the money.

Exit or Abandonment Options

Being stuck in an unattractive business without a viable exit is one of the worst situations for a firm. For instance, a diversified firm owned a coal tar refinery that had operated for over 100 years. The facility was inherited in an acquisition many years earlier. The plant was antiquated and inefficient. Furthermore, the market had

EXHIBIT 14.1 The Growth Option

Problem: You must decide whether to invest $1 million in a research and development program. If the program succeeds, you believe it will generate a business worth $10 million in present value (PV) terms. If it fails, the PV will be zero. You believe the program has only a 20 percent chance of success.

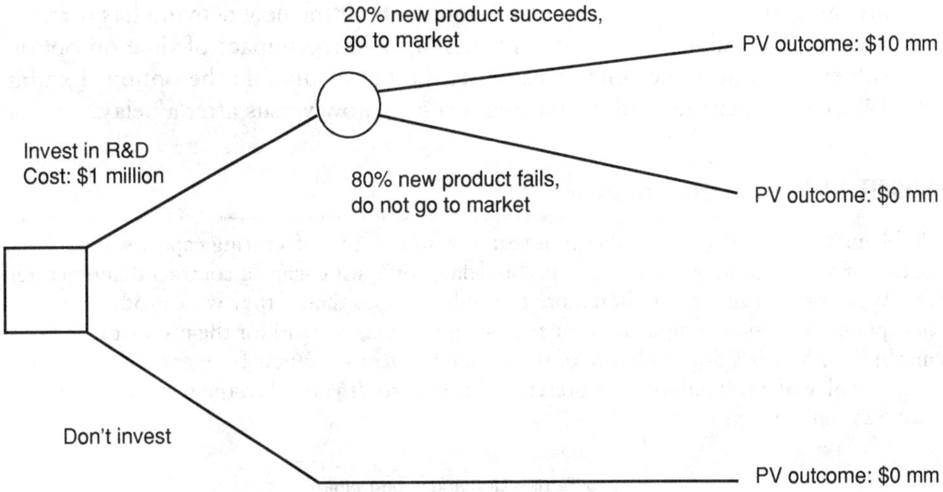

The decision to invest will be decided in this example on the basis of value maximization: invest if value is created. The value of the "invest" branch of the decision can be modeled:

$$\text{Value} = -\$1 + (0.20 \cdot \$10) + (0.80 \cdot \$0) = \$1 \text{ million}$$

turned highly competitive, making the refinery extremely unprofitable. The firm wanted to exit the business, but couldn't because doing so would trigger environmental cleanup obligations from chemical leakage over the years.[5] Nuclear power plants, petrochemical plants, and many manufacturing plants face exit costs that can ruin the economics of a business as it approaches its end. Another example of being stuck is encountered by a minority investor in an underperforming private firm—even if a minority investor wanted to exit, his or her investment could be stranded if the securities are illiquid. Such would be the case until the majority investor decides to sell the entire firm.

The right to sell an asset or abandon a business (*exit or abandonment option*) is valuable—such is the case with all insurance policies, exit or termination clauses in business contracts, and government guarantees of pension obligations. All of these are *put options*, valuable to the option holder and a liability to the counterparty. Put options are discussed in Chapter 10.[6]

Timing Options: Rights to Delay or Accelerate

The rights to delay or accelerate the investment in an asset (*timing options*) are valuable, and exist in an American option, which may be exercised at any point up to expiration. European options are exercisable only at expiration.

- Consider the *right to defer*: Suppose your firm needs to meet growing demand and contemplates construction of a manufacturing plant. Demand is uncertain; you harbor doubts about the firmness of the increased demand and believe that with a year's experience you will learn whether the increased demand is permanent or temporary. By negotiating an outsource manufacturing contract with another firm for the new product, you can essentially buy the right to wait on investing in the new plant until uncertainty about the new demand has been resolved.[7] The value of delay is evident simply in the impact of time on option value: The longer the time to exercise, the more valuable the option. Exhibit 14.2 gives an example of comparing investing now versus after a delay.

EXHIBIT 14.2 The Option to Delay

Problem: You must decide whether to invest now in new manufacturing capacity, for an outlay of $20 million, or wait a year. If you delay, you must engage a contract manufacturer that will cost your firm $1 million more to produce goods than if they were produced at the new plant. To further complicate your reasoning process, demand for the product is uncertain. There is a 50–50 chance of the demand generating a new business with either a present value of $100 million or a present value of zero. If you delay, the new plant will cost $25 million next year.

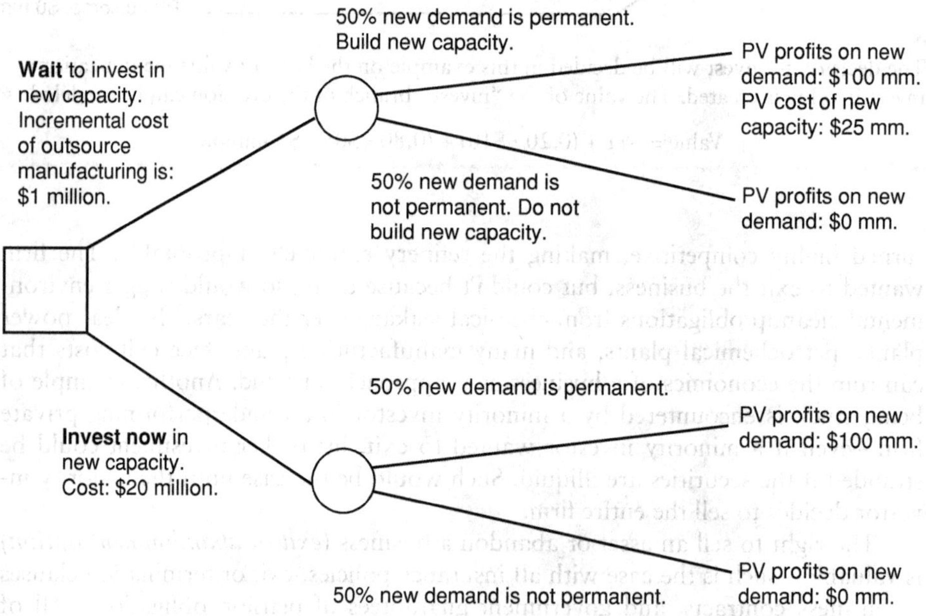

The decision to go now or delay will be decided in this example on the basis of value maximization: delay if value is created. The value of the two branches of the decision can be modeled:

$$\text{Value of "wait"} = -\$1 + [0.50 \cdot (\$100 - \$25)] + (0.50 \cdot \$0) = \$36.5 \text{ million}$$

$$\text{Value of "invest now"} = -\$20 + (0.50 \cdot \$100) + (0.50 \cdot \$0) = \$30 \text{ million}$$

In this example, it pays to wait because of the high uncertainty about the value of the underlying asset (i.e., new demand).

- The *right to accelerate* may be valuable where the underlying asset throws off a high cash flow or is a wasting asset. This is a problem of leakage of value in the underlying asset, and could result from dividends paid out, costs of storage and insurance, taxes, and licensing or royalty fees. Leakage of value is a classic problem in the analysis of options. For instance, suppose that you have an option to purchase a gold mine, and that you strongly believe the price of gold will remain stable over the life of the option. Until you decide to exercise the option, the owner of the gold mine will extract the richest lodes of ore first, imposing on you a cost of the lost opportunity. Depending on the price of gold, it might be rational for you to buy the mine immediately in order to enjoy the high current flow of cash. Exhibit 14.3 offers an example of comparing

EXHIBIT 14.3 The Option to Accelerate

Problem: You already own an option on a gold mine, exercisable at $50 million. You believe the mine has a present value of $100 million if the gold price is high, and $40 million if the gold price is low. The price of gold is uncertain with a 75% chance the price will be high and a 25% chance that the price will be low. The current owner will continue to extract ore worth $10 million during the life of the option.

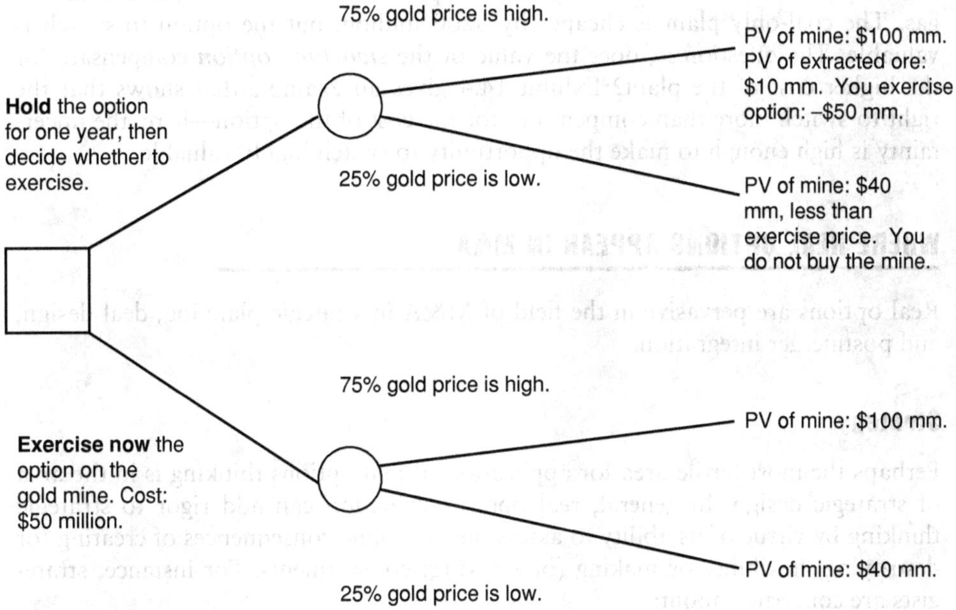

The decision to hold the option or exercise now will be decided in this example on the basis of value maximization: delay if value is created. The value of the two branches of the decision can be modeled:

$$\text{Value of "hold"} = [0.75 \cdot (\$100 - \$10 - \$50)] + (0.25 \cdot \$0) = \$30 \text{ million}$$

$$\text{Value of "exercise now"} = -\$50 + (0.75 \cdot \$100) + (0.25 \cdot \$40) = \$35 \text{ million}$$

In this example, the wasting value of the asset is decisive. Given the relatively high confidence about the value of the underlying asset, it pays to exercise now and appropriate the value of the ore that will be extracted over the next year.

the purchase of the gold mine now versus later. Another example would be where a competitor threatens to enter the same business, by adding new capacity or product features, for instance, and thereby decreasing the attractiveness of that business to your firm. In such a context, early exercise of real options on capacity or product features could serve a strategic purpose of preempting the competitor.

The decision to defer or accelerate a transaction is driven by an assessment of the value of the underlying asset over the life of the option. In the first case, the "asset" is the present value of cash flows—where uncertainty of demand is large enough, it will pay to wait and see how things turn out. In the second case, the "asset" is an ore body that will decline in value with reasonable certainty over the life of the option—the question is who will capture that change in value, you (the option holder) or the current owner?

Switching Options

The flexibility to switch from one operating mode to another can also be valuable.[8] For instance, consider an electric power company that must choose whether to build a plant that runs on coal only, versus a plant that will run on coal and natural gas. The coal-only plant is cheaper by $200 million, but the option to switch is valuable. The question is, does the value of the *switching option* compensate for the higher cost of the plant? Exhibit 14.4 gives an example that shows that the right to switch more than compensates for the cost of the option—here, the uncertainty is high enough to make the opportunity to switch highly valuable.

WHERE REAL OPTIONS APPEAR IN M&A

Real options are pervasive in the field of M&A in strategic planning, deal design, and postmerger integration.

Strategy

Perhaps the most fertile area for application of real options thinking is in the area of strategic design. In general, real options valuation can add rigor to strategic thinking by virtue of its ability to assess the economic consequences of creating (or destroying) flexibility or making (or relaxing) commitments. For instance, strategists are concerned about:

- ***Flexibility versus irreversibility of actions.*** Acquisitions can create or destroy flexibility. Irreversible investments entail commitments that expose the firm to risks. In contrast, flexible investments can be altered as conditions change. Flexibility is an option on an alternative strategy and is enabled, for instance, by holding excess manufacturing capacity, excess inventory, or excess cash. Womack et al. (1990) emphasize that management techniques such as lean manufacturing grant strategic flexibility. The valuation of flexibility using real option theory has been the focus of extensive discussion.[9]

EXHIBIT 14.4 The Option to Switch

Problem: You contemplate investing in a power plant. The question is whether to commit only to coal-fired generation or to another configuration that is fueled by either coal or natural gas. The coal-fired plant requires an investment of $1 billion. The coal/gas plant requires an investment of $1.2 billion. You believe that in half the future states of the world coal will be cheaper, and in the other half, natural gas will be cheaper.

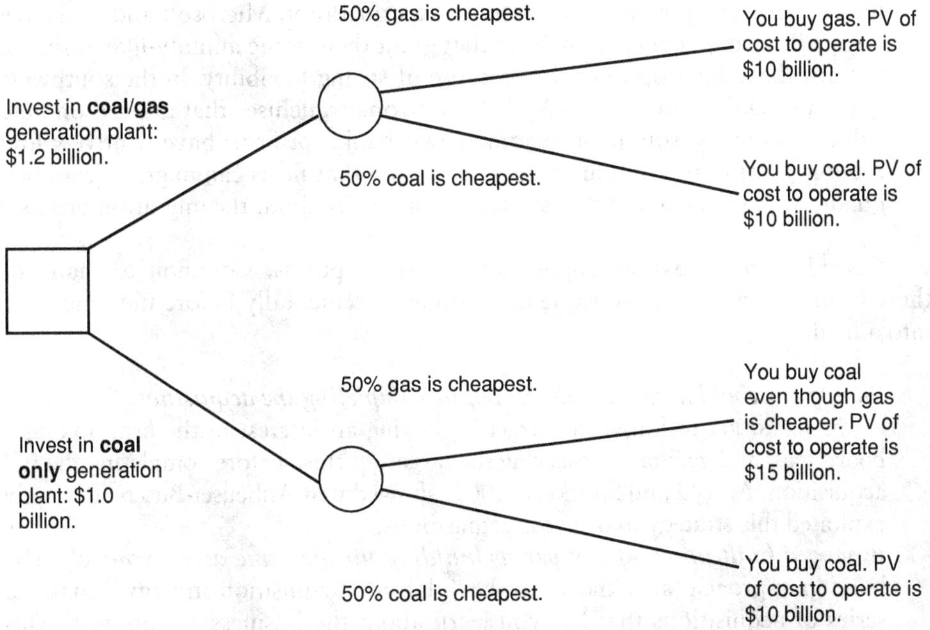

The decision to hold the option or exercise now will be decided on the basis of value maximization—in this case, revenues are assumed to be the same under both alternatives, so we focus only on cash outflows such as investments and operating costs. Thus, the decision reduces to minimizing cash outflows. The value of the two branches of the decision can be modeled:

$$\text{Value of "coal/gas"} = -\$1.2 + (0.50 \cdot -\$10) + (0.50 \cdot -\$10) = -\$11.2 \text{ billion}$$

$$\text{Value of "coal only"} = -\$1.0 + (0.50 \cdot -\$15) + (0.50 \cdot -\$10) = -\$13.5 \text{ billion}$$

In this example, the ability to switch between coal and gas is more valuable than the marginal cost of the right. Given the relatively high uncertainty about the value of the asset underlying the option, it pays to buy the coal/gas configuration.

- ***Insurance.*** Some strategic actions can hedge a firm's exposure to risks. Insurance is analogous to a put option.
- ***Learning and competencies.*** Training and learning by doing create a more flexible workforce, and this flexibility constitutes a valuable real option. Similarly, at the corporate-wide level, gaining more know-how creates strategic competencies that are valuable. Acquiring strategic capabilities through M&A is a common motive for transactions.[10]

- ***Planning.*** Boer (2002), Tufano (1996), and Sahlman (1997) argue that options thinking generally can advance corporate strategic planning. For some firms, the option value as a portion of total value will be high; for others it will be low. The proportion may vary by industry and by phase of the firm's life cycle. For instance, Exhibit 14.5 provides a matrix based on Boer's theories and findings. In the northeast quadrant, eBay and Human Genomics hold rights to unusual new intellectual property that has yet to be fully developed but that has high commercial potential. In the northwest quadrant, Microsoft and Dell have unusually strong market franchises that grant them some annuity-like business, but also have high option value because of strong flexibility. In the southwest quadrant, Duke and General Mills have strong franchises that grant economic value. And in the southeast quadrant, two bankrupt firms have relatively low economic value and option value. Boer argues that firms can migrate from one quadrant to the next and that strategic planning is about the migration process.

Consider these possible applications of real options. Common to many of these is an expression of the value of learning incrementally before jumping fully into a field:

- ***Buying a toehold minority interest before completing the acquisition.*** Some buyers prefer to get to know the target by buying an interest in the firm, taking a board seat, and generally observing the target up close before completing the full acquisition. Arnold and Shockley (2001) showed that Anheuser-Busch effectively exploited this strategy in overseas acquisitions.
- ***Buying a built-up company versus building up the same assets yourself.*** The buildup approach (also known as the "platform acquisition strategy") makes a series of acquisitions that lets you learn about the business as you go.[11] This process of staged investing permits the buyer to decide at each point whether to expand or stop.
- ***The virtue of being a second mover.*** While the "first mover advantage" and "winner take all" were much touted during the Internet bubble, the more sober perspective in recent years has been the benefit of watching someone else make

EXHIBIT 14.5 Matrix of Hypothetical Economic Value and Option Value

	Economic Value	
Option Value	High	Low
High	Microsoft 2002 Dell Computer 2002	eBay 2002 Human Genomics 2002
Low	Duke Energy 2002 General Mills 2002	United Airlines 2002 Bethlehem Steel 2002

Note: This suggests that firms can differ greatly in their composition of assets, that is, between real option value and the value of assets in place.
Source: Author's analysis, after a framework presented by Boer (2002), page 142.

the laborious market discovery—and then following rapidly. Excel followed Lotus and Visicalc. Cottrell and Sick (2001) and Tufano (1989) explore the reputed virtues of the first mover advantage.
- *Rights to exploit an uncertain resource.* This is especially important in fields such as natural resources, talent, and intellectual property. In two separate studies, Weatherford and Bodily (1988) and Bruner (1988) valued the right to drill in a natural gas field using option valuation techniques and illustrated that the value of the right varies directly with the volatility of gas prices.
- *Acquisition search.* Real option theory may offer an avenue for identification of attractive targets based on undervaluation. The equity of a levered firm can be modeled as a call option on the assets of that firm. Rappaport and Mauboussin (2002) use this approach to compare potential and imputed real option values to determine buy and sell strategies.

Deal Design

Transaction structures are usually studded with rights and commitments—these are options.[12] The formal contract is structured as a contingent right: If terms and conditions (i.e., laid out in the representations, warranties and covenants) are satisfied, then the buyer may proceed to acquire the target. Real options in deal design appear in many guises:

- *Exchange offer.* A buyer typically approaches target shareholders with an offer to buy the shares at a stated price, and within a given time—the buyer in effect grants a put option to the target shareholders. The shareholder (typically an arbitrager) must implement a strategy to manage the option value inherent in the offer.
- *Breakup terms.* Topping fees and penalties for not completing the deal are rights to payments in the event of nonperformance by one party or another. These are contingent payments and therefore options.
- *Liquidity and control features.* Chapter 15 argues that the ability to sell an asset on demand is like holding a put option. Having control is like holding a call option on future strategy.
- *Contingent payment schemes.* Chapter 22 describes the use of earnouts. Generally, contingent payments are call options on uncertain future performance.
- *Transaction risk management.* Caps, collars, floors, and contingent value rights are protections given to selling and/or buying investors to limit the uncertainty they may face in concluding the transaction. Chapter 23 describes transaction risk management in more detail.
- *Takeover tactics.* Chapter 33 illustrates that defenses such as poison pills, lockups, and control rights are options.

Postmerger Integration

Many of the options embedded in the transaction structure expire when the deal is consummated. But these are replaced with other options that are created on closing. Chapters 36 and 37 outline practices associated with successful integration efforts. Real options appear in postmerger integration in various guises:

- ***Designing organizational and operational architecture.*** Integration may entail designing a new architecture for a firm. Architecture can create or destroy flexibility and commitment, two overarching dimensions of optionality. An illustration of the creation of flexibility is apparent in the trend toward "modularization" of manufacturing. Complex business processes and products can be organized into subunits, called "modules," that permit specialization, encourage greater innovation, and promote efficiency. Baldwin and Clark (2000) argue that modularity confers flexibility through operators such as splitting a system into two or more modules; substituting one module design for another; augmenting (adding a new module to a system); excluding a module from the system; investing to create new design rules; and porting a module to another system. The innards of any personal computer and the success of Dell Computer illustrate the fruits of modularity: Architectural flexibility pays.
- ***Structuring contracts for human resources.*** Incentive compensation may explicitly employ options, or less directly embed contingent payments into an employment agreement. Investments in training and knowledge transfer systems may create flexibility for the organization.
- ***Selection among competing capabilities.*** Capabilities create flexibility and therefore option value. Especially in mergers of equals, integration planners will face tough choices among business plans, practices, facilities, and so on within the merging firms. Real options analysis may be relevant to illuminating the consequences of alternatives.

IF OPTIONALITY IS SO PERVASIVE, WHY NOT VALUE EVERYTHING AS AN OPTION?

Option valuation is costly to do well and therefore not frequently employed. Other valuation techniques are widely used. And most importantly, not all investment decisions regard options. Real options analysis may not be worth the trouble unless options are clearly present and they are *incremental* to the decision (i.e., when they may make a difference in a go/no-go or either/or choice). Otherwise, DCF or some other valuation technique will probably satisfy the analytic need.

When are options present? The simplistic answer is that an option is present anytime one hears the words "rights," "flexibility," and "commitment." Given that these are such broad terms, it is worthwhile to sharpen our definition of options by considering what options are *not*. Let's distinguish options (where it is appropriate to use our option valuation tools) from opportunities (where it is less useful to do so). Here are five criteria that distinguish an option:

1. *Identifiable underlying asset.* An option is a right regarding some other asset or good. Can you identify it?
2. *Exclusive.* Options give the owner a special right that others do not have. Is this right exclusive to you?
3. *Contingent.* The value of an option derives from the value of an uncertain underlying asset. Can you identify the contingency or uncertainty?

4. ***Costly to acquire.*** Options are valuable, and are costly to acquire. Was the right costly to acquire?
5. ***Time constrained.*** An option has a finite life.

Real options may not affirmatively meet all five criteria, but the closer they come to doing so, the more appropriate it will be to use the valuation techniques outlined in this chapter. Exhibit 14.6 summarizes the differences seen in *options versus opportunities*. To illustrate the logic involved in parsing options from opportunities, consider these two situations. Would you use option valuation in these cases?

1. ***Right to sell lemonade at your street curb.*** Children experiment with this simple act of market entry that is virtually free, unregulated, and with no entry barriers. Cheap and nonexclusive market expansions like these are opportunities, while costly and exclusive market expansions are options. This illustrates the importance of *exclusivity and cost* as distinguishing features of an option.
2. ***Franchising versus generic.*** Exhibit 14.6 sketches two food service situations. One is a costly franchise right, and the other is the regular opportunity to open a generic restaurant. The franchise right is an option: costly, exclusive, finite-lived, and contingent; the right is distinguishable from the eventual investment. In the case of the generic restaurant, there is no cost to acquire the opportunity; it is not exclusive; its life is not finite; and the opportunity is indistinguishable from the underlying investment.

The point is that despite the pervasiveness of choices, not all are options. Some options (such as deep-in-the-money no-brainers) may not even be worth valuing. Real option valuation is challenging but worthwhile when the asset values are uncertain, the rights are exclusive, the decision can be freely and rationally made, and the rights are costly to acquire.

HOW TO ASSESS THE IMPACT OF REAL OPTIONS

This section of the chapter gives a practical overview of real option valuation. The critical first step is to identify real options present in the situation. Next, one values the real options drawing on any of four approaches. Finally, one must interpret the results carefully.

Find and Specify the Option

One of the limitations of discounted cash flow valuation is that it does not necessarily capture well the strategic aspects of capital investment. Such strategic elements include the right to make future investments, the right to sell or liquidate in the future, the right to abandon, and the right to switch investments. All of these rights are indicators of *managerial flexibility*; flexibility is analogous to a long call or long put position: It gives the holder rights to take action.

EXHIBIT 14.6 Comparing Options and Opportunities

	Option	Opportunity
Identifiable underlying asset. An option is a right regarding some other asset or good. Can you identify it?	The underlying asset can be identified and is separate from the option.	The focus of the opportunity can be identified, but is indistinguishable from the right.
Contingent. The value of an option *derives* from the value of an uncertain underlying asset. Can you identify the contingency or uncertainty?	Whether you would exercise the right before expiration is uncertain. The sources of uncertainty are identifiable. The value of the right is contingent.	The value of the opportunity *is* the value of the underlying asset. Whether you will exploit the opportunity depends on whether the NPV > 0.
Exclusive. Options give the owner a special right that others do not have. Is this right exclusive to you?	A right held by one or only a few. Options are exclusive rights.	Opportunities are not exclusive.
Costly to acquire. Options are valuable and are costly to acquire. Was the right costly to acquire?	Resources are deployed to gain the option.	Opportunities are free.
Time constrained. An option has a finite life.	The life of the option is finite and identifiable even with reasonable guesswork.	Opportunities are often not time constrained.
Example	Right to start up a business under an exclusive fast-food franchise that you purchased, that expires within three years unless you open one or more outlets, and that requires further spending to exercise. You are the exclusive franchisee in your territory. Whether and where you exercise the right is contingent on the results of a market survey, on zoning rulings by government, and on actions by competitors.	Opportunity to open a restaurant in your community under a generic name, "Downtown Grille." You didn't pay to acquire this opportunity. There is not much uncertainty: You can rent the perfect location that will deliver a steady clientele. It looks like a good deal already.
Valuation	This is an option-valuation problem. Value the franchise right using an option valuation methodology.	This is an investment-valuation problem. Value the investment opportunity using a conventional method such as DCF.

Another class of strategic elements appears when managers promise to do certain things in response to others—for example, invest more heavily if a competitor enters a market or acquires a new technology, buy if others choose to sell, sell if others choose to buy, and so on. These promises amount to *managerial commitment*; commitment is analogous to a short call or short put position.

Flexibility can be characterized as rights to "get" (i.e., call options) and rights to "give" (i.e., put options). Flexibility creates an economic asset; commitment creates an economic liability. All simple real options can be classified on these two dimensions—Exhibit 14.7 gives a two-by-two matrix that can help the practitioner classify a real option in technical terms. For instance, flexibility to acquire new technology amounts to a long call; flexibility to sell the new technology amounts to a long put. On the other hand, commitment to sell the new technology to someone else whenever the other party desires amounts to a short call position; commitment to buy the new technology from someone else whenever the other party desires amounts to a short put position.

Options and their values can be assessed in general terms for three considerations:

1. ***Direction.*** Who holds the option? Who is the counterparty? Does the option create or destroy value for your position? These questions of *direction* fundamentally seek to establish whether the position is long or short and put or call.
2. ***Materiality.*** Option valuation is complicated, and not something to launch into without a high probability that the answer to the analysis will make a difference. Where the decision is important, the valuation analysis based on discounted cash flow seems close, and/or the assets under option are sizable, the option values will be likely to have *materiality* and make a difference.

EXHIBIT 14.7 Classification of Real Options in Technical Terms

	Flexibility (Long Position)	Commitment (Short Position)
Right to "Get" (Call Option)	You have the flexibility to "get" or buy an asset from someone else at a predetermined price. You have a *long call option position.*	You have committed to someone else the right to "get" or buy at a predetermined price. Thus, you have a *short call option position.*
Right to "Give" (Put Option)	You have the flexibility to "give" or sell an asset to someone else at a predetermined price. You have a *long put option position.*	You have committed to someone else the right to "give" or sell to you at a predetermined price. Thus, you have a *short put option position.*

Note: This table suggests some of the economic consequences of different real option positions. All flexibility creates economic assets (long positions). All commitment creates economic exposure or liabilities (short positions).
Source: Author's analysis.

3. *Key value drivers.* Options are more valuable the deeper in the money, the greater the uncertainty, and the longer the life. Attributes of the assets underlying real options may also create a host of key *value drivers.*

Model and Value the Option

The analyst has four general alternative approaches for valuing real options:

1. ***Value the real option in the framework of an existing equation.*** Equations that solve for option value are partial differential equations. The Black-Scholes equation is the first, simplest in its class, and best known. Using the Black-Scholes model is fairly easy, since with the aid of a standard program in a spreadsheet or handheld calculator, the answer is a few keystrokes away. The problem is that few real options correspond to the assumptions of this venerable model: European call option with a finite life, known value of the underlying asset, and independent of other actions. Since the Black-Scholes model was published in 1973, numerous other equations have been published that correspond more clearly to real options situations. However, most of these newer models will be beyond the reach of the trained business analyst. Therefore, many analysts simply default to using the Black-Scholes model and accept that the resulting estimates may be imperfect. Chapter 10 illustrates the application of the Black-Scholes model to value call options.
2. ***Fit the option in a framework of a binomial lattice.*** Cox, Ross, and Rubenstein (1979) outlined an option valuation approach based on the assumption that the value of the underlying asset follows a *binomial lattice* (branching) process. If the valuation is risk-neutral, the probabilities implied in the branching process permit the analyst to discount the ending values to the present at the risk-free rate, a rather convenient assumption. The binomial approach entails six steps:

    1. Grow the lattice (or "tree") of the underlying asset value over time.
    2. Assess the probabilities of an up or down movement. These will be driven by the risk-free rate of return and the volatility of the underlying asset.
    3. Assess the states in which the options will be exercised.
    4. Estimate the payoffs associated with these end-states.
    5. Calculate the present expected value of future payoffs. This will entail multiplying the probability of up or down movements times the outcomes, and then discounting the expected value back one period at the risk-free rate.
    6. Interpret the results.

    The case study of EM.TV's partial acquisition of SLEC Holdings (later in this chapter) summarizes the steps of the binomial option valuation approach and gives an example of valuing put and call options.
3. ***Fit the option in a decision tree framework.*** A decision tree invites the analyst to look ahead to the full range of ultimate outcomes, and then come back to the present to make the decisions that pursue the optimal outcome. The technical term for this is *dynamic programming.* This is the approach illustrated in the brief examples of Exhibits 14.1, 14.2, 14.3, and 14.4. It is highly versatile

and because of its transparency proves to be a very good discipline on one's thinking. Finally, it permits the analyst to depart from the assumptions of the binomial probability distribution and to custom-tailor an analysis that accounts for the quirks of the option. Exhibits 14.1 through 14.4 give examples of the use of the decision tree framework to value rights.

4. ***Value the option using simulation analysis.*** Boyle (1977) discussed the application of *Monte Carlo simulation* to the valuation of options. For a detailed exposition, see Law and Kelton (1991). Intuitively the executive should understand that a spreadsheet model represents merely one outcome of what might be a wide range of outcomes. Simulation analysis (through spreadsheet add-in programs such as Crystal Ball) instructs the computer to recalculate the spreadsheet model many times, each time using different randomly chosen input parameters—the end result is an entire probability distribution of a key result such as the value of a firm or an option. In essence, software-generated simulation recognizes the unique kind of uncertainty that the decision maker likely faces at each decision point and permits the analyst to visualize the probability that the option will be in the money. Several mini-cases in this book give examples of the use of Monte Carlo simulation to value rights.

Exhibit 14.8 compares and summarizes the four methods. The four methodologies for valuing real options will likely arrive at four different values, which are all approximately similar with one another, but not exactly so—the differences originate from subtle variations in assumptions. This is a telltale about the state of the art in real option valuation: It is a young field with much more analytical development still in progress.

Interpret the Results and Develop Implications

Simply calculating estimates is insufficient. The first step of interpretation is to examine real option estimates against some test of reasonableness. This may entail comparing the estimate to observed values in other cases. Or one could simply test the sensitivity of the result to variations in assumptions or scenarios. And finally, one could backsolve for assumptions that will produce desired outcomes.

Another step of interpretation is to examine one's confidence level in the estimated values. Sensitivity analysis helps in this regard. And simulation analysis can produce formal confidence intervals around means of distributions. But even at a qualitative level, one can take a "gut check" to consider one's relative confidence in results and parameters.

The first two steps will suggest a third: considering how the estimates might be improved through refinements in modeling, sharper assumptions, and so on. This creates an iteration in the estimation process.

Finally, one needs to ask "so what?" Analysis generated purely for its own sake is worthless; it needs to be interpreted within a practical context. One must develop the ability to identify and understand the business implications of the real options analysis *and* consider carefully how to best communicate the analysis and implications to colleagues who may not share one's mastery of real options.

EXHIBIT 14.8 Comparison of the Four Methods of Estimating Real Option Value

	Black-Scholes Equation	Binomial Lattice	Decision Tree	Monte Carlo Simulation
Approach	Choose real option assumptions corresponding to the five parameters of the model: exercise price, underlying asset value, time, risk-free rate, and volatility. Estimate value.	Represent the evolution of option value in simple up or down movements in each period over time. Identify the resulting value at the end of each lattice. Determine the profit or loss from exercise of the option, and calculate the present value of the probability-weighted average.	Model the choices and uncertain events through time (branches) and the outcomes associated with those branches. "Fold back" the outcomes to the present, making optimal choices along the way.	Model the rights and uncertain events, accounting for the probability distribution of uncertain outcomes along the way. Estimate the option value as the present value of expected future outcomes.
Significance and application	The intellectual forebear of all option pricing theory. Useful in valuing European call options on financial assets.	As time periods grow infinitely small, the binomial approach converges into the Black-Scholes model. The big workhorse of real options valuation. Widely applied.	Another tree, like the binomial but that differs in assumptions about uncertainty. Easily applied to real options that are not complex. Excellent for modeling and communicating the framework of a real options analysis.	Most flexible of all methods in handling complexity and various assumptions about uncertainty. Used in the valuation of large capital projects, mines, drilling programs, etc.

Advantages	Simplest to use, drawing on widely available programs.	Uses simple representation of volatility. Relatively easy to describe to clients.	Flexible: can tailor decision tree to the features of the real option. Transparent to the analyst and client. Therefore easy to check logic and results.	Most adaptable to a range of assumptions about uncertainty. Creates appealing visual representations of uncertainty.
Disadvantages	Rigid about assumptions. Not very flexible to adapt to real option features. Can be hard to explain to client.	Can be tedious to use for large problems. Is the binomial uncertainty distribution the best representation of risk for your real option?	Can be tedious for large problems. Requires probability assessments for outcome branches—some of these assessments may be heroic.	Time-consuming to use. Complicated: It can be very difficult to model a stream of decisions, especially distant future ones. Assumptions may be unrelated to markets, arbitrary, and heroic—these risk "garbage-in, garbage-out" results. Challenging to explain to the uninitiated.

Source: Author's analysis.

FOUR MINI-CASES IN THE ANALYSIS OF REAL OPTIONS

This section of the chapter illustrates how one might apply real options valuation techniques in M&A problems, in areas such as spin-offs (Lucent), target valuation (Agouron), staged acquisitions (NCNB), and partial acquisitions (EM.TV).

Spin-off Value of Lucent: Assessing Latent Optionality

Usually the analyst discovers a gap between the actual market value of a target and its intrinsic value. There are many possible reasons for this,[13] but real options value would be a likely suspect. The analyst uses discounted cash flow to value the target, and therefore really assesses only the value of the assets in place. Thus, the valuation gap might be due to the value of growth or other options that DCF does not consider. The solution is to assess the real option value (*optionality*) in the target. As an outsider to a company, you may doubt your ability to produce a detailed analysis of option value. By backsolving for option assumptions that produce the gap value, however, you can begin to envision the conditions under which option value might explain the gap—Rappaport and Mauboussin (2002) offer this approach as one avenue for investment analysis and stock picking. A computer model such as "Option Valuation.xls" (found on the CD-ROM) can afford a basis for this analysis. Through the solver function in Excel, you can highlight assumptions that merit more research.

To illustrate the approach, consider the following case problem. Lucent Technologies was spun off from AT&T in 1996. Shortly after the spin-off, the firm traded at $60 per share. Yet the value of its assets in place was arguably in the neighborhood of $11.[14] What real option assumptions might account for the $49 gap? One begins by assessing the Black-Scholes parameters:

- Current stock price: begin by considering $60 per share, the post spin-off value.
- Life of the option: three years. Since much of Lucent's optionality derived from new technology, and since the design cycle of technology in telecommunications equipment was rapid, one could reasonably assume a life of three years.
- Cost to exercise the option: indicated by Lucent's very high rate of capital spending,[15] about $15 per share annually. At a discount rate of 15 percent, this yields a present value over three years of $34.24.
- Project volatility: uncertain. The volatility of Lucent's equity in its first year was 75 percent. This is probably an understatement of the real option volatility, since stock price volatility will be a weighted average of assets in place and real options.
- Risk-free rate of return: known. The three-year Treasury note yield was 3 percent.

The estimated value of a call option (using the Black-Scholes model and these assumptions) is $38.70 per share. It would appear from this point estimate that real options do not explain entirely the $49 gap. But given the uncertainties surrounding several of the assumptions, it makes sense to backsolve for the kinds of assumptions necessary to produce real option value equal to the $49 gap.

The analysis reveals that for real option value to explain the $49 gap, it must have:

- *A much longer life.* If volatility equals 0.75, the life implied must be 8.5 years. This exceeds the likely life of real options within Lucent, given the rapid rate of technological change.
- *Extremely high volatility.* If the life of the option equals three years, the volatility must be in the neighborhood of 135 percent—compared to the volatility of about 20 percent for the S&P 500 Index.
- *A much lower exercise price* (relative to the resulting economic activity) on the order of $13 per share.
- *Very high value* of the resulting economic activity (relative to the necessary investment).

The last condition is possible, judging from the incredible profitability of some software, hardware, and drug firms. The analysis exposes the aggressive assumptions necessary to justify the high stock price. Taken together, these assumptions seem implausible and should motivate close scrutiny of the technology bets within this firm—or better yet, reexamining beliefs about DCF valuation of Lucent, market efficiency, and rationality. Lucent's share price, along with other telecommunications equipment manufacturers, declined sharply in the market bust of 2000–2001. In December 2002, Lucent's shares were trading around $1.50, well below the $60 level following its spin-off from AT&T. The kind of analysis here, while far from precise, could have raised flags that would have helped prevent disastrous investment.

Agouron Pharmaceuticals: Valuing the Pure Research Firm

In January 1999, Warner Lambert Company acquired Agouron Pharmaceuticals for $2.1 billion. Up to 1997, Agouron had no operating income, and by 1999 was still reporting large negative net income. The target had focused on discovering new molecular entities (NMEs) for treating cancer and HIV. In 1994, the firm had two drugs in Phase I clinical trials and one in preclinical development. Kellogg and Charnes (2000) estimated the value of Agouron shares using decision tree and binomial lattice methods of real option valuation during the period 1994–1996 when the firm's activities were entirely focused on R&D and the firm was almost solely a growth option. Casting their analysis into the framework outlined earlier, the highlighted steps of the valuation are:

1. *Identify the optionality.* Investing in R&D is like buying a call option on uncertain future discoveries. The exercise price equals the investment necessary to commercialize the discovery in the future. In Agouron's case, the firm had three ongoing R&D projects, each with its own stream of options. For instance, a pharmaceutical research project consists of several stages,[16] and at the completion of each stage Agouron faces the decision of whether to terminate the project or invest in further development.
2. *Value the options.* Kellogg and Charnes made a number of assumptions consistent with general industry experience, or specific information about Agouron.

They forecasted the cost, duration, and probability of success at each of the stages. They assigned probabilities and economic outcomes to eventual success of the drug in the marketplace. And they made additional assumptions about the cost of goods sold, marketing costs, general and administrative expenses, tax rates, and working capital. They employed these assumptions in two valuation approaches: decision tree and binomial lattice.

3. ***Interpret the results and develop implications.*** Kellogg and Charnes found that at four out of five points in time, Agouron's share price was materially higher than values estimated by the real options approaches. Exhibit 14.9 gives a summary of the actual and estimated values. These two researchers concluded that real options valued the company reasonably well when all of Agouron's projects were in Phase I or earlier, but that as they approached the successful release, the actual price materially exceeded the estimated value. To explain the difference, the authors backsolved for assumptions that would produce estimated values equal to the actual price: shorter duration of clinical trial phases, higher probabilities of success in clinical phases, and higher revenues for the successful product.

The real options valuation of Agouron reveals the usefulness of this approach in the instance of firms with no revenue, a high proportion of intangible assets, and/or a future that is highly contingent on outcomes of definable processes or events—in such cases, discounted cash flow or multiples-based approaches will poorly capture the economic content of the company.

The case of Agouron also supports the larger truth about valuation: One only *estimates* real option value (that is, with analytical guesses, not facts). But even the mere process of deriving these estimates can yield insights about the drivers of

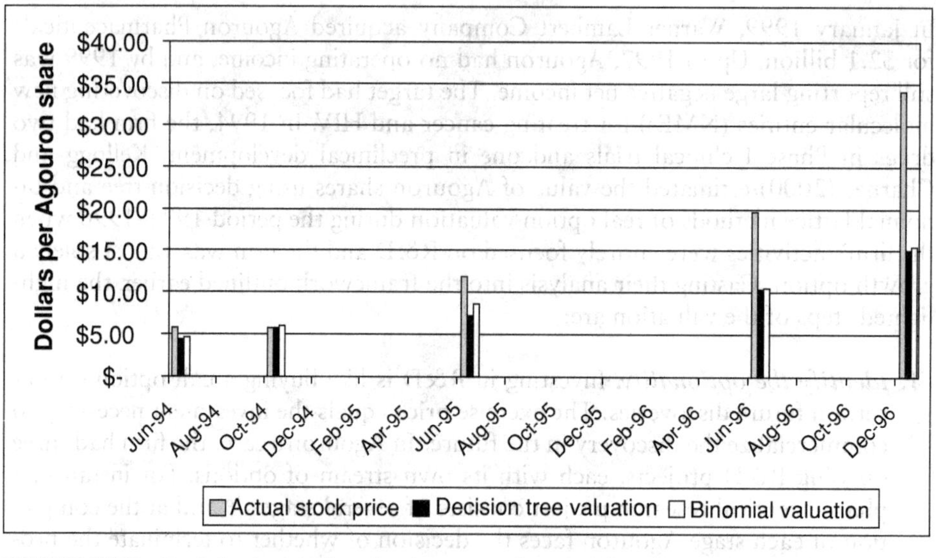

EXHIBIT 14.9 Real Options Values for Agouron Pharmaceuticals (Values in Dollars per Share)
Source of data: Kellogg and Charnes (2000), page 83. Graph prepared by author.

value, which are as important as the insights themselves. Knowledge of these drivers can sharpen one's estimated range of value for a target firm and prepare one for due diligence research and negotiation.

NCNB's Acquisition of First Republic: Valuing the Impact of Staged Investment

In the fall of 1988, North Carolina National Bank (NCNB), an aggressively expanding bank headquartered in Charlotte, announced an agreement to acquire First Republic National Bank of Texas, whose assets had been seized by the Federal Deposit Insurance Corporation (FDIC) following severe loan losses. First Republic had been the victim of an economic "perfect storm" following the collapse of oil prices in 1986 and of Texas real estate values in 1987. The FDIC sought a healthy bank to acquire and operate the branches of First Republic. Three competing buyers surfaced: Citicorp, Wells Fargo, and NCNB. NCNB won the right to acquire First Republic, but sought to hedge the uncertainty about the quality of First Republic's loan portfolio. Accordingly, NCNB negotiated an agreement with the FDIC that had the following features:

- First Republic would be split into a "good bank" (consisting of sound loans and the branch-banking network) and a "bad bank" consisting of a portfolio of defaulted loans. NCNB would acquire the good bank; the FDIC would retain the bad bank.
- At closing, NCNB would acquire 20 percent of the equity of the good bank for \$210 million—this would include 100 percent of the voting control of First Republic. The FDIC's economic interest of 80 percent would be in nonvoting stock.
- NCNB held the exclusive option to acquire the remaining 80 percent economic interest within five years of closing. The exercise price would be:
  - Within the first year after closing: 80 percent of the net book value as of closing, plus 115 percent of the increase in net book value.
  - Within the second year after closing: 80 percent of the net book value as of closing plus 120 percent of the increase in net book value.
  - Within the third, fourth, and fifth years after closing: 80 percent of the net book value as of closing plus 125 percent of the increase in net book value.

NCNB purchased an additional 29 percent of the equity in April 1989, and then the remaining 51 percent in July 1989.

As of the closing date, November 22, 1988, what was the value of NCNB's option to acquire the remaining 80 percent of First Republic's "good bank"? Following the real option analysis steps outlined earlier, this question can be approached through the following process:

1. *Specify the option.* NCNB held a five-year American call option on First Republic stock at exercise prices that rise over time. The rate of increase of the exercise price was not very rapid and probably reflected an expectation on the FDIC's part that First Republic would grow over time; plainly, the FDIC

wanted to participate in that growth for as long as it remained an equity holder. At the same time, the rising exercise price probably created an incentive for NCNB to exercise the option before maturity—this, too, might have reflected FDIC policy (i.e., that it is in the business of insuring bank deposits rather than holding an equity portfolio).

2. ***Value the option.*** The valuation analysis was structured as a Monte Carlo simulation. The economic value and net book value (NBV) of First Republic were forecasted over 260 weeks and varied randomly from the economic value and net book value implied in the closing terms of the acquisition (i.e., $1.05 billion each). Different volatility scenarios were assumed for economic value (10 to 30 percent) and net book value (4 to 8 percent). The volatility for economic value was drawn from a range of equity volatilities for peer banks. The volatility for net book value was drawn from volatilities for investment-grade senior corporate debt. NCNB was assumed to exercise the option when economic value exceeded the exercise price (that is, 80 percent of net book value plus change in NBV times the multiple [1.15, 1.2, or 1.25]). Future payoffs were discounted to the present at the five-year Treasury note yield. Exhibit 14.10 presents the frequency distribution for the present value of payoffs under the option in one scenario: Volatility of economic value is 30 percent, and volatility of net book value is 8 percent. The mean of the distribution is $53.2 million. Exhibit 14.11 summarizes the means for nine volatility scenarios.
3. ***Interpret the results.*** The graph and statistical results reveal that:

   - The option is valuable: In only 8 percent of the cases does the option never pay off. The graph suggests that the mean is influenced by a few outliers that pull the average upward. Still, the median value ($39.9 million) is not far from the mean ($53.2 million).
   - The option value is material, relative to the value of the asset. The implied value of the remaining 80 percent of First Republic at date of closing is $840 million. At an option value of $53.2 million, the option is 6 percent of the total remaining value.
   - The option value is sensitive to variations in volatility (both for economic value and debt value). A 10 percent increase in volatility is associated with an increase in option value of over $10 million.

There are several possible avenues of improving the analysis. First, the methodology assumes that NCNB *can* exercise the option as soon as possible. In fact, NCNB did not have the financial capacity to buy all of First Republic's shares at the outset. It would take time to raise the cash to complete the acquisition. A more sophisticated assessment of the real options here might account for the uncertainty surrounding NCNB's financial capacity. Second, if anything, the volatility estimates are low. The Texas banking market was in disarray, creating great uncertainty in the minds of businesspeople. NCNB's entry into Texas was fundamentally a bet that the market there would bounce back. Rerunning the Monte Carlo simulation to account for higher volatilities reveals, predictably, higher real option values. Third, the volatilities of net book value and economic value were possibly correlated, since they were driven by the same economic fundamentals in the Texas market. The impact of the correlation would merit further analysis.

EXHIBIT 14.10 Estimated Value of NCNB's Call Option on First Republic for a Single Scenario: Volatility of Economic Value of 30% and Volatility of Net Book Value of 8% (Values Are in Millions of U.S. Dollars)

Summary
Certainty level is 39.38%
Certainty range is from $53.3 to +infinity
Display range is from $0.0 to $200.0
Entire range is from $0.0 to $267.2
After 800 trials, the standard error of the mean is $1.7

Statistics	Value
Trials	800
Mean	$ 53.2
Median	$ 39.9
Mode	$ 0.0
Standard deviation	$ 47.4
Variance	$2,244.1
Skewness	1.18
Kurtosis	4.16
Coefficient of variability	0.89
Range minimum	$ 0.0
Range maximum	$ 267.2
Range width	$ 267.2
Mean standard error	$ 1.67

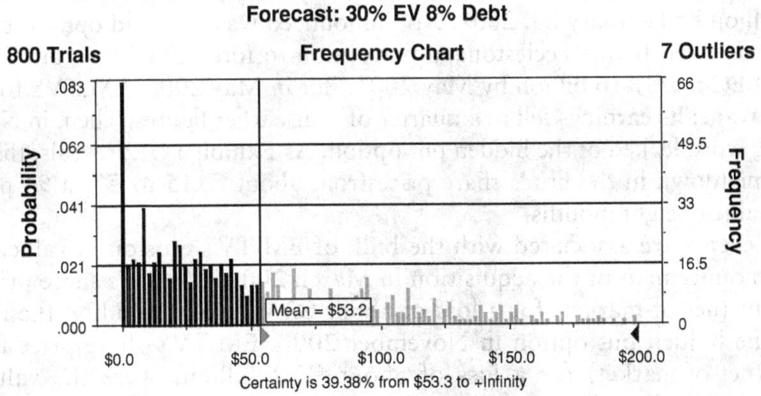

Source: Author's analysis with the assistance of Crystal Ball add-in software.

NCNB's acquisition of First Republic would rank among the most attractive "deals from heaven" in the annals of M&A history. The optionality in the deal design helped to resolve the uncertainty about NCNB's possible exposure to loan losses—the option amounted to a discount of about 6 percent from the stated acquisition price. But the larger benefit was NCNB's discovery of a provision in the U.S. tax code that would allow it to capture First Republic's tax loss carryforwards—these proved to be so large that in the final analysis, NCNB acquired First Republic virtually for free.

EXHIBIT 14.11 Estimated Values for NCNB's Call Option on First Republic (in Millions of U.S. Dollars)

Volatility of Debt	Volatility of Economic Value 10.0%	20.0%	30.0%
4.0%	$22.40	$35.60	$48.70
6.0%	$25.80	$39.30	$50.10
8.0%	$29.80	$40.90	$53.20

Note: The value in each cell is the mean of the simulated distribution of present values of payoffs under NCNB's option to acquire the FDIC's remaining 80 percent interest in First Republic.
Source: Author's analysis.

EM.TV's Partial Acquisition of SLEC: The Long Call and Short Put

In March 2000, EM.TV, a German media company, bought 50 percent of the equity in SLEC Holdings, the operator of the Formula One racing circuit, for €1.88 billion—this implied that the equity value of SLEC was €3.76 billion. At the time, EM.TV's share price was around €115 per share. As part of the deal, EM.TV announced that it also obtained a call option to buy another 25 percent of SLEC for €1.16 billion by February 28, 2001. Not announced was a second option: EM.TV granted the seller, Bernie Ecclestone, a put option to force EM.TV to buy 25 percent of SLEC for €1.16 billion by May 2001. But in May 2000, EM.TV's fortunes began to wane: Its earnings fell to a quarter of year-earlier figures. Then, in November 2000, word leaked of the hidden put option. As Exhibit 14.12 reveals, this triggered a meltdown in the firm's share price from about €115 to €7, a 94 percent drop in value in eight months.

Two events are associated with the bulk of EM.TV's erosion in value. First, at the announcement of the acquisition in March 2000, EM.TV's share price fell 12 percent (net-of-market) for a loss of about €2 billion. Second, at the revelation of the hidden put option in November 2000, EM.TV's share price fell 43 percent (net-of-market) for a loss of about €2.2 billion. Were the values of EM.TV's long call and short put position in SLEC consistent with the size of value destroyed?

The put and call embedded in the EM.TV/SLEC deal can be valued using the binomial valuation approach:

- Value of the underlying asset today: SLEC's equity was the asset underlying both options. We can assume that SLEC's equity was fairly valued in the transaction, and that the value of the firm was €3.88 billion. But the option entailed a claim on only 25 percent of that amount, €0.97 billion.
- Exercise price: €1.16 billion.

EXHIBIT 14.12 Share Price History of EM.TV Compared to DAX Index, Indexed to Starting Value of EM.TV

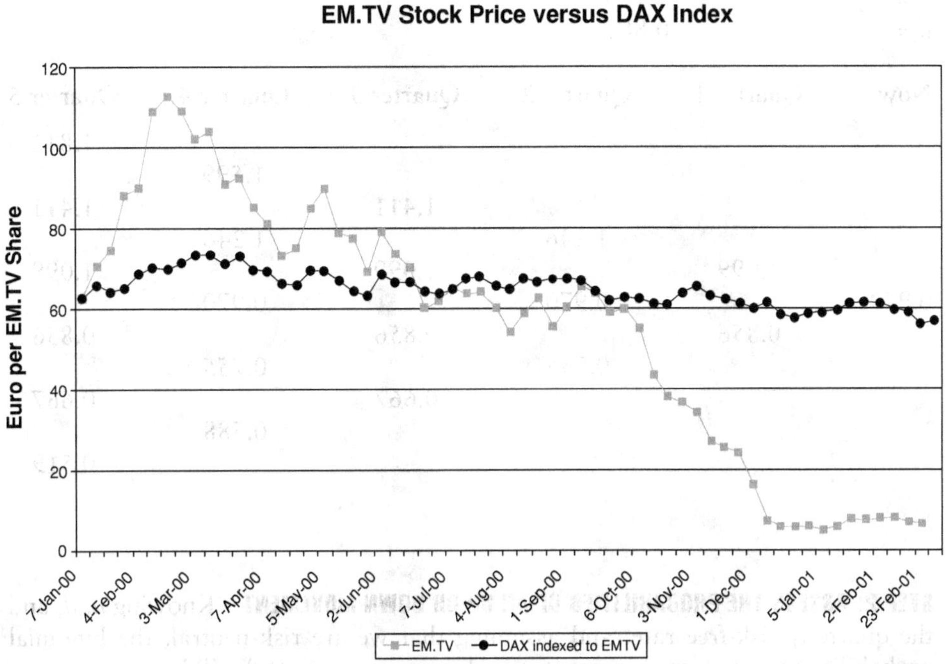

Note: EM.TV announced its deal to acquire 50 percent of SLEC in early March 2000. The put option held by SLEC was first reported on November 22, 2000.
Source: Author's analysis with data obtained from Datastream.

- Volatility: 25 percent. Actually, SLEC was a private company, so the volatility of its share price was unobservable. Yet the firm enjoyed monopoly control over Formula One racing events. Suppose that 25 percent was an appropriate annual volatility level, based on peer comparisons. On a quarterly basis, the volatility would equal the annual volatility times the square root of 1 divided by the number of periods in a year, or $0.25 \cdot (0.25)^{0.5} = 0.125$.
- Life: The options expired in February and May 2001, four and five quarters, respectively, from the date of EM.TV's acquisition of half of SLEC.
- The annualized euro risk-free rate for the next five quarters was 4 percent. On a quarterly basis, this equated to 0.00985 (i.e., almost 99 basis points per quarter).

STEP 1: GROW THE TREE The binomial approach assumes that each quarter, the value of SLEC's equity will move up by u ($u = e^{0.125} = 1.133$) or down by d ($d = e^{-0.125} = 1/u = 0.882$). This means that at the end of the first quarter, a quarter of SLEC's equity will be worth either €1.099 ($u \cdot 0.97$) or €0.856 ($d \cdot 0.97$). One can expand outward in similar fashion for the five-quarter period to yield this expansion tree:

Annual Volatility =	0.25
Quarterly Volatility =	0.125
u =	1.133
d =	0.882

Now	Quarter 1	Quarter 2	Quarter 3	Quarter 4	Quarter 5
					1.812
				1.599	
			1.411		1.411
		1.246		1.246	
	1.099		1.099		1.099
0.970		0.970		0.970	
	0.856		0.856		0.856
		0.755		0.755	
			0.667		0.667
				0.588	
					0.519

STEP 2: ASSESS THE PROBABILITIES OF AN UP OR DOWN MOVEMENT Knowing u, d, and the quarterly risk-free rate, and assuming that we are risk-neutral, the binomial probabilities of an up-movement (p_u) or down-movement (p_d) will be:

$$p_u = \frac{(1+r_f)-d}{u-d} \tag{1}$$

$$p_d = \frac{u-(1+r_f)}{u-d} \tag{2}$$

Under the preceding assumptions, p_u equals 0.508; p_d equals 0.492. These probabilities are constant throughout the tree, and will be used to determine the expected value of the discounted value of future payoffs.

STEP 3: ASSESS THE STATES IN WHICH THE OPTIONS WILL BE EXERCISED One can make a simplifying assumption that neither party will exercise the option early, since this would destroy time value in the option. Therefore, the relevant time for EM.TV is the fourth quarter from now, when it will exercise the call option if the value of one-quarter of SLEC is greater than the exercise price, €1.16 billion. For SLEC, the relevant time is the fifth quarter from now when it will exercise the put option if the value of one-quarter of SLEC is less than the exercise price, €1.16 billion. In the following tree, the boldface numbers indicate where EM.TV will exercise its call; italicized boldface numbers indicate where SLEC will exercise its put.

Now	Quarter 1	Quarter 2	Quarter 3	Quarter 4	Quarter 5
					1.812
				1.599	
			1.411		1.411
		1.246		1.246	
	1.099		1.099		*1.099*
0.970		0.970		0.970	
	0.856		0.856		*0.856*
		0.755		0.755	
			0.667		*0.667*
				0.588	
					0.519

STEP 4: ESTIMATE THE PAYOFFS ASSOCIATED WITH THESE END-STATES This step assesses the consequences for EM.TV. The payoff from a long call option in the end-states will equal *price minus exercise price*. The payoff to EM.TV from a short put option in the end-states will be an outlay equal to *exercise price minus price*. The following tree shows these payoffs:

Now	Quarter 1	Quarter 2	Quarter 3	Quarter 4	Quarter 5
					NM
				0.439	
			—		NM
		—		0.086	
	—		—		*(0.061)*
—		—		0.000	
	—		—		*(0.304)*
		—		0.000	
			—		*(0.493)*
				0.000	
					(0.641)

NM means "not meaningful." If EM.TV has previously exercised its call option, SLEC will not thereafter exercise its put option.

STEP 5: CALCULATE THE PRESENT EXPECTED VALUE OF FUTURE PAYOFFS This final step estimates today's value of the future receipts or payments. For instance, starting with the lower right-hand corner of the table, one would take the expected value of the $p_u(0.493) + p_u(0.641)$ or $(0.508 \cdot 0.493) + (0.492 \cdot 0.641)$ to yield 0.566. Discounting this by one-quarter at the risk-free rate, 0.00985 yields 0.560. This process is repeated for the other cells, folding back to the present, to find a value of €–0.138 billion. The following tree shows the calculated values at each step:

Now	Quarter 1	Quarter 2	Quarter 3	Quarter 4	Quarter 5
					NM
				0.439	
			0.263		NM
		0.111		0.086	
	(0.022)		(0.044)		*(0.061)*
(0.138)		(0.159)		(0.179)	
	(0.261)		(0.281)		*(0.304)*
		(0.371)		(0.393)	
			(0.471)		*(0.493)*
				(0.560)	
					(0.641)

NM means "not meaningful."

STEP 6: INTERPRET THE RESULTS Could the announcement of this hidden put option really have accounted for the meltdown of EM.TV? Hardly. The combination of long call and short put still had a negative value of €138 million—this poorly explains the destruction of over €4 billion surrounding the news about EM.TV's acquisition of SLEC. Separate analysis suggests that the call option alone was worth about €47 million, implying that the short put posed an economic liability to EM.TV of about €185 million. The meltdown was probably due to other factors, such as EM.TV's worsening financial condition and the bursting of the Internet bubble (a name like EM.TV would imply a new economy firm).

SUMMARY AND CONCLUSIONS

This chapter has surveyed the application of real options analysis to M&A. It has discussed four real option valuation methods and offered practical advice for the M&A analyst who must assess the contingencies.

The lessons for the decision maker are perhaps more significant. Chief among these is that the application of options thinking should not be confined to analysts. The first rule, then, should be to *look for real optionality in any business setting*. To look for optionality means to identify the presence of rights and their type of position (put/call, long/short).

The second rule for decision makers should be to *develop a feel for real option value*. At the outset, this means acknowledging that some rights aren't all that interesting or are not easily valued. Recall the distinction between options and opportunities. A feel for option value means understanding the impact of key value drivers.

A third rule is *build or conserve flexibility*. Flexibility appears in large and small ways throughout the design of individual deals and in the management of M&A processes. Real options theory teaches that flexibility is valuable.

NOTES

1. For example, see Hayes and Garvin (1982), Kulatilaka and Marcus (1992), and Nichols (1994).
2. Kester (1984) and Kulatilaka and Perotti (1998) discuss growth options and their valuation.
3. See, for instance, Faulkner (1996) and Grenadier and Weiss (1997) for more discussion of the option valuation of R&D projects.
4. See, for instance, Brennan and Schwartz (1985) for more discussion of the option valuation of natural resources and drilling rights.
5. I studied this situation at AlliedSignal, and found a business unit that had been utterly demoralized—indeed, paralyzed—and was the worst-performing unit in the large conglomerate. In a move to stanch the outflow of cash, AlliedSignal changed managers. The new manager immediately opened negotiations with the environmental authorities, and eventually negotiated a "workout" program in which the refinery would be closed immediately and environmental remediation would be conducted over time, rather than all at once. This was an enormous success for AlliedSignal and the manager, who recognized that not only was the company stuck, but so were the environmental authorities. In this particular case, an exit was in everyone's interest. For more on this, see Bruner, Larson, and Paddack (1996).
6. For a more detailed discussion of the valuation of exit options, see Berger et al. (1996), McDonald and Siegel (1985), Myers and Majd (1990), and Schary (1991).
7. For more discussion of the right to delay, see McDonald and Siegel (1986) and Ross (1995).
8. Margrabe (1978) discusses the right to switch as a call option on the attractive alternative. He argues that in some circumstances switching options can be valued as European calls using the Black-Scholes option pricing model. Moel and Tufano (2002) explored the behavior of mining firms to start and stop production, a decision to switch between operating and mothballed status. They found that option value drivers, such as volatility, had a significant influence on the decisions to open or close mines.
9. For more on the valuation of flexibility, see Brennan and Trigeorgis (1988), Fine and Freund (1990), Kogut and Kulatilaka (1994b), Kulatilaka (1993, 1995), Kulatilaka and Marks (1988), Triantis and Hodder (1990), Trigeorgis (1996), Trigeorgis and Mason (1997), and Upton (1994).
10. For more on the "competencies" perspective on corporate strategy, see Hamel and Prahalad (1994), Hamel (1996), and Kogut and Kulatilaka (1997).
11. For more on buildups as options, see Kogut and Kulatilaka (1994a) and Smit (2001).
12. For detailed discussion of the optionality in M&A agreements, see Chapters 18 ("An Introduction to Deal Design in M&A") and 30 ("Negotiating the Deal").
13. The reasons could include estimation error, synergies, market inefficiencies, and market irrationality.
14. This was estimated using the dividend discount model, where earnings per share were assumed to be \$1.60, perpetual growth rate of the business was 5 percent, and the cost of equity was 20 percent. The resulting figure, \$11.20,

is probably optimistic owing to the absence of assumed investment to sustain growth.

15. A common approach is to view the equity of the firm as a call option with the principal amount of debt outstanding as the exercise price. Lucent's indebtedness was very low, less than $1.00 per share. Such an approach makes no sense here since we are not valuing the whole firm, just the real options. Also, it ignores the very high rate of investment necessary to exercise options to grow—Lucent's profitability was being used to exercise these options.
16. The first stage is *discovery* in which scientists develop concepts for new compounds. The second is *preclinical tests* of the compound in laboratory tests and on animals. Third, *clinical trials* test the compound on humans—these trials consist of three phases: I (tests on a few healthy volunteers focusing on toxicity and safe dosage); II (tests on a larger number of ill patients focusing on efficacy and safety); and III (large-scale trials focusing on safety). Upon successful completion of the research phases, the company files a New Drug Application with the U.S. Food and Drug Administration, which reviews the findings and approves or denies the application for commercial distribution of the drug. Each phase yields an uncertain outcome. Therefore, the decision to make the investment associated with each phase is the acquisition of a call option on the findings of that phase. Collectively, these options form a stream. As a practical matter in valuing a research firm, one cares about the value of the entire stream.

CHAPTER 15

Valuing Liquidity and Control

INTRODUCTION

The simple premise of much M&A valuation analysis is that the target shareholder sells total *control* in the target firm and that the securities or assets being acquired are marketable. This chapter explores the world beyond that premise. The vast majority of M&A deals involve privately owned firms and illiquid stock. Exhibit 15.1 shows the volume of acquisitions involving the purchase of a privately owned target, or the purchase of a minority interest in a company. From 1990 to 2002 acquisitions of minority interests accounted for between 1 and 3 percent of all transactions. During the same period, the purchase of independent entities that were private targets accounted for 40 to 60 percent of all deals. Divestitures by corporations represent the sale of illiquid securities or assets. Exhibit 6.15 in Chapter 6 presents corporate divestitures as a percentage of all M&A activity. From 1990 to 2002, divestitures averaged 33 percent of all transactions. In short, the need to apply illiquidity discounts and control premiums is more the rule than the exception in M&A.

The realm of illiquidity and lack of control is a focus of detailed analysis and lively debate. Shannon Pratt (2001, page 37) wrote:

> *There is often more money in dispute in determining the discounts and premiums in a business valuation than in arriving at the pre-discount valuation itself. Discounts and premiums affect not only the value of the company but also play a crucial role in determining the risk involved, control issues, marketability, contingent liability, and a host of other factors that can make or break a deal.*

This chapter summarizes what we know from research and offers a new framework for valuing *liquidity* and control based on the theory of real options. Learnings include:

- Illiquidity requires a discount from liquid values.
- Minority status requires a discount from value with 100 percent control.
- Liquidity and control are rights, and may be assessed in terms of their option value. This is a new way to think about these effects. This chapter summarizes recent research.

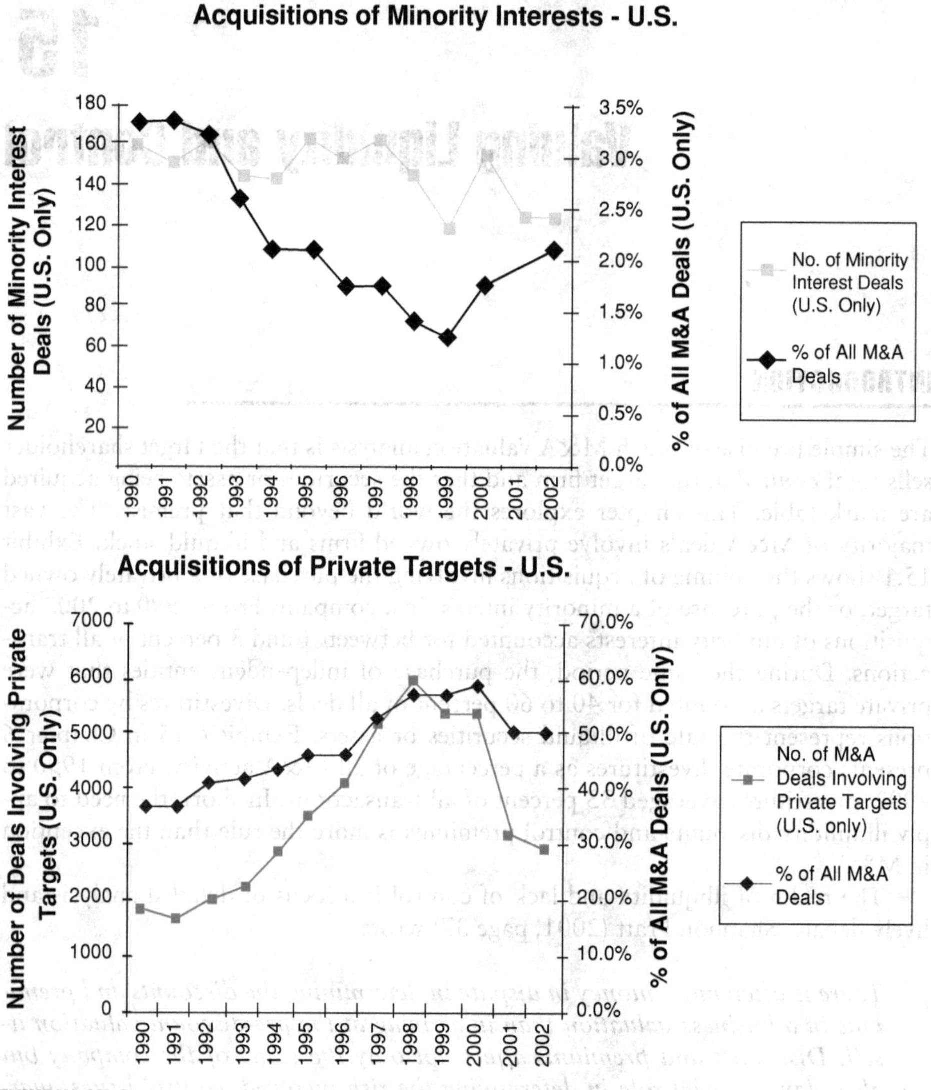

EXHIBIT 15.1 M&A Activity Involving Acquisition of Minority Interests
Source of data: Thomson Financial SDC Database.

- The traditional approach is to assess discounts and premiums based on the analysis of peer deals. This chapter illustrates the calculations under this approach.
- Liquidity and control can have sizable effects on shareholder welfare.

ADJUSTING VALUES FOR DISCOUNTS AND PREMIUMS

The point of departure into the realm of liquidity and control is conventional practice. This section of the chapter surveys the traditional means of adjusting a purchase price for illiquidity and lack of control.

Discounts and Premiums Start from a Base

Whenever liquidity and/or control change, value changes. We can think of the value of the firm as a composite of the stand-alone value of the target plus a *discount or premium* for liquidity and control.

$$\text{Maximum payment for Target} = V_{\text{Stand-alone}} + V_{\text{Synergies}} + \Delta_{\text{Illiquidity and control}} \quad (1)$$

where: Δ is the change in value from the base case resulting from effects of illiquidity and control. This term could be positive or negative.

The "base case" valuation of the stand-alone firm comes from conventional valuation approaches, such as DCF and multiples (described in Chapter 9). These assume, in effect, that you buy a small interest in liquid shares of stock and that the firm continues to operate as is. Chapter 11 recommended valuation of the firm with synergies, to give a sense of the economic upside. The sum of stand-alone value and synergy value form the base case value of the firm.

Base case values estimated with DCF or multiples of earnings implicitly assume that the firm's shares are liquid and that all shareholders are governing; no block of shares retains special control rights over the firm. Deviations from these two assumptions must trigger adjustments in value—this is where the illiquidity discount and *control premium* come in. Exhibit 15.2 sketches an example of possible changes. The base case is in the southeast corner of the diagram, the firm with liquid shares and no *control asymmetries*—this means that there are no

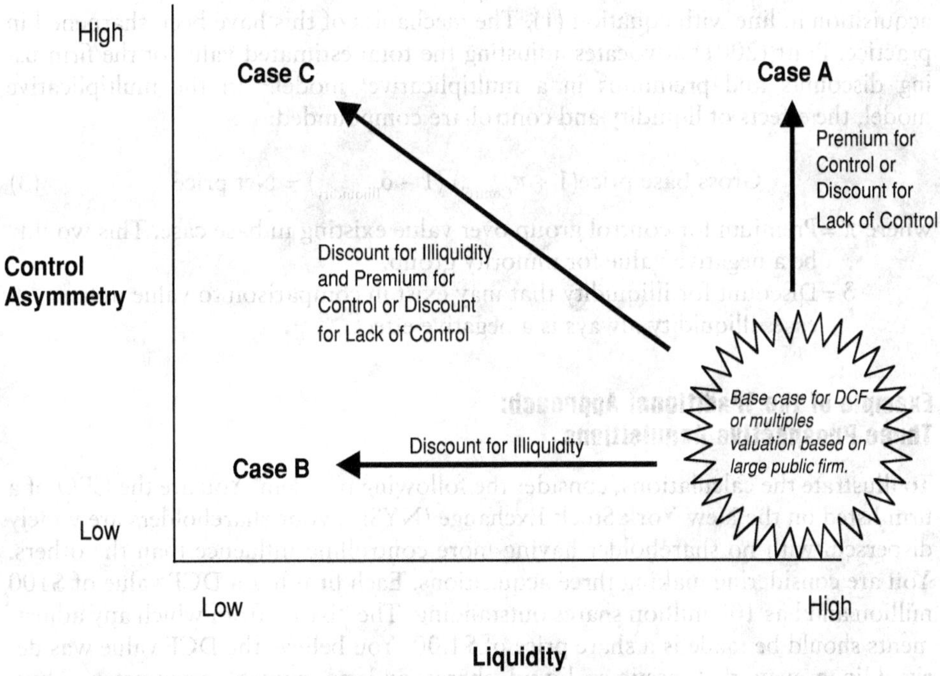

EXHIBIT 15.2 Deviations in Liquidity and Control from Base Case Require a Premium or Discount

groups of shareholders with special control rights. As you move from liquidity to illiquidity, the shareholder must sustain a discount in the value of his or her shares. And as you move from the base case of no control asymmetries to the world where control asymmetries exist, two things happen: The control group gains a premium value to their shares, while the minority shareholders experience a discount—the control group and minority group diverge in value as the control asymmetry grows.

All discussion of premiums and discounts begins with some base case. As a convention in the discussion that follows, the base case will be the value of the firm as if its shares were actively traded on a public exchange (i.e., liquid, and therefore marketable) and as if there were no shareholders with an unusual degree of power over the strategic decisions of the firm—General Electric is a good example of the firm with these qualities. We could just as easily choose a different base case, which would cause us to alter our use of "premium" and "discount" in the discussion of liquidity and control effects.

By the way, premiums and discounts are inversely related. You can convert from one to the other with this formula:

$$\%\ \text{discount} = 1 - \left(\frac{1}{1 + \%\ \text{premium}}\right) \tag{2}$$

The Multiplicative Model—the Traditional Approach

Liquidity and control are valuable. The practitioner must adjust the payment in an acquisition in line with equation (1). The mechanics of this have been sharpened in practice. Pratt (2001) advocates adjusting the total estimated value of the firm using discounts and premiums in a multiplicative[1] model.[2] In the multiplicative model, the effects of liquidity and control are compounded:

$$\text{Gross base price}(1 + \pi_{\text{Control}})\,(1 - \delta_{\text{Illiquidity}}) = \text{Net price} \tag{3}$$

where π = Premium for control group over value existing in base case. This would be a negative value for minority group.

δ = Discount for illiquidity that may exist in comparison to value in base case. Illiquidity always is a negative effect.

Example of the Traditional Approach: Three Prospective Acquisitions

To illustrate the calculations, consider the following problem. You are the CEO of a firm listed on the New York Stock Exchange (NYSE); your shareholders are widely dispersed, with no shareholder having more controlling influence than the others. You are considering making three acquisitions. Each firm has a DCF value of $100 million and has 100 million shares outstanding. The "base" from which any adjustments should be made is a share price of $1.00. You believe the DCF value was derived in a way that assumes liquid shares and no control asymmetry. Thus, illiquidity will impose a discount from the base value and control will command a premium relative to the base case.[3]

- ***Target A: publicly held company with a majority shareholder.*** One shareholder owns 51 percent of the shares of this company. You wonder what share price to offer the majority shareholder, and what price to offer the minority shareholders. Privately, you believe a 40 percent control premium over the base case valuation is justified.
- ***Target B: privately held company with dispersed shareholders.*** Here there is no control asymmetry arising from the existence of a control block and of a group of minority shareholders. But the shares to be purchased are illiquid. Privately you believe a 30 percent discount from the base case for illiquidity is warranted.
- ***Target C: privately held company with a majority shareholder.*** One shareholder owns 51 percent of the shares of this company. All shares are illiquid. You wonder what share price to offer the majority shareholder, and what price to offer the minority shareholders. Privately, you believe a 40 percent control premium and a 30 percent illiquidity discount are justified, relative to the base case valuation.

Note that a control asymmetry will grant a premium to the controlling block and impose a discount on the minority block. Based on the proportions of share ownership, you would be justified in quoting different prices for the control and minority shares.

Exhibit 15.3 computes the adjusted values, showing the impact of the liquidity discount and control premium. This exhibit is drawn from "Liquidity and Control.xls" that is found on the CD-ROM. Exhibit 15.4 summarizes the share price results of the cases in a two-way matrix for liquidity and control that map onto the qualitative presentation in Exhibit 15.2. In the southeast corner is the base case, where all shares command a price of $1.00. In the southwest corner, the shares are subject to a liquidity discount only; in the absence of a control asymmetry all shares command a price of $0.70, reflecting the 30 percent liquidity discount.

The top half of Exhibit 15.4 explores the impact of a control asymmetry. In the northeast corner, shares are liquid, but there is a control asymmetry that causes the control and minority shares to be valued differently. The control block shares are worth $1.40 (reflecting the 40 percent control premium you assumed). And the minority shares are worth $0.58—the majority's gain is the minority's loss! The minority may feel that this discount represents an expropriation of their value. The majority no doubt feels that the premium justly compensates them for the rights of control. But under the conservation of value (one of the deep principles in finance, which can be found in the writings of Modigliani and Miller) the net effect of the control asymmetry must sum to zero.

Finally, in the northwest corner of the table, we have the world of illiquidity and control asymmetry. Here, the control block shares are worth $0.98—barely different from the base case ($1.00) because of the offsetting effects of illiquidity and control. For minority shareholders, however, shares are worth only $0.41: a dramatic discount from the base case and the worst case of all.

This example demonstrates that the impact of liquidity discounts and control premiums on share prices can be dramatic. Also, relatively small changes in the premium and discount can produce material swings in the adjusted share prices.

EXHIBIT 15.3 Three Example of the Multiplicative Approach for Estimating Illiquidity and Control Effects on Value

Assumptions	
% discount for illiquidity	30%
% premium for control	40%
Size of control block	51%
Base case value of the equity; marketable, no control	$100
Number of shares outstanding	100

	Case A	Case B	Case C	Note
Illiquidity? ("Yes" if shares are not liquid)	No	Yes	Yes	
Control asymmetry? ("Yes" if there is a control block)	Yes	No	Yes	
1 Base case value of the equity; marketable, no control asymmetries	$100.00	$100.00	$100.00	A
2 Adjustment for illiquidity	0%	–30%	–30%	B
3 Value of equity adjusted for possible illiquidity	$100.00	$ 70.00	$ 70.00	B
4 % premium for control	40%	0%	40%	C
5 Size of controlling block	51%	0%	51%	D
6 Value of controlling block	$ 71.40	$ —	$ 49.98	E
7 Value of minority block	$ 28.60	$ 70.00	$ 20.02	F
8 Value of equity adjusted for control asymmetry and illiquidity	$100.00	$ 70.00	$ 70.00	G
9 Controlling block price per share	$ 1.40	N/A	$ 0.98	
10 Minority block price per share	$ 0.58	N/A	$ 0.41	
11 Price to all if no control asymmetry	N/A	$ 0.70	N/A	

Notes:

A. Start with the value of the firm with marketable shares but no control blocks—like large, publicly traded corporations. This is the base case from which most valuation adjustment approaches begin.

B. Illiquidity is assumed to affect *all* shares equally. Therefore, the first adjustment must be for illiquidity.

C. The presence of a control block affects the control group and minority differently. Therefore, control must be addressed after liquidity.

D. The size of the control block determines what portion of the equity will receive the control premium.

E. The value of the control block equals the value of equity adjusted for illiquidity (line 3) times (1 + Control premium) (line 4) times % size of control block (line 5).

F. The value of the minority block equals the difference between the value of equity adjusted for possible illiquidity (line 3) and the value of the control block (line 6).

G. The value of minority and control blocks to sum to the value of equity adjusted for possible illiquidity.

Analysts obtain these parameters by studying other M&A transactions that are comparable in terms of size, industry, and other factors. Specialist consultants maintain proprietary databases for the purpose of generating suggested premiums and discounts. But the analysis of comparable transactions leaves considerable room for judgment. For instance, one analyst wrote:

> *It would seem at first glance that control premiums paid in buyouts of public companies would be ideal indicators of the magnitude of discount necessary for proper valuation of a minority interest. Yet it becomes apparent that such data is compiled from such a diverse field that its usefulness is limited. This diversity is caused by differences in the degree of control obtained, the industry of the acquired company, the timing of the buyout, the concentration of control among selling shareholders, the perceived benefits or synergies to be obtained by buyers, the receptiveness of management to the offer, and the presence or absence of competitive bids. Finding enough examples from which to draw a valid discount conclusion for a specific degree of control in a specific industry during a given time period is rarely, if ever, possible. (Pratt 2001, page 20)*

This is a strong and telling statement, which suggests that comparable transactions analysis is helpful, but does not provide definitive answers.

The analyst needs a principled basis for his or her recommendations. Where do discounts and premiums come from? What factors drive them? Does one size fit all cases? And is there any test of reasonableness? The next three sections offer some insights drawn from financial economics, including these:

- Discounts and premiums arise from the optionality embedded in liquidity and control.
- Uncertainty about the value of the target is a significant driver of discounts and premiums. Also, because liquidity and control rights are driven by the same underlying factors, the two options *interact* on the value of each other. Liquidity and control effects are not independent.
- One size does not fit all. Deal makers should not impose a discount or premium in fixed fashion across all transactions. Rules of thumb are likely to be inappropriate.

EXHIBIT 15.4 Summary of Three Case Examples: Offered Share Price as It Varies with Assumptions about Illiquidity and Control Asymmetry

Control Asymmetry	Liquid Shares: No	Liquid Shares: Yes
Yes: Control	$0.98	$1.40
Minority	$0.41	$0.58
No: Price to all	$0.70	$1.00

Note: The dollar values in this exhibit are drawn from the calculations in Exhibit 15.3. Note the correspondence of this exhibit with Exhibit 15.2: The southeast corner corresponds to the base case—the value for the base case is simply the total value, $100, divided by the number of shares, 100, given in the assumptions.

WHERE DO ILLIQUIDITY DISCOUNTS COME FROM? LIQUIDITY IS AN OPTION

First we turn to a consideration of the value of liquidity. This has been the focus of considerable research and recently the useful application of an options perspective.

Liquidity Defined

Illiquidity, or lack of marketability of an asset, commands a discount sufficient to induce investors to buy the nonmarketable asset rather than an identical marketable asset. "Liquidity" and "marketability" are often used interchangeably. However, the terms differ in subtle ways. Liquidity is the ability to exit rapidly, to find a ready price and counterparty. Marketability, on the other hand, is the right to sell (i.e., legally or under the terms of a contract). An asset could be marketable, but not liquid: You may have the legal right to sell a toxic waste dump, but may not find any buyers.

The distinction is crucial for owners of *letter stock*,[4] shares acquired in a private placement of equity under Rule 144 of the SEC. Letter stock is not marketable during the first year after investment. However, the issuer may be publicly listed for trading and generally have a liquid market in its shares. Thus, letter stock issued by this company could be liquid but not marketable. For simplicity of presentation in this chapter, "liquidity" is used in the generic sense of being able to sell. But in specific situations, the M&A professional should determine with competent legal counsel whether assumptions of marketability and liquidity might differ.

Empirical Research on Illiquidity Discounts

Research on government debt, currency options, letter stock, and initial public offerings tells us that liquidity is valuable. For instance, the more liquid Treasury bills offer yields 35 basis points lower than the less liquid Treasury notes.[5] A similar study[6] of Japanese government debt finds a yield difference of 50 basis points. An analysis[7] of liquidity in the euro corporate bond market finds yield differences of as much as 47 basis points. And in the currency options market, the more liquid exchange-traded options sell for about 25 percent more than the less liquid over-the-counter currency options.[8] Equity-linked bonds in the United Kingdom provided the same payoff as investment in an equity index, but were relatively less liquid. Dimson and Hanke (2001) found that over 1989 to 2001 the equity-linked bonds traded at an average 3.35 percent discount to the index.

But of greatest relevance to the analysis of M&A transactions involving illiquid securities is the research on five topics:

1. Discounts associated with *letter stock*, as compared to liquid shares in the market. Studies of letter stock discounts are the most popular points of reference for practitioners. Exhibit 15.5 summarizes these studies and shows average discounts ranging from 13 percent to 45 percent. Silber (1991) finds discounts as high as 84 percent. Finnerty (2002) reports an enormous range, from –47.17 percent (i.e., a *premium*) to 68.3 percent. Plainly, discounts on letter stock vary widely.

EXHIBIT 15.5 Research on Letter Stock Liquidity Discounts

Study	Observations and Time Period	Mean Discount
Studies by Scholars		
Wruck (1989)	N = 99, 1979–1985	13.5%
Silber (1991)	N = 69, 1981–1988	33.75%
Hertzel and Smith (1993)	N = 106, 1980–1987	20.14%
Longstaff (1995)	N/A*	25–35%*
Finnerty (2002)	N = 101, 1991–1997	20.13%
Studies by Government		
SEC (1971)	N = 398, 1966–1969	25.8%
Studies by Practitioners		
Gelman (1972)	N = 89, 1968–1970	33%
Moroney (1973)	N = 146, N/A	35.6%
Trout (1972)	N = N/A, 1968–1972	33.5%†
Maher (1976)	N = N/A, 1969–1973	35.4%
Standard Research Consultants (1983)	N = N/A, 1978–1982	45%†
Willamette Management Associates‡	N = N/A, 1981–1984	31.2%†
Hall and Polacek (1994)	N = 100, 1979–1992	23%
Oliver and Meyers (2000)	N = 53, 1980–1996	27%
Johnson (1999)	N = 72, 1991–1995	20%
Aschwald (2000)	N = 23, 1996–1997	21%
	N = 15, 1997–1998	13%

*Longstaff's result is the estimated *maximum* discount for nonmarketability.
†Median values.
‡Cited in Pratt (1989).

2. Discounts associated with *entrepreneurs' restricted shares*. Founders and managers of companies can be restricted from selling their stock, due to the terms of executive compensation schemes or IPO stock lockups. Illiquidity combined with a lack of portfolio diversification for their personal wealth can impose sizable discounts. Kahl, Liu, and Longstaff (2001) modeled the discounts and found that where stock is restricted for five years and it represents 50 percent of the entrepreneur's wealth, the illiquidity discount could vary between 20 and 70 percent. They find that volatility of stock price and length of restriction period are key drivers of the discount.
3. Discounts implied in *private placements before public transactions*. The letter stock studies consider private placements for securities of public firms. But private placements for private firms grant a different perspective on illiquidity. Emory (2000) found discounts over 1981–2000 averaging 47 percent. Willamette Management Associates, cited in Pratt (2001), found average annual discounts clustering in the 45 to 50 percent range. These pre-IPO transactions are often with insiders; it is possible that special influence or use of the form of these transactions as a form of executive compensation may confound inferences about liquidity.

4. *IPO underpricing and flotation costs* give another perspective on illiquidity. The cost of going public is the price a firm pays to achieve liquidity and other aims.[9] These costs consist of direct costs (i.e., the gross underwriting spread) and indirect costs (the underwriting discount).[10] The literature on these costs is extensive[11] and finds direct costs of about 7 percent and indirect costs of about 15 percent, yielding a total cost of about 22 percent. Like the pre- versus post-IPO comparison, using IPO costs as a measure of liquidity discounts suffers from selection bias: Only the successful issuers are observed; ignored are those firms that must—or choose to—remain private.
5. Comparison of *acquisitions of similar public and private firms* matched for size, industry, and time period. Using a multiples-based approach, Koeplin, Sarin, and Shapiro (2000) estimated an "as-if public" valuation for acquisitions of private firms, 84 in the United States and 108 outside, between 1984 and 1998. Then using the actual transaction prices, they calculated the discount from this public value. Based on EBIT and EBITDA multiples, they found an average discount of 20 to 28 percent for U.S. firms and 44 to 54 percent for foreign firms. Several studies find a sizable announcement day return to bidders when they buy private firms as opposed to public firms.[12] Chang (1998) finds a positive 2.64 percent cumulative average return to bidders who buy private targets with stock. The return in the cases where a new significant shareholder is created in the deal is positive 4.96 percent. Chang hypothesizes that the new block holder will help to monitor the public firm's management. Hansen and Lott (1996) report that in buying a private firm, bidders earn a 2 percent higher cumulative average residual (CAR)[13] than when buying a public firm. Fuller, Netter, and Stegemoller (2002) report a 3.08 percent higher CAR for acquisitions of private companies. Explanations by researchers point to bargaining advantages by public buyers of private firms, the absence of competitive bidding that creates favorable purchase prices, and the creation of new power groups in the buyer company that will motivate the buyer to perform well.

In sum, empirical research finds that illiquidity commands a discount. However, there is little agreement about its size. This is probably due to the variation in kinds of securities, their issuers, government regulations (such as the reduction in the letter stock holding period) and market conditions (such as the opening and closing of the IPO window). Sziklay (2001) summarizes a wide range of factors that practitioners believe to explain cross-sectional variations in letter stock discounts: the size of issue, the time or expense involved in reselling the stock, the existence of a liquid market for the restricted stock, and the size and profitability of issuer.

The Concept of Liquidity as an Option

Options-based thinking provides a framework that can help to guide the practitioner through the range of empirical findings. The right to exit promptly from an investment is equivalent to a put option, of which two drivers are important to the practitioner:

1. *Uncertainty.* The greater the volatility in the value of the underlying stock, the greater will be the value of liquidity. Stated alternatively, the greater the uncertainty, the greater will be the discount for illiquidity.

2. ***Time.*** The longer the delay in exiting from an investment, the greater will be the discount for illiquidity.

Liquidity discounts have been modeled using option pricing theory. Alli and Thompson (1991) estimated the value of liquidity as the value of a European put option with a strike price equal to the share price at date of issue. Chaffe (1993) applied the put option model to the liquidity discount in private company valuations. Longstaff (1995) estimated the analytical upper bound of the value of liquidity as the price of a lookback option. He reported discounts in the range of 25 to 35 percent given typical liquidity restrictions on private placements. Exhibit 15.6 gives selected maximum liquidity discounts implied by his model. Plainly, volatility and time explain wide variation in discounts.

Finnerty (2002) extended this options-based view with a cross-sectional analysis of letter stock discounts. He found that volatility, the length of the restriction period, the riskless rate, and the stock's dividend yield significantly determine the discount. Dividend payments dampen the size and variability of the discount. Other factors he noted are information and the effect on equity ownership concentration. He uses his model to assess the actual premiums, and finds that the options-based model describes well actual premiums that are within a reasonable middle range of volatility (i.e., between 30 and 70 percent). But actual premiums are *overstated* when volatility is low (i.e., under 30 percent), and *understated* when volatility is high (i.e., over 70 percent). This result is consistent with blind application in practice of a fixed discount regardless of risk.

WHERE DO CONTROL PREMIUMS COME FROM? CONTROL IS AN OPTION

In this section, the spotlight shifts to the valuation of control. Here, too, an options perspective lends useful traction to the analyst.

Control and Control Premium

"Control" is the *right* to direct the strategy and activities of the firm, to allocate resources, and to distribute the economic wealth of the firm. Defined in the sense of

EXHIBIT 15.6 Longstaff's Upper Bounds for Percentage Discounts Because of Lack of Marketability (Percentage Discounts from Marketable Values)

Marketability Restriction Period	Volatility = 10%	Volatility = 20%	Volatility = 30%
180 days	5.768	11.793	18.082
1 year	8.232	16.984	26.276
2 years	11.793	24.643	38.605
5 years	19.128	40.979	65.772

Source: This is a small subset of results from Longstaff (1995), Table II.

rights, control is a call option on alternative strategies and policies of the firm. Thinking of control this way yields two fundamental ideas:

1. ***The value of control is contingent, not fixed.*** When the current strategy is working well, the option to switch strategies is out of the money. When the current strategy is working poorly, the option to switch will be in the money. Thus, the value of control will vary, depending on the economic success of the current strategy.
2. ***The drivers of the value of control are based on the volatility of those values,*** for the firm under current and alternative strategies, and the uncertainty or volatility of those values. This suggests that control will be worth more the greater the uncertainty.

Following this logic, "control premium" is the *price* of the control right. In casual conversation, for instance, one often hears "control premium" used to describe the *purchase premium*[14] with which the buyer induces the seller to sell. It is inappropriate to mingle the two ideas or to use the purchase premium as a proxy for the control premium. One should not use the average purchase premium for a sample of companies as the basis for recommending a premium for control.[15] The purchase premium reflects both the value of the control right and the value of expected synergies.

Where one shareholder has controlling power and the others do not, the value of the controller's equity interest will rise by the control premium; the value of the minority shareholders will suffer a minority discount—this is illustrated in the examples given in Exhibits 15.3 and 15.4. The wealth transfers resulting from the changes in the distribution of controlling power among shareholders are a prime reason for studying the value of control.

Control Right Is Derived from *Relative* Power

A simplistic view is that *controlling power* is conferred by owning or being able to direct the votes of 50.1 percent or more of the firm's shares. However, when shares are widely dispersed among shareholders, none of whom own more than 50 percent of the stock, effective control may be achieved with a block of shares of as little as 20 or 30 percent. The issue is not simply the size of the voting groups, but rather how often any of those groups might become *decisive* in the event of a vote. Once you think in terms of winning shareholder votes, you begin to grasp that *voting power is contingent*—votes are relevant only in the context of some game. This can be illustrated by calculating an index for voting power, called the Shapley Value. This value measures the number of times each player in a contest will be pivotal to the voting outcome. Power is found to be a nonlinear function of votes—this is the breakthrough insight of Lloyd Shapley.[16] A related insight is that the percentage of the shares that is truly dispersed (i.e., "atomistic" or "free-floating") is an important determinant of the control contest—quite simply, the distribution of votes prophesies outcomes.

The *Shapley Value* (SV_i) is the ratio of the number of combinations of voting groups in which shareholder i is pivotal to the outcome, divided by the number of all possible combinations. To be "pivotal" is to decide the outcome of the voting contest:

$$SV_i = \frac{n_i^{\text{Pivotal}}}{n!} \tag{4}$$

The larger the Shapley Value is, the more powerful is shareholder *i*. Intuition suggests that the more votes shareholder *i* has, the more likely that shareholder will be pivotal. Voting power is generally related to the number of votes one has. But how the rest of the votes are distributed among voters also affects the power of the individual shareholder. Here's where the measurement of the Shapley Value becomes complicated to model (and beyond the scope of this discussion).[17] Nevertheless, the insights that the Shapley Values afford about voting power are fascinating. Consider, for instance, a setting in which there are two competing raiders soliciting proxies for a takeover of one target. The question is, how powerful is the "ocean" of atomistic voters? The atomistic voters are all the nonaligned shareholders—the use of "atomistic" is game theory jargon to suggest that none of these voters is *individually* powerful. The big insight of the game modeling is that these voters can become very powerful as a group in some circumstances. Exhibit 15.7 presents Shapley Values for the ocean of atomistic voters over a range of scenarios in a setting where two larger shareholders are competing for control, such as a proxy contest. The atomistic shareholders are relatively powerful in the absence of powerful voting blocks—see the northwest corner of the table where each of the control-seeking shareholders or proxy contestants has only 10 percent of the votes; there, the atomistic voters are most powerful. As the proxy contestants gain votes, the power of the atomistic voters subsides. Generally, the more votes you have, the more powerful you are. But there is an interesting exception to this rule: in the southeast corner of the table, the power of the atomistic voters rises sharply. This is consistent with intuition. If you are the swing voter in a contest, even though you may have relatively few votes, you can be powerful.

EXHIBIT 15.7 Sensitivity Analysis of Shapley Values for the Ocean in a Hypothetical Proxy Contest

Votes of Control Shareholder #2	Votes of Control Shareholder #1			
	10	20	30	49
10	0.78	0.65	0.50	0.05
20	0.65	0.56	0.48	0.06
30	0.50	0.48	0.50	0.09
49	0.05	0.06	0.09	0.50

Comment: In this table, the higher the Shapley Value, the greater the power of the oceanic voters. The model assumes 100 votes are outstanding. Each cell estimates the power of the atomistic voters where the number of votes held by each of the competing proxy contestants is indicated in the row and column headings.
Source: See the spreadsheet file "Power.xls" on the CD-ROM.

Potential Private Benefits May Drive the Value of Control

One reason that control might be valuable is that it presents the opportunity for the majority to expropriate wealth of the minority. Thus, control confers the option to steal. Benefits not shared by all shareholders are private benefits. Dyck and Zingales (2001) examined a large sample of M&A transactions across 39 countries and found that the premium paid for control is higher in countries that protect investors less and thus permit extraction of private benefits. An extension of the private benefits findings is an emerging body of research on forms of intercorporate investing that achieve effective voting control. Examples of these forms are cross-shareholding arrangements and *pyramid* arrangements. The concern is that controlling corporate shareholders might expropriate wealth of the minority (called "tunneling").

Pyramids are a way to extract private benefits. Bebchuk, Kraakman, and Triantis (1998) showed that for relatively small investments in a pyramidal firm or a group with extensive cross-shareholdings, a controller might gain control rights disproportionately greater than cash flow rights from any one of the individual enterprises in the group or pyramid. Exhibit 15.8 illustrates that if it takes only a 25 percent voting block to control a corporation, then an initial investment can be leveraged rapidly to control value that is many times the initial outlay. Marco and Mengoli (2001) found that stock pyramiding among Italian firms is associated with wealth transfers toward entities located at higher levels of the organization. The wealth recipients reported significantly positive CARs; the minority reported losses. Similar results were reported for firms in Korea (Bae, Kang, and Kim 2002), China (Liu and Lu 2002) and India (Bertrand, Mehta, and Mullainathan 2000). Parsons, Maxwell, and O'Brien (1999) found that the rise of major investors in a number of

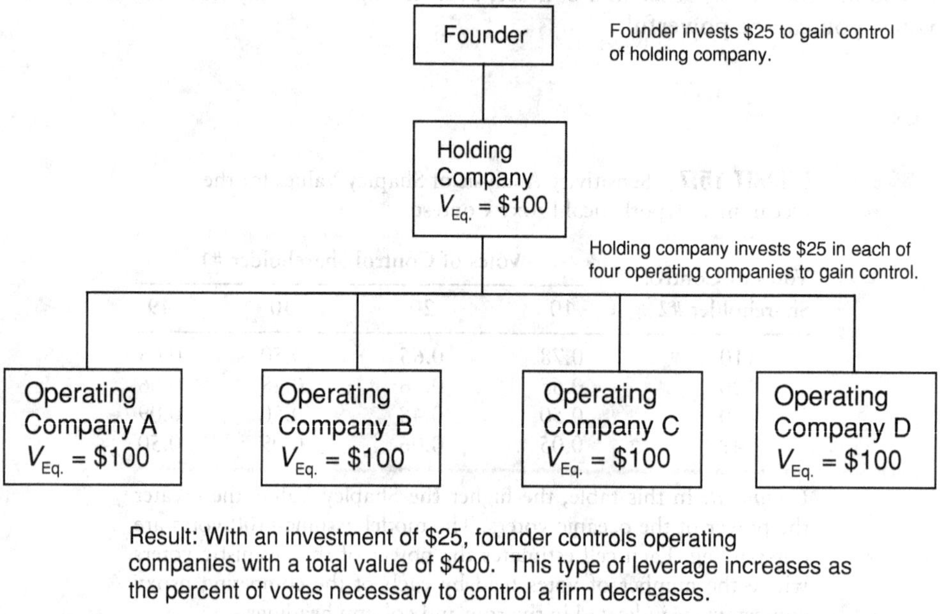

EXHIBIT 15.8 Simple Illustration of the Control Economics of a Pyramid Holding Company

firms in the same industry can change the competition and move the industry toward monopoly.

Strategic Flexibility May Drive the Value of Control

A complementary hypothesis to private benefits (the option to steal) is that control confers the option to direct the strategy of the firm in ways that always maximizes value for shareholders. The controller of this corporation always does what is economically right. Where the expropriation of private benefits always results in a wealth transfer from the minority to the controller, the strategic flexibility aspect of control increases the value of the whole firm. Control is a right to determine the future strategy of the firm, a switching option. Margrabe (1978) and others have explored the valuation of switching options in industrial settings.[18] While Myers (1977, 1984), Kester (1981, 1984), and others studied the value of rights to decide in corporate resource allocation decisions, rights to control the entire enterprise remain relatively unexplored. An example of a controlling shareholder who uses that control not to steal but rather to exercise wisely the rights of strategic direction would be Warren Buffett, CEO of Berkshire Hathaway. Arguably, Buffett has done what is economically right, since for the past 40 years an investment in Berkshire Hathaway has beaten the appropriate investment benchmarks by a wide margin.

What is interesting about strategic flexibility as a driver of the value of control is what happens to the value of a firm when the right to change strategies is constrained or squandered. The overarching power of unions (as in the case recently of United Airlines), or a fixed commitment to obsolete technology (the U.S. integrated steel industry), or a dedication to "the way we've always done things" (the mom-and-pop retail establishment) would be examples of enterprises without strategic control. Such enterprises should sell at a discount compared to firms that have and use strategic flexibility.

The concept of strategic flexibility expands our understanding of control beyond insights afforded by the private benefits hypothesis. In a world where control always leads to the expropriation of private benefits, it will be true that the controller's gain equals the minority's loss. But strategic flexibility enriches that story; with flexibility, it *may* be possible that the controller does not expropriate private benefits, but rather, runs the firm in the interests of all owners—this is what the legal systems in most developed countries seek to promote.

Empirical Findings on the Value of Control

Research tells us that owning a controlling interest commands a premium; owning a minority (i.e., opposite of controlling) interest commands a discount relative to the controller.

RESEARCH ON DUAL-CLASS SHARES Studies of firms that have two classes of common stock outstanding show that the class with superior voting rights trades at a material premium relative to the other class. These *dual-class shares* structures arise as antitakeover devices or where a founding family seeks to exert control of a firm with a large shareholder base. In 1999, 219 out of 1,900 large publicly traded firms in the United States had dual-class structures.[19] Bergstrom and Rydkvist (1990) note that over 70 percent of the firms listed on the Stockholm exchange had dual-class structures in the late 1980s. Zingales (1994) reported that 40 percent of the firms listed on the Milan exchange had dual-class structures. And Hauser and Lauterbach (2000) note that 40 percent of the firms on the Tel Aviv stock exchange had dual-class structures in 1989.

Exhibit 15.9 summarizes the findings of 11 studies of the premium at which senior voting shares traded over junior shares and shows a significant but widely varying premium between 5 and 80 percent. Hauser and Lauterbach (2000) found that reversions by dual-class firms back to one share, one vote structures were accompanied by positive excess returns. Bruner (1999) found that in the case of Renault's attempted acquisition of Volvo, Volvo's voting premium fell from 46.6 percent to 2.3 percent when Renault acquired a significant block of Volvo's stock. Nenova (2003) finds that control premiums in dual-class structures vary significantly across countries according to the legal protections for minority shareholder rights.

Nenova (2001) reports dramatic fluctuations in dual-class premiums in Brazil during a period of market and regulatory reform that strengthened the rights of minority shareholders. A study by Doidge (2003) suggests that variations in shareholder protection among countries may explain some of the variation in the dual-class premium: firms from countries with poor protection to minority investors have higher voting premiums.

RESEARCH ON BLOCK TRADES The trades of large blocks of stock (where a "block" is commonly defined as in excess of 10,000 shares) can alter the ownership structure of a firm. Barclay and Holderness (1989) studied trades of blocks of more than 5 percent of a public firm's shares and found that the blocks traded at a 20 percent premium relative to the post-transaction price. The authors argued that the premium reflected the voting power of the block.

EXHIBIT 15.9 Summary of Research on the Control Premium of Senior Voting Shares over Junior Voting Shares in Dual-Class Share Structures

Study	Country	Average Premium
Rydkvist (1996)	Sweden	12.0%
Lease, McConnell, and Mikkelson (1983)	United States	5.4%
DeAngelo and DeAngelo (1985)	United States	5.0%
Doidge (2003)	United States (foreign firms cross-listed into the U.S.)	8.0%
Levy (1982)	Israel	45.5%
Biger (1991)	Israel	74.0%
Megginson (1990)	Britain	13.3%
Smith and Amoako-Adu (1995)	Canada	10.4%
Zingales (1994)	Italy	80.0%
Horner (1988)	Switzerland	10.0%
Kunz and Angel (1996)	Switzerland	18.0%

RESEARCH ON M&A TRANSACTIONS Chapter 3 discusses numerous studies that find sizable premiums paid to shareholders of target firms in M&A transactions. Henry Manne (1965) argued that these premium payments reflect the value of control of the target, that control is valuable, and that an active market for corporate control exists. Hanouna, Sarin, and Shapiro (2000) argued that the true control premium needs to be separated from the premium driven by other considerations (such as synergies). They analyzed a very large sample of transactions comparing those in which the buyer acquired a minority position, versus the ones where the buyer acquired a controlling position. They found that a majority position commands a 20 to 30 percent premium compared to the price paid for a minority position.

If the control right is an option, then the wide variation in control premiums and voting premiums is attributable to the two key drivers of option value: volatility and duration of the right. It remains for empirical researchers to explore the ability of volatility to explain the cross-sectional variation in the value of control.

INTERACTION OF LIQUIDITY AND CONTROL

Under the conventional method, the analyst selects the relevant discount and premium as if they are independent. But there are four reasons why liquidity and control may interact:

1. ***Liquidity may bring with it transparency, which may reduce the value of control.*** For instance, registration requirements under U.S. law and securities regulations, and listing requirements on the NYSE mandate procedures of governance and reporting that may constrain the ability of controllers to extract private benefits and not operate the firm in the interests of all shareholders. An emerging body of research on the relation between governance and share value underscores the benefits of transparency; see, for instance, La Porta et al. (1999). Lerner and Schoar (2001) argue that the need for control will vary with liquidity.[20] It may be that if shares are highly liquid, investors may have less incentive to oversee firms.[21] A liquidity discount may be more severe in the instance of more asymmetric information (less transparency), such as young firms with no track record and incomplete reporting infrastructure or divided equity investors who don't communicate (e.g. cross-border investors). Lerner and Schoar examine the case of American Research and Development to understand why a venture capitalist would place restrictions on the transferability of partnership interests. Their conclusion is that these restrictions bar "hot money" investors from entering the pool and instead admit only the more patient, well-capitalized investors.
2. ***Liquidity may be associated with more dispersed shareholdings.*** This may increase the power of controllers (see Milnor and Shapley 1978) and therefore increase their ability to extract private benefits and operate the firm in nonvalue-maximizing ways. This would suggest a direct relationship between liquidity and control.
3. ***Control positions tend to be sticky.*** Controlling shareholders amass their positions with difficulty, tend not to trade shares actively, and if they decide to sell

control intact, may experience delays in selling. Heaney and Holmen (2002) find that senior voting shares in Sweden are much less liquid than junior shares.

4. ***With control, any decision to liquidate is complicated by the right to choose the most attractive strategy.*** Thus, liquidation occurs only after you have tried to create value through strategic choice. This time sequencing of control and liquidation choices suggests that the decision to liquidate depends on the prior choice of strategy.

If rights to market and control interact, then they form a *compound* option. This would imply two key insights. First, it is inappropriate to study liquidity in the absence of control, and vice versa. Second, compound options are very difficult to model analytically. As a practical matter, researchers must resort to numerical option pricing methods to explore the valuation of these rights.

Using option pricing methods to value control rights is in its infancy. While the valuation of liquidity rights is a little more advanced, much more work remains to be done before the practitioner will be able to estimate premiums and discounts through option pricing. Still, the early results are promising and consistent with intuition. Bruner and Palacios (2003) estimated the joint discounts from loss of liquidity and control using Monte Carlo simulation.[22] Under conventional assumptions, they obtained estimated discounts in a range consistent with those typically seen in practice: 10 to 50 percent. But importantly, they found that the size of the discounts was very sensitive to time (i.e., length of illiquidity and of minority status) and to uncertainty about the value of the underlying asset (i.e., volatility). Generally, the discounts were large in scenarios of longer time and greater uncertainty. Their modeling offers five insights:

1. ***One size does not fit all.*** Their modeling confirmed that the use of a standard "haircut" for illiquidity or lack of control might leave money on the table.
2. ***Control and liquidity options interact.*** These two effects on value are not merely additive.
3. ***Volatility is the major driver of discounts.*** While volatility cannot be observed, one can "trade on volatility" in negotiations. The options investor can examine options prices for their consistency with the trader's own assessment of the appropriateness of the volatility implied in the price: This is called "trading on volatility."[23]
4. ***The options view provides a benchmark*** for testing the reasonableness of discounts and premiums.
5. ***Lack of control trumps lack of liquidity.*** The modeling suggests that if you had to sacrifice one of the two options, you should give up liquidity first. This is because with control you have more flexibility to create value than without.

MINI-CASE: ATTEMPTED ACQUISITION OF VOLVO BY RENAULT, 1993

The attempted merger of Volvo and Renault in 1993 illustrates the possible significance of synergies and discounts for illiquidity and minority status. Building on equation (1), we can think of the postannouncement value per share as a composite of three quantities: a base case valuation of the firm on an as-is basis, the present value of cash flows arising from synergies, and a premium or discount for change in liquidity and control.

$$P_{\text{After}} = \frac{(V_{\text{Base case, firm before}} + V_{\text{Synergies}})(1 + \%\Delta_{\text{Liquidity and control}})}{\text{Number of shares}_{\text{Before}} + \text{Change in number of shares}} \quad (5)$$

Modeling the share price in this way emphasizes that the market reaction following the announcements of acquisitions, financings, and restructurings is a reflection of three anticipated changes in the firm: (1) in operations and synergies, (2) in share ownership, and (3) in liquidity and control. This has important implications for the inferences one might draw about the operating benefits derived from these transactions.

The economic motivations for the Volvo/Renault deal were sizable synergies. Bruner (1999) estimated these to have a maximum present value of SEK 17.95 billion, quite large in comparison to AB Volvo's equity value on September 6, 1993, of SEK 37.5 billion. Many investors questioned the estimated synergies, simply on the basis of past experience: Volvo's CEO had consummated previous acquisitions that failed to live up to past expectations. And yet industry experts agreed with the basic logic of consolidation in the auto business: Achieving economies of scale in purchasing and new product development was the sure route to survival and profitability. One reading of the demise of the proposed merger was that investors did not believe in the merger synergies or the expressed motivations for the deal.

Consistent with the framework offered here, a second consideration can complement the analysis of the deal: rights of liquidity and control. The proposed deal would reduce *both* Volvo's control and liquidity of its automotive business. Regarding liquidity, the new firm, Renault-Volvo (RVA), would be privately held by two shareholders (the government of France and the holding company, AB Volvo). The French government had announced that it intended to privatize Renault in 1994, though many observers regarded the timing as figurative—strong unions within Renault, the Socialist party in France, and a French political consensus that favored having a French national champion in the automobile industry would likely delay meaningful privatization.

Regarding control, the government of France would own 65 percent of the new firm, and Renault's executives would dominate the upper ranks of the firm. The French government and AB Volvo agreed not to sell or pledge their respective share holdings until the privatization of Renault-Volvo. Each also agreed to give the other a right of first refusal on the sale of shares, and not to sell shares to a competitor. The French government announced that it intended to privatize Renault-Volvo by selling its shares principally to a circle of friendly French corporations, such as defense contractors and French state-owned banks and insurance companies. The French government would retain an unusual right, a "golden share" that retained for the government the ability to prevent an investor from acquiring (or voting) more than a 17.85 percent direct interest in the new firm. Like a poison pill or control share antitakeover amendment, the golden share could change the voting power of sizable shareholders such as AB Volvo. The French had discretion in using the golden share, however, as the limitation was not automatic. Golden shares have been a common feature in the privatization of state-owned enterprises. This right would last indefinitely.

In summary, the merger proposal offered Volvo's shareholders participation in the benefits of potential new synergies in exchange for worsened liquidity and control (in technical terms, a short position in a bundle of control options, including the golden share, a privatization option concerning the timing and magnitude of any public offering of RVA shares, as well as an option concerning the targeted purchasers of any shares offered).

Volvo's board had endorsed the merger proposal. From the standpoint of Volvo shareholders, this agreement would sharply limit the liquidity of their investment and their control. Volvo, the holding company, would lose some control from being a full, 100 percent owner of its automotive business to a minority holder of a larger automotive business. The government of France would dominate the shareholder group and determine the date and pricing of its privatization. Even after going public, the government would continue to hold a golden share, in effect, a veto over future strategic decisions of the automotive firm.

Volvo's share prices fell dramatically following the announcement of the merger proposal. Bruner (1999) reports that abnormal returns on September 6–7, 1993, were –6.04 percent for Volvo's superior-voting A shares, and –6.64 percent for the junior-voting B shares. Over the following seven weeks, abnormal returns accumulated to –21.99 percent for the A shares and –22.04 percent for the B shares. This cumulative abnormal return represents a decline in equity value of about SEK 8.3 billion (US$ 1.055 billion). A large portion of this wealth destruction occurred on dates of the release of detailed information about the merger terms.

Securities analysts estimated the market value of AB Volvo's investments (enterprise value) in the automotive business on a stand-alone basis to be SEK 32.92 billion. The projected value of Renault-Volvo without synergies was SEK 85 billion. The 22 percent cumulative market-adjusted loss (SEK 8.3 billion) in AB Volvo shares following the announcement of the deal equates to a discount of 23 percent from the estimated value of Volvo's interest in Renault-Volvo with full synergies (SEK 36.03 billion); assuming zero synergy value, the discount increases to 27.9 percent (on a base value of SEK 29.75 billion). These discounts suggest that the rejection of the deal by Volvo's investors was founded on the expectation of material delays in AB Volvo's ability to liquidate its interest and loss of flexibility to switch strategy.

Were these losses in value consistent with the erosion of Volvo shareholders' liquidity and control rights? Bruner and Palacios (2003) simulated the mean discount for minority control and illiquidity under the assumption of conventional parameters prevailing in 1993 and found that discounts in the range of 22 to 28 percent are fully explained by the loss in control and an illiquidity delay of one year. When illiquidity increases to five years, the discount increases to 39 percent.

The case of Volvo and Renault underscores the potentially large impact of liquidity and control on shareholders' wealth. Also, option valuation techniques afford a benchmark test of reasonableness for observed discounts. Finally, as noted earlier the analyst should take care in assessing the purchase premium: It is an amalgam of synergy value and discounts or premiums for liquidity and control effects.

CONCLUSION

This chapter has explored some of the properties of liquidity and control rights in M&A and illustrated the traditional multiplicative method for adjusting for premiums and discounts.

- Illiquidity and control asymmetry can affect transaction prices. These effects are traditionally modeled multiplicatively. The example offered here showed that illiquidity and control produced sharply different share values from the base case.
- The traditional approach draws on prices in comparable transactions. Option pricing techniques (especially simulation) can offer a benchmark test of reasonableness of premiums and discounts, though the application of these techniques in this area is still in its infancy.
- Liquidity and control are options, driven significantly by uncertainty about the value of the underlying assets.
- The value of these rights varies. The optionality in these rights helps explain the range of findings about their effect on value of equities. Volatility and time produce material variations in estimates of the premiums and discounts. It remains for future research to enhance the ability of practitioners to estimate the discounts for illiquidity and control. One property of liquidity and control rights has received little attention: the interaction between these rights. The interaction arises because these rights can combine to form a compound option.

NOTES

1. The alternative would be an *additive* model in which the effects of liquidity and control would simply be summed. The multiplicative approach is more consistent with the interaction between liquidity and control rights—this interaction is discussed in the section on Volvo and Renault later in this chapter.
2. Instead of adjusting the purchase price, one could adjust the discount rate in a DCF analysis to account for the value effects of liquidity and control. For instance, Arzac (1996) suggests that the premium to be added to the discount rate can be estimated using the following formula, where d = illiquidity discount, k = cost of equity or WACC, and g = perpetual growth rate:

   $$\text{Risk premium for illiquidity} = \frac{d(k-g)}{(1-d)}$$

   Whether one adjusts the discount rate or the total value of the firm for illiquidity, one must still have an estimate for d, the illiquidity discount. Pratt's approach gives a more transparent presentation of the effect of these adjustments and therefore seems more useful in the context of negotiation, deal design, and communication with investors.
3. The alert reader will notice the semantic emphasis here. This chapter defines "premium" and "discount" relative to a base case valuation. Some analysts

might casually define a control premium relative to the value of minority shares, rather like a percentage spread between shares with voting rights and those without. The problem with this second definition is that in most settings the value of control and minority shares is what you are trying to determine. Thus, it makes no sense to define a control premium over the junior shares. The semantic emphasis here is for analytic convenience, since one generally can get a base value of the firm as defined here. As the text emphasizes, all discounts and premiums start from a base.

4. Letter stock derives its name from the requirement that investors in securities issued under Rule 144 of the SEC must certify that their investment will be held and not resold. Before 1997, the SEC imposed a two-year minimum holding period on letter stock after which the stock could be sold with certain restrictions; in the third year, the stock could be sold without restrictions. On February 20, 1997, the SEC reduced the minimum holding period to one year, and the unrestricted holding period to two years.
5. See studies by Amihud and Mendelson (1991) and Kamara (1994).
6. See Boudoukh and Whitelaw (1991).
7. See Houweling, Mentink, and Vorst (2002).
8. See Brenner, Eldor, and Hauser (2001).
9. Indirect IPO costs also reflect investors' expectations about the profitability of future investment by the issuer. Therefore using IPO costs possibly confounds marketability with other effects.
10. The gross spread is the sum of the management fee, underwriting fee, and selling concession as a percentage of the amount offered. Indirect costs are measured by initial returns or underpricing (i.e., the day *n* close price divided by the offer price minus 1).
11. The following sources offer a cross section of the research on IPO costs: Chaplinsky and Ramchand (2000); Chen and Ritter (2000); Loughran and Ritter (2002); Loughran, Ritter, and Rydkvist (1994); Ritter (1987); and Ritter (1984).
12. Chang (1998) finds a positive 2.64 percent cumulative average return to bidders who buy private targets with stock. The return in the cases where a new significant shareholder is created in the deal is positive 4.96 percent. Chang hypothesizes that the new block holder will help to monitor the public firm's management.
13. Cumulative average residuals are the accumulated daily excess returns over a benchmark like the return on the equity market portfolio. These useful statistics are measures of wealth creation or destruction around an announcement; hence, they are often called "event returns." See Chapter 3 for further discussion of CARs.
14. Purchase premium is typically estimated as the bid price divided by the prebid price minus 1.
15. This practice is, unfortunately, common. For more discussion on the inappropriateness of this practice, see Pratt (2001), pages 33 to 36 and 317.
16. A complete discussion of the analytics of power in the framework of Shapley is beyond the scope of this chapter. See Milnor and Shapley (1978) for a full exposition. The mathematical literature on power is extensive.

17. A fuller expression of equation (3) is this:

$$SV_i = \left(\frac{1}{n!}\right)\sum_{t=1,\ldots,n}(t-1)!(n-t)!\,k_t$$

where n is the total number of possible combinations, t is the number of shareholders in winning coalitions that feature shareholder i as pivot, and k_t is the number of times shareholder i is pivotal in winning coalitions of t shareholders.
18. See, for instance, Kogut and Kulatilaka (1994), Kulatilaka (1993), Triantis and Hodder (1990), Trigeorgis (1996), Trigeorgis and Mason (1987), and Upton (1994).
19. V. Rosenbaum, *Corporate Takeover Defenses*, Washington D.C.: Investor Responsibility Research Center Inc., 1999.
20. In a related study, Lerner and Schoar (2002) find that the reverse is also true: The need for liquidity will vary with control and transparency that private equity investors have with regard to their portfolio firms—liquidity becomes a variable of choice, a method of screening out investors who don't have deep pockets.
21. There may be less incentive or greater barriers to monitoring. Grossmann and Hart (1980) argue that it may be harder to exercise effective capital market discipline in cases of highly liquid shares held by widely dispersed (atomistic) shareholders.
22. This follows the work of Boyle (1977) and others who have used simulation to value complex options.
23. To "trade on volatility" is to make investment (buy or sell) decisions based on the volatility implied in options prices. One compares implied volatility to the volatility that would be justified by one's view of the asset.

CHAPTER 16

Financial Accounting for Mergers and Acquisitions

INTRODUCTION

This chapter surveys the accounting issues in M&A. In the context of designing a particular deal, one should explore these issues with the assistance of an accounting professional. Success and professionalism in M&A depend on the mastery of some essential knowledge that will permit better interaction with accounting professionals and more insightful design of deals. This survey offers lessons in six areas:

1. ***Overview of accounting rules and choices.*** Accounting rules can shape the conduct of firms in M&A. Even though the rules constrain what firms can do in reporting the results of M&A transactions, firms retain a fair amount of latitude in their application of the rules. This chapter will outline some of the areas of latitude, especially in regard to the treatment of *goodwill.* Also relevant for executives is the *Sarbanes-Oxley Act (SOA)*, which imposes harsh penalties for failing to report financial results that are fair and accurate.
2. ***Mechanics of purchase accounting for business combinations.*** This should include *purchase accounting* for both complete and partial acquisitions. This chapter will walk you through these mechanics with a simplified example. The appendix sketches the mechanics of pooling-of-interests accounting for business combinations and why *pooling of interests* has been eliminated.
3. ***Interpretation of reported financial results under alternative accounting choices.*** The chapter will define the concept of *dilution* and explore other measurable results. We will examine the effect of cash and stock payments on net income, earnings per share, cash flow per share, and financial leverage.
4. ***Linkage of accounting choices with form of payment, financing, and price*** in the design of M&A transactions. We will explore how this linkage occurs and its effect on the overall transaction design.
5. ***Financial accounting for M&A*** can become an instrument for an adverse earnings management game in which players seek to enhance the appearance of Newco and thus disguise economic reality. Examples of gaming behavior are allocating the purchase consideration in advantageous ways and/or writing off values of intangible assets. In extreme circumstances the game amounts to *fraud.* The chapter sketches the case of WorldCom Inc. as an example of fraudulent earnings management in M&A.

6. ***Think like an investor.*** Ideally, M&A accounting would clarify our focus on the true economics of deals. But gaming behavior, the wide latitude of choice, and overwhelming attention to EPS dilution can cloud rather than clarify our analysis. Both the deal analyst and the senior executive must exercise caution in the interpretation of historical and pro forma financial results surrounding an acquisition.

OVERVIEW OF PURCHASE ACCOUNTING

Insights into the effects of accounting choices on M&A transactions must start from an understanding of the rules of M&A accounting. This section surveys the rules of purchase accounting and illustrates their application.

Financial Accounting Standards 141 and 142

The Financial Accounting Standards Board (FASB) issued *FAS 141 and 142*[1] that became effective after June 30, 2001. These landmark rules changed the method of accounting for mergers and acquisitions in significant ways.

MANDATES PURCHASE ACCOUNTING All business combinations must be accounted for by the purchase method of accounting. The FASB banned the alternative method of M&A accounting, the pooling-of-interests[2] method, which is summarized in Appendix 16.1. The FASB believed that the purchase method best reflected the economic reality of acquisitions. The purchase method is described in detail later in this chapter.

ELIMINATES AMORTIZATION OF GOODWILL, BUT REQUIRES TESTING FOR IMPAIRMENT When a buyer pays a premium to acquire a target, purchase accounting requires the recognition of goodwill as an asset. Goodwill arises as the difference between the purchase price of the target company and the fair market value (FMV) of the assets[3]—goodwill is the premium paid over and above the value of identifiable assets of the firm. Previous accounting rules had required *amortization* of goodwill over a period no longer than 40 years under the theory that goodwill is an asset that wastes away as it generates revenues. But FAS 142 argued that this imposed a finite life on an asset that could have an *indefinite* useful life.[4] Instead of amortizing goodwill, the FASB required that goodwill be tested at least annually[5] for *impairment* or loss of value. To do this, goodwill first must be allocated to a *reporting unit.* One analyst wrote, "The single most critical choice a company makes in implementing FAS no. 141 and 142 is likely to be its initial choice of reporting units. Goodwill assigned to a poorly performing reporting unit may have to be written down immediately, or at least soon. Conversely, goodwill assigned to a highly profitable reporting unit may never face an impairment write-down." (King 2001, page 2) FAS 142 requires a two-step test for impairment:

1. Compare the FMV of a reporting unit with its carrying value of assets, including goodwill. If carrying value exceeds FMV, then proceed to the second step to determine the amount of impairment loss.

2. Compare the FMV of the reporting unit's goodwill with its carrying value. If the carrying value exceeds the FMV of goodwill, the excess must be recognized that year as an impairment loss against earnings.

Practitioners have greeted this new treatment of goodwill as a mixed blessing. On one hand, the absence of the arbitrary goodwill amortization improves the transparency of reported earnings. But on the other hand, goodwill impairment tests could deliver some negative surprises to company earnings, perhaps at a time when a company least wants them. A final detail is that a company cannot write up, or increase, goodwill at some later date; its maximum value is set at the consummation of the M&A transaction.

TIGHTENS THE RECOGNITION OF INTANGIBLE ASSETS The new accounting standards clarified the recognition of *intangible assets* as a separate asset category. In purchase accounting, one must allocate the price paid to various tangible and intangible asset categories—anything left over from this allocation process must be classified as goodwill. The new standards clarified how value might be allocated between intangibles and goodwill. FAS 141 required the intangible assets should be recognized apart from goodwill if they meet two criteria:

1. *The contractual-legal criterion* held that some intangible assets arise from contractual rights, such as licensing the use of a patent.
2. *The separability criterion* allowed that the intangible asset is capable of being separated from the target firm and sold, licensed, rented, or exchanged, then it may be recognized. Customer and subscriber lists, customer deposits, trademarks, secret formulas, and know-how that accompany a trademark meet this criterion and may be recognized.

Exhibit 16.1 gives a listing of types of intangible assets that meet either of the criteria for recognition apart from goodwill. Intangible assets that are subject to amortization must be disclosed in notes to the financial statements, including the amounts assigned, the amount of any significant residual value, and the weighted-average amortization period. Intangible assets that are *not* subject to amortization must be disclosed in notes, indicating the amounts assigned. For goodwill, notes must disclose the total amount assigned and the amount expected to be deductible for tax purposes. Also, goodwill must be reported by a business reporting unit.

AMORTIZATION OF INTANGIBLE ASSETS, AND CHARGES FOR IMPAIRMENT Intangible assets may have indefinite useful lives and need not be amortized under the new rules. However, intangible assets whose lives are finite must be amortized over their useful lives. Also, any impairment of intangible asset value must be charged to earnings that year.

In sum, the rules for M&A accounting embed several points of judgment for the M&A practitioner (and with concurrence of the firm's auditor), including the determination of:

- Fair market values of tangible and intangible assets.
- Useful lives of tangible assets and, as a consequence, their annual depreciation charge to earnings.

EXHIBIT 16.1 Intangible Assets That Meet the Criteria for Recognition Apart from Goodwill

Marketing-Related Intangible Assets	Customer-Related Intangible Assets	Artistic-Related Intangible Assets	Contract-Based Intangible Assets	Technology-Based Intangible Assets
• Trademarks, trade names. • Service marks, collective marks, certification marks. • Trade dress (unique color, shape, or package design). • Newspaper mastheads. • Internet domain names. • Noncompetition agreements.	• Customer lists. • Order or production backlogs. • Customer contracts and related customer relationships. • Noncontractual customer relationships.	• Plays, operas, ballets. • Books, magazines, newspapers, other literary works. • Musical works such as compositions, song lyrics, and advertising jingles. • Pictures, photographs. • Video and audiovisual material, including motion pictures, music videos, television programs.	• Licensing, royalty, standstill agreements. • Advertising, construction, management, service, or supply contracts. • Lease agreements. • Construction permits. • Franchise agreements. • Operating and broadcast rights. • Use rights such as drilling, water, air, mineral, timber cutting, and route authorities.	• Patented technologies. • Computer software and mask works. • Unpatented technologies. • Databases. • Trade secrets such as secret formulas, processes, recipes.

Source of data: FAS 141.

- Useful lives of intangible assets and, as a consequence, their annual amortization charge to earnings.
- Value of goodwill as part of the annual impairment test.

Judgments made in areas such as these will affect the buyer's reported balance sheet, earnings per share, tax expense, and free cash flow.

Illustration of Basic Purchase Accounting: Acquisition of 100 Percent of the Target

The key idea of purchase accounting is that the buyer should recognize an acquisition at the *cost of the transaction* as if the buyer were purchasing a bundled set of assets and liabilities on the open market. The target firm is recorded on the buyer's books at the purchase price, which is assumed to be fair market value of the entire entity acquired. Purchase accounting requires that the purchase price, the total consideration paid, be allocated among the various accounts of current assets and fixed assets according to the FMV of each. Consider the possible implications:

- ***Inventory*** could be substantially restated in value (this restatement could be especially significant when the target uses LIFO accounting in an inflationary economic environment). Also, the cost of goods sold for the newly acquired operation could be significantly different from the past, due to the restated value of inventory. This may have a significant effect on the subsidiary's gross margin.
- ***Accounts receivable*** will be recorded by the buyer at the cash flows it expects to realize. Note that the buyer and the target might have differing opinions as to the realizability of those receivables, based on their differing perspectives about allowances for doubtful accounts. Bad debts that the target should have recognized may not have been reported previously and must now be recognized as part of the purchase price allocation.
- ***Fixed assets*** would be restated to fair market value. Land, and plant or equipment, which the target had purchased many years ago and carried for many years at historical cost, would likely be stepped up to a higher value through purchase accounting of an acquisition. As a result, annual depreciation expense will increase—the buyer retains discretion over the economic life over which to depreciate the stepped-up basis of fixed assets. Also, purchase accounting in effect eliminates the target firm's historical accumulated depreciation and restarts the depreciation clock.
- ***Goodwill*** may be created. This is the difference between purchase price and FMV of the target's identifiable assets.[6] It reflects asset value not readily recognized in other asset categories and can be thought of as the economic premium over the FMV of the bundle of assets and liabilities. As long as the value of goodwill is not impaired, goodwill has no impact on the reported earnings of the firm.[7]
- ***Liabilities*** are recorded at their fair market value. If interest rates and dividend yields in the capital markets have changed significantly from the date of original issue, fixed income securities might need to be recorded at a significant variance from face value.

No retroactive restatement of the buyer's past financial results is permitted under purchase accounting—the treatment here is no different from the buyer acquiring any other asset on the open market. But as a result, it will be difficult to compare the buyer's financial statements from before and after the transaction: If ExxonMobil buys Microsoft, is ExxonMobil the same company after the deal as it was before? Hardly; the portfolio of ExxonMobil's real economic activities and its financial statements will change dramatically, particularly showing very large growth in assets, sales, and net income that year. The purchase accounting method for M&A may present the illusion of growth even where the buyer and target firms are mature or in decline. The illusion arises if one focuses on size rather than *economic efficiency*.[8] But accounting standards require disclosures that should allow the reader of the statements to assist the reader in gauging the economic impact of the transaction. Unfortunately, those disclosures only deal with data from the current year and the year immediately preceding. Also, the detail in these disclosures can vary from one company to the next, leaving the outside analyst generally wanting more information about the accounting results of M&A.

Acquisition of Less Than 100 Percent of the Target Firm

Partial acquisitions (including the acquisition of a major portion of the stock of a target, or a division or certain assets of a target) will use some variation of purchase accounting. The specific accounting approach correlates with the degree of ownership and control, as suggested in this table:

Method of Accounting	*Ownership Percentage of Shares*	*Implied Degree of Control*
Consolidation method	Greater than 50%	Majority voting control
Equity method	20 to 50%	Material voting power without majority control
Cost method	Less than 20%	Less significant voting power

The intent of the rules is that the parent should consolidate the partially owned target when the parent effectively controls it. The parent could effectively control the target with less than 50 percent ownership through, for instance, the right to appoint the target's management and the control of key resources. Also, Chapter 15 showed that your voting power is not simply a matter of the percentage of votes you hold, but also the concentration of votes among other shareholders. Under election of directors by the cumulative voting method, a holder of a block of 19 percent of the votes in a firm whose shares are otherwise widely dispersed among shareholders could have significant influence over the board and the firm. You should use the *consolidation method* when you effectively control the partially owned firm.

Unfortunately, one has no discretion in the other direction. Golden shares,[9] standstill agreements,[10] and dual-class[11] shareholding structures can cause influence or control to be lower than would be indicated by an equity interest. Even if a holder of 51 percent is deemed not to have control, then the consolidation method still must be used.

CONSOLIDATION METHOD The valuation of assets acquired and liabilities assumed in an acquisition of more than 50 percent of the outstanding stock of a target company should be based on a pro rata allocation of fair market values and historical carrying values. The buyer should record the target company's assets it has acquired at fair market values and recognize goodwill. The remaining portion of the target company's assets and liabilities represents the minority interests' ownership in the target company and, is also carried at fair market values.

Consider an example in which the buyer acquires 60 percent of the assets and liabilities of the target under the purchase method of accounting. Assume that the buyer is an investment vehicle composed of $6,000 in cash and $6,000 in shareholder's equity. The target is a manufacturing company with a book value of assets of $8,000 and an enterprise value of $10,000, for which the fair market value of identifiable assets is estimated to be $9,000. The buyer uses its $6,000 to purchase 60 percent of the target's stock (the target has no debt, so equity value equals enterprise value). Exhibit 16.2 summarizes the change in the buyer's balance sheet. The buyer should record the following consolidating changes in the buyer's balance sheet:

- Credit cash $6,000.
- Debit identifiable assets $9,000, reflecting the acquisition of the target's identifiable assets.

EXHIBIT 16.2 Consolidation of a Partial But Majority Interest in a Target

Percentage of target acquired by buyer			60%
Price paid			$6,000
			Company B
Enterprise value of target			$10,000
FMV of identifiable assets of target			$ 9,000
Carrying (book) value of assets of target			$ 8,000
		Buyer's Balance Sheet	
	Before	**Transaction Adjustments**	**After**
Assets			
Cash	$6,000	$(6,000)	$ —
Identifiable assets	$ —	$ 9,000	$ 9,000
Goodwill	$ —	$ 1,000	$ 1,000
Total assets	$6,000	$ 4,000	$10,000
Liabilities			
Minority interest	$ —	$ 4,000	$ 4,000
Shareholder's equity	$6,000	$ —	$ 6,000
Total	$6,000	$ 4,000	$10,000

- Debit goodwill $1,000 (the purchase price, $10,000, less the FMV of identifiable assets, $9,000).
- Credit minority interests $4,000 ($10,000 value of the enterprise less the $6,000 acquired by the buyer).

The notable outcome with consolidation is that the value of the whole target is carried on the buyer's balance sheet.

All of the target's income statement flows would be added to the buyer's income statement, less a deduction for the minority investors' interest in the profits or losses of the target.

EQUITY METHOD Significant influence, but not majority control, of a target company requires the buyer to recognize its interest in the target using the *equity method* of accounting. Under this method, the buyer recognizes its investment in the target at the cost of purchasing those shares. In addition, the buyer's implied percentage ownership interest in the net earnings of the target will be reflected as an increase in its balance sheet account "Investment in Target Company." Earnings of the target are reflected pro rata as flows through the buyer's income statement. In effect, net undistributed pro rata earnings by the target are simply added to the investment account. Dividends of the target are reflected as a return of invested capital, as a reduction in the account "Investment in Target Company," and as an increase in cash.

COST METHOD Where the buyer has insignificant control of the target, the buyer would account for the acquisition under the *cost method.* Under the cost method, the buyer simply recognizes the investment in the securities of the target firm at the cost of acquisition. Typically, this amount would be reflected on the balance sheet in an account named "Investment in Affiliate(s)." On an ongoing basis, however, the FASB requires fair value accounting for securities that are readily marketable.

COMPARISON OF CONSOLIDATION AND EQUITY METHODS The consolidation and equity methods of accounting for partial acquisitions can produce significantly different effects on the reported financial results of the buyer. Both methods produce the same net income and net worth of the buyer.[12] Under consolidation, the target's assets, liabilities, revenues, expenses and cash flows are included in the accounts of the buyer—less, of course, the interest of the minority investors. Under the equity method, however, the target affects only the buyer's investment account and net income. Cash flows are similarly affected. Under consolidation, many of the buyer's cash flow items can be affected by the target's performance. Under the equity method, only the actual cash flows between the target and buyer will be reflected in the cash flow statement. The chief difference between consolidation and equity methods is whether the target appears *on- or off-balance sheet* of the buyer. Thus, the buyer's accounting-data leverage ratios and returns on assets and equity could vary significantly between the two methods.

HOW TO INTERPRET REPORTED FINANCIAL RESULTS IN AN M&A TRANSACTION

It makes sense to reflect on the basis on which one could compare alternative accounting choices. Very often, seasoned finance and accounting professionals will reduce the complex comparison to only one dimension, such as the impact on earnings per share (EPS). But doing so poorly serves the decision-making process. The best decision makers will *weigh trade-offs* among competing costs and benefits of the different alternatives. In order to highlight the trade-offs, one must inventory a full range of effects.

Accounting Dilution and Accretion

Earnings per share (EPS) is an ongoing concern to executives and directors who believe that this single measure is the main focus of attention by investors and the financial community.[13] For acquisitions, the buyer firm typically compares actual expected EPS for the current year to the pro forma EPS for the same year, assuming consummation of the acquisition. A reduction in EPS is *dilution*, and an increase is *accretion*. The deal design alternative that produces less dilution or more accretion than the other is judged the more attractive.

Cash flow EPS (CEPS), defined in its simplest[14] terms, is the sum of net income and noncash charges (such as goodwill amortization), divided by the number of shares outstanding. This is of interest to analysts who believe that share prices are driven by economic reality, and not influenced by accounting cosmetics. For instance, noncash charges do not represent real economic flows of value (unless they have side effects, such as reducing the tax expense of the firm).

The main drawback of EPS and CEPS is that they typically focus on short-term data: one year's future projected results, and perhaps one to three years in the past. Yet the effect of accounting choices will endure for many years. This suggests that one should look at the impact on free cash flow or residual cash flow over the longer term and estimate its effect in present value terms. For instance, asset allocation choices for the purpose of determining goodwill will affect the future depreciation tax shields, which in turn will affect the value of the firm. Valuation techniques such as discounted cash flow can help model how accounting choices may affect the long-term value of the firm.

Other Measures of Financial Performance Related to Financial Statements

Other measures can offer important insights into the financial consequences of accounting choices. Consider the following areas:

- *Financial leverage ratios.* Many firms are debtors. Usually, covenants in their loan agreements dictate minimum interest coverage ratios, and maximum debt/equity and dividend payout ratios or policies. We will see that accounting choices in M&A can affect the results obtained under these covenant tests, and thus the ability of the firm to borrow funds in the future (unless loan agreements are rewritten).

- ***Profit margins: gross margin, operating earnings, and net income.*** Purchase accounting for M&A affects many asset categories, which, in turn, affect items on the income statement. The allocation of the target's purchase consideration to receivables, inventory, and fixed assets will be affected, which will, in turn, alter the cash revenues, cost of goods sold, and gross margin. Intangible asset amortization affects net income, as do goodwill impairment charges.
- ***Asset efficiency and leverage, and returns on equity and assets.*** As noted earlier, the choice among methods of accounting for a partial acquisition can affect whether the target appears on- or off-balance sheet of the buyer. In turn, this affects measures of asset efficiency, leverage, and accounting returns.
- ***Liquidity.*** Other things equal, larger allocations of the FMV of the target purchase price to current assets will enhance the appearance of the liquidity of Newco.

An Illustrative Example

To illustrate the kinds of differences in financial reporting results that one may encounter due to accounting choices, consider the following example,[15] in which financial results are presented for two cases:

1. Purchase accounting: Buyer purchases the target by issuing shares of common stock.
2. Purchase accounting: Buyer purchases the target with cash financed by issuing debt.

For simplicity, the example assumes two firms that have identical expected revenues for the next year, 2004. Their balance sheets and income statements are similar in size. Thus, this could be a merger of equals. The target, however, has been growing more rapidly than the buyer and is expected to do so in the future. The transaction is assumed to take place in early 2004, although for reporting purposes to its shareholders the buyer prepares pro forma results for 2003.

In essence, the transaction contemplates that the buyer will pay a total of $2,000 for the target's stock (a market value of $2.00 per share), either in cash or with 1,000 shares of the buyer's stock (the example will look at the results with both forms of payment). Also, the buyer will assume $946 of liabilities (current and long-term) of the target. In summary, the total value of the deal (total consideration paid) is $2,946.[16] The goodwill created in this purchase transaction is simply the difference between the total consideration paid for the target of $2,946 and the fair market value of identifiable assets of $2,475 (assumed to be allocated $100 to current assets, $500 to intangible assets and $1,875 to gross fixed assets). The amount of goodwill is thus $471.[17] Exhibit 16.3 gives the historical and projected financial results for both the buyer and target. The restatement of the past year's results is offered here merely for illustration. Other than the differences in deal terms and accounting, the assumptions about the two companies will remain the same in both illustrations.

PURCHASE ACCOUNTING: ACQUISITION WITH STOCK First, consider the case in which the buyer purchases the target by issuing common stock as consideration. The

EXHIBIT 16.3 Historical Statements and Financial Forecasts for Buyer and Target

	Buyer Firm						Target Firm					
		Historical			Forecasted			Historical			Forecasted	
Line	2001	2002	2003	2004	2005	2006	2001	2002	2003	2004	2005	2006
1 Current assets	$ 86.4	$ 90.7	$ 95.2	$ 100.0	$ 105.0	$ 110.3	$ 57.9	$ 69.4	$ 83.3	$ 100.0	$ 120.0	$ 144.0
2 Gross fixed assets	$ 1,295.8	$ 1,360.5	$ 1,482.6	$ 1,500.0	$ 1,575.0	$ 1,653.8	$ 868.1	$ 1,041.7	$ 1,250.0	$ 1,500.0	$ 1,800.0	$ 2,160.0
3 Accumulated depreciation	$ (85.5)	$ (153.6)	$ (225.0)	$ (300.0)	$ (378.8)	$ (461.4)	$ (110.4)	$ (162.5)	$ (225.0)	$ (300.0)	$ (390.0)	$ (498.0)
4 Intangible assets	$ —	$ —	$ —	$ —	$ —	$ —	$ 500.0	$ 500.0	$ 500.0	$ 500.0	$ 500.0	$ 500.0
5 Goodwill	$ —	$ —	$ —	$ —	$ —	$ —	$ —	$ —	$ —	$ —	$ —	$ —
6 Assets	$ 1,296.6	$ 1,297.7	$ 1,298.8	$ 1,300.0	$ 1,301.3	$ 1,302.6	$1,315.5	$ 1,448.6	$ 1,608.3	$ 1,800.0	$ 2,030.0	$ 2,306.0
7 Current liabilities	$ 43.2	$ 45.4	$ 47.6	$ 50.0	$ 52.5	$ 55.1	$ 28.9	$ 34.7	$ 41.7	$ 50.0	$ 60.0	$ 72.0
8 Debt	$ 900.7	$ 768.9	$ 619.2	$ 450.0	$ 259.6	$ 46.0	$ 816.6	$ 860.1	$ 904.7	$ 950.0	$ 995.7	$ 1,041.4
9 Equity	$ 352.7	$ 483.4	$ 632.0	$ 800.0	$ 989.2	$ 1,201.4	$ 470.0	$ 553.8	$ 662.0	$ 800.0	$ 974.3	$ 1,192.6
10 Liabilities & equity	$ 1,296.6	$ 1,297.7	$ 1,298.8	$ 1,300.0	$ 1,301.3	$ 1,302.6	$1,315.5	$ 1,448.6	$ 1,608.3	$ 1,800.0	$ 2,030.0	$ 2,306.0
11 Revenues	$ 1,727.7	$ 1,814.1	$ 1,904.8	$ 2,000.0	$ 2,100.0	$ 2,205.0	$1,157.4	$ 1,388.9	$ 1,666.7	$ 2,000.0	$ 2,400.0	$ 2,880.0
12 Cost of materials & labor	$(1,382.1)	$(1,451.2)	$(1,523.8)	$(1,600.0)	$(1,680.0)	$(1,764.0)	$ (925.9)	$(1,111.1)	$(1,333.3)	$(1,600.0)	$(1,920.0)	$(2,304.0)
13 Depreciation	$ (64.8)	$ (68.0)	$ (71.4)	$ (75.0)	$ (78.8)	$ (82.7)	$ (43.4)	$ (52.1)	$ (62.5)	$ (75.0)	$ (90.0)	$ (108.0)
14 Interest expense	$ (90.1)	$ (76.9)	$ (61.9)	$ (45.0)	$ (26.0)	$ (4.6)	$ (81.7)	$ (86.0)	$ (90.5)	$ (95.0)	$ (99.6)	$ (104.1)
15 Profit before taxes	$ 190.7	$ 217.9	$ 247.6	$ 280.0	$ 315.3	$ 353.7	$ 106.4	$ 139.7	$ 180.4	$ 230.0	$ 290.4	$ 363.9
16 Taxes @ 40%	$ (76.3)	$ (87.2)	$ (99.0)	$ (112.0)	$ (126.1)	$ (141.5)	$ (42.6)	$ (55.9)	$ (72.1)	$ (92.0)	$ (116.2)	$ (145.5)
17 Net profit	$ 114.4	$ 130.7	$ 148.6	$ 168.0	$ 189.2	$ 212.2	$ 63.9	$ 83.8	$ 108.2	$ 138.0	$ 174.3	$ 218.3
18 Number of shares	1,000	1,000	1,000	1,000	1,000	1,000	1,000	1,000	1,000	1,000	1,000	1,000
19 Earnings per share	$ 0.11	$ 0.13	$ 0.15	$ 0.17	$ 0.19	$ 0.21	$ 0.06	$ 0.08	$ 0.11	$ 0.14	$ 0.17	$ 0.22
20 Operating cash flow per share	$ 0.18	$ 0.20	$ 0.22	$ 0.24	$ 0.27	$ 0.29	$ 0.11	$ 0.14	$ 0.17	$ 0.21	$ 0.26	$ 0.33
21 Return on equity	32%	27%	24%	21%	19%	18%	14%	15%	16%	17%	18%	18%
22 Net profit margin	7%	7%	8%	8%	9%	10%	6%	6%	6%	7%	7%	8%
23 Asset turns	1.33	1.40	1.47	1.54	1.61	1.69	0.88	0.96	1.04	1.11	1.18	1.25
24 Debt/liabilities & equity	69%	59%	48%	35%	20%	4%	62%	59%	56%	53%	49%	45%
Value per share												
Discounted cash flow	$ 2.43	$ 2.48	$ 2.53	$ 2.58	$ 2.62	$ 2.66	$ 1.72	$ 2.01	$ 2.36	$ 2.78	$ 3.28	$ 3.87
Multiple of earnings	$ 2.04	$ 2.33	$ 2.65	$ 3.00	$ 3.00	$ 3.00	$1.14	$ 1.50	$ 1.93	$ 2.46	$ 2.76	$ 3.09
KO	10%	10%	10%	10%	10%	10%	10%	10%	10%	10%	10%	10%
Earnings multiple	17.9	17.9	17.9	17.9	15.9	14.1	17.9	17.9	17.9	17.9	15.9	14.1

purchase price for the target's equity of $2,000 will be paid with 1,000 shares of the buyer's common stock, with a market value of $2.00 per share.[18] The calculation of pro forma results for the year 2003 just completed, and the forecasted financials for the next three years is given in Exhibit 16.4.

The following entries are made in purchase accounting:

- Note a: Target current assets are added at their fair market value.
- Note b: Target gross fixed assets are added at their fair market value.
- Note c: Target intangible assets of $500 are added at fair market value.
- Note d: Goodwill of $471 is introduced as an asset at closing.
- Notes e and f: Current liabilities and debt for the target are added to liabilities at fair market value.
- Note g: Equity reflects the fair market value of common stock issued in the purchase.
- Notes h, i, and j: Income statement items are simply added together.[19]
- Notes k and l: A new line is introduced to reflect any amortization of intangible asset value. Also, observe line 15 that holds the possibility of write-offs from the impairment of goodwill.
- Note m: The change in number of shares reflects 1,000 shares issued in the transaction.

PURCHASE ACCOUNTING: ACQUISITION WITH CASH, FINANCED BY AN ISSUE OF DEBT Next, consider the case in which the buyer purchases the target for cash financed by debt with an interest rate of 10 percent. Many of the adjustments are similar to those for the stock deal. The key differences in this case are a higher interest expense (and its resulting effect on net income), fewer shares outstanding, and a higher debt burden. Exhibit 16.5 presents the resulting financial statements of this case:

- Note f: Debt added is the previous debt of the target, $905, plus the $2,000 borrowed to finance the cash payment for the target's equity.
- Notes g and m: Equity and shares outstanding do not change because cash, rather than shares, was used to purchase the target.
- Note n: Interest expense leaps by $291, but is shielded by the tax deductibility of interest.

SUMMARY OF THE COMPARISON Exhibits 16.4 and 16.5 provide a comparison of results for the two cases. Exhibit 16.6 gives the EPS dilution percentages over time for the two cases. The purchase using cash, financed with debt, produces the lowest EPS of all in 2003—this reflects the combined impact of amortization of intangible assets and interest expense. First, the acquisition is dilutive to EPS and CEPS immediately, but turns accretive as time passes. The magnitudes of the immediate dilution effect are large. The stock deal is dilutive to 2003 EPS and CEPS by 20 percent. The dilution in EPS reflects the issuance of new shares (for CEPS) and new shares with amortization of intangible assets (EPS). The cash deal is dilutive to 2003 EPS and CEPS by 21 percent. This reflects the burden of added interest expense and intangible asset amortization rather than of the issuance of new shares.

EXHIBIT 16.4 Purchase Accounting Results for Buyer: Stock-for-Stock Deal

	Historical			As If Combined in 2003, Pro Forma			Forecasted		
Line	2001	2002	2003	Entries		New Balance	2004	2005	2006
1 Current assets	$ 86.4	$ 90.7	$ 95.2	$ 100.0	a	$ 195.2	$ 200.0	$ 225.0	$ 254.3
2 Gross fixed assets	1,295.8	1,360.5	1,428.6	1,875.0	b	3,303.6	3,000.0	3,375.0	3,813.8
3 Accumulated depreciation	(85.5)	(153.6)	(225.0)			(225.0)	(390.2)	(540.2)	(708.9)
Intangible assets	—	—	—	500.0	c	500.0	428.6	357.1	285.7
4 Goodwill	—	—	—	471.3	d	471.3	471.3	471.3	471.3
5 Assets	1,296.6	1,297.7	1,298.8	2,946.3		4,245.1	3,709.7	3,888.3	4,116.1
6 Current liabilities	43.2	45.4	47.6	41.7	e	89.3	100.0	112.5	127.1
7 Debt	900.7	768.9	619.2	904.7	f	1,523.9	680.5	467.5	228.3
8 Equity	352.7	483.4	632.0	2,000.0	g	2,632.0	2,929.2	3,308.3	3,760.7
9 Liabilities & equity	1,296.6	1,297.7	1,298.8	2,946.3		4,245.1	3,709.7	3,888.3	4,116.1
10 Revenues	1,727.7	1,814.1	1,904.8	1,666.7	h	3,571.4	4,000.0	4,500.0	5,085.0
11 Cost of material & labor	(1,382.1)	(1,451.2)	(1,523.8)	(1,333.3)	i	(2,857.1)	(3,200.0)	(3,600.0)	(4,068.0)
12 Depreciation	(64.8)	(68.0)	(71.4)	(93.8)	j	(165.2)	(165.2)	(150.0)	(168.8)
13 Synergies	—	—	—	—		—	—	—	—
14 Amortization of intangibles	—	—	—	—	k	—	(71.4)	(71.4)	(71.4)
15 Goodwill impairment	—	—	—	—	l	—	—	—	—
16 Interest expense	(90.1)	(76.9)	(61.9)	(90.5)		(152.4)	(68.1)	(46.8)	(22.8)
17 Profit before taxes	190.7	217.9	247.6			396.7	495.3	631.8	754.0
18 Taxes @ 40%	(76.3)	(87.2)	(99.0)			(158.7)	(198.1)	(252.7)	(301.6)
19 Net profit	$ 114.4	$ 130.7	$ 148.6			$ 238.0	$ 297.2	$ 379.1	$ 452.4
20 Number of shares	1,000	1,000	1,000	1,000	m	2,000	2,000	2,000	2,000
21 Earnings per share (EPS)	$ 0.114	$ 0.131	$ 0.149			$ 0.119	$ 0.149	$ 0.190	$ 0.226
22 Cash flow per share (CFPS)	$ 0.114	$ 0.131	$ 0.149			$ 0.119	$ 0.184	$ 0.225	$ 0.262
23 Return on equity	32%	27%	24%			9%	10%	11%	12%
24 Net profit margin	7%	7%	8%			7%	7%	8%	9%
25 Asset turns	1.33	1.40	1.47			0.84	1.08	1.16	1.24
26 Debt/liabilities & equity	69%	59%	48%			36%	18%	12%	6%
Accretion (Dilution) in Buyer's EPS and CEPS									
27 EPS without the acquisition						$ 0.149	$ 0.168	$ 0.189	$ 0.212
28 EPS after the acquistion						$ 0.119	$ 0.149	$ 0.190	$ 0.226
29 EPS dilution by year						−20%	−12%	0%	7%
30 CEPS without the acquistion						$ 0.149	$ 0.168	$ 0.189	$ 0.212
31 CEPS after the acquisition						$ 0.119	$ 0.184	$ 0.225	$ 0.262
32 CEPS dilution by year						−20%	10%	19%	23%

EXHIBIT 16.5 Purchase Accounting Results for Buyer: Cash-for-Stock Deal, Financed with Debt

	Historical			As If Combined in 2003, Pro Forma			Forecasted		
Line	2001	2002	2003	Entries		New Balance	2004	2005	2006
1 Current assets	$ 86.4	$ 90.7	$ 95.2	$ 100.0	a	$ 195.2	$ 200.0	$ 225.0	$ 254.3
2 Gross fixed assets	1,295.8	1,360.5	1,428.6	1,875.0	b	3,303.6	3,000.0	3,375.0	3,813.8
3 Accumulated depreciation	(85.5)	(153.6)	(225.0)			(225.0)	(390.2)	(540.2)	(708.9)
Intangible assets	—	—	—	500.0	c	500.0	428.6	357.1	285.7
4 Goodwill	—	—	—	471.3	d	471.3	471.3	471.3	471.3
5 Assets	1,296.6	1,297.7	1,298.8	2,946.3		4,245.1	3,709.7	3,888.3	4,116.1
6 Current liabilities	43.2	45.4	47.6	41.7	e	89.3	100.0	112.5	127.1
7 Debt	900.7	768.9	619.2	2,904.7	f	3,523.9	2,808.2	2,731.0	2,636.2
8 Equity	352.7	483.4	632.0	—	g	632.0	801.5	1,044.8	1,352.7
9 Liabilities & equity	1,296.6	1,297.7	1,298.8	2,946.3		4,245.1	3,709.7	3,888.3	4,116.1
10 Revenues	1,727.7	1,814.1	1,904.8	1,666.7	h	3,571.4	4,000.0	4,500.0	5,085.0
11 Cost of material & labor	(1,382.1)	(1,451.2)	(1,523.8)	(1,333.3)	i	(2,857.1)	(3,200.0)	(3,600.0)	(4,068.0)
12 Depreciation	(64.8)	(68.0)	(71.4)	(93.8)	j	(165.2)	(165.2)	(150.0)	(168.8)
13 Synergies	—	—	—	—		—	—	—	—
14 Amortization of intangibles	—	—	—	—	k	—	(71.4)	(71.4)	(71.4)
15 Goodwill impairment	—	—	—	—	l	—	—	—	—
16 Interest expense	(90.1)	(76.9)	(61.9)	(290.5)	n	(352.4)	(280.8)	(273.1)	(263.6)
17 Profit before taxes	190.7	217.9	247.6			196.7	282.6	405.5	513.2
18 Taxes @ 40%	(76.3)	(87.2)	(99.0)			(78.7)	(113.0)	(162.2)	(205.3)
19 Net profit	$ 114.4	$ 130.7	$ 148.6			$ 118.0	$ 169.5	$ 243.3	$ 307.9
20 Number of shares	1,000	1,000	1,000	—	m	1,000	1,000	1,000	1,000
21 Earnings per share (EPS)	$0.114	$0.131	$ 0.149			$ 0.118	$0.170	$ 0.243	$ 0.308
22 Cash flow per share (CFPS)	$0.114	$0.131	$ 0.149			$ 0.118	$0.241	$ 0.315	$ 0.379
23 Return on equity	32%	27%	24%			19%	21%	23%	23%
24 Net profit margin	7%	7%	8%			3%	4%	5%	6%
25 Asset turns	1.33	1.40	1.47			0.84	1.08	1.16	1.24
26 Debt/liabilities & equity	69%	59%	48%			83%	76%	70%	64%
Accretion (Dilution) in Buyer's EPS and CEPS									
27 EPS without the acquisition						$ 0.149	$ 0.168	$ 0.189	$ 0.212
28 EPS after the acquisition						$ 0.118	$ 0.170	$ 0.243	$ 0.308
29 EPS dilution by year						–21%	1%	29%	45%
30 CEPS without the acquisition						$ 0.149	$ 0.168	$ 0.189	$ 0.212
31 CEPS after the acquisition						$ 0.118	$ 0.241	$ 0.315	$ 0.379
32 CEPS dilution by year						–21%	43%	66%	79%

EXHIBIT 16.6 Comparative EPS and CEPS Dilution Associated with Share-for-Share and Cash-for-Share Deals

	2003a	2004f	2005f	2006f
EPS, stock deal	–20%	–12%	0%	7%
CEPS, stock deal	–20%	10%	19%	23%
EPS, cash deal	–21%	1%	29%	45%
CEPS, cash deal	–21%	43%	66%	79%

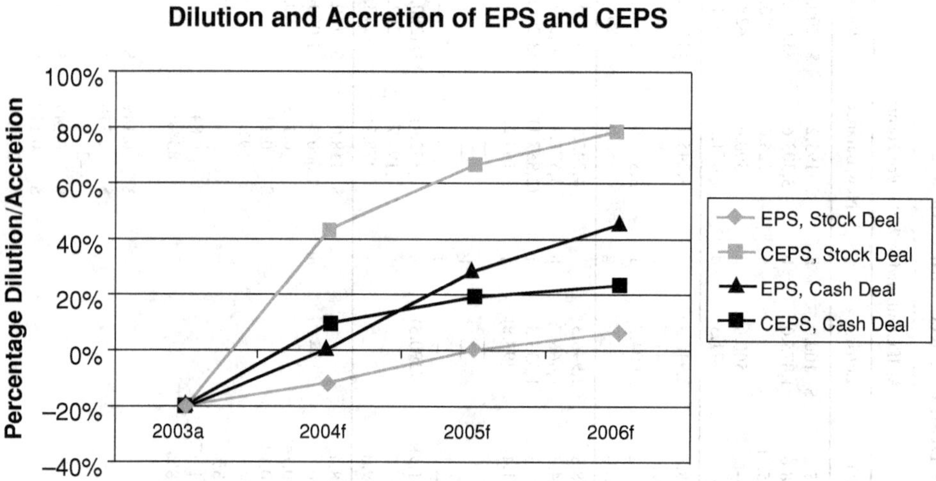

Source: Author's analysis.

Many securities analysts are not surprised to find that an acquisition is immediately dilutive; the large question for them is how fast it will turn accretive. Exhibit 16.6 shows that for both EPS and CEPS, the cash deal is more rapidly accretive.

The allocation of purchase price is significantly a matter of judgment and can have a material effect on EPS dilution and accretion. This is because allocations to identifiable assets result in charges to earnings, whereas goodwill does not. Exhibit 16.7 illustrates the impact on EPS dilution of different asset allocation schemes. This exhibit takes the base case forecasts of EPS from the previous examples and varies the initial asset allocation according to how much the values of fixed assets will be stepped up from their preexisting book values: The greater the step-up, the larger will be the allocation to identifiable assets, and the smaller to goodwill. Exhibit 16.7 shows the basic result that the larger allocations to identifiable assets result in greater dilution to EPS.

Can buyers adopt any allocation scheme they want? No. The allocation scheme must be approved by an auditing firm and the audit committee of the buyer's board of directors, all of whom must be concerned with the "fairness and accuracy" of financial reports as required in professional standards and laws such as the Sarbanes-Oxley Act. Thus, the results of Exhibit 16.7 ignore the constraining influence of the auditor.

EXHIBIT 16.7 Effect of Different Asset Allocations in Purchase Accounting for an Acquisition

Step Up in Asset Value	EPS, Stock	EPS, Cash
0.75	–10%	–1.6%
1.00	–14%	–7.9%
1.25	–17%	–14.2%
1.50	–20%	–20.6%
1.75	–23%	–26.9%

Note: This table gives the EPS dilution in the first year, associated with heavier or lighter allocation of the purchase price to fixed assets. EPS dilution increases as the values of gross fixed assets are stepped up from their book values before the merger. This creates more depreciation expense and lower reported EPS.
Source: Author's analysis.

Senior executives focus much of their thinking on the impact of the accounting method on EPS. Accounting dilution (or reduction in EPS) often becomes the single metric by which the choice is made. This book argues at several points that value creation, not cosmetic measures such as EPS, should be the guide for management decision making. Executives may choose a particular accounting policy because of its beneficial effects on EPS. But concerns over accounting treatment can easily distract executives from focusing on value creation, the real economic effects of the deal, and the mission of the firm.

Practical Insights about Accounting Dilution

The dilutive effects of a deal upon the buyer's reported EPS is a focus of intense analysis. The example here raises three important considerations. First, the extent of dilution (or accretion) can be influenced by accounting choices. Managers who focus on reported earnings as a measure of deal success will feel some incentive to manage EPS and the accounting choices in ways to minimize dilution—more is said about this in the section on the dangers of earnings management later in this chapter.

Second, synergies can trump accounting dilution. A detailed discussion of synergy is given in Chapter 11. But it is important to see that synergies can offset the impact of additional shares issued, interest expense, and goodwill. One can backsolve for the synergies needed to eliminate EPS dilution—doing so may be dangerous for the firm if it leads to imposing performance targets on managers; one should estimate synergies from the bottom up rather than the top down.

Third, other kinds of dilution may be more important. Chapter 18 distinguishes accounting dilution from economic dilution (i.e., NPV) and control dilution (i.e., percentage voting position). Best practitioners give greater weight to economic dilution than to accounting dilution.

LINKAGE AMONG ACCOUNTING CHOICES, FORM OF PAYMENT, FINANCING, AND PRICE

As the preceding example reveals, the reported financial results are affected by accounting choices. Thus, accounting choices can have a material effect on various deal terms. Consider the influence on just these three aspects:

1. *Form of payment.* Accounting choices and form of payment can both affect the buyer's earnings dilution. If the accounting treatment required by the buyer's auditors increases the dilution in the buyer's earnings per share, it could discourage the use of stock as a form of payment, since payment with stock will tend to worsen earnings dilution.
2. *Financing.* The presentation of pro forma and forecasted financial results can influence creditors and major investors. Accounting choices may affect judgments about the buyer's creditworthiness or investment attractiveness.
3. *Price.* Other things equal, higher prices will be associated with more goodwill. The desire to avoid, or the willingness to accept, goodwill on the buyer's balance sheet may affect the premium that the buyer offers.

The executive and M&A professional should think critically about these linkages: They may have more to do with accounting cosmetics than economic reality. Furthermore, these points serve to illustrate ways in which accounting choices might influence deal design.

DANGERS OF EARNINGS MANAGEMENT

The thrust of the discussion thus far in this chapter is that accounting for M&A transactions poses many choices for which careful judgment is required. This next section reviews the dark side of these choices: earnings management and fraud.

Types of Earnings Management

One of the most important insights of the discussion so far is that the financial accounting for business combinations offers some latitude for choices and judgments by executives and M&A professionals. *If* perceptions of performance stemming from accounting choices really affect the value of the firm's securities (this assumption is questioned in the next section), then executives may be motivated to manipulate the financial accounting for combinations to give it the best appearance. This kind of manipulation is gaming behavior, in which the buyer uses the system of generally accepted accounting principles to achieve outcomes that serve the buyer's self-interest, but may conflict with the intent of the system of principles. In a world of gaming behavior there may be losers as well as winners—thus, it will pay M&A practitioners, investors, creditors, and analysts to sharpen their awareness of this kind of behavior and defend against its adverse consequences. There are at least four broad categories of games:

1. ***Earnings and EPS enhancement games.*** Many executives believe that stable and consistently growing EPS is the foundation of a high valuation multiple for the firm. Accordingly, many buyers make accounting choices that help EPS to conform to a desired trend. There is a growing body of scientific research that suggests that it is cash flow, not EPS, that the investors care about. Under the *earnings enhancement* game, managers and some shareholders[20] may win at the expense of other shareholders who permit themselves to be fooled by EPS figures. Chapter 17 discusses this game in more detail.
2. ***Credit enhancement games.*** Lenders judge the creditworthiness of buyers based on the strength of their earnings and cash flow, and the size and quality of their asset base. Choices in the accounting for business combinations can affect these indicators. Bankers are trained to see through these *credit enhancement* effects, but the unwary may not catch the effect of accounting choices and may grant the debtor more credit than its company financial condition merits. The notable illustration of this game was the use by Enron of special purpose entities (SPEs), off-balance sheet enterprises that held assets and debt of Enron and were not included in the consolidated financial statements of the firm. SPEs are used widely in business and are permissible under laws and accounting rules. Enron's very aggressive use of SPEs had the effect of hiding liabilities and making the firm seem less levered than it was. It will be the focus of civil and criminal litigation for years. The rules on consolidation of SPEs are currently in revision and will probably be tightened substantially.
3. ***Price maximization games.*** Target companies can make accounting choices that help to realize a high selling price: "Big bath" *write-offs* of sour assets (or the deferral of such write-offs), tapping reserves, and careful timing of the recognition of revenues, expenses, and expenditures can help justify a higher selling price. A careful due diligence effort on the part of the buyer should expose *price maximization* abuses. In 1998, Symbol Technologies walked away from acquiring Telxon when it questioned whether $14 million in revenues booked by Telxon were bona fide sales.[21] After CUC International and HFS, Inc., merged to form Cendant Corporation in late 1997, Cendant discovered an estimated $500 million in fraudulent revenue booked at CUC over the previous three years.
4. ***Tax management games.*** This chapter has focused on financial accounting rather than tax accounting. However, any short list of accounting-related games should include some mention of *tax management* games. Tax avoidance is approached by most firms in the spirit of expense management, a spirit at the core of good practice. Governments exploit this spirit through the tax code in seeking to motivate businesses in ways consistent with government policies. The tax code creates opportunities for firms to alter their operations in ways that reduce taxes. For instance, the location of plants and offices can expose the firm to higher or lower tax rates.[22] The timing of recognition of receipts and expenses can affect a tax bill: Selling inefficient assets at a loss or using net operating loss carryforwards can be timed to offset the tax expense on temporarily high profits. At many firms, managing tax exposure is within the intent of the tax laws and GAAP. But pursued aggressively, it can lead to two adverse outcomes. First, tax exposure can drive the fundamental economic direction of the business, rather than the other way around; tax strategy could obscure the

larger mission of the firm. Second, a culture of aggressive tax management can morph into a culture of tax fraud. Managers must remain vigilant in their observance of ethical norms, laws, and the mission of the firm.

These various games can be played simultaneously, though quite often the accounting choices involve trade-offs among taxation, EPS, and credit and price enhancement. To illustrate the games and some of their trade-offs, consider the impact of choices regarding *allocation of purchase price*, amortization of purchase price, and EPS growth management.

ALLOCATION OF THE PURCHASE PRICE Under purchase accounting, the total consideration paid for the target is allocated to the assets that were purchased. Purchase accounting permits a step-up in basis of the assets to reflect their fair market value. The excess of the consideration over the fair market value of the assets is allocated to goodwill.

- ***Goodwill minimization: a cash flow strategy.*** Some executives detest goodwill in the belief that it confuses investors. Others fear possible future goodwill impairment charges. As a result of these concerns, buyers will seek to allocate as much of the purchase price to fixed assets that are depreciated and intangibles that are amortized—the net effect is to shield the firm from tax expense, which is beneficial to shareholders of the buyer.
- ***Goodwill maximization: an EPS strategy.*** If one is confident about the future value of goodwill and believes that impairment is unlikely, then maximizing the allocation to goodwill reduces the allocations to other assets. This, in turn, results in lower depreciation, amortization, and higher reported earnings.

AMORTIZATION AND WRITE-OFFS Buyers have some discretion over the rate at which the newly purchased assets can be depreciated, depleted, expensed, or amortized. For tax purposes, any acceleration of income-deductible expenses will increase the present value of tax shields to shareholders from the use of those assets. Reduction of tax expense is a benefit to shareholders. From a financial reporting standpoint, acceleration may reduce EPS. Management that is oriented to cash flow will want to accelerate the use of the assets; management oriented to EPS will want to slow the use of the assets.

Aggressive write-offs of capitalized in-process R&D expense received heightened attention from the Financial Accounting Standards Board and Securities and Exchange Commission (SEC) in 1998 and 1999. They observed a pattern in a number of high technology and pharmaceuticals deals of allocating a material percentage of the purchase amount to in-process R&D, and then writing it off shortly after the consummation of the deal. The buyers claimed that technological developments had rendered the R&D of little or no value, when, in fact, the R&D projects continued. A study[23] by Baruch Lev of New York University found that 400 firms had written off part of their acquisitions as in-process R&D during the 1990s, compared with only three in the 1980s. In the 1990s, the average write-off was 72 percent of the entire purchase price. Lev suggested that buyers may have assigned higher values to purchased R&D in order to lower the amount assigned to goodwill. For example, Excite paid $70 million for a share in a joint venture with

Netscape Communications in 1998, and quickly wrote off $58 million of it. One analyst applauded "the company's creativity and chutzpah. . . . It is an aggressive accounting choice that distorts future operating earnings by making costs vanish like a puff of smoke."[24] In July 1998, Lycos bought three firms for $104 million and wrote off 87 percent of the allocation to in-process R&D.

EPS AND MOMENTUM If growth of EPS is a key driver of stock prices, purchase accounting in the context of an aggressive acquisition program can give the appearance of rapid growth when the firm's ongoing operations may, in fact, be stagnant. Purchase accounting does not require restatement of prior years' financial statements (unlike pooling). Thus, it might be possible for a buyer with no growth to acquire other no-growth firms and produce a time series of rapidly growing EPS.[25]

Exhibit 16.8 suggests some of the possibilities of producing a managed EPS trajectory through the acquisition over time of no-growth firms A, B, and C. Because purchase accounting does not require restatement, *any accretive acquisition will give the appearance of growth.* The dashed line, showing that EPS is growing sharply, gives this illusion. In reality, the fairest benchmark of growth would be to compare the buyer's EPS after any of the combinations against the sum of the EPSs of the separate firms before the deal. Analysts, however, almost never make this comparison.

An extension of managed EPS growth through acquisition is the creation of momentum in the share price of the buyer through reporting a sequence of positive EPS surprises over time. The momentum game is discussed more fully in Chapter

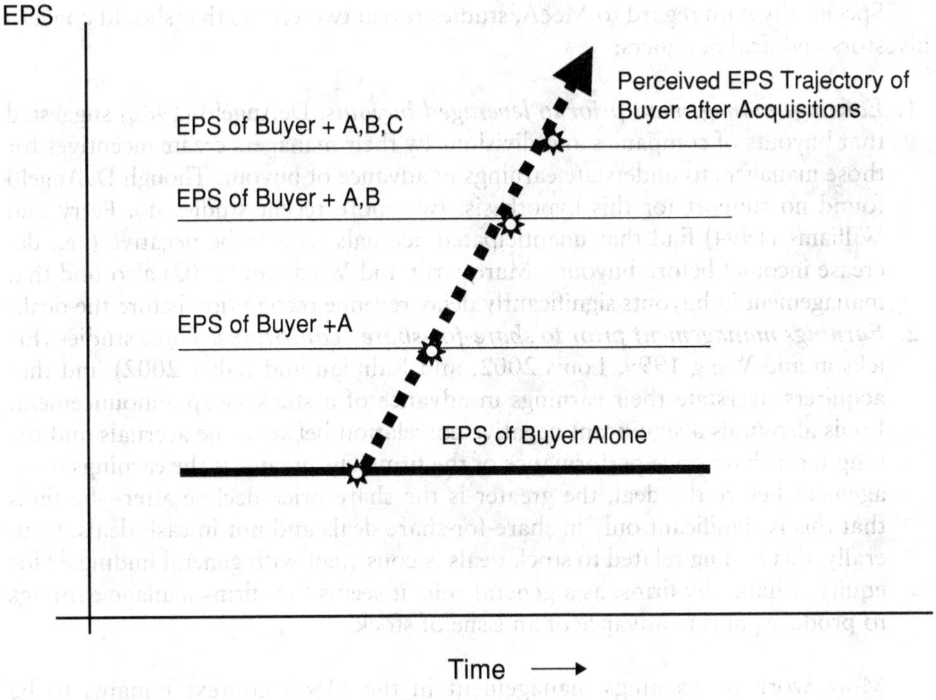

EXHIBIT 16.8 Hypothetical Managed EPS Trajectory

17. The flaws here are the assumptions that EPS growth drives stock prices, that EPS gains from momentum are sustainable indefinitely, and/or that at least some investors are easily fooled. Accordingly, the game exists between early equity investors and late equity investors. The gamble involves how rapidly the market will conclude that the beneficial economics have ended. Winners in this game are the early-arriving and early-departing investors; losers are the late-arriving and late-departing investors.

Research on Earnings Management

Practitioners, regulators, and some scholars believe that earnings management is pervasive and is a source of material costs to the investing public. Arthur Levitt, former chairman of the SEC, criticized the "widespread but too little challenged custom: earnings management." (Levitt 1998) He cited, among other practices, "big bath" accounting charges, creative acquisition accounting, and the creation of miscellaneous "cookie jar" reserves. Walter Schuetz, former chief accountant at the SEC, told the U.S. Senate that "earnings management is a scourge in this country. . . . We need to put a stop to earnings management."[26] Scholars have wrestled with problems about definition and measurement of earnings management, though recent studies suggest that earnings management is widespread and that its effect on investors is material.[27] At issue has been the question of whether sophisticated investors in financial markets are fooled by earnings management. The conventional wisdom had been that investors see through efforts to manage earnings. Perhaps in the wake of recent large accounting scandals, however, conventional wisdom and research findings have shifted.

Specifically with regard to M&A, studies reveal two effects that should concern investors and deal designers:

1. ***Earnings management prior to leveraged buyouts.*** DeAngelo (1988) suggested that buyouts of companies and divisions by their managers create incentives for those managers to understate earnings in advance of buyout. Though DeAngelo found no support for this hypothesis, two more recent studies do. Perry and Williams (1994) find that unanticipated accruals tend to be negative (i.e., decrease income) before buyouts. Marquardt and Wiedman (2002) also find that management in buyouts significantly delay revenue recognition before the deal.
2. ***Earnings management prior to share-for-share acquisitions.*** Three studies (Erickson and Wang 1999, Louis 2002, and Rahman and Bakar 2002) find that acquirers overstate their earnings in advance of a stock swap announcement. Louis also finds a significant negative correlation between the accruals and the long-term share price performance of the firm: The greater is the earnings management before the deal, the greater is the share price decline after—he finds that this is significant only in share-for-share deals and not in cash deals. Generally, this finding related to stock deals is consistent with general findings[28] for equity issuance by firms; as a general rule, it seems that firms manage earnings to produce gains in advance of an issue of stock.

More work on earnings management in the M&A context remains to be done. Of particular interest would be the use of accounting reserves, write-offs, transaction structures, and earnings guidance to analysts in advance of, and following, transactions.

Earnings management has been defined as "non-neutral financial reporting" (Nelson et al. 2000, page 1), "a purposeful intervention in the external financial reporting process with the intent of obtaining some private gain (as opposed to, say, merely facilitating the neutral operation of the process)" (Schipper 1989, page 92), and "to either mislead some stakeholders about the underlying economic performance of the company or to influence contractual outcomes that depend on reported accounting numbers" (Healy and Wahlen 1999, page 6). These definitions differ thinly from *financial fraud*, defined as the "deliberate misrepresentation of the financial condition of an enterprise accomplished through the intentional misstatement or omission of amounts or disclosures in the financial statements to deceive financial statement users." (Certified Fraud Examiners 1993, cited in Dechow and Skinner 2000, page 6) Dechow and Skinner (2000) note that earnings management can constitute fraud, but that some forms of earnings management are within the bounds of generally accepted accounting principles (GAAP). They cite the example of the deferral of revenue recognition by a software company: Revenue is not "earned" until customer support is given. This has the effect of smoothing the recognition of revenues over time. From the practitioner's standpoint, it is not entirely clear whether revenue deferral is "conservative" or "aggressive"—indeed, "earnings management" could be either. Exhibit 16.9 surveys other accounting choices across a spectrum of earnings management practices: from conservative accounting to *neutral earnings*, to aggressive accounting, to fraud. Nelson et al. (2000) surveyed auditors and found earnings management spanned 22 subject areas.[29]

Earnings management could be motivated by the desire to meet earnings targets tacitly advised by the company and published by Wall Street analysts (Healey and Wahlen 1999) or to sustain earnings momentum (Skinner and Myers 1999).

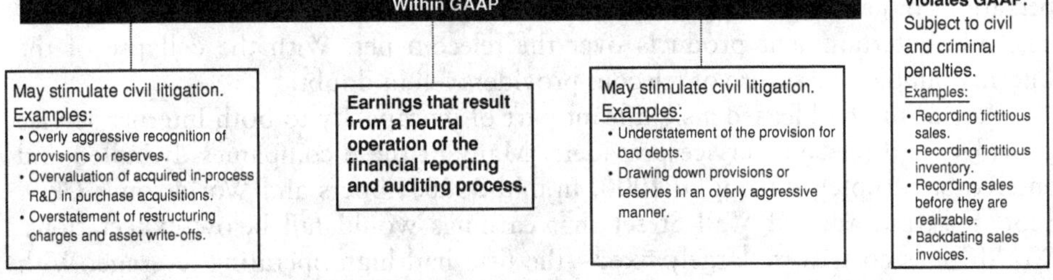

EXHIBIT 16.9 A Spectrum of Earnings Management Choices and Fraud
From Patricia M. Dechow and Douglas J. Skinner, 2000, "Earnings Management: Reconciling the Views of Accounting Academics, Practitioners, and Regulators," *Accounting Horizons* 14(2, June):235–250.

Watts (2003) notes that managers have limited tenure and liability, which perhaps encourages risk taking in accounting choices. Nelson et al. (2000, 2001) found that auditors were influenced in their judgments about earnings management attempts by managers according to size of the client (the larger, the more lax), materiality of the adjustment, and the imprecision of the rules. They found that auditors tended to waive earnings management attempts when the accounting rules were imprecise and the transaction was unstructured.

GAAP permits and generally encourages the exercise of managerial and auditor judgment under broad principles, such as conservatism of results. This encouragement arises from two considerations. First is flexibility: No rules-based system can anticipate all conditions at any point in time, or as conditions change over time. A good accounting system adapts to innovations in business and managerial behavior. Most importantly for M&A, a flexible system helps to promote the structuring of transactions in economically efficient ways. Second is measurability: Accounting seeks to represent economic reality, a task that is riddled with judgment. As Chapter 9 emphasizes, we cannot observe intrinsic value, we can only *estimate* it. A world of "no earnings management" would also be a world of no judgments and zero flexibility—this, in turn, would sacrifice the usefulness, relevance, and timeliness of financial reports as gauges of economic activity. Some practitioners have argued for an abandonment of accrual accounting in favor of mark-to-market accounting. But mark-to-market is at least as laden with opportunities for judgment and measurement error as accrual accounting.

Financial Fraud: Mini-Case on WorldCom Inc.

The largest corporate fraud in history entailed the alleged falsification of $11 billion in profits at WorldCom Inc.[30] WorldCom was among the three largest long-distance telecommunications providers in the United States, the creation of a roll-up acquisition strategy by its CEO, Bernard Ebbers. Its largest acquisition, MCI Communications in 1998, capped a momentum-growth story. This, combined with the buoyant stock market of the late 1990s, enlarged the firm's share price dramatically.

In early 2001, it dawned on analysts and investors that the United States was far oversupplied with long-distance telecommunications capacity. A Merrill Lynch analyst estimated that only 3 percent of the fiber-optic telecom capacity in the U.S. was actually in use. Much of that capacity had been put in place under inflated expectations of growing use by the Internet that would deliver a vast expanse of business and entertainment products over the telecom net. With the collapse of the Internet bubble, the future of telecom providers fell in doubt.

WorldCom had leased a significant part of its capacity to both Internet service providers and telecom service providers. Many of these companies dwindled and entered bankruptcy starting in 2000. In mid-2000, Ebbers and WorldCom's CFO, Scott Sullivan, advised Wall Street that earnings would fall below expectations. WorldCom's costs were largely fixed—the firm had high operating leverage. With relatively small declines in revenue, earnings would decline a lot. In the third quarter of 2000, WorldCom was hit with $685 million in write-offs as its customers defaulted on capacity lease commitments. In October 2000, Sullivan pressured three midlevel accounting managers in WorldCom to draw on reserve accounts set aside for other purposes to cover operating expenses—this would reduce the reported operating expenses and increase profits. The transfer violated rules regarding the independence and purpose of reserve accounts. The three accounting managers acquiesced and later regretted their action. They considered resigning but were persuaded to remain with the firm through its earnings crisis. They hoped or believed that a turnaround in the firm's business would make this action an exception.

Conditions worsened in the first quarter of 2001. Revenue fell further, producing a profit shortfall of $771 million. Sullivan prevailed again on the three accounting managers to shift operating costs—this time to capital expenditure accounts. Again, the managers complied, this time backdating entries in the process. In the second, third, and fourth quarters of 2001, they transferred $560 million, $743 million, and $941 million, respectively. In the first quarter of 2002, they transferred $818 million.

The three accounting managers experienced deep emotional distress over their actions. When, in April 2002, they discovered that WorldCom's financial plan for 2002 implied that the transfers would continue to at least the end of the year, the three managers vowed to cease making transfers, and to look for new jobs. But inquiries by the SEC into the firm's suspiciously positive financial performance triggered an investigation by the firm's head of internal auditing. Feeling the heat of an investigation, the three met with representatives from the SEC, FBI, and U.S. Attorney's office on June 24, 2002. The next day, WorldCom's internal auditor disclosed to the SEC the discovery of $3.8 billion in fraudulent accounting. On June 26, the SEC charged WorldCom with fraudulent accounting.

In addition to the $3.8 billion fraud from reallocating operating expenses to reserves and capital expenditures, WorldCom shifted another $7.2 billion to its MCI subsidiary, affecting the tracking stock on that entity.

From its peak in late 2000 until WorldCom filed for bankruptcy in July 2002, about $180 billion of WorldCom's equity market value evaporated. In March 2003, WorldCom announced that it would write off $79.8 billion in assets following an impairment analysis: $45 billion of this arose from the impairment of goodwill.

The three accounting managers had hoped that they would be viewed simply as witnesses. On August 1, they were named by the U.S. Attorney's office as unindicted co-conspirators in the fraud. WorldCom fired them immediately. Unable to cope with the prospect of large legal bills for their defense, they pleaded guilty to securities fraud and conspiracy to commit fraud. The charges could carry a maximum of 15 years in prison.

Bernard Ebbers and Scott Sullivan, CEO and CFO respectively, were charged with fraud. A study later done by the bankruptcy examiner concluded that Ebbers played a role in inflating the firm's revenues. One example cited by the report was the firm's announcement of the acquisition of Intermedia Communications Inc. in February 2001 even before the WorldCom board had approved the deal—the firm's lawyers made it look as if the board had approved the deal by creating false minutes.

This case carries a number of implications for corporate executives, M&A professionals, and investors. First, fraud gets caught. Second, fraud is costly to companies, investors, and employees and damages investor confidence and trust. Third, fraud and earnings management share a common soil: a culture of aggressive growth. Though growth is one of the foremost aims in business, a mentality of growth at any price can warp the thinking of honorable people. And fourth, the shields against fraud are a culture of integrity, strong governance, and strong financial monitoring.

Sarbanes-Oxley Act

President George W. Bush signed the Sarbanes-Oxley Act into law on July 30, 2002, citing the need to end "corporate corruption [that] . . . has struck at investor confidence, offending the conscience of our nation." He said that SOA was one of "the most far-reaching reforms of American business practices" since the enactment of laws in the 1930s that regulated securities markets and practices. SOA had overwhelming legislative support, passing the Senate without a dissenting vote. The context for this legislation was a sense of alarm and outrage stemming from 22 major events of accounting irregularities by large corporations that were committed from 1998 to the signing of SOA.[31]

Yet, Bloomenthal (2002) writes that "the Act in some respects is poorly drafted, reflecting to some extent last-minute amendments . . . and revisions. . . . There are overlapping certification provisions. . . . Since [the Act] takes the form of an amendment to the criminal code, the [SEC] has no rulemaking authority notwithstanding it relates to the same periodic reports filed with the Commission. There are also overlapping provisions relating to a company's internal controls." (Pages xi, xii) Bloomenthal also noted possible unintended consequences arising from the Act's prohibition on "personal loans" to corporate officers, vagueness about who can bring an action to enforce provisions against "misconduct" by corporate officers, the apparent application of the Act to events occurring before enactment, and the potential for private lawsuits under the Act.

The SOA is a bundle of individual legislative remedies reacting to the disclosures of alleged corporate earnings management and fraud. These include:

- *Establishing the Public Company Accounting Oversight Board* (PCAOB), which would be charged with overseeing the audit of public companies. Public accounting firms would need to register with PCAOB; any accountant not registered could not perform an audit of a public company. PCAOB would make accounting rules and periodically inspect auditing firms' adherence to them. Finally, it would enforce compliance with SOA and with accounting rules and conduct disciplinary proceedings.
- *Prohibiting auditors from providing ancillary services* such as bookkeeping, consulting, corporate financial advisory services, and legal services. This sought to enhance auditor independence and to correct what was widely perceived as the role of nonaudit services in influencing the audit activities.
- *Requiring public companies to appoint independent directors* to audit committees within their boards of directors. These committees were charged with overseeing the work of public auditors.
- *Requiring certification of financial reports by the CEO and CFO*. These officers must submit signed statements that they have reviewed the financial reports and that the reports did not contain any "untrue statement of a material fact or omit to state a material fact necessary in order to make the statements

made . . . not misleading." Also, the officers would need to certify that internal controls exist to reveal "material information" each reporting period. It became illegal to "influence, coerce, manipulate, or mislead" a public auditor. Accounting restatements due to "misconduct" would trigger reimbursement by the CEO and CFO of any incentive compensation received in the previous 12 months, and of any profits realized from the sale of securities.

- ***Prohibiting insider trading during periods of "blackout"*** in pension funds, when pension investors are unable to trade.
- ***Requiring enhanced financial disclosures by corporations.*** These disclosures would include "all material correcting adjustments" identified by the public accounting firm and all material off-balance sheet transactions and obligations.
- ***Prohibiting personal loans to corporate executives.***
- ***Directing the SEC to adopt rules "reasonably designed to address conflicts of interest*** that can arise when securities analysts recommend equity securities in research reports and public appearances."
- ***Authorizing an increased appropriation of funds to the SEC*** to support enlarged activities.
- ***Stiffening the fines and jail terms*** as criminal penalties under the Exchange Act of 1934. Mail and wire fraud jail terms were increased from five years to 20 years. Penalties for willful violations of the Exchange Act or any rule under it were increased from 10 to 20 years and from $1 million to $5 million for a natural person (and from $5 million to $25 million for a corporation).

SUMMARY AND CONCLUSIONS

This chapter has reviewed the mechanics of purchase accounting in M&A and the larger context for accounting today. The chapter argues that financial accounting in M&A is not like an engineering problem with well-defined rules and relationships. Rather, it is a field laden with judgments and uncertain effects. Executives, analysts, and M&A deal practitioners should focus attention on eight aspects raised by this chapter:

1. Judgments in asset allocations, especially in determining intangible asset value and goodwill.
2. Judgments in choice of reporting unit.
3. Judgments in valuation that support asset allocation and impairment tests.
4. Scrutiny of the effect of accounting choices on earnings before and after the deal.
5. Trade-offs among aspects of deal design such as accounting, form of payment, price, and financing.
6. Avoidance of fraud.
7. Observance of the Sarbanes-Oxley Act and other laws.
8. The need to think like an investor.

Decisions in the area of financial accounting for M&A should be made with counsel of competent professional advice.

APPENDIX 16.1
Mechanics of Pooling-of-Interests Accounting

Pooling accounting was prohibited for U.S. mergers beginning in 2001, and is of interest here mainly to understand historical accounting behavior and to compare with purchase accounting. (See Exhibit 16.10.) This method arose for use in special cases of a merger of equals where the companies were about the same size and where it was unclear who was buying whom. In these instances, purchase accounting seemed less appropriate. Over time, companies were successful in arguing that their transactions were almost mergers of equals, and eventually the size criterion was abandoned. Pooling accounting was available to any transaction that met certain regulatory rules.

Pooling simply adds the balance sheets and income statements of the two firms, line by line. No goodwill is created, thus reducing the penalty to reported earnings from goodwill amortization. Also, asset values are not restated. Under pooling, historical values are simply carried over to the new firm. With pooling accounting, anytime the buyer presents an income statement or a series of income statements for any past periods, those statements must be restated to reflect the results of the pooled entities. Thus, it permits an examination of trends over a historically consistent set of financial statements. This method was called "dirty pooling" by some critics because it improved[32] the cosmetic appearance of transactions that were, in substance, purchases. In 1970, the Accounting Principles Board (APB) issued a famous opinion (Opinion 16) in which it limited the use of pooling of interests. Under the most prominent rules, pooling would be allowed only where:

- Target shareholders maintained a continuing ownership interest in the new firm. This test eliminated outright purchase transactions where the target shareholders departed.
- There would be no change in the basis for accounting for the target's assets.
- The combining firms must have been autonomous entities and independent from each other for at least two years. "Independence" here is defined as less than a 10 percent intercorporate ownership. This test prevented treating as a pooling those acquisitions that began as purchases.
- Combination occurred in a single transaction or was completed in accordance with a specific deal within one year. This test prevented treating as a pooling those slow, creeping acquisitions over time that are in substance purchases.
- Buyer issued only voting common stock in exchange for substantially all (90 percent) of the voting common stock of the target. Contingent payments were not permitted. This test prohibited preferential forms of payment to target shareholders, and was consistent with the notion of combining of interests.
- Neither the buyer nor the target could change the equity interests of the common shareholders for the year prior to the transaction, and Newco was not allowed to repurchase shares or dispose of major assets for up to two years after the transaction. This rule prevented delayed cash payments to selling shareholders, or the exchange of assets for shares—either of those could be substantially purchases rather than true mergers with continuity of ownership.[33]

EXHIBIT 16.10 Summary Comparison of Purchase and Pooling Accounting

	Pooling of Interests	Purchase Accounting
Transaction viewed as?	Combination of equals. Unclear who is buying whom.	A purchase of the target by the buyer. Target being viewed as just another asset being purchased. Assets and liabilities are received into the buyer's balance sheet at fair market value.
Record of payment?	Does not record what the buyer paid since the deal is a mere blending of the balance sheet items of firms. Suppresses the true cost of the acquisition. May present unrealistically low carrying value of assets; upon sale of assets, firm may book unrealistically large gains.	Records what the buyer paid.
Time perspective?	Backward-looking. No change in historical cost basis. No step-up in basis. No goodwill. Timing of the acquisition may matter.	Current-looking. Purchase price allocated on the basis of current market values. Possible step-up in basis. Goodwill possible but not amortized. Past does not matter. Timing of the deal does not matter—impact of the target starts from date of purchase.
Effect on net income compared to sum of two firms?	Net income is unchanged.	Net income may be lower, because asset value increases, resulting from the merger/due to the merger, must be amortized.
Effect on cash flow (net income plus noncash charges)?	Cash flows are unchanged compared to the sum of the two firms.	Cash flows are higher or unchanged, to the extent of the tax deductibility of the increased asset amortization.
Effect on leverage?	No change in leverage beyond a blend of the two capital structures.	Leverage is lower, if stock is used to acquire, leverage is higher if cash is used to acquire, and financed either from unused debt capacity or excess cash.

(Continued)

EXHIBIT 16.10 *(Continued)*

	Pooling of Interests	Purchase Accounting
Effect on historical financial results?	Requires historical restatement for all years presented. May imply credit to buyer's management for the target's prior financial performance.	Requires no historical restatement. Pre- and postacquisition financial results are difficult to compare. Buyer's statements reflect target only from date of transaction. Possible illusion of growth.
Effect on postmerger restructuring?	Limits asset sales and stock repurchases for two years.	No limitation.
Effect on terms of payment?	Requires stock-for-stock transaction.	No limitation.
Effect on assets?	No change.	Higher to the extent of difference between purchase price and target's historical book value.
Effect on bid premiums?	Associated with higher bid premiums.	Associated with lower bid premiums.
Effect on buyer's stock price?	Little stock price reaction.	Positive stock price reaction, perhaps reflecting higher cash flow.

Poolings as a percentage of all transactions increased from 14 percent in 1994 to 22.9 percent in 1996, on the basis of the dollar value of transactions. On the basis of numbers of transactions, poolings represented 7.8 percent in 1994 and 9.1 percent in 1996.[34] This percentage shows a tendency to vary with capital market conditions, having reached a peak of nearly 40 percent for poolings in 1969 and fallen since then.

The former rules regarding pooling accounting for mergers and acquisitions were set forth in APB Opinions 16 and 17, published in 1970. Practice has changed significantly since that time and accountants, analysts, managers, and even politicians have clamored for change:

> *The present rules . . . are approaching their twentieth anniversary—an event many believe should never occur. Most recognize that these rules were a convenient compromise, not rules of reason and logic. Their survival is only at the cost of shortcomings in financial statement presentation.*[35]

Globalization of business has been one important driver for change. Across the industrialized world, there has been a wide variety of acceptable accounting methods for business combinations. In most countries outside the United States, the use of pooling accounting was severely limited and was applied only to true mergers of equals. In many countries, it was acceptable to write off goodwill at the time of the transaction. Other countries have agreed that goodwill could be allowed to remain on the balance sheet indefinitely, subject only to an ongoing challenge to realizability. Still other countries have required that goodwill be amortized to income over very short periods. Under pressure from the securities regulators around the world, the accounting profession sought to establish one set of accounting standards that would be followed throughout the world. The International Accounting Standards Committee (IASC) completed its set of core standards, including a standard on business combinations. That new standard limits the use of pooling accounting to true mergers of equals, where there is no obvious buyer, and requires that goodwill from purchases be written off over no more than 20 years.

The U.S. Securities and Exchange Commission was one of the regulatory bodies that pushed for the IASC core standards program and made clear its dislike of pooling accounting—if for no other reason than that its staff spent a disproportionate amount of time working with registrants who wanted to qualify a transaction for pooling accounting. The implementation rules for poolings had become very complex. That concern and the establishment of a new standard on business combinations by the IASC have pushed the FASB to reconsider the status of APB Opinions 16 and 17. Although the business community remained divided, the call for greater comparability across firms and transactions was impetus for changing the rules.

Finally, financial innovation required modification in the rules. New securities and more complex forms of combination were difficult to handle within the existing framework. In August 1996, the FASB agreed to add a special project to its agenda to address the subject of accounting for business combinations and intangible assets. On September 7, 1999, the FASB issued its exposure draft of the new accounting standards for business combinations. These new standards, FAS 141 and 142, became effective for M&A deals consummated after June 30, 2001, and eliminated pooling accounting for mergers.

NOTES

1. The discussion in this section is adapted from FAS 141 and 142.
2. In essence, pooling combines two firms at their *historical*, not exchanged, values. This led to a number of abuses and was derided as "dirty" pooling. In contrast, purchase accounting records the combination on the basis of exchanged values.
3. The FMV of goodwill is determined by allocating the purchase price of a target company across its tangible and intangible assets; what is left over is goodwill. The FMV of tangible or intangible assets is the amount at which they could be sold in a transaction between willing parties.
4. Goodwill cannot be assigned to any specific intangible asset such as a trademark or patent, but is apparent in the loyal customer franchise a company may enjoy. Examples of this franchise with an indefinite life would be Disney in theme parks and animated films, Johnson & Johnson in personal health-care products, and Microsoft in software.
5. The test for impairment should also be made at times other than annually—for instance, after a significant adverse change in business.

6. Goodwill can also be negative, where the purchase price is less than FMV of the target's identifiable assets.
7. The focus of this chapter is on *financial reporting*. The impact of goodwill from a tax accounting standpoint may be different. For tax accounting, goodwill arising from an *asset purchase* must be amortized over 15 years and recognized as a deductible expense in computing the annual tax payment. But if the transaction is a *stock purchase*, goodwill is not deductible unless the buyer takes a Section 338 election. A Section 338 election occurs in an acquisition of stock where the buyer elects to have it treated for tax purposes like an acquisition of assets, where the basis of the target firm is stepped up and depreciated or amortized. See Chapter 19 for more on the tax aspects of acquisitions.
8. To focus on economic efficiency is to measure value creation with such indicators as net present value and economic value added (EVA); these are economic, rather than accounting, measures of performance. The change in the value of reported results such as assets, sales, and earnings is a poor measure of value creation because historical accounting values may not reflect economic reality. Also, bigger is not necessarily better. Even the change in earnings per share is a poor measure of value creation, for reasons explained in Chapter 17.
9. Governments often retain a "golden share" when state-owned enterprises are privatized. These single shares grant veto rights over large asset sales, major strategic changes, and changes in control of the enterprise.
10. Standstill agreements commit buyers not to acquire further shares (or even vote their shares), usually in return for cooperation by the target in providing confidential information about the target.
11. In dual-class share structures, common stock is subdivided into senior (high voting power) and junior (low voting power) shares. In these cases it may be possible for a shareholder to hold a minority of shares outstanding, but a majority of votes.
12. This assumes equivalent tax rates for both target and buyer and positive net income for both.
13. Scholarly research is at best of mixed agreement with this view; some research is hostile to it. In efficient capital markets, investors will "see through" reported EPS and will focus on cash flow, which better reflects economic reality. Investors like Warren Buffett claim to do just that (see Chapter 9). Still, other research (Andrade 1999; Dechow 1994) finds that changes in EPS help to explain variations in stock prices. Some of this research is summarized in a later section of this chapter. My own view is that change in EPS is important mainly as a signal of real economic phenomena, useful but imperfect and susceptible to earnings manipulation. My recommendation to executives and M&A practitioners is to view EPS with skepticism and caution.
14. As Chapter 9 discusses, "cash flow" has many possible definitions. The "cash EPS" presented in this chapter—Cash EPS = (Net income + Goodwill amortization)/Number of shares—is emerging as a measure of the operating health of the firm, untainted by the impact of purchase accounting goodwill. Ideally, one would also examine such measures as free cash flow and residual cash flow—these other measures better approximate the economic reality of flows of cash to investors.

15. The details of this example may be found in spreadsheet form in "Purchase Accounting.xls" on the CD-ROM.
16. For brevity the figures are rounded to whole numbers in the discussion of this example.
17. Again, the calculation is: Equity cost + Liabilities assumed = Purchase price; purchase price – FMV of identifiable assets = Goodwill or $2,000 equity + $946 debt = $2,946 purchase price; $2,946 – $2,475 = $471.
18. Note that once the number of shares to be given in consideration is agreed upon in a stock purchase deal and the purchase price is established, the buyer may wind up paying (and the seller receiving) a higher or lower purchase price because of changes in the market value of the buyer's shares. The two companies may in this situation agree to put a cap, floor, or collar on the price of the buyer's stock, outside of which the deal will be terminated.
19. The purchase accounting cases show clearly the impact of the step-up in basis of gross fixed assets, but the case glosses over the potential impact of a step-up in the value of current assets. As more costly inventory flows through the income statement, cost of goods sold will rise.
20. Managers may benefit from EPS enhancement games if their incentive compensation is tied to EPS growth. Some shareholders might benefit at the expense of others if sophisticated shareholders (who recognize the fruitlessness of EPS manipulation) sell their shares at high prices to other shareholders who are fooled by EPS figures.
21. Steven Lipin, "Telxon Is Probed by the SEC," *Wall Street Journal*, February 22, 1999.
22. Tyco International relocated its headquarters from New Hampshire to Bermuda to reduce tax expense.
23. This study was reported in Elizabeth MacDonald, "FASB Weighs Killing Merger Write-Off," *Wall Street Journal*, February 23, 1999.
24. Quoted in Kara Swisher and Leslie Scism, "Internet Firm's Fast Write-Off Draws Notice," *Wall Street Journal*, August 27, 1998, page C1.
25. For this to work most credibly, there needs to be some genuine growth early in the buyer's history on which an efficient stock market could base expectations of future gains.
26. Cited in Arya et al. (2003), page 112.
27. For reviews of academic research on earnings management, see Schipper (1989), Healey and Wahlen (1999), and Watts (2003). Marquardt and Wiedman (2002) summarize costs of earnings management to firms. Significant negative abnormal returns to shareholders are associated with announcements of SEC enforcement actions, earnings restatements, shareholder litigation for securities fraud, and qualified audit reports.
28. See Shivakumar (2000), Teoh, Welch, and Wong (1998a, 1998b), Teoh, Wong, and Rao (1998), and Rangan (1998).
29. These areas included reserves (general and restructuring), revenue recognition, business combinations, non-R&D intangibles, fixed assets, investments, leases, accounting changes, prior period adjustments, compensation, taxes, consolidations and the equity or cost method of accounting, transfers of receivables, cash flows and working capital, long-term debt, pensions and other postretirement

benefits, segment reporting, R&D, foreign currency, EPS, related party disclosures, and nonmonetary transactions.

30. The facts on which this case is based were drawn from Pulliam (2003), Blumenstein and Pulliam (2003), Blumenstein and Solomon (2003), and Solomon (2003).
31. The companies and their alleged or admitted accounting issues were Adelphia (loans and looting), Bristol-Myers (improper inflation of revenues through use of sales incentives), CMS Energy (overstatement of revenues through "round trip" energy trades), Computer Associates (inflation of revenues), Dynegy (artificial increase of cash flow), Elan (use of off-balance sheet entities), Enron (inflation of earnings and use of off-balance sheet entities), Global Crossing (artificial inflation of revenues), Halliburton (revenue recognition), Kmart (accounting for vendor allowances), Lucent Technologies (revenue accounting and vendor financing), Merck (revenue recognition), MicroStrategy (backdating of sales contracts), Network Associates (revenue and expense recognition), PNC Financial Services (accounting for transfer of loans), Qwest (revenue inflation), Reliance Resources (revenue inflation through "round trip" energy trades), Rite Aid (inflation of earnings), Tyco International (improper use of "cookie jar" reserves and acquisition accounting), Vivendi Universal (withholding information about liquidity troubles), WorldCom (revenue and expense recognition), Xerox (revenue and earnings inflation). These cases and their points of controversy are summarized in Bloomenthal (2002), pages App. E-1 and E-2.
32. The "improvement" occurred because pooling booked acquisitions, not at their actual purchase price, but at the typically lower historical book values.
33. This rule was extended following the SEC's rejection of First Bank System, Inc.'s attempted takeover of First Interstate Bancorp on the basis that FBS announced plans to buy back shares as part of the deal. The SEC issued a bulletin in March 1996, following the rejection, restricting a pooler's ability to make major stock repurchases for up to 24 months surrounding a transaction. In response, some companies limited stock buyback programs in order to preserve their future ability to pool.
34. These are the findings of Securities Data Company as reported in Ian Springsteel, "Say Goodbye to Pooling," *CFO Magazine*, February 1997.
35. Richard Dieter, "Is Now the Time to Revisit Accounting for Business Combinations?," *CPA Journal Online*, July 1989.

CHAPTER 17

Momentum Acquisition Strategies: An Illustration of Why Value Creation Is the Best Financial Criterion

INTRODUCTION: FOUR CAUTIONARY TALES

This chapter considers the implications of an acquisition strategy that is driven by the desire to maintain the momentum of financial performance of the firm. This *momentum acquisition strategy* has swung in and out of favor over the years, and appeared again in the merger wave of the late 1990s. Momentum acquiring is a seductive strategy to be avoided, and practitioners should understand why. Here are four arresting tales.

"Automatic" Sprinkler[1]

Harry E. Figgie was an ambitious manager, eager to exploit estimable skills in reducing costs within manufacturing operations. With degrees in engineering, law, and business, he joined Booz Allen and Hamilton in 1953, where he rose to partner within six years and specialized in cost reduction techniques. In early 1962, he left Booz Allen to join A. O. Smith Corporation as a group vice president. In less than two years, the business sector he managed increased its revenues 100 percent and its profits by 400 percent. In late 1963, Figgie quit A. O. Smith to buy "Automatic" Sprinkler Corporation for $5.85 million, nearly $1.4 million less than its book value. In calendar year 1964, the firm's revenues increased by 11 percent, but its earnings tripled to $1.2 million—all without acquisitions, but due instead to operational improvements.

Figgie was eager to maintain the spectacular one-year improvement in earnings. In 1965, his firm acquired four companies. In 1966, it acquired another four. Most of these early acquisitions were concentrated in construction equipment and fire protection equipment manufacturing. The firm's revenues rose to $45.9 million in 1965, and $90.7 million in 1966. In November 1965, the firm offered shares to the public in an IPO, at $7.80 each, almost 100 times the price paid by Figgie's financial backers.

Figgie's rationale for his early acquisitions was the "nucleus theory" of business expansion. Acquisitions would be clustered around an industry nucleus company in order to shape a dominant player in the field. Figgie restructured his targets through a process of business process reengineering, R&D, and market development. But starting in 1967, the firm showed more appetite for acquiring companies with internal problems that would need to be turned around—nothing in the "nucleus theory" dictated whether a target might be too sick to acquire. In mid-October 1967, the firm's share price peaked at $57, about eight times its IPO price less than two years earlier.

In 1967, "Automatic" Sprinkler acquired 11 firms, and sales rocketed to $242.3 million. Figgie announced in November 1967 that the firm's earnings per share (EPS) growth would exceed 40 percent in 1967, suggesting, he said, an EPS between $1.70 and $1.90 per share. He also announced a belief that the firm's EPS would reach $2.75 in 1968. Upon this expectation, investors bid up the firm's shares to $74. But reflecting operating difficulties within some of the business units and Figgie's own finite span of attention, the firm's profit growth began to subside. In February 1968, "Automatic" Sprinkler announced an EPS of $1.43, an improvement over the $1.15 of a year earlier, but well below forecast. Following the news, the firm's share price tumbled to the low $30s. The earnings shortfall was due entirely to surprising operating problems that had developed within several business units of the firm. While none of these was individually a serious problem for the firm, they aggregated to a major challenge.

In 1968, "Automatic" Sprinkler acquired three more companies. Its revenues grew to about $325 million, but its profits fell again, reflecting extraordinary charges and operating losses in various divisions. EPS fell to $0.10. By the end of 1968, the firm's share price had fallen to $18. All but one of the 24 mutual funds that had invested in "Automatic" Sprinkler's growth expectations abandoned ship. In reflecting on this episode, Rukeyser (1969, page 89) wrote:

> *For the first few years, profits rose even more dramatically than sales. Expectations that such a growth pattern could be sustained were fed by the company's hyperoptimistic projections of sales and earnings. To justify those projections, Automatic Sprinkler had to make mergers at a frantic clip. . . . The pace was too fast to allow for thorough investigation of merger partners before deals were made, or for proper assimilation of newly acquired companies before management's attention was diverted to other negotiations.*

Ling-Temco-Vought

James Ling built the conglomerate Ling-Temco-Vought (LTV) starting from nothing in 1948 to the twenty-second largest U.S. firm by 1968. Ling's approach was to grow the firm largely by acquisition. It was described in these terms:

> *The secret? An acquisition-plus-spin-off technique that some people suggest Jim Ling should patent. In general, it works this way: LTV borrows cash to acquire control of another company. That company then merges with LTV through an exchange of securities. Next, it is split into operating divisions along product lines. These divisions are then reorganized as individual corporations with their own managements. But that's not all. In the final stage, there are public offerings of stock in the new LTV subsidiary corporation; LTV sells 20% to 30% of their shares to the public and keeps the remaining 70% to*

> 80%. LTV capitalizes on the willingness of investors to value a company's common stock at a price higher than its "book value," or net worth after subtracting liabilities and the cost of redeeming preferential stock from assets. *The difference represents a kind of profit for LTV—a profit it uses to help repay the money borrowed to get control of the subsidiaries in the first place. . . . Such increases magnify the assets of LTV, which keeps a majority stock interest in the subsidiaries, and the increases provide more collateral for loans—so that LTV can borrow still more money to purchase control of still more companies.*[2] (Emphasis added.)

Fruhan (1972, pages 1 and 2) described LTV's typical targets this way:

> *The companies selected by LTV as acquisition targets generally had (a) low price-to-earnings ratios, (b) substantial unused borrowing capacity, and (c) one or more easily separable operating divisions which competed in industries characterized by relatively higher price-to-earnings ratios. . . . The goal of a complete transaction cycle was to leave LTV with a large ownership fraction of some highly leveraged subsidiary companies at no (or very little) cost to LTV. At the conclusion of each transaction, LTV would have the use of an increased reserve of borrowing power generated by its growing portfolio of marketable securities of subsidiary companies. LTV's increased borrowing power could then be used to finance the acquisition of additional and generally larger companies.*

LTV's earnings per share, revenues, and assets grew spectacularly under this program until 1969, when the firm tendered for Jones & Laughlin Steel. In that year, the Antitrust Division of the U.S. Justice Department obtained a restraining order preventing LTV from consolidating/breaking up/spinning off Jones & Laughlin. Theorizing that the conglomerate form of organization represented a new antitrust threat that required regulation and seeking a court opinion consistent with this view, the Antitrust Division chose to sue the most aggressive conglomerateur, LTV. The antitrust suit was like a cannon shot across the bow of all conglomerates, and helped signal the end of the conglomeration movement, though arguably the movement had already peaked and would have been stymied by the recessions of 1970 and 1974 whether or not the Justice Department had intervened.

Unfortunately for LTV, the injunction left the firm in the middle of its transaction cycle, with no hope of immediate consummation. The courts took three years to resolve the case (LTV lost), during which time Jones & Laughlin required large cash infusions from LTV to carry it through the trough of the recession of 1970. In the resulting financial distress, creditors assumed control of LTV, declared the acquisition program at an end, began to sell assets, and fired James Ling.

U.S. Office Products

In 1994, Jonathan Ledecky began what is popularly called an "industry roll-up" in the office supply business, a consolidation of firms in what was a previously fragmented industry. This well-known acquisition strategy has been pursued in industries as disparate as garbage disposal (Waste Management and Browning-Ferris), hospitals (Hospital Corporation of America), funeral homes (Loewen and Service Corporation of America), as well as medical and dental practices, temporary help agencies, and health insurance plans.

The industry that sold office supplies to businesses and households through retail outlets had been highly fragmented. Typically, a few privately owned firms serviced each local market, each having one or two stores. While these small retailers enjoyed a loyal customer base, their size prevented them from exploiting economies of scale in purchasing, advertising, inventory management, and employee costs. In the 1980s, chains of megastores (Office Depot and Staples) penetrated the major urban markets in the United States, and began to threaten the retailers in smaller cities. This industry turbulence helped to stimulate consolidation.

Ledecky offered retailers a solution to two problems: the rising risks of being a small competitor against the megastore chains, and the illiquidity of ownership of a private business. In every acquisition he undertook, local management remained in place. New information systems were installed at the target firm, and advertising and supply contracts were consolidated with the parent for greater purchasing power. Ledecky believed that by improving margins of the target operations he could realize rapid earnings growth in what was a mature industry growing at a nominal rate of about 5 percent per year.

Beginning in 1993, Ledecky undertook a program of acquisition in which the deal volume and annual value acquired grew exponentially. Most of the deals were stock-for-stock acquisitions, accounted for on a pooling-of-interests basis. In 1995, the firm went public in an IPO giving its investors the benefits of a buoyant price/earnings multiple and liquid trading in their shares.

By early 1998, Ledecky had consummated more than 230 acquitions, and the revenues of U.S. Office Products (USOP) amounted to $3.6 billion, representing a spectacular compound growth rate from its founding four years earlier. Unfortunately, an agreement with some early investors required the firm to repurchase their shares in the company. At the time, accounting rules prohibited the use of pooling-of-interests accounting within 18 months of share repurchases. Accordingly, the firm had to restate its financial statements to reflect purchase accounting instead. This restatement lowered the firm's earnings growth trend. At about the same time, Ledecky announced that he would leave U.S. Office Products to start all over again with a new roll-up in a different industry. Within a year of going public in 1995, U.S. Office Products' price had increased two and a half times; but by year-end 1998 it was at a quarter of the IPO price. A class-action lawsuit claimed that Ledecky had deceived investors in public statements and in the design of the most recent deals (i.e., by consummating pooling transactions when he anticipated that USOP would have to repurchase shares anyway). Ledecky vigorously denied the claim.

Tyco International, Ltd.

On January 22, 2002, Dennis Kozlowski, CEO of Tyco International, Ltd., announced a radical restructuring plan for the firm that would break Tyco into four segments. The transaction would entail three spin-offs. Kozlowski argued that the firm would be worth 50 percent more after the restructuring: "Acquisitions have become far less important. The model for the future is far more for organic growth."[3]

Securities analysts were mystified by the announcement. Tyco had been the target of SEC accounting investigations—so far, these had turned up nothing. But a new spate of rumors had dogged the firm since late fall 2001. More importantly, the firm's strategy for 20 years had been to grow by acquisition. Exhibit 17.1 shows the pattern of Tyco's M&A activity by number and volume of deals. This had delivered steadily growing EPS and a buoyant stock price. An analyst was quoted as saying,

To me, it smells a little bit fishy. If you are a public company and people are pointing the finger at you, I wouldn't think your first reaction would be to split

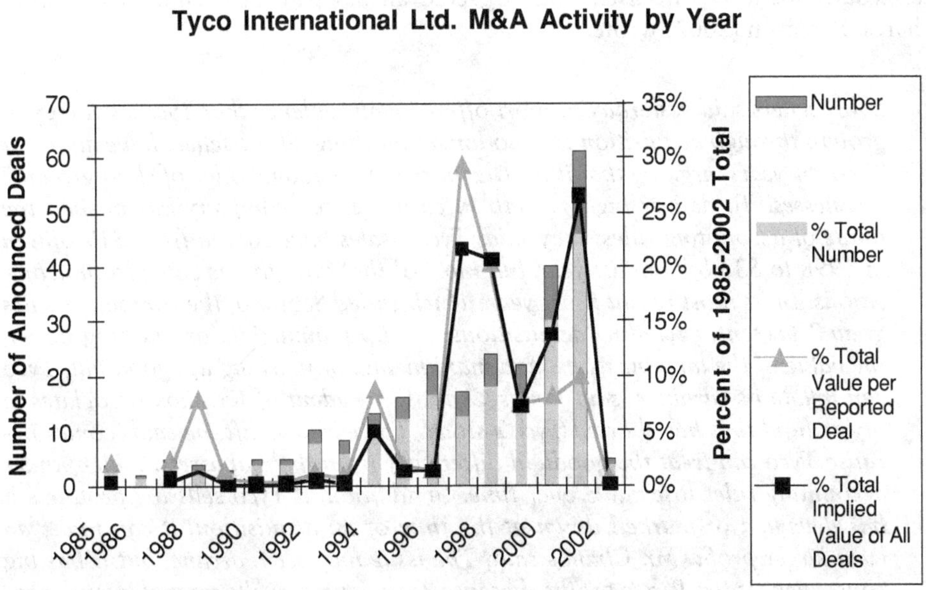

EXHIBIT 17.1 Tyco International Ltd. M&A Activity 1985–2002
Note: The displayed variables are defined as follows:
Number is the number of announced M&A transactions reported in the Thomson Financial SDC Platinum database for Tyco International each year. It has been reported that Tyco did not report numerous transactions. If it can be assumed that Tyco's unreported volume of deals followed a similar distribution over time, then this series is useful mainly as an indicator of the total activity.
% Total Number is the number of announced deals each year as a percentage of the total number of Tyco deals over 1985–2002, 226 deals.
% Total Value per Reported Deal is the dollar value of reported deals each year, divided by the total value of reported deals, 1985–2002.
% Total Implied Value of All Deals is the product of the number of deals each year times the average value of reported deals each year divided by the total for all years. The value of all deals each year is implied rather than actual and is meaningful if the actual value per reported deal each year is a reasonable proxy for the actual value per unreported deal each year.
Source of data: Thomson Financial SDC Platinum M&A database.

up and make things confusing for investors. Here is a clear effort to break up one company and make it a more complicated company. . . . Their goal is to show revenue and earnings momentum. . . . *The first quarter had a questionable earnings outlook going forward. They use it [stock] as a currency to make acquisitions, so the timing [of the split] is certainly questionable.*[4] (Emphasis added.)

Other observers speculated that Tyco's profitability was declining and would create problems in trying to service its huge debt load, built up during its acquisition program. The sale of stakes in operating units would generate about $8 billion in cash to service and pay down some of the debt.

Just a week earlier, Tyco had announced that its earnings for the current quarter would not meet forecasts. This triggered an 8.5 percent decline in the firm's shares. Berenson (2002) wrote:

Short sellers said yesterday's report offered new evidence that Tyco's strategy of growth through acquisition was no longer working. Short sellers have aimed at Tyco for years, arguing that it is little more than a hodgepodge of slow-growing businesses. To deliver high growth in earnings, the company has pushed the limits of accounting rules, they said. Tyco's sales have soared from $19 billion in 1998 to $36 billion last year, but most of that growth has come from acquisitions. In its most recent fiscal year, which ended Sept. 30, the company's sales grew 3 percent, excluding acquisitions. . . . By minimizing, or marking down, the value of the tangible assets and maximizing, or marking up, goodwill, Tyco can inflate its earnings, said James Chanos, president of Kynikos Associates, a hedge fund that has shorted Tyco's stock. The earnings lift, he said, comes because Tyco can treat the goodwill differently from the real assets, which under accounting rules lose value over time. In addition, if Tyco sells the products it has devalued or marked down at the time of an acquisition, it can make an even larger profit, Mr. Chanos said. The issue may seem arcane, but it has big consequences for Tyco's profits, because Tyco generally allocates almost the entire price of an acquisition to goodwill, Mr. Chanos said. Over the last three years, Tyco has spent about $30 billion on acquisitions and created the same amount of goodwill.

The spin-off announcement triggered a sell-off in the firm's shares, sending the price to $18 from $43, where it had been just before the announcement. But this was only the beginning of a dramatic unraveling of a strategy of growth by acquisition. The highlights of the slide included these:

- February 2002: Tyco revealed that it had not disclosed 700 acquisitions over the past three years, worth about $8 billion. The company argued that individually, these deals were immaterial and unworthy of disclosure.[5]
- July 2002: Kozlowski and CFO Mark Swartz were fired. Edward Breen was hired as the new CEO.

- September 2002: Kozlowski and Swartz were indicted on grounds that they looted $170 million from Tyco in unauthorized compensation and $430 million in fraudulent stock sales. The two executives claimed innocence.
- December 2002: Tyco released a report of the results of an internal investigation that revealed that the company had systematically managed its accounting to inflate earnings. Specifically cited were tapping reserves to cover unrelated expenses, and booking current charges as long-term expenses. The aggressive creation of reserves by Tyco's targets before acquisition was also cited as a means of inflating Tyco's postacquisition performance. The investigation, led by David Boies, found no "systemic or significant fraud" and that the practice had been to bend rather than break the accounting rules. The investigators acknowledged that they did not study all transactions and might have missed something.
- Spring 2003: CEO Breen continued to investigate. Tyco announced that it would take charges against earnings to cover more accounting problems. The write-offs for accounting-related problems accumulated to $2.3 billion. The investment community seethed at the apparent inability of Tyco to put its problems behind it. Of particular concern was the overhang of goodwill on the firm's balance sheet. Maremont and Weil (2003) noted that as of March 31, 2003, Tyco's book value of equity was $25.39 billion and that its goodwill was $26.03 billion, "meaning the company's shareholder equity would be negative without the goodwill. Any substantial write-down in goodwill would send shareholder equity plunging, potentially putting Tyco in default" of a credit agreement; they quoted Professor Abraham Briloff as opining that Tyco's goodwill was "severely excessively overstated."

At the core of these acquisition-growth stories are a buoyant stock market that creates a high-priced acquisition currency and a *feedback effect* that together create perceived *momentum* in the financial performance of the firm. The feedback is illustrated in Exhibit 17.2. The observed rate of growth of EPS influences investors to value the firm more highly—this increases the price/earnings multiple. The firm issues new (higher-priced) shares in an acquisition. If the acquisition is accretive, the EPS grows further, and the cycle continues. The exhibit is a simple representation of the feedback effect as a driver of momentum.

In addition to feedback, the four stories offer some other themes: low organic rate of growth offset by rapid growth from acquisition, earnings management, unexpected trouble, a rapid fall in reported financial performance and stock price, and a change in management. Momentum acquiring rarely ends with a gradual adjustment of investor expectations; the outcome is generally sudden and painful to investors.

MOMENTUM ACQUISITION STRATEGIES

Creating unexpected growth is the foundation for the momentum cycle. Momentum strategies can focus on a variety of targets for momentum growth. Two targets stand out with the most frequency: *EPS momentum* and *revenue momentum.*

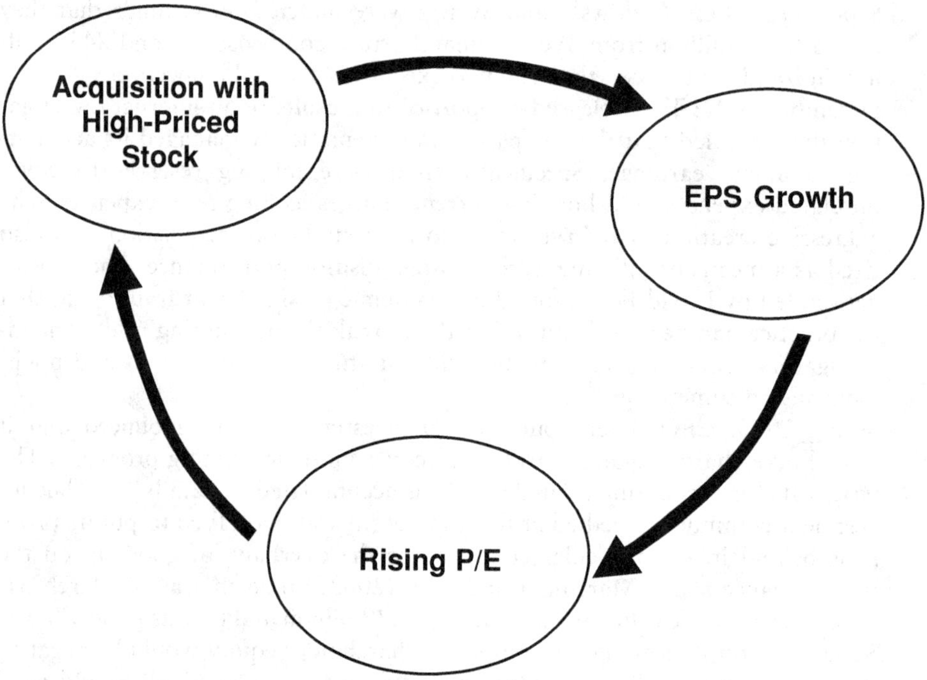

EXHIBIT 17.2 Feedback Effect in Momentum Acquiring

EPS Momentum

Earnings per share (EPS) growth is the focus of momentum acquirers, who believe that stock prices are driven by changes in EPS and that therefore steady and aggressive growth in EPS will result in high stock prices (and high P/E multiples). In the context of an acquisition program, EPS can be managed through the design of deals in ways that avoid EPS dilution. The avoidance of dilution motivates a focus on buying target firms that have lower P/E ratios than the buyer firm. Dilution could also be avoided or reduced through earnings management and aggressive accounting choices. Above all, negative earnings surprises are to be avoided in order not to impair the buyer's P/E ratio. The core implication of this approach for senior management is the need to establish, and continually justify, the acquirer's high P/E multiple. Rather than give fundamental information to investors to justify the firm's share value, the momentum acquirer sends signals about the firm's value through the path of EPS growth.

Revenue Momentum

In some industries, the momentum focus is on revenues instead of earnings per share. Firms in some industries, such as biotechnology, computing, and software, may be difficult to value using more traditional approaches, since their net earnings are depressed by large R&D expenses, new product introductions, and other temporary costs associated with young firms or firms with a large portfolio of new products. A significant portion of the market value of these firms derives from their *growth options*, which are ordinarily quite difficult to value using standard techniques such as discounted cash flow. In these instances, some analysts advocate using revenue multiples as a basis for valuing the firm. Perceiving this, managers of these firms may focus on acquisition strategies that lift the firm's revenues and create momentum. They view building revenue momentum with the assistance of an acquisition program as a logical supplement to internal growth efforts.

ARGUMENTS FOR AND AGAINST MOMENTUM ACQUIRING

The chief claim in favor of momentum acquiring is that stock market investors appear to value it. First, firms with momentum seem to enjoy higher *valuation multiples* than firms without. But what is the chain of causation? Does momentum create high multiples, or do high multiples stimulate momentum acquiring? The four stories earlier in the chapter associate momentum with a buoyant, or overvalued, stock market. Chapters 3 and 20 argue that "hot" markets stimulate very different behavior compared to "cold" markets. The mere association of momentum and high valuations is not enough to persuade one of causality.

One argument in favor of causation is the appearance of *momentum investors*. The 1990s saw the emergence of professional money managers who invested on the basis of earnings or share price momentum. These investors were the financial analogue to sports fans who believe that athletes can have a "hot hand" or a winning streak that is sustainable over some period. Richard H. Dreihaus, the founder of Dreihaus Capital Management, was regarded to be one of the leaders of the momentum investing approach. He described this style in these terms:

> *We are looking for earnings growth, earnings acceleration. After all, momentum investing is an acknowledgment that things in motion tend to stay in motion. We say that the most successful companies are those which have been able to demonstrate strong, sustained earnings growth. We look for many different variations of earnings growth. We look for accelerating sales and earnings. We look for positive earnings surprises. We look for sharp upward earnings revisions. And finally, we look for a company that is showing very strong, consistent, sustained earnings growth.*[6]

Scott Sterling Johnson, another institutional investor with the momentum style, focused on the *S curve*:

> *I want to be in the sweet spot of the "S curve," which is the point of maximum rate-of-change, acceleration, momentum. I want to own companies that are undergoing the greatest upward rate of change in earnings, sales, discovery, ownership change, brokerage sponsorship, and relative price strength. There are five things I specifically look for . . . dramatically accelerating earnings . . . strong balance sheet . . . strong relative price strength . . . industries that are doing well . . . low institutional ownership . . . dynamic trends. We concentrate on finding the small company before it's been discovered. I know that some small-cap managers keep their winners going even as they grow to large-caps. We sell them when they get too large. Why? Because as I said before, we want*

to be in the sweet spot of the "S curve"—the discovery, the momentum, the period of biggest change.[7]

The existence of momentum-style investment managers is not persuasive evidence that investors especially value momentum. Thousands of investment management companies, hedge funds, and specialty boutiques exist to invest on the basis of unusual themes or strategies, but the vast bulk of them fail to beat benchmark returns with any consistency. A profitable momentum strategy is inconsistent with the existence of rational investors and an efficient market. Any success from momentum investing is just as plausibly due to luck, or the possibility that the momentum style inadvertently exploits investment drivers that *do* matter, or the ability to find a temporary anomaly in the stock market—but none of these proves that investors will pay a premium for momentum. The burden of proof is on momentum investors to show that momentum pays.

Evidence That Momentum-Investing Strategies Are Not Superior

Research suggests that momentum-style investing pays no better than other investing strategies, and may pay worse. The test is whether the strategy of buying stocks with winning momentum and selling with losing momentum earns positive "alpha" returns (i.e., returns in excess of a suitable benchmark). Like other investing strategies, momentum-style investing *may* generate a small positive alpha that turns negative when one considers taxes and transaction costs.[8] And the precosts positive alpha return from momentum investing is almost entirely explained by *industry momentum* rather than firm momentum[9]; this finding is consistent with the industry shocks hypothesis discussed in Chapter 4: Perhaps it isn't momentum that investors value, but rather the occurrence of positive developments that affect an entire industry. If true, then CEOs should be less concerned with creating earnings momentum through acquisition and more concerned about creating real economic value by responding appropriately to industry shocks.

Momentum Is Unsustainable Indefinitely

It is difficult to find an episode of momentum acquisition that did not end in some or all of the following: sharp loss in stock price, dashed expectations among investors and securities analysts, bankruptcy or financial distress, and sacked managers. All of this is virtually inevitable. Producing a steady rate of growth through a program of acquisitions is ultimately unsustainable, for at least three reasons.

1. ***The annual volume must get bigger.*** A fixed percentage growth target each year dictates that the acquisition volume must grow from year to year. A growing acquisition program becomes more challenging to implement and probably stimulates the search for bigger targets, both of which expose the firm to more risk.
2. ***The world is finite.*** *Any* acquisition growth target in excess of the rate of real growth plus inflation, if extended long enough, will result in the momentum acquirer owning the entire world economy.

3. ***Stuff happens.*** Unblinking expectations of steady growth fail to account for possible adversities, such as the operational foul-ups that ultimately plagued "Automatic" Sprinkler, the antitrust suit against LTV, the shot-in-the-foot share repurchase by U.S. Office Products, or the SEC investigations and restructuring proposal at Tyco.

Against factors like these, it seems inevitable that the momentum acquirer will be thrown from the game, like a player in musical chairs. In theory a soft landing is possible, though eventually investors settle up with momentum managers.

Specifically regarding M&A, studies by Rosen (2002) and Ang and Cheng (2003) give evidence consistent with the unsustainability of momentum benefits. Rosen found some evidence of merger momentum; buyer's share prices showed larger increases at deal announcements when the market for mergers was hot or if the general equity market was buoyant. But these increases were not permanent: Over the long run, buyer returns were *worse* for deals announced in hot markets. Ang and Cheng found that acquirers tend to be more overvalued than their targets. As overvaluation increases, it is more likely that a firm will acquire another firm, and that stock-paying buyers are more overvalued than buyers in cash deals. But the benefits of this overvaluation are brief. The long-run returns following the overvalued stock deals are negative. As a target shareholder in these deals, it is best to bail out quickly from the buyer's stock. The unsustainability of momentum benefits is consistent with the information asymmetry theories discussed in Chapters 4 and 20. It seems that firms tend to acquire when they have an inflated currency with which to do so. Momentum helps to create the inflated currency.

Momentum Invites a Focus on Accounting Cosmetics Rather Than Economic Reality

Central to the momentum acquisition approach is the maintenance of a steady path of growth in EPS, revenues, or assets.[10] Because of the difficulties of maintaining the growth trajectory, the incentives increase to use *accounting cosmetics*. Chapter 16 described earnings management techniques that are permitted within generally accepted accounting principles but can be used to misrepresent the performance of the firm. The fixation on accounting dilution to EPS, rather than *economic reality*, can distort managers' M&A decision making.

Exhibit 17.3 presents an example of how *dilution/accretion* occurs. Suppose that a buyer and target agree to a stock-for-stock purchase acquisition. Before the deal, the buyer and target are equal in size of earnings, number of shares, price/earnings ratio, and EPS. Also suppose that the buyer feels justified in offering a 25 percent premium for the target (Line 9), equal to a bid of $31.25 (Line 8). Line 2 of this exhibit shows that net income of the buyer will increase by 95 percent, thanks to the acquisition. But the buyer's shares outstanding will increase by even more, 125 percent (see Line 3). The net result is a 13 percent decrease in EPS. *Shares outstanding increased faster than did earnings; this caused the dilution.* This relationship between shares, income, and dilution is fundamental to understanding the behavior of momentum acquirers.

A second important insight has to do with the price/earnings ratio embedded in the offer for the target, and the buyer's price/earnings ratio. This insight is illustrated

EXHIBIT 17.3 Example of EPS Dilution and Accretion

	Before		After Share-for-Share Acquisition	
	Buyer	Target	Newco	% Change
Financial Data of Merging Firms				
1 Purchase-related charges 5%			(50)	
2 Net income	$1,000	$1,000	$1,950	95%
3 Number of shares	1,000	1,000	2,250	125%
4 Earnings per share (EPS)	$ 1.00	$ 1.00	$ 0.87	−13%
5 Current stock price	$25.00	$25.00		
6 Price/earnings ratio	25.00	25.00		
7 Ratio of earnings of target to buyer		1.00		
Terms of Share-for-Share Offer				
8 Dollar value of bid			$ 31.25	
9 Premium over target's prebid price			25%	
10 Ratio of P/E paid to P/E of buyer			1.25	
Dilution to the Buyer Resulting from the Deal				
11 Dollar accretion (dilution) in buyer EPS			$ (0.13)	
12 Percentage accretion (dilution)			−13%	

Source: Author's analysis.

through a sensitivity analysis of the example in Exhibit 17.3. Exhibit 17.4 gives a sensitivity analysis of the dilution/accretion percentage with variations in the relative P/E ratio of the bid and buyer (Line 10), along with the relative size of earnings of the target to the buyer (Line 7). Momentum acquirers will be highly sensitive to the factors that drive EPS dilution:

- ***Growth in earnings and shares.*** Generally, dilution occurs where the buyer's shares grow faster than the buyer's earnings as a result of acquisition. Momentum buyers will aim to give away no more shares (in percent) than the growth rate in earnings due to acquisition of the target.
- ***Relative size of P/E ratios.*** The P/E ratio also has an influence. Generally when the P/E ratio of the acquisition exceeds the buyer's P/E ratio, dilution is amplified. Momentum buyers will tend to seek out targets who will accept relatively lower P/E bids—this may explain why momentum acquirers seek to acquire mature firms.
- ***Size of target relative to size of bidder.*** Bigger targets amplify the effect of dilution or accretion.

Dilution matters only if there is a *feedback effect*: Lynch (1970) and Reinhardt (1972) described this in their critiques of the conglomeration wave of the 1960s. Appendix 17.1 gives an analytic exposition of EPS dilution in acquisitions, based on the work of Reinhardt (1972).

EXHIBIT 17.4 Sensitivity Analysis of EPS Dilution by Variations in Relative Size of Earnings and Relative Size of Acquisition P/E to Buyer's P/E

Ratio of Offered P/E to P/E of Buyer	Stock-for-Stock Deal Relative Size (Earnings of Target/Buyer)					
	0.50	0.75	1.00	1.25	1.50	1.75
0.05	41%	64%	86%	107%	128%	148%
0.25	29%	43%	56%	68%	78%	88%
0.50	16%	24%	30%	35%	40%	44%
0.75	5%	9%	11%	14%	15%	17%
1.00	–3%	–3%	–3%	–2%	–2%	–2%
1.25	–11%	–12%	–13%	–14%	–15%	–15%
1.50	–17%	–20%	–22%	–23%	–25%	–26%
1.75	–23%	–26%	–29%	–31%	–32%	–34%
2.00	–28%	–32%	–35%	–37%	–39%	–40%

Note: Shading indicates result found in the base case example.

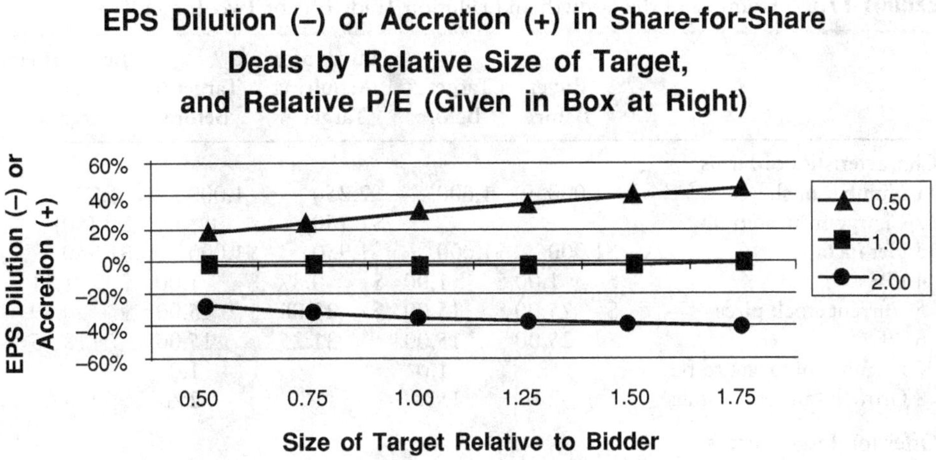

Source: Author's analysis.

Momentum Strategies Can Promote Uneconomic Deals and Reject Good Ones

The most serious criticism of momentum acquiring is that it offers a flawed benchmark for evaluating the desirability of acquisition opportunities. For instance, the momentum acquirer would say that the decision criterion is simple: Accept all deals that build momentum, and reject deals that diminish momentum. It is relatively straightforward to show that this rule can hurt the firm and its shareholders. Consider the example in Exhibit 17.5. The acquirer contemplates a mutually exclusive choice between two targets that are alike in terms of number of shares (Line 1), net income (Line 3), EPS (Line 4), current stock price (Line 5), and price/earnings ratio (Line 6). They differ in two important respects: expected growth of EPS (Line 8) and the P/E multiple at which they would have to be acquired (Line 6; see the shaded areas of Exhibit 17.5). Target A offers high growth (15 percent) and a very high acquisition multiple, 31.25. Because the target's takeover multiple is higher than the buyer's P/E, the deal is *dilutive* to the buyer's EPS (–13 percent). Target B offers low growth (2 percent), and an acquisition multiple that is relatively low, 18.75—because this multiple is below the buyer's multiple, the deal with Target B is *accretive* (+11 percent).

The trade-off facing the buyer is stark: Accept the pain of dilution today in return for faster growth in the future, or accept the pleasure of accretion today in return for slower growth in the future. Exhibit 17.6 shows that in about four years, Target A will yield the higher EPS.

Under some simplifying assumptions, one can show that Target A yields the highest value creation for the buyer firm today. Yet the momentum acquirer's rule would reject this alternative. Surely momentum acquiring is fundamentally flawed if it rejects economically attractive transactions.

EXHIBIT 17.5 Example of the Growth and Dilution Trade-offs of Two Target Firms

	Buyer Before	Target A Before	Buyer after Acquiring Target A	Target B Before	Buyer after Acquiring Target B
Characteristics of Firms					
1 Number of shares	1,000	1,000	2,250	1,000	1,750
2 Charge from step-up			$ (50)		$ (50)
3 Net income	$1,000	$1,000	$1,950	$1,000	$1,950
4 EPS	$ 1.00	$ 1.00	$ 0.87	$ 1.00	$ 1.11
5 Current stock pirce	$ 25.00	$ 15.00	$ 27.08	$ 15.00	$ 20.89
6 P/E	25.00	15.00	31.25	15.00	18.75
7 Earnings of target to buyer		1.0		1.0	
8 Growth rate of earnings	7%	15%	11%	2%	5%
Offer for Target Shares					
9 Aggregate			$ 31.25		$ 18.75
10 Premium			108%		25%
11 Ratio of P/E paid to P/E of buyer			1.25		0.75
Resulting Accretion (Dilution)					
12 Dollar accretion (dilution) in buyer EPS			$ (0.13)		$ 0.11
13 Percentage accretion (dilution)			–13%		11%

Note: Line 2, "Charge from step-up," reflects the added depreciation expense charged to earnings from a step-up in the book value of the target's assets following the purchase.
Source: Author's analysis.

EXHIBIT 17.6 EPS Trajectories of the Buyer Alone with Two Target Firms: Firm A Offers Accretive EPS and Slow Growth; Firm B Offers Dilutive EPS and High Growth

	At Closing	Years from Closing										Compound Average
	0	1	2	3	4	5	6	7	8	9	10	Growth Rate
Buyer alone	$1.00	$1.07	$1.14	$1.23	$1.31	$1.40	$1.50	$1.61	$1.72	$1.84	$1.97	7.0%
Buyer with Target A	$0.87	$0.96	$1.07	$1.19	$1.32	$1.46	$1.62	$1.80	$2.00	$2.22	$2.46	11.0%
Buyer with Target B	$1.11	$1.16	$1.22	$1.27	$1.33	$1.39	$1.45	$1.52	$1.58	$1.66	$1.73	4.5%

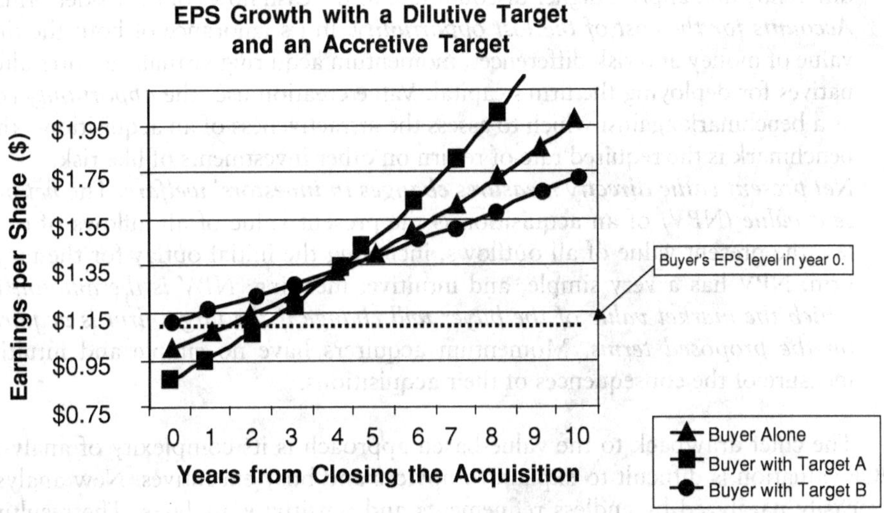

Source: Author's analysis.

VALUE CREATION IS THE BEST CRITERION FOR EVALUATING ACQUISITION STRATEGIES

The antidote to the vagaries of momentum acquiring is to base the acquisition strategy on *value creation*, rather than momentum. Value creation and its associated measure, discounted cash flow (DCF), respond to the defects of momentum discussed earlier and carry a number of strengths.

- *Focus on the longer-term future,* as opposed to just the present or the near-term future. Valuation analysis requires one to account for consequences to investors whenever they might occur in time.
- *Accounts for the time value of money.* It is exceptional for a momentum acquirer to discuss the present value of future performance. What appears to matter is the trajectory of growth, rather than today's value of that trajectory. The value creation criterion explicitly considers the present value of that trajectory.
- *Focus on economic reality: Cash is king.* Momentum acquiring focuses on the cosmetic results of acquisition, such as earnings per share (EPS). But what matters

to investors is the economic reality of a transaction, the cash flow consequences. The focus on EPS almost fatally ignores the investment in assets necessary to produce the EPS. The cash flow used in valuation analysis explicitly considers this investment.

- ***Focus on risk and return.*** The momentum acquirer ignores the risks incurred to produce the EPS growth. Assume two acquisition targets that are identical in all respects (especially their EPS trajectories) except for their risks: One firm operates toxic waste disposal sites that are threatened with lawsuits and closure by the government; the other firm simply holds a portfolio of U.S. government bonds. To the momentum acquirer, a dollar of EPS from one firm is as good as a dollar of EPS from another firm. The value-oriented approach would view these two firms quite differently and apply a higher discount rate to the cash flows of the riskier firm.
- ***Accounts for the cost of the lost opportunity.*** In its ignorance of both the time value of money and risk differences, momentum acquiring virtually ignores alternatives for deploying the firm's capital. Value creation uses the *opportunity cost* as a benchmark against which to assess the attractiveness of an acquisition—that benchmark is the required rate of return on other investments of like risk.
- ***Net present value directly measures changes in investors' welfare.*** The *net present value (NPV)* of an acquisition is the present value of all inflows of cash, less the present value of all outflows, including the initial outlay for the target firm. NPV has a very simple, and intuitive, meaning: *NPV is the amount by which the market value of the buyer will change if the target firm is acquired on the proposed terms.* Momentum acquirers have no simple and intuitive measure of the consequences of their acquisitions.

The chief drawback to the value-based approach is its complexity of analysis. DCF valuation is difficult to explain to novices and busy executives. New analysts are easily paralyzed by endless refinements and sensitivity analyses. The resulting values are themselves uncertain, and almost surely measured with error.

Though not perfect, value-based acquisition strategies have the ultimate virtue of weeding out bad deals more effectively than other approaches. In addition, the value approach highlights good deals more prominently. Regardless of the temporary robustness of momentum acquisition approaches, value creation better promotes the survival and prosperity of the firm.

CONCLUSION: MOMENTUM STRATEGIES VERSUS VALUE STRATEGIES

The key lesson of this discussion must be that momentum-acquiring is a dangerous path, for both corporate managers and their investors. It is a strategy premised on the mistaken belief that the *appearance* of growth matters more than economic reality. Some of the telltales of this strategy are a focus on EPS (or revenues), earnings management, the manipulation of goodwill and dilution, a relatively large number of acquisitions increasing in size over time, and an aggressive trajectory of performance. This chapter has argued that value creation is a superior foundation for acquisition planning. A summary comparison of the momentum and value approaches is given in Exhibit 17.7.

EXHIBIT 17.7 Comparison of Momentum Acquisition Strategy and Value-Oriented Strategy

	Momentum Acquiring Strategy	Value-Oriented Acquiring Strategy
Focus	Contribution to earnings or revenue momentum; size, reported financial results.	Price to acquire target versus its intrinsic value. Net present value of the acquisition.
Implicit assumptions	Reported results matter. Investors are driven by accounting reality: EPS is king.	Value matters to investors. Investors are driven by economic reality: Cash is king.
Approach	Estimate the target's contribution to earnings or revenue momentum. Avoid dilution and goodwill charges.	Estimate the intrinsic value of the target. Negotiate a price. Price ≠ value. Tell investors about value.
End game	Bubble bursts.	Value created.

APPENDIX 17.1
An Analytic Model of EPS Dilution

The economics of dilution in mergers was discussed by Uwe Reinhardt (1972). He showed that the extent of the initial dilution (or accretion) in earnings per share experienced by the buyer upon the acquisition of a target firm can be described by equation (1) and its more compact version, equation (2). Given these variables:

Y_i = Current earnings after taxes for firm i.
N_i = Number of shares outstanding for firm i.
E_i = Earnings per share for firm i.
P_i = Market price per share for firm i.
P/E_i = Price/earnings ratio for firm i.
G_i = Expected annual growth rate of earnings in the absence of a merger.
R_i = Exchange ratio, number of buyer shares issued for target shares.
ΔN = Number of newly issued buyer shares exchanged for target shares (i.e., $R \cdot N_B$).
A = Y_{Target}/Y_{Buyer} the ratio of the acquired company's total earnings to the total earnings of the buyer.
B = Ratio of the P/E ratio paid for the target company to the P/E ratio of the buyer.
D = Immediate percentage dilution or accretion in the EPS of buyer as a result of acquisition of target.

$$D = \frac{\dfrac{(Y_{Buyer} + Y_{Target})}{(N_{Buyer} + \Delta N_{Buyer})}}{\left(\dfrac{Y_{Buyer}}{N_{Buyer}}\right)} - 1 \qquad (1)$$

$$D = \frac{A(1-B)}{1+AB} \tag{2}$$

Reinhardt concluded from an examination of these equations that:

> *D will be negative whenever B is greater than 1, or whenever AB is greater than A. [These equations] therefore lead to the following more intuitively appealing rule: In a stock-for-stock transaction, the acquiring company will suffer immediate dilution in its earnings per share whenever the P/E ratio paid for the acquired earnings exceeds the P/E ratio implicit in the market price of the acquirer's own stock.*
>
> *An alternative statement of this rule is that: in a stock-for-stock transaction, the acquiring company will suffer immediate dilution in its earnings per share whenever the merger causes the acquirer to increase the number of its shares outstanding by a greater percentage than are the acquired earnings as a percentage of the premerger earnings.*[11]

NOTES

1. This account is based substantially on Rukeyser (1969), one of the classics in the practitioner literature on mergers and acquisitions.
2. James C. Tanner, "LTV Keeps Expanding on Borrowed Money, Stock Price Increases," *Wall Street Journal*, August 18, 1967, page A1.
3. Quoted in Sorkin (2002).
4. A quotation of Ron Taylor, Schaeffer Investments in Cincinnati, in Fakler (2002).
5. Reported in Moore (2002).
6. Quoted in Tanous (1999), page 58.
7. Quoted in Tanous (1999), pages 155–160.
8. See, for instance, Lesmond, Schill, and Zhou (2002).
9. See Moskowitz and Grinblatt (1999).
10. The discussion in this section and the next draws a number of expository points from the classic discussion by Reinhardt (1972).
11. Reinhardt (1972), page 20.

PART Four

Design of Detailed Transaction Terms

CHAPTER 18

An Introduction to Deal Design in M&A

You name the price. I'll name the terms. (And I'll do better than you every time.)

—Old Saying

INTRODUCTION

As the old saying suggests, designing a deal is more than setting a price. The aim of this chapter is to describe a way to think about optimizing across the various terms in a deal. Designing a deal is more like fixing a complicated meal: One strives for a good blend of ingredients and a balanced delivery. This chapter presumes that one's research and analysis are complete and that one is ready to prepare for bargaining or bidding. Here we address the crucial linkage between analysis and action. This is a challenging topic because, as most experienced M&A practitioners will say, this is an area of tacit knowledge.[1] Very little has been written about M&A deal design; it is a subject typically learned by the apprentice at the elbow of the master.

While virtually all of the chapters in this book lend insights about deal design, Chapters 18 to 24 present the core discussion. This chapter offers a conceptual foundation for the later chapters and emphasizes some key foundational ideas:

- Deal design is in part an engineering problem, optimizing across objectives and constraints. Be clear on your priorities: Price is not the only dimension of a deal. You may find several attractive deal structures that meet your goals—in this sense, there may be no single best deal (but there may be many bad ones).
- Deal design is in part a bargaining problem, seeking the structure that satisfies both sides. Look for *trade-offs* among the many dimensions of a deal. Manage the feedback process carefully.
- Think of a deal as a system where each component interacts with the others—this is the *"whole deal" view.* If you change one dimension of a deal, watch out for ripple effects to other dimensions. Because a *deal is a system*, practice multi-issue bargaining (dealing with a bundle of dimensions simultaneously) rather than single-issue bargaining (dealing with issues serially).

DEAL STRUCTURES ARE SOLUTIONS TO ECONOMIC PROBLEMS

The point of departure must be to consider how deal structures arise. One possibility is that they arise from random forces, or the caprice of decision makers. This is the "stuff happens" view of deal design. This first view is like a null hypothesis in science; it says that nothing explains the structure of deals. If true, this would be a short chapter.

The alternative view about deal structures is that they can be viewed as solutions to an economic problem existing between two or more players. This view is consistent with the pathbreaking writing of Ronald Coase (1937) and Michael Jensen and William Meckling (1976), who argued that contracts can be regarded as bridges over potential market failures arising from risk, moral hazard, and so on. The important implication of this view is that if you can perceive the problem, then you can understand the solution and design the deal terms.

Deal structures are a financial engineering response to a problem: one aims to optimize one or more key objectives subject to constraints. Designing specific terms is the means of accomplishing this. In theory, the optimal deal could be found using mathematical modeling.[2] In practice, the analytic work in M&A amounts to searching, by trial and error,[3] through different potential deal structures for one that seems to meet the decision maker's objectives. In practice, there may be many feasible solutions to an economic problem. As I have argued elsewhere in this book, there are no "right" deals, but there are lots of wrong ones. William Sahlman (1989) calls this the "contractual impossibility theorem," which says there exists no perfect deal that dominates all others.

Viewing deal terms as solutions to economic problems, gives the foundation for a means of studying deal drivers. The following sections will use it to survey the classic dimensions of the deal design problem, the terms or tools at the designer's disposal, and the implications of this point of view for how the deal design process is managed.

POSSIBLE DESIRABLES IN DESIGNING A DEAL

Price is a necessary but not sufficient basis for a deal. Other "*desirables*" matter, too. Chapter 1 highlights a number of outcomes, the achievement of which conduct and structure affect. In this chapter we must revisit these outcomes because one must optimize across a range of goals and within a series of constraints. The classic objectives of M&A deal design include these:

- ***Create value.*** Good transactions create value. The classic sources of value creation are synergies, discussed in Chapter 11. Also, value may be created for some parties at the expense of others—this is a *value transfer*. The objective of careful analysis should be to avoid *value destruction*. The consequences of persistently destroying value are higher capital costs, declining access to capital, and ultimately, hostile raids on the firm. Decision makers know that estimates of value are uncertain. Therefore, the analyst must aim to identify the sources of value creation, transfer, or destruction as a foundation for effective negotiation and, later, management after the deal is struck.

- ***Improve reported financial results; avoid EPS dilution.*** Managers seek to avoid dilution, though they are often confused about its meaning or effect. In its most common usage, "dilution" refers to a reduction in reported earnings per share following an equity issuance or stock-for-stock acquisition; this is *accounting dilution*, a change in reported results (without necessarily a reduction in economic value). Accounting dilution arises because target shareholders are often paid proportionally more than the target's contribution to the earnings of the combined firm. *Economic dilution* is quite simply a reduction in shareholder wealth. *Voting dilution* is a reduction in voting power (i.e., the percentage of total votes held by the investor). The point of distinguishing among these is to suggest that the three dilutions do not necessarily move together. The opposite of dilution is *accretion*.
- ***Improve control; avoid voting dilution.*** Decision makers are highly sensitive to the ways in which deals can limit their actions. The classic focus is voting control by common shareholders. But lenders and preferred stockholders can impose limits on managerial action (e.g., through loan covenants). Managers, of course, can fight back with instruments such as antitakeover provisions (e.g., poison pills), changes in bylaws (which are the rules by which shareholders vote), and lawsuits. As Chapter 15 discussed, *control is valuable.* One can think of control as an option on the strategy of the firm.
- ***Build financial flexibility.*** Managers seek to enhance flexibility and minimize its reduction. Acquisitions have financial side effects. Cash deals draw down the cash balance of the acquirer and/or require the issuance of debt or equity securities. Stock-for-stock deals explicitly entail equity issuance. Some complex deals may entail the issuance of mezzanine securities. The implication is that the acquisition may affect the firm's *future* ability to raise financing simply because of the way the deal was financed. Most senior executives wish to preserve the firm's financial flexibility. Financial flexibility is like a call option on future financing; when the firm has a lot of flexibility, the call option value can be substantial. Here we see an interaction between financial flexibility and value creation in a deal. The classic example of the destruction of financial flexibility is the leveraged buyout of Revco Drug Stores in 1986, outlined in Chapter 13. The firm was so highly levered and so dependent on asset sales to meet financial commitments that it was unable to absorb the shock of a slow retail season in 1987. The firm went bankrupt 19 months after the closing.
- ***Manage risk.*** Mergers expose investors of both sides to the risk of adverse movements in security prices. Typically, M&A transactions take months between initial design and consummation. In the interim, capital markets can move adversely. For instance, in a stock-for-stock transaction, share prices of the two firms could move well beyond the levels that prevailed at the initial discussion—usually if the prices move in tandem, the exchange ratio could remain justifiable. But the worst case is if prices of the target and acquirer move in opposite directions. A similar risk may affect debt securities. If the two parties span international borders, currency fluctuations may pose a risk to the transaction. The topic of risk management is explored more extensively in Chapter 23.

- ***Preserve and improve competitive standing.*** Chapter 6 outlines strategic considerations that can motivate a deal. Reaching strategic objectives will be a key aim. This may entail designing the transaction in ways that retain good retail locations, customer relationships, assets, and talent—these can lay the foundation for strategic success.
- ***Manage signals to the capital markets.*** Chapter 4 summarizes research suggesting that some structures convey hints to investors about what insiders believe regarding the outlook for the firm. Specifically, issues of equity are associated with significant declines in share prices. One interpretation is that share-for-share structures signal that buyers believe their firm to be overvalued. Managers try to anticipate the reception of merger announcements in the marketplace, and frame those announcements to send the best signals about the firm's prospects.
- ***Manage incentives.*** Transactions create incentives for managers, both deliberately and inadvertently. The aim of careful deal doers is to keep and properly motivate employees who contain the best intellectual capital of the firm. The challenge is how to achieve this when negotiating with the managers (who may not represent the best intellectual capital) the terms of acquisition. The careful deal designer needs to ensure that the incentives created in a transaction are consistent with the overall culture of a company that the new management wishes to prevail, and with management's vision for the future.
- ***Enhance the governance and management structure.*** M&A could be a device for resolving thorny problems stemming from the composition of the shareholder group, board of directors, or management team. Acquiring new talent and putting in place new procedures and bylaws could help to resolve CEO succession problems, infuse new energy into a management team, and/or break deadlocks among the directors.
- ***Shape impact on employees and communities.*** Executives may wish to ensure the continuity of employment of target shareholders, protect pension assets, minimize the impact of plant closings or restructurings, and build employee morale. In other settings and situations, deal designers may want to shape the deal in ways that build motivation in a moribund organization or alert the outside community to deal more fairly with Newco than it had with the target.

One could extend this list further. The large implication of this list is that simply focusing on value (the main focus of many deal designers) could ignore other legitimate concerns of the decision maker. Instead, the deal designer needs to regard all of these objectives in arriving at a desirable outcome.

THE DESIGN OF TERMS CAN HELP ACHIEVE OBJECTIVES

The deal designer has a relatively broad range of building blocks or "terms" with which to promote and achieve objectives such as those outlined in the preceding section. These include:

VALUE TO BE DELIVERED (I.E., PRICE) This is the first among equals of any term sheet—but often it is negotiated near the end, after social issues have been resolved.

Chapters 9 through 15 discuss the valuation of firms that is necessary for setting a pricing strategy. Price is *the* blunt instrument of deal design; it can be used to achieve many objectives but usually does so gracelessly, expensively, and with more than a few side effects. One of the most important insights generated from academic research into negotiations in the past 40 years is that multi-issue bargaining generally leads to more successful outcomes than does single-issue bargaining. The lesson for merger deal designers is that it is useful to envision terms that go well beyond price.

FORM OF PAYMENT Many practitioners regard choosing the form of payment to be the real art in deal design. One can define form of payment in terms of the securities delivered. Chapter 20 summarizes data on the use of cash, stock, and other securities in transactions over time. The mix of cash and stock used in M&A varies over time. To gain greater insight into practice, it is useful to abandon the categories of cash, stock, and debt from a deal design standpoint, as these categories are arbitrary[4] and not very descriptive of the economic implication of the choices made. Of more use are descriptive names for different *payment choices, such as "fixed," "semifixed," "contingent," and "side."* These help illuminate the considerable richness of choice available to designers.

- *Fixed payments:* cash and senior debt securities. There is little uncertainty to the buyer or target about the value being conveyed in these payments. The use of these securities is aimed at *resolving uncertainty* about the transaction. These can be used to assure target investors about the value they will receive and the seriousness of the buyer's offer. Fixed payments can also have an adverse signaling effect: Their use could be interpreted as a lack of confidence by target shareholders in the buyer's future management of the enterprise (i.e., thus prompting them to demand fixed payments).
- *Contingent payments:* mezzanine or "junk" debt securities, preferred stock, and common stock. The value of these securities is simply less certain than cash or senior debt. While the common share price of a publicly listed buyer is known with certainty today, the price might change upon the announcement of the merger or upon the arrival of other news between now and the consummation of the deal. Common stock is not a fixed form of payment; at best, it is semifixed. Chapter 20 surveys research that finds a negative investor reaction to the announcement of share-for-share deals: The buyer's share price falls significantly. The short-term effects notwithstanding, semifixed forms of payment are used to permit target investors to participate in an optimistic future foreseen for the combined firm. Another reason for these semifixed payments is that they may be a response to financial constraints; perhaps the buyer does not have the cash or senior debt capacity to finance the acquisition. Earnouts, warrants, convertible bonds, contingent value rights, puts, guarantees, caps, collars, floors are almost always used to resolve strong disagreements about the value of the target firm. Usually, the target sees itself as more valuable than does the buyer. The contingent payment is structured such that if the target performs well in the future, the target shareholders will receive some extra payoff. Earnouts, warrants, and convertible bonds capitalize on the uncertainty about the future—as option

pricing theory suggests, the greater the uncertainty, the greater will be the estimated value of these securities. The other function of contingent payments is to hedge risk for one or both sides of the transaction. For instance, caps, collars, and floors can be used to limit the adverse effect of stock price changes between the announcement and consummation of a deal. Contingent value rights are, in effect, two- to three-year put options that protect target shareholders in the event of a slump in the combined firm's share price; they entail a contingent payment that makes the target shareholder "whole" in the event of adversity. Chapters 10, 14, 15, and 23 discuss in more detail the possible application of contingent forms of payment.

- *Side payments:* These are payments to parties other than the owners of the target firm, parties who may have some influence in the design and consummation of the transaction or in its success postmerger. Examples of side payments are golden parachutes, warrants, bonuses, buyouts of employment contracts, and consulting commitments to managers of the target firm. Unions might receive guarantees of work rules, jobs, and training. Municipalities and state governments might receive guarantees against plant closing or in favor of continued investment. National governments have been known to demand a "golden share" or veto over future strategic actions by the firm. Bank lenders[5] might be offered enhanced terms (such as a higher interest rate). Finally, outright bribes[6] would be classed as side payments. Too often, side payments are ignored as costs to the buyer. Chapter 24 argues that careful analysis of the economic attractiveness of a deal should account for these *social issues* as well as the usual direct payments to investors.

FINANCING How the transaction is financed affects Newco in numerous ways, particularly signaling to the capital markets, exploitation of debt tax shields, influencing default risk, and affecting the financial flexibility of the firm. Financing is intimately linked to choices about price and form of payment. Chapter 20 surveys the dimensions of financing choice.

TIMING AND DEADLINES Managers know that time is money. The speed of closing and creation of deadlines to action will affect the present value of cash flows to investors. Nowhere is the effect of timing more apparent than in the choice of *immediate versus deferred* payments. The use of immediate payments resolves uncertainty about the deal. The use of deferred payments may reflect the buyer's financial constraints. Acquisition might be full and immediate, or partial and staged over time. Deferring payment and investment essentially grants the payer an option to renege at some future date. This option will be more valuable the greater the uncertainty about the future value of the asset being acquired.

COMMITMENTS Deal structures often explicitly address the assumption of environmental liabilities, product liabilities, and potential liabilities arising from lawsuits in progress. The buyer may be asked to honor product warranties. Some deal structures commit the seller to maintain and hand over at closing brand names, patents, trademarks, customer lists, and other intangible assets that might affect the prosperity of the resulting firm. The transfer of tangible assets such as retail locations might also be addressed. And if the transaction is to cause knowledgeable executives to leave the firm, the transaction structure might include noncompete clauses. Warranties are commitments from either side to the other that certain conditions exist and that, if not true, reparations will be made. Commitments are nothing less than short positions in options—the more uncertain the parties to the transaction are, the more valuable will be the commitments.

CONTROL AND GOVERNANCE Agreements or their implementation can affect the distribution of voting power among the shareholders of the firm, as well as the degree of managerial discretion. Terms of the agreement can dictate the composition of Newco's board of directors, limit voting power (through standstill agreements), tighten or relax financial covenants, create fixed income securities with high demands on the firm's cash flow,[7] appoint operating executives,[8] and so on. These provisions resolve a class of economic problems known as "agency costs." An agency cost arises when the agent takes actions that are beneficial to the agent, but costly to the owner. By restructuring the board of directors, for instance, the shareholders may obtain better monitoring of the managers' actions and policies. Chapter 26 surveys voting control and governance issues in more detail.

RISK MANAGEMENT Buyers and sellers face risks that the transaction may not be consummated. Often, deal designers put in place special terms that mitigate these risks. One example is the deterioration in the buyer's share price (i.e., in a share-for-share exchange)—this risk can be mitigated through the use of a collar. Another source of transaction risk is the possible entry of a competing bidder—this can be minimized through lockup provisions, toehold equity positions, and "topping fees." A third category of risk is that of the fickle counterparty—that either side would walk away from the deal simply because it changed its mind. This third kind of risk could be mitigated by walk-away fees and guarantees to pay the counterparty's costs associated with the development of the aborted transaction. Chapter 23 discusses the assessment of transaction risk and its remedies.

ACCOUNTING CHOICES Chapter 16 argues that though accounting for M&A is based on rules and principles, managers retain some latitude of choice in presenting the financial results of the new firm. The accounting choices in a deal may affect efforts to create value and the firm's access to capital. Accounting choice is linked directly to choices about price, form of payment, and form of transaction.

FORM OF TRANSACTION AND TAX EXPOSURE TO THE PARTIES There are eight alternative forms of transaction, each bearing different implications for tax exposure, exposure to liabilities, control, and value creation. Chapter 19 discusses these in more detail. Choices about form of transaction will affect choices about price, form of payment, and accounting.

SOCIAL ISSUES Practitioners use this euphemism to refer to the interplay of titles, compensation, and ego in establishing the governance and managerial hierarchy of the new organization. Many merger agreements explicitly state the new positions that the CEOs of the combining firms will hold. Side agreements or understandings may state the salaries, perquisites, and responsibilities of these executives. Under this category would fall the composition of the board of directors of Newco and their compensation. Chapter 24 discusses social issues in more detail.

SOCIAL WELFARE AND COMMUNITY ISSUES Though rarely stated in the formal merger agreement, understandings may be created about plant or branch closings, employee layoffs, continuation of charitable contributions, headquarters locations, and the like. Sellers of privately held companies may be highly sensitive about the welfare of their former employees. Companies in certain countries may be subject to social welfare obligations as part of their corporate charters.

The list could be lengthened considerably. The core task of the deal designer is to choose terms that optimize across the entire range of desirables.

EACH DEAL IS A SYSTEM: THE "WHOLE DEAL" PERSPECTIVE

Exhibit 18.1 summarizes the substance of the preceding three sections: It lists possible deal goals (the desirables), the menu of possible terms, and the modes of assessment of those terms. Three very important insights (presented in this section and the next) change what would otherwise be a rather dry taxonomy of considerations into a living understanding of deal design.

The first of these is that *deal terms are linked to one another; in other words, the deal is a system.* The nature of this system is explored in this section. This is the

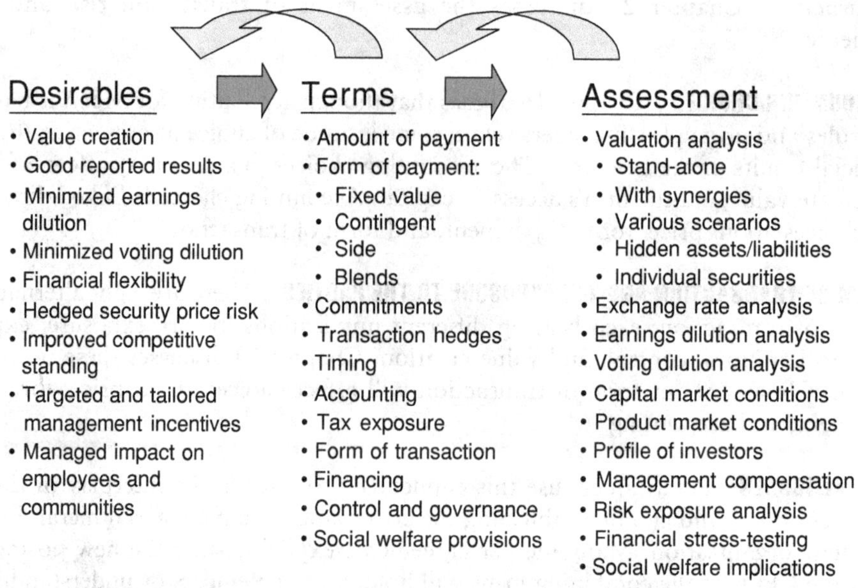

EXHIBIT 18.1 General Framework of Deal Design

"whole deal" perspective mentioned in Chapter 13. Viewing M&A deals this way yields numerous insights into the development and assessment of terms. These implications are summarized in the next section.

Exhibit 18.2 transforms the list of terms we have developed into an influence diagram that sketches the *linkages among terms* and the possible direction of influence. The diagram suggests at least nine ways in which deal terms interact:

1. ***Price, form of payment, accounting choices, form of transaction.*** Cash payment dictates that the deal will be taxable, which typically results in a higher price to compensate the seller for immediate tax payment. Price affects the amount of goodwill that must be recognized on the buyer's balance sheet.
2. ***Price, transaction risk hedging, form of payment.*** Payment in cash presents no transaction risk to the seller; payment in stock exposes the seller to transaction risk, which can be hedged through the use of a collar.
3. ***Form of payment, financing, timing.*** Cash payments tend to be quicker to finance and to pay. This is because cash can be raised through loans (bridge or permanent) from bankers. Payment in shares of stock often entails registration of those shares with the SEC, and possibly requires a vote of the shareholders to authorize those shares. Shareholder votes can require four to six months to obtain.
4. ***Financing, timing, form of transaction.*** Taxable cash deals require less time to close; nontaxable stock deals generally require more time.
5. ***Form of payment, control.*** Payment in cash or stock affects the resulting voting control of Newco in very different ways and exposes selling shareholders to differing tax expense.

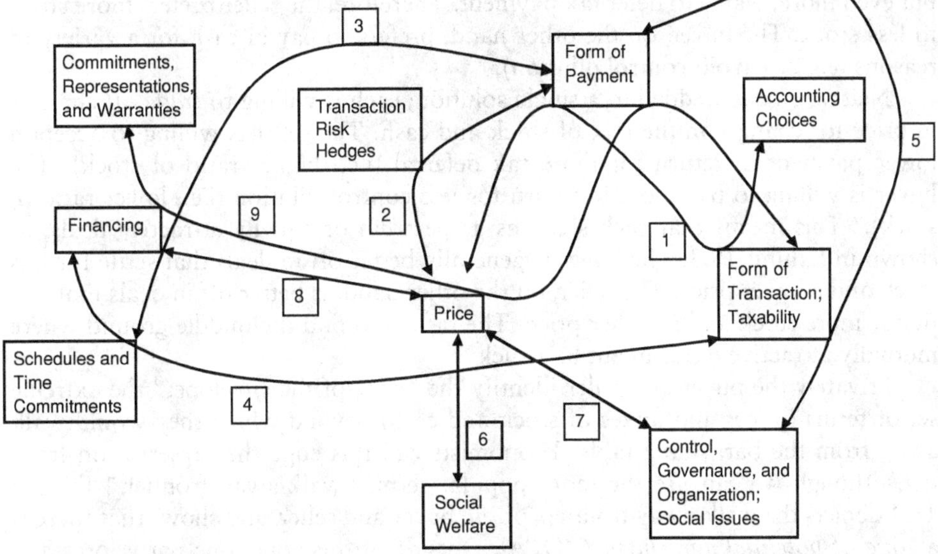

EXHIBIT 18.2 Some Linkages That Make M&A Deals a System

6. ***Price, social welfare.*** Social welfare commitments are costly and should be included in the buyer's valuation of the target and price.
7. ***Price, social issues.*** Social issues can be costly to settle and also may influence price. Control is valuable and therefore will influence the price the buyer might pay. Ordinarily, outright control of a firm commands a premium price. A weak minority interest might be purchased at a discount.
8. ***Financing, price.*** Financing influences price through the cost of capital.
9. ***Commitments, price, form of payment, form of transaction.*** Commitments to assume liabilities and/or representations and warranties are costly to the buyer and will influence the price the buyer will pay and the financing the buyer can obtain. Form of payment and transaction dictate the exposure to the target's known and hidden liabilities.

One could extend this list much further. The chief insight is that *terms of an M&A transaction cannot be set independently of each other.* They are linked and must be fashioned to optimize the entire bundle of terms. The "whole deal" perspective is to see these linkages and to understand how changes in one dimension can ripple through the system to affect the other dimensions.

SOME IMPLICATIONS FOR THE DEAL DESIGNER

Characterizing deal design as a problem of optimizing a system offers a number of important insights to the designer. To illustrate these, consider a simple deal design problem in which the buyer and seller must agree on just two dimensions: price and form of payment. On the issue of price, the seller wants more and the buyer wants less. Form of payment is simply the percentage mix of stock as a total package of stock and cash—the ratio varies from all stock (100 percent) to all cash (0 percent). On the issue of form of payment, the seller wants the liquidity that cash affords, but even more, wants to defer tax payment. Therefore, the seller prefers more stock to less stock. The buyer, on the other hand, prefers to pay in cash for a variety of reasons (e.g., to avoid control dilution).

Neither side is wedded to a single solution; each is willing to *trade off* changes in price for changes in the mix of stock and cash. The seller is willing to accept a lower payment in return for more tax deferral (i.e., higher ratio of stock). The buyer is willing to pay more in return for less control dilution (i.e., lower ratio of stock).[9] This means that each side has a spectrum of equally attractive deals, as shown in Exhibit 18.3. The buyer is generally better off in deals that settle for less stock and a lower price. The seller, on the other hand, is better off in deals that settle for more stock and a higher price. The task is to find the middle ground where mutually attractive terms might be struck.

Privately the buyer and seller identify the "edge of the envelope," the extreme set of terms (prices and mixes of stock and cash) beyond which they would walk away from the bargaining table. Economists call this edge the "reservation frontier," though we can use the more popular term, "walk-away frontier." Exhibit 18.4 depicts the walk-away frontiers of the buyer and seller, and shows that there is a *zone of potential agreement (ZOPA).* Outside of this zone, one party loses and the other wins—this is the Darwinian zero-sum world. But within the ZOPA both

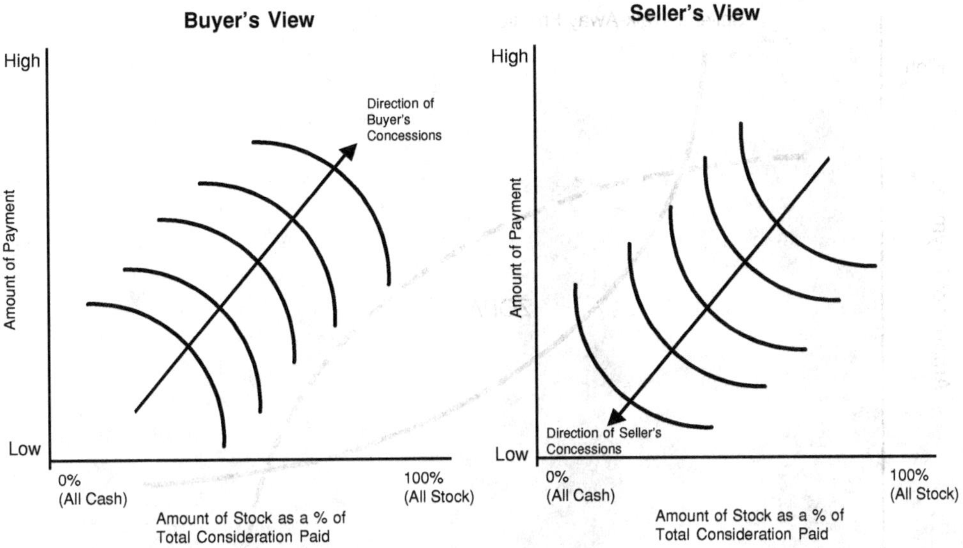

EXHIBIT 18.3 Spectrum of Attractive Deals

sides win—the deals here are mutually beneficial. Seen from the perspective of Exhibit 18.4, the deal designer faces a number of important implications.

There Is No Single *Best* Feasible Deal

The ZOPA describes an area within which a number of *feasible deal* structures exist. The best deals for the buyer would be along the lower side, since this consists of all combinations of lowest price/lowest stock—the buyer would be indifferent among these deals. The best deals for the target are on the opposite side. All feasible deals are in the middle—these are "pretty good" deals. The main implication here is that there is no optimal point, no single best feasible outcome.

This is good news. Settings in which there exists only a unique feasible deal or one best deal are settings in which intractable design deadlocks are bound to arise. Expecting that there are many good solutions to a design problem liberates the deal designer. It also complicates life for those who want a simple solution.

Trade-offs Are Driven by Constraints and Dominance

The process of optimization is simply a matter of comparing the desirability of one set of terms against another. Desirability is measured in terms of the value attached to each attribute. In economic parlance, this value is indicated by a *shadow price*, the implied amount of one good that one would be willing to forgo in return for an amount of another good. The seller likes both a higher price and more stock, and therefore prefers deals that offer these—such deals are said to dominate the rest. The buyer prefers deals that offer both lower prices and less stock. The search for better deals is almost always constrained, at the very least, by the walk-away frontiers of the counterparties. Thus, the best feasible deal is bound to be a mixture of

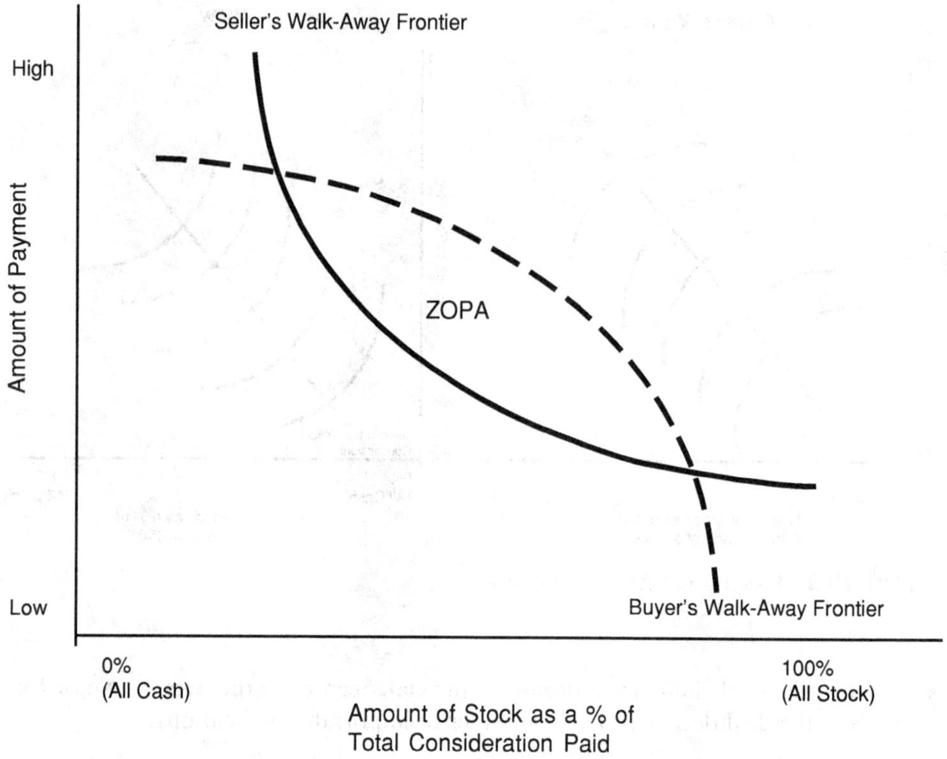

EXHIBIT 18.4 Walk-Away Frontiers and Zone of Potential Agreement (ZOPA)

terms in the middle. Knowing your own and your counterparty's shadow prices, dominance, and constraints assumes huge importance in the deal design effort.

Deal Design Is a Learning Process

Rate of learning is of crucial importance. It determines the efficiency and effectiveness of the deal design effort. Ideally, buyers and sellers converge over the course of a deal negotiation toward a mutually agreeable outcome. Based on my observation of hundreds of simulated and actual deal design efforts, this process of convergence is rarely direct and simple. Typically, it is indirect and meandering, much like the paths depicted in Exhibit 18.5. The buyer opens with a proposal well within his walk-away frontier. The seller counters with a set of terms well within his frontier. The two sides explain their reasoning behind their opening positions. The learning begins. New facts emerge. Assumptions are challenged and revised. Unanticipated side effects come to light. Persuasion takes root. Perhaps the shadow prices of the two sides change. These learning steps occur both directly as trial-and-error offers and counteroffers are made and indirectly through comments made by one side to the other. The field of systems dynamics offers a number of important insights about learning processes:

- *Feedback is key.* If learning is the substance of deal design, then simply being open to new ideas and *feedback* is essential. One rarely observes a successful

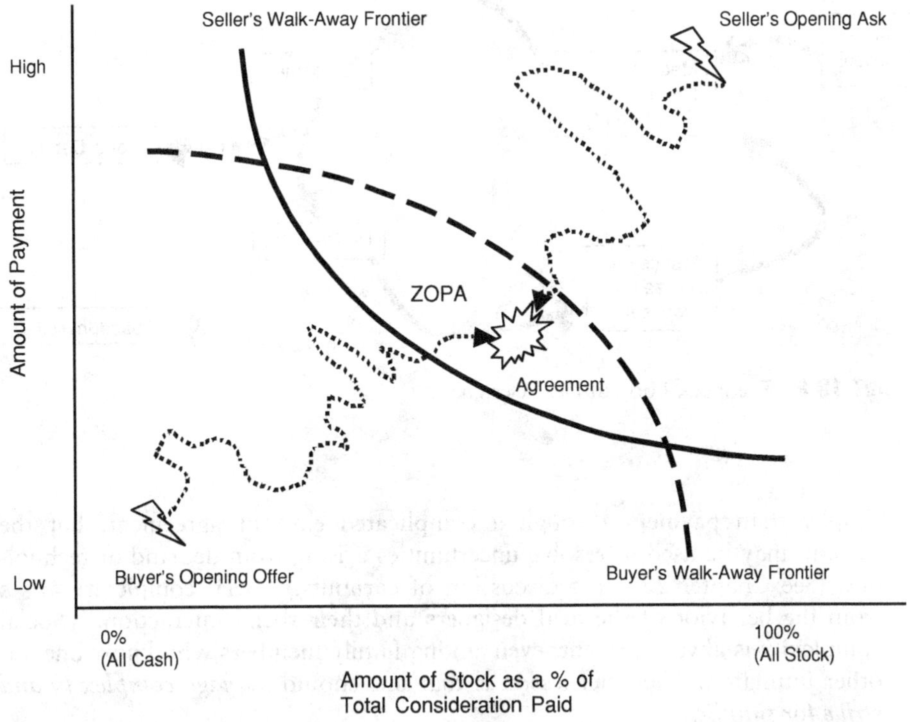

EXHIBIT 18.5 The Meandering Path toward Agreement

negotiator who simply made an offer and then dug in, ignoring new information and sticking tenaciously to the position. Instead, from the buyer's or seller's point of view, the learning process forms a *cycle* through which the proposal is optimized subject to the constraints of the counterparty. Exhibit 18.6 for instance, gives a diagrammatic representation of the cycle.

- ***Speed and momentum: virtues and vices.*** If deal design is a learning process, then one measure of the effectiveness and efficiency of the process is the speed at which learning occurs. Assume that there is a given set of information to be acquired before a mutually agreeable design is developed. If time is money, then learning faster is better. But the dark side of speed is psychological momentum: The frenzy to do a deal arises from the very exhilaration of speed and sense of approaching closure. Chapter 17 describes the adverse consequences of momentum-induced behavior. The deal designer is properly counseled toward *patient haste*: to press forward in the learning process with a focus on speed of learning without being caught up in the mentality of momentum.
- ***Simplicity and complexity.*** Process engineering teaches that all else equal, simple processes tend to be more efficient and effective than complex processes. Complexity seems to work its way inexorably into human affairs, and breaks down into two broad categories. Technical complexity arises from the economics of the deal problem and from the constraints imposed on it by laws, regulations, and capital-market conditions. A cash payment is unquestionably

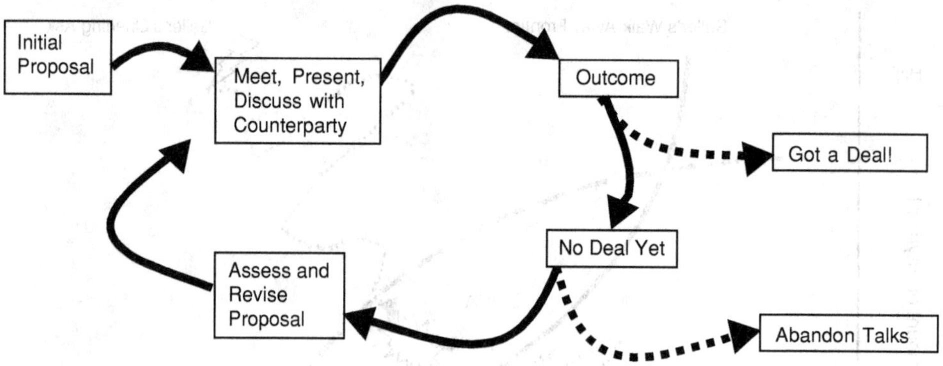

EXHIBIT 18.6 Feedback Loop of Deal Design

simpler than payment through a complicated earnout agreement, but the earnout may be used to resolve uncertainties arising from demand or technology. (See Chapter 22 for a discussion of earnouts.) Social complexity arises from the behavior of the deal designers and their social interaction.[10] Social complexity is always present, even among family members who know one another intimately. The chief lesson is that one should *manage complexity and strive for simplicity.*

- ***Vicious and virtuous cycles: reinforcing and balancing linkages.*** Negotiations can unravel or move toward convergence quickly. The pace and direction of deal design can be explained by the *type* of feedback loop in the minds of the designers.
  - *Balancing feedback strives to achieve a goal.* A thermostat, for instance, gives feedback to the furnace and air conditioner that aims to keep the room temperature at a constant setting. Balancing feedback in deal design would focus on changes in specific terms that would achieve a "pretty good" deal, a Goldilocks outcome—not too hot, not too cold.
  - *Reinforcing feedback amplifies a trend.* This is the self-fulfilling prophecy in which a trend builds on itself. For instance, rumors and an occasional product stock-out might motivate panic buying and hoarding among consumers, which leads to more stock-outs. Mass behavior like this has occurred with fad toys (Pound Puppies, Pokemon), food (visit any supermarket in the South before a snowstorm), and gasoline (in the 1970s rationing reinforced fears of shortage). In deal design, reinforcing feedback is seen explicitly in competitive bidding settings. The buyer makes an opening offer; the seller's agent replies that the offer is inadequate and that a bid X percent higher is necessary to get "into the hunt." The buyer raises the bid and is told that it is getting warm, but that a competitor is higher. The buyer raises again and is encouraged further. How far this goes depends on the buyer's resources and discipline. Plainly, the agent's feedback is aimed at reinforcing the trend of rising bids and the buyer's expectation of winning. This kind of reinforcing feedback creates a vicious cycle for the buyer and a virtuous cycle for the seller.

SUMMARY AND CONCLUSIONS

Deal design is economic problem solving. Therefore, the careful design process should start with a detailed understanding of the problem: the desirables and constraints under which the designer must operate. Much of the analytic work described in this volume serves in some way to illuminate the economic problem.

Solutions to the design problem involve choices in at least nine areas. Designing a deal is not a matter of price only. Indeed, the nine choices interact with one another, suggesting that *a deal is a system*. This chapter advocates that you adopt a "whole deal" view of deal design. Thus, to improve upon a deal means that one must improve upon the bundle of terms simultaneously—this is achieved by trade-offs among terms, giving a little here to get more there. This complexity is daunting to novices and gratifying to seasoned deal designers. It liberates the designer from the fixation on just one feasible outcome, and grants considerable flexibility. This perspective is emphasized by Bruce Wasserstein, one of the leading M&A practitioners:

> *Implementing a deal is a blend of psychology, business judgment, and technical dexterity. While taxes, accounting, and corporate law provide the skeletal frame of a transaction, optimizing position is the purpose of direct negotiation.*[11]

Effective deal design is a learning process. Learning is incorporated through feedback loops in the deal design effort. Speed and simplicity of the learning process are desirable. But delays and complexity are natural companions of deal designers. Complexity arises through the nature of the economic problem and through the behavior of the negotiators. It may be unreasonable to expect to eliminate all delay and complexity, but sound leadership can minimize their effects.

NOTES

1. The distinction between tacit and objective knowledge in M&A is profoundly important to professionals who care about teaching their skills to others. Objective knowledge is easily described in writing, easily lectured about. Examples of objective knowledge are how to change the oil in a car or build a financial spreadsheet model. Tacit knowledge is best learned by direct observation: how to knead bread dough and know when it is ready for the oven, or how to close a sale.
2. Technical engineers will recognize this as an exercise in linear programming. While the analogy is exact, I know of no instance in which mathematical programming techniques have been applied to deal design. The reasons probably have to do with the difficulty of applying these techniques and the fuzziness of the inputs. For instance, values in M&A are estimated with uncertainty.
3. The French have a word for this: *tatonnement* (tapping one's way along as if in the dark of night).

4. One is reminded of the Red Queen in *Alice in Wonderland*, who said, "A thing is what I choose to call it." The Red Queen can call it what she wants, but we do not have to believe her. For instance, in a leveraged buyout, junior debt securities actually bear many of the characteristics of equity. Practitioners know that convertible bonds can trade like debt or like equity at different points in time. Common stock that is sold in units with a put or contingent valuation right is less risky than simple common stock. Preferred equity redemption contingent securities (PERCS) are a financially engineered clone of debt.
5. Banks often incorporate covenants into their loan agreements restricting the ability of the debtor to sell assets or change control. This gives banks the right to renegotiate loan terms in anticipation of a sale of a firm.
6. National laws (such as the U.S. Foreign Corrupt Practices Act) and personal ethics sharply restrict the payment of bribes. Excellent deal designers carefully observe the limitations of both.
7. Professor Michael Jensen (1986) has offered the notion that highly leveraged transactions bind the firm to an operating and financial strategy that prevents the waste of the firm's free cash flow by managers.
8. In the merger of Travelers and Citicorp, announced in April 1998, the terms included the appointment of "co-CEOs." Generally, it is not unusual that merger terms will include the future title of the target CEO.
9. Economists would call these radiating concave and convex lines "iso-utility curves." All of the combinations of price and mix that fall on one line offer the same benefit in the eyes of the target and buyer respectively.
10. Perhaps social complexity is most obvious in cross-border deal negotiations. The classic example involves negotiations between Americans and Japanese. The Japanese word *hai* means different things to each side. Americans tend to interpret *hai* as equivalent to "yes" and assume that it signals agreement on a point. But the Japanese word *hai* actually means "I hear you."
11. Quoted from Bruce Wasserstein, *Big Deal*, New York: Free Press, 1998, page 561.

CHAPTER 19

Choosing the Form of Acquisitive Reorganization

INTRODUCTION: FIVE KEY CONCERNS FOR THE DEAL DESIGNER

Mergers and acquisitions often result in a legal *reorganization* of one or both of the partners to the deal. There are several forms of reorganization, each with peculiar advantages and qualifying conditions. Transactions are designed in ways to meet those qualifying conditions and to achieve desired outcomes. This chapter surveys the forms of reorganization, the pros and cons of each, and the qualifying conditions. Through an understanding of the forms of organization, one can see that transaction design has big implications for issues that concern deal designers and senior executives. These implications fall into five large categories:

1. *Taxation.* Is this proposed deal *taxable* or *tax deferred*? To whom is it taxable? What are the tax consequences for the buyer and seller? How large is the tax exposure? Will the seller be subject to double taxation?
2. *Risk exposure.* Will this structure isolate the hidden liabilities of the target from the buyer?
3. *Control.* Will this require a vote of shareholders of the target and/or the buyer? How will the voting control of Newco be affected by this structure?
4. *Continuity.* Which, if any, firm survives as an ongoing entity? What implications does this firm's *continuity* have for the ability to assign leases and licenses, for corporate identity, and for social issues such as headquarters location?
5. *Form of payment.* What form of payment is required to achieve objectives for taxation, risk exposure, control, and continuity?

In the interest of brevity, this chapter will provide the barest answers to these questions. The intent here is to prepare the reader to speak more confidently with tax, accounting, and legal advisory professionals, who should always be consulted for insights on specific problems.

THE FORM OF REORGANIZATION HAS IMPORTANT IMPLICATIONS

The design of mergers and acquisitions has many dimensions of which one of the more complicated is the choice of the form of reorganization. At the outset, it seems odd to call M&A transactions "reorganizations" since that is a term more generally associated with bankruptcies and liquidations. The term is derived from the U.S. *Internal Revenue Code*, which establishes the tax rules for these transactions. The predominance of tax law in this area explains why many analysts and general managers understand reorganization choices so poorly: The tax code is complex.

This aspect of M&A design is important. Tax planning considerations are the focus of considerable professional time and talent in M&A. Hayn (1989) found that about half of all acquisitions are designed to be *tax-free* or only partially taxable. Form of reorganization showed a strong relationship to the abnormal return at the merger announcement: In taxable deals, the acquisition premium is more than twice as high (see Exhibit 19.1). Two effects might explain this, though the explanations are not entirely satisfying: (1) in taxable deals, target company shareholders' taxes are immediate rather than deferred, thus creating a demand for higher payment stimulated by the time value of money; or (2) in taxable deals, the buyer is allowed to step up the tax *basis* of the acquired assets, thus affording a larger depreciation tax shield. This lifts the ceiling amount that the buyer could afford to pay. Perhaps because of the target's bargaining power or a "winner's curse" effect, the buyer *does* pay more in taxable deals.

Hayn found that two tax effects were significant in explaining the size of announcement returns. In tax-free deals, net operating loss carryforwards and tax credits expiring within two years of acquisition were positively related to the announcement returns of target and buyer. In taxable acquisitions, the most significant variable was the *step-up in basis* of the assets to fair market value.

The evidence suggests that an even greater percentage of acquisitions of privately held companies tend to be structured to defer paying tax.[1] Even the elimination or deferral of a relatively small percentage of tax exposure can materially affect internal rates of return to investors. Research suggests that tax effects figure importantly in all segments of all M&A transactions.

EXHIBIT 19.1 Cumulative Abnormal Returns to Buyers and Targets According to Tax Status of the Deal (Days –1,0)

	Taxable	Tax-Free	Partially Taxable
Target firms	18.6% n = 178	8.2% n = 181	11.1% n = 116
Buyer firms	2.2% n = 308	1.1% n = 134	2.1% n = 76

Note: All cumulative abnormal returns were significantly positive at the 0.95 level.
Source of data: Reprinted from the *Journal of Financial Economics*, 1989, Carla Hayn, Table 3, Cumulative Abnormal Returns to Buyers and Targets According to Tax Status of the Deal (Days –1,0), from "Tax Attributes as Determinants of Shareholder Gains in Corporate Acquisitions," pp. 121–153. Copyright © 1989, with permission from Elsevier.

It remains a question of active debate whether tax considerations *cause* acquisitions. Scholes and Wolfson[2] analyzed changes in the volume of merger and acquisition activity before and after changes in the tax laws passed in 1981 and 1986, and concluded that the evidence "very strongly" suggested that these changes affected M&A activity. M&A is associated with three possible tax benefits:

1. The exploitation of net operating loss (NOL) tax carryforwards and other tax credits.
2. The step-up, or increase, in the basis or value of assets on which such tax shields as depreciation expense are computed.
3. The exploitation of debt tax shields through increased financial leverage.

Scholes and Wolfson argue that each of these benefits can be realized through means other than M&A, possibly at lower transactional cost. However, targeted studies by Auerbach and Reishus (1988a,b,c) suggest that NOLs, basis step-up, and leverage changes are probably significant in only a small number of mergers.

The fundamental conclusion must be that tax exposure probably matters immensely in the detailed design of individual transactions even though the macroeconomic impact of the exploitation of tax shields through mergers may not be large.

Internal Revenue Code Creates Choices

Before surveying the various forms of acquisition, it is useful to consider the general drivers or considerations that create these alternatives. The following six items will be the most important in the deal designer's work, though the Internal Revenue Code admits a wide range of possible considerations.

1. ***Tax liability: immediate or deferred.*** Tax deferral is usually referred to as "tax free" though this is clearly not the economic reality of the tax code. The basic rule is that where a gain occurs, there is either tax today or tax tomorrow, but generally not "no tax." Tax-deferred transactions require stock-for-stock deals. If only cash or debt is used, selling shareholders generally have an immediate tax liability. With a blend of stock, cash, and debt, the tax liability is more complicated. Tax deferral also matters to the buyer: Generally where the seller gains the benefit of deferral, the buyer forgoes the depreciation tax shield created by the step-up in basis. This trade-off in benefits for the buyer and seller sets up a tussle for negotiatiors.
2. ***Exposure to the target's liabilities.*** Some buyers want the target's assets, but not the target's known (and unknown) liabilities. Transactions can be structured in ways to shield the buyer from the target's liabilities.
3. ***Need for a shareholder vote.*** Usually the sale of a company entails the vote of the target's shareholders. Mergers require a vote of the buyer's shareholders, too. Also, the buyer's shareholders may have to authorize new shares needed to consummate a transaction.[3] Shareholder votes complicate life for deal designers, as they add yet one more dimension of transaction risk (i.e., that the buyer's shareholders will not approve the deal). Generally, deal designers seek to avoid buyer shareholder votes.
4. ***Survival of the target company.*** In some circumstances, it is important that the target company survive as a corporate entity. In many instances, key contracts,

warranties, and choice retail leaseholds are not assignable to another company, even if that other company is the new owner. In these cases, it will be important for the target company to continue to exist, even if in name only.

5. *Permissible form of payment.* Deal designers often prefer to tailor the payment as a blend of cash, debt, and/or stock. The tax code offers some flexibility to deal designers, though the implications of different blends should be understood before undertaking the transaction.
6. *Limitations on other actions.* Managers want more flexibility rather than less, other things equal. The choice of form of transaction can affect flexibility. For instance, there can be no tax-free deals within two years of a spin-off (i.e., before or after) without incurring tax on the distribution of the stock of the entity spun off or meeting a narrow exception.[4]

How to Choose?

As a road map of the alternatives available to the deal designer, Exhibit 19.2 shows how these choices must result from decisions on the first three dimensions (tax exposure, exposure to liabilities, and the need for a vote). The other three (survival, form of payment, and limitations) are more complex and will be discussed in the text that follows. The main implication of Exhibit 19.2 is that the choice of form of transaction will emerge from the needs and constraints of the buyer and seller. Knowing the goals of the counterparties in the negotiation is indispensable.

DEALS THAT ARE IMMEDIATELY TAXABLE TO THE SELLING SHAREHOLDERS

From the seller's standpoint, a sale of stock is preferable to selling assets. This is because a sale of assets incurs tax liabilities at two levels (one, a gain at the corporate level, and the other at the shareholder level when securities are sold or liquidated). A sale of stock incurs tax only at the shareholder level. Also, a sale of stock may be easier since some asset purchases may entail bills of sale or deeds for each asset or class of assets.

Purchase of Assets, Substantially Using Cash or Debt Securities

In a *cash purchase of assets* (see Exhibit 19.3), the buyer exchanges its cash for the assets of the target. The target's liabilities are not transferred to the buyer without explicit agreement (one example would be the transfer of the commitment to honor product warranties). After the transaction, the target may liquidate or remain as a holding company for other contemplated investments.

The tax consequences to the seller from an asset purchase are to realize an immediate gain or loss on assets equal to the difference between the allocated sale price and book value of each asset. Arguably, shareholders are taxed twice on any gain: once when the corporation pays a tax on the gain, and again if the proceeds are distributed to shareholders in the form of a dividend or liquidating distribution.[5] This double taxation is avoided by structuring the transaction as a pur-

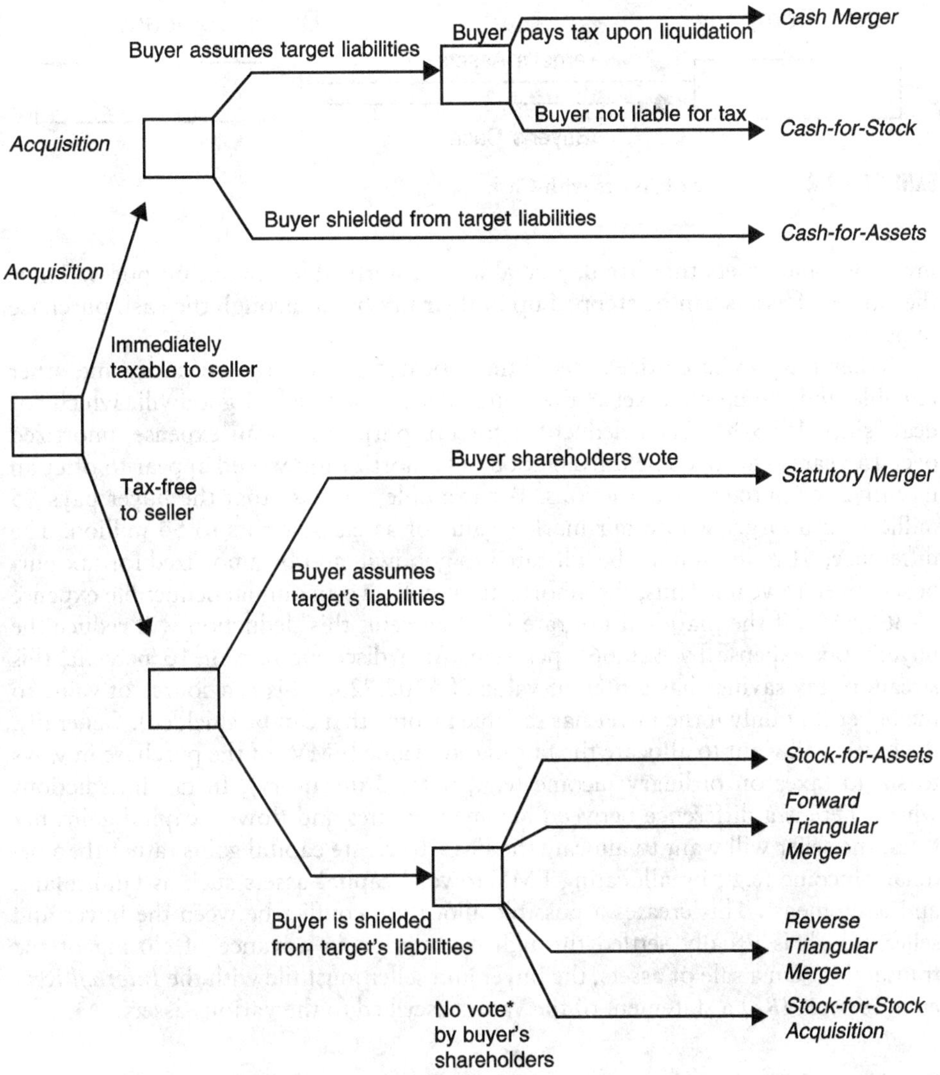

EXHIBIT 19.2 Decision Tree of Choice of Form of Transaction

*Merger statutes ordinarily do not require buyer's shareholders to vote upon a merger between a buyer's *subsidiary* and a target. However, the rules of stock exchanges and legal counsel may prompt buyers to seek the concurrence of their shareholders where such mergers are material. Also, buyer shareholders may be required to vote to authorize the creation of new shares of stock to be offered in the transaction.

chase of stock (described in the section on voting stock-for-assets acquisition later in this chapter).

From the buyer's standpoint, the taxable purchase of assets has no immediate tax consequences. The taxable basis of the assets becomes the fair market value of consideration paid for the assets. Typically, the fair market value is allocated among all asset classes, including intangibles. The buyer will maximize its tax shields from the purchase if the purchase price can be allocated substantially to

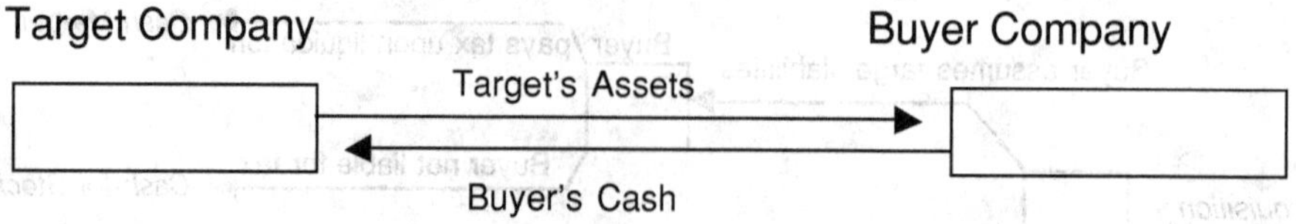

EXHIBIT 19.3 Purchase of Assets with Cash

inventory and assets that are depreciable or amortizable for tax purposes. Thus, the values of assets can be stepped up in their tax basis through the cash purchase of assets.

When the purchase price exceeds the allocated basis of the inventory and other tangible and intangible assets,[6] the remainder is allocated to goodwill, which for deals since 1993 has been deductible for tax purposes, as an expense amortized over 15 years. This tax shield from goodwill amortization would appear to offer an incentive for purchase transactions. For example, suppose that the buyer pays $5 million for a target whose fair market value of assets amounts to $4 million. The difference, $1 million, must be allocated to goodwill and be amortized for tax purposes[7] over 15 years. Thus, the amortization will give an annual deductible expense of $66,666[8]; if the marginal tax rate is 40 percent, this deduction will reduce the buyer's tax expense by $26,666 per year. At a discount rate of 10 percent, this stream of tax savings has a present value of $202,823—this is a source of value to the buyer (but only if the buyer has taxable income that can be shielded). Generally, the buyer will want to allocate the fair market value (FMV) of the purchase in ways to shield taxes on ordinary income (e.g., toward inventory). In tax jurisdictions where there is a difference between income tax rates and (lower) capital gains tax rates, the seller will want to allocate the FMV to create capital gains rather than ordinary income (e.g., by allocating FMV toward capital assets such as land, plant, and equipment). This creates a possible allocation conflict between the buyer and seller, which is usually settled through negotiation in advance of closing of the transaction. On a sale of assets, the buyer and seller must file with the *Internal Revenue Service (IRS)* a statement of the values ascribed to the various assets.

Purchase of Stock, Substantially Using Cash or Debt Securities

In a *cash purchase of stock* (see Exhibit 19.4), the buyer exchanges its cash for shares of the target's voting common stock. The target company remains in existence. The buyer will be shielded from the target's known and unknown liabilities unless a claimant can penetrate the separation of entities (i.e., the corporate veil that separates parent and subsidiary).

There is no "double taxation" in this transaction, as it occurs directly between the buyer and the target company's shareholders. The selling shareholder recognizes a gain or loss on the sale of stock, equal to the difference between the fair market value of consideration received and the stockholder's investment basis.

The buyer can treat the purchase as a straightforward purchase of stock, or can elect to treat it as a purchase of assets by declaration to the Internal Revenue Service. This special election alternative (called a "Section 338 election") has results

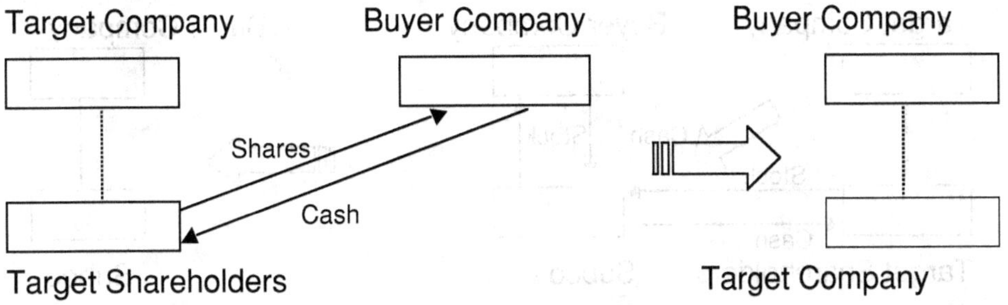

EXHIBIT 19.4 Purchase of Stock with Cash

Note: With the transaction structures in Exhibits 19.4 and 19.5, the buyer may step up the tax basis of the target company assets by making a Section 338 election. By this means, a purchase of stock can produce the tax benefits to the buyer of a purchase of assets.

similar to an outright purchase of assets including an allocation of purchase price, increased by taxes paid upon the election, and the liabilities assumed in the transaction. This election may increase the actual cost to the buyer from possible gains in liquidation by the target company. Knowledgeable buyers will anticipate this added cost in their negotiation of the purchase price.

Triangular Cash Mergers

An alternative to the direct purchase of either stock or assets is for the buyer to form a subsidiary (called "Subco"), capitalize it with cash sufficient to acquire the target's stock, and have the target merge with Subco in either of two structures:

1. ***Reverse triangular merger.*** In a *reverse triangular cash merger* (see Exhibit 19.5), Subco merges into the target. The target company survives, as do its tax attributes and liabilities. The IRS views the transaction as a simple purchase of shares.
2. ***Forward triangular merger.*** In a *forward triangular cash merger* (see Exhibit 19.6), the target merges into Subco. The target company ceases to exist, along with its tax attributes, although its liabilities have been transferred to Subco. The final target company tax return reflects the sale of assets, the gain on which is taxed at the company level. The IRS views this as a purchase of assets. A step-up in asset basis follows to the buyer.

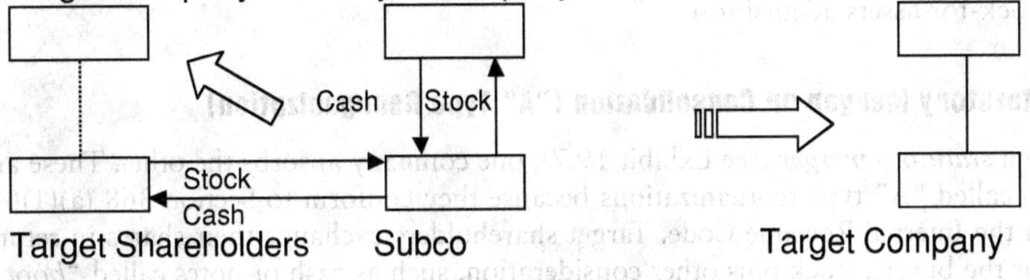

EXHIBIT 19.5 Reverse Triangular Cash Merger (Buyer Purchases Target Stock with Cash)

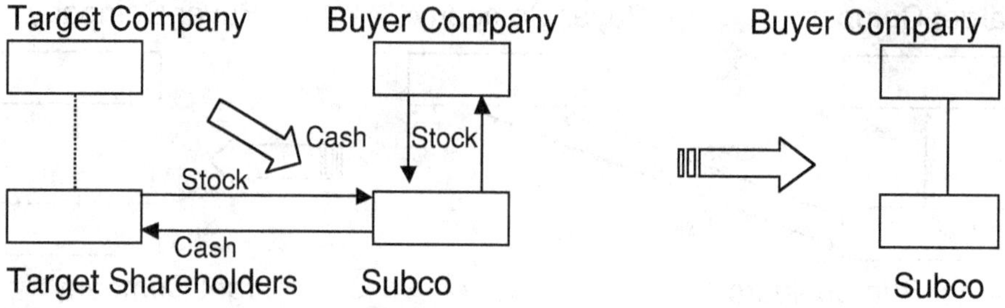

EXHIBIT 19.6 Forward Triangular Cash Merger (Viewed by the IRS as Equivalent to a Sale of Assets)

Cash mergers have one advantage over direct purchases of stock: No minority shareholders remain. Absent a merger, minority shareholders cannot be forced to change their status (though it is possible to do a *minority "freeze-out"*[9] if the buyer owns over 90 percent of the shares). As long as they remain in existence, Subco must submit annual reports to shareholders, hold shareholder meetings, elect a board of directors by formal shareholder voting, and so on—all of these are opportunities for nettlesome intervention by dissident shareholders. As long as the buyer can attract a voting majority of the target's shareholders, the merger can be effected and the dissenting shareholders forced to exit (though many states permit appraisal rights for dissenting shareholders to determine whether they received fair value for their shares).

One disadvantage to the seller of the forward cash merger is that the proceeds of the transaction are, in effect, taxed twice.[10] The buyer must know who is paying taxes on the proceeds of the sale. Also, the buyer must consider the length of time required to publish a merger proxy statement and hold a meeting of the shareholders—these are virtually always required for target firms because merger alters the legal identity of the firm.[11] This may take six months. In contrast, a direct purchase of shares or assets could be consummated in considerably less time, such as a period of one to three months.

DEALS THAT DEFER TAX TO THE SELLING SHAREHOLDERS

The Internal Revenue Code recognizes three classes of transactions as eligible for the deferral of tax expense to the selling shareholder. These are (1) statutory merger or consolidation, (2) voting stock-for-stock acquisition, and (3) voting stock-for-assets acquisition.

Statutory Merger or Consolidation ("A" Type Reorganization)

In a *statutory merger* (see Exhibit 19.7), one company absorbs the other. These are so-called "A" type reorganizations because they conform to Section 368 (a)(1)(A) of the Internal Revenue Code. Target shareholders exchange their shares in return for the buyer's stock plus other consideration, such as cash or notes called *"boot."* The payment in stock is tax deferred to the target shareholders, but boot is immedi-

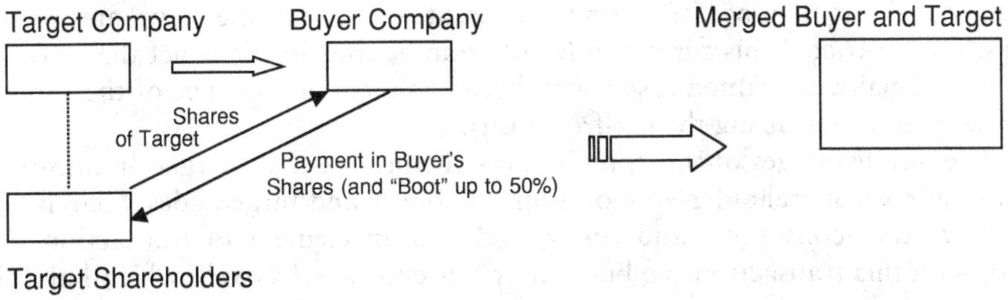

EXHIBIT 19.7 Statutory Merger

ately taxable to the extent of any taxable gain. The target company ceases to exist. The buyer assumes the liabilities of the target. Asset ownership is transferred relatively cost effectively. Under merger statutes in most states, a majority vote of the shareholders is required to approve the merger. Once approved, all shares in the target company become buyer shares—target shareholders turn in their old shares to the buyer's transfer agent and receive new shares in return. No minority target shareholders remain, though they do have appraisal rights in most states.

In a statutory *consolidation* (see Exhibit 19.8), two or more corporations combine into one new corporation ("Newco").[12] The preexisting corporations cease to exist as legal entities. The formation of a completely new entity may be warranted by business and legal reasons. For instance, in a so-called "merger of equals" it may be impolitic for one company to survive and the other to cease.

The statutory merger or consolidation is thought to be the most flexible of the tax-free structures from a deal design point of view. The IRS recognizes these as tax free as long as there is sufficient "continuity of interest" by the selling shareholders, which requires that at least 50 percent of the merger consideration is paid in stock of the acquiring company (preferred, common, voting, or nonvoting)—the balance is boot. The selling shareholder will be taxed immediately on any gain represented in the transaction to the extent of the boot. This structure will be attractive where the buyer seeks to pay only partially with stock, the seller needs cash, and minority or dissident shareholders must be eliminated. Statutory mergers were often the form of transaction underlying hostile tender offers, structured as a cash "front-end" payment for the first 50 percent of shares tendered, and

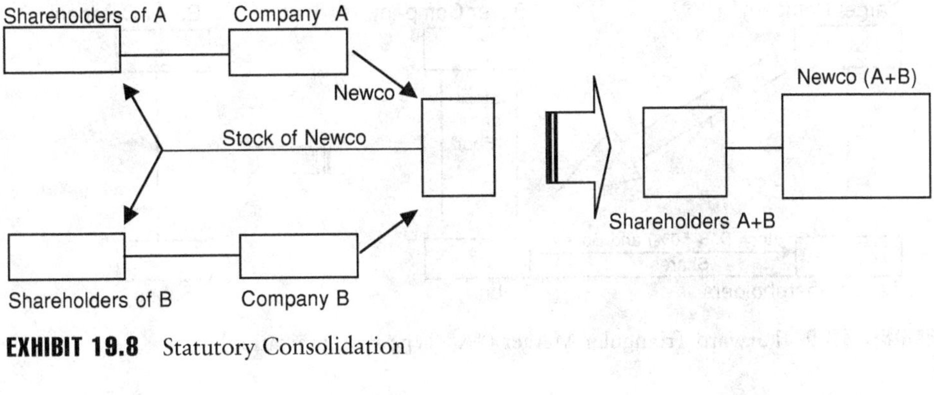

EXHIBIT 19.8 Statutory Consolidation

shares for the remaining 50 percent. In recent years, securities laws and regulations have restricted this format in hostile transactions in the belief that they are coercive. Finally, unwanted assets may be sold shortly in advance of the transaction without jeopardizing the tax-free status.

The disadvantages of this transaction structure are that merger or consolidation requires a shareholder vote on both the buyer and target sides. Shareholder votes are time-consuming and costly, and add an element of transaction risk. Also, with this transaction the buyer may not choose selectively which liabilities to assume.

Forward Triangular Merger ("A" Type Reorganization)

As with the cash forward triangular merger described earlier, the *forward triangular merger ("A")* (see Exhibit 19.9) entails the merger of the target company into a subsidiary of the buyer (Subco). To qualify as a tax-free transaction, the subsidiary must acquire "substantially all" of the target's assets (e.g., at least 70 percent of the fair market value of gross assets and 90 percent of the FMV of net assets). Under this rule, asset sales just prior to the transaction may threaten favorable tax treatment. Also, there can be no tax-free deals within two years of a spin-off (i.e., before or after). As with the statutory merger, payment must consist of at least 50 percent of the parent corporation stock. The balance, or boot, may be tailored to meet the requirements of selling shareholders.

This structure has two advantages over the statutory merger. First, it insulates the buyer company from the target's liabilities by isolating those liabilities in a subsidiary. Second, it does not require a vote of the buyer's shareholders (though shareholders of the target must still approve the transaction).

Reverse Triangular Merger ("A" Type Reorganization)

As with the cash reverse triangular merger, the tax-free form of *reverse triangular merger ("A")* (see Exhibit 19.10) entails the merger of the buyer's subsidiary into the target, leaving the target company in existence as a subsidiary of the buyer and eliminating minority shareholders of the target. In order to qualify as a tax-free transaction, at least 80 percent of the consideration must be paid in

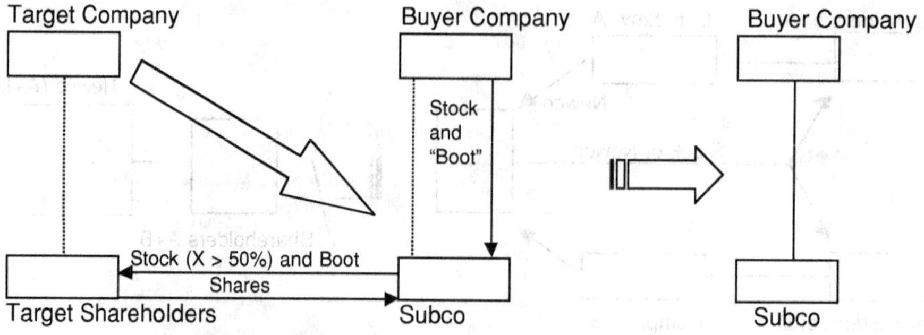

EXHIBIT 19.9 Forward Triangular Merger ("A" Type Reorganization)

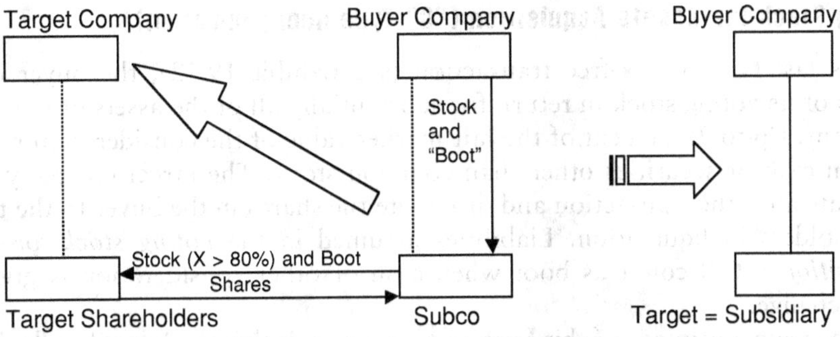

EXHIBIT 19.10 Reverse Triangular Merger ("A" Type Reorganization)

the buyer's parent corporation *voting stock* (either common or preferred). Also, the buyer must control "substantially all" of the target's assets. This form of transaction limits the buyer's use of spin-offs and asset sales just prior to the transaction. As with the other mergers, a vote of the target's shareholders is required, though a vote of the buyer's is not necessary. The liabilities of the target are isolated in a subsidiary.

Voting Stock-for-Stock Acquisition ("B" Type Reorganization)

To qualify as a tax-free transaction in a stock-for-stock deal (see Exhibit 19.11), the buyer must exchange only voting, common, or preferred stock, and after the transaction must control at least 80 percent of the votes. No boot payments are allowed. No merger occurs, as the target is retained as a wholly (or partially) owned subsidiary. The target survives as an entity. Therefore, the target's liabilities are isolated from the buyer. Also, no shareholder votes are required. Given the 80 percent rule, the *voting stock-for-stock acquistion ("B")* permits the existence of minority shareholders in the target company. The purchaser need not acquire control at once; this form permits a "creeping acquisition." In comparison, the reverse triangular merger gives results similar to the stock-for-stock acquisition, but permits boot and eliminates minority shareholders.

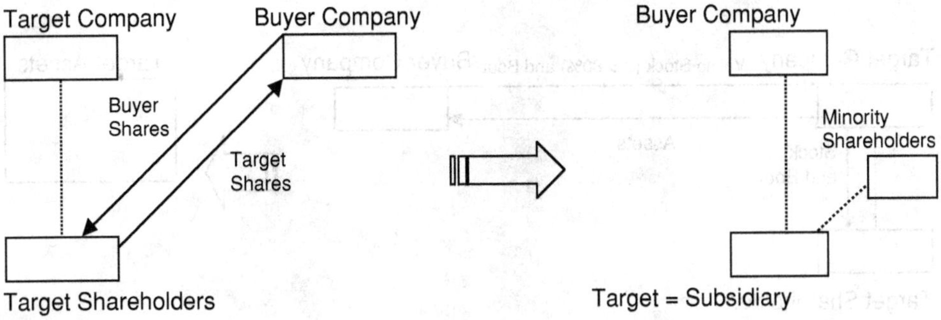

EXHIBIT 19.11 Voting Stock-for-Stock Acquisition ("B" Type Reorganization)

Voting Stock-for-Assets Acquisition ("C" Type Reorganization)

In this last type of tax-free transaction (see Exhibit 19.12), the buyer offers shares of its voting stock in return for substantially all of the assets of the target company. Up to 20 percent of the fair market value of the consideration may be paid in cash or securities other than common stock. The target company must liquidate after the transaction and distribute the shares in the buyer to the target shareholders in liquidation. Liabilities assumed in the *voting stock-for-assets acquisition ("C")* count as boot when cash or other consideration is given in the exchange.

The main advantage of this form of transaction is that the buyer has flexibility about the medium of payment, subject to the 20 percent rule. Also, the buyer has flexibility in choosing whether to assume any of the target's liabilities. The buyer's shareholders do not necessarily need to vote to approve the transaction, unless the buyer's stock is listed on an exchange or additional stock must be authorized to complete the acquisition. As with the other types of reorganizations, a Subco may be used.

The stock-for-assets acquisition may incur sizable legal and administrative costs to transfer numerous individual assets. Tax-free status requires that at least 70 percent of the fair market value of the gross assets, and 90 percent of the FMV of net assets of the target company be transferred. Finally, to the extent that the target shareholders receive boot they will recognize an immediate tax on the gain, if any.[13]

SUMMARY AND IMPLICATIONS FOR THE DEAL DESIGNER AND SENIOR EXECUTIVE

As the discussions of the various forms of transaction reveal, the deal designer faces a varied menu of possible structures. Each has advantages and disadvantages. Therefore, the decision maker will need to weigh the trade-offs associated with each type of transaction as they apply to the situation at hand. Exhibit 19.13 summarizes some salient points of each transaction type for the reader.

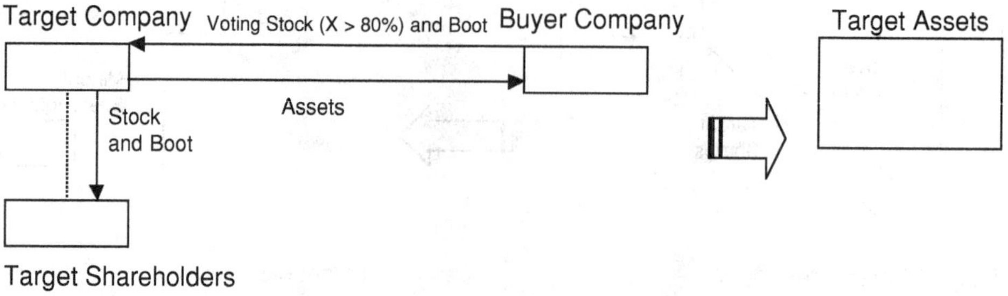

EXHIBIT 19.12 Voting Stock-for-Stock Acquisition ("C" Type Reorganization)

EXHIBIT 19.13 Summary of Features of Various Transaction Types

	Tax Implications for Seller and Buyer	Buyer's Exposure to Target's Liabilities	Need for Target Shareholder Vote	Need for Buyer Shareholder Vote	Minority Freeze-Out?*	Does the Target Company Survive?	Form of Payment
Cash purchase of assets	Immediately taxable to seller. Step-up for buyer.	Low	Maybe	No	No minority	Uncertain	No restriction. Usually cash.
Cash purchase of stock	Immediately taxable to seller. Step-up for buyer.	High	No	No	No	Yes	No restriction. Usually cash.
Cash merger	Immediately taxable to seller. Step-up for buyer.	Low if target merged into a sub	Yes	Maybe	Yes	No if forward triangular merger. Yes if reverse triangular merger.	No restriction. Usually cash.
Statutory merger or consolidation ("A" Reorganization)	Tax-free to seller.† No step-up for buyer.	High	Yes	Yes	Yes	No	Buyer's stock and typically no more than 50% boot

(Continued)

EXHIBIT 19.13 *(Continued)*

	Tax Implications for Seller and Buyer	Buyer's Exposure to Target's Liabilities	Need for Target Shareholder Vote	Need for Buyer Shareholder Vote	Minority Freeze-Out?*	Does the Target Company Survive?	Form of Payment
Forward Triangular Merger ("A" Reorganization)	Tax-free to seller.† No step-up for buyer.	Low—limited by sub	Yes	No‡—unless need to authorize more shares	Yes	No	Buyer's stock and typically no more than 50% boot.
Reverse Triangular Merger ("A" Reorganization)	Tax-free to seller.† No step-up for buyer.	Low – limited by sub	Yes	No‡—unless need to authorize more shares	Yes	Yes	Buyer's voting stock of at least 80% and the rest in boot.
Voting Stock-for-Stock ("B" Reorganization)	Tax-free to seller.† No step-up for buyer.	Low—limited by sub	Maybe	No‡—unless need to authorize more shares	No	Yes	100% in buyer's voting stock.
Voting Stock-for-Assets ("C" Reorganization)	Tax-free to seller.† No step-up for buyer.	High for liabilities that convey with the assets	Maybe	No‡—unless need to authorize more shares	No minority	No	At least 80% buyer's voting stock in value and the rest in boot.

*A minority freeze-out seeks to eliminate *direct* interests in the target firm held by a minority of shareholders (who are possibly dissidents) following the completion of the deal. This is ordinarily accomplished by merging the target into the buyer.

†"Tax-free" is common usage for "tax deferred until disposition or sale of the stock." Also, any boot in the "tax-free" transactions may create an immediate tax liability to the extent of any gain implicit in the boot.

‡Stock exchanges and legal counsel may require a vote of the buyer's shareholders on material transactions. Asset sales and spin-offs could create adverse tax consequences.

This survey raises several large implications for the deal designer and senior executive:

- ***Transaction choice can affect control.*** The buyer's flexibility in operating Subco can be affected by the structure of the transaction. Many seasoned acquirers avoid structures that create minority shareholders in a newly acquired subsidiary—laws and court decisions in most developed countries protect the rights of the minority in ways that may limit the freedom of the majority (the buyer).
- ***Transaction choice can affect exposure to risk.*** Known and unknown risks embedded in the target can be contained through careful deal design.
- ***Transaction choice is interdependent with the choice about form of payment.*** To achieve the tax-deferred status of the deal, it will usually be necessary to pay substantially in stock.
- ***Transaction choice can create (or destroy) value.*** In the give-and-take of bargaining, the choice of transaction structure can capture benefits and impose costs on the buyer and target. Exhibit 19.14 invites the reader to consider the valuation effects of transaction choice. Some transaction types offer tax savings—the value of these can be estimated using standard discounted cash flow methodology. Other transactions offer great flexibility, in the form of voting control, designing the transaction payment, and/or in freeing the buyer from liabilities of the seller. These are various kinds of embedded options, and will tend to be more valuable the greater the uncertainty under which the deal designer is working. Option pricing theory is not easily adapted to estimating the value of these options, but it is sufficient to know that options are always valuable, even if out of the money.

EXHIBIT 19.14 Transaction Choice and Valuation Analysis of Acquisitions

The fundamental rule for buyers is to accept a transaction proposal if the target company is worth more than what the buyer pays.

$$V_{\text{Firm}} \geq V_{\text{Payment}}$$

Transaction choice would add factors to each side of the inequality. On the left-hand side, one could add an estimate of the value of transaction-specific benefits, such as the present value of tax savings and the value of hidden options. On the right-hand side, one could add a factor that recognizes possible change in payment *incremental* to the specific transaction alternative—for instance, this might reflect higher payment to cover the seller's immediate tax obligation. The enhanced rule for buyers is:

$$V_{\text{Firm basic}} + V_{\text{Transaction benefits}} \geq V_{\text{Base payment}} + V_{\text{Payment due to this transaction form}}$$

Since the basic estimates of value and payment do not vary with transaction choice, the transaction designer can simplify the decision rule about transactions: *Accept a transaction alternative if its benefits are greater than its costs.*

$$V_{\text{Transaction benefits}} \geq V_{\text{Payment due to this transaction form}}$$

But since there are at least eight types of transactions to choose from, the deal designer needs to *choose the transaction alternative that creates the most value.*

$$\text{Value created through transaction choice} = V_{\text{Benefits specific to this transaction form}} - V_{\text{Incremental transaction payment}}$$

In short, transaction choice is riddled with value-creating effects. Well-informed counterparties in a merger negotiation may attempt to appropriate some (or all) of the value created by transaction choice. To some extent, this reflects the zero-sum nature of U.S. tax policy: Sooner or later, someone has to pay the tax on profits. Sellers know this, and may ask for a higher payment from the buyer if their gain is immediately taxable. *Buyers should be cautioned not to overpay for the benefits of a specific transaction type. Choose the form of transaction that maximizes value creation.*

- ***A careful understanding of the buyer's and seller's goals should drive transaction choice.*** None of the eight transaction forms reviewed here is best in any absolute sense. What matters is their reasonableness in light of the wants and needs of the counterparties in the merger negotiation. This implies that the careful deal designer must observe the classic "commandment" of negotiation, *know thy counterparty.*
- ***Obtain counsel.*** This is a complex aspect of M&A. Laws, regulations, and practices change steadily. *No transaction should be consummated without prior review by tax and legal experts.*

NOTES

1. An article in *Mergerstat Review* (1989) argued that "a privately held business has one owner or a handful of shareholders, usually members of the owner's family. Hence, their concern for tax liability is much greater. Furthermore, in many instances, management owners remain with the company, expecting to contribute to the future growth of the newly merged entity, and thereby profiting from the stock's appreciation." (Page 51)
2. See Scholes and Wolfson (1992), page 515.
3. Active buyers will often seek advance authorization of new shares from their shareholders, well before a specific transaction is contemplated. Where buyers have sufficient shares in treasury, a vote to authorize new shares will be unnecessary.
4. The buyer should always determine whether the target has been party to a spin-off within the two-year window before or after the transaction, and if so should perform an analysis as to whether a taxable event may take place.
5. Historically, the double taxation could be avoided if the corporation liquidated and distributed all assets to shareholders within a 12-month period. However, the Tax Reform Act of 1986 eliminated this treatment.
6. The value of intangible assets such as patents and R&D is amortizable over 15 years for tax purposes.
7. Tax treatment of goodwill stands in contrast to accounting treatment. Under FAS 141 and 142, goodwill is not amortized for financial reporting purposes, though it must be tested annually for impairment and written off as necessary.
8. This is equal to $1 million divided by 15 years.
9. In a minority freeze-out, the buyer obtains shareholder approval for a merger of the target into Subco, thus eliminating a minority interest in the target.
10. In a forward cash merger, the target company, in effect, sells its assets and liquidates. Taxes are paid by the target on any gain in the sale, and again by the

shareholder upon receipt of the liquidating dividend. In a reverse cash merger, the buyer receives stock in the target, and shareholders are exposed only once to a gain on the sale of the stock. But the buyer can elect to have the transaction treated as a purchase of assets—in which case the buyer must be responsible to pay the tax on the inherent gain on the underlying assets.

11. Whether a proxy statement and shareholder vote are required of the buyer will depend on various considerations, driven largely by size. For transactions that are large relative to the size of the buyer, stock exchange rules and some state laws will require a vote of the shareholders.
12. Throughout this book, "Newco" is used generically to indicate the firm that emerges from a merger or acquisition. In Exhibit 19.8, "Newco" is used in the narrow legal sense to indicate an entirely new legal entity.
13. Boot is commonly thought of as cash or notes. Stock warrants are a form of boot as well. But these are deemed to have zero value for tax purposes, and therefore carry no tax liability.

CHAPTER 20

Choosing the Form of Payment and Financing

INTRODUCTION

Form of payment and *financing mix* are two of the major deal design dimensions outlined in Chapter 18. In comparison to setting price or value boundaries, research and practice have much less to say about form and financing. This chapter illuminates the complexities and offers frameworks for thinking through the choices. Lessons include these:

- ***Form of payment and financing practices vary with the economic cycle.*** Changes in interest rates and stock prices are strongly associated with changes in M&A deal design over time.
- ***Form of payment matters.*** Research shows large differences in outcomes for shareholders according to whether a deal is based on cash or stock.
- ***Choice of form of payment is heavily influenced by factors outside the firm.*** The chapter discusses how differing perspectives, information, costs, tax exposure, and so on affect the choice. The key implication of this is that the deal designer needs to think well outside the firm to gain a proper perspective on the problem.
- ***Form of payment, financing, and price are tightly linked.*** Decisions about how to pay the seller are implicitly decisions about financing. The deal designer is well advised to consider the financing side effects of the choice of form of payment.
- ***Financing choice also benefits from thinking from several perspectives.*** The chapter discusses the view of the investor, creditor, competitor, and CEO—these capture very different views about the implications of financing alternatives. Six criteria help to parse out the advantages and disadvantages of financing alternatives: flexibility, risk, income, timing, control, and other (*FRICTO*).

PATTERNS AND TRENDS IN FORM OF PAYMENT

Exhibit 20.1 gives information on the number and dollar value of deals by form of payment over time. Several important insights may be gleaned from this table.

EXHIBIT 20.1 Volume of M&A Transactions Broken Down by Form of Payment

	1990	1991	1992	1993	1994	1995	1996	1997	1998	1999	2000	2001	2002
Panel A: Number of *all deals* classified as cash, stock, or a blend													
Cash only	4,174	4,704	4,725	5,429	6,587	7,351	8,157	9,115	9,756	10,281	10,116	7,942	6,968
Stock only	383	529	666	818	959	1,098	1,220	1,453	1,438	1,554	2,063	1,243	842
Hybrid	234	311	398	498	691	645	940	1,228	1,183	1,153	1,433	953	663
Total	4,791	5,544	5,789	6,745	8,237	9,094	10,317	11,796	12,377	12,988	13,612	10,138	8,473
Panel B: Percentage distribution of number of *all deals* classified as cash, stock, or a blend													
Cash only	87%	85%	82%	80%	80%	81%	79%	77%	79%	79%	74%	78%	82%
Stock only	8%	10%	12%	12%	12%	12%	12%	12%	12%	12%	15%	12%	10%
Hybrid	5%	6%	7%	7%	8%	7%	9%	10%	10%	9%	11%	9%	8%
Total	100%	100%	100%	100%	100%	100%	100%	100%	100%	100%	100%	100%	100%
Panel C: Dollar value of *all deals* classified as cash, stock, or a blend ($MM)													
Cash only	$267,740	$208,772	$187,901	$208,803	$321,717	$413,630	$478,013	$ 726,714	$ 801,416	$1,048,193	$1,052,959	$ 673,732	$597,306
Stock only	$ 47,330	$ 29,855	$ 32,735	$ 58,364	$ 59,618	$193,256	$225,407	$ 360,575	$1,000,643	$1,067,675	$1,067,275	$ 277,799	$164,055
Hybrid	$ 15,570	$ 30,729	$24,824	$ 59,924	$ 50,080	$ 74,422	$146,872	$ 240,821	$ 236,156	$ 594,203	$ 450,151	$ 362,144	$108,224
Total	$330,640	$269,356	$245,460	$327,091	$431,414	$681,309	$850,292	$1,328,110	$2,038,215	$2,710,071	$2,570,385	$1,313,675	$869,585
Panel D: Percentage distribution of dollar value of *all deals* classified as cash, stock, or a blend													
Cash only	81%	78%	77%	64%	75%	61%	56%	55%	39%	39%	41%	51%	69%
Stock only	14%	11%	13%	18%	14%	28%	27%	27%	49%	39%	42%	21%	19%
Hybrid	5%	11%	10%	18%	12%	11%	17%	18%	12%	22%	18%	28%	12%
Total	100%	100%	100%	100%	100%	100%	100%	100%	100%	100%	100%	100%	100%
Panel E: Number of *jumbo deals* classified as cash, stock, or a blend													
Cash only											1		
Stock only						1	1		10	9	6	1	1
Hybrid								1		3	3	1	
Total	0	0	0	0	0	1	1	1	10	12	10	2	1

(Continued)

EXHIBIT 20.1 *(Continued)*

	1990	1991	1992	1993	1994	1995	1996	1997	1998	1999	2000	2001	2002
Panel F: Percentage distribution of number of *jumbo deals* classified as cash, stock, or a blend													
Cash only						—	—	—	—	—	10.0%	—	—
Stock only						100.0%	100.0%	—	100.0%	75.0%	60.0%	50.0%	100.0%
Hybrid						—	—	100.0%	—	25.0%	30.0%	50.0%	—
Total						100.0%	100.0%	100.0%	100.0%	100.0%	100.0%	100.0%	100.0%
Panel G: Dollar value of *jumbo deals* classified as cash, stock, or a blend													
Cash only											25,065		
Stock only						33,788	30,090		516,391	551,518	353,703	25,263	59,515
Hybrid								41,907		165,873	112,814	72,041	
Total						33,788	30,090	41,907	516,391	717,390	491,581	97,305	59,515
Panel H: Percentage distribution of dollar value of *jumbo deals* classified as cash, stock, or a blend													
Cash only						—	—	—	—	—	5.1%	—	—
Stock only						100.0%	100.0%	—	100.0%	76.9%	72.0%	26.0%	100.0%
Hybrid						—	—	100.0%	—	23.1%	22.9%	74.0%	—
Total						100.0%	100.0%	100.0%	100.0%	100.0%	100.0%	100.0%	100.0%

Note: This table excludes all deals for which financing was classified as "other" by SDC. "Jumbo" deals are in excess of $25 billion. Percentage totals may reflect rounding.
Source of data: Thomson Financial Corporation, SDC Platinum database.

First, as shown in Panels A through D, cash is king: Cash deals account for 75 to 85 percent of all deals on a numbers-of-deals basis and about 40 to 80 percent on a dollar-value basis.

Second, form of payment is related to size of the deal. The prevalence of cash payment probably reflects the fact that cash is the predominant form of payment in smaller acquisitions and that small acquisitions account for the bulk of deal volume. As shown in Panels E through H, stock payment is far more prevalent in very large deals ("jumbo" deals defined here as greater than $25 billion).

Third, the use of stock varies with the economic cycle: Stock is used in greater volume when the stock market is buoyant (as it was in 1998–2000). The high stock market and the surge in jumbo deals at that time are associated with higher dollar value of stock deals to dominate cash in buoyant times. This relationship of stock payment to buoyant market conditions is a fact cited in support of overvaluation theories that companies use stock as payment when they believe their shares are richly valued in the market. This is discussed at more length later in the chapter and in Chapter 4.

The time patterns of form of payment challenge the practitioner: Is this simply a random variation or are there serious explanations for these changes? More importantly, is the form of payment choice associated with significant outcomes?

DOES FORM OF PAYMENT MATTER?

Research finds that the decision about financing and form of payment is associated with large differences in outcomes. Several varieties of research offer insights here.

EVENT STUDIES OF NEAR-TERM INVESTOR REACTIONS TO ANNOUNCEMENTS Chapter 3 discusses the event study methodology and argues that it can lend insights into the expected profitability of transactions for the buyer and target. Exhibit 20.2 summarizes 12 studies of announcement returns segmented by form of payment. The consistent result across these studies can be summarized in the following points:

- ***Returns to target shareholders.*** Consistent with the results summarized in Chapter 3, target shareholders earn generally large positive announcement returns. But these returns differ materially by form of payment:
  - *Payment in cash:* Target shareholder returns are materially higher.
  - *Payment in stock:* Target shareholder returns are significantly positive but materially lower than those for the cash deals.
- ***Returns to buyer shareholders.*** As shown in the general results of Chapter 3, buyer shareholders basically break even at announcement. But form of payment produces an important difference in returns:
  - *Payment in cash:* Buyer shareholder returns are zero to positive, in some cases significantly positive.
  - *Payment in stock:* Buyer returns are significantly negative.
- ***Tender offers amplify the cash versus stock effect:*** with *tender offers* paid in cash, the returns to buyers are even higher and the returns from offers paid in stock are even lower.

EXHIBIT 20.2 Summary of Shareholder Return Studies for M&A: Returns to Acquiring Firm Shareholders

Study	Cumulative Abnormal Returns to Targets	Cumulative Abnormal Returns to Buyers	Sample Size	Sample Period	Notes
Wansley, Lane, Yang (1983)	Securities: 17.47%* (–40,0) Cash: 33.54%† Combination: 11.77%†	N/A	102	1970–1978	
Asquith, Bruner, Mullins (1987)	*All Observations (–1,0)* Stock: +13.85%† Cash: +27.47% Stock & cash: +32.18%† *Tender Offers Only (–1,0)* Stock: N/A Cash: +24.58% Stock & cash: +37.57%† *Merger Offers Only* Stock: +13.85%† Cash: +28.77%† Stock & cash: +27.69%†	*All Observations (–1,0)* Stock: -2.40%† Cash: +0.20% Stock & cash: -1.47%† *Tender Offers Only* Stock: N/A Cash: +1.21% Stock & cash: –2.35%† *Merger Offers Only* Stock: –2.58%† Cash: +0.91% Stock & cash: –0.20%	343	1973–1983	U.S. targets and buyers. Mergers and tender offers.
Travlos (1987)	N/A	Stock: –1.47%† Cash: +0.24%	60	1972–1981	
Eckbo, Giammarino, Heinkel (1990)	N/A	Stock: +2.72%* Cash: +1.43% Stock & cash: +5.68%†	182	1964–1982	Canadian companies.

Masse et al. (1990)	*Over −1,0* Stock: +7.38%† Cash: +11.37%† *Over −10, +10* Stock: +2.94% Cash: +23.45%	*Over −1,0* Stock: +2.39%† Cash: +1.59%* *Over −10, +10* Stock: +3.83%‡ Cash: +5.89%†	80	1984–1987	Canadian companies.
Franks, Harris, Titman (1991)	N/A	Stock: +0.42% Cash: +1.08%* Other: +1.21%*	399	1975–1984	Returns difference between cash and equity is significant.
Servaes (1991)	Stock: +20.47%† Cash: +26.67%† Mix: +21.05%† (from announcement date to effective date)	Stock: −5.86%† Cash: +3.84%† Mix: −3.74%†	704	1972–1987	Mergers and tender offers; segment data by payment method.
Sullivan et al. (1994)	Stock: +12.94%* Cash: +21.56%*	Stock: −0.62% Cash: +0.24%	84	1980–1988	Sample of merger offers that were eventually terminated.
Han, Suk, Son (1998)	N/A	All stock: −2.2%* All cash: −0.5% Mergers stock: −2.3%† Mergers cash: −1.0% Tender offers stock: +0.3% Tender offers cash: −0.3%	126	1974–1980	

(Continued)

EXHIBIT 20.2 *(Continued)*

Study	Cumulative Abnormal Returns to Targets	Cumulative Abnormal Returns to Buyers	Sample Size	Sample Period	Notes
Emery, Switzer (1999)	N/A	Stock: –2.02%† Cash: –0.18%	347	1967–1987	Sample of successful mergers and tender offers.
Yook (2000)	N/A	Stock (whole sample): –1.51%* Stock, debt upgrade: +2.32%* Stock, debt downgrade: –4.61%† Stock, no rating change: –1.62%* Cash (whole sample): –0.71% Cash, debt downgrade: –0.09% Cash, no rating change: –1.21%	311	1985–1996	Considers interaction of form of payment and debt rating changes.
Heron, Lie (2002)	Stock: +17.1%† Cash: +25.4%† Mix: +19.3%†	Stock: –1.9% Cash: +0.6% Mix: +0.3%	859	1985–1997	

Note: Unless otherwise noted, event date is announcement date of merger/bid.
*Significant at the 0.05 level or better.
† Significant at the 0.01 level or better.
‡Significant at the 0.10 level or better.

CROSS-SECTIONAL STUDIES OF THE DRIVERS OF EVENT RETURNS The arresting disparity in event returns between cash and stock deals has stimulated further research into its origins. Han et al. (1998) and Asquith et al. (1987) find that relative size significantly interacts with the cash versus stock choice: Large cash deals have more positive returns, and large equity deals have more negative returns. Emery and Switzer (1999) found that tax, size, "Q,"[1] and the amount of cash or unused debt capacity were significant drivers. Hayn (1989) compared the returns to bidders and targets in taxable and nontaxable deals—taxable deals are often for cash; nontaxable deals are almost always for stock. Hayn found a pattern of returns to bidders that mirrors well the pattern associated with form of payment—this implies that taxes are a factor in the choice. Yook (2000) found that changes in the firm's bond ratings were significantly associated with these returns—this emphasizes the financing dimension of the choice of medium of exchange.

STUDIES OF LONG-TERM PERFORMANCE AFTER THE DEAL IS DONE Focusing on reported financial results, two studies found no evidence that operating performance varied by form of payment. But focusing on investor returns, Loughran and Vijh (1997) found a sizable difference over the five years following the deal: Share-for-share deals yielded average excess returns of +14.5 percent to investors, while cash deals yielded +90.1 percent. The disparity between the two sets of studies is a clue that the use of stock could be opportunistic—that is, to exploit overvaluation of the buyer's shares in the market.

FACTOR ANALYSES REVEALING CHARACTERISTICS OF THOSE WHO PAY WITH CASH OR STOCK Several studies lend insights here. The studies reveal that *stock* tends to be used when:

- ***A deal is friendly.*** Zhang (2001) finds that cash payment is strongly associated with tender offers, which tend to be hostile.
- ***Buyer's stock price is buoyant.*** The better performing the buyer's stock is, the greater the likelihood of a share-for-share deal. The typical measure here is the firm's "Q" ratio (market value divided by book value). Several studies identify this effect: Zhang (2001), Heron and Lie (2002), Chang and Mais (2000), and Martin (1996). Carleton et al. (1983) and Martin (1996) find that the acquiring firm's investment opportunities are an important determinant of the form of payment: Acquirers with high "Q" are significantly more likely to issue stock than cash or a blend.
- ***Ownership is not concentrated.*** Two studies, Chang and Mais (2000) and Yook et al. (1999), find that if the ownership of the target and/or the buyer is concentrated, the deal tends to be settled in cash. By not paying with stock, the buyer possibly avoids bringing a new significant shareholder into the equity ownership of the buyer, with the potential to destabilize the internal politics of the equity ownership group. When Time-Warner acquired Turner Enterprises for stock, it made Ted Turner the largest single shareholder of the firm. Turner, known for his temper and outspoken views, must have contributed to lively board meetings until he resigned in disagreement.
- ***Deals are larger in size.*** The larger the size of the target relative to the buyer, the greater the likelihood that the buyer will pay with stock. This may be re-

lated to the next point, the ability to simply "write a check." See Hansen (1987) and Zhang (2001).

- *Buyer has less cash.* Zhang (2001), Heron and Lie (2002), and Chang and Mais (2000) find that the ability of the buyer to pay with cash (measured as the buyer's cash balance relative to the size of the target deal) was a significant determinant of whether the form of payment was cash or stock.

This research leads to three general explanations for why form of payment has such a big effect on returns to shareholders. These are not mutually exclusive, though in the research papers they compete for primacy. The first is an explanation based on *minimization of costs.* In general, the theory of capital structure choice from Modigliani and Miller (1963) to the present is a study in how firms can minimize their cost of capital. This entails the classic trade-off between bankruptcy costs and the benefits of debt tax shields. But taxes have an effect in M&A that extends well beyond the cost of capital. For instance, some deal structures may be more tax-efficient than others: All else equal, deals that allow the buyer to reduce tax expense create value for shareholders.[2] Tax-efficient deals from the buyer's standpoint will most likely be cash deals.

Second, *agency costs* and monitoring may explain the impact of form of financing. If the firm must borrow to finance a cash deal, then the intervention of creditors binds managers to delivering targeted levels of performance; they cannot divert the free cash flow of the firm for private benefits, and instead must discipline the firm to meet its future obligations. This discipline presumably yields higher performance and better share prices. Bharadwaj and Shivdasani (2003) report that bidders' announcement returns in tender offers are positively related to the fraction of the acquisition value financed by bank debt. Creditors appear to play an important certification and monitoring role.

The third explanation is based on *information asymmetry*, the possibility that managers have a clearer view of the true value of the firm than do public shareholders. This asymmetry means that market prices may deviate from intrinsic value of the firm and present interesting arbitrage opportunities. Myers and Majluf (1984), for instance, have used this to argue that firms will follow a *pecking order* in their financing, preferring to use inside funds before raising funds in the capital market, and then preferring to raise debt before equity. Thus, Myers and Majluf hypothesize that managers will issue new equity only when the firm is overvalued and that therefore equity issues will be a negative signal to public investors about the private beliefs of the insiders. Consistent with this, event studies have documented that the announcement of equity issues by firms is associated with significant negative event returns.[3] Shleifer and Vishny (2001) and Rhodes-Kropf and Viswanathan (2003) use this logic to explain the appearance of merger waves. Market booms will be times of overvaluations; these overvaluations trigger a rise in M&A activity and the use of stock as a medium of payment. Ang and Cheng (2003) find empirical evidence that overvaluation is an important motive for the use of stock as a medium of payment. Buyers are more overvalued than targets and nonbuyers; successful acquirers (those who actually consummate announced deals) are more overvalued than unsuccessful acquirers.

CONSIDERATIONS IN SELECTING THE FORM OF PAYMENT

The systemic nature of M&A deal design is one of the important themes of this book. Chapter 18 emphasizes this message and illustrates the linkages among the various dimensions of a deal. Nowhere does the linkage among the elements emerge so clearly as in the question of which form of payment to choose for an offer. Theoretical research on this question highlights a number of considerations that are significant for the practitioner. The challenges here arise from several sources.

Different Perspectives

To the selling shareholder, form of payment is an *investment* issue; to the buyer, form of payment is a *financing* issue. As a result of a transaction, the seller's portfolio of investments will change. This raises the four classic considerations of portfolio allocation decisions: risk, return, liquidity, and taxes. Also, the seller may have derived benefits from a control position, which may change with the transaction. How the buyer finances the acquisition only indirectly affects the seller's thinking, through risk and return. The form of payment one chooses has an impact on the buyer's post-merger capital structure and may trigger the issuance of securities. From a managerial perspective, form and financing are identical to the buyer. Thus, the first implication is that the deal designer should think strategically: Consider the perspective of the counterparty as well as your own. The viable deal will satisfy both perspectives.

Possibility of Competing Bidders

This amplifies the need to think strategically, taking into account the likely reactions of the counterparty, but also of competitors (actual and potential). Chapters 31, 32, and 33 discuss the deal-design implications of competitors. But much of the theoretical work emphasizes that choosing the right form of payment can strongly influence the target and thus preempt competing bidders. Hostile tender offers are predominantly cash deals, reflecting the investment appetites of arbitrageurs and removing any contingency about the assessment of the value of the bid. Thus, the practical implication here is to choose a form of payment consistent with the probability of entry by competitors.

Taxes

Cash and stock deals differ significantly in their tax exposures for the target shareholders and buyer firm. Chapter 19 describes the various forms of reorganization and their tax implications. In a cash-for-stock deal, the target's shareholders must pay taxes immediately on their capital gains, and recognize any losses. The buyer firm may step up the tax basis of the assets to reflect the acquisition premium provided it executes the appropriate election to do so (see Chapter 19 for details on elections). This increases the depreciation tax shield of the target postacquisition, and creates value for the buyer. In a stock deal, neither of these effects happens: the target's shareholders' taxes are deferred until the shares of Newco are sold, and the buyer firm does not get to step up its tax basis.[4] Hayn (1989) shows that abnormal returns to target shareholders are higher for taxable than tax-deferred deals, which is consistent with the findings summarized in Exhibit 20.2. In cash deals the target shareholders may receive greater payment because of their immediate tax exposure and perhaps because buyers can pay more thanks to the larger tax shield they enjoy. Tax effects must be traded off against other costs and benefits.

Control

Cash and stock may differ materially in their impact on the voting control of Newco after the transaction. A cash transaction will not affect the composition of the buyer's equity ownership. But a stock transaction could impose a large change, depending on the size of the target relative to the buyer. Control is valuable, as Chapter 15 discusses. Control effects must be traded off against other costs and benefits.

Reported Financial Results

The choice of stock or cash payment will affect Newco's balance sheet, EPS, returns, and measures of leverage. Chapters 16 and 17 detail some of the effects of a merger on reported financial results. EPS dilution occurs where the buyer's shares outstanding increase faster than net income—this means that using equity as a form of payment will generally[5] be more dilutive than cash. However, the decision maker should give more weight to economic dilution than accounting dilution.

Financing

In general, paying with stock will create financial flexibility, and paying with cash will consume it. Exhibit 20.3 illustrates the linkage between form of payment and financing. A deal might create or consume excess cash or unused debt capacity (commonly called *"financial slack"*) depending on whether it is able to draw on internal resources or must turn to external financing, and on whether the financing is in the form of debt or equity. The pecking order theory of corporate financing suggests that managers will have a preference to use internal resources before seeking external financing. Shares of stock held in treasury are a form of internal finance because these shares have already been approved and do not require a shareholder vote, as is typically the case with an issue of new shares. Various practical considerations in weighing the financial implications of different deal designs are discussed in this chapter.

Transaction Costs

Different forms of payment may entail a wide variety of frictional costs. They may be nil in the case of a cash payment made directly from the buyer's cash account or a stock payment made directly from the buyer's shares held in treasury. A cash payment financed by a bank loan or an issue of bonds might entail underwriting or closing costs of 1 to 3 percent of the face amount of the funds. A stock payment financed by shares repurchased in the market would incur brokerage fees. And a stock payment financed by the issue of new equity might incur fees for preparation of a proxy statement, an extraordinary shareholder meeting to approve the share

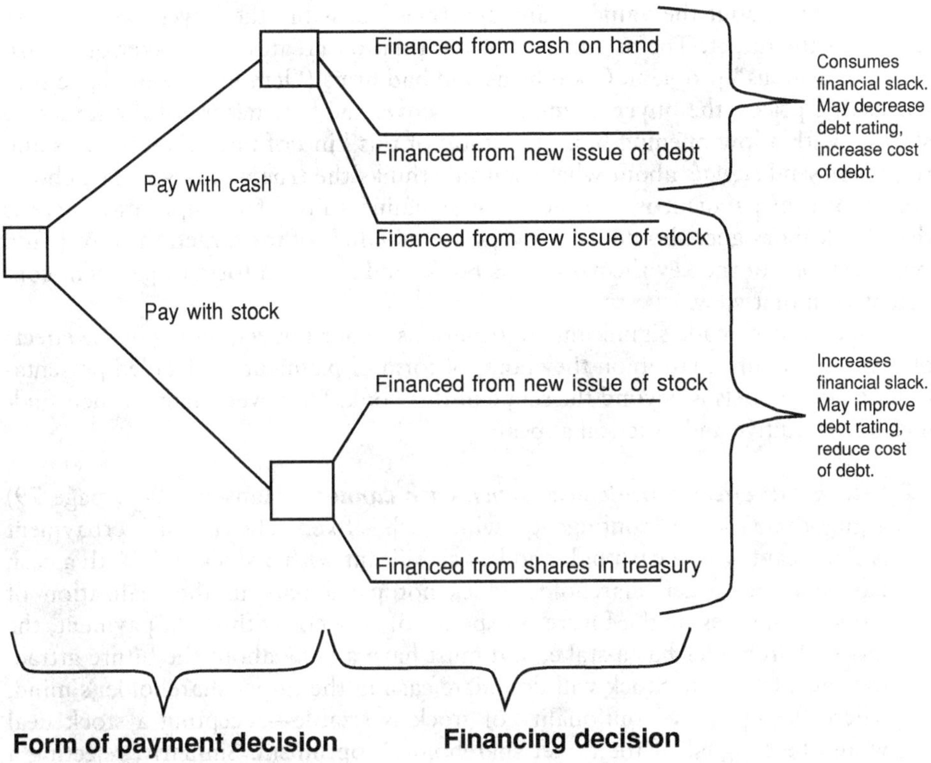

EXHIBIT 20.3 Illustration of Linkage between Form of Payment and Financing: Decision Tree and Outcomes

issue, and registration—for a large issue, these can run into the millions of dollars. Though transaction costs are not usually a primary consideration in the choice of form of payment, they can be decisive when the choice hangs in the balance.

Size, Both Absolute and Relative

Size matters for reasons of financing, control, and strategic positioning. Larger buyers have deeper pockets than smaller buyers—in practice, many large buyers prefer to "write a check" or issue shares from treasury for smaller deals; this is the influence of transaction costs. But when the target is large *relative to the buyer*, the effects of transaction costs, financing, control, and expected synergy value are amplified. More importantly, larger relative size may give greater bargaining power to extract more of the synergy value for the benefit of target shareholders.

Asymmetric Information

The target managers usually have a clearer idea of the target's intrinsic value than the buyer's management has. And this asymmetry doubles where the buyer's managers have a clearer idea of the buyer's intrinsic value compared to what the target's management knows. The buyer and target managers may have their own private views about the value of any synergies—possibly the buyer has a clearer idea than the target. The asymmetry of information creates what Akerlof (1970) called a "lemons" problem: Good firms and bad firms ("lemons") could have similar asking prices; the buyer attempts to discover the true nature of the target by starting with a low opening bid. In a world of this kind of uncertainty, offers and responses send *signals* about what each side thinks the true values are. The choice about form of payment is one means of signaling value. The implication here is that the deal designer should have a view about values of the target, the buyer, and synergies (one of the key themes of this book) and choose a form of payment consistent with that view.

Four studies[6] made significant contributions to our understanding of the effects of asymmetric information on the choice of form of payment. A detailed presentation of their models is beyond the scope of this book. However, many of their findings have intuitive and practical appeal:

- ***"Stock can effect a trade even when cash cannot."*** Hansen (1987, page 79) argues that stock is "contingent," while cash is fixed. The risk of overpayment is significant with a cash bid, and less significant with a stock bid. With a cash payment the target shareholder does not participate in the realization of merger synergies or the future prosperity of Newco; with stock payment, the target shareholder has a stake, and must have a view about the future attractiveness of Newco. Stock will dominate cash in the target shareholder's mind, where the upside or optionality of stock is sizable—accepting a stock deal would be a signal of the target shareholder's optimism. Similarly, rejecting a stock deal would be a signal of pessimism. From the buyer's standpoint, a stock offer is part of a process of price discovery. "When a target firm knows its value better than a potential acquirer, the acquirer will prefer to offer stock, which has desirable contingent-pricing characteristics, rather than cash." (Hansen 1987, page 75)
- ***Buyers tend to offer stock when they believe their shares are overvalued and cash when undervalued.*** This reflects the asymmetric knowledge held by the buyer, and is generally consistent with theories and empirical findings about equity issuance and merger waves. In all of the studies bidders who believe they are undervalued and/or are optimistic about the value of merger synergies will tend to offer cash. This signal of optimism with the cash offer is used to argue why the stock prices of bidders react positively at the announcement of cash deals, and negatively at the announcement of stock deals. Berkovich and Narayanan (1989) explore the situation of the target and argue that we should observe the same pattern in target returns. Chapter 4 also discusses the impact of overvaluation on M&A activity.
- ***Stock is used less often where the target is small relative to the buyer.*** Hansen argues that the attractiveness of stock depends on its contingent-pricing feature, the ability of Newco's share price to reflect future synergies arising from the acquisition of the target. "Contingent pricing" means that target shareholders who receive Newco stock will receive total payments that are higher or lower in proportion to the merger benefits realized. These benefits are uncertain. Thus, the use of stock is a hedge against the buyer's uncertainty. When the target is small the effect of this uncertainty on Newco's

shares may be negligible and the risk-management benefit of paying with stock not important.

- ***The probability of a stock offer increases with the buyer's indebtedness and decreases with the target's indebtedness.*** This grows out of Hansen's size argument: The bigger the target's equity is relative to the buyer's stock, the more attractive it will be because of its contingent nature. One could add that the relation with the buyer's indebtedness would also be consistent with a process of capital structure optimization.
- ***A cash offer preempts competitors better than securities.*** Fishman (1989) explores the presence of competitors and finds that form of payment is as important a signal as price. When the buyer offers securities, the expected value of the target must be lower than if cash were offered, and the likelihood of rejection by the target will be higher. Competitors will have a greater likelihood of entering after an initial offer of securities than after an initial offer of cash. And the more costly the buyer's acquisition of information about the target, the more likely the buyer will offer cash and the less likely that competitors will enter. Fishman (1989, page 53) writes, "This is an interesting rationale for firms to continually release information. It can make preemptive bids more costly and thus raise a firm's expected payoff in the event it becomes a candidate for acquisition." Berkovich and Narayanan (1989) find that the fraction of synergy captured by target shareholders will increase with a cash deal and with increasing competition and that the cash portion of an offer will increase with competition.

The thrust of this research is that the practitioner should view form of payment, price, and financing as *jointly determined* in settling on terms of a deal. Exhibit 20.4 combines the choices about price, form of payment, and financing to demonstrate how they might be bundled to present very different propositions to target shareholders. Consider two alternative strategies:

1. ***Preemption strategy.*** In 1995, IBM mounted a hostile tender offer of $3.5 billion in cash for all shares of Lotus Corporation. This was the biggest takeover attempt seen in the software industry up to that time, and the price represented one of the largest acquisition premiums, 100 percent, in the computer technology field. The payment was practically funded from IBM's cash on hand.[7] Lotus capitulated within one week. This was a *preemptive strategy*. Industry observers noted that IBM needed Lotus for strategic positioning versus Microsoft and may have feared a competitive bid from that firm. By offering a very full price, cash, and payment from internal funds, IBM made a convincing offer to Lotus shareholders that held *no contingencies*: no doubts about financing, no doubts about the value of securities, and no efforts to establish the credibility of future synergies. IBM effectively thwarted the entry of other bidders.
2. ***Contingency strategy.*** On January 27, 1997, Hilton offered to pay $55 a share in cash for 50.1 percent of ITT shares and $55 a share in stock for the rest. The bid was a 29 percent premium to ITT's share price before, and amounted to a $6.5 billion equity bid, large in comparison to Hilton's market capitalization of about $5 billion. The cash portion of the bid would be financed by loans from banks. The issue of common shares would require approval from Hilton's

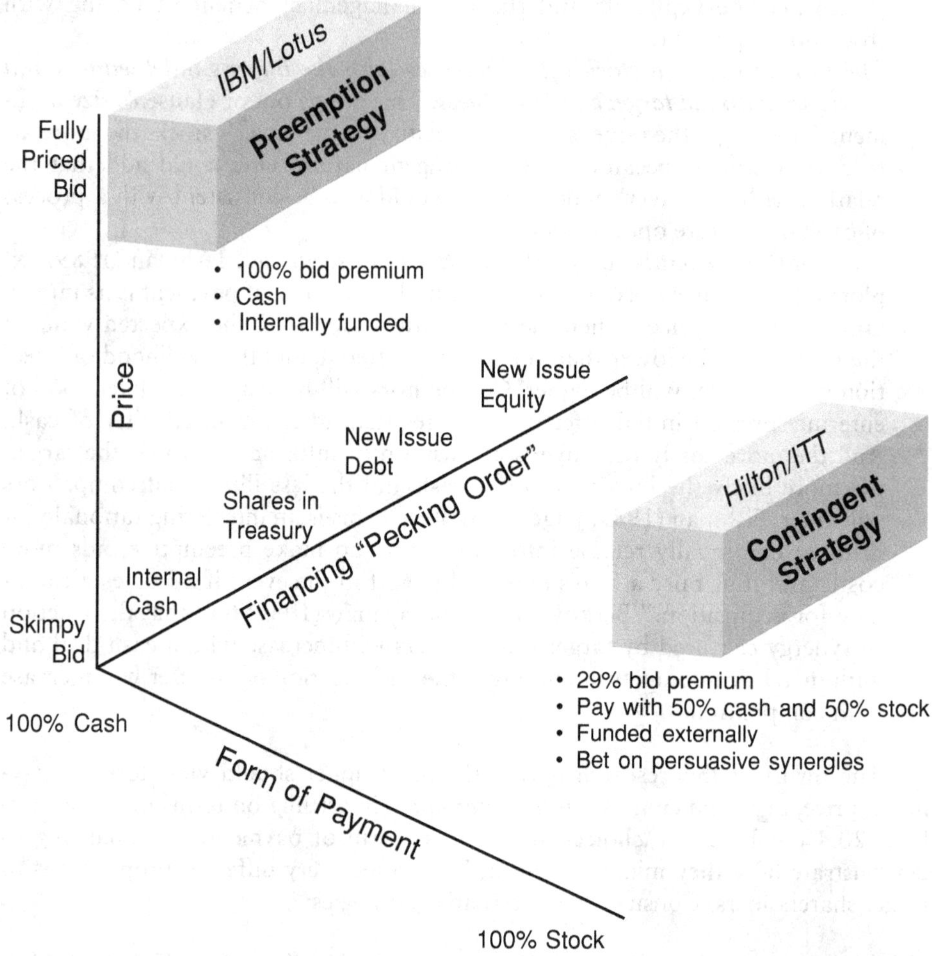

EXHIBIT 20.4 Classification of Deal Structures in Terms of Price, Form of Payment, and Financing

shareholders and registration with the SEC. Whereas Hilton was regarded as an efficient firm with rising financial performance, ITT had performed poorly in recent years. Hilton's view was that value would be created by restructuring operations to make them more efficient, and by exploiting synergy opportunities worth perhaps another $1 billion in present value terms; see Bruner and Vakharia (1998).

Both Hilton and ITT operated prominent chains of hotels and gambling casinos. Hilton was appealing to institutional shareholders of ITT to accept the shares and participate in the value creation. Hilton was probably also cognizant of the share holdings by arbitrageurs who prefer payment in cash rather than securities. It was not apparent to Hilton's CEO that other bidders could come forward with the industry expertise and credibility of Hilton. By mounting a low-premium bid, a blend of cash and shares, and financing from external borrowings, Hilton was pursuing a *contingent strategy*, appealing to investors' view of the future, and generally starting low so as not to suffer from overpayment. In response to the hostile bid, ITT mounted a recapitalization program and then persuaded Starwood Corporation, a real estate investment trust (REIT), to enter the bidding. Owing to its tax-advantaged status, Starwood was able to bid more (a 98 percent premium over ITT's pretakeover price) and thereby acquired ITT.

ASSESSING THE FINANCING ASPECTS OF A DEAL

Thus far, this chapter has focused mainly on the choice of form of payment. Here, the focus turns to an assessment of the financing of the deal.

Seven Dimensions of M&A Transaction Financing

Occasionally, a chief financial officer will say, "All I do is get the best deal I can whenever we need funds." In all probability, CFOs are more determinate than that. The range of choice is captured in the following seven levers that executives can manipulate to find an appropriate transaction financing structure: mix, maturity, basis, currency, exotica, control, and distribution.

MIX OF TYPES OF FINANCING The mix of classes of capital (such as debt versus equity) is perhaps the most prominent choice in acquisition financing. Mix may be analyzed through capitalization ratios, debt-service coverage ratios, and the firm's sources and uses of funds statement (where the analyst should look for the origins of the new additions to capital in the recent past). Many firms exhibit a pecking order of financing: They seek to fill their funds needs through retentions of profits, then through debt, and, finally, through the issuance of new shares. As outlined in Chapter 13, the effect of leverage on the value of the firm is curvilinear: there is likely to be an optimal mix at which the present value of debt tax shields and the present value of expected distress and bankruptcy costs just trade off to produce a maximum value. In addition to this value optimization approach, CFOs display preferences for kinds of financing. The theory of the pecking order, originated by Stewart Myers, supposes that managers have a preference for using internal sources of capital first before going to the capital markets—and when they have to do so, they prefer issuing debt before equity. The mix may also be influenced by opportunistic response to hot, cold, or segmented markets. There may be good moments to issue debt or equity. Finally, the asset base of the firm may influence its decision about the mix of debt and equity. Lenders are prone to lend money against assets in place, but not against assets they can't see.

MATURITY *Maturity structure of financing* refers to the life of securities issued. This is measured in years and ranges significantly across commercial paper (short-term), notes (intermediate-term), and bonds (long-term). Maturity structures can be summarized by statistics such as average maturity and duration.[8] But the key idea is that different financing proposals often have rather different implications for the maturity structure of liabilities; they can expose the firm to different kinds of risks. A *risk-neutral maturity structure* would equate the life of the firm's assets to the life of the firm's liabilities. Most firms accept an inequality in one direction or the other. A structure in which the maturity of liabilities is greater than the maturity of the firm's assets creates *reinvestment risk*, the risk that management will not be able to deploy the cash released by the firm's assets to achieve returns sufficient to service the liabilities. In the opposite case, where the maturity of assets is greater than the maturity of liabilities, the firm is exposed to *refinancing risk*, the risk that the firm will not be able to roll over its maturing liabilities on favorable terms. Most firms do not have risk-neutral maturity structures. The absence of a perfect maturity hedge might reflect managers' better-informed bets about the future of the firm and markets.

BASIS FOR THE YIELDS: FIXED OR FLOATING In simplest terms, *yield basis* addresses the choice between *fixed or floating rates* of payment and is a useful tool in fathoming management's judgment regarding the future course of interest rates. Whether to lock in a fixed rate of interest now rather than agree to a floating rate of interest will depend in part on one's outlook for interest rates. There is also a second consideration: whether the issuer's returns vary with fluctuations in interest rates. Much like the matching of maturities, one can try to match the type of interest rate to the type of asset returns. This is relatively easy to do for financial institutions, and considerably more difficult for commercial and industrial firms. For those firms, basis will be a less important consideration.

CURRENCY *Currency* addresses the global aspect of a firm's acquisition financing opportunities. These opportunities are expressed in two ways: (1) management of the firm's exposure to foreign exchange rate fluctuations, and (2) exploitation of unusual financing possibilities in global capital markets. Exchange rate exposure arises when a firm earns income (or pays expenses) in currencies other than its operating income. Whether and how a firm hedges this exposure can reveal bets that management is making about the future movement of exchange rates and the future currency mix of the firm's cash flows. Chapter 12 discusses the effect of foreign currency exposure on valuation.

EXOTIC TERMS Every firm faces a spectrum of financing alternatives, ranging from plain vanilla bonds and stocks to hybrids and one-of-a-kind, highly tailored securities.[9] Where a firm positions itself on this spectrum of *exotic terms* can shed light on management's openness to new ideas, intellectual originality, and, possibly, opportunistic tendencies. As a general matter, option-linked securities often appear in corporate finance where there is some disagreement between issuers and investors about a firm's prospects. For instance, managers of high-growth firms will foresee rapid expansion and vaulting stock prices; bond investors, not having the benefit of inside information, might only see high risk—issuing a convertible bond might be a way to allow the bond investors to capitalize the risk[10] and enjoy the creation of value through growth in return for accepting a lower current yield. Also, the circumstances under which exotic securities were issued are often fascinating episodes in a company's history. Exotic securities can serve the firm and M&A deal in a second important way: They can tap pools of capital and thus perhaps lower the firm's cost of capital.

CONTROL FEATURES Any management team probably prefers little outside control. With regard to *control features*, one must recognize that, in any financial structure, management has made choices about subtle control trade-offs, including *who* might exercise control (e.g., creditors, existing shareholders, new shareholders, or a raider); *degree* of control exercised by various players, and the control *trigger* (e.g., default on a loan covenant, passing a preferred stock dividend, a shareholder vote). How management structures these control triggers (e.g., the tightness of loan covenants) or forestalls changes of control (e.g., through the adoption of poison pills and other takeover defenses) can reveal insights about management's fears and expectations. Clues about external-control choices may be found in credit covenants, collateral pledges, the terms of preferred shares, the profile of the firm's equity holders, the voting rights of common stock, corporate bylaws, and antitakeover defenses. A second interesting dimension of control resides in who will own the securities. Whether or not an investor has outright control over the firm, the inclinations of that investor can influence directors and managers. Knowing who will own the securities issued in an M&A financing will influence one's assessment of the control implications of a financing.

DISTRIBUTION This final design lever affects (1) the way the firm markets its securities (i.e., acquires capital) and (2) the way the firm delivers value to its investors (i.e., returns capital). Regarding marketing, insights emerge from knowing where a firm's securities are listed for trading, how often shares are sold, and who advises the sale of securities (the adviser a firm attracts is one indication of its sophistication). Regarding delivery of value, the two generic strategies involve dividends or capital gains. Some companies will pay low or no dividends and force their shareholders to take returns in the form of capital gains. Other companies will pay material dividends, even borrowing to do so. Still others will repurchase shares, split shares, and declare extraordinary dividends. Managers' choices about delivering value yield clues about management's beliefs about investors and about the company's ability to satisfy investor needs. The choices about *distribution* of securities include retail versus institutional, domestic versus international, and full commitment versus best efforts.

Key Perspectives for Analysis of the Financing Choice

The seven levers of financing suggest many avenues for analysis. Exhibit 20.5 summarizes the issues raised by each dimension. In themselves the seven dimensions have no normative content. Thus, the deal designer must have in mind some benchmarks against which to evaluate the structural alternatives. Here are four perspectives that will yield useful insights about the relative merits of alternative financing structures.

THINK LIKE AN INVESTOR The definition of a good capital structure would be one that maximizes shareholder value. This structure will also minimize the weighted average cost of capital and maximize the share price and value of the enterprise. Chapter 9 discusses what it means to think like an investor.

EXHIBIT 20.5 Using the Seven Elements to Assess M&A Financing Choices

	Issues in M&A Finance	Tests of Effects and Design Solutions
Mix	Form of payment: stock, debt, cash (negative debt).	The effect of different mix choices can be tested through valuation analysis and sensitivity analysis. The most advanced test of the appropriateness of a mix uses Monte Carlo simulation to estimate the probability of default. Here one would consider how well the mix exploits the benefits of debt tax shields and avoids effects of default risk.
Maturity	How rapidly to repay acquisition debt.	Comparing the duration of debt with hypothetical duration of firm's assets can test the effect of different maturity choices. Determined by strength of target cash flows and buyer's alternative uses for cash.
Basis	Is the exposure to debt and equity market volatility acceptable? How will the value of the deal vary with capital market volatility?	Can be tested by examining the duration of the debt, or with Monte Carlo simulation. Exposure hedged with caps, floors, and collars on stock-for-stock exchange ratios; interest rate hedges can minimize exposure to rate volatility.
Currency	Is the exposure to foreign currency exchange rate volatility acceptable?	Can be tested with sensitivity analysis or more advanced value at risk (VAR) analysis. Currency hedges (options, futures, foreign currency loans) can be used to minimize this exposure.
Exotica	Will tailoring pay? Do special capital market segments exist that have an appetite for tailored securities from this deal?	The potential advantage from tailoring cannot be measured rigorously without being able to compare the exotic and plain-vanilla alternatives. Financial advisers who are actively engaged in the distribution of securities can offer general insights in the opportunities here: mezzanine debt and equity, hybrid securities, options, warrants, earnouts.
Control	What degree of control do the different players in the deal have? How is it represented? How can it be exercised? What incentives for cooperation in financial distress does the financial design create?	Test for the tightness of loan covenants, the distribution of shareholder votes, and seats on the board of directors. Tailor control through design of securities.
Distribution	To whom will the target's cash flows go? Through what channels will the securities in this deal be distributed?	One can test for potential wealth transfers among participants in the deal through valuation analysis. The appropriateness of financial advisers can be considered with the help of league tables, reputations, core competencies, and fee scales.

THINK LIKE A CREDITOR Lenders and investors in firms are quite conscious of this risk of default, and set their required returns in reference to that risk. Beyond some reasonable level of indebtedness, lenders and investors will sense that the firm is assuming more and more default risk, and will raise the required returns (the interest rate) on their loans and on their equity investments. The required rate of return is set through a process of credit analysis. Credit analysis could be as complicated as using an advanced credit scoring model[11] or simulating the risk of default (see the mini-case on Revco Drug Stores in Chapter 13), or as simple as making qualitative judgments on a set of standard criteria such as the "*Six C's of Credit*:"

1. *Cash flow:* Is the firm's expected cash flow large enough to meet the principal and interest payments?
2. *Collateral:* If we have to foreclose on the loan, are there sufficient assets in the firm that we could sell to repay the loan?
3. *Capital:* Is there enough other capital ranking in priority below this loan to withstand a reasonable cyclical downturn in this firm's business?
4. *Conditions:* Do the current economic conditions favor timely debt payments?
5. *Course:* Is the use to which these funds will be put appropriate? Is the general strategy of this firm on course?
6. *Character:* Are the managers involved not only sufficiently intelligent and skilled, but also inclined to honor the repayment commitment?

For many long-term bonds, creditworthiness is summarized in a bond rating. As the firm borrows more, the rating will decline. As the rating declines, the return that investors require will rise.

A special concern of *unsecured* creditors is whether the surviving firm is to be adequately capitalized in the face of ordinary business adversities. Failure to do so exposes secured lenders, directors, selling shareholders, and professional advisers to a variety of penalties[12] under *fraudulent conveyance*[13] litigation. The incidence of fraudulent conveyance lawsuits has risen over time, along with the volume of highly leveraged transactions. It should remain a concern for the deal designer, however, in virtually all transactions.

To mitigate exposure to possible fraudulent conveyance litigation, deal designers will seek to obtain an *opinion of solvency* from a qualified independent consultant. Typically the opinion will be based on independent due diligence, valuation analysis, and analysis of forecasts. This may entail field investigations of the company and the industry, discussions with industry experts, and the use of advanced analytical techniques. The opinion may consist of a one-page letter that summarizes the analytic work of the consultant, the conclusions, and finally the opinion itself. Frequently, the opinion will be accompanied by a bound report describing the detailed analysis; the purpose of this is to document the consultant's work for possible use in future litigation.

THINK LIKE A COMPETITOR The competitive perspective matters to transaction designers and senior executives for two important reasons. First, it tests a proposed financial structure against standard practice in the industry and the strategic position of the firm relative to the competition. Second, it explores the competitive implications of a financial structure, giving particular attention to the reaction of competitors in the future and the resources with which a firm might respond. This perspective takes for granted the firm's financial strategy, and explores how it is likely to play in the competitive arena.[14] Chapter 6 discusses the competitive and strategic perspective.

THINK LIKE THE CEO Senior managements' vision for the firm is the final major benchmark for assessing a firm's financial structure. This screen accounts for the consistency of the firm's financial structure with the profitability, growth, and dividend goals of the firm. The classic tools of internal analysis are the forecast cash flow and financial statements. The essence of this perspective is a concern for (1) the preservation of the firm's *financial flexibility*, (2) the *sustainability* of the firm's financial policies, and (3) the *internal consistency* of the firm's strategic goals. For instance, the long-term goals may call for a doubling of sales in five years. The business plan for achieving this goal may call for the construction of a greenfield plant in year 1, then regional-distribution systems in years 2 and 3. Substantial working-capital investments will be necessary in years 2 through 5. How this growth is to be financed has huge implications for your firm's financial structure *today*. Typically, an analyst addresses this problem by forecasting the financial performance of the firm, experimenting with different financing sequences and choosing the best one, then determining the structure that makes the best foundation for that financing sequence. This analysis implies the need to maintain future financial flexibility. Financial flexibility is easily measured as the excess cash and unused debt capacity on which the firm might call. In addition, there may be other reserves such as unused land or excess stocks of raw materials that could be liquidated. All reserves that could be mobilized should be reflected in an analysis of financial flexibility. A shorthand test for sustainability and internal consistency is the self-sustainable growth model. This model is discussed in Chapter 6.

TRIANGULATE ACROSS THESE PERSPECTIVES All four perspectives are not likely to offer a completely congruent assessment of financial structure. The investor's and creditor's views look at the *economic* consequences of a financial structure; the competitor's view considers *strategic* consequences; the internal view addresses the *mission and objectives* of the firm. The four views ask entirely different questions; an analyst should not be surprised when the answers diverge. The judgment about what constitutes an appropriate financial structure will depend on blending these various perspectives through a process of triangulation much as is discussed in Chapter 9 with regard to valuation.

A Summary Framework: FRICTO

A widely used approach to evaluating financing alternatives is the FRICTO framework. The framework can help to identify trade-offs along six dimensions:

1. *Flexibility:* the ability to meet unforeseen financing requirements as they arise. Flexibility may involve liquidating assets or tapping the capital markets in adverse market environments or both. Flexibility can be measured by bond ratings, coverage ratios, capitalization ratios, liquidity ratios, and the identification of salable assets.

2. ***Risk:*** This is the predictable variability in the firm's operating cash flow. Such variability may be due to both macroeconomic factors (e.g., consumer demand) and industry- or firm-specific factors (e.g., product life cycles, biannual strikes in advance of wage negotiations). To some extent, past experience may indicate the future range of variability in earnings before interest and taxes (EBIT) and cash flow. High leverage tends to amplify the impact of these predictable business swings—this amplification is what is commonly called leverage. In theory, beta should vary directly with leverage. The firm's debt rating will provide a second external measure of risk of the firm.
3. ***Income:*** This compares financial structures on the basis of value creation. Measures such as DCF value, projected ROE, EPS, resulting price/earnings ratio, and cost of capital indicate the comparative value effects of alternative financial structures. Finance theory tells us that (all else equal) the value-maximizing capital structure is also that which minimizes the weighted average cost of capital. Thus, the analyst can devote attention to the capital cost resulting from the different financial structures. Finally, economic profit, or EVA, summarizes the joint impact of capital structure, investment, and operating profit effects.
4. ***Control:*** Alternative financial structures may imply changes in control or different control constraints on the firm as indicated by the percentage distribution of share ownership and by the structure of debt covenants. Significant investors will be sensitive to the dilution in their voting position in the firm, implied by different acquisition financing alternatives.
5. ***Timing:*** This asks the question of whether the current capital market environment is the right moment to implement any alternative financial structure, and what the implications for future financings will be if the proposed structure is adopted. The current market environment can be assessed by examining the Treasury yield curve, the trend in the movement of interest rates, the existence of any windows in the market for new issues of securities, P/E multiple trends, and so on. Chiefly, one wants to look for evidence of over- or undervaluation of securities in the capital market. Sequencing considerations are implicitly captured in the assumptions underlying alternative DCF value estimates and can be explicitly examined by looking at annual EPS and ROE streams under alternative financing sequences.
6. ***Other:*** Since no framework can anticipate all possible effects, the "O" reminds the analyst to consider potential idiosyncratic influences on the decision. Two such items are investment liquidity of the owners and estate planning considerations. As these examples suggest, such considerations tend to be more influential in smaller and privately held firms. However, a major "other" consideration for large publicly traded firms is the signaling content of their financial choices. The issuance of equity is typically accompanied by decreases in share prices; issuance of debt is accompanied by increases. One interpretation of this result is that the type of financing signals optimism or pessimism about the future by insiders in the firm.

This framework can be used to indicate the relative strengths and weaknesses of alternative financing plans. To use a simple example, suppose that your firm is considering two alternatives for financing an acquisition: a new issue of debt to fund a cash payment or a new issue of equity in exchange for the target's shares.

Your financial analyst offers a comparison of the two structures, as shown in Exhibit 20.6. Looking across each row, the decision maker can determine which alternative dominates on each criterion. The debt structure is favored on the grounds of income (perhaps reflecting debt tax shields and no share dilution), the absence of voting dilution, and today's interest rate conditions. The equity structure is favored on the grounds of flexibility, risk, absence of covenants, today's equity market conditions, and the long-term financial sequencing benefits. This example boils down to a choice between "eat well" and "sleep well." One should always think like an investor in making this choice. The other perspectives mentioned in this chapter (creditor, competitor, CEO) may add further richness to the analysis.

SUMMARY AND CONCLUSIONS

This chapter explores the complexities of choosing form of payment and financing in the design of a deal. Each has implications for the other. Therefore, it is appropriate to consider the choices simultaneously. When price is added into consideration, one has the core building blocks of a bidding strategy. The chapter sketches how price, form of payment, and financing combine to form two classic bidding strategies: preemption and contingency.

Research suggests that the choice of form of payment is heavily influenced by

EXHIBIT 20.6 Comparison of Two Hypothetical Acquisition Financing Alternatives Using the FRICTO Framework

M&A Transaction	New Issue $250 Million in Bonds; Acquire Target Equity with Cash	New Issue $250 Million in Shares for Target Equity
Flexibility	Low flexibility. BBB debt rating. $50 million unused debt capacity remains.	High flexibility remains. AA debt rating. $300 million unused debt capacity remains.
Risk	Book debt/assets = 0.60. Exposure is high. EBIT/interest coverage = 3.0.	Book debt/assets = 0.30. Exposure is medium. EBIT/interest coverage = 6.0.
Income	Reported EPS = $1.50. WACC = 10%. DCF value = $20/share.	Reported EPS = $0.90. WACC = 11.9%. DCF value = $17/share.
Control	Covenants become tighter, but no voting dilution.	Covenants not as tight. Voting dilution occurs.
Timing	Interest rates low today. Risky sequence for future financing: must issue equity for next major financing, which makes Newco dependent on future equity market conditions.	Equity multiples high today. Low risk sequence for future: more flexibility for form of financing in the future; less dependent on future equity market conditions.
Other	Signal of optimism and that shares may be underpriced.	Signal that shares may be overpriced or that management prefers a conservative financing strategy.

the role of information. As is usually the case in merger negotiations, each side has information that the other side does not. Because of this information asymmetry, the choice of form of payment carries important signals about what each side thinks the values of the two firms really are, and how valuable the synergies might be. Thus, a key practical implication of this chapter is to think carefully about the messages that form of payment sends to the counterparty and the public shareholders.

The chapter also surveys the buyer's financing decision that is embedded in a deal. There are at least seven levers of design of financings: mix, maturity, basis, currency, exotica, control, and distribution. These should prompt thoughtful comparisons among financing alternatives. The chapter also summarizes the FRICTO framework that enables one to summarize and weigh trade-offs among financing alternatives.

Research suggests that the form of payment choice is associated with large differences in returns to shareholders—for this reason alone it merits careful analysis. Given the wide variations over time in the selection of methods of payment, the thoughtful practitioner should focus less on what the standard methods of payment have been in recent years, and more on trying to understand the fundamental drivers of this choice. This chapter outlines a number of these drivers as have been revealed by research. Future research will continue to refine our understanding.

NOTES

1. Tobin's Q is typically measured as the ratio of market value to book value of equity.
2. See Hayn (1989), Sullivan et al. (1994), and Auerbach and Reishius (1988).
3. See Asquith and Mullins (1986) and Masulis and Korwar (1986).
4. There is an exception to this mentioned in Chapter 19: The acquirer with stock may make a Section 338 election that permits a share-for-share acquisition to be treated like a cash purchase with step-up to the buyer and immediate taxability to the seller.
5. If a cash payment is financed with costly debt, the interest burden could prove to be more dilutive than payment with shares. The dilution effect of alternative forms of payment should be modeled under assumptions appropriate to each case.
6. See Hansen (1987), Fishman (1989), Berkovitch and Narayanan (1990), and Eckbo, Giammarino, and Heinkel (1990).
7. IBM held $10.5 billion in cash, cash equivalents, and marketable securities at the end of 1994. Also, the firm's net cash flow in 1994 was $2 billion.
8. "Average maturity" is the mean number of years of the life of liabilities, weighted by the outstandings in each year. "Duration" is mean number of years weighted by the *present value* of outstandings in each year.
9. Examples of highly tailored securities include exchangeable and convertible bonds (such as those issued by Chubb Company), hybrid classes of common stock (such as General Motors' class E and H shares), and contingent securities (such as Eli Lilly's contingent payment unit, a dividend-paying equity issued in connection with an acquisition).

10. In general, the call options embedded in a convertible bond will be more valuable the greater the volatility of the underlying asset.
11. This technique employs discriminant analysis to build a predictive model of financial failure. Altman (1968) first estimated this model:

$$Z = 1.2X_1 + 1.4X_2 + 3.3X_3 + 0.6X_4 + 0.99X_5$$

where X_1 = Working capital/total assets ratio, a measure of the net liquid assets of the firm.
X_2 = Retained earnings/total assets, a measure of cumulative profitability over time.
X_3 = Earnings before interest and taxes/total assets, a measure of asset productivity.
X_4 = Market value of equity/total liabilities, a measure of equity cushion beneath liabilities.
X_5 = Sales/total assets, measuring the sales-generating ability of the firm's assets.

Altman finds that any firm with a Z score below 1.8 is a strong candidate for bankruptcy; generally, the lower the score, the higher the probability of failure. The model was over 90 percent accurate in classifying bankrupt firms correctly prior to failure, and over 80 percent accurate in *ex post* tests. Altman has modified the model and reestimated the coefficients over time. The revised model is proprietary to Zeta Services Incorporated. In general, credit scoring is useful where the analyst needs to survey the default risk of a number of firms quickly.
12. Secured lenders might be forced to take credit losses pari passu with unsecured lenders (i.e., they might forfeit their absolute priority in the event of liquidation of the bankrupt debtor). Directors might be assessed damages and punitive penalties. Selling shareholders may be compelled to return the payment they received for the firm. Advisers may be assessed damages and punitive penalties, and be required to disgorge fees received.
13. In fraudulent conveyance, unsecured creditors have been defrauded by secured creditors, shareholders, and advisers. The fraud can be either *deliberate* or *constructive*. The law defines constructive fraud to have occurred where the debtor received less value than the obligation assumed, and either was insolvent on the date of transfer, was inadequately capitalized from that time forward, or assumed debts beyond its ability to repay. Almost all highly leveraged transactions would fail the "reasonably equivalent value" test because the proceeds of the loan do not remain with the company (i.e., the borrowings are used to purchase assets or repurchase shares). Thus, it is crucial for deal designers to determine in advance whether the debtor can be judged to be insolvent or inadequately capitalized after the transaction. The solvency letter is obtained for this purpose.
14. For a discussion of finance as a competitive instrument, see William E. Fruhan Jr., *Financial Strategy: Studies in the Creation, Transfer, and Destruction of Shareholder Value*, Homewood, IL: Irwin, 1979.

CHAPTER 21

Framework for Structuring the Terms of Exchange: Finding the "Win-Win" Deal

INTRODUCTION

The *exchange ratio* in a share-for-share deal is the number of buyer shares offered per target share. Cash deals also have an exchange ratio: The *cash exchange ratio* is the number of dollars exchanged per target share. This chapter presents a framework for determining an exchange ratio in mergers and acquisitions.

In essence, the design of terms of exchange should be driven by an assessment of the gains or losses imposed on the two parties through any particular deal structure.

- *Cash deals.* With deals in which payment is in cash, this assessment is straightforward: For either party, one compares the cash payment to the intrinsic value of the asset. The question for each side in a *cash-for-stock deal* is whether the deal will create, or at least conserve, value.
- *Stock deals.* In *stock-for-stock deals*, the logic is the same, though the analysis is a bit more complicated. In stock deals, the crucial design feature that governs the wealth of the buyer and seller is the exchange ratio, the number of shares of the buyer's stock to be received for each share of the target firm's stock. In concept, the buyer does not want to give away more value (expressed in shares of its stock) than the target share is worth; and the target shareholder does not want to settle for less of the buyer's stock than the target is worth. Plainly, the adequacy of an exchange ratio (and the resulting determination of winners and losers) boils down to some notion about the worth of the buyer and target shares.

The focus on exchange ratio raises an important tool for assessing price and form of payment: the exchange ratio determination model. This chapter will present analytic models for critically assessing the exchange ratio in both stock-for-stock deals and cash-for-stock deals. The overarching implication of these models is that one must have a view about the value of the new firm ("Newco") arising from the deal. These models show, especially, the important effect of synergies on terms of exchange. The models also reveal that the choice of terms of exchange potentially creates winners and losers. Deal makers (especially buyers) who intend to participate in M&A transactions repeatedly will want to design transactions that are mutually beneficial to both parties. The models presented here offer insights into the win-win terms of exchange: the *"sweet spot"* of M&A deal design.

A MODEL FOR CRITICALLY ASSESSING EXCHANGE RATIOS

Deal boundaries are the limits within which a mutually agreeable deal (*"win-win" deal*) deal is possible: Such a deal is above the minimum acceptable ratio for the seller and below the maximum acceptable ratio for the buyer. Larson and Gonedes (1969) derived these boundaries based on an analysis of *price-earnings ratios*—their derivation of these boundaries is given in Appendix 21.1. Yagil (1987) derived the boundaries based on the discounted dividend growth model. Drawing on Larson and Gonedes, I derived the share-exchange boundaries based on general discounted cash flow (DCF) estimates of value (see Appendix 21.2 for the derivation). I also derived the boundaries for the *cash* exchange (see Appendixes 21.3 and 21.4).

The key foundation for these models is the reasonable assumption that neither the buyer nor the seller wants to be poorer after the deal than before. This suggests that the buyer will set a *maximum exchange ratio* below which the buyer will be willing to acquire the target. Similarly, it suggests that the target shareholders will have a *minimum exchange ratio* above which it will be willing to be acquired. A deal rationally should be consummated somewhere in the range between the buyer's maximum and target's minimum. It should be simple enough to identify this range, except for one detail: The maximum and minimum depend on the estimated value of the new firm arising from the deal ("Newco"). Because the value of Newco is uncertain, the analyst needs to assess the minimum and maximum exchange ratios across a range of possible values for Newco. In the models that follow, this is accomplished in two ways: (1) by focusing on the likely price/earnings (P/E) ratio of Newco, and (2) more directly, by estimating the likely DCF value of equity of Newco.

The boundaries defining the value-creating and value-destroying deals are summarized in Exhibit 21.1. The terms in these equations are defined as follows—the subscript "1" indicates the buyer; the subscript "2" indicates the target; and subscript "12" indicates Newco:

ER_1 = Maximum acceptable exchange ratio (buyer shares per target share) from the buyer's viewpoint.

ER_2 = Minimum acceptable exchange ratio (buyer shares per target share) from the target's viewpoint.

P_1 = Price per share of the buyer today, before the transaction.

P_2 = Price per share of the target today.

S_1 = Number of buyer shares outstanding today, before the transaction.

S_2 = Number of target shares outstanding today.

E_1 = Net income of the buyer, next year,[1] stand-alone basis.

E_2 = Net income of the target, next year, stand-alone basis.

$E_{Synergies}$ = The change in net income of the combined firm arising from synergies.

DCF_{12} = Discounted cash flow value of the equity of the combined firm.

PE_{12} = Price/earnings ratio of the combined firm, based on leading estimates of earnings.

EXHIBIT 21.1 Formulas for the Deal Boundaries

	Buyer's Maximum Acceptable Exchange Ratio	Target's Minimum Acceptable Exchange Ratio
Shares for shares (P/E boundaries) (Larson and Gonedes 1969)	$ER_1 = \frac{S_1}{S_2} + \frac{E_1 + E_2 + E_{\text{Synergies}}}{P_1 S_2} PE_{12}$ (a)	$ER_2 = \frac{P_2 S_1}{PE_{12}(E_1 + E_2 + E_{\text{Synergies}}) - P_2 S_2}$ (b)
Shares for shares (DCF boundaries)	$ER_1 = \frac{DCF_{12} - P_1 S_1}{P_1 S_2}$ (c)	$ER_2 = \frac{P_2 S_1}{DCF_{12} - P_2 S_2}$ (d)
Cash for shares (P/E boundaries)	$ER_1 = \frac{\text{Cash}}{S_2} = \frac{PE_{12}(E_1 + E_2 + E_{\text{Synergies}}) - P_1 S_1}{S_2}$ (e)	$ER_2 = \frac{\text{Cash}}{S_2} = P_2$ (f)
Cash for shares (DCF boundaries)	$ER_1 = \frac{\text{Cash}}{S_2} = \frac{DCF_{12} - P_1 S_1}{S_2}$ (g)	$ER_2 = \frac{\text{Cash}}{S_2} = P_2$ (h)

USES OF THESE MODELS

Though seemingly complex, the exchange rate determination models have three simple but important potential applications:

1. *With an informed, rational view about the DCF value or the P/E ratio of Newco, one can identify a negotiation range and some likelihood of agreement.* Within these boundaries, one can proceed to define more specific boundaries of various possible deal outcomes: (1) a win-win outcome for acquirer and target, (2) lose-lose, and (3) one wins and the other loses.
2. *Given a proposed exchange ratio, one can identify P/E or DCF breakeven assumptions necessary to permit a mutually beneficial deal.* The formula is easily solved by trial and error (or with the "Data Table" function in Excel) for the P/E ratio or DCF value at which $ER_1 = ER_2$; this value identifies the minimum P/E or value of Newco necessary to achieve a win-win outcome. Having a good idea of whether one is in win-lose or win-win territory is indispensable for developing a negotiating strategy.
3. *Given both a proposed exchange ratio and view of DCF value or P/E of Newco, one can evaluate the adequacy of a proposal.* An offer (in cash or number of shares) can easily be compared to the maximum or minimum deal boundaries (depending on your side) as a basis for responding to an offer.

AN ILLUSTRATION

The spreadsheet model "Deal Boundaries.xls," which can be found on the CD-ROM, offers the following example. Consider a share-for-share exchange proposal with the parameters given in Exhibit 21.2; the most important assumptions are that Newco will have a P/E ratio of 20 and a DCF value of $12,000. Consistent with these assumptions, the maximum acceptable exchange ratio to the buyer is 0.83 buyer shares per target share based on the P/E model, and 0.83 shares based on the DCF model (see Exhibit 21.3). The minimum acceptable exchange ratio to the target is 0.57 shares based on the P/E model, and 0.57 shares based on the DCF model. A *zone of agreement* (or range of exchange ratios over which a mutually ac-

EXHIBIT 21.2 Assumptions Used in the Illustration of Deal Boundaries

	P/E Model Assumptions		DCF Model Assumptions	
Buyer's share price	P_1	$ 60	P_1	$ 60
Target's share price	P_2	$ 40	P_2	$ 40
Buyer's net income	E_1	$300		
Target's net income	E_2	$250		
Net Income from synergies	E_s	$ 1		
Buyer's share outstanding	S_1	100	S_1	100
Target's shares outstanding	S_2	100	S_2	100
Expected P/E ratio/DCF of Newco	PE_{12}	20	DCF_{12}	$12,000

EXHIBIT 21.3 Estimates of the Maximum and Minimum Exchange Ratios Used in the Example

Results Based on P/E of Newco			Results Based on Equity DCF Value of Newco		
PE_{12}	Maximum Acceptable ER_1	Minimum Acceptable ER_2	DCF_{12}	Maximum Acceptable ER_1	Minimum Acceptable ER_2
12.70	0.17	1.33	$ 7,000	0.17	1.33
14.52	0.33	1.00	$ 8,000	0.33	1.00
16.33	0.50	0.80	$ 9,000	0.50	0.80
18.15	0.67	0.67	$10,000	0.67	0.67
19.96	0.83	0.57	$11,000	0.83	0.57
21.78	1.00	0.50	$12,000	1.00	0.50
23.59	1.17	0.44	$13,000	1.17	0.44

ceptable deal might be struck) exists in this example—the target's minimum exchange ratio is well below the buyer's maximum.

The attractiveness of the deal depends to a large extent on the P/E ratio and/or DCF value for the buyer's shares expected to prevail after the transaction. To a large extent, the attractiveness of the deal depends on the P/E ratio and/or the DCF value expected from the future value of the buyer's shares, after the transaction. Some analysis of the deal boundaries is required in order to determine the sensitivity of the zone of agreement to the assumed posttransaction value. Using the Data Table function in Excel, one can readily generate the boundaries given different P/E and DCF values. Extending this example, the buyer's maximum (ER_1) and target's minimum (ER_2) acceptable exchange ratios are given in Exhibit 21.3. The exchange ratios in these tables offer an interesting insight: Over some ranges of P/E or DCF value, *there is no feasible deal for one or both parties.* A feasible deal for each side simply meets the requirement of not being poorer after the deal than before. There are, in fact, four possible states of the world:

1. ***Both win.*** This is the win-win outcome where an exchange ratio can be chosen that is below the buyer's maximum and above the target's minimum.
2. ***Target wins, buyer loses.*** Here, an exchange ratio is chosen that is above the target's minimum *and* above the buyer's maximum. In this outcome *the buyer has overpaid.*
3. ***Both lose.*** This outcome destroys value for both sides, the "deal from hell."
4. ***Buyer wins, target loses.*** Here, an exchange ratio is chosen that is below the target's minimum *and* below the buyer's maximum. In this outcome *the target has undersold.*

Graphing the results of the data tables reveals each of these four regions. Graphs of the P/E and DCF results are given in Exhibits 21.4 and 21.5. These graphs reveal that the minimum and maximum boundaries create "zones" of outcomes. Insights into the size and location of the zones are enormously useful in the identification of bargaining strategies.

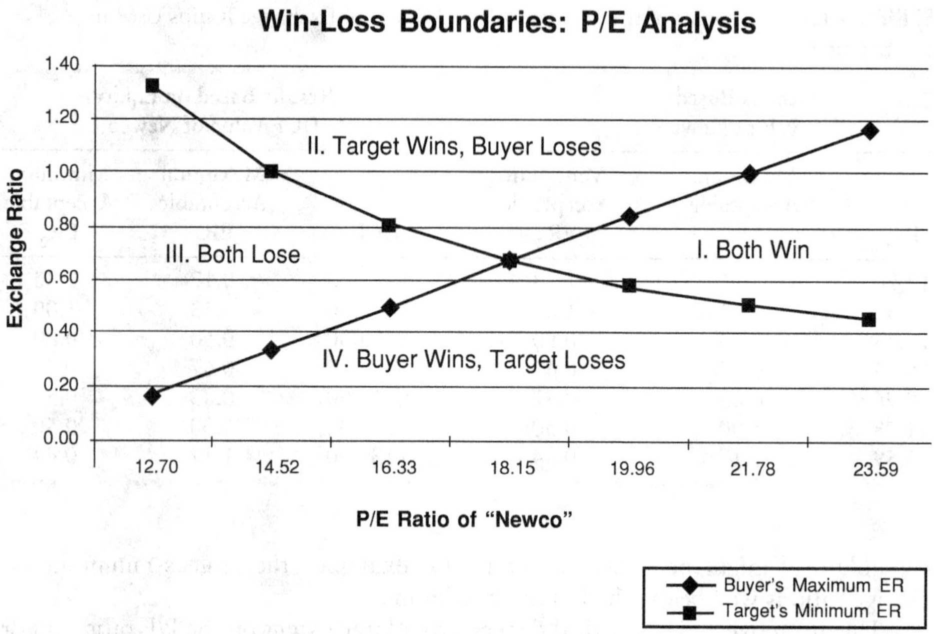

EXHIBIT 21.4 Estimated Deal Boundaries Based on Price/Earnings Ratios; Hypothetical Case Example: Share-for-Share Deal

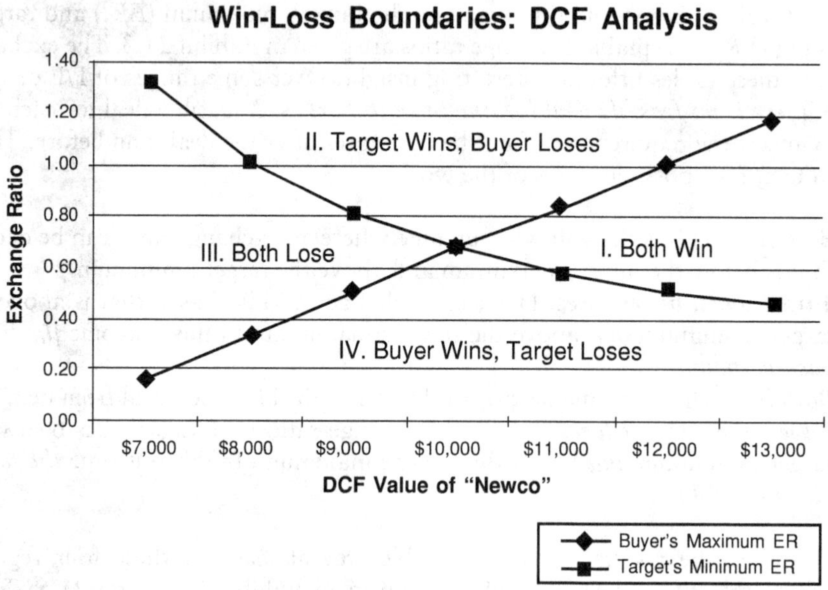

EXHIBIT 21.5 Estimated Deal Boundaries Based on Discounted Cash Flow; Hypothetical Case Example: Share-for-Share Deal

The first insight is the point of crossover between the target and buyer deal boundaries—the value at this point is the minimum P/E or DCF value necessary to permit a mutually agreeable deal. Knowing this minimum allows the deal designer to conduct a sensitivity analysis of valuation assumptions necessary to achieve this minimum value. Gaining insight into the breakeven values is the second potential application of this model.

The third application would simply be to position any particular offered exchange ratio on the diagram to see whether the bid was good, and for whom. For instance, if a postmerger P/E ratio for Newco were 23.6 times, an exchange ratio offer of 1:1 would be attractive to both buyer and seller.

EXTENSION TO CASH-FOR-STOCK DEALS

The logic of the stock-for-stock model can be extended easily to cash-for-stock deals (see Appendixes 21.3 and 21.4). Here, the exchange ratio is expressed literally in dollars per share of target stock. Unlike the stock-for-stock scenario, in cash deals the target's minimum is quite simple: To avoid destroying value, the target shareholders should not sell for less than the value per share before. This results in the same four zones. Exhibits 21.6 and 21.7 give the results for our example, but assuming a cash deal.

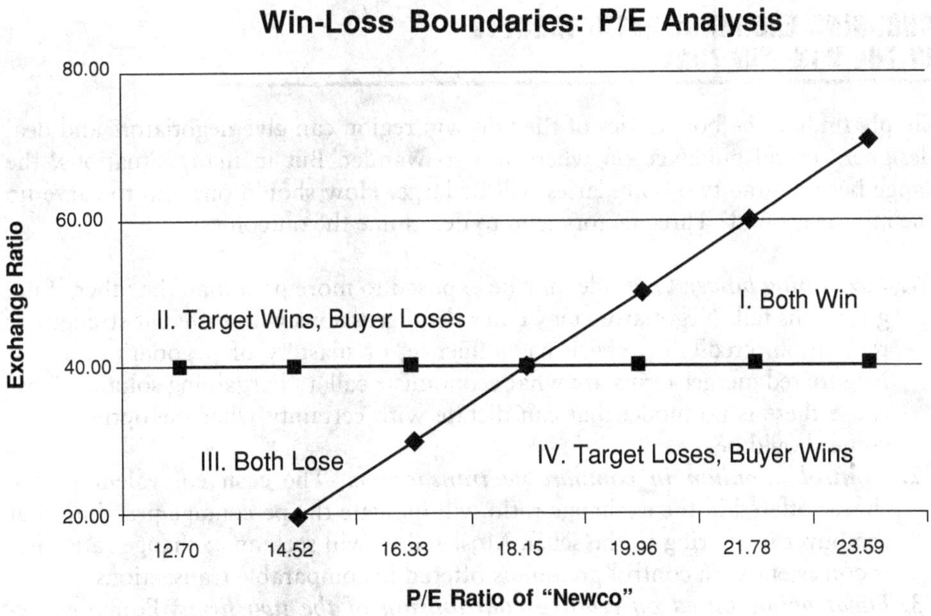

EXHIBIT 21.6 Estimated Deal Boundaries Based on Price/Earnings Ratios; Hypothetical Case Example: Cash-for-Share Deal

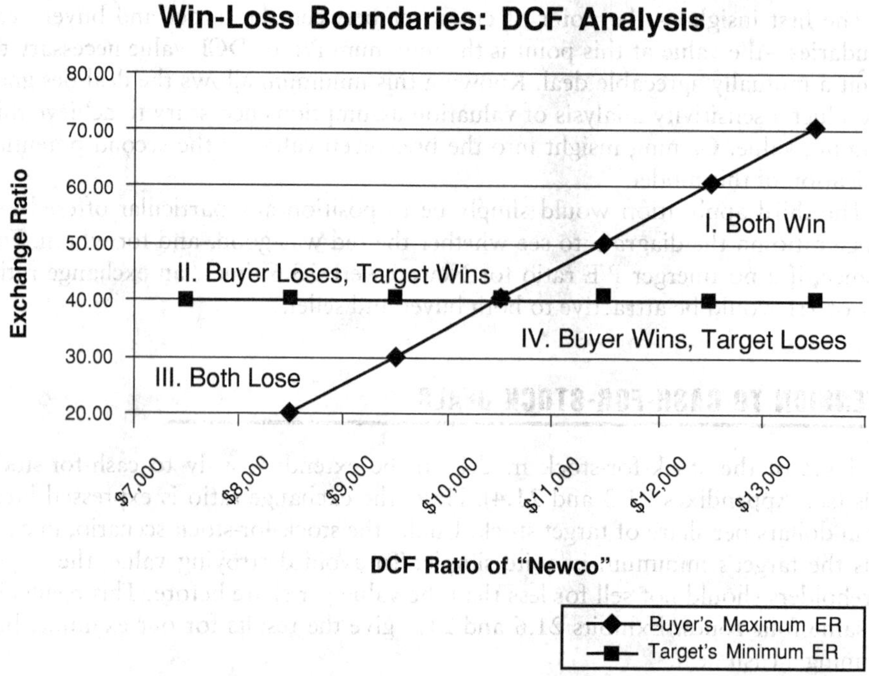

EXHIBIT 21.7 Estimated Deal Boundaries Based on Discounted Cash Flows; Hypothetical Case Example: Cash-for-Share Deal

CHOOSING EXCHANGE RATIO TARGETS IN THE WIN-WIN ZONE

Simply finding the boundaries of the win-win region can give negotiators and deal designers useful guidance on where *not* to wander. But in many situations, the range between the two boundaries will be large. How should one aim to carve up the middle ground? Three factors tend to determine the outcomes:

1. ***Bargaining power.*** One side may be exposed to more pain than the other, if negotiations fail. Negotiators may enter the discussions with different strength of reputation, credibility, charisma, influence, or mastery of negotiating tactics. Negotiated merger terms are what economists call a "bargaining solution," because there is no model that can dictate with certainty what the optimal outcome should be.
2. ***Control premium in comparable transactions.*** The cash equivalent of the shares offered in the exchange ratio will indicate the percentage premium that the buyer is offering to the seller. Most sellers will seek an exchange ratio that is consistent with control premiums offered in comparable transactions.
3. ***Focal points based on relative contribution of the two firms.*** Equitable exchange ratios would be those that reward the respective sides for their contributions to the value of Newco. There are many possible means of measuring the relative contribution of the two sides to Newco—it must be emphasized

that all measures of relative contribution are only signposts toward what is ultimately a matter of judgment, the contribution to the expected value of a firm that does not as yet exist. Thus, the task for the deal designer is to abstract an equitable exchange ratio from a variety of imperfect measures of contribution, such as:

- *Share prices of the two firms before the deal.* The buyer must offer the number of shares (S) at whose current share price (P) the total value is equal to the market capitalization of the target as shown in equation (1).

$$P_{\text{Target}} \times S_{\text{Target}} = P_{\text{Buyer}} \times \Delta S_{\text{Buyer}} \tag{1}$$

Rewriting this equation to show the ratio of shares offered to target shares (which is the exchange ratio) is equal to the ratio of the price per target share to the buyer's share price.

$$ER = \frac{\Delta S_{\text{Buyer}}}{S_{\text{Target}}} = \frac{P_{\text{Target}}}{P_{\text{Buyer}}} \tag{2}$$

- *Other measures of contribution.* In negotiations between private firms, or where the current share prices might reflect temporary exuberance or depression in one side's share price, the negotiators should look toward more fundamental indicators of contribution to the value of the enterprise. Such indicators could include operating profits, assets, unit sales, revenues, or number of employees—these are only useful as proxies for the generation of shareholder value by the buyer relative to the target.

Applying contribution analysis to the bargaining setting is relatively straightforward. First, one compares the relative contribution percentages on a variety of dimensions, and from them chooses a hypothetical contribution percentage. Second, the hypothetical contribution is converted into an exchange ratio using this formula, where S is the number of shares of the buyer or target before the deal and C is the hypothetical contribution percentage of the buyer:

$$ER = \frac{\dfrac{S_{\text{Buyer}}}{C} - S_{\text{Buyer}}}{S_{\text{Target}}} \tag{3}$$

Note that the numerator in this formula represents the number of shares of Newco to be offered to the target firm that is consistent with the relative contributions of the two firms. See Appendix 21.5 for the derivation of equation (3).

To illustrate how one uses equations (2) and (3) to settle on a focal point for carving up the win-win zone, consider the merger of Fleet Financial Group and BankBoston Corporation in early 1999. Exhibit 21.8 gives a range of data for the two firms, and their contribution ratios—these data can be used with the equations to estimate exchange ratios:

- ***Focal point based on share prices.*** Exhibit 21.8 gives the ratios of the share prices of BankBoston and Fleet at various points in time from October 1998 to

EXHIBIT 21.8 Contribution Analysis for the Fleet Financial Group/BankBoston Merger

	Fleet Financial	BankBoston	Ratio of BKB/FLT	Ratio of BKB to BKB + FLT
Ticker symbol	FLT	BKB		
Assets	$104,382	$73,513	70%	41%
Deposits	$ 69,678	$48,500	70%	41%
Loans and lease financing	$ 67,844	$42,806	63%	39%
Equity (book value)	$ 9,409	$ 4,817	51%	34%
Net interest income	$ 3,869	$ 2,147	55%	36%
Net income	$ 1,532	$ 792	52%	34%
Dividends	$ 587	$ 350	60%	37%
Average common shares				
Basic	568,059	293,873	52%	34%
Fully diluted	587,769	296,663	50%	34%
Number of employees	35,481	24,519	69%	41%
Share prices				
2/26/99	$42.94	$40.44	94%	NM
1/29/99	$44.31	$36.94	83%	NM
12/31/98	$44.69	$38.94	87%	NM
11/30/98	$41.69	$41.63	100%	NM
10/30/98	$40.69	$36.81	90%	NM
Market value of equity				
2/26/99	$25,237	$11,996	48%	32%
1/29/99	$26,046	$10,958	42%	30%
12/31/98	$26,266	$11,551	44%	31%
11/30/98	$24,503	$12,349	50%	34%
10/30/98	$23,915	$10,921	46%	31%

Note: "NM" stands for not meaningful.
Sources of data: Company annual reports, and SEC filings and Bloomberg Financial Services.

February 1999. Consistent with equation (2), these would suggest an exchange ratio varying between 0.83 and 1.00. At prices as of the most recent date, the exchange ratio would be 0.94.

- ***Focal point based on contribution ratios.*** The right-hand column of Exhibit 21.8 gives the contribution ratios for BankBoston based on various measures (the comparable ratios for Fleet would simply be 100 percent minus the BankBoston ratio). These percentages could be inserted into equation (3), along with the Fleet shares outstanding (about 568 million) and the BankBoston shares outstanding (about 294 million) to produce a range of estimated exchange ratios. The resulting estimates vary from 1.36 (using a contribution percentage based on assets) to 0.99 (using a contribution percentage based on book value of equity); these two exchange ratio estimates are based on financial accounting estimates rather than on market values and therefore might be given somewhat less weight. Using a contribution percentage based on market value of equity produces exchange ratios closely consistent with share prices.

The merger agreement between the two firms called for an exchange ratio of 1.1844 shares of Fleet to be given for each share of BankBoston—this implied a payment of $53 per BankBoston share, a premium of 31 percent over its price at the end of February 1999. This gave greater weight to BankBoston than suggested by the relative market values or share prices of the two firms. Backsolving equation (3) for the contribution ratio that produces an exchange ratio of 1.1844 reveals a BankBoston contribution ratio of 38 percent, within the range (but toward the higher end) of contribution ratios given in Exhibit 21.8.

SUMMARY AND IMPLICATIONS OF THE EXCHANGE RATIO FRAMEWORK

This chapter has presented a framework for considering cash and stock exchange ratios from the standpoints of both the buyer and seller in a merger transaction. The framework is founded on the straightforward idea that neither side wants to be poorer after the deal (than before). This implies the existence of deal boundaries for exchange ratios. These deal boundaries can form an extremely useful foundation for analysis of proposed terms and setting targets for negotiators.

Perhaps the most important implication of exchange ratio analysis is that the value of the combined firm (PE_{12} or DCF_{12}) has an immense influence on the flexibility or constraint under which the deal designer works. In addition, this analysis highlights the importance of fundamental valuation analysis as a driver for deal design. In this regard, the models reveal that *synergies create bargaining flexibility for the buyer and target deal designers.* Value creation through synergies has the effect of raising the buyer's maximum exchange ratio boundary and lowering the target's minimum. Thus, synergies increase the area of Zone I and thereby increase the probability of finding a mutually agreeable exchange ratio.

Exhibit 21.9 depicts the impact of synergies on the deal boundaries of the buyer and target. Looked at with P/E ratio on the horizontal axis, synergies widen the win-win zone. The key crossover point shifts lower, permitting a wider range of possible exchange ratios at any particular firm value. Exhibit 21.10 shows the effect of synergies on the deal boundaries when DCF of Newco is on the horizontal axis—here, synergies simply move the expected value of Newco further to the right on the axis, enlarging the negotiation window.

A second important implication is that the chance of consummating a value-destroying deal for one or both parties is not trivial, as shown by research summarized in Exhibit 21.11. Conn and Nielsen (1977) used the P/E model to test the distribution of share exchange deals that occurred in 131 mergers in the 1960s and 1970s. They found that 60 percent of transactions occurred in Zone I, the win-win region. This exhibit also presents summary data from a studies by Conn, Lahey, and Lahey (1991); by Cook, Gregory, and Pearson (1994) using observations from the United Kingdom; and by Bruner (2003) using transactions involving U.S. banks in the 1990s. Three important points emerge from these findings:

1. ***A high proportion of deals are unattractive to one or both sides.*** The high proportion of deals (40 to 51 percent) that occurred outside the region of mutual gains (i.e., outside Zone I) should caution deal designers about transaction analysis.
2. ***Buyers make more errors than targets.*** The transactions outside of the win-win zone fall disproportionately *against* buyers. For instance, at announcement, buyers destroy value in 36 to 48 percent of the cases (the sum of Zones II and III), while targets destroy value in 13 to 14 percent of the cases (Zones III and IV). This result is consistent with the survey of findings in Chapter 3. This asymmetry calls to mind the "winner's curse" described by Thaler (1992) and others—more about this is in Chapter 31.
3. ***Optimism dwindles.*** Over the weeks following announcement of the deals, the percentage of deals remaining in Zone I declines. This might be due to the use of overvalued equity by buyers. Conn and Nielsen speculated that this might be due to an initial gush of optimism about the deals. The difficulty of sustaining investor support for M&A transactions should caution deal designers about the importance of communications to investors, and the need to manage investor expectations.

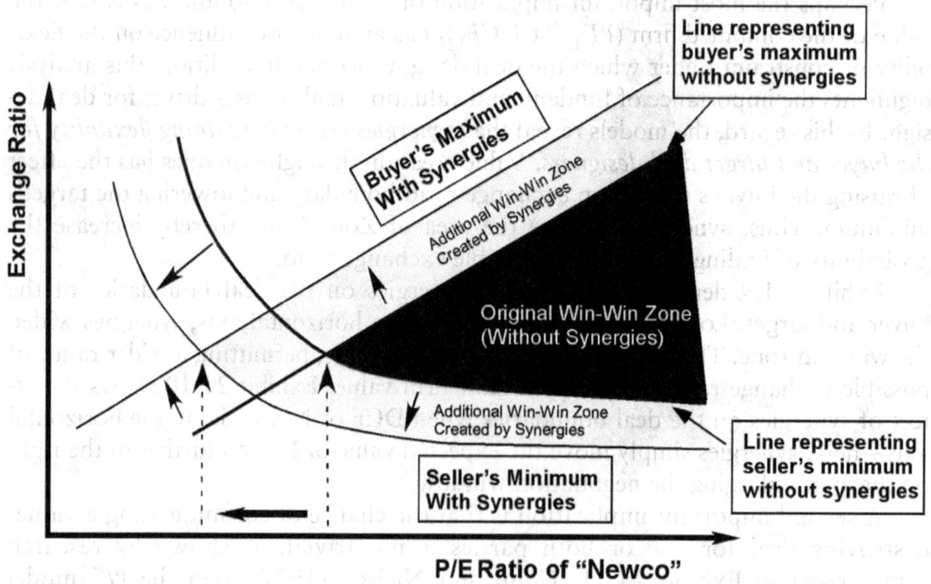

EXHIBIT 21.9 Effect of Synergies on Deal Boundaries: The P/E Approach

Note: The chart depicts the impact of earnings synergies on the deal boundaries of the buyer and target. The win-win zone increases in the presence of synergies. If the estimation of P/E remains the same but the earnings are higher due to synergies, both parties will be willing to adjust their maximum and minimum requirements, resulting in a wider range of possible exchange ratios.

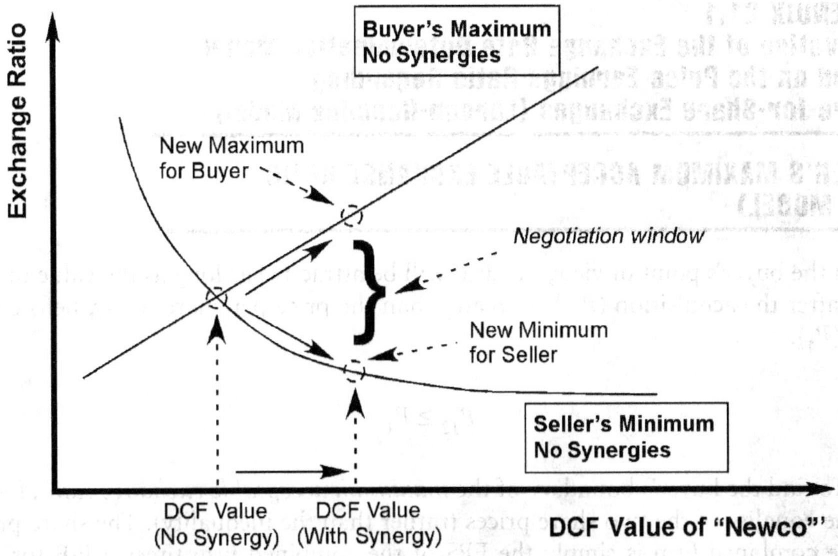

EXHIBIT 21.10 Effect of Synergies on Deal Boundaries: The DCF Approach
Note: The chart depicts the impact of synergies on the deal boundaries of the buyer and target. The DCF value of Newco increases, enabling both parties to move to the right along their respective lines—the seller reduces its minimum exchange ratio requirement, and the buyer raises the maximum exchange ratio it is willing to give. As a result, the negotiation window widens.

EXHIBIT 21.11 Percentage Distribution of Transactions by Deal Boundaries Zones as Found in Studies

	Conn and Nielsen (1977) (U.S. Firms, Various Industries, 1960s and 1970s)	Conn, Lahey, and Lahey (1991) (U.S. Firms, Various Industries, 1960–1979)	Cook, Gregory, and Pearson (1994) (U.K. Firms, Various Industries, 1980s)	Bruner (2003) (U.S. Commercial Banks, 1990s)
Zone I	60%	56%	49%	51%
Zone II	27%	32%	38%	35%
Zone III	9%	8%	10%	12%
Zone IV	4%	4%	3%	2%

Note: The results will vary somewhat by the point in time at which measurement was taken. The findings reported here were as of the announcement date of the merger. The studies report that, when measured at date of consummation or later, the percentage of observations in Zone I declines on the order of 5 percent.

APPENDIX 21.1 Derivation of the Exchange Rate Determination Model Based on the Price-Earnings Ratio Regarding Share-for-Share Exchanges (Larson-Gonedes Model)[2]

BUYER'S MAXIMUM ACCEPTABLE EXCHANGE RATIO (P/E MODEL)

From the buyer's point of view, the deal will be attractive as long as the value of the firm after the acquisition (P_{12}) is greater than the price per share today, before the deal (P_1).

$$P_{12} \geq P_1$$

To find the buyer's boundary of the *maximum acceptable exchange ratio*, focus on the equality of the two share prices (rather than the inequality). The share price of the combined firm is simply the EPS of the combined firm times a P/E for the combined firm.

$$P_{12} = (PE_{12})(EPS_{12})$$

Also, the EPS of the combined firm is simply the sum of the net incomes of the two firms (plus any synergy[3]) divided by the shares of the firm postmerger—these shares will be the sum of the preexisting number of shares plus any shares issued in an exchange offering.

$$EPS_{12} = \frac{E_1 + E_2 + E_{\text{Synergies}}}{S_1 + S_2 ER_1}$$

Inserting the equations for P_{12} and EPS_{12} into the first equation and setting the two sides equal gives a formula for the break-even condition:

$$P_1 = \frac{(PE_{12})(E_1 + E_2 + E_{\text{Synergies}})}{S_1 + S_2(ER_1)}$$

Solving for ER_1 gives the formula cited earlier in the chapter (Exhibit 21.1) for the maximum acceptable exchange ratio of buyer's shares per target share above which the buyer's shareholders lose:

$$ER_1 = -\frac{S_1}{S_2} + \frac{E_1 + E_2 + E_{\text{Synergies}}}{P_1 S_2} PE_{12}$$

TARGET'S MINIMUM ACCEPTABLE EXCHANGE RATIO (P/E MODEL)

The target seeks to accept deals that preserve or create value for target investors. Thus,

$$P_{12} \geq \frac{P_2}{ER_2}$$

To find the target's boundary of the *minimum acceptable exchange ratio*, ER_2, focus on the equality of the two share prices (rather than the inequality). The share price of the combined firm is simply the EPS of the combined firm times a P/E for the combined firm.

$$P_{12} = (PE_{12})(EPS_{12}) = \frac{P_2}{ER_2}$$

Also, the EPS of the combined firm is simply the sum of the net incomes of the two firms (plus any synergy[4]) divided by the shares of the firm postmerger—these shares will be the sum of the preexisting number of shares plus any shares issued in an exchange offering.

$$EPS_{12} = \frac{E_1 + E_2 + E_{\text{Synergies}}}{S_1 + S_2 ER_2}$$

Inserting the equations for P_{12} and EPS_{12} into the first equation gives this expanded formula for the postmerger share price:

$$P_{12} = \frac{P_2}{ER_2} = \frac{(PE_{12})(E_1 + E_2 + E_{\text{Synergies}})}{S_1 + S_2(ER_2)}$$

Solving for ER_2 gives the formula cited earlier in the chapter (Exhibit 21.1) for the target's minimum acceptable exchange ratio of buyer's shares per target share:

$$ER_2 = \frac{P_2 S_1}{(PE_{12})(E_1 + E_2 + E_{\text{Synergies}}) - P_2 S_2}$$

APPENDIX 21.2
Derivation of the Exchange Rate Model Based on Discounted Cash Flow Regarding Share-for-Share Exchanges

BUYER'S MAXIMUM ACCEPTABLE EXCHANGE RATIO (DCF MODEL)

From the buyer's point of view, the deal will be attractive as long as the value of the firm after the acquisition (P_{12}) is greater than the price per share today, before the deal (P_1).

$$P_{12} \geq P_1$$

To find the buyer's boundary of the *maximum acceptable exchange ratio*, focus on the equality of the two share prices (rather than the inequality). Also, recognize that the value of the firm postmerger will simply be the DCF value of equity (DCF_{12})[5] divided by the shares of the firm postmerger—these shares will be the sum of the pre-existing number of shares plus any shares issued in an exchange offering. Thus,

$$P_{12} = \frac{DCF_{12}}{S_1 + S_2(ER_1)} = P_1$$

Solving for ER_1 gives the formula cited earlier in the chapter (Exhibit 21.1) for the buyer's maximum acceptable exchange ratio of buyer's shares per target share:

$$ER_1 = \frac{DCF_{12} - P_1 S_1}{P_1 S_2}$$

TARGET'S MINIMUM ACCEPTABLE EXCHANGE RATIO

The target seeks to accept deals that preserve or create value for target investors. Thus,

$$P_{12} \geq \frac{P_2}{ER_2}$$

To find the target's boundary of the *minimum acceptable exchange ratio*, ER_2, focus on the equality of the two share prices (rather than the inequality). The share price of the combined firm is simply the DCF of equity of the combined firm divided by the number of shares of the combined firm.

$$P_{12} = \frac{P_2}{ER_2} = \frac{DCF_{12}}{S_1 + S_2(ER_2)}$$

Solving for ER_2 gives the formula cited earlier in the chapter for the target's minimum acceptable exchange ratio of buyer's shares per target share:

$$ER_2 = \frac{P_2 S_1}{DCF_{12} - P_2 S_2}$$

APPENDIX 21.3
Derivation of the Exchange Rate Determination Model Based on the Price/Earnings Ratio Regarding Cash-for-Share Exchanges

BUYER'S MAXIMUM ACCEPTABLE EXCHANGE RATIO (P/E MODEL)

From the buyer's point of view, the deal will be attractive as long as the value of the firm after the acquisition (P_{12}) is greater than the price per share today, before the deal (P_1).

$$P_{12} \geq P_1$$

To find the buyer's boundary of the *maximum acceptable exchange ratio*, focus on the equality of the two share prices (rather than the inequality). The share price of the combined firm is simply the EPS of the combined firm times a P/E for the combined firm.

$$P_{12} = (PE_{12})(EPS_{12})$$

Also, the EPS of the combined firm is simply the sum of the net incomes of the two firms (plus any synergy[6]) divided by the shares of the firm postmerger—these shares will be equal to the buyer's preexisting number of shares.

$$EPS_{12} = \frac{(E_1 + E_2 + E_{\text{Synergies}})}{S_1}$$

Inserting the equations for P_{12} and EPS_{12} into the first equation and setting the two sides equal gives a formula for the break-even condition:

$$P_1 = \frac{(\text{Newco equity value} - \text{Cash paid})}{\text{Number of buyer's shares}}$$

$$P_1 = \frac{[PE_{12}(E_1 + E_2 + E_{\text{Synergies}})] - \left(\frac{\text{Cash}}{S_2} S_2\right)}{S_1}$$

Solving for ER_1 gives the formula cited earlier in the chapter (Exhibit 21.1) for the maximum acceptable exchange ratio of buyer's shares per target share above which the buyer's shareholders lose:

$$ER_1 = \frac{\text{Cash}}{S_2} = \frac{PE_{12}(E_1 + E_2 + E_{\text{Synergies}}) - P_1 S_1}{S_2}$$

TARGET'S MINIMUM ACCEPTABLE EXCHANGE RATIO (P/E MODEL)

The target seeks to accept deals that preserve or create value for target investors. Thus, the target's boundary of the *minimum acceptable cash exchange ratio* is:

$$\frac{\text{Cash}}{S_2} = P_2$$

The target's shareholders will be unwilling to accept any cash price per share less than the prevailing price in the market. Because they are not retaining an equity claim in Newco's equity, the target's minimum acceptable exchange ratio is unaffected by the P/E ratio expected to prevail after the transaction is consummated.

APPENDIX 21.4
Derivation of the Exchange Rate Model Based on Discounted Cash Flow Regarding Cash-for-Share Exchanges

BUYER'S MAXIMUM ACCEPTABLE EXCHANGE RATIO (DCF MODEL)

From the buyer's point of view, the deal will be attractive as long as the value of the firm after the acquisition (P_{12}) is greater than or equal to the buyer's price per share before the deal (P_1).

$$P_{12} \geq P_1$$

To find the buyer's boundary of the *maximum acceptable exchange ratio*, focus on the equality of the two share prices (rather than the inequality). Also, recognize that the value of the firm postmerger will simply be the DCF value of equity (DCF_{12})[7] divided by the shares of the firm postmerger—these shares will be the preexisting number of buyer's shares. Thus,

$$P_{12} = \frac{DCF_{12} - \left(\frac{\text{Cash}}{S_2} S_2\right)}{S_1} = P_1$$

Solving for ER_1 gives the formula cited earlier in the chapter (Exhibit 21.1) for the buyer's maximum acceptable exchange ratio of buyer's shares per target share:

$$ER_1 = \frac{\text{Cash}}{S_2} = \frac{DCF_{12} - P_1 S_1}{S_2}$$

TARGET'S MINIMUM ACCEPTABLE EXCHANGE RATIO

The target seeks to accept deals that preserve or create value for target investors. Thus, the target's boundary of the *minimum acceptable cash exchange ratio* is:

$$\frac{\text{Cash}}{S_2} = P_2$$

The target's shareholders will be unwilling to accept any cash price per share less than the prevailing price in the market. Because they are not retaining an equity claim in Newco's equity, the target's minimum acceptable exchange ratio is unaffected by the P/E ratio expected to prevail after the transaction is consummated.

APPENDIX 21.5
Derivation of Equation (3) Exchange Ratio Consistent with Buyer's Percentage Contribution to Newco

The buyer's percentage claim (C) on Newco is initially expressed as the number of shares held by the buyer's shareholders (S_{Buyer}), divided by the total number of shares of Newco:

$$C = \frac{S_{\text{Buyer}}}{S_{\text{Buyer}} + (ER \times S_{\text{Target}})}$$

Whereas the *ex ante* number of shares of the buyer and target are known, the exchange ratio, *ER*, is to be negotiated. But with a simplifying assumption, it should be possible to solve for *ER*: Assume that shares are distributed, C, proportional to the real economic contribution of the buyer to Newco. We could use the DCF values of the buyer, target, and Newco to compute C, or we could use proxies,[8] such as those mentioned in the text of the chapter, including revenues, assets, and so on. Thus, given a proxy for C, we can rearrange the contribution equation to solve for *ER*:

$$S_{\text{Buyer}} + (ER \times S_{\text{Target}}) = \frac{S_{\text{Buyer}}}{C}$$

$$(ER \times S_{\text{Target}}) = \frac{S_{\text{Buyer}}}{C} - S_{\text{Buyer}}$$

$$ER = \frac{\frac{S_{\text{Buyer}}}{C} - S_{\text{Buyer}}}{S_{\text{Target}}}$$

[Equation (3) in the text.]

NOTES

1. The theory would dictate that the next year's earnings be used, consistent with the general notion that security prices are the present value of expected future cash flows. This would suggest that the P/E ratio be used on leading, rather than trailing, earnings. Some practitioners would use the most recent year's earnings (and a trailing P/E) for both companies either for simplicity or in the belief that the future is unknowable. Either way, it is important that the P/E and net income for buyer and target be consistent.
2. As summarized from J. Fred Weston and Thomas Copeland, *Corporate Financial Theory and Policy*, 2d edition, Reading, MA: Addison-Wesley, 1983, pages 623–627.
3. The synergy term was not contained in the original Larson-Gonedes derivation. It is inserted here by the author for clarity.
4. The synergy term was not contained in the original Larson-Gonedes derivation. It is inserted here by the author for clarity.
5. Presumably DCF_{12} reflects any synergies created in the merger.
6. The synergy term was not contained in the original Larson-Gonedes derivation. It is inserted here by the author for clarity.
7. Presumably DCF_{12} reflects any synergies created in the merger.
8. Proxies are always noisy and imperfect—and those based on accounting data can be even more imperfect. But in the absence of other measures of economic contribution, they may be the best alternative for estimating ER.

CHAPTER 22

Structuring and Valuing Contingent Payments in M&A

OVERVIEW AND SUMMARY

This chapter explores the use and analysis of *contingent payments* in M&A deal design. Contingent forms of payment to the seller are pegged to the future performance of the target firm. They are "contingent" because the size of the payment *depends* on uncertain future performance. Much of the discussion in M&A presumes that the payment to the seller is fixed and known with certainty. This chapter and the next relax that assumption and explore its implications for the practitioner.

"Contingent payment" covers a variety of payment arrangements to the seller, including *earnouts*, *escrow funds*, stock options, and *holdback allowances*. But for simplicity and because of its widespread recognition among practitioners, this chapter will focus particularly on the earnout, an arrangement under which a portion of the purchase price in an acquisition is contingent on achievement of financial or other performance targets after the deal closes. Economically, the earnout is a legally binding financial agreement among two or more parties and is a claim on future value—it is described variously as an "instrument," "agreement," or "contract." Escrows and holdbacks are economically similar to earnouts. Stock options are also similar, but because of their tradability they are covered in Chapter 10. What distinguishes these kinds of payments is that they *resolve disagreement about an optimistic future* and *create incentives* for the target company management. For simplicity, I will use "earnout" generically to refer to contingent payments that create incentives. The technicalities of contingent payments, however, should not obscure five points that are important to the practitioner:

1. ***Contingent payment plans are options.*** This implies that earnouts are more valuable the longer the term of the instrument, and the greater the uncertainty about the underlying asset. Indeed, it is this uncertainty that can make an earnout so valuable and useful.
2. ***The right way to value a contingent payment instrument is to account for its optionality.*** The approach recommended here is to model, and value, the earnout using Monte Carlo simulation. The wrong way to value an earnout is to project a "most likely" stream of expected cash flows and discount it to the present. The latter approach is a widespread practice that probably *underestimates* the value of the earnout instrument.

3. ***Earnouts are challenging instruments to structure.*** They raise daunting issues of performance measurement and can create unintended consequences in human behavior. Ultimately, they require a fair amount of trust among honorable parties to the agreement.
4. ***The contingent payment plan can be an extremely useful device for breaking deadlocks in deal negotiations.*** The same instrument can be worth very different amounts to an optimistic seller and a pessimistic buyer.
5. ***The earnout can be an important device for retaining and motivating talent.*** People who hold special know-how, such as researchers, artists, and operational managers, may have a more optimistic view about the prospects of the target firm and thus may be willing to accept payment tied to that view. This enables the buyer to retain talent more successfully. Also, the prospect of an attractive future payment can motivate the target company management to bring the optimistic future to fruition.

CONTINGENT PAYMENTS IN M&A

Contingent payments are elements in many M&A transactions and can take many forms, including these:

- ***Bonus payments to sellers*** (especially if the sellers are managers who stay on with the target firm).
- ***Escrow funds.*** Part of the total payment is set aside in an escrow account, and released to the seller when the target firm satisfies some condition, such as completion of a new product.
- ***Holdback allowance.*** Part of the total payment is allowed to be withheld at closing and paid later upon satisfaction of some condition in the buyer. With holdback allowances, no escrow account is involved.
- ***Stock options.*** These are rights to acquire shares in the buyer. The exercise price is usually set at a level above the buyer's share price at closing, and is aimed at reflecting the value the target will hopefully bring to the buyer.
- ***Targeted stock.*** The buyer can issue to the target's shareholders or managers shares of stock whose dividends are pegged to the performance of the target. This can minimize accounting dilution imposed on the buyer's shareholders. Esty (2001) argues that targeted stock creates value by facilitating acquisitions.
- ***Earnout plan.*** The previous plans involve simple triggers on payments to the seller. In the case of earnouts, the triggers may be determined by complicated formulas and agreements for measuring progress. The earnout plan takes the form of a legally binding contract.

In common usage, "earnout" often refers to all of these types of contingent payments.

Several notable deals have included contingent features:

- In 1998, Seagate Technology completed an earnout deal in its acquisition of Quinta Corporation, a small technology company. The deal was structured such that Seagate paid Quinta $230 million at closing and could potentially pay an additional $95 million over the next three years. The portion, if any, of the $95 million that will be paid in the future is contingent upon Quinta achieving certain technological milestones.

- In December 1996, Unocal sold its subsidiary, 76 Products Company, to Tosco for $2.05 billion in cash, common stock, and an earnout.
- In November 1996, Resort Condominiums International was acquired by HFS Corporation for $550 million in cash, $75 million in common stock, and an earnout worth about $200 million.
- In June 1996, Rouse Company acquired Hughes Corporation for $176 million in stock and an earnout.
- In 1996, Inco won a bidding contest against Falconbridge to acquire Diamond Fields Resources. Inco paid Diamond Fields shareholders a package of cash, Inco common stock, and shares of stock that tracked Diamond Fields and stock that tracked a nickel-mining project in which Inco and Diamond Fields had been co-owners. One observer wrote, "Traditional corporate finance valuation techniques are difficult to apply to exploration potential, so a separate security allows stockholders of the target company to share in any upside gained from the exploration rights it owned."[1]
- In August 1996, Atlantic Energy of New Jersey and Delmarva Power of Delaware announced a merger in which Atlantic shareholders would receive a class of stock in Newco that would track Atlantic's performance. "No deal would ever have been announced had the targeted stock technique not been applied; the differences in expectations of how Atlantic Electric would perform—the valuation gap was too wide," said an observer.[2]

Notwithstanding these public-company deals, earnouts have been used predominantly in small, private company acquisitions. The targets in these deals typically have a short and/or volatile operating history and substantial uncertainty about future performance.

Exhibit 22.1 summarizes the trend and volume of earnout deals. Several insights emerge from the data:

- Earnouts are featured in a small portion of all publicly announced deals. Depending on how the volume of earnouts is measured, they vary from 0.4 to 2.5 percent (based on dollar volume) or 1.1 to 3.5 percent (based on deal volume) of the total flow of deals.
- The absolute volume of earnout deals has risen. This increase probably is due to the buoyancy in M&A activity, but also to the acceptability of the earnout structure in larger deals.
- In deals where they occur, earnouts are a material portion of the consideration reported by the parties to the deal. The rightmost column in Exhibit 22.1 shows that earnouts account for between 19 and 88 percent of total consideration paid in the deals in which they are used.

Kohers and Ang (2000) studied 938 acquisitions using earnouts from 1984 to 1996, and concluded that the use of earnouts was consistent with two explanations. First, earnouts may help to manage the buyer's risk. And second, earnouts

EXHIBIT 22.1 Volume of Deals Involving Earnouts by Year, and in Comparison to All Deals

	Earnout Deals				
Year	Total Value ($ Mil)	% All Deals	Number	% All Deals	% Payment Due to Earnout
1985	$ 447.4	0.4%	8	1.3%	51%
1986	$ 2,081.6	0.9%	15	1.2%	26%
1987	$ 1,697.3	0.9%	15	1.1%	44%
1988	$ 1,795.3	0.7%	26	1.5%	54%
1989	$ 2,774.9	0.9%	52	2.4%	24%
1990	$ 1,438.5	0.8%	53	2.6%	21%
1991	$ 2,254.4	1.8%	55	2.8%	30%
1992	$ 1,272.6	1.1%	61	2.7%	40%
1993	$ 4,332.0	2.5%	89	3.4%	21%
1994	$ 1,990.1	0.7%	92	2.7%	88%
1995	$ 7,150.4	1.8%	86	2.3%	27%
1996	$ 8,831.7	1.5%	85	2.0%	19%
1997	$11,711.1	1.7%	144	3.1%	29%
1998	$ 9,845.1	0.8%	167	3.5%	28%
1999	$13,562.4	0.9%	163	1.7%	21%
2000	$26,028.3	1.6%	174	1.9%	23%
2001	$15,644.7	2.2%	151	2.4%	27%
2002	$ 8,089.3	2.1%	150	2.6%	29%

Source of data: Securities Data Company, Merger & Acquisition database.

help to retain management. Also, their study offered a profile of the use and impact of earnouts:

- ***Types of targets.*** Earnouts are used predominantly in two kinds of deal situations: divestitures of corporate divisions and acquisitions of privately held targets. Two-thirds of the sample consisted of deals with privately held targets. Thirty percent of the deals consisted of acquisitions of divested subsidiaries. Tests show that the use of earnouts is more likely for private targets. About a fourth of the private company acquisitions emanate from high-tech industries. Statistical tests show that high-tech deals have a significantly greater tendency to use earnout structures. Service industries are another arena in which use of earnouts is significantly more likely. Earnouts are more likely the smaller the stockholder group of the target firm.
- ***Types of buyers.*** Smaller acquirers are more likely to use earnouts than larger acquirers. Foreign buyers from countries with common law traditions (similar to the United States) are more likely to use earnouts than foreign buyers from countries with civil code traditions (e.g., France). Kohers and Ang point out that the similarity in legal traditions underscores the importance of the enforcement of earnout contracts, an argument advanced in La Porta et al. (1997).
- ***Pairing of buyers and targets.*** Earnouts are more likely to be used where the buyer and target are from different industries.
- ***Portion of total payment.*** As a percentage of total consideration paid, the earnout component is larger in private transactions (45 percent of total) as

compared to the divested subsidiary acquisitions (33 percent of total). The size of the earnout payment in deals is driven by many of the same elements that drive the likelihood of using an earnout.

- *Acquisition premium.* The acquisition premiums were larger in earnout deals than in straight cash or stock deals. The premiums in earnout deals tend to be higher for private targets than for divested subsidiaries.
- *Returns to the buyer.* The abnormal returns to buyers at the announcement of earnout transactions are significantly positive, 1.4 percent. The returns are significantly higher than for straight cash or stock deals for private firms and where there is evidence of large information asymmetry between the buyer and target. Also, the buyer's returns are significantly more positive where management stays and where a payout is actually made under the earnout. Most of the gains from these acquisitions appear to be captured at the announcement, since over the three to five years after the deal the buyers' share prices perform in line with the market.
- *Structure.* The average performance horizon for earnout contracts is between two and five years. The earnouts tend to be structured around the profits of the target firms. And the targets of earnout deals usually exist as subsidiaries of the buyer, which facilitates performance measurement against the terms of the earnout.
- *Payout.* In 91 percent of the cases, some payment was made under the earnout arrangement. In half the cases, the full payment was made. On average across all cases, about 62 percent of the stated earnout amounts were actually received by target shareholders.
- *Retention of managers.* In about two-thirds of the cases, target managers stayed with the buying firm after the earnout period ended. The retention of management was highly correlated with the size of the actual earnout payment.

Datar, Frankel, and Wolfson (1998) reported similar profiles and conclusions for a sample of earnouts.

EARNOUTS CAN BE USEFUL; BUT IF SO, WHY AREN'T THEY UBIQUITOUS?

The relative rarity of earnouts questions their relevance. The advantages and disadvantages of earnouts create trade-offs that mean the deal designer should be selective in the application of this form of payment.

Potential Benefits of Using Earnouts

An earnout can provide a number of benefits to both parties if it is properly structured. For the seller, an earnout can provide additional payments if the acquired business does as well as expected. For the buyer, the earnout is acceptable because additional payments will be necessary only if the business does significantly better than expected. Three typical reasons explain the use of earnouts in merger and acquisition transactions.

1. ***Bridging the valuation gap.*** The most common reason for using an earnout is to bridge the gap between the buyer's and seller's evaluations of the intrinsic value of the target. When both parties agree that a higher valuation would be justified if the target met future performance goals, then the parties can make the differential between their valuations subject to an earnout.
2. ***Retention of shareholder/managers.*** Earnouts can also allow the buyer to induce key managers of the target, who are also shareholders, to remain with the target after the sale. If a portion of the purchase price is subject to performance goals after the closing, the target's shareholder/managers have an incentive to remain with the target in order to participate in the potential future payments.
3. ***Motivation of shareholder/managers.*** A third reason to use earnouts is to motivate the target's shareholder/managers to continue the target's aggressive growth after closing the sale. Earnouts are most effective for this purpose if the target can substantially increase its sales price by achieving its performance goals.

Potential Disadvantages of Earnouts

Despite the economic attractiveness of earnouts, they carry a variety of complications that must be considered before the negotiating parties decide to use an earnout deal structure. As the growing number of public deals that include earnouts suggests, these complications can be resolved through diligent attention to details by both parties. When problems occur from using earnouts, they generally fall into one or more of the following categories:

- ***Postacquisition integration.*** Earnouts are least likely to be effective when the target is totally integrated into the buyer. The more the target's operations are integrated into the buyer's, the less control the target's management will have over achieving performance goals. In an integrated company, revenue, expense, and profit decisions may be made to benefit the combined entity instead of the target, which could demotivate the target management. To avoid this problem, it is important to choose performance goals that will not be adversely affected by integration or to assure the target's operating independence during the earnout period.
- ***Complexity of definition.*** It is difficult to create effective earnout formulas. While the earnout concept may be simple, objective numerical definitions can easily become complex. It is important that the parties agree on simple performance goals that are unambiguous and easy to measure.
- ***Overly aggressive performance goals.*** In order to get the highest target valuation, the target's management may be tempted to base the earnout on overly aggressive performance goals. Most companies rarely predict their future performance with any accuracy. Earnouts can demotivate the target's management if it becomes likely that the target will miss its performance goals. The best way to ensure the continued motivation of the target management is to choose realistic performance goals, make progress payments for partial performance, and provide a fair mechanism to adjust performance goals to reflect changing business circumstances.

- ***Managers don't own a significant earnout claim.*** Earnouts may not sufficiently motivate target management if they do not receive a sizable earnout claim on future performance. For instance, suppose that the target is a large publicly held corporation in which management owns 1 percent of the shares, and that the earnout instruments are distributed pro rata to shareholders. Because of their small claim on the total earnout benefits, the payoff to management of exceeding the earnout targets might be small. To avoid this problem, it may be necessary to provide additional incentive compensation for the target's key managers.

Given the practical difficulties of earnouts, the parties may conclude that it is preferable not to use them. Even if negotiations lead to a nonearnout structure, consideration of an earnout is still valuable. Negotiations about earnouts frequently bring the parties closer together on price, performance expectations, and operating philosophies.

EARNOUTS ARE OPTIONS ON FUTURE PERFORMANCE

The key to understanding how earnouts can be structured and valued lies in seeing them as a type of financial option. An option is the right, not the obligation, to do something; for instance, a call option traded on the Chicago Board Options Exchange (CBOE) is the right to buy shares of the underlying common stock. The only circumstance in which a rational person would exercise the call option is if the value of the underlying stock exceeds the exercise price of the call option. In other words, the value that the investor receives from an option is contingent on the performance of an underlying asset; the option value derives from the value of another asset—hence, the name "derivative security."

Earnout provisions are a type of call option on the benefits of future performance by the target firm. Like the more straightforward CBOE call option, the earnout can be described in terms of some of its key value drivers shown in Exhibit 22.2—it hints at the possible application of option pricing techniques to the valuation of earnouts. However, earnouts are more complicated than financial options. And unlike financial options, earnouts are not standardized or exchange traded. But even if the analogy is imperfect, the options perspective still yields a number of extremely important implications for deal doers:

- *Earnouts are likely to be valuable, even if they are out of the money today.* The key question about all options is not whether it would be profitable to exercise them right now, but rather, how likely it is that the option will become in the money sometime in its remaining life?
- *Earnouts are not free to the buyer; they are costly.* Quite often, the buyer structures an earnout so that it is out of the money today. Thus, the buyer might assume that the earnout is a costless trinket, given away to placate the seller in the negotiations. But if out-of-the-money options (i.e., with some time remaining) are generally valuable, then the earnout is costly to the buyer and may convey value to the seller.
- *Earnouts are tailor-made for situations of great uncertainty.* Remember that options are more valuable the greater the uncertainty or volatility of the underlying

EXHIBIT 22.2 Comparison of Earnouts and Call Options on Common Stock

	Call Options on Common Stock	Earnouts	Implications for Value of the Earnout
Underlying asset	Shares of common stock.	Some index or measure of financial or operating performance; whatever the earnout is pegged to: revenues, earnings, cash flow, even market share or product introductions.	The earnout is a derivative security.
Exercise price	The stated strike price of the options contract.	Any benchmark, hurdle, or triggering event, beyond which the earnout provision starts paying off.	The lower the levels of performance of the benchmark or target, the greater the value of the earnout.
Price of the underlying asset	Share price of the underlying common stock.	The level of the index or measure of performance: revenues, earnings, cash flow, and so on to which the earnout is tied.	The higher the performance of the underlying index to which the earnout is pegged, the greater the value of the earnout.
Interim payouts	Dividends.	Any interim cash flows associated with the earnout.	The higher the interim payout, the lower the value of the earnout after payment.
Term of the option	At original issue, contracts are for three, six, or nine months.	Typically as long as five years.	The longer the remaining life of the earnout, the more valuable. This is generally the second most important driver of option value.
Uncertainty	Volatility of returns on the underlying asset.	Uncertainty about the performance of the underlying index to which the earnout is pegged.	The greater the uncertainty (or volatility), the more valuable the earnout. This is generally the most important driver of option value.

asset. In other words, earnouts will be seen as conveying material value if there is uncertainty about the target company. How much value and uncertainty remains for the analyst to determine. But in general, one should instinctively consider using earnouts in settings such as high technology, rapid growth, and/or sharp turbulence in the economic environment. In contrast, earnouts may not help much in settings involving mature firms and industries and a quiet economic environment.

- *Earnouts will be helpful in bridging the differences in outlook between an optimistic seller and a pessimistic buyer.* Highly disparate outlooks are simply another form of uncertainty. Indeed, it is the existence of pessimists and optimists that makes the options market. Options investors are said to "trade on risk" (i.e., on the differences in beliefs about future volatility)—both the buyer and seller of options willingly enter into the transaction in the belief that they will gain as their view of the world unfolds. So it is with parties to an M&A transaction: earnouts can be structured in ways that will favor each side if that side's view of the future actually occurs. Thus, at the time when the transaction is consummated, both parties are likely to be satisfied.[3]

STRUCTURING AN EARNOUT

The following section looks at each of the key elements to consider when structuring an effective earnout. In addition, this section outlines the negotiating positions that the buyer and the target are likely to take and suggests mechanisms to bridge potential conflicts.

Earnout Amount

The parties must determine what portion of the target's purchase price will be paid to its shareholders at closing and what portion will be subject to the earnout. Each will attempt to reduce its risk in the acquisition: the buyer by trying to increase the earnout ratio,[4] the target by trying to get more cash at closing.

The earnout percentage is usually a function of the negotiation price gap. That is, there is usually some portion of the purchase price on which both parties can agree. This becomes the noncontingent or fixed portion of the purchase price. The difference between the fixed portion and what the seller desires to receive is the "price gap" and is the basis for the earnout. When determining the earnout percentage, both parties need to consider that any earnout payments are contingent in nature and will not be paid until a later date. The contingent nature of the payments makes valuing an earnout more complicated than merely discounting the future earnout payments. Rather, the earnout is comparable to an option where the value of the earnout increases with additional uncertainty about future cash flows.

It is important that the parties strike an appropriate balance between the payments at closing and the amount of the earnout. The proper balance will depend on how strong the target's position is, the total risk in the earnout, and the parties' objectives. There may be little incentive effect if the earnout ratio is small (such as less than 20 percent). In contrast, if the earnout ratio is large (such as more than 70 percent), the target may be assuming too much risk in the transaction. Most earnouts range from 20 to 70 percent of the total purchase price.

Earnout Period

Earnouts typically run for a period of between one and five years, with an average of three years. The earnout period is usually determined by the earnout ratio (the percent of total payment derived from the earnout). In general, the larger the earnout ratio, the longer the earnout period.

Some managers might conclude that since "time is money," the seller will want shorter earnout periods to increase the present value of an expected payment. In contrast, the buyer would want to stretch the earnout payments over a longer period in order to reduce the present value of these payments. Also, a longer earnout will extend the period that the target's shareholder/managers will be retained and motivated.

The options analogy produces a rather different conclusion about earnout periods. Quite simply, longer-lived options are more valuable since with more time the likelihood is greater that the option will pay off. Thus, option theory would suggest that the seller would want longer-running earnouts, all else equal. In contrast, the buyer would want shorter earnout periods. The conventional wisdom makes the mistake of viewing the earnout as a sure thing when in reality it is highly uncertain. Given the uncertainty, the options perspective on the earnout period is more appropriate.

Performance Goals

Earnout payments can be based on any number of measurable performance criteria. To be effective, performance goals must be clearly defined, mutually understood, attainable, and easily measurable. Common performance criteria used in earnouts raise numerous issues that both parties should consider when evaluating the appropriateness of those criteria for its earnout:

- ***Revenues.*** Revenue-based earnouts are seen in situations in which the buyer wishes to integrate the operations of the two companies. When the target is fully integrated into the buyer, it becomes difficult to measure future results other than revenues from the former target products. Using revenue-based earnouts also appears in those situations where the target management does not intend to remain with the company after the deal. In these cases, the earnout provides both parties with a way to value the brand equity that the former managers of the target built.

  The main risk to the buyer in using a revenue-based earnout is that the target will sell product on liberal credit terms in order to boost revenues. The buyer can mitigate this risk by directly managing credit extension to customers. On the other hand, the target may be concerned that the buyer's manufacturing or distribution capacity will not be sufficient to meet customer demand for the target's products. To avoid this problem, the target will want the earnout formula to specify what resources the buyer must dedicate to support the target's revenue goals.
- ***Gross margin.*** The buyer may prefer to base the earnout on the target's gross margin because it forces the target to be profitable. However, if the target is subject to the buyer's control, the target's management may worry that the buyer will dictate its expenses to the detriment of the earnout. To address this concern, the earnout formula should specify how the parties would determine overhead, burden rate, purchasing requirements, and similar factors affecting gross margin.
- ***Pretax profit.*** Using pretax profit as the earnout measure requires the target's business to perform well in all respects. It also prevents any meaningful operating integration of the target into the buyer during the earnout period. To ensure that the target has a fair opportunity to achieve its earnout objectives, an earnout based on pretax profit needs to provide the target with adequate operating freedom.

- ***Cash flow or EBITDA.*** When parties have used an EBITDA multiple to value the target at closing, it can be useful to base the earnout formula on a similar measure to highlight the importance of providing future cash, and hence future value, to the buyer. A cash flow type metric is also particularly useful if the buyer is cash-short or if the buyer wants to impose discipline on a target that has historically been a large cash consumer.
- ***Milestones.*** Earnout payments can also be contingent upon attaining nonfinancial milestones, such as completion of some specified critical product development, product shipment, or contract execution. These types of performance criteria are particularly common in the technology sector where a new product development can greatly enhance the value of the target.

It is also not uncommon to incorporate more than one of these performance criteria into the earnout formula by assigning each criterion a separate weight, allowing the goals to be achieved independently. For example, each year's earnout payment could be based 50 percent on revenues and 50 percent on EBITDA.

After determining which goals to use in the earnout, the parties must decide how the payout will be computed. In the majority of transactions, performance goals are measured on an annual basis. A mathematical formula should be developed that determines the exact amount of cash or shares to be distributed to the target's shareholders.

Payment Schedule

There are a number of ways to structure the payment schedule in an earnout. To balance risk and reward, the earnout should provide rewards for significant partial performance by the target, even if it does not completely meet its performance goals. For example, a sliding scale could be used whereby the target would receive some partial payment if it attains at least 50 percent of the performance goal. The payment amount would then increase linearly thereafter up to the performance goal.

The payment schedule must also account for instances in which the target exceeds its performance goal. In some cases, earnout formulas pay bonuses if the target exceeds its performance goals. Another way to treat excess performance is to allow the target to use any excess performance in a given year to offset any periods in which it fails to meet its goals. To eliminate the annual volatility of the earnout payment, some companies prefer to structure one lump-sum payment at the end of the earnout that accounts for the cumulative performance of the target relative to the annual performance goals.

Due to the unpredictability of future performance, buyers almost always cap the payments that can be earned in an earnout. If the buyer caps the total payments that can be earned, the target could seek minimum annual payments and the right to bonus payments if it exceeds its performance goals.

Operational Integration

Another issue that impacts the potential effectiveness of an earnout is the extent to which the buyer intends to integrate the operations of the target. The earnout contract must clearly define the business unit being measured in the earnout and establish who will control the target's major corporate decisions. Earnouts frequently require that the target cooperate with the buyer's operations or integrate products. The target needs to evaluate its control over those integrated factors and determine what impact they will have on the design and payout of the earnout. For example, if the buyer intends to provide the target with additional products to manage, will those revenues be included in the earnout? If the buyer is to be the target's major customer, will the target attain the same level of profitability that it would if it were selling its products to third parties?

If the target retains operating control, it is less likely to claim that the buyer has interfered with its attainment of its earnout performance goals. Since acquisitions with low operating integration after the closing generally produce the most effective earnouts, the target should negotiate to retain its operating independence during the earnout. Since the buyer frequently acquires the target to accomplish operating integration, this issue must be carefully handled. One possibility is to choose the target performance goals that allow necessary integration. Alternatively, a shorter earnout period may permit the parties to be integrated after the earnout, but within a reasonable period. The earnout must be structured to allow attainment of the strategic as well as the financial and earnout objectives of the acquisition.

Accounting Rules and Performance Measurement

Earnouts require a clear understanding of the applicable financial accounting policies by which performance will be measured. The buyer and the target may have different financial reporting policies before the acquisition; the target generally will be required to conform its accounting system to the buyer's after the closing. The earnout agreement should specify the accounting policies that will be followed when measuring the target's performance. An agreement that requires numbers to be computed according to generally accepted accounting principles (GAAP) is not sufficient because of the variety of accounting treatments that are within the range of GAAP.

Items to be deducted from the target's financial statements to obtain performance results should be clearly specified. Of particular importance is the way the buyer treats interest, goodwill or other intangibles, earnout payments, and corporate allocations and expenses related to the transaction. These items normally should not be treated as the target operating expenses in determining its performance.

The acquisition contract needs to incorporate accurate and timely ways to monitor performance goal results. It should require an independent annual audit of the target and provide a method to resolve numerical disputes. A subcommittee of the target's former board of directors, representing the target's shareholders, frequently will be asked to negotiate any disputes with the buyer during the earnout period. If this subcommittee and the buyer are unable to reach accord, the contract should provide for arbitration or determination by some independent accounting firm.

Additional Issues

In addition to the issues previously addressed, several other issues should be kept in mind when negotiating an earnout:

- ***Availability of financing.*** The target will want to ensure that the buyer can and will provide the capital the target will need to achieve its performance goals. On the other hand, the buyer will be concerned that the target could become a cash drain. When the target is not in a position to fund its growth internally, it is common for the buyer to provide capital and charge the target's income statement for the buyer's cost of capital. If the buyer will not commit to providing necessary capital, the target needs authority to obtain funds from outside sources.
- ***Management process.*** Both parties must agree on how the target will conduct business after the closing. The parties must establish an approval process for the target's annual operating plans. While this process generally will mirror the buyer's own business planning process, it is important to structure a planning process for the earnout period that will not adversely affect the target's ability to achieve its performance goals.
- ***Change in control.*** There is always a risk that the buyer may sell the acquired business in the future or that the buyer will itself be bought by another entity. The seller should ensure that any future changes in control do not adversely affect the target's ability to obtain its future earnout payments. Some earnout agreements will provide for any acquiring company to pay the target the maximum amount due under the earnout as part of the purchase.
- ***Liquidity.*** Some earnout agreements will permit the earnout instrument to be sold, assigned, or transferred. Generally, this is a feature that should add some value to the earnout, as it confers greater liquidity on the investment value latent in the earnout. Some earnout instruments may be detached from the common shares of public firms and/or listed separately for trading on a stock exchange—in this instance, the deal designer should prepare for lengthy discussions with securities regulators on even the most fundamental question of whether the instrument is a debt security or an equity security.
- ***Impact on the buyer's financial structure.*** Earnouts, like other contingent liabilities, have historically been presented in footnotes to the buyer's financial statements. The accounting profession is debating their possible presentation directly on the balance sheet, as a contra-equity account or an outright liability. Economically speaking, earnouts are claims that are senior to the common shareholders. Therefore, earnouts will tend to increase the financial leverage of the buyer (in comparison with payment in shares of common stock) and should be assessed for their possible impact on the debt rating and general creditworthiness of the buyer.

TAX AND ACCOUNTING CONSIDERATIONS

An earnout is just the payment mechanism for some portion of the purchase price in an acquisition. The parties still need to decide how they want to structure the acquisition given the legal and accounting implications of using an earnout. Earnouts are complex and must be carefully crafted to reduce future friction between the parties. Both parties need to thoroughly read and understand the documentation that will govern their working relationship and profits during the earnout period. The following legal and accounting considerations are the most common and critical issues that must be considered. Earnout proposals should be evaluated with the counsel of competent tax and accounting advisers.

Tax Implications of Earnout Structures

Use of an earnout does not limit flexibility in structuring acquisitions. Earnouts can be included in tax-free and taxable transactions and in mergers, stock-for-stock acquisitions, or asset acquisitions. The earnout can be paid in stock or in cash.

Both parties must carefully consider the tax implication of using stock versus cash to make earnout payments. Any cash will, of course, be taxable, so the target may want stock from the buyer because taxes can be deferred. It is worth noting that the target generally can defer the tax due on cash payments until the payments are received by reporting the earnout payments on an installment sale basis. The buyer also has an incentive to use stock because it may want to conserve cash and/or provide the shareholder/managers of the target with a continuing interest in the growth and prosperity of the buyer after the closing of the transaction.

When structuring an earnout as a tax-free transaction, the tax rules regarding the allowable form of payment vary depending on the type of transaction chosen by the parties. If the purchase transaction is structured as a merger-type reorganization, cash earnout payments will be fully taxable and, if large enough, may defeat tax-free reorganization treatment. Specifically, a straight or forward triangular tax-free merger must have at least 50 percent of the total consideration paid in stock, while a reverse triangular tax-free merger must have at least 80 percent of the total consideration paid in stock. If the transaction is a tax-free stock-for-stock acquisition, all of the consideration paid must be in stock. In a tax-free stock-for-assets acquisition, consideration in the form of cash or the assumption of liabilities must be less than 20 percent of the total consideration.

Currently, in a tax-free acquisition, the earnout ratio should not be more than 50 percent and the earnout period should not exceed five years. The IRS will impute interest on deferred payments, whether stock or cash, unless the agreement specifically provides for adequate interest.

Financial Accounting

Under purchase accounting for M&A, the earnout must be included as part of the total consideration paid to acquire the target. Some portion of the purchase price will be contingent upon the target's meeting its performance goals after the closing. As a result, any excess of the purchase price over the fair market value of the target's assets at closing will be treated as goodwill. Since earnout payments are part of the purchase price, they may create or increase the amount of goodwill in the transaction.

GENERIC APPROACH TO VALUING EARNOUT INSTRUMENTS

In order to design effective earnouts, it is important to understand how to value them and their possible alternative structures. Some practitioners believe that the appropriate way to value these instruments is to forecast a "most likely" stream of cash flows, and discount them to the present. Unfortunately, this ignores the uncertainty of the underlying index and the optionality of the instrument itself. This approach will often *underestimate* the value of the earnout instrument. The correct approach to valuing earnouts is to recognize their optionality—that is, to value them as instruments with contingent payments rather than as fairly certain streams of cash.

Although it may be possible to design a theoretical model to value earnouts, there is a simpler and equally effective numerical valuation approach: Monte Carlo simulation. Numerical simulations can be designed that allow users to change the key drivers of future value and estimate today's value of the target. The buyer and seller will have different distributions for the key value drivers and this will lead to different valuations of the same earnout structure for the two parties. Monte Carlo simulation yields useful negotiating and structuring insights from a review of the payout distributions. For example, the buyer can determine the probability that the earnout has no value as well as the maximum earnout amount and the likelihood of that payment.

A template model for valuing earnouts, "Earnout.xls," is contained in the CD-ROM. The user must have installed Microsoft Excel and Crystal Ball or similar compatible software to execute a simulation using this model.

Valuing an Earnout with Monte Carlo Simulation

The following example illustrates a Monte Carlo simulation of the present value of the earnout payment based on variations of sales growth and profit margins. For the purposes of this example, let's assume that the buyer plans to acquire the target that has $10 million in sales. The buyer has completed a DCF analysis that yielded an enterprise value of $3 million for the target, while the target values itself at $5 million. The parties decide to use an earnout to bridge this valuation gap. The earnout will last for five years and will have earnout targets starting at $250 thousand and increasing by that amount each year. The consideration paid at closing should not exceed the buyer's enterprise valuation of the target. A price of $2 million is agreed upon for this transaction—the key question is whether this is a fair price.

A Monte Carlo simulation valuing this earnout is based on models given in Exhibits 22.3 and 22.4, presenting a separate model for the buyer and the seller. This permits us to value the identical earnout from the perspective of both parties. An earnout that is valuable to one side may not be valuable to the other.

The first step in creating a Monte Carlo simulation to value this earnout is to determine the probability distribution of key forecast assumptions. These are probability distributions of the assumptions that drive the forecast. In this simple example, we will focus only on sales growth and profit margins. These must be determined for both the buyer and the seller points of view. The analyst can choose among a variety of possible distributions: normal, uniform, and triangular, to name three common forms. In this example, we will focus on the triangular distribution for simplicity. The amounts chosen as the minimum, maximum, and most likely will be used as the basis to create a triangular distribution of future values for the key drivers from the perspective of each party. In this case, the buyer expects values

EXHIBIT 22.3 Buyer's Forecast and Valuation Model: Generic Evaluation of an Earnout

		Year 1	Year 2	Year 3	Year 4	Year 5
Base year sales	$10,000					
Earnout period, in years	5					
Sales growth rate		$10,500	$11,025	$11,576	$12,155	$12,763
Minimum	0%					
Most likely	5%	5%	5%	5%	5%	5%
Maximum	10%					
Operating income profit margin		$ 525	$ 551	$ 579	$ 608	$ 638
Minimum	0%					
Most likely	5%	5%	5%	5%	5%	5%
Maximum	10%					
Earnout target		$ 250	$ 500	$ 750	$ 1,000	$ 1,250
Annual earnout value		$ 275	$ 51	$ —	$ —	$ —
Present value of earnout, discounted at 5%		$ 308				
Dollars at closing		$ 2,000				
Valuation of proposed total payment		$ 2,308				

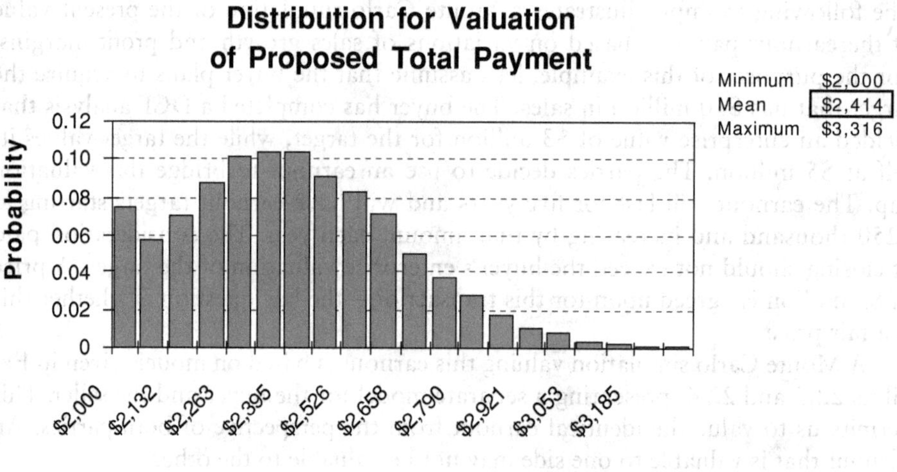

ranging from 0 percent to 10 percent for both sales growth and profit margins (with a "most likely" estimate of 5 percent for each), while the seller has higher and more volatile expectations for these values.

After the expected distributions for the key value drivers are entered into the respective buyer and seller portions of the valuation model, the following steps should be taken to complete the valuation of the proposed earnout using the model "Earnout.xls," found on the CD-ROM.

EXHIBIT 22.4 Seller's Forecast and Valuation Model: Generic Evaluation of an Earnout

		Year 1	Year 2	Year 3	Year 4	Year 5
Base year sales	$10,000					
Earnout period, in years	5					
Sales growth rate		$11,500	$13,225	$15,209	$17,490	$20,114
Minimum	10%					
Most likely	15%	15%	15%	15%	15%	15%
Maximum	20%					
Operating income profit margin		$ 1,150	$1,323	$1,521	$ 1,749	$ 2,011
Minimum	5%					
Most likely	10%	10%	10%	10%	10%	10%
Maximum	15%					
Earnout target		$ 250	$ 500	$ 750	$ 1,000	$ 1,250
Annual earnout value		$ 900	$ 823	$ 771	$ 749	$ 761
Present value of earnout, discounted at 5%		$ 3,482				
Dollars at closing		$ 2,000				
Valuation of proposed total payment		$ 5,482				

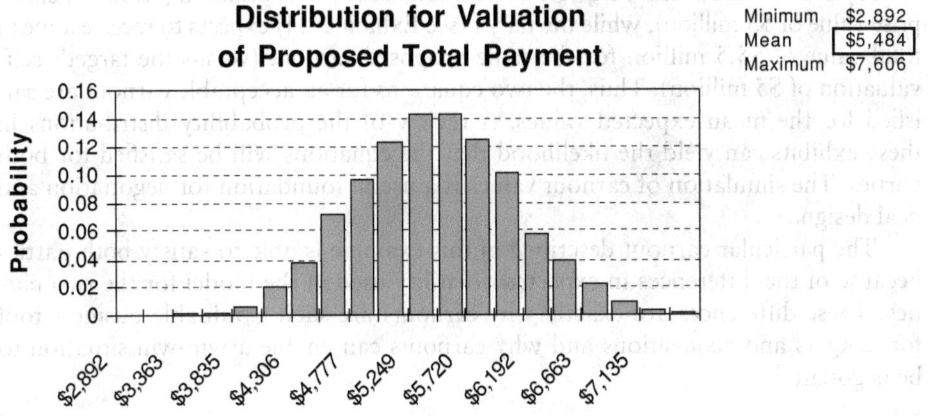

1. Enter the current sales figure of $10 million for the target company into the appropriate cell on the spreadsheet. This amount serves as the basis from which future sales and profits will be derived.
2. Input the earnout period as five years.
3. Enter the earnout targets for each year starting with $250,000 and increasing by that amount each year. The model is designed to compare these annual earnout targets to the annual operating income that results after each iteration of the simulation. Any excess of the projected operating income over and above the earnout target will result in a positive amount in the annual earnout value

line. It is also important to note that the annual earnout line will never be less than zero because the call option nature of an earnout prohibits a negative value. The annual payments expected from the earnout are discounted to account for the time value of money at the risk-free rate of return.[5]

4. Enter the fixed amount of dollars that will be paid out at closing, $2 million in this case. The model adds this figure to the present value of the earnout to arrive at an enterprise valuation of the proposed earnout structure.
5. Select the enterprise valuation cells on both the buyer and the target portion of the model as the outputs of a Monte Carlo simulation and run a simulation to determine the distribution of payouts that can be expected.

Valuation Results of the Hypothetical Example

Monte Carlo simulation offers insights about the value of the earnout to both the buyer and the target. An acceptable earnout will satisfy both sides. To the buyer, the acceptable earnout and fixed payment will be *equal to or less than* the value of the target to the buyer. To the seller, the acceptable earnout and fixed payment will be *equal to or greater than* the target's value. A satisfactory deal should meet both equations simultaneously:

Enterprise value according to buyer ≥ Dollars at closing + Buyer valuation of earnout
Enterprise value according to seller ≤ Dollars at closing + Seller valuation of earnout

A review of the distributions of expected values for this proposed deal shows that the buyer (see Exhibit 22.3) expects a mean total cost of $2.4 million (versus an enterprise value of $3 million), while the target (see Exhibit 22.4) expects to receive a mean total value of $5.5 million for the same proposed earnout (versus the target's self-valuation of $5 million). Thus, the two equations for an acceptable earnout are satisfied for the mean expected values. A review of the probability distributions in these exhibits can yield the likelihood that the equations will be satisfied for both parties. The simulation of earnout values is a useful foundation for negotiation and deal design.

The particular earnout described in this example is able to satisfy both parties because of the differences in expected volatility used in the model for the two parties. These differences are exactly why earnouts are such a valuable business tool for mergers and acquisitions and why earnouts can enable a win-win situation to be negotiated.

CASE EXAMPLE: ELI LILLY'S CONTINGENT PAYMENT UNITS

In September 1985, Eli Lilly announced its intention to acquire Hybritech Inc.[6] Lilly, a leading manufacturer of pharmaceuticals and therapeutics, was founded in 1901. Hybritech, founded in 1978, was a biotechnology research boutique leading the field in the development and marketing of new products in monoclonal antibody (MoAb) research. The acquisition announcement signaled a serious move by Lilly into biotechnology. Between the first announcement of the acquisition and the final announcement of the detailed terms of acquisition, Lilly's share price rose 36 percent (compared to 17 percent for the S&P 500 index). Plainly, investors applauded Lilly's new strategic direction.

The Challenge of Differing Outlooks and Its Solution

Hybritech and Lilly had been discussing a possible combination for over a year. In 1984, Hybritech's shares had traded at prices ranging from $11.00 to $22.75. In February 1985, Hybritech's CEO, Ted Greene, believed that the market had been undervaluing Hybritech, which he believed was worth about $30 per share. Lilly's negotiators disagreed, suggesting that $20 per share was more appropriate. Negotiations broke off, but on friendly terms. Then, from February to September, the market value of most biotechnology and pharmaceutical companies, including Hybritech and Lilly, rose.

When negotiations commenced again in late summer, discussions quickly moved to price and form of payment. Though the two firms had similar expectations about profit margins and sales growth in two product lines, Hybritech and Lilly differed substantially over the likelihood that the target would successfully introduce major new therapeutic drugs. Hybritech believed that it would receive Food and Drug Administration (FDA) approval to launch new drugs in 1988, while Lilly believed it would be 1991. But Lilly believed that once the new drugs were launched, their revenues would grow faster than Hybritech believed they would grow.

When the two sides agreed to a payment of $32 per share in mid-September 1985, the deal reflected the belief of Lilly that Hybritech was worth $29, and the belief of Hybritech that it was worth $32. The form of payment was structured in a way to allow each side to meet its expectations. The payment of $32 per share was comprised of:

- Twenty-two dollars per share to be paid in cash, or at the choice of the shareholder, in $22 of Lilly convertible notes bearing interest of 6.75 percent and a conversion price of $66.31 per share one year after the date of merger. Lilly could call the notes after March 31, 1989, at a premium that would decrease to par by the maturity date, March 31, 1996. The Hybritech shareholder could elect to receive any combination of cash and convertible notes equal to $22 per share.
- Seven dollars in 1.4 warrants to purchase Lilly stock at an exercise price of $75.98 until March 31, 1991. The warrants would be listed for trading on the New York Stock Exchange. Lilly believed that each warrant would have an initial trading value of $5, thus producing a value of $7 for the package of 1.4 warrants.
- Three dollars in value attributed to the *contingent payment units (CPUs)* issued by Lilly. In a private fairness opinion, Hybritech's investment bankers estimated the value of the CPU to be $3. The units would be listed for trading on the American Stock Exchange.

The principal Lilly negotiator of this deal told me that the three components corresponded roughly to Lilly's valuation of Hybritech's three business segments. Hybritech produced diagnostic test kits, a mature product line that would fit easily into Lilly's product line. The diagnostics business was the most valuable component to Lilly, and was worth the equivalent of $22 per Hybritech share to Lilly. A second segment, based on imaging technology, was worth $7 per share to Lilly—this was a more speculative business with a less immediate payoff. The third segment was Hybritech's therapeutics research effort. It was possible that Hybritech would make a dramatic breakthrough in product development, though the prospect of this was highly uncertain to Lilly. Hybritech's staff seemed confident that such a breakthrough would occur.

The contingent payment units (CPUs) offered a means of bridging the expectations of the two sides. The CPUs provided for annual cash payments based on the operating results of Hybritech as a wholly owned subsidiary of Lilly for each of the 12-month periods ending December 31, 1986, through December 31, 1995. The cash payments with respect to each CPU for each calendar year would be equal to:

- Six percent of Hybritech's sales,
- Plus 20 percent of Hybritech's gross profits,
- Minus a deductible amount that was to be $11 million for 1986 and which would increase at a compound rate of 35 percent annually for each of the calendar years 1987 through 1995;
- This total divided by 12,933,894, which was the number of Hybritech shares, fully diluted.

The maximum amount that Lilly offered to pay with respect to each CPU was $22. The CPUs would be canceled when dividends paid per unit had accumulated to $22, or on March 31, 1996, whichever occurred first.

The CPUs would be issued under an indenture as unsecured obligations of Lilly and would rank equally with all other unsecured indebtedness of Lilly. In addition, Lilly would not be obligated to support Hybritech as an operating subsidiary in order to generate payments on the CPUs. Holders of CPUs would have no equity interest in Lilly or Hybritech, and would not derive any economic benefit from Lilly's general business activities.

Lilly had made two acquisitions using some form of contingent payments in the two previous years. On May 31, 1984, it purchased Advanced Cardiovascular Systems for 2.8 million shares with a possibility of issuing up to 1.25 million more to ACS's shareholders. By December 31, 1984, Lilly had issued 41,000 more shares as a result of ACS's performance, and by December 31, 1985, it had issued 160,000 more. Also, Lilly acquired Intec Systems in May 1985 for $47.7 million in cash and $500,000 in convertible debentures, with the possibility of paying up to $85 million more. By early 1985, no such contingency payments had been made.

Valuation of the Contingent Payment Units

It is straightforward to construct a model that will forecast Hybritech's revenues and gross profit. Exhibits 22.5 and 22.6 present the spreadsheets of forecasts from Hybritech and Lilly's standpoints.[7] The forecasts recognize that Hybritech would derive uncertain revenues from three business segments:

1. *Diagnostics products.* These were test kits that could diagnose diseases quickly, cheaply, and in the doctor's office. The FDA had approved these kits for sale, so there was little uncertainty about their commercial possibilities. Lilly foresaw that the diagnostic products would fit easily into their broad product line.

EXHIBIT 22.5 Model Used for the Valuation of the Contingent Payment Units: Lilly's Perspective

		Base Year	1985	1986	1987	1988	1989	1990	1991	1992	1993	1994
Sales growth rate, diagnostic tests kits		$ 15,000	$ 21,750	$ 31,538	$ 45,729	$ 66,308	$ 96,146	$139,412	$202,147	$ 293,113	$ 425,014	$ 616,270
Minimum	30%											
Most likely	45%		45%	45%	45%	45%	45%	45%	45%	45%	45%	45%
Maximum	60%											
Sales growth rate, imaging products		$ —	$1	$ 1,000	$ 1,833	$ 3,361	$ 6,162	$ 11,297	$ 20,711	$ 37,971	$ 69,613	$ 127,624
Minimum	62%											
Most likely	75%		83%	83%	83%	83%	83%	83%	83%	83%	83%	83%
Maximum	113%											
Sales growth rate, therapeutic products		$ —	$ —	$ —	$ —	$ —	$ —	$ —	$ 8,000	$ 17,280	$ 37,325	$ 80,622
Minimum	65%											
Most likely	98%		116%	116%	116%	116%	116%	116%	116%	116%	116%	116%
Maximum	185%											
Contract revenues			$ 16,000	$ 21,000	$ 23,000	$ 15,000	$ 12,000	$ 4,000	$ 3,000	$ 3,000	$ 3,000	$ 3,000
Total revenues			$ 37,751	$ 53,538	$ 70,563	$ 84,669	$114,308	$154,709	$233,858	$ 351,364	$ 534,952	$ 827,516
Gross profit margin			$ 29,949	$ 42,473	$ 55,980	$ 67,171	$ 90,684	$122,736	$185,528	$ 278,749	$ 424,395	$ 656,496
Minimum	65%											
Most likely	78%		79%	79%	79%	79%	79%	79%	79%	79%	79%	79%
Maximum	95%											
Six percent of total revenues			$ 2,265	$ 3,212	$ 4,234	$ 5,080	$ 6,858	$ 9,283	$ 14,031	$ 21,082	$ 32,097	$ 49,651
20 percent of gross profits			$ 5,990	$ 8,495	$ 11,196	$ 13,434	$ 18,137	$ 24,547	$ 37,106	$ 55,750	$ 84,879	$ 131,299
Hurdle		$(11,000)	$(14,850)	$(20,048)	$(27,064)	$(36,537)	$ (49,324)	$ (66,588)	$ (89,894)	$(121,356)	$(163,831)	$(221,172)
Total annual payment of CPU			$ —	$ —	$ —	$ —	$ —	$ —	$ —	$ —	$ —	$ —
Present value of the CPU payments, discounted at 9%			$ 0.00									
Value of cash and warrants			$ 29.00									
Value of Lilly's offer			$ 29.00									

EXHIBIT 22.6 Model Used for the Valuation of the Contingent Payment Units: Hybritech's Perspective

		Base Year	1985	1986	1987	1988	1989	1990	1991	1992	1993	1994
Sales growth rate, diagnostic test kits		$ 15,000	$ 28,000	$ 38,873	$ 53,969	$ 74,927	$104,024	$144,420	$200,503	$ 278,365	$ 386,463	$ 536,540
Minimum	30%											
Most likely	38%		39%	39%	39%	39%	39%	39%	39%	39%	39%	39%
Maximum	49%											
Sales growth rate, imaging products		—	—	$ 2,000	$ 3,593	$ 6,456	$ 11,599	$ 20,840	$ 37,443	$ 67,272	$ 120,866	$ 217,155
Minimum	62%											
Most likely	75%		80%	80%	80%	80%	80%	80%	80%	80%	80%	80%
Maximum	102%											
Sales growth rate, therapeutic products		$ —	$ —	$ —	$ —	$ 8,000	$ 14,853	$ 27,578	$ 51,203	$ 95,066	$ 176,506	$ 327,713
Minimum	70%											
Most likely	88%		86%	86%	86%	86%	86%	86%	86%	86%	86%	86%
Maximum	99%											
Contract revenues			$ 16,000	$ 21,000	$ 23,000	$ 15,000	$ 12,000	$ 4,000	$ 3,000	$ 3,000	$ 3,000	$ 3,000
Total revenues			$ 44,000	$ 61,873	$ 80,562	$104,383	$142,477	$196,838	$292,148	$ 443,703	$ 686,835	$1,084,408

Gross profit margin			$ 34,907	$ 49,086	$ 63,913	$ 82,811	$113,031	$156,158	$231,771	$ 352,004	$ 544,889	$ 860,297
Minimum	65%											
Most likely	78%		79%	79%	79%	79%	79%	79%	79%	79%	79%	79%
Maximum	95%											
Six percent of total revenues			$ 2,640	$ 3,712	$ 4,834	$ 6,263	$ 8,549	$ 11,810	$ 17,529	$ 26,622	$ 41,210	$ 65,064
20 percent of gross profits			$ 6,981	$ 9,817	$ 12,783	$ 16,562	$ 22,606	$ 31,232	$ 46,354	$ 70,401	$ 108,978	$ 172,059
Hurdle		$(11,000)	$(14,850)	$(20,048)	$(27,064)	($36,537)	$ (49,324)	$ (66,588)	$ (89,894)	$(121,356)	$(163,831)	$(221,172)
Total annual payment of CPU			$ —	$ —	$ —	$ —	$ —	$ —	$ —	$ —	$ —	$ 15,952
Hybritech's view of present value of CPU payments, discounted at 9%			$ 3.01									
Value of cash and warrants			$ 29.00									
Hybritech's view of value of Lilly's offer			$ 32.01									

2. ***Imaging products.*** These products used radioisotopes to form a clearer photographic image of an internal site than might be available through more conventional means such as X-rays. These products were in development, but were relatively close to commercialization. As a result, the imaging segment was riskier than the diagnostic segment, but not regarded as being totally speculative.
3. ***Therapeutic products.*** These products represented the cures for major diseases, and were years from release into the marketplace. If, however, a discovery occurred, it was likely to be major and highly successful.

Lilly and Hybritech held approximately similar expectations for margins and growth rates for the diagnostics and imaging products. They differed substantially in their outlook for therapeutics. Hybritech expected that new therapeutic products would launch in 1988 and grow at 86 percent annually. Lilly expected delays; the launch would occur in 1991, and the new products would grow at 116 percent. Lilly believed that the difficult FDA drug approval process in the United States could slow the launch of therapeutics.

The revenue growth and gross margin assumptions were modeled as triangular distributions, notable for their ease of use (one merely needs to specify a "high," "low," and "most likely" value). There are numerous other distributions one can choose from (such as the normal distribution), but in the absence of information that would justify using another distribution, good practice probably dictates that one should use the simplest form.

From the forecasts of revenues and gross margin, the model calculated the total CPU dividend each year using the formula expressed in the acquisition agreement. These annual payments were discounted to the present using the yield on 10-year U.S. Treasury securities. Two rationales for using a 10-year risk-free rate of return are that (1) it matches the life of the earnout instrument and (2) if the risk has already been accounted for in the cash flow, it would be inappropriate to double-count it by also using a higher, risk-adjusted discount rate.[8] The resulting present value was divided by the number of Hybritech shares to give an estimate of the value of one CPU. The chief analytical question was whether the CPU was worth $3 as advertised.

The model used 10,000 draws to simulate the distribution of the value per CPU. Exhibit 22.7 presents the distribution of CPU value simulated from the Hybritech and Lilly perspectives. The mean of the Hybritech distribution (what statisticians call the "expected value") was $3.10 per share, consistent with the fairness opinion of the investment banker. The Hybritech graph reveals nearly a 99 percent probability that the CPU would payoff. Regarding the simulation from the Eli Lilly perspective, the mean was $0.26, and there was only a 21 percent likelihood that the CPU would pay off.

The disparity in results between the two perspectives is arresting, but it illustrates the economic role that earnouts can play in resolving disagreements about the future. Hybritech was optimistic; its shareholders wanted to be paid for value derived from future uncertain growth. Lilly was much less optimistic and less willing to pay for potential future value. From Lilly's perspective, the CPU would protect Lilly from overpaying.

EXHIBIT 22.7 Probability Distribution of CPU Values from the Perspectives of Hybritech and Lilly

	Hybritech's View	Lilly's View
Minimum value	$0.00	$0.00
Maximum value	$8.84	$7.83
Mean value	$3.10	$0.26
Standard deviation	$1.28	$0.55
Probability of $ > 0	99%	21%

Hybritech's View of the Likelihood of Payoff

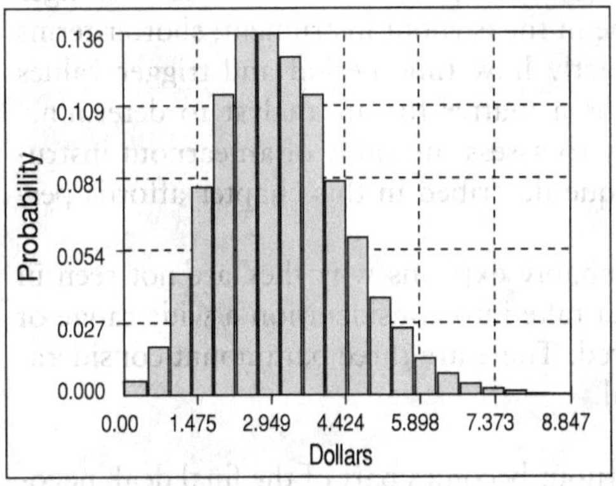

Lilly's View of the Likelihood of Payoff

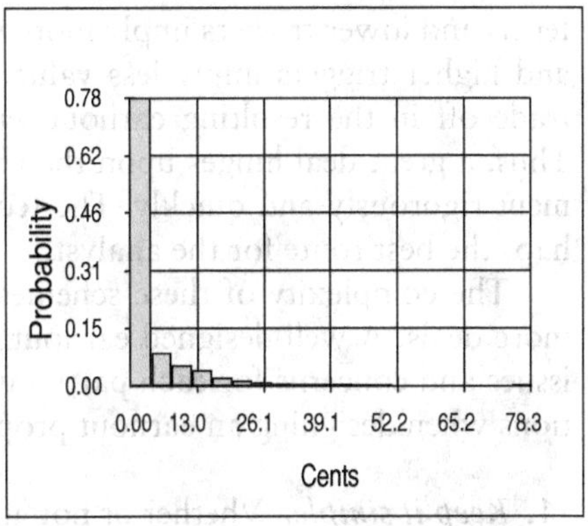

Epilogue

At the end of the first month (March 1986) the CPUs traded for $4.50 each, suggesting that investors leaned toward (indeed, beyond) the outlook of Hybritech's management, rather than Lilly's. But by the end of 1986, the CPUs traded at $2.375; at the end of 1987, they traded at $0.50. The CPUs never paid a dividend. In 1995, Lilly sold Hybritech for $10 million, well below the $374 million in cash, debt, and warrants that it paid to acquire Hybritech.

Postmortems[9] on Lilly's acquisition of Hybritech note a variety of problems. The medicine based on monoclonal antibody technology had material side effects. Abbott Labs introduced a superior competing product in the diagnostic test kit line. Employee morale at Hybritech plummeted. Lilly hesitated to increase its funding for Hybritech research, and abandoned a number of research projects. Senior management at Hybritech quit, to be replaced by middle managers from Indianapolis. On the other hand, Lilly managers told me that Lilly benefited in ways that the financial performance does not reflect, such as the successful application of process and research technologies elsewhere within Lilly.

With benefit of hindsight, the CPU was a very successful application of an earnout structure. It bridged a value gap in the negotiations and enabled the parties to agree on a total price that was generally consistent with other transactions of the day and with internal valuation analyses of the two sides. Ultimately, the CPU was a form of insurance that protected Lilly from overpayment when Hybritech's optimistic outlook for the future did not occur. The CPU performed its function.

CONCLUSION: PROPOSING AND NEGOTIATING EARNOUTS AND OTHER CONTINGENT PAYMENTS

This chapter has argued that contingent forms of payment are highly useful to deal designers. They allocate risk to those most willing to bear it and provide incentives to retain and motivate managers. Yet contingent payments are complex to structure and challenging to value. The key idea to doing both is to remember that *earnouts are options.* As discussed in Chapters 10, 14, 15, and 23, the option framework offers a powerful conceptual approach to deal structuring. The option analogy highlights two important design aspects that are worth careful attention by the negotiators: the time period and triggers (exercise prices) for the earnout. Longer terms and lower triggers imply more value in the earnout instrument; shorter terms and higher triggers imply less value. Exactly how time period and trigger values trade off in the resulting earnout value is a matter for an analyst to determine. Thus, a great deal hinges upon the ability to assess the value of an earnout instrument rigorously and quickly. The technique described in this chapter affords perhaps the best route for the analyst.

The complexity of these schemes probably explains why they are not seen in more deals. A well-designed earnout must take into consideration a wide range of issues and concerns for each party involved. There are three paramount considerations when designing an earnout proposal.

1. ***Keep it simple.*** Whether or not an earnout becomes part of the final deal, negotiating a *simple* earnout structure is the most productive use of time. If negotiations shift toward a nonearnout transaction, the effort to develop complex formulas will have been wasted. If the earnout formula is retained, the seller will want it to be clearly defined, mutually understood, and easily measurable.
2. ***Focus on key issues.*** Many earnout negotiations fail because both sides press their positions on all points. Each party should save its design efforts for its performance value issues.
3. ***Be realistic.*** To maximize the earnout's chance of success, the seller must be realistic and have a detailed understanding of how the target will operate within the buyer. Performance several years into the future is always difficult to forecast, and it is useful to consider both upside and downside scenarios. The main focus of discussion should be on near-term performance since it is the most predictable.

Given an earnout's inherent complexity, attention to detail is required by both parties to avoid future disputes. Although the parties will never be able to foresee every future issue, the written earnout agreements must address at a minimum the issues discussed in this chapter. Despite the potential headaches, a successful earnout can bring parties together on value, provide incentives for management, and generally create a win-win situation for the parties involved.

NOTES

1. Matthew Ball, "Equity Tailored to Suit the Strategy," *Corporate Finance*, October 1996, page 20.

2. Quoted in *ibid.* See also Esty et al. (1998) for a detailed discussion of the use of tracking stock in this deal.
3. Obviously, in a zero-sum world one party's gain must come at the expense of another. The joint satisfaction is probably temporary, as suggested by the operative phrase here, "at the time when the transaction is consummated."
4. The earnout ratio is defined as the percentage of the total maximum payout that is attributed to the earnout rather than the fixed portion of the purchase price.
5. In theory, the risk-free rate of return (the yield on a U.S. Treasury bond of a term equal to the life of the earnout) is the appropriate discount rate because risk has been already recognized in the probability distributions of the forecast assumptions. One does not want to double-compensate for risk. But the practitioner should be warned that simply using the risk-free rate assumes that *all* risk has been accounted for in the analysis. This assumption should be scrutinized carefully since uncertainty permeates business forecasts and may be difficult to reflect completely in the probability distributions of the forecast assumptions.
6. This case example draws upon Bruner and Opitz (1988).
7. The analysis derives from field research and forecasts provided with the cooperation of Eli Lilly & Company. Some of the simulation parameters, such as the variance of growth rates and margins, are assumed from general knowledge rather than estimated from detailed analysis.
8. Generally one needs to reflect on whether indeed all of the risks in the cash flows have been modeled with uncertain distributions. If not, it is necessary to include a risk premium in the discount rate that would account for these remaining unaccounted risks.
9. See, for instance, Burton and Rundle (1995).

CHAPTER 23

Risk Management in M&A

INTRODUCTION AND SUMMARY

The expense of exploring a deal (measured in cash, time, and attention) can be significant. Fortunately, a variety of deal features can limit the buyer's and/or seller's exposure to transaction risks. Though seemingly arcane, these features can have enormous influence on the economic attractiveness of a proposed deal. This chapter surveys these features and their economic impact.

Risk management begins with choosing a level of risk that is prudent and acceptable to your investors, and then tailoring the M&A deal terms to contain and not exceed that targeted exposure. This chapter assumes an ability to judge and choose risk levels, and instead devotes the bulk of attention to the various means for managing risk in M&A transactions.[1] Key lessons include these:

- *Risk management is costly, like insurance.* In an acquisition bargaining situation, one should expect to give something up in order to extract some risk reduction from the counterparty. Conversely, one should not blithely give risk reduction to the counterparty without getting something else in return.
- *Risk management devices are* options *in various guises.* Thus, these devices will be more valuable the longer their lives and the greater the uncertainty about the value of the underlying asset. See Chapter 10 for more discussion of option valuation. An implication of this options perspective is that one should expect to see these features where there is more uncertainty.
- *One can (and should) price risk management.* M&A deals are negotiated transactions; there is no competitive bidding with which to set an equilibrium price for risk management. Accordingly, one needs to gauge independently whether the price is appropriate. Option valuation techniques such as Monte Carlo simulation can help to price these features.
- *The true value of a bid will be equal to the sum of consideration paid and the value of any risk management features.* This is consistent with the "whole deal" perspective advocated in this book (see Chapter 18 for more on this).

This chapter gives an overview of risk management devices and their valuation. The dominant features discussed here are the *collar* and the *contingent value right.* Chapter 22 discusses earnouts and other kinds of contingent payments, which also are important forms of risk management.

VALUE AT RISK WHEN A DEAL FAILS

Any discussion of risk or its management should start from an understanding of the nature of the exposure. The value at risk before consummation include: research expenses; legal, accounting, and financial advisory fees; management time; damage to reputation; and the cost of the lost opportunity. The value at risk grows over the time period of a deal transaction, reaching its maximum at the closing. The opportunity cost can be massive where there are solid synergies or strategic options that might have been created. Strategic options, synergies, and other opportunity costs amplify the value at risk. If the buyer is a frequent participant in M&A activity, reputation considerations will amplify the value at risk.

Some firms are able to self-insure against losses through some combination of deep financial pockets (i.e., to bear the costs of research and advice); large internal staffs (i.e., to shoulder the work that would otherwise fall on senior managers); strategic planning (i.e., approaching the next-best target in an industry if the attempt to acquire the first choice fails); and public relations (i.e., to control any damage to reputation). However, many players in M&A turn to the design of the transaction itself as a means of mitigating the risks of deal failure. This chapter focuses on the deal design features that help to manage merger transaction risk.

TRANSACTION RISK: TYPES AND SOURCES

In order to illuminate the risk-management features in deals, it is useful first to consider the threats to a transaction—*transaction risk and its sources.*

Decline in Buyer's Share Price or Financial Performance

In share-for-share deals, the buyer's share price drives the monetary value of the bid. However, the buyer's share price is not fixed: It can vary after the date of the announcement. One cause would be the announcement itself, which in some cases could lead investors to conclude that the buyer was *overpaying* for the target and to bid downward the buyer's share price. This amounts to a vote of disbelief in the value of synergies to be created in the deal and/or a vote of "no confidence" in the rationality of the buyer's management and board. A second cause was highlighted in Chapters 4 and 20: The use of stock as a transaction currency is typically accompanied by a drop in the buyer's share price, which is interpreted as a signal from insiders that the *buyer's shares have been overvalued.* Third, whether or not the deal itself is attractive, the transaction could be threatened by a *deterioration in the buyer's own financial performance* between the dates of announcement and consummation.

In June 1999, Lockheed Martin Corp. announced a sharp downward revision in projected earnings through the end of 2000. Lockheed's share price fell 14 percent in the wake of the announcement. This—along with other deterioration in Lockheed's share price—threatened its merger with Comsat Corp., announced in September 1998.[2] Another illustration is the cancellation of the merger agreement between Corel and Inprise. The CEO of Inprise backed away when Corel reported a surprising quarterly loss and disclosed that it would run out of cash within three months if the merger did not go through.[3] A fourth cause would be *volatility in the capital markets*, which is usually unrelated to any specific buyer company but is rather a symptom of macroeconomic factors. A leveraged buyout for WestPoint Stevens Inc. was canceled in the face of rising interest rates.[4] In the two weeks after the terror attacks of September 11, 2001, 20 companies canceled mergers, with an aggregate (dollar) value of $15 billion.[5]

Preemption by Competing Bidder

A target goes in play with any public disclosure of merger talks, an unsolicited bid, or a definitive agreement. This can elicit a competing bid and ultimately loss of the opportunity to acquire the target. In June 2003, Oracle launched a hostile bid for PeopleSoft following the announced friendly merger of PeopleSoft and J. D. Edwards; many analysts believed that Oracle's bid was merely an attempt to spoil the PeopleSoft/Edwards deal. In April 2000, Singapore Telecommunications and News Corp. considered making a competing bid for Cable & Wireless HKT to preempt a bid by Pacific Century, whose stock price had fallen 53 percent after its bid.[6] Chapter 32 discusses at more length the dynamics and analysis of competition in bidding. A high offering price is the best deterrent to entry by a competitor. But bidding high easily leads to overpayment.

Disappointed Sellers

When the announced price in a friendly merger is below the seller's expectations, target shareholders can balk and threaten the consummation of the deal. In February 2001, the shares of Hughes Electronics fell 11 percent on the announcement of the preliminary acquisition terms offered by News Corp. The controlling owner of Hughes shares, General Motors, had promised shareholders that they would receive a large premium in any sale of Hughes, and had announced its intention to divest. One shareholder had expected a 30 percent premium, well above the 2 percent premium that was ultimately offered by News Corp. The slump in the technology sector in 2000 and the emergence of only one buyer accounted for the thin premium.[7] Next Hughes sought to be acquired by DirectTV, only to be forestalled by the Federal Communications Commission. In the final event, News Corp. became the merger partner.

Appearance of Formerly Hidden Product Liabilities

American Home Products backed away from a $35 billion acquisition of Monsanto in October 1998, reflecting growing concern about the market reaction and potential liability in Monsanto's line of genetically modified corn seed. Monsanto's share price fell 40 percent in just two days after the announcement.[8] Similarly, in February 1999, Cargill Inc. announced that its deal to sell its seed business to Schering AG and Hoechst AG had collapsed because some of the seeds it sold contained genetically engineered material covered under trade secrets held by Pioneer Hi-Bred International. The day before, Pioneer had sued its rival, Monsanto, for stealing trade secrets. Monsanto and Cargill were partners in a biotechnology joint venture. Schering and Hoechst feared that by buying the Cargill seeds business they would expose themselves to expensive trade-secrets litigation.[9]

Loss of Key Customers by the Target

On June 3, 1998, Tellabs announced plans to acquire Ciena Corp. In August, Ciena announced disappointing third-quarter results. A week later, AT&T announced that it would not purchase a Ciena product, a scheduled deal on which analysts and investors had been counting. On September 10, Digital Teleport, Inc., awarded a $100 million contract to a competitor of Ciena, again disappointing the expectations of investors and analysts. In late August, Tellabs revised downward the terms of its acquisition offer from $6.9 billion to $3.98 billion. In September 1998, Tellabs canceled its acquisition plans entirely. By the date of cancellation, Ciena's share price had fallen 77 percent since the day before the bid.[10]

Problems in Target's Accounting Statements

A leveraged buyout of North Face Inc. in March 1999 was delayed indefinitely by the discovery of accounting problems that might have required restatement of the firm's results as far back as 1997.[11] For another example, in January 1997, Raytheon won a bidding war for some of the defense industry assets of Hughes Electronics. The acquisition agreement gave Raytheon the right to adjust the purchase price after inspecting the balance sheets for the target business after the December 1997 closing. Five months later, Raytheon sent Hughes notice of 144 errors in financial information and claimed an adjustment in the price by $1 billion, more than 10 percent of the total deal value. Frequently, acquisition agreements permit post-transaction price adjustments, particularly where the target is a privately held firm; usually those adjustments are in the range of 2 to 3 percent of the deal value. Raytheon sought arbitration. Hughes sued Raytheon to obtain a court-ordered judgment.[12]

Regulatory Intervention

PennCorp's acquisition of Washington National Corp. was scuttled in November 1997 when the U.S. Securities and Exchange Commission announced an investigation into PennCorp's acquisition accounting practices, particularly the appropriateness of assumptions used in creating reserves. PennCorp's share price fell 90 percent in the following nine months. Analysts credited the failure of PennCorp to promptly integrate earlier acquisitions, and the impact of high leverage created in those acquisitions, to the financial downfall of the firm.[13] In 1999, Barnes & Noble dropped its plans to acquire Ingram Book Group, the largest book wholesaler in the United States, when the Federal Trade Commission opposed the combination.[14]

Litigation by Competitors

Lawsuits filed by Crane Company (in December 1998) and AlliedSignal Corporation (in March 1999) sought to block the merger between B. F. Goodrich Company and Coltec Industries Inc. Goodrich and Coltech competed with Crane and AlliedSignal in the manufacture of aircraft landing gear. The suits alleged that the merger violated U.S. antitrust laws, as it would reduce or eliminate competition in various products.[15]

Disagreements over Social Issues

Chapter 24 discusses the role of social issues in deal design—typically, these are the first and most sensitive terms to be decided. Failure to reach agreement on them usually derails friendly negotiations. In 1999, Texaco (the third-largest oil company in the United States) and Chevron (the fourth-largest oil company) talked for about a month about a potential merger. Then Texaco abruptly canceled the talks out of a belief that Chevron's proposal was "unacceptable for reasons including complexity, feasibility, risk, and price." Some observers suggested that the main barrier to concluding a deal was a disagreement over social issues (e.g., executive titles in Newco).[16] In November 1998, talks on combining the media-buying businesses of Leo Burnett Co. and MacManus Group ended over a dispute about who would run the new firm, someone from Burnett or MacManus.[17] SmithKline Beecham PLC held merger talks with American Home Products Corp. and Glaxo Wellcome PLC that ended with disagreements over management roles and other issues.[18]

Failure to Get Shareholder Approvals

In August 1998, Crescent Real Estate Equities Company backed out of its agreement to buy Station Casinos Inc., claiming that Station had failed to obtain necessary shareholder approvals for the sale. Crescent sued Station seeking $54 million in breakup fees.[19]

Controversy or Lack of Credibility

In June 1999, Park Place Entertainment received a middle-of-the-night all-cash offer to buy eight Caesars hotels and casinos for $3.8 billion. The bidder was Ocean Fund, a Virgin Islands firm that operated the largest pornography site on the Internet. The unusual mode of delivery, numerous misspellings in the document, and the failure to completely establish the identity of the buyer made a laughingstock of the offer. Park Place declined to respond to the bid.[20] In June 1999, Bank of Scotland dropped plans to invest in a U.S. telephone-banking service with evangelist Pat Robertson. This followed public statements by Robertson that proved too provocative for the bank.[21]

These vignettes illustrate various transaction risks associated with mergers and acquisitions. Because no one can foresee with certainty how the threats will appear or play out, risk management devices become very relevant to the deal designer.

TYPES OF RISK MANAGEMENT

The range of risk management devices that are available to the deal designer are best understood from the perspective of three stages of the deal transaction:

Before the Public Announcement of the Deal

In this time period, the buyer and the target anticipate the reaction of investors and competitors to news about the prospective deal. The initial investment in cash and attention given by each side is relatively small.

- ***Toehold stake.*** In the United States, a buyer may acquire up to 4.99 percent of the stock of a public target without revealing its ownership to the public. In the event that another firm in a bidding contest acquires the target, the profit earned on this *toehold stake* may mitigate the expenses incurred by the disappointed buyer. The disadvantage of this tactic is that it is surreptitious and may erode trust between the buyer and target when the acquisition of the toehold stake becomes known.
- ***Antitakeover defenses.*** Large public corporations tend to put *antitakeover defenses* in place well before any contemplated M&A activity. These may give the managers and directors of the target some flexibility in negotiation with one or more buyers. See Chapter 33 for more on defenses that can be mounted before a deal is announced.

Between Announcement and Consummation

The investment of the two sides grows dramatically during this period. Many of the following devices are included in the merger agreement:

- ***Termination fees.*** These are awarded to the party left standing at the altar. *Breakup fee* is another generic name for this risk management device. A *topping fee* is a form of breakup fee awarded to the buyer in the event that another buyer successfully acquires the target with a higher bid, one that has topped the buyer's offer. Termination fee arrangements are simply options that can be valued using the techniques of Chapters 10 and 14. Termination fees are discussed in more detail in Chapters 29 and 33.
- ***Lockup options.*** The merger agreement may include a lockup option, *the right of the buyer to acquire 19.9*[22] percent of the target's stock or certain key assets of the target in the event a competitor crosses a threshold in trying to acquire the target.
- ***Exit clauses.*** These specify the conditions under which the buyer may terminate the deal without having to pay termination fees. Exit provisions hedge against the uncertainty of what the buyer may discover in due diligence research. The target will seek conditions that limit the ability of the buyer to disengage; the buyer will seek less restrictive conditions. *Exit clauses,* too, are options.
- ***Representations, warranties, covenants, and closing conditions.*** *Representations and warranties* are clauses in the definitive merger agreement that establish the required condition of the buyer and target firms at the time of signing the agreement, and again at the closing. Failure to meet these conditions will usually trigger a renegotiation of price, or even cancellation of the deal. See Chapter 29 for more discussion about the definitive agreement.
- ***Due diligence research.*** Chapter 8 characterizes *due diligence research* as a risk management device, like buying a call option on knowledge about the firm. The greater the uncertainty about the target, the more valuable this option. This research helps deal designers to negotiate the final merger agreement and to prepare for postmerger integration. Thus, due diligence helps the buyer hedge against several kinds of uncertainty in the transaction.
- ***Caps, floors, and collars.*** In a share-for-share transaction, the target shareholders assume some risk regarding movements in the buyer's share price until they receive the shares at deal closing (which is the earliest time they can possibly

sell them). Target shareholders may seek to mitigate this risk by putting a *floor* on their exposure. Similarly, buyer shareholders may resent the unlimited upside—what if the market loves the proposed deal and the buyer's share price rises? Thus, the buyers may want to "*cap*" the number of shares they must give away for the target. The combination of cap and floor creates a collar. These risk management devices are discussed further later in this chapter.

After Consummation

Only after the transaction is completed does the buyer *really* learn what is inside the target. In an all-cash deal, the risks during this phase accrue completely to the buyer. But the risk can be shared through artful deal design, such as the stock-for-stock structure,[23] or using the following kinds of features:

- ***Escrow accounts and post-transaction price adjustments.*** In crafting the merger agreement, the buyer may seek to hold back some part of the payment in an *escrow account* pending a detailed audit of the target postmerger. Targets with complicated accounts frequently agree to some mechanism of price adjustment. But these adjustments are used mainly where there is one definable seller (e.g., as in a purchase transaction of selected assets). They are rarely seen in stock-for-stock mergers because of the difficulty of *ex post* settling up[24] and the potentially negative signals they send to the target shareholders.
- ***Contingent value rights.*** In stock-for-stock deals, the target shareholders may be concerned about the value of the buyer's shares over a two-to-three-year time frame. The buyer may grant these rights to target shareholders in order to provide a partial or complete guarantee of a minimum value. This risk management device is discussed further later in this chapter.
- ***Earnouts and other contingent payments.*** The use of earnouts, warrants, and other forms of contingent payments address the opposite concern: the desire to participate in the benefits to be created by the target firm. Chapter 22 discusses these in more detail.
- ***Staged investing.*** Venture capitalists (VCs) know well the advantages of making "milestone investments"[25] in support of a risky venture. In essence, the VC buys a series of call options on the risky firm; with each round of financing, the VC gains the right to participate in the next round, until the target firm either emerges as a brilliant success or fails. Investing in stages reduces the capital at risk during the most uncertain stage of the firm's existence. This risk management device is discussed in the section on *staged acquiring* later in this chapter.
- ***Cash payment.*** From the standpoint of target shareholders, cash payment is the ultimate hedge against uncertainty postacquisition.

Exhibit 23.1 indicates the relatively low frequency with which some of these risk management devices are used. Exhibit 23.2 estimates the correlations between use of collars, for instance, and volatility of the S&P 500 Index. These exhibits suggest that risk management devices are used more frequently in transactions that are (1) large, (2) between public firms, and (3) in times of relatively greater volatility. Fuller (2003) found that collars are more likely to be used where there is uncertainty about the value of the buyer.

EXHIBIT 23.1 Use of Risk Management Devices as a Percentage of Deal Volume (1992–2000)

	All Deals	Percentage	Big Deals	Percentage
Total deals	100,972	100.00%	1,599	100.00%
Deals that featured				
Collars	591	0.59%	95	5.94%
Breakup fees	2,472	2.45%	474	29.64%
Topping fees	118	0.12%	34	2.13%
Lockups	950	0.94%	195	12.20%
Toehold stakes	24	0.02%	2	0.13%
Earnouts	1,213	1.20%	15	0.94%

Source of data: Thomson Financial Securities Data Corporation.

TYPES OF COLLARS AND THEIR ANALYSIS

The collar is worthy of detailed study, not because of its frequency of use (which is typically low) but rather because it affords a range of important insights that can be extended to all risk management devices. A collar is simply a way to hedge against uncertainty about the value of the buyer. Not only does it transform payment, but it often grants either or both of the merging firms the right to renegotiate the deal if the buyer's stock price falls outside the bounds of either strike price—in this sense, a collar may be viewed as an option to cancel a merger. But this right to revise is either granted infrequently or, if granted, is used infrequently: Fuller (2003) found that of 83 collar options, only 12 exceeded the boundaries at expiration. Of these only three offers were revised. Three other findings by Fuller are noteworthy. First, collar offers are significantly more likely to succeed (i.e., to close) than are straight stock or cash offers. Second, the announcement returns to the buyer's shareholders are not significantly enhanced by the use of collars. Finally, bidders' announcement day abnormal returns are lower (and targets' returns higher) with floating collars than fixed collars. To understand why investors might care about the difference it is necessary to consider the varieties of share payment in M&A.

Four Classic Profiles

Consider the four classic profiles of payment in M&A given in Exhibit 23.3. In each case, the graph shows the values paid by the buyer for four stock-for-stock deals—the horizontal axis gives the share price of the buyer, and the vertical axis gives the value received by target shareholders.

- *Fixed exchange ratio deal* (Panel A of Exhibit 23.3). In a *fixed exchange ratio deal*, as the buyer's share price rises or falls, the shareholder of the target feels the value of its expected payment in shares grow and shrink. The buyer knows for sure how many shares must be issued to consummate the deal. But neither the buyer nor the seller may be very happy with the uncertainty about how much the deal is *really* worth. For all the reasons outlined earlier, the buyer's stock price could fall, leaving the target shareholders with less value than they

EXHIBIT 23.2 Use of Collars by Year and Size of Deal, and Correlated with Volatility in the Market

Year	No. of All Deals	No. of Stock-for-Stock Deals	No. of Big Stock Deals*	No. of All Deals with Collars	No. of All Stock Deals with Collars	No. of Big Stock Deals with Collars	Collars (%) Used in All Deals	Collars (%) Used in All Stock Deals	Collars (%) Used in Big Stock Deals	% Collars Used 1992–2000	Annualized Volatility of S&P 500 Index
1992	6,862	577	41	21	20	1	0.31%	3.47%	2.44%	3.55%	0.087
1993	7,721	704	59	50	49	3	0.65%	6.96%	5.08%	8.46%	0.077
1994	9,334	849	114	90	85	8	0.96%	10.01%	7.02%	15.23%	0.088
1995	10,951	864	125	60	56	5	0.55%	6.48%	4.00%	10.15%	0.073
1996	12,554	964	178	50	46	6	0.40%	4.77%	3.37%	8.46%	0.106
1997	13,249	1,119	237	87	77	18	0.66%	6.88%	7.59%	14.72%	0.164
1998	14,994	1,151	263	76	75	18	0.51%	6.52%	6.84%	12.86%	0.183
1999	13,083	1,031	287	89	83	19	0.68%	8.05%	6.62%	15.06%	0.162
2000	12,224	1,197	295	68	61	17	0.56%	5.10%	5.76%	11.51%	0.198
Sum	100,972	8,456	1,599	591	552	95				100.00%	
Correlation between use of collars and volatility of S&P 500 Index							–1.69%	–4.20%	58.52%	50.45%	

*"Big stock deals" are defined as those deals with a deal value equal to 1 billion U.S. dollars in 2000, adjusted for inflation.
Source of data: Thomson Financial SDC Platinum Database.

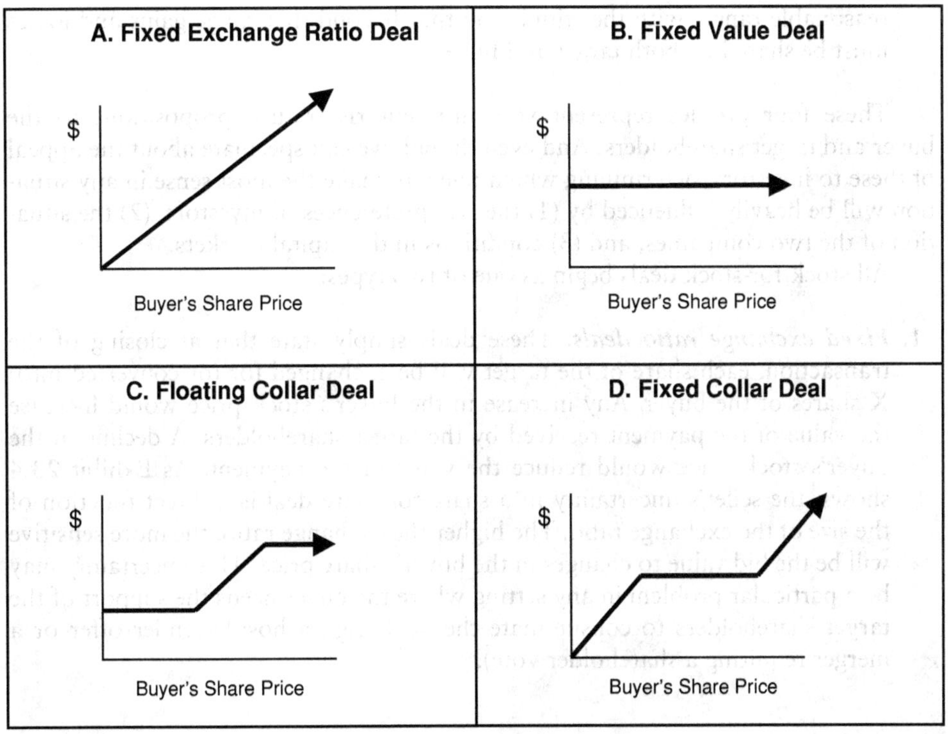

EXHIBIT 23.3 Classic Profiles of Payoffs with and without Collars: Payment Received by Targets as a Function of Buyer's Stock Price

may have thought they would receive. Or the buyer's share price could rise at the announcement, making this a more expensive deal than anticipated from the buyer's perspective.

- *Fixed value deal* (Panel B). There is no doubt in a *fixed value deal* about the value to be paid or received. But there is great uncertainty about the number of shares to be issued, since, as the buyer's share price falls, the exchange ratio must rise in order to keep the value constant (and vice versa for when the price rises). The dollar figures in this graph hide a lot of potential control dilution. From the standpoint of selling shareholders, this is a very conservative bet. Recall the discussion of trade-offs in Chapter 22: For a buyer to give a relatively riskless deal to the sellers, the buyer might reasonably require something in return (e.g., a lower purchase price).
- *Floating collar* (Panel C). One solution might be to settle for a little uncertainty within a reasonable range, with firm boundaries on the top and bottom (*floating collar*). Downside losses are limited from falling below a predesignated floor (which pleases target shareholders) and upside gains are capped (which pleases buyer shareholders). This looks much like a conservative bet (how conservative will depend on the size of the spread between the cap and floor). The resulting payoff diagram resembles the well-known bull spread[26] used by options traders.
- *Fixed collar* (Panel D). Another solution might be a *fixed collar*, where no doubt is left about the payment as long as the buyer's share price remains in a

reasonable range, with the stipulation that beyond that range gains and losses must be shared by both target and buyer.

These four profiles represent very different risk-return propositions to the buyer and target shareholders. And even though we can speculate about the appeal of these to investors, determining which one will make the most sense in any situation will be heavily influenced by (1) the risk preferences of investors, (2) the situation of the two companies, and (3) conditions in the capital markets.

All stock-for-stock deals begin as one of two types:

1. ***Fixed exchange ratio deals.*** These deals simply state that at closing of the transaction, each share of the target will be exchanged for (or converted into) X shares of the buyer. Any increase in the buyer's stock price would increase the value of the payment received by the target shareholders. A decline in the buyer's stock price would reduce the value of the payment. As Exhibit 23.4 shows, the seller's uncertainty in a share-for-share deal is a direct function of the size of the exchange ratio. The higher the exchange ratio, the more sensitive will be the bid value to changes in the buyer's share price. This uncertainty may be a particular problem in any setting where the buyer needs the support of the target shareholders to consummate the deal (e.g., a hostile tender offer or a merger requiring a shareholder vote).

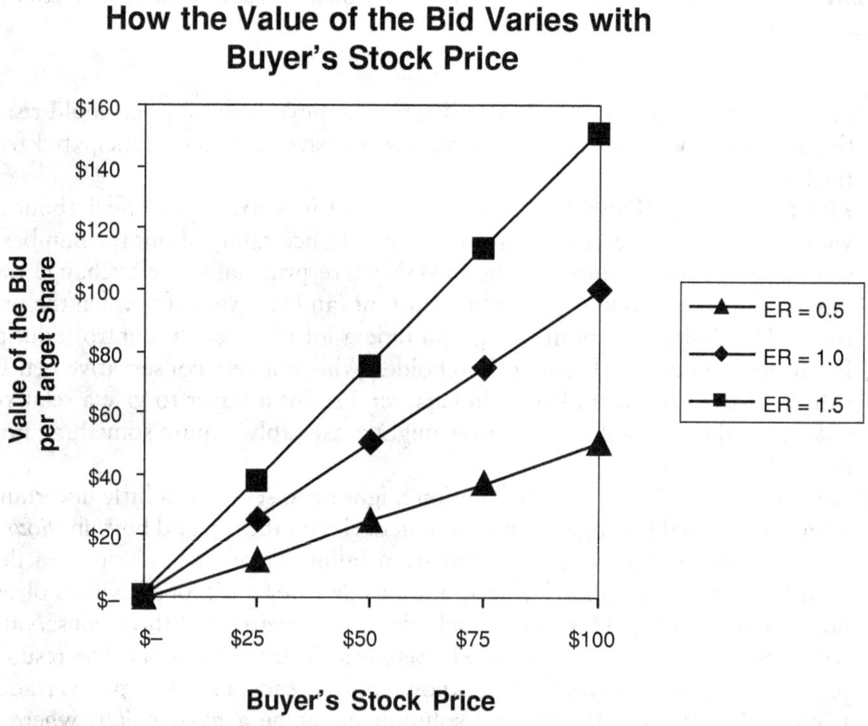

EXHIBIT 23.4 Illustration of Value Paid to Seller as a Function of Buyer's Stock Price

2. ***Fixed value deals.*** These deals simply state that at closing of the transaction, each share of the target will be exchanged for (or converted into) shares of the buyer determined by dividing the payment amount per share by the previous day's closing stock price for the buyer. In this kind of deal, a decline in the buyer's share price would raise the number of shares required to consummate the deal, thus imposing greater accounting dilution and control dilution[27] on the buyer's shareholders. An increase in the buyer's stock price would shift dilution onto the target shareholders.

A collar mitigates the impact of uncertainty about the buyer's share price through either a transfer of cash or an adjustment in the exchange ratio. The form of this adjustment will differ between the fixed exchange ratio and fixed value deals. Consider these two scenarios:

COLLAR FOR FIXED EXCHANGE RATIO DEALS Beyond the high and low trigger points, the collar converts the fixed exchange ratio deal into a minimum or maximum fixed value deal. For example, suppose the fixed exchange ratio in a deal is 1:1, and that at the time of agreement the buyer's share price is \$20. A collar might strike triggers at \$15 on the low side and \$25 on the high side, outside of which the number of shares paid would adjust.[28] Thus, the agreement would state that the exchange ratio is one-for-one, *unless* the buyer's stock price is less than \$15, in which case the exchange ratio will be equal to \$15 divided by the buyer's share price at closing, and *unless* the buyer's share price is greater than \$25, in which case the exchange ratio will equal \$25 divided by the buyer's share price at closing. Exhibit 23.5 gives a table illustrating the results of this example, the total shares issued by the buyer, and total consideration paid. Exhibit 23.6 gives graphs of the value and shares paid for the stock portion alone (Panels A and B), the collar alone (Panels C and D), and the combination of stock and the collar (Panels E and F). Panel C shows that the collar for a fixed exchange rate deal essentially consists of a long put option (with a low strike price) and a short call option (with a higher strike price). When combined with the stock position (graphed in Panel A) the payoff presented to the target shareholders corresponds to the *floating collar* described earlier (Panel E). How attractive this collar will be to the target shareholders will depend on their relative optimism or pessimism, the width of the collar, and on where the buyer's stock price falls within the boundaries of the collar. The greater the range between the two strike prices in the collar, the greater the uncertainty for the target shareholders. If the buyer's stock price is near the high strike on the collar, target shareholders mainly face a risk of loss. If the buyer's stock price is near the low strike on the collar, the target shareholders mainly face a chance of gain.

COLLAR FOR FIXED VALUE DEALS Outside of the high and low trigger points, the collar converts the fixed value deal into a fixed exchange ratio deal. For example, suppose the fixed value deal specifies that the exchange ratio will be determined by \$20 (the fixed value) divided by the share price of the buyer at closing. A collar might strike triggers at \$15 on the low side and \$25 on the high side. Thus, the agreement would state that the exchange ratio will equal \$20 divided by the buyer's share price at closing *unless* the buyer's stock price is less than \$15, in which case the exchange ratio will be equal to 1.33 shares of stock, or *unless* the buyer's stock price

EXHIBIT 23.5 Illustration of Impact of Collar on Value Paid and Shares Issed to Seller in Fixed Exchange Ratio Deal

		Buyer's Stock Price	Value of Bid without Collar	Value of Collar	Value of Bid with Collar	Payoff on Upper Strike	Payoff on Lower Strike	Number of Buyer Shares Issued per Target Share		
								Without Collar	Stock Collar	With Stock Collar
"Fixed" exchange ratio	1.00	$ 0.01	$ 0.01	$ 14.99	$15.00	$ —	$14.99	1.00	1,499.00	1,500.00
Collar upper strike	$25.00	$ 5.00	$ 5.00	$ 10.00	$15.00	$ —	$10.00	1.00	2.00	3.00
Exchange ratio above upper strike	Upper strike/ Buyer's stock price	$10.00	$10.00	$ 5.00	$15.00	$ —	$ 5.00	1.00	0.50	1.50
Collar lower strike	$15.00	$15.00	$15.00	$ —	$15.00	$ —	$ —	1.00	0.00	1.00
Exchange ratio below lower strike	Lower strike/ Buyer's stock price	$20.00	$20.00	$ —	$20.00	$ —	$ —	1.00	0.00	1.00
		$25.00	$25.00	$ —	$25.00	$ —	$ —	1.00	0.00	1.00
		$30.00	$30.00	$ (5.00)	$25.00	$ (5.00)	$ —	1.00	–0.17	0.83
		$35.00	$35.00	$(10.00)	$25.00	$(10.00)	$ —	1.00	–0.29	0.71
		$40.00	$40.00	$(15.00)	$25.00	$(15.00)	$ —	1.00	–0.38	0.63

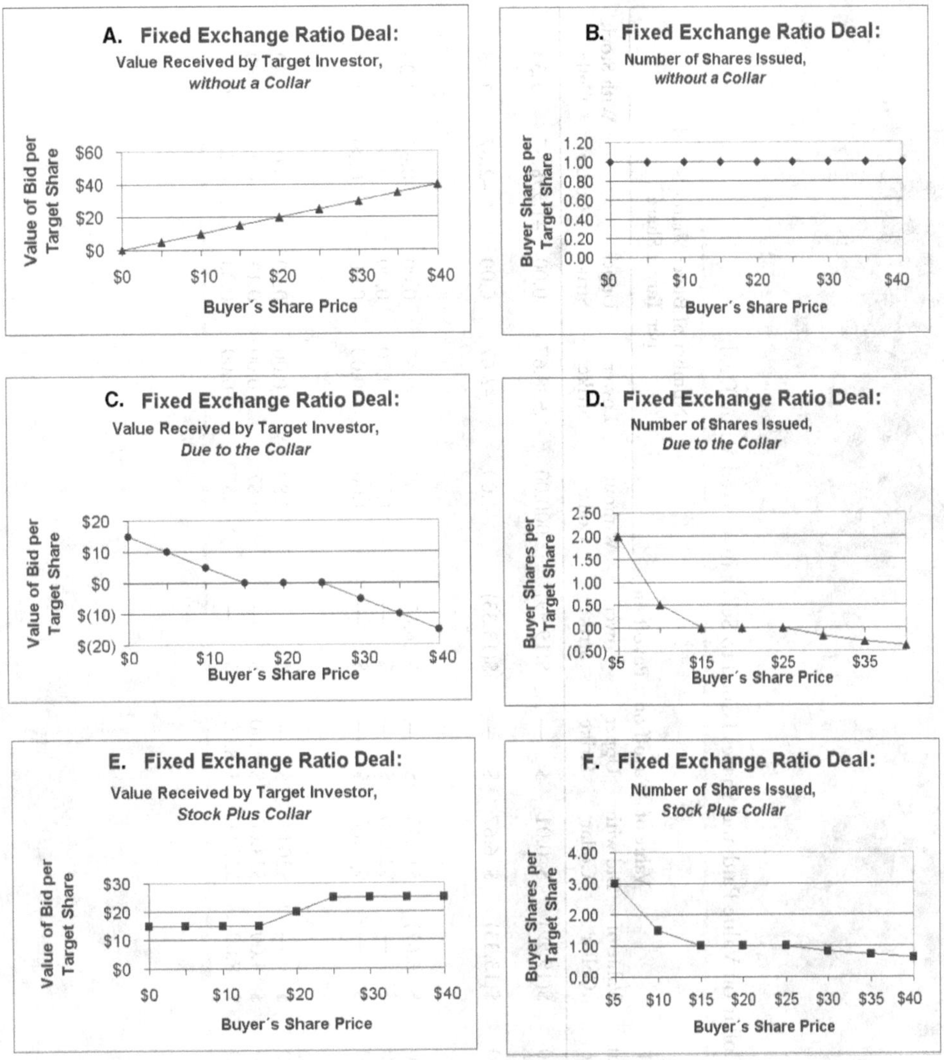

EXHIBIT 23.6 Graphs of the Value and Number of Shares Paid to Target Shareholders

is greater than $25, in which case the exchange ratio will equal 0.80 shares of stock. Exhibit 23.7 gives a table illustrating the results of this example, the total shares issued by the buyer, and total consideration paid. Exhibit 23.8 gives graphs of the value and shares paid for the stock portion alone (Panels A and B), the collar alone (Panels C and D), and the combination of stock and the collar (Panels E and F). The diagram of the combined position given in Panel E corresponds to the *fixed collar* described earlier. Again, the attractiveness of this combination will depend on the relative optimism of the target shareholders, the width of the collar, and the level of the buyer's stock price relative to the collar strike prices. The greater the range between the two strike prices, the less the uncertainty to the target share-

EXHIBIT 23.7 Illustration of the Impact of Collar on Value Paid and Shares Issued to Seller in a Fixed Value Deal

		Buyer's Stock Price	Value of Bid without Collar	Value of Collar	Value of Bid with Collar	Payoff on Upper Strike	Payoff on Lower Strike	Number of Buyer Shares Issued per Target Share				
								Without Collar	Lower Strike	Upper Strike	Collar	With Stock Collar
"Fixed" value per target share	$20.00	$ 0.01	$20.00	$(19.99)	$ 0.01	$ —	$(19.99)	2,000.00	–1,998.67	0.00	–1,998.67	1.33
Collar upper strike	$25.00	$ 5.00	$20.00	$(13.33)	$ 6.67	$ —	$(13.33)	4.00	–2.67	0.00	–2.67	1.33
Exchange ratio above upper strike	0.8	$10.00	$20.00	$ (6.67)	$13.33	$ —	$ (6.67)	2.00	–0.67	0.00	–0.67	1.33
Collar lower strike	$15.00	$15.00	$20.00	$ —	$20.00	$ —	$ —	1.33	0.00	0.00	0.00	1.33
Exchange ratio below lower strike	1.33	$20.00	$20.00	$ —	$20.00	$ —	$ —	1.00	0.00	0.00	0.00	1.00
		$25.00	$20.00	$ —	$20.00	$ —	$ —	0.80	0.00	0.00	0.00	0.80
		$30.00	$20.00	$ 4.00	$24.00	$ 4.00	$ —	0.67	0.00	0.13	0.13	0.80
		$35.00	$20.00	$ 8.00	$28.00	$ 8.00	$ —	0.57	0.00	0.23	0.23	0.80

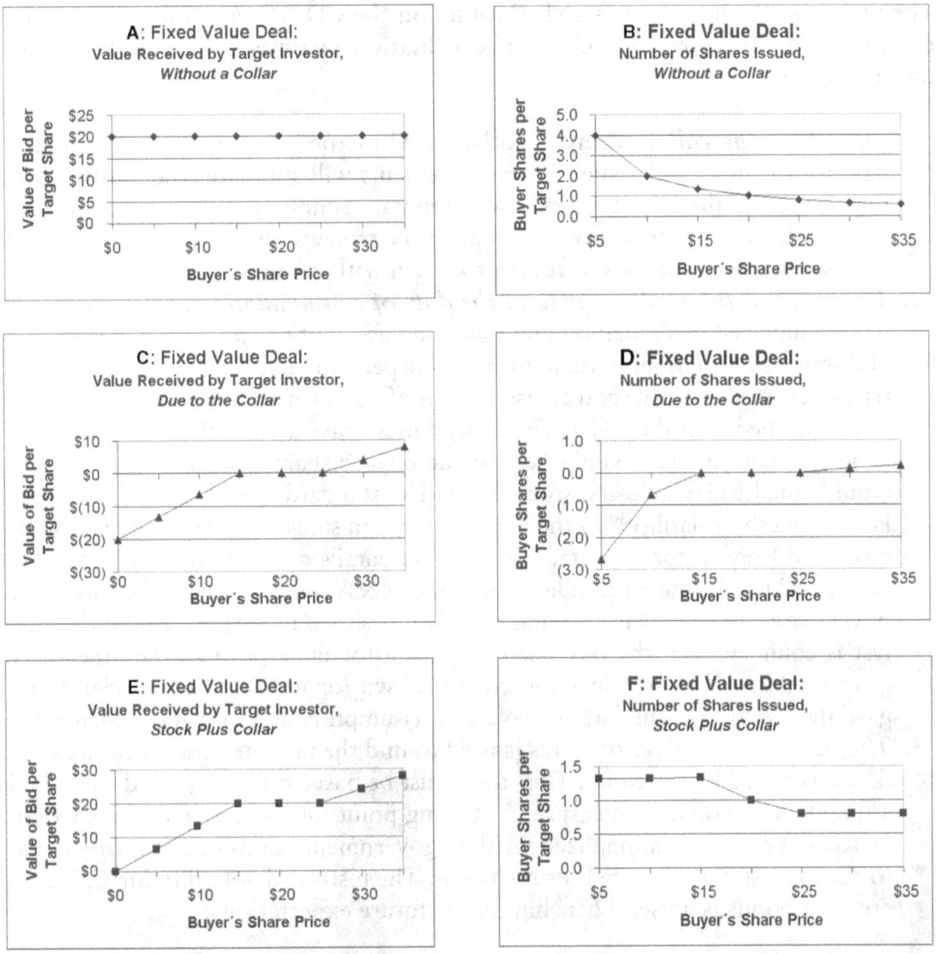

EXHIBIT 23.8 Graphs of the Impact of Collar on Value Paid and Shares Issued to Seller in a Fixed Value Deal

holder. The closer the buyer's stock price is to the lower strike, the greater the target shareholder's downside risk will be.

Valuing a Collar: The Case of AT&T/MediaOne

Collars can and should be valued as a routine aspect of deal evaluation. The simplest approach is to decompose the collar into two (or more) component options, then value the options separately, and finally sum the values. Chapter 10 gives more detail about option valuation. The spreadsheet model found on the CD-ROM ("Option Valuation.xls") provides a Black-Scholes valuation model for options. This approach would be appropriate for valuing simple options that are independent of each other, which assumption is violated in the collar.[29] For more complex collars, the best approach is to simulate the value of the collar using a computer-based spreadsheet and add-in simulation software.

The program "Collars Analysis.xls," found on the CD-ROM, affords a template for valuing more complex collars. The valuation analysis must simulate three uncertainties:

1. *The life of the collar.* Many negotiators will express a target consummation date for the deal, and some merger agreements will stipulate a definitive deadline. But given the uncertainties associated with simply completing the due diligence research, antitrust reviews, regulatory reviews, and so on, the practical fact is that the life of the collar is not known with certainty.
2. *The expected future share price at the date of consummation of the deal.* This will be modeled in simulation analysis using assumptions about the mean value and standard deviation. Both, in turn, will depend on macroeconomic and industry drivers of share price and an assessment of the investors' likely reaction to the deal over the life of the collar. The analyst must have a view about this likely reaction—a neutral view would be that the buyer's share price at consummation would equal today's closing stock price. The standard deviation may be calculated using the volatility[30] of the buyer's common stock. This volatility is usually estimated from historical data, but doing so entails one important bet: that the future will be like the past. Indeed, once the M&A transaction is announced, the buyer's stock price may gyrate significantly more than in the past. And if the analyst is confident that the buyer is overpaying (or underpaying), then the share price might make a step-function change down (or up). Options specialists regard the selection of the forecast volatility assumption as a matter of judgment.
3. *The risk-free rate of return.* This is used to find the present value of future cash flows triggered by the collar. This, too, must be based on an expected value and a quantifiable volatility measure. A starting point for these assumptions would be to use yesterday's annualized yield on government bonds of a maturity equal to the longest date assumed for the collar. The historical volatility for U.S. government bonds is a useful benchmark for future expectations.

The terms of the collar itself are known, and can be modeled by breaking the collar into its components and calculating payouts under any of the four well-known option positions—long call, short call, long put, and short put.

To illustrate the valuation process, consider the case of AT&T's collar on its share-for-share offer to acquire MediaOne in 1999.[31] In essence, AT&T offered the shareholders of MediaOne two alternatives: either $85 cash per share of MediaOne or 1.4912 shares of AT&T common stock, plus a collar. The collar would "top up" the proceeds to MediaOne shareholders in the event AT&T's share price declined. Specifically, the collar required that if AT&T's share price was less than $57, MediaOne shareholders would receive cash equal to 1.4912 times the difference between $57 and the AT&T share price, with a maximum cash payment of $8.50 per MediaOne share.

The question facing every MediaOne shareholder was whether these two alternatives were equivalent in value and which deal to accept. Was the stock-plus-collar deal worth more or less than $85?

The stock being offered could easily be valued by analysts; $57 was AT&T's share price before the announcement of the deal. At 1.4912 AT&T shares per

MediaOne share, the bundle of AT&T shares offered was worth $84.99. The first step in valuing the collar is to observe that it consists of two option components:

1. Long put, struck at $57.
2. Short put, struck at $51.30, equal to $57 – ($8.50/1.4912).

The long put would lift the payout to the shareholder if AT&T share price fell. But the short put would cap the payout at $8.50. The life of the collar was uncertain, and would depend on how long it took AT&T and MediaOne to gain the necessary regulatory approvals and the support of both firms' shareholders. One might reasonably guess that the minimum life would be 90 days, the maximum would be 360 days, and a "best guess" life would be 180 days. At the time of the deal, the prevailing short-term yield on U.S. government debt (the risk-free rate) was about 5 percent and the volatility of AT&T shares was about 15 percent. The worksheet for the valuation model is given in Exhibit 23.9.

A graph of the probability distribution of possible collar payment values is given in Exhibit 23.10. From 5,000 trials (draws), the mean of the distribution is $1.57 (with a standard deviation of $2.54). In 64 percent of the cases, the payout was zero. Given that each MediaOne shareholder would receive collar payments in proportion to the number of AT&T shares received, the collar was worth $2.34 per MediaOne share (equal to 1.4912 times $1.57). At the exchange ratio of 1.4912 AT&T shares per MediaOne share, and at AT&T's share price of $57.00, the shares component was worth $84.99. With the collar valued at $2.34 per MediaOne share, the total offer was worth $87.33.

The shares-plus-collar offer was arguably more valuable than the cash offer of $85 because it added a "kicker," an alternative feature that would perhaps win the support of those shareholders who were sophisticated enough to see the positive value embedded in the collar—most likely, these were large institutional investors and traders of financial securities.

CONTINGENT VALUE RIGHTS: RHÔNE-POULENC'S ACQUISITION OF RORER

Contingent value rights (CVRs) may be regarded as fixed collars that live well beyond the closing dates of the transactions. Usually they are listed for trading on an exchange, and they may be traded separately from the shares with which they were originally associated. These are relatively rare but have appeared in a number of prominent deals in the past decade. Exhibit 23.11 lists the largest of these. Like collars, CVRs merit attention because they are handy tools that may help deal makers surmount challenging deal design problems.

Contingent payments have tended to appear in acquisitions involving large potential differences between the target transaction prices of buyers and sellers or when the sellers were seeking some protection for the remaining minority shareholders who might be vulnerable to unfair treatment by the acquirers. Acquisitions in the pharmaceutical industry have featured some of the most innovative forms of these contingent-payment schemes.

EXHIBIT 23.9 Worksheet from "Collars Analysis.xls" Illustrating the Assumptions for the Analysis of the AT&T Collar

Life of the collar	
Best guess days	180
Maximum days	360
Minimum days	90
Forecast of life of collar	185.1365
Structure of the collar	
If one component is a long call:	
Strike price	$—
Payoff formula (text)	Maximum of (stock price minus strike price) or zero
Payoff calculated	0
If one component is a short call:	
Strike price	$—
Payoff formula (text)	Zero minus the maximum of (stock price minus strike price) or zero
Payoff calculated	$—
If one component is a long put:	
Strike price	$57.00
Payoff formula (text)	Maximum of (strike price minus stock price) or zero
Payoff calculated	$2.20
If one component is a short put:	
Strike price	$48.50
Payoff formula (text)	Zero minus the maximum of (strike price minus stock price) or zero
Payoff calculated	0
Buyer's share price today	$57.00
Annualized volatility of buyer's share price	15%
Forecast of return of buyer's share price at closing of deal	−3.9%
Forecast of buyer's share price at closing of deal	$54.80
Risk-free rate of return today	5%
Annualized volatility of risk-free rate of return	15%
Standard deviation of annualized risk-free rate of return	0.8%
Forecast of risk-free rate of return	4%
Calculated value of the collar (sum of four payoffs)	$2.15

Note: The calculated value indicated in this exhibit is simply the estimate of *one* draw of the model. The mean of the entire distribution is $1.57, indicated in Exhibit 23.10.

Chen, Chen, and Laiss (1994) describe the CVR as a *bearish put spread* that functions like puttable stock, liquid yield option notes (LYONs),[32] and transferable put stock. CVRs may be inserted into transaction designs for any of several reasons, including to:

- Protect minority shareholders from economic expropriation.
- Permit the buyer to acquire control without having to acquire 100 percent of the shares.

EXHIBIT 23.10 Probability Distribution of Payments under AT&T's Collar Offered to Shareholders of MediaOne

Statistics	Value
Trials	5,000
Mean	$1.57
Median	$0.00
Mode	$0.00
Standard deviation	$2.54
Variance	$6.45
Skewness	1.49
Kurtosis	3.89
Coefficient of variability	1.62
Range of minimum	$0.00
Range of maximum	$8.40
Range width	$8.40
Mean standard error	$0.04

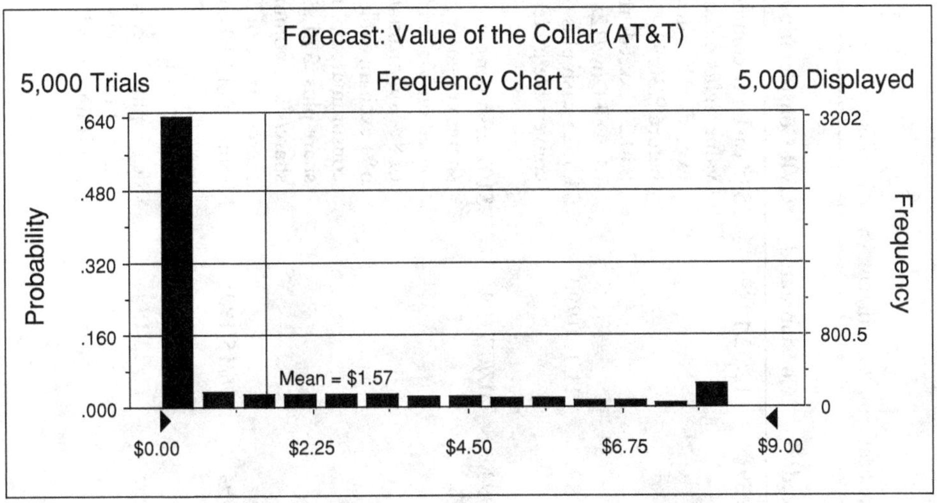

Note: The horizontal axis of this graph is measured in dollars, the vertical axis in percentage probability. The mean of the distribution is $1.57 and standard deviation $2.54. In 64 percent of the drawings, the payout was zero.

- Signal optimism on the part of the buyer, and thus reduce agency costs.
- Obtain some operating flexibility for the buyer.

CVRs have been used as merger vehicles since 1985, although they did not gain widespread recognition until 1989, when they were featured in the takeover of Marion Laboratories, Inc. by Merrill-Dow, the pharmaceutical subsidiary of Dow Chemical Co. The creation of Rhône-Poulenc Rorer (RPR) in August 1990 was modeled on the Marion/Merrill-Dow deal.

EXHIBIT 23.11 Some Landmark Acquisitions Featuring Contingent Value Rights

Buyer	Target	Date Announced	Date Consummated	CVR Considerations
Dow Chemical Co.	Marion Laboratories, Inc.	07/17/1989	12/02/1989	$38 cash per common share for 58.5 million shares, plus contingent value rights maturing on 9/30/91 at the amount by which $45.77 exceeds the value of Marion Merrell Dow (MMD) for the 90 days before 9/30/91, or maturing on 9/30/92 at the amount by which $50.23 exceeds the value in the 90 days prior to 9/30/92, and Merrell Dow/128 million newly issued Marion shares.
National Intergroup, Inc.	Permian Partners LP	12/20/1989	11/13/1990	$3.5625 cash plus one contingent value right/cumulative convertible preference unit representing limited partnership units.
Viacom Inc. (National Amusements)	Paramount Communica-tions	09/09/1993	07/07/1994	$107 cash per common share for 51% interest; .93065 class B shares common plus .93065 Viacom contingent value rights valued based on Viacom's future share price plus $17.5 in principal amount of 8% subordinated debentures exchangeable at Viacom's option into 5% exchangeable preferred stock if the Blockbuster merger is not consummated plus .5 3-year warrant for class B shares at $60 per share plus .3 of a 5-year warrant for class B shares at $70 per share/share common for remaining 49% and options minus average exercise price of $42.38.
MacAndrews & Forbes Holdings	Abex Inc. (Mafco Consolidated)	11/21/1994	06/15/1995	Minimum of $10 contingent value rights per common share.
Gensia, Inc.	Aramed, Inc.	06/16/1995	11/22/1995	$8 cash plus $3 common plus $1 contingent value rights/share common; subject to a collar requiring the exact share ratio to fall between .6061 and .9091 shares of common stock per common share.

Allianz AG	AGF	11/17/1997	05/12/1998	320 French francs ($55.20 US) cash/share ordinary, for at least 51% of Assurances Generales de France (AGF); or a put warrant with contingent value right of 360 francs ($62.10) exercisable in 28 months' time per ordinary share of common stock, for not more than 49% of AGF.
AXA-UAP	Royal Belge SA	05/05/1998	07/28/1998	21,513 Belgian francs (3,491.559 French francs/$589.026 US) cash, plus 5 new shares of ordinary common stock, plus a contingent value right per 3 shares of ordinary common stock.
Tembec, Inc.	Crestbrook Forest Industries Ltd	01/11/1999	04/02/1999	Each Crestbrook shareholder would receive a contingent value right, which would entitle the holder to receive a one-time payment on March 31, 2000, of up to a maximum of $1.50 per Crestbrook share depending on the amount by which the average price of NBSK pulp for calendar 1999 exceeds US$549/tonne. The current quoted price for these purposes is approximately US$500/tonne.
Elan Corporation, plc	Liposome Company	04/13/2000	05/12/2000	Each share of Liposome common stock outstanding immediately prior to the consummation of the merger will be converted into the right to receive 0.385 share of ELN American depositary shares (ADS), plus one contingent value right (CVR). The maximum payment on the contingent value rights would be $1.19 per Liposome share in the case of the approval milestone payment, and $0.97 per Liposome share in the case of the revenue milestone payment. The maximum payment on the contingent value rights would be $2.16 per Liposome share.
Apex Oil Co.	Crown Central Petroleum Corp.	08/24/2000	11/30/2000	Cash tender offer for all Crown stock for $10.50 per share. Stockholders not accepting the $10.50 tender offer would retain their stock and receive a $12.50 contingent value right.

The $3.2 billion combination of Rorer Group with Rhône-Poulenc (RP) coincided with a wave of mergers in the pharmaceutical industry, including the following: Merrill-Dow and Marion Laboratories, Genentech and Hoffman–La Roche, SmithKline and Beecham, Bristol-Myers and Squibb, and major joint ventures between Sanofi and Sterling Drug and between DuPont and Merck.

The merger was consummated in a three-stage transaction by which Rhône-Poulenc obtained 68 percent of Rorer's common stock (91.6 million shares), which was enough to permit Rhône-Poulenc to consolidate Rorer's results for financial reporting.[33]

1. Rhône-Poulenc would tender for 50.1 percent (43.2 million shares) of Rorer's common stock for $36.50 cash per share. (Rhône-Poulenc, by borrowing the funds to finance the tender offer, increased its debt/capital ratio to 45 percent, well above competitors' capitalizations of 20 to 30 percent.)
2. Rorer assumed $265 million of RP debt (guaranteed by RP), made a $20 million cash payment to RP, and issued 48.4 million new common shares to RP in exchange for RP's HPB division.[34] Observers believed that Rorer's bylaws would require at least 85 percent of all shares be voted in favor of the issuance of new shares and, more generally, of this entire transaction.
3. Rhône-Poulenc issued the 41.8 million CVRs to the remaining minority shareholders in Rorer. A CVR entitled the holder to the right, at the end of three years (July 31, 1993) or four years, at RP's option, to a cash payment of US$49.13 (or $53.06 if the payment were made at the end of four years) reduced by the higher of the value of the RPR share at that date or $26. Thus, if the value of the RPR share exceeded $49.13 (or $53.06), there would be no payment. The maximum amount of RP's liability on December 31, 1990, was 5,165 million French francs at the date of the issuance of the rights.[35] The maximum amount of RP's liability at the date of issuance was hedged. Any changes in the value of the CVRs resulting from fluctuations in exchange rates, as well as the amortization of the cost of the hedge, were recorded directly into the consolidated equity of RP. The CVRs were quoted on the American Stock Exchange and traded independently of the shares of RPR, which were listed on the New York Stock Exchange.

Rorer and Rhône-Poulenc jointly announced that they believed that the package of CVR and minority share in RPR was worth $36.50 and thus equal to the price at which RP was tendering for shares of RPR. Rorer investors responded favorably to the announcement of an agreement in principle to merge. During the week of the announcement (January 12–19, 1990), Rorer shares increased by 28 percent net of the changes in the Standard & Poor's 500 index over the week. This gain equaled about $632 million in new value. Meanwhile, RP's shares lost 4.4 percent net of market during the announcement week, or about $175 million.

Much of this transaction's complexity can be understood in light of one basic fact: Rhône-Poulenc's financing constraint. Rhône-Poulenc desperately wanted to acquire Rorer as a way to establish critical mass for its own strategic entry into pharmaceuticals, but it could not buy the company using either cash or shares for the following reasons:

- Rhône-Poulenc could not pay with internally generated cash. Around the date of the acquisition, RP was a net cash user because of its huge capital-spending requirements and the severe recession in chemicals.

- Rhône-Poulenc had limited ability to pay with borrowed cash. It was more highly levered than its peer group of companies. Indeed, it did borrow for the cash portion of the deal, but it was reluctant to borrow all the cash for fear of the impact on its balance sheet.
- Rhône-Poulenc could not pay with cash raised from selling equity or pay with RP common shares. Management's perception was that its own share price was depressed; to the extent that this perception was true, a share-based deal would mean economically diluting the old shareholders. More importantly, however, as a state-owned enterprise, Rhône-Poulenc could offer only an odd, nonvoting "certificate of investment" rather than standard common stock, of which it had none. The appetite of Rorer shareholders for this odd paper can only be imagined.
- Rhône-Poulenc could not pay with debt securities. If it were too highly levered to borrow and pay cash, then it was also too highly levered to swap debt securities for shares.

In short, Rhône-Poulenc probably wanted to issue equity for part of the deal but could not do so. The design of the transaction resolved its financing dilemma. That design monetized the firm's human pharmaceuticals business and raised equity by persuading Rorer's shareholders to remain minority equity investors in the new firm.

The CVR could be valued similarly to a collar. It contains a long put, struck at \$49.13, and a short put, struck at \$26.00. In early August 1990, the current share price was \$24.65, volatility of Rhône-Poulenc was 0.176, the term period was two to three years, and the risk-free rate was 6.85 percent. The worksheet for this calculation is reproduced in Exhibit 23.12.

Exhibit 23.13 gives the probability distribution of present values of payouts under the CVR, based on a Monte Carlo simulation from 5,000 draws. The mean is \$15.49 (standard deviation is \$5.36). In about 3.7 percent of the drawings, the payout was zero. The simulation analysis suggests that the CVR was a material inducement to hold shares: The total value of the stock-plus-CVR package is estimated to be \$40.14.[36] This is more than the cash-only alternative of \$36.50—Rhône-Poulenc asserted that the two alternatives were equal in value.

Following the acquisition, RPR exceeded its forecast performance because of larger-than-expected cost savings, new-product introductions, and aggressive introduction of Rorer's over-the-counter drugs into Europe. RPR's share price, however, did not significantly exceed the put exercise price of \$49.13 during the period leading up to the three-year expiration of the CVR on July 31, 1993. The terms of the CVR had required a cash payment equal to the difference between \$49.13 and the average closing price of RPR's stock between April 27 and July 25, 1993, about \$49.08. Thus, on July 26, 1993, Rhône-Poulenc announced that it would pay \$2.3 million to the holders of the CVR (roughly \$0.05 per CVR). This payment permitted Rhône-Poulenc to realize an increase in shareholders' equity of 2.3 billion francs (about \$418 million), the difference between the cash payment and the contingent liability carried on the firm's balance sheet.

In June 1997, Rhône-Poulenc announced a tender offer for the 31.9 percent of Rorer shares that it did not own. The preliminary cash offer was \$92 per share, although Rhône-Poulenc subsequently raised the offer to \$97 per share. The acquisition was consummated on October 1, 1997.

EXHIBIT 23.12 Worksheet from "Collars Analysis.xls" Illustrating Assumptions for Analysis of Rhône-Poulenc Contingent Value Right

Life of the collar	
Best guess days	720
Maximum days	1,080
Minimum days	720
Forecast of life collar	965.2403
Structure of the collar	
If one component is a long call:	
Strike price	$—
Payoff formula (text)	Maximum of (stock price minus strike price) or zero
Payoff calculated	0
If one component is a short call:	
Strike price	$—
Payoff formula (text)	Zero minus the maximum of (stock price minus strike price) or zero
Payoff calculated	$—
If one component is a long put:	
Strike price	$49.13
Payoff formual (text)	Maximum of (strike price minus stock price) or zero
Payoff calculated	$17.91
If one component is a short put:	
Strike price	$26.00
Payoff formula (text)	Zero minus the maximum of (strike price minus stock price) or zero
Payoff calculated	$—
Buyer's share price today	$24.65
Annualized volatility of buyer's share price	17.6%
Forecast of return of buyer's share price at closing of deal	23.6%
Forecast of buyer's share price at closing of deal	$31.22
Risk-free rate of return today	6.85%
Annualized volatility of risk-free rate of return	15%
Standard deviation of annualized risk-free rate of return	1.0%
Forecast of risk-free rate of return	6.78%
Calculated value of the collar (sum of four payoffs)	$15.06

Note: The calculated value indicated in this exhibit is simply the estimate of *one* draw of the model. The mean of the entire distribution is $15.49, indicated in Exhibit 23.13.

STAGED ACQUIRING: THE CASE OF GENZYME'S INVESTMENT IN GELTEX[37]

A final form of risk management is one that specifically stages the outlays by the acquirer to occur with the successful achievement of targets. So-called staged investing is a widely used tactic in venture capital and in R&D spending by corporations. Gompers and Lerner (1999, page 130) wrote,

One of the most common and potent features of venture capital is the meting out of financing in discrete stages over time. Prospects for the firm are periodically reevaluated. The shorter the duration of an individual round of financing, the more frequently the venture capitalist monitors the entrepreneur's progress and the greater the need to gather information. Staged capital infusion keeps the owner/manager on a "tight leash" and reduces potential losses from bad decisions. Because venture capital financings are costly to negotiate and structure, funding is provided in discrete stages.

Similar logic applies in M&A settings. The case of Genzyme's joint venture investment in GelTex illustrates the economics of staged acquiring. In 1997, Genzyme Corporation sought to negotiate the terms of a joint venture with GelTex to

EXHIBIT 23.13 Probability Distribution of Payments under Rhône-Poulenc's Contingent Value Right Offered to Shareholders of Rorer Group

Statistics	Value
Trials	5,000
Mean	$15.49
Median	$17.56
Mode	$0.00
Standard deviation	$5.36
Variance	$28.71
Skewness	−1.26
Kurtosis	3.81
Coefficient of variability	0.35
Range minimum	$0.00
Range maximum	$21.71
Range width	$21.71
Mean standard error	$0.08

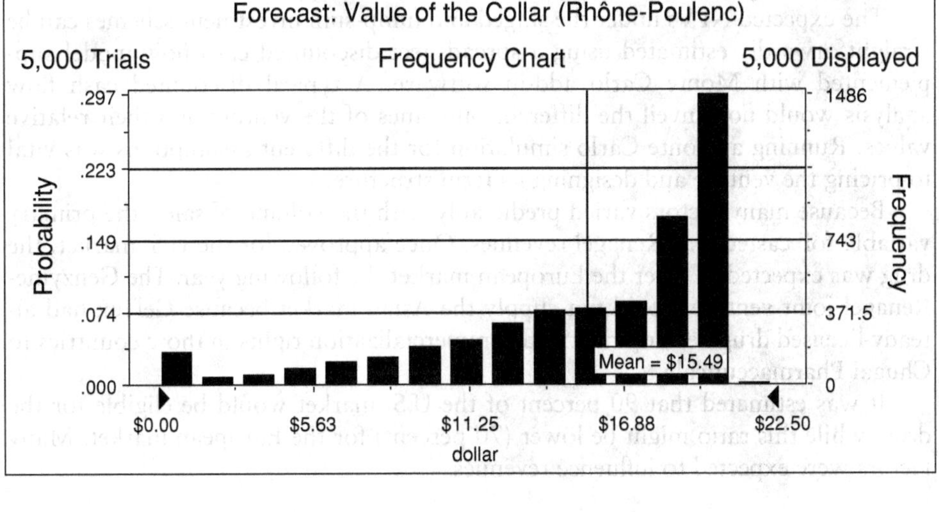

produce a new therapeutic drug to treat kidney failure. At the time, Genzyme was a large biotechnology firm that had grown significantly through the use of joint ventures and alliances, and GelTex was an early-stage biotech research company with only two products in development. One of these projects was the development of Renagel, a treatment for kidney failure—and the focus of Genzyme's interest. This drug was in clinical trials for approval by the U.S. Food and Drug Administration. The business tasks for the Genzyme corporate development team were to assess the timing and $27 million outlay for a 50 percent interest. How to deal with the uncertainty about FDA approval was the major business issue in the design of the joint venture. Genzyme management addressed the concern by considering the use of *staged investing* (as opposed to lump-sum investing) as a means of hedging the risk associated with FDA approval. By tying the payment by Genzyme to the clearance of successive FDA approvals, the risk to Genzyme could be reduced—indeed, the investment interest was transformed into a sequence of contingent payments. Monte Carlo simulation of a staged investment scheme for the joint venture revealed an expected net present value that was about $8 million, as opposed to an expected NPV of negative $4 million associated with a lump-sum investment scheme.

What made the deal so interesting was the staged investment to which Genzyme actually committed. The deal left Genzyme with the option to not invest further in the joint venture after a $2.5 million equity investment *if the FDA did not approve Renagel for sale to the public*. In other words, Genzyme had the right but not the obligation to pay the $15 million and the $10 million milestone investments in each of the following years. Genzyme captured some value by structuring the deal in staged investments that granted the option to invest, wait, or divest in response to new information about Renagel's potential success.

This kind of staged investment deal has become popular in the biotech industry. One recent example is the deal between Amgen, the leading biotech company in the United States, and Guilford Pharmaceuticals to commercialize drugs for Alzheimer's and Parkinson's diseases. The deal granted that Guilford would receive $35 million upon closing, plus $13.5 million over three years to support research activities, and an additional $392 million in milestone payments if all 10 indications of the drug were successfully developed to FDA approval.

The expected NPVs under the staged and lump-sum investment schemes can be straightforwardly estimated using a spreadsheet discounted cash flow model supplemented with Monte Carlo add-in software. A typical discounted cash flow analysis would not unveil the different outcomes of the venture and their relative values. Running a Monte Carlo simulation for the different assumptions was vital to pricing the venture and designing its term structure.

Because many factors varied predictably with the volume of sales, the primary variable forecasted was Renagel revenues. Once approved for the U.S. market, the drug was expected to enter the European market the following year. The Genzyme-Renagel joint venture would not supply the Asian market because GelTex had already licensed drug development and commercialization rights in those countries to Chugai Pharmaceuticals.

It was estimated that 90 percent of the U.S. market would be eligible for the drug, while this ratio might be lower (70 percent) for the European market. Many factors were expected to influence revenues.

- ***Peak penetration rate in the market.*** Based on different marketing analyses and analysts' reports, the best guess was a 50 percent peak penetration rate at year 5, with a range from 20 percent to 59 percent (giving an average of 43 percent). Whatever the value of this peak rate, one could assume that the pattern of penetration over time would be similar and thus the market penetration at any time would be proportional to the peak.
- ***Compliance.*** Not all patients who used the drug would do so faithfully, even with a doctor strongly recommending its use. One could assume that the most likely compliance rate would be 92 percent, with a low of 75 percent and a high of 94 percent. Based on these numbers, the average compliance would be 87 percent.
- ***Price per patient.*** The annual price of the drug per patient would depend on many things, including how many pills the patient used and competitive pressures on the price that could be charged for the pill. The joint-venture team had worked up a figure of $1,000 as the average annual price per patient. This figure was based on an estimate of $1,100 as the most likely outcome, with a range from $600 to $1,300.

Influencing profits were two key assumptions:

1. ***Average industry gross profit margin of 70 percent.*** Genzyme's management also believed that a gross profit margin for Renagel could not be pinpointed but that the standard deviation around that number would be about 5 percent.
2. ***Marketing costs.*** The total estimated market for Renagel was 200,000 patients. Instead of targeting patients with chronic renal failure, however, the joint venture would target doctors with the largest patient populations. In essence, these doctors composed Renagel's target market. A sales force of 45 people would be enough to serve the market. Each member of the sales force would cost $200,000, rising at 5 percent a year. The marketing costs could turn out to be higher or lower than this schedule. The costs could be as low as 87 percent of the schedule or as much as 20 percent higher, and the most likely outcome was that they would be 93 percent of the schedule (which produced an average of exactly 100 percent). General and administrative costs were assumed to be 40 percent of the cost of the sales force.

A final consideration was regulatory risk. Past experience showed that a drug such as Renagel, which was in Phase III of the FDA approval process, had a 65 percent probability of being approved for launch into the market. As a drug progressed through the different clinical stages, the revenue stream generated through market launch drew closer. It took several years for a drug in Phase III to reach the market. The uncertainty surrounding FDA approval was compounded by the impact of changing regulations and governmental policies as well as by the arrival of competing compounds in the drug marketplace. With regard to Renagel, an expeditious response from the FDA would occur one year after filing, that is, in 1998. Because of the encouraging results of Renagel's Phase III studies, management believed that Renagel would be launched in the United States at the beginning of 1999 and in Europe at the beginning of 2000. The team assumed a 20 percent probability of a one-year launch delay in the United States (and therefore in Europe) beyond those dates and a 10 percent probability of a two-year delay.

Monte Carlo simulation generated the forecasted free cash flows for the joint venture and discounted them to produce an estimated net present value. Uncertain variables were modeled as distributions.[38] Exhibits 23.14 and 23.15 give the probability distributions for the two investment schemes that emerged from the simulation analysis. The lump sum scheme shows an expected NPV that is considerably worse than that for the staged investment scheme.

The source of improvement in NPV is due to the contingent staging of the outlays by Genzyme. In a world of uncertainty, waiting can be valuable.

CONCLUSION: WHERE AND WHEN TO MANAGE RISK

This chapter has surveyed types of risk management features in M&A deals. Their effect on the payment to the target shareholders can be illustrated graphically and numerically with valuation analysis. The tools of option valuation are useful in the valuation of risk management features. The concepts and examples in this chapter show that risk management comes at a price; it should not be freely given.

The discussion in this chapter emphasizes the optionality present in risk management features. The use and design of these features hinges fundamentally on your view about the risk of the buyer's shares and the target's future performance. Always develop an informed view before undertaking to design risk management features. The value of risk management features will be directly related to the uncertainty one sees and the duration of that uncertainty: Time and the degree of risk are always important drivers of option value.

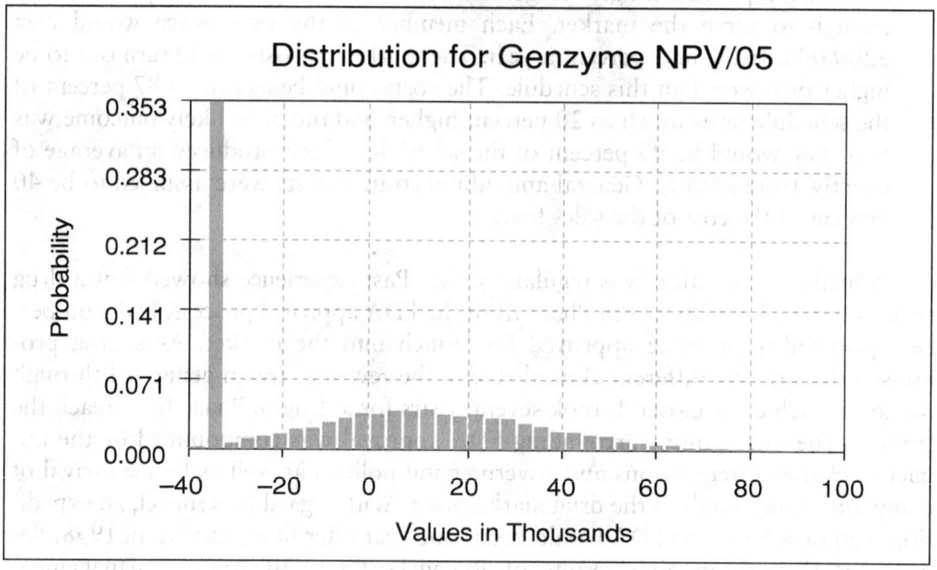

EXHIBIT 23.14 Probability Distribution of NPV under a Lump-Sum Initial Payment of $27 Million by Genzyme to GelTex

Note: The average NPV of this distribution is –$4.135 million. "NPV/05" stands for the net present value of cash flows through 2005.

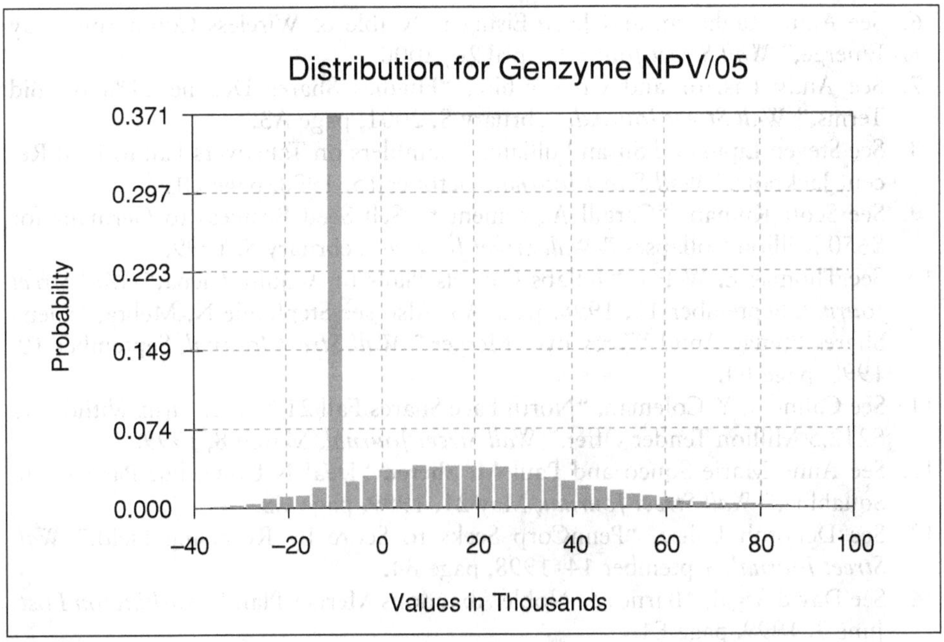

EXHIBIT 23.15 Probability Distribution of NPV under a Stage Investment Plan of $27 Million by Genzyme to GelTex

Note: The average NPV of this distribution is $8.037 million. "NPV/05" stands for the net present value of cash flows through 2005.

Finally, the discussion here underscores the need for a "whole deal" perspective in thinking about even small details such as risk management features. As Chapter 18 argues, one should look for trade-offs. Buyers who provide collars should expect to seek something else in return, such as a more advantageous price. This use of risk management features as a bargaining chip is a matter of "best practice" and remains a fertile area for research.

NOTES

1. How to choose the appropriate level of risk is beyond the scope of this discussion. But in designing risk management devices, one must consider the potential losses associated with adverse outcomes and gauge one's ability to bear those losses.
2. See Anne Marie Squeo, "Lockheed Bid for Comsat Hits Obstacles," *Wall Street Journal*, June 11, 1999, page A3.
3. See Elena Cherney and Mylene Mangalindan, "Corel and Inprise Agree to Call Off Plans for Merger," *Wall Street Journal*, May 17, 2000.
4. See Rick Brooks and Carrick Molenkamp, "WestPoint Says Rising Rates Ruined Buyout," *Wall Street Journal*, May 23, 2000.
5. "Wait and See," *The Economist*, September 29, 2001, page 64.

6. See Anita Raghavan and Jesse Eisinger, "Cable & Wireless Counterbid May Emerge," *Wall Street Journal*, April 26, 2000.
7. See Andy Pasztor and Greg White, "Hughes Shares Decline 11% on Bid Terms," *Wall Street Journal*, February 8, 2001, page A3.
8. See Steven Lipin and Susan Pulliam, "Gamblers on Takeovers Fail to Find Recent Jackpots," *Wall Street Journal*, October 15, 1998, page C1.
9. See Scott Kilman, "Cargill Agreement to Sell Seed Business to Germans for $650 Million Collapses," *Wall Street Journal*, February 5, 1999.
10. See Thomas E. Weber, "Tellabs Cancels Plans to Acquire Ciena," *Wall Street Journal*, September 15, 1998, page A3. Also see Stephanie N. Mehta, "Ciena Shares Plunge Amid Worry over Merger," *Wall Street Journal*, September 10, 1998, page B4.
11. See Calmetta Y. Coleman, "North Face Shares Fall 21% after Firm Withdraws $212.5 Million Tender Offer," *Wall Street Journal*, March 8, 1999.
12. See Anne Marie Squeo and Paul M. Sherer, "Deal Is Done, but Parties Still Squabble," *Wall Street Journal*, May 21, 1999, page C2.
13. See Deborah Lohse, "PennCorp Seeks to Score by Reversing Field," *Wall Street Journal*, September 14, 1998, page B4.
14. See David Segal, "Barnes & Noble Abandons Merger Plan," *Washington Post*, June 3, 1999, page E1.
15. See Paul M. Sherer, "AlliedSignal Files Suit to Block Merger of B. F. Goodrich and Coltec Industries," *Wall Street Journal*, March 1, 1999, page A1.
16. See Frank Swoboda, "Texaco Spurns Chevron: Oil Merger Talks End on Sour Note," *Washington Post*, June 3, 1999, page E1.
17. See Sally Beatty, "Talks between Burnett and MacManus Fail Due to 'Fundamental Differences,'" *Wall Street Journal*, November 19, 1998.
18. See Steven Lipin and Robert Langreth, "SmithKline Is Expected to Sell Two Units," *Wall Street Journal*, February 9, 1999.
19. See Neal Templin, "Crescent Is Becoming Serial Balker, Leaving Trail of Jilted Partners," *Wall Street Journal*, November 2, 1998.
20. See Stacy Kravetz, "From Out of the Blue, Web Pornographer Makes Casino Bid," *Wall Street Journal*, June 16, 1999, page B2.
21. See "Bank of Scotland Calls Off Plans for U.S. Service with Evangelist," *Wall Street Journal*, June 7, 1999, page A6.
22. The 19.9 percent amount is just below the 20 percent threshold at which most stock exchanges in the United States require firms to gain approval of shareholders for a sale of shares.
23. The exchange ratio will determine how the risks and rewards are shared in a stock-for-stock deal.
24. This difficulty is attributable to the fact that seeking to get cash back from thousands or millions of individual shareholders will prove to be costly and contentious.
25. A "milestone investment" is made when the target passes a milestone of performance such as product development, obtaining regulatory approvals, meeting cash flow targets, and so on.
26. Chapter 10 introduces the bull spread, which gains its name from the bullish (optimistic) bet on share prices implicit in the design of the position. Typically, traders structure this position with the stock price near the lower of the two

strike prices—thus, upward movements in stock prices will reward the investor. The cap is placed on the position (by selling a call option) as a means of defraying the cost of the long call embedded in the floor of the collar.

27. The extent of any economic dilution would be determined by the relation of the payment amount to the estimated intrinsic value of the target.
28. This collar, based on cash rather than shares, would simply call for cash payments instead of adjustments in the exchange ratio.
29. Simply summing the two option values assumes there is no interaction between them. Yet in a collar, the payoff on the long and short option positions are correlated, violating the assumption of independence of the two positions—if one of the options pays off, it must be true that the other option does not.
30. As described in Chapter 10, "volatility" is the annualized standard deviation of returns on a share of stock.
31. For brevity, this discussion simplifies the terms of the deal in some respects in order to illuminate the economics of collars and the process of analysis.
32. Liquid yield option notes are zero-coupon debt securities convertible into common stock.
33. RPR split its common shares 2:1 on May 17, 1991. To avoid unnecessary confusion, all share numbers and prices reported in this case are given on a post-split basis. Actually, the acquisition terms involved half the number of shares and twice the share price reported here.
34. The transfer of RP's health sector excluded RP's business units in veterinary products, serums, and vaccines and the firm's minority interest in a French pharmaceutical concern, Roussel-Uclaf.
35. In general, the disclosure of contingent liabilities by a firm depends on whether the likelihood of realizing the liability is probable, possible, or remote. If the probability of realization is less than 50 percent, accounting conventions require that the liability be disclosed in the footnotes to the financial statements. The accounting rules contain no prescribed way, however, to estimate the magnitude of contingent liabilities.
36. The value of the total package is the sum of the CVR value ($15.49) and the *ex ante* share price in Rorer Group ($24.65).
37. This section and Exhibits 23.14 and 23.15 draw upon a case study by Jacquet, Bruner, and Bodily (1999). My co-authors' contributions are so material as to warrant recognizing them as co-authors of this section.
38. For more detail on the simulation analysis, see Jacquet et al. (1999).

CHAPTER 24

Social Issues

INTRODUCTION: THE IMPORTANCE OF SOCIAL ISSUES IN M&A

This chapter considers the nature and impact of "*social issues*" in an M&A transaction. The term "social" is meant to distinguish a set of issues and deal terms from "economic" issues such as price, form of payment, and generally the returns to shareholders. These issues define the management and governance of Newco, including designation of the CEO and senior management team, makeup of the board of directors, and location of the headquarters. The term is sometimes misunderstood to refer to social welfare concerns such as treatment of the environment, community relations, and the effect of layoffs, plant closings, and the like. Also, social issues are sometimes supposed to regard the problems of integrating two merging cultures—Chapter 36 addresses these. In fact, social issues usually relate to only a narrow group of people, including senior management, the board of directors, and influential middle managers, all of whom may have a decisive role in the acceptance of a bid by a target firm.

Social issues are usually the first to be addressed in M&A talks. Failure to resolve social issues can torpedo a deal that in other respects seems attractive. And conversely, the field of M&A is full of rumors about transactions that were consummated because of attractive social terms despite their unattractiveness to shareholders; such cases are examples of how side payments may overcome target managers' duty to their shareholders. Settlement of social issues directly affects the probability of successful consummation of a deal. This chapter will review the impact of social issues on the deal design.

Social issues can have an economic impact: Often they impose a direct cost on either or both the buyer and target shareholders. But the economic cost may be offset by an incentive effect on the managers of Newco that creates a benefit for Newco's shareholders. For this reason, the economic impact of social issues is difficult to assess. Research is beginning to illuminate the impact of social issues. But conventional wisdom among practitioners is that their impact is significant. Negotiation over social issues raises rather starkly the prospect of *agency costs* in M&A deal design. Since the landmark discussion of agency costs by Jensen and Meckling (1976) practitioners and scholars have grown to realize the size and ubiquity of costs arising from the separation of ownership and control of the firm. This chapter aims to highlight the presence of these costs for the M&A practitioner. Because social issues may address the desires of individuals rather than the interests of the entire firm and its shareholders, social terms in a deal sometimes carry the cachet of a side payment. Executives and deal designers must be extremely careful to observe not only the law but also the spirit of business norms in order to avoid the taint of bribery. Social issues typically stimulate side payments and complex trade-offs of the sort discussed in Chapter 18. But social terms can have a positive economic function: to recognize the sometimes hidden value of know-how, core competencies, working cultures, and long-standing informal practices.

SURVEY OF SOCIAL ISSUES FREQUENTLY ADDRESSED IN MERGER NEGOTIATIONS

As a foundation to considering the economic impact of social issues and their place in deal design, it is useful to gain a sense of the variety of these concerns. Social issues cluster into at least nine categories:

1. Management team.
2. *Retention payments.*
3. *Severance payments.*
4. *Leadership succession.*
5. Organization design.
6. Board composition.
7. Structure of transaction.
8. Corporate name.
9. Headquarters location.

Management Team of Newco: Who Stays, Who Leaves

Turnover of senior managers increases significantly following acquisitions. CEO tenure is unusually short—on average five years. Warren Bennis and James O'Toole (2000) describe the use of top leadership talent by major corporations as "CEO churning." To be the CEO of a target firm in an M&A transaction is risky for one's career, as attested by research:

- The churning effect increases significantly following takeovers of underperforming firms.[1]
- Between half and three-quarters of target top management turns over within four years of the deal[2]—the turnover rate increases sharply within the first year, and thereafter declines to more normal levels. In comparison, North (2001) reports an expected turnover rate of 26.6 percent for peer firms that are not the targets of acquisitions.
- There is no significant difference in top management turnover between friendly and unfriendly deals, according to Martin and McConnell (1991).
- What *does* matter in CEO turnover is performance of the target firm before acquisition. Martin and McConnell report that top management turnover increases significantly following the transaction. Most of these firms were underperformers. The study found that the degree of underperformance and management change were associated. The finding suggests that CEO turnover

is an indication of capital market discipline at work on poorly performing firms.

- Complaints about lack of autonomy and culture differences between buyer and target firms explain significant variation in the top management turnover rate in the first year (Lubatkin et al. 1999).
- More visible executives (such as CEOs) turn over sooner than less visible executives (such as division executives), according to Walsh (1988).
- Target managers who leave are replaced by *outsiders* 93 percent of the time; 78 percent of these changes are disciplinary, associated with an underperforming firm (North 2001).
- CEOs who lose their jobs following a takeover fail to find another within three years, according to Agrawal and Walkling (1994).

Very early in the negotiations, usually when they are at the informal stage, the two senior negotiators (usually CEOs) will reach agreement on the management structure of Newco at the most senior levels: board chair, CEO, COO, CFO, and so on. Designation of middle managers is usually left to be determined during the planning for postmerger integration. It may seem self-serving for the most senior leaders to look after their own positions first, though doing so serves to unblock discussion of other material issues.

Nominally it would seem that decisions about who stays and who leaves are determined by *power*—that is, if one views transactions as contests for control, then the winning side exercises the power it won in the contest, and looks after its own team. But often the decision is influenced by economic considerations such as:

- ***Financial performance record*** of the buyer and target management teams. For instance, the premise of most hostile takeovers is that buyers believe that they can run the target better than its own management. However, management turnover following hostile takeovers is no higher than following friendly acquisitions. Research *does* show that management turnover is greater following takeovers of *underperforming* firms.
- ***Core competencies*** and/or the possible contribution of managers to the realization of synergies, which could make them even more important after the transaction.
- ***Fit with the strategy of Newco.*** Generally, an M&A transaction will be associated with some strategic change in the target firm. Business units and individuals not contributing to the core strategy of Newco stand a greater chance of separation from the firm.

Retention Payments: Terms of Compensation for Continuing Managers

Retention payments may take the form of ordinary salary and bonuses or an extraordinary retention bonus that pays the manager for fulfilling some terms of employment over a period of time such as three years. Retention payments are typically used in acquisitions of firms where employees have valuable skills, know-how, and/or customer relationships. The choice of size of payment and period of time is typically determined by the market value of the executive's skills outside the firm,[3] and by the importance of that executive to the success of an integration program or effort to realize synergies.

Research has found a strong relationship between size of a firm and the absolute compensation of its senior managers: Larger firms pay more. Thus, it should be no surprise that managers of Newco tend to receive increased compensation—both the target managers who stay on with Newco, as well as the buyer's executives. Murphy (1998) reviewed the evidence on executive compensation and reports a strong linkage between compensation and the size of the firm—in contrast to theories that CEO compensation is generally tied to performance of the firm. Murphy suggests that large firms simply consider the compensation policies of their peers in setting executive pay; size will be an important consideration in determining the firm's peer group. Bliss and Rosen (2001) found that mergers lift executive compensation—mainly through the effect of firm size, even if the merger causes the firm's stock price to fall.

Severance Payments: Terms for Departing Managers

Severance payments are lump-sum gifts typically determined according to a formula such as a month's salary for every year worked with the firm. *Golden parachute payments* are typically triggered by change of control of a target firm. Golden parachutes are adopted by corporate boards of directors as an inducement for managers to act in the interests of shareholders[4] and as a potential discouragement to buyers.[5] These payments are lump sums determined at the time of adoption by the board. *Consulting agreements* may be negotiated with managers who hold important skills or knowledge. Often these agreements are paired with *noncompete agreements* that prevent the employee from working for a competitor. *Perquisites* include the use of a company office, car, airplane, secretarial support, and country club membership. Termination of a senior or middle manager is often accompanied by a severance payment, golden parachute, or other exit cost, which may be spread over time.

Leadership Succession

It is not unusual for an M&A transaction to raise the issue of management succession within the buyer or target firm. Executives who are nearing the mandatory retirement age of 65 may wish strongly to complete their term of service, at least through the integration of the two firms. But thereafter the leadership of Newco may be uncertain unless resolved in the early stage of negotiations. Spelling out succession in the merger agreement has the virtue of keeping the successor within the firm. But if the heir apparent has similarly talented rivals, the anointment would almost certainly trigger their departure.

The economic impact of new succession plans on either Newco or the value of the transaction to the buyer is difficult to assess. The effect could be positive (if the transaction brings in value-creating leadership to Newco) or negative (if the succession plan triggers infighting or the departure of talented employees). Talent, or human capital, has an economic value to investors in the firm, conceivably modeled as an option. Leadership succession remains an area ripe for rigorous research.

Organization Design of Newco

Degree of autonomy of the target firm within Newco will be an important consideration to the target firm's management. More generally, lines of reporting and accountability will convey the sense of independence of the target.

Board Composition and Control Options

The composition of Newco's board, derived from the directors of the buyer and target, will be a major point of interest for all directors, and will signal the relative influence of the two shareholding groups in Newco. Often the board seats are allocated on the basis of:

- Relative sizes of buyer and target.
- Relative percentage of shares held in Newco by the shareholders of the former buyer and target.
- Bargaining power. The discussion of board composition often reflects the concerns of major shareholders, such as wealthy individuals, foundations, or governments. M&A transactions among recently privatized firms often carry with them control options, such as golden shares or veto rights of governments over major actions such as plant closings, asset sales, and so on.

In large friendly transactions, the CEO of the target is often granted a seat on Newco's board.

Structure of Transaction: "Merger of Equals"

The *merger of equals (MOE)* combines partners of roughly equal influence without the payment of a premium by one party to the other. These deals are typically mergers effected by an exchange of shares with a low or zero implied acquisition premium. Exhibit 24.1 presents data comparing bid premiums on MOEs and non-MOE deals. It shows that despite variation over time, MOE premiums are typically much smaller than those in non-MOE deals. Exhibit 24.2 summarizes abnormal returns to buyers and targets around the announcements of MOEs. Wulf (2001) and Becher and Campbell (2002) find that in MOEs:

- Buyers earn zero-to-positive abnormal returns. This contrasts with non-MOEs where buyers earn significantly negative returns. The difference between MOE and non-MOE returns is significant.
- Targets earn significantly positive abnormal returns that are, however, significantly smaller than those in non-MOEs.

Wulf (2001, page 28) concluded, "The findings generally support the hypothesis that target CEOs trade 'power for premium.' Specifically, they negotiate control rights in the merged firm (both board and management) in exchange for a lower premium for their shareholders."

It is said that in a true merger of equals the two sides should share equally in the benefits of combination, such as from synergies. Payment of an acquisition premium

EXHIBIT 24.1 Comparison of Acquisition Premiums, Mergers of Equals (MOEs) versus Non-MOEs

	1997	1998	1999	2000
MOEs	15	14	9	23
Non-MOEs	9,661	10,747	8,577	9,032
Total Mergers	9,676	10,761	8,586	9,055
Mean Bid Premiums				
MOEs				
1 day prior	5.8	19.3	13.0	9.4
1 week prior	8.5	18.7	23.1	10.0
4 weeks prior	13.3	19.8	14.7	10.1
Non-MOEs				
1 day prior	16.0	97.4	23.7	29.3
1 week prior	19.0	104.2	29.0	34.6
4 weeks prior	22.8	92.5	38.0	42.3
Difference in Bid Premiums (MOEs – Non-MOEs)				
1 day prior	(10.18)	(78.19)	(10.75)	(19.87)
1 week prior	(10.49)	(85.47)	(5.93)	(24.54)
4 weeks prior	(9.57)	(72.61)	(23.36)	(32.25)

Source of data: Thomson Securities Data Corporation.

EXHIBIT 24.2 Summary of Research on Abnormal Returns to Target and Buyer Firm Shareholders at the Announcement of Mergers of Equals (MOEs) and Non-MOEs

	Combined Firms	Buyer Firms	Target Firms
Wulf (2001) (Table 5) 53 MOEs, 1,677 acquisitions 1991–1999	1.97%* MOEs 0.80% non-MOEs 1.17% difference	0.60% MOEs –4.36%* non-MOEs 4.96%* difference	3.89%* MOEs 9.44%* non-MOEs –5.55%* difference
Becher and Campbell (2002) (Table 3, Panel E) 23 MOEs, 418 acquisitions, Banking Industry 1990–1999	4.07%* MOEs 0.76%* non-MOEs 3.31%* difference	0.31%† MOEs –1.50%* non-MOEs 1.81%‡ difference	6.74%* MOEs 17.35%* non-MOEs –10.61%* difference

*Significant at 0.99 confidence level.
†Significant at 0.90 confidence level.
‡Significant at 0.95 confidence level.

would tilt the division of benefits toward the target shareholders. Others note that the MOE structure signals an absence of dominance of one side over the other—this helps to quell fears in the target company and to build a general sense of teamwork that can pay off in faster postmerger integration. Therefore, the MOE structure is believed to reduce resistance among target managers; it increases the probability of successfully consummating the deal.

A more cynical interpretation is to view the lower MOE bid premium as equal to the present value of side payments to the managers of the target firm—the buyer refuses to pay more than the target is worth and persuades the target firm's management to accept a lower offering price in return for better social terms. Thus, social terms impose an agency cost on target company shareholders. According to this view, few MOEs are true mergers of equals. Analysts and industry specialists often claim to see in the MOE terms a clear dominance of one firm (the buyer) over the other (the target). However, this subject warrants more scientific study.

As Exhibits 24.1 and 24.2 imply, target shareholders may bear the cost of the MOE structure. This cost can be estimated as the difference between the acquisition premium under the MOE and the premium that would have been necessary to consummate the deal without the MOE, times the market capitalization of the target *ex ante.*

Corporate Name of Newco

Corporate identity matters to managers. Using the target's name as the name for Newco can lend the appearance of continuity even when other elements are changing radically. The appearance of equality, or at least neutrality, may be enhanced by adopting a name for Newco that is different from either the buyer or target. Strength of brand identity is also a major consideration in naming Newco. The four alternatives are:

1. ***Target name retained.*** "Citigroup" emerged from the acquisition of Citicorp by Travelers Insurance. This transaction was actually advertised as a merger of equals.
2. ***Buyer name is retained.*** "Hewlett-Packard" was retained after its merger of equals with Compaq.
3. ***Blended name.*** Recent examples include "ExxonMobil" and "DaimlerChrysler."
4. ***New name.*** "Cendant" emerged from a combination of HFS Corporation and CUC Inc.

Name changes are expensive affairs, entailing not only costs of signage and stationery and of corporate identity advertising, but also legal expenses associated with redrawing contracts under the name of the new entity.

Headquarters Location

Another telltale of dominance is location of Newco's headquarters. Relocation costs and inconvenience are so sizable that buyers are discouraged from moving, and instead tend to seek savings by closing the target firm headquarters. But in the instance of a true MOE, the two firms may share headquarters functions. In the case of the merger of Pharmacia and Upjohn Pharmaceuticals, the new firm wound up with *three* regional headquarters: London, Milan, and New York (which eventually proved untenable). The sale or purchase of real property, quit-rent payments, and relocation costs represent flows of value to or from Newco that will affect the NPV of the deal to the buyer. These flows should be tax-adjusted and discounted to determine their present value.

Other

The list of potential social terms is limitless. The adroit analyst and negotiator will remain sensitive to the possibilities, such as use of a common language in Newco (where the transaction crosses borders and cultures), union relations, and support for charities. To the extent that these other terms involve flows of cash, their effect on the economics of the deal should be valued similarly to the other social terms.

IMPACT OF SOCIAL ISSUES ON ATTRACTIVENESS OF THE DEAL

How social issues affect the economics of a deal—and who pays and who benefits—deserve careful scrutiny. Fortunately the valuation tools outlined in previous chapters can lend some analytic structure to the evaluation of social terms.

Avenues of Economic Impact

Social terms should matter to the deal designer because they can affect the success of the transaction in virtually all of the outcomes sketched in Chapter 1. To illustrate the impact of social issues, consider five ways in which they can affect the economic outcomes, whether the deal creates value:

1. *Direct costs.*
2. *Incentive effects.*
3. *Price impact.*
4. *Competitive effect.*
5. *Signaling effect.*

DIRECT COSTS Increased cash costs of social terms will reduce the NPV of the transaction to the buyer. These flows of cash should be estimated as the *marginal new payments* to (or on behalf of) the executives that are triggered by the transaction, adjusted for taxes. The discount rate for this valuation is reasonably estimated as Newco's cost of debt, since compensation payments are an expense of the firm and if structured as a multiyear contract would rank in liquidation along with other creditors and ahead of stockholders.

INCENTIVE EFFECTS Spending on social terms might increase the motivation of employees, resulting in higher growth and profits. For instance, many leveraged buyouts are predicated on managers running a leaner firm, which inevitably means working longer hours with less support staff. This harder work is the incentive effect from the prospect of personal wealth gains in the LBO. It is difficult to isolate and value incentive effects beyond assuming, say, higher growth or profit margins in a DCF calculation. And one should take care not to double-count the incentive effect in acquisitions—it may have been reflected already in estimates of synergy cash flows.

PRICE IMPACT There may be an adjustment in price (or other terms) resulting from adding social terms to the deal. The MOE is the clearest illustration of a possible trade-off between price and social terms.

COMPETITIVE EFFECT To the extent that social terms induce insiders to endorse the transaction, their support may discourage other bidders from entering a higher competing bid. This imposes an *opportunity cost* on the target company shareholders. Lower competition in bidding for the target may translate to a lower price, another linkage between social terms and price.

SIGNALING EFFECT Social issues might convey signals of intent to parties beyond the shareholders and employees. Decisions about headquarters location and commitment to local charities might reduce local political opposition. Payment of retention bonuses to key individuals might signal to competitors some strategic intent.

One might identify other effects as well, but these are sufficient to suggest that social terms can have a complicated impact on deal design.

Who Pays for Social Terms? The Matter of Trade-Offs

Thus far, the discussion has referred generically to the present value of social costs without specifying to whom the present value belongs. The short answer is that it depends on form of payment and price.

Form of payment determines ownership of Newco. And whoever owns Newco pays for social terms:

- In cash-for-stock or cash-for-assets deals, the buyer owns Newco. Therefore, in these deals, the buyer pays for social terms.
- In mergers, stock-for-stock, or stock-for-assets deals, the shareholders of both the buyer and target own Newco. Thus, they jointly pay for social terms.

But price also determines who pays, because it could be used as a bargaining chip to trade off a lower price for higher social terms. For instance, consider a merger of equals with a zero percent acquisition premium and a handsome step-up in compensation for the target firm's managers. It would seem that the buyer and target shareholders would share pro rata in bearing the social terms—until one considered the opportunity cost to the target shareholders from not selling in a straight acquisition with a premium of, say, 10 to 25 percent. In such deals, it can be fairly argued that the target shareholders effectively bear the cost of the social terms. The MOE effects a wealth transfer from target shareholders to beneficiaries of the social terms.

It would seem that the cost of a deal's social terms would simply equal the sum of the present values of the various cash flow streams. The challenge is greater than it seems.

Some of the effects are practically impossible to measure. Incentives, signaling, and bidding are largely a matter of guesswork. The best one can do is to construct a model and backsolve for the benefits in these areas that would be necessary to bring the deal to a break-even level of attractiveness for the buyer. One can evaluate the resulting values for reasonableness against intuition, and the judgment of operating managers. As outlined in Chapter 9, one should still attempt to value the known cash flows and reflect them in your total assessment of the deal. But the measurement problem implies that there will be a band of uncertainty surrounding any estimate, not to be ignored.

CASE STUDIES IN THE ROLE OF SOCIAL ISSUES

Individual M&A transactions illustrate the variety of ways in which social issues crop up and the wide range of terms crafted to resolve them. The merger prospectus, filed with the SEC in connection with the combination of two publicly held corporations in which a vote of shareholders is required, contains the merger agreement. This document will disclose major social terms, and must disclose financial or titular arrangements that benefit the most senior executives of the buyer and target firm. The following case studies suggest the terms that an analyst might see in an assessment of social issues.

Daimler and Chrysler: Cross-Border Merger of Equals

Between January and May 1998, secret meetings of senior executives of Daimler-Benz A.G. and Chrysler Corporation negotiated the terms of a merger of equals of the two corporations. Social issues were the first to be discussed, in private meetings between Jürgen Schrempp (CEO of Daimler-Benz) and Robert Eaton (CEO of Chrysler). Specifically, they discussed governance, organizational structure, composition of Newco's management, country of incorporation, and the ways to foster integration of the two entities. With a rough sketch in hand, their representatives turned to pricing and other terms of merger, though they continued to work on social issues in greater detail. Much of the structure of the merger was influenced by the need to win approval of shareholders, regulators, and unions in the United States and Germany.

The terms of combination that were finally agreed on by Schrempp and Eaton included prominent social issues:

- ***Transaction structure:*** merger of equals. Actually, Daimler was larger in total revenues ($69 billion) than Chrysler ($61 billion), though Chrysler was larger in the automobile segment. Some observers believed that Daimler was buying Chrysler, a suspicion that subsequent history supports.
- ***Joint name:*** DaimlerChrysler. In interviews afterward, Jürgen Schrempp said that the name remained unresolved until the end of the discussions. Schrempp held out for Daimler-Benz as the name for Newco. Eaton insisted that Chrysler be reflected somehow in the name, and intimated that successful

conclusion of the merger depended on this point. Realizing that a rose by any other name would *not* smell as sweet to Eaton, Schrempp conceded to name the firm DaimlerChrysler. The joint name would seem consistent with the merger-of-equals structure.

- *Country of incorporation:* Germany. This was consistent with various legal constraints on Daimler-Benz, and perhaps the reality that this may not have been a true merger of equals.
- *Operational headquarters:* Germany and United States.
- *Common language:* English. English is widely used as a language for business in Europe. The language concession proved to be controversial among DaimlerChrysler's German employees.
- *CEO:* a structure of two co-CEOs, Schrempp and Eaton. It was understood that Eaton would serve as co-CEO for only two years.
- *Board seats:* Chrysler executives would hold half the board seats of the management board of Newco. But the supervisory board would yield only about one-third of its seats to Chrysler directors—owing to German law, which requires that unions must hold 49 percent of the seats on boards of directors.
- *Executive compensation:* Compensation for German executives was significantly lower than for their American counterparts. Executive pay in German firms had to be reviewed by the supervisory board of a company. In addition, German companies were not required to disclose executive pay to the same extent as U.S. companies (to the U.S. Securities and Exchange Commission). Daimler disclosed pay only on an aggregate basis, and reported that in 1997 the 10 executives on the management board received total remuneration of DM20 million,[6] or $11.3 million. Schrempp made about $2.5 million a year. In comparison, Chrysler chairman and CEO Robert Eaton made $16 million in 1997. The merger agreement called for large lump-sum payments to the top five Chrysler executives to compensate for their holdings in Chrysler, golden parachutes for them, and employment continuation agreements for the top 30 executives worth $96 million over two years. The agreement placed a moratorium on executive compensation changes for two years.

The epilogue to the merger-of-equals design occurred two years later. Kirk Kerkorian, who had been a significant minority investor in Chrysler, sued DaimlerChrysler A.G., alleging that the company committed fraud by claiming that the deal was a merger of equals. The company's share price had hit a high of $108 in January 1999, and then fallen steadily to about $40 in November 2000 when Kerkorian sued. The suit noted the departure of most of Chrysler's senior executives since the merger and said, "Had Mr. Kerkorian known the truth [he] would never have agreed to vote all of [his] shares for the merger."[7] Business law experts dismissed the chances of the suit. One said that "soft assurances about the fate of managers and the whole concept of a 'merger of equals' are probably too vague to prompt court action."[8]

First Union and Wachovia versus SunTrust

In April 2001, Wachovia Corporation agreed to a merger of equals with First Union Corporation—both were major U.S. bank holding companies headquartered in North Carolina. First Union's bid was $12.5 billion. This included a relatively low premium over Wachovia's previous trading price, and a "lockup option"[9] that allowed First Union to acquire 19.9 percent of Wachovia's shares. The announcement of this transaction followed earlier merger discussions between Wachovia and SunTrust Banks, Inc., of Florida. Following the announcement, SunTrust appealed directly to Wachovia's shareholders with an unsolicited tender offer of $13.69 billion, a 6 percent premium over First Union's bid (subsequently raised to $14.54 billion, a 16.3 percent premium). Notwithstanding the higher offer, Wachovia's management backed the First Union bid. Journalists and securities analysts noted First Union's incentive to preempt competing bidders (such as SunTrust) and suspected strong influence on Wachovia of social issues:

- The name Wachovia Corporation to be retained for Newco.
- The appointment of Wachovia's CEO, L. M. "Bud" Baker Jr., as chairman of Newco's board of directors.
- Payment to Baker of $2 million per year for the rest of his life. Should his wife outlive him, she would receive 60 percent for the rest of her life. In addition, Baker would receive $200,000 per year after taxes for life, for transportation, secretarial support, and office space. SunTrust claimed that these terms were negotiated by Baker with First Union without the knowledge of Wachovia's board, a charge he denied.

The low purchase premium for Wachovia's shares and sizable compensation to Mr. Baker upset some institutional investors, and raised demands to know what happened to the earlier SunTrust negotiations. A newspaper account recounted how the Wachovia-SunTrust negotiations derailed:

> *At the last minute, Mr. Baker balked. SunTrust executives say Mr. Baker's only concern had been that Wachovia's wealth-management business reports to a centralized business unit while SunTrust's wealth management specialists report on the basis of geography. SunTrust's CEO, L. Phillip Humann, told Mr. Baker there wasn't a practical difference between the two approaches, but SunTrust was willing to adopt the Wachovia approach. Still, the day before Wachovia's Dec. 15 board meeting, Mr. Baker told Mr. Humann that Wachovia was backing out. SunTrust executives were dumbstruck.*
>
> *People familiar with Wachovia's thinking say disagreements over asset management were simply the final straw and symptomatic of larger disagreements. The Wachovia side found it had a profoundly different view of how the combined company should be run and felt that the SunTrust executives had proposed a merger of equals but were really engineering a takeover with their viewpoints expected to prevail. There was an increasing feeling among several top managers at Wachovia that SunTrust was simply not the right partner and that merging would create a big regional bank with little upside.*[10]

Hewlett-Packard and Compaq: Retention Bonuses and CEO Compensation

In 2001, HP and Compaq announced that they would combine their two companies as a merger of equals. HP's CEO, Carly Fiorina, would become the CEO of Newco. Compaq's CEO, Michael Capellas, would become the chief operating officer of Newco. The companies disclosed that they would pay retention bonuses to employees to keep them within the firm if the deal were consummated. HP expected to pay $337 million to 6,000 employees, of which $33.1 million would be paid to 10 senior executives. Compaq would pay $242 million to "several thousand executives" with $22.4 million being paid to the top seven.

The transaction was soon contested by dissident shareholders. One of them, Walter Hewlett, a member of HP's board of directors, divulged the terms of compensation for the CEOs of HP and Compaq just three weeks before the shareholders would vote on the deal.[11] He had been a member of HP's board compensation committee, in which capacity he reviewed the prospective compensation for Fiorina and Capellas given in Exhibit 24.3. HP denied having agreed to any postdeal employment contracts and pointed out that in 2001 both Carly Fiorina and Michael Capellas had turned down deal-related executive retention bonuses valued at $14.4 million (for Fiorina) and $8 million (for Capellas), to indicate faith in the deal.

Fleet Financial Group and BankBoston

In 1998, Fleet Financial Group was the ninth-largest bank holding company in the United States with total assets of $104.4 billion. BankBoston was the fourteenth largest bank holding company with total assets of $73.5 billion. Both firms were headquartered in Boston and had substantial banking operations in New England.

At the end of February 1999, the CEOs of the two banks sketched the outline

EXHIBIT 24.3 Executive Compensation for Fiorina and Capellas Disclosed by Walter Hewlett

	Carly Fiorina (Hewlett-Packard)		Michael Capellas (Compaq)	
	Compensation Before (HP)	Compensation After (Newco)	Compensation Before (Compaq)	Compensation After (Newco)
Employment contract	Not reported	Two years	Not reported	Two years
Base salary	$1.0 million	$1.6 million	$3.8 million (includes loan forgiveness)	$1.0 million
Annual targeted bonus	$1.25 million	$4.8 million	None	$3.8 million
Stock purchase plan	None	None	10-year plan valued at $13.2 million (assuming 10% appreciation in share price)	None
Stock options granted	3 million received since date of employment	6 million, estimated value of $57 million	Not reported	4 million, estimated value of $38 million

Source of data: Pui-Wing Tam and Gary McWilliams, "Hewlett Sees Postdeal Pacts for Two CEOs," *Wall Street Journal*, February 27, 2002, page A3. *Wall Street Journal*. Eastern Edition [staff produced copy only] by Pui-Wing Tam and Gary McWilliams.

of governance, management, and strategy for a new firm that would combine the banks' operations. They contemplated a merger of equals to recognize the important contribution of each bank to the new organization that would emerge to be the eighth largest commercial bank in the United States. A merger between Fleet Financial Group and BankBoston was announced March 12, 1999. The social terms in the agreement included these:

- Headquarters to be located in Boston.
- Name: "Fleet Boston Corporation."
- Titles and management succession: Terrence Murray, CEO of Fleet, would become CEO for two years; Chad Gifford, CEO of BankBoston, would be chief operating officer of the new firm, and would become CEO in 2001 upon Murray's retirement.
- Safeguards to ensure succession: As part of the deal, Fleet would amend its corporate charter to require that a majority of 80 percent of the board should be required for any change of the CEO succession plan. This supermajority provision would prevent the 12-to-10 majority of Fleet over BankBoston directors from reneging on the succession plan. Not long after NationsBank merged with Bank of America, the former CEO of Bank of America was ousted, leaving the NationsBank executive firmly in control.
- Directors: 12 from Fleet and 10 from BankBoston. Following the transaction, Fleet shareholders would own 62 percent of the company; BankBoston shareholders would own 38 percent.
- A retention plan worth $800 million for employees of BankBoston Robertson Stephens. The retention plan would pay key Robertson Stephens employees the amount in the plan if they remained with the firm by the third anniversary of the closing of the merger. The intent of this plan was to retain key "rainmaker" employees on whose skills and contacts the success of Robertson Stephens depended. When BankBoston acquired Robertson Stephens two years earlier, it put in place a retention plan worth $200 million that would pay off within 18 months of the Fleet/BankBoston deal. The sizable increase in the retention plan reflected both the growth of Robertson Stephens and the desire to retain employees who would benefit under the previous plan.
- Employee benefit plans for Fleet and BankBoston would remain in effect until replaced by Newco.

SUMMARY AND CONCLUSIONS

The survey of social issues and four mini-cases reviewed in this chapter reveal that social issues can have large implications for top managers of merging firms, as well as their shareholders. Careful analysis of these transactions should include a rigorous assessment of the economic impact of social terms. The cases and discussion reveal:

- ***Primacy.*** Social terms are usually negotiated first and thus represent the gateway to structuring the other terms of the transaction.
- ***Variety of terms.*** There are many ways to address social issues. The chapter surveys nine dimensions. Many details of social terms need not be disclosed publicly. Therefore, the design and impact of social terms are poorly understood and warrant further research.

- *Valuation.* The economic implications of social terms are estimated with difficulty, owing to their complexity, lack of transparency, and potential interactions among the terms. Some impacts may be impossible to estimate.
- *Materiality.* The cases suggest that in absolute terms the economic impact of social terms can be huge. Some of the recent research on mergers of equals suggests that the effects of social terms are economically significant for shareholders of the buyer and target firms.

NOTES

1. See, for instance, Martin and McConnell (1991), North (2001), Walsh (1988), and Walsh and Ellwood (1991).
2. Martin and McConnell (1991) report a turnover rate of 55 percent, using deals between 1958 and 1984. But using deals from the 1990s, North (2001) reports the higher turnover rate of 70.6 percent. Walsh (1989), using a different sample, reports a 74 percent five-year turnover rate among targets of hostile takeovers, and a 62 percent turnover rate for friendly deals.
3. The market value of an employee's skills is typically determined by peer comparison, studies of the compensation paid to comparable employees in other firms.
4. Managers might resist takeovers if they believed that their jobs were threatened. Golden parachutes typically enrich managers, relieving them of economic adversity following the loss of a job.
5. Golden parachutes, if activated, add to the cost of acquisition for the buyer. Most parachutes, however, require not only a change in control, but also departure of the manager within a predetermined amount of time. Thus, managers who choose to stay indefinitely with Newco may forgo payments under golden parachutes.
6. Jay Palmer, "Shake-up Artist: Daimler-Benz Chairman Jürgen Schrempp Has Knocked the Dust off Mercedes, Restoring Hope for European Manufacturers," *Barron's*, March 23, 1998, page 35.
7. Jeffrey Ball and Scott Miller, "Kerkorian Sues Daimler, Calls Deal a Fraud," *Wall Street Journal*, November 28, 2000, page A3. *Wall Street Journal*. Eastern Edition [staff produced copy only] by Jeffrey Ball and Scott Miller. Copyright 2000 by Dow Jones & Co. Inc. Reproduced with permission of Dow Jones & Co. Inc. in the format textbook via Copyright Clearance Center.
8. Ibid.
9. Generally, a lockup option grants a buyer the right to purchase a percentage of the target's shares, sizable enough to block a takeover by a competing bidder. See Chapters 23 and 35 for more about lockup options.
10. Nikhil Deogun and Carrick Mollenkamp, "Wachovia Chief Has Some Explaining to Do," *Wall Street Journal*, May 16, 2001, page C1. *Wall Street Journal*. Eastern Edition [staff produced copy only] by Nikhil Deogun and Carrick Mollenkamp. Copyright 2000 by Dow Jones & Co. Inc. Reproduced with permission of Dow Jones & Co. Inc. in the format textbook via Copyright Clearance Center.
11. Pui-Wing Tam and Gary McWilliams, "Hewlett Sees Postdeal Pacts for Two CEOs," *Wall Street Journal*, February 27, 2002, page A3. *Wall Street Journal*. Eastern Edition [staff produced copy only] by Pui-Wing Tam & Gary McWilliams. Copyright 2000 by Dow Jones & Co. Inc. Reproduced with permission of Dow Jones & Co. Inc. in the format textbook via Copyright Clearance Center.

PART Five

Rules of the Road: Governance, Laws, and Regulations

CHAPTER 25

How a Negotiated Deal Takes Shape

INTRODUCTION

This chapter gives an overview of the process of making an M&A deal, paying attention to the laws, regulations, and court precedents that form the "rules of the road." Knowing these rules is vitally important to the success of an M&A practitioner, but it does not guarantee good outcomes.

The key to understanding best practice in shaping a deal is the concept of *risk management*. The shaping process is riddled with uncertainties. Anecdotal evidence from seasoned M&A professionals suggests that only a small percentage of M&A proposals results in a consummated deal. The process of striking a deal is more like a game of poker than an engineering problem. Law structures the game. Economics adds powerful incentives and motivates strategic behavior. Psychology influences how the game is played. Best practitioners recognize the risky nature of M&A deal doing, and use the legal framework to hedge risk exposure and stimulate good behavior.

This chapter and the next four survey the legal framework within which deals are done, and elaborate on the risk management point of view.

OVERVIEW OF THE DEAL SHAPING PROCESS

The deal process can be decomposed into several stages for closer examination. Exhibit 25.1 gives a time line of these stages:

1. ***Strategic planning, search, and target identification.*** Best practice companies in M&A think strategically, rather than opportunistically, about the opportunities they encounter. This lends discipline to their deal analysis and design. Of special importance is clarity about motives, why acquisition is desirable. This is achieved through a rigorous analysis of strengths, weaknesses, opportunities, and threats that the firm may face. In addition, the firm must analyze the possible alternatives to M&A, such as joint ventures, strategic alliance, minority interests, supply chain contracts, and simply doing nothing at all. A buyer can approach M&A opportunistically, and snap up attractive targets as they appear. But this can diminish the odds of success to the extent that it makes the buyer prone to fads, deal frenzy, and the winner's curse. Advocated here is a much more disciplined and strategic approach.

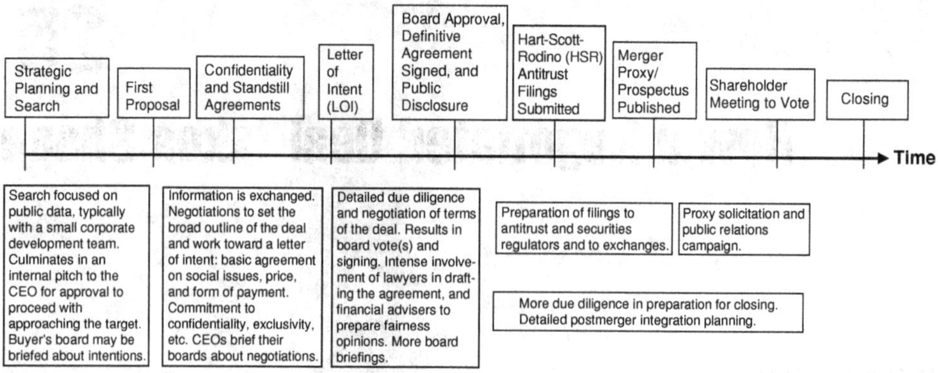

EXHIBIT 25.1 Time Line of a Deal (Time on Horizontal Axis, Not According to Scale)

2. ***The initial contact.*** The presentation of an initial proposal (or "pitch") must give a compelling reason for the combination of two firms that speaks to the needs of target shareholders and management. Where the target is of a substantial size in comparison to the buyer, the presentation might be made by the CEO of the buyer. Where the target is relatively small, the first approach might be made by a vice president, development officer, or operating manager within the buyer firm.
3. ***Confidentiality agreement and related documents.*** Brief agreements are typically negotiated between buyer and target that outline the behavior of the two sides in the early stage of the deal shaping process. These agreements address respect for the confidentiality of information (*confidentiality agreement*), exclusivity of discussions (*exclusivity agreement*), *standstill* in the purchase of target shares, and the conditions for terminating discussions (*termination agreement*). The target firm may form a *special guidance committee* of the board of directors to advise management. And both firms may engage investment bankers or other advisors using an *advisory engagement letter*.
4. ***Term sheet and letter of intent.*** When the two sides reach a sufficient degree of alignment on the general terms of a deal, they may memorialize their understanding in a *term sheet* and/or a *letter of intent*. These serve to confirm a growing level of commitment and guide the lawyers in drafting a definitive agreement.
5. ***Due diligence and negotiation of a definitive agreement.*** The next phase entails drafting a definitive agreement that will depend on detailed assertions about the condition of the target and, perhaps, the buyer. The definitive agreement binds the two sides to consummate a transaction. Due diligence research becomes a vital step underlying both the definitive agreement and the closing. Due diligence is in-depth research *at the target company*; the target permits this scrutiny because of the confidentiality agreement signed earlier and because of a desire to conclude the deal. The buyer's due diligence may have commenced much earlier, drawing on public information and industry experts.
6. ***Affirmative vote by the board of directors.*** The definitive agreement likely requires an *affirmative vote* by the target's board of directors, and may require approval by the buyer's board as well. If a vote of the shareholders is required, the board can only recommend that they approve the deal. Usually by this stage, the merger negotiations are disclosed to the public and to regulators.

7. ***Disclosure to the public and to regulators.*** Securities regulations and court decisions require firms to disclose to shareholders news about events that are material and probable. When to make the announcement and what to say are matters of judgment, and therefore *disclosure* is one of the most delicate issues faced in managing the deal shaping process.
8. ***Antitrust filings and permission.*** Part of the process of releasing information about the deal entails required disclosure to antitrust authorities as part of gaining their permission to consummate the transaction. Filings under the *Hart-Scott-Rodino* Act (HSR) must reveal the likely degree of the Newco's industry concentration following the deal.
9. ***Informing the shareholders and gaining an affirmative vote.*** Merger proposals and/or the sale of significant assets usually require approval by the target's shareholders. The buyer, too, may need to gain approval from its shareholders to create new shares of stock necessary to consummate a stock-for-stock deal. Thus, the target and sometimes the buyer will issue a merger prospectus that informs shareholders about the deal, and a proxy statement that requests their votes in support of the deal. These filings must conform to SEC requirements. It takes 30 to 90 days to prepare a merger prospectus, with the assistance of financial and legal advisers, and another one or two months for the prospectus to be distributed and the votes to be solicited with the aid of a *proxy solicitation* service. Thus, the shareholder vote may be scheduled for three to six months after the announcement of the definitive merger agreement. Typically, the outcome of the voting is known within days of the meeting.
10. ***Closing.*** The M&A agreement commits the two firms to conclude a transaction under various terms and conditions, such as gaining shareholder votes and regulatory approvals. At the *closing*, the two sides document that they have met the *representations*, *warranties*, and *covenants* outlined in the agreement. Payment is made and ownership is assumed by the buyer.
11. ***Postmerger integration.*** Except for terms of the definitive agreement that specifically extend beyond closing,[1] the focus thereafter is on combining the two companies to realize the economic benefits hypothesized at the outset. Indifference to integration is a leading cause of M&A failure. Planning for integration ideally commences early in the process such as at the signing of the letter of intent. Consultants and successful practitioners argue that the bulk of the integration work must be completed within 90 days of closing in order to avoid major pitfalls. Chapter 36 ("Framework for Postmerger Integration") discusses these considerations in more detail.

RISKS TO THE DEAL: HOW THE PROCESS CAN GET DERAILED

Within the time line of a deal, plenty can go wrong. Imagine the range of factors that might derail a deal:

- ***Bad chemistry.*** The two CEOs have their initial meeting and just don't click. One inadvertently offends the other; the other gets defensive. No price is high enough to compensate for ill will.

- *Social issues, control.* There is no intersection in the broad-brush outline of social issues presented by each side: Both CEOs want to be CEO of Newco; both want the headquarters in their hometown; and so on. Fundamentally, each CEO wants to be in control after the closing. Sometimes these problems can be mitigated through artful deal design.
- *Pricing.* The target wants more than the buyer can justify paying. Careful valuation analysis combined with trade-offs on other terms of the deal may justify a slightly higher price (this argument is discussed in more detail in Chapter 18). But valuation differences are a frequent difficulty for deal designers.
- *Adverse move in the stock market or interest rates.* Financing for the deal suddenly gets much more expensive following a sharp move in capital markets. The previously attractive deal cannot be justified in the current market environment. See Chapter 23 for further discussion of ways to mitigate the impact of adverse market movements through the use of caps, collars, and floors.
- *Skeleton in the closet.* Due diligence reveals material adverse conditions within the counterparty that create unexpected liabilities: tax or accounting problems, patent expirations, environmental cleanup costs, labor difficulties, and so on. Chapter 8 suggests the broad range of issues that research might uncover.
- *Material adverse change.* In contrast to the "skeleton" problem, one or both companies may have no problems going into the final stages of the deal, and then encounter a sharp change in the core business that constitutes a "material adverse change" (MAC) allowing the buyer to back out of the deal. Definitive agreements (and occasionally letters of intent) include MAC as one of the conditions under which the agreement might be canceled by the buyer. Triggers of MAC clauses are variously defined. Consider the following examples:
  - *Allegheny Energy/DQE, 1998.* DQE, a Pittsburgh utility holding company, announced in 1997 a deal to be acquired by Allegheny, another utility, shortly after the Pennsylvania legislature passed the Customer Choice Act—this act effectively heightened price competition. DQE, a less efficient power producer, needed to write off assets following this law. In explaining why it was canceling the deal, DQE cited the "material adverse effect" of a decision by the Pennsylvania Public Utility Commission to disallow more than $1 billion in stranded costs claimed by Allegheny.[2]
  - *Tyson Foods/IBP, 2001.* Tyson won a hostile takeover contest to acquire Iowa Beef Processors on January 1, 2001. But accounting problems within IBP caused that firm's share price to collapse to $22.79 per share, well below Tyson's bid price of $30. Tyson delayed the purchase to await the outcome of an SEC investigation into IBP's accounting practices. IBP claimed it had resolved the accounting issues and investigated theft and fraud in a business unit. But in mid-March, IBP reported a quarterly loss and lower earnings expectations. Tyson's CEO became concerned about the ability of Newco to service the acquisition-related debts, and on March 30 canceled the acquisition altogether on the principle of material adverse change. IBP sued Tyson for breach of contract and won in June, forcing Tyson to consummate the deal on the original terms. One lawyer said, "People will start to be more specific with respect to what they mean by material adverse change—a term typically employed to justify use of an escape clause."[3]

- *Dynegy/Enron, 2001.* The proposed merger of Enron into Dynegy was announced on November 9, 2001. A few days later, Enron issued a major restatement of financial results that triggered a sharp erosion in its core trading business. On November 28, Dynegy withdrew, citing the MAC clause. Enron filed for bankruptcy on December 4, and sued Dynegy for breach of contract. The suit was dropped shortly thereafter.

- ***Regulatory or antitrust constraints.*** Governments may decide to oppose the transaction for reasons of public policy.
- ***Competing bidder horns in.*** Competitors may enter a surprise competing bid to the target's board of directors. Once the target is up for sale, the directors have an obligation to maximize shareholder welfare by selling it for the highest price—this is the so-called "Revlon rule."
- ***Shareholders vote "no."*** Particularly in small and family-held businesses, the shareholders may oppose a dream deal for a variety of social and economic reasons.

These elements give a flavor of the M&A deal shaping process. *One should walk away from a bad deal.* But where it appears that a good deal might be had, a failure owing to any of these factors is regrettable; *best practitioners manage the M&A deal shaping process in a way to reduce exposure to these risks.* The following sections of this chapter discuss the phases of a deal in more detail and lend insight into how good process management manages risk.

TRANSACTION PLANNING AND PREPARATION

The first step in risk management of the deal is to lay a groundwork in research, expert support, and governance. The buyer firm will undertake a series of actions to help prepare itself for acquisition. These actions could include:

- ***Informing the board of directors.*** The duty of directors is to remain informed about corporate activities. At the start of an acquisition program, the CEO should brief the board on the motives and direction of the effort, and then follow up subsequently to report on progress.
- ***Formation of special guidance committee.*** The buyer could organize a special team of senior managers and selected directors who could provide guidance on short notice about the direction and process of the acquisition strategy. This smaller group should be more nimble than convening the entire board of directors, and has no official governance capacity other than to advise on activities and to report to the board of directors.
- ***Retaining advisers.*** Successful execution of an acquisition program requires specialized expertise in areas such as law, accounting, investment banking, public relations, and risk management. All but the largest corporations will need to engage specialists for their help; large corporations typically retain such specialists on their in-house staff but may decide to retain outside advisers in the instance of large or complex transactions. Ultimately, the board of directors of a large firm may require the opinion of independent advisers.

- *Corporate review.* The corporate guidance committee and its advisers will conduct a review of the buyer itself to identify any issues that could bar a transaction. These could entail problems across a wide range of considerations including environmental, accounting, and tax issues.

INITIATING DISCUSSIONS: GAINING AN EARLY SENSE OF THE POSSIBILITIES

Friendly negotiations typically begin with a conversation between the CEOs of the buyer and target firms, except where the target is much smaller than the buyer, in which case the buyer may delegate an operating or staff executive to make the approach. The aim of this first conversation is to open the door and gain an agreement to meet again. It presents the concept of the merger, expresses its strategic logic, and frames some possibilities about social issues.

The target's response to the buyer's initial pitch is a crucial inflection point. If the target CEO is neutral or favorably disposed to the pitch, he or she will typically ask for time to consult advisers, and propose a meeting in a few days or weeks. This hiatus will give the target time to engage advisers, do some initial research on the buyer, brief the board, and set strategy. If the target has a strong prior desire to remain independent, or at least not to merge with the buyer, the target CEO will express a strong and clear "no"—this is the famous "*just say no*" defense,[4] and must be grounded in some belief that the transaction is not in the interest of the target's shareholders and/or that the target has some other strategy that dominates the buyer's idea. For instance, the other better strategy may entail a new product launch, deployment of new technology, entry into new geographic markets, investment in R&D, and/or reliance on different forms of combination other than M&A—these alternatives may create more value for the target's shareholders than selling the company to another firm. The tools of strategic analysis (outlined in Chapter 6) and valuation (outlined in Chapters 9 through 15) can help inform the target's decision to say "yes" or "no."

Following a rejection, most merger proposals die. But some buyers may elect to appeal directly to the board of directors in the form of a "bear hug"[5] proposal, or directly to the shareholders in the form of a hostile tender offer.[6]

Following a positive response (i.e., agreement to meet again), the two CEOs may subsequently get together to sketch out social issues, price, and other major terms. After that may come a few more meetings among delegates (such as chief financial officers) to add more detail. The objective of these subsequent meetings is to lend more certainty to the belief that an attractive deal is to be had, and that it is worthwhile for both parties to enter the next phase with a letter of intent.

FIRST-ROUND DOCUMENTS: TERM SHEET, LETTER OF INTENT, AGREEMENTS ABOUT CONFIDENTIALITY, STANDSTILL, AND ENGAGEMENT OF ADVISERS

Up to this point, the two sides have little to show for their efforts but a degree of oral agreement on the possibilities of merger. In order to set an economically attractive price, the buyer needs to gain inside information about the target and perhaps an expression of precommitment to the concept of the deal. The target may find it in its interest to grant these requests, but needs to address two fears: (1) the leakage of its inside information to others, particularly competitors, and (2) the possibility that the buyer will stop negotiating and simply mount a hostile tender offer or buy the target's shares in the open market. The purpose of these first-round documents is to manage risks arising from these needs and fears. Chapter 29 describes these first-round documents in detail, but here's an overview:

- *Term sheet.* This outlines the agreed terms of the deal, often in bullet-point form on a single page.
- *Exclusivity agreement.* This commits the target not to negotiate with other parties, usually for a limited period of time. It is often accompanied by a termination agreement that outlines the conditions under which either side might withdraw from the negotiations.
- *Advisory engagement letter.* Early in the life of a deal, each side will find it desirable to engage expert help. This is done through a letter that outlines the terms and conditions of such help.
- *Confidentiality agreement.* This commits the target to provide confidential information, and the buyer to hold that information in confidence.
- *Standstill agreement.* The buyer will commit not to purchase shares of the target for a specified period of time.
- *Letter of intent.* This is a nonbinding summary of the terms of a deal that will provide the basis for a definitive merger agreement.

Drafting these first-round documents is a matter of strategic choice. Some deals do not feature them simply because the two parties may be in haste and want to proceed directly to a negotiation of the definitive agreement. The target may know and trust the buyer well and therefore be willing to divulge inside information without assurances. Finally, the two sides may wish to continue their discussions in secret, and executing the first-round documents may trigger public disclosure obligations, the news from which might solicit competing bidders or investor reactions.

In other settings, the first-round documents will be vital, and to some extent, interdependent. For instance, in May 2002, Northrop Grumman and TRW Inc. announced the signing of standstill and confidentiality agreements. Grumman had mounted a hostile takeover attempt against TRW. By signing the agreement, Grumman agreed to "stand still"—that is, not purchase TRW shares through a tender offer, but rather attempt to negotiate a friendly transaction. In return, TRW agreed to share with Grumman confidential information that might justify to Grumman a higher offer. Grumman agreed to keep this information private. In general, the linkage of confidentiality and standstill agreements is common.

THE DEFINITIVE AGREEMENT

In contrast to the letter of intent, which is nonbinding, the definitive agreement *is* binding. It sets out the necessary details relevant to consummating the deal, and commits the directors of both companies to take action to bring the deal to a close.

The definitive agreement is clearly a risk management device, limiting and allocating exposures and stimulating good behavior of the players. Chapter 29 gives a more detailed discussion of the merger agreement. The definitive agreement affects the shaping of the deal in four key areas:

1. ***Disclosure of information.*** The agreement sets up a mechanism by which the two sides disclose information about the condition of each other through representations and warranties. A representation (or "rep") is a statement of fact; a warranty is a commitment that a fact is or will be true. The purpose of the representations and warranties is to assist in the due diligence process leading up to the closing and to allocate risks between the two parties.
2. ***Shaping behavior between signing and closing.*** While reps and warranties refer to the condition of a firm at a specific time, covenants refer to the conduct of the firm after the definitive agreement is signed and are a basis for collecting damages if breached. A typical covenant would be the prohibition on extraordinary dividend payments that might effectively loot the target firm. More often, covenants refer to conducting operations on an ordinary basis, limiting indebtedness or the issuance of new securities, and changing compensation or pension plans. The merger agreement specifies actions both sides will take in pursuit of closing the deal. These might include making best efforts to close promptly, seeking a positive recommendation from the board of directors, making all necessary regulatory filings, continuation of target firm employee benefits, indemnification of directors and officers from liabilities arising from the transaction, bringing the target firm's accounting policies into conformity with those of the buyer, and so on. The merger agreement will list the conditions that each side must observe in order to consummate the transaction, such as producing evidence of the accuracy of reps and warranties at closing, shareholder approvals, regulatory approvals, absence of litigation, consents from third parties (such as creditors or landlords), and favorable advisory opinions (e.g., tax, accounting, and fairness to shareholders).
3. ***Shaping the means of exit.*** The merger agreement will list the circumstances under which the parties can unilaterally or mutually terminate the transaction. These may include the failure to receive regulatory or shareholder approvals, the expiration of a completion date, material adverse change in the business, or breach of reps, warranties, or covenants. Some definitive agreements include termination fees that are intended to reimburse the jilted party for expenses related to the merger. Delaware courts have upheld termination fees up to 2 percent of the value of a deal.[7] Barring explicit termination fees or other provisions it is understood that each party bears its own expenses.
4. ***Determining who bears risks, and the consequences.*** The merger agreement must allocate risks between the buyer and seller. Typically, it will specify damages by the target to the buyer for breaches of reps, warranties, and covenants. Occasionally, a portion of the payment to the target will be placed in escrow as a pool from which the buyer might be indemnified in the event of breaches. The use of escrow depends on the nature of the transaction. If you are buying the entity (as opposed to assets), known and unknown liabilities will convey with the target. If you are buying assets and can pick and choose, you may be able to hedge risk through careful selection of assets and therefore may have less need

of escrow. If the economic consequences of a risk occurrence are large (as might be the case with an environmental issue), escrow will be more important. Be sure your attorney is aware of the risk exposure in the acquisition of the target. Finally, the definitive agreement will specify that each side should pay its own expenses. Though this may seem obvious, given that one (or both entities) will be extinguished, it is important to establish in advance who will pay which bills.

DISCLOSURE TO INVESTORS AND REGULATORS

Public disclosure of a deal heightens the risk of interference from competing bidders, lawsuits from cranky shareholders, and opportunistic reactions from competitors. For this reason, many buyers prefer to delay public disclosure of a deal until it is relatively mature, the details have been worked out, synergies have been estimated, board approvals have been received, and the public relations campaign is fully planned. From this perspective, the policy on disclosure would be summed up in the word "delay."

On the other hand, early disclosure is sometimes advocated on the bases of fairness to investors and market competitiveness. It seems unfair for the buyer and target to represent themselves in public as separate firms when their CEOs have committed to a merger; shareholders current and prospective deserve to know about the change in status of the two firms soon after the commitment is reached so that they may make informed investment decisions. And from a more macroscopic perspective, markets function better (i.e., pricing is more efficient) when investors are fully informed.

One other argument in favor of early disclosure is control over the disclosure process. The more mature a deal becomes, the wider the circle of people involved, leading to an increasing risk of leakage of news of the deal. Thus, it is argued that the parties to the deal should go public with the news at a time when they can shape perceptions rather than later when they may be placed in reactive mode.

Between these two extremes is a wide gray area of practice, about which the U.S. Supreme Court has said, "It depends." In *Basic Inc. v. Levinson*,[8] the Court said that the materiality of the news and the resulting obligation to disclose will depend on:

- Significance of the transaction to the company.
- Probability of the transaction occurring.

The court has stated that merger is always a significant event in a corporation's life, therefore, the primary focus is on the *probability* of the transaction occurring. Probability could be indicated by the existence of board resolutions, instructions to investment bankers, and actual negotiations. Highly probable and significant transactions should be disclosed soon. Improbable and insignificant transactions need not be disclosed. This leaves enormous discretion in the middle. One's policy in the middle is best guided by a "duty to update" the public: Where the firm has made previous statements indicating a certain policy (e.g., the company is not for sale), and now has a deviation from that policy (e.g., yes, we will be sold), then the company is obliged to disclose the change in policy.

Once a deal is struck, securities laws and rules of public stock exchanges require public disclosure. The purpose of these is to promote orderly capital markets and a level playing field among investors and to ensure competitiveness of product markets. Obviously, these disclosures are relevant only if one or both parties to the deal are publicly held firms. Of note are five kinds of disclosures:

1. ***Periodic reports under the Securities Exchange Act of 1934.*** Publicly listed firms are required to file with the Securities and Exchange Commission (SEC) annual and quarterly financial reports, and to amend those reports as material new information is released. The prospective release of these reports by either buyer or target will trigger consideration of the materiality of M&A negotiations and perhaps the release of news.
2. ***Responses to questions about unusual trading activity.*** Stock exchanges and regulators may seek information regarding unusual trading activity in a firm's shares. Exchanges may ask for a comment on recent trading activity and an indication of whether there are any material developments in the company that would explain the trading. Firms are obliged to reply and to tell the truth, although a response of "we do not comment on rumors in the market" is perhaps the best policy.[9]
3. ***"Toehold" purchases.*** Securities law requires filing a public disclosure with the SEC of any person's equity ownership exceeding 5 percent. This is intended to signal to investors the accumulation of shares by a potential raider.
4. ***Merger proxy statement.*** When targets (and buyers) seek to gain the approval of shareholders for the deal, they must solicit votes either to be delivered in person or by proxy. The proxy statement is a public filing with the SEC that explains such things as the motives for the deal, the deal structure, payment, and the fairness opinion from outside advisers.
5. ***Registration statement/prospectus.*** In large share-for-share transactions, the buyer will need to register new shares with the SEC, and perhaps seek a vote of approval from shareholders to create these new shares. Registration of new securities is required under the Securities Act of 1933 by filing Form S-4. This document is rich with information about motives, structure, payment, and value of the deal. Often the proxy statement and prospectus are bundled into one document.

The second main area of regulatory disclosure is with antitrust regulators, which in the United States are the Department of Justice (DOJ) and the Federal Trade Commission (FTC). The Hart-Scott-Rodino Act (HSR)[10] requires the approval by the DOJ or FTC *before* a merger can occur. Typically, merging firms will notify the DOJ or FTC about the prospective combination with required forms and voluntary submission of further information. HSR imposes a 30-day waiting period on the merging firms before the deal may be consummated—this gives the DOJ and FTC the time to render an opinion on the legality of the deal.

GAINING APPROVAL FOR THE DEAL

The deal for the sale of a company is not done until shareholders vote to do so; this poses one last stage of risk management. The target's board of directors can bind itself to present the deal to shareholders, and use its best efforts to obtain their approval. Definitive agreements typically require board approval as a condition of the deal, which is why target directors are asked to vote before the CEO signs the merger agreement.

Typically, the board of directors[11] calls a special meeting of shareholders to vote on the transaction. This triggers the preparation of a proxy/prospectus document, which takes between 30 and 90 days. The SEC must approve the document for completeness before it can be sent to shareholders. A key component of the merger proxy/prospectus is the "fairness opinion," a letter opining on the fairness to selling shareholders of the purchase price, form of payment, and other aspects of the transaction.

The meeting itself is scheduled for a month or so after delivery of the prospectus. This affords time for the buyer and target to solicit proxies in favor of the transaction, typically relying on a proxy solicitation firm. Proxy solicitation is a risk management activity. Because of the proxy solicitation, the shareholder meeting often begins with a foregone conclusion in favor of the transaction. The meetings are usually run on parliamentary rules of order: Approval of the deal is moved and seconded; there is discussion, and then a vote. Dissident shareholders may seek to amend the proposed transaction, or defeat it. A competing bidder (who by now probably has a toehold equity interest) may seek to present an alternative proposal. After sufficient discussion, a vote is taken, and if close it is usually audited by an outside agency such as an accounting firm.

The consummation, or formal closing, of the transaction is typically scheduled to occur as soon as possible after an affirmative vote by shareholders. It is in the interests of both sides to push for speedy closing since the buyer wants to get on with integrating the two firms (i.e., further delay is costly), and since the seller wants to sell lest any unforeseen circumstances derail the deal.

For large transactions, the closing would occur in a hotel ballroom and include hundreds of people: senior executives of the two firms; their staffs; the entire range of advisers who will be asked to attest to representations, warranties, and covenants; commercial bankers who may be financing the deal; public-relations professionals; and so on. Lawyers serve as masters of ceremony with the spotlight on CEOs and CFOs as they attest to the deal conditions. In a sale of assets for cash, title to the assets would be exchanged for a check. In a stock-for-stock deal, the closing would trigger a process of canceling the old shares and distributing new shares, a process that might take weeks. Sometimes a lavish party celebrates the conclusion of the deal-making process.

CASE STUDY: DAIMLER-BENZ AND CHRYSLER

To illustrate the process by which a major deal is developed, consider the example of the discussions between Daimler-Benz A.G. and Chrysler Corporation in 1998. This case is an example of a process that did not entail use of a letter of intent. One can surmise why: Given the materiality of the deal, an LOI would have been immediately disclosable to the public. Instead, nearly four months elapsed between the initial contact and a public announcement.

At the Detroit International Auto Show in mid-January, Jürgen Schrempp,

CEO of Daimler-Benz, visited with Robert Eaton, chairman and CEO of Chrysler. Schrempp discussed with Eaton some of his thoughts about the likelihood of consolidation in the worldwide automotive industry and suggested it might be mutually beneficial if Daimler-Benz and Chrysler were to consider a merger or deep strategic alliance between their two firms. In Schrempp's view:

> *The two companies are a perfect fit of two leaders in their respective markets. Both companies have dedicated and skilled work forces and successful products, but in different markets and different parts of the world. By combining and utilizing each other's strengths, we will have a pre-eminent strategic position in the global marketplace for the benefit of our customers. We will be able to exploit new markets, and we will improve return and value for our shareholders.*[12]

Schrempp recalled:

> *I just presented the case, and I was out again. The meeting lasted about 17 minutes. I don't want to create the impression that he was surprised. When the meeting was over, I said, 'If you think I'm naïve, this is nonsense I'm talking, just tell me.' He smiled and said, 'Just give me a chance. We have done some evaluation as well, and I will phone you in the next two weeks.' I think he phoned me in a week or so.*[13]

Independently Eaton had concluded that some type of combination of Chrysler with another major automobile firm was needed: the firm was currently financially healthy, but industry overcapacity and huge prospective investment outlays called for an even larger type of global competitor. Before seeing Schrempp, Eaton had polled investment bankers for their ideas about a major automotive merger, and had spoken with executives from BMW on this topic. Eaton appointed a small task force of business executives and lawyers to represent Chrysler in the detailed negotiations. Eaton challenged this team on several counts: exploit the benefits of combination; preserve and strengthen the Chrysler brands; minimize the adverse effects of combination on employees and executives; and maximize shareholder value. In Eaton's view:

> *My number-one criterion is that [any deal] has got to be a long-term upside with no negative short-term impact. It's got to be good for the shareholders. That's my—and my board's—fiduciary responsibility.*[14]

Toward the end of January, Robert Eaton telephoned Jürgen Schrempp to suggest a meeting early in February. On February 5, 1998, the Chrysler board was briefed on the discussion between Schrempp and Eaton.

The merger proxy/prospectus prepared by the firms outlined the following key events in the development of the transaction.[15] Other than the prospectus, little information about the substance of discussions is in the public domain. Chrysler's objective in giving this historical summary of events is to persuade shareholders that management and the board of directors have been duly loyal and careful in the ex-

> *Comment:* In their first substantive discussions, Eaton and Schrempp brought their lieutenants who would conduct most of the detailed negotiations, but they didn't bring their investment bankers. Why? One speculation is that the most sensitive social issues are addressed here. Privacy would assist the candid discussion of such issues.

ecution of their duties. Given in boxes along the way are comments that highlight likely steps in the development of the deal.

- On **February 12, 1998**, Eaton and Gary Valade, executive vice president and chief financial officer of Chrysler, met with Schrempp and Dr. Eckhard Cordes, the Daimler-Benz board member responsible for corporate development and directly managed businesses, to discuss the possibility of combining the two companies. Following this discussion, they decided to consult with their respective financial advisers and to meet again on February 18, 1998.
- On **February 17 and 18, 1998**, Cordes and representatives of Goldman Sachs (the merger adviser to Daimler) met with Valade and representatives of Credit Suisse First Boston (CSFB, the merger adviser to Chrysler) to discuss various transaction structures. During the course of these discussions, Valade stated that it was important to Chrysler that any potential transaction maximize value for its stockholders, that it be tax free to Chrysler's U.S. stockholders and tax efficient for DaimlerChrysler AG, that it have the post-merger governance structure of a merger of equals, that it have the optimal ability to be accounted for as a pooling of interests, and that it result in the combination of the respective businesses of Daimler-Benz and Chrysler into one public company. Cordes indicated that it was important to Daimler-Benz that any potential transaction maximize value for its stockholders, that it be tax free to Daimler-Benz's German stockholders and tax efficient for DaimlerChrysler AG, and that the surviving entity of any combination be a German stock corporation, thereby enhancing the likelihood of acceptance of the transaction by all important constituencies of Daimler-Benz. During these meetings, various tax, corporate, and management issues were discussed with a view to developing a transaction structure that would accommodate the parties' objectives.

> *Comment:* In mid-February, the investment bankers were brought in, as part of the financial and tax focus of the discussions. In contrast, on March 2, the executives met alone to focus on social issues.

- On **March 2, 1998,** Schrempp and Cordes met with Eaton and Valade in Lausanne, Switzerland, to discuss governance and business organizational structures for a possible combined entity. The organizational issues discussed by the parties included, among other things, the impact of the jurisdiction of incorporation of the combined company on its corporate governance, the composition of the combined company's management, and the most effective way to foster the integration of the two business organizations. Over the course of their discussions, the parties considered various alternative transaction structures for the combination of the two enterprises, including (1) a newly incorporated U.S. company, (2) a company incorporated in the Netherlands, and (3) either a newly organized German *Aktiengesellschaft* or Daimler-Benz itself. The simplest structural solution, a direct merger of Daimler-Benz and Chrysler, was not possible under German law. Instead the parties settled on a consolidation-type[16] structure that was tax efficient for the combined entity on an ongoing basis, could be tax free to Chrysler's U.S. stockholders and to Daimler-Benz's German stockholders, and would enable the elimination of all minority stockholders of Daimler-Benz and Chrysler, thereby creating a parent corporation with one group of stockholders holding a single publicly traded equity security.
- Valade and Cordes met on **March 6, 1998,** to discuss the progress of their respective working teams. They concluded that the working teams should continue to meet in an effort to refine the structural alternatives then under discussion. In addition, Valade requested that Daimler-Benz provide Chrysler with its preliminary thoughts on valuation.
- On **March 5 and 17,** representatives from each party's legal and investment banking teams met in New York to continue their discussion with respect to alternative transaction structures. On **March 19,** representatives of Chrysler and CSFB met with representatives of Daimler-Benz and Goldman Sachs to discuss valuation matters.
- On **March 23,** the Chrysler board was updated concerning the status of discussions with Daimler-Benz. On **March 26,** representatives of Chrysler and Daimler-Benz met at the offices of CSFB to discuss the progress of the working teams, valuation analyses, governance, and structural matters.

> *Comment:* For about the next month, the negotiations focused on valuation and organization structure. Note that negotiators changed meeting locations regularly, probably to minimize leakage of news.

- On **April 7,** the Chrysler board was updated concerning the status of discussions with Daimler-Benz. On **April 9,** at a meeting in London, Schrempp and Eaton agreed that the valuations and preliminary views on the transaction structure being discussed were approaching a point where they could each recommend them to their respective boards, and they discussed a governance structure for the combined company. During late March and the month of April, the legal and investment banking teams, including representatives of the law firm of Bruckhaus Westrick Heller Lober, German counsel to Chrysler, continued to discuss and refine their analysis with respect to the appropriate business combination structure.

- On **April 16, 1998**, Schrempp and Cordes discussed the status of the proposed Chrysler transaction with Hilmar Kopper, the chairman of the Daimler-Benz supervisory board, and on **April 19**, Schrempp and Cordes gave a detailed presentation of the transaction to the Daimler-Benz management board.
- On **April 21, 1998**, Eaton and Valade met with Schrempp, Cordes, and Grube (director of corporate strategy and planning for Daimler-Benz) to refine their thinking with respect to, among other things, valuation and key governance and management positions. In addition, they agreed that the working teams should work with the objective of completing all elements necessary to announce a transaction on **May 7**.
- Between **April 23 and May 6, 1998**, members of the working teams met at various times to negotiate the combination agreement and related documentation.
- On **April 22 and 29**, the Chrysler board was updated concerning the status of discussions with Daimler-Benz. On **May 3**, the Daimler-Benz management board met to review the transactions and unanimously approved the combination agreement and the transactions.
- At meetings on **May 5 and May 6**, the Chrysler board reviewed the proposed combination agreement and the transaction. At the **May 6** meeting the Chrysler board unanimously approved the combination agreement and the transaction. Also on **May 6**, the Daimler-Benz supervisory board met in Stuttgart and received a full briefing and the recommendation of the management board with respect to the proposed combination agreement. Although no resolution was proposed at the meeting, there was substantial discussion and several members indicated their general satisfaction with the proposed transaction. The discussion at the meeting focused on the reasons for the business combination, including, among other things, general consolidation in the automotive industry and the strong potential for synergies between the constituent companies, the company profile of Chrysler, the transaction structure, organizational issues relating to the structure and composition of the Daimler-Chrysler management board and supervisory board, and the prospects for enhancing the value of the combined entity in the future. The Daimler-Benz supervisory board scheduled a second meeting on May 14, 1998, to consider and vote on the proposed combination agreement.
- On **May 6**, in response to newspaper stories about discussions between Chrysler and Daimler-Benz, the companies announced that they were in discussions. Late that evening, in London, all constituent parties signed the combination agreement. The next morning, **May 7**, the signing of the combination agreement was publicly announced. On **May 14, 1998**, the Daimler-Benz supervisory board unanimously approved the combination agreement and the transaction.

On **July 22 and 30, 1998**, respectively, the European Union and U.S. antitrust agencies allowed to lapse without objection the waiting period on consummating the transaction—this amounted to approval of the deal from an antitrust standpoint. On **August 6, 1998**, Chrysler and the newly named DaimlerChrysler AG jointly filed a proxy statement/prospectus and an F-4 registration statement with the U.S. Securities and Exchange Commission. This proxy/prospectus requested shareholder approval for the merger of the two firms. The registration statement would seek shareholder permission for DaimlerChrysler to create the new shares necessary to consummate the transaction. The special shareholder meeting of the two firms was on **September 18, 1998.** The merger was approved by both sets of shareholders. On **September 20, 1998,** the transaction was consummated by Eaton and Schrempp at a formal ceremony.

The elapsed time for the deal was about eight months, relatively short considering its size, complexity, and international nature. Yet the detailed history reveals stages of development consistent with the time line in Exhibit 25.1. As time elapsed, the deal shows:

- ***Widening involvement.*** The circle of people involved in the deal expanded outward from an initial engagement between the two CEOs ultimately to involve lower-level managers and financial advisers.
- ***Growing detail.*** The detailed terms did not emerge from the early talks between Schrempp and Eaton; they evolved through the negotiation process. However, the broad conceptual terms outlined by Schrempp and Eaton guided the detailed work.
- ***Governance.*** The history records regular briefings of the boards of Chrysler and Daimler-Benz, and formal votes of the two boards before signing the definitive agreement. Shareholder votes were the critical and final step in the deal process.
- ***Document focus.*** Though the deal process here did not feature a letter of intent, it was plainly oriented toward a document-centered task: drafting and signing a definitive agreement. This agreement is a formal manifestation of a broader range of understandings surrounding a vision of creating the new firm.

SUMMARY AND CONCLUSIONS

The purpose of this chapter is to survey the process by which a deal takes shape and to highlight some of the "rules of the road" and risks that influence the shaping process. Five key takeaways from this discussion are:

1. ***Let an attitude of* risk management *guide the deal-shaping process.*** Deal development is risky business. The chapter outlines a number of reasons why parties may fail to consummate a deal that seems to be very sensible. The chapter also discusses how the legal framework and adept management of different phases of the process can help manage the risk exposure of the deal.
2. ***Learn the rules.*** Ignorance of the law is no excuse for illegal behavior. Though one must rely on expert advice on fine points, it is essential for the M&A professional to have a basic knowledge of the legal framework surrounding mergers and acquisitions. *Observe the spirit, as well as the letter, of laws, regulations, and court precedents.* There are few "bright lines" that separate acceptable from unacceptable behavior. Managers necessarily must reflect on what they do and why.

3. ***Be aware that project leadership skills are at a premium.*** Shaping the deal is a complex task. Governance requires the satisfaction of procedural steps that come in a certain order. One must focus on good process and trust that, in doing so, a good outcome will emerge. M&A is too important to be left to technicians. The complexity of the process described in this chapter suggests that excellence in deal doing rests fundamentally on diverse skills of process management.
4. ***Get expert professional help.*** The best path forward is not well defined, and the risks to the deal are legion. Some missteps may expose directors and corporate executives to personal financial liability. The chapter outlines the areas of expertise that may be required: law, accounting, investment banking, and public relations, to name a few.
5. ***Stay in charge of the process.*** The Daimler-Chrysler case study illustrates that executives from Daimler and Chrysler were intimately involved with the development of the deal. While they plainly delegated some responsibilities to lower-level managers and financial advisers, they and their boards of directors remained in control of the deal shaping process.

NOTES

1. Covenants such as indemnification provisions and earnout plans usually extend beyond closing.
2. After electricity markets are deregulated, prices may fall, rendering some plants and projects unprofitable. The cost of the investment in these assets is said to be "stranded." Utilities usually seek to recover the lost investment through rate increases, which are subject to approval by regulatory commissions. See Dean Starkman, "DQE Calls Off Its Planned Acquisition by Allegheny Energy, Citing Regulators," *Wall Street Journal*, July 29, 1998.
3. Quoted in Scott Kilman and Robin Sidel, "Judge Rules against Tyson in IBP Takeover Case," *Wall Street Journal*, June 18, 2001.
4. In 1983, First Lady Nancy Reagan advocated a drug abuse prevention program that had the popular slogan, "Just say no." This preceded a series of court decisions that seemed to legitimize the power of CEOs to reject merger proposals without bringing them to the board of directors or shareholders. Thus, the defense of a firm but simple rejection—"just say no"—was born. The effectiveness of this defense relies on the firm's past financial performance and the height of its share price. Poorly performing targets rarely fend off an insistent suitor by just saying no.
5. The "bear hug" is a technique just one step short of a hostile tender offer. The buyer sends a merger proposal directly to the target firm's board of directors—bypassing the CEO. Typically, the financial offer is high enough to warrant serious consideration by the directors, who may elect to appoint a special committee (i.e., excluding the CEO) to negotiate a sale of the target.
6. A "tender offer" invites the target company shareholders to submit ("tender") their shares to the buyer in return for offered payment. Tender offers for public companies are subject to rules of the U.S. Securities and Exchange Commission. A tender offer is judged "hostile" when the target company management and board are opposed to the offer.

7. See *Kysor Indus. Corp. v. Margaux Inc.*, Del. Super., 674 A. 2d 889 (1996) and *Brazen v. Bell Atlantic Corp.*, 695 A. 2d 43 (Del. 1977).
8. 485 U.S. 224 (1988).
9. Most market rumors are patently false. Therefore, it is tempting to quash the false rumors forthrightly. But suppose your firm is in merger negotiations, at a delicate stage where it is early to say that the deal is "probable." If, having quashed earlier false rumors you now reply with "no comment," canny investors will assume that means "yes" and start trading in the target as if it is in play.
10. Hart-Scott-Rodino Antitrust Improvements Act of 1976, Pub. L. No. 94-435, 90 Stat. 1390, 15 U.S.C. §§18a et seq.
11. For simplicity, the discussion refers to one board—usually the target's board must consider the transaction. But in the event of a merger (in which a new legal entity will emerge from the combination of two firms), where new shares are to be authorized, or in any transaction requiring shareholder approvals as outlined in the bylaws of the firm, the shareholders of the buyer may also be required to vote on the transaction.
12. Press release, Daimler-Benz A.G., May 6, 1998.
13. "Gentlemen, Start Your Engines," *Fortune*, June 8, 1998, page 140. © 1998 Time, Inc. All rights reserved.
14. John Pepper, "Why Eaton Cut the Deal," *Detroit News*, May 7, 1998, detnews.com. Reprinted by permission from the *Detroit News*.
15. The following bullet points paraphrase or quote directly from the merger proxy/prospectus and F-4 statement jointly filed by Daimler-Benz and Chrysler with the Securities and Exchange Commission on August 6, 1998.
16. In a consolidation, each entity merges into a third consolidating entity. See Chapter 19 for detail on this.

CHAPTER 26

Governance in M&A: The Board of Directors and Shareholder Voting

INTRODUCTION

After two CEOs negotiate the terms of merger, the deal shaping process turns to gaining approval from the owners of the firm. The perspective of investors can be easily anticipated: They seek the preservation or increase of wealth. The perspective of the corporate director is more complicated, and governed by corporate rules, government regulations, and court opinion. To understand the deal approval process requires understanding the perspectives of directors, and more generally the challenge of corporate governance.

"Governance" is the action of controlling or directing. In a corporate setting, governance entails a system of oversight and delegation of decisions that reaches from the owners of the firm (the shareholders) to the board of directors, and from there to senior, middle, and front-line managers. The board of directors plays a key role of promoting shareholder interests in the management of the firm. Through processes of executive hiring and firing, compensation, auditing, review of financial performance, and approval of major decisions (such as mergers) the board influences management in its conduct of business. The chain of shareholders-directors-managers suggests one other important attribute of governance: It is inherently political, as reflected in the accumulation and exercise of decision-making power. Legislation and court law limit possible abuses of this power, though participants in corporate politics retain wide latitude in their actions. For governance purposes, the law of the firm's state of incorporation applies. About 50 percent of publicly owned corporations in the United States are incorporated in Delaware, which gives Delaware courts unusual influence in establishing doctrine regarding governance.

The M&A professional should understand elements of good governance. These transactions generate a disproportionate volume of litigation, often surrounding the extent to which corporate directors fulfilled their duties. The best hedge against the risk of litigation is scrupulous observance of high standards of governance. Moreover, the collapses of Enron, WorldCom, Tyco, and Adelphia in 2001 and 2002 remind us that positive track record, large size, and prominent position are no guarantee of the effectiveness of governance processes. The professional must be vigilant.

Key lessons of this chapter include these points:

- Governance of the firm entails supervision and control in the interest of shareholders.
- Complexity, size, diffuse ownership, conflicting interests of owners and agents, and moral hazard can frustrate good governance.
- Research finds that good governance pays in the sense of being associated with value creation for shareholders.
- Shareholders rule. In countries with the "Anglo-American" common law legal system, shareholders exercise their will through election of directors, voting on resolutions at annual meetings, *jawboning*, proxy fights, and litigation. In "civil law" countries, shareholders also rule, but often share some power with other stakeholders (e.g., employees).
- Directors are representatives of shareholders and are obliged to govern with care and loyalty to shareholder interests. Courts are reluctant to meddle in business decisions by the board, except in cases of gross negligence. This chapter defines and illustrates gross negligence. Grossly negligent directors expose themselves to litigation and large financial penalties.
- Seeking or giving board approval for an M&A transaction should entail a process of careful and disinterested review of the proposal.

GOVERNING WELL IS HARD TO DO

At the outset, one must acknowledge a gulf between idealized governance and actual practice. Critics point not only to recent prominent business collapses, but also to other firms that underperform their potential consistently, violate laws and accounting principles, respond inadequately to predictable business surprises, permit management to become deeply entrenched, squander excess cash, overcompensate managers, initiate misguided diversification strategies, and consummate bad M&A deals. One asks, "Who was minding the store? What can they have been thinking? Why didn't a rational system of governance intervene?" For instance, Michael Jensen wrote,

> *The problems with internal corporate governance systems start with the board of directors. The board, at the apex of the internal control system, has the final responsibility for the functioning of the firm. Most important, it sets the rules of the game for the CEO. The job of the board is to hire, fire, and compensate the CEO, and to provide high-level counsel. The very purpose of the internal control mechanism is to provide an early warning system to put the organization back on track before difficulties reach a crisis stage.*[1]

Governance systems must surmount a range of challenges to be effective:

- ***Information and expertise.*** Even relatively small firms and M&A deals can exceed the grasp of directors. M&A is fairly specialized, and a typical deal has many dimensions, a bundle of attributes across which the deal designer seeks to find an acceptable blend. Determining what is good is a matter of detailed research, analysis, and judgment. Good governance should accommodate complexity. This may mean delegating some tasks to experts and relying on their opinions. But it may also mean providing sufficient information to decision makers.

- ***Silent investors.*** For virtually all public corporations, and many private ones, ownership of the firm is diffuse and separated from active control of the firm. To pick an extreme example, General Electric's 9.9 billion shares outstanding are held by 2.1 million shareholders. In such a setting, it is impossible for an individual shareholder to have much influence, or even to be heard, in operating decisions. Over 50 percent of public corporate shares, worth $9.7 trillion, are held by large institutional investors, such as insurance companies, pension funds, and mutual funds. Yet these players tend to remain silent and passive. Legal doctrine in the United States and many other countries holds that firms are to be operated in the best interests of shareholders. But if shareholders are dispersed and weak, or concentrated and silent, management and the board of directors may feel little threat of discipline from shareholders.
- ***Agency costs and moral hazard.*** *Agency costs* arise where agents pursue their own interests to the detriment of owners. Such costs include the appropriation of value by managers in the form of salary and perquisites, entrenchment by managers to make their jobs more secure, engagement in risky or unprofitable projects, and so on. Morck, Schleifer, and Vishny (1988) explain: "When managers hold little equity in the firm and shareholders are too dispersed to enforce value maximization, corporate assets may be deployed to benefit managers rather than shareholders."[2] Good governance seeks to minimize these costs to shareholders through schemes of monitoring, control, and executive compensation that align the interests of managers with those of shareholders. These costs arise because of:
    - Information asymmetries that grant insiders (the agents) a better picture of the firm than outsiders (the owners). If information and expertise were readily and cheaply available, owners could easily monitor agents and agency costs would disappear.
    - Less than full ownership of the firm by managers, providing an incentive to consume benefits and perquisites beyond what a sole proprietor would consume.[3]
- ***Board composition and culture.*** Critics point to boards composed significantly of insider-managers, or friends of the CEO. On many major boards, the CEO is also the chairman, effectively setting the agenda for board discussions. Large boards, running to 20 or 30 directors, frustrate frank and intimate counsel for the CEO. Finally, some boards evolve unspoken traditions or norms of politeness and respect that cede to the CEO a presumption that "management knows best."
- ***Incentive problems.*** Many directors hold minuscule financial interests relative to their personal net worth in the corporations they govern. This, combined with sizable potential legal liabilities from lawsuits and adverse media publicity, creates an incentive to minimize risk, rather than maximize value.

Since the landmark article by Jensen and Meckling in 1976, the fields of law and economics have wrestled with the costs that arise from delegation. Good governance reduces agency costs through a variety of mechanisms:

- ***Compensation.*** In the form of equity or equity-like securities (e.g., stock options) executive compensation can help align the interests of managers and shareholders and motivate managers to maximize shareholder wealth.
- ***Monitoring.*** Systems of financial reporting and performance review can help identify the economic results of individual business units and their managers. Metrics such as economic value added (EVA) and discounted cash flow (DCF) can lend insights into actions necessary to improve shareholder wealth.
- ***Financial contracting.*** Binding the managers through contracts aimed at achieving goals can be highly motivational. For instance, earnout payment schemes used in M&A can stimulate a target's management to achieve results necessary to make the deal profitable. Leveraged buyout structures have a similar effect: Binding owner-managers to meet an aggressive debt repayment schedule can motivate them to achieve the cash flow targets required. Jensen (1986), Schleifer and Vishny (1989), and others have argued that in the absence of significant ownership stakes, managers will undertake wealth-destroying strategies to pursue their own goals[4] to the detriment of the firm's owners. Jensen wrote: "The [free cash flow] theory implies managers of firms with unused borrowing power and large free cash flows are more likely to undertake low-benefit or even value-destroying mergers. Diversification programs generally fit this category, and the theory predicts they will generate lower gains."[5]
- ***Jawboning.*** Hirschman (1970) contrasts voice with exit as possible actions by a principal who disagrees with an agent's actions. In the context of institutional investors, exit corresponds to the "Wall Street Rule" (i.e., if you do not like management, sell your shares). Voice, on the other hand, entails a process of exhortation to management and coalition building among investors and directors to influence a firm's board and managers, in response to what Hirschman calls "an objectionable state of affairs." Schleifer and Vishny (1986) discuss voice or jawboning along with tender offers and proxy fights as means by which a large minority shareholder can monitor management. They show that the choice of jawboning versus tender offers and proxy fights will depend on the balance of costs and benefits associated with each.

GOOD GOVERNANCE PAYS

Numerous studies suggest that strong systems of governance result in higher market valuations. Typically, researchers form a governance index to measure the quality of governance practices and test for the significance of a relationship with company valuation using measures such as cumulative returns, price/earnings ratios, or Tobin's Q (the ratio of market value of equity to book value of equity). The general findings are these:

- ***Worldwide, firms with stronger governance practices tend to trade at higher market values.*** Shareholder protections vary significantly among countries. Differences in laws and their enforcement are associated with variations in valuations.[6] Lee and Ng (2002) find that firms from countries with higher levels of corruption trade at lower valuation multiples. More generally, La Porta et al. (2000) note that efficiency of investment, breadth and depth of capital markets, dividend policies, ownership structures, and new security issuance are associated with how well legal systems protect shareholders and creditors. Even a firm in a country with strong governance laws and practices can opt out of certain governance provisions through amendments to the firm's charter and bylaws. Generally,[7] firms with stronger governance practices are more highly valued.

Finally, looking across the entire range of firms and countries, Klapper and Love (2002) find a significant relation between strength of governance and valuation of the firm. This finding extends even to emerging countries where governance institutions at the national level may be relatively weak, but at the firm level, the governance is strong. The study also finds that firm-level governance is weaker in countries with weak legal systems, suggesting that enhancing the legal system should remain a priority for policymakers. Gilson (1994) suggests that corporate governance may be linked to economic performance through its ability to monitor and discipline management, and through its ability to create sufficient stability for a firm to honor implicit contracts necessary to realize internal business transformations through strategies based on lean manufacturing, total quality management, alliance networks, and so on.

- ***Activism by institutional investors is valuable.*** Institutions such as pension funds and life insurance companies are distinct from individual investors by their large size, strong performance orientation, close proximity to markets, ability to withstand transaction costs, and, generally, being well informed. Events in which these investors become active (i.e., in the sense of seeking to influence the board of directors, etc.) are associated with the creation of shareholder value. Black (1992a,b) has argued that institutional voice is potentially valuable because of the need for someone to monitor corporate managers. It can add value by increasing the independence of corporate directors, discouraging bad takeovers, encouraging more efficient governance rules, discouraging cash hoarding, and establishing a more arm's-length process for setting CEO pay.

  The empirical evidence is consistent with the hypothesis that voice is valuable. Nesbitt (1994) finds that intervention by CalPERS, a large pension fund, is associated with excess returns of 41 percent over the five years following intervention. Smith (1996) finds significant positive excess returns associated with activism by CalPERS, but no significant effect on operating performance. Gordon Group (1992) reports excess returns from *institutional activism* of up to 30 percent. Agrawal and Mandelker (1990) discovered that companies with high institutional ownership experience event returns that are much more positive in response to antitakeover amendment proposals. And McConnell and Servaes (1990) concluded that institutional ownership correlates with Tobin's Q and with accounting measures of profitability. Pound (1988), Jarrell and Poulsen (1987), Brickley, Lease, and Smith (1988), and Gordon and Pound (1993) give evidence that the presence of institutional ownership is associated with a higher probability of dissidents winning proxy contests, with lower adoption of value-decreasing antitakeover proposals, and with the success of shareholder-sponsored proposals to change corporate governance structures. Bruner (1999) analyzed share price response to institutional investor resistance to the proposed merger of Volvo and Renault. Abnormal returns associated with institutional activism were positive and significant during the period of active opposition. The case of Volvo-Renault suggests that institutional voice is valuable.

- ***Governance intervention by shareholders is associated with increased shareholder value.*** Investors can influence directors and managers through proxy fights, shareholder resolutions, lawsuits, and jawboning. Generally, these are associated with positive changes in firm value. Ultimately, target company shareholders may support a hostile takeover, the ultimate mechanism of market discipline. Hostile takeovers are associated with creation of value for targets and buyers.[8]
- ***Restructuring to align the interests of managers and shareholders is associated with higher firm valuation.*** Alignment occurs through equity-like compensation systems, and performance measurement based on economic value. Conflicts of interest impose penalties on firm valuations, consistent with the theory of agency costs originally proposed by Jensen and Meckling (1976). Studies of leveraged buyouts,[9] replacement of executives of underperforming firms,[10] and corporate restructurings[11] reveal significant gains in equity value following realignment and improved governance.

HOW SHAREHOLDERS RULE

In the United States and other countries with so-called Anglo-American, or common law legal traditions, shareholders retain ultimate power over the corporation. In countries with code-based law, such as much of continental Europe, corporate governance provides for a much more prominent role for unions and employees in the board of directors. In Japan, banks, suppliers, and customers may have a significant voice in the governance of the firm solemnized through "relationship investing" among industrial and financial firms—the famous *keiretsu*. Exhibit 26.1 summarizes some of the important differences among the Anglo-American, German, and Japanese governance systems. The detailed discussion that follows focuses on the *Anglo-American system*.

Foundational Documents for Shareholder Rule

Much of the M&A analysis and decision making is oriented toward the interests of shareholders. An extensive volume of case law sustains the shareholder orientation. Two key corporate documents afford the foundation for shareholder rule:

1. *Corporate charter also known as articles of incorporation.* When corporations are founded, they must be registered with the secretary of state of the state of incorporation to achieve the status of a "legal person." The *corporate charter* outlines the fundamental information about the firm, such as purpose, location of headquarters, nature of business, powers under state law, authorized classes of securities to be issued, and the rights and liabilities of shareholders and directors.
2. *Corporate bylaws.* The bylaws of a corporation are adopted by shareholders, much like a founding constitution. These state the procedure for voting, number and election of directors, duties of directors, appointment of senior executives, creation of new shares of stock, how shareholder meetings may be called,

EXHIBIT 26.1 Summary Comparison of Anglo-American, German, and Japanese Systems of Corporate Governance

	Anglo-American	German	Japanese
Type	Transactional. Control and performance driven.	Relational through formal kinds of contracts.	Relational through informal contracts and placement of "alumni" officers in firms.
Ownership	Relatively diffuse and fluid; transience based on perception of opportunity. Perhaps 50%+ of shares are held by institutional investors who trade actively. Cross-shareholdings are rare.	Dedicated capital. Relatively concentrated. Investors (typically banks) hold for long periods and advise the firm. Cross-shareholdings are common.	Relatively concentrated. Investors (typically other industrial firms) hold for long periods. *Keiretsu* rule: cross-shareholdings by affiliated companies, including customers and suppliers, centered on a main bank.
Focus	Maximization of shareholder value as measured by stock price.	Perpetuation of the firm, in the belief that this serves interests of shareholders and employees.	Growth in market share and continued employment.
Board election and composition	Shareholder rule. Board elected directly by shareholders; no other groups represented. Board has majority of outsiders.	Two-board system of stakeholder rule: Power-sharing between stockholders and employees. Unions are represented on boards. Intent is to bind together in the board with potential conflicts of interest. Each group holds a veto over election of other group's representatives. Selection process is geared toward building consensus.	Board elected by shareholders. Composed primarily of insiders.

(Continued)

EXHIBIT 26.1 *(Continued)*

	Anglo-American	German	Japanese
Government intervention	Relatively slight. Through securities regulation and civil litigation.	Decreasingly interventionist. Historically active in stimulating the development of "national champions" whose growth they promote through subsidies and trade barriers.	Powerful. Japanese Ministry of Finance (MOF) governs all regulations, even flows of capital through *gyosei shido*, "administrative guidance."
Capital market discipline	Relatively high. Proxy contests, hostile tender offers. Institutional investors become active in periods of declining performance.	Low. Hostile takeovers and proxy contests are rare. Financial institutions influence the board through direct participation on the board.	Low. Hostile takeovers and proxy contests are rare. Institutional investors are relatively quiet. Selective intervention, active monitoring by main banks.
Executive "contract"	Annual bonuses tied to corporate financial performance. Relatively high turnover. Relatively high use of equity-linked compensation (e.g., options).	Modest bonuses, not tied to profits. Relatively low executive turnover. Comparatively modest cash compensation; relatively low equity-linked compensation.	Lifetime employment. Semiannual bonuses. But executive pay not tied tightly to profits. Comparatively modest cash compensation; relatively low equity-linked compensation and turnover.
Criticisms	"Hot money" mentality promotes short-term focus and opportunistic thinking among directors and executives.	Bureaucratic structure and union role distracts directors and managers from focusing on economic efficiency.	*Keiretsu* structure, culture of consensus, and central planning mentality of MOF breed economic inefficiency.

and how resolutions may be presented to shareholders.[12] Rules regarding the amendment of *corporate bylaws* vary by state; for instance, in Delaware, only shareholders get to amend the bylaws unless the charter allows exceptions; in New York, the board of directors has amendment power, but shareholders have power to override the board; in Illinois, the board has exclusive power to amend the bylaws unless the charter makes exception.

Votes per Share

Typically, shareholders vote only at shareholder meetings that are held once a year. Most corporations allocate ballots on the basis of *one share, one vote*, a scheme favored by the New York Stock Exchange from 1926 to 1989 in its requirements for a firm to gain listing on the NYSE. One share, one vote was the widely prevailing view, though some corporations had adopted a *dual-class voting* scheme in which each senior share has more voting power (e.g., 10 votes), and each junior share has less voting power (e.g., one vote). Typically, this reflected the desire of a founder's family to maintain its ongoing influence over the corporation. Then, in the 1980s, a wave of *dual-class recapitalizations* occurred,[13] mainly as an antitakeover defense to concentrate votes in friendly hands. In the typical dual-class recapitalization, the shareholder would swap an ordinary share (with votes) for a nonvoting share that paid a higher dividend. Fearing managerial entrenchment, in 1994 the SEC issued Rule 19c-4 that prohibited the reduction of voting rights to existing shareholders, though it did allow new issues of low- or nonvoting common stock. Then the Business Roundtable successfully sued the SEC to prevent enforcement of this rule.[14] However, the major stock exchanges were pressured by the SEC to adopt rules that mirrored Rule 19c-4. They permitted firms to make dual-class recapitalizations after a majority vote of directors and shareholders and other conditions were met.[15]

Of 1,900 publicly listed firms in 1999, 219 had classes of shares with unequal voting rights.[16] These firms included names well known to investors and consumers: Adolph Coors, Ben & Jerry's Homemade, Berkshire Hathaway, Carmike Cinemas, Coca-Cola Bottling, Dow Jones, Excite@Home, J. M. Smucker, Nike, Polo Ralph Lauren, Times Mirror, Viacom, and Wm. Wrigley. Shares with superior voting power typically trade at higher prices than do their junior siblings. Lease, McConnell, and Mikkelson (1983) observed an average premium of 4 percent. The hypothesis is that the premium reflects the private benefits to holders of superior shares that accrue from higher voting power.

Proxies

It is impractical to expect all shareholders of a large corporation to attend a meeting. Therefore, most corporate bylaws permit voting by *proxy*, a ballot submitted by an absent shareholder to the directors with instructions how to vote on resolutions presented at the meeting. Occasionally, competing parties will submit proposals (such as competing slates for the election of directors) to the shareholders, and will engage in solicitation of proxies or votes, using a firm that specializes in proxy solicitation.[17] Proxy contests present one route for corporate takeover: A raider will seek to replace the target's board of directors by nominating an alternative slate of directors and soliciting votes through a proxy contest. Then the raider would rescind the target's antitakeover defenses, and proceed with a cash tender offer to the shareholders.

Supermajority Provisions

Shareholder will is typically determined by a majority vote (e.g., 50.1 percent) on resolutions presented at the annual meeting. The bylaws may specify, however, that some kinds of resolutions (e.g., to sell the company) require a supermajority vote such as 66, 75, or 85 percent to be approved. *Supermajority provisions* are a standard type of antitakeover defense. As of 1999, 218 companies out of 1,900 listed on major stock exchanges required a supermajority vote to approve a merger.[18]

Cumulative Voting for Directors

On selected issues, such as election of directors, the charter and bylaws may specify either *straight voting* or *cumulative voting*. Under straight voting, the shareholder wields votes equal to the number of shares on each candidate independently. Under cumulative voting, a shareholder is granted votes equal to the number of shares held times the number of directors to be elected, and can allocate votes at will, in the extreme giving all his or her cumulative votes to just one director. The cumulative voting system makes it easier for cohesive, but minority, groups of shareholders to gain representation on the board.

Exhibit 26.2 gives an example of voting for directors under the cumulative and noncumulative schemes. Jay Gould owns 200 shares of Olde Upstate Railroad. A majority group, dominated by Jim Fisk, owns the other 800 shares. Upstate's rules call for cumulative voting for the election of directors. Gould feels threatened by Fisk and wants to elect *at least one* director to the board to protect his interests. Therefore, Gould has nominated one candidate friendly to himself. Meanwhile, Fisk and his group of directors want to fill *all five* empty board seats, and have nominated five candidates sympathetic to Fisk. In straight voting, Gould would elect no directors, as his number of votes (200) would be dominated on voting for each seat by Fisk's votes (800). Gould would be denied representation on the board. But under cumulative voting Gould would have 1,000 votes (200 times 5 seats to be filled) versus Fisk's votes of 4,000 (800 times 5). If Gould concentrates all his votes on one candidate, he will elect at least one of the five, since Fisk must spread his votes among the five directors. Gould's votes will exceed the votes that Fisk can allocate to elect any one director (4,000 divided by 5).

Shareholder Influence through Litigation

A final way in which shareholders can influence a corporation is through lawsuits. M&A transactions generate a significant amount of litigation, typically around the claim that the target's board of directors has neglected its fiduciary duties in some way. For example, the shareholder might claim that directors or management entrenched themselves or manipulated the governance process to deny the shareholder fair standing on some decision. In another example, the shareholder might claim that a proposed transaction would harm the welfare of shareholders. Litigation around takeover defenses frequently entails claims of entrenchment and economic harm.

EXHIBIT 26.2 Example of Voting for Directors, Comparing Cumulative and Noncumulative Voting Schemes

Problem: Jay Gould owns 200 shares and a majority group dominated by Jim Fisk owns the other 800 shares of the Olde Upstate Railroad. Upstate's rules call for cumulative voting for the election of directors. Gould wants to elect at least one director to the board, while Fisk and his group of directors want to fill all five empty board seats. In straight voting, Gould would elect no directors, as his number of votes (200) would be dominated on voting for each seat by Fisk's votes (800). Gould would be denied representation on the board. But under cumulative voting Gould would have 1,000 votes (200 times 5 seats to be filled), versus Fisk's votes of 4,000 (800 times 5). If Gould concentrates all his votes on one candidate, he will elect at least one of the five, since Gould's votes will exceed the votes necessary to elect one director (4,000 divided by 5).

Number of nominees	6
Number of seats to fill	5
Number of shares	1,000

Shareholder		Straight Voting	Cumulative Voting
Fisk (majority)	800	800	4,000
Gould (dissident)	200	200	1,000
Votes per majority nominee		800	800
Votes per dissident nominee		200	1,000
Number of seats the dissident can elect		0.25	1.25

Source: "Cumulative Voting Example.xls" on the CD-ROM.

Lawsuits may be brought in two ways:

1. ***Direct.*** The lawsuit is brought for the benefit of the shareholder-plaintiff, who has control over its direction. The shareholder claims that he or she directly was harmed by some action of the directors.
2. ***Derivative.*** The lawsuit is brought for the benefit of the corporation (i.e., the corporation suing some or all of its own directors). The shareholder initiating the derivative lawsuit claims the corporation was harmed by some action of the directors. Here the control resides in the corporation, which may decide whether and how to pursue the lawsuit.

Lawsuits may be designated as a class action to represent the interests of an entire group of injured claimants who, as of the date of initiating the lawsuit, may not yet be fully identified.

Shareholder Influence through Jawboning

Shleifer and Vishny (1986) cite jawboning to influence a board of directors to abandon a value-destroying course of action. Black (1992a) and others have hypothesized that jawboning or institutional voice is valuable. The case of institutional investor resistance to the proposed merger of Volvo and Renault (see Bruner 1999) reveals a variety of forms that jawboning can take.

- Asking questions/demanding more information.
- Direct communication with the board of directors.
- Public announcements of deferral of support.
- Public announcements of opposition.
- Threats to sue.
- Demand for renegotiation of the merger terms.
- Demand for resignation of the chairman and/or the board.

FIDUCIARY DUTIES OF TARGET DIRECTORS IN CONSIDERING M&A

The target's board typically ratifies the definitive agreement and commits itself to present the deal to shareholders and seek their approval. The board of the target (and probably the buyer if the deal is material) will have been briefed on the progress of merger negotiations. Typically, the definitive agreement requires an affirmative vote of the directors and their recommendation of the deal to shareholders. The actions of directors are measured against three doctrines of rising degrees of intervention by courts: the *business judgment rule*, *enhanced scrutiny*, and *entire fairness*.

First Standard of Review: Business Judgment Rule

Courts are reluctant to second-guess the appropriateness of managerial and board decisions—if you can prove you made a "reasonable judgment" at the time, you cannot be found liable for damages that may have arisen. Judges are not business professionals; business decisions can go wrong for many reasons; and business is generally risky. The "business judgment rule" is court doctrine that discourages intervention in board decisions if directors and officers fulfill their duties in good faith—that is, if they are not conflicted, are informed, and act in rational belief that the transaction serves shareholder interests.[19] Where the business judgment rule applies, directors are protected unless a plaintiff can prove violation of the directors' duties. Thus, at the heart of the business judgment rule are two key duties that govern the deliberations of directors: the duty of loyalty and the duty of care.

1. *Duty of loyalty.* The duty of loyalty requires directors to make decisions in the interests of shareholders and avoid conflicts with other interested parties. In legal actions that challenge directors under the duty of loyalty, the burden of proof is on the plaintiffs to show members of the board engaged in self-dealing transactions. Ordinarily an arm's-length transaction (i.e., where the directors have no personal interest in the outcome) will not present loyalty problems. Where potential conflicts of interest may exist for some directors, the board should grant powers of review to a committee of independent directors. A classic example of the violation of the duty of loyalty is given in the case *Guth v. Loft*.[20] Guth, the president of Loft, Inc., had appropriated for himself the right

to acquire a Pepsi-Cola bottling operation, a right that was judged to belong to the company. The Supreme Court of Delaware opined that "corporate officers and directors are not permitted to use their position of trust and confidence to further their private interests. While technically not trustees, they stand in a fiduciary relation to the corporation and its stockholders."

2. ***Duty of care.*** The duty of care requires directors to be well informed and diligent in considering all aspects of issues before them, including consideration of relevant materials and the opinions of competent advisers. The plaintiff must prove that the directors' conduct has risen to the level of gross negligence. A classic illustration of the duty of care is given in a court decision in the case of *Lutz v. Boas*,[21] in which the plaintiff charged directors with a failure to properly oversee the management of mutual funds. The court agreed that directors gave "almost automatic approval . . . did not examine registration statements . . . did not discuss securities . . . did not know who selected securities for purchase or sale," and so on. The court found the directors in this case to be grossly negligent.

CASES INVOLVING VIOLATION OF DUTIES A famous case illustrating the consequences of failing in a director's duty of care is *Smith v. Van Gorkom*.[22] In 1980, Van Gorkom, CEO of Transcom, sought to take the company private in a leveraged buyout, with himself to be CEO and key investor in the private company. The announcement of the prospective LBO elicited a *higher* bid per share from another firm. The directors of Transcom approved Van Gorkom's bid after a brief meeting, without all directors present, without expert opinion comparing the two deals, and even though Transcom shareholders would receive less money. Disaffected Transcom shareholders sued their directors and were awarded damages equal to the difference of what they would have received under the higher offer—to be paid for by the directors. In the wake of the decision, boards of directors have pursued higher standards of deliberation and disclosure to shareholders. "Smith v. Van Gorkom.pdf" on the CD-ROM gives excerpts from the decision in *Smith v. Van Gorkom*. Some practitioners assign this to novices as required introductory reading in the field of M&A. It highlights a number of practices to avoid and, by implication, good practices to pursue.

In a duty of care lawsuit, the business judgment rule deflects court scrutiny from the substance of the management decision, though the court will tend to look at the *procedure* by which the decision was reached. A classic example of the application of the business judgment rule is given in the case of *Puma v. Marriott*.[23] Here, the plaintiffs challenged the fairness of the acquisition of certain properties by Marriott Corporation from the Marriott family, essentially a claim of insider dealing against the interests of outside shareholders of Marriott. The court did not find a violation of the duties of loyalty or care and concluded that "since the transaction complained of was accomplished as a result of the exercise of independent business judgment of the outside, independent directors whose sole interest was the furtherance of the corporate enterprise, the court is precluded from substituting its uninformed opinion for that of the experienced, independent board members of Marriott."

In *Aronson v. Lewis*[24] the court said, "The business judgment rule is an acknowledgement of the managerial prerogatives of . . . directors. . . . It is a presumption that in making a business decision the directors of a corporation acted on an informed basis, in good faith and in the honest belief that the action taken was in the best interests of the company. . . . Absent an abuse of discretion, that judgment will be respected by the courts. . . . [The business judgment rule] has no role where directors have either abdicated their functions or absent a conscious decision, failed to act."

"Survey of Key Court Cases.pdf" on the CD-ROM summarizes 15 key court cases in the area of directors' duties with which the M&A practitioner should be familiar.

Second Standard of Review: Enhanced Scrutiny

In certain instances, such as hostile tender offers and auctions, the courts have acknowledged that some business problems may warrant a higher level of judicial scrutiny. Before applying the business judgment rule, the court will first examine the directors' decision-making process and the reasonableness of the action; this is "enhanced scrutiny."

In 1985, Mesa Petroleum commenced a hostile tender offer for Unocal Corporation at a bid of $54 per share. Mesa had already purchased 13 percent of Unocal's shares in the open market. Unocal's directors, advised that a fair price for the firm would be $70 to $75 per share, rejected Mesa's bid and commenced a self-tender for its shares at $72—explicitly excluding Mesa from the offer. Mesa sued Unocal, arguing that the discriminatory exchange offer violated duties that Unocal owed to Mesa, a shareholder. Unocal replied that its board approved the exchange offer in good faith, with good information, and exercising care, to protect the firm and its shareholders from Mesa's hostile bid. In *Unocal Corporation v. Mesa Petroleum Co.*,[25] the court opined:

> *When a board addresses a pending takeover bid it has an obligation to determine whether the offer is in the best interests of the corporation and its shareholders. In that respect a board's duty is no different from any other responsibility it shoulders, and its decisions should be no less entitled to the respect they otherwise would be accorded in the realm of business judgment. There are, however, certain caveats to a proper exercise of this function. Because of the omnipresent specter that a board may be acting primarily in its own interests, rather than those of the corporation and its shareholders, there is an enhanced duty that calls for judicial examination at the threshold before the protections of the business judgment rule may be conferred.*

The court imposed two tests under its enhanced scrutiny:

1. The board must show that it had *reasonable grounds for believing a danger to corporate policy and effectiveness existed*, arising from the hostile bid. The basis for this belief must be good faith, reasonable investigation, and deliberation by independent directors. The threat could take the form of:

   - *Structural coercion.* For instance, the two-tier front-end-loaded tender offer[26] is regarded by some practitioners to be a type of offer designed to stampede shareholders to sell to the bidder. Chapters 32 and 33 discuss the dynamics of these offers in more detail.

- *Opportunity loss.* The bid may interrupt a strategy by target management to realize significantly higher shareholder value.
- *Substantive coercion.* The bid may be below the target's intrinsic value. For sound reasons (e.g., avoiding disclosure of sensitive competitive information), management may be unable to present a convincing case to shareholders. The raider's bid exploits the asymmetry to coerce shareholders to sell for less than their shares are intrinsically worth.

2. The defensive response must be *reasonable in relation to the threat posed.* The judgment of reasonableness must be based, again, on careful analysis, the interests of the bid on a variety of constituencies (including subgroups of shareholders such as arbitrageurs), and the value adequacy of the bid.

The following year, the Supreme Court of Delaware extended its oversight of boards by imposing a duty to auction the target firm when the board has decided to sell the firm or control,[27] and when there are competing bidders. This emerged as the famous *Revlon Rule* in an opinion by the Supreme Court of Delaware in *Revlon, Inc. v. MacAndrews & Forbes Holdings.*[28] The raider, Ronald Perelman, had commenced a hostile tender offer against Revlon through his firm, Pantry Pride. Revlon's board, seeking to thwart the offer, agreed to sell the firm to Forstmann & Co., a leveraged buyout firm, and gave Forstmann a lockup option on Revlon and put in place other defenses to repel Pantry Pride. The Court opined:

> *However, when Pantry Pride increased its offer to $50 per share, and then to $53, it became apparent to all that the break-up of the company was inevitable. The Revlon board's authorization permitting management to negotiate a merger or buyout with a third party was a recognition that the company was for sale. The duty of the board had thus changed from the preservation of Revlon as a corporate entity to the maximization of the company's value at a sale for the stockholders' benefit. This significantly altered the board's responsibilities under the* Unocal *standards. It no longer faced threats to corporate policy and effectiveness, or to the stockholders' interests, from a grossly inadequate bid. The whole question of defensive measures became moot. The directors' role changed from defenders of the corporate bastion to auctioneers charged with getting the best price for the stockholders at a sale of the company. . . . The original threat posed by Pantry Pride—the break-up of the company—had become a reality which even the directors embraced. Selective dealing to fend off a hostile but determined bidder was no longer a proper objective. Instead, obtaining the highest price for the benefit of the stockholders should have been the central theme guiding director action. . . . When a board ends an intense bidding contest on an insubstantial basis, and where a significant by-product of that action is to protect the directors against a perceived threat of personal liability for consequences stemming from the adoption of previous defensive measures, the action cannot withstand the enhanced scrutiny which* Unocal *requires of director conduct.*

The Court enjoined the sale of Revlon to Forstmann and required the board to conduct an auction, which Pantry Pride won at a price of $2.3 billion. Perelman significantly restructured Revlon, selling assets for $2.06 billion (but retaining the cosmetics business for which he received a bid of $0.9 billion), suggesting a relatively short-term gain of 29 percent.[29]

Third Standard of Review: Entire Fairness

The highest level of court intervention occurs when an actual conflict of interest affects a majority of directors approving a transaction. In these cases, the defendants (directors) must show that the challenged action was entirely fair to the corporation and its shareholders: fair in terms of fair dealing and fair price. The court raised this standard in *Weinberger v. UOP Inc.*[30] Weinberger, a shareholder, challenged the fairness of terms by which Signal Companies would freeze out minority shareholders of UOP. The Supreme Court of Delaware found that the UOP board was not informed in its decision and imposed an "entire fairness standard."[31] Under this important standard, boards must assess an offer for a target firm from *both* the fairness of price and the fairness of dealing—the latter embraces candor, timing, structure of the transaction, access to information, and disclosure, especially about conflicts of information. The Court opined,

> *The concept of fairness has two basic aspects: fair dealing and fair price. The former embraces questions of when the transaction was timed, how it was initiated, structured, negotiated, disclosed to the directors, and how the approvals of the directors and the stockholders were obtained. The latter aspect of fairness relates to the economic and financial considerations of the proposed merger, including all relevant factors: assets, market value, earnings, future prospects, and any other elements that affect the intrinsic or inherent value of a company's stock. However, the test for fairness is not a bifurcated one as between fair dealing and price. All aspects of the issue must be examined as a whole since the question is one of entire fairness. However, in a nonfraudulent transaction we recognize that price may be the preponderant consideration outweighing other features of the merger.*

The possible need to establish "entire fairness" now motivates boards to obtain fairness opinions from competent outside experts, to conduct arm's-length negotiations (such as between the independent directors of the target and the buyer), and to fully disclose any conflicts of interest to the decision makers who are considering the transaction.

The entire fairness standard arises especially in a *minority freeze-out* where a subsidiary is merged into a parent, forcing any minority shareholders to accept payment at the offered rate. In such situations, controlling shareholders (the parent corporation) have a fiduciary duty to refrain from using control to obtain a special advantage or to cause the corporation to take an action that unfairly prejudices minority shareholders.

PRACTICAL IMPLICATIONS: PREPARING FOR THE BOARD'S REVIEW OF A DEAL

As a practical matter, directors must observe at least four obligations in their deliberations over an M&A transaction. First, the director must be loyal to shareholder interests. Directors, senior managers, and controlling shareholders must not self-deal. Second, directors must give careful analysis and deliberation. Lack of care invites court intervention, despite the business judgment rule. Third, directors must disclose personal interests and news. Shareholders must know all material information and be cognizant of any potential conflicts of interest when they are asked to approve a transaction. And finally, under some circumstances the board must conduct an auction when there are bidders competing to acquire the target. This is the duty of special care when the firm is a takeover target. Courts will apply special scrutiny to directors' actions, especially the decision process and use of any defensive tactics.

A board's review of a recommendation to buy or sell a company should include:

- ***The advice of a lawyer.*** The duties of the board are described here in only general terms. Case law continues to evolve. There are few yes/no answers available. To avoid jail and retain one's personal wealth, it is important to obtain competent legal advice at every step of the way.
- ***The advice of other expert opinion.*** Directors may be familiar with the industry, the target company, and the transaction. But they can hardly master the extensive detail on which the transaction has been based. Also, they may hold subtle (or not so subtle) biases. For these reasons, best practice in board oversight of M&A proposals is to draw on the opinion of experts in law, accounting, operations, human resources, and valuation. A key component of the board deliberations is the "fairness opinion," a letter opining on the fairness to selling shareholders of the purchase price, form of payment, and other aspects of the transaction. The board will present this to shareholders to assert the completeness of the process by which the board of directors evaluated the proposal. Hence, the fairness opinion, though written by financial advisers to the board, is shared with shareholders. The letter typically describes the analytic procedures used, and ends with the opinion that the deal is "fair"—not that the price is "best" or "better than others" or "attractive." As described in the valuation chapters of this book, it is extremely difficult to *observe* true intrinsic value of an asset. Language other than "fair" or "not fair" implies more clarity about intrinsic value than may be warranted. The CD-ROM gives an example of a fairness opinion (see "Lecture: The Merger Proxy Statement: How to Read It and What It Reveals.").
- ***Sufficient time to make an informed decision.*** It is unlikely that a single two- or three-hour meeting will yield enough time to survey all issues and to reflect independently on the interests of shareholders. Therefore, many such meetings are scheduled to occur in series: an evening meeting followed by a morning or daylong meeting the next day. If the M&A transaction is sufficiently complex, the meeting might span a weekend.

- ***Independence and privacy.*** The board should deliberate free of external pressures. It may be desirable to meet without the CEO (or anyone else who has become a strong advocate of the deal) and to *form a subcommittee of independent directors* to review and approve a proposal where there is any possibility of self-interest on the part of some members of the board. Meeting privately not only serves the goal of independent consideration, but also avoids leakage of news of an impending transaction. A gathering of prominent people in a public location can fuel rumors in the capital market. Also, it may make sense to meet after the close of capital markets on Friday, to leave enough time to craft a careful public disclosure of the deal on Monday morning when the market reopens.
- ***Comprehensive agenda.*** The meeting should review all aspects of the proposal and its consequences:
    - A recitation by legal counsel of the obligations of directors, of the decisions the board will be asked to make, and of the disclosures that must emanate from the meeting.
    - A summary by the CEO (and others responsible for negotiations) of the history of the deal, developments since the last board meeting, and structure of the proposed transaction.
    - A presentation of the due diligence research about the deal partner.
    - A presentation of the fairness of the deal to shareholders, given by the financial adviser to the board. This should compare the proposed deal to other offers that may be outstanding.
    - Review by legal counsel of the definitive agreement and regulatory filings.

The shareholder meeting is typically scheduled for a month or so after delivery of the prospectus. This affords time for the buyer and target to solicit proxies in favor of the transaction, typically relying on a proxy solicitation firm. Because of the proxy solicitation, the shareholder meeting often begins with a foregone conclusion in favor of the transaction. The meetings are conducted on formal rules of order: Approval of the deal is moved and seconded; shareholders may seek to amend the proposed transaction; there is discussion, and then a vote. Dissident shareholders may seek to present an alternative proposal. Frustrating such attempts may be devices such as bylaws, long deadlines, large numbers of required signatures (or consents), nominating committees, and special agenda-setting privileges.

CODA: HOW CAN FIRMS BE GOVERNED BETTER?

Following the large corporate failures of 2001 and 2002 (e.g., Enron, WorldCom, Tyco, Adelphia, and Global Crossing) business professionals have reflected intently on changes to be made in governance to forestall future crises. The range of suggestions includes these 15:

1. ***Tie the welfare of managers closely to that of shareholders.*** Aggressive use of option-based compensation was a hallmark of the 1990s. Call options carry

upside gain, and no consequences for loss. It would seem more appropriate to tailor equity-like securities that more fully mirror the gains and losses of shareholders.

2. ***Separate the offices of chairman and CEO.*** The agenda and direction of board meetings should be set by an independent (i.e., not insider) chairman. Separation of board chair from CEO allows the board to set its own agenda apart from that of management.
3. ***Promote transparency*** in the reporting of financial results and of equity ownership of managers and directors. The '34 Act requires officers and directors to file a report listing their holdings and a monthly update of any changes. But with modern information technology, the reporting of option exercises and the purchase or sale of common stock could be made instantaneously to the SEC, which could then convey the news through its EDGAR system or an Internet site.
4. ***Promote discussion among investors.*** Historically, U.S. securities laws have constrained the ability of institutional investors to confer and coordinate their actions. While this may have served its intended effect (limiting market manipulation), it also neuters collective action by shareholders.
5. ***Promote consultation between management and major investors.*** As noted earlier, jawboning by institutional investors enhances share values. But companies may be reluctant to engage candidly with some investors if under the regulations they must disclose to *all* investors any information divulged to a few. The rules of engagement could be modified to make it easier for institutional investors to confer with management on major issues. Lockheed-Martin (see Pound and Skowronski 1997) consults major investors on nominations of new directors.
6. ***Chair the board committees with independent directors.*** Chairs of the audit, nominations, and executive compensation committees set agendas for the entire board and draft policies for adoption. The Sarbanes-Oxley Act mandates that the audit committees of public companies be composed exclusively of independent directors.
7. ***Require that a majority of directors are independent.*** Independence from managerial influence is perhaps the first requisite for making policies consistent with shareholders' interests. For instance, regarding the mix of inside and outside directors, Spencer Stuart recently reported that for the S&P 500 firms in 2001, on average, 77 percent of directors were independent.[32] At issue is the definition of "independence" and the extent to which friendship and other ties might elude these measures.
8. ***Impose term limits on directors' service.*** Long time in service may breed complacency and intimacy with management. Term limits may enhance objectivity and freshness of viewpoint.
9. ***Limit board size*** to promote intimate and direct conversation among all board members.
10. ***Shareholders should be permitted to vote "no confidence"*** of management annually, which surpassing a threshold of the shares would trigger a housecleaning.
11. ***Directors should meet alone*** (i.e., without management) regularly.

12. ***The performance of boards should be audited*** by an outside firm, reporting directly to shareholders.
13. ***Directors should be limited in the number of boards*** on which they can sit.
14. ***Directors should be required to invest*** a significant portion of their own net worth in the equity of firms they direct.
15. ***Financial audits should not be paid for by the audited firms***, but rather by insurance companies or directly by shareholders.

Proposals such as these will warrant considerable debate. First, laws and regulations are imperfect instruments for guiding corporate behavior. Chapter 16 discusses the Sarbanes-Oxley Act and notes areas of inconsistency and ambiguity within it—for example, penalties for CEOs hinge on the proof of "misconduct" though the Act neglects to define the term.

Second, the behavior that new rules elicit is not necessarily what one may want. James Westphal (2002) reports that boards are moving toward many of these proposals already, and that unintended consequences have been increased politicization of board-level deliberations and a decline in cooperative interaction among directors and executives. Evidently, effective governance entails a trade-off between rules and human behavior. Colley et al. (2003) note that punitive taxation of large executive salaries stimulated the shift to compensation by means of options and stock. They speculate that as regulations tighten, going private may become more conducive to good business operations.

Third, independence and transparency in governance may not lead to greater *effectiveness* of decision making. Dahya and McConnell (2002) found that newly independent boards in the United Kingdom make different decisions with respect to CEO appointments—they are more likely to hire CEOs from outside the company and to fire CEOs following poor corporate performance. McConnell (2003, pages 30–31) writes,

> *Why, then, do I urge caution in coercing publicly traded companies to add outside directors? I do so for two reasons. First, as a strong believer in the virtues of a market economy, I am inherently inclined to believe that companies will supply the types of boards that investors demand. If investors demand outside directors, companies will supply them. The second reason I urge caution has to do with the shortcomings of the extant research on corporate boards. In particular, the research supports the conclusion that boards with outside directors make different decisions but the research has not yet demonstrated whether those decisions are better.*

Finally, Holmstrom and Kaplan (2003, page 20) argue that "despite its alleged flaws, the U.S. corporate governance system has performed very well, both on an absolute basis and relative to other countries. It is important to recognize that there is no perfect system and that we should try to avoid the pendulum-like movement so typical of political inspired system redesigns. The current problems arose in an exceptional period that is not likely to happen again soon. After all, it was almost 70 years ago that the corporate governance system last attracted such intervention."

NOTES

1. Michael C. Jensen, "The Modern Industrial Revolution, Exit, and the Failure of Internal Control Systems," in Donald C. Chew, ed., *International Corporate Finance and Governance Systems*, Oxford: Oxford University Press, 1997, page 32.
2. See Morck, Schleifer, and Vishny (1988), page 293.
3. The agency problems described here focus on relations between managers and equity holders of the firm. Another class of agency problems, those arising from relations between creditors and equity holders, describe wealth transfers among classes of providers of capital to the firm. These may be of interest to the M&A professional who seeks to understand nuances of financing contracts, but they will be ignored here for our discussion of shareholder voting and board conduct in M&A.
4. Schleifer and Vishny (1989) suggest that a manager might diversify a firm in a way that increases the firm's demands for his or her particular skills. Amihud and Lev (1981) suggest that diversification may be pursued to reduce the firm's total risk since managers cannot efficiently diversify their risk of employment.
5. See Jensen (1986), page 328.
6. See, for example, La Porta, Lopez de Silanes, Schleifer, and Vishny (1999a,b, and 2000), Claessens, Djankov, and Lang (2000), Berkowitz, Pistor, and Richard (2002), Lombardo and Pagano (2000), and Beck, Demirguc-Kunt, and Levine (2001).
7. Schleifer and Vishny (1997) and Maher and Anderson (2000) survey the recent literature as it pertains to the United States and OECD. Gompers, Ishi, and Metrick (2001) study firm-specific governance practices in the United States.
8. See Brickley, Jarrell, and Netter (1989) and Kaplan (1989).
9. See Baker and Wruck (1989), DeAngelo, DeAngelo, and Rice (1984), Kaplan (1989), Lichtenberg and Siegel (1990), Palepu (1990), and Smith (1990).
10. Warner, Watts, and Wruck (1988) find a significant association between poor stock performance and the frequency of management turnover, but find no significant excess returns to shareholders at the announcement of management change; as they said, "The unimpressive magnitude [of abnormal returns at announcement] raises questions about the gains from such an endeavor." (Page 488) Other studies (Bonnier and Bruner 1988, Furtado and Rozeff 1987, and Weisbach 1988) document significantly positive returns at management change.
11. See Denis and Denis (1993), Denis (1994), Donaldson (1990), Holderness and Sheehan (1991), Murphy and Dial (1992), and Wruck (1994).
12. A generic set of corporate bylaws may be viewed on the Internet without charge at www.renaissancelawyer.com/corporate_bylaws.htm.
13. Ninety-three dual-class recapitalizations occurred between 1980 and 1987, with 43 in 1986 and 1987 alone. For more detail, see Lehn, Netter, and Poulson (1990), Table 1.
14. *The Business Roundtable v. Securities and Exchange Commission*, 905 F. 2d 406 (D.C. Cir., 1990).

15. These rules are not unconditional. A shareholder vote is necessary but not sufficient; other conditions must be met. For a summary of the conditions, see Robert Todd Lang, "Shareholder Voting Rights: The New Uniform Standards," *Insights* 9(2), February 1995.
16. Virginia Rosenbaum, *Corporate Takeover Defenses 2000*, Washington, DC: Investor Responsibility Research Center Inc., page 218.
17. Leading proxy solicitation firms are Georgeson Shareholder and Mellon Investor Services. See their web sites for more explanation of their activities.
18. Rosenbaum, *Corporate Takeover Defenses 2000*, page vii.
19. Thompson (1996), page 147, from which this point is paraphrased, gives an excellent summary of the business judgment rule.
20. *Guth v. Loft, Inc.*, Supreme Court of Delaware, 1939, 5 A. 2d 503.
21. *Lutz v. Boas*, Court of Chancery of Delaware, 1961, 171 A. 2d 381. A more recent example is *Spiegel v. Buntrock*, 571 A. 2d 767 (Del. 1970).
22. *Smith v. Van Gorkom*, Delaware Supreme Court, 1985, 488 A. 2d 858.
23. *Puma v. Marriott*, Court of Chancery of Delaware, 1971, 283 A. 2d 693.
24. *Aronson v. Lewis*, Supreme Court of Delaware, 1984, 473 A. 2d 805.
25. *Unocal Corporation v. Mesa Petroleum Co.*, Supreme Court of Delaware, 1985, 493 A. 2d 946.
26. Such an offer might, for instance, give the first 51 percent of shares $100 in cash per share, and the later 49 percent of shares $90 in stock or junk bonds (whose market value may be materially less than face value). "Two tier" refers to the 51/49 division of payment. "Front-end-loaded" refers to the higher payment to those shareholders tendering early. With such an offer, prompt response is rewarded, thus encouraging a shareholder stampede.
27. Transactions involving sale of control of the corporation are subject to enhanced scrutiny. Sale of control is clear in cash-for-stock deals but is less clear in stock-for-stock mergers, where a "reverse takeover" may be possible.
28. *Revlon, Inc. v. MacAndrews & Forbes Holdings*, Supreme Court of Delaware, 1986, 506 A. 2d 173.
29. This equals [($2.06+$0.9)/$2.3] – 1.
30. *Weinberger v. UOP Inc.*, Supreme Court of Delaware, 1983, 457 A. 2d 701.
31. Other significant cases that deal with this standard are *Kahn v. Lynch*, *Mills Acquisition Co. v. Macmillan, Inc.*, and *Sinclair Oil Corp. v. Levien*.
32. Spencer Stuart Board Index, 2001. This and other research on boards of directors may be downloaded free of charge from www.spencerstuart.com/common/pdflib/ssbi-2001.pdf.

CHAPTER 27

Rules of the Road: Securities Law, Issuance Process, Disclosure, and Insider Trading

INTRODUCTION

The practice of M&A is vastly influenced by securities laws and regulations. These constraints arise in the issuance of new shares by a buyer, in the disclosure of information to prospective investors, and in the prohibitions on insider trading. While there is wide discretion within these and other settings, the consequences for violating laws and regulations can be very costly, in the form of civil and criminal penalties. One attorney quipped, "The first rule of securities law is that investors never sue when they make money—only when they lose it."[1] Since ignorance of the law is no defense, the M&A practitioner must learn the general structure: This chapter is devoted to introducing the subject. The field is complicated; its important nuances easily exceed the scope of discussion here. Thus, you must seek expert legal advice.

Key lessons from this chapter include these:

- You must disclose to markets all material and relevant facts about a proposed M&A transaction between two public companies. The aim of securities laws is to inform investors, produce more efficient markets, and achieve a fair or level playing field. Often, there will be sound economic reasons for telling less, rather than more. The *disclosure* requirements are vague, placing the burden on the practitioner to judge wisely how much to tell. A simple diagnostic will determine whether a fact is "material": Would you want to know about it if you were in the investor's shoes?
- You must control leakage of information about a deal and avoid *insider trading*. The aim of securities laws is to prevent market manipulation by insiders.
- You must observe correct procedures regarding deadlines and filings with regulators. These "rules of the road" limit the practitioner's flexibility in some respects.

OVERVIEW OF KEY SECURITIES LAWS AND RULES IN THE UNITED STATES

Securities regulations arose in response to abuses of investors and markets. The founding laws were enacted in 1933 and 1934, after the stock market crash and

Great Depression exposed the abuses. More constraints were imposed after the rise of the hostile tender offer in the 1960s. "Laws" are enacted by the U.S. Congress or state legislatures. "Rules" are regulations adopted by the Securities and Exchange Commission or state regulatory commissions.

Securities Act of 1933

Referred to as the *'33 Act*, this landmark legislation addresses the issuance of new securities. It requires that the issuer must register new securities with the Securities and Exchange Commission, grants the SEC rule-making authority, and sharply limits the trading of unregistered securities. The significance of this act lies in the concept of *registration*, through which the SEC can impose standards of disclosure of information by means of a *prospectus*. The registration statement is a document filed with the SEC that contains the prospectus—this describes the business of the issuer, the issuer's financial condition, the capitalization, the purposes for raising the new funds, and so on. The SEC deems the registration to be *effective* when it is satisfied with the completeness of disclosure in the prospectus. It is unlawful to "offer to sell or offer to buy" any security for which a registration statement has not been filed with the SEC. The issuer submits a preliminary prospectus to the SEC, called a *red herring*, because the securities have not yet received official registration—a required statement in red ink on the front of the prospectus declares as much. The red herring prospectus is used merely to inform potential buyers of the securities. Upon making any changes requested by the SEC, the registration becomes effective, and the issuer can publish the final prospectus. The issuer submits the prospectus to the SEC in one of these forms:[2]

- *Form S-1.* This is required for companies registered with the SEC less than three years, and permits no incorporation by reference to other documents submitted to the SEC—in short, it will entail the fullest degree of disclosure.
- *Form S-2.* This is a streamlined registration statement for firms registered longer than three years with the SEC. It contains the same transaction-specific information as in the Form *S-1*, but refers to an annual report or Form *10-K* incorporated by reference into the prospectus.
- *Form S-3.* This allows maximum use of incorporation by reference to other reports the firm has filed with the SEC. It requires no material change in the firm's affairs since the submission of any of the reports incorporated by reference.
- *Form S-4.* This registration is specifically used for business combinations and exchange offers, and therefore will be most relevant for M&A practitioners.

Motivated by the belief that "sunlight is the best disinfectant," the SEC never opines of the economic soundness of securities, but rather promotes the disclosure of material information.

Securities Exchange Act of 1934

This second landmark law (also known as the *'34 Act* or the Exchange Act) addressed the regulation of securities exchanges and the securities held or traded in the public markets. This Act also promoted the disclosure of information. Corporations with assets greater than $10 million and more than 500 shareholders are required to register with the SEC—these are called *reporting companies*. All reporting companies are required to submit financial reports to the SEC and shareholders, including these forms:

- *10-K.* This provides the annual report of the company.
- *10-Q.* This is a quarterly report of financial performance in abbreviated form.
- *8-K.* This form provides a report on significant events and material news.
- ***Proxy statement.*** This informs shareholders about the annual shareholders meeting and resolutions to be presented for voting. The *proxy statement* indicates how shareholders can vote without attending the meeting.

A complete list of reports is given in "Documents for Filing with the SEC.pdf" on the CD-ROM. The process of submitting reports gives the SEC a vantage from which to review the reports for completeness of disclosure and to require improvements. Again, the SEC never certifies the reports as "correct" but merely accepts them when they meet standards of disclosure.

Williams Amendment to the Securities Exchange Act of 1934

Prior to the Williams Amendment (also known as the Williams Act), a hostile bidder was not required to disclose any information to target shareholders in connection with a bid. In 1968, Congress amended the '34 Act to extend regulation to tender offers, largely in response to perceived abuses in the 1960s. As further amended in 1970, the Williams Amendment imposes four very important rules of the road on the conduct of hostile tender offers:

1. ***Early warning.*** Upon the accumulation of 5 percent or more of a target firm's shares, the buyer must notify the SEC by filing Form 13(d). The buyer has 10 days from crossing the 5 percent threshold to make the filing—this stimulates the strategy of slowly acquiring the 5 percent toehold in the open market and then aggressively acquiring more shares in the 10-day window. The appearance of sudden aggressive buying of shares has caused many CEOs to anxiously await the announcement of a 13(d) filing. The practical impact of this is to give an early warning to targets, shareholders, and competing bidders about a developing takeover contest.
2. ***Open for 20 days.*** The buyer's tender offer must be open for 20 business days (about 30 calendar days) before shares may be purchased. The practical impact of this is to discourage stampeding the target firm shareholders with offers that have a very short time fuse. This is intended to promote more deliberate evaluation of the buyer's offer. Practically, it also grants a longer window in which competing bidders may respond and/or the target can find a "white knight" buyer.
3. ***Equal treatment.*** The target shareholders must be treated equally by the buyer. There may be no favoritism shown in the purchase of shares. If more than enough shares are tendered to the buyer (e.g., if the buyer offers to purchase 51 percent of shares but receives 70 percent), the buyer must purchase shares pro

rata from all investors. This has the practical effect of preventing preferential deals with some shareholders (e.g., large institutions, family groups, and influential individuals) at the expense of the smaller individual shareholder.

4. *Cash offers, too.* The '33 Act addressed the issuance of securities and was therefore relevant to stock-for-stock offers. But recognizing the rising volume of cash tender offers, the Williams Amendment extended the antifraud and registration requirements of the Act to cash offers as well.

As argued in Chapter 32, hostile takeovers are games; the Williams Amendment rules are important influences on the timing and structure of hostile tender offers.

The Williams Amendment does not define the term "tender offer." Consistent with so much else in the regulation of mergers and acquisitions, the definition was purposely avoided to give the SEC and courts flexibility in the application of the law. Such flexibility is useful in the world of M&A, where practices (and abuses) change continually. Recognizing the absence of definition, some buyers have designed transactions that they believe escape the reach of the Williams Amendment—these include solicitation of members of one family only, privately negotiated transactions (where the counterparties are widely dispersed), and aggressive open-market purchase programs. But the SEC has defined these and other unconventional approaches as "tender offers" and required that the offerors abide by the standards of the Williams Amendment.

Generally, the Williams Amendment was intended to favor neither hostile bidders nor their targets, but rather to balance their interests while promoting market efficiency and integrity. Offsetting this is the potentially dampening effect of takeover regulation. Raiders view themselves as entrepreneurs or inventors: They discover profitable investment opportunities in the market, through which corporate management is improved and investment mistakes are corrected. The effect of the Williams Amendment and other takeover regulation is to dilute the effectiveness of raiders and transfer gains to target shareholders who have done nothing to discover or create the investment opportunity. Thus, raiders argue that the leveling impulse of takeover regulation actually discourages the cleansing activities of the takeover activity.

Exceptions for Private Placements

Registering stock with the SEC is expensive and time-consuming. The '33 Act exempts some kinds of securities (such as annuity contracts and life insurance policies) from registration requirements, some kinds of transactions (such as recapitalizations, in which shareholders exchange "old" shares of the firm for "new" shares), and offerings with limited venues (such as offerings restricted to one state). These are of generally limited importance to M&A practitioners.

Of greater importance in M&A are the exemptions provided by Section 4 of the '33 Act, Regulation D, and Rule 144, regarding private placements—these are especially relevant in transactions involving a closely held target corporation.

- *Section 4 of the '33 Act.*[3] This section exempts from registration those offerings with a small circle of offerees. Imagine, for instance, a group of venture capitalists who are sophisticated, well informed, and can ask the right questions to protect themselves from the kind of disclosure abuses that the '33 Act was meant to remedy.

- *Regulation D ("Reg D")* provides an exception for private offerings.[4] If the issuance meets the conditions of Reg D, the securities do not have to be registered. This is especially attractive in acquisitions of closely held firms. Reg D outlines the size of offering in terms of dollar amount and number of nonaccredited investors. For instance, the regulation allows an offering of up to $5 million to 35 nonaccredited investors and an unlimited number of accredited investors. An accredited investor is basically a high net-worth individual:
  - Minimum net worth of $1 million.
  - Annual income of at least $200,000.
  - Insiders of the issuer: directors, executive officers, general partners.
- *Rule 144* is a resale provision for securities issued in exempt transactions. It requires that privately placed securities must be held for at least one year, and sold in limited amounts in any three-month period thereafter. Breaching these time constraints could expose one to be deemed an underwriter and thereby subject to broader regulations. The rule also says that the investor may resell privately placed securities to other qualified institutional buyers (an investor of sufficient size and sophistication) without restrictions.

State Securities and Takeover Regulations

Section 28 of the '34 Act explicitly permits states to have jurisdiction over securities registration, as long as it does not conflict directly with the provisions of the '34 Act. This leaves considerable leeway for states to permit or bar the sales of securities under "blue sky" laws—the states may bar transactions that the federal laws would permit. This amplifies the task of registering securities. Fortunately, the information requirements at the state level are similar to those at the federal level.

An important element of state regulation in the field of M&A is in the unique defenses against hostile takeovers permitted by the various states. As a general principle, federal law preempts state law. The states, however, have sought to enable takeover defenses for local firms. The experience of the states in finding a means to influence takeovers has been checkered. First-generation statutes were the initial efforts passed in the 1980s—generally, these sought to regulate tender offers straightforwardly but were found to be preempted by the Williams Amendment at the federal level.[5] Second-generation statutes regulated voting control positions, and were not found to be preempted. Third-generation statutes delayed the merger between a target and the unwanted buyer; these statutes also were not preempted. Fourth-generation statutes permit directors to consider the welfare of stakeholders other than shareholders. Fifth-generation statutes call for disgorging greenmail profits, making severance pay to employees laid off after an acquisition, and continuing labor contracts. Here are some examples:

- ***Indiana Control Share Statute.***[6] In 1986, Indiana enacted a statute focused on the acquisition of "control shares" in a public corporation—this was a second-generation statute. In essence, the Indiana Statute requires a majority vote of disinterested shareholders to confer voting rights on shares acquired by a raider. The U.S. Supreme Court upheld this statute, writing, "The Act does not conflict with the provisions or purposes of the Williams Act. To the limited extent that the Act affects interstate commerce, this is justified by the State's interests in defining the attributes of shares in its corporations and in protecting shareholders. Congress has never questioned the need for state regulation of these matters. Nor do we think such regulation offends the Constitution."[7]

- ***Wisconsin Business Combination Statute.***[8] This law requires that unless the target's board agrees to the transaction in advance, the buyer must wait three years to merge with the target or acquire more than 5 percent of its assets. This has the effect of deferring the realization of synergies or other benefits and thus discouraging unwanted advances. Noting that a law may be economic folly and yet constitutional, the court upheld this law.[9] The Delaware Business Combinations Act[10] provided for a similar three-year delay, and was upheld by the court. These are examples of third-generation statutes.
- ***Pennsylvania Anti-Takeover Act of 1990.***[11] This law expanded a target's directors' discretion in determining the best interests of a corporation. First, it focused directors on "long-term interests and plans" rather than merely maximizing shareholder wealth in the face of a premium bid. Second, it stated that directors need not "regard any corporate interest or the interests of any particular group affected by such action as a dominant or controlling interest or factor." The Act denied voting rights in controlling positions except where a majority of disinterested shareholders voted to confer such rights. This is an example of a fourth-generation statute.

Whether target shareholders are helped or harmed by state antitakeover regulation has been the subject of three specific studies. Karpoff and Malatesta (1989) studied the shareholder wealth effects of enactments of second-generation statutes and found a "small but statistically significant" decline in shareholder wealth. Hahera and Pugh (1991) studied the impact of enactment of Delaware's Business Combinations Act and found no significant effect on shareholder wealth. Finally, Szewczyk and Tsetsekos (1992) studied the impact of enactment of Pennsylvania's Anti-Takeover Act and found a significant abnormal return of –9.09 percent for 56 firms (for a total of $4 billion) and a positive abnormal return when shareholders of those firms chose to opt out of the antitakeover legislation.

International Comparison of Securities Law and M&A

Regulation of M&A in countries outside the United States varies dramatically from none to extremely rigid and lengthy processes. This diversity reflects the variation in capital markets and financial practices across the 181 sovereign nations in the world. However, among developed countries, securities law and takeover regulation show strong similarities; they also differ in interesting ways. Exhibit 27.1 compares U.S., European Union, and U.K. merger policies on several dimensions. The comparison reveals:

- Reasonable similarity in corporate disclosure obligations and shareholder rights.
- One important difference is in employee rights. In the European Union, employees retain protections against layoffs and restructurings. In the United States, there are few such protections.

EXHIBIT 27.1 Comparison of Securities Law and Takeover Regulation

	United States	European Union	United Kingdom
Form	Legislation and SEC rules; case law.	"Directives" yet to be implemented uniformly by member states.	"City Code" that does not have the force of law.
Authority	Congress, SEC, states, courts.	European Commission and EU member states.	Panel on Takeovers and Mergers.
Aim	Fairness; market efficiency.		Flexibility, certainty, speed.
Equity for shareholders	All shareholders of same class must be treated similarly by buyer.	All shareholders of same class must be treated similarly by buyer.	All shareholders of same class must be treated similarly by buyer. "Oppression of a minority is wholly unacceptable."
Disclosure	Full disclosure by published proxy/prospectus.	Full disclosure by published proxy/prospectus.	Full disclosure by published proxy/prospectus.
Insider trading	Prohibited.	Prohibited.	Prohibited.
Merger approved by target shareholders	51% unless bylaws or state law require more.	66%.	51%.
Employee rights protected	No.	Yes.	Not specified.
Fairness opinion obtained	Yes, in response to case law.	Yes, by directive.	Yes, if a valuation is given in connection with an offer.
Shareholders have appraisal rights?	Yes, under Delaware and other states' law.		

(Continued)

EXHIBIT 27.1 *(Continued)*

	United States	European Union	United Kingdom
Time to evaluate a tender offer	20 business days.	2–10 weeks.	21 days.
Must be fully financed?	Not required.	Yes.	Yes.
Right of selling shareholders to withdraw shares from tender?	Yes.	Yes.	Yes.
Mandatory bid for all shares?	No.	Yes.	Yes, if acquire 30%+ of voting rights.
Restrictions on target.	None, within bounds of directors' duties of loyalty, care, and the enhanced business judgment rule (Revlon duties).	Target can seek alternative bids, but can take no other actions to frustrate the tender offer.	Target cannot issue new shares or sell assets.
Restrictions on buyer	None.	If offering illiquid securities, must offer a cash alternative.	Must offer to all shareholders the highest price paid to any. Must offer cash or cash alternative to a securities-based bid.
Target board	Duties of loyalty, care, and enhanced business judgment.	Not specified.	Must opine on the offer. Must act only in the interest of shareholders as a whole.

Sources: This table has been abstracted from Thompson (2001), Button and Bolton (2000), and Panel on Takeovers and Mergers (2001).

- A second important difference is in treatment of minority shareholders in a takeover. In the United States, the standard practice is to conduct a two-step strategy in which the buyer acquires voting control, and then completes a full merger with the target through a freeze-out of remaining target shareholders—typically this leaves the minority with shares in the buyer, or other securities. The European Union and United Kingdom require a full mandatory bid that leaves no minority—in effect, these countries prohibit a two-step transaction.
- Finally, the target in the United States is permitted a wide range of evasive maneuvers including asset sales, recapitalization, and restructuring. In the European Union and United Kingdom, a target may seek alternative bids from other firms, but otherwise may take no other actions to frustrate the bid.

A comparison such as this occurs at the most general level. Within the European Union, the recommended policies of the European commissions must be adopted by the respective member countries. Therefore, the practitioner is cautioned to study country-specific laws and regulations. Also, the definitions of terms may vary from one culture to the next. In Germany, companies must disclose a deal as soon as an agreement is made—before then companies have significant latitude. For instance, in August 1999, Vega and Viag denied rumors that the firms were in merger talks. Then, a month later, the two announced a deal to create Germany's biggest energy firm. A spokeswoman for Viag said, "In Germany a denial basically means we don't want to say anything. A 'no comment' amounts to a confirmation of talks."[12]

KEY IMPLICATION: DISCLOSURE

The '33 and '34 Acts impose strict liability for fraud, statement of a false fact, or omission to state a material fact. This liability extends to the issuing firm, its directors, and managers (subject to defenses for due diligence and reasonable care). An important aim of securities regulation is to promote the efficiency of capital markets through enhanced disclosure about the condition of firms underlying the securities. What, then, must one say? How? When?

The disclosure questions are relatively easy to answer in regard to periodic SEC filings and to a proxy and prospectus: Tell as much as the SEC and your lawyers require. Help investors understand the outlook for Newco. But do not hype investor expectations; express caution where warranted. And omit no material facts.

The problem becomes considerably more difficult when the two sides are in negotiation, a deal has not been concluded, and the economic consequences remain uncertain. Rumors will sprout in a setting such as this. Or worse, information will leak out, triggering trading on inside information. Rumors and leakage of facts can destabilize negotiations, embarrass the principals, and perhaps motivate other buyers to enter the scene. There are no clear rules in a setting such as this, though court law directs the decision maker to several considerations:

1. *Materiality.* Avoiding liability under the antifraud and registration requirements of the '33 and '34 Acts requires the issuer to tell the whole story. But

how much is enough? As the Supreme Court acknowledged in the landmark case *TSC Industries, Inc. v. Northway, Inc.*,[13] some information is of dubious significance. Setting the standard too low might "simply bury the shareholders in an avalanche of trivial information—a result that is hardly conducive to informed decision making." Therefore, the Court adopted a general standard of *materiality* as follows: "An omitted fact is material if there is a substantial likelihood that a reasonable shareholder would consider it important in deciding how to vote." In *Basic Inc. v. Levinson*,[14] the Supreme Court extended this standard of materiality to questions of insider trading under Section 10(b) and Rule 10b-5 of the '34 Act.

2. ***Probability.*** Merger negotiations are *highly* material for every target firm. But they may not be very important to investors if a merger is not likely. In *Basic Inc. v. Levinson*, the U.S. Supreme Court did not require disclosure simply because the information was material.
3. ***Commit and disclose.*** Evidence of high probability is the execution of written documents such as a definitive agreement or even a letter of intent. Many practitioners prefer to defer signing documents until the buyer and seller are ready to make a public announcement.
4. ***Expectations in the market.*** If a target has staunchly told investors in the past that "the firm is not for sale," but has recently initiated serious merger negotiations with a buyer, then the firm is obliged to correct the prevailing expectations in the market. A firm has a "duty to update" where recent actions depart from past pronouncements.
5. ***"No comment."*** To avoid spilling the beans under a "duty to update," many firms follow a strict policy of not commenting on market rumors, negotiations in progress, and so on. Carnation failed to do so in the face of rumors about its secret negotiations to be acquired by Nestlé in 1984. The company denied that it was for sale, even though negotiations were serious and ultimately produced a proposed deal. The SEC wrote, "Whenever an issuer makes a public statement or responds to an inquiry from a stock exchange official concerning rumors, unusual market activity, possible corporate developments, or any other matter, the statement must be materially accurate and complete. If the issuer is aware of nonpublic information concerning acquisition discussions that are occurring at the time the statement is made, the issuer has an obligation to disclose sufficient information concerning the discussions to prevent the statements made from being materially misleading."[15]
6. ***Abstain from trading or disclose.*** If a target firm is trading in its own shares, such as executing a standard share repurchase program over time, insider trading laws will require it to disclose to the market material information (such as news of merger negotiations) or else abstain from trading. It is possible that suspending a share repurchase program will become known to the market (through brokers or others), and thereby trigger speculation about material developments at the firm.[16]

In addition to these broad guidelines, two special issues warrant further discussion: forward looking statements and cautionary statements.

Forward-Looking Statements

Under U.S. securities law and case law, the ability to make forward-looking statements about the issuer has historically been limited. The rationale for this is that absent these restrictions, unscrupulous promoters might hype the prospects of an issuer to unsophisticated investors, and thereby exploit them. But as a practical matter, *all* securities are priced and purchased on the basis of expectations. It would appear, then, that the restriction on making forward-looking statements about an issuer would frustrate the effort to promote the efficiency of capital markets.

In 1995, Congress crafted a "safe harbor" with regard to forward-looking statements for issuers in the Private Securities Litigation Reform Act. The Act added new Sections 27A to the '33 Act and 21E to the '34 Act that protected from private litigation forward-looking statements that conformed to the following:

- They are identified as "forward looking."
- They are accompanied by meaningful cautionary statements reminding the reader that actual results could differ materially from projections. The cautions cannot be boilerplate; they must be meaningful.
- The person making the forward-looking statement must not intend to make a false or misleading statement.

Covered here are financial projections, discussion of business plans, and discussion of assumptions underlying projections. However, not covered by this exemption are financial statements prepared in accordance with generally accepted accounting principles (GAAP), tender offers, and initial public offerings.

Caution

Generally, courts have tended to dismiss fraud claims where a company has disclosed risks that might affect future performance—this is the "*bespeaks caution*" doctrine. For instance, Brad Grossman sued Novell, Inc. for falsely assuring investors about its acquisition of WordPerfect Corporation in 1994. The judge dismissed the claim and said, "Securities fraud claims cannot be maintained where defendants have issued detailed cautionary warnings. The 'bespeaks caution' doctrine provides a mechanism by which a court can rule as a matter of law . . . that defendants' forward-looking representations contained enough cautionary language or risk disclosure to protect the defendant against claims of securities fraud." It does not matter "if the optimistic statements are later found to have been inaccurate or based on erroneous assumptions when made, provided that the risk disclosure was conspicuous, specific, and adequately disclosed the assumptions upon which the optimistic language was based."[17]

Manage Leaks of Information

M&A practitioners manage the flow of information very carefully with a view toward forestalling leaks of facts or rumors in the stock market. Some of the typical practices include these four:

1. ***Limited access, no access.*** Information about a deal is limited strictly to those having a need to know. Documents are sequestered under lock and key; digital firewalls limit hackers and inadvertent e-mails. The organization practices a culture of secrecy.
2. ***Small teams.*** The circle of professionals brought in to work on a deal is no larger than necessary.
3. ***Limited time.*** Consistent with the need to know, disclosures to others are withheld until the last minute.
4. ***Encryption and disguises.*** Deals are given code names, the only point of reference in conversations outside the walls of the group.

These practices extend to suppliers to M&A professionals. For instance, a graphic designer who specializes in M&A work said, "We can't afford to trust anyone. . . . We're a self-contained environment. . . . It's a little bit like a loyal cult."[18]

KEY IMPLICATION: INSIDER TRADING

In Section 10(b), the '34 Act prohibits insider trading and has been used to prosecute cases under two theories, both of which the U.S. Supreme Court has upheld. Rule 10b-5 of the SEC implements the section. The Insider Trading and Sanctions Act of 1984 pursues those who trade on information not available to the general public. Penalties under this act include disgorging the illegal profits from insider trading and up to three times the value of those profits. The Insider Trading and Securities Fraud Enforcement Act of 1988 added a section to the '34 Act that requires corporations and brokers to implement systems to prevent insider trading. Finally, the Racketeer Influenced and Corrupt Organizations Act of 1970 (RICO) has been applied to securities trading operations, most famously the junk bond desk of Drexel Burnham Lambert and its chief, Michael Milken. Originally aimed at corrupt unions, RICO has been applied more broadly and has two key criteria for prosecution: (1) conspiracy to defraud and (2) repeated transactions. The penalties include triple damages for successful plaintiffs. In criminal proceedings, RICO authorizes the court to seize the assets of the accused while the case is being tried—even though the defendant might be acquitted, the prospective disruption of business might be so severe as to impose a strong incentive to settle the case in advance of trial.

Classical Theory of Insider Trading Liability

The first basis for prosecution is *deception*, which the classical approach to insider trading prohibits. Insiders, or agents of the owners, are viewed as holding a position of trust. In the landmark case *Dirks v. SEC*, the Supreme Court held that the position entails a "duty to disclose or abstain from trading because of the necessity of preventing a corporate insider from . . . taking unfair advantage of . . . uninformed . . . stockholders." This duty applies not only to permanent insiders of a corporation (such as executives) but also to consultants, accountants, and others who temporarily become fiduciaries. The deception arises from a failure to disclose or abstain from trading.

Misappropriation Theory of Insider Trading Liability

The second basis for prosecution is the *theft* (or misappropriation) of confidential information for the purpose of trading. Doing so denies the principal owner of that information its exclusive use. In *United States v. O'Hagan*, the Supreme Court agreed that misappropriation meets the definition of prohibited conduct under Section 10(b).

Mini-Case: McDermott and Gannon

One of the most infamous cases of insider trading in the 1990s featured an affair between James J. McDermott Jr., former chairman and CEO of Keefe, Bruyette & Woods (KBW), and Kathryn Gannon, an entertainer. The relationship was discovered when KBW was conducting due diligence prior to an initial public offering of its stock in 1999. The SEC immediately began an investigation. KBW forced McDermott to resign two months later, after 21 years with the company.

McDermott had passed to Gannon inside information on pending M&A transactions among banks on which McDermott's firm was advising. Gannon gave the information to Anthony Pomponio, with whom she was having a second affair and who traded on the news. The trading on inside information yielded profits of about $170,000.

In April 2000, a jury convicted McDermott, Gannon, and Pomponio of insider trading, conspiracy, and securities fraud. Gannon and McDermott received jail sentences of three and five months respectively. Pomponio was sentenced to 21 months in prison.

KEY IMPLICATION: OBSERVANCE OF PROCESS

The main caution to M&A deal designers must be to follow the rules of the road—whether defined by courts, legislators, and regulators.

Due Process

The '33 Act outlines a strict process of securities registration with the SEC:

- *Prefiling period.* Before the issuer files a registration statement with the SEC, it is unlawful to offer to buy or sell that security.
- *Waiting period.* This is the time between the filing of a registration statement and the date when the registration becomes effective. One can make oral offers and receive preliminary indications of interest in buying securities. But during the waiting period, it is unlawful to consummate a sale. This is the time in which one circulates a red herring prospectus.
- *Posteffective period.* The securities may be sold, as long as they are accompanied by, or preceded by, a prospectus complying with an effective registration.

No Gun Jumping

The securities issuance process outlined in the '33 Act limits the actions of an issuer until a registration becomes effective. Yet the pressures in an M&A setting to start dealing before the registration is effective (i.e., "gun jumping"[19]) can be immense. In a hostile tender offer setting, moving quickly can determine success or failure. For instance, in 1970, Chris-Craft Industries and Bangor Punta Corporation were competing to acquire Piper Aircraft. Bangor made a tender offer for Piper shares in a share-for-share exchange (i.e., Bangor would be issuing new shares, and thus would be subject to the '33 Act). In support of its offer, Bangor issued a press release that said,

> *Bangor Punta has agreed to file a registration statement with the SEC covering a proposed exchange offer for any and all of the remaining outstanding shares of Piper Aircraft for a package of Bangor Punta securities to be valued in the judgment of The First Boston corporation at not less than $80 per Piper share. The registration statement covering all securities to be issued will be filed as soon as possible and a meeting of the shareholders of Bangor Punta Corporation will be called for approval.*[20]

The SEC declared that this announcement constituted an offer to sell securities and immediately enjoined Bangor and Piper from making further such statements until a registration of Bangor shares became effective. Later, Chris-Craft successfully sued Bangor, claiming that Bangor's acquisition occurred in violation of the '33 Act. The judge noted that Bangor's registration statement had not yet been filed with the SEC (i.e., Bangor had jumped the gun), and that assigning a dollar value to the offered shares constituted an offer to sell. The opinion said, "One of the evils of a premature offer is its tendency to encourage the formation by the offeree of an opinion of the value of the securities before a registration statement and prospectus are filed."[21]

Bespeak Caution

Another pressure in an M&A setting is to express a high degree of optimism in the economic prospects of the deal; such expressions help to win shareholder approval and sustain doubtful employees. But one easily slips from building a positive case for a deal into the kind of unfounded hyping of prospects that the '33 Act and '34 Act discourage. One needs to bespeak caution.

- ***Do your own homework first.*** One needs to base one's optimistic outlook on some rational basis that prior experience or the performance of peers might validate. A gut feeling is an unworthy foundation for expressions of confidence.
- ***Let facts speak for themselves.*** Within the bounds of the law and regulations and of good business practice, let investors see the foundations, rather than the lofty conclusions of your thinking. Also, one can draw on the opinions of outsiders such as consultants, securities analysts, and bankers.
- ***Be frank about risks.*** Candor probably helps one's case; securities analysts grow suspicious when there is no acknowledgement that things might go other than as planned.

- ***Temper the language.*** Moderate the assertive to be more conditional: "This will happen" becomes "We expect this will happen" and so on.
- ***SEC filings require it.*** To win approval from the SEC, the prospectus must contain a listing of possible risks to the future.

Say It Plainly; Make No Omissions

Related to the problem of overly optimistic statements is risk of confounding investors through overly complicated language. The SEC now requires the preparation of filings in "plain English." This includes:

- Short sentences.
- Definite, concrete everyday language.
- Active voice.
- Tabular presentation of complex information.
- No legal jargon.
- No multiple negatives.[22]

This is more than simply empathizing with the reader. One must view plain expression as a mandate on behalf of full disclosure. Courts frown on absent material facts. For instance, in the case *Feit v. Leasco Data Processing Equipment Co.*, the court said,

> *This case raises the question of the degree of candor required of issuers of securities who offer their shares in exchange for those of other companies in takeover operations. Defendants' registration statement was, we find, misleading in a material way. While disclosing masses of facts and figures, it failed to reveal one critical consideration that weighted heavily with those responsible for the issue—the substantial possibility of being able to gain control of some hundred million dollars of assets not required for operating the business being acquired. Using a statement to obscure, rather than reveal, in plain English, the critical elements of a proposed business deal cannot be countenanced under the securities regulation acts. The defense that no one could be certain of precisely how much was involved . . . is not acceptable. The prospective purchaser of a new issue is entitled to know what the deal is all about. Given an honest and open statement, adequately warning of the possibilities of error and miscalculation and not designed for puffing, the outsider and insider are placed on more equal grounds for arm's-length dealing. Such equalization of bargaining power through sharing of knowledge in the securities market is a basic national policy underlying the federal securities law.*[23]

SUMMARY AND CONCLUSIONS

Studying securities law is important for the M&A practitioner because fraud and violation of registration rules can be expensive—whether committed intentionally or inadvertently. The minimum penalty is repayment to investors of their losses. Civil and criminal penalties raise the ante. This chapter has outlined rules of the road in the area of securities law. The spirit of these rules is to suppress abuses arising from information asymmetries and market manipulation—the so-called "level playing field" is the ideal. In some areas the rules set clear limits; in others, the rules remain vague. Overall, the application of the rules continues to evolve. Obtain competent legal counsel for any matters related to the issuance of securities.

NOTES

1. Marc H. Morgenstern, "Private Placement Guidelines—A Lawyer's Letter to a First-Time Issuer," 48, *Business Lawyer* 257 (1992).
2. These descriptions are paraphrased from Securities Act Release No. 33-6383 (March 3, 1982).
3. Section 4(2) is referred to as the "statutory exemption for private offerings." Factors include whether potential purchasers need the protection of registration provisions, their access to information, the size of the group of offerees, and whether the sale has the appearance of a public offering. Section 4(6) covers offerings up to $5 million for accredited investors.
4. Rule 506 under Reg D is referred to as the "private offering safe harbor"—meaning that compliance with the rule provides shelter from statutory interpretation (litigation). Rule 506 permits up to 35 accredited investors in any dollar amount. All nonaccredited investors must be sophisticated in business and finance or employ a knowledgeable representative. Related Rule 504 covers an offering up to $1 million; Rule 505 covers up to $5 million.
5. The U.S. Supreme Court in *Edgar v. Mite Corp.* (1982 102 S.Ct. 2629) concluded that the Illinois Business Take-Over Act "frustrate[s] the congressional purpose by introducing extended delay into the tender offer process," that "Congress intended for investors to be free to make their own decisions," and that "the Illinois Act imposes a substantial burden on interstate commerce which outweighs its putative local benefits."
6. The Indiana Control Share Acquisitions Act; Ind. Code §23-1-42-1 et seq.
7. *CTS Corp. v. Dynamics Corp. of America*, United States Supreme Court, 1987 107 S.Ct. 1637.
8. Wisconsin Statutes W.S.A. 180.726.
9. *Amanda Acquisition Corp. v. Universal Foods Corp.*, United States Court of Appeals, Seventh Circuit, 1989 877 F. 2d 496.
10. Del. Code Ann. 8, §203.
11. 15 Pa. Cons. Stat. Ann. §§2571-75 (West 1995).
12. Dagmar Aalund and Vanessa Fuhrmans, "In German Business-Speak, 'No' Often Means 'Yes,' " *Wall Street Journal*, September 29, 1999, page A18.
13. 46 U.S. 438 (1976).
14. 485 U.S. 224 (1988).
15. *In the Matter of Carnation Company*, Exchange Act Release No. 22214, July 8, 1985.
16. See Conner, Brown, and Talcott (2003), page 13.
17. *Grossman v. Novell, Inc., et al.*, United Stated District Court, District of Utah, 1995, 909 F. Supp. 845.

18. Erin White, "In a Merger Insiders Include the Fellow Doing the Xeroxing," *Wall Street Journal*, March 6, 2000, page A1.
19. This is U.S. slang derived from track-and-field competition where the contestant begins to run before the starter fires the gun.
20. *Chris-Craft Industries, Inc. v. Bangor Punta Corp.*, United States Court of Appeals, 1970, 426 F. 2d 569.
21. Ibid.
22. SEC Division of Corporation Finance, Updated Staff Legal Bulletin No. 7 ("Plain English Disclosure"), June 7, 1999.
23. *Feit v. Leasco Data Processing Equipment Co.*, United States District Court, Eastern District of New York, 1971, 332 F. Supp. 544.

CHAPTER 28

Rules of the Road: Antitrust Law

INTRODUCTION

Antitrust constraints on M&A are among the least well known to practitioners. Laws in this area are complex; the issues are subtle; and the policies and their enforcement continue to evolve. But the issues and requirements here deserve more than passing acquaintance, since violations pose a "showstopper" barrier to mergers and acquisitions, and can lead to fines and treble damages. The aim of this chapter is to lend an introduction to the field. However, detailed analysis on a specific deal will always be warranted, as will be consultation with expert legal counsel on actions contemplated well in advance of their execution.

Key lessons from this chapter include these:

- The law prevents anticompetitive behavior "in restraint of trade." In short, the law seeks to promote competition in the belief that economic efficiency and rising consumer welfare will follow. To most business practitioners, dominating the competition is an important objective. But the law prohibits such an outcome achieved through anticompetitive behavior.
- The courts and enforcement agencies are prone to pursue M&A transactions that have the *potential* for creating market power. In other words, you don't need to engage in anticompetitive behavior to excite regulators. Your deal merely needs to create the conditions typically associated with market dominance and anticompetitive behavior.
- Anticompetitive behavior is associated with market power. Market power is associated with concentration. Regulators use the *Herfindahl-Hirschman Index* as one measure of market power.
- In the United States, antitrust regulators have issued guidelines for horizontal combinations. These indicate the likelihood of a challenge to the deal. Good practice would dictate that early in the development of a deal one should test it against these guidelines.
- You must inform regulators about the deal in advance, and wait a month or two for an indication of clearance or challenge. The Hart-Scott-Rodino filing is one of the important steps in the process of consummating a deal.
- Cross-border antitrust enforcement varies widely. Foreign antitrust authorities should not be taken for granted, as the case of General Electric/Honeywell suggests. Whereas the U.S. antitrust system tends to focus on consumer protection, the antitrust systems of other countries may focus on industrial or trade protec-

tionism. It will be interesting to see how these systems change under pressures for the emergence of a global antitrust standard.

- Antitrust law and economics remain fraught with controversy.
- You must observe correct procedures regarding deadlines and filings with regulators. These "rules of the road" limit the practitioner's flexibility in some respects.

ANTITRUST LAW: HISTORY AND MOTIVES

Antitrust regulation took root in the late nineteenth century as a reaction against anticompetitive behavior of dominant firms in a variety of industries. The focus of antitrust on M&A (among other forms of behavior) rose straightforwardly from the sheer size of the early combinations formed in the first great merger wave in U.S. history. Lamoreaux (1985) notes that from 1894 to 1904, over 1,800 firms disappeared into 93 combinations, called "trusts." A trust was a grouping of competitors in an industry gathered through mergers or informal production agreements—these were often motivated by a desire for stability in prices and volumes.

Standard Oil was the classic trust, organized by John D. Rockefeller in 1870. As of that year, the company held 10 percent of the oil refining capacity in the United States.[1] In 1872 Rockefeller formed an alliance with railroads that would give Standard Oil a strong pricing advantage in shipments of oil, in effect forming a "double cartel" in oil and rails that doubled freight rates for all of Standard Oil's competitors, but not Standard Oil itself.[2] Rockefeller followed a strategy of industry domination that sought to bring order, high prices, and steady output to the industry—all through a process of predatory pricing, discriminatory dealing, and acquisition. In 1906, the federal government sued to break up Standard Oil under the *Sherman Act*. The company was charged with "monopolizing the oil industry and conspiring to restrain trade through a familiar litany of tactics: railroad rebates, the abuse of their pipeline monopoly, predatory pricing, industrial espionage, and the secret ownership of ostensible competitors."[3] By 1907, Standard Oil refined 87 percent of all kerosene sold in the United States. In 1911, the Supreme Court ordered the dismantling of Standard Oil.[4]

The criticism of trusts is that they harm consumers by charging prices higher than those that would prevail in a competitive industry. Of course, shareholders benefit from this, which gave the antitrust movement a populist rallying point: The average man and woman were being exploited for the benefit of capitalists. The socialist ideal of appropriating all profits from shareholders was never seriously promoted in the United States. Rather, the substance of policy has been to preserve and promote competition within industries in the belief that active competition produces efficiency, innovation, and prices that are fair.

The theoretical ideal of a perfectly competitive industry is a rather stark landscape. The product made by one firm is indistinguishable from the next—the product is homogeneous, a commodity like salt. No player in the industry can affect prices—as a practical matter, this suggests that there are no large and dominant firms. All firms are small players. The factor inputs of production (such as labor, intellectual property, and capital) are fluid so that no firm has an advantage. The market knows: There are no asymmetries of information among firms or consumers about prices or product attributes. In a world such as this, managers don't have much choice; the highest price they can charge is the price prevailing in the market. It happens that such a price will yield returns that just cover the firm's cost of capital. There are no economic profits or positive NPVs. This is a world that most managers would want to get out of. Indeed, as the work of Michael Porter (1980) and others suggests, much of modern business management is oriented to delivering products and services that are highly differentiable and difficult to imitate, segments that are difficult to enter, and investments that create value. Invention, product enhancement, and opening up new markets—in short, innovation and entrepreneurial activity—are the positive routes of exit from the grinding conditions of the perfectly competitive industry.

The problem is that the nineteenth century revealed an alternative route: collusion to lift prices artificially. By acting in concert, competitors may approximate the powers of a monopolist. In theory, a pure *monopoly* is characterized by only one player in an industry who sets prices and the volume of output. Typically, the price charged is that which maximizes the firm's profits, a price higher than the price if the industry were purely competitive. Monopolies are also characterized by high barriers to entry (i.e., preventing the entry of new competition) and asymmetric information where the monopolist has good (or perfect) information and consumers and potential competitors are at a disadvantage.

Monopoly has two key defects. First, it allocates resources inefficiently. Capital and labor are not invested in ways that satisfy consumer demand. The monopolist, confident about high profits, may grow less vigilant about quality, efficiency, and innovation. A stark example is the state-owned monopoly. In the Soviet Union, these proved to be so extraordinarily inefficient that with the removal of heavy state subsidies and the opening of trade to foreign firms after 1990, the monopolies virtually collapsed. The second defect is that monopoly redistributes wealth unfairly. The monopolist's high prices have been likened to "a privately imposed and privately collected tax."[5]

Monopolies can arise naturally, as a result, for instance, of a new technology. These so-called *natural monopolies* are not necessarily bad; they may reflect the benefits of a first-mover advantage, patents, or some other economic condition, none of which antitrust policy should necessarily strive to eliminate. Microsoft, for example, established what is arguably a natural monopoly in personal computer operating systems ("Windows"). Had it not been for Microsoft's alleged tying behavior, it seems unlikely that the United States antitrust establishment would have pursued the firm.

A near relative of monopoly is *oligopoly*, which features a few competitors who recognize their interdependence and, with an eye on the behavior of each other, raise prices and reduce output. This is possible because of:

- Differentiated products that allow the competitors a place in the industry.
- Economies of scale that benefit only the large-scale players in the market.
- Barriers that make it difficult for new players to enter.

Collusion among competitors to fix prices and outputs is a primary concern of antitrust regulators. Like monopoly, a successful oligopoly results in inefficient allocation of resources and a private tax on consumers.

Even though an industry has few competitors, oligopoly pricing may not result. Potential competitors may be lurking outside the industry, watching for an economically attractive opportunity (such as rising prices) to come in. The competitors already in the industry know this, and set prices low enough to exclude the potential new entrants. This is a *contestable market*, made possible by low entry and exit barriers and low nonrecoverable outlays.[6] The possibility of contestable markets complicates life for antitrust regulators, since it compels a wider consideration of competition, both existing and potential.

Mergers potentially destabilize effective competition. For instance, the Federal Trade Commission wrote:

> *Most mergers actually benefit competition and consumers by allowing firms to operate more efficiently. But some are likely to lessen competition. That, in turn, can lead to higher prices, reduced availability of goods or services, lower quality of products, and less innovation. Indeed, some mergers create a concentrated market, while others enable a single firm to raise prices.*
>
> *In a concentrated market, there are only a few firms. The danger is that they may find it easier to lessen competition by colluding. For example, they may agree on the prices they will charge consumers. The collusion could be in an explicit agreement, or in a more subtle form—known as tacit coordination or coordinated interaction. Firms may prefer to cooperate tacitly rather than explicitly because tacit agreements are more difficult to detect, and some explicit agreements may be subject to criminal prosecution.*
>
> *When a merger enables a single firm to increase prices without coordinating with its competitors, it has created a unilateral effect. A firm might be able to increase prices unilaterally if it has a large enough share of the market, if the merger removes its closest competitor, and if the other firms in the market can't provide substantial competition.*
>
> *Generally, at least two conditions are necessary for a merger to have a likely anticompetitive effect: The market must be substantially concentrated after the merger; and it must be difficult for new firms to enter the market in the near term and provide effective competition. The reason for the second condition is that firms are less likely to raise prices to anticompetitive levels if it is fairly easy for new competitors to enter the market and drive prices down.*[7]

OVERVIEW OF ANTITRUST REGULATORS AND LAWS AFFECTING MERGERS AND ACQUISITIONS

Antitrust laws are enforced by the U.S. government mainly through two agencies: the *Antitrust Division of the Department of Justice (DOJ)*[8] and the *Federal Trade Commission (FTC)*.[9] The DOJ prosecutes violations of the Sherman Act as criminal felonies. The FTC enforces the Federal Trade Commission Act and parts of the *Clayton Act*—neither of these entails criminal sanctions. The FTC and DOJ coordinate their activities to prevent duplication; each requests clearance from the other before initiating an action. However, the FTC refers any possible criminal violations to the DOJ for prosecution under the Sherman Act.

Regarding selected industries, the DOJ and FTC defer to agencies charged with regulating competition. Examples include the Federal Communications Commission, which regulates the broadcast and telephone industries; the Surface Transportation Board, which regulates railroads; and the Federal Reserve Bank, which regulates banks with national charters.

State attorneys general are authorized by the *Hart-Scott-Rodino Act* to initiate civil antitrust lawsuits on behalf of consumers in their states harmed by allegedly anticompetitive behavior. The National Association of Attorneys General (NAAG) has published merger antitrust guidelines (that parallel the federal guidelines and will, therefore, not be reviewed here). Private individuals may initiate lawsuits for treble damages arising from anticompetitive behavior prohibited under the Clayton Act.

Sherman Act of 1890

The Sherman Act was passed by Congress to address anticompetitive abuses associated with the rise of trusts in the period following the Civil War. The first major victory under this act was the Northern Securities trust decision in 1904, which prevented a famous deal brokered by J. P. Morgan for the combination of the Great Northern and Northern Pacific Railroads. Northern Securities had been formed in March 1902 as a holding company for railroad interests in the northwestern United States. Critics (especially farmers and business shippers) saw it as a monopoly. Within four months, the Justice Department under President Theodore Roosevelt sued to break up Northern Securities Company. This was part of a wave of antitrust lawsuits initiated by Roosevelt that earned him the sobriquet "trustbuster." The famous antitrust lawsuit against Standard Oil was also initiated that year. The Northern Securities case earned its notoriety as the first of a string of landmark decisions in antitrust law. In March 1904, the Supreme Court ordered the dissolution of Northern Securities and thereby gave teeth to the Sherman Act. The historian Vincent Carosso wrote, "A majority of justices (five to four) upheld the appellate court's opinion that even though the company had not violated the law, the fact that it had the power to do so was sufficient to order the corporation's dissolution. . . . The majority opinion, reflecting the public's fear of large, powerful corporations, asserted the federal government's authority to supervise them, and revived the moribund Sherman law, but served no constructive or economic purpose."[10]

Two sections of the Sherman Act outlaw anticompetitive behavior:

- *Section 1:* "Every contract, combination in the form of trust or otherwise, or conspiracy in restraint of trade or commerce among the several States, or with foreign nations is hereby declared to be illegal. Every person who shall make any contract or engage in any combination or conspiracy hereby declared to be illegal shall be deemed guilty of a felony and, on conviction thereof, shall be punished by fine . . . or by imprisonment not exceeding three years, or by both. . . ."
- *Section 2:* "Every person who shall monopolize, or attempt to monopolize, or combine or conspire with any other person or persons, to monopolize any part of the trade or commerce among the several States, or with foreign nations,

shall be deemed guilty of a felony, and, on conviction thereof, shall be punished by fine . . . or by imprisonment not exceeding three years, or by both. . . ."

Court decisions have agreed that these sections extend across a range of trade-restraining combinations, including horizontal, vertical, and conglomerate mergers and acquisitions. Individuals can be fined up to $350,000 and jailed for up to three years under each violation. Corporations can be fined up to $10 million for each violation, and even higher amounts in special circumstances.

Clayton Act of 1914

Congress passed the Clayton Act to extend the powers of the Sherman Act. Section 7 of the Clayton Act specifically addresses mergers and acquisitions. It prohibits combinations that would restrain trade:

> *No person engaged in commerce or in any activity affecting commerce shall acquire, directly or indirectly . . . where in any line of commerce or in any activity affecting commerce in any section of the country, the effect of such acquisition may be substantially to lessen competition or tend to create a monopoly.*

Originally, the Clayton Act regulated acquisitions of shares of stock, not assets. The Celler-Kefauver Act of 1950 amended the Clayton Act to cover both asset and stock acquisitions.

Hart-Scott-Rodino Antitrust Improvements Act of 1976

With this act (also known as HSR), Congress amended the Clayton Act, adding a new Section 7A that required combinations above a certain size threshold to submit information to the DOJ and FTC *in advance* of consummating the deal, and to wait 15 to 30 days[11] for response before consummation. From a public policy standpoint, advance review is vastly preferable to *ex post* review. From a managerial standpoint, this law prevents preemptive action (i.e., the presentation of regulators with a fait accompli that would make government try to undo a completed deal). A later section in this chapter reviews the detailed implications of how HSR affects M&A process. This important law grants the federal government a right of advance regulatory refusal on M&A deals—in essence, this is an option (a long call) on the merger benefits. The counterparty is the buyer (or pair of merging firms) for whom the right of review is a liability (a short call). The greater the uncertainty (volatility) about competitive impact of the deal, the greater is the liability.

United States Antitrust Merger Guidelines

To help business practitioners anticipate the attitude of regulators toward new M&A transactions, the DOJ and FTC have published a consolidated set of guidelines for federal enforcement of Section 7 of the Clayton Act.[12] These have been revised over time, and bear periodic review for ongoing changes.

Horizontal mergers

Horizontal mergers occur among peer competitors in an industry. For instance, Staples, Inc., proposed to acquire Office Depot. Since both were superstore retailers of office supplies, the merger would have reduced the number of superstore competitors. The FTC staff argued that after the merger, Staples would have been able to raise prices an average of 13 percent. The FTC blocked the merger.

The agencies apply a five-step process[13] to assessing whether a deal will create or enhance market power or strengthen Newco's exercise of such power:

1. ***What are the relevant markets and their current concentration levels?*** At the outset of the process, the agencies seek to identify the players in a market, their shares, and the degree of premerger concentration. The market is assessed on the demand side (rather than supply side) and measured by dollar sales or unit sales. Two key measures emerge at this stage:

   A. *Cross elasticity of demand.* This measures the percentage change in demand for one good that coincides with the percentage change in price with another. The formula for *cross-elasticity of demand* is:

   $$\text{Elasticity} = \frac{\text{\% Change in quantity demanded of good B}}{\text{\% Change in price of good A}}$$

   A value of zero would indicate no economic relationship between the two products; values greater than 1.0 indicate elastic demand, a relatively high sensitivity to changes in price. Values less than 1.0 indicate inelastic demand, relatively lower sensitivity. For instance, natural gas and electricity are two key sources of energy for households. As electricity prices rise, consumers will shift away from using electricity for warmth and cooking, and will use natural gas. A high cross-elasticity value indicates that economically these two substitutes exist in a convergent market; a low cross-elasticity value suggests the two substitutes are in separate markets. Values less than zero indicate negative elasticity, suggesting that a price increase in one product results in a decline in the quantity sold of another product. For instance, an increase in the price of pasta might be associated with a decrease in the volume sold of tomato sauce. Negative elasticity suggests that the two products are complements rather than substitutes. The cross-elasticity of demand is used to determine the scope of the relevant market for analysis. The Supreme Court wrote, "The outer boundaries of a product market are determined by the reasonable interchangeability of use or the cross elasticity of demand between the products itself and substitutes for it."[14] For instance, in the famous antitrust case in which the government sued DuPont for dominating the cellophane market, the Supreme Court judged from an analysis of cross-elasticities that the relevant market was actually "flexible packaging material," which included "Pliofilm, foil, glassine, polyethylene, and Saran" and that DuPont did not have monopoly control over the "market" defined in these terms.[15]

B. *Herfindahl-Hirschman Index (HHI).* This is a measure of concentration estimated as the sum of the squares of the market shares of the players in the relevant market.

$$HHI = \sum_{i}^{n}\left(\frac{\text{Sales or output of firm } i}{\text{Total sales or output of market}} \times 100\right)^2$$

The HHI can range from a value of 10,000 for a pure monopoly to a value approaching zero for a market with a large number of insignificant players. The spreadsheet file which can be found on the CD-ROM, "HHI.xls," offers a calculator for computing the HHI.

2. ***What is the concentration ratio for relevant markets, postmerger?*** The guidelines are premised on the belief that increased concentration is associated with anticompetitive behavior. How much concentration is too much? The agencies consider both the postmerger level of concentration, and the change in concentration produced by the transaction. The guidelines divide the postmerger industry into three categories:
   A. *HHI less than 1,000.* The agencies view markets in this range as unconcentrated. An HHI below 1,000 would be associated, for instance, with a market share of the four largest firms of less than 40 percent. Here, the agencies will make no challenge to a merger.
   B. *HHI between 1,000 and 1,800.* This is a moderately concentrated industry and conforms to a four-firm *concentration ratio* of 40 to 70 percent. Mergers producing a change of less than 100 points are unlikely to be challenged. Generally, mergers may be challenged depending on ease of entry by other firms, possible efficiencies to be created, distress of one or both firms, and the impact of possible coordinated or unilateral effects.
   C. *HHI greater than 1,800.* This is viewed as highly concentrated. Mergers yielding this level of concentration and/or producing a change of 50 points or higher are likely to be challenged, subject to an assessment of the likelihood of coordinated or unilateral actions.

   Exhibit 28.1 presents a mini-case problem in estimating the HHI for an industry on a unit output basis and revenue basis. The estimated HHIs reveal the proposed deal to fall in the middle category, suggesting it might be challenged on the basis of industry concentration effects. In this case, successfully avoiding challenge will likely depend on how well one can employ defenses on the next three points.
3. ***Will the merger forestall entry by other firms?*** Entry by other firms is one avenue through which market competitiveness is obtained. Mergers that discourage other potential players from entering could worsen competition. The effect of potential entrants waiting in the wings can be a strong discipline on the behavior of players in the market. This stage of the analysis considers the identity of the potential entrants, their likelihood of entry, and their possible effect on the market.
4. ***Are there alternatives to obtain the merger efficiency gains?*** Here the agencies consider the ability of the merging firms to use assets more efficiently, lower costs, or improve quality—changes that may improve consumer welfare. In

EXHIBIT 28.1 Example of Calculating the Herfindahl-Hirschman Index (HHI)

Here's a hypothetical problem: You want to propose a merger of the sixth- and tenth-largest competitors in a market. How likely is this merger to be challenged by the U.S. antitrust authorities? The answer depends on your estimates of the Herfindahl-Hirschman Indexes for the market before and after the merger and on the basis of revenues and unit outputs.

Analysis

1. You must identify the relevant market for your two firms, including their peer competitors.
2. Load the revenue and unit data for your two firms and their peers into the calculator. Note that in the postmerger scenario, firms 6 and 10 are combined.
3. Compare the postmerger results in the summary (at the top) against the HHI benchmarks offered in the DOJ/FTC merger guidelines:

If HHI < 1,000, challenge is unlikely.
If 1,000 < HHI < 1,800, and change in HHI is 100 points or more, challenge is likely.
If HHI > 1,800, challenge is likely.

Conclusion

On the basis of the example given in the "Model" worksheet, the deal is right on the borderline:

Based on revenues, HHI after the deal is 1,405, and change in HHI is 132. Challenge is likely.
Based on unit output, HHI after the deal is 1,284, and change in HHI is 81. Challenge is unlikely.

Therefore, find a good antitrust lawyer who can work proactively with the antitrust agencies to help them understand your case for why this deal is not anticompetitive. Arguments about efficiencies, potential new entrants, or firm failure may be decisive.

The following calculations support this example.

Summary	Revenues	Unit Output
Market HHI before deal	1,272.7	1,203.0
Market HHI after deal	1,405.3	1,284.5
Change in market HHI	132.6	81.4

EXHIBIT 28.1 *(Continued)*

HHI Indexes before Contemplated Transaction

	Based on Revenues			Based on Unit Output		
Market Players	Revenues	% Market Share	(Market Share)^2	Units Produced	% Market Share	(Market Share)^2
1	100	18.2	330.6	100	17.5	307.8
2	90	16.4	267.8	92	16.1	260.5
3	80	14.5	211.6	79	13.9	192.1
4	70	12.7	162.0	68	11.9	142.3
5	60	10.9	119.0	59	10.4	107.1
6	50	9.1	82.6	49	8.6	73.9
7	40	7.3	52.9	39	6.8	46.8
8	30	5.5	29.8	29	5.1	25.9
9	20	3.6	13.2	28	4.9	24.1
10	10	1.8	3.3	27	4.7	22.4
Total	550	100.0	1,272.7 HHI	570	100.0	1,203.0 HHI

HHI Indexes after Contemplated Transaction

1	100	19.2	369.8	100	17.5	307.8
2	90	17.3	299.6	92	16.1	260.5
3	80	15.4	236.7	79	13.9	192.1
4	70	13.5	181.2	68	11.9	142.3
5	60	11.5	133.1	59	10.4	107.1
6	30	5.8	33.3	39	6.8	46.8
7	20	3.8	14.8	29	5.1	25.9
8	10	1.9	3.7	28	4.9	24.1
Newco (=#6+#10)	60	11.5	133.1	76	13.3	177.8
Total	520	100.0	1,405.3 HHI	570	100.0	1,284.5 HHI

1997, the agencies wrote that they would not challenge mergers where efficiencies could be substantiated and would not result in anticompetitive reductions in output or service: "Efficiencies are difficult to verify and quantify, in part because much of the information relating to efficiencies is uniquely in the possession of the merging firms. Moreover, efficiencies projected reasonably and in good faith by the merging firms may not be realized. Therefore, the merging firms must substantiate efficiency claims so that the Agency can verify by reasonable means the likelihood and magnitude of each asserted efficiency, how and when each would be achieved (and any costs of doing so), how each would enhance the merged firm's ability and incentive to complete, and why each would be merger-specific."[16] Plainly, *credibility of efficiencies* is the key issue in seeking antitrust approval for a deal that increases market concentration. For instance, in the case of *FTC v. Staples, Inc.*, which challenged the proposed merger of Staples and Office Depot, two large retailers of office supplies, the court chastised the defendants' cost savings estimates as "unreliable" and its projection of savings passed on to customers as "unrealistic." On this basis, the court prevented consummation of the merger.

5. ***Is either of the merging partners a "failing firm"?*** Challenging a merger might promote competition, but in the case of failing firms also might trigger other public policy concerns about unemployment, pension liabilities, and loss of tax revenues. For instance, in *United States v. General Dynamics*, the Supreme Court wrote, "The failing-company defense presupposes that the effect on competition and the 'loss to [the company's] stockholders and injury to the communities where its plants were operated' . . . will be less if a company continues to exist even as a part to a merger than if it disappears entirely from the market;" the Court permitted the merger even though it would lessen competition in the market for coal.[17]

Nonhorizontal Mergers: Vertical and Conglomerate

Vertical mergers occur among firms *within the value chain*. The classic example would be the acquisition of Tennessee Coke and Coal (TCC) by U.S. Steel in 1907. TCC supplied one of the key factors of production of steel. Vertical deals are often motivated by a desire to exploit efficiencies in supply and logistics between supplier and customer that would not be possible with both firms on an independent basis. For a more recent example, the merger of Time Warner, Inc., and Turner Corp. promised to create a programming powerhouse that would enjoy its own downstream channel of cable TV distribution. The FTC was worried that this would give Time Warner monopoly power against independent distributors. Thus, the FTC allowed the merger but prohibited discriminatory access to programming.

Conglomerate mergers occur among firms unrelated by value chain or peer competition. The most prominent conglomerate today is General Electric, which has interests in finance, aircraft engines, consumer appliances, broadcast TV, electric generators, and so on. The formation of conglomerates is typically motivated by the belief that the central office has key know-how that can allocate capital and run the disparate businesses better than they can be run independently. Unfortunately, the evidence on this advantage is mostly negative; researchers have yet to observe a conglomerate premium; rather, the majority of studies suggest a discount applied to conglomerates.

The antitrust agencies challenge nonhorizontal mergers under two theories:

1. ***Theory of potential competition.*** Nonhorizontal mergers do not affect the level of concentration in an individual market. However, they can have adverse effects on competition in indirect ways by eliminating potential entrants into a market who might help ensure competition there. For instance, the combination of an existing player in a market with a potential player in effect weakens the threat of potential entry. This might relax the constraint on anticompetitive behavior in the market. The DOJ may challenge nonhorizontal mergers under the theory of harm to *potential competition*.
2. ***Barriers to entry from vertical mergers.*** Some vertical mergers could reduce competition in a market through the erection of significant barriers to entry. Suppose two markets in a value chain are tightly linked, so that entry into one market makes it competitively advantageous to enter the other. The need to enter two markets simultaneously creates an entry barrier in the form of capital

requirements. Vertical combinations can promote this barrier (and also remove a potential entrant).

U.S. PREMERGER REVIEW PROCESS: HART-SCOTT-RODINO AND EXON-FLORIO

Hart-Scott-Rodino Filing Process

The Hart-Scott-Rodino Antitrust Improvements Act of 1976 requires that "persons" (i.e., individuals or corporations, both parties to a merger) exceeding a size threshold must report their intentions to acquire stock or assets (or be acquired) *in advance* of doing so, and provide information to the DOJ and FTC. After submitting the report, the persons must wait a prescribed period of time for either agency to challenge the deal. Absent a challenge within that time, the deal can be consummated.

- ***Size.*** The obligation to file under HSR covers a very wide range of deals, established by size tests. The buyer must have assets or sales greater than $100 million and/or the target must have assets or sales greater than $10 million. Alternatively, the buyer must acquire more than 15 percent of the voting securities or assets of the target.
- ***Information.*** The report sought by the FTC and DOJ is outlined in a "Notification and Report Form" supplied by the agencies. HSR specifies that the report should be "in such form and contain such documentary material and information relevant to a proposed acquisition as is necessary and appropriate to enable the [agencies] to determine whether such acquisition may, if consummated, violate the antitrust laws." This information includes data on revenues categorized on a Standard Industrial Classification (SIC)[18] basis, by product line and geographic area, supplier-customer relationships between buyer and target, acquisitions in the past 10 years, SEC filings, annual reports, internal market share analyses, and control relationships with players in these products and markets. However, antitrust practitioners strongly advise that filing persons take a proactive role in supplying information and building a case in favor of the deal.
- ***Waiting period.*** The delay in consummating the deal starts upon receipt of the report by the FTC and DOJ, and ends 30 days later. However, the agencies may terminate the review earlier than 30 days by informing the firms that they will not challenge the deal. Cash tender offers entail only a 15-day waiting period, conveniently shortened to within the 20-day waiting period for tender offers under securities law. However, the agencies can extend the waiting period another 20 days (10 days for cash tender offers) if a request for information "is not fully complied with."

Exhibit 28.2 gives the total number of HSR filings by year from 1991 to 2000 and the percentage of "second requests for information" that signal material probability of antitrust challenge. Over time, the agencies issue second requests for information in two to three percent of the cases. Exhibit 28.3 shows that the percentage of second requests rises with the size of the deal. The outcome of challenged transactions is usually a change in the deal, either by a consent decree in

EXHIBIT 28.2 Hart-Scott-Rodino Filings and Second Requests for Information as a Percent of Filings, by Year, 1991–2000

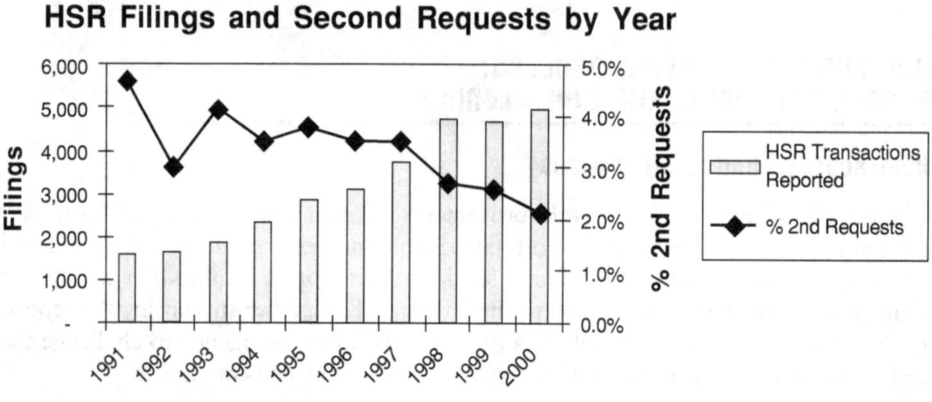

	HSR Transactions Reported	% 2nd Requests
1991	1,529	4.7%
1992	1,589	3.0%
1993	1,846	4.1%
1994	2,305	3.5%
1995	2,816	3.8%
1996	3,087	3.5%
1997	3,702	3.5%
1998	4,728	2.7%
1999	4,642	2.6%
2000	4,926	2.1%

Source: The data for this exhibit are from "Annual Report to Congress Fiscal Year 2000, Pursuant to Subsection (j) of Section 7A of the Clayton Act Hart-Scott-Rodino Antitrust Improvements Act of 1976," 23d Report by Federal Trade Commission and Department of Justice Antitrust Division, downloaded from the FTC web site, September 9, 2002.

which the parties agree to divest certain assets or by a voluntary restructuring. Exhibit 28.4 gives the outcomes of mergers challenged by the FTC and DOJ in 2000. The general insights from these three exhibits include:

- The number of HSR filings varies with the general volume of M&A transactions.
- The proportion of investigations and challenges is relatively small.
- Transactions among larger firms gain more antitrust attention, though even for the largest category of firms, the proportion of investigations is relatively small.
- Once challenged, however, a deal must be either restructured or withdrawn. Antitrust challenges are usually successful. Therefore, *inaction is not an alternative.*

The effect of HSR has been to reduce post-transaction antitrust litigation. Prolonged litigation was seen by some as an effort to hold onto the target's cash flow for as long as possible and defeat the effort to divest the target. Johnson and Park-

EXHIBIT 28.3 HSR Filings and Percent of Second Requests for Information, by Size Category, 2000

Transaction Size Range in $ Millions	HSR Filings		2nd Request Investigations		2nd Request Investigations as % of Filings
	Number	Percent	Number	Percent	
Less than 15	168	3.5%	0	0.0%	0.0%
15 up to 25	959	20.2%	9	9.2%	0.9%
25 up to 50	1,120	23.6%	13	13.3%	1.2%
50 up to 100	845	17.8%	14	14.3%	1.7%
100 up to 150	407	8.6%	7	7.1%	1.7%
150 up to 200	244	5.1%	6	6.1%	2.5%
200 up to 300	244	5.1%	5	5.1%	2.0%
300 up to 500	236	5.0%	7	7.1%	3.0%
500 up to 1,000	238	5.0%	13	13.3%	5.5%
1,000 and higher	288	6.1%	24	24.5%	8.3%
All transaction filings in 2000	4,749	100.0%	98	100.0%	2.1%

Source: The data for this exhibit are from "Annual Report to Congress Fiscal Year 2000, Pursuant to Subsection (j) of Section 7A of the Clayton Act Hart-Scott-Rodino Antitrust Improvements Act of 1976," 23d Report by Federal Trade Commission and Department of Justice Antitrust Division downloaded from the FTC web site, September 9, 2002.

man (1991) studied transactions that generated an antitrust complaint, dividing their sample at September 5, 1978, the date when HSR became effective. The average length of antitrust litigation fell by 50 percent, from 837 days before HSR to 399 after.[19]

Exon-Florio: Acquisitions by Foreigners Affecting National Defense

The *Exon-Florio Amendment* of 1988 creates a process of premerger review that grants the president of the United States wide authority to review and prohibit acquisitions by foreign parties that might "threaten to impair the national security." The act states that this review may consider factors such as:

- Domestic production capacity needed for defense.
- Capabilities and resources needed for defense (e.g., human resources, technology, etc.).
- Control of industries and commercial activity needed for national security.
- Impact of the deal on sales of military goods, equipment, or technology to any country.
- Impact on U.S. technological leadership in areas affecting national security.

The Committee on Foreign Investment in the United States (CFIUS) conducts the reviews under the act, and has tended to show restraint in blocking transactions

EXHIBIT 28.4 Resolution of Antitrust Challenges: Court Status and Outcome

	DOJ	FTC	Sum	Percent
Total challenges in 2000	48	32	80	100%
DOJ filed complaint in court	21		21	26%
Settled by consent decree	18		18	23%
Defendents abandoned the transaction	2		2	3%
Litigation completed, DOJ won	1		1	1%
DOJ threatened to litigate and parties respond	27		27	34%
Parties restructured the transaction to satisfaction of DOJ	16		16	20%
Parties abandoned the proposed transaction	11		11	14%
FCT and parties reached consent agreements for restructuring		18	18	23%
Parties abandoned the proposed transaction after FTC challenge		9	9	11%
FTC sought injunctive relief in court		5	5	6%
Parties abandoned the proposed transaction		3	3	4%
Parties negotiated consent agreement with FTC		1	1	1%
Case still pending		1	1	1%
Summary of results for Both Agencies				
Total			80	100%
Went to court			26	33%
Did not go to court			54	68%
Outcome: Abandoned the deal			25	31%
Restructured voluntarilty			16	20%
Restructured with consent decree or agreement			38	48%
Case still pending			1	1%

Source: The data for this exhibit is from "Annual Report to Congress Fiscal Year 2000, Pursuant to Subsection (j) of Section 7A of the Clayton Act Hart-Scott-Rodino Antitrust Improvements Act of 1976," 23d Report by Federal Trade Commission and Department of Justice Antitrust Division downloaded from the FTC web site, September 9, 2002.

under the otherwise sweeping language of the act. The Committee has tended to block transactions related to the potential transfer of weapons technology.

Any party to a transaction covered by the act can submit a voluntary filing. The chief criterion for filing is that the acquisition is by or with foreign persons, or would result in their control of the target. The review process under Exon-Florio follows three stages:

1. A 30-day *waiting period* in which CFIUS reviews the transaction.
2. A 45-day investigation period, if warranted.
3. A 15-day period in which the president decides whether to prohibit or permit the deal.

ANTITRUST REGULATION OF M&A IN THE EUROPEAN UNION

One of the most interesting antitrust venues today is the European Union. There, new regulatory policies are taking shape that will affect antitrust enforcement and M&A practices in all countries. Thus, the emerging policies in the European Union bear special attention.

Dimensions of Enforcement

In Europe, mergers are regulated by individual countries and by the European Competition Commission of the European Union (EU). The multiple jurisdictions in which business firms operate create headaches for M&A practitioners, and a fervent desire for a "one-stop shop" in regulation. In 1989, the Council of the European Communities issued a regulation on "the control of concentrations between undertakings" that established the foundation for harmonized antitrust enforcement of merger policies among countries in Europe. As amended in 1997, the merger guidelines[20] stipulate the following:

- *Size.* The merger policy covers transactions above size thresholds including these:
  - Worldwide revenues of Newco are greater than €5 billion, and EU revenues are greater than € 250 million.
  - Worldwide revenues of Newco are greater than € 2.5 billion, and there are EU revenues in three member states of € 100 million.
- *Definition.* "Concentration" arises from mergers, acquisitions, formation of joint ventures, and acquisitions of controlling share interests. Excluded are holdings by banks and financial institutions.
- *Prior notification.* Merging firms must report to the Commission within a week of reaching agreement or announcing an unsolicited bid.
- *Commission response.* EU antitrust regulators must respond to the merger report within one month, though this can be increased to six weeks at the request of a member state for more time. The process includes these stages:
  1. Request for information.
  2. Investigation by Commission or member states.
  3. Hearings of merging parties and third persons.
  4. Consultation with antitrust authorities of member states.
  5. Publication of decisions. Fines and penalties imposed as necessary.
  6. Appeal to the Court of Justice.

Mini-Case: General Electric/Honeywell and the European Commission's Perspective

On October 22, 2000, General Electric and Honeywell announced an agreement to merge. The parties filed the HSR report with the DOJ and FTC and received clearance for the transaction, although GE had to commit to divesting certain assets. On February 5, 2001, the firms submitted a report to the European Competition Commission of the EU. After considerable study and request for additional information, the European Commission declared on July 3, 2001, that the merger was "incompatible with the common market." Realizing that this decision would forestall their business dealings in the EU, GE and Honeywell terminated their merger plans.

Four main factors motivated the decision of the European Competition Commission:

1. ***Large beginning market positions.*** Before the merger, GE and Honeywell were already material players in their respective markets. Both were conglomerates, but with strong positions in technology—notably, in this case, aerospace products.
2. ***Factors contributing to dominance.*** The Commission noted GE's past competitive behavior, especially:
   - *Tying.* GE Capital Aviation Services (GECAS) was the largest purchaser of new aircraft. GECAS selected only GE engines in its purchase specifications.
   - *Financing.* GE Capital and GECAS gave GE an advantage in financing costs and in access to capital. GE used this financing as an advantage to close deals.
   - *Vertical integration.* In addition to financing, GE enjoyed competitive advantage from positions in services and engine parts supply.
3. ***Firm size.*** The European Competition Commission noted that both firms were already large in absolute terms, and that General Electric was the largest firm in the world on the basis of market value of equity. Perhaps the Commission felt some bias against the deal because it would make the biggest firm even bigger.
4. ***Horizontal overlap.*** The merger would create a concentration of market power for GE in the engines for regional and corporate aircraft. For instance, GE accounted for 90 percent of the orders for engines in large regional aircraft, and Honeywell for the other 10 percent. Newco would account for 100 percent of the market.

Staff analysts for the EU wrote, "The proposed merger would have led to the creation/strengthening of dominant positions on several markets as a result of horizontal overlaps between some of the parties' products and the combination of Honeywell's leading market positions with GE's financial strength and vertical integration in aircraft purchasing, financing, leasing and aftermarket services. The merged firm's incentive and ability to foreclose competition through, inter alia, bundling/tying and other anti-competitive means would have also contributed to the creation/strengthening of dominant positions on several of the relevant markets."[21]

Mini-Case: General Electric/Honeywell, DOJ's Perspective

Why did the United States clear the merger and the Europeans do the opposite? The analysis by the DOJ reached sharply different conclusions. In a paper prepared after the EU decision, the DOJ offered these comments:[22]

> *The theories of competitive harm relied heavily on the claim that GE was already dominant in the market for large aircraft engines. We found little support for that argument. Under U.S. law, a firm must have "the power to control*

prices or exclude competition" in order to be found to have market power or to be "dominant." While GE currently enjoys a large market share (due largely to its position through its CFMI joint venture with SNECMA as the exclusive supplier of engines for the Boeing 737), we concluded that the market for large aircraft engines is a big market with three strong competitors—GE, Rolls-Royce, and Pratt & Whitney. In such a market, historic market shares are only weakly indicative of future success, as illustrated by the fact that recent contract awards have been quite evenly divided among the three firms, with GE winning 42%, PW 32%, and Rolls-Royce 27% (even including CFMI engines in GE's share). We could see no basis, therefore, for finding that GE would be able impose restrictions on its engines customers (for example, by tying Honeywell avionics to its engine sales) without disadvantaging itself in its battle against Pratt & Whitney and Rolls-Royce to have its engines selected on future platforms. And, in the case of CFMI engines, GE's ability to impose such restrictions would be further constrained by its joint venture partner, SNECMA, who would gain nothing from such restrictions.

We were also unpersuaded that GE would be able to leverage its strong position in engines to gain a decisive competitive advantage in the markets for avionics and non-avionics systems through either mixed bundling or technological tying. . . . The empirical evidence we examined convinced us that mixed bundling, to the extent it may be practiced in aerospace markets, is unlikely to convey a decisive competitive advantage. We found little, if any, evidence that aerospace suppliers have been able to gain significant market share through bundling tactics in the past. With respect to technological tying, we could likewise see no way to determine, ex ante, *whether physically integrating engines and avionics/non-avionics systems together would have any foreclosure effect, much less whether any potential foreclosure effect would outweigh the efficiencies that might be produced by such integration. Even assuming* arguendo *that bundling conferred a competitive advantage, we were unable to find any evidence suggesting that other firms would be unable to match the merged firm's offerings through teaming arrangements of the type that are common in this industry. . . . We also could not believe that large, sophisticated buyers, like Boeing and Airbus, would permit GE/Honeywell to monopolize the market for such important aircraft components as engines and avionics. We also examined the claim that GE uses its aircraft-leasing arm, GE Capital Aviation Services ("GECAS"), to gain an advantage in engine competitions and would be likely, post-merger, to use GECAS similarly to expand Honeywell's market share for avionics and non-avionics systems. This was characterized as vertical foreclosure. . . . We concluded that GECAS's share of aircraft purchases—less than 10% of all planes worldwide—was too small to give rise to a significant foreclosure effect. This being the case, to the extent GECAS is shifting share towards GE by offering more attractive financing deals than its competitors, GE is simply discounting its engines, and it is unclear why GE's competitors should not be able to match these discounts.*

All of the theories of consumer injury from the GE/Honeywell merger were dependent on the argument that the merger ultimately would drive competitors from the market or would decrease their shares to a point where they could no longer effectively constrain GE's competitive behavior. This argument was critical to consumer injury because prices could rise only after GE's competitors were either forced to exit or could no longer compete effectively.

We found no evidence supporting the notion that competitors would not be able to keep up or would be forced to exit as a result of the merger. GE's and Honeywell's rivals are mostly large, financially healthy companies with large shares in many of the relevant markets and ready access to capital. Since the engines and avionics and non-avionics systems have already been selected for all existing airframe platforms, and since very little or no new platform competition is expected in the near term, these competitors have an assured revenue stream for many years and any exit scenario seemed wholly implausible. We found no historical evidence of aerospace firms exiting or withdrawing from the market because they could offer only a narrow range of products, other than through mergers which kept their productive assets in the market.

In summary, we found no factual support for any of the key elements of the range effects theories of competitive harm with respect to the GE/Honeywell merger. To the contrary, we concluded that to the extent those theories were based on the argument that the merged firm would have the ability and incentive to offer customers lower prices and better products, that meant the merger should benefit customers both directly—*through the lower prices and better products offered by the merged firm—and* indirectly—*by inducing rivals to respond with their own lower prices and product improvements. That, in our view, was a reason to welcome the merger, not condemn it.*

In conclusion, this case is an important cautionary tale for business executives: *Foreign antitrust authorities can have a long and powerful reach.* Though there may be some tendency toward harmonization of antitrust policies of different countries, the fact is that differences exist and can torpedo a deal.

CRITICAL PERSPECTIVES ON ANTITRUST POLICY

The thrust of antitrust economics is to promote fair competition in the belief that this will promote economic efficiency and gains in consumer welfare. Critics, however, pose several charges:

1. ***Oligopolies are internally unstable.*** History shows that cartels, production agreements, price-fixing arrangements, and other forms of coordinated behavior are at best temporary because of the *large incentive to cheat.* Often, a financially weak member of the oligopoly will cut prices and increase output without warning, thus gaining higher profits from increased production at least until other members of the oligopoly follow suit. There follows more negotiation and a reallocation of production quotas until the next-weakest player cheats. And so on. Eventually, the strongest players cut prices deeply to take back the share of market they have given up, chaos ensues, survival of firms is threatened, and negotiations begin again. This is hardly a history of high, stable prices. Countering this view is that the most prominent cartel in history, the Organization of Petroleum Exporting Countries (OPEC), was predicted by

Milton Friedman in 1974 to eventually collapse; by 2003 OPEC was still in existence but controlled a smaller share of market and had seen its cohesive discipline atrophy.

2. ***Oligopolies are vulnerable to external turbulence.*** Elsewhere in this book, I describe the influence of economic change induced by globalization, deregulation, new technology, trade liberalization, and demographic change. Just as these forces can motivate individual firms to merge and split up, they can do so to oligopolies and monopolies. The antitrust litigation against IBM in the 1970s for monopolization of the mainframe computer market today seems quaint in light of technological change from distributed computing power in the form of minicomputers and personal computers. This criticism of antitrust enforcement thus charges that antitrust is static, that it tends to fight the last war rather than the future war. Judge Richard A. Posner has criticized the agility of antitrust enforcement, especially in the area of new technology: The cases advance too slowly relative to changes in markets, and practitioners lack the necessary expertise.[23] However, remarks by Robert Pitofsky, chairman of the FTC, recognized the importance of these external forces: "Recently merger review has been an extremely daunting and challenging task. . . . Today's mergers are more likely to be motivated by fundamental developments in the rapidly changing economy and reflect more traditional corporate goals of efficiency and competitiveness. . . . The [FTC] devotes substantial resources to understanding and evaluating issues in this area."[24]
3. ***Competitors can co-opt regulators.*** William F. Schugart wrote, "Antitrust has a dark side. Opposition to mergers, though in theory based on worries that competition may be impaired, often in practice comes not from consumers whose interests antitrust is supposed to defend, but from competitors faced with the prospect of a larger, more aggressive rival. Because they respond to the demands of competitors, labor unions and other well-organized groups having a stake in stopping mergers that promise to increase economic efficiency, the antitrust authorities all too often succeed, not in keeping prices from rising, but in keeping them from falling."[25] Competitors can play a prominent role in the origination and prosecution of antitrust cases. The case against Microsoft was stimulated largely by complaints from AOL and Netscape, Microsoft's main competitors in Web browser technology.
4. ***The relationship between concentration and prices is debatable.*** A core tenet of antitrust economics is that anticompetitive market behavior follows from increased concentration in an industry. Judge Richard Posner complained, however, that there was not enough "empirical guidance from industrial organization economists," that "It is regrettable that antitrust cases are decided on the basis of theoretical guesses," and that the empirical research is "at an early and inconclusive stage."[26] These charges constitute "Posner's lament," and became the focus of substantial discussion. For instance, a common point of evidence is the strong relationship found between concentration ratios and profits: Firms in industries with few players seem to make more money. But as Harold Demsetz argued, this may reflect lower costs and higher efficiency arising, for instance, from a first-mover advantage rather than from fixing high prices. Does *price* rise with competition? This, too, is debatable. Summarizing the views of 47 economists who wrote in response to Posner's lament, Samuel

Thompson found that 21 agreed that higher prices are associated with higher concentration, 11 disagreed, 5 were equivocal, and 10 offered no opinion[27]—this is hardly indicative of professional consensus. A series of studies by Eckbo[28] and others challenge the post–World War II antitrust assumption that horizontal mergers will lead to market power concentration.

5. ***The merger guidelines are arbitrary.*** For many years, a threshold of 66 percent was accepted as indicating a concentrated market. Why not 65 percent? What constitutes a concentrated market is a matter of opinion. Recognizing their own fallibility, the enforcement agencies now admit several other considerations beyond the concentration ratios in seeking to determine whether a market is concentrated.
6. ***Antitrust enforcement shifts with the political tides.*** The senior leaders of the antitrust enforcement agencies are political appointees by the president. As presidential administrations shift from one end of the political spectrum to the other, it is charged that antitrust enforcement policy shifts as well. The resulting inconstancy of merger policy undercuts its credibility. Thomas Leary, FTC commissioner, stated, "Midway through the twentieth century, antitrust policy generally—and merger policy, in particular—was shaped by a mixed stew of economic misconceptions, social and political concerns, and a generous dose of nostalgia for a bygone era."[29] For instance, in 1977, Michael Pertschuk, the newly appointed chairman of the FTC, created an uproar by advocating a "competition policy" based on "environmental harms . . . resource depletion, energy waste, environmental contamination, worker alienation, [and] the psychological and social consequences of producer-stimulated demands."[30] Then, in the 1980s, conventional wisdom had it that antitrust merger policy appeared to be more laissez-faire. But Leary argues that a deepening intellectual linkage between law and economics began to inform merger policy among antitrust authorities. He says, "Merger policy is informed by our best efforts to understand the economics of real markets, not politics or other social concerns."[31]
7. ***Antitrust enforcement is a costly form of protection for small and inefficient businesses.*** This is one of the arguments in Robert Bork's critique, *The Antitrust Paradox: A Policy at War with Itself*.[32] He argues that antitrust policy has been subverted by politicians and administrators seeking to promote policies unintended by the founders of antitrust policy. He writes that antitrust has advanced by the "casual introduction and acceptance of concepts that were neither defined nor tested by rigorous analysis and adversarial debate. This history should constitute a warning about the weaknesses of the adjudicative process and the danger of relying upon courts to evolve major social policy. . . . Law tends to arrive at basic answers before the right questions have been asked."[33]
8. ***Large size is not necessarily an advantage.*** Much of the original impulse for antitrust regulation sprang from an anxious reaction in the nineteenth century to the sudden rise of very large firms. Size suggested the power to override political and social institutions. In recent years, the alleged misbehavior among the largest firms (Enron, WorldCom, Tyco, etc.) seems to suggest that size may have conferred a sense of invulnerability. With economies of large scale go lower costs and higher profits. For these and other reasons, the sense has been in some circles therefore that "big is bad." But is this true? As Clayton Christensen (1997) suggests, size and strong market positions may actually be an in-

dicator of future decline. Wal-Mart, Dell, Home Depot, and others were small firms that entered a field crowded with large firms—and won because they were more efficient. Size knows no efficiency boundaries. Capital flows to good investments and will actually go out of its way to find them, as the active venture capital industry in the United States and Europe attest.

An implication of these criticisms is that antitrust policy should be considerably more flexible than in the past. Robert Bork[34] wrote, "Gigantic mergers are bursting out all over, and we seem headed for a new era of vigorous antitrust enforcement—if we aren't careful. . . . The proper remedy for the government's antitrust enforcers is a large dose of Valium."

SUMMARY AND CONCLUSIONS

Antitrust has been contentious since its establishment as a field in 1890. The evolving policy continues to form part of the constantly shifting landscape for the M&A practitioner. This chapter has emphasized the importance of gaining familiarity with the current attitudes and practices in the field, and especially the implications for M&A *process*. The story of GE/Honeywell should remind the practitioner to take nothing for granted, and instead work diligently with antitrust authorities to explain economic and competitive effects of the deal. Consulting with expert legal counsel in this area is indispensable. Simply put, an antitrust challenge is probably a "showstopper," a dramatic end to a transaction. Anticipating possible objections and creatively working to revise a deal to satisfy regulators is a "show enabler." This chapter has outlined the framework of antitrust analysis and challenge as they apply to M&A.

NOTES

1. Chernow (1998), page 136.
2. Ibid., page 137. Chernow describes the reaction to this as violent—death threats, mob meetings, and vandalism against Standard Oil.
3. Ibid., page 537.
4. Chernow (1998, page 555) captured the significance and controversy surrounding this decision: "The antitrust suit against Standard tested whether the American legal system could cope with the new agglomerations of wealth and curb their excesses. The paradoxical lesson learned was that government intervention was sometimes necessary to ensure unfettered competition. Regulation did not inevitably harm business but could also aid it. The 1911 decision was not an undiluted triumph for reformers by any means, and many of them considered it a shameful betrayal. Senator Robert La Follette, who stood in the courtroom as Judge White read the verdict, told reporters afterward, 'I fear the court has done what the trusts wanted it to do, and what Congress had steadily refused to do.' Echoing this, William Jennings Bryan asserted that Chief Justice White had 'waited 15 years to throw his protecting arms around the trusts and tell them how to escape.' For 15 years, White had vainly advanced a doctrine called the

'rule of reason,' which would not outlaw every combination in restraint of trade, but only those that were unreasonable and violated the public interest. This doctrine vastly expanded judicial discretion and opened a loophole large enough to tolerate many trusts. In lone dissent, Associate Justice John Harlan angrily protested this new principle, banging the bench and accusing his fellow justices of having put 'words into the antitrust act which Congress did not put there.' He added mockingly, 'You may now restrain commerce, provided you are reasonable about it; only take care that the restraint is not undue.' The decision tallied in many ways with Teddy Roosevelt's belief that the government should rein in irresponsible trusts but not meddle with good ones. The more militant reformers were right to consider it, at best, a partial victory."

5. Arnold C. Harberger, *Taxation and Welfare* (1974), page 17.
6. For detailed discussion of the theory of contestable markets, see William J. Baumol, John C. Panzar, and Robert D. Willig, *Contestable Markets and the Theory of Industry Structure*, New York: International Thompson Publishing, 1982; Michael Spence, "Contestable Markets and the Theory of Industry Structure: A Review Article," *Journal of Economic Literature* 21 (1983), page 981; and William G. Shepherd, "Contestability vs. Competition," *American Economic Review* 74 (1984), page 572.
7. This discussion by the FTC was downloaded on September 9, 2002, from the FTC's web site, www.ftc.gov/bc/compguide/mergers.htm.
8. The Antitrust Division of DOJ gives a detailed profile of activities and cases at its web site, www.usdoj.gov/atr/overview.html.
9. One can learn more about the Federal Trade Commission's policies and activities at its web site, www.ftc.gov.
10. Carosso (1987), pages 529–530.
11. Detail on the waiting period is given later in the chapter.
12. See *Horizontal Merger Guidelines* (April 8, 1997, DOJ and FTC) and *Non-Horizontal Merger Guidelines* originally issued by the DOJ (June 14, 1984) and still regarded as standing guidance as of 2002. The guidelines may be downloaded without charge from www.usdoj.gov/atr/public/guidelines/horiz_book/hmg1.html (horizontal) and www.usdoj.gov/atr/public/guidelines/2614.htm (nonhorizontal).
13. This section is built upon Thompson (2001, pages 477–478), which outlines the 1992 DOJ/FTC *Horizontal Merger Guidelines* and lends added legal perspective.
14. *Brown Shoe Co. v. United States*, 370 U.S. 294 (1962) at 325.
15. See *United States v. E.I. Du Pont de Nemours and Co.*, United States Supreme Court, 1956, 76 S. Ct. 994.
16. "1997 Revision of Efficiencies Provision to the 1992 DOJ/FTC Merger Guidelines," April 8, 1997.
17. *United States v. General Dynamics*, United States Supreme Court, 1974, 94 S. Ct. 1186.
18. The SIC code is a system for categorizing industries that is maintained by the United States Commerce Department for statistical purposes.
19. Ronald Johnson and Allen Parkman, "Pre-merger Notification and the Incentive to Merge and Litigate," *Journal of Law Economics and Organization* 7 (1991), page 145.
20. See "Consolidated Text of Council Regulation (EEC) No. 4064/89 of 21 December 1989 on the control of concentrations between undertakings" with

amendments introduced by Council Regulation (EC) No. 1310/97 of 30 June 1997, published by the European Commission.
21. Dimitri Giotakos, Laurent Petit, Gaelle Garnier, and Peter De Luyck, "General Electric/Honeywell—An Insight into the Commission's Investigation and Decision," *Competition Policy Newsletter*, Brussels: European Commission (No. 3, October 2001), page 9.
22. "Range Effects: The United States Perspective" (author unattributed), Department of Justice Antitrust Division Submission for OECD Roundtable on Portfolio Effects in Conglomerate Mergers, October 12, 2001, pages 20–23. Downloaded from www.usdoj.gov:80/atr/public/international/9550.wpd.
23. See Richard Posner, "Antitrust in the New Economy," University of Chicago Law and Economics Olin Working Paper No. 106, November 2000. For Posner's more general critique of antitrust, see *Antitrust Law*, Chicago: University of Chicago Press, 2001.
24. "Statement of the FTC, Presented by Robert Pitofsky, Chairman, before Committee on the Judiciary, United States Senate," June 16, 1998.
25. William F. Shugart II, "The Government's War on Mergers," *Policy Analysis*, Washington, DC: Cato Institute (No. 323), page 1.
26. *United States v. Rockford Memorial Corp.*, 898 F.2d 1278 (7th Cir. 1990) at 1286.
27. Samuel C. Thompson Jr., *Business Planning for Mergers and Acquisitions* 2d ed., Durham: Carolina Academic Press, page 495.
28. See Eckbo (1983, 1985a,b, 1989, 1991, and 1992).
29. Thomas B. Leary, "The Essential Stability of Merger Policy in the United States," January 17, 2002, downloaded from www.ftc.gov/speeches/leary/learyuseu.htm, September 9, 2002.
30. Ibid., page 3.
31. Ibid., page 6.
32. Robert Bork, *The Antitrust Paradox: A Policy at War with Itself*, New York: Free Press, 1993.
33. Ibid., page 16.
34. Robert Bork, "Megamergers," a letter to Eleanor Fox posted on www.slate.com, April 16, 1998.

CHAPTER 29

Documenting the M&A Deal

INTRODUCTION

Writing is a process of crystallizing ideas. Therefore, the drafting of documents that describe the M&A transaction as it emerges is vitally important to the refinement of the deal. This chapter surveys the three rounds of documents that crystallize the transaction. These documents serve three key aims: They lend structure to the *process for shaping* the deal; they *signal* ideas and intentions from one side to the other and from the negotiators to people outside the circle of negotiation; and they *manage risk* in important ways. Excellence in M&A depends on a mastery of the documentation process. The CD-ROM contains three text lectures with annotated examples of important documents:

1. *"Lecture: The First-Round Documents."* This offers detailed comments on the documents prepared early in the process of deal negotiation. The lecture also gives examples of a fee agreement, *confidentiality agreement*, *letter of intent* (LOI), and *term sheet.*
2. *"Lecture: The Definitive Agreement."* This walks you through an actual *definitive* agreement, describing its key features and terminology.
3. *"Lecture: The Merger Proxy Statement: How to Read It and What It Reveals."* This outlines the contents of what is perhaps the single most informative document by offering annotated comments by what is contained and what is missing.

This chapter distills the primary insights from these three lectures into a quick overview of the deal documents. Use this chapter to gain the big picture and then turn to the resources on the CD-ROM for the valuable details.

The negotiation and drafting of M&A documents requires specialized legal expertise. While this chapter gives an overview, the practitioner should seek the advice of qualified legal counsel for a detailed review of proposed documents and/or for drafting documents for presentations to a counterparty.

FIRST-ROUND DOCUMENTS

After preliminary discussion between the buyer and target, the two sides have little to show for their efforts beyond an oral agreement on the possibilities of merger. In order to set an economically attractive price, the buyer needs to gain inside information about the target and perhaps an expression of precommitment to the concept of the deal. The target may find it in its interest to grant these requests, but needs to address two fears: (1) the potential leakage of its inside information to others, particularly competitors, and (2) the possibility that the buyer will stop negotiating and simply mount a hostile tender offer or buy the target's shares in the open market. Thus, the purpose of the first-round documents is to address these and other concerns. These documents set the ground rules for further negotiation. They are *risk management* devices that serve a function parallel to those of due diligence (Chapter 8), contingent payments (Chapter 22), and caps, collars, and floors (Chapter 23). Using these documents is a matter of strategic choice. Many transactions do not feature them. The two parties may be in haste and want to proceed directly to a negotiation of the definitive agreement. The target may know and trust the buyer well and therefore be willing to divulge inside information without assurances. Finally, the two sides may wish to exclude potential competing buyers—some preliminary documents may trigger public *disclosure* that could tip off others to an impending deal.

The initial documents in a deal will embrace seven topics:

1. ***Retention of advisers.*** Successful execution of an acquisition program requires specialized expertise in areas such as law, accounting, investment banking, public relations, and risk management. All but the largest corporations will need to engage specialists for their help—large corporations typically retain such specialists on their in-house staff but may decide to retain outside advisers in the instance of large or complex transactions. Ultimately, the board of directors of a large firm may require the opinion of independent advisers. Note that the *engagement letter* should deal with at least five considerations: the scope and duration of the engagement, compensation for the adviser, *indemnification*, and *termination* of the advisory relationship.
2. ***Confidentiality of information.*** A confidentiality agreement commits the buyer to hold in confidence all nonpublic information received from the target and to use it for no purpose other than consummating the transaction. The agreement outlines the information (e.g. documents, kinds of technical information, and/or access to employees) to be provided and the channels (e.g., a data room or investment banker) through which it is to be accessed. If a definitive merger agreement is not consummated, all non-public information is to be returned. The agreement may commit the buyer not to disclose publicly the merger negotiations without approval of the target. Finally, the agreement will enable the target to seek injunctions or other relief in the event that the information is misused or about to be disclosed.
3. ***Exclusivity of negotiation.*** Typically a buyer requests a period of time (such as 90 days) in which to complete its due diligence research and negotiate a merger agreement; during this period the target agrees not to share information or seek discussions with other potential buyers. By granting this request the target gives a commitment to the buyer, an option. The target's motives for doing so may include to increase the probability of a successful agreement and to deter an undesirable competing buyer. The disadvantage of granting exclusivity to the buyer is that it removes the target from the market during

the exclusivity period, perhaps cools the ardor of other buyers, and may slow the progress of the target's effort to arrange a sale. More importantly, the target gets little in return for exclusivity other than a nonbinding commitment in the form of the LOI.

4. ***Termination of the transaction.*** The alternative to an *exclusivity agreement* is to enter into termination and other agreements such as lockups, golden parachutes, and *breakup fees. Termination agreements* subsume the payment of these other fees. For instance, if an agreement is terminated, payment of the breakup fee is triggered. Thus, the termination agreement creates a contingent claim. The economic purpose of these contingent payments is to raise the entry price for a potential competitor and thereby discourage nuisance bids by competitors, buy time, and focus the attention of the counterparty.
5. ***Standstill on purchasing additional shares.*** The target's final fear is that having divulged its inner secrets to the buyer, the buyer will short-circuit the merger negotiations and proceed to acquire the target through open market purchases or a tender offer directly to target shareholders. A *standstill agreement* precludes the buyer from circumventing the negotiations through these alternate means and may last for as long as five years following the date of agreement.
6. ***Term sheet.*** Perhaps the most significant document in the early stage of a deal is a brief summary of terms of the deal such as price, form of payment, structure, and social issues. In one or two pages, a term sheet outlines the terms in tabular or bullet point form. The term sheet is used to propose terms and to memorialize a *handshake* agreement.
7. ***Letter of intent.*** A letter of intent is an agreement to agree. It describes the basic structure of a transaction and is used to record the intent of the deal negotiations up to that point as guidance for completing the transaction process. Signing an LOI offers only a very weak level of legal commitment, though it remains a means of confirming understanding, expressing commitment, and perhaps publicly disclosing the understanding.

DEFINITIVE AGREEMENT

In contrast to the letter of intent, which is nonbinding, the agreement is definitive; that is, it sets out all the necessary details relevant to consummating the deal, and is a legally *binding* contract, subject to any conditions such as shareholder approval. The definitive agreement may ignore vital aspects of a deal, such as synergies, trade-offs in deal design, plans for integration, details of governance and organization, financing arrangements, executive appointments and compensation, and understandings about the culture of Newco. If, as argued earlier, an M&A deal is a system of economic elements, then why does the key legal document in a deal grasp only a portion of the whole? First, some of these other deal aspects may be disclosed in the merger *proxy* statement. Second, other facts (such as those concerning integration plans, management appointments, and compensation) may be obscured for competitive reasons (such as suppressing the ability of competitors to steal talented employees from the target firm). But finally and most importantly, the limited focus of the definitive agreement can be explained by this key idea: *The definitive agreement is a risk management device focused only on the completion of the transaction.*

Definitive agreements have a number of elements in common, including these:

1. *Parties to the deal.* A contract begins by specifying the various players and their roles.
2. *Recitals.* This section tells the reader what the parties want to accomplish, and is easily identified by clauses that begin with "Whereas." Though not required, these statements of fact help a reader (such as a jurist at some later date) understand the motivations and general idea of the transaction laid out in the agreement. The risk management aspect of the "Recitals" section is to present the general rationale for the deal and assert that it is in the best interests of shareholders.
3. *Definition of terms.* This section confirms a mutual understanding of terminology, which can be especially important in complex transactions and business settings unfamiliar to the general reader.
4. *Description of the basic transaction: purchase or sale of assets or equity, or merger.* Here the agreement specifies exactly what is to be exchanged, by whom, and when.
5. *Representations and warranties.* This section of the agreement gives a mechanism by which the two sides disclose information about the condition of each other. A representation (or "rep") is a statement of fact; a warranty is a commitment that a fact is or will be true. Together, these present a profile of the target (and possibly the buyer) at the date of the transaction.
6. *Covenants.* Here, the agreement manages risks that might arise from the behavior of the parties between signing the agreement and closing the transaction. These risks might arise from opportunistic behavior such as a selling strategy of bait and switch in which the seller loots the firm just before closing. Covenants are promises, forward-looking commitments. They can be affirmative (we promise to do this) or negative (we promise not to do that). Breach of covenants can trigger litigation for damages.
7. *Conditions to closing.* The definitive agreement will list the conditions that each side must observe in order to consummate the transaction. Failure on the part of one party to meet the conditions permits the other party to walk away from the deal without recourse.
8. *Termination.* This section outlines the conditions under which one party will allow the other to exit from the agreement without penalty.
9. *Indemnifications.* The definitive agreement typically specifies damage payments in the event of losses discovered after closing, or even breach of provisions in the agreement.
10. *Miscellaneous items.*

Though some of these items may seem to be routine, cosmetic, or insignificant, each serves a vital purpose for defining the actions of the players and for allocating risk exposure during (and maybe even after) the life of the transaction. In the event of litigation during or after the transaction, these provisions must explain to the court who committed to doing what, and with what consequences.

MERGER PROXY STATEMENT AND PROSPECTUS

The key role of the proxy statement is to disclose the deal to the investors in sufficient detail to enable them to vote on the transaction. These documents are devices for communication to the investing public. A proxy is a document empowering someone to act on behalf of another. In the context of a vote to approve a merger, the proxy statement chiefly aims to disclose the terms, history, and effects of the merger, along with benchmarks against which to evaluate the price being paid. Occasionally a proxy statement is combined with a *prospectus*, the document described in Chapter 27 that informs shareholders in advance of a vote to authorize the creation of new shares of stock. Thus, in share-for-share deals, the buyer may need to publish a prospectus as a step to issuing stock, and the target will need to publish a proxy statement to obtain shareholder approval of a merger or acquisition. In these cases the SEC allows the two documents to be combined into one document (a merger proxy/prospectus).

CONCLUSION

Documenting the deal (that is, writing letters and contracts) can have a huge influence on conduct of deal development. Three contributions to the process are particularly important:

1. ***Shape the process.*** Thus, the first-round documents set some of the ground rules by which the detailed negotiation process will be conducted.
2. ***Control risks.*** The first-round documents and definitive agreement hedge risks of the buyer and target much in the same way as other risk-management devices in M&A.
3. ***Communicate terms and intentions.*** The first-round documents convey terms and commitment to negotiate. The definitive agreement conveys commitment to close the deal. The proxy statement and prospectus inform the investing public about the terms of the deal.

The CD-ROM contains three text lectures that offer detailed notes and actual examples of these documents. To extend your learning beyond the contents of this chapter, please review the text lectures.

PART
Six

Competition, Hostility, and Behavioral Effects in M&A

CHAPTER 30

Negotiating the Deal

INTRODUCTION

The previous chapters have focused largely on analysis and design, the things you can do in the confines of your own office, team, or company. With this chapter the narrative opens outward to consider the impact of counterparties in a negotiation, competing bidders, the constituencies with whom one must communicate, and the organizations to be integrated; this chapter and those following are where the rubber of analysis meets the road of behavior. These chapters teach that it remains important to *think like an investor* but that this thinking can be enriched in important ways with an understanding of the effect of human behavior on decision making.

This chapter turns specifically to the challenge of negotiating the merger agreement. Here, the practitioner needs to manage the tug of at least four kinds of polarities; none of these is an "either/or" choice; instead, one has to find a balance between the poles:

1. ***Analysis versus negotiation.*** It would be simple to assume that the analysis is behind you. But in practice, valuation and due diligence research are ongoing processes of refinement up to the consummation of the deal. The merger negotiation process is a *learning* process in which new information is revealed and must be analyzed in real time. There is no bright line that separates the analytic phase from the negotiation phase; they are linked.
2. ***Rationality versus behavioral "stuff."*** Much of the writing on M&A presumes that once you have an estimate of values and understand the incentives, the negotiation outcome will follow. This view assumes a rational actor, who lets the economic terms of the proposal speak for themselves. Yet M&A practitioners tell a richer story: *How* you present ideas has a big influence on their reception. Thus, when you enter the negotiation phase of deal development, it helps to take the perspective of a behavioralist to understand the actions of others and to anticipate the impact on others of your own actions.
3. ***Strategic versus tactical views of negotiation.*** Strategic motivations for a deal should drive negotiating strategy. Strategy lends discipline to one's participation in the talks. But strategy defines *positions* that can become ends in themselves, when in fact it is one's *interests* that really matter[1]—the dark side of strategy is inflexibility. At the other extreme is the view of negotiations as purely an exercise in bargaining tactics. We know that tactics, the moves by which you implement your strategy, can have a large influence on outcomes. But tactics devoid

of strategy may be little more than opportunism. Best practitioners manage both strategy and tactics.

4. ***Principles versus context.*** The world is messy. Each new merger negotiation presents new challenges and opportunities for lying, strategic misrepresentation, threats, and posturing of all sorts. While adaptation to circumstances is generally a virtue in business, not all adaptations are worth making. One should enter negotiations with a clear internal understanding of the principles that will guide one's own conduct, principles informed by ethical reflection. Here the guidance of ethical analysis sketched in Chapter 2 may help frame one's negotiating principles.

Howard Raiffa, one of the earliest scholars in negotiation, wrote, "It is my belief that many disputes could be more efficiently reconciled if the negotiators were more skillful." (1982, page 2) This chapter aims to enlarge the discussion of M&A deal design with insights about how skillful bargaining can affect outcomes. These insights are relevant to a range of negotiations in M&A, including the terms of an agreement (i.e., between buyer and seller), the financing (with a creditor), social issues (with the target CEO), and antitrust clearance (with the government).

THE RELEVANCE OF NEGOTIATION PROCESS

That bargaining process affects outcomes of negotiations is consistent with a set of findings I obtained from my observation of 161 simulated merger negotiations (Bruner 1992a,b). One of the objects of the research was to examine the extent to which the bargaining outcomes conformed to predictions based on rational expectations, or whether other factors influenced the results.

If rationality strictly determined negotiation outcomes, then it should be true that deals get done if the terms meet the minimum requirements of each side. The buyer and the target enter negotiation with a privately known opening bid or ask price, and a *reservation price*[2] beyond which they will abandon negotiations. For each side, the range from opening to reservation represents the price range of an acceptable deal. If the price ranges of the two sides overlap, there exists a *zone of potential agreement (ZOPA)*—this is the range between the reservation prices. If rationality governs, deal prices should settle in the ZOPA; alternatively, if the price ranges do not overlap there should be no deal.

My study limited the negotiators to discussing price and form of payment, and then adjusted for different values attached to different forms of payment, so that the results could be boiled down to one metric: price. The findings suggest that behavioral considerations influence rational decision making.

- ***Something more than plain rationality.*** *Ex ante* reservation prices[3] explain two-thirds of the outcomes. As shown in Exhibit 30.1, 67 percent of the deals either settled where a ZOPA existed, or did not settle where a ZOPA did not exist. In the social sciences, a factor that explains two-thirds of the outcomes is very strong. But the unexplained part is equally interesting: 25 percent settled even though no ZOPA existed—this means that one or both parties agreed to terms that were worse than their reservation prices; 8 percent did not settle

EXHIBIT 30.1 Results of a Simulated Negotiation: Distribution of Number of Negotiations Partitioned by Settlement and Existence of Zone of Potential Agreement (ZOPA)

	Settled	Did Not Settle	Row Total
ZOPA existed	85 cases (52.8%)	13 cases (8.1%)	98 (60.9%)
ZOPA did not exist	40 (24.9%)	23 14.3%	63 (39.2%)
Column total	125 (77.6%)	36 (22.4%)	161 (100%)

Note: Percentages may not sum to 100 because of rounding.
Source: Bruner (1992a), page 12.

even though a ZOPA did exist—in these cases, the parties could have (should have) come to terms, but did not. Thus, in one-third of the cases, the negotiators did not reach an outcome that was economically rational in light of their *ex ante* reservation prices.

- ***Creativity plays a role.*** Unlike the rigid assumptions of mathematical game theory, bargainers tend to concoct unexpected solutions. The paramount example of this is the use of earnouts and other contingent terms of payment that are used to bridge significant differences in outlooks by the two negotiating sides. The two sides had very different expectations about the future in the negotiation problem for this study. As a result, buyers and targets attached very different values to earnouts and other contingent payments. Thus, buyers believed they were giving away little value in the form of earnouts, whereas targets believed that earnout features were highly valuable. This finding is consistent with the role of contingent payments in bridging the differences between sides in a negotiation.[4]
- ***Buying with abandonment.*** The buyers in merger negotiations tend to abandon their reservation prices much more readily than do targets. Some 44 percent of buyers settled on terms worse than their reservation prices (this is a large departure from economic rationality); only 14 percent of targets did so. Also, where one side abandoned the reservation price and the other did not, the abandoner gave up significant middle ground between the two sides. This finding is consistent with the review of announcement returns in Chapter 3 and of the departures from win-win deal zones in Chapter 21: Buyers destroy value more readily than targets.
- ***Taking ZOPA.*** Buyers give more (and targets take more) of the middle ground. Especially where a ZOPA did not exist beforehand, the buyer tended to give away more value (beyond its reservation) than did the target.
- ***Beliefs, values, and aspirations.*** These vary across negotiators and were found to have a significant influence on outcomes. The more the seller wants to settle, the lower is the buyer's payment. The more optimistic the buyer is, the higher will be the settlement price. The more pessimistic the target is, the lower will be the settlement price. These results are broadly similar to previous research.[5]

- ***Tactics pay.*** Tactics such as "*anchoring*," offering many proposed deals, and simply sticking with the negotiations have a significant influence on outcomes. Anchoring tends to carve up the middle ground to the anchorer's advantage. Making successive offers[6] tends to result in settlements in the counterparty's favor. And giving the negotiations plenty of time increases the odds of settling.
- ***Bad stuff happens.*** My debriefing of teams in laboratory simulations of merger negotiations suggests that some kinds of conduct contribute materially to negotiation failures and/or the agreement to irrational deals. These include misrepresentation of facts and opinions; threats and ultimatums; cross-cultural misunderstandings; verbal abuse; reneging on agreement; stonewalling on information; spying; offers of favors, bribes, and other forms of influence; team infighting; emotional outbursts; walking out.

BEHAVIORAL FINANCE

What makes the findings reported in the previous section so interesting is that they depart somewhat from the predictions of "rational choice," a paradigm that prevails widely in economics and the other social sciences. Rational choice (or "rationality" for short) presumes that individuals are self-interested, that they prefer more wealth as opposed to less, and generally that their preferences are transitive (if you like A better than B, and B better than C, you will like A better than C). The rational decision maker is guided by outcomes and chooses the best. As the economist Jon Elster put it, "To act rationally is to do as well for oneself as one can."[7]

Rationality is an attractive foundation in the social sciences for two reasons. First, it simplifies the world greatly and opens up a number of important and intuitively appealing economic insights. Even the proponents of behavioral theories acknowledge the fundamental tractability of rationalism. Charles Plott (1986) wrote that the real issue is not whether the rational choice paradigm is "true or false, but rather whether the magnitude of error in predicting market phenomena is acceptable. . . . Market models based on rational choice principles . . . do a pretty good job." (Page S302)

Nevertheless, other researchers in behavioral finance point to disorderly patterns in markets that are not consistent with rationality:

- ***Market volatility: manias, panics, and crashes.*** Periodically, securities markets detach themselves from reality. There is no explanation for why or when these will occur, though some work by Robert Shiller (1995) points to "herd mentality" in which investors crowd together and follow trends. The herd mentality is founded on waves of information cascading through the securities market, followed by conversation among investors. More generally, securities prices seem to change not only because of changes in economic fundamentals, but also because of changes in investor sentiment or psychology. Shiller suggests that "prices change in substantial measure because the investing public en masse capriciously changes its mind." (1989, page 1)
- ***Winner's curse.*** In the classic barroom game, someone auctions a jar full of pennies. It is highly probable that the winner will pay more than the value of the jar and pennies. This is the *winner's curse*, a phenomenon first identified

by Capen, Clapp, and Campbell (1971) in their analysis of bidding for oil leases. Oil companies who win auctions of lease rights on oil lands tend to overpay; whether or not they actually lose money on the bidding, the winners will almost always be disappointed that the asset is worth less than they thought. In short, winning buyers tend to make outlying assessments that drive their estimates of value for the target. Capen et al. (1971) warn that "he who bids on a parcel what he thinks it is worth, will, in the long run, be taken for a cleaning."[8] The winner's curse is hugely important in M&A, and has been offered as a possible explanation for the poor returns to buyers; see, for instance, Roll (1986) and Varaiya and Ferris (1987). This phenomenon is revisited in the next chapter.

- ***Loss aversion.*** People view value asymmetrically: the utility of gaining a dollar is less than the disutility of giving one up—this is "*loss aversion.*" This is the outgrowth of pathbreaking research by Kahneman and Tversky (1984), and led to a better understanding of two related phenomena of great importance in M&A: *endowment effect*, in which people tend to ask more in selling an asset than they would offer to buy it, and *status quo bias*, in which people tend to stick with their current situation because the disadvantages of changing seem larger than the advantages.

There are numerous other examples of departure from what economic rationality would predict.[9] These findings imply that economics shares the decision-making stage with other considerations. Skills of bidding and bargaining may matter more than theory presently allows. To the extent this is true, you should not believe that your economic analysis of an M&A transaction will dictate the final result. Perhaps Stewart Myers said it best in commenting on the Bendix/Martin-Marietta takeover fight:

> *And it finally came to me that, in mergers, the ratio of "noise" to "signal" is very high, and that the noise is a helluva lot more fun. . . . They're idiosyncratic things that happen in a particular case, once people get into it, and once people start trying to win . . . the lesson about noise and signal is really very important. If we pose the problem of valuing a merger candidate, what you want to do is find the signal and avoid the noise. The great danger is that you start out trying to be rational and end up as a noisemaker. . . . People start out trying to be rational but they end up making mistakes in the analysis; they end up getting carried away in the heat of the battle, and they lose the kind of rationality, the kind of power, that financial analysis can bring to this kind of a problem. As Pogo used to say, "We've met the enemy and he is us."*[10]

INFLUENCING BARGAINING OUTCOMES: AN OVERVIEW OF THE CHALLENGE

From an economic standpoint alone, the bargaining problem can be summarized with value ranges and ZOPA. Exhibit 30.2 gives some examples. In the first example (1), the range of the buyer is lower than the range of the seller, but they overlap, producing the ZOPA. The buyer's range is lower typically because of the seller's great

EXHIBIT 30.2 Find the ZOPA: Four Distributions of Buyer and Target Negotiation Ranges

The following figure presents four cases of the distribution of the bargaining ranges of the buyer (solid line) and target (dashed line):

1. The buyer has a lower bargaining range than the target, perhaps reflecting pessimism, anchoring, or risk aversion on the part of the buyer, and optimism, anchoring, or better information on the part of the target. This kind of positioning of buyer and target is commonly observed in M&A negotiation. The ZOPA is bounded by the region of overlap between the two negotiation ranges.
2. In this case, the buyer and target are positioned in the classic low/high pattern, but there is no ZOPA, because the reservation price of the buyer is below the reservation price of the target.
3. Occasionally one observes buyers with a *higher* bargaining range than the target has. This may be due to special synergies or greater optimism. The likelihood of settlement should be high in this case.
4. Occasionally one observes that the bargaining range of one side *completely surrounds* the bargaining range of the other. The likelihood of settlement should be high in this case as well.

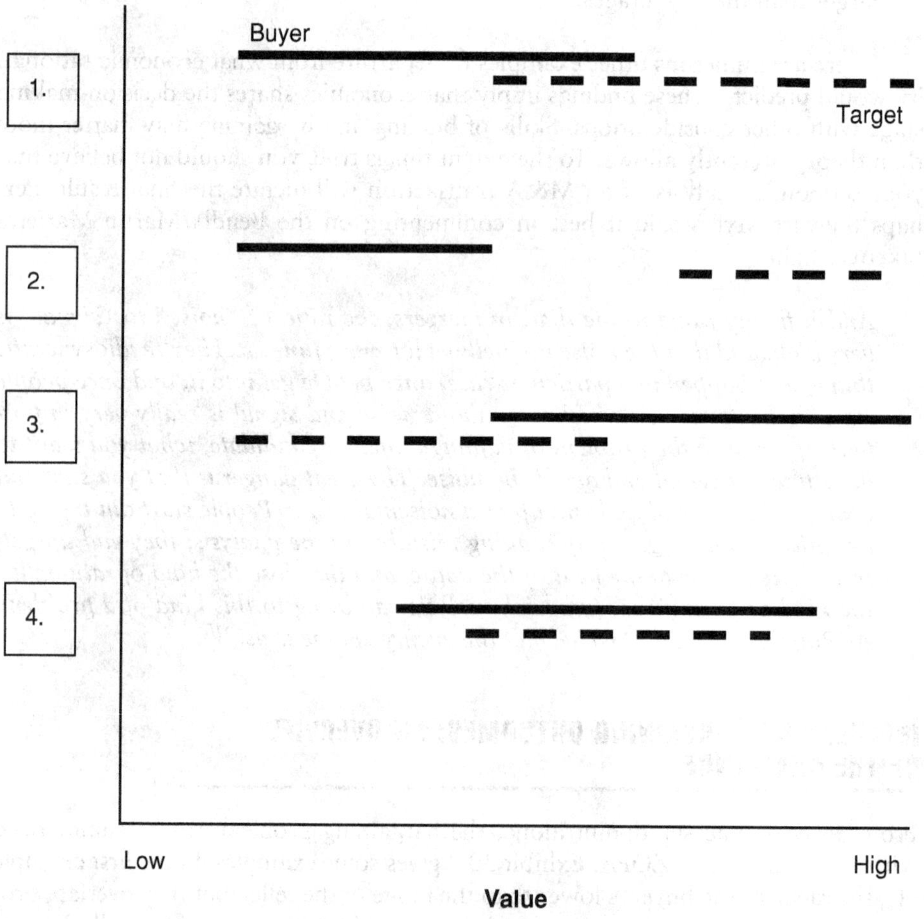

optimism about the company and the buyer's reticent tendency (i.e., with less than perfect information, the buyer suspects that the range in which the intrinsic value of the target is to be found will be less than the target claims). The second example (2) shows no overlap; the two parties have no common ground. In simulated merger negotiations, I have observed the final two examples: in which the buyer has a higher bargaining range than the seller (3), and where one side's range completely surrounds the other side's (4). Psychology intervenes in these neat diagrams through the length and positioning of the negotiation ranges. For instance, the treatment of uncertainty and intangible values may vary dramatically among decision makers.

Uncertainty

Chapter 9 argues that valuation ranges should embrace the range of one's certainty to an acceptable level of confidence. Ultimately, we cannot observe intrinsic value; we can only estimate it. The triangulation process that produces the valuation range is best regarded as choosing a range within a probability distribution that trades off *confidence* that the range likely embraces the true intrinsic value of the firm and *efficiency* of the estimated mean. For instance, by setting the range between zero and infinity we could achieve nearly 100 percent confidence that the range embraces the intrinsic value, but such a range would be useless. We settle for less than 100 percent confidence in order to improve our decision making.

The need for confidence and efficiency will matter to executives in various ways. Psychology can influence this *trade-off*.

Conversion of Multiple Dimensions into a Deal

It would take a heroic effort to reduce the entire assessment of the deal to a single dollar figure. For instance, the sole owner of a target firm may want to structure a deal in a way that takes into account her regret about selling, her self-esteem over the firm she built, her care for the employees she will be leaving behind, and so on. The conversion of intangible concerns such as these into a handshake on price will vary across decision makers—psychology will influence this conversion.

In short, if psychology enters the bargaining process in ways such as these, the practitioner should learn to manage both the economics and the psychology of deal making. To "manage" means to blend both perspectives in a way that promotes successful outcomes such as those outlined in Chapter 1. This includes understanding how one's own actions might affect other party's perception of confidence and efficiency and conversion of multiple dimensions. It also includes recognizing when the counterparty is trying to affect *your* thinking, and how to guard against it. The following sections lend some practical advice on how to work on both realities and perceptions in a negotiation.

PRACTICAL ADVICE: HOW TO PREPARE FOR A NEGOTIATION

Sound prenegotiation homework helps the deal maker anticipate and respond to the other side's tactics and unusual behavior that might otherwise influence or derail the negotiations. Economic and strategic analyses provide vital foundations with which to use, or defend against, behavioral influences.

Assess Buyer and Target Strategy

Assessment of the current strategic position and alternative strategic actions for buyer and target would include mapping the strategic strengths, weaknesses, opportunities, threats, and goals of the buyer and target, studying their goals, and exploring the alternative strategic actions and tactics they might use to pursue their goals. Tools of strategic analysis outlined in Chapter 6 may be useful at this stage.

Value the Target

Use a variety of approaches outlined in Chapter 9. Most of these approaches assume to some degree that the market and its pricing of assets are rational. Sensitivity analysis assumes great importance in negotiation, for the problem is rarely a binary, go/no-go decision, but rather an arbitrage process across different bundles of attributes. The purpose of the sensitivity analysis should be to identify key value drivers and gain some sense of the elasticity of value with respect to small changes in assumptions. While it may help to have negotiation goals, negotiators should never prepare to bargain from point estimates of value, but rather from ranges.

Explore Your Best Alternative to a Negotiated Agreement (BATNA)

BATNA defines your reservation price and therefore defines one end of your negotiation range. Lax and Sebenius (1986, page 48) note that "alternatives limit the bargaining range." If negotiations can deliver only a deal that is worse than the BATNA, then the rational deal doer should walk away or should try to shape the counterparty's perception of BATNA relative to this deal—in short, change the reservation price. Also, clarity about your own BATNA is the first defense against attempts by the counterparty to change your reservation price.

Determine Asking Price and Reservation Price

Refine the strategic and valuation analyses until you converge upon an opening offer or asking price and a reservation price—these are different numbers drawn from different perspectives on the deal. The reservation price becomes an important discipline on one's conduct of negotiations and should be abandoned only with care; obviously, new information may surface in the negotiations that might cause you to revise your reservation price, but the whole point of having one is to limit the impact of psychological tactics, such as anchoring. Because of anchoring, the opening price is important as an influence on the final outcome: Raiffa (1982) found in experiments that the midpoint between the opening and asking prices is a fair predictor of the settlement price for value negotiators, as long as it falls within the ZOPA.

Identify Relevant Players and Their Interests

A "position" is a demand or requirement expressed straightforwardly—an example would be the line drawn in the sand, which becomes a boundary for future conduct. "Interests" are the real aims standing behind the positions. Interests for negotiators in an M&A transaction range across economics (get rich), politics (retain control), and psychology (preserve self-esteem or "face"). Fisher and Ury (1981) urge negotiators to focus on interests rather than positions; Lax and Sebenius (1986) argue that focusing on interests enhances creativity and breaks deadlocks, but that it may be more useful to focus on positions when ideological differences make agreement difficult. Also, it is important to assess actual or potential competitors in the negotiation. One must identify who they are and what their strategy might help for advance thinking on how to present oneself as the best partner for the target.

Anticipate Trade-Offs

Having identified the interests of the players, it is possible to take a further important step of looking for opportunities to give and take that might advance the attractiveness of the whole deal. I have argued that an M&A deal is a system, a bundle of attributes that can be optimized by looking for valuable exchanges where you sacrifice on some dimension that is less valuable to you in order to gain on another dimension that is very valuable. For instance, the seller of a business might be fixated on winning a very high price but be willing to provide generous financing or take contingent payments in return. Lax and Sebenius (1986, page 86) note that "Tradeoffs are as important to interests as proportions are to recipes. To assess tradeoffs among intangible interests, it is sometimes helpful to imagine services one could buy otherwise to satisfy the same interests."

Consider Motivations and Aspirations

How motivated the seller and buyer are to do a deal has a significant influence on outcomes. My research found that the greater the desire, the higher the likelihood of settlement. For the two sides the motivation works symmetrically: For the buyer, a strong desire to settle results in higher prices; for the target, it results in lower prices. Classic motivators for the target to sell are financial distress, the need to settle an estate of a deceased owner, and the private belief that current market conditions are ideal and temporary. Overlaid on the motivation to settle are often some private aspirations about price. One can be highly motivated to settle for a high price, but not so motivated at lower prices. Thus, the homework for negotiators is to reflect on the counterparty's motivation at different price levels. This is just speculation, of course, and can usually be informed only through the negotiations themselves.

Role-Play

Work through possible negotiation scenarios in your mind or with a team to role-play the negotiations: "Suppose I make this move, and the other side responds with

X; then what should I do?" This is a process of thinking several moves ahead, like a master chess player—this is *thinking strategically.*[11] But be very careful not to let these scenarios become scripts—one wants to remain flexible in the face of conditions as they emerge, and not fixed according to some idealized scenario.

Determine Bargaining Costs

Assess the impact of bargaining costs as you enter the negotiations. It is costly to prepare for an M&A negotiation. One must acquire information about the counterparty. Experts (e.g., in law, accounting, and valuation) must be retained. And not least, the investment in time by the deal designer and the executives to whom he or she reports will be considerable. Termination fees, meant to discourage a change of heart and to compensate the counterparty for these expenses, typically amount to 2 to 4 percent of the total deal value. The effect of these costs is manifold:

- *Entry barrier.* They may discourage some parties from making the effort to strike a deal.
- *Sunk cost; deal frenzy.* Bargaining costs represent some "skin in the game," a commitment that becomes a psychological loss of face if the deal does not go through. They can stimulate a strong desire to complete a deal, even a bad one (deal frenzy). However, one of the basic lessons of economics is to reject sunk costs from one's decision making. One should look forward, not backward, in assessing the attractiveness of an investment opportunity.
- *Strategy.* From the buyer's perspective, it is rational to try to reduce bargaining costs by seeking deadlines, asking for termination fees, and looking for other forms of commitment from the target that mitigate the costs. The target, on the other hand, will try to deepen the buyer's commitment by raising the bargaining costs—of course, this has the effect of raising the entry barrier, so the target may try to discriminate among potential counterparties.

Check Your Counterparty Reputation

One prenegotiation influence on outcomes is the set of expectations about the negotiator and his or her firm. Practitioners assert that reputation has an influence on the negotiation process and outcomes. One approaches tough negotiators differently than easy ones. Reputation can play a role of anchoring the expectations of the counterparty. For example, consider the case of Hugh McColl, CEO of NationsBank, a U.S. bank that grew rapidly by acquisitions in the 1980s and 1990s. In an interview, he acknowledged to me that some banks would not discuss deals with him because of his reputation as an aggressive restructurer. He said,

> *There have been many cartoons about me and most of them depict me as sort of a savage attacker, tossing hand grenades into parties. . . . Generally speaking, I earned that reputation in the '80s. And it sort of doesn't reflect the warm and cuddly Hugh McColl of today. I got a lot better as time went by. I got a lot more mellow. And . . . but the image never went away. It's an image that's stayed. And arguably it's well earned.*[12]

Reputations are sticky and can have both positive and negative effects. The role of reputation as an influence on merger negotiations has received little research attention. Experimental research in games suggests that players learn from the counterparty's past behavior and adjust their actions accordingly. For instance, the use of bluffs, threats, and ultimatums in the past can elicit a range of defenses and/or the same behavior. The practitioner should be aware that the counterparty's beliefs about the negotiation process and the likely deal are probably affected by the negotiator's reputation even before the talks begin. The thrust of the effort should be to determine the bargainer's reputation for deal making and any implications it may hold for the forthcoming talks.

Reflect on Persuasion

M&A negotiation is to some extent a persuasive process. Conger (1998) argues that persuasion is more than just argument; it also depends on emotional connection, common ground, evidence, and credibility. Here is where influence counts. Cialdini (1993) argues that the aura of influence a person brings into a transaction can affect the outcome. Influence is the "dark matter" of deals and is gathered through:

- ***Reciprocity.*** For instance, giving gifts can create a sense of indebtedness that sways the judgment of the recipient.
- ***Commitment and consistency.*** For instance, skilled salespeople invite you to try an appliance in your home and then later seek to close the sale. By taking the appliance into your home, you make a (small) commitment that later becomes hard to back away from. Psychologists tell us that humans preserve consistency. Skilled M&A negotiators look to build influence in the negotiations through the establishment of small commitments.
- ***Social proof.*** The conduct of peers is enormously influential, as parents of all teenagers learn. M&A negotiators can point to other firms in the same industry or similar deals as social proof that suggested terms are appropriate.
- ***Familiarity and likability.*** Research finds that people tend to agree with people they like and have known. The success of peer-based sales organizations (e.g., Tupperware and Amway) indicates the influence of familiarity and likability. For this reason, some M&A practitioners seek to build personal positive relationships with counterparties or to hire advisers (e.g., lawyers, investment bankers) who already enjoy such relationships. Raiffa (1982) observed that the foundations for bargaining progress were often more effectively prepared in a tavern or restaurant than in the formal bargaining venue.
- ***Authority.*** Experiments by Stanley Milgram (1974) found that people will defer to authority. Obedience to authority might be heightened through the use of titles, clothing or trappings, and junior staff who give the example of respectful deference.
- ***Scarcity.*** Small numbers and/or short time can elevate the desire to conclude a deal. Cialdini (1993, page 195) notes, "opportunities seem more valuable to us when they are less available."

MANAGE THE NEGOTIATION PROCESS PROACTIVELY

The research and practitioner literatures on negotiation offer a range of recommendations for managing the bargaining process.

Conduct Multi-Issue, Parallel Bargaining, Not Single-Issue, Serial Bargaining

Observing the processes and outcomes of numerous government and business negotiations, Raiffa (1982) concluded that those situations in which multiple issues were negotiated simultaneously and as a package were more likely to avoid deadlock than were the one-issue-at-a-time negotiations. This is because negotiations across many issues simultaneously permit trade-offs that may allow the buyer and target to gain simultaneously. My research found an interdependence between price and terms of payment. Generally, buyers paid more if part of the payment was contingent on future performance. It seems reasonable to speculate that failure to settle would have been higher if the negotiators had been restricted to bargaining on price alone.

Distinguish Claiming Value from Creating Value

Fisher and Ury (1981) argue that one should focus on ways to expand the pie, rather than on how to slice it. Do not assume that your gains must come from the other side. Look for opportunities to create joint value through effective deal design. This is the idea underpinning the discussion of trade-offs in Chapter 18. Stimulating cooperative behavior is possible in a setting of repeated dealings, such as an annual negotiation over a manufacturing contract. But in the M&A setting, the owner of a target may be a person entering retirement for whom this is a one-and-only opportunity to deal. Lax and Sebenius (1986, pages 164–166) offer a range of cooperation-building approaches, including giving principled justifications for all offers, openly attempting to develop joint gains, making the process into a series of small wins rather than just one gigantic outcome, criticizing "claiming" tactics, and socializing with the counterparty in ways that create trust.

Look for Trade-Offs

Identifying possible trade-offs is part of the suggested homework for negotiators *before* coming to the table. But *at* the table, an orientation toward trade-offs can get lost in the hurly-burly of discussion. Bazerman and Neale (1992) give a helpful overview of possible tactics with which to identify possible trade-offs. These include sharing information, asking questions, giving away some information (in hopes of gaining some from the other side), making multiple offers simultaneously, searching for postsettlement settlements, and exploiting differences in expectations, risk aversion, and time preference.[13]

Consider Openness

Raiffa et al. (2002, page 86) describe the virtues of *full open truthful exchange (FOTE)*: "An idealized, collaborative style of deliberation in which they try jointly to solve their problem. . . . They keep no secrets from each other—at least as far as the current negotiations are concerned—and they divulge to each other the truth, nothing but the truth, and the whole truth. (There's the rub—the whole truth.)" They note that many partnerships (and marriages) practice this to great success. Its chief strength is as an antidote to a focus on *claiming* value rather than *creating* value through joint gains. Wessel (1976) offers a code of conduct with which a FOTE strategy is consistent—this is given in Exhibit 30.3. Openness does not absolve the parties from having to struggle with differences in reservation prices, preferences, timing, and power. But it advances the talks quickly to a point where these issues may be engaged, and more importantly, helps the negotiations sail past the minefield of bad stuff that can derail a deal. FOTE may be a risky strategy if only

EXHIBIT 30.3 Rules of Reason, by Milton Wessel

1. Data will not be withheld because they may be "negative" or "unhelpful."
2. Concealment will not be practiced for concealment's sake.
3. Delay will not be employed as a tactic to avoid an undesired result.
4. Unfair "tricks" designed to mislead will not be employed to win a struggle.
5. Borderline ethical disingenuity will not be practiced.
6. The motivation of adversaries will not unnecessarily or lightly be impugned.
7. An opponent's personal habits and characteristics will not be questioned unless relevant.
8. Wherever possible, opportunity will be left for an opponent's orderly retreat and "exit with honor."
9. Extremism may be countered forcefully and with emotionalism where justified, but will not be fought or matched with extremism.
10. Dogmatism will be avoided.
11. Complex concepts will be simplified as much as possible so as to achieve maximum communication and lay understanding.
12. Effort will be made to identify and isolate subjective considerations involved in reaching technical solutions.
13. Relevant data will be disclosed when ready for analysis and peer review—even to an extremist opposition and without legal obligation.
14. Socially desirable professional disclosure will not be postponed for tactical advantage.
15. Hypothesis, uncertainty, and inadequate knowledge will be stated affirmatively—not conceded only reluctantly or under pressure.
16. Unjustified assumption and off-the-cuff comment will be avoided.
17. Interest in an outcome, relationship to a proponent, and bias, prejudice, and proclivity of any kind will be disclosed voluntarily and as a matter of course.
18. Research and investigation will be conducted appropriate to the problem involved. Although the precise extent of that effort will vary with the nature of the issues, it will be concomitant with stated overall responsibility [for] the solution of the problem.
19. Integrity will always be given first priority.

Source: Wessel (1976), presented in Raiffa et al. (2002), page 408.

one of the two sides deals openly—clearly such a strategy requires a fair amount of trust. Raiffa et al. offer a partially open truthful exchange (*POTE*) as an alternative to be considered in setting a negotiating approach.

Don't Let Stalemates Simmer

Standoffs are among the most challenging obstacles to settlement. By definition, the two sides have dug into their positions, and perhaps by *ex post* reasoning justify them on principle. Brandenburger and Nalebuff (1995) offer a framework that suggests three approaches that may yield progress:

1. ***Changing the rules of the game.*** One can possibly change the constraints that influence the two players.
2. ***Changing the players.*** Sometimes stalemates arise because of the psychological investment the sides feel about their respective positions.
3. ***Changing the value-added.*** Perhaps you can change the perceived value that you bring to the table.

Master the Tactics

Bazerman and Neale (1992) emphasize that rational negotiation techniques can help one avoid well-documented losing behaviors. My research highlighted the influence of several tactics on negotiation outcomes:

- ***Anchoring.*** Believing there is a value to letting the other side expose its hand first, many negotiators prefer not to be the first party to offer a price. But this exposes the negotiator to a psychological phenomenon called "anchoring." A seller anchors the buyer's thinking by quoting a high asking price; this has the effect of elevating the range of prices within which the buyer believes a deal is possible. Of course, an exorbitantly high asking price can drive the buyer from the negotiation, having destroyed the buyer's belief that the seller is bargaining in good faith. Opening with "Here's my best offer, and that's final" may be a formula for failure. Thaler (1992) emphasizes that "notions of fairness can play a significant role in determining the outcomes of negotiations." (Page 34)
- ***Making offers: number and rate of change.*** My research found that the number of offers extended during a negotiation was associated with a higher likelihood of settlement and a higher final price. The intuition here is that a high number of offers occurs where the negotiations are arduous: The parties are far apart and require a large number of offers to find common ground. The practical implication of this finding is that negotiation is a dance. You take a step, your counterparty takes a step, and so on. It is important to keep stepping for two reasons: Reciprocity keeps the other side at the bargaining table. And continued movement helps build a sense of momentum toward the goal—this helps motivate the two sides to find common ground. On the other hand, don't overdo it. In one's eagerness to keep up the dance, it is possible for one to submit offers in succession without waiting for the counterparty to respond. Don't do this; you are bidding against yourself and will be exploited by an observant counterparty.

Time Matters

Time invested in the negotiations is a special subset of bargaining costs, but merits special attention. Cross (1969, page 45) argues that "the more distant the agreement, the less its present value." Time bears further consideration for at least three reasons. First, the *length* of time matters. My own research found that the length of time spent in bargaining was associated with a higher likelihood of reaching agreement, and a higher price. I believe these findings tell us about the trade-off between two very important effects: *discovery* and *fatigue*. The impact on likelihood of settlement is straightforward: Given more time (and patience), the two sides are likely to discover *some* set of terms that are mutually satisfactory.

Offsetting the higher creativity associated with more time is the fact that more time allows the two sides to grind each other down with rational arguments or emotional suasion. In the case of M&A, the grinding shows a strong propensity to head in one direction: It is to the seller's advantage and the buyer's disadvantage. My study found that the side more likely to weaken with more time was the buyer—perhaps this is a result of hubris or the winner's curse. Negotiations carried into the wee hours will amplify the fatigue effect. Careful attention to detail, patience, and emotional intelligence, all strain at these times. *Deadlines*, either self-imposed or externally imposed, have an effect similar to ultimatums: They force the hand of the bargainers. The danger arises from stress on the negotiators and therefore provocation of a hasty conclusion to the negotiations. But deadlines are also useful in promoting movement where the two sides have simply been holding firm.

Turn Negotiation into a Corporate Capability

M&A negotiation is an infrequent occurrence for all but the most active serial acquirers, for whom there is enough memory from one negotiation to the next to permit professional learning and development on the job. But for most other professionals, the acquisition and development of negotiation talent as a corporate *capability* must result from a more determined effort. As Raiffa (1982) suggested, the accumulation of *skill* should be a priority. Ertel (1999) outlines four practices of firms that have successfully done this:

1. ***Infrastructure.*** To help align the priorities of the company and its negotiators, the firm should develop a database and knowledge transfer systems, promote active training, and debrief negotiating teams to encourage sharing of successful practices. Chapter 37 offers more detail on how infrastructure can promote the development of negotiation as a corporate capability.
2. ***Evaluation.*** The popular saying is, "What you measure is what you get." Best practitioners realize that a good deal is more than a price—indeed, the thrust of this book is to encourage the view of a deal as a system of attributes. To promote good deals, the negotiator must be evaluated against this richer view of M&A deal structure. Ertel highlights other possible bases for evaluation: development of a deeper relationship with the counterparty, constructive communication, win-win outcomes, creativity, and so on.
3. ***Deal versus relationship.*** Where the buyer is in the market for firms regularly, successful negotiators will understand the importance of each deal for

building a general perception in the market and specific relationships that can help development of future deals—this is a relationship that opens future options.

4. *Okay to walk away.* Best practitioners develop deal cultures based not on closing a high number of deals, but rather on closing *good* deals. This means that the buyer must have the discipline to swallow the cost in time and money of preparing for the negotiations. Generally, such a culture begins with a focus on creating value, a sense of patience and understanding that the firm faces a range of opportunities (expressed in the form of BATNA) and that very few deals are must-haves.

Bridge a Gap

Contingent payments can bridge a gap between two positions. My research found that contingent payment deals look very different in value to the buyer and seller. This is because the two sides bring differing expectations to the bargaining table. By definition, the value of a contingent payment term depends on (i.e., is contingent upon) the realization of the expectations one has. The greater one's optimism, the more attractive an earnout will seem. Bazerman and Gillespie (1999) wrote, "In effect, contingent contracts allow negotiators to be flexible without feeling that they've been compromised."

Culture Counts

Practitioners know that best practice in negotiation is always defined relative to the cultures of the two sides. Thus, in cross-border negotiations it pays to learn the principles of the local culture and anticipate their impact on the bargaining. For instance, negotiators from the United States in Asia are often counseled to be patient with delays; to respect age and status; that a direct "no" may be indelicate; that humility is a virtue; and that saving face is important. If you are unfamiliar with the cultural challenges of cross-border negotiation, consult experienced professionals and some of the commercially available guides to dos and don'ts.[14]

Manage the Politics within Your Own Team

Realistically, negotiating teams are not monolithic. They will harbor differences in attitudes, personalities, aims, and incentives. Lax and Sebenius (1986) note that "Former Secretary of Labor John Dunlop once remarked that any bargain really involves three separate transactions: one across the table and one on each side of it. Making a deal with the 'other' side is normally only part of the process; often the interplay within one's 'own' side is as difficult or even more so." (Page 339) In short, the negotiation team leader is truly stuck in the middle and must find allies within the team. The task of the leader will be to help the team reach alignment so that the members can present a reasonably similar perspective to the counterparty.

SUMMARY AND CONCLUSIONS

The key lesson of this chapter is that success in M&A is not determined solely by excellent analysis. Analysis remains vitally important, but one must also master the processes of negotiation by which deals are obtained. Analysis provides an important grounding, reflected in the walkaway price and an understanding of economic trade-offs. Mastery of negotiation addresses the behavioral aspects of deal design. This chapter has outlined numerous tactical considerations in pursuit of settlement.

One final caution is necessary. Given the relatively high variance of returns to buyers (summarized in Chapter 3), practitioners are well reminded to perfect the ability *simply to walk away* from an acquisition negotiation that appears to have no profitable prospect. Robert Cizik, former CEO of Cooper Industries and an active acquirer, said, "Acquisitions require tremendous discipline, the courage to walk away from an acquisition opportunity that is attractive in every way except price."

NOTES

1. The distinction between positions and interests may be illustrated by this comparison: my *position* is that I want a red Ferrari; my *interest* is in having personal transportation.
2. The reservation price is the value to you of your best alternative to a negotiated agreement (BATNA). At prices above the buyer's reservation price, the buyer will walk away; at prices below the target's reservation price, the target will walk away.
3. *Ex ante* means "before"—these are the reservation prices set by the negotiators before bargaining starts.
4. For more on the role of contingent payments in merger negotiations, see Bazerman and Gillespie (1999).
5. See Siegel and Fouraker (1960), Sawyer and Guetzkow (1965), Raiffa (1982), and Kahneman and Tversky (1979).
6. Successive offers occur where one side makes more offers than the other side.
7. Elster (1989), page 28.
8. For an excellent discussion of the winner's curse, and violations of economic rationality generally, see Thaler (1992).
9. Raiffa, Richardson, and Metcalfe (2002, pages 35 and 38), catalog 48 "decision traps" to which most people will commit themselves some of the time.
10. Stewart Myers, "The Evaluation of an Acquisition Target," in *The Revolution in Corporate Finance*, Joel Stern and Donald Chew, eds. (New York: Basil Blackwell, 1986), page 394.
11. The opposite of thinking strategically is to think *myopically* (i.e., to look ahead no further than one move at a time). Myopic negotiation is a formula for disaster.
12. Bruner et al. (2003).
13. These points are drawn from Bazerman and Neale (1992), pages 91–97.
14. For an introduction, see Morrison et al. (1995), a compendium about doing business in various countries of the world.

CHAPTER 31
Auctions in M&A

INTRODUCTION

The *auction* as a method of purchase or sale is important to the M&A practitioner for three chief reasons. First, in one or another guise, it is widespread in business. Examples include control contests (such as hostile takeovers); privatizations of state-owned enterprises; divestitures; liquidations; sale of assets in bankruptcy; rights to exploit natural resource reserves such as oil, timberland, or broadcast spectrum; rights to assets created by regulation such as import quotas, pollution rights, or airport time slots; rare assets such as art, books, and athletic talent; construction contracts; agricultural products such as raw tobacco in North Carolina and cut flowers in the Netherlands; U.S. Treasury bonds; organized equities exchanges; and commodities markets. This chapter outlines the main types of auctions, one of the most prominent auctions in the history of M&A, and some lessons derived from research on auctions.

Second, auctions are siblings of negotiated transactions; to understand auctions is to reinforce one's understanding of negotiation. As emphasized throughout this book, process affects outcomes. Therefore, mastery of the field of M&A depends on understanding the process drivers of transactions such as auctions. This chapter highlights some key process drivers and their implications for practitioners.

Third, understanding the economic implications of auctions is vital to mastering the subject of hostile takeovers, the source of the most visible, contentious, and high-stakes transactions. Numerous popular misunderstandings about takeovers stem from unfamiliarity with basic ideas in auction theory and behavior.

Important practical lessons in this chapter are:

- Auctions differ markedly from negotiations. If a negotiated deal turns into an auction (seen where the entry of a hostile bidder triggers the target board's Revlon duties), you should prepare for dramatic changes in process and outcomes and adopt a new mind-set.
- Auctions invite strategic thinking. The rules of the auction will shape the strategy one may adopt.
- M&A auctions still involve a large element of negotiation. This complicates the strategy making of both buyer and seller, but also opens fresh opportunities to improve each side's gains in the deal.

- In holding an auction, the seller should express clear rules, adhere to the rules, manage the process to ensure credibility and integrity of the outcome, and seek to increase the number of buyers.
- In participating in an auction, buyers should know the rules and develop strategy in their context. This includes knowing your reservation price. Rules, strategy, and reservation price can help you avoid getting caught by the "*winner's curse.*" It may benefit the buyer to challenge the rules or persuade the seller to abandon the auction and consummate a negotiated deal; the buyer has several possible tactics with which to stimulate such a change.

AUCTION STRUCTURES AND MOTIVES

An auction is a process by which an asset is sold by soliciting bids from buyers; the event is public and governed by rules of conduct that culminate in the sale to the highest bidder. Though this is a conventional definition,[1] auctions in M&A do not strictly conform to this model—they may be neither a single event, truly public, ruly, nor won by the highest bid. But to understand how M&A induces such departures, it is necessary to survey the types of auctions and to place them in the broader spectrum of transactions.

The Auction in the Spectrum of Asset Sales

The formal auction is but one method by which a seller can find a buyer. McMillan (1994) outlines four methods and contrasts them on dimensions such as transparency, flexibility, speed, and pricing. The advantages and disadvantages of these methods suggest the comparative appeal of auctions.

1. *Beauty contest.* This is a purely administrative process by which interested buyers are invited to present themselves to the target's directors. Often the judges will request further information from the competing buyers, leading to a process that is drawn out and vulnerable to lobbying by individual buyers. The choice is made behind closed doors. While the beauty contest preserves great flexibility for the seller (in terms of time, discovery of information, and criteria on which a choice is made), its opacity, slow speed, and potential corruption can discourage potential buyers from tendering offers.
2. *Lottery.* Under this method, the seller simply announces a sale at a specified price, and invites potential buyers to enter a random drawing. At the deadline, a name is drawn randomly (e.g., from a hat), and the deal is consummated. The disadvantage with this is obvious: *There is no price discovery by the seller.* The U.S. government allocated cellular licenses by lottery in the 1980s, virtually giving away spectrum rights; in the 1990s, the government realized that it had simply enriched lottery winners, and switched to auctions as the means of distributing spectrum licenses. Furthermore, the seller almost certainly has other concerns than price (e.g., the technical competence of the buyer to operate the target firm in the future). The only advantage of this method is speed.
3. *First come, first served.* The target directors could simply announce that the target is for sale and then pursue a sale with the first buyer to show up. Some

effort at extracting a higher price may be made, but once a buyer discovers that there is no competition (or that the "first served" rules have driven competitors away), the exercise often reduces to discovering what the buyer will pay. This has the same disadvantages (and advantage) as the lottery. While there is almost no hard evidence on the use of this approach, it seems reasonable to speculate that the bulk of M&A transactions fall in this category. For small and medium-sized firms, the paucity of buyers and sizable costs of the other methods will virtually dictate this relatively passive approach.

4. *Auction.* In contrast to these other methods, a true auction is run by rules and a schedule clearly expressed in advance. Commitment to these rules builds credibility about the process in the minds of potential buyers, thus encouraging a wider draw of bidders. Auctions are transparent and relatively fast. But most importantly, they reveal prices. This is the distinctive difference of the auction versus other methods of sale. For this reason, auctions are ideal for use in the sale of any nonstandard item (e.g., a world-class athlete, the painting *Mona Lisa*, or a company).

These four methods entail competition among buyers and imply some initiative on the part of the owners or directors of the target firm to sell it. To flesh out the types of transactions, consider a fifth:

5. *Friendly noncompetitive negotiation.* Anecdotal evidence suggests that many transactions are initiated by the buyer who persuades the target to sell. Like the beauty contest or first come, first served, this method is relatively unstructured. The key difference is that the buyer retains more power owing to the absence of competing bids and deadlines.

How Negotiations and Auctions Compare

Negotiation is the dominant method for selling a company. Why then are auctions on the M&A landscape at all? A comparison of the two methods (see Exhibit 31.1) suggests the complementary role that they play:

- *Competition.* Negotiation at its simplest is a discussion between two parties devoid of concerns about competition. Many negotiations are conducted under promises of secrecy and exclusive dealing (even though for sellers such promises warrant critical examination). The auction typically involves multiple buyers (and potential buyers), and may even involve multiple sellers.[2] In short, negotiations are typically *exclusive* in spirit if not in fact, and auctions are typically *competitive.* It is the competition among bidders that helps realize higher prices for sellers in auctions as compared to negotiated transactions.[3]
- *Structure.* M&A negotiations have few rules and deadlines. It may be uncertain whether the target will be sold at all. Auctions, on the other hand, are governed by rules, procedures, and deadlines. Simply by establishing the auction, the target board of directors commits to a high probability that the firm will be sold; typically this is not absolutely certain since the board must reserve for itself the right to take the firm off the market if an economically fair bid is not forthcoming.

EXHIBIT 31.1 Comparison of Negotiation and Auction

	Negotiation	Auction
Competition	Low or no competition unless target and buyer can convince each other that they have strategic alternatives to a negotiated transaction (e.g., LBO, liquidation, etc.).	Highly competitive.
Structure	Few rules and deadlines. Some uncertainty about whether target will be sold at all.	Clear rules and deadlines. Strong probability that the target will be sold.
Goals and control	Controlled by target management. Social issues important.	Independent directors control. Price important.
Flexibility	High.	Low.
Speed	Slow.	Fast.

- ***Goals and control.*** In negotiations, the target's management leads the structuring of the deal, often asserting the importance of social issues in tandem with price and other terms. In auctions, a special committee of independent directors of the board will control the process, and typically will seek to maximize revenue over other objectives (see Chapter 26 that discusses the duties of directors).
- ***Flexibility in transaction design.*** For the foregoing reasons, a deal is more easily tailored in negotiations than in auctions. Negotiations may be able to accommodate multiple objectives more easily than can auctions.
- ***Speed.*** Auctions are typically consummated more rapidly than negotiations.

For reasons such as these, the experience of deal makers will differ markedly between negotiation and auction. The comparison suggests that as a deal process moves from negotiation to auction, the buyer (seller) should be alert to three key effects:

1. ***Rules and deadlines.*** What are they? Can I relax them? (How can I police and enforce them?)
2. ***Control.*** Who is in charge?
3. ***Competition.*** What can I do to decrease (increase) the competition? Is it possible to return to (resist returning to) negotiation?

Types of Auctions

Auctions can be classified on a number of grounds:

- ***Open versus sealed.*** In an open auction, the bidders are able to observe the prices and number of other bidders. Tactics such as collusion, bluffing, and threats to leave may have some influence where bidders can observe each other. In a *sealed bid* auction, the range of bids is observable only by the seller.

- ***Single versus double.*** In a *single auction*, only the buyers bid. In a *double auction*, the buyers bid, as well as the sellers who offer prices at which they would be willing to consummate a deal. Some organized stock exchanges and commodity markets are, in effect, double auctions.
- ***Common value versus private value.*** This distinction was originally the focus of research by theorists but has since proved to be of huge significance to practitioners as well. *Common value* auctions exist where the asset being sold has similar use to all potential buyers. A bushel of wheat, for instance, would be viewed by a range of buyers as a factor in production of food products. An acre of land, on the other hand, might have very different values to a farmer, an industrial developer, and an extractor of natural resources. Where values differ by use, the auction is said to be a *private value* auction. The distinction is important because price discovery by the seller is much easier in the case of common value auctions, and much harder in private value auctions. In the common value setting, bidders care to know the other bids because it provides added information about the intrinsic value of the asset. In the private value setting, the other bids convey information about the value of the asset to the respective bidders, but less about the value to you as an individual bidder. It would seem that the vast majority of M&A auctions are the private value type. Yet Cramton and Schwartz (1991) have argued that auctions among horizontal competitors are common value, whereas only auctions to conglomerate or vertical buyers are private value.

McAfee and McMillan (1987) outlined four classic kinds of auctions:

1. *English auction.* This is the classic open auction one observes at art auction houses. The bidding is open for observation by all. It starts at the reservation price of the seller, and rises until no other bids are made. The asset is sold to the highest bidder.
2. *Dutch auction.* This method is used most prominently in the sale of cut flowers in the Netherlands. Here the seller begins with an arbitrarily high price and reduces it until a bidder accepts the offer.
3. *First price sealed bid auction.* This is similar to the English auction, except that each bidder has only one chance to offer, and it takes place outside of the view of the other bidders. The asset is sold to the bidder offering the highest price. The U.S. government uses this method in the sale of rights to exploit natural resources.
4. *Second price sealed bid auction.* This is like the first price sealed bid auction, but the winner pays the second-highest price, rather than the winning highest price. Vickrey (1961) first offered this as a theoretically attractive auction model, though it is rarely used. This auction structure might mitigate the impact of the "winner's curse" among buyers in M&A and thus encourage more buyers and higher prices. More is said about the winner's curse later.

The possible auction structures go well beyond these four types. Mathematical economists have studied numerous variations. As McAfee and McMillan (1987) report in their survey, a surprising result of these studies is that the choice of auction structure does not matter under certain general conditions. The revenue to the seller will, on average, be the same regardless of structure choice as long as (1) bidders are risk-neutral, (2) the auction is a private values type, (3) bidders have similar assessments as to the uncertainty of the asset's value,[4] and (4) payment of the bid is not contingent.

ADVANTAGES AND DISADVANTAGES OF AUCTIONS

Price discovery is the first and most important reason for structuring an asset sale as an auction. In the absence of an auction, the buyer and seller approach each other with private information. Each side knows more about its own assessment of the intrinsic value of the asset (and of the price it would be willing to pay or receive) than about the other side. This information asymmetry raises the possibility that the seller will not maximize revenue from the sale. An active and competitive auction can help to reveal the buyers' assessments of value for the target.

The second important reason is that auctions motivate buyers to bid in ways that are desirable for the seller (i.e., with speed and some determination to win the asset by bidding at the high end of the buyer's feasible range). Clear deadlines and rules by which the auction will be resolved help potential buyers assess the costs of participating in the auction.

McMillan (1994) has outlined other general advantages of auctions in the context of the sale of broadcast spectrum by governments: transparency, fairness, revenue generation, speed and efficiency of process, and flexibility for incorporating a wide range of public policy goals. If auctions are so advantageous, why aren't they ubiquitous? The answer lies in a range of fears and practical considerations:

- ***Reduced discretion in the selection process.*** In an auction, the seller commits to a process for selecting a buyer—usually based on price. But the seller may have other criteria that count, and that cannot be described publicly (e.g., management's desire for job security, compensation, and other social issues). Furthermore, the auction process may reveal more information about the various bidders. But by precommitting to a process, the seller may be unable to respond to the new information in a way other than canceling the auction.
- ***Always a test of wills.*** McMillan (1994, page 14) wrote, "The rules of the auction must not have gaps, for bidders will seek ways to outfox the mechanism." It is in the bidder's interest to drive the auction back toward a negotiation format. Thus, bidders will strive to cancel the auction through a direct appeal to the target board in the form of a "bear hug" letter, or even threatening not to participate at all. Other strategies will include requesting time extensions and requesting exceptions from the qualifying conditions of a bid.
- ***Reputation risk from canceling the auction or deviating from the rules.*** Any other outcome than a sale of the target company can result in a loss of reputation to the target. Cancellation or departure from the rules may suggest to skeptics that the target is in much worse shape than originally implied.
- ***Discourages entry by prospective bidders.*** Because auctions are so successful in maximizing revenue to the seller, some buyers decline to participate in auctions as a matter of policy. Also, since auctions are relatively public events, some buyers may be reluctant to participate simply out of a fear of damage to

their reputation should they lose. These concerns may reduce the economic efficiency of the auction by reducing the number of bidders. From a macroeconomic perspective, the debate over the discouragement of bidders has implications for the effectiveness with which capital markets monitor managers, and the structure of corporate law. Gilson and Black (1995, page 1174) note that "the development of Delaware law . . . has been decidedly pro-auction" in the sense that it permits the use of poison pills and other defenses, and requires waiting periods within which a target can find alternative bidders and start an auction.

AUCTIONS IN PRACTICE: THE CASE OF RJR NABISCO

In actual practice, firms are auctioned in a first price sealed bid structure, but then followed by a negotiation over terms other than price. The seller typically reserves the right to cast off the winner of the auction in the event that the parties are unable to agree on detailed terms in the negotiation. But since casting off the winner of the auction would be a very negative signal to other potential buyers, this rarely happens. In short, the "auction" of a firm is really a hybrid between a classic auction and a negotiation.

Wasserstein (2000) describes the typical auction process:

1. ***Selling memorandum.*** The process starts with the preparation of a "pitch book" and prospectus, prepared by the seller rather than the buyer.
2. ***Initial contact.*** A list of prospective bidders is prepared: These buyers are identified for possible reasons that are strategic (e.g., peer competitor) or financial (e.g., LBO prospects). The prospects are contacted. If interested, they are asked to sign a confidentiality agreement. Upon signing, the prospective buyers receive the information book.
3. ***Indication of interest.*** The book is mainly an appetizer, intended to elicit the interest of bidders in learning more. They may be given more information, or they may be asked to submit a nonbinding value range in which they would be willing to do a deal.
4. ***Second round.*** From the firms who submit nonbinding indications, a subset is chosen to enter a second round of the auction. Here, management of the target will give presentations and tours to the bidders, and access to a data room containing detailed information. Formal rules outline the procedure in this second round: These will state deadlines and the nature of bids that will be deemed to be contenders in the final competition. For instance, the seller may dictate that only cash bids with a firm financing commitment by the buyer will be acceptable. At the deadline, directors of the target will examine the bids and declare a winner.
5. ***Third round.*** Occasionally the seller will return to the few highest bidders in the second round, using the high bid to elicit even higher bids. Wasserstein calls this the *"dripping wax" auction.* It can be an effective tactic in maximizing revenue to the seller, but it can also contribute to a negative reputation that in future auctions might prompt buyers to bid relatively low in anticipation of the dripping wax tactic.

6. ***Final negotiations.*** After the auction, negotiations over the definitive agreement begin. New issues may surface. Crafting the definitive agreement invites heightened scrutiny of the target and buyer that could reveal concerns and negotiable issues not previously identified.

A process much like this culminated in the acquisition of RJR Nabisco by Kohlberg, Kravis, and Roberts (KKR) in 1988. The history[5] of the auction began on October 19, 1988, when Ross Johnson, CEO and Chairman of RJR Nabisco, issued a press release announcing his intent to take the firm private in a leveraged buyout. At the bid of $75 per share, the deal would amount to $17.6 billion, the largest LBO in history. In January of that year, Johnson had requested the firm's CFO to undertake a study of possible LBO structures and prices. His chief motivation was that the firm was undervalued, trading at nine times earnings, a value that ignored the profitable Nabisco foods business whose peers traded at 22 times earnings. In July 1988, Johnson had commissioned Shearson Lehman to study the LBO and recommend strategy. In early October, Johnson informed the board of directors of his intent to submit a proposal; thereupon they formed a committee of independent directors to evaluate the proposal. Johnson's LBO proposal was remarkable for two reasons. First, though the bid premium was a respectable 34 percent (RJR Nabisco's shares had traded around $55.875 before the bid), quick analyses suggested that the breakup value of the firm was between $80 and $90 per share. Second, the LBO gave control of the firm to Ross Johnson and his team with no cash investment required of them—most LBOs required cash investments by key managers and gave control to the financial investors.

Within days, four more competing groups surfaced:

1. ***Kohlberg, Kravis, and Roberts (KKR)*** offered $90 per share, for a total deal of about $20.3 billion. The package included a payment of $79 in cash and $11 in pay-in-kind (PIK) preferred stock.
2. ***Hanson Trust and Salomon Brothers*** entertained making a bid. But when the lofty KKR bid was announced, Hanson backed out.
3. ***Forstmann, Little and Goldman Sachs*** explored making a bid, but backed away after concluding that the financing would be too difficult.
4. ***Pritzker Interests and First Boston*** were the last to enter the competition and eventually made a surprising bid.

In October, the special committee of directors organized a due diligence research process for interested groups. In addition, the committee commenced research on the value that might be delivered to shareholders through an internal restructuring—this was a signal to potential bidders that the directors were setting a floor based on the value that the firm could deliver on its own. During October, the special committee sought to determine who else might enter the bidding. KKR and the management group explored the possibility of a joint bid, but separated in a disagreement over control of Newco. In a reply to KKR on November 3, the Ross Johnson/Shearson group offered $92 per share for the firm.

Confident that the firm would be sold, and no doubt counseled by lawyers about the Revlon duties, on November 7 the special committee declared an auction with bids due on November 18. This would be a first price sealed bid auction, intended to be resolved in a single round of bidding. The rules for the auction were:

- Asset sales could not be a condition for the offer. This meant that a bidder could not try to line up purchasers for key assets of the firm, and then, failing to find a buyer, walk away from the deal.
- RJR Nabisco shareholders should retain a "substantial common-stock related interest." The directors wanted shareholders to have the opportunity to participate in the possible gains from restructuring the firm.
- The proposals needed to describe financing for the offer, present commitments for financing (such as commitment letters from banks), and give details on any securities to be offered (e.g., convertible bonds).
- The board of directors of the bidding firm must have approved the bid. This would eliminate any uncertainty about the intent of the buyer.
- The special committee retained the power to revise the rules and to reject any or all bids.

On November 18, the special committee received a number of bizarre offers from unanticipated bidders. Burroughs and Helyar reported that these included a bid of $123 per share from a Toronto banker (who offered each independent director $7 million for his vote), $126 from an individual in Maryland, and $127 from a stockbroker in Winston-Salem (who wrote that though he did not have financing arranged, he was confident that he could find financing in the event that the bid was accepted). The independent committee rejected these bids as lacking credibility to consummate the deal. The more credible bidders raised their offers:

- ***KKR*** offered $94 per share, or a total of $21.62 billion. The KKR bid carried a full financial commitment from banks.
- ***Ross Johnson/Shearson*** offered $100 per share, or $23 billion. This bid also carried a financial commitment from banks.
- ***Pritzker/First Boston*** entered the competition very late and surprised the committee by offering $105 to $118 per share. This bid was accompanied by no financing commitment.

Rather than resolving the situation as the high bidder, the Pritzker/First Boston bid created confusion. The offer was based on a complex tax provision. None of the directors or their advisers were qualified to render an opinion on the bid. In addition, First Boston's proposal gave no detail about financing. Though First Boston's bid was the highest, it was also the most uncertain. Anticipating shareholder lawsuits if they rejected the First Boston bid, the special committee declared a second round of bidding mainly to give First Boston more time to provide more detail. One director argued that it was in the shareholders' best interests to extend the contest and create more competition. The deadline for the second round would be November 29.

Over the intervening period, KKR nearly dropped out of the competition, though accounts of their behavior suggest that their statements to this effect merely bluffed, in an effort to dampen the tendency of the other teams to bid higher. George Roberts said, "Let's just lay low. We'll put out the word we don't know what we're going to do. It's the truth. There's no reason to say we're really going to go after this deal. Let's let the world know we may not be there."[6]

On November 29, the bids returned:

- Johnson/Shearson team returned with a bid of $101 per share, up modestly from its previous bid of $100. The bid included giving 15 percent of Newco's stock to RJR shareholders. The team would not guarantee the value of its PIK preferred and bonds. And the securities were to be placed on a "best efforts" basis.
- The First Boston team did not return to the bidding, unable to line up a financing commitment satisfactory to the special committee.
- KKR surprised everyone with a bid of $106. The proposal included leaving 25 percent of Newco's stock in the hands of RJR shareholders. The placement of the securities would be fully underwritten.

The next day, the special committee invited KKR to negotiate a definitive agreement. When the Johnson/Shearson team learned this, they exploded in anger, believing they had been deceived by KKR's demurrals. Pressuring the special committee to reopen the bidding, the Johnson/Shearson team gave an unsolicited offer of $108 per share, consisting of $84 in cash, $20 in PIK preferred stock, and $4 in convertible bonds; this bid was divulged to the press. When KKR learned about it from the news ticker, they threatened to walk out of the bidding, unless the special committee guaranteed their expenses. The board agreed to do so, in an effort to buy time with which to analyze the competing bids. At that point the special committee reopened the bidding one more time.

At the deadline for the third round, the Johnson/Shearson team offered $112 per share. The only uncertainty was that their financing included securities that might have a doubtful market that would cause the market value of the securities to fall below the face value—how much the market would discount these securities was uncertain to the special committee. In contrast, KKR boosted its bid to $108 per share, consisting of a mix of $80 in cash, $18 in PIK preferred, and $10 in convertible bonds. Henry Kravis believed this to be a more credible bid and that in market value terms, KKR and Johnson/Shearson were about even. When the Johnson/Shearson team refused to strengthen the terms of their securities (i.e., relieving uncertainty about their demand in the market), the special committee awarded the deal to KKR. But the directors wanted KKR to pay one more dollar (i.e., bid $109), which KKR agreed to do if the directors also returned a signed merger agreement committing themselves to consummate the deal with KKR; Henry Kravis wanted the bidding to stop. The special committee returned shortly thereafter with a signed agreement, and the auction finally closed. KKR consummated its acquisition of RJR Nabisco on February 9, 1989, at a premium more than 100 percent above RJR's trading price before the bidding began.

The case of RJR Nabisco illustrates a number of important lessons about auctions:

1. Auctions are one part of a deal spectrum. Exhibit 31.2 depicts the phases of this case, ranging from negotiation to unsolicited biddings, and concluding in a formal auction. Where one segment ends and another begins is typically fuzzy;

EXHIBIT 31.2 Deal Spectrum: History of Bidding in the Case of RJR Nabisco

Negotiation	Unsolicited Bidding	Auctions

October 19, 1988: Seeking a negotiated deal, a team of Ross Johnson and Shearson Lehman extends a private offer of $75 per share to the directors of RJR Nabisco.

October 23: KKR makes an unsolicited tender offer of $90 per share.

November 3: Johnson/Shearson offers $92 per share.

November 7: Special committee of directors declares an auction for the firm.

November 18: 1st round
KKR bids $94.
Johnson/Shearson: $100.
Pritzker/First Boston: $105–118.

November 29: 2d round
KKR bids $106.
Johnson/Shearson: $101.
Pritzker/First Boston: exit.

November 30: 3d round
KKR bids $108.
Johnson/Shearson: $112 (face value), $108 (estimated market value).

November 30: Johnson/Shearson offers $108.

November 30: KKR and special committee quickly negotiate the final terms of a definitive agreement. Board demands that KKR raise its bid by $1 to $109 in order to dominate the Johnson/Shearson bid. KKR agrees.

the segments link and blend in many ways. Indeed, as the detailed accounts of RJR Nabisco suggest, negotiations continued as a strong undercurrent throughout the entire episode.

2. Consistent with the review of research insights, this case reveals that:
   - Sellers seek to reduce uncertainty about the process (i.e., make rules, enforce discipline), and draw many bidders into the contest.
   - Buyers seek to bend or break the rules to gain some special advantage in the process—in this case, special pressure applied on the committee, the aggressive bids, use of the press, and tactics such as bluffing and threats. The attempted collusion between pairs of bidders was an effort to dampen the bidding dynamics.
3. Psychology remains a potent influence on bidders in an auction. The detailed accounts of RJR Nabisco suggest that deal frenzy amplified the bidding. The special committee was conscious of this psychological effect, and sought to manage it to the shareholders' advantage. Most auctions close when the bidding gets too high for all but one party—reopening the bidding twice, and asking for one more dollar in value were only possible in a context of psychological momentum that could be exploited by the committee.

THE "WINNER'S CURSE" IN M&A: IS IT REAL?

The closing stage of the case of RJR Nabisco suggests psychological momentum, sometimes called "deal frenzy," that can detach the bidder from reality, spurring one to win at any price. This is one of the behavioral dangers to avoid in M&A negotiation. In its simplest terms, the winner's curse implies overpayment for an asset in an auction. McAfee and McMillan (1987) argue that the winner's curse arises in common value auctions. They write, "Each bidder in a sealed-bid auction makes his own estimate of the true value of the item. The bidder who wins is the bidder who makes the highest estimate. Thus there is a sense in which winning conveys bad news to the winner, because it means that everyone else estimated the item's value to be less." (McAfee and McMillan 1987, page 721) Also, the true value of the asset is also probably less if one assumes that the assessments of value are distributed around the true value.

How prevalent is the winner's curse? Evidence of the winner's curse has been found in auctions for publishing rights (Dessauer 1981); offshore oil leases (Capen, Clapp, and Campbell 1971); baseball players (Cassing and Douglas 1980); uncertain technology (Quirk and Terasawa 1984); and takeovers (Roll 1986; Varaiya and Ferris 1987). Thaler's review of the experimental and field research led him to conclude that "the winner's curse may be a common phenomenon." (1992, page 52)

McAfee and McMillan (1987) examined the same studies and challenged Thaler's conclusion. They said that the problem with the hypothesized winner's curse is that it implies repeated violations of rationality in the sense that bidders are regularly surprised with auction results. They argued that if a bidder believed in the pervasiveness of the winner's curse, would it not be rational to *underbid* regularly if one believed one were likely to win? Thaler (1992, pages 61–62) replied, "It is important to keep in mind that rationality is an assumption in economics, not a demonstrated fact. . . . If you react by optimally reducing your bids, then you will avoid paying too much for leases, but you will also win very few auctions. In fact, you may decide not to bid at all! Unless you want to switch businesses, this solution is obviously unsatisfactory."

SOME PRACTICAL ADVICE TO SELLERS IN AUCTIONS

This review of research and of the RJR Nabisco case affords some significant insights for the M&A practitioner. Consider these from the standpoint of the seller (the implications for the buyer are in most cases the exact opposite):

- Choose to auction the asset if the number of assets is limited—in the M&A world, most companies are fairly unique. But if the target company has a closely comparable set of peers, negotiation may be the better path of sale.
- Strive to increase the number of bidders in the auction. You can accomplish this by reducing information and other auction costs to the buyer. This encourages entry. A well-managed data room and due diligence process are vital. Also, it helps to commit to rules and stick by them. This tends to increase the confidence of bidders in the integrity of the auction and thereby attracts bidders.
- Discriminate among bidders (within the rules). For instance, strategic and financial buyers may have different favored deal structures. Permit each to bid from strength.
- If bidders know one another or are affiliated, structure the sale as a first price sealed bid auction—the inability to communicate in real time may promote competition.

SUMMARY AND CONCLUSIONS

An understanding of the basics of corporate auctions is vital to understanding the general behavior of buyers and sellers, and specifically important as a foundation to mastering the subject of hostile takeovers. Furthermore, auction behavior helps illuminate behavior in friendly negotiations and vice versa—this is because in most cases an auction is an important alternative to a negotiated agreement.

It is naive to view auctions as rational processes driven by strict rules and settled solely by price. The price paid is but one consideration within the bundle of attributes that constitutes the M&A deal. In other words, the effective M&A practitioner must master the art of *multi-attribute* bidding in auctions.

In addition, the effective practitioner must master two other major considerations: strategy and psychology. Strategy matters because most auctions in M&A are not settled in one round. Thus, one must think a few moves ahead in entering every bid. Henry Kravis's "head fake" in the bidding for RJR Nabisco is a preeminent example of how strategic signaling can influence the behavior of competitors and win the contest. Strategy is important also because the auction phase is typically ended with an episode of intense negotiation—thus the auction merely gains the buyer the right to deal exclusively with the seller. One's bidding and behavior during the auction phase can frame the expectations of the seller during the final negotiations.

Just as in negotiations, psychology matters significantly in auctions. Again, the case of RJR Nabisco suggests that the special committee of the board sought to create and manipulate a climate of scarcity and competition in order to extract high offers from the bidders. The aversion to losing the competition, and thus sustaining a loss to reputation, supercharged the bidding. Deal frenzy is a behavioral phenomenon well known to experienced M&A practitioners.

NOTES

1. The classic conventional definition is "A public sale in which each bidder offers an increase upon the price offered by the preceding, the article put up being sold to the highest bidder," as given in the *Oxford English Dictionary*, 2d edition, Oxford: Clarendon Press, 1989, Vol. 1, page 778. From an economist's standpoint, this is inadequate: It describes the English auction and ignores others.
2. In a double auction, there are multiple buyers and sellers. But even in the usual practice of auctions, the bidders might set their own reservation prices based on what they *believe* they might be able to buy elsewhere, in different times and places.
3. Competition is one of the factors that produces higher acquisition premiums for targets of hostile takeovers compared to friendly deals (see Chapters 3 and 34). Another driver is affordability: To the extent that targets of hostile takeovers are poorly managed firms, the buyer can afford to pay more as a result of improved efficiency after takeover.
4. McAfee and McMillan (1987) explain that foreign and domestic bidders could look at an asset's uncertainty very differently owing to cost exposures of the two kinds of firms.
5. This section draws substantially on the account in *Barbarians at the Gate: The Fall of RJR Nabisco*, by Burrough and Helyar—I strongly recommend this book to students of M&A.
6. Quoted from Burrough and Helyar, *Barbarians at the Gate*, page 421.

CHAPTER 32

Hostile Takeovers: Preparing a Bid in Light of Competition and Arbitrage

INTRODUCTION: TAKEOVERS ARE GAMES

A hostile tender offer ("takeover") begins with an unsolicited offer by a *bidder* to purchase a majority or all of the *target* firm's shares. The bidder will set the offer for a particular period of time, at a price, and with a form of payment, and may attach conditions to the offer. The target will ordinarily undertake evasive maneuvers. Takeovers are *games*: This lends the foundation for understanding, analyzing, and designing or repelling hostile tender offers. One can understand these events and the behavior of their participants by studying them as a game:

- Gain the perspective of the various players in the takeover scenario, their motives and behaviors.
- Master important rules and defenses that constrain the players.
- Anticipate the paths that outcomes may take.

Takeover attempts are bets on uncertain outcomes. The analytics of hostile tender offers significantly entail the assessment of probabilities. The players' strategies are aimed at tilting the odds in one's favor. Of course, understanding the game is no assurance of likely success—it also takes skill. As John McDonald said in his classic discussion of poker, "A knowledge of mathematical probabilities will not make a good poker player, but a total disregard for them will make a bad one."[1]

Profile of the Target of a Hostile Bid

The conventional view has been that targets of hostile takeovers are underperforming firms that have attracted capital market discipline. Henry Manne wrote: "The lower the stock price, relative to what it could be with more efficient management, the more attractive the takeover becomes to those who believe that they can manage the company more efficiently. And the potential return from the successful takeover and revitalization of a poorly run company can be enormous."[2] This perspective leads to the *inefficiency hypothesis* that takeovers are motivated by a desire to correct, and profit from, target company inefficiency. An implication of this view is that takeover defenses merely frustrate the realization of welfare gains for the entire economic community. The bidder is an entrepreneur who should be entitled to a healthy incentive for performing the reallocation function. Takeover defenses create *free rider*[3] problems, interfere with allocation of resources, and entrench management. Some research evidence about target firms supports the view that takeover targets have been poorly run:

- Targets of *hostile bids* show lower sales growth, debt, returns on equity, insider ownership, and price/earnings ratio; they also show higher liquidity and unused debt capacity.[4] Schwert writes that the differences in performance are "consistent with the notion that targets of hostile offers suffer disproportionately from entrenched management . . . [and] inefficient use of corporate assets."[5] He also notes that resistance might allow target shareholders enough time to learn about the value of the assets of their firm.
- In advance of the hostile bid, institutional investors have been defecting from the target firm; see Ambrose and Megginson (1992).
- Studies of the likelihood of takeover find numerous predictive factors consistent with underperformance. Hasbrouck (1985) found that high market/book ratios and large size reduced the probability of takeover. Palepu (1986) found that high sales growth, high leverage, and large size reduce the probability. Morck et al. (1988) confirmed the effect of size and market/book ratio. Medium or small size might predict takeover if these firms are followers or otherwise at a size-induced competitive disadvantage. Trimbath concludes that "relatively inefficient firms have a higher probability of being taken over."[6]
- Comparisons of targets in hostile and friendly deals reveal that hostile targets show higher management turnover, lower profitability, and lower indebtedness.[7]
- Management and board turnover increases following hostile takeovers, as does corporate restructuring; see Dahya and Powell (1998) and Shivdasani (1993).

But a competing hypothesis suggests that targets simply present attractive investment opportunities, owing, for instance, to strong growth prospects or synergies—this is the *investment opportunities hypothesis*. Some evidence suggests that targets are not particularly different from other firms, and not less efficient; see Ravenscraft and Scherer (1987) and Schwert (2000). Franks and Mayer (1996) found that "there is little evidence of poor performance prior to bids." McWilliams (1990) found that the exploitation of synergies better explains returns from takeovers than does the replacement of entrenched managers or redirection of underperforming firms. Models that attempt to predict likelihood of takeover do not select measures of valuation such as market/book or price/earnings; see, Ambrose and Megginson (1992), Shivdasani (1993), and Comment and Schwert (1995).

The evidence is mixed on the question of whether takeover targets tend to be inefficient firms. They seem not to be basket cases—but also they are not stellar performers. One has the sense that these firms have middling-to-mediocre performance in which the bidder sees a profitable opportunity for takeover. A thread through many of these studies has less to do with efficiency than with governance: the entrenchment of target management. Bidders resort to forceful entry when target managers reject friendly entreaties.

A PROFILE OF HOSTILE TAKEOVERS

Hostile takeovers offer an unusual blend of risk and return. Judged against the strategic alternatives that were outlined in Chapter 6, the hostile bid is an unusual tactic.

Uncertain Outcomes

Exhibit 32.1 summarizes the outcomes of 371 U.S. and 190 foreign hostile takeover attempts from 1975 to 2000. In a hostile bid, the target's directors officially oppose the offer in the face of the bidder's advances.[8] *Unsolicited bids* account for 1.2 percent of all completed deals in the United States (0.3 percent outside the United States)—plainly, these are rare events. Of the unsolicited bids, about 32 percent were hostile according to Thomson Securities Data Corporation. Of the U.S. bids that were hostile, the hostile bidder consummates a deal about 25 percent of the time. In about 30 percent of the cases, the target is acquired by another, usually friendly, firm. And in about 45 percent of the cases, the target remains independent. In other countries, the results are less benign for the target. There, the hostile bidder wins in 37 percent of the cases; a "white knight" wins in 25 percent; and the target remains independent in 38 percent. Whether in the United States or elsewhere, the odds tilt against the hostile bidder. At the same time, the odds run against the target remaining independent. Plainly, the hostile bid triggers an episode of high uncertainty for all participants. These contests are hardly

EXHIBIT 32.1 Summary of Outcomes of Hostile Takeover Attempts: Breakdown of Deal Attitude and Takeover Results from 1975 to 2000

	Bids for U.S. Targets by U.S. or Foreign Bidders		Bids for Foreign Targets by U.S. or Foreign Bidders	
Total M&A done deals	93,312	100%	147,971	100%
Total confirmed, unsolicited	1,151	1.2%	451	0.3%
Of those that were unsolicited:				
Friendly	111	9.7%	147	25.3%
Neutral*	669	58.1%	114	42.1%
Hostile	371	32.2%	190	32.6%
Total	1,151	100.0%	451	100.0%
Of those that were hostile:				
Target sold to hostile bidder	91	24.5%	71	37.4%
(over competing bids)	(28)	(7.5%)	(11)	(5.8%)
Target sold to another bidder	114	30.7%	47	24.7%
Successful defense, target not sold	166	44.8%	72	37.9%
Total	371	100%	190	100%

*Neutral is defined as either (1) the bid is independent of the board of directors or (2) the board of directors neither accepts the initial bid as friendly nor rejects the bid as hostile.
Source of data: Thomson Securities Data Corporation. The observations run from January 1, 1975, to November 1, 2000.

sure things, a fact that should heighten the importance of professional counsel and mastery of the process for decision makers in these scenarios.

Attractive Returns

Given the low rate of success for hostile bidders, what would induce them to take action? The summary of event returns to bidders in hostile takeovers given in Chapter 3 reveals that bidders win significantly positive abnormal returns of about 2 to 4 percent.[9] Target shareholders win as well, receiving higher acquisition premiums in hostile deals than in friendly deals. When a target successfully rejects a bidder, the target's share price falls but to a price level higher than prevailed *ex ante*—the takeover attempt typically stimulates a restructuring that unlocks value for shareholders. Further evidence presented in Chapter 20 shows that when the bidder offers cash, the returns are more positive still.

Bargaining Tactic

Looking at the similarity of targets in hostile and friendly deals, Schwert (2000) concluded that hostility was merely in the eyes of the beholder and that "hostility reflect[s] strategic choices made by the bidder or the target firm to maximize their respective gains from a potential transaction. . . . Strategic bargaining is the motivation for hostility." (Page 2639) This is consistent with the two previous chapters that characterized negotiation, auction, and hostile bids as segments of a *spectrum* of bargaining approaches to a deal.

BE AWARE OF THE PLAYERS, BOTH ON THE FIELD AND OFF

It is useful to enter a game by surveying all the players. Here is a brief rundown of the usual suspects. It is naive to see the hostile tender offer as a contest simply between bidder and target. The field is considerably more complicated. Viewed through the lens of economics, the contest embraces six kinds of players:

1. *Attacker (or in street parlance, a bidder).* The popular press and halls of government view bidders rather harshly, for it is the bidders who propose to wrest control, close plants, lay off workers, and take other actions to enrich themselves. A more benign view is that bidders are *entrepreneurs* who through research and initiative discover profitable opportunities. The hostile tender offer is the action taken to begin to harvest the profit.
2. *Defender or target is* the profitable opportunity. The bidder may see synergies, hidden or underutilized assets that could be sold, or businesses that are draining cash and could be restructured or closed.
3. *Various free riders.* Free riders are shareholders who may not be well informed but who suspect that the bidder knows something they don't, and who are tempted to participate in some of the profits flowing to the bidder. These shareholders seek to ride free in harvesting the profitable opportunity. The bidder would like to quell the free riders, because they reduce the bidder's profit.

4. ***Groups within the target.*** One of the worst mistakes is to view the target as a solid block of decision makers. In reality, the target harbors important divisions that the bidder can exploit:
   - ***Managers versus directors.*** Usually senior target company managers lose their jobs following a successful hostile takeover. Even if they do not lose them, salaries and perquisites tend to be distributed less freely. In short, target managers have a strong incentive to oppose a hostile bid. A firm's directors, however, are bound by legal doctrines of the duties of care and loyalty to maximize the welfare of shareholders. Failing to do so exposes directors to micromanagement by courts of law, and possible personal liability for past errors. Obviously, the interests of managers and directors can diverge. The target's board of directors is at the fulcrum of pressure and can reverse management's strategy in the game through such means as rescinding the firm's antitakeover defenses and declaring an auction for the firm.
   - ***Insiders versus outside directors.*** The board itself may consist of subgroups that harbor divergent interests. Inside directors are usually also managers. Other directors who side with the manager-directors may have links by marriage or work experience that tie them by loyalty more closely to managers than to shareholders.
   - ***Large shareholders versus small shareholders.*** Not all target shareholders are equal; their relative voting power can have an influence on the board of directors.
5. ***Other potential buyers***, who would have an interest in acquiring the target, but have yet to enter a bid. These might include friendly buyers (also called "white knights"), and friendly investors in special controlling securities (also called "white squires"[10]).
6. ***Arbitrageurs*** make a living betting on price movements in takeovers. Once a takeover is announced, the "arbs" (as they are more popularly known) practically absorb all loose shares sloshing around in the stock market, and almost certainly become the crucial deciders of any contest; for this reason they deserve careful examination.

THE ARB IS THE CONSUMMATE ECONOMIC ACTOR

The arbs' outlook is rationalistic, impatient, and always oriented toward value maximization. Appeals to loyalty, tradition, or some vague plan will have little influence over them. They like immediate cash profits. *Arbitrageurs* are short-term investors driven only by economic motives. They invest funds in takeover situations and recapitalizations and try to limit the exposure to the likelihood of a deal not being consummated. They often provide liquidity to investors who do not wish to wait out a battle for corporate control. More usually, risk arbitrageurs will play both sides of a hostile tender offer, taking a long position in the shares of the target and a short position in the shares of the bidder. This long/short position is a hedged play on the outcome of the deal—the short position hedges against a downward movement in equities generally, as well as possible failure of the deal to be consummated. (When a deal fails to consummate, the buyer's share price typically rises.) One of the leading arbs, Guy Wyser-Pratte, has written,

> *An arbitrageur is not an investor in the formal sense of the word: i.e., he is not normally buying or selling securities because of their investment value. He is, however, committing capital to the "deal"—the merger, tender offer, recapitalization, etc.—rather than to the particular security. He must thus take a position in the deal in such a way that he is at the risk of the deal, and not at the risk of the market.*[11]

Consider the example[12] of a target company that receives an offer of $60 per share for all the shares of the company. If the shares are trading at $40 per share when the offer is announced, one could make a profit of $20 by buying instantaneously and holding until the transaction is completed. Unfortunately, the stock exchange would probably suspend trading in the stock as investors flood the market with orders to buy or sell. When order has been regained, the stock will resume trading at a point where there are both buyers and sellers at the same price. At that point, the shares may be trading at $57 or $58 a share. Institutions and private investors would be able to sell shares immediately to the arbs at $57, reaping a $17 gain. The $3 difference or spread can be viewed as compensation to the arbs for any remaining uncertainty about whether the transactions will be consummated, and for the time remaining to closing of the deal. Suppose that the bidder's share price declines $3 upon the announcement to close at $50. Your view is that the bidder's price will decline to $49 by the end of the holding period.

Exhibit 32.2 presents an example of the calculation of the return to the arb in this transaction. In brief, the calculation divides the dollar return for the holding period by the capital employed. Apparent in the exhibit is the role of leverage, both as a cost in calculating the dollar return and as a source of funds in calculating the net capital employed. The *annualized return* on capital of 195 percent from this 40-day investment seems extremely high in absolute terms, though most arbs would argue that they take large risks in pursuit of such returns. The exhibit also shows that if the takeover is resolved in 20 rather than 40 days, the annualized return rises to 414 percent.

Exhibit 32.3 shows that the arb's annualized return on investment is very sensitive to small variations in waiting period and dollar return. Apparently small variations (e.g., $2.00) in expected payoffs produce sizable swings in returns; returns vary directly with payoffs. The exhibit also shows that returns vary inversely with holding period—the longer the period, the smaller the returns.[13] Plainly, a takeover consummated in 20 days results in dramatically higher returns than those taking 40 and 80 days. The implication of Exhibits 32.2 and 32.3 is that the arb will be extremely sensitive to variations in time and payoff. This sensitivity means that bidders and targets that seek the support of arbs must tailor their tactics to exploit this sensitivity.

INTERPRETING ARBITRAGE SPREADS

Of paramount interest to the arb is the difference between today's share price for the target and the offer price by the bidder—this difference is called the *arbitrage spread*.[14] When arbitrage spreads are negative, the target's share price is *above* the bidder's offer. It means that arbs and other investors expect a higher offer to be

EXHIBIT 32.2 Example of Estimating the Return to the Arbitrageur

Example: The target receives a bid at $60 per share, when its shares were trading in the market at $40. The price instantaneously leaps to $57. The $3 difference or spread (i.e., $60 minus $57) can be viewed as compensation to investors for any remaining uncertainty about whether the transaction will be consummated, and for the time remaining to closing of the deal. The bidder's share price declines $3 upon the announcement to close at $50, and remains there until the end of the arb's holding period, judged to be 40 days. Your view is that at the end of the holding period, the bidder's price will fall to $49. Here is the calculation of prospective return to the arbitrageur from a combined long position in 100 target shares and short position in 100 bidder shares:

		Days in Holding Period	
Assumptions		40	20
Position and Payoff in Target Shares			
Buy target shares at		$ 57.00	$ 57.00
Value of target shares at end of holding period		$ 60.00	$ 60.00
Gross spread per share on target shares		$ 3.00	$ 3.00
Total value of gross spread on target shares (times # shares =)	100	$ 300.00	$ 300.00
Position and Payoff in Buyer Shares			
Short buyer shares at		$ 50.00	$ 50.00
Value of buyer shares at end of holding period		$ 49.00	$ 49.00
Gross spread per share on buyer shares		$ 1.00	$ 1.00
Total value of gross spread on buyer shares (times # shares =)	100	$ 100.00	$ 100.00
Total assets of the arbitrage position		$ 5,700.00	$ 5,700.00
Short position in buyer shares		$ 5,000.00	$ 5,000.00
Borrowed shares of buyer		$(5,000.00)	$(5,000.00)
Debt @ % assets	70%	$ 3,990.00	$ 3,990.00
Capital employed		$ 1,710.00	$ 1,710.00
Total liabilities and capital of the arbitrage position		$ 5,700.00	$ 5,700.00
Net Spread Calculation			
Gross spread		$ 400.00	$ 400.00
–Interest @	10%	$ (43.73)	$ (21.86)
–Short dividends forgone		$ (20.00)	$ (20.00)
+Long dividends received		$ 30.00	$ 30.00
Net spread		$ 366.27	$ 388.14
Days in holding period		40	20
Results			
Return on capital for holding period only		21%	23%
Return on capital annualized		195%	414%

Source: Author's analysis, based on the spreadsheet file on the CD-ROM, "Arbs.xls."

EXHIBIT 32.3 Sensitivity Analysis of Annualized Rate of Return to Variations in Length of Holding Period and Expected Payoff from Investment

Days in Holding Period	Expected Value per Share								
	$55	$57	$59	$60	$61	$63	$65	$67	$69
20	–119%	94%	308%	414%	521%	734%	948%	1,161%	1,375%
25	–100%	71%	241%	327%	412%	583%	754%	924%	1,095%
30	–87%	55%	197%	268%	340%	482%	624%	766%	909%
35	–78%	44%	166%	227%	288%	410%	532%	654%	776%
40	–71%	35%	142%	195%	249%	356%	462%	569%	676%
45	–66%	29%	124%	171%	219%	313%	408%	503%	598%
50	–62%	24%	109%	152%	194%	280%	365%	451%	536%
55	–58%	19%	97%	136%	175%	252%	330%	407%	485%
60	–55%	16%	87%	123%	158%	229%	300%	372%	443%
65	–53%	13%	78%	111%	144%	210%	275%	341%	407%
70	–51%	10%	71%	102%	132%	193%	254%	315%	376%
75	–49%	8%	65%	93%	122%	179%	236%	293%	349%
80	–47%	6%	59%	86%	113%	166%	219%	273%	326%

Note: Shaded cell indicates example case in text.
Source: Author's analysis, based on the spreadsheet file on the CD-ROM, "Arbs.xls."

forthcoming soon. When the arbitrage spreads are positive, it is because the target's share price is *less than* the bidder's offer. It indicates that arbs think it unlikely that the offer will be topped. Of course, if the arbitrage spread is large, it may suggest that the arbs doubt that the deal will be consummated at all. Thus, the arbitrage spread is an indicator of the probability of consummation. To see this, consider that the current share price is the average of two outcomes weighted by their probabilities: (1) the deal is consummated and the shareholder receives the bidder's offering price; or (2) the takeover attempt fails and the target's share price subsides back to its value on a stand-alone basis—here the prebid price is a useful guess as to what that stand-alone value might be. In mathematical terms:

$$P_{Current} = (\text{Prob} \times P_{Bid}) + [(1 - \text{Prob})P_{Stand\text{-}alone}] \quad (1)$$

In public company takeover situations, the prices, P, are readily observable. It is easy, therefore, to solve for "prob," the probability that the takeover succeeds and the arbs receive P_{Bid}. A calculator in the spreadsheet file "Arbs.xls" (found on the CD-ROM) does that for you. To see the insight gained from this calculation, consider four takeovers that were pending on July 18, 2003: Oracle's bid for PeopleSoft, Berkshire Hathaway's bid for Clayton Homes, ArvinMeritor's bid for Dana, and Palm Computing's bid for Handspring. Arbitrage spreads on pending deals are readily obtained from the Internet (a good source is found at www.thedeal.com). Exhibit 32.4 summarizes the calculations. The results show that the market thinks that the bids for Clayton Homes and Dana are likely to be topped—this is apparent in the negative spreads. Oracle's bid for PeopleSoft has a 63 percent implied probability of success. And Palm's bid for Handspring has only

EXHIBIT 32.4 Estimated Probabilities of Deal Closing Based on an Analysis of Arbitrage Spreads: Four Pending Deals at July 18, 2003

				Target's Price			
Target	**Bidder**	**Dollars**	**Percent**	**Current**	**Bid Price**	**Prebid***	**Probability of Closing**
PeopleSoft	Oracle	$ 1.68	9.4%	$17.82	$19.50	$15.00	63%
Dana	ArvinMeritor	$(0.55)	–3.5%	$15.54	$14.99	$11.50	Expect higher bid
Clayton Homes	Berkshire Hathaway	$(0.51)	–3.9%	$13.01	$12.50	$11.00	Expect higher bid
Handspring	Palm	$ 0.46	46.4%	$ 0.99	$ 1.45	$ 0.85	24%

*Using the prebid price in this calculation assumes that it is a fair estimate of the target's value per share if the deal does not close.
Note: See calculator in "Arbs.xls" on the CD-ROM.

a 24 percent likelihood of closing. These probabilities are significant influences on whether and what type of position an arb might take in a deal.

THE ARB ASSESSES A RECAPITALIZATION PROPOSAL IN TERMS OF BLENDED VALUE

Assume that in response to the hostile tender offer, the target company decides to mount its own recapitalization plan by buying back 35 percent of its shares at $85 per share. Furthermore, assume that the *stub share*[15] will be estimated to trade at approximately $55 per share afterward.

$$\text{Blended value} = (35\% \cdot \$85) + (65\% \cdot \$55) = \$65.50 \quad (2)$$

Note that an arb would prefer a *blended value* of $65.50 from the recap to the hostile bid of $60 if that value could be delivered on a timely basis.

In deciding where to tender their shares in a contest for corporate control, the arbs will determine which offer (the hostile bid or the recapitalization) gives them the highest annualized return on their invested capital. Thus, an arb would probably prefer $60 cash on July 10 as opposed to cash and securities of $65.50 received on October 10. With capital costs of 30 to 40 percent per year, the timing of cash flows received is crucial to the arbs' decision.

Understanding the arbs' mode of thought, much of the strategies of hostile bidders and defensive targets is oriented to modifying the arbs' beliefs about the target's value, the likelihood of a successful takeover, and the length of the holding period. Tactics of attack and defense are best understood as efforts to shift the arbs' thinking in your firm's favor—more is said about this in Chapter 33.

GOVERNMENT CONSTRAINTS ON THE GAME

Government intervention in hostile takeovers influences the takeover process considerably. At the federal government level in the United States, securities law has been oriented toward creating a level playing field in the spirit of enhancing competition among bidders. Antitrust law has been oriented toward protecting consumers and generally enhancing competition in product markets. At the state government level, antitakeover laws have been oriented toward simply preventing unwanted takeovers. These and other laws and regulations (surveyed in Chapters 26, 27, and 28) constrain the behavior of bidders and targets and affect the odds of successful acquisition:

1. The acquisition of shareholdings in excess of 5 percent of a target's shares must be disclosed within 10 days to the Securities and Exchange Commission (Rule 13-D). Arbitrageurs, major trading houses, and financial institutions employ runners to transmit copies of these 13-D filings with the SEC immediately to their employers. Disclosures of major changes in shareholding become rapidly impounded in share prices. The effect of this requirement is to telegraph the intentions of a bidder to the target and the rest of the market, well in advance of acquiring control through open market purchases.

2. A tender offer must remain open 20 business days in accordance with Rule 14e-1(a). Before the *Williams Act*, raiders could set a relatively short time to expiration of the offer, compelling hasty decision making on the part of the target shareholders and preventing action by target management. The effect of this rule is to give the target a window in which to organize a defense or a counterproposal to the arbs.
3. The bidder must honor all shares tendered into the offering pro rata, rather than on a first come, first served basis (Rule 14d-8). This relieves some of the target shareholders' compulsion to decide quickly in order to get in line early—offers for a controlling interest (e.g., 51 percent) rather than 100 percent of shares might be intended to induce a shareholder stampede. Two-tier offers are still permissible, though now less effective under Rule 14d-8.
4. Target shareholders may withdraw their tenders for any reason in the first 15 days of a tender offer in accordance with Rule 14d-7(a)(1). This permits shareholders greater flexibility in responding to competing offers, should they appear.
5. Rule 14d-7(a)(1) also extends tender offer time periods by 10 days if a competing offer appears.
6. Directors must exercise duties of care and loyalty to the shareholders, as Chapter 26 discussed. This is case law, legal doctrine created by courts.
7. Directors and managers must disclose *material* information about the company to the public (as discussed in Chapter 27). For instance, receipt of a bona fide[16] certain offer to buy a company that is communicated to management under some circumstances must be communicated to shareholders. However, what is "material" is a key matter of judgment. If management receives an offer, then they must determine, with or without the assistance of an investment banker, if the offer is bona fide. For instance, an offer made by someone without financial support may not be deemed to be bona fide. If the offer is deemed to be bona fide, then at the very least the board of directors should be notified. At that point, legal counsel should be sought to make a determination of the disclosability of the offer. Company officials should never lie to the press, because to do so would make them liable to charges of fraud. They may elect, as a matter of corporate policy, not to comment on market rumors.
8. If it is determined that the company is to be sold, the directors must sell it to the highest bidder. (Case law, the "*Revlon duties.*" See Chapter 26.)
9. The courts are disinclined to intervene in, or second-guess, management decision making unless gross negligence or fraud can be proved. This is the "business judgment rule" doctrine in U.S. federal courts (see Chapter 26). This puts the burden of proof on the bidder if the bidder seeks to have a court invalidate a target's antitakeover defenses.
10. In the event that the board of directors conducts an auction for the company, director's must be careful to maintain a level playing field during the auction process. They can give no bidder a preferred advantage in the bidding process. These are the enhanced scrutiny and entire fairness doctrines in case law (see Chapter 26).

SELLING SHAREHOLDERS FACE A PRISONER'S DILEMMA

The decision of whether to sell into a tender offer creates an unusual conflict of interest for the selling shareholders of target companies. On one hand, by waiting and not tendering, shareholders may receive a higher offer down the road—or management might reveal some hidden value justifying a higher share price and bid offer. On the other hand, selling now locks in a certain value. The only way to find out whether there is more value in the target firm is for target shareholders to band together, delay in tendering into the bidder's offer, and wait to see if a higher value (or bid) emerges. The problem is that unified action among a highly atomistic shareholder group is difficult, if not impossible, to engineer.

This is the classic problem of the "*prisoner's dilemma*."[17] In this hypothetical case, two suspects are arrested by the police in the belief that they acted together in committing a crime. The prisoners are separated in different cells and interrogated independently. The prosecutor encourages each to confess and implicate the colleague. If neither prisoner confesses, the prosecutor believes the court can be convinced to send the suspects to jail for five years each. If both prisoners confess *and* implicate each other, the court will send the suspects to jail for 10 years each. If one prisoner confesses and implicates the other and the other neither confesses nor implicates, the one who confesses will get three years (time off for assisting the prosecution), and the other will get eight years. The prisoner's dilemma is whether to confess, and offers four possible outcomes, represented in Exhibit 32.5.

Plainly, Quadrants II and III are the best outcomes for prisoners B and A respectively, since these result in lower jail terms for each. But if *both* prisoners take the incentive offered, they will wind up with the longest sentences, 10 years each. The safest course of action is for neither to confess, since it results in a jail term materially shorter than 8 or 10 years, and not much longer than 3 years. Unfortunately, with the prisoners separated and unable to communicate, the collaboration and mutual assurances necessary to achieve Quadrant I are unlikely.

The prisoner's dilemma illustrates how opportunism and the absence of joint action result in least-desirable outcomes. The model has been used to explain a wide range of phenomena in business and finance. The key here is in anticipating the probabilities and actions of other players in the game.

EXHIBIT 32.5 Overview of the Payoffs in the Classic Prisoner's Dilemma

	Prisoner B	
Prisoner A	Doesn't Confess	Confesses
Doesn't Confess	I. A gets 5 years. B gets 5 years.	II. A gets 8 years. B gets 3 years.
Confesses	III. A gets 3 years. B gets 8 years.	IV. A and B get 10 years each.

The decision facing target shareholders (especially arbs) is similar. Exhibit 32.6 recasts the prisoner's dilemma into a takeover setting. Here, two shareholders contemplate a two-tier tender offer of $80 cash paid per share for the first 51 percent of shares, and $60 in securities for the rest. Target shareholders face the payoffs shown in the cells of Exhibit 32.6 associated with either tendering immediately or waiting. With an immediate tender, the investor accepts the raider's offer. If both wait, the offer is defeated and the raider must raise its offer. If only one waits, the waiting shareholder becomes a minority investor in the firm, and eventually sells to the raider at a much-reduced price.

If the target shareholders act in concert and wait, they may obtain better information and a better price for their firm (Quadrant I). If some sell into the tender offer while others wait, those who sell may obtain a better deal than those who wait and wind up being minority shareholders in a firm that is dominated by the bidder. Absent joint action and communication, if all shareholders sell into the tender offer, the bidder takes the firm at the price offered (Quadrant IV).

To the extent that takeovers conform to this model, the prisoner's dilemma has important implications for bidders and target shareholders:

- Bidders benefit, and target shareholders lose by the asymmetric structure of payoffs and the difficulty of taking joint action among target shareholders.
- To heighten the bidder's benefit (and achieve Quadrant IV), the bidder could structure the asymmetry of incentives to the target shareholders in a way that motivates all to "defect" to accept the bid. This might be achieved by offering one high and relatively certain price to those who tender early, and another lower and less certain payment to those who tender late. Also, the bidder might send signals consistent with a likely future "minority shareholder freeze-out."[18] The classic achievement here is the two-tier tender offer: Cash is offered to shareholders who participate in the bidder's offer for 51 percent of the firm, to be followed by shares or high-yield bonds for the shareholders who delay and tender late, participating in the last 49 percent of the purchase. A minority that holds out entirely might see the assets of the firm stripped and sold piecemeal

EXHIBIT 32.6 Example of the Prisoner's Dilemma as Applied to Target Company Shareholders in the Face of a Coercive Two-Tier Hostile Tender Offer

	Investor B	
Investor A	**Waits**	**Sells into Offer**
Waits	I. A gets $100/share. B gets $100/share.	II. A gets $60/share. B gets $80/share.
Sells into Offer	III. A gets $80/share. B gets $60/share.	IV. A and B get $70 each.*

*The $70 payoff in Quadrant IV assumes proration of the front-end and back-end payments, 50% times $80 plus 50% times $60.

to the bidder, in essence liquidating the target. In 1997, Hilton Hotels Corporation bid $55 per share for ITT Corporation: For the first 50.1 percent of shares, Hilton would pay cash; for the rest of the shares outstanding, Hilton would pay $55 in shares of stock. The consideration was structured to be equivalent in value, though the cash payment appealed much more to arbitrageurs.

- A key problem for arbs and other target firms' shareholders is to assess the probability of other shareholders' actions. Nowhere does the gamelike nature appear in takeovers more clearly than in this fact: Like the cardplayer who must assess the hands and probabilities of other players, the arb in this situation must assess the likely actions of other investors.
- Collaboration among selling shareholders may pay. This perhaps explains the appearance of ad hoc committees of target shareholder groups, and the appeals to take action together.
- Securities regulation regimes that favor equitable treatment of all shareholders and level playing field conditions will discourage asymmetric incentives that lead to Quadrant IV outcomes.
- Time is very valuable to the target shareholders, and is the enemy of the bidder. Searching for a white knight buyer, developing a recapitalization plan, or mounting defenses takes time. To the extent that the bidder can hasten the target shareholders' decision process, the target management's evasive action is bound to be less effective.

TO SET A BID PRICE: THINK LIKE AN INVESTOR

Given that arbitrageurs are the significant decision makers in a hostile tender offer, it is reasonable to assume that the highest price offered takes the company. The bidder presumably will offer to purchase shares at a premium to the preexisting share price. The key issue is how large the premium should be. The range of choice for the bid premium will be bounded on the high side by the bidder's most optimistic estimate of the target's intrinsic value (e.g., accounting for the most optimistic estimate of synergy value to achieve this high value). At first glance, it would seem that the low end of the premium range would be determined by the preexisting share price. But the bidder needs to assume the possibility that the target might undertake a self-initiated restructuring that would release value to its shareholders in excess of the current share price—a leveraged restructuring would be an example of such an action. Since it is reasonable to assume that members of target management want to keep their jobs and that restructuring is the only alternative available if a white knight cannot be induced to enter the bidding, then in effect, this restructuring value becomes the other bound in the range of bid premiums. Exactly where, within this range, the bidder will choose to make its offer is a matter of how likely the bidder believes a competing bidder will enter the action.

The advice to a bidder in a situation like this is to *think like the target shareholder*. Gilson and Black (1995) implement this perspective by reducing the decision to tender to a simple comparison of shareholder wealth. Accept the tender offer if:

$$\text{Value of tendering} > \text{Expected value of not tendering} \quad (3)$$

Since the value of the bidder's offer can be reasonably estimated, the core of the analysis lies in estimating the *expected value of not tendering (EVNT)*. EVNT is an average weighted by probabilities of share prices under two uncertain outcomes: (1) no shares are tendered to the raider, the takeover fails, and share prices subside to the *ex ante* price[19]; and (2) no shares are tendered to the raider, but they are tendered to a higher competing bidder who buys the firm. These prices are multiplied times their probability, "prob," of occurrence, and summed:

$$\text{EVNT} = (\text{Share price}_{\text{No competing bid}} \cdot \text{Prob}) + [\text{Share price}_{\text{Competing bid}} \cdot (1 - \text{Prob})] \quad (4)$$

Thus, to succeed in the bidding, the raider must set the bid price somewhat higher than EVNT. Of course, this requires estimates of probabilities and the dollar offer of a competing bidder. If a decision maker is uncomfortable with this judgment, the EVNT formula could be solved in reverse for those probabilities and competing bid prices that yield outcomes just better or worse than the bidder's possible offers. Then, the bidder can make some judgment about the reasonableness of the range of competing offers and probabilities as a final step to preparing a bid price.

To illustrate how the EVNT equation can be used to help frame a bidder's analysis, consider the following example. A hostile bidder wants to prepare an initial bid for ABC Corp. ABC's current share price is $45. Under an aggressive restructuring plan (calling for asset sales and a leveraged recapitalization), ABC would be worth $65 per share. The hostile bidder envisions some synergies with ABC, which, if applied entirely to the value of ABC, would justify a maximum bid of $77 per share. Plainly, the hostile bidder would like to appropriate as much of the middle range for itself as possible. At what price should the bidder commence the hostile offer?

As discussed earlier, the bidder's strategy will be heavily influenced by the target's ability to counter with a value-creating restructuring plan. Thus, the bidder could consider two scenarios:

- ***Possibility A: Target does not restructure.*** In this instance, if the bidder's bid fails to attract the requisite number of shares, the target's share price could be presumed to fall back to the *ex ante* level, $45.
- ***Possibility B: Target announces a restructuring.*** Here the shareholders would be unlikely to part with their shares for less than $65, if they were highly confident of the target's ability to deliver this value. For simplicity, let's assume that the restructuring value is highly likely.

An Excel model, "EVNT.xls," found on the CD-ROM, automates the analysis of these scenarios.

Exhibit 32.7 gives EVNT for various combinations of competing bid prices and probabilities in the first scenario, Possibility A. The shaded region indicates the EVNTs that lie between the bidder's maximum value of $77 and the target's stand-alone value of $45. In any one of these cells, the bidder must offer *more* than the EVNT if he or she intends to win the contest. For instance, at a competing bid of $70 and a 50 percent probability, the bidder must offer *more* than $57.50 to motivate the arbs to tender their shares to the bidder. The task of the

EXHIBIT 32.7 Sensitivity of the Estimated Values of the Expected Value of Not Tendering, Varying by Bid Price and Probability of Competing Entry, and Assuming the "Default Value" Is the Target's *Ex Ante* Share Price (Possibility A)

	Value of Competing Bid									
Probability of a Competing Bid	$45.00	$50.00	$55.00	$60.00	$65.00	$70.00	$75.00	$80.00	$85.00	$90.00
10%	$45.00	$45.50	$46.00	$46.50	$47.00	$47.50	$48.00	$48.50	$49.00	$49.50
25%	$45.00	$46.25	$47.50	$48.75	$50.00	$51.25	$52.50	$53.75	$55.00	$56.25
50%	$45.00	$47.50	$50.00	$52.50	$55.00	$57.50	$60.00	$62.50	$65.00	$67.50
75%	$45.00	$48.75	$52.50	$56.25	$60.00	$63.75	$67.50	$71.25	$75.00	$78.75
90%	$45.00	$49.50	$54.00	$58.50	$63.00	$67.50	$72.00	$76.50	$81.00	$85.50

Note: Shaded region indicates EVNTs for scenarios that are below the bidder's maximum ($77) and above the stand-alone value of the target ($45).
Source: Author's analysis, based on the spreadsheet file on the CD-ROM, "EVNT.xls."

bidder must be to assess whether any other firm could possibly afford \$70 per share, which is the same as asking whether the probability of a bid at \$70 is really 50 percent.

Exhibit 32.8 summarizes the results for the second scenario, Possibility B. The chief insight from this exhibit is that the target's restructuring considerably reduces the buyer's room to maneuver—one can see this by comparing the size of the shaded areas in Exhibits 32.7 and 32.8.

The analysis of probabilities and competing bids shows the advantage that accrues to the first mover in hostile tender offers. Arbs must weigh the concrete offer by the first bidder against uncertain offers by potential competing bidders. Uncertainty discounts the value of these potential competitors such that it requires a relatively high probability of a high bid to dissuade arbs from tendering into a certain offer.

The practitioner (bidder or target) can use EVNT analysis to:

1. Bound the bidding range on the low side by either the *ex ante* share price or the value per share produced by any restructuring plan.
2. Set an upper limit on the bidding range, determined by the value of the target firm reflecting all synergies and optimistic assumptions about operations and the ability to use financial leverage aggressively.
3. Estimate the EVNTs for various combinations of competing bids and probabilities—this is equivalent to the shaded areas in Exhibits 32.7 and 32.8.
4. After reflecting on competing bidders, their bid prices, and the likelihood of their entry into the contest, set an offering price that slightly exceeds the EVNT for that cell in your table.

Finally, EVNT offers general insights on two classic competing strategies: (1) start with a high bid; and (2) start with a low bid. Each has advantages and disadvantages:

- ***Bid high.*** A high initial bid is known in M&A parlance as a "bear hug"—presumably referring to the apparent expression of affection that kills all resistance. This strategy deters competitors and pressures the target's directors to accept the offer. Knowing this, and seeing the high offer, arbs will tend to support the bid. Accordingly, the high bid strategy probably wins the contest. The chief disadvantage of this strategy is that it gives value to target shareholders that might have been retained by the bidder with a lower-priced opening bid. Generally, this strategy is appropriate where the bidder fears other competitors or is impatient.
- ***Bid low.*** This has the advantage of saving the gains from takeover for the bidder. But it may attract competing bidders, and almost certainly invites the target to announce an internal restructuring. This approach probably leads to a longer contest. The risk to the bidder is higher. Generally, this strategy is appropriate where the bidder is patient and/or confident of there being no or few other competing bidders.

EXHIBIT 32.8 Sensitivity Analysis of EVNT Assuming a Credible Restructuring Proposal by the Target Firm (Possibility B)

	Value of Competing Bid									
Probability of a Competing Bid	$45.00	$50.00	$55.00	$60.00	$65.00	$70.00	$75.00	$80.00	$85.00	$90.00
10%	$63.00	$63.50	$64.00	$64.50	$65.00	$65.50	$66.00	$66.50	$67.00	$67.50
25%	$60.00	$61.25	$62.50	$63.75	$65.00	$66.25	$67.50	$68.75	$70.00	$71.25
50%	$55.00	$57.50	$60.00	$62.50	$65.00	$67.50	$70.00	$72.50	$75.00	$77.50
75%	$50.00	$53.75	$57.50	$61.25	$65.00	$68.75	$72.50	$76.25	$80.00	$83.75
90%	$47.00	$51.50	$56.00	$60.50	$65.00	$69.50	$74.00	$78.50	$83.00	$87.50

Note: Shaded region indicates EVNTs for scenarios that are below the bidder's maximum ($77) and above the value of the target assuming a restructuring occurs ($65).
Source: Author's analysis, based on the spreadsheet file on the CD-ROM, "EVNT.xls."

CONCLUSION: THE GAME HAS IMPLICATIONS FOR DESIGN AND DEFENSE OF TAKEOVERS

The discussion in this chapter suggests that practitioners need to assess and exploit uncertainty in the design and execution of hostile offers. Specific implications include these:

- *Valuation is key.* Clarity about the value of the target is an absolutely essential foundation for takeover attack and defense. Value should be estimated from a variety of perspectives: current stand-alone status, status if restructured or recapitalized, value to the primary hostile bidder with synergies, and value to potential competing bidders with their synergies. At the very least, this valuation effort anticipates the likely analysis of arbitrageurs who will figure importantly in deciding the contest.
- *Think like an arb.* The focus of both *attacker* and *defender* should be the investor, particularly the arbitrageur. The arb is unimpressed with appeals to loyalty, tradition, or vague strategies. Cash value delivered in timely fashion will be decisive. Winning the game, then, is largely a matter of maximizing value.
- *Focus on payoffs, probabilities, time, and players.* The hostile bidder should take actions that shorten the time to outcome, that forestall collaboration among target shareholders, that preempt potential competitors, that reduce investor uncertainty about the value of the bid, and that generally pressure the target board to cooperate. The target firm should do the opposite: delay, explore restructuring and white knight bidders, cast uncertainty on the hostile bidder and its bid, and generally pressure the target board not to cooperate.
- *Know the rules; anticipate the rulings.* Laws, regulations, and previous court opinions have an immense influence on the takeover game (see Chapters 26 through 29). Courts and government agencies can intervene in the game often in unpredictable ways.

NOTES

1. John McDonald, *Strategy in Poker, Business & War*, New York: W. W. Norton, 1989, page 22.
2. Manne (1965), page 113. See also Grossman and Hart (1980).
3. A free-rider is someone who does not pay for the benefit of transportation. In M&A parlance, this term signifies a stockholder who benefits from the efforts of the hostile bidder who does all the work: research and due diligence about the target, mounting the attack, sustaining various expenses, and risking a loss of all this investment if the takeover bid fails. Free riders dilute the returns to the hostile bidder and thus may discourage takeover activity.
4. From a study by the Conference Board reported in "Merger, Takeovers Increasing Pressure on Outside Board Directors," *Securities Regulation and Law Reporter*, August 16, 1985, page 1479.
5. Schwert (2000), page 2616.
6. Trimbath (2002), page 71.
7. See Dahya and Powell (1998) and Kennedy and Limmack (1996).

8. The hostile bid may be distinguished from other *deal attitudes*. For instance, SDC Platinum, the well-known M&A database, offers these definitions: "Friendly (the board recommends the offer); Hostile (the board officially rejects the offer but the acquirer persists with the takeover); Neutral (the management of the target has nothing to do with the transaction); Unsolicited (the offer is a surprise to the target's board and has not yet given a recommendation)."
9. Numerous studies report positive significant returns to bidders in hostile transactions: Gregory (1997), Loughran and Vijh (1997), Rau and Vermaelen (1998), Lang, Stultz, and Walkling (1989), and Jarrell and Poulsen (1989).
10. Warren Buffett has played the white squire to several firms, most notably Gillette. He has purchased convertible preferred stock, which if converted would represent a material minority of shares outstanding. The shares represented in these white squire positions require added investment on the part of a hostile bidder and thus have a deterrent effect.
11. Quoted from Guy P. Wyser-Pratte, *Risk Arbitrage II*, New York: New York University, Salomon Brothers Center for the Study of Financial Institutions, Monograph 1982-3-4, page 7.
12. This example was drawn from "Takeover 1997 (A)," a Darden case study, UVA-F-1170, co-authored by Robert Bruner, John P. McNicholas, and Edward Rimland.
13. The inverse relationship between holding period and return is true for all but the left-most column, in which the return is less negative, the longer the period. This is because, at short holding periods, the annualization multiple (365 divided by days in holding period) has a huge effect in amplifying a negative return to be even more negative. For longer periods, the annualization impact is less pronounced.
14. Arbitrage spread = $\text{Price}_{\text{Offered}} - \text{Price}_{\text{Current}}$.
15. Like a ticket stub remaining after a movie, the shareholder has a stub share of the common stock remaining after the recapitalization.
16. *Bona fide* is Latin for "in good faith."
17. The prisoner's dilemma was first discussed in Anatol Rapoport and A. M. Chammah, *Prisoner's Dilemma*, Ann Arbor: University of Michigan Press, 1965.
18. In a "freeze-out," minority shareholders (i.e., those who remain stockholders in the target after the buyer has acquired control) are forced out of the target through the mechanism of a merger. In a merger, the former target entity ceases to exist and target shareholders receive payment for their shares. The freeze-out serves to reduce costs (e.g., associated with reporting and regulatory responsibilities) and dispatch dissident shareholders.
19. When a hostile tender offer is successfully deflected, we observe that the target share price tends to subside back toward the level prevailing *ex ante*. Whether it returns to the *ex ante* price exactly will depend on expectations of further takeover bids or possible changes in management policies.

CHAPTER 33

Takeover Attack and Defense

INTRODUCTION

This chapter presents a tactical perspective on hostile takeovers. This complements earlier chapters focused on the influence of economics, laws or regulations, and bidding behavior in M&A.[1] The tactical perspective enriches the picture of how the structure of the takeover problem and the conduct of players influence M&A results. Though contested acquisitions are a small fraction of the total volume of M&A activity, these cases illuminate lessons that have wider significance to the M&A practitioner:

- *Use of defensive tactics is widespread.* Most large firms have erected some form of antitakeover defense. This reflects the fact that the first, and perhaps most important, role of defenses is to discourage potential bidders from making an attempt. If defenses are the rule rather than the exception, the practitioner must anticipate the impact of defenses on the contest.
- *Tactics derive their power by influencing speed of closure, costs to the buyer, and perceptions about certainty to the investor.* The preceding chapter emphasizes the great sensitivity of hostile bidders and arbitrageurs to profit, delays, and uncertainty about the outcome. Through the use of these tactics, the buyer seeks to accelerate the consummation and increase certainty; conversely, the target seeks to delay the process and create uncertainty. In effect, these tactics attempt to tilt the payoffs and probabilities in one's favor—in the parlance of Chapter 32, tactics can affect one's assessment of the important benchmark, EVNT (expected value of not tendering).
- *Tactics create or neutralize* control options. Defensive tactics give discretionary rights to the target management and board. Tactics of attack seek to offset those rights. The discussion of control as an option outlined in Chapter 15 underpins some of the insights developed here: These tactics create or destroy value; the value will be contingent on uncertainty and time.
- *Whether defensive tactics create or destroy value for target shareholders depends on governance and uncertainty.* The options perspective gives a framework for anticipating the creation or destruction of value associated with defensive tactics. The effect depends on the degree of uncertainty about the target's intrinsic value, and the quality of corporate governance (i.e., whether it truly aligns management and shareholders).

- *A high offering bid is the most persuasive attack. A high stock price is the best defense.* While some defenses are stronger than others, the most effective means of repelling a bidder is to offer no incentive in the first place—executives afraid of takeovers should attend to running their firms well enough to create value for shareholders. For the same reason, attackers who truly want to win should exploit the desire of shareholders to maximize value, and offer a high bid.

PREVALENCE AND DISSUASIVE INFLUENCE OF ANTITAKEOVER DEFENSES

Exhibit 33.1 reveals that the use of antitakeover defenses is widespread, with the most popular defenses employed in more than 80 percent of public companies. Some defenses, such as golden parachutes, show a marked increase during the 1990s; other defenses remain relatively constant. Coates (2000b) suggests that most of the defenses were emplaced in the 1980s, but argues that some of these defenses (such as the *poison pill*) can be emplaced on short notice by the board of directors. Therefore, such data may understate the influence and role of defenses on the moves of players in the hostile takeover scenario.

The high rate of placement of antitakeover defenses is remarkable in light of the fact that most public corporations have not participated in a hostile takeover contest (either as buyer or as target). Why, then, are defenses so prevalent? First, they seem to give target boards and management some flexibility in their efforts to maximize shareholder value during a takeover—evidence for this is surveyed later in this chapter. Second, they raise the ante for bidders, thus forestalling "nuisance" bids and discouraging all but the stouthearted from making an assault.

The dissuasive power of defenses derives from their influence on timing, likelihood of success, and cost or profit to the bidder. To illustrate, consider the logic of the bidder: Attack if it is likely to be profitable. "Profitable" literally means the difference between the intrinsic value of the target and the price paid for it plus the transaction costs that the bidder is likely to incur. "Likely" reminds us that the bidder can fail to acquire the target. These elements can be reduced to a simple equation. Attack if:

$$[\text{Prob}(\text{Intrinsic value} - \text{Price} - \text{Transaction costs})] - [(1 - \text{Prob})\text{Transaction costs}] > 0 \quad (1)$$

where *"prob"* is the probability of a successful takeover. In words, this equation says that the bidder should attack if the expected payoff is positive. The equation gives an overview of tactical thinking for the attacker and defender. For instance, the implications for the defender are as follows (those for the attacker are the opposite):

- Use defenses to decrease "prob," the probability of the attacker's success. Likelihood of success is affected by time delays, the entry of friendly parties (*white knights*, *white squires*, etc.), and the preparation of alternatives to takeover, such as restructuring programs.

EXHIBIT 33.1 Percentage of Firms Employing Takeover Defenses

	1999	1997	1995	1993	1990
Number of companies in sample	1,900	1,922	1,500	1,483	1,487
Blank check preferred stock	89%	88%	85%	N/A	N/A
Golden parachutes	65%	56%	53%	N/A	N/A
Advance notice requirement	62%	49%	44%	N/A	N/A
Classified board	59%	58%	60%	58%	57%
Poison pill	56%	52%	53%	54%	51%
Limit right to call special meeting	37%	34%	31%	29%	24%
Limit action by written consent	35%	32%	31%	28%	24%
Fair price	25%	26%	32%	33%	32%
Supermajority vote to approve merger	15%	15%	18%	18%	17%
Dual class stock	11%	11%	8%	8%	8%
Confidential voting	10%	9%	12%	9%	3%
Cumulative voting	10%	11%	14%	16%	18%
Eliminate cumulative voting	9%	8%	10%	10%	9%
Consider nonfinancial effects of merger	7%	7%	7%	7%	6%
Antigreenmail	4%	5%	6%	6%	6%
Unequal voting rights	2%	2%	2%	2%	2%

Source of data: Virginia K. Rosenbaum, *Corporate Takeover Defenses 2000*, Investor Responsibility Research Center, October 1999, page viii.

Comment: The sample consists of publicly held firms in the United States, especially the larger and more prominent corporations, including the "Super" S&P 1500 plus another 400 firms chosen on the basis of large market capitalization and high levels of institutional ownership. Many of the defenses listed in this exhibit are defined in the chapter text or in other chapters. Defenses not elsewhere described in this book are:

- *Blank check preferred stock.* The ability of the board of directors to issue preferred stock to friendly shareholders. Like the poison pill, this raises the cost of takeover to the hostile bidder.
- *Advance notice requirement.* Imposes a window for submission of nominations of directors and resolutions to be brought before a shareholder meeting. Failure to meet the window requirements grants the board the right to disregard the nomination or resolution.
- *Limit right to call special meeting.* This constrains the hostile bidder's ability to demand a special meeting of shareholders (that is, a meeting at which the bidder might try to disable takeover defenses).
- *Limit action by written consent.* This constrains the hostile bidder's ability to obtain a vote of the shareholders by means of proxy solicitation in lieu of a meeting.
- *Consider nonfinancial effects of merger.* This permits the board of directors to widen its scope of consideration from simply a focus on shareholder welfare to include, possibly, impact on employees, community, and so on.
- *Unequal voting rights.* Like dual-class stock, this provision triggers super-voting rights of some shareholders for those who have held the stock for a long period of time, such as four years, or in special circumstances, such as a proposed takeover.

- Use defenses to decrease the perception of intrinsic value of the target to the attacker. Spin-offs, special dividends, asset sales, and options to sell "crown jewels" might accomplish this. Threats of union opposition or of customer defections[2] may decrease intrinsic value. If the attacker and target are in the same industry it may be possible to present arguments to antitrust regulators that would prevent the attacker from acquiring the entire target firm. Finally, any delays imposed by defenses must reduce the intrinsic value of the target—intrinsic value is the present value of expected future cash flows. Synergies and other benefits may only become available following a thorough takeover of operations, restructuring, and integration with the buyer. If these benefits are delayed by, say, a staggered board, supermajority provision, or waiting period imposed by law or regulation, the present value of these benefits must be smaller than if realized quickly.

- Use defenses to raise the price paid by the attacker. Payments required under *golden parachutes*, poison puts, and topping or breakup agreements have the effect of directly raising the price to the attacker. Less directly, target management may have knowledge of hidden values not known to the investing public, such as dormant land carried at historical cost rather than market value on the target's books. Disclosure of these hidden values might help to persuade target shareholders that the attacker's bid is inadequate. The best defense that raises the price to the attacker is the poison pill.
- Use defenses to increase transaction costs. For instance, defensive litigation and defensive appeals to regulators may increase the cost of the legal work necessary to support the transaction. Protracted defenses will generally raise the cost of advisers.

INVESTOR REACTION TO ANNOUNCEMENTS OF ANTITAKEOVER DEFENSES

One gauge of the economic impact of defenses is the reaction of investors to the announcement of takeover defense placements. Several studies suggest that the strength of the target's governance mechanisms is a strong determinant of the market reaction to takeover defenses: where the board of directors is strong and independent, and where the CEO's interests are strongly aligned with those of shareholders, the reaction is positive; where governance is poor and/or the CEO is poorly aligned with shareholders, the reaction is negative.

- Governance strength is positively associated with the investor reaction to the announcement of takeover defenses (see McWilliams 1990, 1993)—strong governance is associated with positive reaction of investors at the announcement of antitakeover defenses; weak governance is associated with negative reaction. Bhaghat and Jefferis (1991) found that voting power of ESOPs and the CEO play a prominent role in whether a firm will adopt antitakeover charter amendments.
- Targets of hostile bids have lower percentages of insider shareholdings; see Song, Stulz, and Walkling (1990) and Mikkelson and Partch (1989). For contrasting findings, see Ambrose and Megginson (1992).
- CEO shareholdings are inversely related to resistance to a tender offer and positively related to the likelihood of bidder success; see Cotter and Zenner (1994). Models estimated to predict takeover find that larger CEO shareholdings reduce the likelihood of a hostile bid; see Mikkelson and Partch (1989) and Shivadasani (1993). And the percentage of ownership held by insiders is negatively related to the number of takeover defenses (Boyle et al. 1998).

- Size is directly associated with the likelihood of receiving a hostile bid. Schwert (2000) suggests that this could reflect a tendency toward greater managerial entrenchment within large firms.
- The number of takeover defenses placed by a firm is inversely related to the percentage of shares held by insiders (Boyle et al. 1998). And the more shares that managers own, the more reluctant they are to support of the repeal of antitakeover provisions (Sundaramurthy and Lyon 1998).
- The announcement of takeover defenses benefits shareholders where internal governance mechanisms work well; see Malekzadeh and McWilliams (1995) and Malekzadeh et al. (1998).

The net implication of these findings is that defenses can help shareholders of good firms by enhancing the bargaining power of management to extract high prices from bidders; this is the argument of Coates (2000b). But defenses also may harm shareholders of bad firms by entrenching managers who disrespect their duty to shareholders. To make sense of market responses to announcements about takeover defenses, one must have a view about the efficiency and governance of the target firm.

ECONOMIC EFFECTS OF ATTACK AND DEFENSE

Why defensive tactics can affect the target's value[3] and why the impact varies cross-sectionally or across time are among the most interesting research questions in M&A. It would seem, after all, that defenses are merely intangible and innocuous, and have an impact at best some point distant in the future. Why might we anticipate *any* market reaction to the announcements of defenses?

Consider, for instance, the basic aims of tactics of attack and defense:

- Defense tactics seek to delay the outcome and increase uncertainty about whether the target will be sold, and if so, at what price. Recall from the Chapter 32 that arbitrageurs hate delays and uncertainty. Defense tactics are particularly discouraging to arbs and thus may help to suppress the stampede to tender shares into the bidder's offer.
- Attack tactics seek to accelerate the outcome and resolve uncertainty. These tactics serve the interests of arbitrageurs and thereby improve the fluidity in the exchange of votes.

There are at least two ways to think about the economic effect of tactics. One way is the traditional perspective of the arb: Anything that creates uncertainty or delay reduces the present value of the payoff on a risk arbitrage position. Thus, it might seem that defenses would destroy value. But if the defense buys time for the target to look for higher bidders or negotiate with the bidder for a higher price, then defenses might create value. This is consistent with the perspective developed in Chapter 32.

The second way to think about the impact of tactics is in terms of the *optionality*[4] created in their design and implementation.

- *Defenses are control options* (i.e., call options on the strategy of the target firm). They grant management and directors discretion (i.e., rights or options) to determine whether, how, and when the transaction will be struck. Chapter 15 discusses the optionality in control and its effect on share values.
- Defenses will be more valuable *the longer the delay, and the greater the uncertainty* about the value of the underlying asset (i.e., the enterprise). This is consistent with option pricing theory: Time and uncertainty drive option value.
- *Tactics of attack aim to negate defenses* and thereby destroy the option value that the defenses create. The logic of hedging explains how this occurs: One acquires an option with payoffs that are countervailing to the risks one faces. In effect, the attack seeks to prevent the exercise of the control option.

From this perspective, hostile takeover battles are significantly contests over option value.

The options perspective might explain the apparently conflicting findings about the value impact of defenses:

- ***Variations in uncertainty about the target firm's value.*** The classic drivers of option value, such as time and uncertainty, could vary significantly from one company to the next and from one data set to the next. For instance, announcement of new defenses by a firm probably would not have much effect where there is a tight consensus among analysts, investors, company management, and potential bidders about the intrinsic value of the firm. But where there is wide disparity in the assessment of intrinsic value, the economic impact of announcing defenses could be material.[5]
- ***Variations in governance.*** These would suggest who captures the option value of defenses. As a practical matter, management and the directors retain the exercise rights on control options. In the absence of a proxy contest or consent solicitation in the bidder's favor, shareholders have relatively little say in the disposition of their firm. The economic impact of these rights on shareholder welfare hinges on whether management seeks to maximize shareholder welfare (in which case the control options will be exercised in their interest) or whether management is entrenched (in which case the control options will be exercised in management's interest).
  - In the case of management alignment, shareholders benefit from defenses (i.e., they share in the option value created by the defenses). The counterparty, or loser, is the bidder—intuitively, this is because the defenses extract from the bidder high payment.
  - In the case of management entrenchment, shareholders lose when defenses are put in place; they are the counterparty from whom option value is extracted.

Combining these effects, the analyst can derive an economic framework regarding defenses that encompasses the entire range of market reactions to the announcement of defenses: gains, losses, and no change. Exhibit 33.2 casts these into a two-dimensional space with quality of governance represented on the horizontal axis, and degree of uncertainty about the intrinsic value of the firm on the

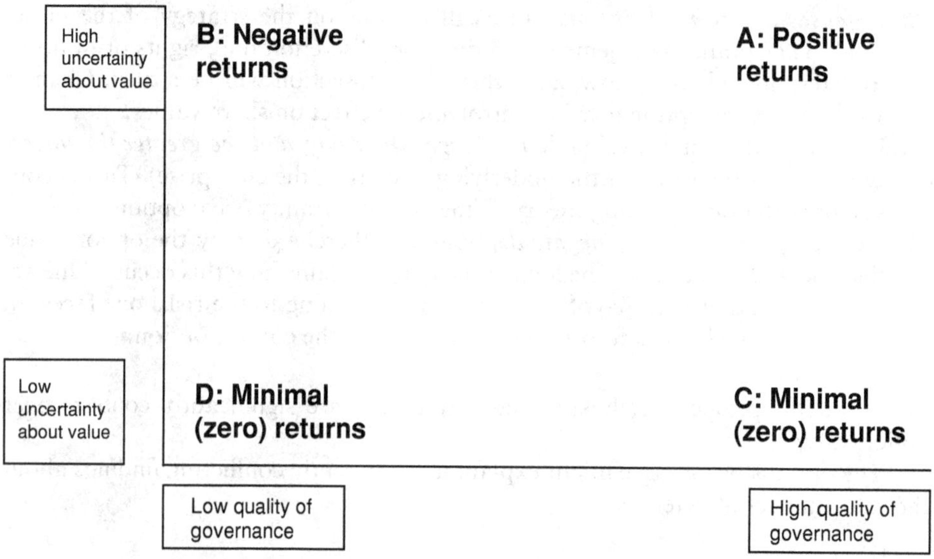

EXHIBIT 33.2 Gains or Losses in Wealth to Target Firm Shareholders According to Uncertainty about the Target's Intrinsic Value and Quality of Governance

vertical axis. While the space so defined is continuous, the figure gives four illustrative cases:

A—High uncertainty/good governance. Here defenses arguably create value. Defenses grant management rights to delay and bargaining power to negotiate, all of which would serve the maximization of shareholder value. Comment and Schwert (1995), for instance, found a reaction to the announcement of poison pill defenses consistent with creation of value.

B—High uncertainty/bad governance. Here defenses arguably destroy value. Defenses simply entrench management, thereby imposing an opportunity cost on shareholders. Bruner (1991) explored this case with simulation analysis and determined that antitakeover defenses were materially costly when management is entrenched.

C—Low uncertainty/good governance and D—Low uncertainty/bad governance. In these two final cases, the announcement of defenses has a negligible effect on value—it neither creates nor destroys value. This does not mean that there is no optionality in defenses, but rather that the option value is immaterial.

From this perspective, the reaction of investors to the announcement of takeover defenses is significantly an indication of investor assessment of management's relative alignment or entrenchment: Positive reactions are associated with alignment; negative reactions are associated with entrenchment. Larger reactions are associated with longer delays and greater uncertainty about value.

Some writers have argued that antitakeover defenses are "free."[6] The options perspective lends a more nuanced conclusion: Defenses are never free, though under some circumstances they may be inexpensive, such as to those firms that are governed well. Options theory teaches that rights are valuable even when out of the money. Thus, the issue of whether defenses are free or costly hinges on quality of governance and the degree of alignment of interests between management and shareholders.

TACTICS OF TAKEOVER ATTACK

The hostile bidder typically seeks to consummate the acquisition quickly, before other bidders can enter or the target can mount stronger defenses. The tactics of the bidder aim for speed and closure.

- ***Purchase of shares directly in the market.*** In the absence of any constraints (such as takeover defenses or government regulations), a buyer could simply purchase control of a target on the open market. This is called a *street sweep*. A *drop and sweep* is a street sweep that follows the withdrawal of a buyer's tender offer—it seeks to exploit the panic selling by arbitrageurs. A *block purchase* or *toehold* purchase of target shares in the market seeks to obtain a sizable position in order to signal the seriousness of the bidder's intent, to influence the target board, to fend off other possible bidders, and to earn a "consolation profit" in the event that the target is won by another, higher, bidder. Still, the purchase of the target directly in the market is rarely used. Under the Williams Act, the bidder must notify the SEC upon surpassing a 5 percent stake in the target; this sacrifices the element of surprise. And it can be time-consuming to amass shares from the daily trading float in the market.
- ***Offer directly to the target board of directors.*** Some buyers will seek to gain the endorsement of the board of directors in an effort to persuade the target to drop its defenses. The price, publicity, and life of the offer are varied to heighten the pressure on the board. The *Saturday night special* is a surprising offer to the target board left open for only a brief period of time; the name alludes to a pistol that is "cheap and [goes off] quickly."[7] The *bear hug* is an offer made to the board without a concurrent public announcement. The *strong bear hug* includes a public announcement and a call for negotiations. A *super-strong bear hug* threatens to reduce the offering price in the event of opposition or delay. A *godfather offer* is a cash offer so high that the directors feel unable to refuse it.
- ***Tender offer directly to target shareholders.*** This is an invitation to shareholders to tender or submit their shares for sale to the buyer. The offer typically expresses a price, form of payment, and length of time that the offer will be outstanding (in the United States, the length of time is governed by SEC rules). Some tender offers can be friendly, following mutual agreement between managements of the buyer and target firm. Other tender offers are called *unsolicited* until the intentions of the buyer and the attitude of the target are known. A *hostile* tender offer is simply unwanted by the target firm, and if successful usually entails firing the senior management of the target firm.
- ***Coercive tender offer structures.*** As described in the preceding chapter, the two-tier, front-end-loaded tender offer is designed to exploit the prisoner's

dilemma problem facing target shareholders. Bradley (1980) and Grossman and Hart (1980) argue that this offering structure creates an incentive to tender early into the bidder's offer and penalizes free-riding shareholders who would hold back from the offer on the chance that higher bids might be forthcoming. The target has the option of implementing a fair price provision antitakeover defense; this aims to negate two-tier offers by requiring that the same price be paid to all shareholders. Comment and Jarrell (1987) found that two-tier offers were relatively rare in their sample, but that they more frequently resulted in negotiation between the parties than did any-or-all offers. They also found that the average blended premium for two-tier offers was insignificantly different from the average premium in any-or-all offers. They concluded that target shareholders are not disadvantaged by the seemingly coercive two-tier structure.

- *Proxy contest and consent solicitation.* In advance of the target's annual meeting, the buyer may submit an acquisition proposal for approval by the target shareholders, and then seek to obtain the votes ("proxies" are legal documents by which shareholders vote an absentee ballot). A *proxy contest* can resemble a political election campaign, run by investment bankers and proxy solicitation firms who contact shareholders directly. Some corporate charters and bylaws permit changes in the board of directors by written consent of the shareholders, thus bypassing a shareholder meeting. Like the proxy contest, this strategy is essentially a political campaign. In some legal jurisdictions, it may be possible for the bidder to obtain a faster resolution of the contest by *consent solicitation* than by a proxy contest. A critical difference between the proxy contest and consent solicitation lies in the basis for determining a winning majority: For the proxy contest it is judged in terms of the number of shares voted at the meeting of shareholders; for the consent solicitation, it is judged in terms of all shares outstanding. Given that some shareholders never vote, it may be harder for a raider to win by means of a consent solicitation than by a proxy contest.
- *Challenge the target's defenses through litigation.* Courts have disallowed some takeover defenses put in place during a contest. Arbitrageurs and institutional investors are easily encouraged to participate in litigation aimed at invalidating the target's defenses. Occasionally, the courts go along. In 2000, the Delaware Chancery Court disallowed a supermajority amendment that had been approved by the directors of Shorewood Packaging Corporation during a hostile bid by Chesapeake Corporation. The Court objected to the use of the defense without a vote of the shareholders and to the directors' hasty vote during the contest.

The choice among forms of attack is influenced by at least four considerations:

1. *Attitude of target management and board.* The strength with which target management is likely to resist the unsolicited offer will dictate how much time and effort will be devoted to trying to win their support. For instance, a bear hug offer to the board might be warranted where sentiment is neutral or only mildly opposed to the bidder. An appeal directly to shareholders would be warranted where the attitude of management and the board is strongly opposed to the bidder.

2. ***Distribution of voting power.*** A few large shareholders with relatively high voting power (e.g., large institutional investors or founding families) know one another and communicate during a control contest. These voters are probably well informed and sophisticated. In appealing to them, the bidder would be well advised to undertake a direct, in-person vote solicitation campaign such as seen in a proxy contest or consent solicitation. On the other hand, atomistic dispersion of a large number of voting shareholders would warrant a tender offer—as suggested in the previous chapter, this exploits the "prisoner's dilemma" phenomenon to the bidder's advantage.
3. ***Strength of target defenses in place.*** Of particular interest is the poison pill defense, which, as is discussed later in this chapter, many practitioners view as a "showstopper." The pill is placed and rescinded by action of the board of directors. Therefore, takeover attempts against targets with pills will typically entail a bear hug approach to the board, a tender offer contingent on removing the pill, or efforts to change the composition of the board through a proxy contest or consent solicitation.
4. ***Presence of competing bidders and/or a white knight.*** The entry by a competitor into the bidding, especially a bidder favored by management and directors, will necessitate an appeal directly to shareholders through a tender offer, proxy fight, or consent solicitation.

TACTICS OF TAKEOVER DEFENSE

The numerous tactics available to a target firm can be described along many dimensions. But the analyst and deal designer may find it helpful to characterize the tactics by degree of focus or tailoring to a specific situation—this is associated with the typical timing of announcement of the tactic and its impact. Exhibit 33.3 outlines a hypothetical distribution of these defenses across the time frame of a bid. A key distinction among the defenses is in their degree of tailoring to the identity of the hostile bidder.

- ***Proactive defenses*** typically are put in place in response to a general concern about a potential takeover attempt. Their aim is to discourage or deter potential bidders from attacking. They do not discriminate among potential bidders. By implicitly challenging all potential bidders, these defenses signal the intent of management and directors to preserve the independence of the firm or at least the discretion of its leaders in determining the firm's future control.
- ***Deal-embedded defenses*** may or may not discriminate among bidders. These appear as features of definitive agreements and are intended to raise the ante for an intruder. Generally, these defenses are intended to deter potential competing bidders.
- ***Reactive defenses*** respond directly to the identity of the hostile bidder and/or the characteristics of the hostile bid. In contrast to the preceding two classes of defense, reactive defenses are aimed at repelling known specific bidders.

The following sections outline the specific defenses within each category. The impact on value and the efficacy of the individual defenses varies widely. However,

EXHIBIT 33.3 Placement of Takeover Defenses across a Deal Episode

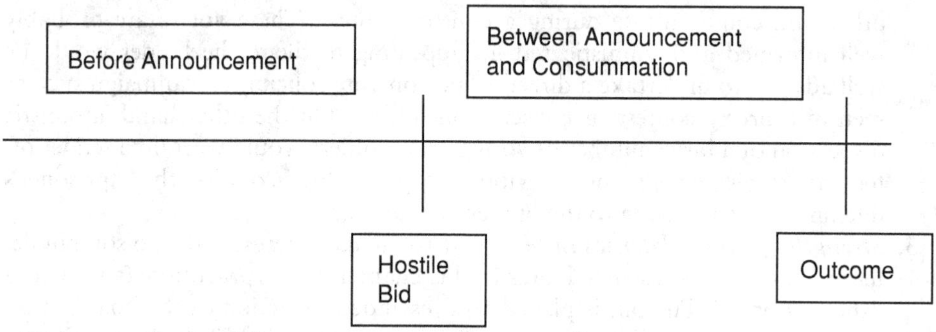

Proactive Tactics (Before a Hostile Bid)	Tactics Embedded in a Friendly Deal	Reactive Tactics (After a Hostile Bid)
Charter amendments:	Breakup or topping fees	Litigation
1. Classified board		Regulatory protection
2. Supermajority	Asset lockups	Legislative protection
3. Fair price	Equity lockups	Countertender (Pac-Man)
4. Dual-class recap	Toehold stakes	Asset restructuring
Golden parachute		White knight/squire
ESOPs and labor agreements		Share repurchase/greenmail
Poison pill		Leveraged recapitalization
Dual-class recapitalization		Going private/LBO

the modern use of defenses is to employ combinations, or "cocktails," of tactics, about which more is said after the survey of individual defensive tactics.

Proactive Defenses: Charter Amendments, Golden Parachutes, Poison Pills

CHARTER AMENDMENTS Changes can be made to a corporation's charter that limit the ability of an attacker to gain control of the firm.[8] This class of defense is obtained only by shareholder vote.[9] The role of a shareholder vote is vital in assessing the desirability of this class of defense, since the outcome of such a vote is uncertain. However, the advantages of charter amendment defenses may override the risk of a shareholder vote.

- A favorable vote signals a likely resolute defense by shareholders, board, and management. The shareholders, having committed through the voting process, suggest that they are likely to resist aggressively an attack.
- The defense itself will impede takeover by a control-oriented bidder and frustrate a creeping buyer.
- Some provisions (e.g., fair price) may extract a higher total payment from the buyer, and thereby impede a financially weak attacker. These provisions also protect the interests of a minority of shareholders who hang onto their shares in the face of an attack—this frustrates an attempted minority freeze-out.

- A shareholder vote protects directors under the business judgment rule from their recommendation of charter amendments.

Generally, research finds that charter amendments are only mildly effective[10] in reducing the likelihood of takeover bid. Charter amendments include four varieties: classified board, supermajority, fair price, and dual-class recapitalization.

1. ***Classified board.*** In an unclassified board, all directors are elected annually by shareholders. In contrast, classified (or staggered) boards are elected fractionally each year (e.g., one-third of the board each year over a span of three years). This amendment delays the bidder's ability to control the board and thereby rescind defenses (such as the poison pill), replace management, implement a restructuring, and so on. In general, the announcement of adoption of a staggered board has little impact on either shareholder wealth or firm performance.[11] When a staggered board is announced as a takeover defense, investors react neutrally—unless the staggered board is accompanied by material share ownership by insiders and directors, in which case the reaction is positive.[12] Firms with a staggered board are slightly less likely to attract a takeover bid.[13] Nevertheless, shareholder rights activists have been increasing the pressure on companies with staggered boards to eliminate them in favor of yearly board elections.[14] A study by the National Association of Corporate Directors found that the incidence of one-year board terms is increasing due to pressure from institutional investors and corporate governance activists.[15] In contrast, as of 2000, 40 states had enacted antitakeover laws that affect board composition.[16]
2. ***Supermajority provision.*** This charter amendment typically specifies that mergers must be approved by an extra-large majority of votes (e.g., 85 or 67 percent versus a simple majority of 51 percent). The intent of this amendment is to give a minority of shareholders a stronger voice with which to protect their interests in the face of a strong attack. At the very least this has the effect of delaying the bidder's consummation of a deal (i.e., it takes more time to amass a supermajority). And it may grant a relatively small minority disproportionate power to block a deal. Typically, supermajority amendments include a "board-out" clause that gives directors discretion to rescind the supermajority requirement, which is intended to favor friendly bids. Linn and McConnell (1983) found that the announcement reduces stockholder wealth by 5 percent. But over the longer term, Johnson and Rao (1999) found that the supermajority decision, along with other antitakeover charter amendments, had no adverse consequences for the firm or the shareholders. Ambrose and Megginson (1992) found that firms with supermajority amendments are insignificantly less likely to attract a takeover bid.
3. ***Fair price provision.*** The fair price amendment requires that all selling shareholders receive the same price from a buyer. This prevents a discriminatory offer from a bidder that seeks to stampede the target shareholders into selling (e.g., the two-tier or freeze-out tender offer in which a controlling block of shares is purchased at a premium and the remaining minority is purchased at a discount). This is a mildly effective takeover defense but plays a crucial role in thwarting two-tier takeover attempts.[17] Many states in the United States now require a takeover bid to carry a "fair price" for all shareholders. Early

research suggested that the stock price effect of adopting a fair price amendment is negligible, but slightly negative. More recent research found a still negligible but now positive effect from implementing a fair price amendment.[18] Ambrose and Megginson (1992) found that firms with fair price amendments are insignificantly more likely to attract a takeover bid.

4. ***Dual-class recapitalization.*** As described in Chapter 26, this amendment creates two classes of stock with different voting rights. For instance, the lower class will have one vote per share, and a higher class will have 10 votes per share. The superior voting shares are typically held by management and shareholders friendly to management who thereby retain strong voting power and can block propositions at shareholder meetings that are hostile to management. Research on dual-class recapitalization shows a statistically significant negative impact on shareholder wealth due to the loss of voting rights.[19] Shum, Davidson, and Glascock (1995) found no overall market reaction to the announcement of a second class of stock. They did find that the stock market reacts negatively when original shareholders lose voting power and are not compensated for the loss of control. However, when shareholders who lose voting power receive compensation (e.g., through increased dividends) the market reacts positively. Bacon, Cornett, and Davidson (1997) found that the market reaction to the announcement of dual-class recapitalizations is associated with composition of the board of directors: Boards with a large component of independent directors are associated with positive announcement returns; boards dominated by insiders are associated with negative returns. Finally, Ambrose and Megginson (1992) found that dual-class recapitalization does not decrease the likelihood of an eventual takeover bid.
5. ***Other charter amendments.*** The range of charter amendments extends further and will not be discussed in detail here other than to identify its reach. Amendments can limit the ability of dissident shareholders (or an attacker) to call special meetings of shareholders, to take action by consent without a shareholder meeting, and to pay *greenmail* or otherwise eliminate a hostile bidder through repurchasing shares. Further, some amendments can require a board of directors to consider other factors beyond price in evaluating a hostile bid; these could include the possible impact on employees, community, creditors, customers, and others, effectively liberalizing the range of considerations guiding the board's actions.

GOLDEN PARACHUTES Golden parachutes grant target management generous severance payments if they are fired following an acquisition that changes control[20] of the target. Parachutes are granted by the board of directors and unlike the charter amendments do not need a vote of the shareholders. Positive motives for the golden parachute include increasing employee retention during a takeover fight, motivating employees to focus on shareholder interests rather than personal concerns, and improving the company's ability to recruit new talent. Critics of the golden parachute regard it as a reward for failure in that it generously compensates managers for allowing the company to be a target of a takeover. Research concerning the effect of adopting golden parachutes on shareholder wealth and the probability of attracting takeover bids had been split. In the 1970s, announcement of a golden parachute was associated with positive stock returns; in the 1980s, the reaction had turned from positive to negative.[21] But in the 1990s, adoption of golden parachutes was associated with zero returns—and when golden parachutes were adopted by boards consisting of insiders or affiliated outsiders, the reaction tended to be more negative than with a board of independent outsiders.[22]

Timing of the golden parachute adoption also affects returns to shareholders. Born, Trahan, and Faria (1993) found that when golden parachutes are announced and a company is already engaged in a takeover bid, the wealth effects are neutral, but they are wealth increasing when the firm is not in play. In contrast, Hall (1998) found that the wealth effects of parachute announcements are negative when a firm is in play, but neutral when a firm is not in play. Both studies agree that the wealth effect is zero when firms adopt a golden parachute as a preemptive measure. This is supported by Schnitzer (1995) who suggests that the wealth effect of golden parachutes is neutral with positive returns for efficiently managed firms. Born, Trahan, and Faria (1993) found that the adoption of a golden parachute increases the probability that a firm will receive a takeover bid, perhaps because it is a sign of weakened management. But Schnitzer (1995) concluded that the likelihood would be lower for firms with efficient management teams.

EMPLOYEE STOCK OWNERSHIP PLANS (ESOPs) AND LABOR AGREEMENTS Targets can exploit agreements with employees for the sake of takeover defense. One avenue is to deploy retirement funds into the firm's own shares, effectively creating a large block of insider ownership. An example would be an *employee stock ownership plan (ESOP)* that borrows to buy the firm's shares, and then uses the stream of pension payments by the firm to service the debt. Bruner and Brownlee (1990) describe perhaps the most famous use of the ESOP to deter takeover, by Polaroid Corporation in the face of a bid by Shamrock Holdings. A supermajority provision in Polaroid's charter required an 85 percent vote of shareholders to approve a business combination. Polaroid established an ESOP with a 14 percent interest in the firm and with the Polaroid CEO as trustee of the ESOP; the CEO therefore had the right to vote unvested shares. Shamrock backed out of the bid when the Delaware Supreme Court refused to grant an injunction against the defense.

Agreements with labor unions may place union representatives on the target firm's board of directors or raise other provisions that prevent a takeover. In 1990, UAL Corporation struck such a collective bargaining agreement with the machinists' union in order to thwart a hostile bid by a raider acting in concert with the pilots' union. Federal courts invalidated the UAL defensive agreement, calling it a "doomsday bomb," that is, out of proportion to the threat posed by the raider as judged under the standard of "enhanced scrutiny" defined by the court (see Chapter 26 for a discussion of this standard).

POISON PILL The poison pill is arguably one of the most significant financial innovations in recent decades and is probably the single most effective defense in the target's arsenal. The apparent infallibility of the pill derives from the fact that since 1982 (when the first pill was placed) no pill has been triggered by any hostile bidder.[23] Indeed, the SEC has argued that this defense is adopted with the intention of not implementing it[24]—rather like a nuclear weapon. Most large U.S. corporations have a poison pill defense in place. The pill figures in litigation in almost all hostile takeovers—but the courts have yet to deny the placement of any pill. On the other hand, many firms with poison pill defenses do get sold; the pill is not a showstopper defense in the face of a truly compelling bid from a hostile buyer.

Proponents of this defense argue that it simply prevents a raider from acquiring a substantial position without approval of the target's board. The pill forestalls tender offers for the whole firm as well as creeping acquisitions and street sweeps. Since the board has the power to rescind the pill,[25] it encourages the bidder to negotiate with the board. Generally, the pill preserves time and flexibility for the board to negotiate a more advantageous deal with the raider—as well as with other potential buyers.

The pill has several disadvantages. First, it is a magnet for litigation during a hostile takeover attempt; legal challenges are inevitable. Second, it potentially alienates some investors, including arbitrageurs and institutions, as it appears to entrench management and deny value to investors. Annually, the shareholder-meeting season features shareholder proposals to rescind the pill defense. In the 1990s poison pills came under increasingly heavy opposition from shareholder rights groups as pills originally placed in the 1980s began coming up for renewal. After a wave of poison pill renewals in 1997–1998, shareholder voting to rescind poison pills increased, especially in the volatile technology sector. Designs, Inc. directors voted to drop a poison pill after shareholders approved a resolution calling for the pill's removal; and in an unusual move, Oregon Steel Mills disclosed that its board had chosen not to adopt a pill due to shareholder concerns. In 1998, AlliedSignal Inc. was able to acquire control of AMP Inc. after a Pennsylvania court ruled that AMP had to allow its shareholders the right to vote to repeal the poison pill.

The poison pill is a nondetachable shareholder right to obtain common shares at nominal cost upon the occurrence of a triggering event. All shareholders participate in the right except for an "interested person" who triggers the rights by acquiring more than the threshold percentage of shares allowed under the rights plan. Thus, the plan discriminates against an unwanted acquirer in favor of all other shareholders, making the acquisition more expensive (e.g., 25 to 50 percent more) than otherwise. Typically the right is effective for 10 years unless extended by the board of directors. Nondetachable rights are distributed pro rata to all common stockholders as a stock dividend. The rights are automatically transferred with the shares of common stock to which they relate but do not become exercisable (and indeed are not even represented by separate instruments) until the occurrence of the triggering event. At that point, separate instruments representing the rights are distributed to shareholders. The rights detach from the common shares and become separately tradable.

- ***Triggering event, "interested person."*** The triggering event is defined as the acquisition by any person (or group of persons acting in concert) of a certain percentage (today, typically 10 percent) of outstanding common stock without the prior consent of the firm's board of directors. Such an acquirer is known as an "interested person." An interested person may not exercise the rights.
- ***"Flip in" and "flip over" provisions.*** The rights plan may contain "flip in" and/or "flip over" provisions. The latter apply only when the interested person, having acquired voting control of the firm, attempts to merge the firm into the buying firm. At that point, holders of the rights become entitled to purchase common shares of the surviving firm at nominal value. "Flip in" provisions en-

title the holders to purchase common shares of the target firm at nominal value. Both the "flip in" and "flip over" provisions impose significant economic dilution on the interested person.

- ***Redemption.*** The board of directors may redeem the rights at any time prior to the triggering event and for 10 days thereafter at a negligible redemption price such as $0.01 per right. The rights become irredeemable after a 10-day window.
- ***Qualified offer, "dead hand" provision.*** The board may also choose to exempt a qualified offer from the operations of the rights plan. A "qualified offer" might be defined as an all-cash, any-and-all-shares tender offer or a merger proposal that has been approved by the board. After a change of control, defined as the replacement of 50 percent of the board in a proxy contest, the rights may be redeemed only by a majority of (at least two) "continuing directors." A "continuing director" is defined as a person who was a member of the target board at the time the rights plan was adopted or was nominated by a majority of the directors then in office or their nominees.
- ***Chewable poison pills.*** A variant of the poison pill, the chewable pill is similar to the straight pill, except that it "dissolves" in the face of a very high bid. The chewable pill will become void if a certain event occurs, such as a fully financed offer at a generous premium to the current price; or it can shift the decision from the board of directors to the shareholders, who can vote by a supermajority to accept the bid. The prime case of the use of a chewable pill was that of Pennzoil Co., which adopted such a pill in response to Union Pacific Resources Group's unsolicited bid for the company. The Pennzoil chewable pill dissolved in the face of a more attractive offer from Quaker State Corp.

An example of how a "flip in" poison pill imposes dilution on the bidder is presented in Exhibit 33.4. The example assumes that for each old share of common stock in the firm, the nonraider shareholders may purchase common stock worth $100 for an exercise price of $10, if a raider acquires 20 percent of the shares outstanding. Given other assumptions in the example, triggering the pill has three main effects:

1. ***Voting dilution.*** Triggering the pill dilutes the raider's voting percentage from 20 percent down to 5 percent of all shares outstanding (compare lines 17 and 18).
2. ***Economic dilution.*** The raider's economic interest falls by 69 percent, regardless of whether the bid succeeds or the pill exercise cash flow is "dividended" back to shareholders (see lines 22 and 29).
3. ***Cost to acquire.*** Triggering the pill makes the remaining shares 14 percent more expensive to acquire (line 30).

Sensitivity analysis of the model suggests that the key drivers of variations in dilution imposed on the bidder are the trigger percentage, the discount, and the exercise price multiple (exercise price of the rights plan divided by the bidder's bid price).[26] This example illustrates the conventional wisdom that the poison pill is potentially very costly to the raider.

Shareholder returns associated with the announcement of poison pills have

EXHIBIT 33.4 Illustration of the Dilution Imposed upon a Hostile Bidder after Triggering a Poison Pill

Assumption		
1 Stock price of target before pill is triggered	$ 25.00	
2 Number of shares outstanding before attempted raid	1,000,000	
3 Discount at which nonraider shareholders have the right to purchase shares	90%	
4 Purchase shares worth	$ 100	
5 By paying	$ 10	
6 Poison pill trigger	20%	
7 Assumption about whether pill exercise proceeds will be dividended to shareholders	**No Dividend**	**Dividend**
8 Market value of equity before trigger	$ 25,000,000	$25,000,000
9 Cash received upon exercise of poison pill rights	$ 8,000,000	$ 8,000,000
10 Dividend paid	$ —	$ (8,000,000)
11 Market value of equity after trigger	$ 33,000,000	$25,000,000
12 Number of shares held by the raider when the pill is triggered	200,000	200,000
13 Number of shares held by investors other than the raider after the pill is triggered	4,000,000	4,000,000
14 Total number of shares outstanding after the pill is triggered	4,200,000	4,200,000
15 Price per share after trigger	$ 7.86	$ 5.95
16 Dilution in price per share	69%	76%
Analysis of Voting Dilution Imposed on Raider		
17 Raider voting interest just before pill is triggered	20%	
18 Raider voting interest after pill is triggered	5%	
Economic Dilution Imposed on Raider If Pill Is Triggered and Bid Fails		
19 Change in raider's value of shares after pill is triggered	$ (3,428,571)	$ (3,809,524)
20 Raider's share of dividend from pill exercise proceeds	$ —	$ 380,952
21 Raider's total economic dilution after pill is triggered	$ (3,428,571)	$ (3,428,571)
22 Raider's total economic dilution as a percent of outlay	–69%	–69%

Economic Dilution Imposed on Raider If Pill Is Triggered and Bid Succeeds			
23 Value of nonraider shares before pill is triggered	$20,000,000		
24 Value of nonraider shares after pill is triggered	$31,428,571		
25 Change in raider's cost to acquire rest of shares		$(11,428,571)	$ (3,809,524)
26 Raider's share of dividend from pill exercise proceeds			$ 380,952
27 Raider applies cash from rights toward purchase price		$ 8,000,000	$ —
28 Raider's total economic dilution after pill is triggered		$ (3,428,571)	$ (3,428,571)
29 Raider's total economic dilution as a percent of outlay pretrigger		–69%	–69%
30 Change in cost to acquire remaining: 80%		14%	14%

Note: This example estimates in lines 28 and 29 the economic dilution to the hostile bidder (raider) from triggering a poison pill. Lines 1 to 6 give the underlying assumptions. The reader may consult the Excel spreadsheet accompanying this book, "Poison Pill Dilution.xls," for more detail, and try different sets of assumptions. The model estimates economic dilution in two scenarios:

1. The "no dividend" column simply assumes that the pill is triggered, the rights are exercised, and the cash received by the target from the rights exercise simply sits in its bank account. This is like buying a car that has a large wad of cash in the glove compartment. The cash balance defrays the cost of acquisition (see line 27).
2. The "dividend" column assumes a more rational scenario: The target simply dividends the cash back to all shareholders before the raider proceeds to acquire the target. Thus, the raider gets a small dividend (line 26).

The comparison reveals that disposition of the cash proceeds has no economic effect on the raider.

Line 13: Equal to the percentage of shares held by shareholders other than the raider (1 minus line 6) times the number of shares before the raid (line 2), times one plus the purchase amount (line 4) times the current stock price (line 1).

varied over time. For instance, Jarrell and Poulsen (1987) found statistically significant negative stock prices following announcements of poison pill amendments in the 1980s. In contrast, several studies have found that in the 1990s the effect of poison pills on shareholder value was nil.[27] Comment and Schwert (1995) observed larger negative returns before 1985 and smaller negative returns after 1985—as an earlier section of this chapter argues, the event returns at the announcement of poison pills are reasonably related to the quality of the target firm's governance and attention to shareholder value creation. Ambrose and Megginson (1992) found that the pill strongly deters takeover bids. Danielson and Karpoff (2002) examined earnings before interest and taxes (EBIT) and operating margin for five years after the adoption of a pill and found that the operating performance of firms improved after pill adoptions; based on cross-sectional analysis, they concluded that the pill has little relation to a firm's operating performance. The adoption of pills seems to occur at a time when insiders anticipate improved fortunes.

POISON PUTS Poison puts trigger the repayment of debt at or above par value in the event of a change in control. These deter bids by forcing the bidder to arrange more financing, and possibly to pay a premium for the target's debt. The poison put was a response by institutional lenders to the aggressive use of leverage by some bidders—such use typically destroyed value for incumbent bondholders. Thus, the poison put simultaneously provides a sense of security to bondholders (by hedging some of the risk of devaluation) and triggers an immediate cash drain for the bidder. This has been seen as a moderately effective antitakeover provision, especially when combined with other cash and asset provisions. The research finds that the issuing of bonds with poison puts attached has a statistically significant negative impact on stockholder wealth and a statistically significant positive impact on bondholder wealth.[28] Finally, Ambrose and Megginson (1992) find that event risk covenants ultimately have a small, negative impact on the frequency of bid offers.

Embedded Defenses

Some antitakeover defenses appear as provisions in an announced definitive agreement. These terms anticipate the possible intrusion of one or more competing buyers, and either make it more costly for the intruder or diminish the attractiveness of the target to the intruder.

TERMINATION FEES Termination fees award a payment (usually sufficient in size to cover expenses) to the jilted party. A *breakup fee* is triggered if one party exits from the pending transaction. A *topping fee* is a form of breakup fee awarded to the buyer in the event that another buyer successfully acquires the target with a higher bid, one that has topped the buyer's offer. Termination fees have averaged around 3.5 percent of the deal value. Perhaps the record payment of a termination fee was $1.8 billion, triggered by Pfizer's abandonment of American Home Products (AHP) for Warner Lambert (WL) in 1999. AHP had bid $75 billion for WL and was topped by Pfizer's eventual $90 billion bid; Pfizer agreed to pay WL's termination fee. Coates and Subramaniam (2000) reported a rising trend in the use of termination fees. They found that in the late 1990s, two-thirds of deals contained breakup fees, but that on average from 1988 to 1998 just over one-third of all deals contained this provision. They also revealed that the completion of deals with the friendly bidder is higher in the presence of breakup fees. Lemmon and Bates (2002) reported that in the late 1990s, more than 60 percent of deals contained a termination fee payable by the target to the bidder, while in only 13 percent of deals were fees payable by the bidder to the target.

Including a termination fee in a deal could have several motives. Some fees are structured as if to reimburse expenses of deal negotiation. These fees also help deter nuisance bids that are just a small amount above the buyer's bid: a nuisance bidder who wins will be saddled with paying the breakup, or topping, fee. Also, termination fees may be a means of locking in the deals with friendly bidders and preempting hostile bids. Officer (2003) rejected the notion that termination fees are management entrenchment devices and concluded from an empirical study that target termination fees serve to motivate the bidder to invest in deal development. He found that takeover premiums to target shareholders are on average 4 percent *higher* in the presence of target fees than without and that they increase the likelihood of successful consummation of the deal. Lemmon and Bates (2002) find that the incorporation of a target termination fee is associated with a higher probability of completion of a deal. They note that target fees are likely to be used in larger deals, stock deals, and where targets have large growth opportunities. They find that returns to target shareholders are unaffected by the inclusion of target fees in a deal. But the deal premiums *are* affected by bidder fees: Premiums are negatively correlated with the presence of bidder termination fees, suggesting that targets make a concession on price in return for the risk reduction of a bidder termination fee provision.

TOEHOLD STAKES Here, the target permits the friendly buyer to acquire shares of the target, possibly in excess of the poison-pill trigger (i.e., without triggering the pill). This gives the buyer a head start in accumulating a majority stake in the target. Ravid and Spiegel (1999) hypothesize that bidders will purchase toeholds when they fear intrusion by a rival bidder. But surprisingly, Jarrell and Poulsen (1989) find that only about 40 percent of bidders do acquire a *toehold stake* in their targets. Two studies (Betton and Eckbo 1999; Walkling and Edmister 1985) report that toeholds are associated with lower tender offer premiums to target shareholders. But Walkling (1985) found that toeholds are associated with a higher probability of success for the tender offer.

ASSET LOCKUP OPTIONS: THE "CROWN JEWEL" DEFENSE The merger agreement may include the right of the buyer to acquire certain key assets of the target in the event a competitor successfully acquires the target. One of the prominent cases featuring an asset lockup was the bidding in 1986 to acquire Revlon. The target had granted Forstmann, Little, the friendly buyer, an option to purchase two of Revlon's divisions if another bidder acquired 40 percent of Revlon's shares. The purchase price of $525 million was claimed to be at a 20 percent discount from intrinsic value. The Delaware Supreme Court enjoined the lockup on grounds that it would destroy competition rather than enhance it. In 1989, the Delaware Supreme Court struck down another prominent lockup provision in the deal between Kohlberg, Kravis, and Roberts and the Macmillan Publishing Company, which sought to fend off Robert Maxwell, the unwanted intruder. The Court applied the *Unocal* test to the use of asset lockups and required directors to ask whether the use of this tactic was proportional to the threat, whether the price was fair, when was the lockup granted, and whether the board was maximizing shareholder value. The use of the *crown jewel defense* is not per se illegal, but is such a showstopper to a competing bidder that target boards must meet the enhanced scrutiny of these tests. Since *Macmillan*, the asset lockup has virtually disappeared as a defensive tactic.

STOCK LOCKUP OPTIONS The target may grant the buyer rights to accumulate more target shares at an attractive price. In effect, a *stock lockup option*[29] is similar to a poison pill, but with benefits that flow to the friendly buyer rather than the target shareholders. Similar to the pill, exercise of the options dilutes the return to the intruder. Coates and Subramaniam (2000) found that the median stock lockup is priced slightly in the money, and that it represents a right to buy 19.9 percent of the target's stock, just below the 20 percent trigger of most major exchanges at which a target firm would be required to gain a shareholder vote on the sale. A prominent example of the use of a lockup option to thwart an intruder occurred in 1993 in the competition between Viacom and QVC Network to acquire Paramount Communications. Paramount granted Viacom the right to buy 24 million shares (compared to 120 million outstanding) in the event that QVC acquired Paramount, and then to sell the shares to QVC. Though the Delaware Supreme Court invalidated the Paramount lockup, this defense later appeared prominently in the agreement between Conrail and CSX and in other large transactions. The research on share lockups suggests that they are used infrequently—on the order of 8 to 13 percent of all deals.[30] Burch (2001) reported finding that lockup options appear to discourage competing bidders and that returns to target shareholders are larger in deals that contain lockups. As with the asset lockup, target boards should anticipate the possibility of enhanced scrutiny of stock lockups (as opposed to mere application by the courts of the business judgment rule)[31] in terms of their proportionality, timing, and use of terms that would heavily compensate the favored buyer.

Reactive Defenses

LITIGATION Litigation is a common tactic in takeover defense, raising the transaction costs to the buyer (especially if the litigation is conducted in many venues), delaying the buyer's ability to consummate the deal, raising uncertainty about the final outcome, increasing the disclosure of material information by the bidder, heightening the publicity of the defense, and generally demonstrating a scorched-earth level of resistance. Bidders can respond in kind, countersuing to neutralize the target's litigation. Litigation creates a bargaining chip in the sense that lawsuits can be suspended in return for friendly dealings and an increased bid price. On the other hand, litigation is surprisingly costly, rising into the millions of dollars for defenses of even limited duration and narrow geographical scope.

A target's defensive litigation can cover a number of possible claims:[32]

- Violation of Section 13(d): failing to disclose promptly a share interest greater than 5 percent, intent to control, and full membership of a group of investors.

- Failure to comply with tender offer disclosure requirements, especially regarding the bidder's plans or proposals for operation or restructuring of the target company, the bidder's financial condition, and its source of financing.
- Use of inside information and/or breach of confidentiality commitments to the target.
- A purchase program seen as the equivalent of a tender offer. For instance, an accumulator who has approached many shareholders privately may have substantially breached rules on tender offers.
- Violations of antitrust law, or of rules and laws specific to regulated industries. For instance, the target could seek to enjoin the hostile tender offer on grounds that a combination of the firms would unduly concentrate an industry and produce anticompetitive results. A court has ruled, "If the effect of a proposed takeover may be substantially to lessen competition, the target company is entitled to fend off its suitor and preserve its separate existence."[33] Successful antitrust litigation is a showstopper defense.

The impact of defensive litigation on shareholder welfare is mixed. Jarrell (1985) found that where the target was sold, litigation was associated with a final price that was 17 percent higher than where there was no litigation. But where the target remained independent, target shareholders lost the entire bid premium plus the costs of litigation. Also, the use of legal maneuvers to stop a takeover does not necessarily decrease the probability of attracting a takeover bid in the future.[34]

REGULATORY AND/OR LEGISLATIVE PROTECTION Similar to the "white knight" defense, governments can give external protection to the target—but in the case of government the mechanism is through the implementation of discriminatory laws and regulations. When James Goldsmith mounted a hostile bid for Goodyear Tire in 1986, the target lobbied the state legislature to enact an antitakeover law favorable to the in-state firm. In 1989, the Pennsylvania legislature enacted an antitakeover law at the behest of Armstrong World Industries, which was fighting a takeover bid from the Belsberg family. In both cases the defenses succeeded.

Dahya and Powell (1998) found that 42 states had adopted some form of antitakeover legislation, with many having more than one form on the books. In 1987, the U.S. Supreme Court upheld an Indiana antitakeover law in the case of *CTS Corporation v. Dynamics Corporation of America.* Antitakeover laws also provide a kind of "political defense." Karpoff and Malatesta (1989) found that in 40 antitakeover bills passed by various states in the late 1980s, 75 percent of these cases were introduced on behalf of at least one large firm headquartered in the state and having noticeable goodwill with the constituents. This use of both the existing legal system and the political system to create laws has proven a very effective defense, but it has had some unforeseen outcomes.

Karpoff and Malatesta also found a small but significant negative return to shareholders of firms headquartered in states that enacted antitakeover laws between 1982 and 1987. Ryngaert and Netter (1988) reported a significant decline in value for firms headquartered in Ohio upon enactment of the Ohio legislation; Szewczyk and Tsetsekos (1992) found significant losses to shareholders of Pennsylvania firms at the time of enactment. Comment and Schwert (1995) revealed that the laws did not materially alter the probability of takeover of protected firms, but that the takeover bid premiums tended to be higher. Hoi, Lessard, and Rubin (2000) found that following the enactment of state antitakeover laws, protected firms also increased the number of independent directors. As for the wealth generation effect of antitakeover legislation, Karpoff and Malatesta (1989) reported that the announcement of antitakeover legislation negatively affected stock price of firms in the state (small and significant change). They went on to find that firms with preexisting takeover defenses suffered no significant stock price reactions. The effects of antitakeover laws have also had some effects outside of shareholder wealth. Garvey and Hanka (1999) found that legal barriers erected by antitakeover laws might be increasing managerial slack. They found that managers in states where these laws are available reduce their use of financial management strategies such as debt management. In a completely different arena, Bertrand and Mullainathan (1999) revealed that the enactment of antitakeover laws is associated with an increased annual wage expense of 1 to 2 percent. They reason that these laws entrench managers who then pay higher wages.

Just as targets can lobby legislatures for protection, they can also seek protection from regulatory agencies. For instance, the Federal Communications Commission (FCC) was lobbied energetically by two competing bidders for DirectTV, the satellite television business of Hughes Electronics, a subsidiary of General Motors. EchoStar, the second-largest operator in the United States, had negotiated a friendly deal to acquire DirectTV. But Rupert Murdoch's News Corporation also sought to acquire DirectTV. Several journalists reported heavy or intense lobbying with the FCC.[35] On October 10, 2002, the FCC denied the EchoStar/DirectTV deal.

COUNTERTENDER OFFER: "PAC-MAN" The "*Pac-Man*" defense entails an effort by the target to simultaneously seek to acquire the bidder. The name was drawn from a computer game in which each of two players seek to eat up the opponent's resources before being eaten themselves. It first appeared in 1980 in the hostile takeover attempt on Midway Manufacturing Company. In 1982 five[36] contests featured this defense. Since then, the defense has been rarely used. The advantages of the countertender offer are that it demonstrates aggressive resistance, raises the possibility of success by the target, and affords yet one more bargaining chip in dealings with the hostile bidder. The countertender offer has three chief disadvantages: It may appear to acknowledge the desirability of a combination between the two firms, thus eliminating a range of claims and defenses that the target otherwise might make; it exposes the original target to the same range of defenses as outlined in this chapter; and there is little clarity about how this defense gains closure. Fleischer and Sussman (1995) wrote, "Unresolved is the question of how counter tender offers, each pursued to the end, would be unwound by courts in the absence of an agreement among the parties; if both bidder and counter-bidder own a majority of the other, who controls whom when the contest concludes?"[37]

Successful execution of this tactic depends on being able to buy and take control first, or at least claim to be the first buyer. Delays could spring from other defenses such as a staggered board or the ability to call a special meeting, and from state law regarding the ability of a subsidiary to vote shares held in the parent corporation. This last is a particularly nettlesome point that probably explains the limited use of this tactic. The most famous example of this problem was the Bendix/Martin-Marietta takeover fight in 1982. Bendix, the attacker, had opened with a bid for Martin-Marietta. Martin responded with a counterbid for Bendix, financed in part by a white squire, Allied Corporation. At the end, Martin and Bendix owned a majority of shares of each other. The laws in Maryland (where Martin was incorporated) and Delaware (where Bendix was incorporated) forbade the voting of shares by a subsidiary in a parent—and it seemed that each was the subsidiary of the other. The impasse was broken by Allied Corporation, which, through a complicated stock swap, acquired Bendix and then swapped the Martin shares owned by Bendix back to Martin in return for Martin shares owned by Bendix. Allied remained a substantial shareholder in Martin but agreed to a standstill provision that would limit further acquisition of Martin shares.

SHARE REPURCHASES AND LEVERAGED RECAPITALIZATION A *leveraged recapitalization* by the target entails borrowing heavily and paying a large one-time dividend to target shareholders. This can be an attractive defense in that it delivers cash to shareholders (i.e., arbitrageurs) and leaves in its wake a more highly levered company that presumably earns higher returns on equity. Thus, the tactic tends to raise the target's share price. Also, it means that the attacker would assume a large debt burden from the target. Some debt provisions in highly leveraged recapitalizations include poison puts that make the debt immediately payable upon a change of control of the target firm. Thus, the bidder must be prepared to refinance the target's debt upon acquisition. Denis and Denis (1993) found that stockholders incur losses of about 1 percent around the time that a leveraged recapitalization is announced. Walker (1998) found that leverage, when used as a takeover defense, is associated with improved managerial performance later.

Share repurchase[38] plans act as a defense by levering the target firm and raising its return on equity. Investors react favorably to this tactic. It should be noted that this is often used as a preoffer defense to stay out of the takeover market; but it can also be used as part of a postoffer defense in the form of a counteroffer to stockholders by the target firm or a targeted repurchase of a selective group of shares such as those already owned by the bidder. Many companies conduct share repurchase programs in lieu of dividend payments. As a postoffer defense, share repurchases financed by a combination of debt financing and asset sales can be quite effective, as illustrated earlier in the Hilton-ITT case. Research on the effect of stock repurchases on shareholder wealth finds gains to shareholders.[39] Kirch, Bar-Niv, and Zucca (1998) report that size of repurchase matters: Buying back at least 5 percent of the shares has a larger effect than smaller repurchase programs. Ambrose and Megginson (1992) find that a stock repurchase plan is associated with a lower likelihood of takeover bid, although the effect is not statistically significant.

An example of the financial analysis of a leveraged recapitalization is given in Chapter 13. Also, Chapter 34 discusses in detail the leveraged recapitalization defense of American Standard in a hostile takeover.

ASSET RESTRUCTURING The defending target could dispose of assets through spinoffs, divestiture of tangible assets or subsidiaries, or complete liquidation. These alter the attractiveness of the target to the bidder by disposing of key assets (e.g., crown jewels) or ruining opportunities for synergies between the target and buyer. The sale of undervalued assets (e.g., unused land, operating rights, patents, etc.) may monetize resources that the bidder had hoped to exploit. Of course, any sale of assets could provide the cash to fund an extraordinary dividend, share repurchase, greenmail payment, or other defense. Research has found that the announcement of asset restructuring is associated with a significant decline in shareholder wealth of about 2 percent.[40]

In March 2000, International Security Products (ISP) made a hostile bid to purchase Dexter Inc. Dexter immediately began a plan to sell off both tangible assets as well as subsidiary companies. The sales of various parts of the company enabled Dexter to fight off ISP until a friendly acquirer was found. In 1978, UV Industries took the more draconian asset restructuring strategy of liquidating completely in the face of a hostile bid,[41] which generated a dramatically higher value to shareholders than given in the bid.

Asset *purchases* are another form of defensive restructuring. The target could acquire assets to make the company a less desirable target. Examples of this would be assets pertaining to a regulated industry where regulations limit horizontal acquisitions—such regulations have prevailed from time to time in industries such as banking, broadcasting, and transportation. In other settings, asset purchases could forestall hostile takeovers on grounds of national defense concerns (the "Pentagon play")—for more on this, see the discussion of the Exon-Florio Amendment in Chapter 28.

WHITE KNIGHT, WHITE SQUIRE The target company seeks a friendly buyer with which to merge, a white knight. This friendly company typically agrees not to break the company up or lay off employees. Often a white knight is a horizontal or vertical peer of the target firm and is motivated to bid by the prospect of synergies in the combination and/or the desire to preserve a strategic relationship or deny such a relationship to a competitor. But a white knight can also be motivated by purely financial considerations. One example is Berkshire Hathaway's acquisition of Scott & Fetzer in 1986. The managers of Scott & Fetzer had attempted a leveraged buyout of the company in the face of a rumored hostile takeover attempt. When the U.S. Department of Labor objected to the company's use of an employee stock ownership plan to assist in the financing, the deal fell apart. Soon the company attracted unsolicited proposals to purchase it, including one from Ivan F. Boesky. Warren Buffett, CEO of Berkshire Hathaway, offered to buy the company for $315 million (compared to its book value of $172.6 million). Following the acquisition, Scott & Fetzer yielded a return on investment for Berkshire Hathaway of about 36 percent.[42] Buffett noted that in terms of return on book value of equity, Scott & Fetzer would have easily beaten the Fortune 500 firms.[43]

A white squire merely purchases a large block of stock in the target, but does not take control. The white squire typically agrees to vote in alignment with target management and not purchase more stock for a specified period of time. The white knight/squire defense succeeds by preempting the hostile bidder of control. In the hostile fight for control of Polaroid, the target solicited an investment from corporate partners that, in combination with Polaroid's ESOP, locked up a block of 33 percent of Polaroid's voting shares and stopped the hostile bid.[44] Warren Buffett has acted as a white squire in a number of cases where a hostile bid existed or was threatened—these included Gillette, First Empire State, USAir, Salomon Brothers, and Champion International.

GOING PRIVATE TRANSACTION/LEVERAGED BUYOUT (LBO) Management could simply acquire the target company and continue to operate it as a private entity. Typically this entails significant use of debt financing to purchase the shares, as well as the participation of a financial partner to contribute equity financing. Kohlberg, Kravis, and Roberts and Forstmann, Little are two of the largest and best-known leveraged buyout practitioners. The bid premium in a leveraged buyout is derived from the aggressive exploitation of debt tax shields, reduced costs (i.e., from being a private, as opposed to public, company), and operating efficiencies. Whether this premium is sizable enough to outbid the hostile bidder depends on the synergies that the intruder had hoped to exploit. While LBOs were a common defensive tactic in the 1980s, they receded significantly in the 1990s as strategic buyers exploited synergies to outbid the LBO proposals. Furthermore, the LBO raises questions of self-dealing on the part of the target management, necessitating heightened scrutiny by independent directors.[45] See Chapter 13 for more discussion of the going private alternative.

GREENMAIL OR TARGETED SHARE REPURCHASE Here, the target buys back shares from the acquirer at a premium to the current asking price. As the name implies, greenmail, like blackmail, pays the intruder to go away. This defense has prompted sharp criticism and legal disputes with stockholders who did not obtain the premium price for their shares. In reaction, several states now prohibit or discourage paying greenmail. Some companies have amended their charters to prohibit greenmail payments. And the U.S. Congress imposed a 50 percent tax on the gain received by the greenmailer. While greenmail succeeds in repelling the intruder and buying a little time for target management to implement a restructuring, it does not protect the company from further takeover attempts, as do other kinds of defenses. Chapter 2 offers a detailed discussion of the greenmailing of Walt Disney Company in 1984.

The research findings on the announcement effects of greenmail use show a significant negative response of 2 to 3 percent.[46] On the other hand, Eckbo (1990) found that in the three months leading up to the proxy mailing date, the greenmail announcement culminated in positive returns to shareholders. Also, companies who are engaged in a takeover fight and have a stated precommitment not to pay greenmail have abnormally positive returns as well. In contrast, Ang and Tucker (1988) found that target firms paying greenmail and remaining independent realized a zero abnormal return over time. It would seem that targets that pay greenmail would attract follow-on hostile bids, much as happened in the case of Walt Disney Company. But the empirical evidence on this is mixed. Mikkelson and Ruback (1991) suggest that there is no correlation between the use of greenmail and future takeover bids. Ambrose and Megginson (1992) claim the opposite, that there is a strong positive correlation between greenmail and future bids.

Combinations of Defenses

The inference from Exhibit 33.1 is that a given firm probably employs a number of defensive tactics. Bebchuk, Coates, and Subramaniam (2002) examined a set of hostile bids occurring between 1996 and 2000, and found that a combination of staggered board and poison pill was associated with sharply higher defense success. The odds of remaining independent rose from 34 percent to 61 percent, and the odds that a first bidder would be successful declined from 34 percent to 14 percent. Target shareholder wealth, though, declined between 8 and 10 percent associated with the use of this defense. Key to this heightened defense is a staggered board structured so that the bidder must win two successive elections rather than just one in order to rescind the poison pill defense. This imposes costly delay on the bidder. The interaction between the two tactics, a defensive "cocktail," produces a powerful joint defense. Bebchuk, Coates, and Subramaniam write,

> *A pill provides relatively weak takeover protection if the target is vulnerable to a rapid proxy fight, because the target's board can redeem the pill at any time; a staggered board without a pill is likewise ineffective against a bid, given the unlikelihood that target directors will continue to resist if a bidder has acquired a majority of the target's stock. In combination with an effective staggered board, however, a pill provides significant antitakeover protection: the pill blocks any stock acquisition beyond the trigger level, and the staggered board forces the bidder to go through two proxy contests in order to gain control of the board and redeem the pill.*[47]

The case of Hilton Hotels' attempted takeover of ITT[48] illustrates the strategic role of the "cocktail" defense. On January 27, 1997, Hilton offered an unsolicited bid of $55 per share of ITT. ITT's board was unclassified, and the company had a poison pill defense in place. Hilton therefore conditioned its bid on the successful outcome of a proxy fight in which Hilton would unseat the entire board, seat new directors friendly to Hilton's offer, rescind the poison pill, and consummate the tender offer. In response, ITT simply refused to call a meeting of the shareholders and for almost a year stonewalled Hilton's attack while implementing a restructuring defense and searching for a white knight. When it appeared that ITT would need shareholder approval for a major breakup of the firm, it simultaneously requested approval for a charter amendment that would stagger the election of its directors. ITT succeeded in finding a friendly buyer who topped Hilton's bid.

How do firms choose their defenses? The chief finding is that there is rather little herdlike behavior: Firms vary in their adoption of defenses. Several studies—Coates (2000), Field and Karpoff (2000), and Daines and Klausner (2001)—looked at the adoption of defenses "at birth," when firms go public. Daines and Klausner (2001) found that half the firms adopt strong defenses; another 18 percent adopt mild defenses; and the balance adopt no defenses at all at the initial public offering (IPO). Daines and Klausner found support for no hypothesis about defense adoption. Field and Karpoff (2000) found that 53 percent of the IPOs had at least one antitakeover defense in place and that managers who were not tightly monitored by pre-IPO investors (such as venture capitalists) tended to deploy more defenses. Also, Coates (2000) found that firms advised by larger law firms with more takeover experience adopted more defenses at the IPO, that firms with high-quality venture backers and financial advisers also adopted more defenses, and that the adoption of defenses at the IPO generally increased during the 1990s. Generally Coates' findings agreed with the conclusions of the other studies: There is a high variance in defensive practices among firms that go public. Hannes (2001, 2002) argues that the divergence in adoptions of takeover defenses is rational as a means of differentiating targets from one another.

SUMMARY AND IMPLICATIONS FOR THE PRACTITIONER

No public company is immune from hostile attack. To be sure, the greatest incidence of attack is among smaller and midsized firms. But large size gives no sure defense, as large hostile bids in industries such as banking, oil, and defense demonstrated in the 1990s. This chapter focuses on the effectiveness and valuation results of various takeover tactics. What makes defenses effective is their ability to delay, raise prices and transaction costs, and increase uncertainty for the transaction. Tactics of attack seek to offset these effects.

Do takeover tactics pay? The overwhelming evidence is "yes." But how and how much they pay, and to whom remain topics of considerable interpretation. This chapter offers a way to think about the disparate answers. One could start by regarding defense tactics as control options and attack tactics as attempts to neutralize the control options. Option theory lends at least two immediate insights from this perspective: tactics will be more valuable (1) the greater the uncertainty about the intrinsic value of the target and (2) the longer the defenses can run. But as a practical matter in many firms it is the target firm's managers, not the shareholders, who hold these control rights. Therefore, whether the rights are used to enhance shareholder value determines who benefits from the rights. Here, the effectiveness of the target firm's governance is decisive: good governance aligns managers and shareholders and is associated with the effective use of tactics to create value. This perspective offers some useful implications for managers, investors, and M&A advisers:

- Antitakeover defenses are costly to shareholders of underperforming companies with entrenched managers. Defenses impose a sizable opportunity cost on shareholders of firms that could use some capital market discipline.
- Antitakeover defenses are beneficial to shareholders of well-performing firms with managers whose interests are aligned with those of shareholders. For these firms, defenses give good managers the time and flexibility to negotiate attractive deals on behalf of their shareholders.
- The size of costs or benefits from antitakeover defenses is likely related to the extent of disagreement or uncertainty about intrinsic value of the target.

In short, research offers no blanket conclusion about the profitability and efficacy of takeover tactics. The M&A professional should ask instead about the quality of the firm's governance and the uncertainty about the firm's intrinsic value—these can guide the analyst to some reasonable conjectures about the impact of the firm's antitakeover defenses.

The chapter also outlines numerous tactics along with what we know from research about their impact and efficacy. This survey offers more implications for managers:

- Whatever feelings of helplessness a target CEO must feel upon the announcement of a hostile bid, the target is not defenseless. The target can call upon a rich range of tactics that can be deployed across time (before a hostile bid, embedded in a friendly deal, and in reaction to the hostile bid itself).

- While the efficacy of individual tactics may vary, these tactics may gain strength when combined into "cocktails" of defense. Thus, the architect of takeover defenses should attend to the ways in which the defensive tactics can combine to greatest effect.
- Defenses can be emplaced across time: well in advance of a hostile bid, embedded in the terms of a friendly deal, and in reaction to a bid. The implication here is that the defensive strategy is not merely a matter of what is done in advance; agile response to a hostile bid may matter as much as premeditated defense.
- Still, planning one's defenses makes a large difference in quality of execution at the time of a hostile bid. Fleischer and Sussman (1997, pages 2-3 to 2-5) note that such planning could cover a range of actions: retain counsel and investment bankers; put in place a comprehensive range of proactive defenses; study your shareholder base, giving attention to key block holders, turnover among holders, and monitoring of daily stock trading; survey any restrictive covenants in debt issues that might limit actions such as spin-offs or asset sales; check liability insurance policy for officers and directors for coverage of takeover costs; form a contingency team of decision makers; and prepare a "black book" manual with lists of key coordinates, procedures for discussions with press and analysts, means of calling an emergency board meeting, items to be reviewed at board meeting, and means of contacting shareholders.
- At the end of the day, the single best defense against a hostile raid is a high stock price. Defenses already in place should not lull you into indifference about a potential raid—or worse, indifference toward the welfare of your own shareholders.

This survey offers some practical implications for bidders as well. As the preceding chapter shows, the raider succeeds only about one-third of the time. This is because antitakeover defenses, while not perfect, are material.

- Remember that your key audience consists of arbitrageurs and other sophisticated players. The object of your attacking strategy should be to win their support through a succession of moves. Takeovers are games.
- The point of tactics of attack should be to reduce time and uncertainty about value and success of your bidding.
- Research and expert legal counsel are enormously important in crafting a strategy of attack.
- At the end of the day, the single tactic that best ensures successful takeover is to offer a high bid. Money talks—but within reason. As emphasized elsewhere in this book, one must set limits on what one will bid in order not to destroy value for the bidder's shareholders.

NOTES

1. See Chapters 26, 27, 31, and 32.
2. For instance, in 2003 PeopleSoft enlisted customers to publicly express their resistance to Oracle's proposed takeover of the firm.

3. For reasons suggested in this section, one could hypothesize that the use of tactics has a symmetric effect (adjusted for relative size) on the bidder.
4. Optionality is the right to take action, the triggering of which is contingent on some other event.
5. It would be natural to extend this framework into a third direction, intrinsic value or "moneyness." The defensive option is "out of the money" if the firm is an unlikely target and the probability of attack is low. A defensive option is "in the money" if the firm is under hostile attack or close to it. Case law suggests that the emplacement of defenses *during* an attack may warrant the enhanced scrutiny of the court. This discussion will not complicate the presentation with this third dimension, moneyness, simply because logic suggests that it is likely to be an amplifier: Where the defense can buy time for a well-governed firm to negotiate a higher price, the placement of the defense is likely to have a positive effect. But where there is no hostile attack, the immediate benefit (or cost) of a defense is likely to be smaller.
6. "The [poison pill] right has no economic value" in Arthur Fleischer Jr. and Alexander R. Sussman, *Takeover Defense*, 5th ed., Aspen Law and Business, 1997, page 5-7.
7. A quotation of publicist Richard Cheney, referring to a hostile offer by Colt Industries, the maker of firearms, in Larry Gurwin, "The Scorched Earth Policy," *Institutional Investor*, 34 (June 1979), page 33.
8. For more information on charter amendment defenses, see Fleisher and Sussman (1997), from which this discussion abstracts selected points.
9. In some states it may be possible to obtain these defenses by amending the corporation's *bylaws* instead of its charter. Some states permit amendment of bylaws without a vote of shareholders.
10. See Johnson and Rao (1999), Born and Ryan (2000), Linn and McConnell (1983), and Ambrose and Megginson (1992).
11. See Bhagat and Black (1999).
12. See Markides (1992) and Bacon, Cornett, and Davidson (1997).
13. See Garvey and Hanka (1999).
14. See Bhagat and Black (1999).
15. See *Investor Relations Business* (2000).
16. See Hoi, Lessard, and Robin (2000).
17. See Linn and McConnell (1983), McWilliams (1990, 1993), and Markides (1992).
18. See Linn and McConnell (1983), McWilliams (1990, 1993), and Markides (1992).
19. See Heron and Lewellen (1998), McWilliams (1990), Malezadeh and McWilliams (1995), Sundaramurthyu and Lyton (1998), Brickley and Lease (1998), and Sridaram (1997).
20. "Change of control" can be defined in many possible ways, including number or percentage of shares, turnover in board directors, shareholder vote approving sale or merger, and triggering of the poison pill.
21. See Mogavero and Toyne (1995).
22. Davidson, Pilger, and Szakmary (1998).
23. In fact, the only instance of a pill ever being triggered occurred in September 1990 when the management of Instron Corporation inadvertently triggered the

company's poison pill when they announced that a bloc of management and founding family members owned 39 percent of Instron stock.

24. Cited in Friedman and Sussman (1995), page 5-16.
25. It's not clear who can rescind the pill generally. But lawyers and practitioners believe that the board actually controls both the implementation and removal of the pill.
26. The percentage dilution can be estimated using the following equation, where X is the trigger percentage, D is the percentage discount, and Y is the purchase multiple (the value of shares to be purchased under one right divided by the current share price of the target):

$$\text{Percentage dilution} = \frac{X \times Y \times D(1-X)}{1+Y(1-X)}$$

27. See Lee and Pawlukiewicz (2000), Datta and Iskandar-Datta (1996), and Brickley, Coles, and Terry (1994).
28. See Roth and McDonald (1999), Perumpral, Davidson, and Sen (1999), Cook and Easterwood (1994), and Bjorn and Ryan (2000).
29. Coates and Subramaniam (2000) note that "lockup" implies a degree of efficacy that is not accurate (i.e., not all deals with lockups are completed in favor of the desired buyer) and would likely be illegal if it were so completely successful.
30. Burch (2001) reports the 8 percent average over 1988 to 1995. Coates and Subramaniam (2000) report 12.9 percent of the deals contain share lockup provisions from 1988 to 1998.
31. For a more detailed discussion of the business judgment rule and enhanced scrutiny by the courts, see Chapter 26.
32. This list is abstracted from Chapters 11 and 12 in Fleishman and Sussman (1997).
33. *Consolidated Gold Fields PLC v. Minorco, S.A. 871 F.2d 252* (2d Cir. 1989)
34. See Markides (1992) and Berkovitch and Khanna (1990).
35. "Derailing the agreement would be a huge victory for Mr. Murdoch's News Corporation, which has lobbied intensively to halt the merger." ("Murdoch Wins Second Chance to Gain DirectTV," MediaGuardian.co.UK, September 25, 2002; http://media.guardian.co.uk /rupertmurchoch/story/0,11136,798646,00.html).
36. Fleischer and Sussman (1995) call 1982 the peak year for countertender offers, and cite these contests: American General/NLT, Cities Service/Mesa Petroleum, Olympia Brewing/Pabst, Heublein/General Cinema, and Bendix/Martin-Marietta.
37. Fleischer and Sussman (1995), pages 9-29 and 9-30.
38. A variation on the share repurchase defense is the share *issuance* defense. This is typically connected with a white squire defense, discussed later in the chapter.
39. See Bagnoli, Gordon, and Lipman (1989), Stulz (1988), and Sinha (1991).
40. See Ambrose and Megginson (1992) and Dann and DeAngelo (1983, 1986).
41. See Bruner (1980), "UV Industries" (Harvard Business School Publishing case study 4-280-072).
42. See Bruner (1995), "Warren E. Buffett, 1995" and associated teaching note for details of this calculation.

43. This exempts from the comparison firms emerging from bankruptcy in recent years. Buffett's observation was made in Berkshire Hathaway's 1994 annual report.
44. See Bruner and Brownlee (1990) for a detailed discussion of the Polaroid defense.
45. See Bruner and Paine (1988) for a detailed discussion of the potential conflicts of interests in LBOs, and a possible remedy.
46. See Dann and DeAngelo (1983), Mikkelson and Ruback (1985, 1986, 1991), Bradley and Wakeman (1983), Eckbo (1990), and Ang and Tucker (1988).
47. Bebchuk, Coates, and Subramaniam (2002), page 899.
48. See Bruner and Vakharia (1998) for a detailed discussion and analysis of the Hilton/ITT contest.

CHAPTER 34

The Leveraged Restructuring as a Takeover Defense: The Case of American Standard

INTRODUCTION

The aim of this chapter is to illustrate the execution of a restructuring strategy as a takeover defense. It differentiates the defensive features of the *leveraged recapitalization* and leveraged buyout. Thus, it complements Chapters 32 and 33 dealing with hostile takeovers and Chapter 13 dealing with highly levered transactions. The essence of the contest is captured in the following three statements:

> *Over the past several months, I have tried to arrange a meeting with you to discuss a combination between the Black & Decker Corporation and American Standard. I was hopeful that you would meet with me to discuss this combination and was disappointed that you were not even willing to listen to a plan that will serve the best interests of our companies and their constituencies. . . . Our only alternative is to take our proposal directly to American Standard's stockholders. . . . We believe the combined company would be a highly competitive consumer and commercial products company with a strong market position.*
>
> —Letter from Nolan Archibald, CEO, Black & Decker, January 27, 1988

> *There are no obvious synergies. Black & Decker is a consumer company turning into a conglomerate. This [bid] muddies the waters.*
>
> —Guy Nielsen, securities analyst, Brown Brothers, Harriman & Co.

> *We certainly liked the basic business at American Standard. When we saw their proposed recapitalization with its ESOP, we saw that the end result would have the characteristics of the leveraged buyouts we do.*
>
> —Joseph Schuchert, managing partner, Kelso & Company

On January 27, 1988, Black & Decker Corporation announced a hostile tender offer for the shares of American Standard, Inc. The contest for control of American Standard lasted for two months; ultimately, the attack failed. The target emerged from the contest a very different company, reflecting a dramatic leveraged restructuring. The story of the takeover attempt is more than a colorful tale; it is an illustration of the relative effectiveness of various defensive tactics. More importantly, it raises a number of insights for the senior corporate manager:

1. The uses and limitations of defensive strategies based on golden parachutes, poison pills, and litigation.
2. Why defenses based on financial restructuring can stop an attack, and the circumstances under which such defenses are likely to work.
3. The evolving role of outside advisers and the white knight, and what the senior corporate manager should expect from each.

The main conclusion is that contests for corporate control are not set-piece battles using formalized preestablished defenses; instead, *these are contests of strategic agility in which winners exploit their natural advantages to the fullest and respond flexibly to changes in the course of the contest.*

The following section describes the circumstances of Black & Decker's hostile tender offer for American Standard, and its outcome. The next section analyzes American Standard's initial responses and what they accomplished. The final section focuses on the later phase of American Standard's defense, based on leveraged restructuring. This compares *management buyouts* (MBOs) and leveraged recapitalizations, and develops a profile of the type of company in which these tactics might be effective. The chapter concludes with some caveats about leveraged restructuring as a takeover defense.

THE AMERICAN STANDARD CASE

Consistent with the argument in Chapter 32, consider the attempted takeover of American Standard as a competitive game. One begins the assessment of the game with a profile of the players and their positions at the start.

The Target

A global manufacturer of air conditioning, plumbing, and transportation products, American Standard (AS) had more than $3 billion in sales, with 90 manufacturing facilities in 16 countries in 1987. It was the world's largest producer of bathroom fixtures, and ranked number one in the production of truck braking systems in Europe and in railcar braking systems in the United States. Its Trane subsidiary was the largest domestic producer of air-conditioning systems used in high-rise buildings, and was number two or three in most of the other domestic air-conditioning submarkets. Historically, about 60 percent of operating profits had been generated outside the United States.

With the exception of acquiring Trane, Standard had been paring down its operations over the prior 15 years by cutting costs and divesting marginal divisions. In 1985, the company took a $100 million after-tax restructuring charge, and began a program that resulted in the disposal of businesses accounting for 20 percent of sales. Standard also slimmed down its railcar braking business. In 1986, the company sold its Mosler Safe security products group and American Bank Stationery check printing operations. In 1987, the company disposed of a small commercial printing operation and its bus air-conditioning group. The company used the proceeds of these sales to repurchase common stock, reducing the total number of outstanding common shares from 39 million to 31.2 million. By 1987, American Standard began to realize the payoff from its restructuring. Fiscal year 1987 operating income was 17 percent higher than in 1986.[1]

The Situation

In summer 1987, American Standard's management felt the company was undervalued by the equity markets. Based on management forecasts and recent takeovers in the building industry, internal analysis suggested a stock value of up to $78 a share, at a point in time when the stock had been trading between $40 and $52. Management believed that part of this undervaluation was due to the market's failure to realize the lower risk associated with the replacement and remodeling market in which a growing portion of the company's building products sales occurred. The October 1987 market crash was believed to have removed any immediate takeover threats. Furthermore, the diverse nature of American Standard was thought to be a deterrent to many potential buyers. Management was reluctant to undertake a management-led LBO, which might create a conflict of interest given management's inside information. Both legal advice and top management philosophy kept the company from installing significant takeover defenses in the absence of a bid.

On January 27, 1988, Black & Decker Acquisition, Inc. (a wholly owned subsidiary of the Black & Decker Corp.) announced a hostile $56 per share tender offer for control of American Standard, a substantial premium over the $38 price at which the stock had closed on the previous day. The offer was set to expire at midnight, February 24. Exhibit 34.1 provides a chronology of subsequent events and of American Standard's stock price, along with a chart of the share price movements for American Standard, Black & Decker, and the S&P 500.

The Bidder

Headquartered in Towson, Maryland, Black & Decker (B&D) was the world's largest manufacturer of power tools and small household products, with production facilities in 10 countries and distribution networks in more than 100 nations. B&D also owned replacement parts and service centers around the world. In 1987, B&D's business position was spread across power tools, air conditioning, building products, and transportation. Projected operating income of $313 million for 1988 would come $100 million from air conditioning, $118 million from building, and $95 million from transportation. Power tools accounted for 41 percent of the company's $1.9 billion in sales, with household items representing 34 percent of sales.

In 1985, Black & Decker's plants were aging and inefficient. Its marketing efforts were weak. And the line of small household appliances, which Black & Decker had just acquired from General Electric, was floundering. Faced with high overhead costs and manufacturing overcapacity, B&D was losing market share to offshore competition.

In September 1985, Nolan D. Archibald, 44, became president and CEO of Black & Decker. A Harvard MBA with an impressive history of turning around

EXHIBIT 34.1 Chronology of American Standard's (AS) Defense against Black and Decker (B&D)

Date		AS Price
8/87	AS internal analysis suggests market undervaluation.	
10/87	Market crash thought to remove takeover threat.	
1/26/88		$38.0
1/27/88	B&D announces hostile $56 bid.	$58.8
	AS retains Goldman Sachs to develop response.	
2/1/88	AS announces higher than expected 1987 EPS	$60.5
2/4/88	AS board meeting—delays vote on proposals to 2/8	$63.2
2/5/88	B&D increases offer to $65.	$63.8
2/9/88	AS board announces rejection of B&D offer and adoption of interim rights plan.	$67.0
2/10/88	B&D announces consent solicitation in attempt to unseat board and files separate suits in Delaware challenging AS rights plan and Delaware takeover law.	$67.3
2/18/88	AS board ratifies golden parachute, amends interim rights plan, and approves leveraged recap proposal valued at $68 to $70 (see Exhibit 34.6).	$67.5
2/23/88	B&D increases bid to $68.	$68.2
3/3/88	AS boosts cash payout of recap to $64 (value $74–$75).	$68.6
3/4/88	B&D responds with $73 bid.	$72.5
3/15/88	Delaware judge disarms golden parachute and says AS under Revlon duties.	$75.1
3/17/88	AS announces merger agreement with Kelso at $78.	$76.3
	B&D responds, upping bid to $77.*	
3/22/88	B&D terminates offer (Kelso pays B&D $25 million*).	$76.6
3/27/88	ASI (Kelso is general partner) purchases 95% of AS shares at $78 ($2.3 billion).	
6/29/88	Effective date of merger under Section 253 of Delaware corporate law.	

*Since B&D's $77 bid amount would be paid 20 days earlier than Kelso's $78 bid, the bid differential of $1 would make B&D's offer attractive at required returns greater than about 27% per year: $(1 + 1/77)^{365/20} = 1.266$.

struggling divisions, he came from Beatrice, where he headed the consumer durables group. His new management team included executives from marketing driven firms such as Emerson and Beatrice. Archibald's management team focused their attention on sales, emphasizing customer service, marketing, and technological innovation. The product mix was redirected toward top line, longer life products with higher margins. The operating results for the first quarter of 1988 were released two days before the tender offer announcement. Earnings jumped 40 percent to $31.1 million as sales rose 16 percent to $672.3 million. Analysts at Prudential Bache commented, "Mr. Archibald's management team has clearly done an outstanding job in turning around Black & Decker over the past three years."

This dramatic turnaround made Black & Decker a prime candidate for a takeover, according to analysts at First Boston Company.

Archibald had been looking for acquisitions since he assumed control of the

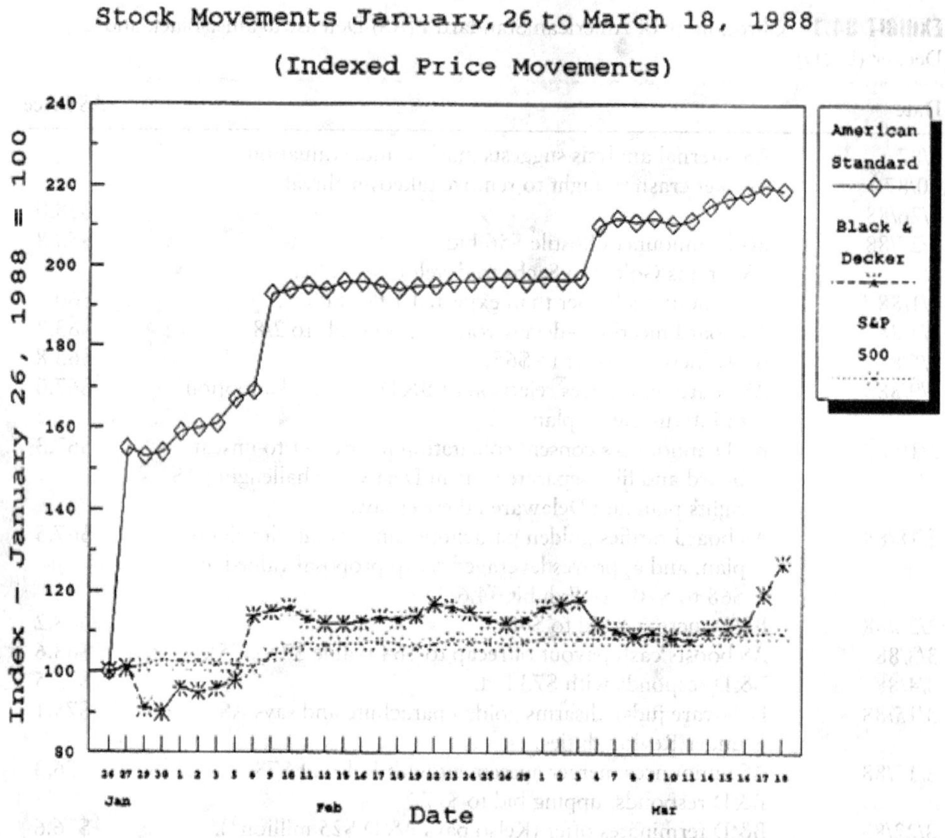

EXHIBIT 34.1 *(Continued)*

company. For six months, Black & Decker had been studying American Standard as a way to broaden its earnings base and achieve its goal of being a global marketer and manufacturer of products for use in and around the home and for commercial applications. Black & Decker could use Standard's strong plumbing fixture lines to complement its building products for do-it-yourselfers and professionals. Although the acquisition of American Standard would increase Black & Decker's long-term debt from $250 million to $1.5 billion, B&D planned to sell Standard's Manhattan headquarters (estimated to be worth $48 million) and the transportation group to reduce its debt load.

THE RESPONSE

The game of takeover attack and defense proceeded in five stages.

Stage One: The Reaction

Once Black & Decker announced its $56 per share hostile bid on January 27, the officers and directors of American Standard were united in their opposition to the bid. On the day the takeover plans were announced, American Standard retained Goldman Sachs & Co. as its investment adviser to work on a response plan with the law firm of Sullivan & Cromwell, American Standard's counsel. The agreement authorized Goldman Sachs to help AS explore numerous alternatives to B&D's takeover offer, including reorganization, purchase of another company, or sale to a white knight. Goldman Sachs would act as AS's exclusive private placement agent. In addition to a $750,000 retainer, Goldman Sachs was to receive $4.25 million if B&D's offer were withdrawn or certain other conditions were met, $17.5 million if specified recapitalizations occurred, and other compensation based on the value of securities issued in a recap or on the value of a takeover by AS.

Publicly, American Standard lashed out at Black & Decker. William B. Boyd, 64, chairman and CEO of AS, was quoted in the *Wall Street Journal* as calling Black & Decker "acquisition and transaction-oriented," as contrasted with his "operations-oriented" team, claiming that "the results we have gotten are quite superior to what he [Archibald] has gotten . . . we have a return on equity at 16.2% after-tax. That puts us back in the top quartile of companies. Black & Decker has a return on equity of about 8.8%. That puts them in the lowest quartile."

Stage Two: The Poison Pill

On February 9, 1988, CEO Boyd announced that the AS board of directors had rejected Black & Decker's bid as inadequate (based on Goldman Sachs' analysis), and that they had adopted an interim rights plan (poison pill) granting existing shareholders the right to purchase five shares of American Standard common stock[2] for each share presently held. The rights would become redeemable when a hostile party acquired 15 percent of American Standard's outstanding common stock. In an accompanying SEC filing, American Standard reported that its options under review included adopting a staggered board; a recapitalization or restructuring; a management-led LBO; the sale of the company or a portion of assets; or a merger with a third party (white knight).

Black & Decker's response on February 10 was to announce a *consent solicitation*[3] to reduce from 10 to 5 the number of seats on American Standard's board, and to seat three of its own directors on the board. If successful, the new board would move to redeem the interim rights plan and move ahead with the acquisition. In addition, Black & Decker filed separate suits in Delaware, challenging both the poison pill and the Delaware antitakeover law.[4]

Stage Three: Revisions and New Steps

As the American Standard board met on February 18, Black & Decker's amended bid stood at $65 per share for all outstanding shares (aggregate value $2.163 billion). To bolster its defensive position further, the board:

1. Ratified a golden parachute amendment to accelerate payments under the retirement and savings plan if management employment was terminated within three years of a change in control of the company.
2. Approved a recapitalization plan initially discussed at the February 8 board meeting, which offered shareholders approximately $68 to $70 per share,

while providing insiders the opportunity to increase their percentage ownership (see Exhibit 34.2).

3. Amended the interim rights plan so that only directors elected at a regularly scheduled annual meeting could terminate the pill (if this was decided to be in the shareholders' best interests), and extended the expiration date of the pill to the earlier of June 30, 1988, or the date on which the shareholders voted on the recapitalization plan.[5]

As of the close of business on February 22, only 47,900 shares had been tendered. This response implied that arbitrageurs were buying up large blocks of American Standard stock in anticipation of higher bids. On February 23, Black & Decker responded by increasing its bid to $68 per share for any and all outstanding common shares, and extended the expiration date of the offer until March 7.

Stage Four: Increasing the Leveraged Recapitalization

On Thursday evening, March 3, the American Standard board voted to boost the cash package of their recapitalization proposal to $64 per share, giving the total re-

EXHIBIT 34.2 Initial Leveraged Recapitalization Proposal (Approved February 18, 1988)

In exchange for each share of common stock outstanding, American Standard will offer a package consisting of:

- A $59 cash dividend.
- A new issue of Series A junior debentures due 2003, with a face value of $10.80, and a market value of approximately $5.
- One share of common stock in the new company with a market value of approximately $6.

The market value of the package was approximately $68 to $70 per share. Instead of taking this package, insiders and savings plan ownership would trade each old share of AS stock for 11.7 shares of Newco stock, thus upping their percentage ownership. In addition, an ESOP would be established, which would purchase $80 million worth of equity in the new company. The lending syndicate will provide a bridge loan to the ESOP to finance its purchase of the common stock. The ESOP facility will be fully payable nine months after closing.

Debt Financing

Total:	$1.84 billion
Lead banks:	Chemical, Citicorp, Manufacturers Hanover, Sumitomo
Credit facilities:	• $250 million, 5-year revolving working credit. Interest rate: prime plus 1%, or LIBOR plus 2%. • $80 million, 9-month bridge to the ESOP. Interest rate: prime plus 1.25 %. • $1.51 billion, 8.5-year term. Interest rate: prime plus 1.25%, or LIBOR plus 2.25% (funded in British pounds, Canadian dollars, U.S. dollars, and/or German marks). *Dollar equivalent limits* British pounds $50 million Canadian dollars $150 million German marks $550 million (balance of $1.51 billion term loan funded in U.S. dollars)

cap package a value of approximately $74–$75 per share. The recap included an arrangement with Emerson Electric, who would provide to AS $160 million in cash financing in exchange for junior subordinated debentures, warrants,[6] and a supplier contract for air-conditioner motors.[7] The announcement on Friday morning sent American Standard's stock soaring from $69 to $72 per share. Black & Decker, responding quickly, raised the ante to $73 cash per share. The offer was conditioned, however, on the absence or elimination of any material obligations of American Standard resulting from its recapitalization proposal.[8] Although Black & Decker had not yet lined up the additional financing, senior managers were confident that it would be provided by their lending syndicate.

On Tuesday, March 8, American Standard stated that it planned to provide confidential information to Black & Decker and to meet with other potential purchasers of the company. On Sunday morning, March 13, advisers at Goldman Sachs informed American Standard's board of directors that they were in discussions for the sale of the company with credible buyers and expected to be able to obtain a price in excess of $75 cash per share.

The AS board of directors then agreed to furnish Black & Decker with the same information as other potential bidders. In addition, they revoked the poison pill stipulation in the event that more than 50 percent of the company's shares were purchased pursuant to a formal tender offer. If less than 50 percent of the shares were tendered, then the pill would remain in effect in order to prevent Black & Decker from executing a "drop and sweep"[9] which might cut short the ongoing auction process and prevent stockholders from obtaining a higher third-party bid.

Stage Five: Court Rulings and the LBO

On March 15, Judge Joseph Longobardi granted Black & Decker's request for a temporary injunction, disarming American Standard's golden parachute and amendments to its retirement and savings plans. In addition, he ruled that the board of American Standard fell under the jurisdiction of the "*Revlon duties*,"[10] and that the structure of American Standard's ESOP, combined with the shares already controlled by members of the board, gave them effective voting control of the company. Thus, none of those shares would fall under the two-thirds calculation in meeting the requirements of the Delaware statute.

On March 17, American Standard announced that it had signed a merger agreement with Kelso & Company for $78 per share. This announcement came as a surprise both to Black & Decker and to analysts on the street. Until this announcement, Kelso's largest deal was its 1984 LBO of Blue Bell, Inc., for $658 million. In coming as a white knight, Kelso brought previous experience with American Standard and with ESOPs.

In 1986, Kelso had purchased the Mosler Safe Company and the Lebanon Valley Offset divisions from American Standard for a total of $182 million. This had provided a close working relationship with senior American Standard management and a familiarity with American Standard's operations. This new deal was not a leveraged ESOP, but rather an LBO with an ESOP investment funded by excess pension assets. Kelso was a buyout sponsor with strong experience in ESOP financings.

Following the March 17 announcement, Black & Decker responded by raising its bid to $77 per share. B&D announced that it would give American Standard shareholders a residual cash distribution of $4 per share, the source of which would be the additional $130 million that would have otherwise been distributed under American Standard's golden parachute plan.[11]

Under the Kelso proposal, American Standard would become a wholly owned subsidiary of ASI Holding Corporation. The price for the shares purchased pursuant to the tender offer was about $2.3 billion, plus related fees and expenses. Proceeds were provided as follows:

- $1.55 billion of a $1.8 billion credit agreement led by Bankers Trust.
- A bridge loan of $920 million provided by First Boston, to be taken in two subordinated debt issues.
- $180 million in equity provided by the sale of 180,000 shares to ASI Partners.

As a part of this agreement, General Electric Capital Corporation received $75 million in private placement of pay-in-kind preferred stock, which was to prepay $75 million of the bridge loan. In exchange, GE and ASI extended and modified their existing agreements for GE to supply motors for the air-conditioning segment (see Exhibit 34.3 for a summary of the Kelso LBO).

On March 22, Black & Decker announced that it was terminating its tender offer for American Standard and was returning the shares that had been tendered. In exchange, Kelso agreed to pay Black & Decker $25 million to cover its tender offer expenses, provided that Black & Decker did not reenter the contest.

In making this announcement, Black & Decker CEO Nolan Archibald said, "We made a commitment to our stockholders that when the bidding reached the level where it was not consistent with Black & Decker's aggressive EPS and ROE growth objectives, we would not pursue it."

PARACHUTES, PILLS, AND LITIGATION

As part of its defense, American Standard emplaced two defenses, a golden parachute and an interim rights plan (or poison pill). The large question is: Why did these defenses fail to preserve the company *status quo ante*?

The Parachute

The golden parachute specified that any officer of the company (there were 29 officers) would receive a payment if terminated within three years of a change in control of the company. The payment would be equal to three times the officer's annual salary plus one times the annual bonus. The total payment was estimated at about $50 million. In addition, a change in control would trigger distribution of the excess assets in the company's pension plan (estimated at $80 million). The pension lockup, plus golden parachutes, would reduce the value of American Standard's stock by about $4 per share if all incumbent management left the company, or about 5 percent of the $78 final bid.

More than 350 firms of the Fortune 500 have golden parachutes in place, though there is no instance in which a parachute has defeated a hostile bid.

EXHIBIT 34.3 Summary of the Kelso LBO

Name	Shares Owned	% Ownership
Kelso ASI Partners, LP (including principals of Kelso & Co.)	180,000	72%
American Standard ESOP	50,000	20%
Concurrent offering to American Standard Officers*	20,000	8%

*The concurrent offering would be available to the following individuals at a price of $1,000 per share: William B. Boyd (chairman, president, and CEO), Nicolas M. Georgitsis (senior vice president, transportation products), Emmanuel A. Kampouris (senior vice president, building products), James C. Workman (senior vice president, air conditioning products), and all executive officers of American Standard (as a group). In a modification of the original proposal for 250,000 shares shown above, 400 American Standard employees had the opportunity to buy $20 million of stock at $1,000 per share, bringing the total shares outstanding to 270,000. To finance the purchase, employees were allowed to borrow up to half their annual salaries, although no employee could purchase stock beyond the equivalent of two-thirds of his or her annual salary.

Capitalization (in Millions)	Historical	Pro Forma for the Tender Offer and Merger	Pro Forma for the Transaction
Short-term debt:			
Loans payable to banks	$139.9	$26.9	$26.9
Funding notes	-0-	920.0	-0-
Current maturities of long-term debt	16.7	291.0	200.0
Total short-term debt	156.6	1,237.9	226.9
Long-term debt:			
9.25% sinking fund	150.0	150.0	150.0
8.25% promissory notes	77.0	-0-	-0-
Other loans	142.5	31.6	31.6
Term loan facility	-0-	1,550.0	1,459.0
Revolving credit	-0-	216.0	216.0
12.875% senior sub debt	-0-	-0-	550.0
14.25% sub discount debt	-0-	-0-	275.0
Less current maturities	16.7	291.0	200.0
Total long-term debt	352.8	1,656.6	2,481.6
Exchangeable preferred stock (pay-in-kind preferred)	-0-	-0-	75.0
Stockholders' equity:			
American Standard, Inc.	871.4	-0-	-0-
New common stock	-0-	180.0	250.0
Total stockholders' equity	871.4	80.0	250.0
Total capitalization	$1,380.8	$3,074.5	$3,033.5
Long-term debt total capitalization	25.6%		81.8%

Source: June 30, 1988, prospectus for American Standard, Inc.

American Standard illustrates why: the primary effect of parachutes and pension lockups is to raise, marginally, the takeover cost. In a close contest, this may provide the margin of success; but such costs are generally not large enough to dissuade a determined bidder.

Black & Decker sued to disarm the golden parachute. In response, a judge temporarily enjoined American Standard from exercising the parachute on March 15.

The Poison Pill

American Standard's poison pill consisted of special rights distributed to shareholders that would entitle them to purchase shares at half of Black & Decker's offer price. The rights would be exercisable when any person acquired 15 percent or more of American Standard's common stock. The rights were nontransferable and could be amended or rescinded by the board of directors without shareholder approval.[12]

To illustrate the effect of the pill, suppose that Black & Decker acquired 55 percent of American Standard's shares in the tender offer at $65 per share, or $1.1 billion in aggregate. This would trigger the rights agreement, flooding the market with 69.75 million shares, diluting Black & Decker's interest from 55 percent to 16.9 percent, and destroying $765 million in the value of B&D's investment. Another effect of the poison pill would be to prevent Black & Decker from conducting a "drop and sweep" plan, in which the tender offer would be dropped, and shares purchased on the market at fire sale prices.

There is no instance in which the target of a hostile raid has swallowed a poison pill. Like nuclear armaments, the pill is not used. Nor, however, is it invulnerable.

On February 10, Black & Decker initiated a two pronged assault on American Standard's poison pill. First, it announced a consent solicitation to reduce from 10 to 5 the number of directors on American Standard's board, and to seat three new directors. In such a reconstituted board, Black & Decker's three nominees would move to rescind the poison pill.

In addition, Black & Decker filed suit to challenge the poison pill. On March 16, the court struck down this defense on the grounds that an auction had been triggered by the firm's leveraged recapitalization proposal, which allowed insiders and the ESOP to roll over their shares (not taking cash) and hence increase their percentage ownership. The court held that in an auction it was management's responsibility to seek the highest price for the shares under the Revlon rule.

Summary

Of the three defenses—golden parachute, pension lockup, and poison pill—the poison pill was a showstopper, an extremely effective defense, which if left in place would have deflected the unfriendly advances of Black & Decker (or any other suitor). The reason why these defenses were vulnerable and ultimately failed is because such defenses are subject to judicial review. Given the predilection of the courts in recent years, one must conclude that the primary value of defenses such as poison pills and golden parachutes is that they buy time for management to develop alternatives to the raider's bid.

RESTRUCTURING DEFENSES: MANAGEMENT BUYOUT AND LEVERAGED RECAPITALIZATION

In American Standard's case, management used the relatively brief life of its initial defenses to propose and then revise plans for a leveraged restructuring. The initial proposal was to execute a leveraged recapitalization; later it was revised to be a management buyout to be financed by an employee stock ownership plan and a white knight investor, Kelso & Company.

Management Buyouts and Leveraged Recaps

In a management buyout, insider managers purchase the company with funds that are mainly borrowed. Buyouts have become more common in the hostile takeover context, and generally have become prominent features on the corporate landscape. The period from 1984 to 1988 was the peak of the first LBO wave of activity: Going private transactions average about one-quarter of all public takeovers.[13]

In a leveraged recapitalization ("recap") the firm itself borrows and pays a large one-time dividend, and the equity remains in the hands of the original owners. Most often leveraged recaps have been spurred by the threat of a hostile takeover and represent one of the newer devices in the takeover defense arsenal. During the period January 1984 to April 1989, at least 42 U.S. firms publicly proposed leveraged recaps in response to active or potential bids by unwanted suitors. Of these, 26 firms actually implemented the recap and remained independent firms. Twelve firms were acquired though not necessarily by the unwanted bidder, and the remainder abandoned the proposal but still were independent as of May 1989.

Both of these restructuring schemes considered by American Standard's management have several features in common:

1. Preexisting shareholders receive a large one-time disgorgement of cash value from their investment in the company.
2. The cash payment is financed by a dramatic releveraging of the company.
3. The restructuring is accompanied by a dramatic rearrangement of incentive compensation for management.
4. Management retains operational control of the firm.
5. The restructuring is usually followed by significant operational tightening to increase operating cash flow.

Because of these similarities, one can view the leveraged recapitalization as a "synthetic management buyout (MBO)," a way to generate the benefits to shareholders without actually taking the firm private. There are, however, important differences between the two forms of reorganization, as summarized in Exhibit 34.4. The key points are:

- Management buyouts lead to private companies, whereas recaps leave the company publicly traded with shareholders receiving "stub" equity in addition to the cash payout. Under the MBO the company saves on public reporting costs,[14] but its equity shares remain illiquid securities. The recap preserves equity liquidity but exploits no (or few) savings on reporting.

EXHIBIT 34.4 Comparison of MBO and Recap

	MBO	Recap
Equity clientele	Owner-insiders	Insiders and outsiders
Ownership status	Private firm	Public firm
Control	Revlon duties trigger auction	Revlon duties may not apply
Potential for conflicts	High	Moderate/low

- Under the MBO, owners are insiders; even a white knight such as Kelso would have board representation and be closely involved in setting management policies of the firm. The MBO gives managers the freedom from having to second-guess the reactions of public shareholders. Under the recap, some equity investors remain, in effect, outsiders.
- With the MBO, the control of the firm changes. This prospective change of control will almost surely trigger auction rules under the Revlon duties. With the recap, control may not necessarily change since the stub equity of the company remains in the hands of public shareholders. As the American Standard case illustrates, however, the recap form may also trigger the Revlon duties when insiders are allowed to increase their percentage ownership by taking more shares instead of cash. In theory, the recap does not forestall another hostile bid. What matters is the effectiveness of the recap in disgorging cash value to investors.
- The MBO may create strong conflicts of interest, requiring the board to actively represent shareholders in the buyout negotiations and to seek a fairness opinion of the buyout terms.[15] Under the recap, the ordinary business judgment rule applies.

Wealth Effects of Leveraged Restructurings

Given the substantial target premiums paid in acquisitions, evaluation of takeover defenses requires close analysis of the effects on shareholders. In fact, many critiques of defenses often point to significant share price declines that accompany announcements of *shark repellent defenses*, such as staggered boards, supermajority provisions, fair price provisions, and rights plans (poison pills).[16] Such declines are interpreted as a sign that incumbent management is adopting such steps to protect their own interests as opposed to furthering the interests of owners.

The available evidence on MBOs and leveraged recaps, on the other hand, shows substantial share price increases. For MBOs research suggests that premiums paid to shareholders are comparable to those paid in third-party transactions.[17] Announcements of leveraged recaps are also typically accompanied by substantial share price increases. Studying 42 leveraged recap proposals in the June 1984 to April 1989 period, Handa and Radhakrishnan (1991) report the results in Exhibit 34.5. Firms announcing leveraged recaps prior to a hostile bid (potential targets) experience substantial share price run-ups of 11.65 percent in the two days around the announcement. Even when a takeover bid was already on the table (31 active targets), the leveraged recap announcement was accorded a 3.35 percent share price boost. Clearly, leveraged recap channels value to shareholders.

EXHIBIT 34.5 Average Wealth Gains to Shareholders over Various Periods around the Announcement of a Leveraged Recap Proposal

Windows in Days Relative to Announcement	All 42 Firms	31 Active Targets	11 Potential Targets
–20 to +20	14.34%	15.35%	11.49%
–5 to +5	8.64%	7.17%	12.80%
–1 to 0	5.52%	3.35%	11.65%

Source of results: Handa, Puneet, and A. R. Radhakrishnan, "An Empirical Investigation of Leveraged Recapitalizations with Cash Payout as Takeover Defense," *Financial Management*, Fall 1991, Vol. 20, No. 3, pages 58–69. Reprinted from *Financial Management*, by permission of the Financial Management Association International, College of Business Administration #3331, University of South Florida, Tampa, FL 33620-5500, Phone (813) 974-2084, Fall 1991, Vol. 20, No. 3.

Why should the wealth results for shark repellent and leveraged restructurings be so different? The key lies in the very tangible effects of these restructurings.

- The MBO or recap involves a substantial *increase in corporate leverage*. Such leverage can increase value in a number of ways, including tax savings from the deductibility of interest and an information signal that incumbent management and new lenders view the future cash flows of the firm as sufficient to service debt. A third benefit of debt may follow if, as Jensen (1986) argues, the burden of debt service commits management to manage cash flow carefully and to improve efficiency of operations. The recap may, however, require less leverage than an MBO to take the company private (often with accompanying asset sales).
- The MBO or recap involves a *direct cash payout* to shareholders. As a result, shareholders have a tangible way to assess the value of the company. Such valuation will reflect the financial package that management has been able to arrange and hence may replace prior equity market valuation with figures based on management or lender projections and incorporating important information not previously priced by the market. At the same time, the cash payout itself may bind management to a program of enhanced performance, reducing the temptation to squander capital on new low return projects or acquisitions.
- The MBO or recap typically involves a *realignment of ownership* interest as one or more groups (often management and an ESOP) take shares in lieu of cash. For instance, Bruner (1986) found that CEO equity interest (fully diluted, including options) rose from 13.8 percent before buyouts to 30.1 percent after. Kleiman (1988) found that insider ownership rises from an average of 6.4 percent before recaps to 29.5 percent thereafter. In a recap, such ownership realignment typically requires prior shareholder votes. As a result, shares may reside with those having the most favorable outlook for the company. To the

extent that management increases its ownership stake, investors may feel more secure in sharing management's confidence for the future and may feel that management has greater incentive structure to run the firm profitably.

- The sharp increase in debt may increase value to shareholders at the expense of *wealth transfers from existing debt owners* who are not protected by covenants. Such wealth transfers have attracted considerable attention from professional money managers spurred by massive slides such as the 15 to 20 percent drop in RJR Nabisco's bond prices after its buyout proposal.
- A leveraged restructuring may serve to *raise the bid* prices for a firm, possibly forestalling a hostile raid.

WHEN DOES A RESTRUCTURING DEFENSE MAKE SENSE?

Exhibit 34.2 details the leveraged recap initially proposed by American Standard's management; Exhibit 34.6 compares it to other recap proposals. As shown in Exhibit 34.6, the AS recap involved a substantial leverage increase, larger than in three-fourths of recaps. Its cash payment is also well above the average for recap proposals. Furthermore, the board upped the initial proposal by $5 during the bidding.

Apparently the leveraged recap was effective in spurring Black & Decker's bidding for American Standard. The final bid of $78 was 20 percent higher than the $65 offer on the table prior to the recap announcement, and similar to an 18.5 percent average increase for eight other recaps abandoned in favor of takeover reported by Handa and Radhakrishnan (1991). Yet, in the end, a leveraged buyout by a white knight replaced the AS recap proposal. This case illustrates what we believe are key requirements for a leveraged recap as well as its merits compared to an MBO.

First, the target company needs to have substantial *unused debt capacity*. Good candidates for recaps must have low current debt relative to their debt capacity. Such candidates are thus characterized by (1) a clean balance sheet with little debt; (2) predictable, safe cash flows that can provide for debt service; (3) assets that can be pledged as debt collateral; and (4) excess assets that can be sold. These characteristics often rest with companies that have strong market positions in mature product markets, a low rate of technological change, and no need for large expenditures on capital improvements or R&D. An experienced, competent management team is also essential to meet the postreorganization requirements.

The description fits American Standard well. Prior to Black & Decker's bid, American Standard's capital structure was less than 30 percent debt. Despite this low debt level, American Standard had relatively stable operating flows well suited for debt service. Indeed, debt capacity may have been increasing over time in line with management's view of reduced cyclicality in the building products segment with heavier reliance on the replacement remodeling business. Having recently invested heavily in capital expenditures, management believed that necessary capital expenditures would be lower for the next few years, providing a further boost to service debt. Furthermore, even prior to Black & Decker's bid, American Standard was looking at disposal of assets such as its landmark headquarters in New York.

Part of American Standard's challenge in issuing new debt involved the use of foreign debt that could serve as a currency hedge for its substantial foreign rev-

EXHIBIT 34.6 American Standard Recap Proposal Compared to 42 Leveraged Recap Proposals

	Proposed Leverage Change*	Proposed Payout Change†
American Standard	93.5%	87.4%
Average of 42 recaps	66.2%	60.4%
First quartile‡	30.7%	27.9%
Median	57.9%	57.0%
Third quartile‡	93.5%	88.9%

**Proposed leverage change* is measured as fresh debt divided by market value of equity one week prior to announcement.

†*Proposed payout change* is measured as cash dividend (or buyback) divided by market value of equity one week prior to announcement.

‡*Quartile* figures are based on those of the 42 companies with available information. One quarter of companies have value at or below the first quartile figure.

Source: Handa, Puneet, and A. R. Radhakrishnan, "An Empirical Investigation of Leveraged Recapitalizations with Cash Payout as Takeover Defense," *Financial Management*, Fall 1991, Vol. 20, No. 3, pages 58–69. Reprinted from *Financial Management*, by permission of the Financial Management Association International, College of Business Administration #3331, University of South Florida, Tampa, FL 33620-5500, Phone (813) 974-2084, Fall 1991, Vol. 20, No. 3.

enues, and provide tax-deductible expenses abroad where the company had substantial tax liabilities. Company management developed an innovative set of transactions, selling equity in foreign subsidiaries to holding companies that borrowed, a process that allowed the proceeds of such borrowings to be channeled back to the United States in a tax-efficient manner. The general structure of these borrowings, which would have been used in the recap, was later employed in the Kelso buyout.

Other requirements and merits are:

- *The proposed restructuring must be able to capture all the gains available from the takeover.* A leveraged restructuring can create value, but this value will not likely be great enough to dissuade a bidder who brings substantial synergies to a takeover. If the company survives as an independent entity it cannot reap these synergies, and hence cannot produce this extra value. While Black & Decker perceived a fit between its products and American Standard's building products, American Standard saw little business fit in the distribution channels, and this perceived lack of synergy was echoed by market analysts. Consistent with this, the market price of Black & Decker plummeted by 11 percent upon its initial announcement of a hostile bid. As a result, the leveraged recap could generate values that competed with those justifiable to Black & Decker.

- *The leveraged recap may be especially effective when the initial hostile bid is low and/or the bidder is perceived as relatively weak.* Black & Decker's initial bid of $56 was clearly viewed as inadequate by both American Standard and the market. On the day of the $56 bid, the stock closed at $58.88 reflecting the market's anticipation of higher bids. American Standard management had already done internal analysis as early as the summer of 1987 suggesting a share value of $78 per share based on an LBO. Having already established such value estimates, it was clear to American Standard that the bid was inadequate.
- *The leveraged restructuring must be a credible alternative in terms of management talent.* In American Standard's case, management had a good reputation in the industry and the continuation of operational policies was viewed as a favorable option.
- *Other defensive maneuvers can be coordinated with a recap to provide additional time.* In this case, AS employed both an interim rights plan and a golden parachute proposal, which, though subject to legal challenge, helped provide time as the leveraged recap was developed. In retrospect AS may have been better served to remove the consent solicitation option from its charter at an earlier date.
- *Management must be able to finance the equity portion of the recap and be willing to assume the attendant risks.* A recap could simply pay out cash pro rata to all stockholders, thus reaping tax advantages of the leveraging employed. It would not, however, necessarily prevent a takeover since the bidder could then purchase the new stub shares. Importantly, such a pro rata distribution does not serve the same important role of conveying a credible signal to the market about management's confidence in the company's future. In this case, management felt the company was substantially undervalued in the market prior to the Black & Decker bid. An effective way of showing this optimism was to take a higher stake in this company. Such a stake also ensures incentives for future performance. American Standard's recap proposal involved a substantial shift of ownership to management and an ESOP. This shift required a shareholder vote subjecting it to further scrutiny. Also, the vote required a 30-day period, which, in the bidding process, gave Black & Decker a time advantage as to when it could actually pay for the shares.[18]
- *The court's position on takeover defenses has a large effect on strategy.* The Delaware courts made a number of important decisions that affected the AS case. Of prime importance to AS was the court's March 15 ruling to disarm the golden parachute and put AS under the Revlon duties. As discussed earlier, one of the possible advantages of a recap over an MBO is that a recap need not trigger the Revlon auction requirement. After the proposed AS recap, management would own 24 percent, the ESOP 30 percent, and public shareholders 46 percent. AS argued that management would not acquire control of the company since the ESOP would be independent of management. The Court found, however, that the transaction would constitute a sale; hence the Revlon duties applied. In effect, the court decision implied that it was the combination of the management and ESOP position that triggered Revlon.[19] Quickly on the heels of the court decision, AS announced its merger agreement with Kelso.

CONCLUSION

The American Standard case shows that leveraged restructurings can be much more effective[20] responses to hostile takeover bids than other defenses. The reason is that many repellents are subject to judicial review and legislative intervention. In essence the state tests repellents on behalf of individual shareholders and enjoins defenses that are apparently self-serving and entrenching. The sophistication and ideology of the state change over time, so it is to be expected that the effectiveness of shark repellent will vary. In contrast, *leveraged restructurings are evaluated in the market*: shareholders "vote" with their shares, in effect granting control to the highest bidder. While the leveraged restructuring is not an ironclad defense, either,[21] this defense at least compensates shareholders for the value latent in the firm's unused debt capacity, and thus, from the standpoint of effectiveness, helps ensure a wealth maximizing outcome from the contest.

Another general conclusion is that many repellents and other legal maneuverings are of tactical, rather than strategic, value; they buy time for managers to search for the most effective outcome of the contest. Of course, in a close contest where time and credibility matter, any tactical advantage is not to be minimized. The main managerial implication of this is that defenses based in law and litigation must ultimately be accompanied by responses based on *true economic transformation.*

A third conclusion is that the nature of that transformation (i.e., the choice between management buyout and leveraged recapitalization) will depend on both the economic opportunities for disgorging cash and the complexities of the law regarding control. Such economic opportunities may reside in a firm's excess cash, unused debt capacity, excess pension assets, salable assets, or relatively large payroll (which would make an ESOP attractive). The choice of either going private in an MBO (and thus triggering auction rules under the Revlon duties) or remaining public with a recap will depend on how much value can be unleashed in the restructuring, thus granting management bidding power over the raider.

Finally, American Standard shows that a contest for control should not be viewed as simple bilateral competition: *Effective defenses create and employ a range of stakeholders on the side of the defender.* Suppliers or customers (e.g., in American Standard's case, Emerson Electric and General Electric) may have an interest in the continuing independence of the target. The loyalty and self-interest of employees may be harnessed through an ESOP. White knights may be attracted from the ranks of operating companies as well as "boutiques" (e.g., Kelso) specializing in specific types of restructurings and willing to commit their own capital in support. Even the interests of outside advisers (e.g., Goldman Sachs) can be aligned with the company through contingent fees to stimulate the search for specific outcomes. From this standpoint, an important managerial implication is that one valuable aspect of advance preparation for the possibility of a contest for control would be to identify these stakeholders and how they might help.

The rising popularity of leveraged restructurings in response to takeovers masked the difficulties associated with these responses. Leveraged restructurings are not appropriate for all takeover targets. Moreover, restructuring proposals are time-consuming to develop; one should expect a raider to do everything possible to preoccupy management and foreshorten the time to outcome. Finally, the most elegant (and effective) restructurings, which employ a range of stakeholders, are complicated to orchestrate and require many types of specialized expertise to fashion. As deal complexity rises, so does the possibility that it will snag or unravel in untimely fashion.

The many difficulties notwithstanding, the leveraged restructuring warrants serious consideration as a strategy, whether in response to a hostile bid or as a unilateral action to increase value.

SPECIAL NOTE

This chapter is a slightly edited version of an article by Benson, Bruner, and Harris (1990) that appears here by the kind permission of my co-authors and the editors, J. O'Donoghue and D. Grunewald, of the journal and book in which this article appeared.

NOTES

1. Based on projections for 1988, sales would be $3.7 billion.
2. The exercise price for these rights would be $32.50 per share.
3. A consent solicitation is similar to a proxy fight in that shareholder approval is required, but a shareholder meeting is not.
4. The *Delaware Anti-Takeover Statute* was designed not as an antitakeover provision per se, but rather to encourage full and fair offers and to discourage freeze-outs and other "abusive takeover tactics." The law provided that a Delaware corporation may not combine with any "interested stockholder" for a period of three years unless (1) the board of directors approves the combination, (2) the interested stockholder owns at least 85 percent of the common stock outstanding, or (3) at least 66.67 percent of the shares outstanding not owned by the interested stockholder are voted in favor of a combination.
5. The effect of this action was to prevent B&D terminating the pill by gaining control of American Standard through B&D's current consent solicitation.
6. The warrants would allow Emerson at any time during the first five years of the recapitalization to purchase approximately 9.4 percent of the outstanding common stock on a fully diluted basis at an exercise price of 105 percent of the average of the closing prices of the common shares during the third and fourth weeks following the recapitalization, provided that the exercise price was between $5.50 and $7.00 per share.
7. Up until then, American Standard bought $50 million to $70 million worth of motors annually from General Electric for their air-conditioning unit. This agreement meant that American Standard would buy air-conditioning components for its residential units from Emerson and shift its motor orders from GE to Emerson.
8. An obvious reference to the Emerson agreement, as Emerson's "Skil" line of power tools competed directly with Black & Decker.
9. A type of "street sweep" that occurs when a tender offer (hostile) is outstanding, and the bidder drops the tender but within hours buys up stock in the mar-

ket from arbitrageurs who have accumulated large blocks of the target stock in anticipation of rising prices.

10. As explained in Chapter 26, "Revlon duties" originated from a 1986 case in which Revlon's directors sought to sell the company to Forstmann, Little at a lower price to stop a hostile takeover bid by Ronald Perelman. The court ruled that when a company puts itself up for sale, all other interests, including those of the employees and the community, can be considered only in light of increasing shareholder value. This imposes a duty to auction the target firm when the board has decided to sell the firm or "control," and when there are competing bidders.
11. This bid under the $78 bid that was currently on the table was believed to be effective by Black & Decker because of the time value of money. B&D's offer would become effective within 10 days, while Kelso's would require 30 days to become effective. Because a large percentage of shares were currently being held by arbitrageurs with high required return, this was viewed as an effective bidding ploy.
12. Each right entitled the shareholder to purchase five shares at $32.50 per share. American Standard had 31 million shares outstanding.
13. *Mergerstat Review*, Merrill Lynch & Co., 1988, page 91.
14. By going private, a company can reduce the costs of communicating information to its public shareholders, and more importantly, eliminate the need to manage the company with one eye on the reaction of the shareholders. Analysts on Wall Street estimate that companies spend between $5 and $35 per year per shareholder on printing and mailing costs for proxies, 10-Ks, and annual reports.
15. The famous Trans Union case, *Smith v. Van Gorkom* (excerpted in a lecture contained on the CD-ROM) established the precedent for objective evaluation of buyout terms and active board involvement. In that case, Van Gorkom (CEO of Trans Union) effected a management buyout of the firm in the face of a hostile bid at a higher price. The court required the Trans Union executives to pay shareholders the difference between their actual purchase price and the forgone bid.
16. See Ruback (1989), Malatesa and Walking (1988), Ryngaert and Jarrell (1986), and Ryngaert (1988).
17. See Amihud (1989), Chapter 1 and references therein.
18. Black & Decker had to leave a tender bid revision open for only 10 days under the Williams Act. Given the high required return of arbitrageurs holding the stock, the 20-day gap provided some advantages to Black & Decker (see Exhibit 34.1).
19. A July 1988 ruling by the Delaware Chancery Court case of *Robert M. Bass Group v. Evans* held that a proposed recap would come under the Revlon duties even though management would control only 39.2 percent of the outstanding stock. Case history is still evolving.
20. We measure effectiveness of a response first in terms of its implications for shareholder wealth, and second for its consistency with management policies for maximizing shareholder wealth over the long run.
21. As discussed earlier, the raider may be able to exploit significant operational synergies, thus permitting a higher bid than the leveraged restructuring.

PART

Seven

Communication, Integration, and Best Practice

CHAPTER 35

Communicating the Deal: Gaining Mandates, Approvals, and Support

INTRODUCTION

Effective communication is a pervasive challenge in M&A. Previous chapters have touched upon it regarding searching for targets (Chapter 7), due diligence (Chapter 8), negotiating (Chapter 30), and dealing with investors, bankers, and arbs (Chapters 9, 20, and 32). This chapter complements the others and turns inward to the company to consider how deals can be effectively communicated in order to:

- Gain a mandate from the CEO and senior management to approach a target company.
- Win approval for a proposed deal from your firm's board of directors.
- Inform employees and gain their support.
- Tell the public in a way that shapes the right expectations.

Given all the other stresses of M&A deal development, communication often becomes an afterthought. Yet failure to communicate well plants the seeds of later failure, measured in terms of lost credibility, diminished employee morale, destroyed value, and investor lawsuits. Effective deal communication promotes good corporate governance, good stakeholder relations, and good postmerger integration.

The aim of this chapter is to survey six important challenges to effective communication, and to offer some principles for responding to these challenges. The chapter reviews features of four classic kinds of deal communications: a "concept" presentation to a CEO or senior executive seeking approval to begin negotiations; a formal presentation to a firm's board of directors seeking approval for negotiated terms; communication of the deal to employees; and an announcement of the deal to the financial markets. From these perspectives, the chapter strives to synthesize a general view on the communication challenge.

CHALLENGES AND GUIDING PRINCIPLES FOR COMMUNICATING THE DEAL

Simply saying what you think, or what you want others to learn, is never easy, and sometimes impossible. In preparing to present a deal to any audience, one should first reflect on the following challenges:

Conflicting Aims

In the abstract, it would seem that communication of M&A deals could be guided by a few simple maxims: Tell people what they *need to know*. Preserve the decision maker's flexibility. Inspire the organization. Tell the truth. The straightforward application of these axioms *simultaneously* is difficult, for they can conflict. You should be able to state in a few points what you want to accomplish with this presentation.

The Reality of the Transaction May Hinge on One's Perspective

A classic exercise in training professional negotiators is to invite each negotiator to keep a journal of impressions and beliefs during practice negotiations, and then compare that record with the counterparty. In the early stages of negotiation, the perceptions can be widely divergent (and not infrequently, they can be divergent up to the consummation of the deal). Research on merger negotiation finds that perceptions about negotiations are influenced by factors such as desire to consummate, time urgency, a sense of momentum, advance preparation, and so on.[1] If we view transactions through imperfect lenses, then it will be difficult to assert what the truth about the transaction is. You should reflect on the *perspective* of your audience as they listen to your message.

The Need to Balance Secrecy and Disclosure

Most transactions are born in a climate of utter secrecy. The discussions are limited to a few professionals on each side of the transaction. Organizational "firewalls" exist between those professionals and the rest of their organizations. These firewalls prevent the dissemination of news about the transaction beyond the immediate deal developers. Firewall features include code names for transactions and players; separate offices for the deal developers that are physically removed from the rest of the organization and secured with special locks or card access systems that restrict entry by the casual passerby; deal documents and analyses that are numbered and tagged for restricted distribution; and so on. In organizations where these firewalls work effectively, the announcement of a transaction is almost always a surprise. This basic fact would seem to give the deal developer an unusual advantage in presenting a deal except for human nature: People dislike economic surprises because of the volatility they create in their cognitive environment. Thus, the challenge is to ease and shape the sense of surprise, within the bounds of truthfulness.

Secrecy is appropriate, especially in the early stages of transaction development. First, one wants to preempt business competitors. Professor Michael Jensen has likened transaction developers to financial entrepreneurs. They invest their time and other resources in acquiring information on which to strike a profitable deal. In a completely transparent environment, competitors might learn of the impending deal, and seek to appropriate the profit by entering a competing bid, or at least to do things to prevent your firm from appropriating the profits. From this perspective, secrecy should be maintained until a transaction is mature enough to withstand a competitor's predatory actions.

Second, one wants to manage capital market expectations. A considerable volume of research suggests that investors quickly impound news about firms into their security prices. But the concern of senior executives is that the *volatility* of the market response to news increases as one ranges across a spectrum of news from solid fact to rank rumor. Early *disclosure* about merger negotiations might do the firms' shareholders more harm than good. The desire to limit unnecessary volatility in their firms' securities explains why executives pay for investor relations departments. Given the uncertainties that attend the development of a deal, news about a transaction in the early stage of development is hardly fact. At the same time, it can be costly to impose a veil of extreme secrecy, say until after the transaction had been consummated. First, it may abuse investors and deny them the opportunity to express their views of the deal and/or make a fully informed assessment. Second, it may violate securities laws. Chapter 27 surveys the laws and regulations dealing with the disclosure of information. In essence, target firms should disclose the transaction at the point in time that the consummation of the deal looks probable. Buyers should make disclosure when the consummation looks probable and the target is of material size relative to the buyer.

Third, a policy of disclosure helps to manage the risk of leaks, which increases with time. When news of a transaction leaks, the parties to a transaction lose the element of surprise and must react rather than proactively shape the news. They turn from being proactive to reactive. Also, not infrequently, leaks are accompanied by investigations of trading on inside information that can be distracting and costly for the target and buyer, even if they are completely innocent of charges. Leaks are the result of inadvertent actions by parties to a deal. Also, parties outside the firm can "synthesize" a leak by piecing together information on the buyer and target. In the movie *Wall Street*, the protagonist played by Charlie Sheen observes the arrival and departure of executives of two firms, and concludes that a deal is being negotiated.

Finally, many deals require disclosure before consummation. Transactions requiring a vote of the shareholders of public firms to approve the deal require the firm to give shareholders a merger prospectus and proxy voting form a minimum number of days in advance of the vote (in the United States, the minimum is 30 days). The date for such a vote (and meeting) will ordinarily need to be set and advertised months before. In these cases, it is not possible to prevent early disclosure. You should reflect on the balance of need for secrecy and disclosure in the presentation you must give. This is an issue with ethical implications. Consider examining these implications using the frameworks presented in Chapter 2.

The Constraints of "Bandwidth"

The fourth major challenge confronting the deal presenter is the asymmetry in knowledge between those who developed the deal and those who are learning about it. The reality is that the "pipeline" between presenter and audience is invariably narrow and unsuited to the task—humans are limited in their ability to absorb a mass of detailed information. To borrow a term from the communications engineering field, this is a problem of "*bandwidth*," the size of the information pipeline. Assuming the bandwidth constraint cannot be changed, it has two classic solutions: lengthen the time of the transmission, or reduce the size or complexity of the message. For most of the audiences considered in this chapter, the first solution is impractical. An important responsibility of a professional is to edit information about the deal, and focus the audience on aspects that matter. This places a large responsibility on the presenter (and exposes the presenter to possible liability if after the fact it appears that material facts were not presented), and it depends on a sense of trust by the audience in the expertise and intent of the presenter. As preparation for your presentation, you should profile the characteristics of your audience: How sophisticated are they? What background do they have that will help or hinder the understanding of your presentation?

The Need to Balance Objectivity and Advocacy

Successful governance resides in making good decisions repeatedly over time. Deal presenters often ignore this basic truth, and instead become invested in the goal of gaining acceptance for their particular deal. In the context of these tendencies, the presenter needs to balance faithfulness to the deal with faithfulness to the governance process. Reflecting back on your main aims for the presentation, consider carefully whether you are in "selling mode" or "judging mode" and why you are in either.

The Opportunity to Manage Expectations of Stakeholders

Major corporate financial transactions that are surprises send signals about management's expectations of performance to the capital markets. To ignore this in a transaction announcement is to forfeit an opportunity to communicate with investors, clarify the message, and shape expectations in the public arena. One must be careful to avoid aggressive attitudes here: management of expectations can morph into fraud. Legal counsel should vet all public announcements. Whether expectations management is an important consideration in public communications of a deal depends on the extent to which one believes that capital markets are strongly efficient, an assumption probably violated where one or both of the transaction participants are privately held. In advance of your presentation, you should consider carefully the degree of adjustment in expectations your presentation may trigger, and the communications challenge that adjustment poses.

In conclusion, approach the task of communication considering carefully the audience, the message, and the opportunity. Communicate when the deal and the audience are ready and when the audience needs to know. The timing of public disclosure is a judgment call, driven mainly by an assessment of probabilities of actually doing the deal. Directors of the two firms will need to be briefed in advance of that disclosure. Focus on action needed. A core organizing theme of deal communication is what is required of the audience: CEO to give a mandate for negotiations, the corporate directors to approve terms of a negotiated deal, the employees to support the integration efforts, or the shareholders to vote in favor of a merger. Remember the problem of bandwidth. Your task is not to present every detail, but only the most important ones. Be an educator: Shape the learning for your audience.

PRESENTING THE "CONCEPT PROPOSAL" TO SENIOR MANAGEMENT OF THE BUYER (INTERNAL ONLY)

Very early in the life of a deal, a corporate development team will approach senior managers of their firm to gain the mandate to approach a target. At this stage, there is no deal, but only the possibility of one. Therefore, the focus of the entire presentation is on likely values, probabilities, themes, opportunities, and idealized outcomes.

At this presentation, the CEO's decision is one of resource allocation: Does it make sense to incur expense and to divert the time and attention of the CEO and corporate development staff toward the development of this deal? From the resource allocation perspective, the *concept proposal* can be evaluated in terms of whether its potential benefits exceed the potential costs. Thus, the concept proposal needs to be framed around the balance of costs and benefits.

A presentation of benefits should emphasize the strategic motivations for the deal. See Chapter 7 for the range of analyses and considerations one might incorporate into the presentation. The issue of organizational fit should be addressed at this phase of the presentation. Then the presentation should turn to how a deal might translate into financial results. A forecasting model should be developed that shows the estimate of synergies and the likely impact on the buyer's financial performance into the future. A preliminary valuation of the target should be presented, focusing chiefly on the estimated high and low valuation range of the target firm. This segment of the presentation should highlight "key value drivers," any sources of uncertainty, and capital market conditions that might influence the development of pricing and terms. Transaction costs (e.g., fees to auditors, lawyers, and financial advisers) will be another dimension to review at this stage of the presentation. The presentation should suggest a walkaway value beyond which the buyer team would abandon negotiations. Finally, the presentation should aim to clarify deal design objectives, especially regarding form of payment, tax exposure, financing, and earnings dilution. The presenter could conclude with a hypothetical term sheet, which the CEO could affirm or modify.

In presentations such as these, the presenters will prepare a briefing book (called a *pitch book* in M&A slang) for the CEO and others in the audience. Some firms have a standard format for these books and/or a file containing especially good presentations—one might consult this in advance of preparing the presentation. Such a book contains hard copies of slides, followed by a textual discussion covering the anticipated benefits and costs, and supported by a section of exhibits containing financial forecasts, valuation analysis, and market data to which the audience can refer if interested. These books are typically distributed in advance for the audience to review, so that the meeting itself can proceed on a fairly high level of information. The length of the book is a matter of the time available for the audience to prepare and for the presenter to actually speak. A 20-slide presentation will take perhaps an hour to give, counting questions from the audience. The length of materials in the appendixes is a matter of choice and company culture. Absent any corporate guidelines, guard against the natural tendency to include everything possible: Too much material can obscure the message you want to give. An example of a pitch book may be found in Bruner et al. (2001) and follows the outline given in Exhibit 35.1.

In conclusion, the distinguishing feature of the concept presentation is its focus on opportunities rather than a deal in place. The decision to be made at the presen-

EXHIBIT 35.1 Contents of a Hypothetical Pitch Book

Section	Possible Contents
Presentation The aim of this section is to *briefly summarize* the deal concept, with the expectation that questions from the audience and the appendixes will flesh out the details. Length: about 20 pages. Given in slide format using Microsoft PowerPoint or equivalent; summary statements in bullet-point format with graphic illustrations.	1. Strategic rationale for the deal including organizational fit and sources of synergy value. 2. Description of target company. 3. Description of target company's industry. 4. Comparison of target company with peers. 5. Historical financial performance of target company. 6. Summary of target company ownership. 7. Valuation of target based on comparable firms (multiples), comparable transactions, DCF. Looked at on stand-alone basis, and with synergy value. Identification of key value drivers from sensitivity analysis. 8. Impact on buyer company projected financial performance. 9. Identification of possible risks to the deal and to the long-term success of the acquired company. 10. Hypothetical term sheet: price range, form of payment, form of transaction, social issues, etc. (See Chapter 18.) 11. Strategy for negotiation.
Appendixes The aim of this section is to give detail to support the assertions in the presentation section. This should be paginated and organized into tabbed sections for easy reference during the meeting.	1. Detailed information on market size, growth, and profitability. 2. Detailed information on possible synergies: sources, size, benchmarks for comparison. 3. Detailed information on material risks. 4. Financial forecasts of target company performance. 5. Valuation analysis of target company, with sensitivity and scenario analyses. 6. Financial forecast of buyer company financial performance assuming the acquisition occurs. The focus here is on the likely impact on economic, accounting, and voting dilution.

Source: Author's research.

tation has been characterized as an investment problem: whether the benefits of the deal development effort outweigh the costs. More accurately, the concept approval is like the decision to buy an *option* to purchase a firm. Indeed, concept development is like a corporate R&D effort. The actual benefits of acquiring the target are uncertain at this stage; investing in efforts to develop a deal (purchasing an option on the deal) buys the information necessary to decide whether to exercise the option. The value of the mandate is similar to the value of search efforts and due diligence research (see Chapters 7 and 8) and will be driven by the decision maker's assessment of the probability of a profitable payoff. The objective of this presentation should be to crystallize a mandate to proceed with research and negotiations. Closure on this discussion should aim for agreement on motives and bargaining goals as fully as possible.

COMMUNICATING THE DEAL TO A BOARD OF DIRECTORS

Perhaps the most challenging deal communication is to the directors of the target and/or buyer firm. Chapter 26 outlines the obligations of directors in evaluating a merger proposal. This audience is exposed to personal liability for failing to execute faithfully their duties as directors, particularly the duty of loyalty and duty of care.

In contrast to the concept proposal to management, the board presentation debuts a deal in finished form. The chief aim of this presentation must be to gain the final approval of the board for the proposed terms, for a public announcement, and for consummation of the deal. Typically, a briefing book will be prepared and distributed to directors for their reading in advance of the presentation. A careful board discussion could last several days and may entail private meetings of only the independent directors. Chapter 26 describes the legal considerations entailed in such meetings, not the least of which is to disclose promptly news of material and probable deals.

In all probability, the directors will have been briefed by the CEO by telephone in advance of the meeting. The board meeting of the target firm will follow a careful agenda: briefing by lawyers on the duties of the directors and other legal considerations; presentation of the deal by the CEO; and presentations by outside experts opining particularly on the fairness of the proposed terms to shareholders. In a large merger, the board meeting of the buyer may follow a similar agenda, but for smaller transactions, the buyer's board meeting will have less participation by outside advisers.

The deal presentation by the CEO or other senior managers should follow the outline of strategy, organization, valuation, and terms that was sketched in the discussion of the pitch book. But because of the legal obligations of directors, the presentation should fully disclose the implications of the deal for shareholders and any "key bets" that may underlie them. This presentation is very different from the initial "pitch" in that a detailed agreement is in hand, the first round of due diligence has been performed, and much more can be said about the risks and benefits of a possible combination. In short, the CEO's presentation to the board is likely to be long and more detailed. The briefing book to directors could include hard copies of presentation slides, appendixes containing detailed valuations and strategic analyses, a copy of the definitive agreement, opinions of advisers, and drafts of public announcements.

The questions that directors raise could cover a broad range of issues, and might include these:

- Assessment of synergies. Synergy value is inevitably one of the key bets underlying the approval of the deal.
- Analysis of earnings and economic dilution and tests of sensitivity.
- Valuation and identification of key value drivers; comparison to pricing of this deal versus others in the industry or current market.
- Critical scrutiny of the strategic rationale for the deal.
- Justification of this deal in comparison to other *hypothetical* deals (e.g., joint ventures or strategic alliances; buying the next competitor).
- Survey of tax, financial reporting, and shareholder control implications.
- Detailed review of key provisions in the merger agreement.
- Anticipation of likely reactions of investors, customers, suppliers, employees, competitors, and the community.
- Need for any apparently complex terms in the agreement.
- Assessment of contingencies that might delay or prevent the deal, such as regulatory approvals.
- Potential liability for the directors.
- Generally, the impact on shareholder welfare and the financial health of the buyer following the transaction.
- Proposed news release to the public.
- Time line and schedule of steps to consummation.

ANNOUNCING THE DEAL TO THE PUBLIC

The first impulse of drafting a public announcement will be to say as little as possible. News releases about mergers and acquisitions should be prepared with legal counsel to minimize possible claims of misrepresentation in the announcement—chief among these would be promises about future benefits, synergies, or anticipated performance deriving from the combination. In addition, since all mergers and some acquisitions are consummated by shareholder votes and the disclosure of considerable information through the merger prospectus, many executives will be inclined to save the details for later.

But the minimal announcement loses the opportunity to shape the thinking of the sophisticated investor (the kind of "*lead steer*" who leads in the setting of prices in the securities market). This investor will respond to the announcement quickly by buying or selling securities of the buyer and target firm. *An aim of the first public announcement should be to inform the lead steer, and to the extent possible within legal advice, advocate the deal.*

The first public announcement is typically a two- to three-page typewritten statement that exploits numerous opportunities to help the lead steer:

- Give details on the terms of payment and timing for consummating the transaction.
- Express the strategic motives for this combination, and show how it fits into the evolution of the two firms. This section should at least hint at the expected benefits of combination. If the transaction is motivated by special strategic considerations, these might be described in the announcement.
- Describe the impact of the transaction on expected earnings per share, voting blocs, and product market position.
- Explain any contingencies that might delay or prevent the consummation of the deal. These could include government regulatory approvals, court decisions, and completion of an audit or negotiations about environmental liabilities.
- Convey strong determination to consummate the deal. Lead steers and potential competing bidders will look for expressions of commitment in this announcement, and may be influenced by them. One strong signal of commitment would be to announce that the financing for this transaction has already been obtained. Another would be that a major shareholder and management of the target firm support the transaction.

The sophisticated investor will absorb this information and form a probabilistically weighted average of the share price of the target (and buyer) firm based on assessments of the share price in the bid, and the share price if the deal is not consummated. Chapter 32 suggests that arbs consider share prices to be a weighted average of outcomes:

$$\text{New target price} = \text{Prob(Bid value)} + (1 - \text{Prob})(\text{Target share price if bid fails})$$

$$\text{New buyer price} = \begin{array}{l}\text{Prob(Buyer price if bid succeeds)} \\ + (1 - \text{Prob})(\text{Buyer share price if bid fails})\end{array}$$

In this framework, the public announcement seeks to shape (increase) the probability, "prob," that the bid will succeed, justify the bid value to the target, and explain benefits of the bid to the buyer. If successful, the new target and buyer share prices should rise upon the announcement of the deal.

COMMUNICATING WITH EMPLOYEES

The aim of communications with employees is to build support for the deal and smooth the postmerger integration of the two firms. Achieving these is a nontrivial challenge, for as Chapter 36 emphasizes, the prospect of merger triggers a concern for "*me issues*" among employees of a merging firm: job security, compensation, reporting relationships, prospect for promotion (or demotion), and generally one's sense of identity with the company. Compounding the challenge are legal restrictions on what may be publicly disclosed and, simply, uncertainties that may persist in advance of closing.

Ainspan and Dell (2000) surveyed companies that had recently completed an acquisition or merger and conducted in-depth interviews with selected companies. They profiled strategies for communicating with employees that differed by point in time, either before the consummation of the deal or after. A summary of these two perspectives is given in Exhibit 35.2—the main insight from this comparison is that communications with employees need to be tailored to the time setting. The difference in strategy is governed mainly by legal restriction on what can be said publicly about a pending deal and, more importantly, by uncertainty.

Research and anecdotal evidence[2] suggest that best practice in the implementation of a communications strategy directed toward employees has these features:

- Be prompt and factual. Rumors fester in the absence of clear information—respond quickly to rumors before they spread.
- Get close. The best channels of communication are personal, from people whom the employees know and respect. Supervisors and/or unit managers are important conduits. For this to work requires a cascade of briefings down through the organization, so that the supervisors and unit managers can speak knowledgeably about the merger.
- Use supporting channels. Though personal communications are best, other channels such as newsletters, "town meetings," and video or Internet presentations can lend important new information in timely fashion. Broadcast media are inflexible and scripted; interactive media (such as videoconferences and ceremonial visits from senior managers) may afford more response to employee concerns.

EXHIBIT 35.2 Strategies for Communicating with Employees during Mergers

	Before Merger Is Consummated	After Merger Is Consummated
Audience	Employees and investing public need to know.	Employees of company, stakeholders, stockholders, and customers need to know.
Content	Investor relations, due diligence, etc.	Strategic direction and operating decisions.
Style	Factual and controlled.	Motivational and openly informative, with a sense of progression.
Time frame	Fast, unplanned, short duration.	Continuous, planned, long-term.
Media	Broadcasts through public media and press releases, closed meetings, internal e-mail, and fax.	Broadcasts through company media, open meetings, managers' communicating one on one and in diverse groups, intranet postings, etc.

Source: Ainspan and Dell (2000), Table 1, page 7.

EXHIBIT 35.3 Summary Comparison of Types of Deal Communications

	Concept Proposal	Board Presentation	Public Announcement	Employee Communication
Key audience	CEO.	Independent directors.	"Lead steer" investors.	Managers, supervisors, rank-and-file employees.
Predominant interest of audience	Fit with his/her vision; resource allocation.	Execute well duties of loyalty and care.	Economic insight on which to base trading intentions.	"Me issues"; rationale for the deal: Why us? Why now?
Focus of communication	An opportunity; themes; the payoff. Key issues are strategy, valuation, and setting negotiation goals.	A definitive agreement. Key issues are valuation, implications for stakeholders, and strategy.	Either letter of intent or definitive agreement. Key issues are deal terms, motives, and probabilities.	Letter of intent or definitive agreement; eventually followed by integration plan for the two organizations; maintaining a customer focus during the transition.
Objective	Gain a mandate to proceed, with targets for negotiation.	A board vote to consummate the deal.	Shape capital market reaction.	Resolve uncertainty; build support for the merger; motivate.
Special challenges	Balance analysis and advocacy: Presenter needs approval and joint thinking on goals.	Can't say too much; limited bandwidth; risk of lawsuit for carelessness, disloyalty.	Can't say enough; risk of lawsuit for misrepresentation.	Greed and fear: dealing with threats and opportunities to employees posed by the merger. Rumors. Distraction caused by the deal, and resulting effect on productivity.
Tactics	Focus on the optionality in the concept development effort: explore uncertainty and its drivers, along with valuation.	Focus on the board's stakeholder perspectives, and their natural concern for risk exposure.	Speak to concerns of the lead steers, not just the average investor, or other interested groups.	Build trust. Address concerns of employees through many channels; intervention by direct managers. Respond promptly to rumors. Be proactive in communicating facts.

Source: Author's analysis.

- Tailor the message. Different employee groups will have different needs for information. Anticipate the needs of the specific audience and respond to them.
- Use behavior and symbolic gestures to communicate. Subtleties such as tone of voice, appearance of confidence, and setting of trust can strongly affect how the news is received. Gestures of respect in treatment of the senior managers of the target company convey a tone for the deal that words cannot. The first day after consummation of the deal is particularly loaded with signals to target company employees and should be managed carefully to ensure that the proper tone is communicated. Cultural differences between the buyer and target may help or hurt; be careful about the unintended messages that behavior sends.

CONCLUSION

Presenting deals well is crucial to effective corporate governance. Yet, simple goals of honesty, leadership, directness, and empathy for the decision maker are challenged by the characteristics of the deal (i.e., typically very complex), nature of the audience (e.g., limited bandwidth), the unusual position of the presenter (the need to be both analyst and advocate), and the presence of competing "goods" (e.g., be honest, but create no unrealistic expectations). This chapter has argued that despite these constraints, deal presenters can pursue the goals through careful tailoring of the presentation. The various kinds of deal presentation must be tailored to the needs of respective audiences as summarized in Exhibit 35.3.

NOTES

1. See, for instance, the research reported in Bruner (1992).
2. The list is derived from the author's field research (see especially the cases in Chapter 36) and Ainspan and Dell (2001).

CHAPTER 36

Framework for Postmerger Integration

INTRODUCTION

Postmerger integration is where expectations are fulfilled or broken. M&A transaction design and transaction terms set the stage for this crucial phase of a deal. Failing to recognize integration issues at the bargaining table or in the analytic phase of the work can create enormous problems later on. More importantly, knowing what to do after the definitive agreement is signed is vital to the success of the deal. The aim of this chapter is to highlight integration issues for the executive to consider. Key lessons of this chapter are these:

- ***Integration strategy should flow from the business rationale for the deal.*** This strategy sets the grand plan for integration, based on an assessment of the need for *autonomy*, *interdependence*, and *control* in attaining the goals of the deal. Decisions to be made in these areas should be viewed comprehensively, not independently. The unifying thread that must run through all the strategic choices should be a vision of the benefits that motivated the deal in the first place. The broad categories of benefits (outlined in Chapter 1) include financial benefits such as measurable synergies, strategic benefits, and organizational benefits such as enhancements to culture, workforce, and know-how.
- ***Integration implementation: Speed and determination are your friends.*** Almost everything in the postmerger environment begs for delay, careful planning, and working out the details before moving. But a deliberate approach is a trap. Delay breeds uncertainty among managers, line employees, customers, suppliers, and investors. This uncertainty paralyzes the ordinary course of business and the eventual implementation of an integration plan. The cost can be measured in terms of employees and customers who defect to competitors, suppliers who raise prices, and investors who run out of patience. Make haste—some consultants argue that the merger is won or lost within the first 90 days after consummation.
- ***Remember the employees' "me issues."*** These issues are captured in questions such as, "Will I have a job?" "Will my pay and benefits change?" "Who will I report to?" "Will I have to move?" "What will 'they' be like to work for?" "How will my title and status change?" These issues are highly distracting and affect productivity. And they trigger employee defections; often it is the most

talented employees who leave first. Delay in responding to the "*me issues*" will be costly in organizational terms.

- ***Integration is transformation.*** Postmerger integration is not simple. It should be approached as one would any major corporate transformation, based on an understanding of the competitive turbulence of the new firm, management of the entire system of the firm, and with leadership at all levels of the organization. Anticipating integration should be part of all aspects of the transaction development.

INTEGRATION STRATEGY

Much of the writing about postmerger integration focuses on the detailed workout of the process without giving much consideration to the guiding approach, or strategy, that the executive may have, when instead it seems appropriate to attend to strategy first, and tactics or implementation afterward. The integration task is chaotic, distracting, and stressful. One needs strong guiding principles to stay on course and to achieve the targeted goals of the deal.

Integration strategy should originate from the rationale for the merger. *Integration strategy follows business strategy.* There is no single blueprint appropriate for all acquisitions; indeed, one of the aims of this chapter is to suggest the variety in approaches. If successful integration of the target is contingent on the characteristics of the deal, then starting with a clear sense of the aims of the acquisition is vital to tailoring the integration. As the old saying puts it, if you don't know where you are going, any road will take you there. And there are many "roads" or strategic choices that the executive will face.

The key idea is that the business rationale for the merger will dictate important objectives, such as to improve efficiency, create new capabilities, and manage risks (Chapter 6 outlines a number of these classic motives). In turn, these objectives will suggest important features of organizational design for the target, linkages with the buyer, and elements of control. In their landmark study, Haspeslagh and Jemison (1991) illuminated two important dimensions of integration strategy: *autonomy* and *interdependence*. My own study of integration cases suggests a third consideration, *control*. There may be other important considerations. But these three suffice to illustrate the range of strategic choices and the thinking necessary to prepare an integration strategy. Exhibit 36.1 offers an overview of the approach: One begins by reflecting on the environment, business strategy, and rationale for the deal. Next, one assesses the range of choices about autonomy, interdependence, and control. Finally, one crafts a strategy that optimizes the reach toward the aims of the transactions, subject to its constraints. With this overview in mind, consider in more detail the strategic dimensions of autonomy, interdependence, and control.

Autonomy: Culture, Leadership, and Decision Making

Will the acquisition target exist on its own? Genuine autonomy is more than the continuation of a brand name, a manufacturing plant, or head office. It resides first in the preservation of a culture, "the way we do things." Second, it is often re-

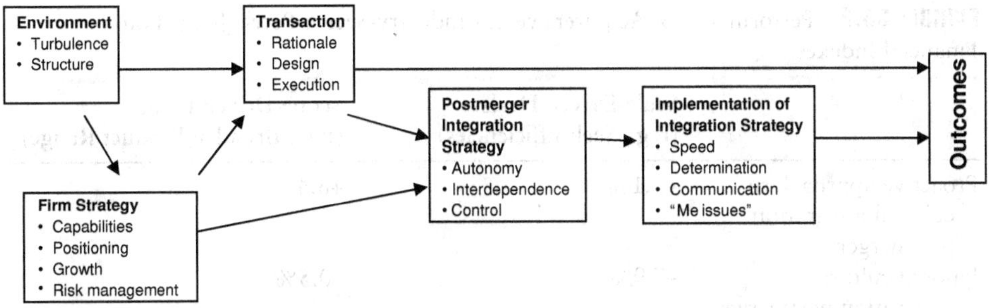

EXHIBIT 36.1 Role of Postmerger Integration in Achieving M&A Goals

flected in the continuation of a leadership team. Third, autonomy is reflected in independence of decision making.

Autonomy matters if the preservation of culture, leadership, and decision making are vital to achieving the strategic aims of the acquisition. A high degree of autonomy might be warranted to preserve attributes that depend greatly on culture and leadership and that understands unique know-how, such as a craft tradition (e.g., beer brewing), creative skill (e.g., animated film production), or R&D capability (e.g., biotechnology laboratory).

Decisions about autonomy are among the most emotionally charged because they affect norms of power and culture. For instance, the decision by Citigroup to merge the cultures of Salomon Brothers and Smith Barney led to the high-profile firing in 1999 of Frank Maturo, a talented veteran of the Salomon firm. A journalist reported that

> *Maturo's dismissal is the most recent evidence that the co-mingling of Salomon's bare-knuckle trading house with Smith Barney's more genteel investment banking and high-end retail businesses hasn't completely bridged the cultural chasm that still has many employees working like Jets among Sharks. "He's Salomon" was the shorthand explanation some company insider gave for Maturo's firing. Others explain away the tumultuous situation saying, "Frank had trouble with the Smith Barney way."*[1]

Avoiding the cultural friction postmerger is probably not an alternative. A study by researchers at Bain & Company considered the impact of taking a proactive approach to dealing with cultural integration (i.e., versus ignoring culture). Their results, given in Exhibit 36.2, suggest that active attention to issues of culture and autonomy pays: Companies that followed proactive integration strategies outperformed sector indexes and the do-nothing strategies. The researchers concluded that in scale-driven deals (typically focused on improving efficiency), the successful acquirers attended to cultural integration and did so by "imposing their culture on the target company; if they adjust their own culture to accommodate that of the acquired company, it is only to a very limited degree."[2] In contrast, the best-performing acquirers in scope-driven deals (i.e., focused on broadening a product range) "gained ground in one of two ways: either by intentionally keeping the merged companies cultures separate or by creating an altogether new culture. The key was the degree of

EXHIBIT 36.2 Performance of Acquirers versus Industry-Sector Peers, Judged on Financial Indexes

	Scale-Driven Deals (E.g., Seek Efficiencies)	Scope-Driven Deals (E.g., Broaden Product Range)
Proactive approach to cultural integration postmerger	+5.1%	+6.4%
Ignored cultural integration postmerger	–7.9%	–0.5%
Strategies of successful acquirers	Impose the buyer's culture on the target company.	Either keep target company as a separate culture or create an altogether new culture.

Note: The numbers in the cells are percentage changes in indexes of financial performance. The indexes were not further described by the authors.
Source of data: Till Vestring, Brian King, and Ted Rouse, "Should You Always Merge Cultures?," *Harvard Management Update* (May 2003), page 10.

overlap in the businesses. When there was significant but not complete overlap—in customer segments, for example—building a new culture was critical to achieving an organizational sum that was greater than its component parts. But when there was a very limited overlap, it made more sense to keep the cultures separate."[3]

Interdependence: Business Processes and Value Chain

How closely must the target mesh with the buyer's value chain and business processes in order to attain the acquisition aims? A buyer pursuing a careful strategy of vertical or horizontal integration might find the issue of interdependence to be vitally important—the extent of this importance will depend on synergies obtained through scale and scope.

On the other hand, a conglomerate pursuing a strategy of unrelated portfolio diversification or a private equity investment firm that seeks to grow the target for resale in a few years may find it unnecessary to engineer any interdependence of the target with the buyer firm. In some acquisitions, synergies might be achieved simply by transferring know-how from one party to the other, or through the exercise of purchasing power—these might be examples of somewhat low interdependence. Parent corporations with low strategic interdependence among their business units probably view themselves as financial portfolio managers.

Control: Finance, Quality, and Reporting

What are the strategic risks and how should they be managed? Risk controls typically appear in the imposition of new control systems that permit closer monitoring, faster response, and/or better hedging. It would be unusual for a buyer to believe that the target entailed *no* risks; rather, the judgments here consist in identifying the risks, and assessing the adequacy of the existing risk control systems. A concern for risks might entail the appointment of a CFO from the home office, installation of a new financial reporting system, introduction of Total Quality Management, and application of the buyer firm's policies and procedures. In the instance of substantial risks (e.g., as with a target firm purchased out of bankruptcy), the changes might be wholesale.

Control deserves special recognition apart from autonomy and interdependence. It captures a dimension of merger integration strategy that is not easily grasped in the other two dimensions. A merging target firm could be granted high autonomy and either high or low control. Control could either worsen the sense of autonomy (because of the intrusiveness of these systems) or enhance it (if the control systems work they may encourage the buyer to leave the target alone). Similarly, the target could be tightly controlled without strong links of interdependence.

FRAMEWORK FOR INTEGRATION STRATEGY

Exhibit 36.3 arrays autonomy, interdependence, and control in three-dimensional space, which suggests the rich range of choice in designing an integration strategy. Viewed this way, developing an integration strategy is a matter of thinking rigorously about these (and other) considerations. The answer to "What strategy is best?" will depend on the suitability of the strategy to meet the acquisition aims. Looking across a sample of deals, different integration strategies could be warranted. To consider the varieties of choice, consider two pairwise comparisons of integration strategy, drawn from banking and conglomerate firms.

Integration Strategies in Banking

In the 1980s and 1990s, the U.S. banking industry witnessed a dramatic consolidation. Two aggressive acquirers, Banc One and NationsBank, shared an appetite for targets but differed markedly in their strategies for integration.

CONFEDERATION: BANC ONE Between 1967 and 1992, Banc One acquired 60 banks. Its integration strategy with these was to leave in place the leadership, culture, and lending decision making of the local organizations, but to impose on them the "best practice" management processes of the best performers in the confederation, and to apply a management information system that communicated financial results and risk exposure information to the headquarters. The information system computed 40 performance ratios that prompted the various local organizations to compare themselves with each other. Local unit heads were "encouraged" to communicate with the best performers in an effort to transfer best practices among the units. The process of sharing information and comparing results stimulated attention to performance within the target organizations. Regarding chain of command, local banks reported to state bank headquarters, which in turn reported to the central headquarters. The CEO of Banc One said:

> *Our objective is to interfere as little as possible with the operation of a bank we acquire. We have found that people instinctively want to excel, they yearn for*

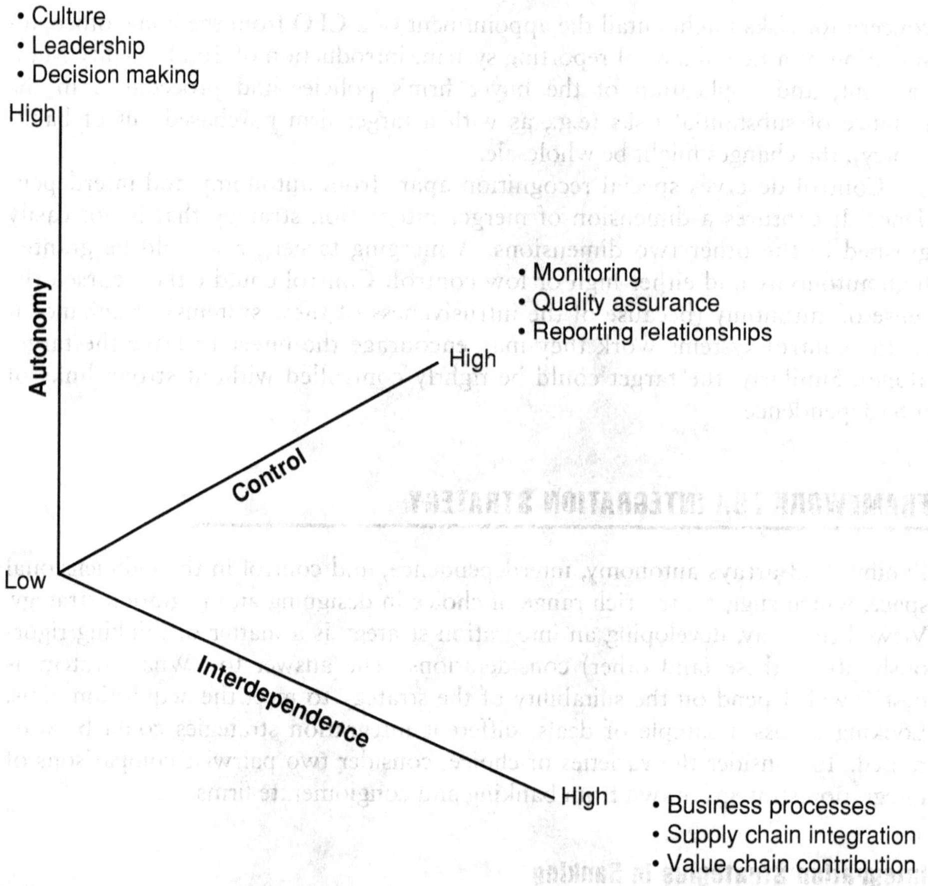

EXHIBIT 36.3 The Space for Integration Strategy: Autonomy, Interdependence, and Control
Source: Author's analysis.

> *standards against which to measure themselves. Our job is to provide these yardsticks in an environment of nondestructive competition.*[4]

Another profile of Banc One said,

> *The Banc One culture blends opposing tendencies that reflect the McCoy*[5] *style: autonomy and control, individuality and uniformity. Acquired banks are encouraged to operate their businesses their own way, unless they fail to meet Banc One's ambitious ROA targets; then they are quickly taken in hand. Banc One will try almost any experiment, as long as the stakes are low and the potential fallout from failure is limited.*[6]

The Banc One example illustrates an integration strategy of *confederation*. The target is given relatively high autonomy, subject to high controls and to low links of interdependence.

ABSORPTION: NATIONSBANK In almost all of its acquisitions, NationsBank replaced the target's brand name, leadership, control systems, and business processes with its own. One journalist described this integration strategy as follows: "But all these banks do know one thing. They'd rather not be taken over by Hugh McColl.[7] McColl has a reputation as a ruthless, cost-minded taskmaster who chews up everything in his path. When he takes over a bank, his lieutenants descend on the town in one of the company's 11 jets, and almost before you can say 'disintermediation,' they've booted out the local management, ripped down the signs, fired workers, and seamlessly absorbed the hapless victim. McColl then parachutes in more new troops who remold the newly merged rank and file into NationsBank's losing-just-isn't-an-option mindset."[8] The clearest example of this was NationsBank's acquisition in 1988 of FirstRepublic, an insolvent bank acquired from the U.S. Federal Deposit Insurance Corporation. With demoralized staff, FirstRepublic needed new leadership and culture. With departing customers and depositors, First Republic needed a new brand name and identity. With a major portion of its loan portfolio in default, First Republic needed new controls. NationsBank's aims were to stabilize the target and return it to profitable operation.

In commenting on the general comparison between Banc One and NationsBank, former CEO Hugh McColl told me in an interview,

> *I've been asked many times why we didn't do as others did and have a confederation of banks and preserve some of the grand traditions and the old names and all the goodwill that goes with that. And wasn't I guilty of destroying goodwill? And the answer to that is yes. We destroyed the old goodwill. But we created new goodwill. But there was a more logical reason behind it. First, we had learned . . . [that if] you do everything the same way, then your management becomes cogs in the machinery that can go anywhere. . . . [It] meant that you could put them down anywhere and they knew how to run the bank. They didn't have a different set of products, a different set of rules or whatever. So first, it's a tremendous management tool to develop general managers that can run the whole place.*
>
> *The second thing is it's more efficient. And from a customer point of view . . . if you want to do business with a bank, you want your account to look the same. You want your information to come out of one account. You know, it's logical from a customer's point of view to have one institution. And then when you get to advertising, it's pretty straightforward. . . . You know when you see McDonald's with the golden arches, they only have to advertise one name and everybody knows their menu. And so the point is it's very expensive to try to operate more than one brand name. It in fact makes no sense whatsoever. In fact, it was such a stupid argument I don't know why anyone ever had it. But the real cost [of] that was . . . you end up with systems that don't talk to each other. And one of the arguments Bank One liked to make, and they trumpeted that they were a great . . . a great technology company . . . was that we could have the same technology. We just market it under different names. Well, that was all well and good, but they didn't. In other words, they could not actually run the same software for 30 different applications in 70 different locations. . . . Which we could. And the difference in cost savings was staggering.*[9]

The NationsBank example illustrates an integration strategy of *absorption*. Low autonomy, high control, and high interdependence of business processes combine to eliminate variation and distinction of the target from the buyer.

Integration Strategies in Conglomerate Firms

Conglomerates pursue a strategy of diversification and growth by acquisition—the very name "conglomerate" suggests an aggregate of different businesses, a lower emphasis on relatedness in business activities among the target firms. Yet closer examination suggests material differences in integration approaches for two conglomerates.

PRESERVATION: BERKSHIRE HATHAWAY Warren Buffett built Berkshire Hathaway into an unusual conglomerate with interests as disparate as furniture retailing, razor blades, ice cream, and jewelry. Reflecting his value-oriented investing style, the firm has earned one of the best corporate performance records since he took it over in the 1960s. His acquisition strategy, unrelated diversification, reflects his financial investment approach to building Berkshire Hathaway, that is, as an investor in an equity portfolio. His integration strategy is to leave the target firms alone, virtually preserving them as they were before the acquisition. One journalist, summarizing this approach, wrote,

> *Buffett insists that his CEOs run their companies as they did before he acquired them. He asks only that they follow his management philosophy, which Hagstrom, author of* The Essential Buffett *and* The Warren Buffett Way, *sums up as "acting rationally about capital allocation, being candid at all times and resisting the lemming tendency of companies to imitate one another for no good reason." . . . Berkshire Hathaway CEOs operate with minimum oversight and a generous budget. "The only part Buffett plays is managing asset allocation, and we're small enough that he doesn't do much there. We spend capital pretty freely," [manager Melvyn] Wolff says. "Sometimes I stop and remind myself I don't own the company anymore." . . .*
>
> *Likewise, when Buffett acquired Helzberg Diamond Shops, "Mr. Buffett said that I should run the company as I saw fit," [Helzberg CEO Jeffrey] Comment recalls. "Two days later he called to apologize. 'Jeff,' he said, 'I do want you to change one thing. Call all your friendly bankers and tell them to go away. I'm your bank now.' And he has been ever since." Helzberg Diamonds has grown from 150 stores in 1995 when Buffett acquired it to 245 today.*[10]

The Berkshire Hathaway example illustrates an integration strategy of *preservation*. The target firm enjoys high autonomy, relatively low control, and low interdependence with the business processes of the parent.

LINKING: GENERAL ELECTRIC POWER SYSTEMS DIVISION Linking is the approach to business development described in Chapter 37 by executives at GE's Power Systems division (GEPS). GEPS pursues a strategy of related diversification though it tailors the integration strategy somewhat to fit the particular acquisition. In one case example, the acquisition of Alpha Company, executives outlined an integration strategy for a target firm that was a supplier to the division. The owners of Alpha were at retirement age and looked for a sale of the company for estate planning purposes. Yet the technology of the company was a creation of the management team. GEPS chose to integrate Alpha by leaving in place its identity and leadership, but also by installing GE operating controls and business processes and tightly linking Alpha to the GEPS value chain.

The GEPS example illustrates an integration strategy of *linking*. The target enjoys considerable autonomy, subject to high controls and high interdependence through business process alignment.

Exhibit 36.4 illustrates the hypothetical positioning of these four examples in the three-dimensional strategic space of autonomy, interdependence of business processes, and control. Preservation and absorption appear in the figure as polar opposites: they differ completely on the three dimensions. Confederation is a polar strategy of its own: high on autonomy and controls, but low on interdependence. Linking is a fourth classic alternative: high on control systems and business process

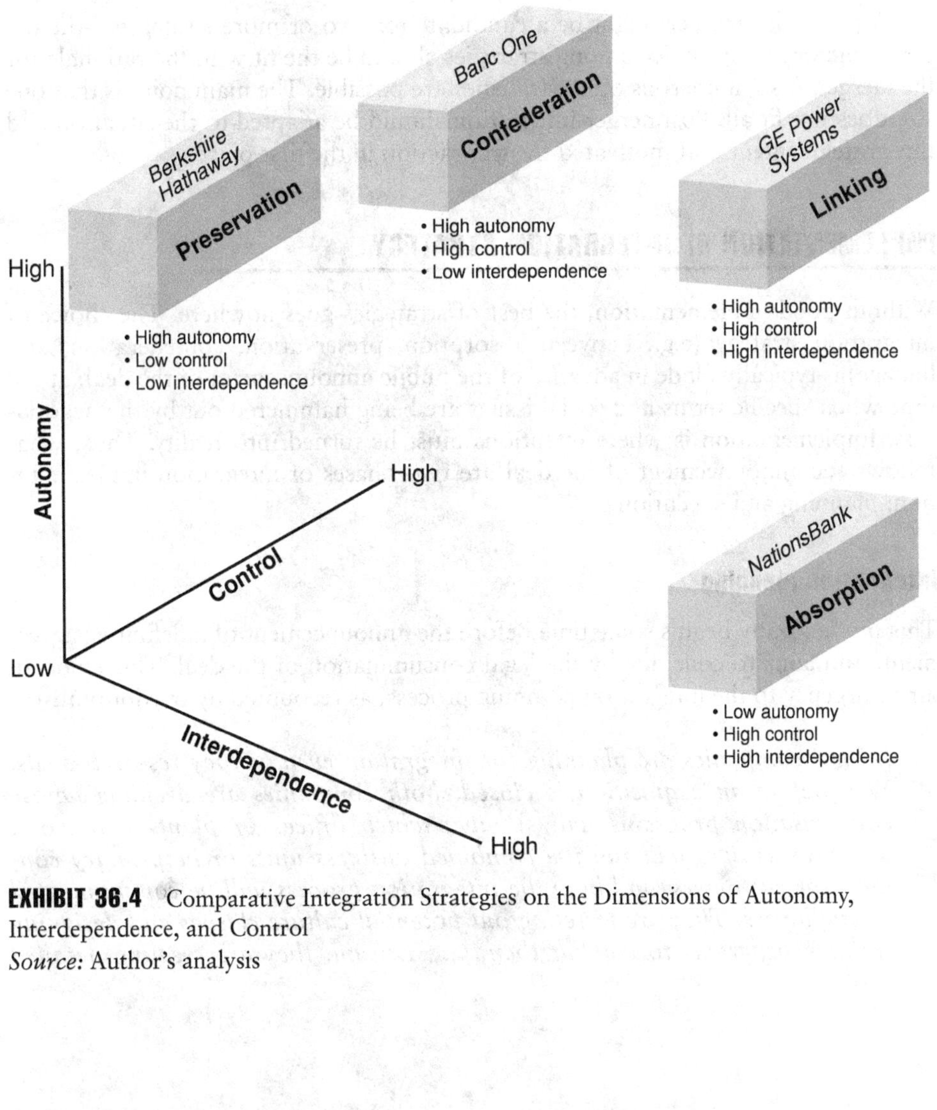

EXHIBIT 36.4 Comparative Integration Strategies on the Dimensions of Autonomy, Interdependence, and Control
Source: Author's analysis

integration, and high on autonomy. The four classic strategies might be seen in the following kinds of situations:

1. ***Preservation.*** Where the need for integration is very low, such as acquisitions of unrelated businesses, pure financially motivated deals, and cases where the need to preserve the entity is extremely high, as with creative artists or research boutiques with highly specialized know-how.
2. ***Confederation.*** Where there is a need to control risks while preserving the unique qualities of the target because of artists or researchers, or to maintain the traditional identity of the business for the sake of retaining a customer franchise. This is often seen in industry roll-ups.
3. ***Linking.*** Where it is desirable to maintain the culture of the target but also to establish the buyer's controls and link the target to the buyer's business processes and value chain. This is seen in vertical mergers and many horizontal mergers.
4. ***Absorption.*** Where the aim is to exploit economies of scale and/or to remove capacity out of the industry.

A particular merger might be a candidate for two or more strategies—the deciding factor in any choice among strategies should be the fit with the rationale for the merger. Also, numerous other strategies are possible. The main point is that one size does not fit all. Postmerger integration should be adapted to the situation and the strategic intent that motivated the transaction in the first place.

IMPLEMENTATION OF INTEGRATION STRATEGY

Without good implementation, the best of strategies goes nowhere. The choice of integration strategy (e.g., between absorption, preservation, confederation, and linkage) is typically made in advance of the public announcement of the deal, at the time when specific terms and social issues are being hammered out by the negotiators. Implementation is where intentions must be turned into reality. Thus, what follows the announcement of the deal are two phases of integration implementation: planning and execution.

Integration Planning

This phase ideally begins some time before the announcement of a definitive agreement, and aims to conclude by the legal consummation of the deal. This lends an air of urgency to the integration planning process, as recounted by one journalist:

> *[More] companies are planning for integration even as they research deals. Well before an acquisition is closed, both companies are deciding whose compensation programs will survive, which offices or plants will close, which executives will run the combined business units or be primary contacts for customers, and how the integration process will be communicated to employees. They are ferreting out potential culture clashes and designing training programs to combat them. . . . In sum, they are creating detailed*

implementation plans, complete with milestones, for making the merger work—and fast.[11]

Arguably, the postmerger integration process begins when an integration leader is appointed. Usually this happens between the letter of intent and signing of the definitive agreement. In this phase, managerial appointments are announced, information technology (IT) platforms are chosen, efficiency programs are specified, and layoffs, if any, are sketched out. In most countries, it is not permissible to implement any of these plans until antitrust authorities give permission, the shareholders have voted, and the merger agreement has been consummated through the exchange of consideration and observance of representations, warranties, and covenants. To begin the integration process in advance of regulatory approval is called "gun jumping" and can expose the merging parties to fines and penalties.

The range of integration planning issues covers a wide spectrum of topics:

- ***Appointment of an integration leader and team.*** The planning process necessarily starts with the identification of a process owner, someone whose interests are aligned with seeing the goals attained. This might entail plucking a general manager from his or her routine to accept a special (temporary) assignment as integration leader. But at some companies that are active acquirers, the job of integration leader is permanent and high-profile. A key role of the integration team is to extend attention to process and momentum for the integration through the organization. A report by KPMG said, "A purely top-down approach engineered by a small group typically results in limited buy-in and minimal ability to implement change. Organizations can harness energy, generate momentum, and identify problem areas early by involving as many staff as possible (without hampering day-to-day operations). Integration team members should have credibility, and they should be on the project full-time to ensure focus and momentum."[12]
- ***Communications.*** The integration process should include communications with employees that impart a vision for the deal, progress reports, the role of the employees in success of the integration, and future milestones. Repetition of the messages and the use of a variety of media are necessary to spread the message.
- ***Deadlines and work plans.*** Target completion dates and lists of tasks to be completed form the essence of a *project management* approach to integration planning. Once established, these are easily tracked using information technology systems. Also, the tasks and deadlines form a ready agenda for discussion with managers and employees.
- ***Retention of talent.*** It is said that for many service firms, the assets walk out the door each evening. The challenge for all merging firms is to motivate those assets to return the next morning. Too often, integration teams focus on layoffs and redundancies necessary to achieve synergies and economies from the combination. Less often do they consider the other side: retention of talent, key employees, and the knowledge base they carry with them. Key to retention efforts are decisions about compensation, titles, and work assignments. Disparities in compensation between the buyer and target were a major hurdle for the merger of Daimler-Benz and Chrysler: The Chrysler managers were more

richly compensated than at Daimler. Adjusting the Chrysler compensation downward might have triggered mass defections. Adjusting Daimler compensation upward would have ruined the synergy forecasts. The CEO of the merged firm aimed to overcome the disparity with a low basic salary and a large performance-based bonus.

- ***Production, logistics, and supply chain management.*** The heart of most expected synergies lies in expected cost economies of supply and production. The integration planners may need to reconsider the manufacturing focus of facilities: broad line versus narrow line; variety of technologies versus narrow concentration. Integration planners may want to reconsider the flow of materials among facilities, and between plants, warehouses, and suppliers. The acquisition of Snapple by Quaker Oats Company foundered on mistaken assumptions about the willingness of Snapple's independent distributors to shift their focus to Quaker's Gatorade brand.
- ***Intangible capital.*** Integration planners will face issues regarding the continuation of brand names, leases, corporate names, the preservation of patents, and strategic options. Because these assets are invisible, they are often neglected; yet, they are often the source of considerable market value.
- ***Work space.*** The integration of office and plant space sends signals that may help or defeat integration. Size, location, and amenities are qualities of work space with which the integration planner can work.
- ***Management information systems.*** Information and reporting systems often reflect the structures of their firms: flat versus vertical; centralized versus decentralized; geographic-focused versus product-focused, and so on. Thus, dilemmas about optimizing information reporting and control may well mirror larger issues posed in the design of the new organization.

Integration Execution

Starting shortly after consummation, the new organization chart goes into effect, with new responsibilities and lines of reporting authority. New corporate identities are announced in the media. Technology platforms are established or converted, including e-mail, data processing, customer service, and telecommunications. The cost savings and layoff programs are implemented. Each of these activities will have a targeted completion ranging widely from a day or two (e-mail and telecommunications) possibly to months (layoffs). The progress in all of these activities is monitored through a detailed project management system.

The implementation of integration strategies shows a strong consistency among "best practitioners": successful implementations have in common speed, determination, and good communication.

SPEED AND DETERMINATION "Speed" refers to the pace of execution. "Determination" is the adherence to the *intent* of a deal and the refusal to be distracted by politicking, unexpected problems, and so on, that an integration effort summons up. Michael F. Spratt and Mark L. Feldman of PricewaterhouseCoopers wrote, "The plain fact is that implementation is everything. Words must be translated into action, action into early wins, and early wins into profitable growth. Yes, early wins.

In a technology-driven, globally competitive environment where the speed of information transfer and thus, competitive intelligence, is measured in nanoseconds, if you're not implementing at the speed of light your opportunities will dissolve before you can extract the rewards."[13] They argued that speed and decisiveness are often sacrificed by seven common errors:[14]

1. *"Obsessive list-making."* Simply identifying tasks drives out making decisions.
2. *"Content-free communications."* Chirpy exhortations do nothing to relieve uncertainty and anxiety, and may amplify them.
3. *"Creating a planning circus."* Excessive planning dulls accountability and delays decision making.
4. *"Respecting barnyard behavior."* Most societies observe some kind of pecking order—yet these hierarchies may not be optimal or desirable from the standpoint of success of integration of the new firm.
5. *"Preaching vision and values."* Endless focus on lofty ideals does nothing to resolve thorny issues in the trenches.
6. *"Putting turtles on fence posts."* Establishing a meritocracy is messy. The tendency in most integration efforts is to resort to quotas or some kind of representativeness from the two sides in a merger. This results in putting turtles on fence posts: If you see a turtle on a fence post, someone must have put it there, for it didn't climb up there on its merits.
7. *"Rewarding the wrong behaviors."* Incentive systems are often established on tradition, culture, peer practices, and so on—but not always on the basis of motivating employees to stretch for the goals that motivated the merger to begin with.

COMMUNICATION Chapter 35 offered some practical suggestions for communicating the deal to various constituencies. Studies of postmerger integration programs by the Conference Board (Ainspan and Dell 2000; Booz-Allen and Hamilton 1999, 2001; and KPMG 1999a) agreed that communication was a key determinant of success. The objective of the communication effort should be to combat what the Conference Board calls the "FUD" factor (fear, uncertainty, and doubt). In studying M&A success, KPMG found that,

> *Companies which gave priority to communications were 13% more likely than average to have a successful deal. When we drilled down to understand this better, poor communications with own employees appeared to pose the greatest risk to deal success, more so than poor communication to shareholders, suppliers, or customers.*[15]

In the Booz-Allen report, communication was the first of four leading principles of successful integration. The report said,

> *We have no doubt that every company goes into a merger with a one- or two-sentence description of what the deal is all about. . . . However, we suggest that the senior leadership team dig even deeper, beyond the immediate rationale to the real and sustainable sources of value they hope to unleash in the merger, and then be aggressive and open in quantifying and communicating those*

sources of value to vested parties—employees, customers, and shareholders. A true shared vision for value creation:

- Specifically identifies sources of value.
- Sets high aspirations for financial growth and synergy.
- Is shared by both companies' senior teams.
- Is communicated broadly and constantly.[16]

INTEGRATION STRATEGY MINI-CASE: THE MERGER OF UNION BANK OF SWITZERLAND AND SWISS BANK CORPORATION, 1998

The challenges of merger integration—and their resolution—are revealed in detailed case studies. The transaction that created UBS A.G. in 1998 affords a close consideration of postmerger integration.

Merger Motives and Integration Strategy

In 1987, the management of Swiss Bank Corporation (SBC) committed itself to a vision for the firm that became the foundation for a profound transformation of the bank: from a Swiss-focused commercial bank to a globally integrated financial services firm. The aim expressed in this vision included to become ranked among the best in its peer group, to increase shareholder value 10 percent per year, and to achieve premier credit ratings. Several acquisitions by SBC during the 1990s transformed the organization culturally, financially, and strategically. The merger in 1998 with Union Bank of Switzerland (ex-UBS)[17] was the culmination of SBC's strategic transformation process.

Ex-UBS had for years been the largest financial service institution in Switzerland, and SBC the third largest (after Credit Suisse). SBC had grown mostly by acquisition; ex-UBS had grown over the years largely through an organic buildup. SBC's culture was more oriented toward trading and capital markets; ex-UBS had more of a traditional "credit culture." Both firms reported losses at year-end 1996 owing to commercial loan write-downs, and ex-UBS had been particularly hit by derivatives-related losses. The two institutions also saw themselves confronted with the controversy over Holocaust-related dormant accounts.

The proposed merger took root in discussions between Peter Wuffli and Marcel Ospel, respectively CFO and CEO of SBC, during a train ride on December 11, 1996. Ospel, who had been named CEO of SBC the previous May, argued that a merger between SBC and UBS was a matter of necessity. Wuffli expressed concerns about the cultural differences between the two banks, and the weaknesses of SBC. The SBC executive committee met on January 2–3, 1997, to explore various merger alternatives, ranging across dimensions such as cross-border versus domestic, and banking versus insurance. UBS emerged as the superior merger partner alternative.

After lengthy negotiations that endured a three-month breakup, the two organizations announced a deal on December 8, 1997. The press release explained that large size would be a key determinant of success in the future—this merger would create an institution with CHF 1.32 trillion in assets under management, making it the largest asset manager in the world. Greater size would provide the firm with critical mass in investment banking. The merger would also permit the rationalization of operations in the domestic Swiss retail and commercial banking segments.

The combined firm, to be named UBS A.G., would have dual headquarters, in Zurich and Basel. Its Private and Corporate Clients division (consumer and corporate banking) would be headquartered in Zurich; its Private Banking division in Basel; UBS Brinson, the institutional asset management division, in Chicago; and UBS Warburg Dillon Read, the investment banking division, in London.

Through better market positioning and economies of scale, the two firms expected to create synergy value of CHF 20 to 25 billion—almost one-third of the premerger market value of the two firms combined. This value would be derived from sizable cost savings by eliminating duplicate activities in the overlapping businesses (e.g., Swiss retail and commercial banking, and investment banking), notably in areas such as operations, infrastructure, trading rooms, Swiss branch networks, and corporate staffs. Also, the executives envisioned accelerated revenue growth. Sources would include market growth in private banking and the realization of benefits from a "bulge bracket" (or leading) position in investment banking. And finally, the merger would free up excess capital, which could be profitably redeployed. The CEOs targeted return on equity in the range of 15 to 20 percent, improving financing with the aim of reducing cost of capital, and improving transparency and disclosure.

Against these economic benefits would be netted expenses related to realizing the synergies, such as the cost of personnel layoffs, new information technology, and changes in real estate. Anticipating these expenses, UBS A.G. would reserve a restructuring charge of CHF 7.0 billion.

In a presentation to analysts in April 1998, the CEOs of the merging firms, Mathis Cabiallavetta (ex-UBS) and Marcel Ospel (SBC), outlined strategies for integration that varied across the main divisions. The choice of strategy was dictated in part by the relative strengths of the merging divisions.

- ***Consumer and corporate banking: absorption.*** This would entail a merger of the Swiss lending businesses of the two firms. The integration here was projected to take from three to four years, reflecting (1) the need to select the best IT platform for the two organizations, migrate the client base to the platform, and maintain a high level of service; (2) the complexities of rationalizing the branch banking networks of the two firms in Switzerland; and (3) the layoff process of 5,000 employees to be pursued, as Cabiallavetta and Ospel said, "with strong social responsibility and fairness."
- ***Private banking: new model.*** UBS A.G.'s private banking division would be built from combining elements from both sides, which would be absorbed into the development of a new business model. Implementation of the integration plan would take one to two years, reflecting the need to ensure continuity in client relationships and to maintain a high level of service.
- ***Institutional asset management: linking.*** Here, the integration would take 12 months. SBC's Brinson division was the fourth largest institutional asset manager in the world, and would be the platform on which UBS A.G.'s institutional asset management business would be built. Nonetheless, parts of the ex-UBS

asset management group would be granted a large degree of autonomy. Both the SBC Brinson and ex-UBS groups were value-style managers.

- ***Investment banking: absorption.*** The integration would take 12 months. SBC Warburg Dillon Read was the leading investment banking operation in Europe. The ex-UBS corporate finance activities would be absorbed by the SBC Warburg division. But in the fixed income area the combination was more of a merger of equals, as ex-UBS was perceived to have a better product platform in that category.
- ***Private equity: absorption.*** The private equity businesses of the two firms would be built upon the ex-UBS private equity group. SBC's private equity activity was small. Management targeted an integration process of three months, reflecting the relatively smaller scale and complexity of the private equity operations of the two merging firms.

Implementation of the Integration Strategy

The announcement of senior management appointments was staggered through time, stretching from early December 1997 through February 1998. Keeping employees informed of key management changes and the progress of the integration was supported by the launch of a joint web site. The integration took place in the context of a very tight labor market due to the booming financial industry. This factor increased the importance of fast and clear-cut decisions during the integration process. Moreover, the time pressure to integrate was acute for UBS A.G.'s Swiss business as the merger (notably the technical migration) had to be finished early enough in 1999 in order to prepare for Y2K technology concerns.

The implementation was fast, meritocratic, and focused on absorbing best practices from each partner to the other. Michael Sweeney, at the UBS Leadership Institute, said, "The success or failure of a merger is determined within its first 100 days," noting a report by A. T. Kearney on merger processes.[18] He argued that "me issues" dominate the thinking of employees to such an extent that speed was necessary to forestall paralysis in the organization—these issues included, "Will I have a job?" "Will my pay and benefits change?" "Who will I report to?" "Will I have to move?" "What will 'they' be like to work for?" These issues draw the organization's focus away from the customer, sacrifice productivity, and trigger the departure of key talent. Marcel Ospel agreed, "Speed is the key for successful execution of a merger. But each deal creates uncertainties. Clients want a new value proposition; shareholders want benefits; and staff want new roles. You have to move quickly to deal with the expectations created in a merger."[19]

Michael Sweeney outlined 14 maxims for successful implementation of an integration strategy:

1. ***Board level structure must be defined at announcement.*** UBS A.G.'s press release of the merger also announced the board of directors and senior management of the new firm. Failure to do this, most observers believed, creates intense uncertainty and political positioning that tends to drive out regular business activities.
2. ***Publish and communicate an integration plan.*** Exhibit 36.5 presents the integration process as foreseen by management at the announcement of the deal.

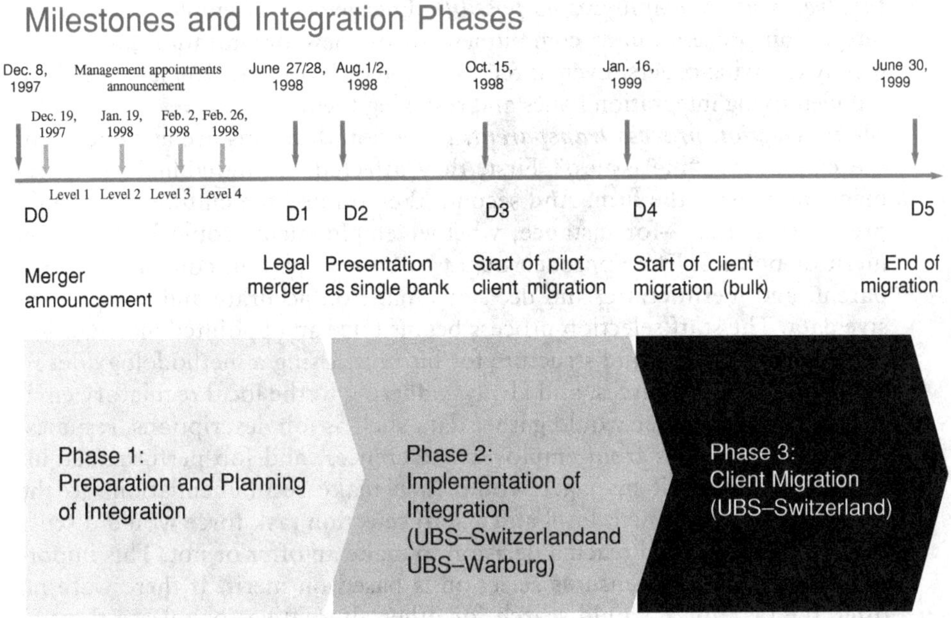

EXHIBIT 36.5 Postmerger Integration Time Line: Merger of Union Bank of Switzerland and Swiss Bank Corporation

This entailed five phases of activity that would aim to complete the integration planning by May 1998, the earliest likely date at which the merger would receive regulatory approval. Sweeney quoted a survey by Watson Wyatt in which 91 percent of managers believed that communication was crucial to successful integration, but only 43 percent said it had been successful in their firms. The survey found several reasons why communications were ineffective: inadequate resources, slow process, inadequate senior management attention, uneven attention to various groups in the firm, inconsistency of messages, late launch, poor planning, infrequent communication, and early termination of the communication effort.[20]

3. ***Have very clear business and financial targets.*** Consistently in the public presentations about the merger, senior managers repeated strategic and financial aims.
4. ***Keep integration time as short as possible.*** Most observers of mergers and acquisitions note that efforts to realize synergistic benefits are easily paralyzed by integration uncertainties. The aim of UBS A.G.'s integration plan was to resolve these uncertainties by the date of consummation.
5. ***Make decisions swiftly—speed is critical.*** The corollary to the preceding point is that lengthy decision processes tend to worsen uncertainty. Also, delays encourage jockeying for advantage by individual managers and lengthen the window during which competitors cherry-pick talented employees to greatest advantage.

6. ***Involve as many employees as possible.*** Engagement of employees with the integration process builds commitment to the new organization faster than merely receiving orders. Even at relatively junior levels, involvement could entail identifying integration issues and resolving them.
7. ***Make selection process transparent.*** Retention decisions are at the core of the employees' "me issues." First, they affected the individual's employment status with the firm. And second, they framed the culture that would prevail thereafter—for instance, whether employment would be based on merit or politics. The approach ought to be seen as fair, consistent, transparent, and meritocratic, and decisions made on accurate and comprehensive data. The staff selection process begins once an appointed manager has developed a strategy and structure for his unit. Using a methodology developed by human resources, and always adhering to the local regulatory environment, the manager would gather data such as job descriptions, resumes, position preferences from employees, references, and job performance information. The unit manager would then make recommendations to the next higher management level and a staff selection task force would discuss the appointments and reach a decision to make an offer or not. This important governance step ensures selection is based on merit. If there were no offer, the task force would search for other alternatives or release the employee into the social plan pool. If the offer was made, the staff selection process would begin to assist the newly appointed manager with selecting staff in his or her domain.
8. ***Release those who cannot culturally adjust.*** Part of the transformation that mergers entail is change in culture. For instance, SBC had explicitly sought to change its own culture to be more rigorous and performance-oriented through its acquisitions of O'Connor Associates and Brinson Partners. In acquiring the investment bank S. G. Warburg, SBC sought to extend its culture to the target. Culture change requires that incumbent employees must adapt—those who do not may threaten the success of the integration effort.
9. ***Do not prolong life of integration project teams.*** The risk of forming integration teams is that they might become new layers of bureaucracy, imped-

SEVEN DEADLY SINS TO AVOID

- Have poor due diligence (financial and human capital).
- Delay the start of integration and drag out the finish.
- Allow divergent initiatives.
- Take too long to answer "me issues."
- Undercommunicate.
- Put no one in charge.
- Ignore project management disciplines.

Source: UBS A.G. internal document, Michael Sweeney, May 31, 2000.

ing the work of the regular business units. At the start of the integration effort, "sunset" expectations and deadlines should be established for the integration teams.

10. ***Move to a common systems platform.*** Information technology defines reality for most organizations. Systems are often the pets of the respective merging organizations, reflecting their values and cultures. Often these systems spark heated debates within integration teams over the selection of one system over the other—or even the continued operation in parallel of both systems. UBS A.G. believed that a common systems platform was vital to the establishment of a newly integrated organization and necessary to efficiently tackle the Y2K issue.
11. ***Manage the integration process as a project.*** Viewing the integration effort as a project meant that it would have finite goals, milestones, and life—all apart from the ordinary course of business. UBS A.G. believed that integration management needed to be separate and distinct—viewed as a special project whose responsibilities and authority spanned functions and hierarchies. An integration stress-tests most systems and processes in an organization and exposes many of the weak links that exist in all organizations. Although much of the integration process can be planned, assisting the organization in handling unexpected events becomes a major factor in determining the successful outcome of the integration. This is where managing the integration as a project and not as a unique event that one wants to get completed as soon as possible adds real value.
12. ***Manage each transitional phase; celebrate victories.*** Successes helped to create momentum for the integration process, building confidence in the capacity of the entire organization to successfully achieve the merger goals.
13. ***Consider the influence of the press.*** Press relations would need to be managed through the integration process, for the simple reason that the press influences perceptions of employees, customers, investors, and competitors. To "manage" press relations is not to dictate what is to be written, but rather to cooperate with journalists such that they understand the firm's point of view. Statements by disgruntled parties make interesting copy but may be a poor reflection of the reality or benefits of a deal.
14. ***Allow organizations time to develop new culture.*** Sweeney noted that "one cannot impose a culture on someone else," and that "business culture clashes are a necessary ingredient of prosperity and creativity." Within a framework of alignment around common goals, clearly defined responsibilities, and decision-making processes, managers need to allow each business unit to grow first of all together in the new environment within an overall cultural framework.

Consistent with this philosophy, the UBS A.G. integration planning effort completed the IT platform decisions within 46 days of the announcement, and all staffing decisions within 15 weeks. Also, by April 1998, Cabiallavetta and Ospel could report that decisions had been made and announced regarding the name and logo for the group and its divisions; pending were decisions about downsizing the Swiss branch network, migration of clients to new systems, allocation of premises worldwide, legal structure abroad, and detailed business plans to realize strategic goals. By the date of consummation of the merger, June 29, 1998, integration planning was complete. Thereafter, management of the consumer and corporate banking division looked forward to a client migration process that would occur over a year, first in a pilot project and then in a series of batches over various weekends.

Execution of Postmerger Integration in Consumer and Corporate Banking (Private and Corporate Clients Division)

Of all the business segments of the new firm, the integration of activities in consumer and corporate banking (Private and Corporate Clients division) were viewed by many as the most daunting. While the opportunities for synergistic cost savings were sizable, the layoffs would be greatest here, and the cultural changes would be substantial. This business division included the old Swiss commercial banking segment for which client relationships were important and cultures were well embedded. The gradual decline of commercial banking within both firms (contrasting with the rise of investment banking, asset management, and private banking), and the rise of a global (rather than a domestic) focus would challenge the integration effort. Stephan Haeringer, member of the ex-UBS group executive board, CEO of ex-UBS Switzerland, and former division head of Private Banking, was appointed to be the division head of Private and Corporate Clients in which capacity he would be directly responsible for consumer and corporate banking. He said,

> *I wanted to learn from the other side. . . . I told my managers to take it fast. Don't fool around. Our management principle was "just do it." Of course, the key here was strict project control and close oversight. It's very important not to get arrogant in a merger integration. You have to keep close to the managers out in the field; to live the standards. Don't preach water and drink wine. It's all about credibility. Leaders must be totally committed to the deal; they have to sign on. And you have to create a vision with which employees can identify.*[21]
>
> *. . . We faced three main challenges during the integration process. First of all, there was the human dimension. We had to bring together two different management teams and two rather different cultures, which was quite difficult. One should not forget that from one day to the next, former competitors had suddenly become colleagues, and had to work closely with each other. This created a potential for intra-staff and intra-managerial friction. . . .*
>
> *Secondly, we had to act very quickly on the selection of the new IT platform, and the conversion of the redundant platform, as we had to be ready for the upcoming Y2K. . . . Thirdly . . . due to the "merger of equals" nature of the transaction within [banking] we had to deal with the duplication of products, pricing HR policies, etc., which often looked similar but rarely were the same. This situation forced us not only to make a selection decision on one of these above issues, but also to train the other 50% of the staff from the merged organization who were unfamiliar with these.*
>
> *I would identify the following as the key success factors regarding integration for PCC [Private and Corporate Clients]:*
>
> - *Strong leadership: we received from the start unconditional support in our goals from UBS AG's top management, notably Marcel Ospel. And*

we (PCC senior managers) delivered throughout the integration process a unified and consistent message that was effectively driven down through the ranks of the division.

- *Sustaining staff motivation: by breaking-up the seemingly enormous list of integration tasks into more-manageable sub-tasks, thereby helping to create for staff deliverables that were relatively more "easy wins" and/or more measurable. This supported the momentum of the integration process by keeping employees narrowly focused on their objectives, rewarding them for their efforts, and pushing them to "deliver" more.*
- *Comprehensive integration capabilities: a full-time integration office provided a critical coordinating and control role regarding the project management of the integration process. One particularly effective integration tool developed by the integration office was the launch and circulation of the integration newsletter, a bi-weekly and then monthly magazine that featured lead articles on new appointments within PCC and the wider Group, HR policies, and other relevant information affecting staff.*[22]

Execution of Postmerger Integration in the Investment Banking Division

The integration process within the investment banking division varied somewhat by area (corporate finance, equities, fixed income, etc.). For instance, in fixed income, both sides brought strengths to the new operation and the integration was more of a merger of equals. John Costas (the current chairman and CEO of UBS Warburg) became Global Co-Head of Fixed Income, rising from the ex-UBS side. In corporate finance, the SBC Warburg side dominated the ex-UBS side. Robert Gillespie, Joint Global Head of Investment Banking for UBS Warburg, described the integration challenges and process in corporate finance:

> *UBS did not run its CF [corporate finance] business as SBCWDR [SBC Warburg Dillon Read] did, and was also significantly smaller and rather more staff-intensive. . . . The processes between SBCWDR and UBS in CF also differed sharply. . . . It was obvious that the bulk of the new CF platform would be provided by SBCWDR. Therefore, we decided not to favor a merger of equals in this area and "beauty parade" the top 30–40 jobs, as it would have created too much instability across both banks. Furthermore, we realized that some significant staff reductions would have to be made in the former UBS CF area. . . .*
>
> *Once the necessary staff reductions in CF had been made, a single European business had to be forged from both the former SBCWDR and UBS entities. The decision was taken that all Managing Directors had to meet once a month across different main European centers, which we felt would help strengthen bonds and relationships within the business. . . . Another initiative that facilitated the integration process on both sides was the introduction of a mentoring system providing an early warning of dissatisfied key personnel. This helped us to act pre-emptively and try to address disaffection early on prior to actual staff departure. . . . Lastly, I would add that a key success factor for the UBS-SBC merger . . . was the natural pre-selection of the managers*

responsible for the integration process. Most of these . . . had other serious professional options to be elsewhere . . . but rather stayed on for other reasons to try to make the deal work.[23]

CONCLUSION: INTEGRATION IS TRANSFORMATION

This chapter argues three main ideas:

1. ***Strategy.*** The business rationale for the merger should be the foundation for integration strategy. The chapter outlines three dimensions along which integration strategy could be modeled: autonomy, interdependence, and control.
2. ***Implementation*** succeeds through a process of planning and execution. Speed, determination, and communication are vital attributes of successful implementation phases since employees, customers, suppliers, and investors focus on the personal implications of the deal—this internal focus can have a deadening influence on the integration efforts. "Me issues" cannot be ignored but should be dealt with quickly.
3. ***Integration is transformation.*** Planning for postmerger integration must begin with the recognition that the changes needed are not marginal, small, or casual. Instead, they demand the same skills that one observes in major corporate makeovers.

   Transformation is driven by strategic turbulence. To really understand the drivers and challenges of postmerger integration, start by understanding the strategic turbulence that motivated the acquisition effort in the first place. As argued in Chapter 4, merger activity is motivated not by opportunism, but by a need to respond to a strategic problem or opportunity. Begin by understanding the forces that shaped that problem or opportunity. The related insight is that transformation is best managed as a change of the entire *system*. Absorption of one firm into another is radical change, not change at the margin. Numerous case studies of transformation efforts illustrate the importance of the interplay of elements within the system that is the firm. Inevitably, tinkering with only one part of the system perturbs other parts. From this perspective, piecewise, marginal, corporate change may leave the enterprise worse off than before.

   Finally, transformation requires being sustained by leadership from the top, middle, and bottom. This serves as a useful reminder to planners and managers of postmerger integration: Patience and perseverance matter immensely in the successful conclusion of these efforts.

NOTES

1. Gregg Wirth, "At Salomon Smith Barney, Making Enemies the Old-Fashioned Way," thestreet.com, March 31, 1999, 1:07 P.M. Used with permission © 1999 TheStreet.com, all rights reserved.
2. Till Vestring, Brian King, and Ted Rouse, "Should You Always Merge Cultures?," *Harvard Management Update*, May 2003, page 10.

3. Ibid., pages 10 and 11.
4. *The World of Banking*, July–August 1992, page 18, quoted in Jeanne Liedtka, "Banc One Corporation: The Evolution of Partnership," Darden Case Collection, Darden Graduate Business School (e-mail: dardencases@virginia.edu; UVA-BP-0335).
5. John B. McCoy was the CEO of Banc One during its period of growth by acquisition.
6. "The Magnificent McCoys: Running America's Best Bank," *Institutional Investor*, July 1991, quoted in Liedtka, "Banc One Corporation."
7. Hugh McColl was CEO of NationsBank during its period of growth by acquisition. For a profile of McColl, see the digital case study, "Hugh McColl and NationsBank: Building a National Footprint through Acquisition," Darden Case Collection (e-mail: dardencases@virginia.edu; UVA-F-1398-M).
8. Linda Grant and Suzanne Barlyn, "Here Comes Hugh," *Fortune*, August 21, 1995, page 42.
9. Interview of Hugh McColl with Robert Bruner, June 18, 2002.
10. Russ Banham, "The Warren Buffett School," *Chief Executive*, December 2002, downloaded from www.robertpmiles.com/BuffettSchool.htm, May 19, 2003.
11. Claudia H. Deutsch, "The Deal Is Done: The Work Begins, Practicing the Steps Even before the Dance," *New York Times*, April 11, 1999, Section 3, page 1. Copyright © 1999 by the New York Times Co. Reprinted with permission.
12. "The New Art of the Deal: How Leading Organizations Realize Value from Transactions," KPMG white paper, 1999, page 15.
13. Michael F. Spratt and Mark L. Feldman, *Five Frogs on a Log*, New York: HarperCollins, 1999, page 22.
14. These seven points are abstracted from Spratt and Feldman, ibid. The ensuing discussion of each point is my own.
15. KPMG (1999), page 3.
16. Booz-Allen and Hamilton (2001), page 4.
17. "UBS" hereafter refers to Union Bank of Switzerland, one of the two parties to the merger. "UBS A.G." hereafter refers to "Newco," the new company emerging from the merger.
18. Quotation and the following 14 points are abstracted from UBS A.G. internal document by Michael Sweeney, "Cross-Border Merger Management: Lessons from UBS AG," Master Class, Lucerne, May 31, 2000. The ensuing discussion of each point is mine.
19. Interview of Marcel Ospel by Robert Bruner, March 3, 2003.
20. Michael Sweeney, quoting "Mergers and Acquisitions Survey" by Watson Wyatt, May 4, 1999.
21. Interview, March 3, 2003.
22. Interview of Stephan Haeringer by Klaus Durrer and David Remmers, November 15, 2002, and January 16, 2003, UBS A.G. archives, pages 4–8.
23. Interview of Robert Gillespie, Joint Global Head of Investment Banking at UBS Warburg by Klaus Durrer and David Remmers, July 30, 2002, UBS A.G. archives.

CHAPTER 37

Corporate Development as a Strategic Capability: The Approach of GE Power Systems

INTRODUCTION

Active buyers show increasing attention to the codification of skills, the retention of learnings, and the conscious creation of a talent pool that actively seeks to implement the development strategy of the firm. This is a significant direction in the field of M&A. Such a trend succeeds if the development activity itself assumes the importance of a *strategic capability*. This is a radically different view of business development and corporate M&A. A strategic capability is a set of skills, know-how, or special insight that generates competitive advantage and high returns, creates organizational agility, and is difficult to imitate. Chapter 6 discusses strategic capabilities in more detail.

This chapter addresses the possibility that the corporate business development activity could assume the status of a strategic capability for a firm. Researchers have argued that various elements of the M&A process—such as due diligence, negotiation, and valuation—should be developed for their capability potential. Leading companies are pursuing such a goal. This chapter offers a profile of an active acquirer that exemplifies many of the practices suggested throughout this book and, more importantly, *integrates* its various business development processes well. This example offers a number of lessons for business development practitioners.

BUSINESS DEVELOPMENT AT GE POWER SYSTEMS

As of 2003, the Power Systems division (GEPS) was one of the largest business units of General Electric, accounting for $23 billion in revenues in 2002. Its strategy was to span the whole energy chain "from wellhead to consumer," focusing on oil and gas, power generation, and energy management technologies. John Rice, CEO of GEPS, reported to Jeffrey Immelt, CEO of the company. David Tucker, general manager of business development for GEPS, reported to John Rice and oversaw a staff operation of professional employees. From 1995 to 2000, GEPS acquired 45 firms, adding $4 billion in revenue contribution to the core business. In 2001 alone, GEPS completed 25 transactions: 17 acquisitions, 3 minority buyouts, and 5 equity investments. The pace of acquisition reflected growth goals for GEPS set by Rice and Immelt: Growth by acquisition was used to complement organic growth of the business units. In 2002, GEPS approached 253 firms and ultimately closed nine transactions. Tucker determined that 70 percent of GEPS's acquisitions were successful judged on the basis of meeting both strategic and financial goals in the years after closing. Some 95 percent of the deals met their strategic goals. In Tucker's mind, the key criterion for success was whether GEPS would be willing to do the deal again. This reflected close involvement with the deals and their operating managers, attention to outcomes, integration activities, and the performance of audits on all deals.

Business development at GEPS featured several attributes:

- *Consistency of processes.* Dave Tucker emphasized that a foundation of the business development processes at GEPS was consistency of approach, reflected in the use of standardized valuation models and presentation templates, as well as the use of a common decision framework that required standard information and certain criteria applied consistently.
- *Active knowledge management.* Through digitization and various process tools, GEPS business development leaders shared knowledge across the staff and across time. A data retrieval system stored data, analyses, and presentations for future use and comparison. This permitted better use of repetitive M&A expertise. Web-based tools helped to manage *deal process* and better integrate work efforts. They also deepened business development planning and oversight.
- *Continuous improvement mind-set.* Dave Tucker sought to focus quality improvement efforts on six areas: deal origination, deal cycle time, due diligence, acquisition integration, and synergies. He hired Joe Such, a master black belt[1] in Total Quality Management, to map processes and leverage the six sigma approach to transaction process improvement. This resulted in better tools and models, and linkage among data and pitch books. Joe Such told me, "Six sigma looks at everything you do as a process. This is straightforward to do in manufacturing operations. But to apply it to commercial activities is revolutionary. In Business Development we measure our process activities in terms of life cycle (how long it takes to develop each deal), stages of review and approval, integration success, and analysis of failures (e.g., on valuation, technical synergies, and integration). In the past, Business Development was not process-focused; each professional was a sole operator and there was a lower volume of deals. Dave Tucker wanted to operationalize the Business Development function and operate at a higher pace. Now, 5 percent of the staff is focused on process improvement. The payback has been unbelievable."
- *Top-down and bottom-up deal pipeline.* Jerry Miller, business development leader, said, "We used to rely on ideas from the sales force and marketing. This only produced low-hanging fruit. Now, by defining competitive spaces from a top-down view and by making our own contacts, we can produce a richer set of ideas."
- *Senior management engagement.* The GEPS senior leadership spent three to four hours every Friday reviewing the deals in progress. These meetings focused on new deal origination, transaction reviews of information from due

- diligence research, ownership from the operating managers, signing of agreements, and reviews of postacquisition integration and subsequent progress. GE CEO Jeffrey Immelt reviewed the business development activities of GEPS once each month.

Dave Tucker hired 28 new staff members to do the front-end work in business development; these were people most familiar with the industry and opportunities faced by the operating units and also brought transaction experience in law and tax. The GEPS Business Development staff was organized into three levels, business development leaders (such as John Cataldo and Jerry Miller who reported directly to Dave Tucker and had measurable growth targets in terms of revenues and operating margin contribution), managers, and associates.

DEAL PROCESS AT GE POWER SYSTEMS

Transaction management followed roughly four stages: setting strategy, developing the deal, integrating the target, and auditing the results.

Setting Strategy for M&A: Goals and Criteria

The process of discovering new acquisition opportunities originated from either of two sources. First, the Business Development staff could assess a current business unit and design a broad new vision for it. The staff would meet with the operating unit managers in "workout," a business meeting at which they talked through the issues. John Cataldo said, "We have three people from Business Development and six from the operating business unit. We say, 'Here's the strategy. Here's where we think we might get growth.' Then we identify business segments where we know enough to make intelligent decisions, and where we don't know enough. We highlight the players in the relevant segments. This generates a list of maybe 20 to 40 firms. We'll already know many of them. We prioritize the list. That is one way to set the agenda."

Second, the business development process could emerge from the annual planning cycle of the firm. John Cataldo said, "The whole GE culture is centered on establishing a strategy and plan, and signing up for commitments. Commitments take the form of numerical targets as well as qualitative goals regarding operations and strategy. John Rice likes to see the operating leader and lieutenants 'sign up' for goals. In January of each year, operating managers begin a 'bottom-up' planning process with John Rice that looks at each business over the next three years. This generates a lengthy document for each business that sets the organic and inorganic growth goals for revenues and profits. These growth goals in turn set targets for the business development effort, in terms of industry focus, geographic focus, and the staffing necessary to achieve goals." Notable was the high level of interaction between senior leadership and division managers: Their conversations formed an iterative planning cycle.

The planning cycle focused on using acquisitions to supplement strategic needs. The GEPS current business units were represented in a matrix showing industry segments and product or service offerings in each. Exhibit 37.1 gives an abstraction

EXHIBIT 37.1 Example of Analytical Grid Used for Identifying Targets for Business Development at GE Power Systems

This diagram illustrates the matrix approach to framing acquisition search priorities at GE Power Systems. The two left-hand columns give industry segments of GEPS and subsegments. Each subsegment could be subdivided further, but for simplicity is shown at this level of detail. Arrayed across each subsegment is the range of products and services that might reach a customer. These might include equipment, field service, software, information services, and so on. On the right half of the diagram, numbered rectangles indicate eight acquisition search priorities derived from a strategic assessment of market attractiveness and GE's position. The blank regions represent areas where there is no product or service offering.

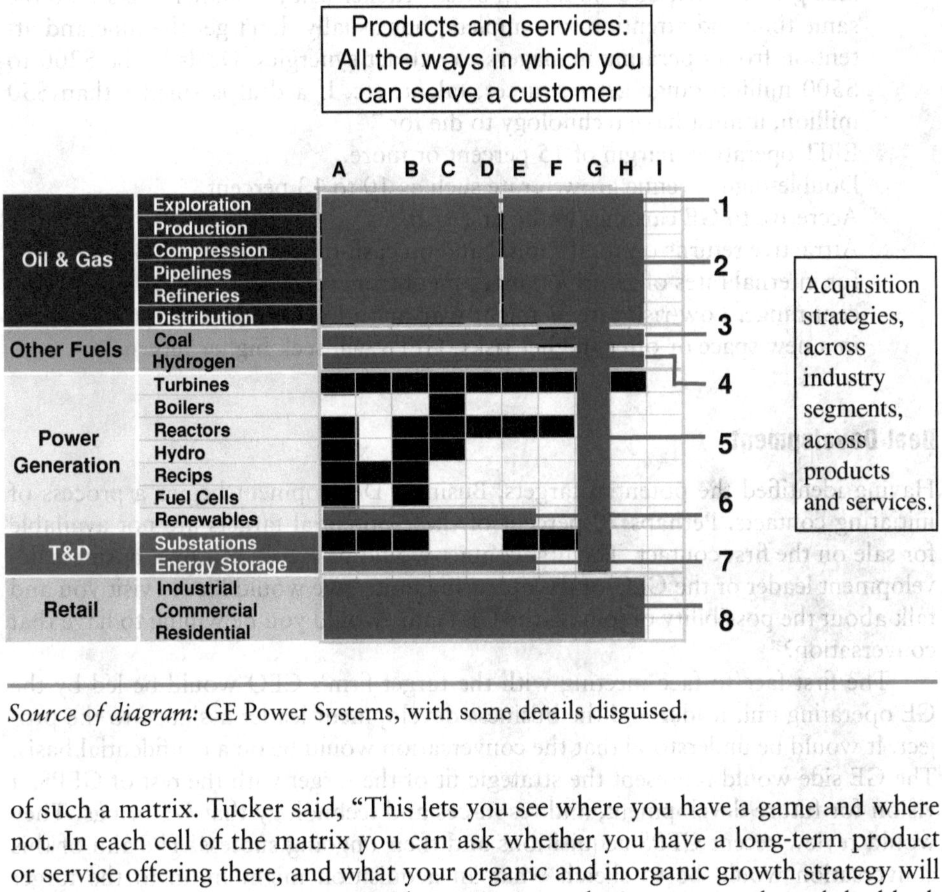

Source of diagram: GE Power Systems, with some details disguised.

of such a matrix. Tucker said, "This lets you see where you have a game and where not. In each cell of the matrix you can ask whether you have a long-term product or service offering there, and what your organic and inorganic growth strategy will be to achieve a serious position." The strategic marketing team evaluated the blank spaces in the matrix, and studied the desirability of competing there. Business Development focuses on helping to fill in the targeted cells.

GEPS cited a number of criteria that formed the basis for screening acquisition opportunities:

- *Strategic fit* with objectives for growth, profitability, and global positioning. The target should be in a current market segment of GEPS or an adjacent segment. As John Rice said, "I don't acquire to get bigger; I acquire to get better."

The target would need to show competitive leadership in a niche segment, and had to do at least one thing well. The target must be very focused.

- *Technology.* GEPS would not simply buy a book of business. A target had to offer a deeper rationale, as in providing a technology or service extension. Dave Tucker said, "We buy technology that expands our game."
- *People.* Talent, experience, and know-how were intangible assets that would augment the attractiveness of a target firm. Quality of people in the target would seriously influence the acquisition decision.
- *Financial considerations.* Finally, the target would be screened against a variety of quantitative criteria.
  - Size greater than $50 million in sales. Tucker said, "Smaller deals take the same time and attention to complete, but usually don't get the time and attention from operating managers to extract synergies. Deals in the $200 to $500 million range get resources, talent, etc. If a deal is smaller than $50 million, it must have technology to die for."
  - EBIT operating margin of 15 percent or more.
  - Double-digit revenue growth rate such as 10 to 13 percent.
  - Accretive to GE earnings in the first year.
  - Attractive returns on total capital and on cash-on-cash returns. GEPS looked for internal rates of return on investment from the upper teens to the 30 percent range. Low-risk targets might warrant a lower IRR. But if the target is in a new space or offers higher risks, GEPS will seek higher returns.

Deal Development

Having identified the potential targets, Business Development begins a process of initiating contacts. Perhaps 70 percent of these potential targets are not available for sale on the first contact. The first contact would be a cold call by a business development leader or the CEO of the operating unit: "We would like to visit you and talk about the possibility of joining the GE team. Would you be willing to have that conversation?"

The first face-to-face meeting with the target firm's CEO would be led by the GE operating unit leader and the business development leader assigned to the project. It would be understood that the conversation would be on a confidential basis. The GE side would represent the strategic fit of the target with the rest of GEPS, a vision for future development, and resources and technology that GE brings. They would review recent GEPS acquisitions and their ongoing success. The aim of this conversation would be to sketch what an acquisition might mean to the target owners in terms of value paid and strategic fit. Also, the first meeting aims to help the target owner surmount the emotional hurdle of selling. Jerry Miller says, "We try to build relationships and know what's important to the seller."

Perhaps another three or four meetings would occur in which GE seeks to build the target's familiarity with GE and comfort with a possible acquisition. John Cataldo says, "We seek to create a relationship and get them comfortable with the GE culture. We invite them to come to GE and meet all our people. We lay out our vision and fit between GE and the target, and ask them to tell us their issues."

Dave Tucker notes that GEPS would seek information from the target firm in three "buckets":

1. An initial request for information about the target firm that would fit on one page. This would be compact enough to avoid overwhelming the target firm managers.
2. At the due diligence stage, the request for information would be substantial, enough to cover the range of deal risks and considerations that might shape the terms.
3. After signing the definitive agreement, GEPS would request information targeted toward integration planning. For instance, this might focus specifically on organization structure and control systems.

As discussions proceed toward development of the first-round documents, Jim Waterbury, senior counsel, and his staff will become involved. He says, "We tend to be involved early in transactions. Our lawyers are an integral part of the BD team; indeed, all functional experts are part of the team. Other companies rely more on outside counsel, and tend to involve them later in the process. Before we enter the letter of intent (LOI) stage, we look for showstoppers such as difficult regulatory problems, restrictions imposed by some other agreement, etc."

When a comfort level is reached, GE and the target firm sign a confidentiality agreement. GE requests basic information about the target, including financials, customer data, technology and patents, organization, head count, and workforce. The target firm may take three weeks to collect the data. Then the business development leader and the CEO of the operating unit visit the company to have a full discussion about the data.

If the information confirms GE's vision for the target, the business development leader and the CEO of the operating unit give a presentation to John Rice, CEO of GEPS. This consists of a summary of the target's lines of business, technology, market size, segments, competitors, strategic fit, synergies, projected financial performance, and valuation based on comparable firms. John Cataldo says, "The point of this presentation is to build a groundswell of support for the acquisition at this early stage. But also, the commitment by the CEO of the operating unit comes here. This is where the operating guys sign up."

With an expression of internal support from John Rice, the business development leader and the CEO of the operating unit proceed to negotiate and sign a LOI. This may take two weeks to three months, and is focused on a term sheet describing the contemplated transaction. Features may include parties to the deal, structure, form of payment, price, adjustments to net asset values, noncompete agreements, amounts to be held in escrow, representations and warranties, applicable law, and exclusivity for GEPS for a period of two to four months.

During the development of the LOI, leadership of the postmerger integration plan is appointed. These appointments represent part of the commitment process and generally frame the tasks that lie ahead. Jerry Miller, business development leader, says, "The integration team always wants to get involved very early in the process. But I like to see them involved later; they often get in the way during due diligence. You can't gun-jump anyway, only plan. They can ask for information that will help with the integration process, but they are less useful in the due diligence phase. There are all kinds of sensitivities with the owners. People say things they shouldn't. This can negatively impact the negotiations. The less they see the integration folks the better. Of course, it's different for every deal."

With a signed letter of intent in hand, GE begins an intense due diligence effort involving a visit by 5 to 50 GE people for one to two weeks at the target firm—the team size and amount of time would depend on the complexity of the target firm opportunity. These people are experts in intellectual property, environmental issues, human resources, finance, law, sales, technology, sourcing, and manufacturing. In addition, GE may bring in outside experts in accounting and law. The target creates a data room[2] that includes the entire list of employees and their demographic information, customer lists with sales histories, detailed financials, work-in-process inventory, and financial information around specific projects with attention given to revenue recognition and to expensing versus capitalizing. This due diligence visit includes interviews with key managers.

Upon the completion of a favorable due diligence report, the deal cycle enters the phase of negotiating the definitive acquisition agreement. GE's business development leader, a GE M&A lawyer, and outside counsel begin with the framework of a standard contract and tailor it to the particular needs of the transaction. This may take one to two weeks of elapsed time. Then the document is delivered to the seller—sometimes this is done in person in order to walk the seller through the contract. Over the next one to four weeks, the document will go through several rounds of markups as the two sides negotiate specific terms.

Before the definitive agreement is signed, the business development leader and operating unit head present the deal again to John Rice. They review the key terms and the due diligence research process and findings, and outline a postmerger integration plan that assigns responsibilities and sets a timetable for integration. GE CEO Jeffrey Immelt and GEPS CEO John Rice approve execution of the definitive agreement, and the deal is signed.

With completion of the definitive agreement, antitrust and other regulatory filings are submitted to the U.S. federal government, state governments, and any foreign governments as may be required. It takes two to three weeks to pull the data together. Then when submitted, a 30-day waiting period ensues for the Hart-Scott-Rodino review. During this period, other details, such as negotiating employment agreements, may be attended to.

Due diligence research informs the postmerger integration challenge. Integration planning becomes rigorous between signing the definitive agreement and closing. It covers topics as disparate as human resources; benefits planning; plans for communications with customers, employees, and the public; a commercial plan; and a celebration kickoff.

The closing of the agreement occurs between the sellers and the business development leader and a GE lawyer. Funds are wired to the bank accounts of the sellers.

The cycle-time target is 19 weeks from the start of serious discussions through signing of the definitive agreement. Progress through the deal cycle would be monitored for flagging problem areas and failures in understanding. The range of deal cycles extends up to 30 weeks. Deal monitoring seeks to understand the drivers of this range, with the aim of minimizing the variance. If a deal has to be killed, it is preferable for it to fail fast.

Postmerger Integration

Dave Tucker argued that "more than half the success in any deal will be due to integration. It starts with getting the integration leadership into the deal early on, and identifying resources early. The deal doesn't close unless you have leadership identified." He convened an Acquisition Integration Council to ensure that all GEPS deals were employing consistent processes. Business Development provided deal resources in the form of a team of 50 to 60 professionals. This team spanned strategic planning, marketing, finance (for postintegration control), legal, and human resources areas. An *integrity briefing* was scheduled early in each integration process. Tucker said, "There is not one target we've bought that hasn't adopted our *"Spirit & Letter" compliance* policies and practices, and our GE-wide initiatives on quality, globalization, and management practices."

Well before closing the integration leader would be assigned. The integration team leader was not the business leader for the reason that the business leader could not be distracted from running the entire business. The integration leader would be given a one-week intensive training course covering the tasks, assignments, and measurement of progress, including use of the "e-integration" Web-based tool for monitoring progress against goals. This showed the status of progress in the integration on 6,500 measured items, and indicated in colors the attention they deserved: red for less than 95 percent of goal, yellow for 95 to 99 percent, and green for 100 percent. John Rice and Dave Tucker follow integration progress each week.

Business Development organized Centers of Excellence (COEs) that focused on guiding integration in each function. Tucker said, "We looked at past deals and found repetitive activities, such as getting on the GE payroll, connecting with benefits, getting on the intranet, etc. So we organized small teams in each function that go through and hook up the pipes. The COEs take out the bulk of the work."

Postaudit

The business development cycle did not end with the close of the deal or the integration process. The BD unit performed postacquisition audits on all deals, focusing on whether the integration was completed and the extent to which the new unit was following all policies and procedures. Of special interest was reporting transparency (i.e., the avoidance of special reserves or slush funds). Also of careful attention was observance of GE's Integrity Policy, that training had occurred, that the new employees understood it, and that they were following it.

Mini-Case: The Acquisition of Alpha Company

In February 2002, GEPS closed the acquisition of Alpha Company.[3] GEPS had been watching the company for many years and respected its technology. Alpha was used as a supplier to two of the GEPS operating units. The company was privately held and growing smoothly. The history of this acquisition illustrates the timing and phases of the acquisition process.

In 1998, business development leaders of GEPS had first approached the owner of Alpha. He was over 70 years old and the original inventor of the proprietary technology used by the firm. The response by the owner was negative, so the deal development process was suspended.

In 2001, GEPS approached again. A follow-up contact revealed that one of the two co-owners was interested in now exploring a possible sale to GEPS. The GEPS leadership team developed a strategy for educating the owner about GEPS, the benefits of a deal with GEPS, GE's technology position, and Alpha's future with GEPS. This began a sustained wooing process in which John Cataldo emphasized that GE was a technology company, like the target firm.

GEPS began a full-court press in June 2001. It flew the target company principal and his lawyer to GE's Global Research Center in Schenectady to show them the firm's R&D programs and then took them to manufacturing plants in Schenectady and Greenville, South Carolina. Finally, they flew them to visit a service facility for remote monitoring and diagnostics. John Rice told them, "You need to decide: Is now the time? Are we the people? If so, give us your thoughts on price and structure." The sellers wanted to be bought at a multiple like GE's, which suggested a price of $500 million. John Rice replied that GE was willing to pay for value and would need to get closer to Alpha's numbers in order to prepare an offer.

In August 2001, GEPS signed a confidentiality agreement with Alpha and launched a preliminary due diligence effort. Business development leaders spent a day with Alpha's owner, technology leader, COO, CFO, and lawyer. Tucker, Cataldo, and a senior GE technology executive assessed Alpha's strategy and built pro forma forecasts of financial performance. The analysis suggested a value of $350 to $400 million for the firm.

In August 2002, John Cataldo presented the deal to John Rice for his pre-LOI approval. Cataldo also presented the transaction to GE's CEO, Jeffrey Immelt. Dave Tucker recalled, "We got Immelt's buy-in early in the deal cycle. Immelt approved a value range to work with and possible terms." From GEPS's side the value of the proposal was $350 million; from Alpha's side the value looked more like $425 million. John Rice and the principals of Alpha signed a letter of intent that month.

In October 2001, the GEPS business development team conducted due diligence research on the company and negotiated the definitive agreement. John Rice said that usually GE floods the target firm with 20 to 40 due diligence researchers. But in this instance, he was reluctant to scare the seller with a demanding due diligence process. Furthermore, GEPS knew the target well from years of a supplier relationship; this gave John Rice comfort about the target. Accordingly, he assigned five people the task of finding any major deal breakers within a space of five days.

In November 2001, the two sides signed the definitive agreement. The elapsed time from LOI to signing the agreement was 19 weeks, the target. The signing set in motion two new efforts. First was the submission of regulatory documents in the United States and 10 foreign countries. The process of seeking regulatory clearance lasted from April to July. The second process was the integration planning effort—this was formally launched on expiration of the 30-day Hart-Scott-Rodino waiting period.

The agreement was consummated in late February 2002, about six months after the serious contact.

THE M&A "FACTORY": OPERATIONALIZING BUSINESS DEVELOPMENT

Rob de Michiei, finance manager of the business development unit at GEPS, said, "Unless you do deals every day, it's very difficult to do things right. You learn something from every deal and need to pour it back into the next deal. Most acquisitions are poorly done and thought out, and that's why. We built a factory for business development that eliminates variation. Our deals use the same templates and metrics. Business development is not just a series of one-off transactions, but rather is a process that you use every day."

Dave Tucker was especially proud of the digitization process for business development at GEPS. He described four resources that this initiative had developed:

1. ***E-deal room.*** This Web-based system tracked deal progress, showing their progress against cycle targets, status, and facts and financials. It offered chat rooms for professionals to compare and inquire.
2. ***Company tracker.*** This Web-based system showed a wish list of companies and their competitors, and when a company's value might be in a feasible range for affordability.
3. ***Equity tracker.*** This Web-based system permitted executives to follow minority equity investments made by GEPS. It gave summaries of board meetings and financial progress of companies.
4. ***Due diligence tools.*** This system offered key questions to ask early in the company contact process as well as questions for deeper research during the formal due diligence period. Good due diligence also afforded the information necessary to support good integration efforts.

The other aspect of the operationalization of business development at GEPS was the use of Centers of Excellence to perform functions that are common and repeatable across transactions. For instance, audit, tax, and valuation analyses were required in every deal and could therefore be conducted by a dedicated team who would bring standard best practice to each transaction.

Finally, business development at GEPS relied on frequent meetings that shared information and helped to build alignment of the BD staff. Every Thursday was a "Quick Market Intelligence" meeting. On Fridays, Dave Tucker and John Rice met to review progress of deals and of postmerger integrations.

IMPLICATIONS FOR BEST PRACTICE

This profile of GE Power Systems' business development unit suggests some attributes of business development as a strategic capability.

- ***Process focus.*** Many business development managers are charged with finding targeted amounts of new earnings each year. This readily leads to a quota-fulfilling mentality that impairs the quality of thinking and of deals. One response is to systematize a process of checking in the form of meetings with business development leaders, research guidelines, and so on. GEPS's focus on process improvement is a telltale about the importance of a process orientation. To devote a black belt in Total Quality Management to assessing and improving the deal development process is evidence of a process focus.

- ***Discipline.*** This reflects itself in at least two areas. First is the adherence to a consistent process approach for business development. Dave Tucker emphasized that the process discipline lent great flexibility toward the creative design of deals. He said, "We use the discipline to solve the seller's problem." The discipline signals what is important, such as the five key drivers of success outlined in Chapter 1: strategy, value creation, organizational development, law, and ethics. Best practitioners build in checks and balances to fight deal frenzy and the winner's curse.
- ***Having a view of the world.*** Best practice business development is not opportunistic, seeking to acquire any target simply because it is available or has an attractive price. Capable business development begins with a strategic view that motivates the entire process. The view becomes a benchmark against which the target is evaluated, the deal is designed, and the process assessed. In the case of GE Power Systems this view is manifest in the strategic grid and the aim to assert that certain cells are attractive and others not.
- ***Integrated teams, not silos of expertise.*** Consistent with the numerous drivers of M&A success, a "best practice" business development approach is to integrate the efforts of many specialties in the development of transactions. Under CEO Jack Welch, GE became a proponent of the "boundaryless" organization. Consistent with a focus on process and integration of effort, a "best practice" business development approach will be team-based. The requisites for well-functioning teams have been discussed extensively elsewhere, though one aspect is worth highlighting: Good teams are led, not managed. Leaders, in particular, are needed to constantly set vision, communicate, build teams, and shape the processes.
- ***Sufficient infrastructure.*** Another dimension of good practice is the provision of support in the form of information technology, analytic talent, and expertise. The combination of *infrastructure* and teams gives the business development activity its agility.
- ***Commitment.*** This plays a central role. It has been said that an obligation that is owned by many is owned by none. The problem in many firms is that an acquisition gains only the vague acquiescence of what many individuals must do to make it a success. The good business development process is one of special commitment-building and commitment-giving. Due diligence research plays a central role in providing the fact basis for commitments. Approvals go forward only with the name(s) of managers who will be responsible for delivering on those outlooks.
- ***An early start for integration of the target.*** At GEPS, planning begins shortly after the operating manager gives commitment to performance goals, which is about the time of the LOI. Early integration efforts can raise questions that motivate due diligence research, and in any event proceed to resolve the open issues that can stall realization of synergies.
- ***Knowledge management.*** Finally, what makes a business development unit into a capability is the capacity of a firm to learn across successive deals, to build

best practice from the learnings, to share new information in real time, to access specialized expertise when needed, and to think critically about past successes and failures.

These criteria set a high standard for the management of the business development function within a firm. But are they applicable to all firms? Some things to think about are:

- Capability development is costly in terms of time, money, and talent. Do you have these resources? Can you get them?
- Is the capability model scalable? Given the higher costs and resources required, perhaps this model is relevant for only the most active acquirers. Yet we have seen in other industries the scalability of models that are focused mainly on processes. It remains to be seen whether smaller buyers can follow this model.
- The capability model may be more valuable where you have a focused strategy, as in GEPS's focus on power systems and technology. Perhaps it is less relevant for business development operations where focus is not so important (e.g., a holding company, pure conglomerate, or LBO shop).
- Focus really is the key. Do you *have a view* that permits a sharp focus? How confident are you that it is right?

NOTES

1. Six sigma was developed by Motorola in the mid-1980s as a method of improving manufacturing quality based on careful statistical measurement and business process reengineering. "Black belts" are full-time Total Quality Management practitioners trained and certified in the six sigma techniques.
2. See Chapter 8 for more discussion of the data room and the due diligence process.
3. Names and some dates have been disguised.

CHAPTER 38

M&A "Best Practices": Some Lessons and Next Steps

INTRODUCTION

The premise for this book is fundamentally (although cautiously) optimistic: Good M&A practices can be identified and adopted—and if employed well they can become part of a masterful repertoire of *best practices*. This final chapter aims to revisit some good practices highlighted in previous chapters and to synthesize them into a view about best practice in M&A. The field is too complicated and rapidly changing to offer a definitive expression. But this chapter aims to focus the work of practitioners in ways to promote success.

A second objective of this chapter is to acknowledge frankly some things we know and others that we don't understand yet. Both practitioners and scholars should appreciate the limits of our knowledge and how these constrain advancement of the field. I will highlight this with 10 examples.

The final goal of this chapter is to direct the reader to other resources that, in my experience, have proved to be especially useful in training good practitioners. The literature about M&A is vast and enormous. Described here are a number of worthwhile readings in M&A, the "classics," which offer lessons that an M&A professional should strive to absorb.

SOME ELEMENTS OF M&A BEST PRACTICE

There may be many maxims that outline what actually constitutes a "best practice" in M&A. The following are my nominees for the top 10. These have been argued in the preceding chapters.

1. *Think like an investor.* Unsuccessful deals have many causes, but I believe the most common is to forget whom you are working for and what you are trying to achieve. Chapter 9 outlines what it means to think like an investor. Doing so brings rigor and discipline to analysis, negotiation, and deal design. The essence of this view is to focus on the creation of value for shareholders in a way that is consistent with integrity. Numerous other chapters have echoed this theme. Whenever you get confused about deal evaluation, this is a useful point from which to refocus.

2. ***Take a "whole deal" perspective.*** Chapter 1 invites the practitioner to look at a range of effects of a deal; wealth creation should top the list, but others should include strategic benefits, a strengthened organization, and so on. Just as I recommend taking a wide-angle view, I strongly warn the M&A practitioner against focusing too narrowly on one or two items in a deal. Instead, it is advisable to look at the entire package and strive to find trade-offs that make both the buyer and seller better off—this is an idea conveyed in Chapter 18. Chapter 13 presents the argument that the "whole deal" perspective should bid one to study the payoffs and costs to *all* the participants in a deal—this is a way to guard against hidden wealth transfers. To be a best practitioner is to adopt a rigorous and comprehensive point of view.
3. ***Aim to create value rather than claim value.*** Some assume that each M&A deal is merely a wrestling match for value: a zero-sum game in which any value for your side comes out of the pockets of the other side. An alternative view—espoused in Chapters 18, 21, and 30—is that it is possible to design deals that create value for *both* sides—these are the so-called win-win transactions. To look for joint gains takes strong analytical capabilities and a creative mind-set. In the long run, the best reputations are associated with win-win deals.
4. ***Develop a "view" and play the game.*** Best practitioners understand the competitive nature of M&A. How should one compete? Start with an understanding of one's mission and strategy, informed by careful assessment of the environment. Next, think about one's counterparts in the merger setting: What are their current positions and interests? Then identify the key bets or assumptions in the setting—these are expected changes in the environment or in the operating prospects of the firm that have the potential to be the most significant drivers of expected outcomes. Do the research necessary to form your own opinion, your view, about how these factors are likely to play out. Taking a view is one of the hardest steps of all: It feels risky. But can you really be an agnostic? As Harvey Cox said, "Not to decide is to decide." To *not* take a view is to decide passively to put yourself in the hands of your counterparty or at the will of the larger economic forces. Effective management begins with having a view or outlook to lend discipline to your thinking.
5. ***Find and use optionality.*** Options thinking is a powerful lens through which to view M&A. Though more complicated than other kinds of analysis surveyed in this book, it yields some extremely valuable insights about how to manage risk and difference of opinion. Chapters 10, 14, 15, 22, 23, and 33 illustrate a number of practical applications. Because options thinking is in its infancy in M&A and not widely applied, thoughtful practitioners who can wield options concepts in framing their M&A strategies may gain a meaningful advantage over those who don't.
6. ***Resist earnings management and momentum-acquiring.*** Chapters 16 and 17 explore the choices that CEOs can make in reporting the results of individual deals, and entire growth programs. The policies allowable under GAAP are wide enough to permit reporting the firm's financial results under very aggressive assumptions. While some of these practices may be technically legal, they can contribute to the creation of unsustainable expectations. As Mark Twain said, "Tell the truth. It will aggravate your enemies, and astonish the rest." After Sarbanes-Oxley, there may be less ability to do otherwise.

7. ***Temper determinism with behaviorism.*** Beginning with Chapter 1, the book emphasizes that M&A success resides not entirely "in the numbers." Outcomes are driven not just by structural issues like strategy, economics, and law—they are also influenced by *conduct* or behavioral factors. Whereas the NPV in a spreadsheet may be comfortingly positive, actually realizing it will depend on issues, such as recruiting, organizing, motivating, compensating, monitoring, and leading employees.
8. ***Focus on process, then outcome.*** This is especially relevant for team leaders, business development professionals, and CEOs. Many chapters emphasized that deal design is a creative activity. To focus on outcomes is to leap to conclusions before all the facts are known and all possible solutions have been explored. The process management of M&A development can even become a strategic capability for a company, as Chapter 37 illustrates. The framework developed throughout the text is that effective deals arise from a process that begins with listening to markets and companies, followed by episodes of research, due diligence, valuation, deal design, and negotiation. The adept deal leader sees the opportunities to leverage the possibly beneficial *interactions* among all of these processes.
9. ***Master the tools and concepts, but also get help.*** The level of technical mastery varies greatly across M&A professionals. People at the front line of M&A deal development should have a command of the tools and concepts in this book. But even those who are technically proficient should call on the assistance of specialists in fields such as tax, accounting, strategy, integration, negotiation, and valuation when necessary.
10. ***Practice with integrity.*** M&A is loaded with opportunities to improve your own standing through unethical behavior. The book sketches some of these, including earnings management (Chapters 2 and 16), self-dealing (Chapter 26), lying in negotiations (Chapter 30), and managerial entrenchment (Chapters 32 and 33). Sometimes this is met with a shrug of the shoulders and a "That's business!" attitude. But the point of best practice is not to confirm the way things are, but rather to show who we might become. And it should elevate the profession by example.

These practices return us to the framework of deal success discussed in Chapter 1. As Exhibit 38.1 suggests, the practices operate mainly on the conduct of M&A, the part of the problem where you have the most influence. The big lesson of these practices and of the diagram is that the best practitioners take the world on their terms: They operate according to insights garnered from experience and research rather than "the way it's always done."

WHERE THE SIDEWALK ENDS

Chapter 13 uses the phrase "terra incognita" to refer to a region beyond our knowledge. Arguably, most of M&A is on the border between *cognita* and *incognita*—best practitioners understand that they always go together: What we know raises more questions. The implication of this is to retain an openness to new ideas,

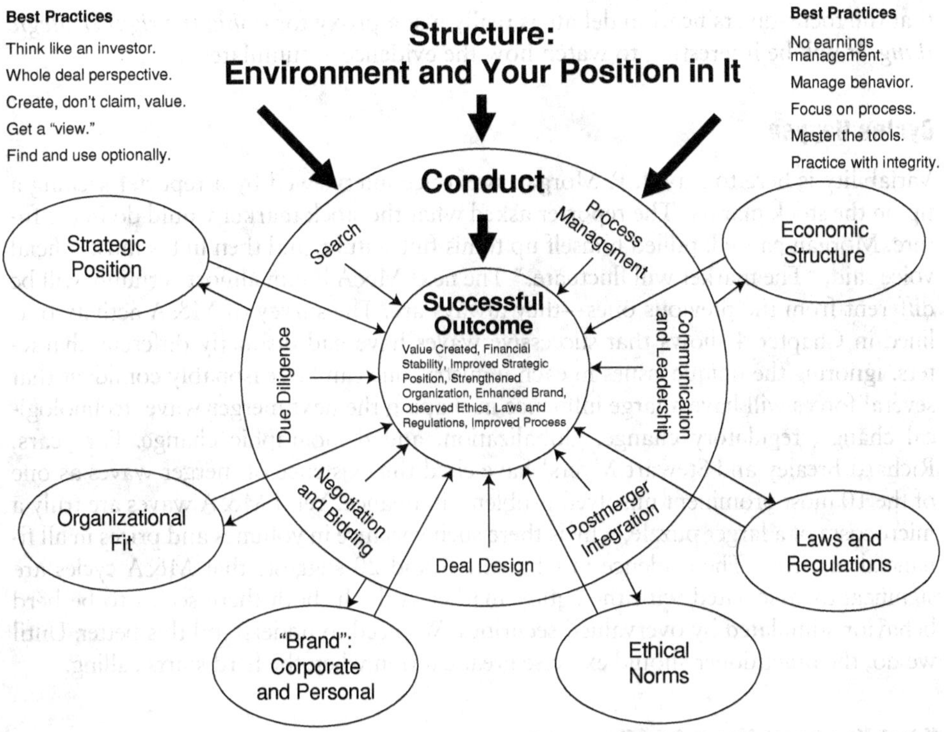

EXHIBIT 38.1 Best Practices Help Drive M&A Success

a critical view of them, and ultimately a sense of humility to remind us that at best, one sees the field through a glass darkly. To illustrate the point, here are my nominations for the most interesting areas for future contribution to the evolution of best practice—each is rooted in something we know and invites more research.

Yes, M&A Pays, But . . .

Chapter 3 summarizes the findings of 134 surveys and studies and concluded that, in contrast to the claim of many pundits, M&A pays buyers about as well as other forms of corporate investment. That is, most deals appear to at least cover the cost of capital. Yet this is based on averages, around which one sees a relatively wide variance of outcomes. What causes the good, the bad, and the ugly? And though we know about the failures, who are the exemplars? What can we learn from *them*?

Focus Is Good, But . . .

Chapter 6 discusses the debate over the profitability of strategies of focus versus strategies of diversification. Conventional wisdom has held that focusing the activities of the firm pays better than diversifying. Yet interesting new evidence questions the measurements that produced the conventional wisdom, and raises the possibility that the focus-diversification debate is really just a proxy for *doing the right strategic thing*. It will be interesting to watch how the evidence accumulates here.

Cycles Happen

Variability is here to stay. J. P. Morgan was once interviewed by a reporter seeking a tip on the stock market. The reporter asked what the stock market would do in the future. Morgan paused, pulled himself up to his full stature, and then in his most official voice said, "The market will fluctuate." The next M&A boom almost certainly will be different from the previous ones—they always are. The survey of M&A activity outlined in Chapter 4 shows that successive waves have had distinctly different characters. Ignoring the unique issues in each industry, one can be reasonably confident that several forces will have a large influence in shaping the next merger wave: technological change, regulatory change, globalization, and demographic change. For years, Richard Brealey and Stewart Myers[1] have cited the existence of merger waves as one of the 10 most prominent unsolved problems in finance. Yet if M&A waves are truly a microcosm of a larger puzzle, why is there such variance in volumes and prices in all financial markets? The evidence in Chapters 6 and 20 suggests that M&A cycles are significantly associated with the equity market cycle. In both there seems to be herd behavior stimulated by overvalued securities. We need to understand this better. Until we do, the practitioner should exercise great caution when the herd starts calling.

What You Don't Know Can Hurt You

"Information asymmetry" appears at several points in this book to explain:

- Why markets get overheated (Chapter 4).
- Why buyers may choose to pay with equity rather than cash (Chapter 20).
- How wealth gets transferred from some suppliers of capital to others (Chapter 13).
- The motives for risk management (Chapter 23).
- The philosophy of rules for information disclosure (Chapter 27).
- How representations and warranties are used (Chapter 29).
- How buyers can get burned in negotiations and auctions (Chapters 30 and 31).
- How access to information can affect the target search process (Chapter 7), due diligence (Chapter 8), and communication of the deal (Chapter 35).

The very strong emphasis in this book is on the value of research and analysis: *Do your homework*. The best practitioners are inherently good fundamental analysts. Still, understanding how to deal with information asymmetry is still in its infancy. The 2002 Nobel Prize in Economics was awarded to the founders of signaling theory, and may offer a continuing stimulus for research on the effect of information asymmetry in fields such as M&A.

Negotiators Trade Off

Consistent with arguments in Chapters 13, 18, and 23, we have evidence that a deal is a system: Having more of some features (like risk management devices or social issue payments) results in having less of another part of the deal (such as price). We do not know much about the efficiency of these trade-offs. One might expect fair trades. But is that what actually happens? If not, why not? Does behavior intervene in helpful or perverse ways? If so, what are the implications for practitioners? The structural design of transactions is as yet a new focus for research in financial economics.

Earnings Get Managed

Research reveals what many practitioners discuss freely, that the use of reserves, write-offs, special purpose entities, and changes in accounting policy can create the appearance of stability or growth when there may be little of either. We need to understand better why this has been such a common (but certainly not "best") practice. Perhaps the most frequent explanation is that executives and boards of directors manage earnings because they are fixated on reported earnings per share (EPS) as a measure of performance. Business schools have been teaching for decades that *cash flow* is a much better criterion for evaluating performance and making resource allocation decisions. What, then, explains the longevity of EPS?

Good Governance Pays. But What Is Good Governance?

Chapters 5 and 26 offer evidence that share prices are higher when firms are managed in the interests of shareholders and when the rule of law ensures the sanctity of contracts and protections for minority shareholders. Yet there is much less consensus on what actually constitutes good corporate governance. How does one judge the elements and functions of corporate governance: board composition and practices; management compensation and incentive systems; shareholder rights to intervene in board and management decisions, and so on? Currently CEOs and regulators are considering a wide range of proposals for changing the governance of firms. Which of these will actually make corporate governance more efficient and effective?

Getting Defensive

Chapter 33 surveys the plethora of antitakeover defenses that firms adopt and acknowledged that we do not have a very clear idea about how and why firms adopt them. They seem to be moderately effective, but at what cost or benefit to their shareholders?

How Much Regulation Is Appropriate?

The system of rules and laws dealing with governance, securities issuance, and antitrust seems to have worked reasonably well, though we will never know how it might have functioned with less regulation. Any such system evolves much more slowly than markets change and than entrepreneurs invent new techniques. The current trend of the past 30 years toward deregulation has been checked, if only temporarily, by the landmark events of recent years. What is the cost and/or benefit of merger regulation? Is a continued policy of liberalization warranted?

"What Is the Cost of Capital?"

This question has attained cult status as a joke among scholars and MBA students. Though the models outlined in Chapters 9 and 12 offer guidance, there remains enough room for varying assumptions and judgments in the estimation of capital costs that any two Wall Street analysts are more likely to differ than agree. Most practitioners simply strive to get "close enough" and then turn their focus to issues they can actually resolve. "Close enough" may be acceptable for valuing assets where risk is moderate and well understood. But Chapters 11, 12, and 13 highlight the need to derive capital costs for important special tasks such as valuing synergies, assets across borders, and debt tax shields—here there may be more risk and judgment involved. What is the best practice for estimating the cost of capital?

DEVELOPING BEST PRACTITIONERS

Experience is an excellent teacher, although it often gives the tests first, and the lessons after. In the field of M&A, the lessons can be very costly. Therefore, it makes sense to supplement one's "*learning by doing.*" One of the icons of M&A, Bruce Wasserstein, described the deal development process this way: "What a confused, halting, fumbling spectacle it is. All participants are one-legged men because there is no blueprint, no clarity, and a lot of motion. These are decisions under uncertainty, with high stakes, immature data, and a cyclicality of the views of informed opinion."[2] Most professional managers want to avoid the "confusing, halting, fumbling spectacle," and therefore could benefit from an alternative to trial and error.

First, there is "*learning by watching*": Seek out and develop a working relationship with a professional mentor and watch that person do deals. In addition, you could learn by osmosis by simply hanging around with other active deal doers and listening carefully to what insights they might offer. Another recommended option is to plan and attend professional engagements with the best advisers. Short educational experiences can lend a coherent exposition to the substance of the M&A field. They can also supplement and reinforce your mastery of tools. Many leading business schools offer short courses on M&A for executives (in addition to full-time students).

Second, there is "*learning by reading.*" If you have made it this far in *Applied Mergers and Acquisitions*, you are well down this path. But don't stop here. Exhibit 38.2 gives my list of favorites along with some notes on each. Start a reading program that takes you through these classics. Perhaps you could do this with a friend or team of colleagues. In the professional setting, you could try obtaining the files on some past successes (and failures) at your firm and try to determine why things turned out the way they did.

Finally, there is "*learning from current events.*" A grasp of recent news in M&A is valuable for building a frame of reference for your own development. The daily financial press and/or web sites offer the means for this kind of framing. Several leading newspapers, such as the *Wall Street Journal* and *New York Times*, have online editions that can be set up to send you e-mail about big announcements. Web sites such as www.thedeal.com offer valuable insights into pending deals and

EXHIBIT 38.2 "Best Bet" Readings Relevant to Best Practice in M&A

Introduction

These readings were selected for their readability, content, and practitioner-orientation. Because of the self-imposed constraint of space, it was not possible to include many other worthy citations. Absent are articles written for an audience of scholars, but which, nevertheless, contain many insights for the practitioner. The list of references at the end of the book directs the reader to these valuable resources. The thoughtful practitioner should regard this list as a point of departure, rather than a destination.

Practice

Burrough, B., and J. Helyar, *Barbarians at the Gate: The Fall of RJR Nabisco*, New York: HarperCollins, 1990. This is the riveting story of the auction of RJR Nabisco. It illustrates well the dynamics of contested acquisitions.

Carosso, V., *The Morgans: Private International Bankers, 1854–1913*, Cambridge: Harvard University Press, 1987. J. P. Morgan was arguably the first merchant banker to employ M&A on an industry-wide scale. The history of his rationalization of industries offers an instructive example of the role of M&A in industrial renewal and of the role of deal leadership in effective implementation.

Swisher, K., and L. Dickey, *There Must Be a Pony in Here Somewhere*, New York: Crown Business, 2003. This story about the merger of AOL and Time Warner holds important lessons for strategy, deal design, and integration.

Wasserstein, B., *Big Deal 2000: The Battle for Control of America's Leading Corporations*, New York: Warner Books, 2000. A valuable survey of recent M&A history and practice by a leading practitioner.

Wolf, Michael, *Burn Rate: How I Survived the Gold Rush Years on the Internet*, New York: Simon & Schuster, 1998. M&A from the standpoint of the seller, with very illuminating comments on the difficulties of deal development.

The M&A Setting

Baker, George P., and George David Smith, *The New Financial Capitalists*, Cambridge: Cambridge University Press, 1998. The authors focus on Kohlberg, Kravis, and Roberts and the determinants of their success as private equity investors. A fresh counterpoint to arguments offered elsewhere that M&A does not pay.

Jensen, M., "The Modern Industrial Revolution, Exit, and the Failure of Internal Control Systems," *Journal of Finance* 48, July 1993, pages 831–880. Also published in *The New Corporate Finance*, Donald Chew, ed., Burr Ridge, IL: Irwin McGraw-Hill, 1999.

Lamoreaux, N. R., *The Great Merger Movement in American Business, 1895–1904*. Cambridge: Cambridge University Press, 1985.

Valuation

Amram, M., and N. Kulatilaka, *Real Options: Managing Strategic Investment in an Uncertain World*, Boston: Harvard Business School Press, 1999. This is an excellent introduction to the subject of real options.

Copeland, T., T. Koller, and J. Murrin, *Valuation: Measuring and Managing the Value of Companies*, New York, NY: John Wiley & Sons, 1994. This is a classic introduction to the subject of valuing firms. Highly readable with intuitively appealing illustrations.

Hull, John C., *Options, Futures, and Other Derivatives*, 3d ed., Englewood Cliffs, NJ: Prentice-Hall, 1997. This is a comprehensive introduction to option pricing theory and the valuation of options.

Rappaport, A., *Creating Shareholder Value*, New York: Free Press, 1998. This is a highly readable and compelling introduction to the logic of thinking like an investor.

(Continued)

EXHIBIT 38.2 *(Continued)*

Scholes, M., and M. Wolfson, *Taxes and Business Strategy: A Planning Approach*, Englewood Cliffs, NJ: Prentice-Hall, 1992.

Sirower, M. L., *The Synergy Trap: How Companies Lose the Acquisition Game*, New York: Free Press, 1997. This book is a valuable caution against overblown synergy expectations.

Stewart, G. B., III, *The Quest for Value*, New York: HarperBusiness, 1991. This is a comprehensive introduction to economic value added (EVA), a measure of value creation.

Wyser-Pratte, G., *Risk Arbitrage II*. New York: Salomon Brothers Center for the Study of Financial Institutions, Graduate School of Business Administration, New York University, Monograph 1982-3-4. This is one of the rare discussions of risk arbitrage in M&A by a leading practitioner.

Deal Design and Negotiation

Bazerman, M., and J. Gillespie, "Betting on the Future: The Virtues of Contingent Contracts," *Harvard Business Review*, September–October 1999, pages 155–160.

Bazerman, M., and M. Neale, *Negotiating Rationally*, New York: Free Press, 1992.

Lax, D., and J. Sebenius, *The Manager as Negotiator*, New York: Free Press, 1986. This is a highly readable introduction to the general topic of negotiation and how managers should organize for bargaining success.

Raiffa, H., J. Richardson, and D. Metcalfe, *Negotiation Analysis: The Science and Art of Collaborative Decision Making*, Cambridge: Belknap Press of Harvard University Press, 2002. This complements the book by Lax and Sebenius with a more analytic presentation of the challenges encountered in bargaining toward a solution.

Rappaport, A., and M. Sirower, "Stock or Cash? The Trade-offs for Buyers and Sellers in Mergers and Acquisitions," *Harvard Business Review*, November–December 1999, pages 147–158.

Thaler, R., *The Winner's Curse: Paradoxes and Anomalies of Economic Life*, Princeton: Princeton University Press, 1992.

General Management, Ethics, and Governance

Colley, J., J. Doyle, G. Logan, and W. Stettinius, *Corporate Governance*, New York: McGraw-Hill, 2003. This gives a good overview of the current issues in governing a firm and their implications for general managers.

Gladwell, M., *The Tipping Point: How Little Things Can Make a Big Difference*, Boston: Little, Brown, 2000. This book is a good introduction to the subject of social networks, the "small world" phenomenon, and the role of intermediaries. It will offer some general background relevant to M&A search.

Haspeslagh, Philippe C., and David B. Jemison, *Managing Acquisitions: Creating Value through Corporate Renewal*, New York: Free Press, 1991. An excellent blending of strategic, organizational, and financial perspectives in M&A. Thoughtful, with excellent examples of principles. Contains an international perspective.

Nash, L. L., "Ethics without the Sermon," *Harvard Business Review*, November–December 1981, pages 79–90. This is a highly useful framework for reasoning through ethical dilemmas.

Rukeyser, W., "Why the Rain Fell on 'Automatic' Sprinkler," *Fortune*, May 1969, 79, 88–91, 126–129.

EXHIBIT 38.2 *(Continued)*

Legal Issues

Fleischer, A., and Sussman, A. R., *Takeover Defense*, 5th ed., New York: Aspen Law & Business, 1997. This is more of a reference work rather than a summary presentation. But the authors summarize well the issues of takeover attack and defense.

Freund, James C., *Anatomy of a Merger: Strategies and Techniques for Negotiating Corporate Acquisitions*, New York: Law Journal Press, 1975. This is a classic introduction to legal issues in M&A.

Gilson, Ronald J., and Bernard S. Black, *The Law and Finance of Corporate Acquisitions*, 2d ed., Westbury, NY: Foundation Press, 1995. This gives readable access to case law and regulations; widely used in law schools.

Thompson, Samuel C., Jr., *Business Planning for Mergers and Acquisitions*, 2d ed., Durham: Carolina Academic Press, 2001. This gives readable access to case law and regulations; widely used in law schools.

information about arbitrage spreads. One should also focus on recently completed mergers: As deals come along, they almost inevitably leave a trail of informative paper with regulators. Proxy statements, especially, give a good glimpse into the guts of current practice. See the SEC's web site, www.sec.gov, to download these documents. Consider drawing together a discussion group of teammates or peers to discuss current events. Seven key questions to ask about a new deal announcement between public companies are:

1. ***What are the terms?*** A useful exercise at the outset is to sketch the term sheet of the deal in as much detail as you can. See Chapters 7, 18, and 29 for more about term sheets and what one might include in them.
2. ***What is the bid premium?*** Compare the bid price to the target's price prevailing before the bid—you might scrutinize the time-trend of the target's share price leading up to the bid. If there was leakage of information or rumors before the deal, you may need to go back in time to get a true *ex ante* share price for calculating the bid premium.
3. ***What are the espoused motivations and synergies in this deal?*** How realistic are they? Many merger announcements express some quantitative targets for synergy value. You could produce a quick DCF valuation of these (for a template see the model, "Valuing Synergies.xls," found on the CD-ROM) and then compare the synergy values to the total preannouncement market capitalization of the two firms. Where the synergy value is relatively large, you should scrutinize its sources closely.
4. ***Does the deal create value for the buyer?*** The best way to answer this is with a detailed valuation analysis. But you can get reasonably close to the answer with a quick calculation. In essence, value is created for the buyer if the "gets" are greater than the "gives." The buyer gives a premium over the *ex ante* share price to get the target and have a shot at gaining synergies. Thus, the deal is economically attractive for the buyer if:

$$V_{\text{Stand-alone}} + V_{\text{Synergies}} > (P_{\text{Ex ante}} \times N_{\text{Shares}}) + \Pi_{\text{Bid}} \quad (1)$$

Where V is the DCF value of the target and synergies respectively, P is the share price, N is the number of shares, and Π is the bid premium.

In efficient markets for securities, the stand-alone value of the firm should equal its market capitalization. If this assumption is reasonable in the deal you are studying, then the test for value creation for the buyer reduces to:

$$V_{\text{Synergies}} > \Pi_{\text{Bid}} \quad (2)$$

5. ***Are there competitors or the likely intervention from governments or regulatory bodies that might affect the development of the deal?*** To determine the probability of success for consummation (refer back to Chapter 32 for more on this), you can backsolve from the arbitrage spread.
6. ***How has the market reacted to the deal?*** Look at the share price response for both the buyer and target. If there are competing bidders, look at their price reactions as well. Ideally, the price reaction should be net of the market movement that day—in effect, your calculations will generate a cumulative abnormal return around the announcement of the deal, similar to the methodology outlined in Chapter 3. Here, too, consider the arbitrage spread and what it tells you.
7. ***What is your view of the announced deal?*** If you take into account your answers to the foregoing questions, you should be able to develop your own view. Reflect on Exhibit 1.2 of Chapter 1: What are the strengths, weaknesses, opportunities, and threats in the environment surrounding the buyer and target? How have these developed the deal? What are the prospective outcomes? Can these companies reasonably generate good outcomes?

THE END OF IT ALL

Writing a book aimed at shaping best practices has a great deal in common with teaching and managing. It is said that teaching is like sending a letter to a moving addressee; you never know when and where the message will arrive. General managers will understand this as a core challenge in developing business leaders. To M&A professionals I would advise patience and continued efforts to observe, learn, and exercise the best practices. My own experiences from 30 years of professional work suggest that sooner or later the message does indeed arrive. Once a group of friends decided to write to Mark Twain, who was lecturing abroad. Not knowing exactly where he was, they mailed a letter addressed to "Mark Twain, God knows where." A few months later, a reply arrived from Twain, simply stating, "He does."[3]

NOTES

1. See Richard Brealey and Stewart Myers, *Principles of Corporate Finance*, 7th ed., New York: McGraw-Hill/Irwin, page 1003.
2. Bruce Wasserstein, *Big Deal: The Battle for Control of America's Leading Corporations*, New York: Time-Warner, page 348.
3. This anecdote is abstracted from *Bartlett's Book of Anecdotes*, Clifton Fadiman and André Bernard, eds., Boston: Little, Brown and Company, 2000, page 545.

About the CD-ROM

INTRODUCTION

The CD-ROM for *Applied Mergers and Acquisitions* contains:

- **Generic templates.** These are 25 spreadsheet programs written in Microsoft Excel, readily adaptable by you for hands-on experimentation and learning. A description of these models is given in the following table. These templates are found in the subdirectory "Templates."
- **Questions and Answers.** The "Questions" document has chapter-by-chapter questions to accompany the text, while the "Questions and Answers" document has the questions plus their answers. These files are found in the subdirectory "Questions and Answers."
- **Supplemental readings.** For select chapters, supplemental readings are provided, such as "Smith vs. Van Gorkom.pdf," "Survey of Key Court Cases.pdf," "Documents for Filing with the SEC.pdf," "Lecture: The First Round Documents.pdf," "Lecture: The Definitive Agreement.pdf," and "Lecture: The Merger Proxy Statement—How to Read It and What It Reveals.pdf." These files are found in the subdirectory "Supplemental Readings."
- **Crystal Ball simulation add-in software.** This is useful for valuing real options as discussed in Chapters 14, 16, 22, and 23. This software is found in the subdirectory "Crystal Ball."
- **Key Spreadsheets from the Questions and Answers.** These include 11 spreadsheets that show you derived solutions from the Questions and Answers, provided here to enable students to study the underlying Excel functions and formulae. These hidden functions and formulae can be useful to readers who ultimately wish to develop their own spreadsheets. These spreadsheets are found in the subdirectory "Key Spreadsheets from the Questions and Answers."
- **Key Spreadsheets from the Workbook.** These are 16 spreadsheets from the *Applied Mergers and Acquisitions Workbook* (to be purchased separately), provided here to enable students to study the underlying Excel functions and formulae. These hidden functions and formulae can be useful to readers who ultimately wish to develop their own spreadsheets. These spreadsheets are found in the subdirectory "Key Spreadsheets from the Workbook."

DESCRIPTION OF GENERIC TEMPLATES

The following table gives a description of each of the spreadsheet programs.

Program Name	*Description*
Growth Share.xls	Automates the preparation of a growth-share matrix, useful in strategic analysis of market positions.
Learning Curve.xls	Automates the preparation of a learning curve graph, useful in comparison of strategic cost positions.
Strategic Canvas.xls	Automates the preparation of a strategic canvas graph, useful in analysis of market positions.
Strategic Map.xls	Automates the preparation of a strategic map chart, useful in the analysis of market positions.
Value Merge.xls	A general valuation template that forecasts cash flows and produces DCF valuations and estimates of EPS dilution.
Triangulation Graph.xls	Automates the preparation of a triangulation graph, useful in comparing the value ranges produced by different estimators and in triangulating toward a single value range.
Option Valuation.xls	An option pricing model using the Black-Scholes formula. Useful for valuing European call and put options.
Valuing Synergies.xls	Gives general valuation templates for estimating the DCF values of cost savings, revenue enhancements, asset restructurings, and financial synergies.
Country IRP.xls	Illustrates the concept of Interest Rate Parity and the conversion of foreign currency cash flows to home currency using IRP-generated forward exchange rates.
Real versus Nominal.xls	Illustrates DCF valuation under the Real/Real and Nominal/Nominal approaches outlined in Chapter 12.
MediMedia Whole Deal Assessment.xls	Illustrates the whole deal analysis of a leveraged buyout, using the case of MediMedia presented in Chapter 13.
EMTV Option Analysis.xls	Illustrates real option valuation, focusing on the case of EMTV presented in Chapter 14.
Power.xls	Estimates Shapley values, measures of voting power.
Discounts and Premiums.xls	Estimates the joint percentage discount due to illiquidity and lack of control, and converts discounts to premiums.
Liquidity and Control.xls	Estimates the value of equity adjusted for illiquidity and/or lack of control using the multiplicative method outlined in Chapter 15.

Program Name	*Description*
Purchase Accounting.xls	Illustrates the effect of purchase accounting choices on reported financial results.
Momentum.xls	Illustrates the illusion of EPS momentum created by terms of deal design and financial reporting.
Deal Boundaries.xls	Automates the analysis of the buyer's maximum and seller's minimum prices, and the identification of the win-win zone.
Earnout.xls	Values earnout proposals from the perspectives of the buyer and the seller using Monte Carlo simulation. Must be opened in Crystal Ball add-in software.
Collars Analysis.xls	Values caps, floors, and collars, as risk management in M&A deals, using Monte Carlo simulation. Must be opened in Crystal Ball add-in software.
Cumulative Voting.xls	Illustrates the comparison of straight and cumulative shareholder voting.
HHI.xls	Estimates the Herfindahl-Hirschman Index of industry concentration based on dollar revenues and/or unit sales. The HHI is one measure of market power and is used in antitrust enforcement.
EVNT.xls	Estimates the expected value of not tendering (EVNT), a benchmark for setting bidding strategy in a hostile takeover.
Arbs.xls	Estimates the returns to arbitrageurs and the probability of a deal being consummated, as implied by the arbitrage spread.
Poison Pill Dilution.xls	Estimates the economic and voting dilution imposed on the hostile bidder by triggering a poison pill antitakeover defense.

MINIMUM SYSTEM REQUIREMENTS

Make sure that your computer meets the minimum system requirements listed in this section. If your computer doesn't match up to most of these requirements, you may have a problem using the contents of the CD.

Equipment required to access this software includes the following minimum configuration:

Hardware:

Pentium II computer with a minimum of 32 MB of RAM.

Monitor capable of displaying 256 colors with a resolution of 800×600.

Operating system:

Windows 98, Windows 2000, or Windows NT 4.0.

Web browser:

Microsoft Internet Explorer 4.0 (higher version preferred).

Spreadsheet software:

Microsoft Excel 4.0 or higher.

USING THE CD WITH WINDOWS

To install the items from the CD to your hard drive, follow these steps:

1. Insert the CD into your computer's CD-ROM drive.
2. A window appears with the following options: Install, Explore, Links, and Exit.

   Install: Gives you the option to install the supplied software and/or the author-created samples from the CD-ROM onto your hard drive.

   Explore: Enables you to view the contents of the CD-ROM in its directory structure.

   Exit: Closes the autorun window.

If you do not have autorun enabled, or if the autorun window does not appear, follow these steps to access the CD:

1. Click Start, then Run.
2. In the dialog box that appears, type ***d*:\setup.exe, where *d*** is the letter of your CD-ROM drive. This brings up the autorun window described in the preceding set of steps.
3. Choose the Install, Explore, or Exit option from the menu. (See Step 2 in the preceding list for a description of these options.)

TROUBLESHOOTING

If you have difficulty installing or using any of the materials on the companion CD, try the following solutions:

- ***Turn off any antivirus software that you may have running.*** Installers sometimes mimic virus activity and can make your computer incorrectly believe that it is being infected by a virus. (Be sure to turn the antivirus software back on later.)
- ***Close all running programs.*** The more programs you're running, the less memory is available to other programs. Installers also typically update files and programs; if you keep other programs running, installation may not work properly.

- ***Reference the ReadMe.*** Please refer to the ReadMe file located at the root of the CD-ROM for the latest product information at the time of publication.

If you still have trouble with the CD-ROM, please call the Wiley Product Technical Support phone number: (800) 762-2974. From outside the United States, call (317) 572-3994. You can also contact Wiley Product Technical Support at www.wiley.com/techsupport. Wiley Publishing will provide technical support only for installation and other general quality control items; for technical support on the applications themselves, consult the program's vendor or author.

To place additional orders or to request information about other Wiley products, please call (800) 225-5945.

References and Suggestions for Further Reading

Abarbanell, J., B. Bushee, and J. Raedy. 1998. The effects of institutional investor preferences on ownership changes and stock prices around corporate spin-offs. Unpublished working paper.

Abernathy, W. J., and K. Wayne. 1974. The limits of the learning curve. *Harvard Business Review* 52(5, September–October):109–119.

Abrahams, J. 1999. *The Mission Statement Book: 301 Corporate Mission Statements from America's Top Companies*, 2d ed. Berkeley, CA: 10-Speed Press.

Abuaf, Niso, and Quyen Chu. 1994. The executive's guide to international capital budgeting: 1994 update. New York: Salomon Brothers, Global Financial Strategy Series.

Achampong, F., and W. Zemedkun. 1995. An empirical and ethical analysis of factors motivating managers' merger decisions. *Journal of Business Ethics* 14:855–865.

Adler, Michael, and Bernard Dumas. 1983. International portfolio choice and corporation finance: A synthesis. *Journal of Finance* (June).

Admati, Anat R., and Paul Pfleiderer. 1994. Robust financial contracting and the role of venture capitalists. *Journal of Finance* 49:371–402.

Adolph, G., I. Buchanan, J. Hornery, B. Jackson, J. Jones, T. Kihlstedt, G. Neilson, and H. Quarls. 2001. Merger integration: Delivering on the promise. Company report. New York: Booz-Allen & Hamilton.

Aggarwal, R., and A. Samwick. 2003. Why do managers diversify their firms? Agency reconsidered. *Journal of Finance* 58:71–118.

Agmon, T., and D. R. Lessard. 1977. Investor recognition of corporate international diversification. *Journal of Finance* 32:1049–1055.

Agrawal, A., and G. Mandelker. 1990. Large shareholders and the monitoring of managers: The case of anti-takeover charter amendments. *Journal of Financial and Quantitative Analysis* 25:143.

Agrawal, A., and R. A. Walkling. 1994. Executive careers and compensation surrounding takeover bids. *Journal of Finance* 985–1014.

Agrawal, A., J. Jaffe, and G. Mandelker. 1992. The postmerger performance of acquiring firms: A re-examination of an anomaly. *Journal of Finance* 47(4, September):1605–1621.

Agrawal, Anup, and Gershon N. Mandelker. 1987. Managerial incentives and corporate investment and financing decisions. *Journal of Finance* 42(4, September):823–837.

Ahn, S., and D. Denis. 2001. Internal capital markets and investment policy: Evidence from corporate spin-offs. Working paper, downloadable from http://papers.ssrn.com/abstract=291527.

Ainspan, Nathan D., and David Dell. 2000. *Employee Communication during Mergers*. New York: Conference Board. Research report no. 1270-00-RR.

Akerlof, G. 1970. The market for lemons: Qualitative uncertainty and the market mechanism. *Quarterly Journal of Economics* 89:488–500.

Alchian, A. 1969. Corporate management and property rights. In Henry Manne, ed., *Economic Policy and the Regulation of Corporate Securities.* Washington, DC: American Enterprise Institute.

Alexander, G., P. Benson, and J. Kampmeyer. 1984. Investigating the valuation effects of announcements of voluntary corporate sell-offs. *Journal of Finance* 39:503–517.

Alexandrou, G., and S. Sudarsanam. 2001. Shareholder wealth experience of buyers in corporate divestitures: Impact of business strategy, growth opportunities, and bargaining power. Cranfield University working paper. Available by e-mail from p.s.sudarsanam@cranfield.ac.uk.

Allen, J. 1998. Capital markets and corporate structure: The equity carve-outs of Thermo Electron. *Journal of Financial Economics* 48:99–124.

Allen, J., and J. McConnell. 1998. Equity carve-outs and managerial discretion. *Journal of Finance* 53(1):163–186.

Allen, J., and G. Phillips. 2000. Corporate equity ownership, strategic alliances, and product market relationships. *Journal of Finance* 55(6):2791–2816.

Allen, J., S. Lummer, J. McConnell, and D. Reed. 1995. Can takeover losses explain spin-off gains? *Journal of Financial and Quantitative Analysis* 30(4):465–477.

Alli, Kasim L., and Donald J. Thompson II. 1991. The value of the resale limitation on restricted stock: An option theory approach. *Valuation* 36:22–34.

Altman, E. 1968. Financial ratios, discriminant analysis and the prediction of corporate bankruptcy. *Journal of Finance* (September):589–609.

Ambrose, Brent W., and William L. Megginson. 1992. The role of asset structure, ownership structure, and takeover defenses in determining acquisition likelihood. *Journal of Financial and Quantitative Analysis* 27:575–589.

Amess, K. 2002. Management buyouts and firm-level productivity: Evidence from a panel of UK manufacturing firms. *Scottish Journal of Political Economy* 49:304–317.

Amihud, Y., and B. Lev. 1981. Risk reduction as a managerial motive for conglomerate mergers. *Rand Journal of Economics* 12:605–618.

Amihud, Y., and Haim Mendelson. 1991. Liquidity, maturity, and the yields on U.S. Treasury securities. *Journal of Finance* 46:1411–1425.

Amihud, Y., J. Kamin, and J. Ronen. 1979. Revenue vs. profit maximization: Differences in behavior by the type-of-control and by market power. *Southern Economic Journal* 45:838–846.

Amihud, Yakov. 1989. *Leveraged Management Buyouts: Causes and Consequences.* Homewood, IL: Dow Jones/Irwin.

Amobi, Tuna N. 1998. Price protections in stock-swap transactions. *Mergers & Acquisitions* (September–October):22–28.

Amram, Martha, and Nalin Kulatilaka. 1999. *Real Options: Managing Strategic Investment in an Uncertain World.* Boston: Harvard Business School Press.

Amram, Martha, and Nalin Kulatilaka. 2000. Strategy and shareholder value creation: The real options frontier. *Journal of Applied Corporate Finance* 13(4, Summer): 15–28.

Anderson, A. 2002. Selecting the key to unlock hidden value. University of Arizona working paper. Copy may be obtained by e-mail from anea@mailbpa.arizona.edu.

Andrade, G. 1999. Do appearances matter? The impact of EPS accretion and dilution on stock prices. Working paper, Harvard University. Downloaded from http://papers.ssrn.com/paper.taf?abstract_id=172868.

Andrade, G., and S. Kaplan. 1998. How costly is financial (non-economic) distress? Evidence from highly leveraged transactions that became distressed. *Journal of Finance* 53(5, October):1443–1493.

Andrews, W., and M. Dowling. 1998. Explaining performance changes in newly privatized firms. *Journal of Management Studies* 35(5):601–618.

Ang, J., and Y. Cheng. 2003. Direct evidence on the market-driven acquisitions theory. (March). Downloaded from http://papers.ssrn.com/sol3/papers.cfm?abstract_id=391569.

Ang, J. S., and A.L. Tucker. 1988. The shareholder wealth effects of corporate greenmail. *Journal of Financial Research* 11(4):265–280.

Anslinger, P. L., and T. E. Copeland. 1996. Growth through acquisitions: A fresh look. *Harvard Business Review* (January–February):126–135. Reprint 96101.

Arnold, Tom, and Richard Shockley. 2001. Value creation at Anheuser-Busch: A real options example. *Journal of Applied Corporate Finance* 14(2, Summer):52–61.

Arthur Andersen & Co. 1998. *Guide to Mergers and Acquisitions*. St. Charles, IL: Arthur Andersen & Co.

Arya, A., J. Glover, and S. Sunder. 2003. Are unmanaged earnings always better for shareholders? *Accounting Horizons* 17:111–116.

Arzac, E. 1996. Valuation of highly leveraged firms. *Financial Analysts Journal* 52(4, July/August).

Aschwald, K. F. 2000. Restricted stock discounts decline as result of one-year holding period. *Shannon Pratt's Business Valuation Update* (May):1–5.

Ashby, W. R. 1956. *An Introduction to Cybernetics*. New York: John Wiley and Sons.

Ashkenas, Ronald N., Lawrence J. DeMonaco, and Suzanne C. Francis. 1998. Making the deal real: How GE Capital integrates acquisitions. *Harvard Business Review* (January–February). Reprint 98101.

Asquith, P. 1983. Merger bids, uncertainty, and stockholder returns,. *Journal of Financial Economics* 11(1, April):51–83.

Asquith, P., and D. Mullins. 1986. Equity issues and offering dilution. *Journal of Financial Economics* 15:61–89.

Asquith, P., R. Bruner, and D. Mullins Jr. 1983. The gains to bidding firms from merger. *Journal of Financial Economics* 11(1, April):121–139.

Asquith, P., R. Bruner, and D. Mullins Jr. 1987. Merger returns and the form of financing. Proceedings of the Seminar on the Analysis of Security Prices 34(1, May):115–146.

Auerbach, A. J., and David Reishus. 1988a. Taxes and the merger decision. Chapter 19 in J. C. Coffee Jr., L. Lowenstein, and S. Rose-Ackerman, eds., *Knights, Raiders and Targets*. New York: Oxford University Press.

Auerbach, A. J., and David Reishus. 1988b. The effects of taxation on the merger decision. Chapter 6 in A. J. Auerbach, ed., *Corporate Takeovers: Causes and Consequences*. Chicago: University of Chicago Press.

Auerbach, A. J., and David Reishus. 1988c. The impact of taxation on mergers and acquisitions. Chapter 4 in A. J. Auerbach, ed., *Mergers & Acquisitions*. Chicago: University of Chicago Press.

Auerbach, Alan J., ed. 1988. *Mergers and Acquisitions*. Chicago: University of Chicago Press.

Bacon, C. J., M. M. Cornett, and W. N. Davidson III. 1997. The board of directors and dual-class recapitalizations. *Financial Management* 26(3):5–22.

Bae, K., J. Kang, and J. Kim. 2002. Tunneling or value added? Evidence from mergers by Korean business groups. *Journal of Finance* 57(6):2695–2740.

Bagnoli, M., R. Gordon, and B. Lipman. 1989. Stock repurchase as a takeover defense. *Review of Financial Studies* 2(3):423–443.

Bagwell, S., and J. Zechner. 1993. Influence costs and capital structure. *Journal of Finance* 48:975–1008.

Bahree, B. 1999. Oil mergers often don't live up to the hype. *Wall Street Journal* (July 23):A10.

Baker, G., and G. Smith. 1998. *The New Financial Capitalists*. Cambridge: Cambridge University Press.

Baker, G., and K. H. Wruck. 1989. Organizational changes and value creation in leveraged buyouts: The case of the O. M. Scott & Sons Company. *Journal of Financial Economics* 25(December):163–190.

Baker, George, and Karen Wruck. 1997. Lessons from a middle market LBO: The case of OM Scott. In Donald H. Chew, ed., *Studies in International Corporate Finance and Governance Systems*. New York: Oxford University Press.

Baker, S. 2000. Telefonica: Takeover escape artist? *BusinessWeek* (April 10):58–60.

Baldwin, Carliss, and Kim B. Clark. 2000. *Design Rules: The Power of Modularity*. Cambridge, MA: MIT Press.

Barabba, Vincent P., and Gerald Zaltman. 1991. *Hearing the Voice of the Market: Competitive Advantage through Creative Use of Market Information*. Boston: Harvard Business School Press.

Baradwaj, A., and A. Shivdasani. 2003. Valuation effects of bank financing in acquisitions. *Journal of Financial Economics* 67:113–148.

Barclay, M., and C. Holderness. 1989. Private benefits from control of public corporations. *Journal of Financial Economics* 25:371–395.

Barclay, M., and C. Holderness. 1992. The law and large-block trades. *Journal of Law and Economics* 35:265–294.

Barclay, M. J., C. W. Smith, and R. L. Watts. 1995. The determinants of corporate leverage and dividend policies. *Journal of Applied Corporate Finance* 7(Winter):4–19.

Bar-Gill, O., and L. Bebchuk. 2003. Misreporting corporate performance. Harvard Law School working paper, downloaded from http://papers.ssrn.com/sol3/papers.cfm?abstract_id=354141.

Barnea, Amir, Robert A. Haugen, and Lemma W. Senbet. 1985. *Agency Problems and Financial Contracting*. New York: Prentice-Hall.

Barney, J. 1995. Looking inside for competitive advantage. *Academy of Management Executive* 9(4):49–61.

Barth M. E., G. Clinch, and T. Shibano. 1999. International accounting harmonization and global equity markets. *Journal of Accounting and Economics* 26(1–3):201–235.

Bathel, J., J. Porter, and T. Opler. 1998. Block share purchases and corporate performance. *Journal of Finance* 53(2):605–634.

Baumol, William J., John C. Panzar, and Robert D. Willig. 1982. Contestable markets and the theory of industry structure. New York: International Thompson Publishing.

Bazerman, Max H., and James J. Gillespie. 1999. Betting on the future: Virtues of contingent contracts. *Harvard Business Review* (September–October):155–160.

Bazerman, Max H., and Margaret A. Neale. 1992. *Negotiating Rationally*. New York: Free Press.

Beatty, A. 1994. An empirical analysis of the corporate control, tax and incentive motivations for adopting leveraged employee stock ownership plans. *Managerial and Decision Economics* 15:299–315.

Beatty, A. 1995. The cash flow and informational effects of employee stock plans. *Journal of Financial Economics* 38:211–240.

Bebchuk, L., and A. Guzman. 1999. An economic analysis of transnational bankruptcies. *Journal of Law and Economics* 17:775–808.

Bebchuk, L., J. Coates, and G. Subramaniam. 2002. The powerful anti-takeover force of staggered boards: Theory, evidence, and policy. *Stanford Law Review* 54(5):887–951.

Bebchuk, L., R. Kraakman, and G. Triantis. 1998. Stock pyramids, cross-ownership, and dual class equity: The creation and agency costs of separating control from cash flow rights. Working paper, SSRN Electronic Library: http://papers/ssrn.com/paper.taf?abstract_id=147590.

Becher, D. A., and T. L. Campbell III. 2002. Merger of equals. Working paper, Northern Illinois University and University of Delaware (October).

Beck, Thorsten, Asli Demigirc-Kunt, and Ross Levine. 2001. Law, politics, and finance. World Bank working paper 2585.

Becketti, S. 1986. Corporate mergers and the business cycle. *Federal Reserve Bank of St. Louis Economic Review* 13–26.

Beitel, P., D. Schiereck, and M. Wahrenburg. 2002. Explaining the M&A—success in European bank mergers and acquisitions. Working paper, University of Witten/Herdecke, Germany (January).

Bekaert, Geert. 1995. Market integration and investment barriers in emerging equity markets. *World Bank Economic Review* 9:75–107.

Bekaert, G., C. Erb, C. Harvey, and T. Viskanta. 1997. What matters for emerging equity market investments. *Emerging Markets Quarterly* (Summer):1–30.

Bekaert, G., C. Harvey, and R. Lumsdaine. 2002. Dating the integration of world equity markets. *Journal of Financial Economics* 65:203–247.

Bekaert, Geert, and C. R. Harvey. 1995. Time-varying world market integration. *Journal of Finance* 50(June):403–443.

Bekaert, Geert, and C. R. Harvey. 1997. Emerging equity market volatility. *Journal of Financial Economics* 43:29–77.

Bennis, W., and J. O'Toole. 2000. Don't hire the wrong CEO. *Harvard Business Review* (May–June).

Benson, D., R. Bruner, and R. Harris. 1990. The leveraged restructuring as a takeover defense: The case of American Standard. *Journal of Merger and Acquisition Analysis* (Fall):51–82. Reprinted in J. O'Donoghue and D. Grunewald, eds., *How to Resist Hostile Takeovers.* White Plains: International University Press, 1991.

Benson, D., R. Harris, and R. Saylor. 1989. *American Standard (A and B Cases).* Charlottesville, VA: Darden Graduate School of Business, UVA-F-870, 871.

Berenson, A. 2002. Tyco shares fall as investors show concern on accounting. *New York Times* (January 16). Downloaded from http://query.nytimes.com/search.restricted/article?res=F50D14FC385C0C758DDDA80894DA404.

Berger, P. G., and E. Ofek. 1995. Diversification's effect on firm value. *Journal of Financial Economics* 37(1, January):39–65.

Berger, P .G., and E. Ofek. 1999. Causes and effects of corporate refocusing programs. *Review of Financial Studies* 12(2, Summer):311–345.

Berger, P., E. Ofek, and I. Swary. 1996. Investor valuation of the abandonment option. *Journal of Financial Economics* 42(2):257–287.

Bergstrom, C., and K. Rydqvist. 1990. Ownership of equity in dual-class firms. *Journal of Banking and Finance* 14:255–269.

Berkovitch, E., and N. Khanna. 1990. How target shareholders benefit from value-reducing defensive strategies in takeovers. *Journal of Finance* 45(1):137–157.

Berkovitch, E., and M. Narayanan. 1990. Competition and the medium of exchange in takeovers. *Review of Financial Studies* 3(2):153–174.

Berkovitch, E., and M. P. Narayanan. 1993. Motives for takeovers: An empirical investigation. *Journal of Financial and Quantitative Analysis* 28(3):347–362.

Berkowitz, Daniel, Katharina Pistor, and Jen-Francois Richard. 2003. Economic development, legality, and the transplant effect. *European Economic Review* 47(1):165–195.

Berman, P. 1999. Tom Lee is on a roll. *Forbes* (November 17):127–131.

Bertrand, M., and S. Mullainathan. 1999. Is there discretion in wage setting? A test using takeover legislation. *RAND Journal of Economics* 30(3):535–554.

Bertrand, M., and S. Mullainathan. 2002. Pyramids. Massachusetts Institute of Technology working paper no. 02-32.

Bertrand, M., P. Mehta, and S. Mullainathan. 2000. Ferreting out tunneling: An application to Indian business groups. Working paper, Massachusetts Institute of Technology.

Best, R. W., R. J. Best, and A. M. Agapos. 1998. Earnings forecasts and the information contained in spin-off announcements. *Financial Review* 33:53–67.

Betton, S., and B. E. Eckbo. 2000. Toeholds, bid-jumps, and expected payoffs in takeovers. *Review of Financial Studies* 13:841–882.

Bhagat, S., and B. Black. 1999. The uncertain relationship between board composition and firm performance. *Business Lawyer* 54:921–963.

Bhagat, S., and R. H. Jefferis. 1991. Voting power in the proxy process: The case of antitakeover charter amendments. *Journal of Financial Economics* 30:193–226.

Bhattacharyya, S., and R. Singh. 1999. The resolution of bankruptcy by auction: Allocating the residual right of design. *Journal of Financial Economics* 54(3):269–294.

Bhide, A. 1993. The hidden costs of stock market liquidity. *Journal of Financial Economics* 34:31–51.

Bhide, A., and H. H. Stevenson. 1990. Why be honest if honesty doesn't pay. *Harvard Business Review* (September–October):121–129.

Bielinski, Daniel W. 1992. Putting a realistic dollar value on acquisition synergies. *Mergers & Acquisitions* (November/December):9–12.

Biger, N. 1991. Market recognition of the value of control. Unpublished manuscript, University of Haifa.

Billett, M., and D. Mauer. 2000. Diversification and the value of internal capital markets: The case of tracking stock. *Journal of Banking and Finance* 24: 1457–1490.

Billett, M., and A. Vijh. 2002. The wealth effects of tracking stock restructurings. University of Iowa working paper, downloadable from www.biz.uiowa.edu/faculty/mbillett/billett.html.

Billett, M., T. King, and D. Mauer. 2003. Bondholder wealth effects in mergers and acquisitions: News evidence from the 1980s and 1990s. Working paper. *Journal of Finance*, forthcoming.

Bing, Gordon. 1996. *Due Diligence Techniques and Analysis.* Westport, CT: Quorum Books.

Bisnaire, J. 1999. Hostile or friendly, Canadian M&A remains active. *International Financial Law Review* 18(6):15–16.

Biswas, R., D. R. Fraser, and A. Mahajan. 1997. The international market for corporate control: Evidence from acquisitions of financial firms. *Global Finance Journal* 8:33–54.

Bizjak, J. M., and C. J. Marquette. 1998. Are shareholder proposals all bark and no bite? Evidence from shareholder resolutions to rescind poison pills. *Journal of Financial and Quantitative Analysis* 33(4):499–521.

Black & Decker Corp. v. American Standard Inc., 679 F. Supp. 1183 (D. Del. 1988).

Black, Bernard S. 1992a. Agents watching agents: The promise of institutional investor voice. *UCLA Law Review* 39:811–892.

Black, Bernard S. 1992b. The value of institutional investor monitoring: The empirical evidence. *UCLA Law Review* 39:895–939.

Black, Bernard S. 2001. Fiduciary duties of outside directors. Stanford Law School working paper no. 219.

Black, Fischer, and J. Cox. 1976. Valuing corporate securities: Some effects of bond indenture provisions. *Journal of Finance* 17:351–367.

Black, Fischer, and Myron Scholes. 1973. The pricing of options and corporate liabilities. *Journal of Political Economy* 18:637–659.

Blackwell, D. W., M. W. Marr, and M. F. Spivey. 1990. Plant-closing decisions and the market value of the firm. *Journal of Financial Economics* 26:277–288.

Bleeke, J., and D. Ernst. 1995. Is your alliance really a sale? *Harvard Business Review* (January–February):97–105.

Bliss, R. T., and R. J. Rosen. 2001. CEO compensation and bank mergers. *Journal of Financial Economics* 61:107–138.

Bloomenthal, Harold S. 2002. *Sarbanes-Oxley Act in Perspective.* St. Paul, MN: West Group.

Blumenstein, R., and D. Solomon. 2003. MCI is expected to pay massive fine in SEC deal. *Wall Street Journal* (May 19). Downloaded from http://online.wsj.com/article_print/0,,SB105329362774148600,00.html.

Blumenstein, R., and S. Pulliam. 2003. WorldCom report finds Ebbers played role in inflating revenue. *Wall Street Journal* (June 6). Downloaded from http://online.wsj.com/article_print/0,,SB105485251027721500,00.html.

Boardman, N., and M. Pescod. 1999. Issues affecting UK M&A activity in 1999 and beyond. *International Financial Law Review* 18(6):72–73.

Boatright, J. R. 1999. *Ethics in Finance.* Oxford: Blackwell Publishers.

Bodnar, G., B. Dumas, and R. Marston. 2003. Cross-border valuation: The international cost of capital. Fontainebleau, France: INSEAD. Working paper (June).

Boer, F. Peter. 2002. *The Real Options Solution.* New York: John Wiley & Sons.

Bolten, Steven E. 1990. Discounts for stocks of closely held corporations. *Trusts & Estates* 47–48.

Bonnier, Karl-Adam, and Robert Bruner. 1989. An analysis of stock price reaction to management change in distressed firms. *Journal of Accounting and Economics* 11:95–106.

Boone, A. L., and J. H. Mulherin. 2001. Valuing the process of corporate restructuring. Penn State University working paper. (January). Available by e-mail from aboone@psu.edu.

Boone, A. L., and J. H. Mulherin. 2002. Corporate restructuring and corporate auctions. Working paper, College of William and Mary (November). Available from the first author at audra.boone@business.wm.edu.

Booz-Allen and Hamilton. 1999. *Making Acquisitions Work: Capturing Value after the Deal.* (Authorship attributed to John R. Harbison, Albert J. Viscio, and Amy T. Asin.) New York: Booz-Allen and Hamilton.

Booz-Allen and Hamilton. 2001. *Merger integration: Delivering on the Promise.* (Authorship attributed as "A viewpoint by Gerry Adolph, Ian Buchanan, Jennifer Hornery, Bill Jackson, John Jones, Torbjorn Kihlstedt, Gary Neilson, and Harry Quarls.) New York: Booz-Allen and Hamilton.

Borer, J., and J. Hohn. 2000. Hostile takeovers. *International Financial Law Review* 19:29–32.

Bork, Robert. 1993. *The Antitrust Paradox: A Policy at War with Itself.* New York: Free Press.

Born, J. A., and H. E. Ryan Jr. 2000. Capital expenditure announcements and antitakeover barriers. *Quarterly Review of Economics and Finance* 40(2):205–228.

Born, J. A., E. A. Trahan, and H. J. Faria. 1993. Golden parachutes: Incentive aligners, management entrenchers, or takeover bid signals? *Journal of Financial Research* 16(4):299–308.

Bouchard, P. J., and Lizz Pellet. 2000. *Getting Your Shift Together: Making Sense of Organizational Culture and Change*. Chandler, AZ: CCI Press.

Boudoukh, J., and R. F. Whitelaw. 1991. The benchmark effect in the Japanese government bond market. *Journal of Fixed Income* 1:52–59.

Bowie, N. E. 1999. A Kantian approach to business ethics. In R. E. Frederick, ed., *A Companion to Business Ethics*. Malden, MA: Blackwell.

Boyle, G. W., R. B. Carter, and R. D. Stover. 1998. Extraordinary antitakeover provisions and insider ownership structure: The case of converting savings and loans. *Journal of Financial and Quantitative Analysis* 33(2):291–304.

Boyle, P. 1977. Options: A Monte Carlo approach. *Journal of Financial Economics* 4(May):323–338.

Bradley, M. 1980. Interfirm tender offers and the market for corporate control. *Journal of Business* 53(4, October):345–376.

Bradley, M., and L. M. Wakeman. 1983. The wealth effects of targeted share repurchases. *Journal of Financial Economics* 11:301–329.

Bradley, M., A. Desai, and E. H. Kim. 1982. Specialized resources and competition in the market for corporate control. Working paper, Ann Arbor: University of Michigan.

Bradley, M., A. Desai, and E. H. Kim. 1983. The rationale behind interfirm tender offers: Information or synergy? *Journal of Financial Economics* 11(1–4, April): 183–206.

Bradley, M., A. Desai, and E. H. Kim. 1988. Synergistic gains from corporate acquisitions and their division between the stockholders of target and acquiring firms. *Journal of Financial Economics* 21(1, May):3–40.

Bradley, Michael, and Gregg Jarrell. 2003. Inflation and the constant-growth valuation model: A clarification," Working paper (February). Downloaded from http://papers.ssrn.com/sol3/papers.cfm?abstract_id=356540.

Brams, Steven J. 1985. *Rational Politics, Decisions, Games, and Strategy*. Boston: Academic Press.

Branch, B., and T. Yang. 2002. Predicting successful takeovers: Cash, stock swap, and collar mergers. University of Massachusetts working paper, available from the authors at Brancdhb@oitunix.oit.umass.edu.

Brandenburger, Adam M., and Barry J. Nalebuff. 1995. The right game: Use game theory to shape strategy. *Harvard Business Review* (July–August):57–71.

Bratic, Walter, Patricia Tilton, and Mira Balakrishman. 1997. Navigating through a biotechnology valuation. *Journal of Biotechnology in Healthcare* 4:207–216.

Brealey, R., and S. Myers. 1996. *Principles of Corporate Finance*, 5th ed. New York: McGraw-Hill.

Brennan, M., and E. Schwartz. 1985. Evaluating natural resource investment. *Journal of Business* 58(2):135–157.

Brennan, M., and L. Trigeorgis, eds. 1998. *Flexibility, Natural Resources and Strategic Options*. Oxford: Oxford University Press.

Brennan, Michael J., and Eduardo S. Schwartz. 1977. Savings bonds, retractable bonds and callable bonds. *Journal of Financial Economics* 5(1):67–88.

Brennan, Michael J., and Lenos Trigeorgis. 2000. *Project Flexibility, Agency, and Competition*. New York: Oxford University Press.

Brenner, M., R. Eldor, and S. Hauser. 2001. The price of options illiquidity. *Journal of Finance* 56:789–805.

Brickley, J. A., and R. C. Lease. 1988. Ownership structure and voting on antitakeover amendments. *Journal of Financial Economics* 20:267–289.

Brickley, J. A., J. L. Coles, and L. R. Terry. 1994. Outside directors and the adoption of poison pills. *Journal of Financial Economics* 35(3):371–391.

Bris, A., and C. Cabolis. 2002. Corporate governance convergence by contract: Evidence from cross-border mergers. Yale ICF working paper no. 02-32.

Brown, M. M., and P. S. Bird. 1999. SEC rules on cross-border offers and rights offerings. *International Financial Law Review* 18(12):22–25.

Bruner, R. 1982. Brown-Forman Distillers Corporation. Charlottesville VA: Darden Case Collection (UVA-F-541) and associated teaching note (UVA-F-541TN), University of Virginia.

Bruner, R. 1986a. Management buyouts and shareholder welfare: Self-dealing versus financial signaling. Working paper, University of Virginia.

Bruner, R. 1986b. Chrysler's warrant, September 1983. Darden Case Collection (UVA-F-682) and associated teaching note (UVA-F-682TN), University of Virginia.

Bruner, R. 1987a. Yield premia on leveraged buyout debt. *Southern Business Review* 13:1–15.

Bruner, Robert F. 1987b. Walt Disney Productions, June 1984. Darden Case Collection (UVA-F-676) and associated teaching note (UVA-F-676TN), University of Virginia.

Bruner, R. 1988a. The use of excess cash and debt capacity as a motive for merger. *Journal of Financial and Quantitative Analysis* 23(2, June):199–217.

Bruner, R. 1988b. Sprigg Lane (B). Darden Case Collection (UVA-F-804) and associated teaching note (UVA-F-804TN), University of Virginia.

Bruner, R. 1989. Hybritech Inc. (B). Case study, Charlottesville: Darden Educational Materials Services, UVA-F-793, University of Virginia.

Bruner, R. F. 1991. The poison pill anti-takeover defense: The price of strategic deterrence. Research Foundation of the Institute of Chartered Financial Analysts, Charlottesville, VA.

Bruner, R. 1992a. Understanding merger negotiation: Testing rational choice and behaviorism in simulated bargaining. *Journal of Financial Practice and Education* (Spring/Summer):55–65.

Bruner, R. 1992b. Understanding merger negotiation. Part 2: Testing rational choice and behaviorism in a simulated setting. *Journal of Financial Practice and Education* (Spring/Summer).

Bruner, R. 1992c. MediMedia International Ltd. Charlottesville, VA: Darden Case Collection (UVA-F-1032) and associated teaching note (UVA-F-1032TN) to MediMedia International Ltd. Charlottesville, VA: Darden Case Collection.

Bruner, R. 1992d. Rhône-Poulenc Rorer, Inc. Charlottesville, VA: Darden Case Collection (UVA-F-1015), University of Virginia.

Bruner, Robert F. 1996. Warren E. Buffett, 1995. Darden Case Collection (UVA-F-1160), and associated teaching note (UVA-F-1160TN), University of Virginia.

Bruner, R. 1999. An analysis of value destruction and recovery in the alliance and proposed merger of Volvo and Renault. *Journal of Financial Economics* 51(1, January):125–166.

Bruner, R. 2000. Kestrel Ventures LLC: August 1999. Charlottesville, VA: Darden Case Collection (UVA-F-1277).

Bruner, R. 2002. "Does M&A pay? A review of the evidence for the decision-maker." *Journal of Applied Finance* 12(Spring/Summer):48–68.

Bruner, R. 2003a. The Merger of Union Bank of Switzerland and Swiss Bank Corporation (A), (B) and (C). (UVA-F-1421, 1422, and 1423) Charlottesville, VA: Darden Case Collection.

Bruner, R. 2003b. Division of value in U.S. banking M&A transactions. Working paper, Charlottesville, VA: Darden Graduate Business School, University of Virginia.

Bruner, R., and E. Brownlee. 1990. Leveraged ESOPs, wealth transfers, and "shareholder neutrality": The case of Polaroid. *Financial Management* 19(1):59–74.

Bruner, R., and J. Chan. 2002. The risk premium for investing in emerging markets: What is it? Where is it? Charlottesville, VA: Darden School, University of Virginia, working paper.

Bruner, Robert F., Jessica Chan, and Melissa Collier. 2003. Hugh McColl and NationsBank: Creating a national footprint through acquisition. Charlottesville, VA: Darden Case Collection, UVA-F-1398-M.

Bruner, Robert F., Jessica Chan, Leslie Glatz, Miguel Palacios, Christopher Stringer, and Karen Whitney. 2001. The M&A "pitch book": Proposed acquisition of Heller Financial by United Technologies Corporation. Charlottesville, VA: Darden Case Collection, UVA-F-1338.

Bruner, R., and S. Chaplinsky. 1998. "Polaroid Corporation, 1996. Charlottesville, VA: Darden Case Collection, UVA-F-1181.

Bruner, Robert, Petra Christmann, and Robert Spekman. 1999. Chrysler Corporation: Negotiations between Daimler and Chrysler. Teaching note for case study, Charlottesville, VA: Darden Educational Materials Services, UVA-F-1240TN.

Bruner, Robert, Petra Christmann, and Robert Spekman. 1998. Daimler-Benz A.G.: Negotiations between Daimler and Chrysler. Case study, Charlottesville, VA: Darden Educational Materials Services, UVA-F-1241.

Bruner, R., M. Davoli, G. Geneletti, M. Ghiotto, and D. Rezende. 1992. Glaxo Italia S.p.A.: The Zinnat marketing decision. Charlottesville, VA: Darden Case Collection, UVA-F-1014.

Bruner, R., and K. Eades. 1992. The crash of the Revco LBO: The hypothesis of inadequate capital. *Financial Management* 21(1, Spring):35–49.

Bruner, R., K. Eades, R. Harris, and R. Higgins. 1998. Best practices in estimating the cost of capital: Survey and synthesis. *Financial Practice and Education* (Spring/Summer):13–28.

Bruner, R., R. Glauber, and D. Mullins. 1979. UV Industries Inc. Boston: Harvard Business School Case Services, 9-280-072.

Bruner, R., and C. Humphries. 1989. Marriott: Frankfurt and Dusseldorf. Charlottesville, VA: Darden Case Collection, UVA-F-928.

Bruner, R., Andrea Larson, and Katarina Paddack. 1996. Tar products: AlliedSignal (A) (UVA-F-0504); Carbon materials technologies (UVA-F-0505); associated teaching note (UVA-F-0504TN). Darden Case Collection, University of Virginia.

Bruner, R., A. Meiman, and R. Menefee. 1996. Westmoreland Energy Inc., power project at Zhangzhe, China. Charlottesville, VA: Darden Case Collection, UVA-F-1155.

Bruner, R., and C. Opitz. 1988. Hybritech Incorporated (B). Charlottesville, VA: Darden Case Collection, UVA-F-793.

Bruner, R., and K. Paddack. 1997. Continental Cablevision's investment in Fintelco. Charlottesville, VA: Darden Case Collection, UVA-F-1149.

Bruner, R., and L. S. Paine. 1988. Management buyouts and managerial ethics. *California Management Review* 30(Winter):89–106.

Bruner, R., and M. Palacios. 2003. Liquidity and control options: Corporate valuation and the interpretation of event returns. University of Virginia working paper.

Bruner, R., and R. Spekman. 1998. The dark side of strategic alliances: Lessons from Volvo-Renault. *European Management Journal* (April).

Bruner, R. F., and S. Vakharia. 1998. The Hilton-ITT Wars. Darden Case Collection case study, UVA-F-1217, and associated teaching note, UVA-F-1217TN.

Buchel, B. 2000. Framework of joint venture development: Theory-building though qualitative research. *Journal of Management Studies* 37(5):637–661.

Buckley, P., and M. Casson. 1976. The future of the multinational enterprise. London and Basingstoke, UK: Macmillan.

Bull, I. 1989. Management performance in leveraged buyouts: An empirical analysis. Chapter 3 in Y. Amihud, ed., *Leveraged Management Buyouts*. Homewood, IL: Dow Jones-Irwin.

Burch, T. R. 2001. Locking out rival bidders: The use of lockup options in corporate mergers. *Journal of Financial Economics* 60:103–141.

Burgelman, R., and A. Grove. 1996. Strategic dissonance. *California Management Review* 38(2):8–28.

Burrough, Bryan, and John Helyar. 1990. *Barbarians at the Gate: The Fall of RJR Nabisco*. New York: HarperCollins.

Burrows, Donald M. 2000. How people problems can sap value from a deal. *Mergers & Acquisitions* (October):36–39.

Burton, Thomas M., and Rhonda L. Rundle. 1995. Lilly gets out of biotechnology and medical diagnostics. *Wall Street Journal* (October 2):B5.

Burzawa, S. 2000. ESOPs in transition: Two companies discuss issues their ESOPs faced over time. *Employee Benefit Plan Review* 55(1):46–49.

Button, Maurice, and Sarah Bolton. 2000. *A Practitioner's Guide to Takeovers and Mergers in the European Union*. London: City & Financial Publishing.

Butz, D. 1994. How do large minority shareholders wield control? *Managerial and Decision Economics* 15(4):291–299.

Byrd, J., and K. Hickman. 1992. Do outside directors monitor managers? Evidence from tender offer bids. *Journal of Financial Economics* 32(2, October):195–214.

Byrne, J. A., and P. Galuszka. 1999. Poison pills: Let shareholders decide. *BusinessWeek* (May 17):104.

Cakici, N., C. Hessel, and K. Tandon. 1996. Foreign acquisitions in the United States: Effect on shareholder wealth of foreign acquiring firms. *Journal of Banking and Finance* 20:307–329.

Callahan, J., and S. MacKenzie. 1999. Metrics for strategic alliance control. *R&D Management* 29(4):365–377.

Camahort, Michael J., and Steven L. Kennedy. 1996. Pricing terms in all stock and cash and stock transactions and other money provisions. Handling mergers & acquisitions in a high-tech environment. New York: Practising Law Institute.

Campa, J., and S. Kedia. 2002. Explaining the diversification discount. *Journal of Finance* 57:1731–1762.

Capen, E. C., R. V. Clapp, and W. M. Campbell. 1971. Competitive bidding in high-risk situations. *Journal of Petroleum Technology* (June):641–653.

Carhart, M. 1997. On persistence in mutual fund performance. *Journal of Finance* 52:57–82.

Carleton, W., D. Guilkey, R. Harris, and J. Stewart. 1983. An empirical analysis of the role of the medium of exchange in mergers. *Journal of Finance* 38:813–826.

Carline, N., S. Linn, and P. Yadav. 2002. The impact of firm-specific and deal-specific factors on the real gains in corporate mergers and acquisitions: An empirical analysis. University of Oklahoma working paper (February).
Carosso, Vincent P. 1987. *The Morgans: Private International Bankers, 1854–1913*. Cambridge: Harvard University Press.
Carow, K. 2001. Citicorp-Travelers Group merger: Challenging barriers between banking and insurance. *Journal of Banking and Finance* 25:1553–1571.
Carr, C. 1999. Globalization, strategic alliances, acquisitions, and technology transfer: Lessons from ICL/Fujitsu and Rover/Honda and BMW. *R&D Management* 29(4):405–421.
Carroll, A. B. 1999. Ethics in management. Pages 141–152 in R. E. Frederick, ed., *A Companion to Business Ethics*. Malden, MA: Blackwell.
Cartwright, Phillip, David Kamerschen, and William Zieburtz. 1987. The competitive impact of mergers, 1930–1979. *American Business Law Journal* 25(1, Spring):33–63.
Cassing, J., and Richard W. Douglas. 1980. Implications of the auction mechanism in baseball's free agent draft. *Southern Economic Journal* 47(1, July):110–121.
Cavaglia, S., R. Hodrick, M. Vadim, and X Zhang. 2002. Pricing the global industry portfolios. Cambridge, NBER, working paper 9344.
Caves, R. 1971. International corporations: The industrial economics of foreign investment, *Economica* 1–27.
Caves, R. 1989. Mergers, takeovers, and economic efficiency. *International Journal of Industrial Organization* 7(1, March):151–174.
Ceneboyan, A. S., G. J. Papaioannou, and N. Travlos. 1991. Foreign takeover activity in the U.S. and wealth effects for target firm shareholders. *Financial Management* 31(3, Spring):58–68.
Chaffe, David B. H., III. 1993. Option pricing as a proxy for discount for lack of marketability in private company valuations. *Business Valuation Review* (December):182–188.
Champion, D. 1999. Finance: The joy of leverage. *Harvard Business Review* 77(4):19–22.
Chan, S. H., J. Martin, and J. Kensinger. 1990. Corporate research and development expenditures and share value. *Journal of Financial Economics* 26:255–276.
Chan, Su H., John W. Kensinger, Arthur J. Keown, and John D. Martin. 1997. Do strategic alliances create value? *Journal of Financial Economics* 46:199–221.
Chandler, A. D. 1977. *The Visible Hand*. Cambridge, MA: Belknap Press.
Chang, S. 1990. Employee stock ownership plans and shareholder wealth: An empirical investigation. *Financial Management* 19:29–38.
Chang, S. 1998. Takeovers of privately held targets, methods of payment, and bidder returns. *Journal of Finance* 53:773–784.
Chang, S., and E. Mais. 2000. Managerial motives and merger financing. *Financial Review* 35:139–152.
Chaplinsky, S., and G. Niehaus. 1990. The tax and distributional effects of leveraged ESOPs. *Financial Management* 19:29–38.
Chaplinsky, S., and L. Ramchand. 2000. The impact of global equity offers. *Journal of Finance* 55(6):2767–2789.
Chatterjee, R., and G. Meeks. 1996. The financial effects of takeover: Accounting rates of return and accounting regulation. *Journal of Business Finance & Accounting* 23(5/6, July):851–868.
Chaudhuri, S., and B. Tabrizi. 1999. Capturing the real value in high-tech acquisitions. *Harvard Business Review* 5(5, September/October):15–21.

Chemmanur, T., and I. Paeglis. 2001. Why issue tracking stock. Unpublished working paper available by e-mail from chemmanu@bc.edu.

Chen, A. H., and J. W. Kensinger. 1988. Puttable stock: A new innovation in equity financing. *Financial Management* (Spring):27–37.

Chen, Andrew H., K. C. Chen, and Barry Laiss. 1994. Pricing contingent value rights: theory and practice. *Journal of Financial Engineering* 2:155–173.

Chen, H., and J. R. Ritter. 2000. The seven percent solution. *Journal of Finance* 55(3):1105–1132.

Chen, H., M. Y. Hu, and J. C. Shieh. 1991. The wealth effect of international joint ventures: The case of U.S. investment in China. *Financial Management* 20:31–41.

Chen, S., K. Ho, C. Lee, and G. Yeo. 2000. Investment opportunities, free cash flow and market reaction to international joint ventures. *Journal of Banking and Finance* 24(11):1747–1765.

Chen, Z., and T. Ross. 2000. Strategic alliances, shared facilities, and entry deterrence. *RAND Journal of Economics* 31(2):326–344.

Chernow, Ron. 1998. *Titan: The Life of John D. Rockefeller, Sr.* New York: Random House.

Chew, D., ed. 1999. *The New Corporate Finance: Where Theory Meets Practice.* Burr Ridge, IL: Irwin McGraw-Hill.

Chew, Donald H., ed. 1997. *Studies in International Corporate Finance and Governance Systems.* New York: Oxford University Press.

Choi, F. D. S., and R. M. Levich. 1991. International accounting diversity: Does it affect market participants? *Financial Analysts Journal* 47(4):73–82.

Choi, Y. K. 2001. Management turnover and executive compensation in synergistic takeovers. *Quarterly Review of Economics and Finance* 223–238.

Chowdhry, B., and V. Nanda. 1993. The strategic role of debt in takeover contests. *Journal of Finance* 2(June):731–745.

Chowdhury, I., and P. Chowdhury. 2001. A theory of joint venture life cycles. *International Journal of Industrial Organization* 19:319–343.

Christensen, Clayton. 1997. *The Innovator's Dilemma.* Boston: Harvard Business School Press.

Chu, Wilson. 1996. The human side of examining a foreign target. *Mergers & Acquisitions* (January/February):35.

Churchill, N. C., and J. W. Mullins. 2001. How fast can your company afford to grow? *Harvard Business Review* (May):135–143.

Cialdini, Robert B. 1993. *Influence: Science and Practice*, 3d ed. New York: HarperCollins.

Claessens, Stijn, Simeon Djankov, and Larry H. P. Lang. 2000. The separation of ownership and control in East Asian corporations. *Journal of Financial Economics* 58:81–112.

Climan, Richard E. 1998. Pricing formulations in "stock-for-stock" mergers. Private manuscript.

Coase, R. 1937. The nature of the firm. *Economica* 4:386–405.

Coates, J. 2000a. Explaining variation in takeover defenses: Failure in the corporate law market. Harvard Law School working paper, downloaded from http://papers.ssrn.com/paper.taf?abstract_id=237020.

Coates, J. 2000b. Takeover defenses in the shadow of the pill: A critique of the scientific evidence. *Texas Law Review* 79(2):271–382.

Coates, J., and G. Subramaniam. 2000. A buy-side model of M&A lockups: Theory and evidence. *Stanford Law Review* 53(2):307–396.

Coles, J. W., and W. S. Hesterly. 2000. Independence of the chairman and board composition: Firm choices and shareholder value. *Journal of Management* 26(2):195–214.

Colley, John L., Jacqueline L. Doyle, George W. Logan, and Wallace Stettinius. 2003. *Corporate Governance*. New York: McGraw-Hill.

Comment, R., and G. Jarrell. 1987. Two-tier and negotiated tender offers: The imprisonment of the free-riding shareholder. *Journal of Financial Economics* 19:283–310.

Comment, R., and G. Jarrell. 1995. Corporate focus and stock returns. *Journal of Financial Economics* 37(1, June):67–87.

Comment, Robert, and G. William Schwert. 1995. Poison or placebo? Evidence on the deterrence and wealth effects of modern antitakeover measures. *Journal of Financial Economics* 39:3–43.

Conger, Jay A. 1998. The necessary art of persuasion. *Harvard Business Review* (May/June).

Conn, R. L., and F. L. Connell. 1990. International mergers: Returns to U.S., and British firms. *Journal of Business Finance and Accounting* 17(5):689–711.

Conn, Robert L., and J. F. Nielsen. 1977. An empirical test of the Larson-Gonedes exchange ratio determination model. *Journal of Finance* (June):749–760.

Conn, Robert L., Karen E. Lahey, and Michael Lahey. 1990. A deterministic model approach to merger analysis. *Managerial Finance* 17(6):35–45.

Conner, Frank M. III, David E. Brown, Jr., and Jonathan H. Talcott. 2003. *Bank Mergers and Acquisitions: Some Practical Guidance*. Washington, DC: Alston & Bird LLP.

Conrad, Jennifer, and Gautam Kaul. 1998. An anatomy of trading strategies. *Review of Financial Studies* 11:489–519.

Cook, D. O., and J. C. Easterwood. 1994. Poison put bonds: An analysis of their economic role. *Journal of Finance* 44(5):1905–1920.

Cooke, Terry, Alan Gregory, and Bernard Pearson. 1994. A UK empirical test of the Larson-Gonedes exchange ratio model. *Accounting and Business Research* 24:133–147.

Coolidge H. C. 1975. Fixing the value of minority interest in a business: Actual sales suggest as high as seventy percent. *Estate Planning* (Spring):141.

Coolidge, H. C. 1983. Survey shows trend toward larger minority discounts. *Estate Planning* (September):282.

Copeland, Tom, and Vladimir Antikarov. 2001. *Real Options: A Practitioner's Guide*. New York: Texere.

Copeland, Tom, Tim Koller, and Jack Murrin. 1994. *Valuation: Measuring and Managing the Value of Companies*, 2d ed. New York: John Wiley & Sons.

Cornu, P. 1997. The deterring role of the means of payment in corporate acquisitions. HEC Universite de Geneve working paper, available from author at cornu@uni2a.unige.ch.

Cotter, J., and S. Peck. 2001. The structure of debt and active equity investors: The case of the buyout specialist. *Journal of Financial Economics* 59:101–147.

Cotter, J. F., and M. Zenner. 1994. How managerial wealth affects the tender offer process. *Journal of Financial Economics* 35:63–97.

Cottrell, Tom, and Gordon Sick. 2001. First mover (dis)advantage and real options. *Journal of Applied Corporate Finance* 14:(2, Summer):41–51.

Courtadon, Georges R., and John J. Merrick Jr. 1983. The option pricing model and the valuation of corporate securities. *Midland Corporate Finance Journal* 1(3, Fall):43–57.

Cox, J., S. Ross, and M. Rubinstein. 1979. Option pricing: A simplified approach. *Journal of Financial Economics* (October):229–264.

Cox, John C., and Mark Rubinstein. 1985. *Options Markets*. Englewood Cliffs, NJ: Prentice-Hall.

Cragle, R. 1998. Replacing poison pills with vitamins. *Global Finance* 12(7):15–16.

Cramton P., and Alan Schwartz. 1991. Using auction theory to inform takeover regulation. *Journal of Law, Economics, and Organization* 27.

Cross, John G. 1969. *The Economics of Bargaining*. New York: Basic Books.

Crutchley, C. E., E. Guo, and R. S. Hansen. 1991. Stockholder benefits from Japanese-US joint ventures. *Financial Management* 20:22–30.

Cusatis, P., J. Miles, and J. Woolridge. 1993. Restructuring through spin-offs: The stock market evidence. *Journal of Financial Economics* 33:293–311.

Dahya, J., and J. J. McConnell. 2002. Outside directors and corporate board decisions. Working paper, Krannert School of Management, Purdue University.

Dahya, Jay, and Ronan Powell. 2001. Ownership structure, managerial turnover, and takeovers: Further U.K. evidence on the market for corporate control. *Multinational Finance Journal* 2:63–85.

Daines, R., and M. Klausner. 2001. Do IPO charters maximize firm value? *Journal of Law, Economics and Organization* 17:83–120.

Daley, L., V. Mehrotra, and R. Sivakuma. 1997. Corporate focus and value creation: Evidence from spin-offs. *Journal of Financial Economics* 45(2):257–281.

Damodaran, Aswath. 2001. *Investment Valuation*, 2d ed. New York: John Wiley & Sons.

Danielson, M. G., and J. M. Karpoff. 2002. "Do pills poison operating performance? Working paper, downloaded from http://papers.ssrn.com/abstract=304647.

Dann, L. Y., and H. DeAngelo. 1983. Standstill agreements, privately negotiated stock repurchases, and the market for corporate control. *Journal of Financial Economics* 11(April):275–300.

Dann, L. Y., and H. DeAngelo. 1986. Corporate financial policy and corporate control: A study of defensive adjustments in asset and ownership structure. Working paper 86-11, Managerial Economics Research Center of the University of Rochester (August).

Das, T., and B. Teng. 1999. Managing risks in strategic alliances. *Academy of Management Executive* 13(4):50–62.

Dasgupta, S., V. Goyal, and G. Tan. 2000. Active asset markets, divestitures, and divisional cross-subsidization. Hong Kong University of Science and Technology working paper, available by e-mail from dasgupta@ust.hk.

Datar, S., R. Frankel, and M. Wolfson. 1998. Earnouts: The effects of adverse selection on acquisition techniques. Working paper, Ann Arbor: University of Michigan.

Datta, D. K., G. E. Pinches, and V. K. Narayanan. 1992. Factors influencing wealth creation from mergers and acquisitions: A meta-analysis. *Strategic Management Journal* 13(1, January):67–86.

Datta, S., and M. Iskandar-Datta. 1995. Corporate partial acquisitions, total firm valuation and the effect of financing method. *Journal of Banking and Finance* 19(1):97–115.

Datta, S., and M. Iskander-Datta. 1996. Takeover defenses and wealth effects on securityholders: The case of poison pill adoptions. *Journal of Banking & Finance* 20(7):1231–1250.

Davidson, K. 1989. Evolution of a new industry. *Journal of Business Strategy* 10 (January/February):54–56.

Davidson, W. N. III, T. Pilger, and A. Szakmary. 1998. Golden parachutes, board committee composition, and shareholder wealth. *Financial Review* 33:17–32.

Davis, A., and M. Leblond. 2002. A spin-off analysis: Evidence from new and old economies. Queen's University working paper, available by e-mail from adavis@business.queensu.ca.

Davis, E., G. Shore, and D. Thompson. 1991. Continental mergers are different. *Business Strategy Review* 2(1):49–70.

Davis, G., and H. Greve. 1997. Corporate elite networks and governance changes in the 1980s. *American Journal of Sociology* 103(1, July):1–37.

Davis, Michael L. 1990. Differential market reaction to pooling and purchase methods. *Accounting Review* 65(July):696–709.

Davis, Michael L. 1996. The purchase vs. pooling controversy: How the stock market responds to goodwill. *Journal of Applied Corporate Finance* 9(Spring):50–59.

DeAngelo, H., and R. Masulis. 1980. Optimal capital structure under corporate taxation. *Journal of Financial Economics* 8(March):5–29.

DeAngelo, H., L. DeAngelo, and E. Rice. 1984. Going private: Minority freezeouts and stockholder wealth. *Journal of Law and Economics* (October):367–402.

DeAngelo, L. 1988. Managerial competition, information costs, and corporate governance: The use of accounting performance measures in proxy contests. *Journal of Accounting & Economics* 10:3–36.

Dechow, P., and D. Skinner. 2000. Earnings management: Reconciling the views of accounting academics, practitioners, and regulators. University of Michigan working paper, downloaded from http://papers.ssrn.com/sol3/papers.cfm?abstract_id=218959. *Accounting Horizons* 16(2):157–168.

Dechow, P. M. 1994. Accounting earnings and cash flows as measures of firm performance: The role of accounting accruals. *Journal of Accounting and Economics* 18:3–42.

DeLong, G. 2001. Stockholder gains from focusing versus diversifying bank mergers. *Journal of Financial Economics* 59(2, February):221–252.

DeLong, G. 2003. Does long-term performance of mergers match market expectations? Evidence from the US banking industry." *Financial Management* (Summer):5–25.

Dempsey, S., G. Labor, and M. Rozeff. 1993. Dividend policies in practice: Is there an industry effect. *Quarterly Journal of Business and Economics* 32:3–13.

Demsetz, Harold, and Kenneth Lehn. 1985. Structure of corporate ownership: Causes and consequences. *Journal of Political Economy* 93(6, December):1155–1177.

Denis, D., D. Denis, and A. Sarin. 1997. Agency problems, equity ownership, and corporate diversification. *Journal of Finance* 52:135–160.

Denis, D., D. Denis, and K. Yost. 2002. Global diversification, industrial diversification, and firm value. *Journal of Finance* 57:1951–1979.

Denis, D. J., and D. K. Denis. 1993. Managerial discretion, organizational structure, and corporate performance: A study in leveraged recapitalizations. *Journal of Accounting and Economics* 16:209–237.

Dennis, D., and J. McConnell. 1986. Corporate mergers and security returns. *Journal of Financial Economics* 16(2, June):143–187.

Deogun, N. 1999. Merger wave spurs more stock wipeouts. *Wall Street Journal* (November 29):C1.

Desai, H., and P. Jain. 1999. Firm performance and focus: Long-run stock market performance following spin-offs. *Journal of Financial Economics* 54(1): 75–101.

Desai, M., C. F. Foley, and J. R. Hines. 2002. International joint ventures and the boundaries of the firm. Harvard University NOM Research Paper no. 02-29 (July), downloaded from http://ssrn.com/abstract_id=324123.

Dessauer, John P. 1981. *Book Publishing*. New York: Bowker.

Deutsch, Claudia H. 1999. The deal is done. The work begins: Practicing the steps even before the dance. *New York Times* (April 11):Section 3:1

Dewenter, K. L. 1995. Does the market react differently to domestic and foreign takeover announcements? Evidence from the U.S. chemical and retail industries. *Journal of Financial Economics* 37:421–441.

Dhillon, U., and G. Ramirez. 1994. Employee stock ownership and corporate control: An empirical study. *Quarterly Journal of Business and Economics* 18:9–26.

Diamond, D. 1991. Debt maturity structure and liquidity risk. *Quarterly Journal of Economics* (August):709–737.

Dickerson, A., H. Gibson, and E. Tsakalotos. 1997. The impact of acquisitions on company performance: Evidence from a large panel of U.K. firms. *Oxford Economic Papers* 49(3, July):344–361.

Diermeier, J., and B. Solnik. 2001. Global pricing of equity. *Financial Analysts Journal* 57(4):37–47.

Dittmar, A., and A. Shivdasani. 2002. Divestitures and divisional investment policies. Working paper, Indian University and University of North Carolina. Downloaded from http://ssrn.com/abstract=363060.

Dixit, Avinash, and Robert S. Pindyck. 1994. *Investment under Uncertainty*. Princeton: Princeton University Press.

Dodd, P. 1980. Merger proposals, management discretion and stockholder wealth. *Journal of Financial Economics* 8(2, June):105–138.

Dodd, P., and R. Ruback. 1977. Tender offers and stockholder returns: An empirical analysis. *Journal of Financial Economics* 5(3, December):351–374.

Doherty, J. 1998. Allied victory? *Barron's* 78(38, September 21):13.

Doidge, C. 2003. U.S. cross-listings and the private benefits of control: Evidence from dual class shares. University of Toronto working paper, downloaded from http://ssrn.com/abstract=373740.

Donaldson, G. 1990. Voluntary restructuring. *Journal of Financial Economics* 27: 117–141.

Donaldson, Gordon. 1997. The corporate restructuring of the 1980s—and its import for the 1990s. In Donald H. Chew, ed., *Studies in International Corporate Finance and Governance Systems*. New York: Oxford University Press.

Doukas, J., and N. Travlos. 1988. The effect of corporate multinationalism on shareholders' wealth: Evidence from international acquisitions. *Journal of Finance* 23:1161–1178.

Doukas, J., M. Holmen, and N. Travlos. 2001. Corporate diversification and firm performance: Evidence from Swedish acquisitions. Working paper available by e-mail from jdoukas@odu.edu.

Doyle, B., and H. Ammidon. 1989. *The Anatomy of a Leveraged Buyout*. New York: Salomon Brothers Bond Research.

Doz, Y., and G. Hamel. 1998. *Alliance Advantage: The Art of Creating Value through Partnering*. Boston: Harvard Business School Press.

D'Souza, J., and J. Jacob. 2000. Why firms issue targeted stock. *Journal of Financial Economics* 56:459–483.

Dunning, J. H. 1988. The eclectic paradigm of international production: A restatement and some possible extensions. *Journal of International Business Studies* 1–31.

Dunning, J. H. 1998. Location and the multinational enterprise: A neglected factor? *Journal of International Business Studies* 29:45–66.

Dyck, A., and L. Zingales. 2001. Private benefits of control: An international comparison. Working paper. Boston: Harvard Business School.

Eberhart, A., E. Altman, and R. Aggarwal. 1999. The equity performance of firms emerging from bankruptcy. *Journal of Finance* 54(5):1855–1868.

Eccles, Robert G., Kersten L. Lanes, and Thomas C. Wilson. 1999. Are you paying too much for that acquisition? *Harvard Business Review* (July-August):136–146. Reprint no. 99402.

Eckbo, B. Espen. 1983. Horizontal mergers, collusion and stockholder wealth. *Journal of Financial Economics* 11:241–273.

Eckbo, B. Espen. 1985. Mergers and the market concentration doctrine: Evidence from the capital market. *Journal of Business* 58:325–349.

Eckbo, B. Espen. 1989. The role of stock market studies in formulating antitrust policy towards horizontal mergers. *Quarterly Journal of Business and Economics* 28:22–38.

Eckbo, B. E. 1990. Valuation effects of greenmail prohibitions. *Journal of Financial and Quantitative Analysis* 25(4):491–505.

Eckbo, B. Espen. 1991. Mergers, concentration, and antitrust. Chapter 6 in C. Wihlborg, M. Fratiani, and T. D. Willett, eds., *Financial Regulation and Monetary Arrangements after 1992*. Amsterdam: North-Holland, Contributions to Economic Analysis Series.

Eckbo, B. E. 1992a. Mergers and the value of antitrust deterrence. *Journal of Finance* 47(3, July):1005–1030.

Eckbo, B. Espen 1992b. Mergers and the value of antitrust deterrence. *Journal of Finance* 47(3, July):1005–1030.

Eckbo, B. E., R. Giammarino, and R. Heinkel. 1990. Asymmetric information and the medium of exchange in takeovers: Theory and tests. *Review of Financial Studies* 3:651–675.

Eckbo, B. E., and K. Thorburn. 2000. Gains to bidder firms revisited: Domestic and foreign acquisitions in Canada. *Journal of Financial and Quantitative Analysis* 35(1, March):1–25.

Eckbo, B. Espen, and Peggy Wier. 1985. Antimerger policy under the Hart-Scott-Rodino Act: A reexamination of the market power hypothesis. *Journal of Law and Economics* 28(1, April):119–150.

Eckhouse, John. 1998. To navigate an M&A payoff. *InformationWeek, Manhassett* (November 9):103.

Elder, J., and P. Westra. 2000. The reaction of security prices to tracking stock announcements. *Journal of Economics and Finance* 24(1):36–55.

Elster, Jon. 1989. *Nuts and Bolts for the Social Sciences*. Cambridge: Cambridge University Press.

Emery, G., and J. Switzer. 1999. Expected market reaction and the choice of method of payment for acquisitions. *Financial Management* 28(4):73–86.

Emory, J. D. 1997. The value of marketability as illustrated in initial public offerings of common stock—November 1995 through April 1997. *Business Valuation Review* 16(3, September):125.

Erb, Claude, Campbell R. Harvey, and Tadas E. Viskanta. 1995. Country risk and global equity selection. *Journal of Portfolio Management* (Winter):74–83.

Erickson, M., and S. Wang. 1999. Earnings management by acquiring firms in stock for stock mergers. *Journal of Accounting and Economics* 27:149–176.

Erickson, M., and S. Wang. 2000. The effect of transaction structure on price: Evidence from subsidiary sales. *Journal of Accounting & Economics* 30(1):59–97.

Errunza, V., and D. Miller. 2000. Market segmentation and the cost of capital in international equity markets. Working paper, McGill University.

Errunza, V., and E. Losq. 1985. International asset pricing under mild segmentation: Theory and test. *Journal of Finance* 40:105–124.

Errunza, V., and E. Losq. 1987. How risky are emerging markets? *Journal of Portfolio Management* 14(1):62–68.

Errunza, V., and L. Senbet. 1981. The effects of international operations on the market value of the firm: Theory and evidence. *Journal of Finance* 36(May):401–417.

Ertel, Danny. 1999. Turning negotiation into a corporate capability, *Harvard Business Review* (May–June):55–70.

Esty, Benjamin C. 2001. The information content of litigation participation securities: The case of CalFed Bancorp. Working paper. Boston: Harvard Business School.

Esty, Benjamin C., Mathew Mateo Millett, and Tracy Aronson. 1998. Atlantic Energy/Delmarva Power & Light (A) and (B). Boston: Harvard Business School case studies 9-298-034 and 9-298-066.

Eun, C. S., R. Kolodny, and C. Scheraga. 1996. Cross-border acquisitions and shareholder wealth: Tests of the synergy and internalization hypotheses. *Journal of Banking and Finance* 20(9):1559–1582.

Evans, J., and C. Green. 2000. Marketing strategy, constituent influence, and resource allocation: An application of the Mile and Snow typology to closely held firms in Chapter 11 bankruptcy. *Journal of Business Research* 50(2):225–231.

Evans, Philip, and Thomas S. Wurster. 2000. *Blown to Bits: How the New Economics of Information Transforms Strategy.* Boston: Harvard Business School Press.

Fakler, J. 2002. Splitsville for Tyco, worry for analysts. *South Florida Business Journal* (January 28). Downloaded from http://southflorida.bizjournals.com/southflorida/stories/2002/01/28/story1.html?t=printable.

Fama, E., and K. French. 1992. The cross-section of expected stock returns. *Journal of Finance* 47(June):427–465.

Fama, E., and K. French. 1993. Common risk factors in the returns on stocks and bonds. *Journal of Financial Economics* 33:3–56.

Fama, Eugene. 1965. The behavior of stock market prices. *Journal of Business* 38(January):34–105.

Fan, J., and V. Goyal. 2002. On the patterns and wealth effects of vertical mergers. Hong Kong University of Science & Technology working paper (January).

Fanto, J. 2000. Braking the merger momentum: Reforming corporate law governing mega-mergers. Brooklyn Law School working paper, downloadable from http://papers.ssrn.com/sol3/papers.cfm?abstract_id=223149.

Farrell, Joseph. 1995. Talk is cheap. *AEA Papers and Proceedings* 186–195.

Fatemi, A. M. 1984. Shareholder benefits from corporate international diversification. *Journal of Finance* 39:1325–1344.

Faulkner, T. 1996. Applying "options thinking" to R&D valuation. *Research Technology Management* (May–June):50–56.

Fauver, L., J. F. Houston, and A. Naranjo. 2002. Capital market development, integration, legal systems, and the value of corporate diversification: A cross-country analysis. Working paper, downloaded from http://papers.ssrn.com/sol3/papers.cfm?abstract_id-320220.

Feldman, Spencer G. 1996. The use of ferformance (not economic) earn-outs in computer company acquisitions. *Insights* (August):12.

Feliciano, Z., and R. E. Lipsey. 2002. Foreign entry into U.S. manufacturing by takeovers and the creation of new firms. Working paper 9122, Cambridge, MA: National Bureau of Economic Research.

Fernandez, P. 2001. The value of tax shields is the difference of two present values with different risk. University of Navarra working paper, downloadable from http://papers.ssrn.com/sol3/papers.cfm?abstract_id=294279.

Fernandez, P. 2002a. The correct value of tax shields. An analysis of 23 theories. University of Navarra working paper, downloadable from http://papers.ssrn.com/sol3/papers.cfm?abstract_id=276051.

Fernandez, P. 2002b. Beta levered and beta unlevered. University of Navarra working paper, downloadable from http://papers.ssrn.com/sol3/papers.cfm?abstract_id=303170.

Fernandez, P. 2002c. The value of tax shields is NOT equal to the present value of tax shields. University of Navarra working paper, downloadable from http://papers.ssrn.com/sol3/papers.cfm?abstract_id=290727.

Fernandez, P. 2002d. The correct value of tax shields. University of Navarra working paper, downloadable from http://papers.ssrn.com/sol3/papers.cfm?abstract_id=330541.

Ferrell, O. C., Debbie Thorne LeClair, and Linda Ferrell. 1998. The federal sentencing guidelines for organizations: A framework for ethical compliance. *Journal of Business Ethics* (March):353–363.

Ferris, S., and K. Park. 2001. How different is the long-run performance of mergers in the telecommunications industry. University of Missouri working paper (March).

Ferris, S. P., N. Sen, C. Y. Lim, and G. H. H. Yeo. 2002. Corporate focus versus diversification: The role of growth opportunities and cash flow. *Journal of International Financial Markets, Institutions and Money* 12:231–252.

Field, L. C., and G. Hanka. 2001. The expiration of IPO share lockups. *Journal of Finance* 56:471–500.

Field, L. C., and J. M. Karpoff. 2000. "Takeover defenses of IPO firms. Working paper, Penn State and University of Washington. Downloaded from faculty.washington.edu/~karpoff/IPOpaper.pdf.

Financial Accounting Standards Board. 2001a. *Statement 141: Business Combinations.* Washington, DC: Financial Accounting Standards Board. Downloaded from http://store.yahoo.com/fasbpubs/publications-statements-of-standards—126-150-html.

Financial Accounting Standards Board. 2001b. *Statement 142: Goodwill and Other Intangible Assets.* Washington, DC: Financial Accounting Standards Board. Downloaded fromhttp://store.yahoo.com/fasbpubs/publications-statements-of-standards—126-150-html.

Fine, C., and R. Freund. 1990. Optimal investment in product-flexible manufacturing capacity. *Management Science* 36(3):449–466.

Finnerty, J. E., J. E. Owers, and R. C. Rogers. 1986. The valuation impact of joint ventures. *Management International Review* 26:14–26.

Finnerty, John D. 2002. The impact of transfer restrictions on stock prices. Working paper, Analysis Group/Economics, Cambridge, MA (October).

Firth, M. 1980. Takeovers, shareholder returns, and the theory of the firm. *Quarterly Journal of Economics* 94(2, March):235–260.

Fisher, A. B. 1994. How to make a merger work. *Fortune* (January 24):66–69.

Fisher, Roger, and W. Ury. 1981. *Getting to Yes.* Boston: Houghton Mifflin.

Fishman, M. 1989. Preemptive bidding and the role of the medium of exchange in acquisitions. *Journal of Finance* 44(March):41–57.

Fleischer, A., and A. R. Sussman. 1997. *Takeover Defense*, 5th ed. New York: Aspen Law & Business.

Floreani, A., and S. Rigamonti. 2001. "Mergers and shareholders' wealth in the insurance industry. Working paper, Universita Cattolica del S. Cuore (March).

Fluck, S., and A. Lynch. 1999. Why do firms merge and then divest? A theory of financial synergies. *Journal of Business* 72:319–346.

Frankfurter, G., and E. Gunay. 1992. Management buyouts: The sources and sharing of wealth between insiders and outside shareholders. *Quarterly Review of Economics and Finance* 32(3):82–95.

Franks, J., and C. Mayer. 1996. Hostile takeovers and the correction of managerial failure. *Journal of Financial Economics* 40:163–181.

Franks, J., R. Harris, and S. Titman. 1991. The postmerger share-price performance of acquiring firms. *Journal of Financial Economics* 29 (1, March):81–96.

Franks, Julian, and Colin Mayer. 1990. Capital markets and corporate control: A study of France, Germany and the U.K. *Economic Policy* 10:189.

Frederick, R. E. 1999. *A Companion to Business Ethics*. Oxford: Blackwell Publishers.

Freeman, R. E. 1984. *Strategic Management: A Stakeholder Approach*. Boston: Pittman.

Freiman, H. 1990. Understanding the economics of leveraged ESOPs. *Financial Analysts Journal* 46:51–55.

Freund, James C. 1975. *Anatomy of a Merger: Strategies and Techniques for Negotiating Corporate Acquisitions*. New York: Law Journals Seminar Press.

Friedman, J. 2000. *Dictionary of Business Terms*, 3d ed. Hauppauge, NY: Barron's Educational Series.

Friedman, M. 1962. *Capitalism and Freedom*. Chicago: University of Chicago Press.

Froot, K. A., and J. C. Stein. 1991. Exchange rates and foreign direct investment: An imperfect capital markets approach. *Quarterly Journal of Economics* 106(4):1191–1217.

Fruhan, W. 1972. *Ling-Temco-Vought, Inc.* Boston: Harvard Business School case study 9-272-102.

Frydman, H., R. Frydman, and S. Trimbath. 2002. Financial buyers in takeovers: Focus on cost efficiency. *Managerial Finance* 28:1–13.

Fuld, Leonard M. 1985. *Competitor Intelligence: How to Get It; How to Use It*. New York: John Wiley & Sons.

Fuller, K., J. Netter, and M. Stegemoller. 2002. What do returns to acquiring firms tell us? Evidence from firms that make many acquisitions. *Journal of Finance* 57(4, August):1763–1793.

Fuller, Kathleen P. 2003. Why some firms use collar offers in mergers. *Financial Review* 38:127–150.

Furtado, E. P. H., and M. S. Rozeff. 1987. The wealth effects of company initiated management changes. *Journal of Financial Economics* 18:147–160.

Garvey, G. T., and G. Hanka. 1999. Capital structure and corporate control: The effect of antitakeover statutes on firm leverage. *Journal of Finance* 54(2): 519–546.

Gelman, M. 1972. An economist–financial analyst's approach to valuing stock of a closely held company. *Journal of Taxation* (June)353–354.

Gerard, B., P. Hillion, and F. de Roon. 2002. International portfolio diversification:

Industry, country, and currency effects revisited. Working paper, INSEAD, Fontainebleau, France.

Gerstein, Mark D. 1996. *Earnouts: An Outline of Key Issues, Acquiring or Selling the Privately Held Company.* New York: Practising Law Institute.

Gertner, R., E. Powers, and D. Scharfstein. 2002. Learning about internal capital markets from corporate spin-offs. *Journal of Finance* 57(6):2479–2506.

Ghosh, A. 2001. Does operating performance really improve following corporate acquisitions? *Journal of Corporate Finance* 7(2, June):151–178.

Ghosh, A. 2002. Increasing market share as a rationale for corporate acquisitions. Baruch College working paper (May).

Ghosh, A., and W. Ruland. 1998. Managerial ownership and the method of payment for acquisitions, and executive job retention. *Journal of Finance* 53(2):785–797.

Gil, M., and P. Gonzalez de la Fe. 1999. Strategic alliances, organizational learning, and new product development: The cases of Rover and Seat. *R&D Management* 29(4):391–404.

Gilson, R. 1982. The case against shark repellent amendments: Structural limitations on the enabling concept. *Stanford Law Review* 34(1982):792–804.

Gilson, Ronald. 1984. Value creation by business lawyers: Legal skills and asset pricing. *Yale Law Journal* 94:239ff.

Gilson, Ronald J. 1994. Corporate governance and economic efficiency. Pages 131–141 in Mats Isaksson and Rolf Skog, eds., *Aspects of Corporate Governance.* Stockholm: Juristförlaget.

Gilson, Ronald J. 1997. Regulating the equity component of capital structure: The SEC's response to the one share–one vote controversy. In Donald H. Chew, ed., *Studies in International Corporate Finance and Governance Systems.* New York: Oxford University Press.

Gilson, Ronald J., and Bernard S. Black. 1995. *The Law and Finance of Corporate Acquisitions*, 2d ed. Westbury, NY: Foundation Press.

Gilson, S. 2000. Analysts and information gaps: Lessons from the UAL buyout. *Financial Analysts Journal* (November/December):82–110.

Gilson, S., and C. Escalle. 1998. Chase Manhattan Corporation: The making of America's largest bank. Harvard Business School case study 9-298-016.

Ginsburg, Martin D., and Jack S. Levin. 1996a. *Mergers, Acquisitions and Buyouts: Sample Acquisition Agreements with Tax and Legal Analysis.* Boston: Little, Brown.

Ginsburg, Martin D., and Jack S. Levin. 1996b. *Mergers, Acquisitions and Buyouts: A Transactional Analysis of the Governing Tax, Legal, and Accounting Considerations.* Boston: Little, Brown.

Ginsburg, M., and J. Levin. 1997. Mergers, acquisitions and buyouts. *Aspen Law and Business* (January).

Gish, Al, Z. Gu., and P. Jain. 2003. Price-earnings multiples and sustained earnings and revenue growth. Working paper, downloaded from http://papers.ssrn.com/sol3/papers.cfm?abstract_id=404840.

Gladwell, Malcolm. 1999. Six degrees of Lois Weisberg. *New Yorker* (January 11). Downloaded from http://www.gladwell.com/1999/1999_01_11_a_weisberg.htm.

Gladwell, Malcolm. 2000. *The Tipping Point: How Little Things Can Make a Big Difference.* Boston: Little, Brown.

Gleick, J. 1998. *Chaos: Making a New Science.* New York: Penguin Books.

Godfrey, Stephen, and Ramon Espinosa. 1996. A practical approach to calculating costs of equity for investments in emerging markets. *Journal of Applied Corporate Finance* 9(5):80–89.

Goergen, M., and L. Renneboog. 2003. Shareholder wealth effects of European domestic and cross-border takeover bids. European Corporate Governance Institute (January), Finance working paper no. 08/2003.

Golbe, D., and L. White. 1988. Mergers and acquisitions in the U.S. economy: An aggregate and historical overview. Pages 25–47 in A. Auerbach, ed., *Mergers and Acquisitions*. Chicago: University of Chicago Press.

Golbe, D., and L. White. 1993. Catch a wave: The time series behavior of mergers. *Review of Economics and Statistics* 75(August):493–499.

Goldstein, Marvin M. 1989. How labor audits can reveal added value at a target. *Mergers & Acquisitions* (January/February):51–55.

Gompers, Paul. 1995. Optimal investment, monitoring, and the staging of venture capital. *Journal of Finance* 50:1461–1489.

Gompers, Paul, and Josh Lerner. 1999. *The Venture Capital Cycle*. Cambridge: MIT Press.

Gompers, Paul, Joy Ishi, and Andrew Metrick. 2001. Corporate governance and equity prices. NBER working paper 8449.

Gonzalez, P., G. M. Vasconcellos, and R. J. Kish. 1997. Cross-border mergers and acquisitions: The undervaluation hypothesis. *Quarterly Review of Economics and Finance* 38:(1):25–45.

Goodman, Stephen H. 1979. Foreign exchange rate forecasting techniques: Implications for business and policy. *Journal of Finance* (May):415–427.

Goold, Michael, and Andrew Campbell. 1998. Desperately Seeking Synergy. *Harvard Business Review* (September–October):131–143. Reprint no. 98504.

Gordon Group. 1992. Active investing in the US equity market: Past performance and future prospects. (December 2). Working paper, cited in Robert A. G. Monks and Nell Minow. 1995. *Corporate Governance*. Cambridge, England: Basil Blackwell.

Gordon, Lilli A., and John Pound. 1993. Information, ownership structure, and shareholder voting: Evidence from shareholder-sponsored corporate governance proposals. *Journal of Finance* 68:697–718.

Gordon, Myron J., and Joseph Yagil. 1981. Financial gain from conglomerate mergers. *Research in Finance* 3:103–142.

Gort, M. 1969. An economic disturbance theory of mergers. *Quarterly Journal of Economics* 83(November):624–642.

Gosh, A., Z. Gu, and P. Jain. 2003. Price-earnings multiples and sustained earnings and revenue growth. Carnegie Mellon University working paper, downloaded from http://papers.ssrn.com/sol3/papers.cfm?abstract_id=404840.

Graham, J., and C. Harvey. 2001. The theory and practice of corporate finance: Evidence from the field. *Journal of Financial Economics* 60:187–243.

Graham, J., M. Lemmon, and J. Wolf. 2002. Does corporate diversification destroy value? *Journal of Finance* 57:695–720.

Granovetter, M. 1995. *Getting a Job: A Study of Contacts and Careers*, 2d ed. Chicago: University of Chicago Press.

Granovetter, Mark. 1973. The strength of weak ties. *American Journal of Sociology* 78(6):1360–1380.

Greenberg, Herb. 1998. EBITDA: Never trust anything that you can't pronounce. *Fortune* (June 22):192–194.

Gregory, A. 1997. An examination of the long run performance of U.K. acquiring firms. *Journal of Business Finance & Accounting* 24(7/8, September):971–1002.

Grenadier, S. R., and A. Weiss. 1997. Investment in technological innovations: An option pricing approach. *Journal of Financial Economics* 44(3):397–416.

Grenadier, Steven R. 2000. Option exercise games: The intersection of real options and game theory. *Journal of Applied Corporate Finance* 13(2, Summer):99–107.

Griffin, J., and A. Karolyi. 1998. Another look at the role of the industrial structure of markets for international diversification strategies. *Journal of Financial Economics* 50:351–373.

Grinblatt, M., S. Titman, and R. Wermers. 1995. Momentum investment strategies, portfolio performance, and herding: A study of mutual fund behavior. *American Economic Review* 85:1088–1105.

Grinold, R., A. Rudd, and D. Stefek. 1989. Global factors: Fact or fiction. *Journal of Portfolio Management* (Fall).

Grossman, S., and O. Hart. 1980. Takeover bids, the free-rider problem, and the theory of the corporation. *Bell Journal of Economics* 11:42–64.

Grubb, Thomas M., and Robert B. Lamb. 2000. *Capitalize on Merger Chaos*. New York: Free Press.

Gu, Z., C. Lee, and J. Rosett. 2002. Measuring the pervasiveness of earnings management from quarterly accrual volatility. Carnegie Mellon University working paper, downloaded from http://papers.ssrn.com/sol3/papers.cfm?abstract_id=305764.

Guare, John. 1990. *Six Degrees of Separation: A Play*. New York: Vintage Books.

Gupta, A., and L. Misra. Undated. Regulatory change, profitability, and managerial motives in financial mergers. Bentley College working paper.

Hadlock, C., M. Ryngaert., and S. Thomas. 2001. Corporate structure and equity offerings: Are there benefits to diversification? *Journal of Business* 74(4):613–635.

Hahera, John S., Jr., and William Pugh. 1991. State takeover legislation: The case of delaware. *Journal of Law, Economics, and Organizations* 7:410.

Hall, B. 1991. The impact of corporate restructuring on industrial research and development. NBER working paper W3216.

Hall, L. S., and T. C. Polacek. 1994. Strategies for obtaining the largest valuation discounts. *Estate Planning* (January/February):38–44.

Hall, P. L. 1998. An examination of stick returns to firms adopting golden parachutes under certain conditions. *American Business Review* 16(1):123–130.

Hambrick, D., and L. Crozier. 1985. Stumblers and stars in the management of rapid growth. *Journal of Business Venturing* 1(1):31–45

Hamel, Gary, and C. K. Pralahad. 1994. *Competing for the Future*. Boston: Harvard Business School Press.

Hamel, G. 1996. Strategy as revolution. *Harvard Business Review* (July–August): 69–82.

Hammond, John S., Ralph L. Keeney, and Howard Raiffa. 1998. Even swaps: A rational method for making trade-offs. *Harvard Business Review* (March–April). Reprint no. 98206.

Handa, Puneet, and A. R. Radhakrishnan. 1991. An empirical investigation of leveraged recapitalizations with cash payout as takeover defense. *Financial Management* (Fall):58–69.

Hannes, S. 2001. The missing link in the corporate takeover literature. Stanford/Yale Junior Faculty Forum Research Paper 01-08, downloaded from http://papers.ssrn.com/paper.taf?abstract_id=275474.

Hannes, S. 2002. The hidden virtue of antitakeover defenses. Harvard Law School discussion paper no. 354, downloaded from http://papers.ssrn.com/papers=304389.

Hanouna, P., A. Sarin, and A. Shapiro. 2000. Value of corporate control: Some international evidence. Working paper, Marshall School of Business, University of Southern California.

Hansen, R., and J. Lott. 1996. Externalities and corporate objectives in a world with diversified shareholders/consumers. *Journal of Financial and Quantitative Analysis* 31:43–68.

Hansen, R. G. 1987. A theory for the choice of exchange medium in mergers and acquisitions. *Journal of Business* 60:75–95.

Harberger, Arnold C. 1974; reprint ed. 1978. *Taxation and Welfare*. Chicago: University of Chicago Press.

Harford, J. 1999. Corporate cash reserves and acquisitions. *Journal of Finance* 54(6, December):1969–1997.

Harrigan, K. 1984. Formulating vertical integration strategies. *Academy of Management Review* 9(9):638–652.

Harrigan, K. 1985. *Managing for Joint Venture Success*. New York: Praeger.

Harris, M., and A. Raviv. 1988. Corporate control contests and capital structure. *Journal of Financial Economics* 20:55–86.

Harris, M., and A. Raviv. 1991. The theory of optimal capital structure. *Journal of Finance* 48(March):297–356.

Harris, M., and A. Raviv. 1996. The capital budgeting process: Incentives and information. *Journal of Finance* 51:1139–1174.

Harris, R. S., and D. Ravenscraft. 1991. The role of acquisitions in foreign direct investment: Evidence from the U.S. stock market. *Journal of Finance* 46:825–844.

Harris, Robert S., Julian R. Franks, and Colin Mayer. 1987. Means of payment in takeovers: Results for the U.K., and U.S. Cambridge, MA: National Bureau of Economic Research working paper no. 2456.

Harrison, J. S., and C. H. St. John. 1994. *Strategic Management of Organizations and Stakeholders: Theory and Cases*. St. Paul, MN: West Publishing.

Harrison, Joan. 1999. Finding the ethics soft spots of a target. *Mergers and Acquisitions* (September/October):8–11.

Harvey, C. 1995. Predictable risk and returns in emerging markets. *Review of Financial Studies* 8:773–816.

Hasbrouck, Joel. 1985. The characteristics of takeover targets. *Journal of Banking and Finance* 9:351–362.

Haspeslagh, Philippe, and David B. Jemison. 1991. *Managing Acquisitions: Creating Value through Corporate Renewal*. New York: Free Press.

Hass, J. 1996. Directional fiduciary duties in a tracking stock equity structure: The need for a duty of fairness. *Michigan Law Review* 94:2089–2177.

Hauser, S., and B. Lauterbach. 2000. The value of voting rights to majority shareholders: Evidence from dual-class stock unifications. Working paper. Ramat Gan, Israel: School of Business Administration, Bar Han University.

Haushalter, D., and W. Mikkelson. 2001. An investigation of the gains from specialized equity: Tracking stock and minority carve-outs. University of Oregon working paper.

Hax, A., and N. Majluf. 1984. *Strategic Management: An Integrative Perspective*. Englewood Cliffs, NJ: Prentice-Hall.

Hayes, R., and D. Garvin. 1982. Managing as if tomorrow mattered. *Harvard Business Review* (May–June):71–79.

Hayes, Robert H., and Steven C. Wheelwright. 1979. Link manufacturing process and product life cycles. *Harvard Business Review* 133–140.

Hayn, C. 1989. Tax attributes as determinants of shareholder gains in corporate acquisitions. *Journal of Financial Economics* 23:121–153.

Healey, P., and J. Wahlen. 1999. A review of the earnings management literature and its implications for standard setting. *Accounting Horizons* 14(4):365–383.

Healy, P., K. Palepu, and R. Ruback. 1992. Does corporate performance improve after mergers? *Journal of Financial Economics* 31(2, April):135–175.

Healy, P., K. Palepu, and R. Ruback. 1997. Which takeovers are profitable: Strategic of financial? *Sloan Management Review* 38(4, Summer):45–57.

Heaney, R., and M. Holmen. 2002. Shareholder diversification and the value of control. Working paper. Canberra, Australia: School of Finance and Applied Statistics, Australian National University.

Hearth, D., and J. K. Zaima. 1986. Divestiture uncertainty and shareholder wealth: Evidence from the U.S.A. (1975–1982). *Journal of Business Finance & Accounting* 71–85.

Hellerman, M., and B. Jones. 2000. The would'ves, could'ves, and should'ves of spin-offs. *Journal of Business Strategy* 21(4):10–14.

Hennessy, D. 2000. Corporate spin-offs, bankruptcy, investment, and the value of debt. *Insurance: Mathematics and Economics* 27:229–235.

Herman, E., and L. Lowenstein. 1988. The efficiency effect of hostile takeovers. Pages 211–240 in J. C. Coffee, Jr., L. Lowenstein, and S. Rose-Ackerman, eds., *Knights, Raiders, and Targets*. New York: Oxford University Press.

Heron, R., and E. Lie. 2002. Operating performance and the method of payment in takeovers. *Journal of Financial and Quantitative Analysis* 37:137–155.

Heron, R. A., and W. G. Lewellen. 1998. An empirical analysis of the reincorporation decision. *Journal of Financial and Quantitative Analysis* 33(4):549–568.

Hertzel, M., and R. L. Smith. 1993. Market discounts and shareholder gains for placing equity privately. *Journal of Finance* 48:459–485.

Hertzel, M., M. Lemmon, J. Linck, and L. Rees. 2002. Long-run performance following private placements of equity. *Journal of Finance* 57:6(December):2595–2617.

Heston, S. L., and K. G. Rouwenhorst. 1994. Does industrial structure explain the benefits of international diversification? *Journal of Financial Economics* 36:3–27.

Hevert, Kathleen. 2001. Real options primer: A practical synthesis of concepts and valuation approaches. *Journal of Applied Corporate Finance* 14(2, Summer):25–40.

Hietala, P., S. Kaplan, and D. Robinson. 2002. What is the price of hubris? Using takeover battles to infer overpayments and synergies. NBER working paper no. W9264 (October).

Hirschman, Albert O. 1970. *Exit, Voice and Loyalty*. Cambridge: Harvard University.

Hisey, K. B., and R. E. Caves. 1985. Diversification and choice of country. *Journal of International Business Studies* 16:51–65.

Hite, G., and J. Owers. 1983. Security price reactions around corporate spin-off announcements. *Journal of Financial Economics* 12:409–436.

Hite, G., J. Owers, and R. Rogers. 1987. The market for inter-firm asset sales: Partial sell-offs and total liquidations. *Journal of Financial Economics* 18:229–252.

Hitt, M., E. Levitas, and A. Borza. 2000. Partner selection in emerging and developed market contexts: Resource-based and organizational learning perspective. *Academy of Management Journal* 43(3):449–467.

Hitt, M. A., M. T. Dacin, E. Levitas, J-L. Arregle, and A. Borza. 2000. Partner selection in emerging and developed market contexts: Resource-based and organizational learning perspectives. *Academy of Management Journal* 43(3):449–467.

Hitt, M. A., R. D. Ireland, and R. E. Hoskisson. 1995. *Strategic Management: Competitiveness and Globalization*. St. Paul, MN: West Publishing.

Hitt, M. A., R. D. Nixon, R. E. Hoskisson, and R. Kochhar. 1999. Corporate entrepreneurship and cross-functional fertilization: Activation, process and disintegration of a new product design team. *Entrepreneurship: Theory & Practice* 230:145–167.

Hogan, K., and G. Olson. Undated. A comparison of equity carve-outs and original initial public offers: The differential impact of information asymmetry related variables and underpricing. St. Joseph's University working paper, available by e-mail from Hogan@sju.edu.

Hoi, C., H. Lessard, and A. Robin. 2000. The effect of state anti-takeover laws on board competition. *American Business Review* 18(1):9–18.

Holmstrom, B., and J. Tirole. 1993. Market liquidity and performance monitoring. *Journal of Political Economy* 101:678–709.

Holmstrom, B., and S. Kaplan. 2001. Corporate governance and merger activity in the U.S.: Making sense of the 1980s and 1990s. NBER working paper W8220.

Holmstrom, B., and S. Kaplan. 2003. The state of U.S. corporate governance: What's right and what's wrong? *Journal of Applied Corporate Finance* 15(5):8–21.

Hong, Hai, Robert S. Kaplan, and Gershon Mandelker. 1978. Pooling vs. purchase: The effects of accounting for mergers on stock prices. *Accounting Review* 53(January):31–47.

Horner, Melchior R. 1988. The value of the corporate voting right: Evidence from Switzerland. *Journal of Banking and Finance* 12:69–83.

Hoskisson, R., R. Johnson, and D. Moesel. 1994. Divestment intensity of restructuring firms: Effects of governance, strategy and performance. *Academy of Management Journal* 37:1207–1251.

Houston, J., C. James, and M. Ryngaert. 2001. Where do merger gains come from? Bank mergers from the perspective of insiders and outsiders. *Journal of Financial Economics* 60(2/3, May/June):285–331.

Houston, Joel F., and Michael D. Ryngaert. 1996. The value added by bank acquisitions: Lessons from Wells Fargo's acquisition of First Interstate. *Journal of Applied Corporate Finance* 9(2, Summer).

Howeling, P., A. Mentink, and T. Vorst. 2002. Is liquidity reflected in bond yields? Evidence from the euro corporate bond market. Working paper. Rotterdam: Erasmus University. http://store.yahoo.com/fasbpubs/publications-statements-of-standards—126-150-.html.

Huang, Y., and R. Walkling. 1987. Target abnormal returns associated with acquisition announcements: Payment, acquisition form, and managerial resistance. *Journal of Financial Economics* 19(2):329–350.

Huang, Yen-Sheng, and Ralph A. Walkling. 1987. Abnormal returns associated with acquisition announcements: Payment, acquisition form, and managerial resistance. *Journal of Financial Economics* 19:329–350.

Hubbard, G., and D. Palia. 1999. A re-examination of the conglomerate merger wave in the 1960s: An internal capital markets view. *Journal of Finance* 54:1131–1152.

Huber, P., and J. Trenkwalder. 2000. Austria: Creeping-in regulations. *International Financial Law Review* 19(11):52.

Huiskes, C. 1998. Dutch proposals to restrict anti-takeover devices. *International Financial Law Review* 17(3):29–31.

Hulburt, H., J. Miles, and R. Woolridge. 2000. Value creation from equity carve-outs. *Financial Management* (Spring):83–100.

Hull, John C. 1997. *Options, Futures, and Other Derivatives,* 3d ed. Englewood Cliffs, NJ: Prentice-Hall.

Hyland, D., and J. Diltz. 2002. Why firms diversify: An empirical examination. *Financial Management* (Spring):51–81.

Ingham, H., I. Kran, and A. Lovestam. 1992. Mergers and profitability: A managerial success story? *Journal of Management Studies* 29(2, March):195–209.

Inkpen, A. 2000. Learning through joint ventures: A framework of knowledge acquisition. *Journal of Management Studies* 37(7): 1019–1043.

The Internet bounce for equity carve-outs. 1999. *Mergers & Acquisitions* 33(5):27–34.

Isakov, D., and F. Sonney. 2002. Are practitioners right? On the relative importance of industrial factors in international stock returns. Working paper, HEC-University of Geneva.

Jackson, P. 1982. *The Political Economy of Bureaucracy*. Oxford: Philip Allan.

Jacquet, Pierre, Robert Bruner, and Samuel Bodily. 1999. Genzyme/GelTex Pharmaceuticals joint venture. Charlottesville, VA: Darden Case Collection, University of Virginia, UVA-F-1254 and its associated teaching note.

Jacquillat, B., and B. Solnik. 1978. Multinationals are poor tools for diversification. *Journal of Portfolio Management* 4(Winter):8–12.

Jain, P. 1985. The effect of voluntary sell-off announcements on shareholder wealth. *Journal of Finance* 40:209–224.

Jarrell, G., and A. Poulsen. 1989. The returns to acquiring firms in tender offers: Evidence from three decades. *Financial Management* 18(3, Autumn):12–19.

Jarrell, G., and M. Bradley. 1980. The economic effects of federal and state regulations of cash tender offers. *Journal of Law and Economics* 23(2, October):371–407.

Jarrell, G., J. Brickley, and J. Netter. 1998. The market for corporate control: The empirical evidence since 1980. *Journal of Economic Perspectives* 2(2, Winter): 49–68.

Jarrell, G. A. 1985. The wealth effects of litigation by targets: Do interests diverge in a merger? *Journal of Law and Economics* 28:151.

Jarrell, G. A., and A. B. Poulsen. 1987. Shark repellents and stock prices: The effects of antitakeover amendments since 1980. *Journal of Financial Economics* 19(1):127–169.

Jarrell, G. A., and A. B. Poulsen. 1989. Stock trading before the announcement of tender offers: Insider trading or market anticipation? *Journal of Law, Economics and Organizations* 5:225–249.

Jayaratne, J., and C. Shapiro. 2000. Simulating partial asset divestitures to "fix" mergers. *International Journal of Economics of Business* 7(2):179–200.

Jegadeesh, N., and S. Titman. 1993. Returns to buying winners and selling losers: Implications for stock market efficiency. *Journal of Finance* 48:65–91.

Jensen, M. 1986. Agency costs of free cash flow, corporate finance, and takeovers. *American Economic Review* 76(2, May):323–329.

Jensen, M. 1988. Takeovers: Their causes and consequences. *Journal of Economic Perspectives* 2(Winter):21–48.

Jensen, M. 1989a. The eclipse of the public corporation. *Harvard Business Review* 61–74.

Jensen, M. 1989b. Active investors, LBOs, and the privatization of bankruptcy. *Journal of Applied Corporate Finance* 2(1):35–44.

Jensen, M. 1993. The modern industrial revolution, exit, and the failure of internal control systems. *Journal of Finance* 48(July):831–880. Reprinted in D. Chew, *The New Corporate Finance*. Burr Ridge, IL: Irwin McGraw-Hill. 1999.

Jensen, M., and R. Ruback. 1983. The market for corporate control: The scientific evidence. *Journal of Financial Economics* 11(1–4, April):5–50.

Jensen, M. C., and W. H. Meckling. 1976. Theory of the firm: Managerial behavior, agency costs, and ownership structure. *Journal of Financial Economics* (3):305–360.

John, K., and E. Ofek. 1995. Asset sales and increase in focus. *Journal of Financial Economics* 37:105–126.

Johnson, B. 1999a. Restricted stock discounts, 1991–1995. *Shannon Pratt's Business Valuation Update* (March):1–3.

Johnson, B. 1999b. Quantitative support for discounts for lack of marketability. *Business Valuation Review* (December):152–155.

Johnson, L. Todd, and Bryan D. Yokley. 1997. Issues associated with the FASB project on business combinations. Financial Accounting Series, no. 174-A, Financial Accounting Standards Board (June).

Johnson, M. 1993. *Moral Imagination.* Chicago: University of Chicago Press.

Johnson, M. S., and R. P. Rao. 1999. The impact of anti-takeover charter amendments on expectations of future earnings and takeover activity. *Managerial and Decision Economics* 51(3):75–86.

Johnson, S., D. Klein, and V. Thibodeaux. 1996. The effects of spin-offs on corporate investment and performance. *Journal of Financial Research* 19:293–307.

Johnson, S. A., and M. B. Houston. 2000. A reexamination of the motives and gains in joint ventures. *Journal of Financial and Quantitative Analysis* 35(1, March):67–86.

Jones, E. Phillip, and Scott P. Mason. 1986. Equity-linked debt. *Midland Corporate Finance Journal* 3(4, Winter):46–58.

Jovanovic, B., and P. Rousseau. 2002. Mergers as reallocation. NBER working paper no. 9279 (October).

Kabir, R., D. Cantrijn, and A. Jeunink. 1997. Takeover defenses, ownership structure and stock returns in the Netherlands: An empirical analysis. *Strategic Management Journal* 18(2):97–109.

Kahl, M., J. Liu, and F. Longstaff. 2003. Paper millionaires: How valuable is stock to a stockholder who is restricted from selling it? *Journal of Financial Economics* 67:385–410.

Kahneman, D., and A. Tversky. 1979. Prospect theory: An analysis of decision under risk. *Econometrica* (March):263–291.

Kahneman, D., and A. Tversky. 1984. Choices, values and frames. *American Psychologist* (April):341–350.

Kaiser, K., and A. Stouraitis. 2001. Reversing corporate diversification and the use of the proceeds from asset sales: The case of Thorn EMI. *Financial Management* 4:63–102.

Kale, J. R., T. H. Noe, and G. D. Gay. 1989. Share repurchase through transferable put rights: Theory and case study. *Journal of Financial Economics* (November):141–160.

Kale, P., H. Singh, and H. Perlmutter. 2000. Learning and protection of proprietary assets in strategic alliances: Building relational capital. *Strategic Management Journal* 21:217–237.

Kamara, Avraham. 1994. Liquidity, taxes, and short-term Treasury yields. *Journal of Financial and Quantitative Analysis* 29:403–417.

Kang, J. K. 1993. The international market for corporate control: Mergers and acquisitions of U.S. firms by Japanese firms. *Journal of Financial Economics* 34(3):345–371.

Kaplan, S. 1989a. The effects of management buyouts on operating performance and value. *Journal of Financial Economics* 24(2, October):217–254.

Kaplan, S. 1989b. Sources of value in management buyouts. Chapter 4 in Y. Amihud, ed., *Leveraged Management Buyouts.* Homewood, IL: Dow Jones–Irwin.

Kaplan, S. 1989c. Management buyouts: Evidence on taxes as a source of value. *Journal of Finance* 44:611–633.

Kaplan, S. 1989d. Campeau's acquisition of Federated: Value destroyed or value added. *Journal of Financial Economics* 25(2, December):191–212.

Kaplan, S. 1992. The staying power of leveraged buyouts. NBER working paper, W3653. Printed in Donald H. Chew, ed., *Studies in International Corporate Finance and Governance Systems.* New York: Oxford University Press, 1997.

Kaplan, Steven N. 1997. Corporate governance and corporate performance: A comparison of Germany, Japan, and the U.S. In Donald H. Chew, ed., *Studies in International Corporate Finance and Governance Systems.* New York: Oxford University Press.

Kaplan, S., and G. Andrade. 1997. How costly is financial (not economic) distress? Evidence from highly leveraged transactions that became distressed. Working paper, downloadable from http://papers.ssrn.com/sol3/papers.cfm?abstract_id=29359.

Kaplan, S., M. Jensen, and L. Stiglin. 1992. Effects of LBOs on tax revenues of the U.S. Treasury. *Tax Notes* 42:(6).

Kaplan, S. N., M. L. Mitchell, and K. H. Wruck. 1997. A clinical exploration of value creation and destruction in acquisitions: Organizational design, incentives, and internal capital markets. Center for Research in Security Prices working paper no. 450 (July).

Kaplan, S., and J. Stein. 1992. The evolution of buyout pricing and financial structure in the 1980s. *Quarterly Journal of Economics* 2(May):313–357.

Kaplan, S., and M. Weisbach. 1992. The success of acquisitions: evidence from divestitures. *Journal of Finance* 47:108–138.

Karpoff, Jonathan M., and Paul H. Malatesta. 1989. The wealth effects of second-generation takeover legislation. *Journal of Financial Economics* 25:291.

Kaslow, A. M. 2000. The best defense for takeover pressure: Be prepared. *Community Banker* 9(5):26–29.

Katzenbach, Jon, and Douglas Smith. 1993. *The Wisdom of Teams.* Boston: Harvard Business School Press.

Keck, T., E. Levengood, and A. Longfield. 1998. Using discounted flow analysis in an international setting: A survey of issues in modeling the cost of capital. *Journal of Applied Corporate Finance* 11(3, Fall):82–99.

Kellogg, David, and John M. Charnes. 2000. Real-options valuation for a biotechnology company. *Financial Analysts Journal* (May/June):76–87.

Kelly, J., C. Cook, and D. Spitzer. 1999. *Unlocking Shareholder Value: The Keys to Success.* New York: KPMG LLP.

Kelly, K. 1994. *Out of Control: The New Biology of Machines, Social Systems, and the Economic World.* Reading, MA: Addison-Wesley.

Kenc, T. 2000. Discussion of optimal entrepreneurial financial contracting. *Journal of Business Finance and Accounting* 27:1375–1378.

Kennedy, R. 2000. The effect of bankruptcy filings on rivals' operating performance: Evidence from 51 large bankruptcies. *International Journal of the Economics of Business* 7(1):5–25.

Kester, C. 1981. Growth options and investment: A dynamic perspective on the firm's allocation of resources. Ph.D. dissertation, Harvard University.

Kester, C. 1984. Today's options for tomorrow's growth. *Harvard Business Review* (March-April):153–160.

Kester, W. Carl. 1986. An options approach to corporate finance. In E. I. Altman, ed., *Handbook of Corporate Finance.* New York: John Wiley & Sons.

Kester, Carl. 1997a. Governance, contracting, and investment horizons: A look at Japan and Germany. In Donald H. Chew, ed., *Studies in International Corporate Finance and Governance Systems.* New York: Oxford University Press.

Kester, Carl. 1997b. The hidden costs of Japanese success. In Donald H. Chew, ed., *Studies in International Corporate Finance and Governance Systems.* New York: Oxford University Press.

Khanna, T., and K. Palepu. 1997. Why focused strategies may be wrong for emerging markets. *Harvard Business Review* (July–August):41–51.

Khanna, T., and K. Palepu. 2000. Is group affiliation profitable in emerging markets? An analysis of diversified Indian business groups. *Journal of Finance* 55: 867–891.

Kidder, R. 1997. Ethics and the bottom line: Ten reasons for businesses to do right. *Insights on Global Ethics* (Spring):7–9.

Kim, C., and R. Mauborgne. 2002. Charting your company's future. *Harvard Business Review* (June):77–83.

Kim, E. H., and J. D. Schatzberg. 1987. Voluntary corporate liquidations. *Journal of Financial Economics* 19:311–328.

Kim, Y., and R. McElreath. 2001. Managing operating exposure: A case study of the automobile industry. *Multinational Business Review* 9(1):21–26.

Kindleberger, C. 1969. *American Business Abroad: Six Lectures on Direct Investment.* New Haven: Yale University Press.

King, A. 2001. Applying new M&A accounting rules. *Strategic Finance* 83(3). Downloaded from http://global.factiva.com/en/arch/display.asp.

Kirch, D. P., R. BarNiv, and L. J. Zucca. 1998. Investment strategies based on completion of open market repurchase programs. *Journal of Financial Statement Analysis* 3(2):5–13.

Kiymaz, H., and T. K. Mukherjee. 2000. The impact of country diversification of wealth effects in cross-border mergers. *Financial Review* 35:37–58.

Klapper, Leora, and Inessa Love. 2002. Corporate governance, investor protection, and performance in emerging markets. World Bank working paper.

Kleiman, Robert. 1988. The shareholder gains from leveraged cash-outs: Some preliminary evidence. *Journal of Applied Corporate Finance* (Spring).

Klein, A. 1986. The timing and substance of divestiture announcements: Individual, simultaneous and cumulative effects. *Journal of Finance* 41:685–696.

Klein, A., and J. Rosenfeld. 1988. Targeted share repurchases and top management changes. *Journal of Financial Economics* 493–506.

Klein, P. 2001. Were the acquisitive conglomerates inefficient? *RAND Journal of Economics* 32(4):745–761.

Klein, A., J. Rosenfeld, and W. Beranek 1991. The two stages of an equity carve out and the price response of parent and subsidiary stock. *Managerial and Decision Economics* 12(December):449–460.

Kling, Lou R., and Eileen Nugent Simon. 1995. *Negotiated Acquisitions of Companies, Subsidiaries and Divisions.* New York: Law Journal Seminars Press.

Koedijk, K., and M. Van Dijk. 2000. The cost of capital of cross-listed firms. Rotterdam: Erasmus University, working paper.

Koedijk, K., C. Kool, P. Schotman, and M. Van Dijk. 2002. The cost of capital in international financial markets: Local or global. Centre for Economic Policy Research, working paper, http://'www.cepr.org/pubs/dpsDP3062.asp.

Koeplin, J., A. Sarin, and A. C. Shapiro. 2000. The private company discount. *Journal of Applied Corporate Finance* 12(4)94–101.

Kogut, B., and N. Kulatilaka. 1994a. Options thinking and platform investments: Investing in opportunity. *California Management Review* (Winter):52–71.

Kogut, B., and N. Kulatilaka. 1994b. Operating flexibility, global manufacturing, and the option value of a multinational network. *Management Science* 40(1):123–139.

Kogut, B., and N. Kulatilaka. 1997. Capabilities as real options. Proceedings of the Conference on Risk, Managers, and Options, in Honor of Edward Bowman, Reginald Jones Center, Wharton School of Business, University of Pennsylvania.

Koh. J., and N. Venkataraman. 1991. Joint venture formation and stock market reaction: An assessment in the information technology sector. *Academy of Management Journal* 34:869–892.

Kohers, N., and T. Kohers. 2000. The value creation potential of high-tech mergers. *Financial Analysts Journal* 53(3, May/June):40–48.

Kohers, N., and T. Kohers. 2001a. Takeovers of technology firms: Expectations vs. reality. *Financial Management* (Autumn):35–54.

Kohers, N., and T. Kohers. 2001b. Domestic versus cross-border takeovers of U.S. targets: Why do foreign bidders pay more? Working paper, University of South Florida.

Kohers, Ninon, and James Ang. 2000. Earnouts in mergers: Agreeing to disagree and agreeing to stay. *Journal of Business* 73:445–476.

Koretz, G. 1998. A payoff from failed takeovers. *BusinessWeek* (February 9):30.

Kosedag, A., and W. Lane. 2002. Is it free cash flow, tax savings, or neither? An empirical confirmation of two leading going-private explanations: The case of reLBOs. *Journal of Business Finance and Accounting* 29:257–271.

Kotter, John P. 1995. Why transformation efforts fail. *Harvard Business Review* (March–April).

KPMG. 1999a. *Unlocking Shareholder Value: The Keys to Success.* (Authorship unattributed, but foreword by John Kelly, Colin Cook, and Don Spitzer.) New York: KPMG International.

KPMG. 1999b. The new art of the deal: How leading organizations realize value from transactions. White paper. (Authorship unattributed.) New York: KPMG International.

KPMG International. 2002. KPMG's corporate tax rate survey—January 2002. New York: KPMG International.

Krishnaswami, S., and V. Subramaniam. 1999. Information asymmetry, valuation, and the corporate spin-off decision. *Journal of Financial Economics* 53:73–112.

Kritzman, M., and S. Page. 2002. The hierarchy of investment choice: A normative interpretation. Working paper, Windham Capital Management, Boston.

Krugman, Paul. 1998. *Pop Internationalism.* New York: Norton.

Kruse, T. 2002. Asset liquidity and the determinants of asset sales by poorly performing firms. *Financial Management* 4:107–129.

Kruse, T., H. Park, K. Park, and K. Suzuki. 2002. The value of corporate diversification: Evidence from post-merger performance in Japan. Working paper, University of Arkansas, available by e-mail from tkruse@walton.uark.edu.

Kuipers, D., D. Miller, and A. Patel. 2003. The legal environment and corporate valuation: Evidence from cross-border mergers. Texas Tech University working paper (January).

Kulatilaka, N., and S. Marks. 1988. The strategic value of flexibility: Reducing the ability to compromise. *American Economic Review* 78:574–580.

Kulatilaka, Nalin, and Alan J. Marcus. 1992. Project valuation under uncertainty: When does DCF fail? *Journal of Applied Corporate Finance* 5(3, Fall):92–100.

Kummer D., and R. Hoffmeister. 1978. Valuation consequences of cash tender offers. *Journal of Finance* 33(2, May):505–516.

Kunz, Roger M., and J. J. Angel. 1996. Factors affecting the value of the stock voting right: Evidence from the Swiss equity market. *Financial Management* 24:7–20.

La Porta, R., F. Lopez-de-Silanes, and A. Shleifer. 2002. Investor protection and corporate valuation. *Journal of Finance* (June).

La Porta, R., F. Lopez-de-Silanes, A. Shleifer, and R. Vishny. 1997. Legal determinants of external finance. *Journal of Finance* 52(July):1131–1150.

La Porta, R., F. Lopez-de-Silanes, A. Shleifer, and R. Vishny. 1998. Law and finance. *Journal of Political Economy* 106:1113–1155.

La Porta, R., F. Lopez-de-Silanes, A. Shleifer, and R. Vishny. 1999. Corporate ownership around the world. *Journal of Finance* 54:471–517.

La Porta, R., F. Lopez-de-Silanes, A. Shleifer, and R. Vishny. 2000. Investor protection and corporate governance. *Journal of Financial Economics* 58:3–27.

Lajoux, A. R., and J. F. Weston. 1998. Do deals deliver on postmerger performance? *Mergers & Acquisitions* (2, September–October):34–38.

Lajoux, Alexandra Reed. 1998. *The Art of M&A Integration: A Guide to Merging Resources, Processes, & Responsibilities.* New York: McGraw-Hill.

Lambrecht, B. 2002. The timing of takeovers under uncertainty: A real options approach. University of Cambridge working paper (April).

Lamont, O. 1997. Cash flow and investment: Evidence from internal capital markets. *Journal of Finance* 52:83–110.

Lamont, O., and C. Polk. 2001. The diversification discount: Cash flows versus returns. *Journal of Finance* 56:1693–1721.

Lamoreaux, N. R. 1985. *The Great Merger Movement in American Business, 1895–1904.* Cambridge: Cambridge University Press.

Lang, L., A. Poulsen, and R. Stulz. 1995. Asset sales, firm performance, and the agency costs of managerial discretion. *Journal of Financial Economics* 37:3–37.

Lang, L., R. M. Stulz, and R. A. Walkling. 1989. Managerial performance, Tobin's Q, and the gains from successful tender offers. *Journal of Financial Economics* 24:137–154.

Lang, L., R. Stulz, and R. Walkling. 1991. A test of the free cash flow hypothesis: The case of bidder returns. *Journal of Financial Economics* 29(2, October): 315–335.

Langetieg, T. 1978. An application of a three-factor performance index to measure stockholders gains from merger. *Journal of Financial Economics* 6(4, December):365–384.

Larson, Kermit O., and Nicholas Gonedes. 1969. Business combinations: An exchange ratio determination model. *Accounting Review* (October).

Law, A., and W. Kelton. 1991. *Simulation and Modeling Analysis.* New York: McGraw-Hill.

Lawrence, Gary M. 1999. *Due Diligence in Business Transactions*, revision 8. New York: Law Journal Press.

Lax, David A., and James K. Sebenius. 1986. *The Manager as Negotiator*. New York: Free Press.

Lease, Ronald C., John J. McConnell, and Wayne H. Mikkelson. 1983. The market value of control in publicly-traded corporations. *Journal of Financial Economics* 11:439–471.

Lee, Charles M. C., and David Ng. 2001. Corruption and international valuation: Does virtue pay? Cornell University working paper.

Lee, I., and S. B. Wyatt. 1990. The effects of international joint ventures on shareholder wealth. *Financial Review* 25:641–649.

Lee, S. 1992. Management buyout proposals and inside information. *Journal of Finance* 47(3):1061–1079.

Lee, S. K., and J.E. Pawlukiewicz. 2000. Poison pills: 1980s vs. 1990s. *American Business Review* 18(1):28–32.

Leeth, J., and J. R. Borg. 2000. The impact of takeovers on shareholder wealth during the 1920s merger wave. *Journal of Financial and Quantitative Analysis* 35(2, June): 217–238.

Legale, S. 1999. Italy. *International Financial Law Review* 18:33–37.

Lehn, K., and A. Poulsen. 1989. Free cash flow and stockholder gains in going private transactions. *Journal of Finance* 44:771–787.

Lemmon, M. L., and T. W. Bates. 2002. Breaking up is hard to do? An analysis of termination fee provisions and merger outcomes. University of Delaware College of Business and Economics, Center for Corporate Governance working paper no. 2002-005.

Lerner, J., and A. Schoar. 2001. Transferability constraints in private equity. Working paper, Harvard Business School and Massachusetts Institute of Technology.

Lerner, J., and A. Schoar. 2002. The illiquidity puzzle: Theory and evidence from private equity. Working paper, Harvard Business School and Massachusetts Institute of Technology.

Lerner, J., H. Shane, and A. Tsai. 2003. Do equity financing cycles matter? Evidence from biotechnology alliances. *Journal of Financial Economics* 67:411–446.

Lerner, Josh. 1999. A note on valuation in private equity settings. Harvard Business School Publishing, 9-297-050.

Lesmond, D., M. Schill, and C. Zhou. 2002. The illusory nature of momentum profits. Darden School University of Virginia working paper 03-06. Downloaded from http://papers.ssrn.com/sol3/papers.cfm?abstract_id=256926.

Lessard, D. 1985. Transfer prices, taxes, and financial markets: Implications of international financial transfers within the multinational corporation. Pages 426–447 in D. Lessard, ed., *International Financial Management*. New York: John Wiley & Sons.

Lessard, D., and A. Shapiro. 1983. Guidelines for global financing choices. *Midland Corporate Finance Journal* (Winter):68–80.

Lessard, Donald R. 1976. World, country and industry relationships in equity returns. *Financial Analysts Journal* (January/February).

Lessard, Donald R. 1996. Incorporating country risk in the valuation of offshore projects. *Journal of Applied Corporate Finance* 9(5):52–63.

Lesser, Henry, Ann Lederer, and Charles Steinberg. 1992. Increasing pressures for confidentiality agreements that work. *Mergers & Acquisitions* (March/April):23–27.

Leuz, C., D. Nanda, and P. Wysocki. 2002. Investor protection and earnings management: An international comparison. University of Pennsylvania working paper, downloaded from http://papers.ssrn.com/sol3/papers.cfm?abstract_id=281832.

Levine, David I. 1993. Do corporate executives have rational expectations? *Journal of Business* 271–293.

Levinsohn, A. 2000. Tracking stock. *Strategic Finance* 82(3):62–67.

Levitt, A. 1998. The numbers game. Speech delivered at the NYU Center of Law and Business, cited in Gu et al. (2002).

Levy, Edmond. 1992. Pricing European average rate currency options. *Journal of International Money and Finance* 11:474–491.

Levy, H., and H. Sarnat. 1970. Diversification, portfolio analysis, and the uneasy case for conglomerate mergers. *Journal of Finance* 25:795–802.

Levy, Haim. 1982. Economic evaluation of voting power of common stock. *Journal of Finance* 38:79–93.

Levy, R. 1967. Relative strength as a criterion for investment selection. *Journal of Finance* 22:595–610.

Lewellen, Wilbur. 1971. A pure financial rationale for the conglomerate merger. *Journal of Finance* (May).

Lichtenberg, F., and D. Siegel. 1990. The effects of leveraged buyouts on productivity and related aspects of firm behavior. *Journal of Financial Economics* 27: 165–194.

Lichtenberg, F., and D. Siegel. 1991. The effects of leveraged buyouts on productivity and related aspects of firm behavior. NBER working paper W3022.

Liebowitz, Martin L., and Stanley Kogelman. 1990. Inside the P/E ratio: The franchise factor. *Financial Analysts Journal* (November–December):17–35.

Liedtka, Jeanne. 1993. Banc One Corporation: The evolution of partnership. Darden Case Collection, Darden Graduate Business School, Charlottesville, VA: University of Virginia, UVA-BP-0335, e-mail:dardencases@virginia.edu.

Lindenberg, Eric, and Michael P. Ross. 1999. To purchase or to pool: Does it matter? *Journal of Applied Corporate Finance* 12(Summer):32–47.

Linn, S. C., and J. J. McConnell. 1983. An empirical investigation of the impact of "anti-takeover" amendments on common stock prices. *Journal of Financial Economics* 11:361–400.

Lins, K., and H. Servaes. 1999. International evidence on the value of corporate diversification. *Journal of Finance* 54:2215–2239.

Lins, K., and H. Servaes. 2002. Is corporate diversification beneficial in emerging markets? *Financial Management* (Summer):5–31.

Liu, Q., and J. Lu. 2002. Earnings management to tunnel: Evidence from China's listed companies. University of Hong Kong working paper, downloaded from http://papers.ssrn.com/sol3/papers.cfm?abstract_id=349880.

Loderer, C., and K. Martin. 1990. Corporate acquisitions by listed firms: The experience of a comprehensive sample. *Financial Management* 19(4, Winter):17–33.

Loderer, C., and K. Martin. 1992. Postacquisition performance of acquiring firms. *Financial Management* 21(3, Autumn):69–79.

Logue, D., J. Seward, and J. Walsh. 1996. Rearranging residual claims: A case for targeted stock. *Financial Management* 25:43–61.

Lombardo, Davide, and Marco Pagano. 2000. Legal determinants of the return on equity. Mimeo.

Long, W., and D. Ravenscraft. 1993. LBOs, debt and R&D intensity. *Strategic Management Journal* 14:119–135.

Longhofer, S. 1997. Absolute priority rule violations, credit rationing and efficiency. *Journal of Financial Intermediation* 6:249–267.

Longstaff, Francis A. 1995. How much can marketability affect security values? *Journal of Finance* 50:1767–1774.

Longstaff, Francis A. 2001. Optimal portfolio choice and the valuation of illiquid assets. *Review of Financial Studies* 14:407–431.

Loughran, T., and A. Vijh. 1997. Do long-term shareholders benefit from corporate acquisitions? *Journal of Finance* 52(5, December):1765–1790.

Loughran, T., and J. Ritter. 2002. Why don't issuers get upset about leaving money on the table in IPOs? *Review of Financial Studies* 15:413–443.

Loughran, T., J. Ritter, and K. Rydquist. 1994. Initial public offerings: International insights. *Pacific-Basin Finance Journal* 2(2–3):165–199.

Louis, H. Undated. The causes of post-merger underperformance: Evidence from successful and unsuccessful bidders. Pennsylvania State University working paper.

Louis, H. 2002. Earnings management and the market performance of acquiring firms. Pennsylvania State University working paper, downloaded from http://papers.ssrn.com/sol3/papers.cfm?abstract_id=336180.

Lubatkin, M., D. Schweiger, and Y. Weber. 1999. Top management turnover in related M&A's: An additional test of the theory of relative standing. *Journal of Management.*

Luis, Christopher. 1999. Mating markets with cultures for a better deal. *Mergers & Acquisitions* (January/February):17–21.

Lutz, S. 1994. Epic ESOP participants hit a home run with sale. *Modern Healthcare* 3(January 17).

Lynch, H. 1971. *Financial Performance of Conglomerates.* Boston: Division of Research, Graduate School of Business Administration, Harvard University.

Lyroudi, K., J. Lazaridis, and D. Subeniotis. 1999. Impact of international mergers and acquisitions on shareholder's wealth: A European perspective. *Journal of Financial Management and Analysis* 12(1, January–June):1–14.

Lys, Thomas, and Linda Vincent. 1995. An analysis of value destruction in AT&T's acquisition of NCR. *Journal of Financial Economics* 39(2/3, October/November):353–378.

Madura, J., and A. White. 1990. Diversification benefits of direct foreign investment. *Management International Review* 30:73–85.

Magee, S. 1976. Technology and the appropriability theory of the multinational corporation. In J. Bhagwati, ed., *The New International Economic Order.* Cambridge: MIT Press.

Maher, J. M. 1976. Discounts for lack of marketability for closely held business interests. *Taxes* (September):562–571.

Maher, Maria, and Thomas Andersson. 2002. Corporate governance: Effects on firm performance and economic growth. In J. A. McCahery, P. Moerland, T. Raaijmakers, and L. Renneboog, eds., *Convergence and Diversity of Corporate Governance Regimes and Capital Markets.* Oxford, England: Oxford University Press.

Makino, S., and K. Neupert. 2000. National culture, transaction costs, and the choice between joint venture and wholly owned subsidiary. *Journal of International Business Studies* 31(4):705–713.

Maksimovic, V., and G. Phillips. 2001. "The market for corporate assets: Who engages in mergers and asset sales and are there efficiency gains? *Journal of Finance* 56(6, December):2019–2065.

Maksimovic, V., and G. Phillips. 2002. Do conglomerate firms allocate resources inefficiently across industries? Theory and evidence. *Journal of Finance* 57(April):721–767.

Malatesta, P. 1983. The wealth effect of merger activity and the objective functions of merging firms. *Journal of Financial Economics* 11(1–4, April):155–181.

Malatesta, Paul, and Ralph Walkling. 1988. Poison pill securities: Stockholder wealth, profitability and ownership structure. *Journal of Financial Economics* 20.

Malezadeh, A. R., and V. B. McWilliams. 1995. Managerial efficiency and share ownership: The market reaction to takeover defenses. *Journal of Applied Business Research* 11(4):48–63.

Malezadeh, A. R., V. B. McWilliams, and N. Sen. 1998. Implications of CEO structural and ownership powers, board ownership and composition on the market's reaction to antitakeover charter amendments. *Journal of Applied Business Research* 14(3):53–62.

Mallette, P., and R. Spagnola. 1994. State takeover legislation: The political defense. *S.A.M. Advanced Management Journal* 59(3):15–24.

Mandelker, G. 1974. Risk and return: The case of merging firms. *Journal of Financial Economics* 1(4, December):303–335.

Manne, Henry G. 1965. Mergers and the market for corporate control. *Journal of Political Economy* 73:110–120.

Manoocheri, G., and B. Jizba. 1990. How to use ESOPs as an effective tool in corporate strategy. *Journal of Compensation and Benefits* 4:272–277.

Mansi, S., and D. Reeb. 2002. Corporate diversification: What gets discounted? *Journal of Finance* 57(5):2167–2183.

Manzon, G. B., D. J. Sharp, and N. Travlos. 1994. An empirical study of the consequences of U.S. tax rules for international acquisitions by U.S. firms. *Journal of Finance* 49:1893–1904.

Maquieria, C., W. Megginson, and L. Nail. 1998. Wealth creation versus wealth redistributions in pure stock-for-stock mergers. *Journal of Financial Economics* 48(1, April):3–33.

Marais, L., K. Schipper, and Smith. A., 1989. Wealth effects of going private for senior securities. *Journal of Financial Economics* 23:155–191.

Marber, Peter. 1998. *From Third World to World Class: The Future of Emerging Markets in the Global Economy.* Reading, MA: Perseus Books.

Marco, B., and S. Mengoli. 2001. Sub-optimal acquisition decisions under a majority shareholder system: An empirical investigation. Working paper, Bologna, Italy: University of Bologna.

Maremont, M., and J. Weil. 2003. Tyco's problems on accounting may not be over. *Wall Street Journal* (May 5):C1.

Margrabe, W. 1978. The value of an option to exchange one asset for another. *Journal of Finance* 33(1):177–186.

Markham, J. 1955. Survey of the evidence and findings on mergers. Pages 141–182 in NBER, ed., *Business Concentration and Price Policy*. Princeton: Princeton University Press.

Markides, C. 1998. Strategic innovation in established companies. *Sloan Management Review* 39(3):31–42.

Markides, C. C. 1992. How much-hated takeover defenses can unlock hidden value. *Multinational Business* 21–29.

Markides, C. C., and C. D. Ittner. 1994. Shareholder benefits from corporate international diversification. *Journal of International Business Studies* 25:343–360.

Marks, Mitchell Lee, and Philip H. Mirvis. 1998. *Joining Forces: Making One Plus One Equal Three in Mergers, Acquisitions, and Alliances*. San Francisco: Jossey-Bass Publishers.

Marquardt, C., and C. Wiedman. 2002. How are earnings managed? An examination of specific accruals. New York University working paper, downloaded from http://papers.ssrn.com/sol3/papers.cfm?abstract_id=375660.

Marr, M. W., S. Mohta, and M. F. Spivey. 1992. An analysis of foreign takeovers in the United States. *Managerial and Decision Economics* 14(4):285–294.

Martin, K. 1996. The method of payment in corporate acquisitions, investment opportunities, and management ownership. *Journal of Finance* 51(4):1227–1246.

Martin, K. J., and J. McConnell. 1991. Corporate performance, corporate takeovers, and management turnover. *Journal of Finance* (June):671–687.

Masse, I., R. Hanrahan, and J. Kushner. 1990. The effect of the method of payment on stock returns in Canadian tender offers and merger proposals for both target and bidding firms. *Quarterly Journal of Business and Economics* 29(4):102–124.

Masulis, R., and A. Korwar. 1986. Seasoned equity offerings: An empirical investigation. *Journal of Financial Economics* 15:91–118.

Mata, J., and P. Portugal. 2000. Closure and divestiture by foreign entrants: The impact of entry and post-entry strategies. *Strategic Management Journal* 21:549–562.

Mathur, K, N. Ranmgan, I. Chachi, and S. Sundaram. 1994. International acquisitions in the United States: Evidence from returns to foreign bidders. *Managerial and Decision Economics* 107–118.

Maupin, R., C. Bidwell, and A. Ortegren. 1984. An empirical investigation of the characteristics of publicly-quoted corporations which change to closely-held ownership through management buyouts. *Journal of Business Finance & Accounting* 11:435–450.

McAfee, R. Preston, and John McMillan. 1987. Auctions and bidding. *Journal of Economic Literature* 25(June):699–738

McCabe, G. M., and K. C. Yook. 1996. The effect of international acquisitions on shareholders' wealth. *Mid-Atlantic Journal of Business* 32:5–17.

McCarthy, E. 1999. Stock buybacks: The rules. *Journal of Accountancy* 187(5):91–97.

McCloskey, Donald N. 1990. *If You're So Smart: The Narrative of Economic Expertise.* Chicago: University of Chicago Press.

McCloskey, Donald, and Arjo Klamer. 1995. One quarter of GDP is persuasion. *AEA Papers and Proceedings* (May):191–195.

McCoid J., II. 1996. Discharge: The most important development in bankruptcy history. *American Bankruptcy Law Journal* 70:163–193.

McConnell, J., and T. Nantell. 1985. Corporate combinations and common stock returns: The case of joint ventures. *Journal of Finance* 40:519–536.

McConnell, John J. 2003. Outside directors. *Financial Review* 38:25–31.

McDonald, John. 1996. *Strategy in Poker, Business & War.* New York: W. W. Norton.

McDonald, R., and D. Siegel. 1985. Investment and the valuation of firms when there is an option of shut down. *International Economic Review* 28(2):331–349.

McDonald, R., and D. Siegel. 1986. The value of waiting to invest. *Quarterly Journal of Economics* 101(November):707–727.

McHugh, C. 1996. *The 1996 Bankruptcy Yearbook and Almanac.* Boston: New Generation Research Inc.

McMillan, John. 1992. *Games, Strategies, and Managers.* Oxford: Oxford University Press.

McMillan, John. 1994. Why auction the spectrum? *Telecommunications Policy* (November 22).

McNeil, C., and W. Moore. 2001. Spin-off wealth effects and the dismantling of internal capital markets. Working paper.

McWilliams, V. B. 1990. Managerial share ownership and the stock price effects of antitakeover amendment proposals. *Journal of Finance* 45(5):1627–1640.

McWilliams, V. B. 1993. Tobin's Q and the stock price reaction to antitakeover amendments. *Financial Management* 22(4):16–18.

Mead, W. J., A. Moseidjord, and P. E. Sorenson. 1984. Competitive bidding under asymmetrical information: Behavior and rerformance in Gulf of Mexico drainage lease sales 1959–1969. *Review of Economics and Statistics* 66(3, August):505–508.

Meeks, G. 1977. *Disappointing Marriage: A Study of the Gains from Merger.* Cambridge: Cambridge University Press.

Meese R. A., and K. Rogoff. 1983. Empirical exchange rate models in the seventies: Do they fit out of sample? *Journal of International Economics* 3–24.

Megginson, W., A. Morgan, and L. Nail. 2002. The determinants of positive long-term performance in strategic mergers: Corporate focus and cash. Working paper, University of Alabama (August), available from the authors by e-mail at lnail@uab.edu.

Megginson, W. L., A. Morgan, and L. A. Nail. 2003. Changes in corporate focus, ownership structure, and long-run merger returns. Working paper, available from Social Science Research Network Electronic Paper Collection, http://papers.ssrn.com/paper.taf?abstract_id=250993.

Megginson, William L. 1990. Restricted voting stock, acquisition premiums, and the market value of corporate control. *Financial Review* 25:175–198.

Meisner, James F., and John W. Labuszewski. 1984. Modifying the Black-Scholes option pricing model for alternative underlying instruments. *Financial Analysts Journal* (November–December):23–30.

Melicher, R., J. Ledolter, and L. D'Antonio. 1983. A time series analysis of aggregate merger activity. *Review of Economics and Statistics* 65(August):423–430.

Merton, Robert. 1973. Theory of rational option pricing. *Bell Journal of Economics and Management Science* 4(2):141–183.

Merton, Robert. 1976. Option pricing when underlying stock returns are discontinuous. *Journal of Financial Economics* 3(1):125–144.

Merton, Robert C., and Andre F. Perold. 1993. Theory of risk capital in financial firms. *Journal of Applied Corporate Finance* 6(3, Fall).

Mikhail, S., and H. Shawky. 1979. Investment performance of U.S.-based multinational corporations. *Journal of International Business Studies* 10(Spring/Summer):53–66.

Mikkelson, W. H., and M. M. Partch. 1989. Managers' voting rights and corporate control. *Journal of Financial Economics* 25:263–290.

Mikkelson, W. H., and R. S. Ruback. 1985. An empirical analysis of the interfirm equity investment process. *Journal of Financial Economics* 14(December):523–553.

Mikkelson, W. H., and R. S. Ruback. 1991. Targeted repurchases and common stock returns. *RAND Journal of Economics* 22(4):544–561.

Miles, J., and J. Rosenfeld. 1983. An empirical analysis of the effects of spin-off announcements on shareholder wealth. *Journal of Finance* 38:1597–1606.

Miles, J., and R. Ezzell. 1980. The weighted average cost of capital, perfect capital markets and project life: A clarification. *Journal of Financial and Quantitative Analysis* 15(September):719–730.

Milgram, S. 1974. *Obedience to Authority.* New York: Harper & Row,

Milgram, Stanley. 1967. The small-world problem. *Psychology Today* 1(May):62–67.

Milgrom, Paul. 1987. Auction Theory. Pages 1–32 in Truman Bewley, ed., *Advances in Economic Theory.* Cambridge: University of Cambridge Press.

Milgrom, Paul. 1989. Auctions and bidding: A primer. *Journal of Economic Perspectives* 3(Summer):3–22.

Miller, M., and F. Modigliani. 1961. Dividend policy, growth and the valuation of shares. *Journal of Business* 34(October):411–433.

Miller, M. H. 1977. Debt and taxes. *Journal of Finance* 32(May):261–276.

Millman, Gregory J., and Carol Lippert Gray. 2000. Desperately seeking synergy. *Financial Executive* (March/April):12–17.

Milnor, J., and L. Shapley. 1978. Values of large games II: Oceanic games. Reprinted in *Mathematics of Operations Research* 3:290–307.

Mishra, D., and T. O'Brien. 2001. A comparison of cost of equity estimates of local and global CAPMs. *Financial Review* 36:27–48.

Mitchell, M., and J. Mulherin. 1996. The impact of industry shocks on takeover and restructuring activity. *Journal of Financial Economics* 41(June):193–209.

Mitchell, M. L., and E. Stafford. 2000. Managerial decisions and long-term stock price performance. *Journal of Business* 73(3, July):287–329.

Mobius, Mark J. 1996. *On Emerging Markets*. London: FT Pittman Publishing.

Modigliani, Franco, and Merton Miller. 1963. Corporate income taxes and the cost of capital: A correction. *American Economic Review* 53(June):433–443.

Mody, Ashoka, and Shoko Negishi. 2001. Cross-border mergers and acquisitions in East Asia: Trends and implications. *Finance & Development* 38(1, March); www.imf.org/external/pubs/ft/fandd/2001/03/mody.htm.

Moel, A., and P. Tufano. 2000. When are real options exercised? An empirical study of mine closings. *Review of Financial Studies*.

Moeller, S., F. Schlingemann, and R. Stulz. 2003. Do shareholders of acquiring firms gain from acquisitions? Ohio State University working paper (February). Also presented as NBER working paper W9523 (March).

Mogavero, D. J., and M. F. Toyne. 1995. The impact of golden parachutes on Fortune 500 stock returns: A reexamination of the evidence. *Quarterly Journal of Business and Economics* 34(4):30–38.

Monks, Robert A. G., and Nell Minow. 1995. *Corporate Governance*. Cambridge, England: Basil Blackwell.

Moore, Geoffrey. 1991. *Crossing the Chasm*. New York: HarperCollins.

Moore, R. 2002. Fool on the hill: The breaking point. *The Motley Fool* (February 21). Downloaded from http://222.fool.com/Server.FoolPrint.asp?file=/news/foth/2002/foth020221.htm.

Moore, William T. 2001. *Real Options & Option-Embedded Securities*. New York: John Wiley & Sons.

Morck, R., and B. Yeung. 1991. Why investors value multinationality. *Journal of Business* 64(2):165–188.

Morck, R., and B. Yeung. 1997. Why investors sometimes value size and diversification: The internalization theory on synergy. University of Alberta, Institute for Financial Research working paper no. 5-97.

Morck, R., A. Shleifer, and R. Vishny. 1990. Do managerial objectives drive bad acquisitions? *Journal of Finance* 45(1, March):31–48.

Morck, R. M., A. Shleifer, and R. W. Vishny. 1989. Alternative mechanisms for corporate control. *American Economic Review* 89:842–852.

Morck, Randall M., Andrei Shleifer, and Robert W. Vishny. 1988. Characteristics of targets of hostile and friendly takeovers. In Alan J. Auerbach, ed., *Corporate Takeovers: Causes and Consequences*. Chicago: National Bureau of Economic Research.

Moroney, R. E. 1973. Most courts overvalue closely held stocks. *Taxes* (March): 144–154.

Morrison, T., W. Conaway, G. A. Borden, H. Koehler. 1995. *Kiss, Bow, or Shake Hands: How to Do Business in Sixty Countries*. New York: Adams Media.

Moskowitz, T., and M Grinblatt. 1999. Do industries explain momentum? *Journal of Finance* 54:1249–1290.

Mueller, D. 1979. Testimony before U.S. Senate, Committee on the Judiciary; Subcommittee on Antitrust, Monopoly, and Business Rights; 96th Congress, 1st Session; serial no. 96-26:302–312.

Mueller, D. 1980. *The Determinants and Effects of Mergers: An International Comparison.* Cambridge, MA: Oelgeschlager, Gunn & Hain.

Mueller, D. 1985. Mergers and market share. *Review of Economics and Statistics* 67(2, May):259–267.

Mueller, G., H. Gernon, and G. Meek 1994. *Accounting: An International Perspective,* 3d ed. Burr Ridge, IL: McGraw-Hill/Irwin.

Mulherin, H. 2000. Incomplete acquisitions and organizational efficiency. Working paper, State College, PA: Penn State.

Mulherin, J., and A. Boone. 2000. Comparing acquisitions and divestitures. *Journal of Corporate Finance* 6:117–139.

Murphy, K. 2001. Executive compensation. Working paper, cited in Bliss and Rosen (2001).

Murphy, P. E. 1997. 80 Exemplary ethics statements. Cited in L. H. Newton, A passport for the corporate code: From Borg Warner to the Caux Principles. Pages 374–385 in Robert E. Frederick, 1999. *A Companion to Business Ethics.* Malden, MA: Blackwell.

Muscarella, C., and M. Vetsuypens. 1990. Efficiency and organizational structure: A study of reverse LBOs. *Journal of Finance* 45(5, December):1389–1413.

Myers, S., and N. Majluf. 1984. Corporate financing and investment decisions when firms have information that investors do not have. *Journal of Financial Economics* 13:187–221.

Myers, S., and S. Majd. 1990. Abandonment value and project life. *Advances in Futures and Options Research* 4:1–21.

Myers, S. C. 1993. Still searching for optimal capital structure. *Journal of Applied Corporate Finance* 6:(Spring):4–14.

Myers, Stewart. 1984. Finance theory and financial strategy. *Interfaces* 14 (January–February):126–137.

Myers, Stewart C. 1977. Determinants of corporate borrowing. *Journal of Financial Economics* 5:146–175.

Myerson, T. S., and J. R. Thoyer. 1998. United States. *International Financial Law Review* 17(4):123–126.

Nail, L., W. Megginson, and C. Maquiera. 1998. How stock-swap mergers affect shareholder (and) bondholder wealth: More evidence of the value of corporate "Focus." *Journal of Applied Corporate Finance* 11(3):153–172.

Nanda, V. 1991. On the good news in equity carve-outs. *Journal of Finance* 46:1717–1737.

Nanda, V., and M. Narayanan. 1999. Disentangling value: Financing needs, firm scope, and divestitures. *Journal of Financial Intermediation* 8(3):174–204.

Nasar, S. 1989. The foolish rush to ESOPs. *Fortune* (September 25)120:141–150.

Nash, L. L. 1981. Ethics without the sermon. *Harvard Business Review* (November–December):79–90.

Nelson, M., J. Elliott, and R. Tarpley. 2000a. Evidence from auditors about managers' and auditors' earnings-management decisions. Cornell University working paper, downloaded from http://papers.ssrn.com/sol3/papers.cfm?abstract_id=294688.

Nelson, M., J. Elliott, and R. Tarpley. 2000b. Where do companies attempt earnings management, and when do auditors prevent it? Cornell University working paper, downloaded from http://papers.ssrn.com/sol3/papers.cfm?abstract_id=248129.

Nelson, R. 1959. *Merger Movements in American Industry 1895–1956.* Princeton: Princeton University Press.

Nelson, R. 1966. Business cycle factors in the choice between internal and external growth. In W. Alberts and J. Segall, eds., *The Corporate Mergers.* Chicago: University of Chicago Press.

Nenova, T. 2001. Control values and changes in corporate law in Brazil. Working paper, Washington, DC: World Bank.

Nenova, T. 2003. The value of corporate votes and control benefits: A cross-country analysis. *Journal of Financial Economics* 68:325–351.

Nesbitt, Stephen L. 1994. Long-term rewards from shareholder activism: A study of the "CalPERS effect." *Journal of Applied Corporate Finance* 6:75–80.

Newton, C. 2001. Strategic alliances: Collaborate or evaporate. *Journal of Financial Planning* 14(3):72–80.

Nichols, N. 1994. Scientific management at Merck: An interview with CFO Judy Lewent. *Harvard Business Review* (January–February):88–99.

North, D. S. 2001. Corporate mergers and top management turnover: The 1990s evidence. University of Richmond working paper (October 1).

Nyman, S., and A. Silberston. 1978. The ownership and control of industry. *Oxford Economic Papers* 30:74–101.

O'Brien, T. 1999. The global CAPM and a firm's cost of capital in different currencies. *Journal of Applied Corporate Finance* 12(3, Fall).

Officer, M. S. 2003. Termination fees in mergers and acquisitions. *Journal of Financial Economics* 69(3):431–467.

Ogden, Joan. 1999. Doing it with collars. *Global Finance* (January):50–51.

Oliver, R. P., and R. H. Meyers. 2000. Discounts seen in private placements of restricted stock: The Management Planning, Inc., long-term study (1980–1996). Chapter 5 in R. F. Reilly and R. P. Schweihs, eds., *Handbook of Advanced Business Valuation.* New York: McGraw-Hill.

Opler, T. 1992. Operating performance in leveraged buyouts: Evidence from 1985–1989. *Financial Management* 21(1, Spring):27–34.

Opler, T., and S. Titman. 1993. The determinants of leveraged buyout activity: Free cash flow vs. financial distress costs. *Journal of Finance* 48:1985–1999.

Opler, T., M. Saron, and S. Titman. 1996. Designing capital structure to create shareholder value. *Journal of Applied Corporate Finance* 10(1):21–32.

Paine, L. S. 1994. Managing for organizational integrity. *Harvard Business Review* (March–April):106–117.

Paine, L. S. 1999. Law, ethics, and managerial judgment. Pages 194–206 in R. E. Frederick, ed., *A Companion to Business Ethics.* Malden, MA: Blackwell.

Paine, L. S. 2003. Value shift: Why companies must merger social and financial imperatives to achieve superior performance. New York: McGraw-Hill.

Palepu, Krishna. 1986. Predicting takeover targets: A methodological and empirical analysis. *Journal of Accounting and Economics* 8:3–35.

Panel on Takeovers and Mergers. 2001. *The City Code on Takeovers and Mergers and the Rules Governing Substantial Acquisitions of Shares.* London: Burrups Printing Group.

Parrino, J. D., and R. S. Harris. 1999. Takeovers, management replacement, and post-acquisition operating performance: Some evidence from the 1980s. *Journal of Applied Corporate Finance* 11(4, Winter):88–97.

Parrino, J. D., and R. S. Harris. 2001. Business linkages and post-merger operating performance. Working paper, Charlottesville, VA: Darden Graduate School of Business, University of Virginia.

Parrino, R. 1997. Spin-offs and wealth transfers: The Marriott case. *Journal of Financial Economics* 43:241–274.

Parsons, J., C. Maxwell, and D. O'Brien. 1999. "A paradox in measuring corporate control. Working paper, Charles River Associates, Boston, MA.

Paul, A. 1998. United Kingdom. *International Financial Law Review* 17(4): 116–122.

Pereiro, L., and M. Galli. 2000. La determinacion del costo del capital en la valuacion de empresas de capital cerrado: Una guia practica. Instituto Argentino de Ejecutivos de Finanzas y Universidad Torcuato di Tella, Agosto. The results of this study were reported in L. Pereiro, *Valuation of Companies in Emerging Markets.* New York: John Wiley & Sons, 2002.

Pereiro, Luis, E. 1998. Patterns of foreign direct investment inflows in emerging economies: Recent evidence from Argentina" Ms. Universidad Torcuato Di Tella (November).

Perotti, E., and S. Guney. 1993. The structure of privatization plans. *Financial Management* 22(1):84–98.

Perry, S., and T. Williams. 1994. Earnings management preceding management buyout offers. *Journal of Accounting & Economics* 18:157–179.

Perumpral, S., D. Davidson, and N. Sen. 1999. Event risk covenants and shareholder wealth: Ethical implications of the "poison put" provisions in bonds. *Journal of Business Ethics* 22(2):119–132.

Petersen, M., and R. Rajan. 1997. Trade credit: Theories and evidence. *Review of Financial Studies* 10(3):661–691.

Pettit, B. 2000. The long-horizon performance of acquiring firms: The French evidence. Working paper, American Graduate School of International Management (November).

Pettway, R. H., N. Sicherman, and D. Spiess. 1993. Japanese foreign direct investment: Impacts of purchases and sales of U.S. assets. *Financial Management* 82–95.

Phillips, G. 1995. Increased debt and industry product markets: An empirical analysis. *Journal of Financial Economics* 37:189–238.

Pitt, Harvey L., and Stephen I. Glover. 1997. An Earnout—in which part of the purchase price is contingent on performance objectives—can rescue a stalled merger. *National Law Journal* (January):B05.

Plott, C. R. 1986. Rational choice in experimental markets. *Journal of Business* S301–S327.

Porter, M. 1979. How competitive forces shape strategy. *Harvard Business Review* (March–April):137–145. Reprint no. 79208.

Porter, M. 1985. *Competitive Advantage: Creating and Sustaining Superior Performance.* New York: Free Press.

Porter, M. 1987. From competitive advantage to corporate strategy. *Harvard Business Review* 65(May/June):43–59.

Porter, M. 1990. The competitive advantage of nations. *Harvard Business Review* (March–April):73–91.

Porter, Michael. 1980. *Competitive Strategy: Techniques for Analyzing Industries and Competitors.* New York: Free Press.

Posner, Richard. 2001. *Antitrust Law.* Chicago: University of Chicago Press.

Pound, John. 1988. Proxy contests and the efficiency of shareholder oversight. *Journal of Financial Economics* 20:237–266.

Pound, John, and Walter Skowronski. 1997. Building relationships with major shareholders: A case study of Lockheed. In Donald H. Chew, ed., *Studies in International Corporate Finance and Governance Systems.* New York: Oxford University Press.

Pratt, Shannon. 1990. Discounts and premiums. In Theodore Veit, ed., *Valuation of Closely Held Companies and Inactively Traded Securities.* Charlottesville: Institute of Chartered Financial Analysts.

Pratt, Shannon P. 2001. *Business Valuation Discounts and Premiums.* New York: John Wiley & Sons.

Prezas, A., M. Tarimcilar, and G. Vasudevan. 2000. The pricing of equity carve-outs. *Financial Review* 35:123–138.

Price, Allan, and Jacqueline Sloane. 1998. Global designs: Tough challenges for acquirers. *Mergers & Acquisitions* (May/June):50–54.

Pugh, W. N., J. Jahera, and S. Oswald. 1999. "ESOPs, takeover protection and corporate decision-making. *Journal of Economics and Finance* 23(2):170–185.

Pulliam S. 2003. A staffer ordered to commit fraud balked, and then caved. *Wall Street Journal* (June 23):A1.

Quirk, J., and K. Terasawa. 1984. The winner's curse and cost estimation bias in pioneer projects. Working paper no. 512, California Institute of Technology (April).

Raiffa, Howard. 1982. *The Art & Science of Negotiation.* Cambridge: Harvard University Press.

Raiffa, Howard, John Richardson, and David Metcalfe. 2002. *Negotiation Analysis: The Science and Art of Collaborative Decision Making.* Cambridge: Belknap Press of Harvard University Press.

Rajan, R., H. Servaes, and L. Zingales. 2000. The cost of diversity: The diversification discount and inefficient investment. *Journal of Finance* 55:2537–2564.

Rangan, S. 1998. Earnings management and the performance of seasoned equity offerings. *Journal of Financial Economics* 50:101–122.

Rapoport, Anatol, and A. M. Chammah. 1965. *Prisoner's Dilemma.* Ann Arbor: University of Michigan Press.

Rappaport, Alfred. 1998. *Creating Shareholder Value.* New York: Free Press.

Rappaport, Alfred, and Mark L. Sirower. 1998. Calculating the value-creation potential of a deal. *Mergers & Acquisitions* (July/August):33–44.

Rappaport, Alfred, and Mark L. Sirower. 1999. Stock or cash? The trade-offs for buyers and sellers in mergers and acquisitions. *Harvard Business Review* (November–December):147–158.

Rappaport, Alfred, and Michael J. Mauboussin. 2002. *Expectations Investing: Reading Stock Prices for Better Returns.* Boston: Harvard Business School Press.

Rational economic man: The human factor. 1994. *Economist* (December 24):90–92.

Rau, R. P., and T. Vermaelen. 1998. Glamour, value and the post-acquisition performance of acquiring firms. *Journal of Financial Economics* 49(2, August):223–253.

Ravenscraft, D. 1987. The 1980s merger wave: An industrial organization perspective. In L. Brown and E. Rosengren, eds., *The Merger Boom.* Boston: Federal Reserve Bank of Boston.

Ravenscraft, D., and F. M. Scherer. 1987. Life after fakeovers. *Journal of Industrial Economics* 36(2, December):147–156.

Ravenscraft, D. J., and F. M. Scherer. 1987. *Mergers, Sell-offs, and Economic Efficiency.* Washington, DC: Brookings Institution.

Ravid, A., and M. Spiegel. 1999. Toehold strategies, takeover laws and rival bidders. *Journal of Banking and Finance* 23:1219–1242.

Ravindran, A., D. T. Phillips, and J. J. Solberg. 1987. *Operations Research: Principles and Practice*. New York: John Wiley & Sons.

Reed, William C. 1998. Coping with merger-mania: IT's new role. *Health Management Technology Atlanta* (May):38–41.

Reinhardt, U. 1972. *Mergers and Consolidations: A Corporate-Finance Approach*. Morristown: General Learning Press.

Resende, M. 1999. Wave behaviour of mergers and acquisitions in the U.K.: A sectoral study. *Oxford Bulletin of Economics and Statistics* 61(February):85–94.

Reuer, J., and M. Leiblein. 2000. Downside risk implication of multinationality and international joint ventures. *Academy of Management Journal* 43(2):203–214.

Rhoades, Stephen A. 1998. The efficiency effects of bank mergers: an overview of case studies of nine mergers. *Journal of Banking & Finance* 22,(3):19.

Rhodes-Kropf, M., and S. Viswanathan. 2000. Corporate reorganizations and non-cash auctions. *Journal of Finance* 55(4):1807–1854.

Rhodes-Kropf, M., and S. Viswanathan. 2003. Market valuation and merger waves. (April). Downloaded from http://papers.ssrn.com/sol3/papers.cfm?abstract_id=334944.

Rice, B., and B. Spring. 1989. ESOP at the barricade: Polaroid uses a novel anti-takeover defense. *Barron's* 69(February):38–39.

Rigobon, R. 2002. *International Financial Contagion: Theory and Evidence in Evolution*. Charlottesville, VA: Research Foundation of Association of Investment Management and Research.

Ritchken, Peter. 1987. *Options: Theory, Strategy, and Applications*. Glenview, IL: Scott, Foresman.

Ritter, J. 1984. The "hot issue" market of 1980. *Journal of Business* 32:215–240.

Ritter, J. 1987. The costs of going public. *Journal of Financial Economics* 19:269–281.

Ritter, J. 1991. The long-run performance of initial public offerings. *Journal of Finance* 46:1717–1737.

Robinson, D. T. 2001. Strategic alliances and the boundaries of the firm. Columbia University working paper (November 15). Available by e-mail from dtr2001@columbia.edu.

Robinson, D. T., and T. Stuart. 2002. Financial contracting in biotech strategic alliances. Columbia University working paper, downloadable from http://papers.ssrn.com/sol3/papers.cfm?abstract_id=328881.

Robinson, John R., and Philip B. Shane. 1990. Acquisition accounting method and bid premia for target firms. *Accounting Review* 65(January):25–48.

Rogers, E. M. 1995. *Diffusion of Innovations*, 4th ed. New York: Free Press.

Rogers, P., and C. Altvater. 1998. How to defend a hostile takeover bid in Germany. *International Financial Law Review* 17(2):24–26.

Roll, R. 1986. The hubris hypothesis of corporate takeovers. *Journal of Business* 59(April):197–216.

Rondinelli, D., and S. Black. 2000. Multinational strategic alliances and acquisitions in Central and Eastern Europe: Partnerships in privatization. *Academy of Management Executive* 14(4):85–98.

Rosen, C. 1989. Employee stock ownership plans: Myths, magic and measures. *Employee Relations Today* 16:189–195.

Rosen, C., and M. Quarrey. 1987. How well is employee ownership working. *Harvard Business Review* 106:15–19.

Rosen, R. 2002. Merger momentum and investor sentiment: The stock market reaction to merger announcements. Indiana University working paper, downloaded from http://papers.ssrn.com/sol3/papers.cfm?abstract_id=343600.

Rosenfeld, J. 1984. Additional evidence on the relation between divestiture announcements and shareholder wealth. *Journal of Finance* 39(5):1437–1448.

Ross, S. 1995. Uses, abuses, and alternatives to the net present value rule. *Financial Management* 24(3):96–102.

Ross, Stephen. 1977. The determination of financial structure: The incentive signalling approach. *Bell Journal of Economics* 8.

Rossi, S., and P. Volpin. 2001. The governance motive in cross-border mergers and acquisitions. Working paper, Institute of Finance and Accounting, London Business School.

Roth, G., and C. McDonald. 1999. Shareholder-management conflict and event risk covenants. *Journal of Financial Research* 22(2):207–225.

Rouwenhorst, K. G. 1998. International momentum strategies. *Journal of Finance* 53:267–284.

Rowenhorst, G. 1999. European equity markets and the EMU. *Financial Management* (May/June):57–63.

Ruback, R. 1982. The Conoco takeover and stockholder returns. *Sloan Management Review* 23:13–33.

Ruback, Richard. 1988. An overview of takeover defenses. *Mergers and Acquisitions.* Pages 49–67 in A. J. Auerbach, ed., *Corporate Takeovers: Causes and Consequences.* Chicago: University of Chicago Press.

Rubinstein, Mark E. 1974. A mean-variance synthesis of corporate financial theory. *Journal of Finance* (January).

Rukeyser, William. 1969. Why the rain fell on "Automatic" Sprinkler. *Fortune* 79 (May): 88–91, 126–129.

Rumelt, R. 1974. *Strategy, Structure, and Economic Performance.* Boston: Harvard Business School Press.

Rumelt, R. 1982. Diversification strategy and profitability. *Strategic Management Journal* 3(4, October–December):359–369.

Rumelt, Richard P. 1986. *Strategy, Structure, and Economic Performance.* Boston: Harvard Business School Press. (Reprint of 1974 original.)

Rutenberg, D. 1985. Maneuvering liquid assets. Pages 457–471 in D. Lessard, ed., *International Financial Management.* New York: John Wiley & Sons.

Rydqvist, K. 1992. Dual-class shares: A review. *Oxford Review of Economic Policy* 8(3):45–57.

Rydqvist, K. 1996. Takeover bids and the relative prices of shares that differ in their voting rights. *Journal of Banking and Finance* 20:1407–1425.

Ryngaert, M., and J. Netter. 1988. Shareholder wealth effects of the Ohio anti-takeover law. *Journal of Economics and Organization* (Fall):373–383.

Ryngaert, Michael. 1988. The effect of poison pill securities on shareholder wealth. *Journal of Financial Economics* 20.

Ryngaert, Michael, and Gregg Jarrell. 1986. The effects of poison pills on the wealth of target shareholders. A study by the Office of the Chief Economist, Securities and Exchange Commission (October 23).

Rytherband, D. 1991. The decision to implement an ESOP: Strategies and economic considerations. *Employee Benefits Journal* 16:19–25.

Safieddine, A., and S. Titman. 1999. Leverage and corporate performance: Evidence from unsuccessful takeovers. *Journal of Finance* 54(2):547–559.

Sahlman, W. 1997. How to write a great business plan. *Harvard Business Review* (July–August):98–109.

Sahlman, William. 1989. Note on financial contracting: "Deals." Harvard Business School Publishing, 9-288-014 (June).

Salmon, F. 1999. Mega-mergers bring a new spate of carve-outs. *Corporate Finance* (May):10–11.

Salter, M., and W. Weinhold. 1979. *Diversification through Acquisition: Strategies for Creating Economic Value*. New York: Free Press.

Salter, Malcolm, and Wolf A. Weinhold. 1981. Choosing compatible acquisitions. *Harvard Business Review* (January–February).

Sawyer, J., and H. Guetzkow. 1965. Bargaining and negotiations in international relations. Pages 425–520 in Herbert C. Kelman, ed., *International Behavior: A Social-Psychological Analysis*. New York: Holt, Rinehart & Winston.

Scharfstein, D., and J. Stein. 2000. The dark side of internal capital markets: Divisional rent-seeking and inefficient investment. *Journal of Finance* 55:2537–2564.

Schary, (Amram) M. 1991. The probability of exit. *RAND Journal of Economics* 22(3):339–353.

Scherer, F. M. 1988. Corporate takeovers: The efficiency arguments. *Journal of Economic Perspectives* 2(Winter):69–82.

Schill, M., and C. Zhou. 2001. Pricing an emerging industry: Evidence from Internet subsidiary carve-outs. *Financial Management* (Autumn):5–33.

Schipper, K. 1989. Commentary on earnings management. *Accounting Horizons* (December):91–102.

Schipper, K., and A. Smith. 1983. Effects of recontracting on shareholder wealth: The case of voluntary spin-offs. *Journal of Financial Economics* 15:153–186.

Schipper, K., and A. Smith. 1986. A comparison of equity carve-outs and seasoned equity offerings. *Journal of Financial Economics* 15:153–186.

Schipper, K., and A. Smith. 1989. "Equity carve-outs. In J. Stern, G. Stewart, and D. Chew, eds., *Corporate Restructuring and Executive Compensation*. Cambridge, MA: Ballinger.

Schipper, K., and R. Thompson. 1983. Evidence on the capitalized value of merger activity for acquiring firms. *Journal of Financial Economics* 11(April):437–467.

Schlingemann, F. P., R. M. Stulz, and R. A. Walkling. 2000. Asset liquidity and segment divestitures. Ohio State University working paper.

Schlingemann, F. P., R. M. Stulz, and R. A. Walkling. 2002. Divestitures and the liquidity of the market for corporate assets. *Journal of Financial Economics* 64:117–144.

Schnitzer, M. 1995. "Breach of trust" in takeovers and the optimal corporate charter. *Journal of Industrial Economics* 43(3):229–260.

Schoar, A. 2002. Effects of corporate diversification on productivity. *Journal of Finance* 52:2379–2403.

Schoeffler, S., R. D. Buzzell, and D. F. Heany. 1974. Impact of strategic planning on profit performance. *Harvard Business Review* 52(April):137–145.

Schoenberg, R., and R. Reeves. 1999. What determines acquisition activity within an industry? *European Management Journal* 17(February):93–98.

Scholes, M., and M. Wolfson. 1990. Employee stock ownership plans and corporate restructuring: Myths and realities. *Financial Management* 19:12–28.

Scholes, Myron S., and Mark A. Wolfson. 1992. *Taxes and Business Strategy, a Planning Approach*. Englewood Cliffs, NJ: Prentice-Hall.

Schramm, R., and H. Wang. 1999. Measuring the cost of capital in an international CAPM framework. *Journal of Applied Corporate Finance* 12(3, Fall):63–72.

Schumpeter, J. 1942, 2d ed., 1947. *The Theory of Economic Development*. New York: Harper & Brothers.

Schumpeter, J. A. 1950. *Capitalism, Socialism and Democracy*, 3d ed. New York: Harper & Brothers.

Schut, G., and R. van Frederikslust. Undated. Shareholder wealth effects of joint venture strategies: Theory and evidence from the Netherlands. Working paper, Erasmus Universiteit Rotterdam. Available by e-mail, rfrederikslust@fac.fbk.eur.nl.

Schwert, G. W. 1996. Markup pricing in mergers and acquisitions. *Journal of Financial Economics* 41:153–192.

Schwert, G. W. 2000. Hostility in takeovers: In the eyes of the Beholder? *Journal of Finance* 55(6):2599–2640.

Section of Business Law, American Bar Association. 1995. Model stock purchase agreement with commentary.

Sen, A. 1987. *On Ethics and Economics*. Oxford: Blackwell Publishers.

Senchack, A., and W. Beedles. 1980. Is international diversification desirable? *Journal of Portfolio Management* 6(Winter):49–57.

Servaes, H. 1991. Tobin's Q and the gains from takeovers. *Journal of Finance* 46(1, March):409–419.

Servaes, H., and M. Zenner. 1994. Taxes and the returns to foreign acquisitions in the United States. *Financial Management* 23(4):42–56.

Serwer, A. 1999. The deal of the next century. *Fortune* (September 6):154–162.

Seth, A. 1990. Sources of value creation in acquisitions: An empirical investigation. *Strategic Management Journal* 11(6):431–446.

Shafer, W. 2002. Effects of materiality, risk, and ethical perceptions on fraudulent reporting by financial executives. *Journal of Business Ethics* 38(3):243–263.

Shaked, I., A. Michael, and D. McClain. 1991. The foreign acquirer bonanza: Myth or reality. *Journal of Business Finance and Accounting* 18:431–447.

Shapiro, A. 1999. Corporate strategy and the capital budgeting decision. In D. Chew, ed., *The New Corporate Finance*, 2d ed. Burr Ridge: Irwin McGraw-Hill.

Shapiro, Carl, and Hal R. Varian. 1998. *Information Rules: A Strategic Guide to the Network Economy.* Boston: Harvard Business School Press.

Sharma, D., and J. Ho. 2002. The impact of acquisitions on operating performance: Some Australian evidence. *Journal of Business Finance and Accounting* 29(1, January, March):155–200.

Shelton, L. M. 2000, Merger market dynamics: Insights into the behavior of target and bidder firms. *Journal of Economic Behavior and Organization* 41:363–383.

Sherman, Steven J., and David A. Janatka. 1992. Engineering earn-outs to get deals done and prevent discord. *Mergers & Acquisitions* (September/October): 26–31.

Shiller, R. 1988. Fashions, fads, and bubbles in financial markets. Pages 56–68 in J. C. Coffee, Jr., L. Lowenstein, and S. Rose-Ackerman, eds., *Knights, Raiders, and Targets*. New York: Oxford University Press.

Shiller, Robert J. 1989. *Market Volatility*. Cambridge: MIT Press.

Shiller, Robert J. 1995. Conversation, information, and herd behavior. *AEA Papers and Proceedings* (May):181–185.

Shivakumar, L. 2000. Do firms mislead investors by overstating earnings before seasoned equity offerings? *Journal of Accounting and Economics* 29:339–371.

Shivdasani, Anil. 1993. Board composition, ownership structure, and hostile takeovers. *Journal of Accounting and Economics* 16:167–198.

Shleifer, A., and R. Vishny. 1988a. Value maximization and the acquisition process. *Journal of Economic Perspectives* 2(Winter):7–20.

Shleifer, A., and R. Vishny. 1988b. Management buyouts as a response to market pressure. In A. Auerbach, ed., *Mergers and Acquisitions*. Chicago: University of Chicago Press.

Shleifer, A., and R. Vishny. 2001. Stock market driven acquisitions. University of Chicago working paper, downloadable from http://papers.ssrn.com/sol3/papers.cfm?abstract_id=278563.

Shleifer, Andrei, and Robert Vishny. 1986. Large shareholders and corporate control. *Journal of Political Economy* 94:461–488.

Shleifer, Andrei, and Robert Vishny. 1997. Survey of corporate governance. *Journal of Finance* 52:737–782.

Shughart, W., II, and R. Tollison. 1984. The random character of merger activity. *RAND Journal of Economics* 15(Winter):500–509.

Shum, C. M., W. N. Davidson III, and J. L. Glascock. 1995. Voting rights and market reaction to dual classed common stock. *Financial Review* 30(2):275–288.

Sicherman, N., and R. Pettway. 1987. Acquisition of divested assets and shareholders' wealth. *Journal of Finance* 42(5)(December):1261–1273.

Siegel, D., J. Smith, and J. Paddock. 1987. Valuing offshore oil properties with option pricing models. *Midland Corporate Finance Journal* (Spring):22–30.

Siegel, S., and L. Fouraker. 1960. *Bargaining and Group Decision-Making*. New York: McGraw-Hill.

Sikora, M. 1999. The battle lines on chewable pills. *Mergers & Acquisitions* 34(2): 11–12.

Silber, William L. 1991. Discounts on restricted stock: The impact of illiquidity on stock prices. *Financial Analysts Journal* 47:60–64.

Singh, H., and C. A. Montgomery. 1987. Corporate acquisition strategies and economic performance. *Strategic Management Journal* 8(4, July/August):377–386.

Sinha, S. 1991. Share repurchase as a takeover defense. *Journal of Financial and Quantitative Analysis* 26(2):233–244.

Sirower, Mark. 1997. *The Synergy Trap: How Companies Lose the Acquisition Game*. New York: Free Press.

Sirri, Erik R., and Peter Tufano. 1998. Costly search and mutual fund flows. *Journal of Finance* 53:1589–1622.

Skinner, D., and L. Myers. 1999. Earnings momentum and earnings management. University of Michigan working paper, downloaded from http://papers.ssrn.com/sol3/papers.cfm?abstract_id=161173.

Skycom Corporation v. Telstar Corporation, United States Court of Appeals, Seventh Circuit, 1987, 813 F.2d 810.

Sleuwaegen, L. 1998. *Cross-Border Mergers and EC Competition Policy*. Oxford: Blackwell Publishers.

Slovin, M., M. Sushka, and S. Ferraro. 1995. A comparison of the information conveyed by equity carve-outs, spin-offs, and asset sell-offs. *Journal of Financial Economics* 37:89–104.

Smit, Han T. J. 2001. Option games and acquisition strategies. *Journal of Applied Corporate Finance* 14(2, Summer):79–89.

Smith, A. 1990. Corporate ownership structure and performance. *Journal of Financial Economics* 27(1, September):143–164.

Smith, Adam. 1969. *The Money Game*. New York: Dell.

Smith, B., and B. Amoaku-Adu. 1995. Relative prices of dual class shares. *Journal of Financial and Quantitative Analysis* 30(2):223–239.

Smith, C. 1986. Investment banking and the capital acquisition process. *Journal of Financial Economics* 15:3–31.

Smith, Michael P. 1996. Shareholder activism by institutional investors: Evidence from CalPERS. *Journal of Finance* 51:253–278.

Smith, R., and J. Kim. 1994. The combined effects of free cash flow and financial slack on bidder and target stock returns. *Journal of Business* 67(2, April):281–310.

Solnik, B. 1976. L'internationalisation des places financieres. COB-Universite.

Solnik, B. 1996. *International Investments*, 3d ed. Reading, MA: Addison-Wesley.

Solnik, B., and A. de Freitas. 1988. International factors of stock price behavior. In S. Khoury and A. Ghosh, eds., *Recent Developments in International Finance and Banking*. Lexington, MA: Lexington Books.

Solomon, D. 2003. WorldCom moved expenses to the balance sheet of MCI. *Wall Street Journal* (March 31). Downloaded from http://online.wsj.com/article_print/0,,SB1049070544867901OO,00.html.

Solomon, R. 1999. Business ethics and virtue. Pages 30–37 in R. E. Frederick, ed., *A companion to business ethics*. Malden, MA: Blackwell.

Song, M., R. Stulz, and R. Walkling. 1990. The distribution of target ownership and the division of gains in successful takeovers. *Journal of Finance*, 45(3, July):817–833.

Song, M. H., and R. A. Walkling. 1993. The impact of managerial ownership on acquisition attempts and target shareholder wealth. *Journal of Financial and Quantitative Analysis* (December):439–457.

Sorkin, A. 2002. Marketplace: Investors react negatively to Tyco's new, and abrupt, breakup strategy. *New York Times* (January 24). Downloaded from http://query.nytimes.com/search/restricted/article?res=F70810FE355F0C778EDDA80894DA4044.

Spence, Michael. 1973. Job market signalling. *Quarterly Journal of Economics* 87:335–374.

Sridharam, U. V. 1997. Dual class plans and unequal voting rights plans: A managerial choice. *Journal of Managerial Issues* 9(2):230–245.

Staay, J. W. 2000. Public takeovers in the Netherlands. 19(1):83–86.

Stalk, George, Philip Evans, and Laurence E. Shulman. 1992. Competing on capabilities: The new rules of corporate strategy. *Harvard Business Review* (March–April). Reprint 92209.

Steensma, H., and M. Lyles. 2000. Explaining IJV survival in a transitional economy through social exchange and knowledge-based perspectives. *Strategic Management Journal* 21:831–851.

Stein, J. 1997. Internal capital markets and the competition for corporate resources. *Journal of Finance* 52:111–133.

Steiner, P. 1975. *Mergers: Motives, Effects, and Policies*. Ann Arbor: University of Michigan Press.

Stern, J. 1974. Earnings per share doesn't count. *Financial Analysts Journal* (July/August):39–43.

Stern, Joel. 1989. Lead steer roundtable. *Journal of Applied Corporate Finance* 2:24–44.

Stern, Joel M., and Donald H. Chew Jr., editors. 1998. *The Revolution in Corporate Finance*, 3d ed. Malden, MA: Blackwell Publishers.

Stewart, G. B., and D. M. Glassman. 1999. The motives and methods of corporate restructuring. Part I in D. Chew, ed., *The New Corporate Finance: Where Theory Meets Practice*. Burr Ridge, IL: Irwin McGraw-Hill.

Stewart, G. Bennett, III. 1991. *The Quest for Value*. New York: HarperBusiness.

Stickel, A. I. 1998. Companies get a taste of chewable pills. *Investor Relations Business* (August 31):1.

Stigler, G. 1950. Monopoly and oligopoly power by merger. *American Economic Review* 40(May):23–34.

Stillman, R. 1983. Examining antitrust policy toward horizontal mergers. *Journal of Financial Economics* 11(1–4, April):225–240.

Stulz, R. 1995. Globalization of capital markets and the cost of capital: The case of Nestle. *Journal of Applied Corporate Finance* 8(3):30–38.

Stulz, R. M. 1988. Managerial control of voting rights: Financing policies and the market for corporate control. *Journal of Financial Economics* 20:25–55.

Sudarsanam, Sudi. 1995. *The Essence of Mergers and Acquisitions.* London: Prentice Hall.

Suk, D., K. Han, H. Sung. 1998. The evidence of bidders' overpayment in takeovers: The valuation ratios approach. *Financial Review* 33(2):1–11.

Sullivan, M., M. Jensen, and C. Hudson. 1994. The role of medium of exchange in merger offers: Examination of terminated merger proposals. *Financial Management* 23(3):51–62.

Sumway, T. 2001. Forecasting bankruptcy more accurately: A simple hazard model. *Journal of Business* 74(1):101–124.

Sundaram, A., and B. Yeung. 2001. Divestitures as good news or bad news: The role of creditors and management. Unpublished working paper.

Sundaramurthy, C., and D. W. Lyon. 1998. Shareholder governance proposals and conflict of interests between inside and outside shareholders. *Journal of Managerial Issues* 10(1):30–44.

Sung, C. B., and D. P. Simet. 1998. A comparative analysis of leveraged recapitalization versus leveraged buyout as a takeover defense. *Review of Financial Economics* 7(2):157–172.

Swannell, R., and I. Hart. 1999. How to be aggressive about going on the defensive. *Corporate Finance* 12–15.

Swanson, Z., and C. Mielke. 2000. To what extent are majority shareholders affected by the presence of minority stockholders? Unpublished working paper, 1–21.

Szewczyk, Samuel H., and George P. Tsetsekos. 1992. State intervention in the market for corporate control. *Journal of Financial Economics* 31:3.

Sziklay, B. 2001. Factors affecting discounts for lack of marketability for minority interests. Chapter 8 in Shannon Pratt, ed., *Business Valuation Discounts and Premiums.* New York: John Wiley & Sons.

Tannon, Jay M. 1990. The art of structuring a private company deal. *Mergers & Acquisitions* (September/October):58.

Tanous, P. 1999. *Investment Gurus: A Road Map to Wealth from the World's Best Money Managers.* New York: New York Institute of Finance.

Taylor, Richard W. 1987. Option valuation for alternative instruments with the Black-Scholes model: A pedagogical note. *Journal of Financial Education* (Fall):73–77.

Teoh, S., T. Wong, and G. Rao. 1998. Are accruals during initial public offerings opportunistic? *Review of Accounting Studies* 3.

Teoh, W., I. Welch, and T. Wong. 1998. Earnings management and the long-run underperformance of seasoned equity offerings. *Journal of Financial Economics* 50:63–100.

Texaco, Inc. v. Pennzoil Co., Court of Appeals of Texas, 1987, 729 S.W.2d 768.

Thaler, Richard H. 1992. *The Winner's Curse: Paradoxes and Anomalies of Economic Life.* Princeton: Princeton University Press.

Thompson, A. A., and A. J. Strickland. 1992. *Strategic Management: Concepts and Cases.* Homewood, IL: Richard D. Irwin.

Thompson, Samuel C., Jr. 1996. The merger and acquisition provisions of the ALI corporate governance project as applied to the three steps of the Time-Warner acquisition. *Columbia Business Law Review* 2:145–280.

Thompson, Samuel C. Jr. 2001. *Business Planning for Mergers and Acquisitions*, 2d ed. Durham, NC: Carolina Academic Press.

Thorburn, K. 2000. Bankruptcy auctions: Costs, debt recovery, and firm survival. *Journal of Financial Economics* 58(3):337–368.

Torabzadeh, K. M., J. Roufagalas, and C. G. Woodruff. 2000. Self-selection and the effects of poison put/call covenants on the reoffering yields of corporate bonds. *International Review of Economics & Finance* 9(2):139–156.

Town, R. J. 1992. Merger waves and the structure of merger and acquisition time-series. *Journal of Applied Econometrics* 7(December):83–100.

Toxvaerd, F. 2002. Strategic merger waves: A theory of musical chairs. Working paper, (December).

Transparency International. 2002. Corruption perceptions index 2002. Downloaded from http://www.transparency.org/cpi/2002/cpi2002.en.html.

Travers, Jeffrey, and Stanley Milgram. 1969. An experimental study of the small world problem. *Sociometry* 32(4, December):425–443.

Travlos, N. 1987. Corporate takeover bids, methods of payment, and bidding firm's stock returns. *Journal of Finance* 42:943–964.

Travlos, N., and G. Papaionnaou. 1991. Corporate acquisitions: Method of payment effects, capital structure effects, and bidding firms' stock returns. *Quarterly Journal of Business and Economics* 30:3–22.

Triantis, A., and J. Hodder. 1990. Valuing flexibility as a complex option. *Journal of Finance* 45(2):549–565.

Triantis, Alex, and Adam Borison. 2001. Real options: State of the practice. *Journal of Applied Corporate Finance* 14(2, Summer):8–24.

Trigeorgis, L. 1996. *Real Options—Managerial Flexibility and Strategy in Resource Allocation*. Cambridge: MIT Press.

Trigeorgis, Lenos, and Scott P. Mason. 1987. Valuing managerial flexibility. *Midland Corporate Finance Journal* 5(Spring):14–21.

Trimbath, S. 2002. *Mergers and Efficiency: Changes across Time*. Santa Monica: Milken Institute.

Trout, R. R. 1977. Estimation of the discount associated with the transfer of restricted securities. *Taxes* (June):381–385.

Tufano, P. 1989. Financial innovation and first mover advantages. *Journal of Financial Economics* 25(2):213–240.

Tufano, P. 1996. How financial engineering can advance corporate strategy. *Harvard Business Review* (January–February):136–146.

Tufano, P. 1998. The determinants of stock price exposure: Financial engineering and the gold mining industry. *Journal of Finance* 53:1015–1052.

Tully, K. 2000. The legal skills behind winning deals. *Corporate Finance* 17–20.

U.S. Congress, House. 1971. Discounts involved in purchases of common stock (1966–1969). Institutional Investor Study Report of the Securities and Exchange Commission. H.R. Doc. No. 64, Part 5, 92d Cong., 1st Sess. (1971) 2444–2456.

Unseem, M., and Gager, C. 1996. Employee shareholders or institutional investors? When corporate managers replace their stockholders. *Journal of Management Studies* 33(5):613–632.

Upton, D. 1994. The management of manufacturing flexibility. *California Management Review* (Winter):72–89.

Upton, David M., and Andrew McAfee. 1997. A note on plant tours. Harvard Business School Publishing, 9-697-076.

Vancil, R. F. 1987. *Passing the Baton: Managing the Process of CEO Succession.* Cambridge: Harvard Business School Press.

Varaiya, N. 1985. A test of Roll's hubris hypothesis of corporate takeovers. Working paper, Dallas: Southern Methodist University, School of Business.

Varaiya N., and K. Ferris. 1987. Overpaying in corporate takeover: The winner's curse. *Financial Analysts Journal* 43(May/June):64–70.

Vasconcellos, G. M., and R. J. Kish. 1998. Cross-border mergers and acquisitions: The European-US experience. *Journal of Multinational Financial Management* 8(4):431–450.

Vasconcellos, G. M., J. Madura, and R. J. Kish. 1990. An empirical investigation of factors affecting cross-border acquisitions: U.S. vs. U.K. experience. *Global Finance Journal* 1:173–189.

Vechiolla, R. R., M. Prudom, and R. D. Hamilton. 1998. Exposing the corporate vampires: A shareholder's guided to management entrenchment. *Long Range Planning* 31(5):659–671.

Veit, E. T., ed. 1990. *Valuation of Closely Held Companies and Inactively Traded Securities.* Charlottesville, VA: Institute of Chartered Financial Analysts.

Veld, C., and Y. Veld-Merkoulova. 2002. Do spin-offs really create value? The European case. Working paper, Tilburg University. May be obtained by e-mail at C.H.Veld@kub.nl.

Vernon, R. 1974. Competition policy toward multinational corporations. *American Economic Review* (May):276–282.

Vickrey, W. 1961. Counterspeculation, auctions, and competitive sealed tenders. *Journal of Finance* 16(1, March):8–37.

Vijh, A. 1994. The spin-off and merger ex-date effects. *Journal of Finance* 49(2): 581–609.

Vijh, A. 1999. Long-term returns from equity carve outs. *Journal of Financial Economics* 54, 273–308.

Vijh, A. 2002. The positive announcement-period returns of equity carve outs: Asymmetric information or divestiture gains? *Journal of Business* 75(1): 153–190.

Villalonga, B. 1999. Does diversification cause the "diversification discount"? Working paper, University of California, Los Angeles.

Villalonga, B. 2003a. Diversification discount or premium? New evidence from BITS establishment-level data. *Journal of Finance* (forthcoming). Harvard Business School working paper, downloadable from http://papers.ssrn.com/sol3/papers.cfm?abstract_id=253793.

Villalonga, B. 2003b. Research roundtable discussion: The diversification discount. Social Science Research Network, paper downloadable from http://papers.ssrn.com/sol3/papers.cfm?abstract_id=402220.

Vincent, Linda. 1997. Equity valuation implications of purchase versus pooling accounting. *Journal of Financial Statement Analysis* 2(Summer):5–19.

Walker, M. 2000. Corporate takeovers, strategic objectives, and acquiring-firm shareholder wealth. *Financial Management* 29(1, Spring):53–66.

Walker, M. M. 1998. Leveraged recapitalization, operating efficiency, and stockholder wealth. *Financial Review* 33:88–114.

Walkling, R. 1985. Predicting tender offer success: A logistic analysis. *Journal of Financial Quantitative Analysis* 20:461–478.

Walkling, R., and R. Edmister. 1985. Determinants of tender offer premiums. *Financial Analysts Journal* 41:30–37.

Walkling, R. A., and M. S. Long. 1984. Agency theory, managerial welfare, and takeover bid resistance. *RAND Journal of Economics* (Spring):54–68.

Walsh, J. P. 1988. Top management turnover following mergers and acquisitions. *Strategic Management Journal* 173–183.

Walsh, J. P. 1989. Doing a deal: Merger and acquisition negotiations and their impact upon target company top management turnover. *Strategic Management Journal* 307–322.

Walsh, J. P., and J. W. Ellwood. 1991. Mergers, acquisitions, and the pruning of managerial deadwood. *Strategic Management Journal* (March):201–218.

Wansley, J., W. Lane, and H. Yang. 1983. Abnormal returns to acquired firms by type of acquisition and method of payment. *Financial Management* 12(3, Autumn):16–22.

Wansley, J. W., W. R. Lane, and H. C. Yang. 1983. Shareholder returns to U.S. acquired firms in foreign and domestic acquisitions. *Journal of Business Finance and Accounting* 10:647–656.

Warner, J. B., R. L. Watts, and K. H. Wruck. 1988. Stock price and top management changes. *Journal of Financial Economics* 20:461–492.

Wasserstein, Bruce. 2000. *Big Deal 2000: The Battle for Control of America's Leading Corporations*. New York: Warner Books. Published 1998 as Wasserstein, Bruce. *Big Deal*. New York: Free Press.

Watts, Duncan. 1999. Networks, dynamics, and the small-world phenomenon. *American Journal of Sociology* 105(2, September):493–527.

Watts, R. 2003. Conservatism in accounting. Part I: Explanations and implications. University of Rochester working paper, downloaded from http://papers.ssrn.com/sol3/papers.cfm?abstract_id=414522.

Weatherford, Larry, and Samuel Bodily. 1988. Sprigg Lane (A). Darden Case Collection (UVA-QA-302), and associated teaching note by Larry Weatherford, Samuel Bodily, and Robert Bruner (UVA-QA-302TN). University of Virginia.

Weidenbaum, M., and S. Vogt. 1987. Takeovers and stockholders: Winners and losers. *California Management Review* 29(4, Summer):157–167.

Weir, C., D. Laing, and M. Wright. Undated. Incentive effects, monitoring mechanisms and the market for corporate control at going private transactions in the UK. Aberdeen Business School working paper, downloadable at http://papers.ssrn.com/sol3/papers.cfm?abstract_id=379101.

Weisbach, Michael. 1988. Outside directors and CEO turnover. *Journal of Financial Economics* 20:431–460.

Weisinger, J., and P. Salipante. 2000. Cultural knowing as practicing: Extending our conception of culture. *Journal of Management Inquiry* 9(4):376–390.

Weiss, Barry D. 1998. Information-age acquisitions: Locking up assets, Part I. *Mergers & Acquisitions* (July/August):19–26.

Werhane, P. 1988. Two ethical issues in mergers and acquisitions *Journal of Business Ethics* 7:41–45.

Werhane, P. 1990. Mergers, acquisitions, and the market for corporate control. *Public Affairs Quarterly* 4(1):81–96.

Werhane, P. 1997. A note on moral imagination. Charlottesville, VA: Darden Case Collection, UVA-E-0114.

Werhane, P. 1999. Business ethics and the origins of contemporary capitalism: Economics and ethics in the work of Adam Smith and Herbert Spencer. Pages 325–341 in R. E. Frederick, ed., *A Companion to Business Ethics*. Malden, MA: Blackwell.

Wessel, Milton R. 1976. *The Rule of Reason: A New Approach to Corporate Litigation*. Reading, MA: Addison-Wesley.

Weston, J. 1953. *The Role of Mergers in the Growth of Large Firms*. Berkeley: University of California Press.

Weston, J. F. 1970. The nature and significance of conglomerate firms. *St. John's Law Review* 44:66–80.

Weston, J. F. 1989. Divestitures: Mistakes or learning. *Journal of Applied Corporate Finance* (Summer):68–76.

Weston, J. F., and S. K. Mansinghka. 1971. Tests of the efficiency performance of conglomerate firms. *Journal of Finance* 26(3, September):919–936.

Weston, J. F., K. V. Smith, and R. E. Shrieves. 1972. Conglomerate performance using the capital asset pricing model. *Review of Economics and Statistics* 21(4, November):357–363.

Westphal, James. 2002. The impression management trap. *Wall Street Journal* (August 27):B2.

Wheatley, C., R. Brown, and G. Johnson. 1997. Accounting disclosure and valuation revisions around voluntary corporate spin-offs. Unpublished working paper.

Whipple, J. 2000. Strategic alliance success factors. *Journal of Supply Chain Management* (Summer):21–28.

White, Gerald I., Ashwinpaul C. Sondhi, and Dov Fried. 1994. *The Analysis and Use of Financial Statements*. New York: John Wiley & Sons.

Whited, T. 2001. Is it inefficient investment that causes the diversification discount? *Journal of Finance* 56:1667–1691.

Wicks, A. 2003. A note on ethical decision making. Charlottesville, VA: Darden Case Collection, UVA-E-0242.

Wier, P. 1983. The costs of anti-merger lawsuits: Evidence from the stock market. *Journal of Financial Economics* 11(1–4, April):207–225.

Williamson, O. 1970. *Corporate Control and Business Behavior*. Englewood Cliffs, NJ: Prentice-Hall.

Williamson, O. 1975. *Markets and Hierarchies: Analysis and Antitrust Implications*. New York: Free Press.

Wilson, Robert B. 1992. Strategic analysis of auctions. Pages 227–280 in R. J. Aumann and S. Hart, eds., *Handbook of Game Theory with Economic Applications*, Vol. 1. Amsterdam: North-Holland.

Wolfram, S., and R. Gajraj. 2000. France. *International Financial Law Review* 19:19–21.

Womack, J., D. Jones, and D. Roos. 1990. *The Machine That Changed the World*. New York: HarperPerennial.

WorldCom will write down $79.8 billion in assets value. 2003. *Wall Street Journal* (March 14). Downloaded from http://online.wsj.com/article_print/0,,SB105761115376994600,00.html.

Wright, M. 1984. Auditing the efficiency of the nationalized industries: Exit the comptroller and auditor general. *Public Administration* 62(1):95–101.

Wruck, K. 1991. What really went wrong at Revco? *Journal of Applied Corporate Finance* (Summer):79–92.

Wruck, K. H. 1989. Equity ownership concentration and firm value: Evidence from private equity financings. *Journal of Financial Economics* 23:3–28.

Wulf, J. 2001. Do CEOs in mergers trade power for premium? Evidence from "Mergers of Equals." Working paper, Wharton School, University of Pennsylvania (June).

Wurgler, J. 2000. Financial markets and the allocation of capital. *Journal of Financial Economics* 58:187–214.

Wyser-Pratte, Guy P. 1982. *Risk Arbitrage II*. New York: Salomon Brothers Center for the Study of Financial Institutions, Graduate School of Business Administration, New York University, Monograph 1982-3-4.

Yagil, Joseph. 1987. An exchange ratio determination model for mergers: A note. *Financial Review* 22(1):195–202.

Yeheskel, O. 2001. Arkia Israel Airlines' CEO Israel Borovich on strategic alliances and growth. *Academy of Management Executive* 15(1):12–15.

Yook, K., P. Gangopadhyay, and G. McCabe. 1999. Information asymmetry theory, management control theory, and method of payment in acquisitions. *Journal of Financial Research* 22(4):413–427.

Yook, K. C. 2000. Larger return to cash acquisitions: Signaling effect or leverage effect? Working paper, Baltimore, MD: Johns Hopkins.

You, V., R. Caves, M. Smith, and J. Henry. 1986. Mergers and bidders' wealth: Managerial and strategic factors. Pages 201–221 in Lacy Glenn Thomas III, ed., *The Economics of Strategic Planning: Essays in Honor of Joel Dean*. Lexington: Lexington Books.

Zahra, S. 1995. Corporate entrepreneurship and financial performance: The case of management leveraged buyouts. *Journal of Business Venturing* 10(3):225–247.

Zhang, P. 2001. What really determines the payment methods in M&A deals? Manchester School of Management (UMIST) working paper 2001-0103 downloadable from http://papers.ssrn.com/sol3/papers.cfm?abstract_id=284770.

Zingales, L. 1994. The value of the voting right: A study of the Milan Stock Exchange experience. *Review of Financial Studies* 7:125–148.

Zingales, L. 1995. What determines the value of corporate votes? *Quarterly Journal of Economics* 110:1047–1074.

Zuckerman, A. 2000. Revisiting divestiture. *Health Forum Journal* 43(6):53–54.

Zuta, S. 1999. Diversification discount and targeted stock: Theory and empirical evidence. Unpublished working paper.

Index

For information about the CD-ROM see the About the CD-ROM section on page 939.

Printed in the USA/Agawam, MA
September 15, 2026

910600.002